Objective Questions in
MATHEMATICS
for JEE Main and Advanced

Objective Questions in MATHEMATICS for JEE Main and Advanced

Pratyush Kumar Singh
B.Tech. (Civil Engineering)

OBJECTIVE QUESTIONS IN MATHEMATICS FOR JEE MAIN AND ADVANCED

UNIVERSITIES PRESS (INDIA) PRIVATE LIMITED

Registered office
3-6-747/1/A & 3-6-754/1, Himayatnagar, Hyderabad 500 029, Telangana, India
info@universitiespress.com; www.universitiespress.com

Distributed by
Orient Blackswan Private Limited

Registered office
3-6-752 Himayatnagar, Hyderabad 500 029, Telangana, India

Other offices
Bengaluru / Chennai / Guwahati / Hyderabad / Kolkata
Mumbai / New Delhi / Noida / Patna / Visakhapatnam

501767

ISBN: 978-93-89211-87-0

Typeset in Times Ten LT Std 10/12 *by*
SRS Publishing Services, Puducherry

Printed in India by
Navya Printers, Hyderabad 500 013

Published by
Universities Press (India) Private Limited
3-6-747/1/A & 3-6-754/1, Himayatnagar, Hyderabad 500 029, Telangana, India

Preface

The aim of this book is to give students *intensive* as well as *extensive* practice on every topic covered in the JEE syllabus. The questions have been arranged in order of increasing difficulty.

The number of questions in each chapter has been very rigorously determined such that they are *necessary* and *sufficient*. These problems will help students in testing their comprehension of each topic in depth, and also impart breadth to their numerical problem-solving skills. In preparing this book, I have relied heavily on questions asked in the JEE (Main and Advanced) examinations in the past four decades.

Every chapter begins with a list of key concepts, to give the students perspective and act as a guidepost for the chapter. The key concepts are a summary of the important principles and the key equations in that chapter.

Many students experience difficulty when it comes to solving numerical problems. The only way to overcome this is by having a very clear understanding of the associated concepts. I, therefore, strongly urge the students to read the key concepts before solving the questions.

To get the most out of this book, students should attempt all the questions, without skipping any. Every question tests a different aspect of the topic. Care has been taken so as to not repeat any type of question.

I have taken immense efforts to make the subject as interesting as possible, while also ensuring that students are adequately prepared for their exams. This book is the result of my several decades of experience of classroom teaching. I wish all my readers success in their endeavours.

Pratyush Kumar Singh

Acknowledgements

I would like to thank the reviewers of this text, whose detailed line-by-line comments were of fundamental help to me in preparing this book. It is always a joy and a privilege to express gratitude to my family, my teachers and my students for their support during the writing of this book.

I express my deep gratitude to my student, Srikant Singh, for the assistance and attention that he rendered during the computerisation of this book.

I have spent a lot of time and effort in creating the best problem book I could write, and I hope it will help students learn and improve their problem-solving skills. In turn, please help me by letting me know what still needs to be improved.

I welcome communication from students and teachers, especially concerning any errors or deficiencies that you may find in this book. Please feel free to contact me at pratyushkr123@gmail.com.

Pratyush Kumar Singh

Contents

Preface . . . . *v*
Acknowledgements . . . . *vi*

Part I: Algebra

Chapter 1: Theory of Equations 1.1
Chapter 2: Quadratic Equations 2.1
Chapter 3: Sequences and Series 3.1
Chapter 4: Binomial Theorem 4.1
Chapter 5: Complex Numbers 5.1
Chapter 6: Permutations and Combinations 6.1
Chapter 7: Probability. 7.1
Chapter 8: Matrices 8.1
Chapter 9: Vector Algebra 9.1

Part II: Calculus

Chapter 10: Algebraic Functions 10.1
Chapter 11: Trigonometric Functions. 11.1
Chapter 12: Trigonometric Equations 12.1
Chapter 13: Solution of Triangles 13.1
Chapter 14: Inverse Trigonometric Functions 14.1
Chapter 15: Exponential and Log Functions 15.1
Chapter 16: Limits and Continuity. 16.1
Chapter 17: Investigating Functions 17.1
Chapter 18: Differentiation 18.1
Chapter 19: Application of Derivatives 19.1
Chapter 20: Indefinite Integration 20.1
Chapter 21: Definite Integration 21.1
Chapter 22: Differentiation of an Integral 22.1

Chapter 23: Area Between Curves 23.1
Chapter 24: Sum of a Series and Definite Integral 24.1
Chapter 25: Differential Equations 25.1

Part III: Coordinate Geometry

Chapter 26: Straight Line 26.1
Chapter 27: Circle 27.1
Chapter 28: Parabola 28.1
Chapter 29: Ellipse. 29.1
Chapter 30: Hyperbola 30.1
Chapter 31: 3D Geometry 31.1
Appendix I: Previous Years' JEE Main Questions and Solutions A.1
Appendix II: Previous Years' JEE Advanced Questions and Solutions B.1

Truth Alone Triumphs
—Mundaka Upanishad

To
The Almighty
and
My Parents,
Smt. Sharmishtha Sinha
Dr Shashi Kr. Singh

PART I

ALGEBRA

CHAPTER

1

Theory of Equations

Number System

- **Natural Numbers:** Counting numbers $1, 2, 3, 4, 5, \ldots$ are called natural numbers. The set of natural numbers is represented as $\mathrm{N} = \{1, 2, 3, 4, 5, \ldots\}$.
- **Whole Numbers:** If we include 0 in the set of natural numbers, we obtain the set of whole numbers, which is represented as $\mathrm{W} = \{0, 1, 2, 3, 4, 5, \ldots\}$.
- **Integers:** The set of integers is $\mathrm{Z} = \{\ldots, -4, -3, -2, -1, 0, 1, 2, 3, 4, \ldots\}$. The set of positive integers is $\mathrm{Z}^+ = \{1, 2, 3, 4, \ldots\}$. The set of negative integers is $\mathrm{Z}^- = \{-1, -2, -3, -4, \ldots\}$. Note that 0 is neither positive nor negative.
- **Prime Numbers:** Natural numbers that have exactly two distinct, integral factors, namely, 1 and the number itself, are called prime numbers. For example, $2, 3, 5, 7, 11, 13, 17, \ldots$. Note that 1 is not a prime number because it does not have two distinct factors. Also note that 2 is the only even prime number.
- **Composite Numbers:** Natural numbers that have exactly more than two distinct integral factors are called composite numbers. For example, $4, 6, 8, 9, 10, 12, 14, 15, \ldots$. Note that 1 is neither prime nor composite.
- **Co-prime Numbers:** A pair of natural numbers that has no common factor other than 1 is called a co-prime or relatively prime number. For example, $(1,2), (2,3), (3,4), (3,8), (3,10), (5,6), (7,8), (15,16)$, and so on.
- **Rational Numbers:** Real numbers that can be represented in the form p/q, where p, q are integers and $q \neq 0$, are called rational numbers. All integers, terminating decimal numbers and non-terminating but recurring decimal numbers are rational.

Polynomial Equation

- An equation of the form

$$a_0 x^n + a_1 x^{n-1} + a_2 x^{n-2} + \ldots + a_{n-1} x + a_n = 0, \ (n \in \mathbf{N}),$$

where $a_0 \neq 0$, is called an nth degree polynomial equation; n^{th} degree because the highest degree of the variable x that exists is n.

There will be n values of x, real or imaginary, satisfying the above equation. These values are called the roots of the equation. Imaginary roots always occur in conjugate pairs; if there is an imaginary root $\alpha + i\beta$, then $\alpha - i\beta$ will also be a root, where $i = \sqrt{-1}$.

If $x_1, x_2, x_3, \ldots, x_n$ are the roots, then

$$\text{Sum of the roots taken one at a time} = -\frac{a_1}{a_0}$$

$$\text{Sum of the roots taken two at a time} = +\frac{a_2}{a_0}$$

$$\ldots$$

$$\text{Sum of the roots taken } n \text{ at a time} = (-1)^n \frac{a_n}{a_0}$$

The equation can be written as

$$a_0 (x - x_1)(x - x_2) \cdots (x - x_n) = 0$$

Remainder Theorem

- If a polynomial $P(x)=a_0x^n+a_1x^{n-1}+a_2x^{n-2}+\ldots+a_n$ is divided by $x-k$, then the remainder is $P(k)$. Note that if $P(k)=0$, which means no remainder, then $x-k$ will be a factor of the polynomial.

EXERCISES

1. If $x^2+\frac{1}{x^2}=14$, then the value of $x^3+\frac{1}{x^3}$ is:

(a) ± 26 (b) ± 39
(c) ± 52 (d) $\pm 30\sqrt{3}$

2. The coefficient of x^{99} in the polynomial $(x-1)(x-2)\cdots(x-100)$ is:

(a) -2^{10} (b) -10^4
(c) -5050 (d) 0

3. The polynomial $x^5+ax^4+bx^3+cx^2+dx+4$ has real coefficients. If $1+2i$ and $3-2i$ are two roots of this polynomial, then the value of $|a|$ is:

(a) $\frac{524}{65}$ (b) $\frac{324}{65}$
(c) $\frac{224}{65}$ (d) $\frac{124}{65}$

4. Let $\alpha_1,\alpha_2,\ldots,\alpha_{2007}$ be the roots of the equation $1+x^{2007}=0$. Then the value of $(1+\alpha_1)(1+\alpha_2)\cdots\cdots(1+\alpha_{2007})$ is:

(a) 0 (b) 1
(c) 2 (d) 2007

5. If $\alpha_1,\alpha_2,\ldots,\alpha_6$ are the roots of $x^6+x^2+1=0$, then the value of $(1-2\alpha_1)(1-2\alpha_2)\cdots(1-2\alpha_6)$ is:

(a) 0 (b) 1
(c) 64 (d) 81

6. The polynomial $x^3+ax^2+bx+c=0$ has real coefficients. If α,β,γ are its roots, then $\alpha^2\beta^2+\beta^2\gamma^2+\gamma^2\alpha^2$ is:

(a) b^2-2ac (b) b^2-4ac
(c) b^2+2ac (d) b^2+4ac

7. Consider the equation $x^{2007}-1+x^{-2007}=0$. Let m be the number of distinct, complex, non-real roots and n be the number of distinct, real roots of the above equation. Then the value of $m-n$ is:

(a) 0 (b) 2006
(c) 2007 (d) 4014

8. If α,β,γ are the roots of the equation $x^3-6x-4=0$, then the value of $\alpha^3+\beta^3+\gamma^3$ is:

(a) 0 (b) 12
(c) -4 (d) -13

9. If the polynomial $x^4-6x^3+16x^2-25x+10$ is divided by x^2-2x+k, the remainder is $x+a$. Then the values of k and a are:

(a) $k=-1, a=2$ (b) $k=2, a=-3$
(c) $k=-3, a=4$ (d) $k=5, a=-5$

10. Which among the following should be subtracted from the polynomial $x^3-6x^2-15x+80$ so that it becomes exactly divisible by x^2+x-6:

(a) 12 (b) -38
(c) $-2x+38$ (d) $x-15$

11. When the polynomial $P(x)$ is divided by $x-1$, the remainder is 1, and when it is divided by $x-4$, the remainder is 10. If $R(x)$ is the remainder when it is divided by $(x-1)(x-4)$, then $R(0)$ equals:

(a) 0 (b) 3
(c) -1 (d) -2

12. If a,b,c are the roots of the equation $x^3-px^2+qx-r=0$, then the value of $(a+b)(b+c)(c+a)$ is:

(a) $pq-r$ (b) $pq+r$
(c) pqr (d) $\frac{pq}{r}$

13. The number of positive integers n in the range $12\le n\le 40$ such that $(n-1)!$ is not divisible by n is:

(a) 5 (b) 7
(c) 13 (d) 14

14. The polynomials $P(x)=kx^3+3x^2-3$ and $Q(x)=2x^3-5x+k$ give the same remainder when divided by $x-4$. The value of k is:

(a) 1 (b) 3
(c) -2 (d) -4

ANSWER KEYS

1. (c) **2.** (c) **3.** (a) **4.** (a) **5.** (d) **6.** (a) **7.** (d) **8.** (b) **9.** (d) **10.** (c)
11. (d) **12.** (a) **13.** (b) **14.** (a)

SOLUTIONS

1. (c) We have

$$x^3+\frac{1}{x^3}=\left(x+\frac{1}{x}\right)\left(x^2-1+\frac{1}{x^2}\right)$$

$$=\pm 13\sqrt{x^2+\frac{1}{x^2}+2}=\pm 52$$

2. (c) The given expression is a polynomial of degree 100 in x

$$P(x)=x^{100}+a_1x^{99}+a_2x^{98}+\ldots+a_{99}x+a_{100},$$

whose zeros are $x=1,2,3,\ldots,99,100$.
Hence, from the theory of polynomials, we have

$$a_1=-\text{ Sum of the zeros }=-\frac{100\times 101}{2}=-5050.$$

3. (a) The other roots are $1-2i$, $3+2i$ and, say, α. Product of the roots is 4. Hence

$$\left(1^2+2^2\right)\left(3^2+2^2\right)\alpha=4 \text{ gives } \alpha=\frac{4}{65}.$$

Now $a=-$ Sum of the roots

$$=-\left(2+6+\frac{4}{65}\right)=-\frac{524}{65}$$

4. (a) $\alpha_1,\alpha_2,\ldots,\alpha_{2007}$ are the zeros of the given polynomial. Therefore

$$x^{2007}+1=(x-\alpha_1)(x-\alpha_2)\cdots\cdots(x-\alpha_{2007})$$

Now putting $x=-1$ gives

$$\Rightarrow \quad -(1+\alpha_1)(1+\alpha_2)\cdots\cdots(1+\alpha_{2007})=0$$

5. (d) $\alpha_1,\alpha_2,\ldots,\alpha_6$ are the zeros of the given polynomial. Therefore

$$x^6+x^2+1=(x-\alpha_1)(x-\alpha_2)\cdots(x-\alpha_6).$$

Now putting $x=\frac{1}{2}$ gives

$$\frac{1}{2^6}(1-2\alpha_1)(1-2\alpha_2)\cdots\cdots(1-2\alpha_6)=\frac{1+2^4+2^6}{2^6}$$

$$\Rightarrow \quad (1-2\alpha_1)(1-2\alpha_2)\cdots\cdots(1-\alpha_6)=81.$$

6. (a) The given expression reduces to

$$S=(\alpha\beta+\beta\gamma+\gamma\alpha)^2-2\alpha\beta\gamma(\alpha+\beta+\gamma)=b^2-2ac$$

7. (d) The given equation reduces to

$$x^{4014}-x^{2007}+1=0$$

$$\Rightarrow \quad x^{2007}=\frac{1\pm i\sqrt{3}}{2}$$

There will be 4014 roots, all complex and non-real. Hence $m-n=4014$.

8. (b) We see that $\alpha+\beta+\gamma=0$. In this case

$$\alpha^3+\beta^3+\gamma^3=3\alpha\beta\gamma=12$$

$$\left[a^3+b^3+c^3-3abc=(a+b+c)\left(ab+bc+ca-a^2-b^2-c^2\right)\right]$$

9. (d) On performing division, we obtain the remainder

$$(2k-9)x+10-k(8-k)$$

Comparing with $x+a$, we have

$$2k-9=1\Rightarrow k=5 \text{ and } a=10-k(8-k)=-5.$$

10. (c) Let $ax+b$ be subtracted from the given polynomial. After subtracting, the given polynomial reduces to

$$P(x)=x^3-6x^2-15x+80-ax-b$$

Now $P(x)$ will be exactly divisible by $x^2+x-6=(x+3)(x-2)$ if $P(-3)=0$ and $P(2)=0$. Hence

$$-3a+b=44 \text{ and } 2a+b=34$$

gives $a=-2, b=38$.

11. (d) When $P(x)$ is divided by $(x-1)(x-4)$, let $Q(x)$ be the quotient and $R(x)$ be the remainder. Then by Euclid's lemma

$$P(x)=(x-1)(x-4)Q(x)+R(x)$$

Here $R(x)$ must be linear, one degree less than the divisor $(x-1)(x-4)$. Hence, let $R(x)=ax+b$. Now using the conditions $R(1)=1$ and $R(4)=10$, we have

$$a+b=1 \text{ and } 4a+b=10 \Rightarrow a=3, b=-2$$

Thus $R(x)=3x-2$, and hence $R(0)=-2$.

12. (a) We see that $a+b+c=-p$. The given expression reduces to

$$S=(-p-c)(-p-b)(-p-a)$$

a, b, c are the zeros of the given polynomial. Therefore

$$x^3-px^2+qx-r=(x-c)(x-b)(x-a)$$

Putting $x=-p$, we have

$$(-p-c)(-p-b)(-p-a)=pq-r.$$

13. (b) We see that 12 divides 11! since it contains 2 and 6.

Similarly, we can check that the result is true for all n except the prime numbers.

Between 12 and 40, there are 7 prime numbers, namely, 13, 17, 19, 23, 29, 31, 37.

14. (a) From Remainder Theorem, the remainders are

$$P(4)=64k+45 \text{ and } Q(4)=k+108.$$

According to the question, they are equal. Equating the two, we have

$$64k+45=k+108 \text{ gives } k=1.$$

CHAPTER

2 Quadratic Equations

- **Quadratic Equation:** An equation of the form

$$ax^2+bx+c=0,$$

where $a \neq 0$, is called a quadratic equation. There will be two values of x, real or imaginary, satisfying the above equation. These values are called the roots of the equation:

$$x=\frac{-b\pm\sqrt{b^2-4ac}}{2a}$$

- **Discriminant:** The quantity $D=b^2-4ac$ is called the discriminant of the quadratic equation. The roots are real and distinct if $D>0$, real and identical if $D=0$ and imaginary if $D<0$.

Imaginary roots always occur in conjugate pairs; if $\alpha+i\beta$ is one root, then the other root will be $\alpha-i\beta$, where $i=\sqrt{-1}$. Irrational roots also occur in conjugate pairs; if $\alpha+\sqrt{\beta}$ is one root, then the other root will be $\alpha-\sqrt{\beta}$.

Two quadratic equations $a_1x^2+b_1x+c_1=0$ and $a_2x^2+b_2x+c_2=0$ will have one root in common if

$$(a_1b_2-a_2b_1)(b_1c_2-b_2c_1)=(a_1c_2-a_2c_1)^2$$

and both roots will be common if $\frac{a_1}{a_2}=\frac{b_1}{b_2}=\frac{c_1}{c_2}$.

- **Sum, Product and Difference between Roots:** If α, β are the roots, then

Sum of the roots $\alpha\pm\beta=\frac{-b}{a}$

Product of the roots $\alpha\beta=\frac{c}{a}$

Difference between the roots $|\alpha-\beta|=\frac{\sqrt{D}}{|a|}$

The function $f(x)=ax^2+bx+c$ can be written as $f(x)=a(x-a)(x-\beta)$. Its graph is a parabola with vertex at $\left(\frac{-b}{2a},\frac{-D}{4a}\right)$ and x intercepts α, β. The parabola is concave upwards if $a>0$ and concave downwards if $a<0$.

- **Real Zeros:** If α, $\beta(\alpha<\beta)$ are two real zeros of $f(x)=ax^2+bx+c$, then for any given real number k, we have the following conditions and their corresponding necessary and sufficient equations:

1. Roots lie on opposite sides of k $\Leftrightarrow (\alpha-k)(\beta-k)<0$
2. Roots lie on the same side as k $\Leftrightarrow D\geq 0$ and $(\alpha-k)(\beta-k)>0$
3. Both roots are greater than k $\Leftrightarrow D\geq 0$, $(\alpha-k)(\beta-k)>0$ and $\alpha+\beta>2k$
4. Both roots are smaller than k $\Leftrightarrow D\geq 0$, $(\alpha-k)(\beta-k)>0$ and $\alpha+\beta<2k$

Note that $f(x)=a(x-a)(x-\beta)\Rightarrow(\alpha-k)(\beta-k)=f(k)/a$

EXERCISES

1. The roots of the equation $(p^2-r^2)x^2-(r^2-q^2)x+(q^2-p^2)=0$ are:

(a) $\frac{p^2-q^2}{p^2-r^2}$ (b) $\frac{p^2+q^2}{p^2-r^2}$

(c) $\frac{p^2-q^2}{p^2+r^2}$ (d) -1

2. If $\alpha \neq \beta$, but $\alpha^2 = 5\alpha - 3$ and $\beta^2 = 5\beta - 3$, then the equation whose roots are $\frac{\alpha}{\beta}, \frac{\beta}{\alpha}$ is:

(a) $3x^2-5x+3=0$ (b) $5x^2-3x+5=0$

(c) $3x^2-19x+3=0$ (d) $5x^2-11x+5=0$

3. The difference between the roots for the equations $x^2+ax+b=0$ and $x^2+bx+a=0$ is equal. If $a \neq b$, then:

(a) $a+b+4=0$ (b) $a+b-4=0$

(c) $a-b-4=0$ (d) $a-b+4=0$

4. If the equation $(3x)^2+\left(27\cdot 3^{\frac{1}{k}}-15\right)x+4=0$ has real roots, then k lies in the interval:

(a) $k \leq \frac{1}{2}$ or $k \geq 1$ (b) $k \geq \frac{-1}{2}, k \neq 0$

(c) $k<0$ or $k \geq \frac{1}{2}$ (d) $k \leq -1$ or $k \geq \frac{1}{2}$

5. If $1-p$ is a root of the equation $x^2+px+1-p=0$, then its roots are:

(a) $\frac{1}{2}, 1$ (b) $\frac{-1}{2}, 0$

(c) $0, \frac{1}{2}$ (d) $-1, 0$

6. If the equations $x^2+2x+3=0$ and $ax^2+bx+c=0$ have a common root, then the ratio $a:b:c$ equals:

(a) $1:3:2$ (b) $3:1:2$

(c) $1:2:3$ (d) $3:2:1$

7. If for a positive integer n, the quadratic equation $x(x+1)+(x+1)(x+2)+\ldots+(x+n-1)(x+n)=10n$ has two consecutive integral solutions, then n equals:

(a) 9 (b) 10

(c) 11 (d) 12

8. If α, β are the roots of $x^2+px+q=0$ and γ, δ are the roots of $x^2+px-r=0$, then the value of $\frac{\alpha-\gamma}{\beta-\gamma}\cdot\frac{\alpha-\delta}{\beta-\delta}$ is:

(a) 1 (b) -1

(c) $\frac{q+r}{p+r}$ (d) $\frac{q-r}{p-r}$

9. The sum of the squares of the roots of the equation $x^2+(2-k)x+3-k=0$ will be least for k equal to:

(a) -1 (b) 0

(c) 1 (d) -3

10. Both roots of $(x-b)(x-c)+(x-c)(x-a)+(x-a)(x-b)=0$ are always:

(a) Positive (b) Negative

(c) Distinct (d) Real

11. If α, β are the roots of $(x-a)(x-b)-c=0$, then the roots of $(x-\alpha)(x-\beta)+c=0$ are:

(a) a, b (b) $a-b, ab$

(c) $a+b, a-b$ (d) $a+b, ab$

12. Consider the equation $px^2+qx+1=0$, where $p, q \in \{1, 2, 3, 4\}$. The number of such equations having real roots that can be formed is:

(a) 7 (b) 8

(c) 9 (d) 10

13. If the roots of the equation $x^2-2ax+a^2+a-3=0$ are less than 3, then the interval in which a lies is:

(a) $a>4$ (b) $a<2$

(c) $2 \leq a \leq 3$ (d) $1 \leq a \leq 2$

14. If $\alpha, \beta\ (\alpha<\beta)$ are the roots of the equation $x^2+bx+c=0$, where $c<0<b$, then:

(a) $0<\alpha<\beta$ (b) $\alpha<0<\beta<|\alpha|$

(c) $\alpha<\beta<0$ (d) $\alpha<0<|\alpha|<\beta$

15. If $b > a$, then the equation $(x-a)(x-b)-1=0$ has:

(a) Both roots in (a, b)

(b) Both roots in $(-\infty, a)$

(c) Both roots in $(b, +\infty)$

(d) No root in (a, b)

16. Consider the quadratic function $f(x) = ax^2 + bx + c$, where $a, b, c \in \mathbf{R}$. If $(a+b+c)c < 0$, then the equation $f(x)=0$ has:

(a) One root, definitely negative
(b) Distinct and real roots
(c) Imaginary roots
(d) One root, definitely positive

17. If α, β are the roots of $ax^2+bx+c=0, (a, b, c \in \mathbf{R})$ such that $\alpha < -1$ and $\beta > 1$, then the correct statements from the following are:

(a) $1+\frac{c}{a}+\left|\frac{b}{a}\right|>0$

(b) $1+\frac{c}{a}-\left|\frac{b}{a}\right|>0$

(c) $1+\frac{c}{a}+\left|\frac{b}{a}\right|<0$

(d) $1+\frac{c}{a}-\left|\frac{b}{a}\right|<0$

18. If the equation $x^2-(a-b)x+1-a-b=0, (a, b \in \mathbf{R})$ has distinct real roots for all real values of b, then the interval in which a lies is:

(a) $a > 0$ (b) $a > 1$
(c) $0 < a < 1$ (d) $a\langle 0$ or $a\rangle 1$

19. If $f(x) = ax^2+bx+c$ and $g(x) = -ax^2+dx+c$, $(ac \neq 0)$, then the equation $f(x)g(x)=0$ has:

(a) No real roots
(b) Exactly four real roots
(c) Exactly two real roots
(d) At least two real roots

20. If the equations $x^2+ax+b=0$ and $x^2+bx+a=0$, $(a \neq b)$, have a common root, then the value of $a+b$ is equal to:

(a) –1 (b) 0
(c) 1 (d) 2

21. If $x+y+\frac{x}{y}=\frac{1}{2}$ and $(x+y)\frac{x}{y}=\frac{-1}{2}, (x, y<0)$, then $8(x^2+y^2)$ equals:

(a) 1 (b) 2
(c) 3 (d) 4

22. If α, β are the roots of $x^2-px+r=0$ and $\frac{\alpha}{2}, 2\beta$ are the roots of $x^2-qx+r=0$, then r equals:

(a) $\frac{2}{3}(2p+q)(2q-p)$

(b) $\frac{2}{3}(2p-q)(2q+p)$

(c) $\frac{2}{9}(2p-q)(2q-p)$

(d) $\frac{1}{9}(2p+q)(2q+p)$

23. If $a+b+c=0$, then for any $a, b, c \in \mathbf{R}$, the equation $4ax^2+3bx+2c=0$:

(a) Has identical real roots
(b) Has distinct real roots
(c) Has imaginary roots
(d) Has rational roots

24. If α, β are the roots of $ax^2+bx+c=0$ $(a, b, c \in \mathbf{R}$ and $a \neq 0)$, then the roots of $a^3x^2+abcx+c^3=0$ are:

(a) $\alpha^2+\beta^2, \alpha\beta$

(b) $\alpha^2\beta, \beta^2\alpha$

(c) $\frac{\alpha^3}{\beta}, \frac{\beta^3}{\alpha}$

(d) α^3, β^3

25. For the equation $3x^2+px+3=0, (p>0)$, if one root is the square of the other, then p equals:

(a) –6 (b) –3
(c) 1 (d) 3

26. The equation $\sqrt{x+1}-\sqrt{x-1}=\sqrt{4x-1}$ has:

(a) No solution
(b) One solution
(c) Two solutions
(d) More than two solutions

27. If p, q, r are three positive numbers in arithmetic progression (AP), the roots of $px^2+qx+r=0$ are real for:

(a) $\left|\frac{r}{p}-7\right| \geq 4\sqrt{3}$ (b) $\left|\frac{r}{p}-7\right| \leq \sqrt{3}$

(c) $1 \leq \left|\frac{r}{p}-7\right| \leq \sqrt{3}$ (d) No values of r and p

28. If α, β are the roots of $ax^2+bx+c=0$ such that $\alpha+\beta=2$ and $\alpha^3+\beta^3=26$, then the value of $\left|1+\frac{b}{a}+\frac{c}{a}\right|$ is:

(a) 1 (b) 2

(c) 3 (d) 4

29. Consider a quadratic equation which remains unchanged even when its roots are squared. The number of such quadratic equations is:

(a) 1 (b) 2

(c) 3 (d) 4

30. Product of the real roots of the equation $2\left|\sqrt{x}-3\right|+\sqrt{x}\left(\sqrt{x}-6\right)+6=0$ is:

(a) Does not exist (b) 8

(c) 32 (d) 64

31. If the roots of the equation $bx^2+cx+a=0$ are imaginary, then for all real values of x, the value of the function $f(x)=3b^2x^2+6bcx+2c^2$ is:

(a) Less than $4ab$

(b) Greater than $4ab$

(c) Less than $-4ab$

(d) Greater than $-4ab$

32. Let α, β $(\alpha > \beta)$ be the roots of $x^2-6x-2=0$. If $a_n=\alpha^n-\beta^n$ $(n \geq 1)$, then the value of $\frac{a_{10}-2a_8}{2a_9}$ is:

(a) 1 (b) 2

(c) 3 (d) 4

33. Let α, β be the roots of $375x^2-25x-2=0$. If $a_n=\alpha^n+\beta^n$, then the value of $\lim_{n\to\infty}\sum_{1}^{n} a_n$ is:

(a) $\frac{25}{298}$ (b) $\frac{9}{158}$

(c) $\frac{7}{114}$ (d) $\frac{29}{348}$

34. Let α, β be the roots of $x^2-x-1=0$. Let $a_n=p\alpha^n+q\beta^n$, where p, q are integers and $n \in \mathbf{N}$. If $a_4=28$, then $p+2q$ equals:

(a) 21 (b) 14

(c) 12 (d) 7

35. If α, β are the roots of $ax^2+bx+c=0$, then the roots of the equation $a(x-1)^2+b(x-1)(x-2)+c(x-2)^2=0$ are:

(a) $\frac{\alpha-1}{\alpha-2}, \frac{\beta-1}{\beta-2}$ (b) $\frac{2\alpha-1}{\alpha-1}, \frac{2\beta-1}{\beta-1}$

(c) $\frac{\alpha+1}{\alpha-1}, \frac{\beta+1}{\beta-1}$ (d) $\frac{3\alpha-1}{\alpha+1}, \frac{3\beta-1}{\beta+1}$

36. Let S be the set of all real numbers a such that the quadratic equation $ax^2-x+a=0$ has two distinct, real roots α, β satisfying the inequality $|\alpha-\beta|<1$. The subsets of S from the following are:

(a) $\left(\frac{-1}{2}, \frac{-1}{\sqrt{5}}\right)$ (b) $\left(\frac{-3}{2}, \frac{-1}{\sqrt{5}}\right)$

(c) $\left(\frac{1}{\sqrt{5}}, \frac{3}{2}\right)$ (d) $\left(\frac{1}{\sqrt{5}}, \frac{1}{2}\right)$

37. The product of the real roots of the equation $a^2x^2+|x|+c=0$:

(a) Is always positive

(b) Is positive for $c<0$

(c) Is negative for $c<0$

(d) Does not exist for $c>0$

38. For all $x \in \mathbf{R}$, $x^2+2ax+10-3a>0$, then the interval in which a lies is:

(a) $-5<a<2$ (b) $a<-5$

(c) $2<a<5$ (d) $a>5$

39. If one root of the equation $(a-b)x^2+ax+1=0$ is double the other, then the greatest value of b is:

(a) $2/9$ (b) $9/8$

(c) $3/4$ (d) $1/8$

40. If the equation $x(x+1)+(x+1)(x+2)+\ldots+(x+n-1)(x+n)=10n$ has two consecutive integral solutions, then the value of n is:

(a) $n=9$ (b) $n=10$

(c) $n=11$ (d) $n=12$

41. Consider the functions $f(x)=px^2+px-2$, $g(x)=x^2+(2p+1)x+p+2$ and $h(x)=2x^2+(p+q)x+2q$.

Match the conditions given in the left column with the integral values of p in the right column for which the condition is satisfied:

(a) $f(x) > g(x)$ for all real x — (p) -1

(b) $g(x) = h(x)$ has non-real roots for every real q — (q) 2

(c) $f(x) = h(x)$ has real roots for every real q — (r) No such value

42. Consider the function $f(x) = (a-1)x^2 - (a+1)x + a - 1, (a \neq 1)$. Match the conditions given in the left column with the set of values of a in the right column for which the condition is satisfied:

(a) $f(x) = 0$ has exactly one root in (0, 2) — (p) $(1, 7/3)$

(b) Both roots of $f(x) = 0$ are less than 2 — (q) $(1/3, 1) \cup (7/3, 3)$

(c) The zeros of $f(x)$ lie on opposite sides of 2 — (r) $[7/3, +\infty)$

(d) $f(x) \geq 0$ for all $x \geq 2$ — (s) $(1, 5/3)$

ANSWER KEYS

1. (a), (d) **2.** (c) **3.** (a) **4.** (b) **5.** (d) **6.** (c) **7.** (c) **8.** (a) **9.** (c) **10.** (d)
11. (a) **12.** (a) **13.** (b) **14.** (b) **15.** (d) **16.** (b), (d) **17.** (c), (d) **18.** (b) **19.** (d) **20.** (a)
21. (a) **22.** (c) **23.** (b) **24.** (b) **25.** (d) **26.** (a) **27.** (a) **28.** (d) **29.** (d) **30.** (b), (d)
31. (d) **32.** (c) **33.** (d) **34.** (c) **35.** (b) **36.** (a), (d) **37.** (c), (d) **38.** (a) **39.** (b)
40. (c) **41.** (a)-(r), (b)-(r), (c)-(q) **42.** (a)-(p), (b)-(q), (c)-(p), (d)-(r)

SOLUTIONS

1. (a), (d) The coefficient of x can be written as $r^2 - q^2 = p^2 - r^2 + q^2 - p^2$. The quadratic equation can now be written as

$$(x+1)\left\{\left(p^2 - r^2\right)x + q^2 - p^2\right\} = 0$$

$$\Rightarrow \quad x = -1, \frac{p^2 - q^2}{p^2 - r^2}$$

2. (c) According to the given condition, α, β are the roots of $x^2 - 5x + 3 = 0$. Then

$$\frac{\alpha}{\beta} + \frac{\beta}{\alpha} = \frac{\alpha^2 + \beta^2}{\alpha\beta} = \frac{(\alpha+\beta)^2 - 2\alpha\beta}{\alpha\beta} = \frac{5^2 - 6}{3} = \frac{19}{3}$$

and $$\frac{\alpha}{\beta} \cdot \frac{\beta}{\alpha} = 1$$

Hence, the required quadratic equation is

$$x^2 - \left(\frac{\alpha}{\beta} + \frac{\beta}{\alpha}\right)x + \frac{\alpha}{\beta} \cdot \frac{\beta}{\alpha} = 0$$

$$\Rightarrow \quad x^2 - \frac{19}{3}x + 1 = 0$$

$$\Rightarrow \quad 3x^2 - 19x + 3 = 0 = 0$$

3. (a) If α, β are the roots of $x^2 + ax + b = 0$, then

$$|\alpha - \beta| = \frac{\sqrt{D}}{|a|} = \sqrt{a^2 - 4b}$$

If γ, δ are the roots of $x^2 + bx + a = 0$, then

$$|\gamma - \delta| = \frac{\sqrt{D}}{|a|} = \sqrt{b^2 - 4a}$$

They are given to be equal. Hence

$$a^2 - 4b = b^2 - 4a$$

$$\Rightarrow \quad a^2 - b^2 + 4(a-b) = 0$$

$$\Rightarrow \quad (a-b)(a+b+4) = 0$$

$$\Rightarrow \quad a + b + 4 = 0 \ [a \neq b, \text{given}]$$

4. (b) For real roots, $D \geq 0$. Hence, we have

$$\left(27 \cdot 3^{\frac{1}{k}} - 15\right)^2 \geq 4 \cdot 9 \cdot 4 = 12^2$$

$$\Rightarrow \quad 3^{3+\frac{1}{k}} - 15 \leq -12 \text{ or } 3^{3+\frac{1}{k}} - 15 \geq 12$$

$$\Rightarrow \quad 3^{3+\frac{1}{k}} \leq 3 \text{ or } 3^{3+\frac{1}{k}} \geq 3^3$$

$\Rightarrow \quad 3+\frac{1}{k}\le 1$ or $3+\frac{1}{k}\ge 3$

$\Rightarrow \quad \frac{1}{k}\le -2$ or $\frac{1}{k}\ge 0$

$\Rightarrow \quad \frac{1}{k}\le -2$ or $\frac{1}{k}\ge 0$

$\Rightarrow \quad \frac{2k+1}{k}\le 0$ or $k>0$

$\Rightarrow \quad \frac{-1}{2}\le k\langle 0 \text{ or } k\rangle 0 \Rightarrow k\ge \frac{-1}{2}, k\ne 0.$

5. (d) If $1-p$ is a root of the equation $x^2+px+1-p=0$, then

$$(1-p)^2+p(1-p)+1-p=0$$

$\Rightarrow \quad 2(1-p)=0 \Rightarrow p=1$

The quadratic equation reduces to

$$x^2+x=0$$

$\Rightarrow \quad x=-1, 0$

6. (c) The equation $x^2+2x+3=0$ has imaginary roots. Hence, if one root is common, then the other root, which is the conjugate of the first root, will also be common. This is possible only if the two equations are identical. Hence, we have

$$a:b:c=1:2:3.$$

7. (a) The given equation can be written as

$$\sum_1^n (x+n-1)(x+n)=10n$$

$\Rightarrow \quad \sum_1^n \left(x^2+(2n-1)x+n^2-n\right)=10n$

$\Rightarrow \quad nx^2+\sum_1^n (2n-1)x+\sum_1^n \left(n^2-n\right)=10n$

$\Rightarrow \quad nx^2+\{n(n+1)-n\}x + \left\{\frac{n(n+1)(2n+1)}{6}-\frac{n(n+1)}{2}\right\}=10n$

$\Rightarrow \quad nx^2+n^2x+\frac{1}{3}n\left(n^2-1\right)=10n$

$\Rightarrow \quad 3x^2+3nx+n^2-31=0$

If the roots are consecutive integers, then the difference between them equals 1.

$\Rightarrow \quad \frac{\sqrt{D}}{|a|}=1$

$\Rightarrow \quad \sqrt{9n^2-12\left(n^2-31\right)}=3$

$\Rightarrow \quad n^2=121$ gives $n=11$

8. (a) We have

$$\alpha+\beta=-p \text{ and } \gamma+\delta=-p$$

Subtracting the two equations, we have

$\Rightarrow \quad \alpha+\beta-\gamma-\delta=0$

$\Rightarrow \quad \frac{\alpha-\gamma}{\beta-\delta}=-1$ and also $\frac{\alpha-\delta}{\beta-\gamma}=-1.$

Hence $\frac{\alpha-\gamma}{\beta-\gamma}\cdot\frac{\alpha-\delta}{\beta-\delta}=1.$

9. (c) If α, β be the roots, then

$$\alpha^2+\beta^2=(\alpha+\beta)^2-2\alpha\beta$$
$$=(2-k)^2-2(3-k)$$
$$=k^2-2k-2=(k-1)^2-3,$$

whose least value occurs at $k=1$.

10. (d) The quadratic equation can be written as

$$3x^2-2(a+b+c)x+ab+bc+ca=0.$$

The discriminant is

$$D=4\left[(a+b+c)^2-3(ab+bc+ca)\right]$$
$$=4\left[a^2+b^2+c^2-ab-bc-ca\right]$$
$$=2\left[(a-b)^2+(b-c)^2+(c-a)^2\right]$$

Since $D\ge 0$, the roots are always real. However, nothing can be said about their sign as that depends on the values of a, b, c.

11. (a) The quadratic equation can be written as

$$x^2-(a+b)x+ab-c=0$$

Then $\alpha+\beta=a+b$ and $\alpha\beta=ab-c$

The other quadratic equation now reduces to

$$x^2-(\alpha+\beta)x+\alpha\beta+c=0$$

$\Rightarrow \quad x^2-(a+b)x+ab=0$

$\Rightarrow \quad x=a, b$

12. (a) For real roots, $D\ge 0 \Rightarrow q^2\ge 4p$. Hence, the acceptable pairs (p, q) are

$$(1,2), (1,3), (1,4), (2,3), (2,4), (3,4), (4,4)$$

Hence, we have a total of 7 choices.

13. (b) If the roots are less than 3, then $D \geq 0$, $f(3)/a > 0$, and $\alpha + \beta < 6$.
Thus, we have

$$4a^2 - 4(a^2 + a - 3) \geq 0 \Rightarrow a \leq 3$$

$$9 - 6a + a^2 + a - 3 > 0 \Rightarrow a^2 - 5a + 6 > 0$$

$$\Rightarrow a\langle 2 \text{ or } a\rangle 3$$

and $\quad 2a < 6 \Rightarrow a < 3$

Taking the intersection of all the inequalities, we have $a < 2$.

14. (b) We have

$$\alpha + \beta = -b < 0 \text{ and } \alpha\beta = c < 0$$

$\Rightarrow$ Roots are of opposite signs

$\Rightarrow$ $\alpha\langle 0$ and $\beta\rangle 0$

The abscissa of the vertex of the parabola is $x = \dfrac{-b}{2} < 0$

$\Rightarrow$ Vertex lies to the left of the y-axis. Hence, α lies farther away from the origin than $\beta \Rightarrow |\alpha| > |\beta| = \beta$.

15. (d) Let $f(x) = (x-a)(x-b) - 1$

$$= x^2 - (a+b)x + ab - 1$$

The coefficient of x^2 is +ve, which means that the graph of $f(x)$ is a parabola whose concavity is upward. The axis of the parabola is $x = \dfrac{a+b}{2}$, $f(b) < 0$. From this data, we can observe (see figure) that the roots of the equation lie outside the interval (a, b).

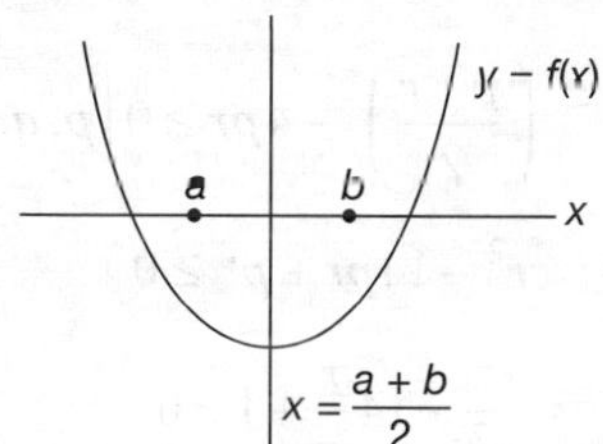

16. (b), (d) We have

$$(a+b+c)c < 0$$

$\Rightarrow$ $f(1)f(0) < 0$

$\Rightarrow$ $f(0)$ and $f(1)$ are of opposite signs

$\Rightarrow$ $f(x)$ cuts the x-axis exactly once at $(0, 1)$

If one root is real, the other root will also be real since imaginary roots always occur in pairs.

17. (c), (d) Let $f(x) = ax^2 + bx + c$.

Roots lie on opposite sides of -1. Hence

$$\frac{f(-1)}{a} < 0 \Rightarrow 1 - \frac{b}{a} + \frac{c}{a} < 0$$

Roots lie on opposite sides of 1. Hence

$$\frac{f(1)}{a} < 0 \Rightarrow 1 + \frac{b}{a} + \frac{c}{a} < 0$$

For both inequalities to be true, we have

$$\Rightarrow \quad \left(1 - \frac{b}{a} + \frac{c}{a}\right)\left(1 + \frac{b}{a} + \frac{c}{a}\right) > 0$$

$$\Rightarrow \quad \left(1 + \frac{c}{a}\right)^2 - \left(\frac{b}{a}\right)^2 > 0$$

$$\Rightarrow \quad \left(1 + \frac{c}{a}\right)^2 > \left(\frac{b}{a}\right)^2$$

$$\Rightarrow \quad \left|1 + \frac{c}{a}\right| > \left|\frac{b}{a}\right|$$

Since both roots are less than -1, their product c/a will be less than -1.

$\Rightarrow$ $1 + \dfrac{c}{a}$ is a negative number.

The above inequality then reduces to

$$-\left(1 + \frac{c}{a}\right) > \left|\frac{b}{a}\right|$$

$$\Rightarrow \quad 1 + \frac{c}{a} + \left|\frac{b}{a}\right| < 0$$

Also, note that

$1 + \dfrac{c}{a} - \left|\dfrac{b}{a}\right| < 0$ (Sum of two negative numbers is negative) $\Rightarrow$ (d) is correct.

18. (b) This is possible if $D > 0$ for all real b. Thus, we have

$$(a-b)^2 - 4(1-a-b) > 0 \text{ for all real } b$$

$$\Rightarrow \quad b^2 - 2(a-2)b + a^2 + 4a - 4 > 0 \text{ for all real } b$$

The above inequality will be true if

$$4(a-2)^2 - 4(a^2 + 4a - 4) < 0$$

$$\Rightarrow \quad -2a + 2 < 0$$

$$\Rightarrow \quad a > 1$$

19. (d) The roots are

$$x = \frac{-b \pm \sqrt{b^2 - 4ac}}{2a}, \frac{-d \pm \sqrt{d^2 + 4ac}}{-2a}$$

We see that whatever be the sign of ac, at least one of the discriminants will be positive. Hence, the equation has at least two real roots.

20. (a) Solving the two equations simultaneously, we have

$$x^2 + ax + b = x^2 + bx + a$$

$$\Rightarrow x = 1$$

Now putting $x = 1$ in any one of the given quadratic equations, we have

$$a + b = -1$$

21. (a) Eliminating $x + y$, we have

$$2\left(\frac{x}{y}\right)^2 - \frac{x}{y} - 1 = 0$$

$$\Rightarrow \quad \frac{x}{y} = \frac{-1}{2}, 1$$

$$\Rightarrow \quad \frac{x}{y} = 1 \, [x, y < 0, \text{given}]$$

$$\Rightarrow \quad x = y$$

Then $x + y = \frac{-1}{2}$. Now solving these two equations gives $x = y = \frac{-1}{4}$. Hence, we have $8(x^2 + y^2) = 1$.

22. (c) We have

$$\alpha + \beta = p \text{ and } \frac{\alpha}{2} + 2\beta = q$$

Solving, we have $\alpha = \frac{2}{3}(2p - q)$ and $\beta = \frac{1}{3}(2q - p)$.

Hence, we have

$$r = \alpha\beta = \frac{2}{9}(2p - q)(2q - p)$$

23. (b) The discriminant is

$$D = 9b^2 - 32ac = 9(a + c)^2 - 32ac$$

$$= 9a^2 - 14ac + 9c^2$$

$$= c^2\left[9\frac{a^2}{c^2} - 14\frac{a}{c} + 9\right],$$

which is positive since the coefficient of $\frac{a^2}{c^2}$ is positive and the discriminant $= 14^2 - 4 \times 81$ is negative; hence, real and distinct roots.

24. (b) We have

$$\alpha + \beta = \frac{-b}{a} \text{ and } \alpha\beta = \frac{c}{a}$$

Let γ, δ be the roots of the other equation. Then, we have

$$\gamma + \delta = \frac{-bc}{a^2} \text{ and } \gamma\delta = \frac{c^3}{a^3}$$

$$\Rightarrow \quad \gamma + \delta = (\alpha + \beta)\alpha\beta \text{ and } \gamma\delta = (\alpha\beta)^3$$

$$\Rightarrow \quad \gamma + \delta = \alpha^2\beta + \beta^2\alpha \text{ and } \gamma\delta = \alpha^2\beta \cdot \beta^2\alpha$$

Hence $\gamma = \alpha^2\beta$ and $\delta = \beta^2\alpha$.

25. (d) Let the roots be α, α^2. Then, we have

$$\alpha + \alpha^2 = \frac{-p}{3} \text{ and } \alpha^3 = 1$$

From the second equation, we have $\alpha = 1, \omega, \omega$. Putting in the first equation, we have

$$p = -3(1 + 1^2), -3(\omega + \omega^2), -3(\omega^2 + \omega^4) = -6, 3, 3.$$

26. (a) Squaring both sides, the equation reduces to

$$2x - 2\sqrt{x^2 - 1} = 4x - 1$$

$$\Rightarrow \quad -2\sqrt{x^2 - 1} = 2x - 1$$

$$\Rightarrow \quad 4(x^2 - 1) = 4x^2 - 4x + 1 \text{ [Squaring again]}$$

$$\Rightarrow \quad 4x - 5 = 0 \Rightarrow x = \frac{5}{4}$$

However, this value of x does not satisfy the given equation. Hence, no solution.

27. (a) For real roots, $D = q^2 - 4pr \geq 0$. Hence, we have

$$\left(\frac{p + r}{2}\right)^2 - 4pr \geq 0 \, [p, q, r \text{ are in AP, given}]$$

$$\Rightarrow \quad r^2 - 14pr + p^2 \geq 0$$

$$\Rightarrow \quad \frac{r^2}{p^2} - 14\frac{r}{p} + 1 \geq 0$$

$$\Rightarrow \quad \left(\frac{r}{p} - 7\right)^2 \geq 48$$

$$\Rightarrow \quad \left|\frac{r}{p} - 7\right| \geq 4\sqrt{3}$$

28. (d) We have

$$\alpha^3 + \beta^3 = 26$$

$$\Rightarrow \quad (\alpha + \beta)^3 - 3\alpha\beta(\alpha + \beta) = 26$$

$$\Rightarrow \quad 8 - 6\alpha\beta = 26 \, [\alpha + \beta = 2, \text{given}]$$

$\Rightarrow \quad \alpha\beta = -3.$

Hence, we have

$$\left|1+\frac{b}{a}+\frac{c}{a}\right| = |1-(\alpha+\beta)+\alpha\beta|$$
$$= |1-2-3| = 4.$$

29. (d) Let the roots be α, β. According to the given condition, α^2, β^2 are also its roots. Thus, we have

$$\alpha^2+\beta^2 = \alpha+\beta$$

and $\quad \alpha^2\beta^2 = \alpha\beta$

$\Rightarrow \quad (\alpha+\beta)^2-(\alpha+\beta)-2\alpha\beta = 0$

and $\quad \alpha\beta(\alpha\beta-1) = 0$

From the second equation, we have $\alpha\beta = 0, 1$. Putting these values in the first equation, we have

for $\alpha\beta = 0,\ (\alpha+\beta)^2-(\alpha+\beta) = 0 \Rightarrow \alpha+\beta = 0, 1$

for $\alpha\beta = 1,\ (\alpha+\beta)^2-(\alpha+\beta)-2 = 0 \Rightarrow \alpha+\beta = -1, 2$

A quadratic equation with roots α, β is $x^2-(\alpha+\beta)x+\alpha\beta = 0.$ Hence, the quadratic equations are $x^2 = 0, x^2-x = 0, x^2+x+1 = 0,$ and $x^2-2x+1 = 0.$

30. (d) Let $\sqrt{x}-3 = u.$ Then the given equation can be written as

$$2|u|+(u-3)(u+3)+6 = 0$$

$\Rightarrow \quad u^2+2|u|-3 = 0$

$\Rightarrow \quad |u|^2+2|u|-3 = 0$ gives $|u| = -3, 1$

The negative value is unacceptable. Hence

$$u = \pm 1$$

$\Rightarrow \quad \sqrt{x}-3 = \pm 1$

$\Rightarrow \quad \sqrt{x} = 2, 4$ gives $x = 4, 16$

Hence, the product of the real roots $= 64$.

31. (d) Roots of the equation $bx^2+cx+a = 0$ are imaginary $\Rightarrow c^2 < 4ab$. The given function can be written as

$$f(x) = 3b^2\left(x^2+\frac{2c}{b}\right)+2c^2$$

$$= 3b^2\left\{\left(x+\frac{c}{b}\right)^2-\frac{c^2}{b^2}\right\}+2c^2 = 3b^2\left(x+\frac{c}{b}\right)^2-c^2$$

$\Rightarrow f(x) \ge -c^2 > -4ab$

32. (c) We have

$$\alpha+\beta = 6 \text{ and } \alpha\beta = -2$$

Then, we have

$$\frac{a_{10}-2a_8}{2a_9} = \frac{\alpha^{10}-\beta^{10}-2\left(\alpha^8-\beta^8\right)}{2\left(\alpha^9-\beta^9\right)}$$

$$= \frac{\alpha^{10}-\beta^{10}+\alpha\beta\left(\alpha^8-\beta^8\right)}{2\left(\alpha^9-\beta^9\right)}$$

$$= \frac{\alpha^9(\alpha+\beta)-\beta^9(\alpha+\beta)}{2\left(\alpha^9-\beta^9\right)}$$

$$= \frac{\alpha+\beta}{2} = 3.$$

33. (d) We have

$$\alpha+\beta = \frac{25}{375} \text{ and } \alpha\beta = \frac{-2}{375}$$

Then $\quad \lim_{n\to\infty}\sum_{1}^{n}\left(\alpha^n+\beta^n\right) = \frac{\alpha}{1-\alpha}+\frac{\beta}{1-\beta}$

$$= \frac{\alpha+\beta-2\alpha\beta}{1-\alpha-\beta+\alpha\beta}$$

$$= \frac{\frac{25}{375}+\frac{4}{375}}{1-\frac{25}{375}-\frac{2}{375}} = \frac{29}{348}$$

34. (c) We have

$$\alpha, \beta = \frac{1\pm\sqrt{5}}{2}$$

Then $\quad p\alpha^4+q\beta^4 = p\left(\frac{1-\sqrt{5}}{2}\right)^4+q\left(\frac{1+\sqrt{5}}{2}\right)^4$

or $p\left(\frac{1+\sqrt{5}}{2}\right)^4+q\left(\frac{1-\sqrt{5}}{2}\right)^4$

$$= p\left(\frac{56-24\sqrt{5}}{16}\right)+q\left(\frac{56+24\sqrt{5}}{16}\right)$$

or $p\left(\frac{56+24\sqrt{5}}{16}\right)+q\left(\frac{56-24\sqrt{5}}{16}\right)$

$$= p\left(\frac{7-3\sqrt{5}}{2}\right)+q\left(\frac{7+3\sqrt{5}}{2}\right)$$

or $p\left(\frac{7+3\sqrt{5}}{2}\right)+q\left(\frac{7+3\sqrt{5}}{2}\right)$

$$=\frac{7}{2}(q+p)+\frac{3}{2}(q\pm p)\sqrt{5}$$

Now $\quad p\alpha^4+q\beta^4=28$

$\Rightarrow \quad \frac{7}{2}(q+p)+\frac{3}{2}(q\pm p)\sqrt{5}=28$

$\Rightarrow \quad 7(q+p)+3(q\pm p)\sqrt{5}=56$

$\Rightarrow \quad 7(q+p-8)+(q\pm p)\sqrt{5}=0$

$\Rightarrow \quad q+p-8=0$ and $q\pm p=0$, gives $q=p=4$ (Only one solution).

Hence $\quad p+2q=12$

35. (b) The given quadratic equation can be written as

$$a\left(\frac{x-1}{x-2}\right)^2+b\left(\frac{x-1}{x-2}\right)+c=0$$

Now α, β are the roots of $ax^2+bx+c=0$. Therefore, we have

$$\frac{x-1}{x-2}=\alpha, \beta$$

$$\Rightarrow \quad x=\frac{2\alpha-1}{\alpha-1}, \frac{2\beta-1}{\beta-1}$$

36. (a), (d) For distinct real roots, we have

$$1-4a^2>0 \Rightarrow |a|<\frac{1}{2}$$

Now $\quad |\alpha-\beta|<1$

$\Rightarrow \quad \frac{\sqrt{D}}{|a|}<1$

$\Rightarrow \quad \sqrt{1-4a^2}<|a|$

$\Rightarrow \quad 1-4a^2<a^2$

$\Rightarrow \quad a^2>\frac{1}{5} \Rightarrow |a|>\frac{1}{\sqrt{5}}$

Taking the intersection, we have $\frac{1}{\sqrt{5}}<|a|<\frac{1}{2}$.

37. (c), (d) The given equation can be written as

$$a^2|x|^2+|x|+c=0$$

$$\Rightarrow \quad |x|=\frac{-1\pm\sqrt{1-4a^2c}}{2a^2}=\alpha, \beta \text{(say)}$$

If $c<0$, then $\sqrt{1-4a^2c}>1 \Rightarrow \alpha\langle 0, \beta\rangle 0$. Here, there are two real solutions, $x=\pm\beta$ and the product of the real roots $=-\beta^2<0$.

If $c>0$, then $\sqrt{1-4a^2c}<1 \Rightarrow \alpha, \beta<0$. Here, there is no solution since $|x|$ cannot be negative.

38. (a) For all $x\in \mathbf{R}$, $x^2+2ax+10-3a>0$ if $D<0$

$\Rightarrow \quad 4a^2-4(10-3a)<0$

$\Rightarrow \quad a^2+3a-10<0$

$\Rightarrow \quad (a+5)(a-2)<0$

$\Rightarrow \quad -5<a<2.$

39. (b) Let the roots be $\alpha, 2\alpha$. Then, we have

$$3\alpha=\frac{-a}{a-b}, 2\alpha^2=\frac{1}{a-b}$$

Eliminating α, we have

$\Rightarrow \quad \frac{1}{9}\left(\frac{a}{a-b}\right)^2=\frac{1}{2(a-b)}$

$\Rightarrow \quad 2a^2=9(a-b)$

$\Rightarrow \quad b=\frac{-2}{9}a^2+a=\frac{-2}{9}\left[\left(a-\frac{9}{4}\right)^2-\frac{81}{16}\right]$

$$=\frac{9}{8}-\frac{2}{9}\left(a-\frac{9}{4}\right)^2\le\frac{9}{8}.$$

40. (c) Simplifying the given equation, we have

$$\sum_1^n(x+n-1)(x+n)=10n$$

$\Rightarrow \quad \sum_1^n\{x^2+(2n-1)x+n^2-n\}=10n$

$\Rightarrow \quad x^2\sum_1^n 1+x\sum_1^n(2n-1)+\sum_1^n(n^2-n)=10n$

$\Rightarrow \quad nx^2+\{n(n+1)-n\}x+\frac{n(n+1)(2n+1)}{6}-\frac{n(n+1)}{2}=10n$

$\Rightarrow \quad x^2+nx+\frac{(n+1)(2n+1-3)}{6}=10$

$\Rightarrow \quad x^2+nx+\frac{n^2-1}{3}-10=0$

$$\Rightarrow \quad x^2 + nx + \frac{n^2 - 31}{3} = 0$$

For $n = 11$, the above equation reduces to

$$x^2 + 11x + 30 = 0,$$

which has two consecutive integral solutions, $x = -6, -5$.

For the other given values of n, the equation does not give two consecutive integral solutions.

41. (a)-(r), (b)-(r), (c)-(q)

(a) We have

$$f(x) > g(x) \text{ for all real } x$$

$\Rightarrow (p-1)x^2 - (p+1)x - (p+4) > 0$ for all real x,

which is possible if $p > 1$

and $D = (p+1)^2 + 4(p-1)(p+4) < 0$

$$\Rightarrow \quad 5p^2 + 14p - 5 < 0$$

$$\Rightarrow \quad -7 - \sqrt{54} < p < -7 + \sqrt{54}$$

There is no value of p satisfying both inequalities.

(b) We have $g(x) = h(x)$ has non-real roots for every real q,

$\Rightarrow x^2 + (q-p-1)x + 2q - p - 2 = 0$ has non-real roots for every real q, which is possible if $D < 0$ for every real q

$\Rightarrow (q-p-1)^2 - 8(2q-p-2) < 0$ for every real q

$\Rightarrow q^2 - 2(p+5)q + p^2 - 2p - 7 < 0$ for every real q, which is not possible since the coefficient of q^2 is positive.

(c) We have

$f(x) = h(x)$ has real roots for every real q

$\Rightarrow$ $(p-2)x^2 - qx - 2(q+1) = 0$ has real roots for every real q, which is possible if $D \geq 0$ for every real q

$\Rightarrow$ $q^2 + 8(p-2)(q+1) \geq 0$ for every real q

$\Rightarrow$ $q^2 + 8(p-2)q + 8(p-2) \geq 0$ for every real q which is possible if

$$\Rightarrow \quad 64(p-2)^2 - 32(p-2) \leq 0$$

$$\Rightarrow \quad (p-2)(2p-5) \leq 0$$

$$\Rightarrow \quad 2 \leq p \leq \frac{5}{2}.$$

The only integer value is $p = 2$.

42. (a)-(p), (b)-(q), (c)-(p), (d)-(r)

(a) The given condition will be satisfied if $f(0)f(2) < 0$

$$\Rightarrow \quad (a-1)(3a-7) < 0$$

$$\Rightarrow \quad 1 < a < \frac{7}{3}.$$

(b) Let α, β be the two zeros of $f(x)$. The given condition will be satisfied if

$$D \geq 0$$

and $\dfrac{f(2)}{a} > 0$

and $\alpha + \beta < 4$.

Now $D \geq 0$

$$\Rightarrow \quad (a+1)^2 - 4(a-1)^2 \geq 0$$

$$\Rightarrow \quad 3a^2 - 10a + 3 \leq 0$$

$$\Rightarrow \quad \frac{1}{3} \leq a \leq 3, a \neq 1$$

and $\dfrac{f(2)}{a} > 0$

$$\Rightarrow \quad \frac{4(a-1) - 2(a+1) + a - 1}{a-1} > 0$$

$$\Rightarrow \quad \frac{3a-7}{a-1} > 0$$

$$\Rightarrow \quad a < 1$$

or $a > \dfrac{7}{3}$

and $\alpha + \beta < 4$

$$\Rightarrow \quad \frac{3a-5}{2(a-1)} > 0$$

$$\Rightarrow \quad a < 1$$

or $a > \dfrac{5}{3}$.

Taking the intersection, we have $a \in \left(\dfrac{1}{3}, 1\right) \cup \left(\dfrac{7}{3}, 3\right)$.

(c) Let α, β be the two zeros of $f(x)$. The given condition will be satisfied if $\dfrac{f(2)}{a} < 0$

$\Rightarrow \quad \frac{3a-7}{a-1} < 0$

$\Rightarrow \quad 1 < a < \frac{7}{3}.$

(d) The given condition will be satisfied if

Coefficient of $x^2 > 0$, vertex lies to the left of $x = 2$, and $f(2) \geq 0$

$\Rightarrow \quad a - 1 > 0$

and $\frac{a+1}{2(a-1)} < 2$

and $4(a-1) - 2(a+1) + a - 1 \geq 0$

$\Rightarrow \quad a > 1$

and $a\langle 1 \text{ or } a \rangle 5/3$

and $a \geq 7/3$

Taking the intersection, we have $a \in [7/3, +\infty)$.

CHAPTER

3 Sequences and Series

- **Arithmetic Progression**: A sequence of numbers $\langle a_n \rangle$ is said to be in arithmetic progression (AP) if the difference between two successive terms $a_n - a_{n-1}$ is a constant. If the first term of an AP is a, and the common difference is d, then the nth term is

$$a_n = a + (n-1)d$$

and the sum to the first n terms is

$$S_n = \frac{n}{2}\left[2a + (n-1)d\right] = n\left(\frac{\text{First term} + \text{Last term}}{2}\right)$$

Note that $a_n = S_n - S_{n-1}$.

Properties related to AP:

1. If $\langle a_n \rangle$ is in AP, then $a_r = \dfrac{a_{r-k} + a_{r+k}}{2}$ for every $0 \le k \le n - r$.
2. If $\langle a_n \rangle$ is in AP, then $\langle a_n + k \rangle$ is in AP, where k is any constant.
3. If $\langle a_n \rangle$ is in AP, then $\langle ka_n \rangle$ is in AP, where k is any constant.
4. If we have to choose a few terms in AP, we choose as follows:

$$a-d,\ a,\ a+d \text{ (three terms)}$$
$$a-3d,\ a-d,\ a+d,\ a+3d \text{ (four terms)}$$
$$a-2d,\ a-d,\ a,\ a+d,\ a+2d \text{ (five terms)}$$

- **Geometric Progression:** A sequence of numbers $\langle a_n \rangle$ is said to be in geometric progression (GP) if the ratio of two successive terms a_n / a_{n-1} is a constant. If the first term of a GP is a, and the common ratio is r, then the nth term is

$$u_n = ar^{n-1}$$

and the sum to the first n terms is

$$S_n = \frac{a\left(r^n - 1\right)}{r - 1}$$

For an infinite GP with $|r| < 1$, the sum of the series is given by

$$S_\infty - \frac{1}{1-r}$$

Properties related to GP:

1. If $\langle a_n \rangle$ is in GP, then $a_r = \sqrt{a_{r-k}a_{r+k}}$ for every $0 \le k \le n - r$.
2. If $\langle a_n \rangle$ is in GP, then $\langle 1/a_n \rangle$ is in GP.
3. If $\langle a_n \rangle$ is in GP, then $\langle ka_n \rangle$ is in GP, where k is any constant.
4. If $\langle a_n \rangle$ is in GP, then $\langle a_n^k \rangle$ is in GP, where k is any constant.
5. If $\langle a_n \rangle$ is in GP, then $\langle \log a_n \rangle$ is in AP.

6. If we have to choose a few terms in GP, we choose as follows:

$$\frac{a}{r}, a, ar \text{ (three terms)}$$

$$\frac{a}{r^3}, \frac{a}{r}, ar, ar^3 \text{ (four terms)}$$

$$\frac{a}{r^2}, \frac{a}{r}, a, ar, ar^2 \text{ (five terms)}$$

- **Harmonic Progression:** A sequence of numbers $\langle a_n \rangle$ is said to be in harmonic progression (HP) if $\langle 1/a_n \rangle$ is in AP. If the first term of an HP is a, and $\frac{1}{a_2} - \frac{1}{a_1} = d$, then the nth term is given by

$$\frac{1}{a_n} = \frac{1}{a_1} + (n-1)d$$

Properties related to HP:

1. If $\langle a_n \rangle$ is in HP, then $\frac{2}{a_r} = \frac{1}{a_{r-k}} + \frac{1}{a_{r+k}}$ for every $0 \le k \le n-r$.
2. If $\langle a_n \rangle$ is in HP, then $\langle ka_n \rangle$ is in HP, where k is any constant.
3. If we have to choose a few terms in HP, we choose as follows:

$$\frac{1}{a-d}, \frac{1}{a}, \frac{1}{a+d} \text{ (three terms)}$$

$$\frac{1}{a-3d}, \frac{1}{a-d}, \frac{1}{a+d}, \frac{1}{a+3d} \text{ (four terms)}$$

$$\frac{1}{a-3d}, \frac{1}{a-d}, \frac{1}{a}, \frac{1}{a+d}, \frac{1}{a+2d} \text{ (five terms)}$$

- **Arithmetic-Geometric Series:** If $\langle a_n \rangle$ is in AP and $\langle b_n \rangle$ is in GP, then $\langle a_n b_n \rangle$ is an arithmetic-geometric sequence. The series has the form

$$S = ab + (a+d)br + (a+2d)br^2 + \ldots + \{a+(n-1)d\}br^{n-1}$$

To find the value of S, we obtain an equation by multiplying the above equation throughout by r and then subtracting the two equations

$$(1-r)S = ab + dbr + dbr^2 + \ldots + dbr^{n-1} - \{a+(n-1)d\}br^n$$

$$\Rightarrow \quad S = \frac{ab}{1-r} + \frac{dbr(1-r^{n-1})}{(1-r)^2} - \frac{\{a+(n-1)d\}br^n}{1-r}$$

- **Arithmetic, Geometric and Harmonic Means:** For any two positive numbers a and b, the n arithmetic means, the n geometric means and the n harmonic means are, respectively,

$$A_1 = a+d,\ A_2 = a+2d, \ldots, A_n = a+nd, \text{ where } d = \frac{b-a}{n+1}$$

$$G_1 = ar,\ G_2 = ar^2, \ldots, G_n = ar^n, \text{ where } r = \left(\frac{b}{a}\right)^{\frac{1}{n+1}}$$

$$\frac{1}{H_1} = \frac{1}{a} + d,\ \frac{1}{H_2} = \frac{1}{a} + 2d, \ldots, \frac{1}{H_n} = \frac{1}{a} + nd, \text{ where } d = \frac{1/b - 1/a}{n+1}$$

We can see that $A_1 + A_2 + \ldots + A_n = n\left(\frac{a+b}{2}\right)$, $G_1G_2 \ldots G_n = (ab)^{n/2}$ and $\frac{1}{H_1} + \frac{1}{H_2} + \ldots + \frac{1}{H_n} = n\left(\frac{1/a + 1/b}{2}\right)$.

For any two positive numbers a and b, the arithmetic mean A, geometric mean G and harmonic mean H are, respectively,

$$A = \frac{a+b}{2},\ G = \sqrt{ab} \text{ and } H = \frac{2ab}{a+b}$$

We can see that $G^2 = AH$ and $A \geq G \geq H$.

For n positive numbers $a_1, a_2, \ldots, a_n$, the arithmetic mean A, geometric mean G and harmonic mean H are, respectively,

$$A = \frac{a_1 + a_2 + \ldots + a_n}{n},\ G = \sqrt[n]{a_1 a_2 \cdots a_n} \text{ and } H = \frac{n}{\frac{1}{a_1} + \frac{1}{a_2} + \ldots + \frac{1}{a_n}}$$

In this case too, the inequality $A \geq G \geq H$ holds true.

- **Some Useful Series**

1. Sum of the first n natural numbers: $\sum_1^n n = \frac{n(n+1)}{2}$.
2. Sum of the squares of the first n natural numbers: $\sum_1^n n^2 = \frac{n(n+1)(2n+1)}{6}$.
3. Sum of the cubes of the first n natural numbers: $\sum_1^n n^3 = \frac{n^2(n+1)^2}{4}$.

EXERCISES

1. If the positive numbers a, b, c, d are in AP, then abc, abd, acd, bcd are in:

(a) AP (b) GP
(c) HP (d) None of these

2. If $\frac{1}{a_1}, \frac{1}{a_2}, \ldots, \frac{1}{a_n}$ are in AP, then the sum $a_1a_2 + a_2a_3 + \ldots + a_{n-1}a_n$ equals:

(a) $(n-1)a_1a_n$ (b) na_1a_n
(c) $(n-1)(a_1 - a_n)$ (d) $n(a_1 - a_n)$

3. An infinite GP has first term x and sum 5. Then:

(a) $x < -10$ (b) $-10 < x < 0$
(c) $0 < x < 10$ (d) $x > 10$

4. Let α, β be the roots of $ax^2 + bx + c = 0$ and D be its discriminant. If $\alpha + \beta, \alpha^2 + \beta^2, \alpha^3 + \beta^3$ are in GP, then:

(a) $cD = 0$ (b) $bc = 0$
(c) $bD = 0$ (d) $D \neq 0$

5. Suppose a, b, c are in AP and a^2, b^2, c^2 are in GP. If $a < b < c$ and $a + b + c = \frac{3}{2}$, then the value of a is:

(a) $\frac{1}{2} - \frac{1}{\sqrt{2}}$ (b) $\frac{3}{\sqrt{2}}$
(c) $\frac{1}{2\sqrt{2}}$ (d) $\frac{1}{2\sqrt{3}}$

6. Let $S_1, S_2, \ldots, S_n$ be squares such that for each $n \geq 1$, the length of a side of S_n equals the length of the diagonal of S_{n+1}. If the length of a side of S_1 is 10 cm, the values of n for which the area of S_n is less than 1 sq. cm is:

(a) 6 (b) 7
(c) 8 (d) 9

7. The first and the $(2n-1)^{\text{th}}$ terms of an AP, a GP and an HP are equal. If their n^{th} terms are A, B, C, respectively, then:

(a) $A \leq B \leq C$ (b) $A \geq B \geq C$
(c) $A + C = B$ (d) $AC - B^2 = 0$

8. For $0 < \theta < \frac{\pi}{2}$ if $x = \sum_0^\infty \cos^{2n}\theta$, $y = \sum_0^\infty \sin^{2n}\theta$ and $z = \sum_0^\infty \sin^{2n}\theta\cos^{2n}\theta$, then:

(a) $xyz = xz + y$ (b) $xyz = xy + z$
(c) $xyz = yz + x$ (d) $xyz = x + y + z$

9. The harmonic mean of two positive real numbers a and b is 4. If p is a real number such that a, 5, p, b form an arithmetic sequence, then $|p - a|$ equals:

(a) 2 (b) 3
(c) 4 (d) 5

10. Let S_n, S_n' denote the sum to n terms of two different APs and a_n, a_n' denote their respective n^{th} terms. If $\frac{S_n}{S_n'} = \frac{3n+8}{7n+15}$, then $\frac{a_n}{a_n'}$ equals:

(a) $\frac{6n+5}{14n+8}$ (b) $\frac{5n+6}{8n+14}$
(c) $\frac{14n+8}{6n+5}$ (d) $\frac{5n+6}{8n+14}$

11. All the terms of an arithmetic sequence are natural numbers. If the ratio of the sum of the first seven terms to the sum of the first eleven terms is 6 : 11 and the seventh term lies between 110 and 130, the common difference of the AP is:

(a) 8 (b) 7
(c) 5 (d) 3

12. The sum of the first n terms of the series $1^2 + 2 \cdot 2^2 + 3^2 + 2 \cdot 4^2 + 5^2 + 2 \cdot 6^2 + \ldots$ is $\frac{n(n+1)^2}{2}$ when n is even. When n is odd, the sum is:

(a) $\frac{n^2(n-1)}{2}$ (b) $\frac{n(n-1)^2}{2}$
(c) $\frac{n^2(n+1)}{2}$ (d) $\frac{n(n^2-1)}{2}$

13. If the harmonic mean and geometric mean of two positive numbers is in the ratio 4 : 5, then the two numbers are in the ratio:

(a) 1 : 4 (b) 4 : 1
(c) 2 : 3 (d) 3 : 2

14. For any odd integer $n \geq 1$, the sum of the series $n^3 - (n-1)^3 + (n-2)^3 - \ldots + (-1)^{n-1} 1^3$ is:

(a) $\frac{1}{4}(n-1)^2(2n+1)$ (b) $\frac{1}{4}(n+1)^2(2n-1)$
(c) $\frac{1}{4}(n-1)^2(n-2)$ (d) $\frac{1}{4}(n+1)^2(n-2)$

15. If $T = \{3, 11, 19, \ldots, 451, 459, 467\}$ and S is a subset of T such that the sum of no two elements of S is 470, then the maximum number of elements in S is:

(a) 28 (b) 29
(c) 30 (d) 31

16. Let p, q be the roots of the equation $x^2 - 2x + A = 0$ and r, s be the roots of the equation $x^2 - 18x + B = 0$. If $p < q < r < s$ are in AP, then:

(a) $A = 5, B = 56$ (b) $A = 7, B = 84$
(c) $A = -3, B = 77$ (d) $A = -2, B = 64$

17. Let $b_i > 1$ for $i = 1, 2, \ldots, 101$. Suppose $\ln b_1, \ln b_2, \ldots \ln b_{101}$ are in AP with common difference $\ln 2$. Suppose $a_1, a_2, \ldots a_{101}$ are in AP such that $a_1 = b_1$ and $a_{51} = b_{51}$. If $T = \sum_1^{51} b_i$ and $S = \sum_1^{51} a_i$, then:

(a) $S > T$ and $a_{101} > b_{101}$
(b) $S > T$ and $a_{101} < b_{101}$
(c) $S < T$ and $a_{101} > b_{101}$
(d) $S < T$ and $a_{101} < b_{101}$

18. If the sum of the first n terms of an AP is cn^2, then the sum of the squares of these n terms is:

(a) $\frac{n(4n^2-1)c^2}{6}$ (b) $\frac{n(4n^2+1)c^2}{3}$
(c) $\frac{n(4n^2-1)c^2}{3}$ (d) $\frac{n(4n^2+1)c^2}{6}$

19. The 288th alphabet of the sequence $a, b, b, c, c, c, d, d, d, d, e, e, e, e, e, \ldots$ is:

(a) w (b) x
(c) y (d) z

20. If $\frac{1}{1^4}+\frac{1}{2^4}+\frac{1}{3^4}+\ldots\infty=\frac{\pi^4}{90}$, then $\frac{1}{1^4}+\frac{1}{3^4}+\frac{1}{5^4}+\ldots\infty$ equals:

(a) $\frac{\pi^4}{96}$ (b) $\frac{\pi^4}{46}$

(c) $\frac{\pi^4}{25}$ (d) $\frac{\pi^4}{5}$

21. The number of terms in an AP is even. The sum of the odd terms is 24, and the sum of the even terms is 33. If the last term is 21/2, then the total number of terms is:

(a) 18 (b) 20

(c) 22 (d) 32

22. If a, b, c, d are in GP such that their sum is 60 and the arithmetic mean of a, d is 18, then the value of bc is:

(a) 86 (b) 102

(c) 128 (d) 142

23. The sum of the first 50 common terms of 15, 19, 23, ... and 14, 19, 24, ... is:

(a) 26620 (b) 25450

(c) 18750 (d) 14870

24. Let S_n denote the sum to n terms of an AP whose first term is 3. For any integer $n(1\le n\le 20)$, if $\frac{S_{5n}}{S_n}$ is constant, then the second term of the series is:

(a) 6 (b) 7

(c) 8 (d) 9

25. A thief running at a uniform speed of 100 m/min crosses a police station at time $t=0$. One minute later, a policeman starts chasing the thief with an initial speed of 100 m/min and increases his speed by 10 m/min after each minute. The time when he will catch up with the thief is:

(a) 4 min (b) 5 min

(c) 6 min (d) 7 min

26. A person is to count 4500 currency notes. Let a_n denote the number of currency notes he counts in n minutes. If $a_1=a_2=\ldots=a_{10}=150$ and $a_{10}, a_{11}, \ldots$ are in AP with common difference –2, then the time taken to count all the notes is:

(a) 14 min (b) 20 min

(c) 24 min (d) 34 min

27. Let $a_1, a_2, \ldots, a_{11}$ be real numbers satisfying $a_1=15, 27-2a_2>0$ and $a_{k+2}=2a_{k+1}-a_k$ for $1\le k\le 9$. If $\frac{a_1^2+a_2^2+\ldots+a_{11}^2}{11}=90$, then the value of $\frac{a_1+a_2+\ldots+a_{11}}{11}$ is:

(a) 0 (b) 9

(c) 11 (d) 99

28. Let $a_1, a_2, \ldots, a_n$ be an arithmetic sequence. Let $S=\sum_1^{30} a_i$ and $S=\sum_1^{15} a_{2i-1}$. If $S-2T=75$ and $a_5=27$, then a_{10} equals:

(a) 47 (b) 42

(c) 57 (d) 52

29. The sum to 10 terms of the series $\frac{1^3}{1}+\frac{1^3+2^3}{1+3}+\frac{1^3+2^3+3^3}{1+3+5}+\ldots$ is:

(a) $\frac{505}{4}$ (b) $\frac{303}{5}$

(c) $\frac{707}{6}$ (d) $\frac{808}{7}$

30. Let A be the first 20 terms and B be the sum of the first 40 terms of the series $1^2+2\cdot2^2+3^2+2\cdot4^2+5^2+2\cdot6^2+\ldots$. If $B-2A=100m$, then the value of m is:

(a) 232 (b) 248

(c) 264 (d) 296

31. The sum of the products of all possible pairs of the first n natural numbers is:

(a) $\frac{n^2(n-1)(4n-1)}{18}$

(b) $\frac{n(n^2-2)(5n-4)}{21}$

(c) $\frac{n(n^2+1)(4n-1)}{30}$

(d) $\frac{n(n^2-1)(3n+2)}{24}$

32. Let $a_1, a_2, \ldots, a_n$ be in AP such that $\sum_0^{12} a_{4k+1}=416$ and $a_9+a_{43}=66$. If $\sum_1^{17} a_k^2=140m$, then the value of m is:

(a) 33 (b) 34

(c) 66 (d) 68

33. If $a_1, a_2, \ldots, a_n$ are positive real numbers whose product is a fixed number c, then the minimum value of $a_1 + a_2 + \ldots + a_{n-1} + 2a_n$ is:

(a) $n(2c)^{1/n}$ (b) $(n+1)c^{1/n}$

(c) $(2n)c^{1/n}$ (d) $(n+1)(2c)^{1/n}$

34. Consider the real numbers $a^{-5}, a^{-4}, 3a^{-3}, 1, a^8, a^{10}$, where $a > 0$. The minimum value of their sum is:

(a) 5 (b) 6

(c) 7 (d) 8

35. If x, y, z are distinct positive numbers, then the minimum value of $\dfrac{x^2(y+z)+y^2(x+z)+z^2(x+y)}{xyz}$ is:

(a) 5 (b) 6

(c) 7 (d) 8

36. The least value of the function $f(x) = 2^{\sqrt{2}\sin x} + 2^{\sqrt{2}\cos x}$ is:

(a) 1 (b) $\sqrt{2}$

(c) $2^{\sqrt{2}-1}$ (d) $2^{\sqrt{2}}$

37. The least value of the function $f(x) = \sin^2 x + \operatorname{cosec}^2 x + \cos^2 x + \sec^2 x + \tan^2 x + \cot^2 x$ is:

(a) 8 (b) 7

(c) 6 (d) 3

38. Let a, b, c be three positive integers in a GP whose common ratio is also an integer. If the arithmetic mean of a, b, c is $b+2$, then the value of $a^2 + a - 35$ equals:

(a) 8 (b) 7

(c) 6 (d) 3

39. If a, b, c are in HP, then $\dfrac{b+a}{b-a} + \dfrac{b+c}{b-c}$ equals:

(a) 1 (b) 2

(c) –1 (d) –2

40. The sum to 10 terms of the series $\dfrac{1^3}{1} + \dfrac{1^3+2^3}{1+3} + \dfrac{1^3+2^3+3^3}{1+3+5} + \ldots$ is:

(a) $\dfrac{505}{4}$ (b) $\dfrac{303}{5}$

(c) $\dfrac{707}{6}$ (d) $\dfrac{808}{7}$

41. If $\Delta_r = \begin{vmatrix} 2^{r-1} & 2\cdot 3^{r-1} & 4\cdot 5^{r-1} \\ \alpha & \beta & \gamma \\ 2^n - 1 & 3^n - 1 & 5^n - 1 \end{vmatrix}$, then the value of $\sum_{1}^{n} \Delta_r$ is:

(a) 0 (b) $\alpha\beta\gamma$

(c) $\alpha + \beta + \gamma$ (d) $\alpha 2^n + \beta 3^n + \gamma 4^n$

42. Let S_k denote the sum of an infinite geometric series whose first term is $\dfrac{k-1}{k!}$ and common ratio is $\dfrac{1}{k}$. Then the value of $\dfrac{100^2}{100!} + \sum_{1}^{100} \left|k^2 - 3k + 1\right| S_k$ is:

(a) 3 (b) 4

(c) 5 (d) 6

ANSWER KEYS

1. (c)	**2.** (a)	**3.** (c)	**4.** (a)	**5.** (a)	**6.** (c),(d)	**7.** (b),(d)	**8.** (b),(d)	**9.** (a),(d)	**10.** (a)
11. (a)	**12.** (c)	**13.** (a),(b)	**14.** (b)	**15.** (c)	**16.** (c)	**17.** (b)	**18.** (c)	**19.** (b)	**20.** (a)
21. (d)	**22.** (c)	**23.** (b)	**24.** (d)	**25.** (c)	**26.** (d)	**27.** (a)	**28.** (d)	**29.** (a)	**30.** (b)
31. (d)	**32.** (b)	**33.** (a)	**34.** (d)	**35.** (b)	**36.** (a)	**37.** (b)	**38.** (b)	**39.** (b)	**40.** (a)
41. (a)	**42.** (a)								

SOLUTIONS

1. (c) We have

a, b, c, d are in AP

$\Rightarrow \quad \frac{abcd}{bcd}, \frac{abcd}{acd}, \frac{abcd}{abd}, \frac{abcd}{abc}$ are in AP

$\Rightarrow \quad \frac{1}{bcd}, \frac{1}{acd}, \frac{1}{abd}, \frac{1}{abc}$ are in AP

$\Rightarrow \quad \frac{1}{abc}, \frac{1}{abd}, \frac{1}{acd}, \frac{1}{bcd}$ are in AP

$\Rightarrow \quad abc, abd, acd, bcd$ are in HP

2. (a) Let $\frac{1}{a_2}-\frac{1}{a_1}=\frac{1}{a_3}-\frac{1}{a_2}=\ldots=\frac{1}{a_n}-\frac{1}{a_{n-1}}=d$

Now $S = a_1a_2 + a_2a_3 + \ldots + a_{n-1}a_n$

$$=\frac{a_1-a_2}{\frac{1}{a_2}-\frac{1}{a_1}}+\frac{a_2-a_3}{\frac{1}{a_3}-\frac{1}{a_2}}+\ldots+\frac{a_{n-1}-a_n}{\frac{1}{a_n}-\frac{1}{a_{n-1}}}=\frac{a_1-a_n}{d}$$

Also $\frac{1}{a_n}=\frac{1}{a_1}+(n-1)d \Rightarrow \frac{a_1-a_n}{d}=(n-1)a_1a_n$

3. (c) Let r be the common ratio. Then, we have

$$\frac{x}{1-r}=5$$

$$\Rightarrow \quad r = 1-\frac{x}{5}$$

For an infinite geometric series

$$|r|<1$$

$$\Rightarrow \quad -1<1-\frac{x}{5}<1$$

$$\Rightarrow \quad 0<x<10.$$

4. (a) We have

$$\left(\alpha^2+\beta^2\right)^2=(\alpha+\beta)\left(\alpha^3+\beta^3\right)$$

$$\Rightarrow \quad 2\alpha^2\beta^2=\alpha^3\beta+\alpha\beta^3$$

$$\Rightarrow \quad \alpha\beta\left(\alpha^2+\beta^2-2\alpha\beta\right)=0$$

$$\Rightarrow \quad \alpha\beta(\alpha-\beta)^2=0$$

$$\Rightarrow \quad \alpha\beta=0 \text{ or } \alpha=\beta$$

$$\Rightarrow \quad c=0 \text{ or } D=0.$$

5. (a) Let d be the common difference. Then, the sequence a, b, c can be written as $b-d, b, b+d$, and we have

$$a+b+c=\frac{3}{2}$$

$$\Rightarrow \quad 3b=\frac{3}{2} \Rightarrow b=\frac{1}{2}$$

and $\quad a^2, b^2, c^2$ are in GP

$$\Rightarrow \quad a^2c^2=b^4 \Rightarrow ac=\pm b^2$$

$$\Rightarrow \quad \left(\frac{1}{2}-d\right)\left(\frac{1}{2}+d\right)=\pm\frac{1}{4} \Rightarrow d=0, \pm\frac{1}{\sqrt{2}}$$

Hence $\quad a=\frac{1}{2}-\frac{1}{\sqrt{2}}$ (since $a<b<c$).

6. (c), (d) The sides of the square are in the following sequence:

$$10, \frac{10}{\sqrt{2}}, \frac{10}{\left(\sqrt{2}\right)^2}, \frac{10}{\left(\sqrt{2}\right)^3}, \ldots, \frac{10}{\left(\sqrt{2}\right)^{n-1}}$$

Now, area of the square less than 1

$$\Rightarrow \quad \left\{\frac{10}{\left(\sqrt{2}\right)^{n-1}}\right\}^2<1$$

$$\Rightarrow \quad 2^{n-1}>100 \Rightarrow n>7.$$

7. (b), (d) Let a, b be the first and the $(2n-1)^{\text{th}}$ terms, respectively. Then

$$A=a+(n-1)d, \text{ where } d=\frac{b-a}{2n-2}$$

$$\Rightarrow \quad A=\frac{a+b}{2},$$

$$B=ar^{n-1}, \text{ where } r=\left(\frac{b}{a}\right)^{\frac{1}{2n-2}}$$

$$\Rightarrow \quad B=\sqrt{ab}$$

and $\frac{1}{C}=\frac{1}{a}+(n-1)d$, where $d=\frac{\frac{1}{b}-\frac{1}{a}}{2n-2}$

$$\Rightarrow \quad C=\frac{2ab}{a+b},$$

Hence, the correct options are (b), (d).

8. (b), (d) We have

$$x=1+\cos^2\theta+\cos^4\theta+\ldots\infty=\frac{1}{1-\cos^2\theta}=\frac{1}{\sin^2\theta},$$

$$y=1+\sin^2\theta+\sin^4\theta+\ldots\infty=\frac{1}{1-\sin^2\theta}=\frac{1}{\cos^2\theta}$$

and

$$z = 1+\sin^2\theta\cos^2\theta+\sin^4\theta\cos^4\theta+\ldots\infty = \frac{1}{1-\sin^2\theta\cos^2\theta}.$$

Hence $z = \dfrac{1}{1-\dfrac{1}{xy}} \Rightarrow xyz = xy + z.$

Also, (d) is correct since $xy = x + y$.

9. (a), (d) We have

$$\frac{1}{a}+\frac{1}{b}=\frac{1}{2} \text{ and } b-a=3(5-a) \Rightarrow b = 15-2a.$$

Eliminating b, we have $2a^2-17a+30=0 \Rightarrow a=\frac{5}{2}, 6.$

The corresponding values for $|p-a|$ are $2|5-a|=5, 2.$

10. (a) We have

$$\frac{S_n}{S_n'} = \frac{3n+8}{7n+15} = \frac{11+3(n-1)}{22+7(n-1)} = \frac{\frac{n}{2}\{11+3(n-1)\}}{\frac{n}{2}\{22+7(n-1)\}}$$

Hence, we have

$$\frac{a_n}{a_n'} = \frac{\frac{11}{2}+3(n-1)}{\frac{22}{2}+7(n-1)} = \frac{6n+5}{14n+8}.$$

11. (a) Let a be the first term and d be the common difference of the AP. Then, we have

$$\frac{\frac{7}{2}[2a+6d]}{\frac{11}{2}[2a+10d]} = \frac{6}{11}$$

$$\Rightarrow \quad \frac{a+3d}{a+5d} = \frac{6}{7} \Rightarrow a = 9d.$$

Now $110 < a+6d < 130$

$\Rightarrow \quad 110 < 15d < 130$

$\Rightarrow \quad \frac{22}{3} < d < \frac{26}{3} \Rightarrow d = 8.$ [d is a natural number]

12. (c) For odd n, we have

$S_n = S_{n-1} + n^2$ [If n is odd, the last term is n^2]

$$= \frac{(n-1)n^2}{2} + n^2 \quad \left[\text{Putting } n-1 \text{ in place of } n \text{ in } \frac{n(n+1)^2}{2}\right]$$

$$= \frac{n^2(n+1)}{2}.$$

13. (a), (b) Let the two numbers be a, ar. According to the given condition, we have

$$\frac{H}{G} = \frac{4}{5}$$

$$\Rightarrow \quad 5\left(\frac{2ar}{1+r}\right) = 4a\sqrt{r}$$

$$\Rightarrow \quad 5\sqrt{r} = 1+r$$

$$\Rightarrow \quad r-5\sqrt{r}-1=0$$

$$\Rightarrow \quad \sqrt{r} = \frac{1}{2}, 2 \text{ gives } r = \frac{1}{4}, 4.$$

14. (b) For odd n, we have

$$S_n = 1^3-2^3+3^3-\ldots-(n-1)^3+n^3$$

$$= \left[1^3+2^3+3^3+\ldots+n^3\right] - 2\left[2^3+4^3+6^3+\ldots+(n-1)^3\right]$$

$$= \left[1^3+2^3+3^3+\ldots+n^3\right] - 2\cdot 2^3\left[1^3+2^3+3^3+\ldots+\left(\frac{n-1}{2}\right)^3\right]$$

$$= \frac{n^2(n+1)^2}{4} - 16\frac{\left(\frac{n-1}{2}\right)^2\left(\frac{n-1}{2}+1\right)^2}{4}$$

$$= \frac{n^2(n+1)^2}{4} - \frac{(n-1)^2(n+1)^2}{4}$$

$$= \frac{(n+1)^2(2n-1)}{4}.$$

15. (b) The total number of elements n in set T is given by

$$3+(n-1)8 = 467 \Rightarrow n = 59.$$

Of these 59 terms, there are 29 pairs, namely, $(3, 467), (11, 459), (19, 451), \ldots$ whose sum equals 470.

For the subset S, the numbers written in pairs should not be chosen together. Hence, the maximum number of elements that can be chosen for S equals

Any one number from each of the 29 pairs + The one unpaired 30th term = 30.

16. (c) Let d be the common difference. Then, the sequence can be written as

$$p, p+d, p+2d, p+3d.$$

Now, we have

$$p+q = 2 \Rightarrow 2p+d = 2$$

and $\quad r+s=18 \Rightarrow 2p+5d=18$

Solving the two equations, we have $p=-1, d=4$.

Thus, the terms of the sequence are $-1, 3, 7, 11$.

Now, we have

$$A=pq=-3 \text{ and } B=rs=77.$$

17. (d) We have

$$\ln b_{n+1}-\ln b_n=\ln 2 \Rightarrow \frac{b_{n+1}}{b_n}=2$$

$\Rightarrow b_1, b_2, \ldots b_{101}$ are in GP with common ratio 2.

Using the condition $a_1=b_1$ and $a_{51}=b_{51}=b_1 2^{50}$, the common difference of the AP $a_1, a_2, \ldots$ is

$$d=\frac{a_{51}-a_1}{50}=\frac{b_1\left(2^{50}-1\right)}{50}.$$

Now $b_{101}=b_1 2^{100}$ and $a_{101}=a_1+100d=b_1+2b_1\left(2^{50}-1\right)=b_1\left(2^{51}-1\right)$.

We see that $a_{101}<b_{101}$.

Now $T=b_1\left(2^{51}-1\right)$ and

$$S=\frac{51}{2}\left[2a_1+50d\right]=\frac{51}{2}\left[2b_1+b_1\left(2^{50}-1\right)\right]$$

$$=\frac{51}{2}b_1\left(2^{50}+1\right)=\frac{51}{4}b_1\left(2^{51}+\frac{1}{2}\right)$$

We see that $S>T$.

18. (c) The nth term of the sequence is given by

$$a_n=S_n-S_{n-1}=cn^2-c(n-1)^2=(2n-1)c$$

Hence, the sum of the squares of these terms is

$$S=\sum_1^n(2n-1)^2c^2=c^2\sum_1^n\left(4n^2-4n+1\right)$$

$$=c^2\left[\frac{4n(n+1)(2n+1)}{6}-2n(n+1)+n\right]$$

$$=\frac{n\left(4n^2-1\right)c^2}{3}$$

19. (b) The first alphabet a appears once, the second alphabet b appears twice, the third alphabet c appears three times, and so on. They will add up to 288 when the nth alphabet appears, where n is given by

$$\frac{n}{2}\{2+(n-1)\}=288$$

$$\Rightarrow \quad n(n+1)=576$$

$$\Rightarrow \quad n>23\ [23\times 24=552]$$

Hence, it is the 24th alphabet, that is, x.

20. (a) We have

$$S=\frac{1}{1^4}+\frac{1}{3^4}+\frac{1}{5^4}+\ldots\infty$$

$$=\left[\frac{1}{1^4}+\frac{1}{2^4}+\frac{1}{3^4}+\ldots\infty\right]-\left[\frac{1}{2^4}+\frac{1}{4^4}+\frac{1}{6^4}+\ldots\infty\right]$$

$$=\left[\frac{1}{1^4}+\frac{1}{2^4}+\frac{1}{3^4}+\ldots\infty\right]-\frac{1}{2^4}\left[\frac{1}{1^4}+\frac{1}{2^4}+\frac{1}{3^4}+\ldots\infty\right]$$

$$=\frac{15}{16}\cdot\frac{\pi^4}{90}=\frac{\pi^4}{96}.$$

21. (d) Let $2n$ be the total number of terms and d be the common difference. The sequence is

$$\frac{21}{2}-(2n-1)d, \ldots, \ldots, \ldots, \frac{21}{2}-3d, \frac{21}{2}-2d, \frac{21}{2}-d, \frac{21}{2}$$

Now, the sum of the even terms is 33

$$\frac{21}{2}-(2n-2)d+\ldots+\ldots+\frac{21}{2}(n \text{ terms})=33$$

$$\Rightarrow \frac{n}{2}\left[\frac{21}{2}-(2n-2)d+\frac{21}{2}\right]=33$$

$$\Rightarrow 21n-2n(n-1)d=66$$

$$\Rightarrow 21n-2n^2d+2nd=66.$$

Now, the sum of the odd terms is 24

$$\frac{21}{2}-(2n-1)d+\ldots+\ldots+\frac{21}{2}-d\,(n \text{ terms})=24$$

$$\Rightarrow \frac{n}{2}\left[\frac{21}{2}-(2n-1)d+\frac{21}{2}-d\right]=24$$

$$\Rightarrow n[21-2nd]=48$$

$$\Rightarrow 21n-2n^2d=48.$$

Subtracting the two equations gives $nd=9$. Putting this value in the first equation, we have

$$\Rightarrow 21n-18n=48$$

$$\Rightarrow n=16.$$

Hence, the total number of terms equals 32.

22. (c) Let r be the common ratio. Then, the sequence can be written as a, ar, ar^2, ar^3. Now, we have

$$a+ar+ar^2+ar^3=60$$

and $\quad a+ar^3=36$

Dividing the two equations, we have

$$\frac{1+r+r^2+r^3}{1+r^3}=\frac{60}{36}$$

$$\Rightarrow \quad 1+\frac{r+r^2}{1+r^3}=\frac{5}{3}$$

$$\Rightarrow \quad \frac{r(1+r)}{(1+r)(1-r+r^2)}=\frac{2}{3}$$

$$\Rightarrow \quad 3r=2(1-r+r^2)$$

$$\Rightarrow \quad 2r^2-5r+2=0 \Rightarrow r=\frac{1}{2},2.$$

Putting the value of r in the second equation gives $a = 32, 4$, respectively. Hence the sequence is 32, 16, 8, 4 or 4, 8, 16, 32. In either case, $bc = 16\times 8 = 128$.

23. (b) The first series 15, 19, 23, 27, 31, 35, 39, 43,…has common difference 4 and the second series 14, 19, 24, 29, 34, 39, 44,…has common difference 5. The common terms 19, 39, 59,… will be in AP with common difference equal to the LCM of 4 and 5, that is, 20. Hence, the sum of the first 50 common terms is

$$25[2\times 19+(50-1)20]=25450.$$

24. (d) Let d be the common difference. Then, we have

$$\frac{S_{5n}}{S_n}=\frac{\frac{5n}{2}[6+(5n-1)d]}{\frac{n}{2}[6+(n-1)d]}=\frac{5[6-d+5nd]}{[6-d+nd]}$$

The above ratio will be independent of n only if $d = 6$. Hence, the second term is $3 + 6 = 9$.

25. (c) After n minutes (measured from the time when the policeman starts chasing), the distance covered by the thief and the policeman, measured from the police station are, respectively,

$$S_{\text{thief}}=100+100n$$

and $$S_{\text{police}}=100+110+120+\ldots n\text{ terms}$$

$$=\frac{n}{2}[200+(n-1)10].$$

The time when the policeman catches up with the thief can be found by equating the two distances:

$$\frac{n}{2}[200+(n-1)10]=100+100n$$

$$\Rightarrow \quad 100n+5n(n-1)=100+100n$$

$$\Rightarrow \quad n^2-n-29=0 \Rightarrow n=5 \text{ (Negative value is unacceptable)}$$

Measured from the start, the time will be 5 min + 1 min = 6 min.

26. (d) In the first 10 minutes, he counts $150\times 10 = 1500$ currency notes. Let n more minutes be required to count the remaining $4500 - 1500 = 3000$ currency notes. Then, we have

$$\frac{n}{2}[2\times 148-2(n-1)]=3000$$

$$\Rightarrow \quad 148n-n(n-1)=3000$$

$$\Rightarrow \quad n^2-149n+3000=0 \Rightarrow n=24, 125.$$

Thus, the total required time is 10 min + 24 min = 34 min.

27. (a) Let the middle term $a_5 = c$ and the common difference be d. Then, the sequence can be written as

$$c-5d, c-4d, \ldots, c, \ldots, c+4d, c+5d$$

Now, we have

$$c-5d=15$$

and $$(c-5d)^2+(c-4d)^2+\ldots+c^2+\ldots+(c+4d)^2+(c+5d)^2=11\times 90$$

$$\Rightarrow \quad 11c^2+110d^2=990$$

$$\Rightarrow \quad c^2+10d^2=90$$

Solving the two equations, we have

$$7d^2+30d+27=0 \Rightarrow d=-3, \frac{-9}{7} \text{ and } c=0, \frac{60}{7}.$$

But $a_2 < \frac{27}{2}$, so the acceptable choice is $d = -3$ and $c = 0$. Now, we have

$$\frac{a_1+a_2+\ldots+a_{11}}{11}=\frac{11c}{11}=c=0.$$

28. (d) Let d be the common difference. Then, we have

$$S=\frac{30}{2}[2a_1+29d]=30a_1+(29\times 15)d$$

and $$T=\frac{15}{2}[2a_1+14(2d)]=15a_1+(14\times 15)d$$

It is given that $S - 2T = 75$ and $a_5 = 27$. Hence, we have

$$15d=75 \text{ and } a_1+4d=27$$

$$\Rightarrow \quad d=5 \text{ and } a_1=7$$

Hence $a_{10}=a_1+9d=52$

29. (a) The nth term of the series is

$$a_n = \frac{\frac{n^2(n+1)^2}{4}}{\frac{n}{2}[2+(n-1)2]} = \frac{\frac{n^2(n+1)^2}{4}}{n^2} = \frac{(n+1)^2}{4}$$

Hence, the required sum is

$$S = \frac{1}{4}\sum_{1}^{10}(n+1)^2$$
$$= \frac{1}{4}\left[2^2+2^2+2^2+2^2+\ldots+11^2\right]$$
$$= \frac{1}{4}\left[\frac{11\times12\times23}{6}-1\right] = \frac{505}{4}$$

30. (b) We have

$$A = \left(1^2+2^2+3^2+\ldots+20^2\right)+\left(2^2+4^2+6^2+\ldots+20^2\right)$$
$$= \left(1^2+2^2+3^2+\ldots+20^2\right)+2^2\left(1^2+2^2+3^2+\ldots+10^2\right)$$
$$= \frac{20\times21\times41}{6}+2^2\left(\frac{10\times11\times21}{6}\right) = 4410$$

and

$$B = \left(1^2+2^2+3^2+\ldots+40^2\right)+\left(2^2+4^2+6^2+\ldots+40^2\right)$$
$$= \left(1^2+2^2+3^2+\ldots+40^2\right)+2^2\left(1^2+2^2+3^2+\ldots+20^2\right)$$
$$= \frac{40\times41\times81}{6}+2^2\left(\frac{20\times21\times41}{6}\right) = 33620.$$

Now $B-2A = 33620-8820 = 24800$. Hence $m = 248$.

31. (d) We have

$$(1+2+3+\ldots+n)^2 = \left(1^2+2^2+3^2+\ldots+n^2\right)+2S,$$

where S is the sum of the products of all possible pairs of the first n natural numbers. Hence

$$S = \frac{1}{2}\left[\left(\sum n\right)^2-\sum n^2\right]$$
$$= \frac{1}{2}\left[\frac{n^2(n+1)^2}{4}-\frac{n(n+1)(2n+1)}{6}\right]$$
$$= \frac{n(n+1)}{12}\left[3n(n+1)-2(2n+1)\right]$$
$$= \frac{n(n+1)}{12}\left[3n^2-n-2\right]$$
$$= \frac{n(n+1)}{12}\left[(3n+1)(n-1)\right]$$
$$= \frac{n\left(n^2-1\right)(3\text{n}+2)}{24}$$

32. (b) Let d be the common difference. Then

$$a_1+a_5+\ldots+a_{49}\,(13\text{ terms}) = 416$$
$$\Rightarrow \quad \frac{13}{2}\left[a_1+a_{49}\right] = 416$$
$$\Rightarrow \quad a_1+a_1+48d = 64$$
$$\Rightarrow \quad a_1+24d = 32 \qquad \ldots(1)$$

and $\quad a_9+a_{43} = 66$

$$\Rightarrow \quad a_1+8d+a_1+42d = 66$$
$$\Rightarrow \quad a_1+25d = 33 \qquad \ldots(2)$$

Solving the above equations, we have $a_1 = 8$ and $d = 1$. Hence

$$\sum_{1}^{17} a_k^2 = 8^2+9^2+\ldots+24^2$$
$$= \frac{24\times25\times49}{6}-\frac{7\times8\times15}{6} = 4760.$$

Hence $m = 34$.

33. (a) Using the inequality AM $\geq$ GM, we have

$$\frac{a_1+a_2+\ldots+a_{n-1}+2a_n}{n} \geq \left(2a_1a_2a_{n-1}a_n\right)^{\frac{1}{n}} = (2c)^{1/n}$$
$$\Rightarrow a_1+a_2+\ldots+a_{n-1}+2a_n \geq n(2c)^{1/n}$$

34. (d) Using the inequality AM $\geq$ GM, we have

$$\frac{a^{-5}+a^{-4}+a^{-3}+a^{-3}+a^{-3}+1+a^8+a^{10}}{8}$$
$$\geq \left(a^{-5}\cdot a^{-4}\cdot a^{-3}\cdot a^{-3}\cdot a^{-3}\cdot 1\cdot a^8\cdot a^{10}\right)^{\frac{1}{8}} = 1$$
$$\Rightarrow a^{-5}+a^{-4}+a^{-3}+a^{-3}+a^{-3}+1+a^8+a^{10} \geq 8.$$

35. (b) The given expression can be written as

$$S = \left(\frac{x}{z}+\frac{z}{x}\right)+\left(\frac{y}{z}+\frac{z}{y}\right)+\left(\frac{x}{y}+\frac{y}{x}\right)$$

Since the value of the terms in each bracket is greater than or equal to 2, $S \geq 6$.

36. (a) Using the inequality AM $\geq$ GM, we have

$$2^{\sqrt{2}\sin x}+2^{\sqrt{2}\cos x} \geq 2\sqrt{2^{\sqrt{2}\sin x}\cdot 2^{\sqrt{2}\cos x}}$$
$$= 2\sqrt{2^{\sqrt{2}\sin x+\sqrt{2}\cos x}}$$
$$= 2\sqrt{2^{2\sin\left(x+\frac{\pi}{4}\right)}} \geq 2\sqrt{2^{-2}} = 1.$$

37. (b) The given function reduces to

$$f(x) = 1+1+2\tan^2 x+1+2\cot^2 x$$

$$\Rightarrow f(x)=3+2\left(\tan^2 x+\cot^2 x\right)$$
$$\geq 3+2\left(2\sqrt{\tan^2 x\cdot\cot^2 x}\right)=7 \text{ [Using the inequality AM} \geq \text{GM]}$$

38. (b) Let the three numbers in GP be a, ar, ar^2, where r is a positive integer. According to the given condition, we have

$$\frac{a+ar+ar^2}{3}=ar+2$$
$$\Rightarrow \quad a\left(r^2-2r+1\right)=6$$
$$\Rightarrow \quad a(r-1)^2=6$$
$$\Rightarrow \quad r=1\pm\sqrt{\frac{6}{a}}$$

For r to be an integer, the only possible value of a is 6. Hence $a^2+a-35=7$.

39. (b) If a, b, c are in HP, then $\frac{1}{a}, \frac{1}{b}, \frac{1}{c}$ are in AP.

Let the three numbers be $k-d, k, k+d$, where $k=\frac{1}{b}$ and d is the common difference. Hence, we have

$$\frac{b+a}{b-a}+\frac{b+c}{b-c}=\frac{\frac{1}{a}+\frac{1}{b}}{\frac{1}{a}-\frac{1}{b}}+\frac{\frac{1}{c}+\frac{1}{b}}{\frac{1}{c}-\frac{1}{b}}=\frac{\frac{1}{a}+\frac{1}{b}}{\frac{1}{a}-\frac{1}{b}}+\frac{\frac{1}{c}+\frac{1}{b}}{\frac{1}{c}-\frac{1}{b}}$$
$$=\frac{2k-d}{-d}+\frac{2k+d}{d}=2.$$

40. (a) The nth term of the series is

$$a_n=\frac{\frac{n^2(n+1)^2}{4}}{\frac{n}{2}[2+(n-1)2]}=\frac{\frac{n^2(n+1)^2}{4}}{n^2}=\frac{(n+1)^2}{4}$$

Hence, the required sum is

$$S=\frac{1}{4}\sum_{1}^{10}(n+1)^2$$
$$\Rightarrow \quad =\frac{1}{4}\left[2^2+3^2+4^2+\ldots+11^2\right]$$
$$\Rightarrow \quad =\frac{1}{4}\left[\frac{11\times 12\times 23}{6}-1\right]=\frac{505}{4}$$

41. (a) We have

$$\Delta_r=A\cdot 2^{r-1}+2B\cdot 3^{r-1}+4C\cdot 5^{r-1},$$

where $A=\beta\left(5^n-1\right)-\gamma\left(3^n-1\right)$,
$B=\gamma\left(2^n-1\right)-\alpha\left(5^n-1\right)$
and $C=\alpha\left(3^n-1\right)-\beta\left(2^n-1\right)$.

Hence, we have

$$\sum_1^n\Delta_r=A\sum_1^n 2^{r-1}+2B\sum_1^n 3^{r-1}+4C\sum_1^n 5^{r-1}$$
$$=A\left(\frac{2^n-1}{2-1}\right)+2B\left(\frac{3^n-1}{3-1}\right)+4A\left(\frac{5^n-1}{5-1}\right)$$
$$=A\left(2^n-1\right)+B\left(3^n-1\right)+C\left(5^n-1\right)$$
$$=\left(2^n-1\right)\left[\beta\left(5^n-1\right)-\gamma\left(3^n-1\right)\right]+\left(3^n-1\right)\left[\gamma\left(2^n-1\right)-\alpha\left(5^n-1\right)\right]+\left(5^n-1\right)\left[\alpha\left(3^n-1\right)-\beta\left(2^n-1\right)\right]$$
$$=0.$$

42. (a) We have

$$S_k=\frac{\frac{k-1}{k!}}{1-\frac{1}{k}}=\frac{1}{(k-1)!}, \text{ where } k=2,3,\ldots \text{ and } S_1=0.$$

Hence, the required sum is

$$S=\frac{100^2}{100!}+\sum^{100}\left|k^2-3k+1\right|S_k$$
$$=\frac{100^2}{100!}+0+1+\sum_3^{100}\frac{k^2-3k+1}{(k-1)!}$$
$$\left[\begin{array}{l}k^2-3k+1=(k-0.38)(k-2.62)\\ \Rightarrow k^2-3k+1>0 \text{ for } k=3,4,5,\ldots\end{array}\right]$$
$$=\frac{100^2}{100!}+1+\sum_3^{100}\frac{(k-1)^2-k}{(k-1)!}$$
$$=\frac{100^2}{100!}+1+\sum_3^{100}\left[\frac{k-1}{(k-2)!}-\frac{k}{(k-1)!}\right]$$
$$=\frac{100^2}{100!}+1+\left[\left(\frac{2}{1!}-\frac{3}{2!}\right)+\left(\frac{3}{2!}-\frac{4}{3!}\right)+\ldots+\left(\frac{99}{98!}-\frac{100}{99!}\right)\right]$$
$$=\frac{100}{99!}+1+\left[\frac{2}{1!}-\frac{100}{99!}\right]=3.$$

CHAPTER

4

Binomial Theorem

- If n is a positive integer and x, y are two complex numbers, then

$$(x+y)^n = {}^nC_0x^n + {}^nC_1x^{n-1}y + {}^nC_2x^{n-2}y^2 + \ldots + {}^nC_ny^n = \sum_{0}^{n} {}^nC_rx^{n-r}y^r$$

Two useful expansions:

1. $(1+x)^n = {}^nC_0 + {}^nC_1x + {}^nC_2x^2 + \ldots + {}^nC_nx^n$
2. $(1-x)^n = {}^nC_0 - {}^nC_1x + {}^nC_2x^2 - \ldots + (-1)^n\, {}^nC_nx^n$

Putting $x = 1$ in the above expansions, we have

$${}^nC_0 + {}^nC_1 + {}^nC_2 + \ldots + {}^nC_n = 2^n \text{ and}$$

$${}^nC_0 + {}^nC_2 + {}^nC_4 + \ldots = {}^nC_1 + {}^nC_3 + {}^nC_5 + \ldots = 2^{n-1}$$

- **Properties Related to ${}^nC_r$:**

1. ${}^nC_r = {}^nC_{n-r}$
2. ${}^nC_r + {}^nC_{r-1} = {}^{n+1}C_r$
3. $\dfrac{n+1}{r+1} \times {}^nC_r = {}^{n+1}C_{r+1}$
4. The greatest value of ${}^nC_r$ is $= \begin{cases} {}^nC_{n/2} \text{ if } n \text{ is even} \\ {}^nC_{n-1/2} \text{ or } {}^nC_{n+1/2} \text{ if } n \text{ is odd} \end{cases}$
5. ${}^nC_0 + {}^nC_1 + {}^nC_2 + \ldots + {}^nC_n = 2^n$ and ${}^nC_0 + {}^nC_2 + {}^nC_4 + \ldots = {}^nC_1 + {}^nC_3 + {}^nC_5 + \ldots = 2^{n-1}$

- **Points to be Noted in the Binomial Expansion:**

1. There are $n+1$ terms in the expansion.
2. The sum of the exponents of x and y is equal to n for every term in the expansion.
3. The binomial coefficients from the beginning and the end are equal since ${}^nC_r = {}^nC_{n-r}$.
4. The term ${}^nC_rx^{n-r}y^r$ is the $(r+1)^{\text{th}}$ term from the beginning; it is denoted as T_{r+1}.
5. The rth from the end is the $(n-r+2)^{\text{th}}$ from the beginning.

- **Remainder Theorem:**

For every $n \in \mathbf{N}$

$$x^n - y^n = (x-y)\left(x^{n-1} + x^{n-2}y + x^{n-3}y^2 + \ldots + y^{n-1}\right)$$

For every odd $n \in \mathbf{N}$

$$x^n + y^n = (x+y)\left(x^{n-1} - x^{n-2}y + x^{n-3}y^2 - \ldots + y^{n-1}\right)$$

Hence, we have the following proposition:

$x^n + y^n$ is divisible by $x + y$ for odd $n \in \mathbf{N}$

$x^n - y^n$ is divisible by $x - y$ for every $n \in \mathbf{N}$

- **Using Differentiation and Integration to Find the Sum of a Series**

Example 1: Find the sum of the series:

(i) $\sum_{0}^{n} r\,{}^nC_r$ (ii) $\sum_{0}^{n} r^2\,{}^nC_r$

Solution:

(i) We have $(1+x)^n = \sum_{0}^{n} {}^nC_r x^r$. Differentiating with respect to x, we have

$$n(1+x)^{n-1} = \sum_{0}^{n} {}^nC_r r x^{r-1} \quad \ldots(1)$$

Now putting $x = 1$ in equation (1), we have the required sum

$$\sum_{0}^{n} r\,{}^nC_r = n2^{n-1}$$

(ii) Multiplying equation (1) by x and then differentiating, we have

$$nx(1+x)^{n-1} = \sum_{0}^{n} r\,{}^nC_r x^r \quad \text{[Multiplying by } x\text{]}$$

and $$n\left[(1+x)^{n-1} + (n-1)x(1+x)^{n-2}\right] = \sum_{0}^{n} r^2\,{}^nC_r x^{r-1} \quad \ldots(2) \quad \text{[Differentiating]}$$

Now putting $x = 1$ in equation (2), we have the required sum

$$\sum_{0}^{n} r^2\,{}^nC_r = n\left[2^{n-1} + (n-1)2^{n-2}\right] = n(n+1)2^{n-2}$$

Example 2: Find the sum of the series:

(i) $\sum_{0}^{n} \frac{{}^nC_r}{r+1}$ (ii) $\sum_{0}^{n} \frac{{}^nC_r}{r+1} 2^{r+1}$

Solution:

(i) We have $(1+x)^n = \sum_{0}^{n} {}^nC_r x^r$. Integrating with respect to x within limits $x = 0$ to $x = 1$, we have

$$\int_0^1 (1+x)^n\,dx = \sum_{0}^{n}\left(\int_0^1 {}^nC_r x^r\right)$$

$$\Rightarrow \quad \left|\frac{(1+x)^{n+1}}{n+1}\right|_0^1 = \sum_{0}^{n}\left({}^nC_r \left|\frac{x^{r+1}}{r+1}\right|_0^1\right)$$

$$\Rightarrow \quad \sum_{0}^{n} \frac{{}^nC_r}{r+1} = \frac{2^{n+1}-1}{n+1}$$

(ii) We have $(1+x)^n = \sum_0^n {}^nC_r x^r$. Integrating with respect to x within limits $x = 0$ to $x = 2$, we have

$$\int_0^2 (1+x)^n\,dx = \sum_0^n \left(\int_0^2 {}^nC_r x^r\right)$$

$$\Rightarrow \quad \left|\frac{(1+x)^{n+1}}{n+1}\right|_0^2 = \sum_0^n \left({}^nC_r \left|\frac{x^{r+1}}{r+1}\right|_0^2\right)$$

$$\Rightarrow \quad \sum_0^n \frac{{}^nC_r}{r+1} 2^{r+1} = \frac{3^{n+1} - 2^{n+1}}{n+1}$$

EXERCISES

1. The sum of the coefficients of all odd degree terms in the expansion of $\left\{x+\sqrt{x^3-1}\right\}^5 + \left\{x-\sqrt{x^3-1}\right\}^5$ is:
   (a) −1 (b) 0
   (c) 1 (d) 2

2. If the sum of the coefficients of $(x+y)^n, n \in \mathbf{N}$ equals 1024, then the value of the greatest coefficient in the expansion is:
   (a) 112 (b) 252
   (c) 280 (d) 390

3. If the ratio of the fifth term from the beginning to the fifth term from the end in the expansion of $\left(2^{1/4}+3^{-1/4}\right)^n$, $n \in \mathbf{N}$ is $\sqrt{6}\cdot 1$, then the value of n is:
   (a) 10 (b) 9
   (c) 8 (d) 7

4. If the second, third and fourth coefficients in the expansion of $(x+y)^n, n \in N$ are in AP, then the value of n is:
   (a) 6 (b) 7
   (c) 8 (d) 10

5. The sum of the rational terms in the expansion of $\left(\sqrt{2}+\sqrt[5]{3}\right)^{10}$ equals:
   (a) 21 (b) 24
   (c) 34 (d) 41

6. The term independent of x in the expansion of $\left(\frac{1}{60}-\frac{x^8}{81}\right)\left(2x^2-\frac{3}{x^2}\right)^6$ is:
   (a) −72 (b) 24
   (c) −36 (d) 12

7. The coefficient of t^{24} in the expansion of $\left(1+t^2\right)^{12}\left(1+t^{12}\right)\left(1+t^{24}\right)$ is:
   (a) $\binom{24}{6}$ (b) $\binom{24}{12}$
   (c) $\binom{12}{2}$ (d) $\binom{12}{6}+2$

8. The coefficient of a^3 in the expansion of $(1+2a)^4(2-a)^5$ is:
   (a) −296 (b) −308
   (c) 92 (d) 42

9. Which of the following expressions will have terms containing x^2:
   (a) $\left(x^{-1/5}+2x^{3/5}\right)^{25}$
   (b) $\left(x^{3/5}+2x^{-1/5}\right)^{24}$
   (c) $\left(x^{3/5}-2x^{-1/5}\right)^{23}$
   (d) $\left(x^{3/5}+2x^{-1/5}\right)^{22}$

10. Let $(1+x^2)^2(1+x)^n = \sum a_k x^k$. If a_1, a_2, a_3 are in AP, then the value of n is:

(a) 11 (b) 7
(c) 4 (d) 3

11. The sum $\binom{n}{3}+\binom{n+1}{4}+\binom{n+2}{5}+\binom{n+3}{6}$ equals:

(a) $\binom{n+4}{6}-\binom{n}{2}$

(b) $\binom{n+4}{7}$

(c) $\binom{n+4}{6}-\binom{n}{4}$

(d) $\binom{n+4}{5}+3\binom{n}{2}$

12. If the coefficient of x^{12} in the expansion of $(x^3+1)^n$ is 210, then the coefficient of x^{15} is:

(a) 242 (b) 252
(c) 272 (d) 282

13. The sum of the coefficients of the integral powers of x in the expansion of $(1-2\sqrt{x})^{50}$ is:

(a) $\frac{1}{2}(3^{50}+1)$

(b) $\frac{1}{2}(3^{50}-1)$

(c) $\frac{1}{2}(2^{50}+1)$

(d) $\frac{1}{2}(2^{50}-1)$

14. The coefficient of x^9 in the expansion of $(1+x)(1+x^2)(1+x^3)(1+x^4)\cdots(1+x^{100})$ is:

(a) 5 (b) 6
(c) 7 (d) 8

15. Let m be the smallest positive integer such that the coefficient of x^2 in the expansion of $(1+x)^2+(1+x)^3+\ldots+(1+x)^{49}+(1+mx)^{50}$ equals $(3n+1)\,^{51}C_3$. Then the value of n is:

(a) 5 (b) 6
(c) 7 (d) 9

16. If $S_1 = \sum_0^n \frac{1}{^nC_r}$ and $S_2 = \sum_0^n \frac{r}{^nC_r}$, then S_2/S_1 equals:

(a) $\frac{n}{2}$

(b) $\frac{n-1}{2}$

(c) $\frac{n}{2}-1$

(d) $\frac{n+1}{2}$

17. If $(1+x+x^2+x^3)^5 = \sum_0^{15} a_k x^k$, then $\sum_0^7 a_{2k}$ equals:

(a) 128 (b) 256
(c) 512 (d) 1024

18. If the fractional part of $\frac{2^{4033}}{15}$ is $\frac{k}{15}$, then k equals:

(a) 1 (b) 2
(c) 7 (d) 13

ANSWER KEYS

1. (d)	**2.** (b)	**3.** (a)	**4.** (b)	**5.** (d)	**6.** (c)	**7.** (d)	**8.** (a)	**9.** (d)	**10.** (c),(d)
11. (a)	**12.** (b)	**13.** (a)	**14.** (d)	**15.** (a)	**16.** (a)	**17.** (c)	**18.** (b)		

SOLUTIONS

1. (d) The given expression is

$$S = 2\left[C_0x^5 + C_2x^3\left(x^3-1\right) + C_4x\left(x^3-1\right)^2\right]$$

$$= 2\left[C_0x^5 + C_2\left(x^6-x^3\right) + C_4\left(x^7-2x^4+x\right)\right]$$

Sum of the coefficients of the odd degree terms is

$$S = 2\left[C_0 - C_2 + C_4 + C_4\right] = 2[1-10+5+5] = 2$$

2. (b) Putting $x=1$ and $y=1$ gives the sum of the coefficients $= 2^n$

Equating it with 1024 gives $n = 10$.

Hence, the greatest term $= \binom{10}{5} = 252$.

3. (a) We have

Fifth term from the beginning $= \binom{n}{4} 2^{(n-4)/4} 3^{-1}$

Fifth term from the end $= \binom{n}{4} 2^1 3^{-(n-4)/4}$

Their ratio is given to be $\sqrt{6}$. Hence

$$\frac{2^{(n-4)/4}3^{-1}}{2^1 3^{-(n-4)/4}} = \sqrt{6}$$

$$\Rightarrow \quad 2^{(n-8)/4} 3^{(n-8)/4} = \sqrt{6}$$

$$\Rightarrow \quad 6^{(n-8)/4} = \sqrt{6} \text{ gives } n = 10.$$

4. (b) We have

$$\binom{n}{1} + \binom{n}{3} = 2 \times \binom{n}{2}$$

$$\Rightarrow \quad n + \frac{n(n-1)(n-2)}{6} = n(n-1)$$

$$\Rightarrow \quad \frac{n(n-1)(n-2)}{6} = n(n-2)$$

$$\Rightarrow \quad n-1 = 6 \text{ gives } n = 7.$$

5. (d) We have

$$\left(\sqrt{2} + \sqrt[5]{3}\right)^{10} = \sum \binom{10}{r} 2^{(n-r)/2} 3^{r/5}$$

The terms will be rational for $r = 0, 10$. The sum of these terms

$$S = \binom{10}{0} 2^5 + \binom{10}{10} 3^2 = 32 + 9 = 41.$$

6. (c) We have

$$\left(\frac{1}{60} - \frac{x^8}{81}\right)\left(2x^2 - \frac{3}{x^2}\right)^6$$

$$= \left(\frac{1}{60} - \frac{x^8}{81}\right) \sum_0^6 {}^6C_r \left(2x^2\right)^{6-r} \left(\frac{-3}{x^2}\right)^r$$

$$= \left(\frac{1}{60} - \frac{x^8}{81}\right) \sum_0^6 {}^6C_r\, 2^{6-r} (-3)^r x^{12-4r}$$

$$= \frac{1}{60} \sum_0^6 {}^6C_r 2^{6-r} (-3)^r x^{12-4r}$$

$$- \frac{1}{81} \sum_0^6 {}^6C_r 2^{6-r} (-3)^r x^{20-4r}$$

The term independent of x

$$= \frac{1}{60}\left\{{}^6C_3 2^3 (-3)^3\right\} - \frac{1}{81}\left\{{}^6C_5 2^1 (-3)^5\right\}$$

$$= -72 + 36 = -36$$

7. (d) We have

$$\left(1+t^2\right)^{12}\left(1+t^{12}\right)\left(1+t^{24}\right)$$

$$= \left(1 + t^{12} + t^{24} + t^{36}\right) \sum_0^{12} \binom{12}{r} t^{2r}$$

$$= \sum_0^{12} \binom{12}{r} t^{2r} + \sum_0^{12} \binom{12}{r} t^{12+2r}$$

$$+ \sum_0^{12} \binom{12}{r} t^{24+2r} + \sum_0^{12} \binom{12}{r} t^{36+2r}$$

The coefficient of t^{24}

$$= \binom{12}{12} + \binom{12}{6} + \binom{12}{0}$$

$$= \binom{12}{6} + 2$$

8. (a) We have

$$(1+2a)^4(2-a)^5$$

$$=\sum_0^4\binom{4}{j}(2a)^j\times\sum_0^5\binom{5}{k}(2)^{5-k}(-a)^k$$

$$=\sum(-)^k\binom{4}{j}\binom{5}{k}2^{5+j-k}a^{j+k}$$

where $j=0\to4, k=0\to5$

Now $j+k=3$ for $(j,k)=(0,3),(1,2),(2,1),(3,0)$

Hence, the coefficient of a^3

$$=-\binom{4}{0}\binom{5}{3}2^2+\binom{4}{1}\binom{5}{2}2^4-\binom{4}{2}\binom{5}{1}2^6+\binom{4}{3}\binom{5}{0}2^8$$

$$=-40+640-1920+1024=-296$$

9. (d) We have

$$\left(x^{-1/5}+2x^{3/5}\right)^{25}=\sum_0^{25}\binom{25}{r}2^r x^{\frac{r-25}{5}+\frac{3r}{5}}$$

$$=\sum_0^{25}\binom{25}{r}2^r x^{\frac{4r-25}{5}}$$

We can see that $\frac{4r-25}{5}$ can never be equal to 2.

Similarly, we have

$$\left(x^{3/5}+2x^{-1/5}\right)^{24}=\sum_0^{24}\binom{24}{r}2^r x^{\frac{72-4r}{5}}$$

We can see that $\frac{72-4r}{5}$ can never be equal to 2.

Similarly, we have

$$\left(x^{3/5}-2x^{-1/5}\right)^{23}=\sum_0^{23}(-1)^r\binom{23}{r}2^r x^{\frac{69-4r}{5}}$$

We can see that $\frac{69-4r}{5}$ can never be equal to 2.

Similarly, we have

$$\left(x^{3/5}+2x^{-1/5}\right)^{22}=\sum_0^{22}\binom{22}{r}2^r x^{\frac{66-4r}{5}}$$

We can see that $\frac{66-4r}{5}$ will be equal to 2 for $r=14$.

10. (c),(d) The given expression is

$$\left(1+2x^2+x^4\right)(1+x)^n$$

$$=\left(1+2x^2+x^4\right)\left(C_0+C_1x+C_2x^2+\ldots\right)$$

Then we have

$$a_1=C_1=n$$

$$a_2=C_2+2C_0=\frac{n(n-1)}{2}+2$$

$$a_3=2C_1+C_3=2n+\frac{n(n-1)(n-2)}{6}$$

The three coefficients are given to be in AP $\Rightarrow a_1+a_3=2a_2$. Hence

$$n+2n+\frac{n(n-1)(n-2)}{6}=n(n-1)+4$$

$$\Rightarrow\quad \frac{n(n-1)(n-2)}{6}=n^2-4n+4$$

$$\Rightarrow\quad n(n-1)(n-2)=6(n-2)^2$$

$$\Rightarrow\quad n^2-7n+12=0 \text{ gives } n=3,4.$$

11. (a) Adding and subtracting $\binom{n}{2}$ in the given series, we have

$$S=\binom{n}{2}+\binom{n}{3}+\binom{n+1}{4}+\binom{n+2}{5}+\binom{n+3}{6}-\binom{n}{2}$$

$$=\binom{n+1}{3}+\binom{n+1}{4}+\binom{n+2}{5}+\binom{n+3}{6}-\binom{n}{2}$$

$$=\binom{n+2}{4}+\binom{n+2}{5}+\binom{n+3}{6}-\binom{n}{2}$$

$$=\binom{n+3}{5}+\binom{n+3}{6}-\binom{n}{2}$$

$$=\binom{n+4}{6}-\binom{n}{2}.$$

12. (b) Coefficient of x^{12} in the expansion of $\left(x^3+1\right)^n$ is $\binom{n}{4}$.

$$\Rightarrow \quad \binom{n}{4} = 210$$

$$\Rightarrow \quad \frac{n(n-1)(n-2)(n-3)}{4!} = 210$$

$$\Rightarrow \quad n(n-1)(n-2)(n-2) = 5040 \text{ gives } n = 10.$$

Now, coefficient of x^{15} in the expansion of $(x^3+1)^{10}$ is $\binom{10}{5} = 252$.

13. (a) We have

$$\left(1-2\sqrt{x}\right)^{50} = \sum \binom{50}{r} (-2)^r x^{r/2}$$

Taking only integral powers of x, the sum of the coefficients is

$$S = C_0 + C_2 2^2 + C_4 2^4 + \ldots + C_{48} 2^{48} + C_{50} 2^{50}$$

$$= \frac{1}{2}\left[(1+2)^{50} + (1-2)^{50}\right] = \frac{1}{2}\left(3^{50}+1\right).$$

14. (d) The process of multiplication involves multiplying one term from each bracket. Thus, the terms involving x^9 in

$(1+x)(1+x^2)(1+x^3)(1+x^4)\cdots(1+x^{100})$ are

$$(1\times 1\times \ldots \times x^9 \times \ldots \times 1) + (1\times 1\times x^3 \times \ldots \times x^6 \times \ldots \times 1)$$

$$+(1\times \ldots \times x^4 \times x^5 \times \ldots \times 1) + (1\times x^2 \times \ldots \times x^7 \times \ldots \times 1)$$

$$+(1\times x^2 \times x^3 \times x^4 \times \ldots \times 1) + (x\times 1\times \ldots \times x^8 \times \ldots \times 1)$$

$$+(x\times 1\times x^3 \times 1\times x^5 \times \ldots \times 1) + (x\times x^2 \times 1\times \ldots \times x^6$$

$$\times \ldots \times 1) = 8x^9$$

Hence $a = 8$.

15. (a) The coefficient of x^2 is

$$S = \sum_{1}^{49} {}^kC_2 + m^2\, {}^{50}C_2$$

$$= \frac{1}{2}\sum_{1}^{49} k(k-1) + m^2 \frac{50\times 49}{2}$$

$$= \frac{1}{2}\sum_{1}^{49}\left(k^2-k\right) + m^2 \frac{50\times 49}{2}$$

$$= \frac{1}{2}\left[\frac{49\times 50\times 99}{6} - \frac{49\times 50}{2}\right] + m^2 \frac{50\times 49}{2}$$

$$= \frac{1}{2}\left[\frac{49\times 50\times 96}{6}\right] + m^2 \frac{50\times 49}{2}$$

$$= \left(m^2+16\right)\frac{50\times 49}{2}$$

Equating it with $(3n+1)^{51}C_3$, we have

$$\left(m^2+16\right)\frac{50\times 49}{2} = (3n+1)\frac{51\times 50\times 49}{6}$$

$$m^2 + 16 = 17(3n+1)$$

$$m^2 = 51n + 1$$

The smallest positive integer value of n satisfying the above condition is 5.

16. (a) We have

$$S_2 = \sum_{0}^{n} \frac{r}{{}^nC_r} = \sum_{0}^{n} \frac{r-n+n}{{}^nC_r}$$

$$= -\sum_{0}^{n} \frac{n-r}{{}^nC_r} + n\sum_{0}^{n}\frac{1}{{}^nC_r}$$

$$= -\sum_{0}^{n} \frac{n-r}{{}^nC_{n-r}} + nS_1$$

$$= -\sum_{0}^{n} \frac{k}{{}^nC_k} + nS_1$$

$$= -S_2 + nS_1$$

$$\Rightarrow 2S_2 = nS_1$$

$$\Rightarrow S_2/S_1 = \frac{n}{2}$$

17. (c) Putting $x = 1$, we have

$$4^5 = a_0 + a_1 + a_2 + a_3 + \ldots + a_{14} + a_{15}$$

Putting $x = -1$, we have

$$0 = a_0 - a_1 + a_2 - a_3 + \ldots + a_{14} - a_{15}$$

Adding the above results, we have

$$4^5 = 2\left[a_0 + a_2 + a_4 + \ldots + a_{14}\right]$$

$$\Rightarrow \quad a_0 + a_2 + a_4 + \ldots + a_{14} = 512$$

18. (b) We can write

$$\frac{2^{4033}}{15} = \frac{2 \times 2^{4032}}{15} = \frac{2 \times 16^{1008}}{15} = \frac{2}{15}(1+15)^{1008}$$

Now, using binomial expansion, we have

$$\frac{2}{15}(1+15)^{1008}$$

$$= \frac{2}{15}\left[C_0 + C_1 15 + C_2 15^2 + \ldots + C_{1008} 15^{1008}\right]$$

$$= \frac{2}{15} + \text{some integer.}$$

We see that the fractional part is $\frac{2}{15}$. Hence $k = 2$.

CHAPTER 5 Complex Numbers

- A complex number z can be represented in two ways.

  Cartesian representation: $z = x + iy$ $(x, y \in \mathbf{R}$ and $i = \sqrt{-1})$

  Here, x is called the real part of z and is denoted as $\text{Re}(z)$, and y is called the imaginary part of z and is denoted as $\text{Im}(z)$.

  Polar representation: $z = re^{i\theta}$ $(r, \theta \in \mathbf{R}$ and $i = \sqrt{-1})$

  Here, r is called the modulus of z and is denoted as $\text{mod}(z)$ or $|z|$, and θ is called the argument of z and is denoted as $\arg(z)$.

- Geometrically complex numbers can be represented as points with Cartesian coordinates (x, y) or polar coordinates (r, θ) referred to a pair of perpendicular axes. The reference frame is called the Argand plane and the axes are called the real (x-axis) and imaginary (y-axis) axes. Remember the conversion

$$(x, y) = \left(\sqrt{x^2 + y^2}, \tan^{-1}\left(\frac{y}{x}\right)\right) \text{ (Cartesian to Polar)}$$

$$(r, \theta) = (r\cos\theta, r\sin\theta) \text{ (Polar to Cartesian)}$$

- Complex numbers can also be represented as free vectors (they can be drawn anywhere in the Argand plane). The number $z = x + iy$ can be treated as a vector, with x and y as its components along the real and imaginary axes, respectively. The number $re^{i\theta}$ can be treated as a vector, with r and θ as its magnitude and direction, respectively.

- **Addition and Subtraction of Two Complex Numbers:** If $z_1 = x_1 + iy_1$ and $z_2 = x_2 + iy_2$ are two complex numbers, then

$$z_1 + z_2 = (x_1 + x_2) + i(y_1 + y_2) \text{ and}$$

$$z_1 - z_2 = (x_1 - x_2) + i(y_1 - y_2)$$

  If $|z_1|$, $|z_2|$ are the respective magnitudes and $\arg(z_1)$, $\arg(z_2)$ are the respective directions, then

$$|z_1 + z_2|^2 = |z_1|^2 + |z_2|^2 + 2|z_1||z_2|\cos\theta \text{ and}$$

$$|z_1 - z_2|^2 = |z_1|^2 + |z_2|^2 - 2|z_1||z_2|\cos\theta,$$

  where $\theta = |\arg(z_1) - \arg(z_2)|$ is the difference between the two directions. Thus, we have the following inequality:

$$||z_1| - |z_2|| \le |z_1 \pm z_2| \le |z_1| + |z_2|$$

  This is known as the triangle inequality since the three complex numbers z_1, z_2 and $z_1 \pm z_2$ represent the three sides of a triangle if they are drawn as vectors; complex numbers add and subtract like vectors.

- **Multiplication of Two Complex Numbers:** If $z_1 = x_1 + iy_1$ and $z_2 = x_2 + iy_2$ are two complex numbers, then

$$z_1 z_2 = (x_1 x_2 - y_1 y_2) + i(x_1 y_2 + x_2 y_1)$$

If $z_1 = r_1 e^{i\theta_1}$ and $z_2 = r_2 e^{i\theta_2}$ are two complex numbers, then

$$z_1 z_2 = r_1 r_2 e^{i(\theta_1+\theta_2)}$$

We see that $|z_1 z_2| = |z_1||z_2|$ and $\arg(z_1 z_2) = \arg(z_1) + \arg(z_2)$.

- **Division of Two Complex Numbers:** If $z_1 = x_1 + iy_1$ and $z_2 = x_2 + iy_2$ are two complex numbers, then

$$\frac{z_1}{z_2} = \frac{x_1 x_1 + y_1 y_2}{x_1^2 + y_1^2} + i\frac{x_2 y_1 - x_1 y_2}{x_2^2 + y_2^2}$$

If $z_1 = r_1 e^{i\theta_1}$ and $z_2 = r_2 e^{i\theta_2}$ are two complex numbers, then

$$\frac{z_1}{z_2} = \frac{r_1}{r_2} e^{i(\theta_1-\theta_2)}$$

We see that $\left|\frac{z_1}{z_2}\right| = \frac{|z_1|}{|z_2|}$ and $\arg\left(\frac{z_1}{z_2}\right) = \arg(z_1) - \arg(z_2)$.

- **Conjugate of a Complex Number:** The complex numbers $x + iy$ and $x - iy$, or $re^{i\theta}$ and $re^{-i\theta}$ are called conjugates of each other. If any one of them is denoted by z, its conjugate is denoted by $\overline{z}$.

Related properties:

1. $z\overline{z} = |z|^2$, $\frac{z+\overline{z}}{2} = \text{Re}(z)$ and $\frac{z-\overline{z}}{2i} = \text{Im}(z)$
2. $\overline{z_1 + z_2} = \overline{z_1} + \overline{z_2}$ and $\overline{z_1 - z_2} = \overline{z_1} - \overline{z_2}$
3. $\overline{z_1 z_2} = \overline{z_1}\,\overline{z_2}$ and $\overline{\left(\frac{z_1}{z_2}\right)} = \frac{\overline{z_1}}{\overline{z_2}}$
4. If $\arg(z) = n\pi$ $(n \in \mathbf{Z})$, then z is purely real and $z - \overline{z} = 0$. If $\arg(z) = (2n+1)\frac{\pi}{2}$ $(n \in \mathbf{Z})$, then z is purely imaginary and $z + \overline{z} = 0$.
5. $|z_1 \pm z_2|^2 = |z_1|^2 + |z_2|^2 \pm 2\text{Re}(z_1\overline{z_2})$

- **Straight Line:** The distance between two points $A(z_1)$ and $B(z_2)$ is given by

$$AB = |z_1 - z_2|$$

The point $P(z)$, which divides the line joining the two points $A(z_1)$ and $B(z_2)$ in the ratio $m : n$, is given by

$$z = \frac{mz_2 \pm nz_1}{m \pm n} \quad (+ \text{ for internal point and } - \text{ for external point})$$

The equation of the straight line joining the points $A(z_1)$ and $B(z_2)$ is given by

$$\begin{vmatrix} z & \overline{z} & 1 \\ z_1 & \overline{z_1} & 1 \\ z_2 & \overline{z_2} & 1 \end{vmatrix} = 0 \text{ or } \begin{vmatrix} \frac{z - z_2}{z_1 - z_2} & \frac{\overline{z} - \overline{z_2}}{\overline{z_1} - \overline{z_2}} \end{vmatrix} = 0$$

The equation of a straight line has the form

$$\bar{a}z + a\bar{z} + b = 0, \text{ where } b \text{ is purely real.}$$

Its slope is $\dfrac{a+\bar{a}}{i(a-\bar{a})}$, which is purely real. It is determined by putting $z = x + iy$ and then rearranging in the slope-intercept form.

- **Circle:** The equation of a circle with centre at $C(z_0)$ and radius r is given by

$$|z - z_0| = r$$

The equation of a circle has the form

$$z\bar{z} + \bar{a}z + a\bar{z} + b = 0, \text{ where } b \text{ is purely real.}$$

Its centre is at $-a$ and the radius is $\sqrt{|a|^2 - b}$.

- **Cube Roots of Unity:** The cube roots of 1 are the roots of the equation

$$z^3 - 1 = 0 \Rightarrow (z-1)\left(z^2 + z + 1\right) = 0 \Rightarrow z = 1, \omega, \omega^2,$$

where $\omega = \dfrac{-1+i\sqrt{3}}{2} = e^{i(2\pi/3)}$ and $\omega^2 = \dfrac{-1-i\sqrt{3}}{2} = e^{-i(2\pi/3)}$. Note that $1 + \omega + \omega^2 = 0$ and $\omega^3 = 1$.

The cube roots of -1 are the roots of the equation

$$z^3 + 1 = 0 \Rightarrow (z+1)\left(z^2 - z + 1\right) = 0 \Rightarrow z = -1, -\omega, -\omega^2$$

Some useful results:

1. $x^2 + x + 1 = (x - \omega)\left(x - \omega^2\right)$
2. $x^2 - x + 1 = (x + \omega)\left(x + \omega^2\right)$
3. $x^2 + xy + y^2 = (x - \omega y)\left(x - \omega^2 y\right)$
4. $x^2 - xy + y^2 = (x + \omega y)\left(x + \omega^2 y\right)$

EXERCISES

1. Area of the triangle formed by z, iz and $z+iz$ is 50 sq. units. Then $|z|$ equals:

(a) 5 (b) $5\sqrt{2}$

(c) 10 (d) $10\sqrt{2}$

2. If $z=1+\cos\frac{2\pi}{3}+i\sin\frac{2\pi}{3}$, then:

(a) $\text{Re}\left(z^5\right)=\frac{\sqrt{3}}{2}$

(b) $\text{Re}\left(z^5\right)=\frac{1}{2}$

(c) $\text{Im}\left(z^5\right)=\frac{\sqrt{3}}{2}$

(d) $\text{Im}\left(z^5\right)=\frac{1}{2}$

3. The real part of $\exp\{\exp(i\theta)\}$ is:

(a) $e^{\cos\theta}\sin(\cos\theta)$

(b) $e^{\cos\theta}\sin(\sin\theta)$

(c) $e^{\cos\theta}\cos(\sin\theta)$

(d) $e^{\cos\theta}\cos(\cos\theta)$

4. The imaginary part of $\frac{\{\sin 2\theta+i\cos 2\theta\}^4}{\{\sin\theta-i\cos\theta\}^3}$ is:

(a) $\sin(11\theta)$ (b) $-\sin(5\theta)$

(c) $\cos(5\theta)$ (d) $-\cos(11\theta)$

5. Let a, b, x, y be real numbers such that $a-b=1$ and $y\neq 0$. If the complex number $z=x+iy$ satisfies $\text{Im}\left(\frac{az+b}{z+1}\right)=y$, then the possible values of x are:

(a) $-1+\sqrt{1-y^2}$

(b) $-1-\sqrt{1-y^2}$

(c) $1+\sqrt{1+y^2}$

(d) $1-\sqrt{1+y^2}$

6. If $\omega(\neq 1)$ is a cube root of unity and a, b, c are integers (not all equal), then the minimum value of $|a+b\omega+c\omega^2|$ is:

(a) 1 (b) $\frac{1}{2}$

(c) $\frac{1}{3}$ (d) 0

7. If z_1, z_2, z_3 are complex numbers such that $|z_1|=|z_2|=|z_3|=1$ and $\left|\frac{1}{z_1}+\frac{1}{z_2}+\frac{1}{z_3}\right|=1$, then the value of $|z_1+z_2+z_3|$ is:

(a) Equal to 3 (b) Greater than 3

(c) Equal to 1 (d) Less than 1

8. Let $z=\cos\theta+i\sin\theta$, then the value of $\sum_{k=1}^{15}\text{Im}\left(z^{2k-1}\right)$ for $\theta=2°$ is:

(a) $\frac{1}{4\sin 2°}$ (b) $\frac{1}{2\cos 2°}$

(c) $\frac{1}{2\sin 4°}$ (d) $\frac{1}{4\cos 4°}$

9. Let $z=x+iy$ be a complex number, where x, y are integers. Then the area of the rectangle formed by the roots of the equation $z\bar{z}^3+\bar{z}z^3=350$ is:

(a) 48 (b) 52

(c) 64 (d) 75

10. Let $\omega=\frac{-1}{2}+i\frac{\sqrt{3}}{2}$. Then the number of distinct complex numbers z satisfying the equation $\begin{vmatrix} z+1 & \omega & \omega^2 \\ \omega & z+\omega^2 & 1 \\ \omega^2 & 1 & z+\omega \end{vmatrix}=0$ are:

(a) 0 (b) 1

(c) 2 (d) 3

11. Let a, b, c be three real numbers satisfying

$$[a\ \ b\ \ c]\begin{bmatrix} 1 & 9 & 7 \\ 8 & 2 & 7 \\ 7 & 3 & 7 \end{bmatrix}=[0\ \ 0\ \ 0].$$

Let ω be a solution of $z^3-1=0$ with $\text{Im}(\omega)>0$. If

$a = 2$, with b and c satisfying the above equation, then the value of $\frac{3}{\omega^a} + \frac{1}{\omega^b} + \frac{3}{\omega^c}$ is:

(a) –3 (b) 3
(c) –2 (d) 1

12. Let $\omega = e^{i\frac{2\pi}{3}}$ and a, b, c, x, y, z be non-zero complex numbers such that $x = a + b + c$, $y = a + b\omega + c\omega^2$ and $z = a + b\omega^2 + c\omega$.

Then the value of $\frac{|x|^2 + |y|^2 + |z|^2}{|a|^2 + |b|^2 + |c|^2}$ is:

(a) $1/3$ (b) 3
(c) $1/4$ (d) 4

13. The vertices of a regular octagon are given by $\frac{1}{a_1 - 2i}, \frac{1}{a_2 - 2i}, \ldots, \frac{1}{a_8 - 2i}$, where $a_1, a_2, \ldots, a_8$ are real numbers. The area of the octagon is:

(a) $\frac{1}{2\sqrt{3}}$

(b) $\frac{1}{6\sqrt{3}}$

(c) $\frac{1}{4\sqrt{2}}$

(d) $\frac{1}{6\sqrt{2}}$

14. If z is a complex number satisfying $|z - 3 - 2i| \le 2$, then the least and the greatest values of $|2z - 6 + 5i|$ are, respectively:

(a) 3,11 (b) 5,13
(c) 3,7 (d) 7,11

15. The complex numbers z_1, z_2, z_3 satisfying $\frac{z_1 - z_3}{z_2 - z_3} = \frac{1}{2} - i\frac{\sqrt{3}}{2}$ are the vertices of a triangle, which is:

(a) Of zero area
(b) Right-angled isosceles
(c) Equilateral
(d) Obtuse-angled isosceles

16. For all complex numbers z_1, z_2 satisfying $|z_1| = 12$ and $|z_2 - 3 - 4i| = 5$, the minimum value of $|z_1 - z_2|$ is:

(a) 1 (b) 2
(c) 3 (d) 4

17. If z, w are complex numbers such that $|z| = 1$ and $w = \frac{z-1}{z+1}, (z \ne -1)$, then $\text{Re}(w)$ is:

(a) $\frac{\sqrt{2}}{|z+1|^2}$ (b) $\frac{-1}{|z+1|^2}$

(c) $\frac{1}{|z+1|^2}$ (d) 0

18. A complex number z is said to be unimodular if $|z| = 1$. Suppose z_1, z_2 are complex numbers such that $\frac{z_1 - 2z_2}{2 - z_1\bar{z}_2}$ is unimoduar and z_2 is not unimodular. Then the point z_1 lies on a:

(a) Straight line of slope 2
(b) Straight line of slope $\sqrt{2}$
(c) Circle of radius 2
(d) Circle of radius $\sqrt{2}$

19. The set $S = \left\{ \text{Re}\left(\frac{2iz}{1-z^2}\right) : z \text{ is a complex number}, |z| = 1, z \ne \pm 1 \right\}$ equals:

(a) $[-1,1] - \{0\}$

(b) $\mathbf{R} - \{0\}$

(c) $(-\infty, -1] \cup [1, +\infty)$

(d) $\mathbf{R} - \{-1, 0, 1\}$

20. If $\frac{w - \bar{w}z}{1 - z}$ is purely real, where $w = \alpha + i\beta$, $\beta \ne 0$ and $z \ne 1$, then:

(a) $z + \bar{z} = 0$ (b) $z - \bar{z} = 0$
(c) $|z| = |w|$ (d) $|z| = 1$

21. Let z_1, z_2 be any two complex numbers and a, b be any two real numbers. Then $|az_1 - bz_2|^2 + |bz_1 + az_2|^2$ equals:

(a) $(a+b)(|z_1|^2 + |z_2|^2)$

(b) $(a^2 + b^2)(|z_1|^2 + |z_2|^2)$

(c) $(a^2 + b^2)(|z_1| + |z_2|)$

(d) $a^2|z_1|^2 + b^2|z_2|^2$

22. If $\left(\sqrt{3}+i\right)^{100}=2^{99}(a+ib)$, then a^2+b^2 equals:

(a) 4 (b) $\sqrt{2}$

(c) 3 (d) $\sqrt{3}$

23. If $\text{Re}(z)+\text{Im}(z)=0$, then:

(a) $\text{Re}\left(z^2\right)=|z|^2$ (b) $\text{Im}\left(z^2\right)=-|z|^2$

(c) $z^2-\bar{z}^2=0$ (d) $\text{Im}\left(ze^{i\frac{\pi}{4}}\right)=0$

24. A man walks a distance of 3 units from the origin towards the north-east direction to reach point *P*. From there, he walks a distance of 4 units towards the north-west direction to reach point *Q*. Finally, he moves through an angle $\frac{\pi}{2}$ in the anticlockwise sense about the origin to reach point *R*. The complex representation of point *R* is:

(a) $(4-3i)e^{i\frac{\pi}{4}}$ (b) $(3-4i)e^{i\frac{\pi}{4}}$

(c) $(4+3i)e^{i\frac{\pi}{4}}$ (d) $(-4+3i)e^{i\frac{\pi}{4}}$

25. Let z_1, z_2 be two distinct complex numbers and let $z=(1-t)z_1+tz_2$, where *t* is a real number such that $0<t<1$. Then:

(a) $|z-z_1|-|z-z_2|=|z_2-z_1|$

(b) $\text{Arg}\left(\frac{z-z_1}{z-z_2}\right)=0$

(c) $\text{Arg}\left(\frac{z-z_1}{z_2-z_1}\right)=0$

(d) $\begin{vmatrix} z-z_1 & \bar{z}-\bar{z}_1 \\ z_2-z_1 & \bar{z}_2-\bar{z}_1 \end{vmatrix}=0$

26. Consider the circle $|z-3-4i|=6$ in the Argand plane. If a straight line through the origin meets the circle at points z_1, z_2, then $|z_1z_2|$ equals:

(a) 7 (b) 11

(c) 12 (d) 16

27. Consider the sets

$$A=\{z:|z-3-4i|=6\}$$

$$B=\{z:\text{Im}(z)\geq 4\}$$

$$C=\{z:\text{Re}\{(4+3i)z\}=0\}$$

If *z* is a point in $A\cap B\cap C$ and *w* is a point in *A*, then the least and the greatest values of $|z|-|w|-3$ are, respectively:

(a) −2 and 9

(b) 3 and 9

(c) −3 and 7

(d) −1 and 9

28. Let z_1, z_2 be two complex numbers satisfying $|z_1-3|\leq 2$ and $|z_2-4|\leq 1$, respectively. Then the least and the greatest values of $|z_1|-|z_2|$ are, respectively:

(a) −4 and 2 (b) 0 and 3

(c) −3 and 7 (d) −1 and 5

29. If $x+\frac{1}{x}=1$, then the value of $x^{2000}+\frac{1}{x^{2000}}$ is:

(a) −1 (b) 1

(c) 0 (d) None of these

30. If α, β are the roots of the equation $x^2+2x+2=0$, then $\alpha^{15}+\beta^{15}$ equals:

(a) −256 (b) 256

(c) −512 (d) 512

31. If *z* and *w* are complex numbers such that $|z|\leq 1, |w|\leq 1$ and $|z+iw|=|z-i\bar{w}|=2$, then $z+w$ equals:

(a) $1-i$ (b) $1+i$

(c) $-1-i$ (d) $-1+i$

32. The value of $\sum_{1}^{6}\left\{\sin\left(\frac{2\pi k}{7}\right)-i\cos\left(\frac{2\pi k}{7}\right)\right\}$ equals:

(a) −1 (b) i

(c) 0 (d) $-i$

33. If the opposite angular vertices of a square are represented by $3+4i$ and $1-i$, the other two vertices are:

(a) $\frac{7}{2}-i\frac{1}{2}$ (b) $\frac{-1}{2}+i\frac{3}{2}$

(c) $\frac{9}{2}+i\frac{1}{2}$ (d) $\frac{-1}{2}+i\frac{5}{2}$

34. If $\omega\neq 1$ is a complex cube root of unity, then the value of the series

$$2(1+\omega)\left(1+\omega^2\right)+3(2+\omega)\left(2+\omega^2\right)+\ldots$$

up to 5 terms is:

(a) 175 (b) 225

(c) 230 (d) 275

35. Let $\omega \neq 1$ be a complex cube root of unity. If $\left(3-3\omega+2\omega^2\right)^{4n+3}+\left(2+3\omega-3\omega^2\right)^{4n+3}+\left(-3+2\omega+3\omega^2\right)^{4n+3}=0$, then the possible values of n are:

(a) 2 (b) 3
(c) 4 (d) 5

36. A and B are two points on a circle centred at the origin, in the complex plane. Tangents to the circle at points A and B intersect at point P. If z_1 and z_2 are the complex representations of A and B, respectively, then the complex representation of P is:

(a) $\dfrac{z_1^2+z_2^2}{z_1+z_2}$

(b) $\dfrac{2z_1z_2}{z_1+z_2}$

(c) $\dfrac{z_1^2+z_2^2+z_1z_2}{z_1+z_2}$

(d) None of these

37. The number of nth roots of unity that are also roots of the equation $z^2+az+b=0$ for some integer a,b is:

(a) 10 (b) 8
(c) 6 (d) 5

38. The locus of points $P(z)$ satisfying the equation $\text{Arg}\left\{\dfrac{(z-z_1)(z_2-z_3)}{(z-z_3)(z_2-z_1)}\right\}=\pi$ for some given points $A(z_1), B(z_2), C(z_3)$ is.

(a) A straight line for any z_1, z_2, z_3
(b) A straight line only if z_1, z_2, z_3 are collinear
(c) A circle for any z_1, z_2, z_3
(d) A circle only if z_1, z_2, z_3 are non-collinear

39. Match the columns:

(a) The set of points satisfying $\left|z-i|z|\right|=\left|z+i|z|\right|$
(b) The set of points satisfying $|z+4|+|z-4|=10$
(c) The set of points satisfying $z=w-\dfrac{1}{w}$, where $|w|=2$
(d) The set of points satisfying $z=w+\dfrac{1}{w}$, where $|w|=1$
(e) The set of points satisfying $z=\dfrac{1}{1+i(2t)}$, where $t\in\mathbf{R}, t\neq 0$

(p) An ellipse whose $e=4/5$
(q) The set of points satisfying $\text{Im}(z)=0$
(r) The set of points satisfying $\text{Im}(z)\leq 1$
(s) The set of points satisfying $|z|\leq 2$
(t) A circle of radius $1/2$

40. Match the columns:

(a) If $\left(\dfrac{1+i}{1-i}\right)^n=1$, then the value of n is
(b) If $\left|z+\dfrac{2}{z}\right|=2$, then the greatest value of $|z|$ is
(c) If $\text{Arg}\left(\dfrac{z-1}{z+1}\right)=\dfrac{\pi}{3}$, then the greatest value of $|z|$ is
(d) If $\log_{\sqrt{3}}\left(\dfrac{|z|^2-|z|+1}{|z|+2}\right)\leq 2$, then the greatest value of $|z|$ is
(e) If $|z|<\sqrt{2}-1$, then $\left|z^2+2z\cos\alpha\right|$ is less than

(p) $1+\sqrt{3}$
(q) $\sqrt{3}$
(r) 5
(s) 4
(t) 1

ANSWER KEYS

1. (c)	**2.** (b)	**3.** (c)	**4.** (d)	**5.** (a),(b)	**6.** (a)	**7.** (c)	**8.** (a)	**9.** (a)	**10.** (b)
11. (c)	**12.** (b)	**13.** (c)	**14.** (b)	**15.** (c)	**16.** (b)	**17.** (d)	**18.** (c)	**19.** (c)	**20.** (d)
21. (b)	**22.** (a)	**23.** (b),(d)	**24.** (d)	**25.** (c),(d)	**26.** (b)	**27.** (c)	**28.** (a)	**29.** (a)	**30.** (a)
31. (a), (d)	**32.** (b)	**33.** (c), (d)	**34.** (c)	**35.** (a), (c), (d)		**36.** (b)	**37.** (b)		

38. (b),(d) **39.** (a)-(q), (b)-(p), (c)-(p), (d)-(s), (e)-(t) **40.** (a)-(s), (b)-(p), (c)-(q), (d)-(r), (e)-(t)

SOLUTIONS

1. (c) The complex numbers z and iz are of the same magnitude and are mutually perpendicular. The three complex numbers z, iz and $z+iz$, when arranged in head-tail fashion, form an isosceles right-angled triangle with $z+iz$ as the hypotenuse. The area of this triangle is $\frac{1}{2}|z|^2$. Equating this with the given area 50, we have

$$\frac{1}{2}|z|^2 = 50 \Rightarrow |z| = 10$$

2. (b) We have

$$z = 1+\cos\frac{2\pi}{3}+i\sin\frac{2\pi}{3}$$

$$= \frac{1}{2}+i\frac{\sqrt{3}}{2} = e^{i\frac{\pi}{3}}$$

Hence

$$z^5 = e^{i\frac{5\pi}{3}} = \cos\frac{5\pi}{3}+i\sin\frac{5\pi}{3}$$

$$= \frac{1}{2}-i\frac{\sqrt{3}}{2}$$

3. (c) We have

$$z = e^{\cos\theta+i\sin\theta} = e^{\cos\theta}e^{i\sin\theta}$$

$$= e^{\cos\theta}\{\cos(\sin\theta)+i\sin(\sin\theta)\}$$

4. (d) We have

$$z = \frac{\{\sin 2\theta+i\cos 2\theta\}^4}{\{\sin\theta-i\cos\theta\}^3} = \frac{\{i(\cos 2\theta-i\sin 2\theta)\}^4}{\{-i(\cos\theta+i\sin\theta)\}^3}$$

$$= \frac{i^4 e^{-i8\theta}}{(-i)^3 e^{i3\theta}} = -ie^{-i11\theta}$$

$$= -i\{\cos 11\theta - i\sin 11\theta\} = -\sin 11\theta - i\cos 11\theta$$

5. (a), (b) We have

$$\text{Im}\left(\frac{az+b}{z+1}\right) = y$$

$$\Rightarrow \quad \text{Im}\left\{\frac{(ax+b+iay)(x+1-iy)}{(x+1+iy)(x+1-iy)}\right\} = y$$

$$\Rightarrow \quad \frac{ay(x+1)-y(ax+b)}{(x+1)^2+y^2} = y$$

$$\Rightarrow \quad a-b = (x+1)^2+y^2$$

$$\Rightarrow \quad x = -1\pm\sqrt{1-y^2} \quad [a-b=1, \text{ given}]$$

6. (a) We have

$$|a+b\omega+c\omega^2|^2 = (a+b\omega+c\omega^2)(a+b\omega^2+c\omega)$$

$$\left[\bar{\omega}=\omega^2 \text{ and } \overline{\omega^2}=\omega\right]$$

$$= a^2+b^2+c^2+(ab+bc+ca)(\omega+\omega^2)$$

$$= a^2+b^2+c^2-ab+bc+ca$$

$$= \frac{1}{2}\left[(a-b)^2+(b-c)^2+(c-a)^2\right].$$

Since $(a-b)^2, (b-c)^2$ and $(c-a)^2$ are all integers and are not all equal, the least value of the above expression is $\frac{1}{2}[1+1+0] = 1$.

7. (c) We have

$$\left|\frac{1}{z_1}+\frac{1}{z_2}+\frac{1}{z_3}\right| = 1$$

$$\Rightarrow \quad |\overline{z_1}+\overline{z_2}+\overline{z_3}| = 1\left[z_1\overline{z_1} = z_2\overline{z_2} = z_3\overline{z_3} = 1, \text{ given}\right]$$

$$\Rightarrow \quad \left|\overline{z_1 + z_2 + z_3}\right| = 1$$

$$\Rightarrow \quad |z_1 + z_2 + z_3| = 1$$

8. (a) We have

$$\sum_{k=1}^{15} \operatorname{Im}\left(z^{2k-1}\right)$$

$$= \operatorname{Im}\sum_{k=1}^{15} z^{2k-1}\left[\operatorname{Im}(z_1) + \operatorname{Im}(z_2) = \operatorname{Im}(z_1 + z_2)\right]$$

$$= \operatorname{Im}\left(z + z^3 + z^5 + \ldots \text{up to 15 terms}\right)$$

$$= \operatorname{Im}\left\{\frac{z\left(z^{30} - 1\right)}{z^2 - 1}\right\}$$

$$= \operatorname{Im}\left\{\frac{z\left(z^{30} - 1\right)}{z^2 - z\bar{z}}\right\} [z\bar{z} = 1, \text{given}]$$

$$= \operatorname{Im}\left\{\frac{z^{30} - 1}{z - \bar{z}}\right\}$$

$$= \operatorname{Im}\left\{\frac{\cos(30\theta) - 1 + i\sin(30\theta)}{i\, 2\sin\theta}\right\}$$

$$= \frac{1 - \cos(30\theta)}{2\sin\theta}$$

For $\theta = 2°$ the value of the above expression is $\dfrac{1}{4\sin 2°}$

9. (a) We have

$$z\bar{z}^3 + \bar{z}z^3 = 350$$

$$\Rightarrow \quad z\bar{z}\left(\bar{z}^2 + z^2\right) = 350$$

$$\Rightarrow \quad \left(x^2 + y^2\right)\left(x^2 - y^2\right) - 175 = 25 \times 7 \text{ or } 35 \times 5$$

Choosing $x^2 + y^2 = 25$ and $x^2 - y^2 = 7$ gives integral solutions $x = \pm 4, y = \pm 3$.

Thus, the vertices of the rectangle are $(\pm 4, \pm 3)$. The lengths of its sides are 8 and 6. Hence, its area equals $8 \times 6 = 48$.

10. (b) We have

$$z\begin{vmatrix} 1 & \omega & \omega^2 \\ 1 & z + \omega^2 & 1 \\ 1 & 1 & z + \omega \end{vmatrix} = 0 \left[C_1 \to C_1 + C_2 + C_3\right]$$

$$\Rightarrow \quad z\left[\left(z^2 - z\right) - \omega z - \omega^2 z\right] = 0$$

$$\Rightarrow \quad z^3 = 0$$

Hence, there is only one solution, $z = 0$.

11. (c) We have

$$a + 8b + 7c = 0, 9a + 2b + 3c = 0 \text{ and } a + b + c = 0$$

The above homogeneous system of equations has infinite solutions $\left(\text{since } |A| = 0\right)$ of the type

$$\frac{a}{1} = \frac{b}{6} = \frac{c}{-7}$$

For $a = 2$, we have $b = 12$ and $c = -14$.

Hence, the value of the given expression is

$$\frac{3}{\omega^2} + \frac{1}{\omega^{12}} + \frac{3}{\omega^{-14}} = 3\omega + 1 + 3\omega^2 = -2$$

12. (b) Here, ω is the cube root of unity. Thus, we have

$$|x|^2 = (a + b + c)\left(\bar{a} + \bar{b} + \bar{c}\right)$$

$$|y|^2 = \left(a + b\omega + c\omega^2\right)\left(\bar{a} + \bar{b}\omega^2 + \bar{c}\omega\right)$$

and $$|z|^2 = \left(a + b\omega^2 + c\omega\right)\left(\bar{a} + \bar{b}\omega + \bar{c}\omega^2\right)$$

$$\left[\bar{\omega} = \omega^2 \text{ and } \overline{\omega^2} = \omega\right]$$

Expanding and adding gives

$$|x|^2 + |y|^2 + |z|^2 = 3\left(|a|^2 + |b|^2 + |c|^2\right)$$

Hence, the required ratio equals 3.

13. (c) All points are of the type

$$\frac{1}{a - 2i} = \frac{a}{a^2 + 4} + \frac{2i}{a^2 + 4}$$

That is, $x = \dfrac{a}{a^2 + 4}, y = \dfrac{2}{a^2 + 4}$

Eliminating a, we see that they lie on the circle $x^2+y^2-\frac{1}{2}y=0$, which has radius $r=1/4$. The octagon can be divided into eight congruent triangles; each triangle is isosceles with two sides of length r and the angle between them as $\theta=2\pi/8=\pi/4$. Hence, the area of the octagon is

$$A=8\left(\frac{1}{2}r^2\sin\theta\right)=\frac{1}{4\sqrt{2}}$$

14. (b) The point z satisfying $|z-3-2i|\le 2$ lies inside a circle centred at $C=(3,2)$ and with radius $r=2$.

Now $|2z-6+5i|=2\left|z-3+\frac{5}{2}i\right|$, where $\left|z-3+\frac{5}{2}i\right|$ is the distance between points z and $P=\left(3,\frac{-5}{2}\right)$.

For points lying inside the circle, this distance lies between $PC-r=\frac{9}{2}-2=\frac{5}{2}$ and $PC+r=\frac{9}{2}+2=\frac{13}{2}$.

Hence, the values of $2\left|z-3+\frac{5}{2}i\right|$ lie between 5 and 13.

15. (c) We have

$$\frac{z_1-z_3}{z_2-z_3}=e^{-i(\pi/3)}$$

$\Rightarrow |z_2-z_3|=|z_1-z_3|$ and $\text{Arg}(z_2-z_3)-\text{Arg}(z_1-z_3)=\frac{\pi}{3}$

Hence, z_1, z_2, z_3 are the vertices of an equilateral triangle.

16. (b) The point z_1 satisfying $|z_1|=12$ lies on a circle centred at $C_1=(0,0)$ and with radius $r_1=12$. The point z_2 satisfying $|z_2-3-4i|=5$ lies on a circle centred at $C_2=(3,4)$ and with radius $r_2=5$. The second circle lies inside the first circle.

Now $|z_1-z_2|$ is the distance between points z_1 and z_2. From the figure, we see that this distance lies between $r_1-(C_1C_2+r_2)=12-(5+5)=2$ and $r_1+(C_1C_2+r_2)=12+(5+5)=22$.

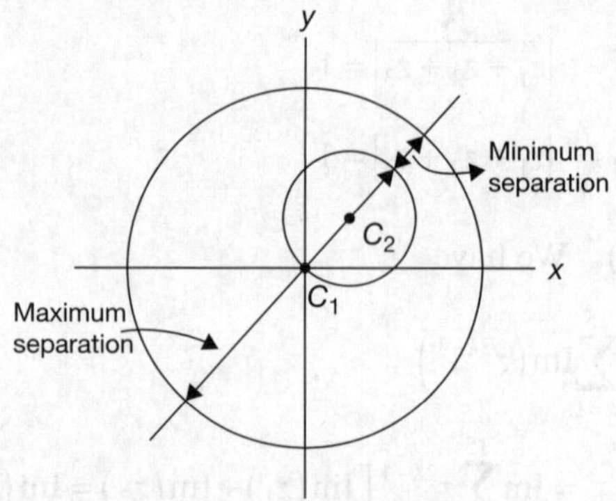

17. (d) We have

$$\text{Re}(w)=\frac{1}{2}\left[\frac{z-1}{z+1}+\frac{\bar{z}-1}{\bar{z}+1}\right]=\frac{z\bar{z}-1}{(z+1)(\bar{z}+1)}=0$$

$$[|z|=1,\text{ given}]$$

18. (c) We have

$$\left|\frac{z_1-2z_2}{2-z_1\bar{z}_2}\right|=1$$

$$\Rightarrow |z_1-2z_2|=|2-z_1\bar{z}_2|$$

$$\Rightarrow (z_1-2z_2)(\bar{z}_1-2\bar{z}_2)=(2-z_1\bar{z}_2)(2-\bar{z}_1z_2)$$

$$\Rightarrow |z_1|^2+4|z_2|^2=4+|z_1|^2|z_2|^2$$

$$\Rightarrow (|z_1|^2-4)(|z_2|^2-1)=0$$

$$\Rightarrow |z_1|^2=4\ [|z_2|\ne 1,\text{ given}]$$

Hence, z_1 lies on a circle of radius 2.

19. (c) We have

$$\text{Re}\left(\frac{2iz}{1-z^2}\right)=\text{Re}\left(\frac{2iz}{z\bar{z}-z^2}\right)[|z|=1,\text{ given}]$$

$$=\text{Re}\left(\frac{2i}{\bar{z}-z}\right)=\text{Re}\left(\frac{-1}{y}\right)=\frac{-1}{y}$$

$$[\text{Putting } z=x+iy]$$

Here, $y\in[-1,1]-\{0\}$ since $|z|=1, z\ne\pm1$. Hence, the values of $\frac{-1}{y}$ will lie in $(-\infty,-1]\cup[1,+\infty)$.

20. (d) We have

$$\operatorname{Im}\left(\frac{w-\bar{w}z}{1-z}\right)=0$$

$$\Rightarrow \quad \frac{w-\bar{w}z}{1-z}=\frac{\bar{w}-w\bar{z}}{1-\bar{z}}$$

$$\Rightarrow \quad (w-\bar{w}z)(1-\bar{z})=(\bar{w}-w\bar{z})(1-z)$$

$$\Rightarrow \quad w+\bar{w}|z|^2=\bar{w}+w|z|^2$$

$$\Rightarrow \quad (w-\bar{w})\left(|z|^2-1\right)=0$$

$$\Rightarrow \quad \beta\left(|z|^2-1\right)=0\ [w=\alpha+i\beta,\text{ given}]$$

$$\Rightarrow \quad |z|=1\ [\beta\neq 0,\text{ given}]$$

21. (b) We have

$$|az_1-bz_2|^2+|bz_1+az_2|^2=(az_1-bz_2)\left(\overline{az_1}-\overline{bz_2}\right)+(bz_1+az_2)\left(\overline{bz_1}+\overline{az_2}\right)$$

$$=\left(a^2+b^2\right)\left(|z_1|^2+|z_2|^2\right)$$

22. (a) We have

$$\left(\sqrt{3}+i\right)^{100}=2^{99}(a+ib)$$

Taking the conjugate of both sides, we have

$$\left(\sqrt{3}-i\right)^{100}=2^{99}(a-ib)$$

Multiplying the above equations, we get

$$4^{100}=2^{198}\left(a^2+b^2\right)$$

$$\Rightarrow \quad a^2+b^2=2^2=4$$

23. (b), (d) According to the given condition, $z=x-ix$

Now, we have

$$z^2=\left(-2x^2\right)i$$

$$\bar{z}^2=\overline{z^2}=\left(2x^2\right)i$$

$$ze^{i\frac{\pi}{4}}=\frac{x}{\sqrt{2}}(1-i)(1+i)=\sqrt{2}x$$

We see that $\operatorname{Im}\left(z^2\right)=-2x^2=-|z|^2$ and $\operatorname{Im}\left(ze^{i\frac{\pi}{4}}\right)=0$ are the correct choices.

24. (d) The complex representations of the paths OP and PQ are, respectively, $3e^{i\frac{\pi}{4}}$ and $4e^{i\frac{3\pi}{4}}$.

Then $OQ=3e^{i\frac{\pi}{4}}+4e^{i\frac{3\pi}{4}}=e^{i\frac{\pi}{4}}(3+4i)$.

Now OQ is rotated by angle $\frac{\pi}{2}$.

Hence $OR=e^{i\frac{\pi}{4}}(3+4i)i=e^{i\frac{\pi}{4}}(-4+3i)$

25. (c), (d) We have

$$z=(1-t)z_1+tz_2$$

$$\Rightarrow \quad z-z_1=t(z_2-z_1)$$

The points z, z_1, z_2 lie in a straight line as shown in the figure.

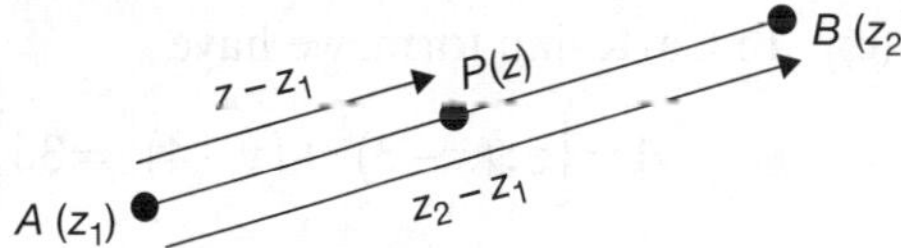

For $0<t<1$, the point z lies between z_1 and z_2. In that case

$$|z-z_1|+|z-z_2|=|z_2-z_1|$$

$\Rightarrow$ Option (a) is incorrect

$$\operatorname{Arg}(z-z_2)-\operatorname{Arg}(z-z_1)=\pi$$

$\Rightarrow$ Option (b) is incorrect

$$\operatorname{Arg}(z-z_1)-\operatorname{Arg}(z_2-z_1)=0$$

$\Rightarrow$ Option (c) is correct

$$\begin{vmatrix} z & \bar{z} & 1 \\ z_1 & \bar{z}_1 & 1 \\ z_2 & \bar{z}_2 & 1 \end{vmatrix}=0\Rightarrow\begin{vmatrix} z-z_1 & \bar{z}-\bar{z}_1 & 0 \\ z_2-z_1 & \bar{z}_2-\bar{z}_1 & 0 \\ z_2 & \bar{z}_2 & 1 \end{vmatrix}=0$$

$$\Rightarrow \begin{vmatrix} z-z_1 & \bar{z}-\bar{z}_1 \\ z_2-z_1 & \bar{z}_2-\bar{z}_1 \end{vmatrix}=0\Rightarrow \text{Option (d) is correct}$$

26. (b) The given equation represents a circle centred at $C=(3,4)$ and with radius $r=6$. The origin O lies inside the circle. If chords drawn from O intersect the circle at points A and B, then from the property of circles, the product $OA\cdot OB$ is the same for any chord. So let us choose the chord through its centre, as shown in the figure.

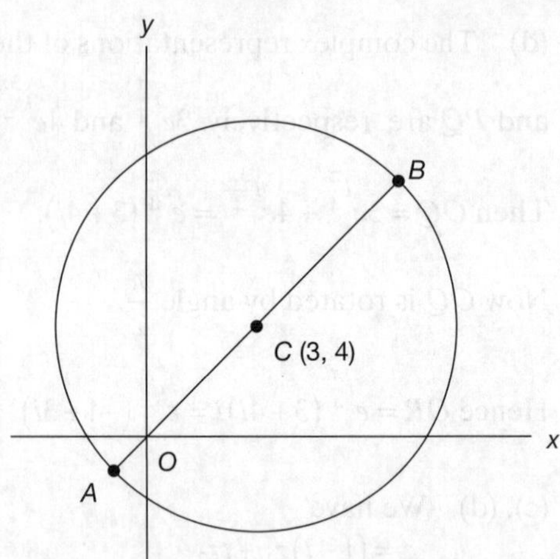

Then $OA = r + OC = 6 + 5 = 11$ and $OB = r - OC = 6 - 5 = 1$.
Hence $OA \cdot OB = 11$.

27. (c) In Cartesian form, we have

$$A = \{z : (x-3)^2 + (y-4)^2 = 36\}$$
$$B = \{z : y \geq 4\} \text{ and}$$
$$C = \{z : 4x - 3y = 0\}$$

Solving equations in set A and C, we obtain two points $P = \left(\frac{33}{5}, \frac{44}{5}\right)$ and $Q = \left(\frac{-3}{5}, \frac{-4}{5}\right)$. Only point P satisfies the condition in set B. Thus, there is only one point in $A \cap B \cap C$, that is, $z = \frac{33}{5} + i\frac{44}{5}$ and hence $|z| = 11$.

The point w belonging to set A lies on the circle whose centre is at C = (3, 4) and with radius $r = 6$ (see figure). For points on this circle, the least and the greatest distance from the origin are, respectively, $r - OP = 6 - 5 = 1$ and $r + OP = 11$. Hence, $1 \leq |w| \leq 11$.

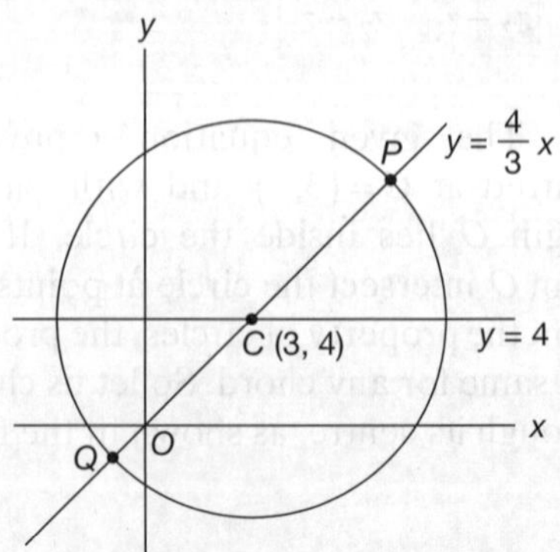

Now $|z| - |w| - 3 = 11 - |w| - 3 = 8 - |w|$, whose values will lie between $8 - 11 = -3$ and $8 - 1 = 7$.

28. (a) The point z_1 lies inside the circle whose centre is at $C_1 = (3, 0)$ and with radius $r_1 = 2$, as shown in the figure. For points on this circle, the least and greatest distance from the origin are, respectively, $OC_1 - r_1 = 3 - 2 = 1$ and $OC_1 + r_1 = 3 + 2 = 5$. Hence $1 \leq |z_1| \leq 5$.

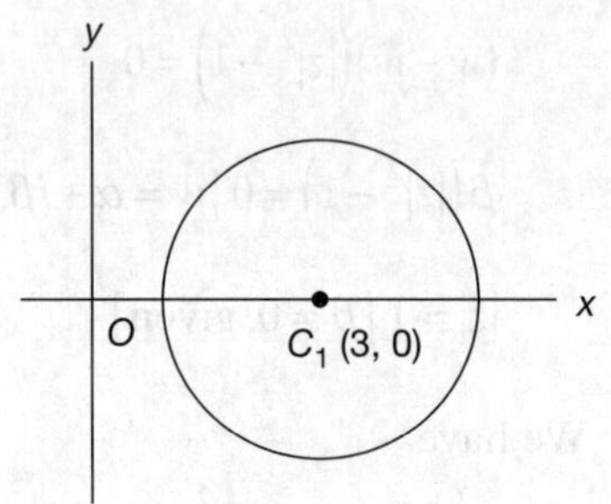

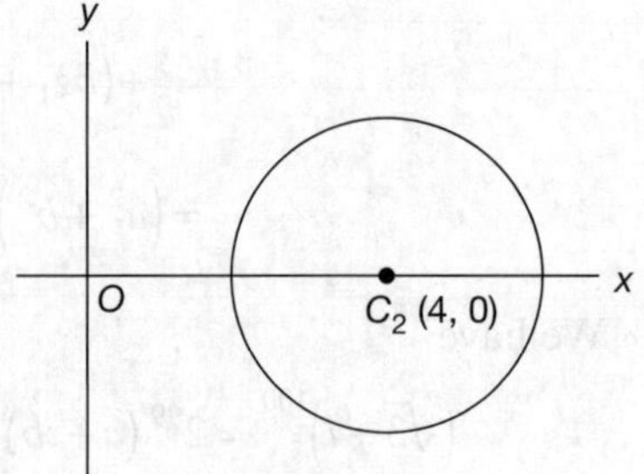

The point z_2 lies inside the circle whose centre is at $C_2 = (0, 4)$ and with radius $r_2 = 1$, as shown in the figure. For points on this circle, the least and greatest distance from the origin are, respectively, $OC_2 - r_2 = 4 - 1 = 3$ and $OC_2 + r_2 = 4 + 1 = 5$. Hence $3 \leq |z_2| \leq 5$.

Hence, the values of $|z_1| - |z_2|$ will lie between $1 - 5 = -4$ and $5 - 3 = 2$.

29. (a) We have

$$x + \frac{1}{x} = 1$$
$$\Rightarrow \quad x^2 - x + 1 = 0$$
$$\Rightarrow \quad x = \omega, \omega^2$$

Now, we have

$$\omega^{2000} + \frac{1}{\omega^{2000}} = \omega^2 + \frac{1}{\omega^2} = \omega^2 + \omega = -1$$

and $$\omega^{4000} + \frac{1}{\omega^{4000}} = \omega + \frac{1}{\omega} = \omega + \omega^2 = -1$$

30. (a) The roots of the equation $x^2 + 2x + 2 = 0$ are

$$x = \frac{-2 \pm \sqrt{-4}}{2} = -1 \pm i = \sqrt{2}e^{\pm i\left(\frac{3\pi}{4}\right)}$$

Hence, we have

$$\alpha^{15} + \beta^{15} = \left(\sqrt{2}\right)^{15}\left[e^{i\left(\frac{45\pi}{4}\right)} + e^{-i\left(\frac{45\pi}{4}\right)}\right]$$

$$= \left(\sqrt{2}\right)^{15}\left[2\cos\left(\frac{45\pi}{4}\right)\right]$$

$$= \left(\sqrt{2}\right)^{15}\left[2\cos\left(11\pi + \frac{\pi}{4}\right)\right]$$

$$= \left(\sqrt{2}\right)^{15}\left[2\cos\left(\pi + \frac{\pi}{4}\right)\right]$$

$$= \left(\sqrt{2}\right)^{15}\left(-\sqrt{2}\right) = -256$$

31. (a), (d) We have

$$|z + iw| = |z - i\bar{w}|$$

$$\Rightarrow \quad (z + iw)(\bar{z} - i\bar{w}) = (z - i\bar{w})(\bar{z} + iw)$$

$$\Rightarrow \quad z\bar{z} - iz\bar{w} + iw\bar{z} + w\bar{w} = z\bar{z} + izw - i\bar{w}\bar{z} + w\bar{w}$$

$$\Rightarrow \quad i\bar{z}(w + \bar{w}) = iz(w + \bar{w})$$

$$\Rightarrow \quad \bar{z} = z \text{ or } \bar{w} = -w$$

$\Rightarrow$ z is purely real or w is purely imaginary.

It is given that $|z| \le 1, |w| \le 1$. Therefore $|z + iw| = 2$ is possible only if

$$|z| = |iw| = 1 \text{ and } \operatorname{Arg}(z) = \operatorname{Arg}(iw)$$

$$\Rightarrow \quad z = iw.$$

Now, since z is purely real, we have

$$z = 1, w = -i \text{ or } z = -1, w = i$$

Thus, we have

$$z + w = 1 - i, -1 + i$$

32. (b) We have

$$S = \sum_1^6 \left\{\sin\left(\frac{2\pi k}{7}\right) - i\cos\left(\frac{2\pi k}{7}\right)\right\}$$

$$= -i\sum_1^6 \left\{\cos\left(\frac{2\pi k}{7}\right) + i\text{isn}\left(\frac{2\pi k}{7}\right)\right\}$$

$$= -i\left\{\sum_0^6 e^{i\left(\frac{2\pi k}{7}\right)} - 1\right\}$$

$$= -i\left\{\frac{e^{i(2\pi)} - 1}{e^{i\left(\frac{2\pi}{7}\right)} - 1}\right\} + i = i$$

33. (c), (d) Let $z_1 = 3 + 4i$ and $z_2 = 1 - i$. If z represents any one of the other two vertices, then

$$z_2 - z = \pm i(z - z_1)$$

$$\Rightarrow \quad z = \frac{z_2 \pm iz_1}{1 \pm i} = \frac{4 + 5i}{1 + i}, \frac{2 + 3i}{1 - i} = \frac{9}{2} + i\frac{1}{2}, \frac{-1}{2} + i\frac{5}{2}$$

34. (c) The given series can be written as

$$S = \sum_1^5 (n + 1)(n + \omega)(n + \omega^2)$$

$$= \sum_1^5 \left(n^3 + 1\right) = \frac{5^2(5 + 1)^2}{4} + 5 = 230$$

35. (a), (c), (d) We have

$$3 - 3\omega + 2\omega^2 = \omega\left(3\omega^2 - 3 + 2\omega\right)$$

$$2 + 3\omega - 3\omega^2 = \omega^2\left(2\omega + 3\omega^2 - 3\right)$$

and $\quad -3 + 2\omega + 3\omega^2 = 1\left(-3 + 2\omega + 3\omega^2\right)$

The given equation reduces to

$$\left(-3 + 2\omega + 3\omega^2\right)^{4n+3}\left[\omega^{4n+3} + \omega^{8n+6} + 1\right] = 0$$

$$\Rightarrow \quad 1 + \omega^n + \omega^{2n} = 0,$$

which is true for $n = 2, 4, 5$.

36. (b) Let O be the origin. Then $\overline{OA} = z_1, \overline{OB} = z_2$. Let $\overline{OP} = z$. Then $\overline{AP} = z - z_1$ and $\overline{BP} = z - z_2$ (see figure)

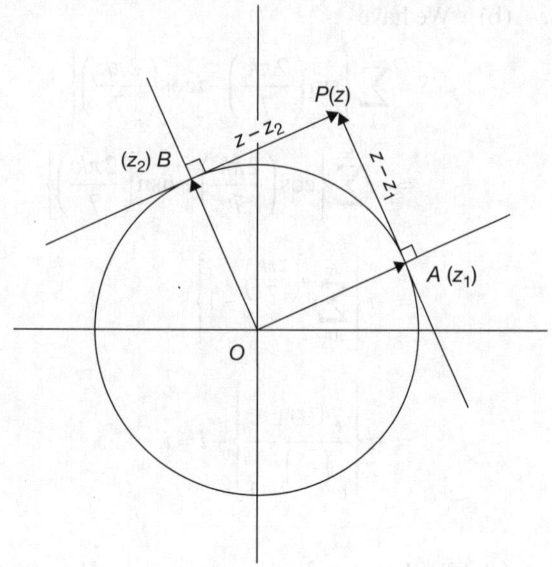

Now $\text{Arg}(\overline{AP}) - \text{Arg}(\overline{OA}) = \pi/2$. Therefore

$$\frac{z-z_1}{z_1} = im, \text{ where } m = \frac{|z-z_1|}{|z_1|} = \frac{AP}{OA}$$

Also $\text{Arg}(\overline{BP}) - \text{Arg}(\overline{OB}) = -\pi/2$. Therefore

$$\frac{z-z_2}{z_2} = -in, \text{ where } n = \frac{|z-z_2|}{|z_2|} = \frac{BP}{OB}$$

Note that $m = n$ since $OA = OB$ (radius) and $AP = BP$ (tangents). Hence, we have

$$\frac{z-z_1}{z_1} = -\frac{z-z_2}{z_2}$$

$$\Rightarrow \quad z = \frac{2z_1z_2}{z_1+z_2}$$

37. (b) We have

$$z^2 + az + b = 0$$

$$\Rightarrow \quad z = \frac{-a \pm \sqrt{a^2-4b}}{2} = \frac{-a}{2} \pm i\sqrt{b - \frac{a^2}{4}}$$

If z is a root of unity, then $|z| = 1$. Thus

$$\frac{a^2}{4} + b - \frac{a^2}{4} = 1 \Rightarrow b = 1$$

Hence $z = \frac{-a}{2} \pm i\sqrt{1 - \frac{a^2}{4}}$, where $\frac{a^2}{4} \le 1 \Rightarrow a = 0, \pm 1, \pm 2$

[a is given to be an integer]

Thus, the possible values of z are $\pm i, \frac{-1}{2} \pm i\frac{\sqrt{3}}{2}, \frac{1}{2} \pm i\frac{\sqrt{3}}{2}, \pm 1 \Rightarrow 8$ solutions.

38. (b), (d) The given equation can be written as

$$\text{Arg}\left(\frac{z-z_1}{z-z_3}\right) + \text{Arg}\left(\frac{z_2-z_3}{z_2-z_1}\right) = \pi$$

$$\Rightarrow \quad \text{Arg}(z-z_1) - \text{Arg}(z-z_3) = \alpha,$$

$$\text{where } \alpha = \pi - \text{Arg}\left(\frac{z_2-z_3}{z_2-z_1}\right)$$

$$\Rightarrow \quad \angle APC = \alpha \text{ (some constant)}$$

If $A(z_1), B(z_2), C(z_3)$ are collinear, then $\text{Arg}\left(\frac{z_2-z_3}{z_2-z_1}\right) = 0$ or π. In that case, $\alpha = 0$ or π, and the locus of $P(z)$ is a straight line.

If $A(z_1), B(z_2), C(z_3)$ are non-collinear, then $\text{Arg}\left(\frac{z_2-z_3}{z_2-z_1}\right)$ is some angle other than 0 or π. In that case, α is some angle other than 0 or π, and the locus of $P(z)$ is a circle.

39. (a)-(q), (b)-(p), (c)-(p), (d)-(s), (e)-(t)

(a) Putting $z = x + iy$, the given equation reduces to

$$x^2 + \left(y - \sqrt{x^2+y^2}\right)^2 = x^2 + \left(y + \sqrt{x^2+y^2}\right)^2$$

$$\Rightarrow \quad 2y\sqrt{x^2+y^2} = 0$$

$$\Rightarrow \quad y = 0 \Rightarrow \text{Option (q) is correct.}$$

(b) By definition, this is an ellipse whose foci are at $(\pm 4, 0)$ and whose major axis equals 10. If a and e represent, respectively, the semi-major axis and the eccentricity of the ellipse, then $2ae = 8$ and $2a = 10$. Hence $e = \frac{4}{5}$ and $b = 3$ $\Rightarrow$ Option (p) is correct.

(c) Let $w = 2e^{i\theta}$. Then

$$z = 2e^{i\theta} + \frac{1}{2}e^{-i\theta} = \frac{5}{2}\cos\theta + i\frac{3}{2}\sin\theta$$

Putting $z = x + iy$, we have

$$x = \frac{5}{2}\cos\theta \text{ and } y = \frac{3}{2}\sin\theta$$

Thus, z lies on an ellipse whose $a=\frac{5}{2}$ and $b=\frac{3}{2}$ and $e=1-\frac{9}{5}=\frac{4}{5}$

$\Rightarrow$ Option (p) is correct.

(d) Let $w=e^{i\theta}$. Then

$$z=e^{i\theta}+e^{-i\theta}=2\cos\theta$$

Putting $z=x+iy$, we have

$$x=2\cos\theta \text{ and } y=0$$

Thus, z lies on the real axis between points –2 and 2

$\Rightarrow$ Option (s) is correct.

(e) Let $z=x+iy$. Then

$$x+iy=\frac{1-i2t}{1+4t^2}$$

$$\Rightarrow \quad x=\frac{1}{1+4t^2} \text{ and } y=\frac{-2t}{1+4t^2}$$

Dividing the above equations gives $t=\frac{-y}{2x}$. Putting this value in the first equation gives

$$x\left(1+\frac{y^2}{x^2}\right)=1\Rightarrow x^2+y^2-x=0$$

It represents a circle of radius $1/2$, centred at $\left(\frac{1}{2},0\right)$

$\Rightarrow$ Option (t) is correct.

40. (a)-(s), (b)-(p), (c)-(q), (d)-(r), (e)-(t)

(a) The given equation can be written as

$$\left(\frac{\sqrt{2}e^{i\frac{\pi}{4}}}{\sqrt{2}e^{l\frac{-\pi}{4}}}\right)^n=1$$

$$\Rightarrow \quad \left(e^{i\frac{\pi}{2}}\right)^n=1$$

$$\Rightarrow \quad i^n=1\Rightarrow n=4$$

$\Rightarrow$ Option (s) is correct.

(b) Using triangle inequality, we have

$$\left||z|-\frac{2}{|z|}\right|\le\left|z+\frac{2}{z}\right|\le|z|+\frac{2}{|z|}$$

$$\Rightarrow \quad \left||z|-\frac{2}{|z|}\right|\le 2\le|z|+\frac{2}{|z|}$$

The RHI $|z|^2-2|z|+2\ge 0$ is always true since $D<0$ and $a>0$.

The LHI reduces to

$$\left(|z|^2-2\right)^2\le 4|z|^2$$

$$\Rightarrow \quad |z|^4-8|z|^2+4\le 0$$

$$\Rightarrow \quad 4-2\sqrt{3}\le|z|^2\le 4+2\sqrt{3}$$

$$\Rightarrow \quad \left(\sqrt{3}-1\right)^2\le|z|^2\le\left(\sqrt{3}+1\right)^2$$

$\Rightarrow$ Option (p) is correct.

(c) The given inequality reduces to

$$\text{Arg}(z-1)-\text{Arg}(z+1)=\pi/3$$

The points z lies on the portion of the circle lying above the x-axis (see figure). The line joining –1 and 1 is a chord which subtends 120° at the centre of the circle. The point P shown on the circle is the farthest point from the origin and this distance is $\cot 30°=\sqrt{3}$

$\Rightarrow$ Option (q) is correct.

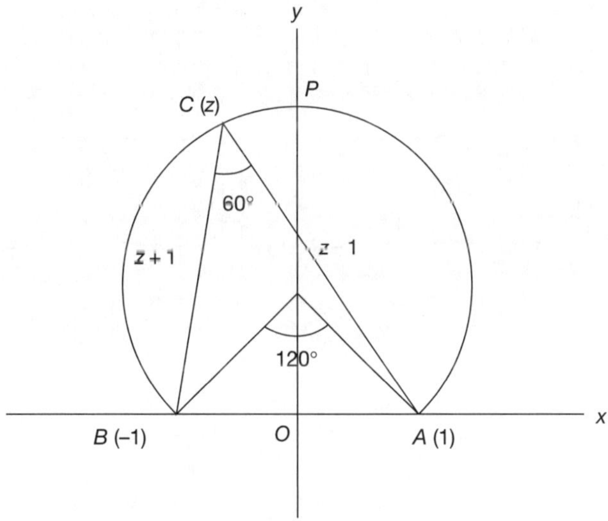

(d) The given inequality reduces to

$$\frac{|z|^2-|z|+1}{|z|+2}\le 3$$

$\Rightarrow \quad |z|^2-4|z|-5\le 0$

$\Rightarrow \quad -1\le |z|\le 5$

$\Rightarrow$ Option (r) is correct.

(e) Using triangle inequality, we have

$$\left|z^2+2z\cos\alpha\right|\le |z|^2+2|z||\cos\alpha|$$

$$\le\left(\sqrt{2}-1\right)^2+2\left(\sqrt{2}-1\right)=1$$

$\Rightarrow$ Option (t) is correct.

CHAPTER 6

Permutations and Combinations

- **Symbols Used:**

1. $n! = n(n-1)(n-2)\cdots 3\cdot 2\cdot 1,\ n \in \mathbf{N}$ and $0! = 1$
2. ${}^nC_r = \dfrac{n!}{r!(n-r)!},\ 0 \le r \le n$
3. ${}^nP_r = r! \times {}^nC_r = \dfrac{n!}{(n-r)!},\ 0 \le r \le n$

- **Properties Related to ${}^nC_r$:**

1. ${}^nC_r = {}^nC_{n-r}$
2. ${}^nC_r + {}^nC_{r-1} = {}^{n+1}C_r$
3. $\dfrac{n+1}{r+1} \times {}^nC_r = {}^{n+1}C_{r+1}$
4. The greatest value of ${}^nC_r$ is $= \begin{cases} {}^nC_{n/2} & \text{if } n \text{ is even} \\ {}^nC_{n-1/2} \text{ or } {}^nC_{n+1/2} & \text{if } n \text{ is odd} \end{cases}$
5. ${}^nC_0 + {}^nC_1 + {}^nC_2 + \ldots + {}^nC_n = 2^n$ and ${}^nC_0 + {}^nC_2 + {}^nC_4 + \ldots = {}^nC_1 + {}^nC_3 + {}^nC_5 + \ldots = 2^{n-1}$

- **Sum Rule:** If A and B are two mutually exclusive events (they never occur together), which occur in m and n ways, respectively, then A or B can occur in $m+n$ ways.
- **Product Rule:** If X is an event comprising two events A and B in succession, which occur in m and n ways, respectively, regardless of the outcome of the other event, then event X can occur in $m \times n$ ways.
- **Combinations:**

1. The number of ways of selecting r things from a set of n different things is
$$ {}^nC_r $$
2. The number of ways of selecting zero or more things from a set of n different things is
$$ {}^nC_0 + {}^nC_1 + {}^nC_2 + \ldots + {}^nC_n = 2^n $$
3. The number of ways of selecting zero or more things from a set of n identical things is
$$ n+1 $$

- **Permutations:**

1. Permutations of n different things taken all at a time is
$$ n(n-1)(n-2)\cdots 3\cdot 2\cdot 1 = n! $$
2. Permutations of n different things taken $r\,(0 \le r \le n)$ at a time without repetition is
$$ n(n-1)(n-2)\cdots(n-r+1) = \frac{n!}{(n-r)!} = {}^nP_r $$

3. Permutations of n different things taken $r(0 \le r \le n)$ at a time with repetition is

$$n \cdot n \cdot n \cdots n(r \text{ times}) = n^r$$

4. Permutations of n things taken all at a time when p of them are alike and of one kind, q of them are alike and of another kind, r of them are alike and of a third kind and the rest $n-(p+q+r)$ are all different is

$$\frac{n!}{p!q!r!}$$

5. The number of circular permutations of n different things is

$$(n-1)!$$

- **Division into Groups:**

1. The number of ways in which $m+n$ different things can be divided into two groups which contain m and $n(m \ne n)$ things, respectively, is

$$^{m+n}C_m \times {}^nC_n = \frac{(m+n)!}{m!n!}$$

2. The number of ways in which $2n$ different things can be divided into two equal groups is

$$\frac{1}{2!}\left({}^{2n}C_n \times {}^nC_n\right) = \frac{(2n)!}{2!(n!)^2}$$

3. The number of ways in which $m+n+p$ different things can be divided into three groups which contain m, n and $p(m \ne n \ne p)$ things, respectively, is

$$^{m+n+p}C_m \times {}^{n+p}C_n \times {}^pC_p = \frac{(m+n+p)!}{m!n!p!}$$

4. The number of ways in which $3n$ different things can be divided into three equal groups is

$$\frac{1}{3!}\left({}^{3n}C_n \times {}^{2n}C_n \times {}^nC_n\right) = \frac{(3n)!}{3!(n!)^3}$$

EXERCISES

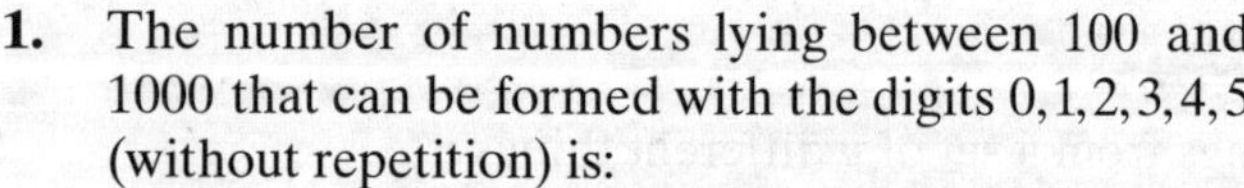

1. The number of numbers lying between 100 and 1000 that can be formed with the digits $0,1,2,3,4,5$ (without repetition) is:
(a) 60 (b) 120
(c) 80 (d) 100

2. Words of length 10 are formed using the letters A,B,C,D,E,F,G,H,I,J. Let m be the number of such words, where no letter is repeated, and let n be the number of such words, where exactly one letter is repeated twice and no other letter is repeated. Then $n/9m$ equals:
(a) 9 (b) 6
(c) 5 (d) 2

3. Let $S = \{1,2,3,\ldots,8,9\}$. Let N_k be the number of subsets of S, each containing 5 elements, of which exactly k are odd. Then $N_1+N_2+N_3+N_4+N_5$ equals:
(a) 106 (b) 126
(c) 210 (d) 252

4. The number of different ways that 4 different prizes can be distributed amongst 5 students so that no one gets all the prizes is:
(a) 620 (b) 600
(c) 400 (d) 380

5. The number of different arrangements that can be made from the letters of the word *PERMUTATIONS* so that there are always four letters between P and S is:
(a) $\frac{10!}{4!}$ (b) $\frac{10!}{2!}$
(c) $\frac{5}{2}\times 10!$ (d) $7\times 10!$

6. The number of numbers greater than 1000000 that can be formed with the digits $1, 2, 0, 2, 4, 2, 4$ is:
(a) 120 (b) 240
(c) 360 (d) 480

7. Words with or without meaning are made using all the letters of the word *AGAIN*. If these words are written as in a dictionary, then the 50th word will be:
(a) *INGAA* (b) *NAAIG*
(c) *NAAGI* (d) None of these

8. A 5-member team is to be selected from a group of 3 girls and 7 boys. The team should have at least 2 girls. If two boys insist that they must be chosen together or not chosen at all, then the number of ways in which the team can be formed is:
(a) 56 (b) 46
(c) 38 (d) 32

9. The number of ways of choosing 10 objects out of 31, of which 10 are identical and the remaining 21 are distinct, is:
(a) $2^{20}-1$ (b) $2^{20}+1$
(c) 2^{21} (d) 2^{20}

10. Consider sets $E=\{1,2,3,4\}$ and $F=\{1,2,3\}$. The number of into and onto functions from $E \to F$ are, respectively:
(a) 54, 27 (b) 48, 33
(c) 45, 36 (d) 42, 39

11. Consider sets $E=\{1,2,3,4\}$ and $F=\{1,2,3,4\}$. The number of one–one, onto functions from $E \to F$ are:
(a) 16 (b) 18
(c) 20 (d) 24

12. Consider sets $E=\{1,2,3,4\}$ and $F=\{1,2\}$. The number of relations that can be defined from $E \to F$ are:
(a) 48 (b) 64
(c) 128 (d) 256

13. Consider set $E=\{1,2,3,4\}$. The number of unordered pairs of disjoint subsets of E is:
(a) 31 (b) 41
(c) 51 (d) 81

14. Triangles are formed by joining the vertices of a regular polygon of 12 sides. The number of triangles having no side in common with the polygon is:
(a) 112 (b) 132
(c) 140 (d) 160

15. There are $2n+1$ consecutively numbered tickets. The number of ways in which three tickets can be chosen so that they form an AP is:
(a) $n(n-1)$ (b) $n(n+1)$
(c) n^2 (d) n^2+1

16. The sum of all numbers that can be formed using all the digits of the number 2334 is:
(a) 39996 (b) 36056
(c) 30246 (d) 30976

17. Four American couples (husband and wife) and one Indian couple are to be seated at a round table. The number of arrangements such that the American couples sit together is:
(a) 1920 (b) 960
(c) 480 (d) 240

18. There are 3 boys and 2 girls standing in a queue such that the number of boys ahead of every girl is at least one more than the number of girls ahead of her. The number of ways in which they can do so is:
(a) 61 (b) 60
(c) 52 (d) 48

19. Bag *I* contains three cards numbered $1, 2, 3$. Bag *II* contains five cards numbered $1, 2, 3, 4, 5$. Bag *III* contains seven cards numbered $1, 2, 3, 4, 5, 6, 7$. One card is drawn from each bag. Let x_i denote the number of the card drawn from the $i^{\text{th}}(i=1,2,3)$ bag. The number of ways the cards can be drawn such that $x_1+x_2+x_3$ is odd is:
(a) 61 (b) 55
(c) 53 (d) 48

20. The number of divisors of 240 of the form $4n+2, n \geq 0$ is:
(a) 3 (b) 4
(c) 5 (d) 7

21. An onto function is to be defined from set A to set B. Set A contains 7 elements and set $B-\{a,b,c\}$. If exactly three of the seven elements in set A have the same image a, then the number of such functions that can be formed is:
(a) 245 (b) 280
(c) 490 (d) 560

22. Let n be the number of ways in which 5 boys and 5 girls can stand in a queue such that all the girls stand consecutively. Let m be the number of ways in which they can stand in a queue such that exactly 4 girls stand consecutively. Then the value of m/n is:
(a) 2 (b) 3
(c) 6 (d) 7

23. Two numbers are said to be relatively prime when they do not have a common prime factor or, in other words, their HCF equals 1. The number of ways in which the number 300300 can be split into two relatively prime factors is:

(a) 2^4 (b) 2^8-2^4
(c) 2^6-4 (d) 2^5

24. The number of ways of distributing 10 distinct balls in 9 identical boxes so that no box remains empty is:

(a) 9 (b) 45
(c) 90 (d) 10!

25. The number of ways in which five prizes, 1st and 2nd in physics, 1st and 2nd in maths and 1st in chemistry, can be distributed amongst 10 students is:

(a) $10^2\times 5!$ (b) $9^2\times 10^3$
(c) $9^2\times 10!$ (d) $9^2\times 10^3\times 5!$

26. There are 4 boxes and 6 balls. The balls are to be placed in the boxes so that no box is empty. Consider the number of ways in which this can be accomplished. Match the columns:

(a) If the boxes and the balls are all different (p) 2
(b) If the boxes are identical but the balls are different (q) 10
(c) If the boxes are different but the balls are identical (r) 65
(d) If the boxes and the balls are all identical (s) 1560

27. Consider all possible permutations of the letters of the word *ENDEANOEL*. Match the columns:

(a) The number of permutations containing word *ENDEA* is (p) 5!
(b) The number of permutations in which the letter *E* occurs in the first and the last positions is (q) $2\times 5!$
(c) The number of permutations in which none of the letters D, L, N occur in the last five positions is (r) $7\times 5!$
(d) The number of permutations in which the letters A, E, O occur only in odd positions is (s) $21\times 5!$

28. The number of different words that can be formed using all the letters of the word *DEEPMALA* if two vowels are together and the other two vowels are also together but separated from the first two is:

(a) 960 (b) 1200
(c) 1440 (d) 2160

29. The sum of all four-digit even numbers that can be formed from the digits 1, 2, 3, 4, 5 is:

(a) 158994 (b) 159984
(c) 159894 (d) 159884

30. A group consisting of 2 Americans, 2 Chinese, and 4 persons of different nationalities are to be seated at a round table such that no two men of the same nationality sit together. The number of ways in which this can be achieved is:

(a) 1584 (b) 1846
(c) 2352 (d) 2404

ANSWER KEYS

1. (d)	**2.** (c)	**3.** (b)	**4.** (a)	**5.** (d)	**6.** (c)	**7.** (b)	**8.** (a)	**9.** (d)	**10.** (c)
11. (d)	**12.** (d)	**13.** (b)	**14.** (a)	**15.** (c)	**16.** (a)	**17.** (a)	**18.** (b)	**19.** (c)	**20.** (b)
21. (c)	**22.** (a)	**23.** (d)	**24.** (b)	**25.** (b)	**26.** (a)-(s), (b)-(r), (c)-(q), (d)-(p)				
27. (a)-(p), (b)-(s), (c)-(q), (d)-(q)			**28.** (c)	**29.** (b)	**30.** (c)				

SOLUTIONS

1. (d) All three-digit numbers will lie between 100 and 1000. The hundred's place can be filled in 5 ways (any digit except zero). The ten's place can now be filled in 5 ways (we have 5 remaining digits). The unit's place can now be filled in 4 ways (we have 4 remaining digits).

Hence, the required number of ways $= 5\times 5\times 4 = 100.$

2. (c) Without repetition, the number of 10-letter words

$$m = 10!$$

We can choose one letter that we wish to repeat (twice) in 10 ways, and the remaining 8 letters in ${}^9C_8 = 9$ ways. Now, these letters can be arranged in $\frac{10!}{2!}$ ways. Hence

$$n = 10 \times 9 \times \frac{10!}{2!} = 45 \times 10!$$

Hence $\frac{n}{9m} = 5.$

3. (b) We have

$$N_1 = n\{1 \text{ odd}, 4 \text{ even}\} = {}^5C_1 \times {}^4C_4 = 5$$
$$N_1 = n\{2 \text{ odd}, 3 \text{ even}\} = {}^5C_2 \times {}^4C_3 = 40$$
$$N_1 = n\{3 \text{ odd}, 2 \text{ even}\} = {}^5C_3 \times {}^4C_2 = 60$$
$$N_1 = n\{4 \text{ odd}, 1 \text{ even}\} = {}^5C_4 \times {}^4C_1 = 20$$
$$N_1 = n\{5 \text{ odd}, 0 \text{ even}\} = {}^5C_5 \times {}^4C_0 = 1$$

Hence $N_1 + N_2 + N_3 + N_4 + N_5 = 126.$

4. (a) Each prize can be distributed in 5 ways. Thus, without restriction, the prizes can be distributed in 5^4 ways. But this also includes those 5 ways in which all the prizes are given to any one student. Hence, the required number of ways $= 5^4 - 5 = 620.$

5. (d) Other than P and S, there are 10 letters, of which 2 are alike (2 Ts).
The letters P and S can be placed at the 1st and 6th places or the 2nd and 7th places, ... or the 7th and 12th places. So, we can arrange the letters P and S in $7 \times 2!$ (P and S can be interchanged) ways.

For each arrangement of P and S, the other 10 letters can be mutually permutated in $\frac{10!}{2!}$ number of ways.
Hence, the required number of ways

$$= \frac{10!}{2!} \times 7 \times 2! = 7 \times 10!$$

6. (c) Without any restriction, we can form $\frac{7!}{3!2!}$ number of numbers.
Numbers with zero at the first place will become smaller than 1000000 and hence they are not allowed. The number of such numbers is $\frac{6!}{3!2!}$.
Hence, the required number of ways $= \frac{7!}{3!2!} - \frac{6!}{3!2!} = 360.$

7. (b) Number of words beginning with $A = 4! = 24$.
Number of words beginning with $G = \frac{4!}{2!} = 12.$
Number of words beginning with $I = \frac{4!}{2!} = 12.$

Hence, the second word beginning with N will be the 50th word, that is, $NAAIG$ (49th word is $NAAGI$).

8. (a) We have three subgroups, namely, $A:2$ boys who insist on being together, $B:5$ remaining boys and $C:3$ girls.
We can form the team in the following ways:
(2 girls) and (3 boys from B)
or (2 girls) and (1 boy from B) and (2 boys from A)
or (3 girls) and (2 boys from B)
or (3 girls) and (2 boys from A)
Hence, the required number of ways

$$= {}^3C_2({}^5C_3 + {}^5C_1) + {}^3C_3({}^5C_2 + 1) = 45 + 11 = 56.$$

9. (d) The 10 objects can be chosen in the following ways:
0 from the 10 identical and 10 from the 21 distinct $= {}^{21}C_{10}$ ways or
1 from the 10 identical and 9 from the 21 distinct $= {}^{21}C_9$ ways or
....
10 from the 10 identical and 0 from the 21 distinct $= {}^{21}C_0$ ways.
Hence, the total number of ways is

$$= {}^{21}C_0 + {}^{21}C_1 + {}^{21}C_2 + \ldots + {}^{21}C_{10}$$
$$= \frac{1}{2}[{}^{21}C_0 + {}^{21}C_1 + {}^{21}C_2 + \ldots + {}^{21}C_{10} + {}^{21}C_{11} + \ldots + {}^{21}C_{20} + {}^{21}C_{21}]$$
$$= \frac{1}{2} \times 2^{21} = 2^{20}$$

10. (c) A function defined from $E \to F$ is the set $\{(1,\_), (2,\_), (3,\_), (4,\_)\}$, where the vacant spaces can each be filled in three ways (either 1 or 2 or 3). This gives $3^4 = 81$ functions.
However, all these functions are not into. For into functions, all the elements in F must not be used. If the vacant spaces are filled using exactly one element (either 1 only or 2 only or 3 only), we can do so in 3 ways.

If the vacant spaces are filled using exactly two elements (either 1,2 or 2,3 or 3,1), we can do so in $3(2^4-2)=42$ ways (subtracting the two ways in which all spaces are filled with 1 only or 2 only because these two ways have already been counted).

Adding these two cases, the required number of into functions is

$$3+42=45.$$

The number of onto functions is

$$81-(3+42)=36.$$

11. (d) A function defined from $E \to F$ is the set $\{(1,\_),(2,\_),(3,\_),(4,\_)\}$. The numbers in the vacant spaces must not be repeated in case of one–one functions.

Hence, the vacant spaces can be filled in $4\times3\times2\times1=24$ number of ways.

12. (d) A relation defined from $E \to F$ is a subset of $E\times F$.

The set $E\times F$ contains $4\times2=8$ elements and hence the total number of its subsets is $2^8=256$.

13. (b) Let us construct two subsets A and B of the given set E. For every element that we pick up from E, we have 3 choices: we choose it for A or for B or we can not choose it at all (we cannot choose it for both since we are constructing disjoint sets).

Thus, we have $3^4=81$ pairs of subsets. This includes $A=\varnothing=B$, and all other choices have been repeated twice.

Hence, the required number of disjoint pairs

$$=\frac{1}{2}(81-1)+1=41.$$

14. (a) We require three vertices to form a triangle. Hence, the total number of triangles $={}^{12}C_3=220$.

Let us name the vertices as $1,2,3,\ldots,12$.

<u>Triangles with one side common with the polygon</u>

If we choose one side formed by the vertices 1 and 2, then we have 8 choices (leaving the two adjacent vertices 3 and 12) for the third vertex. Since there are 12 sides, the total number of such triangles $=12\times8=96$.

<u>Triangles with two sides common with the polygon</u>

The choices are $(1,2,3),(2,3,4),\ldots,(12,1,2)$. The total number of such triangles $=12$.

Hence, the required number of triangles $=220-(96+12)=112$.

15. (c) <u>AP with common difference 1</u>

The choices are

$(1,2,3),(2,3,4),\ldots,(2n-1,2n,2n+1)$.

Total number $=2n-1$.

<u>AP with common difference 2</u>

The choices are

$(1,3,5),(2,4,6),\ldots,(2n-3,2n-1,2n+1)$.

Total number $=2n-3$.

<u>AP with common difference 3</u>

The choices are

$(1,4,7),(2,5,8),\ldots,(2n-5,2n-2,2n+1)$.

Total number $=2n-5$.

....

<u>AP with common difference n</u>

The choices are $(1,n+1,2n+1)$. Total number $=1$.

Hence, the total number of APs

$$=(2n-1)+(2n-3)+(2n-5)+\ldots+1$$

$$=\frac{2n-1+1}{2}\times n=n^2$$

16. (a) The digit 2 will appear at the unit's place $\frac{3!}{2!}=3$ times.

The digit 3 will appear at the unit's place $3!=6$ times.

The digit 4 will appear at the unit's place $\frac{3!}{2!}=3$ times.

The same is true for the other places.

Hence, the sum is

$$[(2\times3)+(3\times6)+(4\times3)][10^3+10^2+10+1]$$

$$=36\times1111=39996.$$

17. (a) Considering each American couple as one person, there are six people to be seated around the table, which can be done in 5! ways, and the American couples can each be permutated in 2! ways.

Hence, the required number of ways

$$=5!\times(2!)^4=1920.$$

18. (b) The ways in which they can queue up are

GGBBB, GBGBB, GBBGB, BGGBB, BGBGB

For each of the above 5 cases, the boys and the girls can be permutated amongst themselves in 3! and 2! ways, respectively.

Hence, the required number of ways $=5(3!\times2!)$

$$=60.$$

19. (c) Bag I contains 2 odd, 1 even numbers.
Bag II contains 3 odd, 2 even numbers.
Bag III contains 4 odd, 3 even numbers.
If we choose 1 from bag I, the other two numbers chosen from bags II and III must be both odd or both even, which can be done in $(3\times4)+(2\times3)=18$ ways.
If we choose 2 from bag I, the other two numbers chosen from bags II and III must be one odd and one even, which can be done in $(3\times3)+(2\times4)=17$ ways.
If we choose 3 from bag I, the other two numbers chosen from bags II and III must be both odd or both even, which can be done in $(3\times4)+(2\times3)=18$ ways.
Hence, the required number of ways $=18+17+18=53$.

20. (b) Prime factors of $240=2^4\times3\times5$.

Numbers of the form $4n+2=2(2n+1)$ are products of one 2 and one odd number, which can be 1,3,5 or 3×5. Hence, there are only four such divisors, namely

$2, 2\times3=6, 2\times5=10$ and $2\times3\times5=30$.

21. (c) Number of ways of choosing three elements from seven elements of set A whose image must be a is ${}^7C_3=35$.
For the remaining four elements of set A, we have two choices for each of them, which equals $2^4=16$ choices. However, two of these choices are unacceptable if the function is to be onto: one in which all the four elements have the same image b, and the other in which all the four elements have the same image c. Subtracting these two cases, the total number of ways $=35(16-2)=490$.

22. (a) Let us treat the 5 girls as one so that we have 6 persons to be arranged in a queue. This can be done in 6! ways. The 5 girls can be permutated amongst themselves in 5! ways. Hence $n=6!\times5!$
In the second case, let us choose any 4 girls, which can be done in ${}^5C_4=5$ ways. Let us treat these 4 girls as one so that we have 7 persons to be arranged in a queue. This can be done in 7! ways and the 4 girls can be permutated amongst themselves in 4! ways. This gives us $7!\times4!$ ways, but these arrangements also include those cases in which all 5 girls are placed consecutively. Subtracting those cases, we have $m=5(7!\times4!-6!\times5!)$

Thus

$$\frac{m}{n}=\frac{5(7!\times4!-6!\times5!)}{6!\times5!}=5\left(\frac{7!\times4!}{6!\times5!}-1\right)=5\left(\frac{7}{5}-1\right)=2.$$

23. (d) The prime factors of 300300 $=2^2\times3\times5^2\times7\times11\times13$.
Relatively prime factors means they should not have a common prime factor. For example, two relatively prime factors are $2^2\times3\times13$ and $5^2\times7\times11$. However, $2\times3\times13$ and $2\times5^2\times7\times11$ are not relatively prime factors. So, while creating the two factors, we must ensure that 2^2 and 5^2 are chosen as one.
Now, we have to create the two factors, say A and B, from a total of six choices, namely, $2^2, 3, 5^2, 7, 11, 13$. Each of them can be chosen in two ways (for any one of the two factors), which gives us 2^6 ways. Note that all the pairs of factors have been repeated twice. Hence, the required number of factors $=2^6/2=2^5$

24. (b) Only one type of group can be formed with 1,1,1,1,1,1,1,1,2 balls. The number of ways in which this group can be formed is $\frac{10!}{(1!)^8\,2!}\times\frac{1}{8!}=45$. Since the boxes are identical, the required number of ways = 45.

25. (b) The physics prize can be distributed in 10×9 ways.
The maths prize can be distributed in 10×9 ways.
The chemistry prize can be distributed in 10 ways.
Hence, the required number of ways $=9^2\times10^3$

26. (a)-(s), (b)-(r), (c)-(q), (d)-(p)
Only two types of groups can be formed: 1,1,2,2 balls or 1,1,1,3 balls.
If the balls are different, the number of ways in which these groups can be formed, are, respectively,

$$\frac{6!}{(1!)^2(2!)^2}\times\frac{1}{2!2!}=45 \text{ and } \frac{6!}{(1!)^3\,3!}\times\frac{1}{3!}=20.$$

If the boxes are different, these groups can now be arranged in the boxes in 4! ways. Hence, the required number of ways $=4!(45+20)=1560$.

If the boxes are identical, the required number of ways $=45+20=65$.

If the balls are identical, the groups can be formed in 2 ways only.

If the boxes are different, these groups can be arranged in $\frac{4!}{2!2!}+\frac{4!}{3!}=10$ ways. If the boxes are identical, the required number of ways = 2.

27. (a)-(p), (b)-(s), (c)-(q), (d)-(q)

Considering *ENDEA* as one letter, there will be 5 distinct letters which can be arranged in 5! ways.

After placing E in the first and last positions, we are left with 7 letters in which there are 2 Ns, which can be arranged in $\frac{7!}{2!}=21\times 5!$ ways.

The first four positions will be filled by $1D, 1L, 2N$ and the last five positions will be filled by $1A, 1O, 3E$, which can be arranged in $\frac{4!}{2!}\times\frac{5!}{3!}=2\times 5!$ ways.

There are 5 odd positions, which will be completely filled by $1A, 1O, 3E$ and the remaining 4 positions will be filled by $1D, 1L, 2N$ (for example, $A\ D\ E\ N\ E\ N\ E\ L\ O$). The number of arrangements $=\frac{5!}{3!}\times\frac{4!}{2!}=2\times 5!$

28. (c) Let V_1 and V_2 represent the two pairs of vowels. Considering V_1 and V_2 as one letter each, we have six letters in total. The number of ways of positioning V_1 and V_2 so that they are not placed adjacent to each other is ${}^6C_2-5=10$.

For each place, the four non-vowel letters can be permutated amongst themselves in $4!=24$ ways, and the four vowels in V_1 and V_2 can be permutated amongst themselves in $\frac{4!}{2!\times 2!}=6$ ways.

Hence, the required number of words $10\times 24\times 6=1440$

29. (b) At the unit's place, only 2 or 4 can appear:

The digit 2 will appear $4\times 3\times 2=24$ times.

The digit 4 will appear $4\times 3\times 2=24$ times.

At the ten's place:

The digit 1 will appear $3\times 2\times 2=12$ times.

The digit 2 will appear $3\times 2\times 1=6$ times.

The digit 3 will appear $3\times 2\times 2=12$ times.

The digit 4 will appear $3\times 2\times 2=6$ times.

The digit 5 will appear $3\times 2\times 2=12$ times.

The same is true for the hundred's and the thousand's places.

Now, we have

Sum of the numbers at the unit's place

$$=(24\times 2)+(24\times 4)=144$$

Sum of the numbers at the ten's place

$$=12(1+3+5)+6(2+4)=144$$

Sum of the numbers at the hundred's place

$$=12(1+3+5)+6(2+4)=144$$

Sum of the numbers at the thousand's place

$$=12(1+3+5)+6(2+4)=144$$

Hence, the sum is

$$144\left[10^3+10^2+10+1\right]=159984$$

30. (c) Total ways of seating, without restriction $=(8-1)!=5040$.

Undesirable cases are those where the two Americans (A_1A_2) or the two Chinese (C_1C_2) are seated together. To count the number of such cases, we use

$$n(A_1A_2\cup C_1C_2)=n(A_1A_2)+n(C_1C_2)-n(A_1A_2\cap C_1C_2)$$

Now, we have

$$n(A_1A_2)=(7-1)!\times 2!=1440$$

$$n(A_1A_2)=(7-1)!\times 2!=1440$$

$$n(A_1A_2\cap C_1C_2)=(5-1)!\times 2!\times 2!\times 2!=192.$$

Hence, the desired number of ways

$$=5040-(1440+1440-192)=2352.$$

CHAPTER

7

Probability

- **Set:** A set is a collection of well-defined objects, called the elements of the set.
- **Properties Involving Sets:**
  1. The union and intersection operations obey commutative and associative law.
  2. $A \cup (B \cap C) = (A \cup B) \cap (A \cup C)$ and $A \cap (B \cup C) = (A \cap B) \cup (A \cap C)$
  3. $A \cup \varnothing = A$ and $A \cap \varnothing = \varnothing$
  4. $A \cup \mathcal{U} = \mathcal{U}$ and $A \cap \mathcal{U} = A$
  5. $A - B = A \cap B'$
  6. $A = (A \cap B) \cup (A \cap B')$
  7. If $A \subset B$, then $B' \subset A'$
  8. De Morgan's laws: $(A \cup B)' = A' \cap B'$ and $(A \cap B)' = A' \cup B'$
- **Random Experiment:** A random experiment is one in which the outcome may not be the same even though the experiment is performed in identical conditions. A set $\mathcal{S}$ of all possible outcomes of a random experiment is called a sample space and each outcome is a sample point. A set of possible outcomes is an event; event is a subset E of the sample space S.
- Since events are sets, statements concerning events can be transformed into the language of sets, and conversely. If A and B are two events, then
  1. $A \cup B$ is the event "either A or B or both".
  2. $A \cap B$ is the event "both A and B".
  3. $A - B$ is the event "A but not B".
  4. A' is the event "not A" and is equal to $\mathcal{S} - A$.

  If sets A and B representing two events are disjoint $(A \cap B = \varnothing)$, we say that the two events are mutually exclusive.
- **Elementary Event:** Let $\mathcal{S} = \{o_1, o_2, o_3, \ldots, o_n\}$. Events consisting of only one outcome are called elementary events. For the given sample space S, there are n elementary events $E_i = \{o_i\}, i = 1, 2, \ldots, n$. Note that elementary events are all mutually exclusive. Now, any other event E is a union of "some" or "all" of these elementary events.

  We shall calculate $P(E)$, the probability of occurrence of an event E, based on the following axioms:
  1. $0 < P(E_i) < 1$
  2. $\Sigma_1^n P(E_i) = 1$
  3. If $E = E_1 \cup E_2 \cup \ldots$, then $P(E) = P(E_1) + P(E_2) + \ldots$.

  If all the outcomes are equally likely, then $P(E_i) = 1/n$. If the event E is a union of m elementary events, then $P(E) = mP(E_i) = m/n$. Hence, in that case, $P(E) = n(E)/n(\mathcal{S})$.

Related properties:

1. $P(A')=1-P(A)$
2. $P(A\cap B')=P(A)-P(A\cap B)$
3. If $A_1, A_2,\ldots$ are mutually exclusive events, then $P(A_1\cup A_2\cup\ldots)=P(A_1)+P(A_1)+\ldots$
4. If A and B are non-mutually exclusive events, then $P(A\cup B)=P(A)+P(B)-P(A\cap B)$
5. $P(A_1\cup A_2\cup\ldots)\le P(A_1)+P(A_1)+\ldots$ and $P(A_1\cap A_2\cap\ldots)\ge 1-P(A_1')-P(A_2')-\ldots$

- If A and B are two events, then
  1. P(at least one of A,B occurs) = $P(A\cup B)$
  2. P(both A,B occur) = $P(A\cap B)$
  3. P(exactly one of A,B occurs) = $P(A\cap B')+P(B\cap A')$
     $= P(A)+P(B)-2P(A\cap B)$
- If A,B and C are three events, then
  1. P(at least one of A,B,C occurs) = $P(A\cup B\cup C)$
  2. P(all of A,B,C occur) = $P(A\cap B\cap C)$
  3. P(at least two of A,B,C occur) = $P(ABC')+P(AB'C)+P(A'BC)+P(ABC)$
     $= P(AB)+P(BC)+P(CA)-2P(ABC)$
  4. P(exactly two of A,B,C occur) = $P(ABC')+P(AB'C)+P(A'BC)$
     $= P(AB)+P(BC)+P(CA)-3P(ABC)$
  5. P(exactly one of A,B,C occurs) = $P(AB'C')+P(A'BC')+P(A'B'C)$
     $= P(A)+P(B)+P(C)-2P(AB)-2P(BC)-2P(CA)+3P(ABC)$
- **Conditional Probability:** If A and B are two events such that $P(A)\neq 0$, then the conditional probability of B given that A has occurred is given by

$$P(B\mid A)=\frac{P(A\cap B)}{P(A)}$$

If $P(B\mid A)=P(B)$, that is, the probability of occurrence of B is unaffected by the occurrence of A, then we say that A and B are independent events; this is equivalent to $P(A\cap B)=P(A)\times P(B)$.

Related properties:

1. If A and B are two events, then
$$P(A\cap B)=P(A)\times P(B\mid A)$$
2. If A, B and C are three events, then
$$P(A\cap B\cap C)=P(A)\times P(B\mid A)\times P(C\mid A\cap B)$$
3. If event A must result in one of the mutually exclusive events $A_1, A_2,\ldots A_n$, then
$$P(A)=P(A_1)P(A\mid A_1)+P(A_2)P(A\mid A_2)+\ldots$$

- **Bayes' Theorem:** Suppose $A_1, A_2,\ldots A_n$ are n mutually exclusive events whose union equals the sample space S. If A is any event that must result in one of the above events, then

$$P(A_k\mid A)=\frac{P(A_k\cap A)}{P(A)}=\frac{P(A_k)P(A\mid A_k)}{\sum_1^n P(A_i)P(A\mid A_i)}$$

- **Binomial Theorem:** If an experiment is repeated n times under similar conditions, we say that n trials of the experiment have been made. Let A be an event such that p is the probability of its occurrence in one trial and $q = 1 - p$ is the probability its of non-occurrence in one trial.
  Let X denote the number of times A occurs. Then the probability that A occurs exactly r times out of n trials is given by
  $$P(X = r) = {}^nC_r\, p^r q^{n-r}$$

EXERCISES

1. Two students Anil and Ashima appear in an examination. The probability that Anil will qualify in the examination is 0.05 and that Ashima will qualify in the examination is 0.10. The probability that both will qualify in the examination is 0.02. Match the columns:

(a) Probability that Anil and Ashima will not qualify in the exam	(p) 0.11
(b) Probability that at least one of them will not qualify in the exam	(q) 0.89
(c) Probability that only one of them will qualify in the exam	(r) 0.87
(d) Probability that both qualify or both do not qualify	(s) 0.98

2. A committee of two persons is selected from two men and two women. Match the columns:

(a) Probability that the committee has no man	(p) 5/6
(b) Probability that the committee has one man	(q) 1/6
(c) Probability that the committee has two men	(r) 1/2
(d) Probability that the committee has at most one man	(s) 2/3

3. Four-digit numbers greater than or equal to 5000 are randomly formed from digits 0, 1, 3, 5 and 7. If repetition of digits is not allowed, the probability of forming a number divisible by 5 is p. If repetition of digits is allowed, the probability of forming a number divisible by 5 is q. Then $8p + 5q$ equals:

(a) 2 (b) 5
(c) 7 (d) 8

4. Seven-digit numbers are randomly formed from digits 1,2 and 3; all digits must appear at least once. The probability of forming a number whose digits add up to 10 is:

(a) $\frac{42}{1806}$ (b) $\frac{42}{2056}$
(c) $\frac{77}{1806}$ (d) $\frac{77}{2056}$

5. A family has two children. The probability that both children are boys given that at least one of them is a boy is:

(a) $\frac{1}{2}$ (b) $\frac{1}{3}$
(c) $\frac{1}{5}$ (d) $\frac{1}{4}$

6. A man is known to speak truth 3 out of 4 times. He throws a die and reports that it is a six. The probability that it is actually six is:

(a) $\frac{1}{4}$ (b) $\frac{3}{8}$
(c) $\frac{2}{3}$ (d) $\frac{3}{5}$

7. Consider the experiment of tossing a coin. If the coin shows heads, toss it again, but if it shows tails, then throw a die. The conditional probability of the event that "die shows a number greater than 4" given that "there is at least one tail" is:

(a) $\frac{1}{2}$ (b) $\frac{3}{5}$
(c) $\frac{2}{9}$ (d) $\frac{3}{7}$

8. Three coins are tossed simultaneously. Consider the events E: three heads or three tails, F: at least two heads and G: at most two heads. Of the pairs $(E,F),(E,G)$ and (F,G), the independent pairs are:

(a) Only (E,G) (b) Only (E,F)

(c) (E,F) and (F,G) (d) All of them

9. Two persons A and B play a game of throwing a pair of dice. A wins if a sum of seven appears and B wins if a sum of ten appears. They keep throwing dice consecutively until one of them wins. If A begins the game, then the probability that he wins is:

(a) $\frac{7}{18}$ (b) $\frac{11}{18}$

(c) $\frac{12}{23}$ (d) $\frac{12}{17}$

10. Given are three identical boxes I, II, III, each containing two coins. In box I, both coins are gold coins, in box II, both are silver coins and in box III, there is one gold and one silver coin. A person chooses a box at random and takes out a coin. If the coin is of gold, then the probability that the other coin in the box is also gold is:

(a) $\frac{1}{4}$ (b) $\frac{1}{3}$

(c) $\frac{2}{3}$ (d) $\frac{3}{5}$

11. A die is thrown three times. Events A and B are defined as follows:

A: 4 on the third throw

B: 6 on the first and 5 on the second throw

The probability of A given that B has already occurred is:

(a) $\frac{1}{2}$ (b) $\frac{1}{3}$

(c) $\frac{1}{6}$ (d) $\frac{1}{4}$

12. A doctor is to visit a patient. From past experience, it is known that the probability that he will come by train, bus, scooter or by other means of transport are, respectively, $\frac{3}{10}, \frac{2}{10}, \frac{1}{10}$ and $\frac{4}{10}$. The probability that he will be late are $\frac{1}{4}, \frac{1}{3}$ and $\frac{1}{12}$ if he comes by train, bus and scooter, respectively. But if he comes by other means of transport, then he will not be late. When he comes, he is late. The probability that he came by train is:

(a) $\frac{1}{5}$ (b) $\frac{3}{10}$

(c) $\frac{1}{2}$ (d) $\frac{3}{5}$

13. A box contains 4 balls. Two balls are drawn and found to be white. The probability that all the balls in the box are white is:

(a) $\frac{2}{3}$ (b) $\frac{4}{9}$

(c) $\frac{3}{4}$ (d) $\frac{1}{3}$

14. A signal which can be green or red with probabilities $\frac{4}{5}$ and $\frac{1}{5}$, respectively, is received by station A and then transmitted to station B. The probability of each station receiving the signal correctly is $\frac{3}{4}$. If the signal received at station B is green, then the probability that the original signal was green is:

(a) $\frac{20}{23}$ (b) $\frac{3}{5}$

(c) $\frac{6}{7}$ (d) $\frac{9}{20}$

15. Let A and B be two urns such that A contains 3 white and 2 red balls, and B contains only 1 white ball. A fair coin is tossed. If heads appears, then 1 ball is drawn from A and put into B. If tail appears, then 2 balls are drawn from A and put into B. Now, 1 ball is drawn from B. Given that the ball drawn from B is white, the probability that heads appeared on the coin is:

(a) $\frac{17}{23}$ (b) $\frac{15}{23}$

(c) $\frac{12}{23}$ (d) $\frac{11}{23}$

16. Let E and F be two independent events. The probability that exactly one of them occurs is $\frac{11}{25}$ and the probability that none of them occurs is $\frac{2}{25}$. Then:

(a) $P(E)=\frac{4}{5}, P(F)=\frac{3}{5}$

(b) $P(E)=\frac{1}{5}, P(F)=\frac{2}{5}$

(c) $P(E)=\frac{2}{5}, P(F)=\frac{1}{5}$

(d) $P(E)=\frac{3}{5}, P(F)=\frac{4}{5}$

17. A student appears for tests I, II and III with probabilities of passing p, q and $\frac{1}{2}$, respectively. The student is successful if he passes in test I and at least one of the other two tests. If the probability of the student being successful is $\frac{1}{2}$, then:

(a) $p+q=1$ (b) $p+q-pq=1$
(c) $p(q+1)=1$ (d) $p(q-1)=1$

18. There are three students who appeared for a test. If their papers may be checked by any one of five teachers, then the probability that their papers are checked by exactly two teachers is:

(a) $\frac{8}{25}$ (b) $\frac{12}{25}$
(c) $\frac{14}{25}$ (d) $\frac{16}{25}$

19. Let m_1 and n_1 be the number of red and black balls, respectively, in box I. Let m_2 and n_2 be the number of red and black balls, respectively, in box II. One of the two boxes was randomly chosen and a ball was randomly drawn. The ball turned out to be red. If the probability that this ball was drawn from box II is 1/3, then the possible values of m_1, n_1, m_2, n_2 are:

(a) $m_1 = 3, n_1 = 3, m_2 = 5, n_2 = 15$
(b) $m_1 = 3, n_1 = 6, m_2 = 10, n_2 = 50$
(c) $m_1 = 8, n_1 = 6, m_2 = 5, n_2 = 20$
(d) $m_1 = 6, n_1 = 12, m_2 = 5, n_2 = 20$

20. Let m_1 and n_1 be the number of red and black balls, respectively, in box I. Let m_2 and n_2 be the number of red and black balls, respectively, in box II. A ball is randomly drawn from box I and transferred to box II. If the probability of drawing a red ball from box I after this transfer is 1/3, then the possible values of m_1, n_1 are:

(a) $m_1 = 4, n_1 = 6$ (b) $m_1 = 2, n_1 = 3$
(c) $m_1 = 10, n_1 = 20$ (d) $m_1 = 3, n_1 = 6$

21. The number of times a fair coin needs to be tossed so that the probability of getting at least two heads is at least 0.96 is:

(a) 5 (b) 6
(c) 7 (d) 8

22. Football teams T_1 and T_2 have to play two matches against each other. The probabilities of team T_1 winning, drawing and losing a match are $\frac{1}{2}, \frac{1}{6}$ and $\frac{1}{3}$, respectively. A team gets 3 points for winning, 1 point for drawing and 0 point for losing a match. Let X and Y denote the total points scored by teams T_1 and T_2, respectively. Then the correct statements from the following are:

(a) $P(X>Y)=\frac{5}{12}$ (b) $P(X<Y)=\frac{7}{12}$
(c) $P(X=Y)=\frac{13}{36}$ (d) $P(X\le Y)=\frac{17}{36}$

23. The probability of getting a sum of 8 in a throw of two dice if at least one of the numbers is not 5 is:

(a) $\frac{13}{36}$ (b) $\frac{7}{36}$
(c) $\frac{1}{7}$ (d) $\frac{1}{5}$

24. Four dice D_1, D_2, D_3, D_4 are thrown simultaneously. The probability that D_4 shows the same number as any one of the other three is:

(a) $\frac{127}{216}$ (b) $\frac{125}{216}$
(c) $\frac{91}{216}$ (d) $\frac{60}{216}$

25. If the probability that a randomly chosen positive divisor of 10^{29} is an integer multiple of 10^{23} is a^2/b^2, then $b-a$ equals:

(a) 8 (b) 15
(c) 21 (d) 23

26. Let E be a set containing n elements, and we randomly select two subsets A and B of E. The probability that $A\cup B=E$ and $A\cap B=\varnothing$ is:

(a) $\frac{1}{2^n}$ (b) $\frac{1}{2^n-1}$
(c) $\frac{2^n}{3^n}$ (d) $\frac{1}{n^2}$

27. A computer producing factory has only two plants T_1 and T_2. Plant T_1 produces 20% and plant T_2 produces 80% of the total computers produced. 7% of the computers produced in the factory are defective. It is known that P (computer is defective | it is from plant T_1) $= 10\times P$ (computer is defective | it is from plant T_2). If a computer is randomly selected and is found to be non-defective, then the probability that it was produced in plant T_2 is:

(a) $\frac{37}{63}$ (b) $\frac{67}{83}$

(c) $\frac{48}{73}$ (d) $\frac{78}{93}$

28. Two balls are drawn from a bag containing 4 white and 3 black balls. Let X denote the case when balls are drawn without replacement and Y when the balls are drawn after replacement. Match the columns:

(a) Probability that both balls are white in case X (p) $\frac{16}{49}$

(b) Probability that the balls are of different colours in case X (q) $\frac{28}{49}$

(c) Probability that both balls are white in case Y (r) $\frac{24}{49}$

(d) Probability that the balls are of different colours in case Y (s) $\frac{14}{49}$

29. A fair die is tossed repeatedly until a six is obtained. Let X denote the number of tosses required. Match the columns:

(a) Probability that $X = 3$ (p) $\frac{1}{6}$

(b) Probability that $X \geq 3$ (q) $\frac{5^2}{6^3}$

(c) Probability that $X \leq 3$ given that $X > 2$ (r) $\frac{5^3}{6^3}$

(d) Probability that $X \geq 6$ given that $X > 3$ (s) $\frac{5^2}{6^2}$

30. An unbiased coin is tossed 5 times. Suppose a variable X is assigned the value k when k consecutive heads are obtained for k = 3, 4, 5; otherwise X takes the value –1. If we define a quantity called the expected value of X as $E(X) = \sum k\,P(X = k)$, then $E(X)$ equals:

(a) $\frac{-3}{16}$ (b) $\frac{3}{16}$

(c) $\frac{-1}{8}$ (d) $\frac{1}{8}$

ANSWER KEYS

1. (a)-(r), (b)-(s), (c)-(p), (d)-(q) **2.** (a)-(q), (b)-(s), (c)-(q), (d)-(p) **3.** (b) **4.** (a) **5.** (b) **6.** (b)
7. (c) **8.** (b) **9.** (d) **10.** (c) **11.** (c) **12.** (c) **13.** (b) **14.** (a) **15.** (c)
16. (a),(d) **17.** (c) **18.** (b) **19.** (a),(b) **20.** (c),(d) **21.** (d) **22.** (a),(c) **23.** (c) **24.** (c) **25.** (d)
26. (b) **27.** (d) **28.** (a)-(s), (b)-(q), (c)-(p), (d)-(r) **29.** (a)-(q), (b)-(s), (c)-(p), (d)-(s) **30.** (d)

SOLUTIONS

1. (a)-(r), (b)-(s), (c)-(p), (d)-(q)

Let A and B be, respectively, the event that Anil qualifies and the event that Ashima qualifies in the exam. It is given that

$$P(A) = 0.05, P(B) = 0.10, P(AB) = 0.02$$

Probability that Anil and Ashima will not qualify

$$P(A'B') = 1 - P(A \cup B)$$
$$= 1 - \{P(A) + P(B) - P(AB)\} = 0.87$$

Probability that at least one of them will not qualify

$$1 - P(AB) = 0.98$$

Probability that only one of them will qualify

$$P(AB') + P(A'B) = P(A) + P(B) - 2P(AB)$$
$$= 0.11$$

Probability that both qualify or both do not qualify

$$P(A'B') + P(AB) = 0.89$$

2. (a)-(q), (b)-(s), (c)-(q), (d)-(p)

Probability that the committee has no man

$$= \frac{2_{C_2}}{4_{C_2}} = \frac{1}{6}$$

Probability that the committee has one man

$$= \frac{2 \times 2}{4_{C_2}} = \frac{2}{3}$$

Probability that the committee has two men

$$=\frac{{}^2C_2}{{}^4C_2}=\frac{1}{6}$$

Probability that the committee has at most one man

$$=\frac{{}^2C_2+2\times 2}{{}^4C_2}=\frac{5}{6}$$

3. (b) Without repetition

Numbers greater than 5000: First place can be filled in 2 ways (by 5 or 7). The remaining places can now be filled in $4\times 3\times 2$ ways. Total of $2\times 4\times 3\times 2=48$ numbers.

Numbers greater than 5000 and divisible by 5: We have two cases. If the first place is filled by 5, the unit's place must be filled with 0 and the remaining places in 3×2 ways. If the first place is filled with 7, the unit's place can be filled in 2 ways (0 or 5) and the remaining places in 3×2 ways. Total of $(3\times 2)+(3\times 2\times 2)=18$ numbers.

Hence probability $p=\frac{18}{48}=\frac{3}{8}$

With repetition

Numbers greater than 5000: The first place can be filled in 2 ways (by 5 or 7). The remaining places can now be filled in $5\times 5\times 5$ ways. Total of $2\times 5\times 5\times 5=250$ numbers.

Numbers greater than 5000 and divisible by 5: The unit's place can be filled in 2 ways (by 0 or 5), first place can be filled in 2 ways (by 5 or 7) and the remaining places in 5×5 ways. Total of $2\times 5\times 5\times 2=100$ numbers.

Hence probability $q=\frac{100}{250}=\frac{2}{5}$

Hence $8p+5q=5$

4. (a) Each place can be filled in 3 ways (by 1, 2 or 3). Total numbers $=3^7=2187$.

Of these numbers, there are three which contain only one digit, and ${}^3C_2\left(2^7-2\right)=378$ numbers which contain exactly two digits (1,2 or 2,3 or 1,3). Subtracting such numbers, the total number of such numbers which contain all the three digits $=2187-3-378=1806$.

Numbers whose digits add up to 10

We have only one choice: five 1s, one 2 and one 3.

Number of such numbers$=\frac{7!}{5!}=42$

Hence, the required probability $=\frac{42}{1806}$

5. (b) The sample space $S=\{GG,GB,BG,BB\}$.

Outcomes favourable to the event "at least one boy"

$$E=\{GB,BG,BB\}$$

Outcomes favourable to the event "both children are boys"

$$F=\{BB\}$$

Outcomes favourable to both F and E

$$F\cap E=\{BB\}$$

Hence, the required probability

$$P(F\mid E)=\frac{P(F\cup E)}{P(E)}=\frac{1/4}{3/4}=\frac{1}{3}$$

6. (b) Let R denote the event "man reports six", T denote the event "man speaks truth" and X denote the event "six appears on the die".

Event R can occur in two mutually exclusive ways, "six appears and man speaks truth" or "six does not appear and man speaks false". Hence, the total probability of reporting six

$$P(R)=P(X)P(T|X)+P(X')P(T'|X')$$

$$=\frac{1}{6}\times\frac{3}{4}+\frac{5}{6}\times\frac{1}{4}=\frac{1}{3}$$

We are required to find the probability that six had actually appeared, given that the man reports six. Hence, the required probability

$$P(X|R)=\frac{P(X\cap R)}{P(R)}=\frac{P(X)P(T|X)}{P(R)}=\frac{1/8}{1/3}=\frac{3}{8}.$$

7. (c) The sample space

$$S=\{HH,HT,T1,T2,T3,\ldots,T6\}$$

Note that the outcomes are not equally likely. Probability of the elementary outcomes $\{HH\}$ and $\{HT\}$ is $\frac{1}{2}\times\frac{1}{2}=\frac{1}{4}$ each, and that of the remaining six elementary outcomes is $\frac{1}{2}\times\frac{1}{6}=\frac{1}{12}$ each.

Outcomes favourable to the event "there is at least one tail"

$$E=\{HT,T1,T2,T3,\ldots,T6\}$$

Outcomes favourable to the event "die shows a number greater than 4"

$$F=\{T5,T6\}$$

Outcomes favourable to both F and E

$$F\cap E=\{T5,T6\}$$

Hence, the required probability

$$P(F\mid E)=\frac{P(F\cap E)}{P(E)}=\frac{2\left(\frac{1}{12}\right)}{\frac{1}{4}+6\left(\frac{1}{12}\right)}=\frac{2}{9}$$

8. (b) Number of elements in the sample space

$$n(S)=2\times2\times2=8$$

Outcomes favourable to the event "three heads or three tails"

$$E=\{HHH,TTT\}$$

Outcomes favourable to the event "at least two heads"

$$F=\{HHT,HTH,THH,HHH\}$$

Outcomes favourable to the event "at most two heads"

$$G=\{TTT,HTT,THT,TTH,HHT,HTH,THH\}$$

Outcomes favourable to (E and F), (F and G) and (E and G)

$$E\cap F=\{HHH\}$$

$$E\cap G=\{TTT\}$$

$$F\cap G=\{HHT,HTH,THH\}$$

The various probabilities are

$$P(E)=\frac{2}{8},\ P(F)=\frac{4}{8},\ P(G)=\frac{7}{8},$$

$$P(E\cap F)=\frac{1}{8},\ P(E\cap G)=\frac{1}{8},\ P(F\cap G)=\frac{3}{8}$$

We can see that only E, F satisfy the condition for independence

$$P(E\cap F)=P(E)\times P(F)$$

9. (d) Number of elements in the sample space

$$n(S)=6\times6=36.$$

Let $E=\{\text{Sum of seven appears}\}$

$$=\{(1,6),(2,5),(3,4),(4,3),(5,2),(6,1)\}$$

and $F=\{\text{Sum of ten appears}\}$

$$=\{(4,6),(5,5),(6,4)\}$$

Then $P(E)=\frac{6}{36}=\frac{1}{6}$ and $P(F)=\frac{3}{36}=\frac{1}{12}$

Now

$$P(E)=P(E)+P(E')P(F')P(E)$$

$$+P(E')P(F')P(E')P(F')P(E)+\ldots$$

$$=\frac{1}{6}+\left(\frac{5}{6}\times\frac{11}{12}\times\frac{1}{6}\right)+\left(\frac{5}{6}\times\frac{11}{12}\times\frac{5}{6}\times\frac{11}{12}\times\frac{1}{6}\right)+\ldots$$

$$=\frac{1}{6}\left(1+\frac{55}{72}+\frac{55^2}{72^2}+\ldots\right)=\frac{1}{6}\left(\frac{1}{1-\frac{55}{72}}\right)=\frac{12}{17}$$

10. (c) Let G denote the event "drawing a gold coin" and B_1, B_2, B_3 denote the events of "choosing boxes I, II, III", respectively.

Event G can occur in two mutually exclusive ways: it can be drawn from box I or from box III. Hence, the total probability of drawing gold

$$P(G)=P(B_1)P(G|B_1)+P(B_3)P(G|B_3)$$

$$=\frac{1}{3}\times1+\frac{1}{3}\times\frac{1}{2}=\frac{1}{2}$$

We are required to find the probability that box I was chosen, given that a gold coin was drawn. Hence, the required probability

$$P(B_1|G)=\frac{P(B_1)P(G|B_1)}{P(G)}=\frac{1/3}{1/2}=\frac{2}{3}$$

11. (c) Outcomes favourable to the event "6 on the first and 5 on the second throw"

$$B=\{(6,5,1),(6,5,2),\ldots,(6,5,6)\}$$

Outcomes favourable to the event "4 appears on the third row"

$$A=\{(x,y,4):x,y=1,2,\ldots,6\}$$

Hence, the outcomes favourable to both A and B

$$A\cap B=\{(6,5,4)\}$$

Hence, the required probability

$$P(A\mid B)=\frac{P(A\cap B)}{P(B)}=\frac{1}{6}$$

12. (c) Let L denote the event "doctor comes late" and T, B, S and O denote the events of coming by "train", "bus", "scooter" and "other transport", respectively.

Event L can occur in three mutually exclusive ways: whether he chooses to come by train, bus or scooter. Hence, the total probability of coming late

$$P(L)=P(T)P(L|T)+P(B)P(L|B)+P(S)P(L|S)$$

$$=\frac{3}{10}\times\frac{1}{4}+\frac{2}{10}\times\frac{1}{3}+\frac{1}{10}\times\frac{1}{12}=\frac{6}{40}$$

We are required to find the probability that the doctor came by train, given that he came late. Hence, the required probability

$$P(T|L)=\frac{P(T)P(L|T)}{P(L)}=\frac{3/40}{6/40}=\frac{1}{2}$$

13. (b) Let A, B, C, D, E denote the events "box contains 4 white balls", "box contains 3 white balls", "box contains 2 white balls", "box contains 1 white ball", "box contains 0 white balls", respectively.

Let W denote the event "2 white balls are drawn from the box". Event X can occur in five mutually exclusive ways:

$$(A \cap W), (B \cap W), (C \cap W), (D \cap W), (E \cap W)$$

Hence, the total probability of drawing 2 white balls is

$$P(W) = P(A)P(W|A) + P(B)P(W|B) + P(C)P(W|C) + P(D)P(W|D) + P(E)P(W|E)$$

$$= \frac{1}{5}\cdot\frac{^4C_2}{^4C_2} + \frac{1}{5}\cdot\frac{^3C_2}{^4C_2} + \frac{1}{5}\cdot\frac{^2C_2}{^4C_2} + \frac{1}{5}\cdot\frac{0}{^4C_2} + \frac{1}{5}\cdot\frac{0}{^4C_2} = \frac{1}{5}\left(\frac{6}{6}+\frac{3}{6}+\frac{1}{6}\right) = \frac{1}{3}$$

We are required to find the probability that the box contained 4 white balls, given that 2 white balls were drawn. Hence, the required probability

$$P(A|W) = \frac{P(A)P(W|A)}{P(W)} = \frac{1/5}{1/3} = \frac{3}{5}$$

14. (a) Let X denote the event "signal received at B is green" and G, R, C denote the events "green signal at source", "red signal at source" and "receiving signal correctly", respectively.

Event X can occur in four mutually exclusive ways:

$$(G, C, C), (G, C', C'), (R, C, C'), (R, C', C)$$

Hence, the total probability of receiving green signal at B

$$P(X) = P(G)P(C)P(C) + P(G)P(C')P(C') + P(R)P(C)P(C') + P(R)P(C')P(C)$$

$$= \frac{4}{5}\cdot\frac{3}{4}\cdot\frac{3}{4} + \frac{4}{5}\cdot\frac{1}{4}\cdot\frac{1}{4} + \frac{1}{5}\cdot\frac{3}{4}\cdot\frac{1}{4} + \frac{1}{5}\cdot\frac{1}{4}\cdot\frac{3}{4} = \frac{46}{80}$$

We are required to find the probability that the original signal was green, given that the signal received at station B is green. Hence, the required probability

$$P(G|X) = \frac{P(G)P(C)P(C) + P(G)P(C')P(C')}{P(X)}$$

$$= \frac{40/80}{46/40} = \frac{20}{23}$$

15. (c) Let X denote the event "ball drawn from B is white" and H and T, respectively, denote the events "heads turns up" and "tails turns up". Event X can occur in the following mutually exclusive ways:

<u>If heads turns up</u>

1 white is transferred and then white is drawn

or 1 red is transferred and then white is drawn

<u>If tails turns up</u>

2 whites are transferred and then white is drawn

or 2 reds are transferred and then white is drawn

or 1 red, 1 white are transferred and then white is drawn

Hence, the total probability of drawing white from B

$$P(X) = P(H)P(X|H) + P(T)P(X|T)$$

$$= \frac{1}{2}\left(\frac{3}{5}\cdot 1 + \frac{2}{5}\cdot\frac{1}{2}\right) + \frac{1}{2}\left(\frac{^3C_2}{^5C_2}\cdot 1 + \frac{^2C_2}{^5C_2}\cdot\frac{1}{3} + \frac{^3C_1\cdot{}^2C_1}{^5C_2}\cdot\frac{2}{3}\right)$$

$$= \frac{12}{30} + \frac{11}{30} = \frac{23}{30}$$

We are required to find the probability that heads had appeared, given that white was drawn from B. Hence, the required probability

$$P(H|X) = \frac{P(X)P(X|H)}{P(X)} = \frac{12/30}{23/30} = \frac{12}{23}$$

16. (a),(d) We have

$$P(EF' + E'F) = \frac{11}{25}$$

$$\Rightarrow \quad P(E) + P(F) - 2P(E)P(F) = \frac{11}{25}$$

and

$$P(E'F') = 1 - P(E \cup F) = \frac{2}{25}$$

$$\Rightarrow \quad P(E) + P(F) - P(E)P(F) = \frac{23}{25}$$

Solving the above equations, we get

$$P(E) + P(F) = \frac{7}{5} \text{ and } P(E)P(F) = \frac{12}{25}$$

There are two options (a), (d) satisfying the above equations.

17. (c) The student can be successful in the following mutually exclusive ways:

Passes in I, II and fails in III

or passes in I, III and fails in II

or passes in I, II and III

Hence, the probability of being successful

$$=\frac{1}{2}pq+\frac{1}{2}p(1-q)+\frac{1}{2}pq=\frac{1}{2}p(q+1),$$

which is given to be $\frac{1}{2}$, and hence the result $p(q+1)=1$.

18. (b) Each test paper can be allotted to any of the five teachers for checking. Hence, the total number of ways in which the three papers can be checked is $5\times5\times5=5^3$.

If the papers are to be checked by exactly two teachers, it can be done in 2^3-2 ways (subtracting the two cases when both papers are allotted to only one of the two teachers). Now two teachers can be selected out of five teachers in ${}^5C_2$ ways. Hence, the number of ways in which the papers can be checked by exactly two teachers $= {}^5C_2\left(2^3-2\right)=60$ ways.

Hence, the required probability $=\frac{60}{5^3}=\frac{12}{25}$.

19. (a),(b) Let R denote the event "red ball is drawn". Let I, II denote the events "ball is drawn from box I" and "ball is drawn from box II", respectively. Event R can occur in two mutually exclusive ways: it is drawn from box I or from box II. Hence, the total probability of drawing a red ball is

$$P(R)=P(I)P(R|I)+P(II)P(R|II)$$

$$=\frac{1}{2}\times\frac{m_1}{m_1+n_1}+\frac{1}{2}\times\frac{m_2}{m_2+n_2}$$

Probability that the ball was drawn from box II if it is known that it is a red ball is

$$P(II|R)=\frac{P(II)P(R|II)}{P(R)}$$

$$=\frac{\frac{1}{2}\times\frac{m_2}{m_2+n_2}}{\frac{1}{2}\times\frac{m_1}{m_1+n_1}+\frac{1}{2}\times\frac{m_2}{m_2+n_2}}$$

$$=\frac{\frac{m_2}{m_2+n_2}}{\frac{m_1}{m_1+n_1}+\frac{m_2}{m_2+n_2}}$$

For the above probability to be equal to $1/3$, we have

$$\frac{m_1}{m_1+n_1}=2\times\frac{m_2}{m_2+n_2}$$

The above condition is satisfied in options (a), (b) only.

20. (c),(d) Let R denote the event "red ball is drawn from box I after transfer".

Event R can occur in two mutually exclusive ways: it is drawn after a red ball is transferred, or it is drawn after a black ball is transferred from box I. Hence, the total probability of event R is

$$P(R)=\frac{m_1}{m_1+n_1}\times\frac{m_1-1}{m_1+n_1-1}+\frac{n_1}{m_1+n_1}\times\frac{m_1}{m_1+n_1-1}$$

$$=\frac{m_1(m_1+n_1-1)}{(m_1+n_1)(m_1+n_1-1)}=\frac{m_1}{m_1+n_1}$$

The above probability equals $1/3$ in options (c), (d) only.

21. (d) Let the required number of tosses be n. Using binomial distribution, the probability of getting at least two heads in n tosses is

$$1-({}^nC_0+{}^nC_1)\frac{1}{2^n}=1-\frac{n+1}{2^n}$$

According to the question, we have

$$1-\frac{n+1}{2^n}\geq0.96$$

$$\Rightarrow\quad\frac{n+1}{2^n}\leq0.04$$

$$\Rightarrow\quad 2^n\geq25(n+1)\text{ gives } n=8.$$

22. (a),(c) Let W, D, L denote the events: team T_1 winning, drawing and losing, respectively.

$$P(X>Y)=P(W)P(W)+P(W)P(D)$$
$$+P(D)P(W)=\frac{1}{4}+\frac{1}{12}+\frac{1}{12}=\frac{5}{12}$$

$$P(X<Y)=P(L)P(L)+P(L)P(D)+P(D)P(L)$$
$$=\frac{1}{9}+\frac{1}{18}+\frac{1}{18}=\frac{2}{9}$$

$$P(X=Y)=P(W)P(L)+P(L)P(W)+P(D)P(D)$$
$$=\frac{1}{6}+\frac{1}{6}+\frac{1}{36}=\frac{13}{36}$$

$$P(X\leq Y)=P(X<Y)+P(X=Y)=\frac{2}{9}+\frac{13}{36}=\frac{21}{36}$$

23. (c) Number of elements in the sample space

$$n(S) = 6 \times 6 = 36$$

Let $E = \{\text{Sum of 8 appears}\}$
$= \{(2,6),(3,5),(4,4),(5,3),(6,2)\}$

and $F = \{\text{At least one number is not 5}\}$
$= \{\text{All pairs except}(5,5)\}$

Then $P(E) = \frac{5}{36}$ and $P(F) = \frac{35}{36}$

Outcomes favourable to both E and F

$$E \cap F = \{(2,6),(3,5),(4,4),(5,3),(6,2)\}$$

Hence, the required probability

$$P(E \mid F) = \frac{P(E \cap F)}{P(F)} = \frac{5}{35} = \frac{1}{7}$$

24. (c) Number of elements in the sample space

$$n(S) = 6 \times 6 \times 6 \times 6 = 6^4$$

Let $E = \{D_4$ shows the same number as any one of the other three$\}$

Let us consider the cases which are unfavourable to event E. The die D_4 has 6 possible outcomes. If all the other dice show a different number, this can happen in $6 \times 5 \times 5 \times 5 = 6 \times 5^3$ ways.

Then $P(E) = 1 - \frac{6 \times 5^3}{6^4} = \frac{91}{216}$

25. (d) The prime factors of 10^{29} are $2^{29} \times 5^{29}$. Forming a divisor from these prime factors is like choosing (zero 2, or one 2,…,or all twenty-nine 2s) and (zero 5, or one 5,…,or all twenty-nine 5s). Thus, the total number of positive divisors of 10^{29} are $n = (1+29)(1+29) = 30^2$.

If we write $10^{29} = 10^{23} \times 10^6$, we see that all factors of $10^6 = 2^6 \times 5^6$, when multiplied by 10^{23}, are integral multiples of 10^{23}. Thus, the number of such factors is $m = (1+6)(1+6) = 7^2$.

The required probability is $7^2 / 30^2$. Comparing with a^2 / b^2, we have $a = 7, b = 30$. Hence $b - a = 23$.

26. (b) To understand the question, let us take an example. Let $E = \{1,2,3\}$. Then its subsets are

$$\{\varnothing,\{1\},\{2\},\{3\},\{2,3\},\{1,3\},\{1,2\},\{1,2,3\}\}$$

There are 2^3 subsets. Any two subsets can be chosen in ${}^{2^3}C_2 = \frac{2^3(2^3-1)}{2} = 2^{3-1}(2^3-1)$ ways. If we have to choose two subsets which satisfy the condition $A \cup B = E$ and $A \cap B = \varnothing$, then we have $\frac{1}{2}(2^3) = 2^{3-1}$ choices.

The required probability $= \frac{2^{3-1}}{2^{3-1}(2^3-1)} = \frac{1}{2^3-1}$

In a set of n elements, the required probability

$$= \frac{2^{n-1}}{2^{n-1}(2^n-1)} = \frac{1}{2^n-1}$$

27. (d) Let D denote the event "selected computer is defective". Let T_1, T_2 denote the events "computer is produced in plant T_1" and "computer is produced in plant T_2", respectively.

Let $P(D \mid T_2) = x$ and hence $P(D|T_1) = 10x$. The total probability of selecting a defective computer is

$$P(D) = P(T_1)P(D|T_1) + P(T_2)P(D|T_2)$$

$\Rightarrow \quad 7\% = (20\%)(10x) + (80\%)x$ gives

$$x = 2.5\%$$

Probability that the computer was produced in plant T_2, given that it is non-defective, is

$$P(T_2|D') = \frac{P(T_2)P(D'|T_2)}{P(D')} = \frac{80\% \times (1-x)}{(1-7\%)}$$

$$= \frac{80\% \times 97.5\%}{93\%} = \frac{78}{93}$$

28. (a)-(s), (b)-(q), (c)-(p), (d)-(r)

<u>Case X: when balls are drawn without replacement</u>

Total number of ways of drawing two balls $= {}^7C_2 = 21$.

Number of ways of drawing both balls as white $= {}^4C_2 = 6$.

Number of ways of drawing 1 white and 1 black ball $= {}^4C_1 \times {}^3C_1 = 12$.

The corresponding probabilities are, respectively, $\frac{6}{21} = \frac{14}{49}$ and $\frac{12}{21} = \frac{28}{49}$

<u>Case Y: when balls are drawn after replacement</u>

Total number of ways of drawing two balls $= 7 \times 7 = 49$.

Number of ways of drawing both balls as white $= 4 \times 4 = 16$.

Number of ways of drawing 1 white and 1 black ball $= 4 \times 3 + 3 \times 4 = 24$.

The corresponding probabilities are, respectively, $\frac{16}{49}$ and $\frac{24}{49}$

29. (a)-(q), (b)-(s), (c)-(p), (d)-(s)

The expression $(X = 3)$ means six appears in the third draw. Hence

$$P(X=3)=\frac{5}{6}\times\frac{5}{6}\times\frac{1}{6}=\frac{5^2}{6^3}$$

The expression $(X \geq 3)$ means $(X=3)+(X=4)$ +.... Hence

$$P(X\geq 3)=P(X=3)+P(X=4)+\dots$$

$$=\frac{5^2}{6^3}+\frac{5^3}{6^4}+\frac{5^4}{6^5}+\dots=\frac{\frac{5^2}{6^3}}{1-\frac{5}{6}}=\frac{5^2}{6^2}$$

Similarly $P(X\leq 3\,|\,X>2)=\dfrac{P(2<X\leq 3)}{P(X>2)}$

$$=\frac{P(X=3)}{P(X\geq 3)}=\frac{\frac{5^2}{6^3}}{\frac{5^2}{6^2}}=\frac{1}{6}$$

Similarly $P(X\geq 6\,|\,X>3)=\dfrac{P(X\geq 6)}{P(X>3)}$

$$=\frac{P(X\geq 6)}{P(X\geq 4)}=\frac{\frac{5^5}{6^5}}{\frac{5^3}{6^3}}=\frac{5^2}{6^2}$$

30. (d) When an unbiased coin is tossed 5 times, the total number of possible outcomes is $2^5 = 32$. Three consecutive heads can occur in 5 ways, namely,

$$HHHTT, HHHTH, THHHT, TTHHH, HTHH$$

Four consecutive heads can occur in 2 ways, namely,

$$HHHHT, THHHH$$

Five consecutive heads can occur in 1 way, namely,

$$HHHHH$$

Hence, we have

$$E(X)=3P(X=3)+4P(X=4)+5P(X=5)$$
$$+(-1)P(X\neq 3,4,5)$$
$$=3P(\text{3 consecutive heads})$$
$$+4P(\text{4 consecutive heads})$$
$$+5P(\text{5 consecutive heads})$$
$$+(-1)P(\text{otherwise})$$
$$=3\left(\frac{5}{32}\right)+4\left(\frac{2}{32}\right)+5\left(\frac{1}{32}\right)$$
$$+(-1)\left(\frac{32-5-2-1}{32}\right)$$
$$=\frac{15+8+5-24}{32}=\frac{1}{8}$$

CHAPTER

8 Matrices

- **Matrix:** A matrix is a rectangular array of numbers (real or complex), called elements, arranged in rows and columns. A matrix A having m rows and n columns is called a matrix of order $m \times n$, and it is denoted as $A = \left[a_{ij}\right](i = 1 \text{ to } m; j = 1 \text{ to } n)$.

  A matrix is said to be **square** when $m = n$. In a square matrix, if all the elements other than the diagonal elements are zero, it is called a **diagonal** matrix. If all the diagonal elements of a diagonal matrix are unity, it is called a **unit** matrix or **identity** matrix.

  Two matrices are said to be **equal** when all the elements are the same. Multiplying a matrix $[a_{ij}]$ by a scalar k is equal to matrix $[ka_{ij}]$.

- **Addition and Subtraction of Two Matrices:** If $A = \left[a_{ij}\right]$ and $B = \left[b_{ij}\right]$ are two matrices of the same order, then $A + B = \left[a_{ij} + b_{ij}\right]$ and $A - B = \left[a_{ij} - b_{ij}\right]$.

  Related properties:
  1. Commutative law: $A + B = B + A$
  2. Associative law: $(A + B) + C = A + (B + C)$
  3. Distributive law: $k(A + B) = kA + kB$

- **Multiplication of Two Matrices:** If $A = \left[a_{ij}\right]$ is a matrix of order $m \times n$ and $B = \left[b_{jk}\right]$ is a matrix of order $n \times p$, then

$$AB = \left[c_{ik}\right] \text{is a matrix of order } m \times p, \text{ where } c_{ik} = \sum_{1}^{n} a_{ij} b_{jk} = \left[a_{i1}\ a_{i2} \ldots a_{in}\right] \begin{bmatrix} b_{1k} \\ b_{2k} \\ \ldots \\ b_{nk} \end{bmatrix}$$

  Related properties:
  1. Commutative law: $AB \neq BA$
  2. Associative law: $(AB)C = A(BC)$
  3. Distributive law: $A(B + C) = AB + AC$
  4. If A is a square matrix, then $AI = IA = A$, where I is a unit matrix of the same order.
  5. $A^m A^n = A^{m+n}\ \forall\ m, n \in \mathbf{N}$

- **Transpose of a Matrix:** If $A = \left[a_{ij}\right]$ is a matrix, then its transpose is matrix $A' = \left[a_{ji}\right]$; it is obtained by interchanging the rows and columns of matrix A.

  Related properties:
  1. $(A')' = A$
  2. $(kA)' = kA'$
  3. $(A + B)' = A' + B'$
  4. $(AB)' = B'A'$, where A and B are conformable for the product AB

  A square matrix A is said to be **symmetric** if $A = A'$ and **skew-symmetric** if $A = -A'$; if a matrix is skew-symmetric, its diagonal elements must be zero.

- **Determinant of a Square Matrix:** If A is a square matrix of order $n \times n$, then its determinant is denoted by the symbol $|A|$. A matrix is said to be singular if $|A| = 0$ and non-singular if $|A| \neq 0$.

Related properties:

1. $|I| = 1$
2. $|AB| = |A||B|$
3. $|kA| = k^n |A|$

- **Adjoint of a Square Matrix:** If $A = [a_{ij}]$ is a square matrix of order $n \times n$, then its transpose is $A' = [a_{ji}]$ and its adjoint is the matrix adj $A = [C_{ji}]$, where C_{ji} is the cofactor of a_{ji}.

Related properties:

1. $A(\text{adj } A) = (\text{adj } A)A = |A| I$
2. $|\text{adj } A| = |A|^{n-1}$ if $|A| \neq 0$
3. $\text{adj}(kA) = k^{n-1} \text{adj } A$
4. $\text{adj}(A') = (\text{adj } A)'$
5. $\text{adj }(AB) = (\text{adj } B)(\text{adj } A)$

- **Inverse of a Square Matrix:** If $A = [a_{ij}]$ is a non-singular square matrix, then its inverse is the matrix

$$A^{-1} = \frac{\text{adj } A}{|A|} \text{ if } |A| \neq 0$$

Useful result: For a 2×2 non-singular matrix $A = \begin{bmatrix} a & \text{b} \\ \text{c} & d \end{bmatrix}$, its inverse is the matrix

$$A^{-1} = \frac{1}{ad - bc}\begin{bmatrix} d & -\text{b} \\ -\text{c} & a \end{bmatrix}$$

Related properties:

1. $(A^{-1})^{-1} = A$
2. $|A^{-1}| = 1/|A|$
3. $(kA)^{-1} = \frac{1}{k}A^{-1}$
4. $(A')^{-1} = (A^{-1})'$
5. $(AB)^{-1} = B^{-1}A^{-1}$
6. $(A^{-1})^n = (A^n)^{-1} \forall n \in \mathbf{N}$

- **Solution of Linear Equations Using Matrices:** Consider the system of n linear equations in n unknowns

$$a_{11}x_1 + a_{12}x_2 + \ldots + a_{1n}x_n = b_1 - (1)$$
$$a_{21}x_1 + a_{22}x_2 + \ldots + a_{2n}x_n = b_2 - (2)$$
$$\ldots$$
$$\ldots$$
$$a_{n1}x_1 + a_{n2}x_2 + \ldots + a_{nn}x_n = b_n - (n)$$

The above system of equations can be written in the form $AX = B$, where A, X and B are the matrices of the coefficients, the unknowns, and the constant terms, respectively. That is

$$A = \begin{bmatrix} a_{11} & a_{12} & \cdots & a_{1n} \\ a_{21} & a_{22} & \cdots & a_{2n} \\ \ldots & \ldots & \ldots & \ldots \\ \ldots & \ldots & \ldots & \ldots \\ a_{n1} & a_{n2} & \cdots & a_{nn} \end{bmatrix}, \; X = \begin{bmatrix} x_1 \\ x_2 \\ \ldots \\ \ldots \\ x_n \end{bmatrix} \text{ and } B = \begin{bmatrix} b_1 \\ b_2 \\ \ldots \\ \ldots \\ b_n \end{bmatrix}$$

The solution to the system of equations is given by

$$X = \frac{(\text{adj.}A)B}{|A|}$$

Case 1: Homogeneous system of equations ($B = O$)

If $|A| \neq 0$, the system of equations has a unique trivial solution $X = O$.

If $|A| = 0$, the system of equations has an infinite number of solutions.

Case 2: Non-homogeneous system of equations $(B \neq O)$

If $|A| \neq 0$, the system of equations has a unique solution.

If $|A| = 0$ and (adj.A) $B = O$, the system of equations has an infinite number of solutions.

If $|A| = 0$ and $(\text{adj}.A)B \neq O$, the system of equations has no solution.

[Note: No two rows of coefficients must be in the same ratio; in that situation, the above rules do not apply, and the system of equations simply has no solution.]

- **Solution of Linear Equations Using Cramer's Rule:** Using Cramer's rule, the solution to the above system of linear equations is

$$x_1 = \frac{D_1}{D}, x_2 = \frac{D_2}{D}, \ldots, x_n = \frac{D_n}{D},$$

where $D = \begin{vmatrix} a_{11} & a_{12} & \ldots & a_{1n} \\ a_{21} & a_{22} & \ldots & a_{2n} \\ \ldots & \ldots & \ldots & \ldots \\ \ldots & \ldots & \ldots & \ldots \\ a_{n1} & a_{n2} & \ldots & a_{nn} \end{vmatrix}$, $D_1 = \begin{vmatrix} b_1 & a_{12} & \ldots & a_{1n} \\ b_2 & a_{22} & \ldots & a_{2n} \\ \ldots & \ldots & \ldots & \ldots \\ \ldots & \ldots & \ldots & \ldots \\ b_n & a_{n2} & \ldots & a_{nn} \end{vmatrix}$,

$D_2 = \begin{vmatrix} a_{11} & b_1 & \ldots & a_{1n} \\ a_{21} & b_2 & \ldots & a_{2n} \\ \ldots & \ldots & \ldots & \ldots \\ \ldots & \ldots & \ldots & \ldots \\ a_{n1} & b_n & \ldots & a_{nn} \end{vmatrix}, \ldots, \ldots, D_n = \begin{vmatrix} a_{11} & a_{12} & \ldots & b_1 \\ a_{21} & a_{22} & \ldots & b_2 \\ \ldots & \ldots & \ldots & \ldots \\ \ldots & \ldots & \ldots & \ldots \\ a_{n1} & a_{n2} & \ldots & b_n \end{vmatrix}$

The system of equations has
- a unique solution if $D \neq 0$.
- an infinite number of solutions if $D = D_1 = D_2 = \ldots = D_n = 0$.
- no solution if $D = 0$ and at least one of $D_1, D_2, \ldots, D_n$ is not zero.

[Note: No two rows of coefficients must be in the same ratio; in that situation, the above rules do not apply, and the system of equations simply has no solution.]

EXERCISES

1. Consider two matrices A, B such that

$$A+B=\begin{bmatrix}2 & 0 & 1\\1 & 1 & 1\\0 & 1 & 2\end{bmatrix} \text{ and } A-B=\begin{bmatrix}1 & 1 & 3\\0 & -1 & c\\1 & 0 & 0\end{bmatrix}.$$

Then $(AB)^{-1}$ exists for:

(a) $c=0$ only (b) $c=-1$ only
(c) Any integer c (d) No value of c

2. Consider two matrices

$$A=\begin{bmatrix}\cos^2\theta & \sin\theta\cos\theta\\ \sin\theta\cos\theta & \sin^2\theta\end{bmatrix} \text{ and}$$

$$B=\begin{bmatrix}\cos^2\phi & \sin\phi\cos\phi\\ \sin\phi\cos\phi & \sin^2\phi\end{bmatrix}.$$

Then $AB=O$ if:

(a) $\theta-\phi=(2n-1)\frac{\pi}{2}$

(b) $\theta+\phi=(2n-1)\frac{\pi}{2}$

(c) $\theta-\phi=(2n-1)\pi$

(d) $\theta+\phi=(2n-1)\pi$

3. The number of 3×3 matrices M with entries from $\{0,1,2\}$, for which the sum of the diagonal entries of $M'M$ equals 5 is:

(a) 126 (b) 378
(c) 630 (d) 882

4. If M is a 3×3 matrix such that $MM'=I$ and $|M|=1$, then the value of $|M-I|$ is:

(a) -1 (b) 0
(c) 1 (d) 2

5. If $B=\begin{bmatrix}-2 & -2\\-1 & 0\end{bmatrix}$ and A is a matrix such that $A^{-1}B=B^{-1}$ and $kA^{-1}=2B^{-1}+I$, where k is some scalar, then the value of k is:

(a) 1 (b) 2
(c) 3 (d) 4

6. Consider the system of equations $x+ay=5$, $3x+by=c$. Then the system has:

(a) A unique solution if $b\neq 3a$
(b) No solution if $b=3a, c\neq 15$
(c) Infinite solutions if $b=3a, c=15$
(d) None of these

7. Let X, Y be two third-order skew-symmetric matrices and Z be a third-order symmetric matrix. Then which of the following is a skew-symmetric matrix:

(a) $Y^3Z^4-Z^4Y^3$ (b) $X^{44}+Y^{44}$
(c) $X^4Z^3-Z^3X^4$ (d) $X^{23}+Y^{23}$

8. If A is a square matrix such that $A^n=I$ for some $n=2,3,\ldots$, then A^{-1} equals:

(a) A (b) I
(c) I^{n-1} (d) A^{n-1}

9. Let A be a square matrix satisfying the equation $A^3-5A^2+4A+kI=O$, where k is a scalar and I is an identity matrix. Then A^{-1} exists if:

(a) $k\neq-1$ (b) $k\neq0$
(c) $k\neq1$ (d) None of these

10. If $A=\begin{bmatrix}i & 0 & 0\\0 & i & 0\\0 & 0 & i\end{bmatrix}$, where $i=\sqrt{-1}$ and I is the identity matrix, then A^{-1} equals:

(a) $-(A+I)$ (b) $-A$
(c) $-I$ (d) None of these

11. If $A^3=O$ (null matrix) and $A^n\neq I$ (identity matrix) for $n=1,2$ then $(I-A)^{-1}$ equals:

(a) $I+A$ (b) $I+A^2$
(c) $I+A+A^2$ (d) None of these

12. If A is a non-singular matrix of order n, then adj(adj A) equals:

(a) $|A|^n A$ (b) $|A|^{n-1} A$
(c) $|A|^{n(n-1)} A$ (d) $|A|^{n-2} A$

13. If $A=\begin{bmatrix}5a & -b\\3 & 2\end{bmatrix}$ and adj $A=A'$, then $5a+b$ equals:

(a) 4 (b) 5
(c) 13 (d) -1

14. The correct statements are:

(a) A is symmetric $\Rightarrow A^n$ is symmetric for all $n\in\mathbf{N}$

(b) A is symmetric $\Rightarrow A^n$ is skew-symmetric for all $n \in \mathbf{N}$
(c) A is skew-symmetric $\Rightarrow A^n$ is symmetric for all $n \in$ even $\mathbf{N}$
(d) A is skew-symmetric $\Rightarrow A^n$ is skew-symmetric for all $n \in$ even $\mathbf{N}$

15. Consider the system of equations:
$$\begin{bmatrix} 1 & a & c \\ 0 & 1 & b \\ 1 & 0 & 1 \end{bmatrix}\begin{bmatrix} x \\ y \\ z \end{bmatrix} = \begin{bmatrix} 0 \\ 0 \\ 0 \end{bmatrix}.$$
If a,b,c can take the values 0 or 1 only, then the number of such equations that have non-zero solutions are:
(a) 6 (b) 4
(c) 3 (d) 0

16. Consider the system of equations $x = cy + bz$, $y = az + cx$, $z = bx + ay$. If the system has non-zero solutions, then the value of $a^2 + b^2 + c^2 + 2abc$ is:
(a) 3 (b) 2
(c) 1 (d) 0

17. Consider the system of equations $x + 2y - 3z = 1$, $(p+2)z = 3$, $(2p+1)y + z = 2$. Then the system has:
(a) A unique solution if $p \neq -2, -1/2$
(b) Infinite solutions if $p = -1/2$
(c) No solution if $p = -2, -1/2$
(d) None of these

18. Let a,b,c be positive real numbers. Consider the system of equations
$$\frac{x^2}{a^2} + \frac{y^2}{b^2} - \frac{z^2}{c^2} = 1, \frac{x^2}{a^2} - \frac{y^2}{b^2} + \frac{z^2}{c^2} = 1, -\frac{x^2}{a^2} + \frac{y^2}{b^2} + \frac{z^2}{c^2} = 1.$$
The above system of equations has:
(a) A unique solution
(b) No solution
(c) Infinitely many solutions
(d) Finitely many solutions

19. Consider the system of equations $x + y + z = 5$, $x + 2y + 3z = 9$, $x + 3y + az = b$. Then the system has:
(a) A unique solution if $a \neq 5$
(b) No solution if $a = 5, b \neq 13$
(c) Infinite solutions if $a = 5, b = 13$
(d) None of these

20. Consider the system of equations
$3x - 2y - az = 10$, $x - 2y - z = 3$, $x + 2y - z = 5b$
Then the system is inconsistent if:
(a) $a = 3, b \in \mathbf{R}$
(b) $a = 3, b \neq 4/5$
(c) $a = 3, b = 4/5$
(d) $a \neq 3, b \in \mathbf{R}$

21. If A is a non-singular symmetric matrix, then:
(a) A^{-1} is skew-symmetric
(b) adj A' is skew-symmetric
(c) $(A^{-1})'$ is symmetric
(d) $(A')^{-1}$ is symmetric

22. Let $P = \begin{bmatrix} 3 & -1 & -2 \\ 2 & 0 & \alpha \\ 3 & -5 & 0 \end{bmatrix}$, where $\alpha \in \mathbf{R}$, and $Q = [q_{ij}]$ be matrices such that $PQ = kI$, where $k \in \mathbf{R}, k \neq 0$ and I is the identity matrix. If $q_{23} = \frac{-k}{8}$ and $|Q| = \frac{k^2}{2}$, then:
(a) $k - 2\alpha = 6$
(b) $k + 6\alpha = 10$
(c) $|Q \text{ adj } P| = 2^{12}$
(d) $|P \text{ adj } Q| = 2^9$

23. Let $P = \begin{bmatrix} 1 & 0 & 0 \\ 4 & 1 & 0 \\ 16 & 4 & 1 \end{bmatrix}$ and $Q = [q_{ij}]$ be matrices such that $P^{50} - Q = I$, where I is the identity matrix. Then $\frac{q_{31} + q_{32}}{q_{21}}$ equals:
(a) 103 (b) 117
(c) 123 (d) 135

24. If the system of equations
$$\begin{bmatrix} 1 & a & a^2 \\ a & 1 & a \\ a^2 & a & 1 \end{bmatrix}\begin{bmatrix} x \\ y \\ z \end{bmatrix} = \begin{bmatrix} 1 \\ -1 \\ 1 \end{bmatrix}$$
has infinitely many solutions, then the value of $1 + a + a^2$ is:
(a) 7 (b) 5
(c) 3 (d) 1

25. If the homogeneous system of equations $x + ky + 3z = 0$, $3x + ky - 2z = 0$, $2x + 4y - 3z = 0$ has a non-zero solution (x, y, z), then $\frac{xz}{y^2}$ equals:
(a) -10 (b) 10
(c) -30 (d) 30

26. If for positive real numbers a, b and c, the system of equations $x = a(y+z)$, $y = b(z+x)$, $z = c(x+y)$ has non-zero solutions, then $\frac{1}{1+a}+\frac{1}{1+b}+\frac{1}{1+c}$ equals:

(a) $3/2$ (b) $1/2$
(c) 3 (d) 2

27. Let $A = [a_{ij}]$ be a matrix of order $n \times n$. If $a_{ij} = \omega^{i+j}$, where $\omega(\omega \neq 1)$ is a cube root of unity, then $A^2 \neq O$ if n equals:

(a) 54 (b) 57
(c) 61 (d) 65

28. If $A^{-1} = \begin{bmatrix} 1 & 0 & -2 \\ -2 & 1 & 0 \\ -1 & 1 & 0 \end{bmatrix}$, then match the columns:

(a) $|2A|$ (p) 2^{-4}

(b) $|\text{adj}(2A)'|$ (q) 2^{-2}

(c) $|(2A)^{-1}|$ (r) 2^2

(d) $|(2A')^{-1}|$ (s) 2^4

29. If $A = \begin{bmatrix} \cos\theta & -\sin\theta \\ \sin\theta & \cos\theta \end{bmatrix}$, then for $\theta = \frac{\pi}{12}$, the matrix A^{-50} equals:

(a) $\frac{1}{2}\begin{bmatrix} \sqrt{3} & -1 \\ 1 & \sqrt{3} \end{bmatrix}$

(b) $\frac{1}{2}\begin{bmatrix} 1 & \sqrt{3} \\ -\sqrt{3} & 1 \end{bmatrix}$

(c) $\frac{1}{2}\begin{bmatrix} \sqrt{3} & 1 \\ -1 & \sqrt{3} \end{bmatrix}$

(d) $\frac{1}{2}\begin{bmatrix} 1 & -\sqrt{3} \\ \sqrt{3} & 1 \end{bmatrix}$

30. Let $\omega(\neq 1)$ be a cube root of unity and S be the set of all non-singular matrices of the form $\begin{bmatrix} 1 & a & b \\ \omega & 1 & c \\ \omega^2 & \omega & 1 \end{bmatrix}$, where a, b, c is either ω or ω^2. The number of matrices in set S is:

(a) 1 (b) 2
(c) 3 (d) 4

ANSWER KEYS

1. (d) **2.** (a) **3.** (d) **4.** (b) **5.** (b) **6.** (a),(b),(c) **7.** (c),(d) **8.** (d)
9. (b) **10.** (b) **11.** (c) **12.** (d) **13.** (b) **14.** (a),(c) **15.** (c) **16.** (c)
17. (a),(b) **18.** (d) **19.** (a),(b),(c) **20.** (b) **21.** (c),(d) **22.** (a),(d) **23.** (a) **24.** (d) **25.** (b)
26. (d) **27.** (c),(d) **28.** (a)-(r),(b)-(s),(c)-(q),(d)-(q) **29.** (c) **30.** (b)

SOLUTIONS

1. (d) We have

$$A = \frac{1}{2}[(A+B)+(A-B)] = \frac{1}{2}\begin{bmatrix} 3 & 1 & 4 \\ 1 & 0 & 1+c \\ 1 & 1 & 2 \end{bmatrix}$$

$$B = \frac{1}{2}[(A+B)-(A-B)] = \frac{1}{2}\begin{bmatrix} 1 & -1 & -2 \\ 1 & 2 & 1-c \\ -1 & 1 & 2 \end{bmatrix}$$

Now $AB = \frac{1}{4}\begin{bmatrix} 0 & 3 & 3-c \\ -c & c & 2c \\ 0 & 3 & 3-c \end{bmatrix}$.

We see that $|AB| = 0$ (since $R_1 = R_2$) for any value of c. Hence, $(AB)^{-1}$ does not exist for any value of c.

Alternative: From the property of determinants, we have

$$|AB| = |A||B| = (-2c)(0) = 0 \text{ for any value of } c.$$

Hence, $(AB)^{-1}$ does not exist for any value of c.

2. (a) We have

$$AB=\begin{bmatrix}\cos^2\theta\cos^2\phi & \cos^2\theta\sin\phi\cos\phi\\ +\sin\theta\cos\theta\sin\phi\cos\phi & +\sin\theta\cos\theta\sin^2\phi\\ \sin\theta\cos\theta\cos^2\phi & \sin\theta\cos\theta\sin\phi\cos\phi\\ +\sin^2\theta\sin\phi\cos\phi & +\sin^2\theta\sin^2\theta\end{bmatrix}$$

$$=\begin{bmatrix}\cos\theta\cos\phi\cos(\theta-\phi) & \cos\theta\cos\phi\cos(\theta-\phi)\\ \sin\theta\cos\phi\cos(\theta-\phi) & \sin\theta\sin\phi\cos(\theta-\phi)\end{bmatrix}$$

We see that $AB=O$ if

$$\cos(\theta-\phi)=0\Rightarrow\theta-\phi=(2n-1)\frac{\pi}{2}$$

3. (d) Let $M=\begin{bmatrix}a & b & c\\ d & e & f\\ g & h & i\end{bmatrix}$, where the entries are from $\{0,1,2\}$. Then

$$MM'=\begin{bmatrix}a & b & c\\ d & e & f\\ g & h & i\end{bmatrix}\begin{bmatrix}a & d & g\\ b & e & h\\ c & f & i\end{bmatrix}$$

$$=\begin{bmatrix}a^2+b^2+c^2 & \dots & \dots\\ \dots & d^2+e^2+f^2 & \dots\\ \dots & \dots & g^2+h^2+i^2\end{bmatrix}$$

According to the given condition, we have

$$a^2+b^2+c^2+d^2+e^2+f^2+g^2+h^2+i^2=5$$

This is possible if we choose (five 1s and four 0s) or (one 2, three 1s, and five 0s) or (two 2s, one 1, and six 0s).

Number of such matrices

$$=\frac{9!}{5!4!}+\frac{9!}{3!5!}+\frac{9!}{2!6!}=126+504+252=882.$$

4. (b) We have $|M-I|=|M-MM'|$ $[MM'=I,\text{given}]$

$=|M||I-M'|=|I-M'|$ $[|M|=1,\text{ given}]$

$=|(I-M)'|=|I-M|$

$=(-1)^3|M-I|$ $[M\text{ is a }3\times3\text{ matrix, given}]$

$=-|M-I|.$

Hence $|M-I|=0$.

5. (b) We have $kA^{-1}=2B^{-1}+I$

$\Rightarrow$ $kA^{-1}B=2I+B$ [Multiplying throughout by B]

$\Rightarrow$ $kB^{-1}=2I+B$ $[A^{-1}B=B^{-1},\text{ given}]$

$\Rightarrow$ $kI=2B+B^2$ [Multiplying throughout by B]

$$\Rightarrow\ kI=\begin{bmatrix}-4 & -4\\ -2 & 0\end{bmatrix}+\begin{bmatrix}6 & 4\\ 2 & 2\end{bmatrix}=\begin{bmatrix}2 & 0\\ 0 & 2\end{bmatrix}\Rightarrow k=2.$$

6. (a),(b),(c)

For the given system of equations, we have

$$D=\begin{vmatrix}1 & a\\ 3 & b\end{vmatrix}=b-3a$$

$$D_1=\begin{vmatrix}5 & a\\ c & b\end{vmatrix}=5b-ac$$

and $$D_2=\begin{vmatrix}1 & 5\\ 3 & c\end{vmatrix}=c-15$$

The system of equations has a unique solution if $b\neq 3a$.

The system of equations has infinite solutions if $b=3a, c=15$.

The system of equations has no solution if $b=3a, c\neq 15$.

7. (c),(d) We have

$$(Y^3Z^4-Z^4Y^3)'=(Y^3Z^4)'-(Z^4Y^3)'$$

$$=(Z')^4(Y')^3-(Y')^3(Z')^4$$

$$=-Z^4Y^3+Y^3Z^4\Rightarrow\text{Symmetric}$$

$$(X^{44}+Y^{44})'=(X')^{44}+(Y')^{44}=X^{44}+Y^{44}$$

$\Rightarrow$ Symmetric

$$(X^4Z^3-Z^3X^4)'=(X^4Z^3)'-(Z^3X^4)'$$

$$=(Z')^3(X')^4-(X')^4(Z')^3$$

$$=Z^3X^4-X^4Z^3=-(X^4Z^3-Z^3X^4)$$

$\Rightarrow$ Skew-symmetric

$$(X^{23}+Y^{23})'=(X')^{23}+(Y')^{23}$$

$$=-X^{23}-Y^{23}\Rightarrow\text{Skew-symmetric.}$$

8. (d) We have $A^n=I$

$\Rightarrow$ $AA^{n-1}=I=A^{n-1}A$

Hence $A^{-1}=A^{n-1}$

9. (b) We have $A^3 - 5A^2 + 4A + kI = O$.

Hence, A^{-1} exists if $k \neq 0$, since if $k = 0$, then the above equation gives $A = O$ and in that case, A^{-1} will not exist. For any other value of k, the above equation will give solutions of the type $A - mI = O \Rightarrow A = mI \Rightarrow |A| \neq 0$.

10. (b) We have $A = iI$.

Hence $A^{-1} = (iI)^{-1} = \frac{1}{i}(I)^{-1} = -iI = -A$.

11. (c) We have $(I - A)(I + A + A^2) = I - A^3 = I$

$\Rightarrow$ $I - A$ and $I + A + A^2$ are inverse matrices of each other.

12. (d) We have adj $A \times$ adj(adj A) = |adj $A|I$

[Using B adj $B = |B|I$; here B = adj A]

$\Rightarrow$ $\text{adj } A \times \text{adj}(\text{adj } A) = |A|^{n-1} I$

$\Rightarrow$ $A \text{ adj } A \times \text{adj}(\text{adj } A) = |A|^{n-1} AI$

[Multiplying both sides by A]

$\Rightarrow$ $|A| I \times \text{adj}(\text{adj } A) = |A|^{n-1} A$

$\Rightarrow$ $\text{adj}(\text{adj } A) = |A|^{n-2} A$

13. (b) We have adj $A = A'$ (given)

$\Rightarrow$ $A \text{ adj } A = AA'$

$\Rightarrow$ $|A| I = AA'$

$$\Rightarrow (10a + 3b)\begin{bmatrix} 1 & 0 \\ 0 & 1 \end{bmatrix} = \begin{bmatrix} 5a & -b \\ 3 & 2 \end{bmatrix}\begin{bmatrix} 5a & 3 \\ -b & 2 \end{bmatrix}$$

$$\Rightarrow \begin{bmatrix} 10a + 3b & 0 \\ 0 & 10a + 3b \end{bmatrix} = \begin{bmatrix} 25a^2 + b^2 & 15a - 2b \\ 15a - 2b & 13 \end{bmatrix}$$

$\Rightarrow$ $10a + 3b = 13 = 25a^2 + b^2, 15a - 2b = 0$.

Solving gives $a = \frac{2}{5}$ and $b = 3$. Hence $5a + b = 5$.

14. (a),(c) If A is symmetric, then $A' = A$. Hence

$$(A^n)' = (A')^n = A^n$$

$\Rightarrow$ A^n is symmetric if A is symmetric $\Rightarrow$ (a) is correct.

If A is skew-symmetric, then $A' = -A$. Hence

$$(A^n)' = (A')^n = (-A)^n = \begin{cases} A^n & \text{if } n \text{ is even} \\ -A^n & \text{if } n \text{ is odd} \end{cases}$$

$\Rightarrow$ A^n is skew-symmetric if A is symmetric is true for even $n \Rightarrow$ (c) is correct.

15. (c) The equation will have non-zero solutions if

$$\begin{vmatrix} 1 & a & c \\ 0 & 1 & b \\ 1 & 0 & 1 \end{vmatrix} = 0 \Rightarrow ab - c + 1 = 0$$

$\Rightarrow$ $c = ab + 1$.

The possible choices for (a, b, c) are (0, 0, 1), (0, 1, 1), (1, 0, 1).

16. (c) The system of equations can be written as

$$-x + cy + bz = 0, cx - y + az = 0, bx + ay - z = 0.$$

The system will have non-zero solutions if

$$\begin{vmatrix} -1 & c & b \\ c & -1 & a \\ b & a & -1 \end{vmatrix} = 0$$

$\Rightarrow$ $a^2 + b^2 + c^2 + 2abc = 1$.

17. (a),(b) For the given system of equations, we have

$$D = \begin{vmatrix} 1 & 2 & -3 \\ 0 & 0 & p+2 \\ 0 & 2p+1 & 1 \end{vmatrix} = -(2p+1)(p+2),$$

$$D_1 = \begin{vmatrix} 1 & 2 & -3 \\ 3 & 0 & p+2 \\ 2 & 2p+1 & 1 \end{vmatrix} = -(2p+1)(p+9),$$

$$D_2 = \begin{vmatrix} 1 & 1 & -3 \\ 0 & 3 & p+2 \\ 0 & 2 & 1 \end{vmatrix} = -(2p+1)$$

and $$D_3 = \begin{vmatrix} 1 & 2 & 1 \\ 0 & 0 & 3 \\ 0 & 2p+1 & 2 \end{vmatrix} = -3(2p+1)$$

The system of equations has a unique solution if $p \neq -2, -1/2$.

The system of equations has an infinite number of solutions if $p = -1/2$.

The system of equations has no solution if $p = -2$.

18. (d) Let $u = \dfrac{x^2}{a^2}, v = \dfrac{y^2}{b^2}, w = \dfrac{z^2}{c^2}$. The system of equations can now be written as

$$u + v - w = 1, u - v + w = 1, -u + v + w = 1$$

Solving the above equations, we get

$$u = 1, v = 1, w = 1$$

$$\Rightarrow \quad x^2 = a^2, y^2 = b^2, z^2 = c^2$$

$$\Rightarrow \quad x = \pm a, y = \pm b, z = \pm c$$

We have two choices for x, y, z. Thus, there are $2 \times 2 \times 2 = 8$ solutions in total.

19. (a),(b),(c) For the given system of equations, we have

$$D = \begin{vmatrix} 1 & 1 & 1 \\ 1 & 2 & 3 \\ 1 & 3 & a \end{vmatrix} = a - 5,$$

$$D_1 = \begin{vmatrix} 5 & 1 & 1 \\ 9 & 2 & 3 \\ b & 3 & a \end{vmatrix} = a + b - 18,$$

$$D_2 = \begin{vmatrix} 1 & 5 & 1 \\ 1 & 9 & 3 \\ 1 & b & a \end{vmatrix} = 2(2a - b + 3)$$

and $$D_3 = \begin{vmatrix} 1 & 1 & 5 \\ 1 & 2 & 9 \\ 1 & 3 & b \end{vmatrix} = b - 13$$

The system of equations has a unique solution if $a \neq 5$.

The system of equations has an infinite number of solutions if $a = 5, b = 13$.

The system of equations has no solution if $a = 5, b \neq 13$.

20. (b) For the given system of equations, we have

$$D = \begin{vmatrix} 3 & -2 & -a \\ 1 & -2 & -1 \\ 1 & 2 & -1 \end{vmatrix} = 4(3 - a),$$

$$D_1 = \begin{vmatrix} 10 & -2 & -a \\ 3 & -2 & -1 \\ 5b & 2 & -1 \end{vmatrix} = 34 - 6a + 10b - 10ab,$$

$$D_2 = \begin{vmatrix} 3 & 10 & -a \\ 1 & 3 & -1 \\ 1 & 5b & -1 \end{vmatrix} = (3 - a)(5b - 3)$$

and $$D_3 = \begin{vmatrix} 3 & -2 & 10 \\ 1 & -2 & 3 \\ 1 & 2 & 5b \end{vmatrix} = 4(4 - 5b)$$

The system of equations has a unique solution if $a \neq 3$.

The system of equations has an infinite number of solutions if $a = 3, b = 4/5$.

The system of equations has no solution if $a = 3, b \neq 4/5$.

21. (c),(d) If A is symmetric, then $A' = A$. Hence, we have

$$(A^{-1})' = (A')^{-1} = A^{-1} \Rightarrow A^{-1} \text{ is symmetric}$$

$\Rightarrow$ (a) is incorrect.

$(\text{adj } A')' = (\text{adj } A)' = \text{adj } A' \Rightarrow \text{adj } A'$ is symmetric $\Rightarrow$ (b) is incorrect.

$$\left((A^{-1})'\right)' = A^{-1} = (A')^{-1} = (A^{-1})'$$

$\Rightarrow (A^{-1})'$ is symmetric (c) is correct.

$\left((A')^{-1}\right)' = (A^{-1})' = (A')^{-1} \Rightarrow (A')^{-1}$ is symmetric $\Rightarrow$ (d) is correct.

22. (a),(d) We have $|P| = 12\alpha + 20$. From the condition $PQ = kI$, we have

$$|P||Q| = k^3 \Rightarrow (12\alpha + 20)\frac{k^2}{2} = k^3 \Rightarrow k - 6\alpha = 10 \ldots (1)$$

Let us find P^{-1}. The matrix of the cofactors of P is

$$R = \begin{bmatrix} \ldots & \ldots & \ldots \\ \ldots & \ldots & \ldots \\ \ldots & -3\alpha - 4 & \ldots \end{bmatrix}$$

Now $$P^{-1} = \frac{\text{adj } P}{|P|} = \frac{R'}{|P|}$$

$$= \frac{1}{2k}\begin{bmatrix} \ldots & \ldots & \ldots \\ \ldots & \ldots & -3\alpha - 4 \\ \ldots & \ldots & \ldots \end{bmatrix}$$

From the condition $PQ = kI$, we have

$$Q = kP^{-1} \Rightarrow q_{23} = k\left(\frac{-3\alpha - 4}{2k}\right) = \frac{-3\alpha - 4}{2}$$

It is given that $q_{23} = \frac{-k}{8}$. Hence

$$\frac{-k}{8} = \frac{-3\alpha - 4}{2}$$

$$\Rightarrow \quad k - 12\alpha = 16 \quad \ldots(2)$$

Solving the two equations gives $\alpha = -1$, $k = 4$.

Then $\quad k - 2\alpha = 6$

and $\quad |Q \text{ adj } P| = |Q||\text{adj } P| = |Q||P|^2$

$$= \frac{k^2}{2} \times (2k)^2 = 2k^4 = 2^9$$

$$\left[|\text{adj } P| = |P|^{n-1}\right]$$

and $\quad |P \text{ adj } Q| = |P||\text{adj } Q| = |P||Q|^2$

$$= 2k \times \left(\frac{k^2}{2}\right)^2 = \frac{k^5}{2} = 2^9$$

23. (a) We have

$$P^2 = \begin{bmatrix} 1 & 0 & 0 \\ 4 & 1 & 0 \\ 16 & 4 & 1 \end{bmatrix}\begin{bmatrix} 1 & 0 & 0 \\ 4 & 1 & 0 \\ 16 & 4 & 1 \end{bmatrix}$$

$$= \begin{bmatrix} 1 & 0 & 0 \\ 4\times 2 & 1 & 0 \\ 16\times(1+2) & 4\times 2 & 1 \end{bmatrix}$$

$$P^3 = \begin{bmatrix} 1 & 0 & 0 \\ 8 & 1 & 0 \\ 48 & 8 & 1 \end{bmatrix}\begin{bmatrix} 1 & 0 & 0 \\ 4 & 1 & 0 \\ 16 & 4 & 1 \end{bmatrix}$$

$$= \begin{bmatrix} 1 & 0 & 0 \\ 4\times 3 & 1 & 0 \\ 16\times(1+2+3) & 4\times 3 & 1 \end{bmatrix}$$

$$P^4 = \begin{bmatrix} 1 & 0 & 0 \\ 12 & 1 & 0 \\ 96 & 12 & 1 \end{bmatrix}\begin{bmatrix} 1 & 0 & 0 \\ 4 & 1 & 0 \\ 16 & 4 & 1 \end{bmatrix}$$

$$= \begin{bmatrix} 1 & 0 & 0 \\ 4\times 4 & 1 & 0 \\ 16\times(1+2+3+4) & 4\times 4 & 1 \end{bmatrix} \ldots$$

Generalising the above result, we have

$$P^{50} = \begin{bmatrix} 1 & 0 & 0 \\ a_{21} & 1 & 0 \\ a_{31} & a_{32} & 1 \end{bmatrix}, \text{ where}$$

$$a_{21} = a_{32} = 4 \times 50 = 200 \text{ and}$$

$$a_{31} = 16 \times (1+2+\ldots+50) = 400 \times 51.$$

$$\text{Now } Q = P^{50} - I = \begin{bmatrix} 1 & 0 & 0 \\ 200 & 1 & 0 \\ 400\times 51 & 200 & 1 \end{bmatrix} - \begin{bmatrix} 1 & 0 & 0 \\ 0 & 1 & 0 \\ 0 & 0 & 1 \end{bmatrix}$$

$$= \begin{bmatrix} 0 & 0 & 0 \\ 200 & 0 & 0 \\ 400\times 51 & 200 & 0 \end{bmatrix}$$

$$\text{Hence } \frac{q_{31} + q_{32}}{q_{21}} = \frac{200 + 400 \times 51}{200} = 1 + 102 = 103.$$

24. (d) For the given system of equations, we have

$$D = \begin{vmatrix} 1 & a & a^2 \\ a & 1 & a \\ a^2 & a & 1 \end{vmatrix} = (a^2 - 1)^2,$$

$$D_1 = \begin{vmatrix} 1 & a & a^2 \\ -1 & 1 & a \\ 1 & a & 1 \end{vmatrix},$$

$$D_2 = \begin{vmatrix} 1 & 1 & a^2 \\ a & -1 & a \\ a^2 & 1 & 1 \end{vmatrix}$$

$$\text{and} \quad D_3 = \begin{vmatrix} 1 & a & 1 \\ a & 1 & -1 \\ a^2 & a & 1 \end{vmatrix}$$

For an infinite number of solutions, all of the above discriminants must be zero. We see that $D = 0$ if $a^2 - 1 = 0 \Rightarrow a = \pm 1$. Putting these values of a, we see that D_1, D_2, D_3 become zero.

Note: Even though $a = \pm 1$ satisfies the conditions for infinite number of solutions, let us put these values of a and see what happens to the system of equations.

For $a = 1$, the equations reduce to

$$x + y + z = 1, x + y + z = -1, x + y + z = 1$$

$$\Rightarrow \quad -1 = 1$$

$\Rightarrow$ No solution.

For $a = -1$, the equations reduce to

$$x - y + z = 1, -x + y - z = -1, x - y + z = 1$$

$\Rightarrow$ $x - y + z = 1$

$\Rightarrow$ Infinite number of solutions since we have only one equation in three unknowns.

Thus, the given system of equations will have an infinite number of solutions only if $a = -1$.

In that case, $1 + a + a^2 = 1$.

25. (b) The system will have non-zero solutions if

$$\begin{vmatrix} 1 & k & 3 \\ 3 & k & -2 \\ 2 & 4 & -3 \end{vmatrix} = 0$$

$\Rightarrow$ $-3k + 8 + 5k + 3(12 - 2k) = 0$ gives $k = 11$.

The equations can now be written as

$$x + 11y + 3z = 0 \quad \ldots(1)$$

$$3x + 11y - 2z = 0 \quad \ldots(2)$$

$$2x + 4y - 3z = 0 \quad \ldots(3)$$

From equations (1) and (2), we get

$$\frac{x}{-55} = \frac{y}{11} = \frac{z}{-22}$$

$\Rightarrow$ $\dfrac{x}{5} = \dfrac{y}{-1} = \dfrac{z}{2}$

We get the same ratios from equations (2) and (3), or from equations (3) and (1). Hence $\dfrac{xz}{y^2} = 10$.

26. (d) The system will have non-zero solutions if

$$\begin{vmatrix} -1 & a & a \\ b & -1 & b \\ c & c & -1 \end{vmatrix} = 0$$

$\Rightarrow$ $-1 + bc + a(bc + b) + a(bc + c) = 0$

$\Rightarrow$ $c(a + b + 2ab) = 1 - ab$

$\Rightarrow$ $c = \dfrac{1 - ab}{a + b + 2ab}$

$\Rightarrow$ $1 + c = \dfrac{1 + a + b + ab}{a + b + 2ab}$

$$= \frac{(1+a)(1+b)}{a + b + 2ab}$$

Now, we have

$$\frac{1}{1+a} + \frac{1}{1+b} + \frac{1}{1+c} = \frac{2 + a + b}{(1+a)(1+b)} + \frac{a + b + 2ab}{(1+a)(1+b)}$$

$$= \frac{2(1 + a + b + ab)}{(1+a)(1+b)} = 2.$$

27. (c),(d) We have $A = \begin{bmatrix} \omega^2 & \cdots & \omega^{1+n} \\ \vdots & \ddots & \vdots \\ \omega^{n+1} & \cdots & \omega^{n+n} \end{bmatrix}$

Now, if $A^2 = \left[c_{ij}\right]$, then

$$c_{ij} = \left[\omega^{i+1} \;\; \ldots \;\; \omega^{i+n}\right] \begin{bmatrix} \omega^{j+1} \\ \ldots \\ \omega^{j+n} \end{bmatrix}$$

$$= \omega^{i+j+2} + \omega^{i+j+4} + \omega^{i+j+6} + \ldots + \omega^{i+j+2n}$$

$$= \omega^{i+j+2}\left(\frac{\omega^{2n} - 1}{\omega^2 - 1}\right)$$

Now $A^2 \neq O$ if $\omega^{2n} \neq 1 \Rightarrow 2n \neq 3k \, (k \in \mathbf{Z})$.

Options (c),(d) satisfy the above condition.

28. (a)-(r),(b)-(s),(c)-(q),(d)-(q)

We have $\left|A^{-1}\right| = 2 \Rightarrow |A| = \dfrac{1}{2}$.

Now, we have

(a) $|2A| = 2^3|A| = 2^2. \left[|kA| = k^n|A|\right]$

(b) $\left|\text{adj}(2A)'\right| = \left|(\text{adj}\, 2A)'\right| = \left|\text{adj}\, 2A\right|$

$$= |2A|^2 = \left(2^3|A|\right)^2 = 2^4$$

(c) $\left|(2A)^{-1}\right| = \left|\dfrac{1}{2}A^{-1}\right|$

$$= \frac{1}{2^3}\left|A^{-1}\right| = \frac{1}{2^3|A|} = 2^{-2}$$

(d) $\left|(2A')^{-1}\right| = \left|(2A^{-1})'\right| = \left|(2A)^{-1}\right| = 2^{-2}$

$$\left[(A')^{-1} = (A^{-1})\right]'$$

29. (c) We have $A^{-50}=(A^{50})^{-1}$. Now

$$A^2=\begin{bmatrix}\cos\theta & -\sin\theta\\ \sin\theta & \cos\theta\end{bmatrix}\begin{bmatrix}\cos\theta & -\sin\theta\\ \sin\theta & \cos\theta\end{bmatrix}$$

$$=\begin{bmatrix}\cos2\theta & -\sin2\theta\\ \sin2\theta & \cos2\theta\end{bmatrix}$$

$$A^3=\begin{bmatrix}\cos2\theta & -\sin2\theta\\ \sin2\theta & \cos2\theta\end{bmatrix}\begin{bmatrix}\cos\theta & -\sin\theta\\ \sin\theta & \cos\theta\end{bmatrix}$$

$$=\begin{bmatrix}\cos3\theta & -\sin3\theta\\ \sin3\theta & \cos3\theta\end{bmatrix}$$

……

$$A^{50}=\begin{bmatrix}\cos50\theta & -\sin50\theta\\ \sin5\theta & \cos50\theta\end{bmatrix}$$

Taking the inverse of the above matrix, we have

$$A^{-50}=\begin{bmatrix}\cos50\theta & \sin50\theta\\ -\sin5\theta & \cos50\theta\end{bmatrix}$$

For $\theta=\dfrac{\pi}{12}$, we have

$$A^{-50}=\begin{bmatrix}\cos\dfrac{25\pi}{6} & \sin\dfrac{25\pi}{6}\\ -\sin\dfrac{25\pi}{6} & \cos\dfrac{25\pi}{6}\end{bmatrix}=\begin{bmatrix}\cos\dfrac{\pi}{6} & \sin\dfrac{\pi}{6}\\ -\sin\dfrac{\pi}{6} & \cos\dfrac{\pi}{6}\end{bmatrix}$$

$$=\frac{1}{2}\begin{bmatrix}\sqrt{3} & 1\\ -1 & \sqrt{3}\end{bmatrix}$$

30. (b) Let A represent the given matrix. Then, we have

$$|A|=1-(a+c)\omega+ac\omega^2$$

We have $2\times2\times2=8$ ways in which matrix A can be formed. The value of $|A|$ is non-zero only when $a=c=\omega$. Since we have two choices for b, the required number is 2.

CHAPTER

9 Vector Algebra

- **Vector:** A vector is a physical quantity having both magnitude and direction. Graphically, a vector is represented by an arrow defining the direction; the length of the arrow is proportional to the magnitude of the vector. A vector will be represented as **a**, and its magnitude is denoted by $|\mathbf{a}|$ or a. The tail of the arrow is called its initial point, and the head is called the final point. If A is the initial point and B is the final point, the vector is denoted by **AB**.

- **Some Fundamental Definitions:**
  1. Two vectors are equal if they have the same magnitude and direction.
  2. A vector having direction opposite to that of **a** but having the same magnitude is denoted by $-\mathbf{a}$.
  3. Two vectors are collinear if they are parallel; having the same direction or opposite direction.
  4. The product of a vector **a** by a scalar m is the vector $m\mathbf{a}$, whose magnitude is $|m|$ times the magnitude of **a**, and whose direction is the same or opposite that of **a**, depending on whether m is positive or negative. If $m = 0$, $m\mathbf{a}$ is a null vector.
  5. A unit vector is a vector of unit magnitude. If **a** is a non-zero vector, then $\hat{\mathbf{n}} = \mathbf{a}/a$ is a unit vector having the same direction as **a**.

- **Addition and Subtraction of Two Vectors:** The sum of vectors **a** and **b** is the vector $\mathbf{c} = \mathbf{a} + \mathbf{b}$, formed by placing the initial point of **b** on the final point of **a**, and joining the initial point of **a** to the final point of **b**; this is known as the triangle law of addition.
  The subtraction of vectors **a** and **b** is the vector $\mathbf{c} = \mathbf{a} - \mathbf{b}$, formed by adding the vectors **a** and $-\mathbf{b}$.

  Related properties:
  1. Commutative law: $\mathbf{a}+\mathbf{b}=\mathbf{b}+\mathbf{a}$ but $\mathbf{a}-\mathbf{b}\neq\mathbf{b}-\mathbf{a}$
  2. Associative law: $(\mathbf{a}+\mathbf{b})+\mathbf{c}=\mathbf{a}+(\mathbf{b}+\mathbf{c})$
  3. Distributive law: $m(\mathbf{a}+\mathbf{b})=m\mathbf{a}+m\mathbf{b}$

- If θ is the smaller angle between the vectors **a** and **b**, then

  $$|\mathbf{a}+\mathbf{b}|^2 = a^2+b^2+2ab\cos\theta \text{ and } |\mathbf{a}-\mathbf{b}|^2 = a^2+b^2-2ab\cos\theta$$

  Thus, we have the following inequality: $|a-b| \le |\mathbf{a}+\mathbf{b}| \le a+b$

  It is known as the triangle inequality since the three vectors **a**, **b** and $\mathbf{a}\pm\mathbf{b}$ represent the three sides of a triangle.

  If $\mathbf{a}=a_1\hat{\mathbf{i}}+a_2\hat{\mathbf{j}}+a_3\hat{\mathbf{k}}$ and $\mathbf{b}=b_1\hat{\mathbf{i}}+b_2\hat{\mathbf{j}}+b_3\hat{\mathbf{k}}$, then

  $$\mathbf{a}+\mathbf{b}=(a_1+b_1)\hat{\mathbf{i}}+(a_2+b_2)\hat{\mathbf{j}}+(a_3+b_3)\hat{\mathbf{k}} \text{ and } \mathbf{a}-\mathbf{b}=(a_1+b_1)\hat{\mathbf{i}}+(a_2+b_2)\hat{\mathbf{j}}+(a_3+b_3)\hat{\mathbf{k}}$$

- **Decomposition of Vectors:** If **a** is a non-zero vector, then any vector **r** collinear with vector **a** can be expressed uniquely as

  $$\mathbf{r}=l\mathbf{a} \text{ for some scalar } l$$

  If **a** and **b** are two non-zero and non-collinear vectors, then any vector **r** coplanar with vectors **a** and **b** can be expressed uniquely as

  $$\mathbf{r}=l\mathbf{a}+m\mathbf{b} \text{ for some scalars } l,m$$

  If **a**, **b** and **c** are three non-zero and non-coplanar vectors, then any vector **r** can be expressed uniquely as

  $$\mathbf{r}=l\mathbf{a}+m\mathbf{b}+n\mathbf{c} \text{ for some scalars } l,m,n$$

- **Position Vector of a Point in Space:** We choose unit vectors $\hat{\mathbf{i}}, \hat{\mathbf{j}}$ and $\hat{\mathbf{k}}$ in three mutually perpendicular directions such that $\hat{\mathbf{i}} \times \hat{\mathbf{j}} = \hat{\mathbf{k}}$; this is the right-handed choice. The position vector **OA** from $O(0,0,0)$ to a point $P(x, y, z)$ is
$$\mathbf{OA} = x\hat{\mathbf{i}} + y\hat{\mathbf{j}} + z\hat{\mathbf{k}},$$
where x, y and z are called the components of vector **r** along $\hat{\mathbf{i}}, \hat{\mathbf{j}}$ and $\hat{\mathbf{k}}$, respectively. The magnitude of this vector is
$$r = \sqrt{x^2 + y^2 + z^2}$$
If the vector **r** makes angles α, β and γ with $\hat{\mathbf{i}}, \hat{\mathbf{j}}$ and $\hat{\mathbf{k}}$, respectively, then $\cos\alpha$, $\cos\beta$ and $\cos\gamma$ are called the direction cosines of the vector. Their values are
$$\frac{x}{r}, \frac{y}{r}, \frac{z}{r}$$
The numbers x, y, z are called the direction ratios of the vector.
- **Section Formula:** The position vector **r** of a point P which internally divides the line joining two points A and B in the ratio $m : n$ is
$$\mathbf{r} = \frac{m\mathbf{b} + n\mathbf{a}}{m+n},$$
where **a** and **b** are position vectors of the points A and B, respectively.
- **Angular Bisectors of Two Vectors:** If **a** are **b** are two vectors along any two directions, then vectors along the directions of their angular bisectors are
$$\frac{\mathbf{a}}{a} \pm \frac{\mathbf{b}}{b}$$
- **Dot or Scalar Product:** The dot product of two vectors **a** and **b** denoted by the symbol $\mathbf{a} \cdot \mathbf{b}$ is a scalar defined as
$$\mathbf{a} \cdot \mathbf{b} = ab\cos\theta,$$
where $\theta (0 \le \theta \le \pi)$ is the angle between the vectors **a** and **b**. If $\mathbf{a} = a_1\hat{\mathbf{i}} + a_2\hat{\mathbf{j}} + a_3\hat{\mathbf{k}}$ and $\mathbf{b} = b_1\hat{\mathbf{i}} + b_2\hat{\mathbf{j}} + b_3\hat{\mathbf{k}}$, then
$$\mathbf{a} \cdot \mathbf{b} = a_1b_1 + a_2b_2 + a_3b_3 \text{ and } \cos\theta = \frac{a_1b_1 + a_2b_2 + a_3b_3}{\sqrt{a_1^2 + a_2^2 + a_3^2}\sqrt{b_1^2 + b_2^2 + b_3^2}}$$
Angle between the vectors **a** and **b** is acute if $\mathbf{a} \cdot \mathbf{b} < 0$; the vectors are perpendicular if $\mathbf{a} \cdot \mathbf{b} = 0$.

  Related properties:
  1. $\mathbf{a} \cdot \mathbf{a} = a^2$
  2. $\mathbf{a} \cdot \mathbf{b} = \mathbf{b} \cdot \mathbf{a}$
  3. $\mathbf{a} \cdot (\mathbf{b} + \mathbf{c}) = \mathbf{a} \cdot \mathbf{b} + \mathbf{a} \cdot \mathbf{c}$
  4. $|\mathbf{a} \pm \mathbf{b}|^2 = a^2 + b^2 \pm 2(\mathbf{a} \cdot \mathbf{b})$
  5. Projection of **a** along $\mathbf{b} = a\cos\theta = \dfrac{\mathbf{a} \cdot \mathbf{b}}{b}$
- **Cross or Vector Product:** The cross product of two vectors **a** and **b** denoted by the symbol $\mathbf{a} \times \mathbf{b}$ is a vector whose magnitude is given by
$$|\mathbf{a} \times \mathbf{b}| = ab\sin\theta,$$
where $\theta (0 \le \theta \le \pi)$ is the angle between the vectors **a** and **b**. The direction of vector $\mathbf{a} \times \mathbf{b}$ is along the perpendicular to the plane containing **a** and **b** such that **a**, **b** and $\mathbf{a} \times \mathbf{b}$ form a right-handed system. If $\mathbf{a} = a_1\hat{\mathbf{i}} + a_2\hat{\mathbf{j}} + a_3\hat{\mathbf{k}}$ and $\mathbf{b} = b_1\hat{\mathbf{i}} + b_2\hat{\mathbf{j}} + b_3\hat{\mathbf{k}}$, then
$$\mathbf{a} \times \mathbf{b} = \begin{vmatrix} \hat{\mathbf{i}} & \hat{\mathbf{j}} & \hat{\mathbf{k}} \\ a_1 & a_2 & a_3 \\ b_1 & b_2 & b_3 \end{vmatrix}$$

Related properties:

1. $\mathbf{a}\times\mathbf{a}=0$
2. $\mathbf{a}\times\mathbf{b}=-\mathbf{b}\times\mathbf{a}$
3. $\mathbf{a}\times(\mathbf{b}+\mathbf{c})=\mathbf{a}\times\mathbf{b}+\mathbf{a}\times\mathbf{c}$
4. Projection of **a** perpendicular to $\mathbf{b}=a\sin\theta=\dfrac{|\mathbf{a}\times\mathbf{b}|}{b}$.
5. A unit vector perpendicular to the plane of **a** and **b** is $\dfrac{\mathbf{a}\times\mathbf{b}}{|\mathbf{a}\times\mathbf{b}|}$.

- **Area of a Triangle and Parallelogram:**
  1. Area of a triangle with sides along vectors **a** and $\mathbf{b}=\dfrac{1}{2}|\mathbf{a}\times\mathbf{b}|$.

     Area of a triangle with vertices represented by position vectors **a**, **b** and **c**
     $$=\frac{1}{2}|(\boldsymbol{b}-\boldsymbol{a})\times(\boldsymbol{c}-\boldsymbol{a})|=\frac{1}{2}|(\mathbf{a}\times\mathbf{b})+(\mathbf{b}\times\mathbf{c})+(\mathbf{c}\times\mathbf{a})|$$
  2. Area of a parallelogram with sides along vectors **a** and $\mathbf{b}=|\mathbf{a}\times\mathbf{b}|$.

     Area of a parallelogram with diagonals **a** and $\mathbf{b}=\dfrac{1}{2}|\mathbf{a}\times\mathbf{b}|$.

- **Test for Collinearity:** Two vectors $\mathbf{a}=a_1\hat{\mathbf{i}}+a_2\hat{\mathbf{j}}+a_3\hat{\mathbf{k}}$ and $\mathbf{b}=b_1\hat{\mathbf{i}}+b_2\hat{\mathbf{j}}+b_3\hat{\mathbf{k}}$ will be collinear if
  $$\frac{a_1}{b_1}=\frac{a_2}{b_2}=\frac{a_3}{b_3}$$
  Three points A, B and C will be collinear if the vectors $\mathbf{AB}=\mathbf{b}-\mathbf{a}$ and $\mathbf{AC}=\mathbf{c}-\mathbf{a}$ are collinear, that is
  $$\frac{b_1-a_1}{c_1-a_1}=\frac{b_2-a_2}{c_2-a_2}=\frac{b_3-a_3}{c_3-a_3},$$
  where $\mathbf{a}=a_1\hat{\mathbf{i}}+a_2\hat{\mathbf{j}}+a_3\hat{\mathbf{k}}$, $\mathbf{b}=b_1\hat{\mathbf{i}}+b_2\hat{\mathbf{j}}+b_3\hat{\mathbf{k}}$ and $\mathbf{c}=c_1\hat{\mathbf{i}}+c_2\hat{\mathbf{j}}+c_3\hat{\mathbf{k}}$ are the position vectors of the three points A, B and C, respectively. An alternative condition for collinearity of the points A, B, C is $(\mathbf{b}-\mathbf{a})\times(\mathbf{c}-\mathbf{a})=0$, which reduces to
  $$(\mathbf{a}\times\mathbf{b})+(\mathbf{b}\times\mathbf{c})+(\mathbf{c}\times\mathbf{a})=0$$

- **Test for Coplanarity:** Three vectors $\mathbf{a}=a_1\hat{\mathbf{i}}+a_2\hat{\mathbf{j}}+a_3\hat{\mathbf{k}}$, $\mathbf{b}=b_1\hat{\mathbf{i}}+b_2\hat{\mathbf{j}}+b_3\hat{\mathbf{k}}$ and $\mathbf{c}=c_1\hat{\mathbf{i}}+c_2\hat{\mathbf{j}}+c_3\hat{\mathbf{k}}$ will be coplanar if
  $$\begin{vmatrix} a_1 & a_2 & a_3 \\ b_1 & b_2 & b_3 \\ c_1 & c_2 & c_3 \end{vmatrix}=0$$
  Four points A, B, C and D will be coplanar if the vectors $\mathbf{AB}=\mathbf{b}-\mathbf{a}$, $\mathbf{AC}=\mathbf{c}-\mathbf{a}$ and $\mathbf{AD}=\mathbf{d}-\mathbf{a}$ are coplanar, that is
  $$\begin{vmatrix} b_1-a_1 & b_2-a_2 & b_3-a_3 \\ c_1-a_1 & c_2-a_2 & c_3-a_3 \\ d_1-a_1 & d_2-a_2 & d_3-a_3 \end{vmatrix}=0,$$
  where $\mathbf{a}=a_1\hat{\mathbf{i}}+a_2\hat{\mathbf{j}}+a_3\hat{\mathbf{k}}$, $\mathbf{b}=b_1\hat{\mathbf{i}}+b_2\hat{\mathbf{j}}+b_3\hat{\mathbf{k}}$, $\mathbf{c}=c_1\hat{\mathbf{i}}+c_2\hat{\mathbf{j}}+c_3\hat{\mathbf{k}}$ and $\mathbf{d}=d_1\hat{\mathbf{i}}+d_2\hat{\mathbf{j}}+d_3\hat{\mathbf{k}}$ are the position vectors of the four points A, B, C and D, respectively.

- **Scalar Triple Product:** The scalar triple product of three vectors **a**, **b** and **c** denoted by the symbol $[\mathbf{a}\ \mathbf{b}\ \mathbf{c}]$ is defined as
  $$[\mathbf{a}\ \mathbf{b}\ \mathbf{c}]=\mathbf{a}\times\mathbf{b}\cdot\mathbf{c}$$
  If $\mathbf{a}=a_1\hat{\mathbf{i}}+a_2\hat{\mathbf{j}}+a_3\hat{\mathbf{k}}$, $\mathbf{b}=b_1\hat{\mathbf{i}}+b_2\hat{\mathbf{j}}+b_3\hat{\mathbf{k}}$ and $\mathbf{c}=c_1\hat{\mathbf{i}}+c_2\hat{\mathbf{j}}+c_3\hat{\mathbf{k}}$, then
  $$[\mathbf{a}\ \mathbf{b}\ \mathbf{c}]=\begin{vmatrix} a_1 & a_2 & a_3 \\ b_1 & b_2 & b_3 \\ c_1 & c_2 & c_3 \end{vmatrix}$$

Related properties:

1. The value of $[\mathbf{a}\ \mathbf{b}\ \mathbf{c}]$ remains unchanged due to interchange in the position of the cross and the dot:
$$\mathbf{a}\times\mathbf{b}\cdot\mathbf{c}=\mathbf{a}\cdot\mathbf{b}\times\mathbf{c}$$
2. The value of $[\mathbf{a}\ \mathbf{b}\ \mathbf{c}]$ remains unchanged due to cylindrical rotation of **a**, **b** and **c**. But a change in sign occurs if any two vectors are interchanged without disturbing the third:
$$[\mathbf{a}\ \mathbf{b}\ \mathbf{c}]=[\mathbf{c}\ \mathbf{a}\ \mathbf{b}]=[\mathbf{b}\ \mathbf{c}\ \mathbf{a}]=-[\mathbf{b}\ \mathbf{a}\ \mathbf{c}]=-[\mathbf{a}\ \mathbf{c}\ \mathbf{b}]=-[\mathbf{c}\ \mathbf{b}\ \mathbf{a}]$$
3. $[\mathbf{a}\ \mathbf{b}\ \mathbf{c}+\mathbf{d}]=[\mathbf{a}\ \mathbf{b}\ \mathbf{c}]+[\mathbf{a}\ \mathbf{b}\ \mathbf{d}]$
4. Three vectors $\mathbf{a},\mathbf{b}$ and $\mathbf{c}$ are coplanar if $[\mathbf{a}\ \mathbf{b}\ \mathbf{c}]=0$.
5. Volume of a parallelepiped with coterminous edges along vectors $\mathbf{a},\mathbf{b}$ and $\mathbf{c}$ = mod of $[\mathbf{a}\ \mathbf{b}\ \mathbf{c}]$.
6. $[\mathbf{a}\ \mathbf{b}\ \mathbf{c}][\mathbf{u}\ \mathbf{v}\ \mathbf{w}]=\begin{vmatrix}\mathbf{a}\cdot\mathbf{u} & \mathbf{a}\cdot\mathbf{v} & \mathbf{a}\cdot\mathbf{w}\\ \mathbf{b}\cdot\mathbf{u} & \mathbf{b}\cdot\mathbf{v} & \mathbf{b}\cdot\mathbf{w}\\ \mathbf{c}\cdot\mathbf{u} & \mathbf{c}\cdot\mathbf{v} & \mathbf{c}\cdot\mathbf{w}\end{vmatrix}$

- **Vector Triple Product:** The vector triple product of three vectors **a**, **b** and **c** is the vector $\mathbf{a}\times(\mathbf{b}\times\mathbf{c})$, which is a vector lying in the plane containing **b** and **c**. It can be expressed as
$$\mathbf{a}\times(\mathbf{b}\times\mathbf{c})=(\mathbf{a}\cdot\mathbf{c})\mathbf{b}-(\mathbf{a}\cdot\mathbf{b})\mathbf{c}$$
- **Equation of a Straight Line**
  1. If $P(\mathbf{r})$ is any point on the line passing through points $A(\mathbf{a})$ and $B(\mathbf{b})$, then
  $$\mathbf{r}=(1-t)\mathbf{a}+t\mathbf{b}\ (t \text{ is a scalar})$$
  2. If $P(\mathbf{r})$ is any point on the line passing through points $A(\mathbf{a})$ and parallel to vector **c**, then
  $$\mathbf{r}=\mathbf{a}+t\mathbf{c}\ (t \text{ is a scalar})$$

EXERCISES

1. Let P,Q,R,S be points on the xy plane with position vectors $-2\mathbf{i}-\mathbf{j}$, $4\mathbf{i}$, $3\mathbf{i}+3\mathbf{j}$, $-3\mathbf{i}+2\mathbf{j}$, respectively. The quadrilateral $PQRS$ must be:
(a) A square
(b) A rectangle but not a square
(c) A rhombus but not a square
(d) None of these

2. Let $\mathbf{p},\mathbf{q},\mathbf{r}$ be three vectors such that $\mathbf{p}+\mathbf{q}=\mathbf{r}$, $|\mathbf{p}-\mathbf{q}|=2|\mathbf{r}|$ and $|\mathbf{p}+2\mathbf{q}|=2|\mathbf{r}|$. The ratio of their magnitudes $|\mathbf{p}|:|\mathbf{q}|:|\mathbf{r}|$ is:
(a) $\sqrt{3}:\sqrt{2}:\sqrt{5}$ (b) $\sqrt{2}:\sqrt{7}:\sqrt{6}$
(c) $\sqrt{6}:\sqrt{5}:\sqrt{3}$ (d) $\sqrt{2}:\sqrt{3}:\sqrt{2}$

3. If the vector $3\mathbf{i}+4\mathbf{j}+7\mathbf{k}=\mathbf{v}_1+\mathbf{v}_2$, where $\mathbf{v}_1$ is parallel to $\mathbf{i}-\mathbf{j}+\mathbf{k}$ and $\mathbf{v}_2$ is perpendicular to $2\mathbf{i}-\mathbf{k}$, then $|\mathbf{v}_1|^2+|\mathbf{v}_2|^2$ equals:
(a) 68 (b) 70
(c) 88 (d) 92

4. Vector **c** is coplanar with vectors $\mathbf{a}=-\mathbf{i}+\mathbf{j}+\mathbf{k}$ and $\mathbf{b}=2\mathbf{i}+\mathbf{k}$. If $\mathbf{a}\cdot\mathbf{c}=7$ and $\mathbf{b}\cdot\mathbf{c}=0$, then $2|\mathbf{a}+\mathbf{b}+\mathbf{c}|^2$ equals:
(a) 68 (b) 70
(c) 72 (d) 75

5. If unit vectors $\mathbf{a},\mathbf{b},\mathbf{c}$ satisfy the conditions $2\mathbf{b}\times\mathbf{a}=\mathbf{c}\times\mathbf{a}$ and $\mathbf{a}\cdot\mathbf{c}=1/4$, then $\mathbf{a}\cdot\mathbf{b}$ equals:
(a) $-7/8$ (b) $7/8$
(c) $-3/4$ (d) $11/16$

6. If $\mathbf{a},\mathbf{b},\mathbf{c},\mathbf{d}$ are unit vectors such that $(\mathbf{a}\times\mathbf{b})\cdot(\mathbf{c}\times\mathbf{d})=1$ and $\mathbf{a}\cdot\mathbf{c}=\frac{1}{2}$, then:
(a) $\mathbf{a},\mathbf{b},\mathbf{c}$ are non-coplanar
(b) $\mathbf{b},\mathbf{c},\mathbf{d}$ are non-coplanar
(c) $\mathbf{b},\mathbf{d}$ are non-collinear
(d) $\mathbf{a},\mathbf{d}$ are parallel and $\mathbf{b},\mathbf{c}$ are parallel

7. If A,B,C,D are four points in space such that $|(\mathbf{AB}\times\mathbf{CD})+(\mathbf{BC}\times\mathbf{AD})+(\mathbf{CA}\times\mathbf{BD})|=k\times$ Area of ΔABC, then k equals:

(a) 1 (b) 2
(c) 3 (d) 4

8. The vertices of a ΔABC are $A(2\mathbf{i}+3\mathbf{j}+5\mathbf{k})$, $B(-\mathbf{i}+3\mathbf{j}+2\mathbf{k})$, $C(a\mathbf{i}+5\mathbf{j}+c\mathbf{k})$. If the median through A is equally inclined to the positive directions of the coordinate axes, then the value of $2a-c$ is:
(a) 4 (b) 3
(c) 2 (d) 1

9. The vertices of a ΔABC are $A(\mathbf{i}+\mathbf{j}+\mathbf{k})$, $B(-\mathbf{i}+3\mathbf{j}+2\mathbf{k})$, $C(4\mathbf{i}+\mathbf{j}-3\mathbf{k})$. Length of the angular bisector through A is:
(a) $\frac{5\sqrt{6}}{8}$ (b) $\frac{3\sqrt{5}}{7}$
(c) $\frac{7\sqrt{3}}{6}$ (d) $\frac{2\sqrt{3}}{5}$

10. If vector $\mathbf{a}=\alpha\mathbf{i}+2\mathbf{j}+\beta\mathbf{k}$ bisects the angle between the vectors $\mathbf{b}=\mathbf{i}+\mathbf{j}$ and $\mathbf{c}=\mathbf{i}-\mathbf{j}+4\mathbf{k}$, then:
(a) $\mathbf{a}\cdot\mathbf{i}+2=0$ (b) $\mathbf{a}\cdot\mathbf{i}-1=0$
(c) $\mathbf{a}\cdot\mathbf{k}+2=0$ (d) $\mathbf{a}\cdot\mathbf{k}-1=0$

11. Let ΔPQR be a triangle such that $\mathbf{QR}=\mathbf{a}$, $\mathbf{RP}=\mathbf{b}$, $\mathbf{PQ}=\mathbf{c}$. If $a=12, b=4\sqrt{3}$ and $\mathbf{b}\cdot\mathbf{c}=24$, then:
(a) $\frac{c^2}{2}-a=24$ (b) $\frac{c^2}{2}+a=30$
(c) $|(\mathbf{a}\times\mathbf{b})+(\mathbf{c}\times\mathbf{a})|=48\sqrt{3}$ (d) $\mathbf{a}\cdot\mathbf{b}=-72$

12. Let $\mathbf{a}=\mathbf{i}-\mathbf{j}, \mathbf{b}=\mathbf{j}-\mathbf{k}$ and $\mathbf{c}=\mathbf{k}-\mathbf{i}$. If $\mathbf{d}$ is a unit vector such that $\mathbf{a}\cdot\mathbf{d}=0=[\mathbf{b}\ \ \mathbf{c}\ \ \mathbf{d}]$, then $\mathbf{d}$ equals:
(a) $\pm\frac{\mathbf{i}+\mathbf{j}-\mathbf{k}}{\sqrt{2}}$ (b) $\pm\frac{\mathbf{i}+\mathbf{j}+\mathbf{k}}{\sqrt{3}}$
(c) $+\frac{\mathbf{i}+\mathbf{j}-2\mathbf{k}}{\sqrt{6}}$ (d) None of these

13. If $\mathbf{a}$ and $\mathbf{b}$ are vectors in space given by $\mathbf{a}=\frac{\mathbf{i}-2\mathbf{j}}{\sqrt{5}}$ and $\mathbf{b}=\frac{2\mathbf{i}+\mathbf{j}+3\mathbf{k}}{\sqrt{14}}$, then the value of $(2\mathbf{a}+\mathbf{b})\cdot(\mathbf{a}\times\mathbf{b})\times(\mathbf{a}-2\mathbf{b})$ is:
(a) 2 (b) 3
(c) 4 (d) 5

14. If $\mathbf{a}=a\mathbf{i}+\mathbf{j}+\mathbf{k}, \mathbf{b}=\mathbf{i}+b\mathbf{j}+\mathbf{k}$ and $\mathbf{c}=\mathbf{i}+\mathbf{j}+c\mathbf{k}$ are coplanar vectors, then the value of $\frac{1}{1-a}+\frac{1}{1-b}+\frac{1}{1-c}$ is:
(a) -2 (b) -1
(c) 1 (d) 0

15. Let $\mathbf{x}, \mathbf{y}$ and $\mathbf{z}$ be three vectors of equal magnitude $\sqrt{2}$ and the angle between each pair be $\pi/3$. If $\mathbf{a}$ is a non-zero vector perpendicular to vectors $\mathbf{x}$ and $\mathbf{y}\times\mathbf{z}$, and $\mathbf{b}$ is a non-zero vector perpendicular to vectors $\mathbf{y}$ and $\mathbf{z}\times\mathbf{x}$, then:
(a) $\mathbf{a}=(\mathbf{a}\cdot\mathbf{y})(\mathbf{y}-\mathbf{z})$ (b) $\mathbf{b}=(\mathbf{b}\cdot\mathbf{z})(\mathbf{z}-\mathbf{x})$
(c) $\mathbf{a}\cdot\mathbf{b}=-(\mathbf{a}\cdot\mathbf{y})(\mathbf{b}\cdot\mathbf{z})$ (d) $\mathbf{a}=(\mathbf{a}\cdot\mathbf{y})(\mathbf{z}-\mathbf{x})$

16. Let $\mathbf{a}, \mathbf{b}, \mathbf{c}$ be three non-coplanar unit vectors such that the angle between each pair is $\pi/3$. If $(\mathbf{a}\times\mathbf{b})+(\mathbf{b}\times\mathbf{c})=p\mathbf{a}+q\mathbf{b}+r\mathbf{c}$, where p,q,r are scalars, then the value of $\frac{p^2+2q^2+r^2}{q^2}$ is:
(a) 4 (b) 5
(c) 6 (d) 8

17. Consider the three vectors $\mathbf{a}=2\mathbf{i}-\mathbf{j}+\mathbf{k}, \mathbf{b}=\mathbf{i}+\mathbf{j}-2\mathbf{k}$, and $\mathbf{c}=\mathbf{i}+2\mathbf{j}-\mathbf{k}$. A vector in the plane of $\mathbf{b},\mathbf{c}$ whose projection on vector $\mathbf{a}$ is of magnitude $\sqrt{2/3}$ is:
(a) $-2\mathbf{i}+\mathbf{j}+5\mathbf{k}$ (b) $2\mathbf{i}-3\mathbf{j}+\mathbf{k}$
(c) $-2\mathbf{i}-\mathbf{j}+5\mathbf{k}$ (d) $2\mathbf{i}+3\mathbf{j}-3\mathbf{k}$

18. If $\mathbf{r}$ is a unit vector such that $\mathbf{r}\times\mathbf{a}=\mathbf{b}$, where $|\mathbf{a}|=\sqrt{3}$ and $|\mathbf{b}|=\sqrt{2}$, then $\mathbf{r}$ equals:
(a) $\pm\frac{2}{3}(\mathbf{a}\times\mathbf{b})\pm\frac{1}{3}\mathbf{a}$ (b) $\pm\frac{1}{3}(\mathbf{a}\times\mathbf{b})\pm\frac{2}{3}\mathbf{a}$
(c) $\pm\frac{1}{3}(\mathbf{a}\times\mathbf{b})\pm\frac{1}{3}\mathbf{a}$ (d) $\pm\frac{2}{3}(\mathbf{a}\times\mathbf{b})\pm\frac{2}{3}\mathbf{a}$

19. Match the columns:

(a) Volume of the parallelepiped whose edges **a**, **b**, **c** satisfy $\mathbf{a}\cdot\mathbf{b}=\mathbf{b}\cdot\mathbf{c}=\mathbf{c}\cdot\mathbf{a}=\frac{1}{2}$	(p) 9
(b) Value of $|\mathbf{a}-2\mathbf{b}|^2+|\mathbf{b}+2\mathbf{c}|^2+|\mathbf{a}+\mathbf{c}|^2$ if **a**, **b**, **c** are unit vectors and $|\mathbf{a}+2\mathbf{b}-\mathbf{c}|=4$	(q) 2
(c) Greatest value of $[\mathbf{u}\ \ \mathbf{i}-\mathbf{j}\ \ \mathbf{i}+\mathbf{k}]$, where **u** is a unit vector	(r) 3
(d) Length of the shorter side of the parallelogram whose diagonals are along $3\mathbf{i}+\mathbf{j}$ and $9\mathbf{i}+\mathbf{j}$	(s) $\frac{1}{\sqrt{2}}$
(e) Value of $(\mathbf{b}-\mathbf{a})\cdot(2\mathbf{c}-\mathbf{a}-\mathbf{b})$ if $|\mathbf{a}-\mathbf{c}|=|\mathbf{b}-\mathbf{c}|$	(t) $\sqrt{3}$
(f) Greatest value of $|\mathbf{a}-\mathbf{b}|^2+|\mathbf{b}-\mathbf{c}|^2+|\mathbf{c}-\mathbf{a}|^2$, where **a**, **b**, **c** are coplanar unit vectors	(u) 0

20. A parallelepiped with coterminous edges along vectors $\mathbf{a} = \mathbf{i} + \lambda\mathbf{k}$, $\mathbf{b} = \mathbf{i} + \mathbf{j}$, and $\mathbf{c} = \mathbf{j} + \mathbf{k}$ has volume equal to 1 unit. Then the area of the triangle whose vertices are represented by position vectors **a**, **b**, **c** can be:

(a) $\frac{1}{\sqrt{2}}$ (b) $\frac{\sqrt{3}}{\sqrt{2}}$

(c) $\frac{\sqrt{5}}{\sqrt{2}}$ (d) $\frac{\sqrt{7}}{\sqrt{2}}$

ANSWER KEYS

1. (d) **2.** (d) **3.** (d) **4.** (d) **5.** (a),(b) **6.** (c) **7.** (d) **8.** (a) **9.** (a)
10. (b),(c) **11.** (c),(d) **12.** (c) **13.** (d) **14.** (c) **15.** (a),(b),(c) **16.** (a) **17.** (c),(d)
18. (c) **19.** (a)-(s),(b)-(q),(c)-(t),(d)-(r),(e)-(u),(f)-(p) **20.** (a), (b)

SOLUTIONS

1. (d) The vectors representing the sides of the quadrilateral are

$$\mathbf{PQ} = 6\mathbf{i} + \mathbf{j},\ \mathbf{QR} = -\mathbf{i} + 3\mathbf{j},$$
$$\mathbf{PS} = -\mathbf{i} + 3\mathbf{j},\ \mathbf{SR} = 6\mathbf{i} + \mathbf{j}$$

This is a parallelogram since $\mathbf{PQ} = \mathbf{SR}$ and $\mathbf{PS} = \mathbf{QR}$. But the adjacent sides are not of equal length since $|\mathbf{PQ}| \neq |\mathbf{SR}|$ and they are not mutually perpendicular since $\mathbf{PQ} \cdot \mathbf{SR} \neq 0$. Hence, *PQRS* is a parallelogram which is neither a rhombus nor a rectangle.

2. (d) Let θ be the angle between **p** and **q**. Then, we have

$$|\mathbf{p} + \mathbf{q}| = |\mathbf{r}|$$
$$\Rightarrow \quad p^2 + q^2 + 2pq\cos\theta = r^2 \quad \ldots(1)$$
$$|\mathbf{p} - \mathbf{q}| = 2|\mathbf{r}|$$
$$\Rightarrow \quad p^2 + q^2 - 2pq\cos\theta = 4r^2 \quad \ldots(2)$$
$$|\mathbf{p} + 2\mathbf{q}| = 2|\mathbf{r}|$$
$$\Rightarrow \quad p^2 + 4q^2 + 4pq\cos\theta = 4r^2 \quad \ldots(3)$$

Adding equations (1) and (2), we get

$$2p^2 + 2q^2 = 5r^2 \quad \ldots(4)$$

Multiplying equation (2) by 2 and adding to equation (3), we get

$$3p^2 + 6q^2 = 12r^2$$
$$\Rightarrow \quad p^2 + 2q^2 = 4r^2 \quad \ldots(5)$$

From equations (4) and (5), we get

$$p^2 = r^2 \text{ and } 2q^2 = 3r^2$$
$$\Rightarrow \quad p = \frac{\sqrt{2}}{\sqrt{3}}q = r \Rightarrow \frac{p}{\sqrt{2}} = \frac{q}{\sqrt{3}} = \frac{r}{\sqrt{2}}$$

3. (d) Let $\mathbf{v}_1 = m(\mathbf{i} - \mathbf{j} + \mathbf{k})$ and $\mathbf{v}_2 = x\mathbf{i} + y\mathbf{j} + z\mathbf{k}$, where $2x - z = 0$.
Now, we have $\mathbf{v}_1 + \mathbf{v}_2 = 3\mathbf{i} + 4\mathbf{j} + 7\mathbf{k}$

$$\Rightarrow \quad (m+x)\mathbf{i} + (-m+y)\mathbf{j} + (m+z)\mathbf{k} = 3\mathbf{i} + 4\mathbf{j} + 7\mathbf{k}$$
$$\Rightarrow \quad m + x = 3, -m + y = 4, m + z = 7$$

Hence, we have $m = -1, x = 4, y = 3, z = 8$, and therefore

$$|\mathbf{v}_1|^2 + |\mathbf{v}_1|^2 = (1^2 + 1^2 + 1^2) + (4^2 + 3^2 + 8^2) = 92$$

4. (d) Since **c** is coplanar with $\mathbf{a} = -\mathbf{i} + \mathbf{j} + \mathbf{k}$ and $\mathbf{b} = 2\mathbf{i} + \mathbf{k}$, it can be expressed as

$$\mathbf{c} = l\mathbf{a} + m\mathbf{b} = (2m - l)\mathbf{i} + (l)\mathbf{j} + (l + m)\mathbf{k}$$

Now, we have

$$\mathbf{a} \cdot \mathbf{c} = 7$$
$$\Rightarrow \quad (l - 2m) + (l) + (l + m) = 7$$
$$\Rightarrow \quad 3l - m = 7 \quad \ldots(1)$$

and
$$\mathbf{b} \cdot \mathbf{c} = 0$$
$$\Rightarrow \quad 2(2m - l) + (l + m) = 0$$
$$\Rightarrow \quad l = 5m \quad \ldots(2)$$

Solving the above equations, we have $l = 5/2$, $m = 1/2$.

Then $\mathbf{c} = \frac{-3}{2}\mathbf{i} + \frac{5}{2}\mathbf{j} + 3\mathbf{k}$ and

$$\mathbf{a} + \mathbf{b} + \mathbf{c} = \frac{-1}{2}\mathbf{i} + \frac{7}{2}\mathbf{j} + 5\mathbf{k}$$

Hence, we have

$$2|\mathbf{a} + \mathbf{b} + \mathbf{c}|^2 = 2\left[\frac{1}{4} + \frac{49}{4} + 25\right] = 2 \times \frac{150}{4} = 75$$

5. (a),(b) The condition $2\mathbf{b} \times \mathbf{a} = \mathbf{c} \times \mathbf{a} \Rightarrow (2\mathbf{b} - \mathbf{c}) \times \mathbf{a} = 0 \Rightarrow$ Vectors $2\mathbf{b} - \mathbf{c}$ and **a** are collinear.

Let $2\mathbf{b}-\mathbf{c}=m\mathbf{a}$.

$\Rightarrow \quad |2\mathbf{b}|=|\mathbf{c}+m\mathbf{a}|$

$\Rightarrow \quad 4b^2=c^2+m^2a^2+2m(\mathbf{a}\cdot\mathbf{c})$

$\Rightarrow \quad 4=1+m^2+m/2$

$\Rightarrow \quad 2m^2+m-6=0$ gives $m=-2, 3/2$

Thus, we have $\mathbf{c}=2\mathbf{b}+2\mathbf{a}$ or $\mathbf{c}=2\mathbf{b}-\dfrac{3}{2}\mathbf{a}$.

Now, we have

$$c^2=4b^2+4a^2+8(\mathbf{a}\cdot\mathbf{b})$$

$\Rightarrow \quad 1=4+4+8(\mathbf{a}\cdot\mathbf{b})$ gives $\mathbf{a}\cdot\mathbf{b}=-7/8$

or $\quad c^2=4b^2+\dfrac{3}{2}a^2-6(\mathbf{a}\cdot\mathbf{b})$

$\Rightarrow \quad 1=4+\dfrac{9}{4}-6(\mathbf{a}\cdot\mathbf{b})$ gives $\mathbf{a}\cdot\mathbf{b}=7/8$

6. (c) Let α be the angle between **a** and **b**. Let β be the angle between **c** and **d**. Let γ be the angle between the plane defined by $\mathbf{a}\times\mathbf{b}$ and $\mathbf{c}\times\mathbf{d}$.

Then, the equation $(\mathbf{a}\times\mathbf{b})\cdot(\mathbf{c}\times\mathbf{d})=1$ reduces to $\sin\alpha\sin\beta\cos\gamma=1$ which is possible only if

$$\sin\alpha=1, \sin\beta=1 \text{ and } \cos\gamma=1 \Rightarrow \alpha=\beta=\frac{\pi}{2} \text{ and } \gamma=0$$

Thus, all the vectors lie in a plane with **a**, **b** mutually perpendicular and **c**, **d** mutually perpendicular. Also, the angle between **a** and **c** is $\dfrac{\pi}{6}$ since $\mathbf{a}\cdot\mathbf{c}=\dfrac{1}{2}$. Thus, **a**, **c** are non-collinear. and hence **b**, **d** are non-collinear.

7. (d) Let **a**, **b**, **c**, **d** be the position vectors of the points A, B, C, D, respectively. Then

$$\mathbf{AB}\times\mathbf{CD}=(\mathbf{b}-\mathbf{a})\times(\mathbf{d}-\mathbf{c})$$
$$=(\mathbf{b}\times\mathbf{d})-(\mathbf{b}\times\mathbf{c})-(\mathbf{a}\times\mathbf{d})+(\mathbf{a}\times\mathbf{c})$$

$$\mathbf{BC}\times\mathbf{AD}=(\mathbf{c}-\mathbf{b})\times(\mathbf{d}-\mathbf{a})$$
$$=(\mathbf{c}\times\mathbf{d})-(\mathbf{c}\times\mathbf{a})-(\mathbf{b}\times\mathbf{d})+(\mathbf{b}\times\mathbf{a})$$

$$\mathbf{CA}\times\mathbf{BD}=(\mathbf{a}-\mathbf{c})\times(\mathbf{d}-\mathbf{b})$$
$$=(\mathbf{a}\times\mathbf{d})-(\mathbf{a}\times\mathbf{b})-(\mathbf{c}\times\mathbf{d})+(\mathbf{c}\times\mathbf{b})$$

Thus, we have

$$|(\mathbf{AB}\times\mathbf{CD})+(\mathbf{BC}\times\mathbf{AD})+(\mathbf{CA}\times\mathbf{BD})|$$
$$=2|(\mathbf{a}\times\mathbf{b})+(\mathbf{b}\times\mathbf{c})+(\mathbf{c}\times\mathbf{a})|=4\times\text{Area of }\Delta ABC$$

8. (a) The vector representing the median through A is given by

$$\mathbf{AD}=\frac{1}{2}(\mathbf{AB}+\mathbf{AC})$$
$$=\frac{1}{2}\{-3\mathbf{i}-3\mathbf{k}+(a-2)\mathbf{i}+2\boldsymbol{j}+(c-5)\boldsymbol{k}\}$$
$$=\frac{1}{2}\{(a-5)\mathbf{i}+2\boldsymbol{j}+(c-8)\boldsymbol{k}\}$$

If it is equally inclined to the positive directions of the coordinate axes, then

$$\frac{a-5}{1}=\frac{2}{1}=\frac{c-8}{1}$$

$\Rightarrow \quad a=7, c=10.$

Hence $2a-c=4$.

9. (a) The vectors representing the sides of the triangle are

$$\mathbf{AB}=-2\mathbf{i}+2\mathbf{j}+\mathbf{k}$$

and $\quad \mathbf{AC}=3\mathbf{i}-4\mathbf{k}$

If **AD** is the angular bisector through vertex A, then D divides side BC in the ratio $|\mathbf{AB}|:|\mathbf{AC}|=3:5$ (see figure).

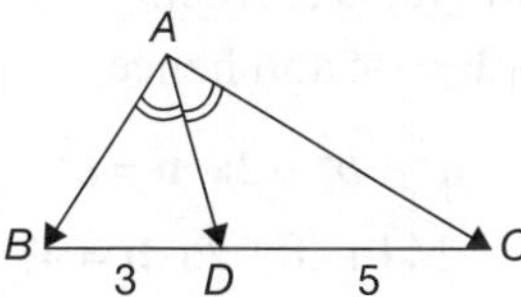

Using section formula, we have

$$\mathbf{AD}=\frac{3\mathbf{AC}+5\mathbf{AB}}{3+5}$$
$$=\frac{1}{8}(-\mathbf{i}+10\mathbf{j}-7\mathbf{k})$$

Hence length of $AD=|\mathbf{AD}|=\dfrac{5\sqrt{6}}{8}$.

10. (b),(c) The angular bisectors of the vectors $\mathbf{b}=\mathbf{i}+\mathbf{j}$ and $\mathbf{c}=\mathbf{i}-\mathbf{j}+4\mathbf{k}$ lie along the vectors

$$\frac{\mathbf{b}}{b}\pm\frac{\mathbf{c}}{c}=\frac{1}{\sqrt{2}}(\mathbf{i}+\mathbf{j})\pm\frac{1}{3\sqrt{2}}(\mathbf{i}-\mathbf{j}+4\mathbf{k})$$
$$=\frac{1}{3\sqrt{2}}(4\mathbf{i}+2\mathbf{j}+4\mathbf{k}) \text{ or } \frac{1}{3\sqrt{2}}(2\mathbf{i}+4\mathbf{j}-4\mathbf{k})$$
$$=\frac{2}{3\sqrt{2}}(2\mathbf{i}+1\mathbf{j}+2\mathbf{k}) \text{ or } \frac{2}{3\sqrt{2}}(\mathbf{i}+2\mathbf{j}-2\mathbf{k})$$

It is given that vector **a** lies along the angular bisectors. Therefore $\mathbf{a}=m(2\mathbf{i}+1\mathbf{j}+2\mathbf{k})$ or $n(\mathbf{i}+2\mathbf{j}-2\mathbf{k})$. Comparing with the given value $\mathbf{a}=\alpha\mathbf{i}+2\mathbf{j}+\beta\mathbf{k}$, we have $m=2$ and $n=1$. Thus

$$\mathbf{a}=4\mathbf{i}+2\mathbf{j}+4\mathbf{k} \text{ or } \mathbf{i}+2\mathbf{j}-2\mathbf{k}$$

Now $\quad \mathbf{a}\cdot\mathbf{i}=4$ or 1 and $\mathbf{a}\cdot\mathbf{k}=4$ or -2

$\Rightarrow$ Options (b), (c) are correct.

11. (c),(d) We have $\mathbf{a}+\mathbf{b}+\mathbf{c}=0$.
Then $\mathbf{b}+\mathbf{c}=-\mathbf{a}$ and hence

$$b^2+c^2+2\mathbf{b}\cdot\mathbf{c}=a^2$$

$$\Rightarrow \quad 48+c^2+48=144 \Rightarrow c=4\sqrt{3}.$$

Then $\dfrac{c^2}{2}-a=12$ and $\dfrac{c^2}{2}+a=36$

$\Rightarrow$ Options (a), (b) are incorrect.
Now $|\mathbf{a}\times\mathbf{b}|=|\mathbf{c}\times\mathbf{a}|=$ Twice the area of the triangle

$$=2\left(\frac{1}{2}\times12\times\sqrt{\left(4\sqrt{3}\right)^2-6^2}\right)=24\sqrt{3}$$

$$\left[a=12, b=c=4\sqrt{3}, \text{given}\right]$$

Hence $|\mathbf{a}\times\mathbf{b}+\mathbf{c}\times\mathbf{a}|=|\mathbf{a}\times\mathbf{b}|+|\mathbf{c}\times\mathbf{a}|$

$$=24\sqrt{3}+24\sqrt{3}=48\sqrt{3}$$

$$[\mathbf{a}\times\mathbf{b} \text{ and } \mathbf{c}\times\mathbf{a} \text{ are collinear}]$$

$\Rightarrow$ Option (c) is correct.
Now $\mathbf{a}+\mathbf{b}=-\mathbf{c}$ and hence

$$a^2+b^2+2\mathbf{a}\cdot\mathbf{b}=c^2$$

$$\Rightarrow \quad 144+48+2\mathbf{a}\cdot\mathbf{b}=48$$

$$\Rightarrow \mathbf{a}\cdot\mathbf{b}=-72$$

$\Rightarrow$ Option (d) is correct.

12. (c) We have $[\mathbf{b}\ \ \mathbf{c}\ \ \mathbf{d}]=0 \Rightarrow \mathbf{b},\mathbf{c},\mathbf{d}$ are coplanar.
Let $\mathbf{d}=x(\mathbf{j}-\mathbf{k})+y(\mathbf{k}-\mathbf{i})$. Then

$$\mathbf{a}\cdot\mathbf{d}=0$$

$$\Rightarrow \quad (\mathbf{i}-\mathbf{j})\cdot\{-y\mathbf{i}+x\mathbf{j}+(y-x)\mathbf{k}\}=0$$

$$\Rightarrow \quad x+y=0$$

Thus $\mathbf{d}=x\mathbf{i}+x\mathbf{j}-2x\mathbf{k}$. Since $\mathbf{d}$ is a unit vector, $x=\pm\dfrac{1}{\sqrt{6}}$. Hence

$$\mathbf{d}=\pm\frac{\mathbf{i}+\mathbf{j}-2\mathbf{k}}{\sqrt{6}}$$

13. (d) Let $\mathbf{c}=\mathbf{a}\times\mathbf{b}$. Then, we have

$$[2\mathbf{a}+\mathbf{b}\ \ \mathbf{c}\ \ \mathbf{a}-2\mathbf{b}]$$

$$=2[\mathbf{a}\ \ \mathbf{c}\ \ \mathbf{a}]-4[\mathbf{a}\ \ \mathbf{c}\ \ \mathbf{b}]+[\mathbf{b}\ \ \mathbf{c}\ \ \mathbf{a}]-2[\mathbf{b}\ \ \mathbf{c}\ \ \mathbf{b}]$$

$$=0+4[\mathbf{a}\ \ \mathbf{b}\ \ \mathbf{c}]+[\mathbf{a}\ \ \mathbf{b}\ \ \mathbf{c}]-0$$

$$=5[\mathbf{a}\ \ \mathbf{b}\ \ \mathbf{c}]$$

$$=5(\mathbf{a}\times\mathbf{b})\cdot(\mathbf{a}\times\mathbf{b})=5|\mathbf{a}\times\mathbf{b}|^2$$

Now, we have

$$\mathbf{a}\times\mathbf{b}=\frac{1}{\sqrt{5}\sqrt{14}}\begin{vmatrix}\hat{\mathbf{i}} & \hat{\mathbf{j}} & \hat{\mathbf{k}}\\ 1 & -2 & 0\\ 2 & 1 & 3\end{vmatrix}$$

$$=\frac{-6\mathbf{i}-3\mathbf{j}+5\mathbf{k}}{\sqrt{70}}$$

Hence $|\mathbf{a}\times\mathbf{b}|=1$ and the value of the above expression is 5.

14. (c) Since $\mathbf{a},\mathbf{b},\mathbf{c}$ are coplanar

$$\begin{vmatrix}a & 1 & 1\\ 1 & b & 1\\ 1 & 1 & c\end{vmatrix}=0$$

$$\Rightarrow \quad a+b+c=abc+2$$

Now, we have $S=\dfrac{1}{1-a}+\dfrac{1}{1-b}+\dfrac{1}{1-c}$

$$=\frac{(1-b)(1-c)+(1-a)(1-c)+(1-a)(1-b)}{(1-a)(1-b)(1-c)}$$

$$=\frac{ab+bc+ca-2(a+b+c)+3}{ab+bc+ca-(a+b+c)-abc+1}$$

$$=\frac{ab+bc+ca-2abc-1}{ab+bc+ca-2abc-1}=1.$$

$$[\text{Putting } a+b+c=abc+2]$$

15. (a),(b),(c) We have $\mathbf{x}\cdot\mathbf{y}=\mathbf{y}\cdot\mathbf{z}=\mathbf{z}\cdot\mathbf{x}=1$. Then

$$\mathbf{a}=m[\mathbf{x}\times(\mathbf{y}\times\mathbf{z})]=m[(\mathbf{x}\cdot\mathbf{z})\mathbf{y}-(\mathbf{x}\cdot\mathbf{y})\mathbf{z}]=m(\mathbf{y}-\mathbf{z})$$

$$\mathbf{b}=n[\mathbf{y}\times(\mathbf{z}\times\mathbf{x})]=m[(\mathbf{y}\cdot\mathbf{x})\mathbf{z}-(\mathbf{y}\cdot\mathbf{z})\mathbf{x}]=n(\mathbf{z}-\mathbf{x})$$

Now $\mathbf{a}\cdot\mathbf{y}=m(\mathbf{y}\cdot\mathbf{y}-\mathbf{z}\cdot\mathbf{y})=m(2-1)=m$. Hence $\mathbf{a}=(\mathbf{a}\cdot\mathbf{y})(\mathbf{y}-\mathbf{z})$.

Similarly $\mathbf{b}\cdot\mathbf{z}=n(\mathbf{z}\cdot\mathbf{z}-\mathbf{x}\cdot\mathbf{z})=n(2-1)=n$. Hence $\mathbf{b}=(\mathbf{b}\cdot\mathbf{z})(\mathbf{z}-\mathbf{x})$.

Now $\mathbf{a}\cdot\mathbf{b}=mn(\mathbf{y}-\mathbf{z})\cdot(\mathbf{z}-\mathbf{x})$

$$=mn(\mathbf{y}\cdot\mathbf{z}-\mathbf{y}\cdot\mathbf{x}-\mathbf{z}\cdot\mathbf{z}+\mathbf{z}\cdot\mathbf{x})=-mn.$$

16. (a) Taking dot product with vectors $\mathbf{a}$, $\mathbf{b}$ and $\mathbf{c}$, we have

$$p+\frac{1}{2}q+\frac{1}{2}r=[\mathbf{a}\ \ \mathbf{b}\ \ \mathbf{c}]$$

$$\frac{1}{2}p+q+\frac{1}{2}r=0$$

$$\frac{1}{2}p+\frac{1}{2}q+r=[\mathbf{a}\quad\mathbf{b}\quad\mathbf{c}]$$

From the first and third equations, we have

$$p+\frac{1}{2}q+\frac{1}{2}r=\frac{1}{2}p+\frac{1}{2}q+r$$

$$\Rightarrow \quad p=r$$

Putting in the second equation, we have $q=-r$.

Hence $\dfrac{p^2+2q^2+r^2}{q^2}=4$.

17. (c),(d) A vector in the plane of $\mathbf{b},\mathbf{c}$ can be chosen as

$$\mathbf{d}=m\mathbf{b}+n\mathbf{c}=(m+n)\mathbf{i}+(m+2n)\mathbf{j}-(2m+n)\mathbf{k}$$

Now $\left|\dfrac{\mathbf{d}\cdot\mathbf{a}}{a}\right|=\sqrt{2/3}$

$$\Rightarrow \quad \frac{|2(m+n)-(m+2n)-(2m+n)|}{\sqrt{6}}=\sqrt{2/3}$$

$$\Rightarrow \quad |m+n|=2$$

$$\Rightarrow \quad m+n=\pm 2=c(\text{say})$$

Hence, we have

$$\mathbf{d}=c\mathbf{i}+(n+c)\mathbf{j}+(n-2c)\mathbf{k}$$

$$=c\mathbf{i}+t\mathbf{j}+(t-3c)\mathbf{k}$$

$$=2\mathbf{i}+t\mathbf{j}+(t-6)\mathbf{k} \text{ or } -2\mathbf{i}+t\mathbf{j}+(t+6)\mathbf{k}, \text{ where } t\in\mathbf{R}.$$

Options (c) and (d) are of this type.

18. (c) Note that $\mathbf{r}$ is coplanar with vectors $\mathbf{a}$ and $\mathbf{a}\times\mathbf{b}$. Let $\mathbf{r}=m(\mathbf{a}\times\mathbf{b})+n\mathbf{a}$. Here $\boldsymbol{a},\boldsymbol{b}$ and $\boldsymbol{a}\times\boldsymbol{b}$ are mutually perpendicular vectors with magnitude $|\mathbf{a}|=\sqrt{3}, |\mathbf{b}|=\sqrt{2}$ and $|\boldsymbol{a}\times\mathbf{b}|=\sqrt{6}$, respectively.

Now, we have

$$\mathbf{r}\times\mathbf{a}=\mathbf{b}$$

$$\Rightarrow \quad m(\mathbf{a}\times\mathbf{b})\times\mathbf{a}=\mathbf{b}$$

$$\Rightarrow \quad |m(\mathbf{a}\times\mathbf{b})\times\mathbf{a}|=|\mathbf{b}|$$

$$\Rightarrow \quad |m|\sqrt{6}\sqrt{3}=\sqrt{2} \text{ gives } m=\pm\frac{1}{3}$$

$\mathbf{r}$ is a unit vector. Therefore

$$m^2|\mathbf{a}\times\mathbf{b}|^2+n^2|\mathbf{a}|^2+2mn(\mathbf{a}\times\mathbf{b})\cdot\mathbf{a}=1$$

$$\Rightarrow \quad 6m^2+3n^2=1 \text{ gives } n=\pm\frac{1}{3}$$

19. (a)-(s),(b)-(q),(c)-(t),(d)-(r),(e)-(u),(f)-(p)

(a) Volume of a parallelepiped is given by $[\mathbf{a}\quad\mathbf{b}\quad\mathbf{c}]$. We have

$$[\mathbf{a}\quad\mathbf{b}\quad\mathbf{c}]^2=\begin{vmatrix}\mathbf{a}\cdot\mathbf{a} & \mathbf{a}\cdot\mathbf{b} & \mathbf{a}\cdot\mathbf{c}\\ \mathbf{b}\cdot\mathbf{a} & \mathbf{b}\cdot\mathbf{b} & \mathbf{b}\cdot\mathbf{c}\\ \mathbf{c}\cdot\mathbf{a} & \mathbf{c}\cdot\mathbf{b} & \mathbf{c}\cdot\mathbf{c}\end{vmatrix}=\begin{vmatrix}1 & \frac{1}{2} & \frac{1}{2}\\ \frac{1}{2} & 1 & \frac{1}{2}\\ \frac{1}{2} & \frac{1}{2} & 1\end{vmatrix}=\frac{1}{2}$$

$$\Rightarrow [\mathbf{a}\quad\mathbf{b}\quad\mathbf{c}]=\frac{1}{\sqrt{2}}$$

$\Rightarrow$ (s) is the correct option.

(b) We have $|\mathbf{a}+2\mathbf{b}-\mathbf{c}|=4$

$$a^2+4b^2+c^2+4\mathbf{a}\cdot\mathbf{b}-4\mathbf{b}\cdot\mathbf{c}-\mathbf{a}\cdot\mathbf{c}=16$$

$$\Rightarrow \quad 4\mathbf{a}\cdot\mathbf{b}-4\mathbf{b}\cdot\mathbf{c}-\mathbf{a}\cdot\mathbf{c}=10$$

Now, we have

$$S=|\mathbf{a}-2\mathbf{b}|^2+|\mathbf{b}+2\mathbf{c}|^2+|\mathbf{a}+\mathbf{c}|^2$$

$$=2a^2+5b^2+5c^2-4\mathbf{a}\cdot\mathbf{b}+4\mathbf{b}\cdot\mathbf{c}+\mathbf{a}\cdot\mathbf{c}$$

$$=12-10=2$$

$\Rightarrow$ (q) is the correct option.

(c) The greatest value of $[\mathbf{u}\quad\mathbf{v}\quad\mathbf{w}]$ is $|\mathbf{v}\times\mathbf{w}|$.

Here $\mathbf{v}\times\mathbf{w}=(\mathbf{i}-\mathbf{j})\times(\mathbf{i}+\mathbf{k})=-\mathbf{i}-\mathbf{j}+\mathbf{k}$

Hence $|\mathbf{v}\times\mathbf{w}|=\sqrt{3}$

$\Rightarrow$ (p) is the correct option.

(d) If the diagonals of a parallelogram are represented by vectors $\mathbf{a}$ and $\mathbf{b}$, then the vectors representing its sides are $\frac{1}{2}(\mathbf{a}+\mathbf{b})=6\mathbf{i}+\mathbf{j}$ and $\frac{1}{2}(\mathbf{a}-\mathbf{b})=3\mathbf{i}$. The smaller magnitude amongst these two is 3

$\Rightarrow$ (r) is the correct option.

(e) The condition $|\mathbf{a}-\mathbf{c}|=|\mathbf{b}-\mathbf{c}|$

$$\Rightarrow \quad a^2-2\mathbf{a}\cdot\mathbf{c}=b^2-2\mathbf{b}\cdot\mathbf{c}$$

$$\Rightarrow \quad 2(\mathbf{b}-\mathbf{a})\cdot\mathbf{c}=b^2-a^2$$

Now, we have

$$S=(\mathbf{b}-\mathbf{a})\cdot(2\mathbf{c}-\mathbf{a}-\mathbf{b})=2(\mathbf{b}-\mathbf{a})\cdot\mathbf{c}+a^2-b^2=0$$

$\Rightarrow$ (u) is the correct option.

(f) We have

$$|\mathbf{a}-\mathbf{b}|^2+|\mathbf{b}-\mathbf{c}|^2+|\mathbf{c}-\mathbf{a}|^2=2(a^2+b^2+c^2)$$

$$-2(\mathbf{a}\cdot\mathbf{b}+\mathbf{b}\cdot\mathbf{c}+\mathbf{c}\cdot\mathbf{a})$$

$$=6-2(\cos+\cos+\cos)$$

Here $\mathbf{a},\mathbf{b},\mathbf{c}$ are coplanar vectors. Therefore $\alpha+\beta+\gamma\le 2\pi$. In that case, $\cos\alpha+\cos\beta+\cos\gamma$ has least value $-3/2$ when $\alpha=\beta=\gamma=2\pi/3$.

$$\text{Hence } |\mathbf{a}-\mathbf{b}|^2+|\mathbf{b}-\mathbf{c}|^2+|\mathbf{c}-\mathbf{a}|^2\le 6-2\left(\frac{-3}{2}\right)=9$$

$\Rightarrow$ (u) is the correct option.

20. (a), (b) Volume of the parallelepiped is given to be 1 unit. Thus, we have

$$\text{mod of } [\mathbf{a}\ \mathbf{b}\ \mathbf{c}] = 1$$

$$\Rightarrow \quad \begin{vmatrix} 1 & 0 & \lambda \\ 1 & 1 & 0 \\ 0 & 1 & 1 \end{vmatrix} = \pm\mathbf{1}$$

$$\Rightarrow \quad \lambda + 1 = \pm 1 \text{ gives } \lambda = 0, -2.$$

Area of a triangle with vertices represented by position vectors **a, b, c** is

$$\text{Area} = \frac{1}{2}\left|(\mathbf{a}\times\mathbf{b})+(\mathbf{b}\times\mathbf{c})+(\mathbf{c}\times\mathbf{a})\right|$$

$$= \frac{1}{2}\left\| \begin{vmatrix} \mathbf{i} & \mathbf{j} & \mathbf{k} \\ 1 & 0 & \lambda \\ 1 & 1 & 0 \end{vmatrix} + \begin{vmatrix} \mathbf{i} & \mathbf{j} & \mathbf{k} \\ 1 & 1 & 0 \\ 0 & 1 & 1 \end{vmatrix} + \begin{vmatrix} \mathbf{i} & \mathbf{j} & \mathbf{k} \\ 0 & 1 & 1 \\ 1 & 0 & \lambda \end{vmatrix} \right\|$$

$$= \frac{1}{2}\left|(-\lambda\mathbf{i}+\lambda\mathbf{j}+\mathbf{k})+(\mathbf{i}-\mathbf{j}+\mathbf{k})+(\lambda\mathbf{i}+\mathbf{j}-\mathbf{k})\right|$$

$$= \frac{1}{2}\left|(\mathbf{i}+\lambda\mathbf{j}+\mathbf{k})\right|$$

$$= \frac{1}{2}\sqrt{\lambda^2+2} = \frac{1}{\sqrt{2}}, \frac{\sqrt{3}}{\sqrt{2}}$$

PART II

CALCULUS

CHAPTER

10 Algebraic Functions

- A function that involves variable x raised to the power of rational numbers ($x^n, n \in \mathbf{Q}$) is an algebraic function. A function that is not algebraic is called transcendental.

  An algebraic function involving only non-negative powers of x is called a polynomial. In general, a function of the type

  $$a_0 + a_1x + a_2x^2 + \ldots + a_nx^n \ (n \in \mathbf{N})$$

  is called a polynomial of degree n; they are defined for $x \in \mathbf{R}$.

  If $P(x)$ and $Q(x)$ are two polynomials, then the function $\frac{P(x)}{Q(x)}$ is called a rational algebraic function; they are defined for $x \in \mathbf{R} - \{x : Q(x) = 0\}$.

- **Some Important Algebraic Functions:**

  1. Constant function $(y = k)$: The graph of this function is a line parallel to the x-axis with y intercept k. It is a many–one function whose domain is $x \in \mathbf{R}$ and whose range is $y \in \{k\}$.

  2. Linear function $(y = ax + b)$: The graph of this function is a straight line with slope a and y intercept b. It is a one–one function whose domain is $x \in \mathbf{R}$ and whose range is $y \in \mathbf{R}$.

     A linear function with $a = 1$ and $b = 0$ is also known as identity function.

  3. Quadratic function $\left(y = ax^2 + bx + c\right)$: The graph of this function is a parabola with the vertex at $\left(\frac{-b}{2a}, \frac{-D}{4a}\right)$, where $D = b^2 - 4ac$ is called the discriminant of the quadratic function. The parabola is concave upwards if $a > 0$ and concave downwards if $a < 0$. It is a many–one function whose

     domain is $x \in \mathbf{R}$ and range is $\begin{cases} y \in \left[\frac{-D}{4a}, +\infty\right) \text{ if } a > 0 \text{(concave upward)} \\ y \in \left(-\infty, \frac{-D}{4a}\right] \text{ if } a < 0 \text{(concave downward)} \end{cases}$

     If $D > 0$, the function $ax^2 + bx + c$ can be written as $a(x - \alpha)(x - \beta)$, where α, β are two real numbers for which the function vanishes; the graph intersects the x-axis at these two points.

     If $D = 0$, the function $ax^2 + bx + c$ can be written as $a(x - \alpha)^2$, where α is the only real number for which the function vanishes; the graph touches the x axis at this point.

     If $D < 0$, the function $ax^2 + bx + c$ does not vanish at all; the graph lies entirely above or below the x axis depending on whether a is +ve or –ve, respectively.

4. Reciprocal function $(y = 1/x)$: The graph of this function is a rectangular hyperbola with coordinate axes as its asymptotes. It is a one–one function whose domain is $x \in \mathbf{R} - \{0\}$ and whose range is $y \in \mathbf{R} - \{0\}$.

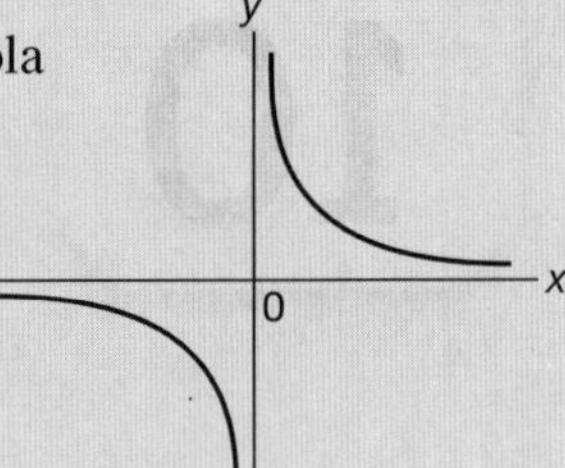

5. Mod function $(y = |x|)$: It is a many–one function whose domain is $x \in \mathbf{R}$ and whose range is $y \in [0, +\infty)$. It returns the magnitude of x:

$$|x| = \begin{cases} -x, & x < 0 \\ x, & x \geq 0 \end{cases}$$

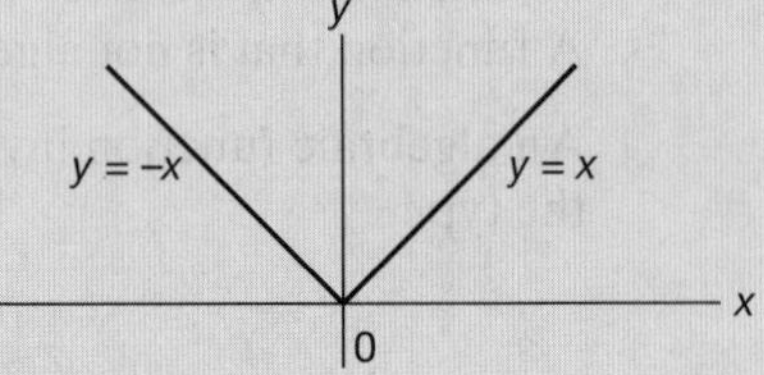

Related properties:

- $||a| - |b|| \leq |a + b| \leq |a| + |b|$. Right-hand equality sign holds when a and b are of the same sign, whereas left-hand equality holds when a and b are of opposite signs.
- $|a| = |b| \Rightarrow a = \pm b$ and $|a| < |b| \Rightarrow -b < a < b$

6. Greatest integer function $(y = [x])$: It is a many–one function whose domain is $x \in \mathbf{R}$ and whose range is $y \in \mathbf{Z}$. It returns the greatest integer less than or equal to x:

$$[x] = \begin{cases} \ldots\ldots \\ -2, & -2 \leq x < -1 \\ -1, & -1 \leq x < 0 \\ 0, & 0 \leq x < 1 \\ 1, & 1 \leq x < 2 \\ 2, & 2 \leq x < 3 \\ \ldots\ldots \end{cases}$$

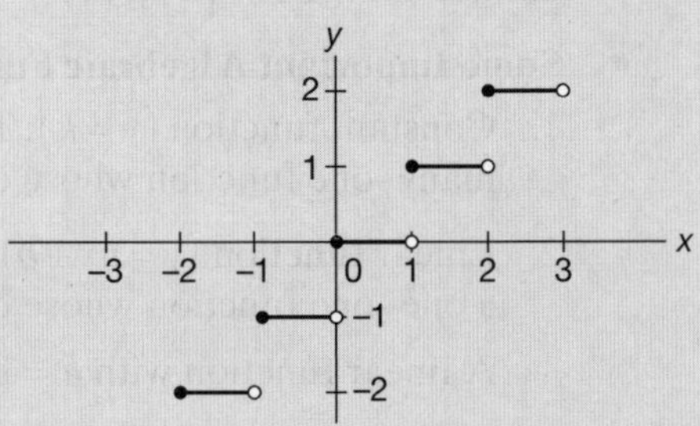

Related property: For any integer k, $[x + k] = [x] + k$.

7. Fractional function $(y = \{x\})$: It is a many–one function whose domain is $x \in \mathbf{R}$ and whose range is $y \in [0, 1)$.

It is a periodic function with period unity. It is defined as $x - [x]$:

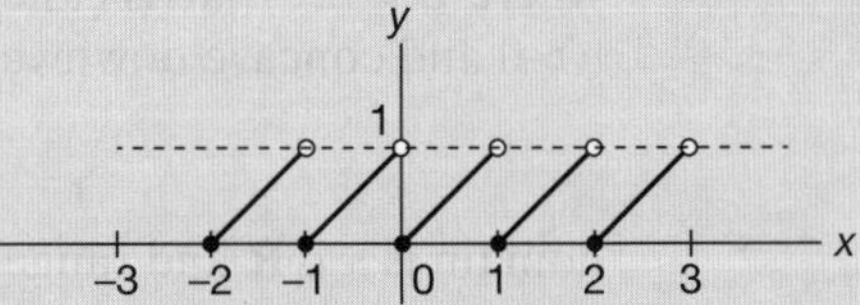

$$\{x\} = \begin{cases} \ldots\ldots \\ x + 1, & -1 \leq x < 0 \\ x, & 0 \leq x < 1 \\ x - 1, & 1 \leq x < 2 \\ \ldots\ldots \end{cases}$$

Related property: For any integer k, $\{x + k\} = \{x\}$.

8. Signum function $(y = \text{sgn}(x))$: It is a many–one function whose domain is $x \in \mathbf{R}$ and whose range is $y \in \{-1, 0, 1\}$. It is defined as

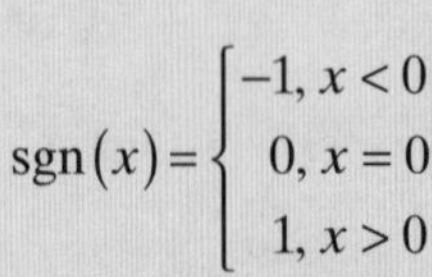

$$\text{sgn}(x) = \begin{cases} -1, & x < 0 \\ 0, & x = 0 \\ 1, & x > 0 \end{cases}$$

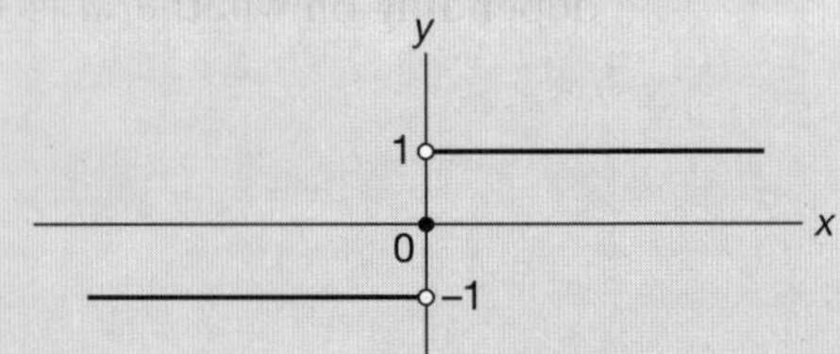

EXERCISES

1. The number of distinct solutions of the equation $||x-3|-3| = \frac{1}{2}x - 1$ is:
(a) 1 (b) 2
(c) 4 (d) Infinite

2. The number of distinct solutions of the equation $|2x-1| = |x-1| + |x-2| + |x-3|$ is:
(a) 0 (b) 1
(c) 2 (d) 3

3. The values of x satisfying the equation $|x^2+6x+6| = |x^2+4x+9| + |2x-3|$ are:
(a) $0 \le x \le 3$ (b) $x \le 0$ or $x \ge 3/2$
(c) $x \ge 3/2$ (d) $x \le -1$ or $x \ge 3$

4. Let $[x]$ denote the greatest integer less than or equal to x. The values of x satisfying the inequality $[x]^2 - 3[x] + 2 \le 0$ are:
(a) $2 \le x \le 4$ (b) $1 \le x < 3$
(c) $x \le -2$ (d) $x \le -1$ or $x \ge 2$

5. Let $[x]$ denote the greatest integer less than or equal to x. The values of x satisfying the inequality $x[x] - x^2 - 3[x] + 3x > 0$ are:
(a) $x < 3, x \ne$ integer (b) $1 < x < 3, x \ne 2$
(c) $0 < x < 3, x \ne 1, 2$ (d) $-1 < x < 1, x \ne 0$

6. Let $\{x\}$ denote the fractional part of x. The values of x satisfying the inequality $\{x\}(x+1) - x - 1 > 0$ are:
(a) $2 \le x < 4$ (b) $1 \le x < 3$
(c) $x < -1$ (d) $x \le -1$ or $x > 2$

7. Let $[x]$ denote the greatest integer less than or equal to x. The number of distinct solutions of the equation $|2x-1| = [x] + 2x$ is:
(a) 1 (b) 2
(c) 3 (d) None

8. Let $[x]$ denote the greatest integer less than or equal to x. The number of distinct solutions of the equation $[x-1] = 2x - 3$ is:
(a) 1 (b) 2
(c) 3 (d) None

9. Let $[x]$ denote the greatest integer less than or equal to x. The value of the series $S = \sum_{1}^{50}\left[\frac{1}{3} + \frac{r}{50}\right]$ is:
(a) 11 (b) 15
(c) 17 (d) 21

10. Let $[x]$ denote the greatest integer less than or equal to x. If $y = 2[x] = 3[x+2]$, then $[x+y]$ equals:
(a) -18 (b) -12
(c) 17 (d) 21

11. The number of points of extrema of the function $f(x) = 2|x| + |x+2| - ||x+2| - 2|x||$ is:
(a) 1 (b) 2
(c) 3 (d) 4

12. Let $[x]$ denote the greatest integer less than or equal to x. The range of the function $f(x) = \left[x + \frac{1}{2}\right] + \left[x - \frac{1}{2}\right] + 2[-x]$ is:
(a) $\{-3, -1\}$ (b) $\{-2, -1, 1\}$
(c) $\{-1, 0, 1\}$ (d) $\{-1, 1, 2\}$

13. The domain of definition of the function $f(x) = \sqrt{2 - x^{2/3} - x^{1/3}}$ is:
(a) $-1 \le x \le 8$ (b) $1 \le x \le 8$
(c) $-8 \le x \le -1$ (d) $-8 \le x \le 1$

14. A quadratic function attains its maximum value 3 at $x = 1$. If the value of the function is 1 at $x = 0$, then its value at $x = 10$ is:
(a) -159 (b) -119
(c) -110 (d) -105

15. The equation $|x^2 - |x| - 2| = k$ will have six distinct solutions if and only if:
(a) $1/4 < k < 1$ (b) $1 < k < 5/4$
(c) $2 < k < 9/4$ (d) None of these

16. The values of x satisfying the inequality $|x^2 - 3x - 1| < |3x^2 + 2x + 1| + |2x^2 + 5x + 2|$ are:
(a) $x \in (-\infty, -2) \cup (-1/2, +\infty)$
(b) $x \in (-\infty, -2) \cup (-3/2, +\infty)$
(c) $x \in (-\infty, -3) \cup (3/2, +\infty)$
(d) $x \in (-\infty, -2) \cup (-1, +\infty)$

17. Match the functions shown in the left column with their ranges shown in the right column:

(a) $6x^2 - 11x + 3$, $x \in \mathbf{R} - [0,1]$ (p) $[-2, 6]$

(b) $4(2-x)^2 - 4|x-2| - 2$, $x \in [1,4]$ (q) $(-\infty, 0) \cup [1, +\infty)$

(c) $||x+1| - |x+2||$ (r) $[-2, +\infty)$

(d) $(3-x)^3 - 2$, $x \in [1,4]$ (s) $[0,1]$

(e) $\dfrac{1}{1-x^2}$ (t) $[-3, 6]$

18. Match the inequalities shown in the left column with their solutions shown in the right column:

(a) $-8x^2 + 10x + 3 \le 0$ (p) $x \langle -1$ or $x \rangle 3$

(b) $3x^2 - x + 1 \ge 0$ (q) $x \le 2$ or $x > 3$, $x \ne 1, 5$

(c) $-2 < x(1-x) \le 1$ (r) $x \le \dfrac{-1}{4}$ or $x \ge \dfrac{3}{2}$

(d) $\dfrac{x+2}{x+1} < \dfrac{2x-1}{x-3}$ (s) $-1 < x < 2$

(e) $\dfrac{(x-2)^3 (x^2 - 3x + 4)}{(3-x)(x^2 - 6x + 5)^2} \le 0$ (t) $x \in \mathbf{R}$

19. Match the inequalities shown in the left column with their solutions shown in the right column:

(a) $x > \sqrt{2-x}$ (p) $x \le \dfrac{-2}{3}$ or $x \ge \dfrac{1}{2}$

(b) $|2x-3| < |3x-2|$ (q) $x \le 0$ or $x \ge \dfrac{2}{3}$

(c) $|x^2 - 3x + 5| < x + 2$ (r) $1 \le x \le 2$

(d) $|x^2 + 3x| + x^2 - 2 \ge 0$ (s) $1 < x < 3$

(e) $|x| + ||x| - |x-1|| \ge 1$ (t) $|x| > 1$

20. A 64-litre solution of 8% boric acid is to be diluted by adding x litres of 2% boric acid solution. If the resulting mixture is to be more than 4% but less than 6% boric acid, then:

(a) $42 < x < 98$ (b) $48 < x < 108$
(c) $64 < x < 114$ (d) $32 < x < 128$

21. For $x \in \mathrm{R} - [0,1]$, let $f(x) = \dfrac{1}{x}$ and $g(x) = 1 - x$ be two functions. If a function $h(x)$ satisfies the condition $gohof(x) = fog(x)$, then $h(x)$ equals:

(a) $\dfrac{1}{1-x}$ (b) $\dfrac{x}{1-x}$
(c) $x(1-x)$ (d) $\dfrac{1-x}{x}$

ANSWER KEYS

1. (b) **2.** (c) **3.** (c) **4.** (b) **5.** (a) **6.** (c) **7.** (a) **8.** (b) **9.** (c) **10.** (a)
11. (c) **12.** (a) **13.** (d) **14.** (a) **15.** (c) **16.** (a) **17.** (a)-(r), (b)-(t), (c)-(s), (d)-(t), (e)-(q)
18. (a)-(r), (b)-(t), (c)-(s), (d)-(p), (e)-(q) **19.** (a)-(r), (b)-(t), (c)-(s), (d)-(p), (e)-(q) **20.** (d) **21.** (a)

SOLUTIONS

1. (b) The given equation can be written as

$$|x-3| - 3 = \pm\left(\frac{1}{2}x - 1\right)$$

$$\Rightarrow \quad |x-3| = \frac{1}{2}x + 2, -\frac{1}{2}x + 4$$

$$\Rightarrow \quad x - 3 = \pm\left(\frac{1}{2}x + 2\right), \pm\left(-\frac{1}{2}x + 4\right)$$

$$\Rightarrow \quad x - 3 = \pm\left(\frac{1}{2}x + 2\right), \pm\left(-\frac{1}{2}x + 4\right)$$

$$\Rightarrow \quad x = 10, \frac{2}{3}, -2, \frac{14}{3}$$

Only two values $x = \dfrac{14}{3}, 10$ are acceptable. This can be checked by inserting the other two values in the given equation. Hence, two distinct solutions.

Alternative: From the graph of the two functions, we can see that they intersect at two points.

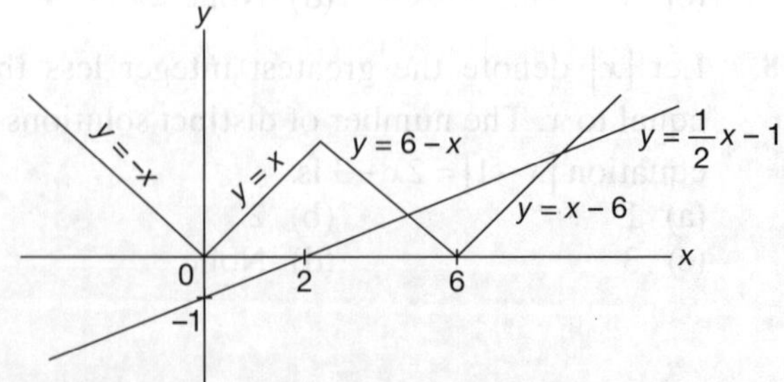

2. (c) For $x < \frac{1}{2}$, the equation reduces to

$$-(2x-1) = -(x-1)-(x-2)-(x-3)$$

$\Rightarrow$ $2x-1 = 3x-6$

$\Rightarrow$ $x = 5$ unacceptable, since it lies outside the interval.

For $\frac{1}{2} \le x < 1$, the equation reduces to

$$2x-1 = -(x-1)-(x-2)-(x-3)$$

$\Rightarrow$ $2x-1 = 6-3x$

$\Rightarrow$ $x = 7/5$ unacceptable, since it lies outside the interval.

For $1 \le x < 2$, the equation reduces to

$$2x-1 = (x-1)-(x-2)-(x-3)$$

$\Rightarrow$ $2x-1 = -x+4$

$\Rightarrow$ $x = 5/3$ acceptable, since it lies inside the interval.

For $2 \le x < 3$, the equation reduces to

$$2x-1 = (x-1)+(x-2)-(x-3)$$

$\Rightarrow$ $2x-1 = x$

$\Rightarrow$ $x = 1$ unacceptable, since it lies outside the interval.

For $x \ge 3$, the equation reduces to

$$2x-1 = (x-1)+(x-2)+(x-3)$$

$\Rightarrow$ $2x-1 = 3x-6$

$\Rightarrow$ $x = 5$ acceptable, since it lies inside the interval.

Hence, there are two distinct solutions $x = 5/3, 5$

3. (c) The equality $|a+b| = |a|+|b|$ is true for $ab \ge 0$
Hence, we have

$$(x^2+4x+9)(2x-3) \ge 0$$

$\Rightarrow$ $(2x-3) \ge 0$

[x^2+4x+9 is always +ve, since $D < 0$ and $a > 0$]

$\Rightarrow$ $x \ge 3/2$

4. (b) The given inequality can be written as

$$([x]-1)([x]-2) \le 0$$

$\Rightarrow$ $1 \le [x] \le 2 \Rightarrow 1 \le x < 3$

5. (a) The given inequality can be written as

$$([x]-x)(x-3) > 0$$

$\Rightarrow$ $-\{x\}(x-3) > 0$

$\Rightarrow$ $\{x\}(x-3) < 0$ $[\{x\} \ge 0$ for all $x]$

$\Rightarrow$ $x < 3, x \ne$ integer $[\{x\} = 0$ for integer $x]$

6. (c) The given inequality can be written as

$$(\{x\}-1)(x+1) > 0$$

$\Rightarrow$ $x+1 < 0$ $[\{x\}-1 < 0$ for all $x]$

7. (a) For $x \le \frac{1}{2}$, the equation reduces to

$$-(2x-1) = [x]+2x$$

$\Rightarrow$ $[x] = 1-4x$,

which has only one solution $x = \frac{1}{4}$ as can be seen from their graphs.

For $x > \frac{1}{2}$, the equation reduces to

$$2x-1 = [x]+2x$$

$\Rightarrow$ $[x] = -1$

$\Rightarrow$ $-1 \le x < 0$,

which means no solution in this interval.

Hence, the given equation has only one solution.

8. (b) The given equation can be written as

$$[x]-1 = 2x-3$$

$\Rightarrow$ $[x] = 2x-2$,

which has two solutions $x = \frac{3}{2}, 2$ as can be seen from their graphs.

9. (c) As long as $\frac{r}{50} < \frac{2}{3} \Rightarrow r < \frac{100}{3} \Rightarrow$ up to $r = 33$, the value of each term is zero. The remaining 17 terms are each equal to 1. Hence $S = 17$.

10. (a) The given equation can be written as

$$2[x] = 3([x]+2)$$

$\Rightarrow$ $[x] = -6$ and $y = 2[x] = -12$

Hence $[x+y] = [x-12] = [x]-12 = -18$

11. (c) The given function can be written as

$$f(x) = \begin{cases} -3x-2-|x-2|, & x < -2 \\ -x+2-|3x+2|, & -2 \le x \le 0 \\ 3x+2-|x-2|, & x > 0 \end{cases}$$

$$= \begin{cases} -2x-4, & x < -2 \\ 2x+4, & -2 \le x < \frac{-2}{3} \\ -4x, & \frac{-2}{3} \le x < 0 \\ 4x, & 0 \le x < 2 \\ 2x+4, & x \ge 2 \end{cases}$$

The function has a minima at $x = -2$, a maxima at $x = \frac{-2}{3}$ and a minima at $x = 0$. Note that there is no extrema at $x = 2$ since the function is increasing on both sides of $x = 2$. Hence, the function has three points of extrema.

12. (a) For any real number $x = I + f$, we have

$$f(I+f) = \left[I+f+\frac{1}{2}\right]+\left[I+f-\frac{1}{2}\right]+2[-I-f]$$

$$= I+\left[f+\frac{1}{2}\right]+I+\left[f-\frac{1}{2}\right]+2(-I-1)$$

$$= \left[f+\frac{1}{2}\right]+\left[f-\frac{1}{2}\right]-2$$

$$= \begin{cases} 0-1-2=-3, & 0 \le f < \frac{1}{2} \\ 1+0-2=-1, & \frac{1}{2} \le f < 1 \end{cases}$$

Hence range is $\{-3,-1\}$.

13. (d) The function is defined for values of x satisfying

$$x^{2/3}+x^{1/3}-2 \le 0$$

$$\Rightarrow \quad (x^{1/3}+2)(x^{1/3}-1) \le 0$$

$$\Rightarrow \quad -2 \le x^{1/3} \le 1$$

$$\Rightarrow \quad -8 \le x \le -1$$

14. (a) The quadratic function is of the type

$$f(x) = a(x-1)^2+3$$

Using the condition $f(0)=1$, gives $a=-2$. Thus, we have

$$f(x) = -2(x-1)^2+3$$

Hence $f(10) = -159$.

15. (c) The function $f(x) = \left|x^2-|x|-2\right|$ is an even function.

For positive values of x

$$f(x) = \left|x^2-x-2\right| = \left|(x+1)(x-2)\right|$$

$$= \begin{cases} -(x^2-x-2), & 0 < x \le 2 \\ x^2-x-2, & x \ge 2 \end{cases}$$

In the interval $0 < x < 1/2$, the value of the function increases from 2 to $9/4$.

In the interval $1/2 < x < 2$, the value of the function decreases from $9/4$ to 0.

In the interval $2 < x < \infty$, the value of the function increases from 0 to ∞.

Now, from the graph of $f(x)$, we can see that the horizontal line $y=k$ will intersect the positive half of the graph three times and its negative half three times (total six times) only if $2 < k < 9/4$.

16. (a) The given inequality can be written as

$$\left|(3x^2+2x+1)-(2x^2+5x+2)\right|$$

$$< \left|3x^2+2x+1\right|+\left|2x^2+5x+2\right|$$

The inequality $|a-b| < |a|+|b|$ is true when a and b are of the same sign, that is, when $ab > 0$. Hence, we have

$$(3x^2+2x+1)(2x^2+5x+2) > 0$$

$\Rightarrow (2x+1)(x+2) > 0$ [$3x^2+2x+1>0$, since $D<0$ and $a>0$]

$\Rightarrow x \in (-\infty,-2)\cup(-1/2,+\infty)$

17. (a)-(r),(b)-(t),(c)-(s),(d)-(t),(e)-(q)

(a) Let $f(x) = 6x^2-11x+3$, $x \in \mathbf{R}-[0,1]$. The function decreases in $(-\infty,0)$ and increases in $(1,+\infty)$. Now $f(-\infty)=+\infty$, $f(0)=3$, $f(1)=-2$, $f(+\infty)=+\infty$.

Thus, the values of the function lie in $[3,+\infty)\cup[-2,+\infty)=[-2,+\infty)$.

(b) Let $f(x) = 4(2-x)^2-4|x-2|-2$, $x \in [1,4]$.

Now $x \in [1,4] \Rightarrow x-2 \in [-1,2] \Rightarrow |x-2| \in [0,2]$.

Putting $|x-2|=t$, the function reduces to $g(t)=4t^2-4t-2$, $t \in [0,2]$. The function $g(t)$ decreases in $\left(0,\frac{1}{2}\right)$ and increases in $\left(\frac{1}{2},2\right)$.

Now $g(0)=-2$, $g\left(\frac{1}{2}\right)=-3$, $g(2)=6$.

Thus, the values of the function lie in $[-3,-2)\cup[-3,6)=[-3,6)$.

(c) The given function can be written as

$$f(x) = \begin{cases} \left|-(x+1)+(x+2)\right|, & x<-2 \\ \left|-(x+1)-(x+2)\right|, & -2 \le x \le -1 \\ \left|(x+1)-(x+2)\right|, & x>-1 \end{cases}$$

$$= \begin{cases} 1, & x<-2 \\ |2x+3|, & -2 \le x \le -1 \\ 1, & x>-1 \end{cases}$$

Now

$x \in [-2,-1] \Rightarrow 2x+3 \in [-1,1] \Rightarrow |2x+3| \in [0,1]$.

Thus, the values of the function lie in $[0,1]$.

(d) Let $f(x) = -(x-3)^3-2$, $x \in [1,4]$. The function strictly decreases in $[1, 4]$. Now $f(1) = 6$, $f(4) = -3$.

Thus, the values of the function lie in $[-3,6]$.

(e) Let $f(x) = \dfrac{1}{1-x^2}$. The function is defined for $x \in \mathbf{R}-\{-1,1\}$.

Now $x \in \mathbf{R} - \{-1, 1\} \Rightarrow 1 - x^2 \in (-\infty, 1] - \{0\}$. Putting $1 - x^2 = t$, the function reduces to $g(t) = \frac{1}{t}, t \in (-\infty, 1] - \{0\}$.

Thus, the values of the function lie in $(-\infty, 0) \cup [1, +\infty)$.

18. (a)-(r),(b)-(t),(c)-(s),(d)-(p),(e)-(q)

(a) The given inequality can be written as

$8x^2 - 10x - 3 \geq 0$

$\Rightarrow 8\left(x + \frac{1}{4}\right)\left(x - \frac{3}{2}\right) \geq 0$

$\Rightarrow x \leq \frac{-1}{4}$ or $x \geq \frac{3}{2}$

(b) Let $f(x) = 3x^2 - x + 1$. Since $D < 0$ and $a > 0$, $f(x)$ will always be +ve.

(c) The given inequality can be written as

$-2 < x - x^2 \leq 1$

$\Rightarrow x^2 - x - 2 < 0 \Rightarrow (x+1)(x-2) \Rightarrow -1 < x < 2$ and $x^2 - x + 1 \geq 0$, which is true for all x since $D < 0$ and $a > 0$.

Thus, the solution set is $-1 < x < 2$.

(d) The given inequality can be written as

$$\frac{x+2}{x+1} - \frac{2x-1}{x-3} < 0$$

$$\Rightarrow \frac{(x^2 - x - 6) - (2x^2 + x - 1)}{(x+1)(x-3)} < 0$$

$$\Rightarrow \frac{-(x^2 + 2x + 5)}{(x+1)(x-3)} < 0$$

$\Rightarrow \frac{1}{(x+1)(x-3)} > 0$ [$x^2 + 2x + 5 > 0$ for all x since $D < 0$ and $a > 0$]

$\Rightarrow x < -1$ or $x > 3$

Thus, the solution set is $x < -1$ or $x > 3$.

(e) The given inequality can be written as

$$\frac{(x-2)^3 (x^2 - 3x + 4)}{(x-3)(x^2 - 6x + 5)^2} \geq 0$$

$\Rightarrow \frac{(x-2)^3}{(x-3)} \geq 0$ [$x^2 - 3x + 4 > 0$ for all x since $D < 0$ and $a > 0$]

$\Rightarrow x \leq 2$ or $x > 3, x \neq 1, 5$ [The denominator becomes zero for $x = 3, 1, 5$]

19. (a)-(r),(b)-(t),(c)-(s),(d)-(p),(e)-(q)

(a) The given inequality can be written as

$x^2 \geq 2 - x$ where $0 \leq x \leq 2$

$\Rightarrow x^2 + x - 2 \geq 0$

$\Rightarrow (x+2)(x-1) \geq 0$

$\Rightarrow x \leq -2$ or $x \geq 1$

Taking the intersection of the two inequalities, we have $1 \leq x \leq 2$

(b) The given inequality can be written as

$(2x-3)^2 < (3x-2)^2$

$\Rightarrow (2x-3)^2 - (3x-2)^2 < 0$

$\Rightarrow (-x-1)(5x-5) < 0$

$\Rightarrow (x+1)(x-1) > 0$

$\Rightarrow x < -1$ or $x > 1$

$\Rightarrow |x| > 1$

(c) The given inequality can be written as

$-x - 2 < x^2 - 3x + 5 < x + 2$

$\Rightarrow x^2 - 2x + 7 > 0$ which is true for all x since $D < 0$ and $a > 0$ and $x^2 - 4x + 3 < 0$

$\Rightarrow (x-1)(x-3) < 0 \Rightarrow 1 < x < 3$

Taking the intersection, the solution set is $1 < x < 3$.

(d) The given inequality can be written as

$|x^2 + 3x| \geq 2 - x^2$

$\Rightarrow x^2 + 3x \leq x^2 - 2$ or $x^2 + 3x \geq 2 - x^2$

$\Rightarrow x \leq \frac{-2}{3}$ or $2x^2 + 3x - 2 \geq 0$

$\Rightarrow (x+2)(2x-1) \geq 0 \Rightarrow x \leq -2$ or $x \geq \frac{1}{2}$

Taking the union, the solution set is

$x \leq \frac{-2}{3}$ or $x \geq \frac{1}{2}$

(e) The given inequality is

$|x| + ||x| - |x-1|| \geq 1$

For $x \leq 0$, the inequality reduces to

$-x + |-x + x - 1| \geq 1$

$\Rightarrow -x + 1 \geq 1$

$\Rightarrow x \leq 0$

For $0 < x < 1$, the inequality reduces to

$x + |x + x - 1| \geq 1$

$\Rightarrow |2x - 1| \geq 1 - x$

$\Rightarrow 2x - 1 \leq x - 1$ or $2x - 1 \geq 1 - x$

$\Rightarrow\ x \le 0$ or $x \ge \frac{2}{3}$,

which means $\frac{2}{3} \le x < 1$ in this interval.

For $x \ge 1$, the inequality reduces to

$x + |x - x + 1| \ge 1$

$\Rightarrow\ x + 1 \ge 1$

$\Rightarrow\ x \ge 0$,

which means $x \ge 1$ in this interval.

Taking the union, the solution set is

$$x \le 0 \text{ or } x \ge \frac{2}{3}$$

20. (d) Amount of boric acid in the mixture $= 8\%(64) + 2\%(x)$. Volume of the mixture $= 64 + x$.

Concentration of boric acid in the mixture $= \frac{8\%(64) + 2\%(x)}{64 + x}$. According to the required condition, we have

$$4\% < \frac{8\%(64) + 2\%(x)}{64 + x} < 6\%$$

Solving the LHI, we have

$$4 \times 64 + 4x < 8 \times 64 + 2x$$

$\Rightarrow\ 2x < 4 \times 64$

$\Rightarrow\ x < 128$

Solving the RHI, we have

$$8 \times 64 + 2x < 6 \times 64 + 6x$$

$\Rightarrow\ 4x > 2 \times 64$

$\Rightarrow\ x > 32$

Hence $32 < x < 128$.

21. (a) Simplifying the given condition, we have

$$gohof(x) = fog(x)$$

$\Rightarrow\ goh\left(\frac{1}{x}\right) = \frac{1}{1-x}$

$\Rightarrow\ 1 - h\left(\frac{1}{x}\right) = \frac{1}{1-x}$

$\Rightarrow\ h\left(\frac{1}{x}\right) = \frac{-x}{1-x}$

Now replacing x with $\frac{1}{x}$, we have

$$h(x) = \frac{-\frac{1}{x}}{1 - \frac{1}{x}} = \frac{1}{1-x}$$

CHAPTER

11 Trigonometric Functions

- Trigonometric functions, also known as circular functions, are periodic functions; they repeat after regular intervals called the period of the function.
  1. Sine function

     It is a many–one function whose domain is $x \in \mathbf{R}$ and whose range is $|y| \le 1$.

     It is an odd function with period 2π.
  2. Cosine function $(y = \cos x)$

     It is a many–one function whose domain is $x \in \mathbf{R}$ do $(y = \sin x)$ and whose range is $|y| \le 1$.

     It is an even function with period 2π.
  3. Tangent function $(y = \tan x)$

     It is a many–one function whose domain is $x \in \mathbf{R} - \left\{(2n+1)\frac{\pi}{2}\right\}, n \in \mathbf{Z}$ and whose range is $y \in \mathbf{R}$.

     It is an odd function with period π.
  4. Cosecant function $(y = \operatorname{cosec} x)$

     It is a many–one function whose domain is $x \in \mathbf{R} - \{n\pi\}, n \in \mathbf{Z}$ and whose range is $|y| \ge 1$.

     It is an odd function with period 2π.
  5. Secant function $(y = \sec x)$

     It is a many–one function whose domain is $x \in \mathbf{R} - \left\{(2n+1)\frac{\pi}{2}\right\}, n \in \mathbf{Z}$ and whose range is $|y| \ge 1$.

     It is an even function with period 2π.
  6. Cotangent function $(y = \cot x)$

     It is a many–one function whose domain is $x \in \mathbf{R} - \{n\pi\}, n \in \mathbf{Z}$ and whose range is $y \in \mathbf{R}$.

     It is neither an even nor an odd function with period 2π.

- **Trigonometric Identities**:
  1. $\sin^2 x + \cos^2 x - 1$

     $1 + \tan^2 x = \sec^2 x$

     $1 + \cot^2 x = \operatorname{cosec}^2 x$
  2. $\sin(x \pm y) = \sin x \cos y \pm \cos x \sin y$

     $\cos(x \pm y) = \cos x \cos y \mp \sin x \sin y$

     $\tan(x \pm y) = \dfrac{\tan x \pm \tan y}{1 \mp \tan x \tan y}$
  3. $\sin 2x = 2\sin x \cos x = \dfrac{2\tan x}{1+\tan^2 x}$

     $\cos 2x = 1 - 2\sin^2 x = 2\cos^2 x - 1 = \dfrac{1-\tan^2 x}{1+\tan^2 x}$

     $\tan 2x = \dfrac{2\tan x}{1-\tan^2 x}$

4. $\sin 3x = 3\sin x - 4\sin^3 x$

   $\cos 3x = 4\cos^3 x - 3\cos x$

   $\tan 3x = \dfrac{3\tan x - \tan^3 x}{1 - 3\tan^2 x}$

5. $2\sin x\cos y = \sin(x+y) + \sin(x-y)$

   $2\cos x\cos y = \cos(x+y) + \cos(x-y)$

   $2\sin x\sin y = \cos(x-y) - \cos(x+y)$

6. $\sin x + \sin y = 2\sin\left(\dfrac{x+y}{2}\right)\cos\left(\dfrac{x-y}{2}\right)$

   $\sin x - \sin y = 2\cos\left(\dfrac{x+y}{2}\right)\sin\left(\dfrac{x-y}{2}\right)$

   $\cos x + \cos y = 2\cos\left(\dfrac{x+y}{2}\right)\cos\left(\dfrac{x-y}{2}\right)$

   $\cos x - \cos y = -2\sin\left(\dfrac{x+y}{2}\right)\sin\left(\dfrac{x-y}{2}\right)$

7. $\sin(x+y)\sin(x-y) = \sin^2 x - \sin^2 y$

   $\cos(x+y)\cos(x-y) = \cos^2 x - \sin^2 y$

EXERCISES

1. If $\tan^2 A = 2\tan^2 B + 1$, then the value of $\cos(2A) + \sin^2 B$ is:

(a) 0 (b) 1/2
(c) –1 (d) 1

2. If $\tan\alpha = \dfrac{1}{7}$ and $\sin\beta = \dfrac{1}{\sqrt{10}}$, where $\alpha, \beta \in \left[0, \dfrac{\pi}{2}\right]$, then $\sin(2\beta + \alpha)$ equals:

(a) $\dfrac{1}{\sqrt{2}}$ (b) $\dfrac{\sqrt{2}}{5}$
(c) $\dfrac{1}{\sqrt{25}}$ (d) $\dfrac{1}{5\sqrt{2}}$

3. If $\cos x = \dfrac{3}{4}$, then the value of $32\sin\left(\dfrac{x}{2}\right)\sin\left(\dfrac{5x}{2}\right)$ equals:

(a) 4 (b) 7
(c) 8 (d) 11

4. If $\cos^6 x$ is identically expressed as $a_0 + a_1\cos x + a_2\cos(2x) + \ldots + a_6\cos(6x)$, then:

(a) $a_0 = \dfrac{5}{16}$ (b) $a_1 = a_3 = a_5 = 0$
(c) $a_6 = \dfrac{1}{16}$ (d) $a_2 = a_4 = a_6 = 0$

5. If $\cos(6x)$ is identically expressed as $a_0 + a_1\cos x + a_2\cos^2 x + \ldots + a_6\cos^6 x$, then:

(a) $a_0 = -1$ (b) $a_1 = a_3 = a_5 = 0$
(c) $a_6 = 16$ (d) $a_2 = a_4 = a_6 = 0$

6. The expression $\tan x\tan 2x + \tan 2x\tan 3x + \ldots + \tan(nx)\tan(n+1)x$ is identically equal to:

(a) $\cot x\left[\tan(n+1)x - \tan x\right] - n$

(b) $\tan x\left[\tan(n+1)x - \tan x\right] - n$

(c) $\cot x \tan(n+1)x - 2n$

(d) $\tan x \tan(n+1)x - 2n$

7. If $|x| \le \frac{\pi}{4}$, the expression $\frac{\sqrt{1+\sin(2x)}+\sqrt{1-\sin(2x)}}{\sqrt{1+\sin(2x)}-\sqrt{1-\sin(2x)}}$ is identically equal to:

(a) $\tan x$ (b) $\cot x$
(c) $\cot x + \tan x$ (d) $\operatorname{cosec} x + \sec x$

8. If the expression $\sin^3 x + \sin^3\left(x+\frac{2\pi}{3}\right)+\sin^3\left(x+\frac{4\pi}{3}\right)$ is identically equal to $a\sin 3x$, then the value of a is:

(a) $\frac{1}{2}$ (b) $\frac{-2}{3}$
(c) $\frac{-3}{4}$ (d) None of these

9. If $1+\cos(x-y)=0$, then:

(a) $\cos x - \cos y = 0$ (b) $\cos x + \cos y = 0$
(c) $\sin x - \sin y = 0$ (d) $\sin x + \sin y = 0$

10. If $A+B=\frac{\pi}{3}$ and $\cos A + \cos B = 1$, then:

(a) $\cos(A-B)=\frac{1}{3}$ (b) $|\cos A - \cos B| = \frac{\sqrt{2}}{\sqrt{3}}$
(c) $\cos(A-B)=\frac{-1}{3}$ (d) $|\cos A - \cos B| = \frac{1}{2\sqrt{3}}$

11. If $A+B+C=\pi$, then the value of $\frac{\sin(2A)+\sin(2B)+\sin(2C)}{\sin A \sin B \sin C}$ is:

(a) $-1/2$ (b) 4
(c) -2 (d) 2

12. If $\frac{x}{\tan(\theta+\alpha)}=\frac{y}{\tan(\theta+\beta)}=\frac{z}{\tan(\theta+\gamma)}$, then the value of $\frac{x+y}{x-y}\sin^2(\alpha-\beta)+\frac{y+z}{y-z}\sin^2(\beta-\gamma)+\frac{z+x}{z-x}\sin^2(\gamma-\alpha)$ equals:

(a) $1/2$ (b) 0
(c) -1 (d) 1

13. If $\frac{\tan(3A)}{\tan A}=k$, then the value of $\frac{\sin(3A)}{\sin A}$ is:

(a) $\frac{k}{k-1}$ (b) $\frac{k}{k+1}$
(c) $\frac{k}{2k-1}$ (d) $\frac{2k}{k-1}$

14. If $\tan(6A)=\frac{p}{q}$, then the value of $p\operatorname{cosec}(2A)-q\sec(2A)$ is:

(a) $\frac{pq}{\sqrt{p^2+q^2}}$ (b) $\frac{2pq}{\sqrt{p^2+q^2}}$
(c) $2\sqrt{p^2+q^2}$ (d) $pq\sqrt{p^2+q^2}$

15. If $\sin(2A+B)=5\sin B$, then the value of $\frac{\tan(A+B)}{\tan A}$ is:

(a) $3/2$ (b) $1/2$
(c) -1 (d) 1

16. If $\cos x - \sin A \cot B \sin x = \cos A$, then $\tan\left(\frac{x}{2}\right)$ equals:

(a) $-\tan\left(\frac{A}{2}\right)\cot\left(\frac{B}{2}\right)$ (b) $\cot\left(\frac{A}{2}\right)\cot\left(\frac{B}{2}\right)$
(c) $\tan\left(\frac{A}{2}\right)\tan\left(\frac{B}{2}\right)$ (d) $-\cot\left(\frac{A}{2}\right)\tan\left(\frac{B}{2}\right)$

17. Let $f_n(x)=\tan\left(\frac{x}{2}\right)(1+\sec x)(1+\sec 2x)(1+\sec 2^2 x)\ldots(1+\sec 2^n x)$. Then:

(a) $f_2\left(\frac{\pi}{16}\right)=\frac{1}{2}$ (b) $f_3\left(\frac{\pi}{32}\right)=\frac{1}{4}$
(c) $f_4\left(\frac{\pi}{64}\right)=1$ (d) $f_5\left(\frac{\pi}{128}\right)=1$

18. If $\cos A+\cos B=x$ and $\sin A+\sin B=y$, then $\sin(A+B)\{1+\cos(A-B)\}$ equals:

(a) $\frac{xy}{x+y}$ (b) $\frac{2xy}{x^2+y^2}$
(c) $xy(x+y)$ (d) xy

19. The value of $\sum_1^3 \frac{1}{\sin\left(\frac{\pi}{4}+\frac{(k-1)\pi}{6}\right)\sin\left(\frac{\pi}{4}+\frac{k\pi}{6}\right)}$ is:

(a) $2(\sqrt{3}-1)$ (b) $2(\sqrt{3}+1)$
(c) $2(3+\sqrt{3})$ (d) $2(3-\sqrt{3})$

20. If $2(\cos B-\cos A)+\cos A\cos B=1$, then:

(a) $\tan\left(\frac{A}{2}\right)+\sqrt{3}\tan\left(\frac{B}{2}\right)=0$

(b) $\sqrt{3}\tan\left(\frac{A}{2}\right)+\tan\left(\frac{B}{2}\right)=0$

(c) $\tan\left(\frac{A}{2}\right)-\sqrt{3}\tan\left(\frac{B}{2}\right)=0$

(d) $\sqrt{3}\tan\left(\frac{A}{2}\right)-\tan\left(\frac{B}{2}\right)=0$

21. If $\theta=\frac{\pi}{2^n+1}$, then $2^n\cos\theta\cos2\theta\cos2^2\theta\ldots\cos2^{n-1}\theta$ equals:

(a) 1 (b) 1/2

(c) −1/2 (d) 0

22. Match the expressions shown in the left column with their values shown in the right column:

(a) $\left(1+\cos\frac{\pi}{8}\right)\left(1+\cos\frac{3\pi}{8}\right)\left(1+\cos\frac{5\pi}{8}\right)\left(1+\cos\frac{7\pi}{8}\right)$	(p) 2^{23}
(b) $\tan9°+\cot9°+\tan117°+\cot117°$	(q) $\frac{1}{8}$
(c) $\tan20°\tan40°\tan80°$	(r) 4
(d) $(1+\tan1°)(1+\tan2°)\ldots(1+\tan45°)$	(s) $\sqrt{3}$
(e) $\sqrt{3}\operatorname{cosec}20°-\sec20°$	(t) $-\sqrt{3}$

23. Using the identity

$$\cos\theta\cos(2\theta)\cos(2^2\theta)\ldots\cos(2^{n-1}\theta)=\frac{\sin(2^n\theta)}{2^n\sin\theta},$$

match the expressions shown in the left column with their values shown in the right column:

(a) $\cos\frac{\pi}{7}\cos\frac{2\pi}{7}\cos\frac{4\pi}{7}$	(p) $\frac{-1}{2}$
(b) $\cos\frac{2\pi}{15}\cos\frac{4\pi}{15}\cos\frac{8\pi}{15}\cos\frac{14\pi}{15}$	(q) $\frac{-1}{8}$
(c) $\sin\frac{\pi}{14}\sin\frac{3\pi}{14}\sin\frac{5\pi}{14}\sin\frac{7\pi}{14}$	(r) $\frac{1}{8}$
(d) $\cos\frac{2\pi}{7}+\cos\frac{4\pi}{7}+\cos\frac{6\pi}{7}$	(s) $\frac{1}{16}$

24. Match the functions shown in the left column with their greatest values shown in the right column:

(a) $2-\sqrt{3\cos x-4\sin x-1}$	(p) −2
(b) $\frac{1}{\sin^2x+3\sin x\cos x+5\cos^2x}$	(q) 0
(c) $1+\sin\left(3x-\frac{3\pi}{4}\right),\ x\in\left[\frac{-\pi}{4},0\right]$	(r) −1
(d) $-2\cos^2x+2\cos x+\frac{3}{2}$	(s) 2

25. Match the functions shown in the left column with their ranges shown in the right column:

(a) $\sin^2x+\cos^4x$	(p) $[-2,4]$
(b) $1+\sin\left(\frac{\pi}{4}+x\right)+2\cos\left(\frac{\pi}{4}-x\right)$	(q) $[1,\sqrt{2}]$
(c) $\frac{\sin(3x)}{\sin x}$	(r) $\left[\frac{3}{4},1\right]$
(d) $\frac{\tan(3x)}{\tan x}$	(s) $[-1,3)$
(e) $\lvert\sin x\rvert+\lvert\cos x\rvert$	(t) $\mathbf{R}-\left[\frac{1}{3},3\right]$

26. If $\sin\theta$, $\tan\theta$, $\cos\theta$ are in GP, $4\sin^2\theta-3\sin^4\theta+\sin^6\theta$ equals:

(a) −1 (b) 1

(c) −2 (d) 2

ANSWER KEYS

1. (a) **2.** (a) **3.** (d) **4.** (a),(b) **5.** (a),(b) **6.** (a) **7.** (b) **8.** (c)
9. (b),(d) **10.** (b),(c) **11.** (b) **12.** (b) **13.** (d) **14.** (c) **15.** (a) **16.** (a),(c)
17. (c),(d) **18.** (d) **19.** (a) **20.** (a),(c) **21.** (a) **22.** (a)-(q), (b)-(r), (c)-(s), (d)-(p), (e)-(r)
23. (a)-(q), (b)-(s), (c)-(r), (d)-(p) **24.** (a)-(s), (b)-(s), (c)-(s), (d)-(s)
25. (a)-(r), (b)-(p), (c)-(s), (d)-(t), (e)-(q) **26.** (b)

SOLUTIONS

1. (a) We have

$$\cos(2A)+\sin^2 B = 2\cos^2 A - \cos^2 B$$
$$= \frac{2\sec^2 B - \sec^2 A}{\sec^2 B \sec^2 A}$$
$$= \frac{1+2\tan^2 B - \tan^2 A}{\sec^2 B \sec^2 A}$$
$$= 0\ [\text{Given } 1+2\tan^2 B = \tan^2 A]$$

2. (a) We have

$$\sin(2\beta+\alpha) = \sin(2\beta)\cos\alpha + \cos(2\beta)\sin\alpha$$
$$= (2\sin\beta\cos\beta)\cos\alpha + (1-2\sin^2\beta)\sin\alpha$$

From the given data, we have

$$\tan\alpha = \frac{1}{7} \Rightarrow \sin\alpha = \frac{1}{\sqrt{50}},\ \cos\alpha = \frac{7}{\sqrt{50}}$$

and $\sin\beta = \frac{1}{\sqrt{10}} \Rightarrow \cos\beta = \frac{3}{\sqrt{10}},\ \tan\beta = \frac{1}{3}$

Now, putting the above values gives

$$\sin(2\beta+\alpha) = \frac{1}{\sqrt{2}}$$

3. (d) We have

$$32\sin\left(\frac{x}{2}\right)\sin\left(\frac{5x}{2}\right) = 16(\cos 2x - \cos 3x)$$
$$= 16(2\cos^2 x - 1) - 16(4\cos^3 x - 3\cos x)$$
$$= 11\left[\text{Putting } \cos x = \frac{3}{4}\right]$$

4. (a),(b) We have

$$\cos^6 x = \left(\frac{\cos 3x + 3\cos x}{4}\right)^2$$
$$= \frac{1}{16}(\cos^2 3x + 6\cos x\cos 3x + 9\cos^2 x)$$
$$= \frac{1}{16}\left\{\frac{1}{2}(1+\cos 6x) + 3(\cos 4x + \cos 2x) + \frac{9}{2}(1+\cos 2x)\right\}$$
$$= \frac{1}{32}\cos 6x + \frac{3}{16}\cos 4x + \frac{15}{32}\cos 2x + \frac{5}{16}$$

5. (a),(b) We have

$$\cos(6x) = 2\cos^2(3x) - 1 = 2(4\cos^3 x - 3\cos x)^2 - 1$$
$$= 32\cos^6 x - 48\cos^4 x + 18\cos^2 x - 1$$

6. (a) We have

$$\tan(2x - x) = \frac{\tan 2x - \tan x}{1+\tan x\tan 2x}$$
$$\Rightarrow\quad 1+\tan x\tan 2x = \cot x(\tan 2x - \tan x)$$
$$\Rightarrow\quad \tan x\tan 2x = \cot x(\tan 2x - \tan x) - 1$$

Similarly, we have

$$\tan 2x\tan 3x = \cot x(\tan 3x - \tan 2x) - 1,$$
$$\tan 3x\tan 4x = \cot x(\tan 4x - \tan 3x) - 1,$$
$$\ldots$$

and

$$\tan(nx)\tan(n+1)x = \cot x\{\tan(n+1)x - \tan(nx)\} - 1$$

Adding the above, we have

$$\tan x\tan 2x + \tan 2x\tan 3x + \ldots + \tan(nx)\tan(n+1)x$$
$$= \cot x[\tan(n+1)x - \tan x] - n$$

7. (b) We have

$$\sqrt{1+\sin 2x} = \sqrt{(\sin x + \cos x)^2}$$
$$= |\sin x + \cos x| = \left|\sqrt{2}\sin\left(x+\frac{\pi}{4}\right)\right|$$

and

$$\sqrt{1-\sin 2x} = \sqrt{(\sin x - \cos x)^2}$$
$$= |\sin x - \cos x| = \left|\sqrt{2}\sin\left(x-\frac{\pi}{4}\right)\right|$$

Now $|x| \le \frac{\pi}{4} \to \frac{-\pi}{4} \le x \le \frac{\pi}{4}$

$$\Rightarrow 0 \le x+\frac{\pi}{4} \le \frac{\pi}{2} \text{ and } \frac{\pi}{2} \le x - \frac{\pi}{4} \le 0$$

Thus, for $|x| \le \frac{\pi}{4}$

$$\sqrt{2}\sin\left(x+\frac{\pi}{4}\right) \ge 0 \Rightarrow \sin x + \cos x \ge 0$$

and

$$\sqrt{2}\sin\left(x-\frac{\pi}{4}\right) \le 0 \Rightarrow \sin x - \cos x \le 0$$

Hence, the given expression reduces to

$$\frac{\sqrt{1+\sin(2x)}+\sqrt{1-\sin(2x)}}{\sqrt{1+\sin(2x)}-\sqrt{1-\sin(2x)}}$$

$$=\frac{(\sin x+\cos x)+(\cos x-\sin x)}{(\sin x+\cos x)-(\cos x-\sin x)}=\cot x$$

8. (c) We have

$$\sin^3 x=\frac{1}{4}(3\sin x-\sin 3x),$$

$$\sin^3\left(x+\frac{2\pi}{3}\right)=\frac{1}{4}\left\{3\sin\left(x+\frac{2\pi}{3}\right)-\sin(3x+2\pi)\right\}$$

and

$$\sin^3\left(x+\frac{4\pi}{3}\right)=\frac{1}{4}\left\{3\sin\left(x+\frac{4\pi}{3}\right)-\sin(3x+4\pi)\right\}$$

Adding the above, we have

$$\sin^3 x+\sin^3\left(x+\frac{2\pi}{3}\right)+\sin^3\left(x+\frac{4\pi}{3}\right)$$

$$=\frac{3}{4}\left\{\sin x+\sin\left(x+\frac{2\pi}{3}\right)+\sin\left(x+\frac{4\pi}{3}\right)\right\}-\frac{3}{4}\sin 3x$$

$$=\frac{-3}{4}\sin 3x$$

Hence $a=\frac{-3}{4}$.

9. (b),(d) We have

$$1+\cos(x-y)=0$$

$$\Rightarrow\quad 2\cos^2\left(\frac{x-y}{2}\right)=0$$

$$\Rightarrow\quad \cos\left(\frac{x-y}{2}\right)=0$$

Now $\cos x+\cos y=2\cos\left(\frac{x+y}{2}\right)\cos\left(\frac{x-y}{2}\right)=0$

Similarly, we can check the other options.

10. (b),(c) We have

$$\cos A+\cos B=1$$

$$\Rightarrow\quad 2\cos\left(\frac{A+B}{2}\right)\cos\left(\frac{A-B}{2}\right)=1$$

$$\Rightarrow\quad \cos\left(\frac{A-B}{2}\right)=\frac{1}{\sqrt{3}}.\ \left[\text{given } A+B=\frac{\pi}{3}\right]$$

Now $\cos(A-B)=2\cos^2\left(\frac{A-B}{2}\right)-1=\frac{2}{3}-1=\frac{-1}{3}$

and $|\cos A-\cos B|=\left|2\sin\left(\frac{A+B}{2}\right)\sin\left(\frac{A-B}{2}\right)\right|$

$$=2\times\frac{1}{2}\times\frac{\sqrt{2}}{\sqrt{3}}=\frac{\sqrt{2}}{\sqrt{3}}$$

11. (b) We have

$$\frac{\sin(2A)+\sin(2B)+\sin(2C)}{\sin A\sin B\sin C}$$

$$=\frac{2\sin(A+B)\cos(A-B)+2\sin C\cos C}{\sin A\sin B\sin C}$$

$$=\frac{2\sin C\cos(A-B)+2\sin C\cos C}{\sin A\sin B\sin C}$$

[Putting $A+B=\pi-C$]

$$=2\left(\frac{\cos(A-B)+\cos C}{\sin A\sin B}\right)$$

$$=2\left(\frac{\cos(A-B)-\cos(A+B)}{\sin A\sin B}\right)$$

[Putting $C=\pi-(A+B)$]

$$=2\left(\frac{2\sin A\sin B}{\sin A\sin B}\right)=4$$

12. (b) We have

$$S=\sum\frac{x+y}{x-y}\sin^2(\alpha-\beta)$$

$$=\sum\frac{\tan(\theta+\alpha)+\tan(\theta+\beta)}{\tan(\theta+\alpha)-\tan(\theta+\beta)}\sin^2(\alpha-\beta)$$

$$=\sum\frac{\sin(\theta+\alpha)\cos(\theta+\beta)+\sin(\theta+\beta)\cos(\theta+\alpha)}{\sin(\theta+\alpha)\cos(\theta+\beta)-\sin(\theta+\beta)\cos(\theta+\alpha)}\sin^2(\alpha-\beta)$$

$$=\sum\frac{\sin(2\theta+\alpha+\beta)}{\sin(\alpha-\beta)}\sin^2(\alpha-\beta)$$

$$=\sum\sin(2\theta+\alpha+\beta)\sin(\alpha-\beta)$$

$$=\sum\frac{1}{2}\{\cos(2\theta+2\beta)-\cos(2\theta+2\alpha)\}$$

$$= \frac{1}{2}\{\cos(2\theta+2\beta)-\cos(2\theta+2\alpha)\}$$
$$+\frac{1}{2}\{\cos(2\theta+2\gamma)-\cos(2\theta+2\beta)\}$$
$$+\frac{1}{2}\{\cos(2\theta+2\alpha)-\cos(2\theta+2\gamma)\}$$
$$=0$$

13. (d) We have

$$\frac{\tan(3A)}{\tan A}=k$$
$$\Rightarrow \quad \frac{3-\tan^2 A}{1-3\tan^2 A}=k$$
$$\Rightarrow \quad \tan^2 A=\frac{k-3}{3k-1}$$

Now $\frac{\sin(3A)}{\sin A}=3-4\sin^2 A=-1+4\cos^2 A$

$$=-1+\frac{4}{1+\tan^2 A}=\frac{2k}{k-1}$$

14. (c) We have

$$p\,\mathrm{cosec}(2A)-q\sec(2A)=\frac{p\cos 2A-q\sin 2A}{\sin 2A\cos 2A}$$
$$=\frac{\sqrt{p^2+q^2}\sin(\alpha-2A)}{\frac{1}{2}\sin 4A}, \text{ where } \tan\alpha=\frac{p}{q}$$
$$=2\sqrt{p^2+q^2}\ \text{[Putting } \alpha=6A]$$

15. (a) Let $s-\frac{\tan(A+B)}{\tan A}$

Then $\frac{s+1}{s-1}=\frac{\tan(A+B)+\tan A}{\tan(A+B)-\tan A}$

$$=\frac{\sin(A+B)\cos A+\cos(A+B)\sin A}{\sin(A+B)\cos A-\cos(A+B)\sin A}$$
$$=\frac{\sin(2A+B)}{\sin B}=5$$

Hence $s=\frac{3}{2}$

16. (a),(c) Let $\tan\left(\frac{x}{2}\right)=t$

Then $\sin x=\frac{2t}{1+t^2}$ and $\cos x=\frac{1-t^2}{1+t^2}$

The given equation reduces to

$(1+b)t^2+2at+(b-1)=0$, where

$a=\sin A\cot B$ and $=\cos A$

$$t=\frac{-a\pm\sqrt{a^2+1-b^2}}{1+b}$$
$$=\frac{-\sin A\cot B\pm\sin A\,\mathrm{cosec} B}{1+\cos A}$$
$$\Rightarrow \quad =\frac{-\sin A}{1+\cos A}\cdot\frac{\cos B\pm 1}{\sin B}$$
$$=-\tan\left(\frac{A}{2}\right)\cot\left(\frac{B}{2}\right),\ \tan\left(\frac{A}{2}\right)\tan\left(\frac{B}{2}\right)$$

17. (c),(d) We have

$$\tan\left(\frac{x}{2}\right)(1+\sec x)=\frac{\sin x}{1+\cos x}\cdot\frac{1+\cos x}{\cos x}=\tan x$$

Similarly, we have

$$\tan x(1+\sec 2x)=\tan(2x),$$
$$\tan 2x\left(1+\sec 2^2 x\right)=\tan\left(2^2 x\right),$$
$$\ldots$$

Eventually, the function reduces to

$f_n(x)=\tan\left(2^n x\right)$. Only (c), (d) are correct.

18. (d) Squaring and adding the given equations, we get

$$(\cos A+\cos B)^2+(\sin A+\sin B)^2=x^2+y^2$$
$$\Rightarrow \quad 2+2\{\cos A\cos B+\sin A\sin B\}=x^2+y^2$$
$$\Rightarrow \quad 1+\cos(A-B)=\frac{x^2+y^2}{2}$$

Dividing the given equations, we get

$$\tan\left(\frac{A+B}{2}\right)=\frac{\sin A+\sin B}{\cos A+\cos B}=\frac{y}{x}$$
$$\Rightarrow \quad \sin(A+B)=\frac{2\left(\frac{y}{x}\right)}{1+\frac{y^2}{x^2}}=\frac{2xy}{x^2+y^2}$$

Hence, we have

$$\sin(A+B)\{1+\cos(A-B)\}=xy$$

19. (a) $S=\sum_{1}^{13}\frac{2}{\cos\left(\frac{\pi}{6}\right)-\cos\left(\frac{\pi}{2}+\frac{(2k-1)\pi}{6}\right)}$

$\left[\text{Using } 2\sin A\sin B=\cos(A-B)-\cos(A+B)\right]$

$$=\sum_{1}^{13}\frac{4}{\sqrt{3}+2\sin\left(\frac{(2k-1)\pi}{6}\right)}$$

For $k=1,2,\ldots,13$, the values of

$2\sin\left(\frac{(2k-1)\pi}{6}\right)=1,2,1,-1,-2,-1,\ldots$ (repeat).

Hence

$$S=5\left(\frac{4}{\sqrt{3}+1}\right)+2\left(\frac{4}{\sqrt{3}+2}\right)+4\left(\frac{4}{\sqrt{3}-1}\right)+2\left(\frac{4}{\sqrt{3}-2}\right)$$

$$=10\left(\sqrt{3}-1\right)+8\left(2-\sqrt{3}\right)+8\left(\sqrt{3}+1\right)-8\left(2+\sqrt{3}\right)$$

$$=2\sqrt{3}-2=2\left(\sqrt{3}-1\right).$$

20. (a),(c) We have

$$2(\cos B-\cos A)+\cos A\cos B=1$$

$\Rightarrow\quad \cos A=\frac{1-2\cos B}{\cos B-2}$

Now $\frac{1-\cos A}{1+\cos A}=\frac{(\cos B-2)-(1-2\cos B)}{(\cos B-2)+(1-2\cos B)}$

$$=\frac{3(1-\cos B)}{(1+\cos B)}$$

$\Rightarrow\quad \tan^2\left(\frac{A}{2}\right)=3\tan^2\left(\frac{B}{2}\right)$

$\Rightarrow\quad \tan\left(\frac{A}{2}\right)=\pm\sqrt{3}\tan\left(\frac{B}{2}\right).$

21. (a) We have

$$S=2^n\cos\theta\cos2\theta\cos2^2\theta\ldots\cos2^{n-1}\theta=\frac{\sin\left(2^n\theta\right)}{\sin\theta}$$

It is given that $\theta=\frac{\pi}{2^n+1}$

$\Rightarrow\quad 2^n\theta+\theta=\pi$

$\Rightarrow\quad 2^n\theta=\pi-\theta$

Hence, we have

$$S=\frac{\sin(\pi-\theta)}{\sin\theta}=1$$

22. (a)-(q),(b)-(r),(c)-(s),(d)-(p),(e)-(r)

(a)

$$\left(1+\cos\frac{\pi}{8}\right)\left(1+\cos\frac{3\pi}{8}\right)\left(1+\cos\frac{5\pi}{8}\right)\left(1+\cos\frac{7\pi}{8}\right)$$

$$=\left(1+\cos\frac{\pi}{8}\right)\left(1+\cos\frac{3\pi}{8}\right)\left(1-\cos\frac{3\pi}{8}\right)\left(1-\cos\frac{\pi}{8}\right)$$

$$=\left(1-\cos^2\frac{\pi}{8}\right)\left(1-\cos^2\frac{3\pi}{8}\right)=\sin^2\frac{\pi}{8}\sin^2\frac{3\pi}{8}$$

$$=\frac{1}{4}\left(1-\cos\frac{\pi}{4}\right)\left(1-\cos\frac{3\pi}{4}\right)$$

$$=\frac{1}{4}\left(1-\frac{1}{\sqrt{2}}\right)\left(1+\frac{1}{\sqrt{2}}\right)=\frac{1}{8}$$

(b) $\tan9^\circ+\cot9^\circ+\tan117^\circ+\cot117^\circ$

$$=(\tan9^\circ+\cot9^\circ)-(\cot27^\circ+\tan27^\circ)$$

$$=\frac{1}{\sin9^\circ\cos9^\circ}-\frac{1}{\sin27^\circ\cos27^\circ}$$

$$=2\left(\frac{1}{\sin18^\circ}-\frac{1}{\sin54^\circ}\right)$$

$$=2\left(\frac{\sin54^\circ-\sin18^\circ}{\sin18^\circ\sin54^\circ}\right)=\frac{4\cos36^\circ\sin18^\circ}{\sin18^\circ\sin54^\circ}=4$$

(c) $\tan20^\circ\tan40^\circ\tan80^\circ$

$$=\tan20^\circ\tan(60^\circ-20^\circ)\tan(60^\circ+20^\circ)$$

$$=\tan20^\circ\times\frac{\sqrt{3}-\tan20^\circ}{1+\sqrt{3}\tan20^\circ}\times\frac{\sqrt{3}+\tan20^\circ}{1-\sqrt{3}\tan20^\circ}$$

$$=\tan20^\circ\times\frac{3-\tan^2 20^\circ}{1-3\tan^2 20^\circ}$$

$$=\frac{3\tan20^\circ-\tan^3 20^\circ}{1-3\tan^2 20^\circ}=\tan60^\circ=\sqrt{3}$$

(d) $(1+\tan1^\circ)(1+\tan44^\circ)=(1+\tan1^\circ)\left(1+\frac{1-\tan1^\circ}{1+\tan1^\circ}\right)=2$

$(1+\tan2^\circ)(1+\tan43^\circ)=(1+\tan2^\circ)\left(1+\frac{1-\tan2^\circ}{1+\tan2^\circ}\right)=2$

…

$$(1+\tan 22^\circ)(1+\tan 23^\circ)=(1+\tan 22^\circ)\left(1+\frac{1-\tan 22^\circ}{1+\tan 22^\circ}\right)=2$$

There are 22 such pairs, and in the end, there is one unpaired term $1+\tan 45^\circ = 2$. Hence, the value of the expression is 2^{23}.

(e) $$\sqrt{3}\ \text{cosec}20^\circ - \sec 20^\circ = \frac{\sqrt{3}\cos 20^\circ - \sin 20^\circ}{\sin 20^\circ \cos 20^\circ}$$

$$= \frac{2\sin(60^\circ - 20^\circ)}{\frac{1}{2}\sin 40^\circ} = 4$$

23. (a)-(q),(b)-(s),(c)-(r),(d)-(p)

(a) $$\cos\frac{\pi}{7}\cos\frac{2\pi}{7}\cos\frac{4\pi}{7} = \frac{\sin\frac{8\pi}{7}}{2^3\sin\frac{\pi}{7}}$$

$$= \frac{-\sin\frac{\pi}{7}}{2^3\sin\frac{\pi}{7}} = \frac{-1}{8}$$

(b) $$\cos\frac{2\pi}{15}\cos\frac{4\pi}{15}\cos\frac{8\pi}{15}\cos\frac{14\pi}{15}$$

$$= -\cos\frac{\pi}{15}\cos\frac{2\pi}{15}\cos\frac{4\pi}{15}\cos\frac{8\pi}{15}$$

$$= -\frac{\sin\frac{16\pi}{15}}{2^4\sin\frac{\pi}{15}} = -\frac{-\sin\frac{\pi}{15}}{2^4\sin\frac{\pi}{15}} = \frac{1}{16}$$

(c) $$\sin\frac{\pi}{14}\sin\frac{3\pi}{14}\sin\frac{5\pi}{14}\sin\frac{7\pi}{14}$$

$$= \cos\frac{3\pi}{7}\cos\frac{2\pi}{7}\cos\frac{\pi}{7}\left[\text{Using } \sin x - \cos\left(\frac{\pi}{2}-x\right)\right]$$

$$= -\cos\frac{4\pi}{7}\cos\frac{2\pi}{7}\cos\frac{\pi}{7}$$

$$= -\frac{\sin\frac{8\pi}{7}}{2^3\sin\frac{\pi}{7}} = -\frac{-\sin\frac{\pi}{7}}{2^3\sin\frac{\pi}{7}} = \frac{1}{8}$$

(d) $$\cos\frac{2\pi}{7}+\cos\frac{4\pi}{7}+\cos\frac{6\pi}{7}$$

$$= 2\cos\frac{3\pi}{7}\cos\frac{\pi}{7} + 2\cos^2\frac{3\pi}{7} - 1$$

$$= 2\cos\frac{3\pi}{7}\left(\cos\frac{\pi}{7}+\cos\frac{3\pi}{7}\right) - 1$$

$$= 4\cos\frac{3\pi}{7}\cos\frac{2\pi}{7}\cos\frac{\pi}{7} - 1$$

$$= -4\cos\frac{4\pi}{7}\cos\frac{2\pi}{7}\cos\frac{\pi}{7} - 1$$

$$= -4\left(\frac{\sin\frac{8\pi}{7}}{2^3\sin\frac{\pi}{7}}\right) - 1$$

$$= -4\left(\frac{-\sin\frac{\pi}{7}}{2^3\sin\frac{\pi}{7}}\right) - 1 = \frac{1}{2} - 1 = \frac{-1}{2}$$

24. (a)-(s),(b)-(s),(c)-(s),(d)-(s)

(a) $$2-\sqrt{3\cos x - 4\sin x - 1}$$

$$= 2 - \sqrt{5\cos(x+\alpha) - 1}, \text{ where}$$

$$\alpha = \tan^{-1}\left(\frac{4}{3}\right)$$

The function will have its greatest value when $\sqrt{5\cos(x+\alpha)-1}$ has the least value, which is 0. Hence, the greatest value of the function is $2-0=2$.

(b) Let $g(x) = \sin^2 x + 3\sin x\cos x + 5\cos^2 x$

$$= \frac{1}{2}(1-\cos 2x) + \frac{3}{2}\sin 2x + \frac{5}{2}(1+\cos 2x)$$

$$= 3 + \frac{1}{2}(4\cos 2x + 3\sin 2x)$$

$$= 3 + \frac{5}{2}\sin(2x+\alpha), \text{ where } \alpha = \tan^{-1}\left(\frac{4}{3}\right)$$

The given function is $\frac{1}{g(x)}$ which will have its greatest value when $g(x)$ has the least value, which is $3-\frac{5}{2}=\frac{1}{2}$. Hence, the greatest value of the function is 2.

(c) When $\frac{-\pi}{4} \le x \le 0$, then $\frac{-3\pi}{2} \le 3x - \frac{3\pi}{4} \le -\frac{3\pi}{4}$.

In this interval

$$\frac{-1}{\sqrt{2}} \le \sin\left(3x - \frac{3\pi}{4}\right) \le 1$$

Hence, the greatest value of the function is $1+1=2$.

(d) The given function can be written as

$$f(x) = -2\left(\cos x - \frac{1}{2}\right)^2 + 2$$

Now, we have

$$-1 \le \cos x \le 1$$

$$\Rightarrow \frac{-3}{2} \le \cos x - \frac{1}{2} \le \frac{1}{2}$$

$$\Rightarrow 0 \le \left(\cos x - \frac{1}{2}\right)^2 \le \frac{9}{4}$$

$$\Rightarrow \frac{-9}{2} \le -2\left(\cos x - \frac{1}{2}\right)^2 \le 0$$

$$\Rightarrow \frac{-5}{2} \le -2\left(\cos x - \frac{1}{2}\right)^2 + 2 \le 2$$

25. (a)-(r),(b)-(p),(c)-(s),(d)-(t),(e)-(q)

(a) $\sin^2 x + \cos^4 x = \frac{1}{2}(1-\cos 2x) + \frac{1}{4}(1+\cos 2x)^2$

$$= \frac{7}{8} + \frac{1}{8}\cos 4x$$

Now, we have

$$-1 \le \cos 4x \le 1$$

$$\Rightarrow \frac{-1}{8} \le \frac{1}{8}\cos 4x \le \frac{1}{8}$$

$$\Rightarrow \frac{3}{4} \le \frac{7}{8} + \frac{1}{8}\cos 4x \le 1$$

Hence, the values of the function lie in

$$\left[\frac{7}{8} - \frac{1}{8}, \frac{7}{8} + \frac{1}{8}\right] = \left[\frac{3}{4}, 1\right].$$

(b) $1 + \sin\left(\frac{\pi}{4} + x\right) + 2\cos\left(\frac{\pi}{4} - x\right)$

$$= 1 + \frac{3}{\sqrt{2}}(\sin x + \cos x) = 1 + 3\sin\left(x + \frac{\pi}{4}\right).$$

Now, we have

$$-1 \le \sin\left(x + \frac{\pi}{4}\right) \le 1$$

$$\Rightarrow -3 \le 3\sin\left(x + \frac{\pi}{4}\right) \le 3$$

$$\Rightarrow -2 \le 1 + 3\sin\left(x + \frac{\pi}{4}\right) \le 4$$

Hence, the values of the function lie in $[-2, 4]$.

(c) $\frac{\sin(3x)}{\sin x} = 3 - 4\sin^2 x$.

Now, we have

$$0 < \sin^2 x \le 1 \ [\sin x = 0 \text{ is not acceptable}]$$

$$\Rightarrow -4 \le -4\sin^2 x \le 0$$

$$\Rightarrow -1 \le 3 - 4\sin^2 x \le 3$$

Hence, the values of the function lie in $[-1, 3]$.

(d) $\frac{\tan(3x)}{\tan x} = \frac{3 - \tan^2 x}{1 - 3\tan^2 x} = y(\text{say})$.

Then $\tan^2 x = \frac{y-3}{3y-1}$. Now

$\tan^2 x > 0$ [$\tan x = 0$ is not acceptable]. Thus, we have

$$\frac{y-3}{3y-1} > 0 \Rightarrow y < \frac{1}{3} \text{ or } y > 3$$

Hence, the values of the function lie in $\mathbf{R} - \left[\frac{1}{3}, 3\right]$.

(e) The function $|\sin x| + |\cos x|$ has period $\frac{\pi}{2}$. In the interval $\left[0, \frac{\pi}{2}\right]$, the function reduces to

$$\sin x + \cos x = \sqrt{2}\sin\left(x + \frac{\pi}{4}\right).$$

When $0 \le x \le \frac{\pi}{2}$, then $\frac{\pi}{4} \le x + \frac{\pi}{4} \le \frac{3\pi}{4}$. In this interval

$$1 \le \sqrt{2}\sin\left(x + \frac{\pi}{4}\right) \le \sqrt{2}$$

Hence, the values of the function lie in $\left[1, \sqrt{2}\right]$.

26. (b) If $\sin\theta$, $\tan\theta$, $\cos\theta$ are in GP, then

$$\tan^2\theta = \sin\theta\cos\theta$$

$$\Rightarrow \quad \tan\theta = \cos^2\theta$$

Hence, we have

$$S = 4\sin^2\theta - 3\sin^4\theta + \sin^6\theta$$

$$= \sin^2\theta(4 - 3\sin^2\theta + \sin^4\theta)$$

$$= \sin^2\theta\{4 - 3(1 - \cos^2\theta) + (1 - \cos^2\theta)^2\}$$

$$= (1 - \cos^2\theta)(2 + \cos^2\theta + \cos^4\theta)$$

$$= (1 - \tan\theta)(2 + \tan\theta + \tan^2\theta)$$

$$= 2 + \tan\theta + \tan^2\theta - 2\tan\theta - \tan^2 2\theta - \tan^3\theta$$

$$= 2 - \tan\theta - \tan^3\theta$$

$$= 2 - \tan\theta(1 + \tan^2\theta)$$

$$= 2 - \tan\theta\sec^2\theta = 2 - 1 = 1$$

CHAPTER

12 Trigonometric Equations

- $\sin x = \sin y$

  $\Rightarrow 2\cos\left(\frac{x+y}{2}\right)\sin\left(\frac{x-y}{2}\right) = 0$

  $\Rightarrow \frac{x+y}{2} = (2m+1)\frac{\pi}{2}$ or $\frac{x-y}{2} = k\pi$, where $m,k \in \mathbf{Z}$

  $\Rightarrow x = (2m+1)\pi + (-1)^{2m+1} y$ or $x = 2k\pi + (-1)^{2k} y$, where $m,k \in \mathbf{Z}$

  $\Rightarrow x = n\pi + (-1)^n y$ where $n \in \mathbf{Z}$

- $\cos x = \cos y$

  $\Rightarrow 2\sin\left(\frac{x+y}{2}\right)\sin\left(\frac{x-y}{2}\right) = 0$

  $\Rightarrow \frac{x+y}{2} = m\pi$ or $\frac{x-y}{2} = k\pi$, where $m,k \in \mathbf{Z}$

  $\Rightarrow x = 2m\pi - y$ or $x = 2k\pi + y$, where $m,k \in \mathbf{Z}$

  $\Rightarrow x = 2n\pi \pm y$, where $n \in \mathbf{Z}$

- $\tan x = \tan y$

  $\Rightarrow \sin x \cos y - \cos x \sin y = 0$

  $\Rightarrow \sin(x-y) = 0$

  $\Rightarrow x = n\pi + y$, where $n \in \mathbf{Z}$

- $\sin x = \cos y$

  $\Rightarrow \cos\left(\frac{\pi}{2} - x\right) = \cos y$

  $\Rightarrow x \pm y = \frac{\pi}{2} + 2n\pi$, where $n \in \mathbf{Z}$

- $\tan x = \cot y$

  $\Rightarrow \tan x = \tan\left(\frac{\pi}{2} - y\right)$

  $\Rightarrow x + y = \frac{\pi}{2} + n\pi$, where $n \in \mathbf{Z}$

- $\sin x = \cos y$ and $\cos x = \cos y$

  $\Rightarrow x = 2n\pi + y$ where, $n \in \mathbf{Z}$

EXERCISES

1. The number of ordered pairs (α,β) satisfying the equations:

$$\cos(\alpha-\beta) = 1 \quad \ldots(1)$$

and $$\cos(\alpha+\beta) = \frac{1}{e} \quad \ldots(2)$$

where $\alpha,\beta \in [-\pi,\pi]$ is:

(a) 4 (b) 2
(c) 1 (d) 0

2. The number of solutions of the pair of equations:

$$2\sin^2 x - \cos(2x) = 0 \quad \ldots(1)$$

and $$2\cos^2 x - 3\sin x = 0 \quad \ldots(2)$$

where $x \in [0,2\pi]$ is:

(a) 4 (b) 2
(c) 1 (d) 0

3. If $4\sin^2 x + 5\cos x + 2 = 0, x \in \left[-\pi, \frac{-\pi}{2}\right]$, then the value of $\tan\left(\frac{x}{2}\right)$ is:

(a) -2 (b) $-\sqrt{3}$
(c) $-\sqrt{5}$ (d) $-\sqrt{7}$

4. If $\sin^4 x + \sin^2 x = 1$, then the value of $\cot^4 x + \cot^2 x$ is:

(a) 1 (b) 2
(c) 4 (d) 8

5. If $\frac{\sin^4 x}{2}+\frac{\cos^4 x}{3}=\frac{1}{5}$, then the value of $500\left(\frac{\sin^8 x}{8}+\frac{\cos^8 x}{27}\right)$ is:
(a) 1 (b) 2
(c) 4 (d) 8

6. Suppose $\alpha_1, \beta_1 (\alpha_1 > \beta_1)$ are the roots of the equation $x^2-(2\sec\theta)x+1=0$ and $\alpha_2, \beta_2 (\alpha_2 > \beta_2)$ are the roots of the equation $x^2+*2\tan\theta)x-1=0$. If θ lies in the fourth quadrant, then $\alpha_1+\beta_2$ equals:
(a) $2(\sec\theta-\tan\theta)$ (b) $2\sec\theta$
(c) $-2\tan\theta$ (d) 0

7. If $a\sin\theta+b\cos\theta=c$, then the value of $b\sin\theta-a\cos\theta$ is:
(a) 0
(b) $\pm\sqrt{(a+b)^2-c^2}$
(c) $\pm\left(\sqrt{a^2+b^2}-c\right)$
(d) $\pm\sqrt{a^2+b^2-c^2}$

8. If $a\sec\theta-c\tan\theta=d$ and $b\sec\theta+d\tan\theta=c$, then:
(a) $a^2+c^2=b^2+d^2$
(b) $a^2+d^2=b^2+c^2$
(c) $a^2+b^2=c^2+d^2$
(d) None of these

9. If $\operatorname{cosec}\theta-\sin\theta=a$ and $\sec\theta-\cos\theta=b$, then:
(a) $a^{2/3}+b^{2/3}=a^{-2/3}b^{-2/3}$
(b) $a^{2/3}+b^{2/3}=a^{1/3}b^{1/3}$
(c) $a^{2/3}+b^{2/3}=a^{-1/3}b^{-1/3}$
(d) None of these

10. Let $S=\left\{x; -\pi<x<\pi, x\neq 0, \frac{\pi}{2}\right\}$. The sum of all distinct solutions of the equation $\sqrt{3}\sec x+\operatorname{cosec}x+2(\tan x-\cot x)=0$ in the set S equals:
(a) $\frac{-7\pi}{8}$ (b) $\frac{-2\pi}{9}$
(c) $\frac{5\pi}{9}$ (d) 0

11. The number of real roots of $\cos^7 x+\sin^4 x=1$ in $[-\pi,\pi]$ is:
(a) 1 (b) 2
(c) 3 (d) 4

12. The number of real roots of $2\sin^2 x+\sin^2(2x)=2$ in $[-\pi,\pi]$ is:
(a) 2 (b) 3
(c) 5 (d) 6

13. The number of real roots of $\sin x+\cos x=1-\sin(2x)$ in $[-2\pi,3\pi]$ is:
(a) 6 (b) 7
(c) 8 (d) 9

14. Let $S=\left\{x; \frac{-\pi}{2}<x<\frac{\pi}{2}, x\neq\frac{n\pi}{5}, n=0,\pm1,\pm2,\ldots\right\}$. The number of values of x satisfying the equations $\tan x=\cot(5x)$ and $\sin(2x)=\cos(4x)$ in the set S is:
(a) 6 (b) 5
(c) 4 (d) 3

15. The inequality $\tan x<\cot x$, is satisfied by:
(a) $x\in\left(\frac{-\pi}{2},\frac{-\pi}{4}\right)\cup\left(0,\frac{\pi}{4}\right)$
(b) $x\in\left(-\pi,\frac{-3\pi}{4}\right)\cup\left(\frac{\pi}{2},\frac{3\pi}{4}\right)$
(c) $x\in\left(\frac{-\pi}{4},\frac{\pi}{4}\right)\cup\left(\frac{\pi}{2},\frac{3\pi}{4}\right)$
(d) $x\in\left(\frac{-\pi}{4},\frac{\pi}{4}\right)$

16. Let $P=\{x:\sin x-\cos x=\sqrt{2}\cos x\}$ and $Q=\{x:\sin x+\cos x=\sqrt{2}\sin x\}$ be two sets. Then:
(a) $P\subset Q$ and $Q-P\neq Q$
(b) $Q\not\subset P$
(c) $P\subset Q$
(d) $P=Q$

17. The number of values of x in $\left[\frac{-\pi}{2},\frac{3\pi}{4}\right]$ satisfying the equation $\sin(2x)-\sin(4x)-\sin(6x)=0$ is:
(a) 3 (b) 4
(c) 5 (d) 6

18. The positive integer value of $n\,(n>3)$ satisfying the equation

$$\frac{1}{\sin\left(\frac{\pi}{n}\right)}=\frac{1}{\sin\left(\frac{2\pi}{n}\right)}+\frac{1}{\sin\left(\frac{3\pi}{n}\right)}$$ is:

(a) 5 (b) 6
(c) 7 (d) 8

19. The number of distinct solutions of the equation $\frac{5}{4}\cos^2 2x+\sin^4 x+\cos^4 x+\sin^6 x+\cos^6 x=2$ in $(0,2\pi)$ is:

(a) 12 (b) 8
(c) 9 (d) 5

20. If $(m+2)\sin\theta+(2m-1)\cos\theta=2m+1$ is identically true for all real m, then $\tan\theta$ equals:

(a) $\frac{3}{4}$ (b) $\frac{2m}{m^2+1}$
(c) $\frac{2m}{m^2-1}$ (d) $\frac{4}{3}$

21. If α,β are the roots of the equation $a\cos\theta+b\sin\theta=c$, then $\sin(\alpha+\beta)$ equals:

(a) $\frac{2c^2}{a^2+b^2}$ (b) $\frac{2c}{(a+b)^2}$
(c) $\frac{2ab}{(a+b)^2-c^2}$ (d) $\frac{2ab}{a^2+b^2}$

22. If $\sin(\pi\cos\theta)=\cos(\pi\sin\theta)$, then $\sin(2\theta)$ equals:

(a) $\frac{1}{4}$ (b) $\frac{-3}{4}$
(c) $\frac{-3}{2}$ (d) $\frac{3}{4}$

23. If $\cos(2x)+2\cos x=1$, then $(2-\cos^2 x)\sin^2 x$ equals:

(a) 0 (b) −1/4
(c) 1 (d) −1

24. The relation $\sec^2\theta=\frac{4xy}{(x+y)^2}$, where $x\in\mathbf{R}, y\in\mathbf{R}$ is true if and only if:

(a) $x+y\neq 0$ (b) $x=y, x\neq 0$
(c) $x=y$ (d) $x\neq 0, y\neq 0$

25. The relation $\operatorname{cosec}\theta=\frac{x^2-y^2}{x^2+y^2}$, where $x\in\mathbf{R}, y\in\mathbf{R}$ is true if and only if:

(a) $x=y\neq 0$ (b) $|x|=|y|\neq 0$
(c) $x+y=0$ (d) None of these

26. If $\tan\left(\frac{\pi}{9}\right), x, \tan\left(\frac{5\pi}{18}\right)$ are in AP and $\tan\left(\frac{\pi}{9}\right), y, \tan\left(\frac{7\pi}{18}\right)$ are also in AP, then:

(a) $2x=y$ (b) $x>y$
(c) $x=y$ (d) None of these

27. If $\tan\left(\frac{\alpha}{2}\right), \tan\left(\frac{\beta}{2}\right)$ are the roots of the equation $8x^2-26x+15=0$, then $\cos(\alpha+\beta)$ equals:

(a) $\frac{-627}{725}$ (b) $\frac{29}{125}$
(c) −1 (d) $\frac{357}{500}$

28. If $\alpha,-\beta$ are the roots of the equation $a\cos\theta-b\sin\theta=c$, then $\cos(\alpha-\beta)$ equals:

(a) $\frac{-a}{b}$ (b) $\frac{a^2-b^2}{a^2+b^2}$
(c) $\sqrt{a^2+b^2}$ (d) $\frac{-2ab}{a^2+b^2}$

29. If $0\le\beta<\alpha\le\frac{\pi}{4}$, $\cos(a+\beta)=\frac{3}{5}$ and $\cos(\alpha-\beta)=\frac{4}{5}$, then $\sin(2\alpha)$ equals:

(a) −1 (b) $\frac{-1}{2}$
(c) 1 (d) 1

30. If $\sin(20°)-\cos(20°)=p$, then $\cos(40°)$ equals:

(a) $-p\sqrt{1+p^2}$ (b) $-p\sqrt{2-p^2}$
(c) $p-\sqrt{1+p^2}$ (d) $-p+\sqrt{2-p^2}$

31. If a, b, c satisfies the system of equations $2a+b=2c, 9c-7a=6b$ and $a^3+b^3+c^3=216$, the number of values of θ in $[0,3\pi]$ satisfying the equation $a\cos\theta+b\sin\theta=c$ is:

(a) 0 (b) 1
(c) 2 (d) 3

32. The number of solutions of $\begin{vmatrix} \sin x & \cos x & 1 \\ \cos x & \sin x & 1 \\ 1 & \sin x & \cos x \end{vmatrix} = 0$ in $[0, 2\pi]$ is:

(a) 4 (b) 5
(c) 6 (d) 7

33. The number of solutions of $\sin(2x) = \cos(3x)$ in $[0, 2\pi]$ is:

(a) 4 (b) 5
(c) 6 (d) 7

34. If $x \in \left(0, \frac{\pi}{2}\right)$, then the function

$f(x) = \cos x\left(\tan^2 x + \operatorname{cosec}^2 x\right) + \tan x\left(\cos^2 x + \operatorname{cosec}^2 x\right) + \operatorname{cosec} x\left(\tan^2 x + \cos^2 x\right)$ cannot take the value:

(a) π (b) e
(c) 6 (d) π^2

35. If $2\cos x(1 - \sin y) + 1 = \left(\tan\frac{x}{2} + \cot\frac{x}{2}\right)\sin^2 x \cos y$, where $-1 < \sin x < -\sqrt{3}/2$ and $\tan x < 0$, then the values of y belong to the set:

(a) $0 < y < \pi/2$

(b) $\pi/2 < y < 4\pi/3$

(c) $4\pi/3 < y < 3\pi/2$

(d) $3\pi/2 < y < 2\pi$

36. If $\frac{\sin\alpha}{\sin\beta} = \frac{\sqrt{3}}{2}$ and $\frac{\cos\alpha}{\cos\beta} = \frac{\sqrt{5}}{2}$, where $0 < \alpha, \beta < \pi/2$, then $\tan(\alpha + \beta)$ equals:

(a) $2 + 3\sqrt{5}$ (b) $3 + 2\sqrt{5}$
(c) $4 + \sqrt{15}$ (d) $2 + 5\sqrt{6}$

37. Match the inequalities shown in the left column with their solutions shown in the right column:

(a) $4\cos^2 x - 1 > 0$ (p) $\frac{-\pi}{12} + n\pi < x < \frac{7\pi}{12} + n\pi$

(b) $2\sin(2x) + 1 > 0$ (q) $\frac{-5\pi}{6} + 2n\pi < x < \frac{-\pi}{6} + 2n\pi$

(c) $\left(\tan x + \sqrt{3}\right)(\tan x - 1) < 0$ (r) $\frac{-\pi}{3} + n\pi < x < \frac{\pi}{3} + n\pi$

(d) $2\sin^2 x - 3\sin x - 2 > 0$ (s) $\frac{-\pi}{3} + n\pi < x < \frac{\pi}{4} + n\pi$

38. If $x \in \left(\frac{\pi}{4}, \frac{\pi}{2}\right)$ and $\sum_{n=1}^{\infty} \cot^n x = \sin x + \cos x$, then $\tan x$ equals:

(a) $\sqrt{2} + 1$ (b) $\sqrt{2}$
(c) $\sqrt{3} + 1$ (d) $\sqrt{3}$

ANSWER KEYS

1. (a)	**2.** (b)	**3.** (d)	**4.** (a)	**5.** (c)	**6.** (c)	**7.** (d)	**8.** (c)	**9.** (a)
10. (d)	**11.** (c)	**12.** (d)	**13.** (a)	**14.** (d)	**15.** (a),(b)	**16.** (a),(c),(d)	**17.** (c)	**18.** (c)
19. (b)	**20.** (d)	**21.** (d)	**22.** (b),(d)	**23.** (c)	**24.** (b)	**25.** (d)	**26.** (a)	**27.** (a)
28. (b)	**29.** (c)	**30.** (b)	**31.** (c)	**32.** (c)	**33.** (c)	**34.** (a),(b)	**35.** (b)	**36.** (b)
37. (a)-(r), (b)-(p), (c)-(s), (d)-(q)	**38.** (d)							

SOLUTIONS

1. (a) From equation (1), we have

$$\alpha - \beta = 2k\pi, k = 0, \pm1, \pm2, \ldots.$$

From equation (2), we have

$$\alpha + \beta = 2l\pi \pm \cos^{-1}\left(\frac{1}{e}\right), l = 0, \pm1, \pm2, \ldots.$$

From the above equations, we have

$\alpha = m\pi \pm \theta, m = 0, \pm1, \pm2, \ldots,$ where $\theta = \frac{1}{2}\cos^{-1}\left(\frac{1}{e}\right)$

and $\quad \beta = \alpha - 2k\pi = \alpha, \alpha \pm 2\pi, \alpha \pm 4\pi, \ldots$

In the interval $[-\pi, \pi]$, the values for α are $\alpha = -\theta, \theta, \pi - \theta, -\pi + \theta$ and the corresponding values for β are $\beta = -\theta, \theta, \pi - \theta, -\pi + \theta$. Thus, there are four ordered pairs of (α, β), namely, $(-\theta, -\theta), (\theta, \theta)$, $(\pi - \theta, \pi - \theta), (-\pi + \theta, -\pi + \theta)$.

2. (b) From equation (1), we have

$$4\sin^2 x - 1 = 0 \Rightarrow \sin x = \pm\frac{1}{2}$$

From equation (2), we have

$$2\sin^2 x + 3\sin x - 2 = 0 \Rightarrow \sin x = -2, \frac{1}{2}$$

The common solution is $\sin x = \frac{1}{2}$, which has two solutions in $[0, 2\pi]$.

3. (d) The given equation can be written as

$$4\cos^2 x - 5\cos x - 6 = 0 \Rightarrow \cos x = -3/4$$

Hence $\quad \tan\left(\frac{x}{2}\right) = -\sqrt{\frac{1-\cos x}{1+\cos x}} = -\sqrt{7}.$

The –ve sign appears because $x \in \left[-\pi, -\frac{\pi}{2}\right]$

$$\Rightarrow \quad \frac{x}{2} \in \left[-\frac{\pi}{2}, -\frac{\pi}{4}\right] \text{(fourth quadrant)}$$

4. (a) From the given equation, we have

$$\sin^2 x = \frac{\sqrt{5}-1}{2} \Rightarrow \operatorname{cosec}^2 x = \frac{\sqrt{5}+1}{2}$$

Hence

$$\cot^4 x + \cot^2 x = \left(\operatorname{cosec}^2 x - 1\right)^2 + \operatorname{cosec}^2 x - 1 = 1.$$

5. (c) The given equation can be written as

$$15\sin^4 x + 10\left(1 - \sin^2 x\right)^2 = 6$$

$$\Rightarrow \quad 25\sin^4 x - 20\sin^2 x + 4 = 0$$

$$\Rightarrow \quad \sin^2 x = \frac{2}{5} \Rightarrow \cos^2 x = \frac{3}{5}$$

Hence $\quad 500\left(\frac{\sin^8 x}{8} + \frac{\cos^8 x}{27}\right) = 4.$

6. (c) We have

$$\alpha_1 = \frac{2\sec\theta + \sqrt{4\sec^2\theta - 4}}{2}$$

$$= \sec\theta + |\tan\theta| = \sec\theta - \tan\theta$$

[θ lies in the fourth quadrant]

and $\quad \beta_2 = \frac{-2\tan\theta - \sqrt{4\tan^2\theta + 4}}{2}$

$$= -\tan\theta - |\sec\theta| = -\tan\theta - \sec\theta$$

[θ lies in the fourth quadrant]

Hence $\quad \alpha_1 + \beta_2 = -2\tan\theta.$

7. (d) Given

$$a\sin\theta + b\cos\theta = c \qquad \ldots(1)$$

Let $\quad b\sin\theta - a\cos\theta = x \qquad \ldots(2)$

From the above equations, we have

$$\sin\theta = \frac{ac+bx}{a^2+b^2} \text{ and } \cos\theta = \frac{bc-ax}{a^2+b^2}$$

Now, using the identity $\sin^2\theta + \cos^2\theta = 1$, we have

$$\left(\frac{ac+bx}{a^2+b^2}\right)^2 + \left(\frac{bc-ax}{a^2+b^2}\right)^2 = 1$$

$$\Rightarrow \quad (ac+bx)^2 + (bc+ax)^2 = (a^2+b^2)^2$$

$$\Rightarrow \quad (a^2+b^2)(x^2+c^2) = (a^2+b^2)^2$$

$$\Rightarrow \quad x^2+c^2 = a^2+b^2$$

$$\Rightarrow \quad x = \pm\sqrt{a^2+b^2-c^2}$$

8. (c) From the given equations, we have

$$\sec\theta = \frac{c^2+d^2}{ad+bc} \text{ and } \tan\theta = \frac{ac-bd}{ad+bc}$$

Now, using the identity $1+\tan^2\theta = \sec^2\theta$, we have

$$1+\left(\frac{ac-bd}{ad+bc}\right)^2 = \left(\frac{c^2+d^2}{ad+bc}\right)^2$$

$$\Rightarrow \quad (ad+bc)^2 + (ac-bd)^2 = (c^2+d^2)^2$$

$$\Rightarrow \quad (a^2+b^2)(c^2+d^2) = (c^2+d^2)^2$$

$$\Rightarrow \quad a^2+b^2 = c^2+d^2$$

9. (a) The given equations reduce to

$$\cos^2\theta = a\sin\theta \text{ and } \sin^2\theta = b\cos\theta$$

Solving the above equations, we get

$$\sin^3\theta = b^2 a \Rightarrow \sin\theta = a^{1/3}b^{2/3}$$

and $\cos^3\theta = a^2 b \Rightarrow \cos\theta = a^{1/3}b^{2/3}$

Now squaring and adding, we get

$$a^{2/3} + b^{2/3} = a^{-2/3}b^{-2/3}$$

10. (d) The given equation reduces to

$$\frac{\sqrt{3}\,\sin x + \cos x}{\sin x \cos x} + \frac{2(\sin^2 x - \cos^2 x)}{\sin x \cos x} = 0$$

$$\Rightarrow \quad \frac{\sqrt{3}}{2}\sin x + \frac{1}{2}\cos x - \cos(2x) = 0$$

$$\Rightarrow \quad \cos\left(x - \frac{\pi}{3}\right) = \cos(2x)$$

$$\Rightarrow \quad x - \frac{\pi}{3} = 2n\pi \pm 2x$$

$$\Rightarrow \quad x = \frac{2n\pi}{3} + \frac{\pi}{9} \text{ or } 2n\pi - \frac{\pi}{3}$$

$$\Rightarrow \quad x = \frac{\pi}{9}, \frac{2\pi}{3} + \frac{\pi}{9}, \frac{-2\pi}{3} + \frac{\pi}{9} \text{ or } \frac{-\pi}{3}$$

$$[\text{In the interval } (-\pi, \pi)]$$

The sum of the above solutions equals 0.

11. (c) The given equation can be written as

$$\cos^7 x + (1-\cos^2 x)^2 = 1$$

$$\Rightarrow \quad \cos^2 x(\cos^5 x + \cos^2 x - 2) = 0$$

$$\Rightarrow \quad \cos x = 0 \text{ or } \cos^5 x + \cos^2 x = 2$$

$$\Rightarrow \quad \cos x = 0 \text{ or } 1$$

$$\Rightarrow \quad x = \pm\frac{\pi}{2} \text{ or } 0\,[\text{In the interval } [-\pi, \pi]]$$

12. (d) The given equation can be written as

$$\sin^2(2x) = 2 - 2\sin^2 x$$

$$\Rightarrow \quad 4\sin^2 x\cos^2 x = 2\cos^2 x$$

$$\Rightarrow \quad \cos x = 0 \text{ or } \sin x = \pm\frac{1}{\sqrt{2}}$$

$$\Rightarrow \quad x = \pm\frac{\pi}{2}, \pm\frac{\pi}{4}, \pm\frac{3\pi}{4}\,[\text{In the interval } [-\pi, \pi]]$$

13. (a) The given equation can be written as

$$(\sin x + \cos x)^2 = \{1 - \sin(2x)\}^2$$

$$\Rightarrow \quad 1 + \sin(2x) = 1 - 2\sin(2x) + \sin^2(2x)$$

$$\Rightarrow \quad \sin^2(2x) - 3\sin(2x) = 0$$

$$\Rightarrow \quad \sin(2x) = 0$$

$$\Rightarrow \quad x = n\frac{\pi}{2} = 0, \frac{\pi}{2}, \pi, \frac{3\pi}{2}$$

$$[\text{In the interval } [0, 2\pi)]$$

However, we can see that $x = \pi, \frac{3\pi}{2}$ does not satisfy the given equation. Hence, there are only two solutions, $x = 0, \frac{\pi}{2}$ in the interval $[0, 2\pi]$.

Now $[-2\pi,3\pi]=[-2\pi,0)\cup[0,2\pi)\cup[2\pi,3\pi]$. Hence, there will be $2+2+2=6$ solutions in the interval $[-2\pi,3\pi]$.

14. (d) From equation (1), we have

$$x+5x=\frac{\pi}{2}+n\pi$$

$$\Rightarrow \quad x=(2n+1)\frac{\pi}{12}=\pm\frac{5\pi}{12},\pm\frac{\pi}{4},\pm\frac{\pi}{12}$$

$$\left[\text{In the interval}\left(\frac{-\pi}{2},\frac{\pi}{2}\right)\right]$$

From equation (2), we have

$$2x\pm4x=\frac{\pi}{2}+2n\pi$$

$$\Rightarrow \quad x=-(4n+1)\frac{\pi}{4}\text{ or }(4n+1)\frac{\pi}{12}$$

$$=\frac{-\pi}{4},\frac{\pi}{12},\frac{5\pi}{12}\left[\text{In the interval}\left(\frac{-\pi}{2},\frac{\pi}{2}\right)\right]$$

Thus, there are three solutions, namely, $\frac{-\pi}{4},\frac{\pi}{12},\frac{5\pi}{12}$, which satisfy both equations.

15. (a),(b) Both functions $\tan x$ and $\cot x$ have the same period π. From their graphs in the interval $[0,\pi]$, we see that $\tan x<\cot x$ for all x satisfying the inequality

$$0<x<\frac{\pi}{4}\cup\frac{\pi}{2}<x<\frac{3\pi}{4}$$

The other intervals in which the inequality is true are

$$n\pi+0<x<n\pi+\frac{\pi}{4}\cup n\pi+\frac{\pi}{2}<x<n\pi+\frac{3\pi}{4}$$

16. (a),(c),(d) The equation representing set P reduces to

$$\tan x=\sqrt{2}+1$$

The equation representing set Q reduces to

$$\tan x=\frac{1}{\sqrt{2}-1}=\sqrt{2}+1$$

Hence, $P=Q$, which also means $P\subset Q$.

17. (c) The given equation reduces to

$$2\cos(3x)\sin x+2\sin(3x)\cos(3x)=0$$

$$\Rightarrow \quad \cos(3x)=0\text{ or }\sin(3x)=\sin(-x)$$

$$\Rightarrow \quad 3x=(2n+1)\frac{\pi}{2}\text{ or }3x+(-1)^n x=n\pi$$

$$\Rightarrow \quad x=(2n+1)\frac{\pi}{6}\text{ or}$$

$$x=\begin{cases}k\frac{\pi}{2}\text{ if }n=2k\\(2k+1)\frac{\pi}{2}\text{ if }n=2k+1\end{cases}=k\frac{\pi}{2}$$

$$\Rightarrow \quad x=\pm\frac{\pi}{6},\pm\frac{\pi}{2},0\left[\text{In the interval}\left[\frac{-\pi}{2},\frac{3\pi}{4}\right]\right]$$

18. (c) The given equation reduces to

$$\frac{1}{\sin\left(\frac{\pi}{n}\right)}-\frac{1}{\sin\left(\frac{3\pi}{n}\right)}=\frac{1}{\sin\left(\frac{2\pi}{n}\right)}$$

$$\Rightarrow \quad \frac{2\cos\left(\frac{2\pi}{n}\right)\sin\left(\frac{\pi}{n}\right)}{\sin\left(\frac{\pi}{n}\right)\sin\left(\frac{3\pi}{n}\right)}=\frac{1}{\sin\left(\frac{2\pi}{n}\right)}$$

$$\Rightarrow \quad 2\cos\left(\frac{2\pi}{n}\right)\sin\left(\frac{2\pi}{n}\right)=\sin\left(\frac{3\pi}{n}\right)$$

$$\Rightarrow \quad \sin\left(\frac{4\pi}{n}\right)=\sin\left(\frac{3\pi}{n}\right)$$

$$\Rightarrow \quad \frac{4\pi}{n}=\frac{3\pi}{n}+2k\pi\text{ or}$$

$$\frac{4\pi}{n}=\pi-\frac{3\pi}{n}+2k\pi,\ k=0,\pm1,\pm2,\ldots$$

$$\Rightarrow \quad n=\frac{1}{2k}\text{ or }\frac{7}{2k+1},\ k=0,\pm1,\pm2,\ldots$$

The only positive integer value for n is 7

19. (b) The given equation reduces to

$$\frac{5}{4}\cos^2 2x+1-2\sin^2 x\cos^2 x+1-3\sin^2 x\cos^2 x=2$$

$$\Rightarrow \quad \frac{5}{4}\cos^2 2x-\frac{5}{4}\sin^2 2x=0$$

$$\Rightarrow \quad \frac{5}{4}\cos 4x=0$$

The function $\cos(4x)$ has period $\frac{2\pi}{4}$. In the interval $\left(0,\frac{2\pi}{4}\right)$, it cuts the x-axis twice. Hence, in the interval $(0,2\pi)$, it will cut the x-axis $4\times2=8$ times.

20. (d) The given equation can be written as

$$(\sin\theta + 2\cos\theta)m + (2\sin\theta - \cos\theta) = 2m + 1$$

The above equation will be identically true for all real m, only if

$$\sin\theta + 2\cos\theta = 2 \text{ and } 2\sin\theta - \cos\theta = 1$$

$$\Rightarrow \frac{1-\cos\theta}{\sin\theta} = \frac{1}{2} \text{ and } \frac{1+\cos\theta}{\sin\theta} = 2$$

$$\Rightarrow \tan\left(\frac{\theta}{2}\right) = \frac{1}{2} \text{ and } \cot\left(\frac{\theta}{2}\right) = 2$$

We see that both results are true for

$$\tan\left(\frac{\theta}{2}\right) = \frac{1}{2} \Rightarrow \tan\theta = \frac{2\left(\frac{1}{2}\right)}{1-\left(\frac{1}{2}\right)^2} = \frac{4}{3}$$

21. (d) We have

$$a\cos\alpha + b\sin\alpha = c \quad \ldots(1)$$

and $$a\cos\beta + b\sin\beta = c \quad \ldots(2)$$

Subtracting the two equations, we get

$$a(\cos\alpha - \cos\beta) + b(\sin\alpha - \sin\beta) = 0$$

$$\Rightarrow \frac{\cos\alpha - \cos\beta}{\sin\alpha - \sin\beta} = \frac{-b}{a}$$

$$\Rightarrow \tan\left(\frac{\alpha+\beta}{2}\right) = \frac{b}{a}$$

$$\Rightarrow \sin(\alpha+\beta) = \frac{2\left(\frac{b}{a}\right)}{1+\left(\frac{b}{a}\right)^2} = \frac{2ab}{a^2+b^2}$$

22. (b),(d) From the given equation, we have

$$\pi(\cos\theta \pm \sin\theta) = \frac{\pi}{2} + 2n\pi$$

$$\Rightarrow \cos\theta \pm \sin\theta = \frac{4n+1}{2}$$

$$\Rightarrow \cos\theta \pm \sin\theta = \frac{1}{2}\left[|\cos\theta \pm \sin\theta| \le \sqrt{2}\right]$$

$$\Rightarrow 1 \pm \sin(2\theta) = \frac{1}{4} \text{ [Squaring both sides]}$$

$$\Rightarrow \sin(2\theta) = \pm\frac{3}{4}$$

23. (d) The given equation can be written as

$$\cos^2 x + \cos x - 1 = 0$$

$$\Rightarrow \cos x = \frac{\sqrt{5}-1}{2}$$

[The other root is less than -1]

Now $$S = (2-\cos^2 x)\sin^2 x$$

$$= \left(2 - \frac{3-\sqrt{5}}{2}\right)\left(1 - \frac{3-\sqrt{5}}{2}\right)$$

$$= \frac{\sqrt{5}+1}{2} \times \frac{\sqrt{5}-1}{2} = 1$$

24. (b) The function $\sec^2\theta$ takes values given by $\sec^2\theta \ge 1$. Hence

$$\frac{4xy}{(x+y)^2} \ge 1$$

$$\Rightarrow (x+y)^2 - 4xy \le 0$$

$$\Rightarrow (x-y)^2 \le 0$$

$$\Rightarrow (x-y)^2 = 0 \left[(x-y)^2 \text{ can never be negative}\right]$$

$$\Rightarrow x = y$$

But both should not be 0 because then the denominator of $\frac{4xy}{(x+y)^2}$ becomes 0.

25. (d) The function $\operatorname{cosec}\theta$ takes values given by $|\operatorname{cosec}\theta| \ge 1$. Hence

$$\left|\frac{x^2-y^2}{x^2+y^2}\right| \ge 1$$

$$\Rightarrow (x^2-y^2)^2 \ge (x^2+y^2)^2$$

$$\Rightarrow 4x^2y^2 \le 0$$

$$\Rightarrow xy = 0 \left[x^2y^2 \text{ can never be negative}\right]$$

$\Rightarrow$ At least one of x, y is 0.

26. (a) We have

$$2x = \tan(20°) + \tan(50°)$$

$$= \frac{\sin(70°)}{\cos(20°)\cos(50°)} = \frac{1}{\cos(50°)}$$

and $$2y = \tan(20°) + \tan(70°)$$

$$= \frac{\sin(90°)}{\cos(20°)\cos(70°)}$$

$$= \frac{2}{\cos(90°)+\cos(50°)} = \frac{2}{\cos(50°)}$$

Hence $2x = y$.

27. (a) We have

$$\tan\left(\frac{\alpha}{2}\right)+\tan\left(\frac{\beta}{2}\right)=\frac{26}{8}$$

and $$\tan\left(\frac{\alpha}{2}\right)\tan\left(\frac{\beta}{2}\right)=\frac{15}{8}$$

Then $$\tan\left(\frac{\alpha+\beta}{2}\right)=\frac{\frac{26}{8}}{1-\frac{15}{8}}=\frac{-26}{7}$$

Hence $$\cos(\alpha+\beta)=\frac{1-\left(\frac{26}{7}\right)^2}{1+\left(\frac{26}{7}\right)^2}=\frac{-627}{725}$$

28. (b) If $\alpha,-\beta$ are the roots of the equation $a\cos\theta-b\sin\theta=c$, then $\sin(\alpha-\beta)$.
We have

$$a\cos\alpha-b\sin\alpha=c \quad ...(1)$$

and $$a\cos\beta+b\sin\beta=c \quad ...(2)$$

Subtracting the two equations, we get

$$a(\cos\alpha-\cos\beta)-b(\sin\alpha+\sin\beta)=0$$

$$\Rightarrow \frac{\cos\alpha-\cos\beta}{\sin\alpha+\sin\beta}=\frac{b}{a}$$

$$\Rightarrow \tan\left(\frac{\alpha-\beta}{2}\right)=\frac{b}{a}$$

$$\Rightarrow \cos(\alpha-\beta)=\frac{1-\left(\frac{b}{a}\right)^2}{1+\left(\frac{b}{a}\right)^2}=\frac{a^2-b^2}{a^2+b^2}$$

29. (c) We have
$\sin(2\alpha)=\sin(\alpha+\beta)\cos(\alpha-\beta)+\cos(\alpha+\beta)\sin(\alpha-\beta)$

$$=\frac{4}{5}\cdot\frac{4}{5}+\frac{3}{5}\cdot\frac{3}{5}=1$$

30. (b) Squaring both sides, we get

$$1-\sin(40°)=p^2$$

$$\Rightarrow \sin(40°)=1-p^2$$

Then $$\cos(40°)=\sqrt{1-(1-p^2)^2}$$

$$=\sqrt{2p^2-p^4}=-p\sqrt{2-p^2}$$

$[p=\sin(20°)-\cos(20°)$ is a negative number$]$

31. (c) From the first two equations, we get

$$b=\frac{4a}{3} \text{ and } c=\frac{5a}{3}$$

Putting in the third equation, we get

$$a^3\left(1+\frac{4^3}{3^3}+\frac{5^3}{3^3}\right)=216\Rightarrow a=3, b=4, c=5.$$

The equation in θ now reduces to

$$3\cos\theta+4\sin\theta=5$$

$$\Rightarrow 5\sin(\theta+37°)=5$$

$$\Rightarrow \theta+37°=90°+n(360°)$$

$$\Rightarrow \theta=53°+n(360°)$$

$$\Rightarrow \theta=53°, 53°+360°$$

[In the interval $[0,3\pi]$]

32. (c) The given equation reduces to

$$\sin^2x(\cos x-1)+\cos x(1-\cos^2x)+\sin x(\cos x-1)=0$$

$$\Rightarrow (\cos x-1)[\sin^2x-\cos x(1+\cos x)+\sin x]=0$$

$$\Rightarrow (\cos x-1)[\sin^2x-\cos^2x+\sin x-\cos x]=0$$

$$\Rightarrow (\cos x-1)(\sin x-\cos x)(\sin x+\cos x+1)=0$$

Now $f(x)=0$ in the interval $[0,2\pi]$ when

$$\cos x=1\Rightarrow x=0,2\pi$$

or $$\tan x=1\Rightarrow x=\frac{\pi}{4},\frac{5\pi}{4}$$

or $$\sin x+\cos x=-1\Rightarrow \sin(2x)=0$$

[Squaring both sides]

$$\Rightarrow x=0,\frac{\pi}{2},\pi,\frac{3\pi}{2}.$$

But $x=0,\frac{\pi}{2}$ does not satisfy the equation $\sin x+\cos x=-1$. Therefore, there are only six zeros of $f(x)$ in the interval $[0,2\pi]$.

33. (c) We have

$$2x\pm 3x=\frac{\pi}{2}+2n\pi$$

$$\Rightarrow x=(4n+1)\frac{\pi}{10} \text{ or } -(4n+1)\frac{\pi}{2}$$

$$\Rightarrow x=\frac{\pi}{10},\frac{5\pi}{10},\frac{9\pi}{10},\frac{13\pi}{10},\frac{17\pi}{10} \text{ or } \frac{3\pi}{2}$$

[In the interval $[0,2\pi]$]

34. (a),(b) The given function reduces to

$$f(x)=\left(\frac{\sin^2 x}{\cos x}+\frac{\cos x}{\sin^2 x}\right)+\left(\sin x\cos x+\frac{1}{\sin x\cos x}\right)$$

$$+\left(\frac{\sin x}{\cos^2 x}+\frac{\cos^2 x}{\sin x}\right)$$

All the expressions in the brackets are of the type $t+\frac{1}{t}, t>0$. In that case, their values will be greater than or equal to 2. Thus $f(x)\ge 6$. Hence $f(x)$ cannot take the values π, e.

35. (b) We have

$$-1<\sin x<-\sqrt{3}/2 \text{ and } \tan x<0$$

$$\Rightarrow \quad -\pi/2<x<-\pi/3$$

Simplifying the given relation, we have

$$2\cos x(1-\sin y)+1=$$

$$\left(\frac{\sin(x/2)}{\cos(x/2)}+\frac{\cos(x/2)}{\sin(x/2)}\right)\sin^2 x\cos y$$

$$\Rightarrow \quad 2\cos x-2\cos x\sin y+1=\left(\frac{1}{\frac{1}{2}\sin x}\right)\sin^2 x\cos y$$

$$\Rightarrow \quad 2\cos x-2\cos x\sin y+1=2\sin x\cos y$$

$$\Rightarrow \quad \sin(x+y)=\frac{1+2\cos x}{2}$$

Since $-\pi/2<x<-\pi/3$

$$0<\cos x<1/2$$

$$\Rightarrow \quad 1/2<\frac{1+2\cos x}{2}<1$$

$$\Rightarrow \quad 1/2<\sin(x+y)<1$$

$$\Rightarrow \quad \frac{\pi}{6}<x+y<\frac{5\pi}{6}$$

$$\Rightarrow \quad \frac{\pi}{6}-x<y<\frac{5\pi}{6}-x$$

$$\Rightarrow \quad \frac{\pi}{6}-x_{\max}<y<\frac{5\pi}{6}-x_{\min}$$

$$\Rightarrow \quad \frac{\pi}{2}<y<\frac{4\pi}{3}$$

36. (c) We have $2\sin\alpha=\sqrt{3}\sin\beta$ and $2\cos\alpha=\sqrt{5}\cos\beta$. Now, squaring and adding, we get

$$3\sin^2\beta+5\cos^2\beta=4$$

$$\Rightarrow \quad 3\sin^2\beta+5-5\sin^2\beta=4$$

$$\Rightarrow \quad \sin^2\beta=1/2$$

$$\Rightarrow \quad \sin\beta=\frac{1}{\sqrt{2}} \text{ and } \sin\alpha=\frac{\sqrt{3}}{2\sqrt{2}}$$

$$\Rightarrow \quad \tan\beta=1 \text{ and } \tan\alpha=\frac{\sqrt{3}}{\sqrt{5}}$$

Hence, we have

$$\tan(\alpha+\beta)=\frac{1+\frac{\sqrt{3}}{\sqrt{5}}}{1-\frac{\sqrt{3}}{\sqrt{5}}}=\frac{\sqrt{5}+\sqrt{3}}{\sqrt{5}+\sqrt{3}}=4+\sqrt{15}$$

37. (a)-(r),(b)-(p),(c)-(s),(d)-(q)

(a) The inequality reduces to

$$\cos^2 x>\frac{1}{4}\Rightarrow|\cos x|>\frac{1}{2}$$

The function $|\cos x|$ has period π. From the graph of $|\cos x|$ in the interval $\left[\frac{-\pi}{2},\frac{\pi}{2}\right]$, we see that the above inequality is satisfied by

$$\frac{-\pi}{3}<x<\frac{\pi}{3}$$

The other intervals in which the inequality is true are

$$n\pi+\frac{-\pi}{3}<x<n\pi+\frac{\pi}{3}$$

(b) The inequality reduces to

$$\sin(2x)>\frac{-1}{2}$$

From the graph of $\sin\theta$ in the interval $\left[\frac{-\pi}{2},\frac{3\pi}{2}\right]$, we see that the above inequality is satisfied by

$$\frac{-\pi}{6}<2x<\frac{7\pi}{6}$$

The other intervals in which the inequality is true are

$$2n\pi+\frac{-\pi}{6}<2x<2n\pi+\frac{\pi}{6}$$

$$\Rightarrow \quad n\pi+\frac{-\pi}{12}<2x<n\pi+\frac{7\pi}{12}$$

(c) The inequality is true for

$$-\sqrt{3} < \tan x < 1$$

From the graph of $\tan x$ in the interval $\left[\frac{-\pi}{2}, \frac{\pi}{2}\right]$, we see that the above inequality is satisfied by

$$\frac{-\pi}{3} < x < \frac{\pi}{4}$$

The other intervals in which the inequality is true are

$$n\pi + \frac{-\pi}{3} < 2x < n\pi + \frac{\pi}{4}$$

(d) The inequality reduces to

$$\left(\sin x + \frac{1}{2}\right)(\sin x - 2) > 0$$

$$\Rightarrow \sin x < \frac{-1}{2}.[\sin x - 2 < 0]$$

From the graph of $\sin x$ in the interval $[-\pi, \pi]$, we see that the above inequality is satisfied by

$$\frac{-5\pi}{6} < x < \frac{-\pi}{6}$$

The other intervals in which the inequality is true are

$$2n\pi + \frac{-5\pi}{6} < x < 2n\pi + \frac{-\pi}{6}$$

38. (d) If $x \in \left(\frac{\pi}{4}, \frac{\pi}{2}\right)$, then $\cot x \in (0, 1)$. Thus, the given equation reduces to

$$\sum_{n=1}^{\infty} \cot^n x = \sin x + \cos x$$

$$\Rightarrow \quad \frac{\cot x}{1 - \cot x} = \sin x + \cos x.$$

$$\Rightarrow \quad \frac{\cos x}{\sin x - \cos x} = \sin x + \cos x$$

$$\Rightarrow \quad \cos x = \sin^2 x - \cos^2 x$$

$$\Rightarrow \quad \cos x = 1 - 2\cos^2 x$$

$$\Rightarrow \quad 2\cos^2 x + \cos x - 1 = 0 \text{ gives } \cos x = -1, 1/2$$

Only $\cos x = 1/2$ is the acceptable solution since $x \in \left(\frac{\pi}{4}, \frac{\pi}{2}\right)$. Hence, $\tan x = \sqrt{3}$.

CHAPTER

13 Solution of Triangles

- If a, b and c represent the lengths of the sides of a triangle and A, B and C represent the internal angles opposite the three sides, respectively, then

$$\frac{a}{\sin A} = \frac{b}{\sin B} = \frac{c}{\sin C} = 2R \text{ (Law of sines)}$$

$$\cos A = \frac{b^2 + c^2 - a^2}{2bc} \text{ (Law of cosines)}$$

Here, R is the radius of the circumcircle of the triangle.

- If $s = \frac{a+b+c}{2}$ is the semi-perimeter of the triangle, then

$$\sin\left(\frac{A}{2}\right) = \sqrt{\frac{(s-b)(s-c)}{bc}}$$

$$\cos\left(\frac{A}{2}\right) = \sqrt{\frac{s(s-a)}{bc}}$$

$$\tan\left(\frac{A}{2}\right) = \sqrt{\frac{(s-b)(s-c)}{s(s-a)}}$$

These are called the half-angle formulas.

- Area of the triangle is given by

$$\text{Area} = \frac{1}{2} bc \sin A = \frac{abc}{4R} = rs = \sqrt{s(s-a)(s-b)(s-c)}$$

Here, r is the radius of the incircle of the triangle.

- Some other useful formulae:

1. $\tan\left(\frac{A}{2}\right) = \frac{r}{s-a}$
2. $\tan\left(\frac{A-B}{2}\right) = \frac{a-b}{a+b} \tan\left(\frac{A+B}{2}\right) = \frac{a-b}{a+b} \cot\left(\frac{C}{2}\right)$
3. Length of the median through $A = \frac{1}{2}\sqrt{2b^2 + 2c^2 - a^2}$

EXERCISES

1. In ΔABC, if $\sin A:\sin B:\sin C=1:\sqrt{3}:\sqrt{2}$, then $\cos C$ equals:

(a) $\frac{1}{\sqrt{3}}$ (b) $\frac{1}{2\sqrt{3}}$

(c) $\frac{2}{\sqrt{5}}$ (d) $\frac{1}{\sqrt{2}}$

2. In ΔABC, if $(a^2+b^2)\sin(A-B)=(a^2-b^2)\sin(A+B)$, then the triangle may be:

(a) Isosceles
(b) Right-angled
(c) Isosceles right-angled
(d) None of these

3. In ΔABC, if $\frac{1}{a+c}+\frac{1}{b+c}=\frac{3}{a+b+c}$, then $\angle C$ equals:

(a) $\frac{\pi}{6}$ (b) $\frac{\pi}{3}$

(c) $\frac{\pi}{4}$ (d) $\frac{\pi}{2}$

4. In ΔABC, if angles A, B, C are in AP, then $\frac{a}{c}\sin 2C+\frac{c}{a}\sin 2A$ equals:

(a) 1 (b) $\sqrt{2}$
(c) $\sqrt{3}$ (d) 2

5. In ΔABC, if sides $a=6, b=10$, $\angle C$ is obtuse and area $=15\sqrt{3}$, then the radius of its incircle is:

(a) 1 (b) $\sqrt{2}$
(c) $\sqrt{3}$ (d) 2

6. In ΔABC, $\angle C=\frac{\pi}{2}$, if r is the inradius and R is the circumradius of the triangle, then $2(r+R)$ equals:

(a) $a+b$ (b) $b+c$
(c) $c+a$ (d) $a+b+c$

7. Consider three circles of radius 3, 4, 5 units touching each other externally. Let P, Q, R be their contact points and T be the point of concurrency of the common tangents drawn at points P, Q and R. The length TP equals:

(a) $2\sqrt{5}$ (b) $3\sqrt{2}$
(c) $2\sqrt{3}$ (d) $\sqrt{5}$

8. In ΔABC, if $\frac{b+c}{11}=\frac{c+a}{12}=\frac{a+b}{13}$, then $\cos A$ equals:

(a) $\frac{1}{\sqrt{3}}$ (b) $\frac{1}{3}$

(c) $\frac{1}{5}$ (d) $\frac{1}{\sqrt{2}}$

9. In ΔABC, if $\cos B+\cos C=4\sin^2\left(\frac{A}{2}\right)$, then $\frac{b+c}{a}$ equals:

(a) 1 (b) 2

(c) $\frac{1}{3}$ (d) $\frac{1}{\sqrt{2}}$

10. In ΔABC, if $\sin A\sin B=\sin C$ and $3b=5c$, then $\cot\left(\frac{A}{2}\right)$ equals:

(a) 5 (b) 4
(c) 3 (d) 2

11. In a triangle, the sum of two sides is x and the product of the same two sides is y. If $x^2-c^2=y$, where c is the third side of the triangle, then the ratio of the inradius to the circumradius of the triangle is:

(a) $\frac{3y}{2x(x+c)}$ (b) $\frac{3y}{2c(x+c)}$

(c) $\frac{3y}{4x(x+c)}$ (d) $\frac{3y}{4c(x+c)}$

12. In ΔABC, if $a=2, b=3$ and $\angle C=\pi/3$, then the length of the internal angle bisector through vertex C is:

(a) $\frac{6\sqrt{3}}{5}$ (b) $\frac{3\sqrt{3}}{7}$

(c) $\frac{\sqrt{19}}{2}$ (d) $\sqrt{7}$

13. In ΔABC, the sides a, b and $\angle A$ are given. If c_1, c_2 are the two possible lengths of the third side of the triangle, then the sum of the areas of the two triangles is:

(a) $ab\sin A$ (b) $\frac{1}{2}ab\sin(2A)$

(c) $\frac{1}{2}a^2\sin(2A)$ (d) $\frac{1}{2}b^2\sin(2A)$

14. In ΔABC, $AB = 20$, $AC = 12$ and $\angle C = \pi/2$. If the perpendicular bisector of AB meets BC at point E, then the area of ΔACE equals:
(a) 24 (b) 22
(c) 21 (d) 18

15. If P is a point on the altitude AD of ΔABC such that $\angle DBP = B/3$ and if $AP = \lambda c \sin\left(\frac{B}{3}\right)$, then λ equals:
(a) 1 (b) 2
(c) 3 (d) 4

16. In ΔABC, if $2(a^2 - b^2) = c^2$ and $\lambda = \frac{\sin(A-B)}{\sin C}$, then the possible values of n for which $\cos(n\pi\lambda) = 0$ is:
(a) 1 (b) 2
(c) 4 (d) 5

17. In ΔABC, if $1 + \cos(2A) - 2\cos(2B) = 2\sin A \sin B$, then the possible values of $\frac{a}{b}$ are:
(a) 1 (b) 2
(c) 4 (d) 5

18. In ΔABC, if $\frac{s-a}{4} = \frac{s-b}{3} = \frac{s-c}{2}$ and the area of its incircle is $\frac{8\pi}{3}$, then:
(a) Area of $\Delta ABC = 8\sqrt{6}$
(b) Radius of the circumcircle $= \frac{35\sqrt{6}}{24}$
(c) $\sin\frac{A}{2}\sin\frac{B}{2}\sin\frac{C}{2} = \frac{4}{35}$
(d) $\sin^2\left(\frac{A+B}{2}\right) = \frac{2}{5}$

19. In ΔABC, AD is the angular bisector of $\angle A$. If $AB = CD$ and $\angle B = 2\angle C$, then $\angle A$ equals:
(a) 36° (b) 27°
(c) 72° (d) 54°

20. The sides of a triangle ΔABC are a, b, c and its area is Δ. If a^2, b^2, c^2 are the roots of $x^3 - px^2 + qx - k = 0$, then:
(a) $\frac{\cos A}{a} + \frac{\cos B}{b} + \frac{\cos C}{c} = \frac{p}{2\sqrt{k}}$
(b) $\frac{\cos A}{a} + \frac{\cos B}{b} + \frac{\cos C}{c} = \frac{2p}{\sqrt{k}}$
(c) $a\sin A + b\sin B + c\sin C = \frac{2p\Delta}{\sqrt{k}}$
(d) $a\sin A + b\sin B + c\sin C = \frac{p\Delta}{2\sqrt{k}}$

21. In ΔABC, l, m, n are the lengths of the medians through A, B, C, respectively. If $\sin^2 A, \sin^2 B, \sin^2 C$ are in AP, then l^2, m^2, n^2 are in:
(a) AP (b) GP
(c) HP (d) None of these

22. In ΔABC, the median AD divides $\angle A$ into angles 30° and 45°. If the length of the median is $\frac{1}{\sqrt{11 - 6\sqrt{3}}}$, then the length of side BC is:
(a) 1 (b) 2
(c) 3 (d) 4

ANSWER KEYS

1. (a)	**2.** (a),(b),(c)	**3.** (b)	**4.** (c)	**5.** (c)	**6.** (a)	**7.** (d)	**8.** (c)	**9.** (b)
10. (c)	**11.** (b)	**12.** (a)	**13.** (d)	**14.** (c)	**15.** (b)	**16.** (a),(d)	**17.** (a)	**18.** (b),(c)
19. (c)	**20.** (a),(c)	**21.** (a)	**22.** (b)					

SOLUTIONS

1. (a) From the law of sines, we have $a:b:c = 1:\sqrt{3}:\sqrt{2}$. Now, we may choose $a = x, b = \sqrt{3}x$ and $c = \sqrt{2}x$.
From the law of cosines, we have

$$\cos C = \frac{a^2+b^2-c^2}{2ab} = \frac{1x^2+3x^2-2x^2}{2\sqrt{3}x^2} = \frac{1}{\sqrt{3}}$$

2. (a),(b),(c) We have

$$\frac{a^2+b^2}{a^2-b^2} = \frac{\sin(A+B)}{\sin(A-B)}$$

$$\Rightarrow \quad \frac{a^2}{b^2} = \frac{\sin(A+B)+\sin(A-B)}{\sin(A+B)-\sin(A-B)}$$

$$\Rightarrow \quad \frac{\sin^2 A}{\sin^2 B} = \frac{\sin A\cos B}{\cos A\sin B} \text{ [Using the law of sines]}$$

$$\Rightarrow \quad \sin A\cos A = \sin B\cos B$$

$$\Rightarrow \quad \sin 2A = \sin 2B$$

$$\Rightarrow \quad 2A = 2B \text{ or } 2A = \pi - 2B$$

$$\Rightarrow \quad A = B \text{ or } A+B = \frac{\pi}{2}$$

3. (b) We have

$$1+\frac{b}{a+c}+1+\frac{a}{b+c} = 3$$

[Multiplying throughout by $a+b+c$]

$$\Rightarrow \quad b(b+c)+a(a+c) = (a+c)(b+c)$$

$$\Rightarrow \quad a^2+b^2-c^2 = ab$$

$$\Rightarrow \quad \frac{a^2+b^2-c^2}{2ab} = \frac{1}{2} \Rightarrow \cos C = \frac{1}{2}$$

4. (c) Let S denote the given expression. Then

$$S = \frac{\sin A}{\sin C}\sin 2C + \frac{\sin C}{\sin A}\sin 2A \text{ [Using the law of sines]}$$

$$= 2\sin A\cos C + 2\sin C\cos A = 2\sin(A+C)$$

Since angles A, B, C are in AP, we can choose them as $60°-\theta, 60°, 60°+\theta$. Then $A+C = 120°$ and hence $S = 2\sin(120°) = \sqrt{3}$.

5. (c) Using area $= \frac{1}{2}ab\sin C$, we have

$$15\sqrt{3} = 30\sin C \Rightarrow C = 120° \text{ [}C\text{ is given to be obtuse]}$$

Now, we have

$$c = \sqrt{a^2+b^2-2ab\cos C} = \sqrt{6^2+10^2+60} = 14$$

The semi-perimeter of the triangle

$$s = \frac{a+b+c}{2} = 15$$

Now, using area $= rs$ gives the radius of the incircle $r = \sqrt{3}$.

6. (a) For a right-angled triangle, the hypotenuse is the diameter of its circumcircle. In the given triangle, $\angle C = \frac{\pi}{2}$. Hence, the hypotenuse length is c, and the circumradius is $R = \frac{c}{2}$.
The inradius

$$r = (s-c)\tan\left(\frac{C}{2}\right) = (s-c)\tan\left(\frac{\pi}{4}\right) = s-c$$

Hence $2(r+R) = 2s-c = a+b$.

7. (d) Let A, B, C be the centres of three circles. Then $AB = 8, AC = 9, BC = 7$. Then the semi-perimeter of the triangle is $s = \frac{8+9+7}{2} = 12$.

Note that TP is the inradius of triangle ΔABC. Hence

$$TP = (s-a)\tan\left(\frac{A}{2}\right) = (s-a)\sqrt{\frac{(s-b)(s-c)}{s(s-a)}}$$

$$= (12-7)\sqrt{\frac{(12-9)(12-8)}{12(12-7)}} = \sqrt{5}$$

8. (c) From the given equations, we have

$$11a-12b = c \text{ and } -a+12b = 13c$$

$$\Rightarrow \quad a = \frac{7}{5}c, b = \frac{6}{5}c$$

$$\Rightarrow \quad \frac{a}{7} = \frac{b}{6} = \frac{c}{5}$$

Now $\cos A = \frac{b^2+c^2-a^2}{2bc} = \frac{5^2+6^2-7^2}{2\cdot5\cdot6} = \frac{1}{5}$

9. (b) We have

$$2\cos\left(\frac{B+C}{2}\right)\cos\left(\frac{B-C}{2}\right) = 4\sin^2\left(\frac{A}{2}\right)$$

$$\Rightarrow \quad \cos\left(\frac{B-C}{2}\right) = 2\sin\left(\frac{A}{2}\right)$$

$$\left[\cos\left(\frac{B+C}{2}\right) = \sin\left(\frac{A}{2}\right)\right]$$

Now, we have

$$\frac{b+c}{a}=\frac{\sin B+\sin C}{\sin A} \text{ [From the law of sines]}$$

$$=\frac{2\sin\left(\frac{B+C}{2}\right)\cos\left(\frac{B-C}{2}\right)}{2\sin\left(\frac{A}{2}\right)\cos\left(\frac{A}{2}\right)}$$

$$=\frac{\cos\left(\frac{B-C}{2}\right)}{\sin\left(\frac{A}{2}\right)}\quad\left[\cos\left(\frac{B+C}{2}\right)=\sin\left(\frac{A}{2}\right)\right]$$

$= 2$ [From the given relation]

10. (c) From the law of sines, we have

$$3b=5c \Rightarrow 3\sin B=5\sin C$$

Using the relation $\sin A\sin B=\sin C$ and the above relation, we have

$$\sin A=\frac{3}{5}\Rightarrow \cos A=\frac{4}{5}$$

Hence $\cot\left(\frac{A}{2}\right)=\sqrt{\frac{1+\cos A}{1-\cos A}}=3.$

11. (b) We have

$$(a+b)^2-c^2=ab$$

$$\Rightarrow\quad a^2+b^2-c^2=-ab$$

$$\Rightarrow\quad \frac{a^2+b^2-c^2}{2ab}=\frac{-1}{2}$$

$$\Rightarrow\quad \cos C=\frac{-1}{2} \text{ gives } C=120°$$

Using relations $A=rs$ and $A=\frac{abc}{4R}$, we have

$$\frac{r}{R}=\frac{\frac{A}{s}}{\frac{abc}{4A}}=\frac{4A^2}{abcs}=\frac{a^2b^2\sin^2C}{abcs}$$

$$=\frac{ab\sin^2C}{cs}=\frac{3y}{2c(x+c)}$$

12. (a)

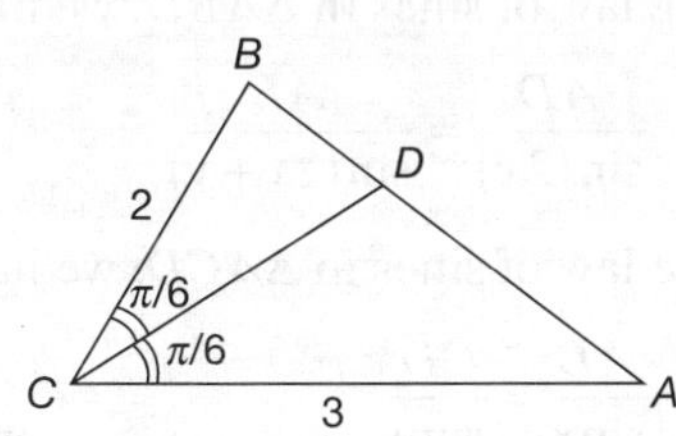

From the figure, we see that

$$AB=\sqrt{2^2+3^2-12\cos 60°}=\sqrt{7}$$

and $$\cos B=\frac{2^2+\left(\sqrt{7}\right)^2-3^2}{2\cdot 2\cdot\sqrt{7}}=\frac{1}{2\sqrt{7}}$$

Now $BD=\frac{2}{5}AB=\frac{2\sqrt{7}}{5}$, and hence

$$CD=\sqrt{BC^2+BD^2-2\cdot BC\cdot BD\cos B}$$

$$=\sqrt{4+\frac{28}{25}-\frac{8\sqrt{7}}{5}\cdot\frac{1}{2\sqrt{7}}}=\frac{6\sqrt{3}}{5}$$

13. (d) If c is the length of the third side, then

$$\cos A=\frac{b^2+c^2-a^2}{2bc}$$

$$\Rightarrow\quad c^2-(2b\cos A)c+b^2-a^2=0$$

If the roots of this equation are c_1, c_2, then the sum of the areas of the two possible triangles are

$$S=\frac{1}{2}bc_1\sin A+\frac{1}{2}bc_2\sin A$$

$$=\frac{1}{2}b(c_1+c_2)\sin A=\frac{1}{2}b(2b\cos A)\sin A$$

$$=\frac{1}{2}b^2\sin(2A)$$

14. (c)

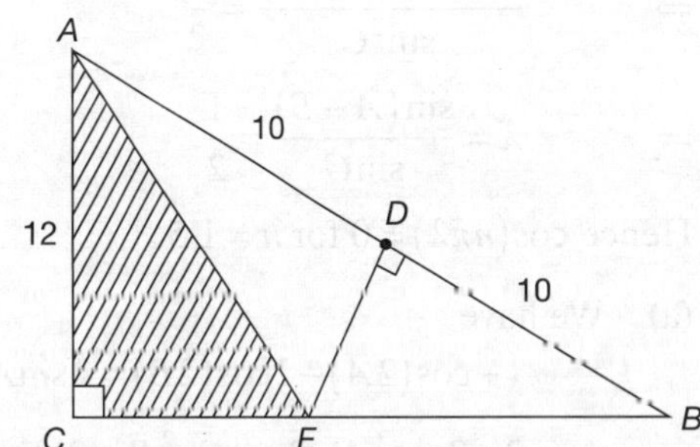

From the figure, we see that

$$BC=\sqrt{20^2-12^2}=16$$

$$BE=BD\sec B=10\times\frac{AB}{BC}=10\times\frac{20}{16}=\frac{25}{2}$$

$$CE=BC-BE=16-\frac{25}{2}=\frac{7}{2}$$

Now, area of

$$\Delta AEC=\frac{1}{2}(AC\times CE)=\frac{1}{2}\left(12\times\frac{7}{2}\right)=21$$

15. (b)

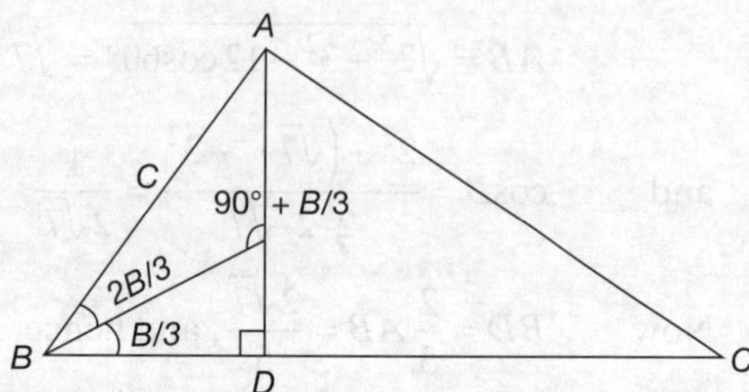

Using the law of sines in ΔABP (see figure), we have

$$\frac{AP}{\sin\left(\frac{2B}{3}\right)} = \frac{c}{\sin\left(90° + \frac{B}{3}\right)}$$

$$\Rightarrow \quad AP = 2c\sin\left(\frac{B}{3}\right)$$

Hence $\lambda = 2$.

16. (a),(d) We have

$$\frac{a^2 - b^2}{c^2} = \frac{1}{2}$$

$$\Rightarrow \quad \frac{\sin^2 A - \sin^2 B}{\sin^2 C} = \frac{1}{2}$$

$$\Rightarrow \quad \frac{\sin(A-B)\sin(A+B)}{\sin^2 C} = \frac{1}{2}$$

$$\Rightarrow \quad \frac{\sin(A-B)\sin C}{\sin^2 C} = \frac{1}{2}$$

$$\Rightarrow \quad \lambda = \frac{\sin(A-B)}{\sin C} = \frac{1}{2}.$$

Hence $\cos(n\pi\lambda) = 0$ for $n = 1, 5$.

17. (a) We have

$$1 + \cos(2A) - 2\cos(2B) = 2\sin A \sin B$$

$$\Rightarrow \quad 2 - 2\sin^2 A - 2 + 4\sin^2 B = 2\sin A \sin B$$

$$\Rightarrow \quad \sin^2 A + \sin A \sin B - 2\sin^2 B = 0$$

$$\Rightarrow \quad x^2 + x - 2 = 0 \quad \left[\text{Putting } \frac{\sin A}{\sin B} = \frac{a}{b} = x\right]$$

$$\Rightarrow \quad x = 1$$

18. (b),(c) We have

$$\frac{s-a}{4} = \frac{s-b}{3} = \frac{s-c}{2} = \frac{3s-(a+b+c)}{4+3+2} = \frac{s}{9}$$

$$\Rightarrow \quad a = \frac{5s}{9}, b = \frac{6s}{9}, c = \frac{7s}{9}$$

The radius r of the incircle is given by

$$\pi r^2 = \frac{8\pi}{3} \Rightarrow r = \frac{2\sqrt{2}}{\sqrt{3}}$$

The value of s is given by

$$rs = \sqrt{s(s-a)(s-b)(s-c)}$$

$$\Rightarrow \quad \frac{8}{3}s^2 = \frac{24}{9^3}s^4 \Rightarrow s = 9$$

Hence, area of ΔABC is $rs = 6\sqrt{6}$

$\Rightarrow$ Option (a) is incorrect.

The radius R of the circumcircle is given by

$$R = \frac{abc}{4 \times \text{area}} = \frac{5 \times 6 \times 7s^3}{9^3 \times 24\sqrt{6}} = \frac{35\sqrt{6}}{24}$$

$\Rightarrow$ Option (b) is correct.

Now $\quad \sin\frac{A}{2} = \sqrt{\frac{(s-b)(s-c)}{bc}} = \sqrt{\frac{3 \times 2}{6 \times 7}}$

$$\sin\frac{B}{2} = \sqrt{\frac{4 \times 2}{5 \times 7}}, \sin\frac{C}{2} = \sqrt{\frac{4 \times 3}{5 \times 6}}$$

Hence $\quad \sin\frac{A}{2}\sin\frac{B}{2}\sin\frac{C}{2} = \frac{4 \times 3 \times 2}{5 \times 6 \times 7} = \frac{4}{35}$

$\Rightarrow$ Option (a) is correct.

Now

$$\sin^2\left(\frac{A+B}{2}\right) = \cos^2\left(\frac{C}{2}\right) = 1 - \frac{4 \times 3}{5 \times 6} = \frac{3}{5}$$

$\Rightarrow$ Option (d) is incorrect.

19. (c) Let $\angle C = x$ and $\angle B = 2x$. Let $\angle BAD = \angle CAD = y$ (see figure).

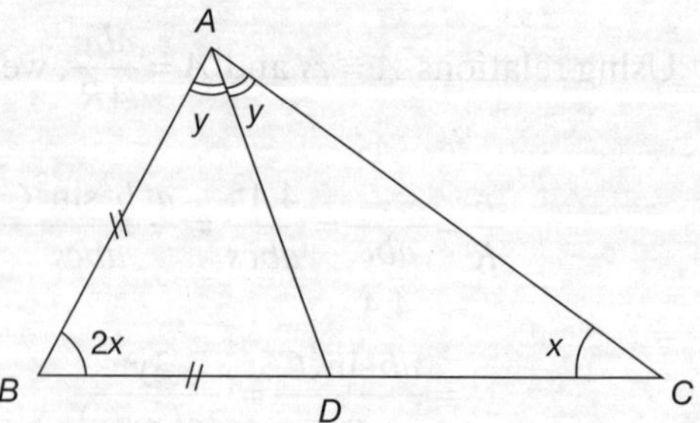

Using the law of sines in ΔABD, we have

$$\frac{AD}{\sin(2x)} = \frac{AB}{\sin(2x+y)}$$

Using the law of sines in ΔACD, we have

$$\frac{AD}{\sin x} = \frac{CD}{\sin y}$$

Dividing the two equations, we get

$$\frac{\sin(2x+y)}{\sin y}=\frac{\sin(2x)}{\sin x}\ [\text{Given } AB=CD]$$

$$\Rightarrow \quad \frac{\sin\left(90^\circ-\frac{1}{2}x\right)}{\sin\left(90^\circ-\frac{3}{2}x\right)}=\frac{\sin(2x)}{\sin x}$$

$$[3x+2y=180^\circ \Rightarrow y=90^\circ-\frac{3}{2}x]$$

$$\Rightarrow \quad \sin x\cos\left(\frac{x}{2}\right)=\sin(2x)\cos\left(\frac{3x}{2}\right)$$

$$\Rightarrow \quad \sin\left(\frac{3x}{2}\right)+\sin\left(\frac{x}{2}\right)=\sin\left(\frac{7x}{2}\right)+\sin\left(\frac{x}{2}\right)$$

$$\Rightarrow \quad \sin\left(\frac{3x}{2}\right)=\sin\left(\frac{7x}{2}\right)$$

$$\Rightarrow \quad \frac{7x}{2}=2n\pi+\frac{3x}{2},\ 2n\pi+\pi-\frac{3x}{2}$$

$$\Rightarrow \quad x=n\pi,\ (2n+1)\frac{\pi}{5}$$

$\Rightarrow \quad x=36^\circ$ (Only possible solution).

Hence $\angle A=2x=72^\circ$.

20. (a),(c) We have $a^2+b^2+c^2=p$ and $a^2b^2c^2=k$. Now, we have

$$\frac{\cos A}{a}+\frac{\cos B}{b}+\frac{\cos C}{c}=\frac{b^2+c^2-a^2}{2abc}+\frac{a^2+c^2-b^2}{2abc}+\frac{a^2+b^2-c^2}{2abc}=\frac{a^2+b^2+c^2}{2abc}=\frac{p}{2\sqrt{k}}$$

and

$$a\sin A+b\sin B+c\sin C=a\left(\frac{2\Delta}{bc}\right)+b\left(\frac{2\Delta}{ac}\right)+c\left(\frac{2\Delta}{ab}\right)=\frac{2\Delta\left(a^2+b^2+c^2\right)}{abc}=\frac{2p\Delta}{\sqrt{k}}.$$

21. (a)

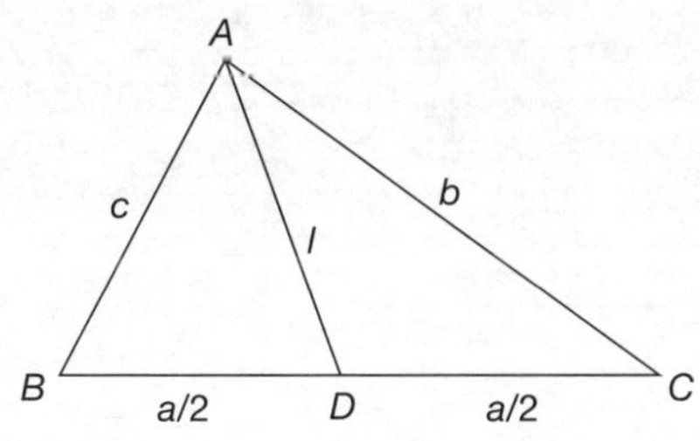

From the figure, we see that the length l of the median through A is given by

$$l^2=c^2+\frac{a^2}{4}-ac\cos B$$

$$\Rightarrow \quad l^2=c^2+\frac{a^2}{4}-\frac{a^2+c^2-b^2}{2}$$

$$\Rightarrow \quad l^2=\frac{2b^2+2c^2-a^2}{4}$$

$$\Rightarrow \quad l^2=\frac{2a^2+2b^2+2c^2-3a^2}{4}$$

$$\Rightarrow \quad l^2=\frac{1}{2}\left(a^2+b^2+c^2\right)-\frac{3}{4}a^2$$

Thus, the sequence l^2, m^2, n^2 equals

$$p-\frac{3}{4}a^2,\ p-\frac{3}{4}b^2,\ p-\frac{3}{4}c^2$$

Now $\sin^2 A, \sin^2 B, \sin^2 C$ are in AP

$\Rightarrow \quad a^2, b^2, c^2$ are in AP.

$\Rightarrow \quad p-\frac{3}{4}a^2,\ p-\frac{3}{4}b^2,\ p-\frac{3}{4}c^2$ are in AP.

22. (b) Let $BC=2x$ and angle $\angle ADC=\theta$ (see figure).

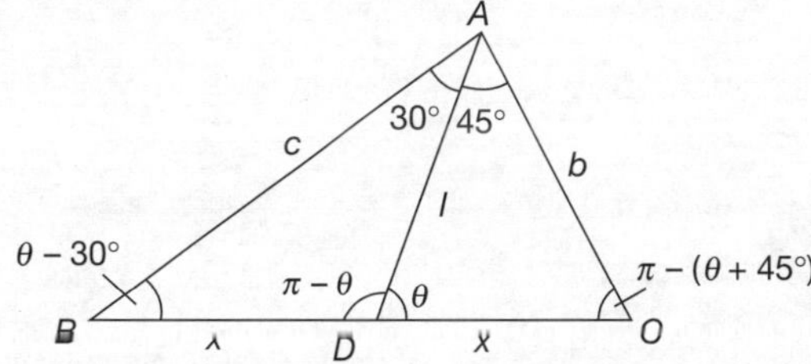

Using the law of sines in ΔABD, we have

$$\frac{l}{\sin(\theta-30^\circ)}=\frac{x}{\sin(30^\circ)}$$

Using the law of sines in ΔACD, we have

$$\frac{l}{\sin(\theta+45^\circ)}=\frac{x}{\sin(45^\circ)}$$

Dividing the two equations, we get

$$\frac{\sin(\theta+45^\circ)}{\sin(\theta-30^\circ)}=\frac{\sin(45^\circ)}{\sin(30^\circ)}$$

$$\Rightarrow \quad \frac{1}{\sqrt{2}}\sin\theta+\frac{1}{\sqrt{2}}\cos\theta=\sqrt{2}\left(\frac{\sqrt{3}}{2}\sin\theta-\frac{1}{2}\cos\theta\right)$$

$$\Rightarrow \quad \sin\theta+\cos\theta=\sqrt{3}\sin\theta-\cos\theta$$

$$\Rightarrow \quad \left(\sqrt{3}-1\right)\sin\theta=2\cos\theta$$

$$\Rightarrow \quad \tan\theta=\sqrt{3}+1$$

$$\Rightarrow \quad \sin\theta=\frac{\sqrt{3}+1}{\sqrt{5+2\sqrt{3}}} \text{ and } \cos\theta=\frac{1}{\sqrt{5+2\sqrt{3}}}$$

Thus, we have

$$x=\frac{\sin(45^\circ)l}{\sin(\theta+45^\circ)}=\frac{l}{\sin\theta+\cos\theta}$$

$$\Rightarrow \quad x=\frac{l\sqrt{5+2\sqrt{3}}}{2+\sqrt{3}}=l\sqrt{5+2\sqrt{3}}\left(2-\sqrt{3}\right)$$

$$\Rightarrow \quad x=l\sqrt{5+2\sqrt{3}}\times\sqrt{7-4\sqrt{3}}=l\sqrt{11-6\sqrt{3}}$$

Putting the value of l gives $x=1$. Hence $BC=2x=2$.

CHAPTER 14 Inverse Trigonometric Functions

- Inverse trigonometric functions are one–one and non-periodic functions:

1. Sine inverse function $\left(y = \sin^{-1} x\right)$

   It is an odd function whose domain is $|x| \le 1$ and whose range is $y \in \left[\frac{-\pi}{2}, \frac{\pi}{2}\right]$.

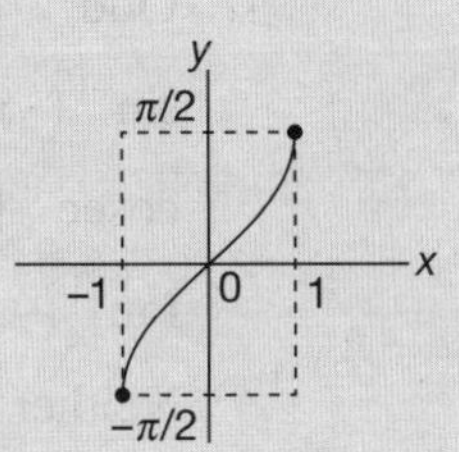

2. Cos inverse function $\left(y = \cos^{-1} x\right)$

   It is neither an even nor an odd function whose domain is $|x| \le 1$ and whose range is $y \in [0, \pi]$.

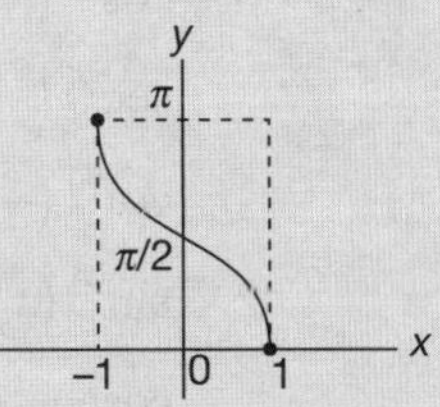

3. Tan inverse function $\left(y = \tan^{-1} x\right)$

   It is an odd function whose domain is $x \in \mathbf{R}$ and whose range is $y \in \left(\frac{-\pi}{2}, \frac{\pi}{2}\right)$.

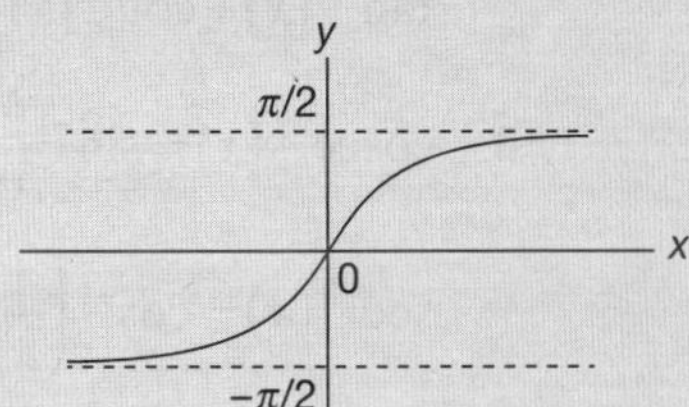

4. Cosec inverse function $\left(y = \operatorname{cosec}^{-1} x\right)$

   It is an odd function whose domain is $|x| \ge 1$ and whose range is $y \in \left[\frac{-\pi}{2}, \frac{\pi}{2}\right] - \{0\}$.

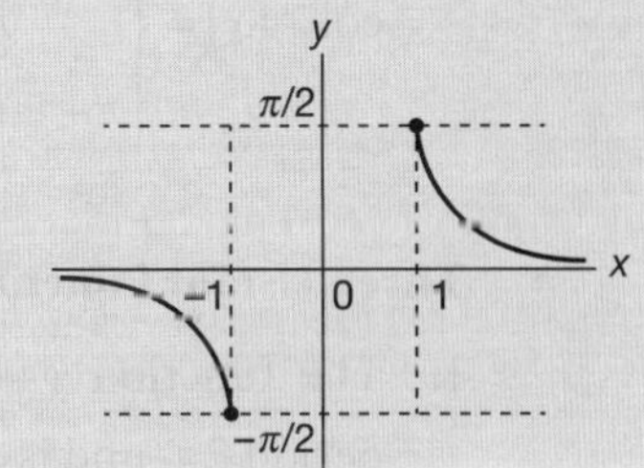

5. Secant function $\left(y = \sec^{-1} x\right)$

   It is neither an even nor an odd function whose domain is $|x| \ge 1$ and whose range is $y \in [0, \pi] - \left\{\frac{\pi}{2}\right\}$.

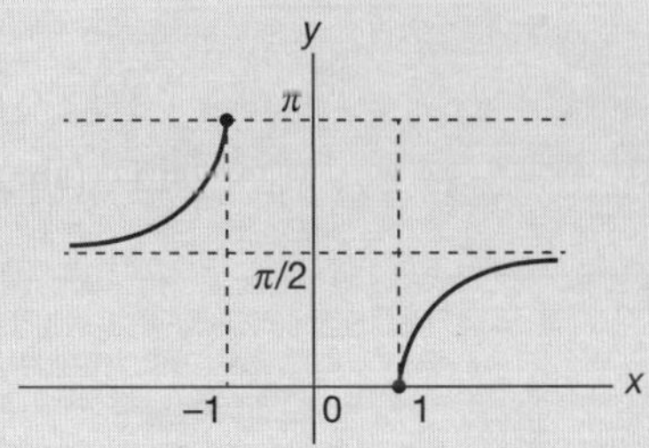

6. Cotangent function $\left(y=\cot^{-1}x\right)$

   It is neither an even nor an odd function whose domain is $x \in \mathbf{R}$ and whose range is $y \in (0, \pi)$.

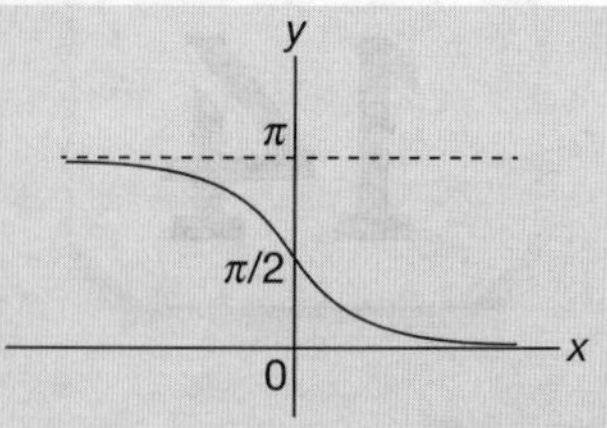

- **Inverse Trigonometric Identities**

1. Odd

   $\sin^{-1}(-x) = -\sin^{-1}x$

   $\operatorname{cosec}^{-1}(-x) = -\operatorname{cosec}^{-1}x$

   $\tan^{-1}(-x) = -\tan^{-1}x$

   Neither Even nor Odd

   $\cos^{-1}(-x) = \pi - \cos^{-1}x$

   $\sec^{-1}(-x) = \pi - \sec^{-1}x$

   $\cot^{-1}(-x) = \pi - \cot^{-1}x$

2. $\sin^{-1}(x) + \cos^{-1}(x) = \pi/2$

   $\operatorname{cosec}^{-1}(x) + \sec^{-1}(x) = \pi/2$

   $\tan^{-1}(x) + \cot^{-1}(x) = \pi/2$

3. $\operatorname{cosec}^{-1}(x) = \sin^{-1}\left(\dfrac{1}{x}\right)$

   $\sec^{-1}(x) = \cos^{-1}\left(\dfrac{1}{x}\right)$

   $$\cot^{-1}(x) = \begin{cases} \tan^{-1}(1/x) \text{ if } x > 0 \\ \pi/2 \text{ if } x = 0 \\ \pi + \tan^{-1}(1/x) \text{ if } x < 0 \end{cases}$$

4. $\sin^{-1}(x) = \cos^{-1}\left(\sqrt{1-x^2}\right)$

   $= \tan^{-1}\left(\dfrac{x}{\sqrt{1-x^2}}\right)$ if $0 \le x < 1$

5. $\sin^{-1}x + \sin^{-1}y = \sin^{-1}\left\{x\sqrt{1-y^2} + y\sqrt{1-x^2}\right\}$

   $\cos^{-1}x + \cos^{-1}y = \cos^{-1}\left\{xy - \sqrt{1-x^2}\sqrt{1-y^2}\right\}$

   $\tan^{-1}x + \tan^{-1}y =$

   $$\begin{cases} \tan^{-1}\left(\dfrac{x+y}{1-xy}\right) \text{ if } xy < 1 \\ \pi/2 \text{ if } xy = 1 \\ \pi + \tan^{-1}\left(\dfrac{x+y}{1-xy}\right) \text{ if } x, y > 0, xy > 1 \end{cases}$$

- **Three Useful Functions**:

1. The function $y = \sin^{-1}(\sin x)$ is a periodic function with period 2π, and is defined as

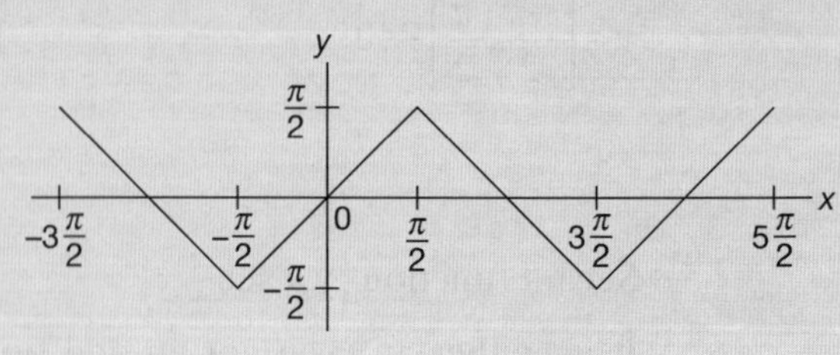

$$\sin^{-1}(\sin x) = \begin{cases} \ldots\ldots \\ x, \quad \dfrac{-\pi}{2} \le x \le \dfrac{\pi}{2} \\ \pi - x, \quad \dfrac{\pi}{2} \le x \le \dfrac{3\pi}{2} \\ \ldots\ldots \end{cases}$$

Its domain is $x \in \mathbf{R}$ and its range is $y \in \left[\dfrac{-\pi}{2}, \dfrac{\pi}{2}\right]$.

2. The function $y = \cos^{-1}(\cos x)$ is a periodic function with period 2π, and is defined as

$$\cos^{-1}(\cos x) = \begin{cases} \ldots\ldots \\ x, & 0 \le x \le \pi \\ 2\pi - x, & \pi \le x \le 2\pi \\ \ldots\ldots \end{cases}$$

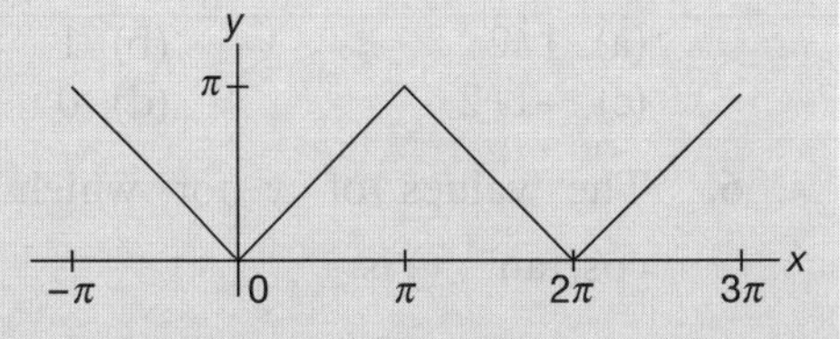

Its domain is $x \in \mathbf{R}$ and its range is $y \in [0, \pi]$.

3. The function $y = \tan^{-1}(\tan x)$ is a periodic function with period π, and is defined as

$$\tan^{-1}(\tan x) = \begin{cases} \ldots\ldots \\ x, & \frac{-\pi}{2} < x < \frac{\pi}{2} \\ x - \pi, & \frac{\pi}{2} < x < \frac{3\pi}{2} \\ \ldots\ldots \end{cases}$$

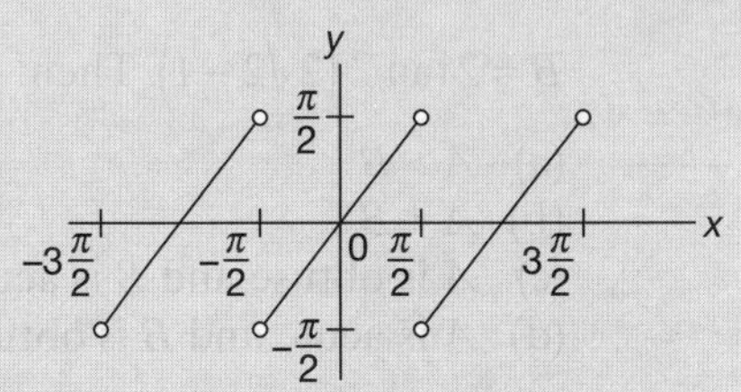

Its domain is $x \in \mathbf{R}$ and its range is $y \in \left(\frac{-\pi}{2}, \frac{\pi}{2}\right)$.

EXERCISES

1. Match the columns:

(a) $\sin^{-1}\left(\frac{\sqrt{3}+1}{2\sqrt{2}}\right)$ (p) $\frac{5\pi}{6}$

(b) $\cot^{-1}\left(\tan\frac{17\pi}{3}\right)$ (q) $\frac{5\pi}{12}$

(c) $\cos^{-1}\left\{\frac{1}{\sqrt{2}}\left(\cos\frac{9\pi}{10} - \sin\frac{9\pi}{10}\right)\right\}$ (r) $\frac{17\pi}{20}$

(d) $\tan^{-1}\left(\frac{1+\tan\frac{7\pi}{12}}{1-\tan\frac{7\pi}{12}}\right)$ (s) $\frac{-\pi}{6}$

2. The value of $\sin^{-1}\frac{1}{\sqrt{5}} + \cos^{-1}\frac{3}{\sqrt{10}} + \tan^{-1}\frac{4}{3}$ equals:

(a) $\cos^{-1}\left(\frac{-1}{5\sqrt{2}}\right)$ (b) $\tan^{-1}(-7)$

(c) $\sin^{-1}\left(\frac{-7}{5\sqrt{2}}\right)$ (d) $\pi - \tan^{-1}(7)$

3. If $0 < x < 1$, then

$$\sqrt{1+x^2}\left[\left\{x\cos\left(\cot^{-1}x\right) + \sin\left(\cot^{-1}x\right)\right\}^2 - 1\right]^{1/2}$$

equals:

(a) $\frac{x}{\sqrt{1+x}}$ (b) $\sqrt{1+x^2}$

(c) x (d) $x\sqrt{1+x^2}$

4. The number of real solutions of the equation $\tan^{-1}\sqrt{x(x+1)} + \sin^{-1}\sqrt{x^2+x+1} = \frac{\pi}{2}$ is:

(a) 0 (b) 1

(c) 2 (d) Infinite

5. If $\sin^{-1}\left\{\sum_{1}^{\infty} x^{k+1} - x\sum_{1}^{\infty}\left(\frac{x}{2}\right)^k\right\} + \cos^{-1}\left\{2\sum_{1}^{\infty}\left(\frac{-x}{2}\right)^{k+1} + x\sum_{1}^{\infty}\left(\frac{-x}{3}\right)^k\right\} = \frac{\pi}{2}$ is identically true for $|x| < 1$, then x equals:

(a) $1/2$ (b) 1
(c) $-1/2$ (d) 0

6. The values of x for which $\sin\left(\cot^{-1}(1+x)\right) = \cos(\tan^{-1} x)$ is:

(a) $1/2$ (b) 1
(c) $-1/2$ (d) -1

7. Consider angles $A = 3\sin^{-1}\left(\frac{1}{3}\right) + \tan^{-1}\left(\frac{1}{3}\right)$ and $B = 2\tan^{-1}\left(2\sqrt{2}-1\right)$. Then:

(a) $A > B$
(b) $A < B$
(c) A is obtuse and B is acute
(d) A is acute and B is obtuse

8. Consider angles $A = 3\sin^{-1}\left(\frac{6}{11}\right)$ and $B = 3\cos^{-1}\left(\frac{4}{9}\right)$. Then:

(a) $\cos A > 0$ (b) $\sin B < 0$
(c) $\cos(A+B) > 0$ (d) $\cos B < 0$

9. Given $f(x) = \cos^{-1}(\cos x), x \in [0, 4\pi]$ and $g(x) = \frac{10-x}{10}$. The number of solutions of the equation $f(x) = g(x)$ is:

(a) 1 (b) 2
(c) 3 (d) 4

10. The value of $\tan^{-1}\frac{4}{7} + \tan^{-1}\frac{4}{19} + \tan^{-1}\frac{4}{39} + \ldots \infty$ terms equals:

(a) $\frac{\pi}{2} - \tan^{-1}\left(\frac{1}{4}\right)$ (b) $\frac{\pi}{4} + \tan^{-1}\left(\frac{1}{4}\right)$

(c) $\frac{\pi}{2} - \tan^{-1}\left(\frac{1}{2}\right)$ (d) $\tan^{-1}(2) - \frac{\pi}{4}$

11. The value of $\cot^{-1}2 + \cot^{-1}8 + \cot^{-1}18 + \ldots \infty$ terms equals:

(a) $\frac{\pi}{2} - \tan^{-1}\left(\frac{1}{4}\right)$ (b) $\frac{\pi}{4} + \tan^{-1}\left(\frac{1}{4}\right)$

(c) $\frac{\pi}{4}$ (d) $\tan^{-1}(2) - \frac{\pi}{4}$

12. If $\sum_{1}^{n} \cot^{-1}\left(n^2 + n + 1\right) = \frac{1}{2}\cos^{-1}\left(\frac{24}{145}\right)$, then n equals:

(a) 11 (b) 10
(c) 9 (d) 8

13. The values of a for which the equation $\left(\tan^{-1}x\right)^2 + a\tan^{-1}x - \pi\cot^{-1}x = 0$ has no real solution lie in:

(a) $\left(\frac{\pi}{2}, \frac{3\pi}{2}\right)$ (b) $\left(\frac{-\pi}{2}, \frac{\pi}{2}\right)$

(c) $\left(\frac{\pi}{4}, \frac{3\pi}{4}\right)$ (d) $\left(\frac{-3\pi}{2}, \frac{-\pi}{2}\right)$

14. The values of the function $f(x) = \cos^{-1}x + \cos^{-1}\left(\frac{x+\sqrt{1-x^2}}{\sqrt{2}}\right), \frac{1}{\sqrt{2}} < x < 1$ lie in:

(a) $\left(\frac{\pi}{4}, \frac{\pi}{2}\right)$ (b) $\left(\frac{\pi}{4}, \frac{3\pi}{4}\right)$

(c) $\left\{\frac{\pi}{4}, \frac{3\pi}{4}\right\}$ (d) $\left\{\frac{\pi}{4}\right\}$

15. If $\cos^{-1}x = \begin{cases} a\pi - b\cos^{-1}\left(2x^2-1\right), & -1 \le x \le 0 \\ c\cos^{-1}\left(2x^2-1\right), & 0 \le x \le 1 \end{cases}$, then the value of $a+b+c$ equals:

(a) 1 (b) 2
(c) 3 (d) 4

16. If $\sin^{-1}a + \sin^{-1}b + \sin^{-1}c = 3\pi/2$ and $f(1) = 2$, $f(x+y) = f(x)f(y)$ for all $x, y \in \mathbf{R}$, then the value of $\{f(1)\}^a + \{f(2)\}^b + \{f(3)\}^c$ equals:

(a) 1 (b) 14
(c) 9 (d) 81

17. If $\cos^{-1}\left(\frac{2}{3x}\right) + \cos^{-1}\left(\frac{3}{4x}\right) = \frac{\pi}{2}, x > \frac{3}{4}$, then x equals:

(a) $\frac{\sqrt{145}}{12}$ (b) $\frac{\sqrt{145}}{11}$

(c) $\frac{\sqrt{145}}{10}$ (d) $\frac{\sqrt{145}}{9}$

18. Match the identical relations in the two columns:

(a) $\sin^{-1} x + \sin^{-1} y = \pi$ (p) $xy = 1$

(b) $\cos^{-1} x + \cos^{-1} y = 0$ (q) point (1, 1)

(c) $\operatorname{cosec}^{-1}(xy) + \sec^{-1} 1 = \frac{\pi}{2}$ (r) $x^2 + y^2 = 1$

(d) $\sin^{-1} x - \cos^{-1} y = 0$ (s) $x - y = 0$

19. If (x, y) satisfies $\sin^{-1}(ax) + \cos^{-1} y + \cos^{-1}(bxy) = \frac{\pi}{2}$, then match the columns:

(a) if $a = 1$ and $b = 0$ then (x, y) (p) lies on $x^2 + y^2 = 1$

(b) if $a = 1$ and $b = 1$ then (x, y) (q) lies on $(x^2 - 1)(y^2 - 1) = 0$

(c) if $a = 1$ and $b = 2$ then (x, y) (r) lies on $y = x$

(d) if $a = 2$ and $b = 2$ then (x, y) (s) lies on $(4x^2 - 1)(y^2 - 1) = 0$

20. Match the identical functions in the two columns:

(a) $\cos\left[\tan^{-1}\left\{\sin\left(\cot^{-1} x\right)\right\}\right]$ (p) $\frac{1}{2}x$

(b) $\frac{1}{2}\cos^{-1}\left(\frac{1-x}{1+x}\right), 0 \le x \le 1$ (q) $\frac{\pi}{4} - \frac{1}{2}\cos^{-1} x$

(c) $\cot^{-1}\left(\frac{\sqrt{1+\sin x} + \sqrt{1-\sin x}}{\sqrt{1+\sin x} - \sqrt{1-\sin x}}\right), 0 < x < \frac{\pi}{4}$ (r) $\sqrt{\frac{x^2+1}{x^2+2}}$

(d) $\tan^{-1}\left(\frac{\sqrt{1+x} - \sqrt{1-x}}{\sqrt{1+x} + \sqrt{1-x}}\right), \frac{-1}{\sqrt{2}} \le x \le 1$ (s) $\tan^{-1}\sqrt{x}$

21. Match the equations with their corresponding solutions:

(a) $2\tan^{-1}(\cos x) = \tan^{-1}(2\operatorname{cosec} x)$ (p) $1/2$

(b) $\tan^{-1}\left(\frac{1-x}{1+x}\right) = \frac{1}{2}\tan^{-1} x$ (q) 0

(c) $\sin^{-1}(1-x) - 2\sin^{-1} x = \frac{\pi}{2}$ (r) $\pi/4$

(d) $\tan^{-1}\left(\frac{2}{3}x\right) + \tan^{-1}(x) = \frac{\pi}{4}$ (s) $1/\sqrt{3}$

22. If $\tan^{-1}\left(\frac{\sqrt{1+x^2} - \sqrt{1-x^2}}{\sqrt{1+x^2} + \sqrt{1-x^2}}\right) = \alpha$, then:

(a) $\alpha \in \left[0, \frac{\pi}{4}\right]$ (b) $\alpha \in \left[-\frac{\pi}{4}, \frac{\pi}{4}\right]$

(c) $\alpha \in \left[-\frac{\pi}{2}, \frac{\pi}{2}\right]$ (d) $\alpha \in \left[-\frac{\pi}{4}, \frac{3\pi}{4}\right]$

23. If a, b, c are positive numbers, then $\sum \tan^{-1}\sqrt{\frac{a(a+b+c)}{bc}}$ equals:

(a) $\frac{\pi}{2}$ (b) π

(c) $\frac{2\pi}{3}$ (d) $\frac{3\pi}{4}$

24. The values of x for which the function $f(x) = \cos^{-1}\left(\frac{x^2}{2} + \sqrt{1-x^2}\sqrt{1-\frac{x^2}{4}}\right)$ is identical to the function $g(x) = \cos^{-1}\left(\frac{x}{2}\right) - \cos^{-1} x$ are:

(a) $|x| \le 1$

(b) $0 \le x \le 1$

(c) $|x| \le 1/2$

(d) $-1 \le x \le 0$

25. If $\sin^{-1}a+\sin^{-1}b+\sin^{-1}c=\pi$, then the value $a\sqrt{1-a^2}+b\sqrt{1-b^2}+c\sqrt{1-c^2}$ equals:

(a) abc (b) $2abc$

(c) $\frac{1}{2}abc$ (d) $\frac{1}{3}abc$

26. The values of the function $(\sin^{-1}x)^2+(\cos^{-1}x)^2$ lie in the interval:

(a) $\left[\frac{\pi^2}{8},\frac{5\pi^2}{4}\right]$ (b) $\left[\frac{\pi^2}{4},\frac{5\pi^2}{4}\right]$

(c) $\left[\frac{\pi^2}{4},\frac{3\pi^2}{4}\right]$ (d) $\left[\frac{\pi^2}{8},\frac{3\pi^2}{8}\right]$

ANSWER KEYS

1. (a)-(q), (b)-(p), (c)-(r), (d)-(s) **2.** (a),(d) **3.** (d) **4.** (c) **5.** (c),(d) **6.** (c) **7.** (b),(d) **8.** (b),(c),(d) **9.** (c) **10.** (c) **11.** (c) **12.** (a) **13.** (d) **14.** (d) **15.** (b) **16.** (b) **17.** (a) **18.** (a)-(q), (b)-(q), (c)-(p), (d)-(r) **19.** (a)-(p), (b)-(q), (c)-(p), (d)-(s) **20.** (a)-(r), (b)-(s), (c)-(p), (d)-(q) **21.** (a)-(r), (b)-(s), (c)-(q), (d)-(p) **22.** (a) **23.** (b) **24.** (b) **25.** (b) **26.** (a)

SOLUTIONS

1. (a)-(q),(b)-(p),(c)-(r),(d)-(s)

$$\sin^{-1}\left(\frac{\sqrt{3}+1}{2\sqrt{2}}\right)=\sin^{-1}\left(\frac{1}{\sqrt{2}}\cdot\frac{\sqrt{3}}{2}+\frac{1}{\sqrt{2}}\cdot\frac{1}{2}\right)$$

$$=\sin^{-1}\left(\sin\frac{\pi}{4}\cos\frac{\pi}{6}+\cos\frac{\pi}{4}\sin\frac{\pi}{6}\right)$$

$$=\sin^{-1}\left(\sin\frac{5\pi}{12}\right)=\frac{5\pi}{12}$$

$$\cot^{-1}\left(\tan\frac{17\pi}{3}\right)=\cot^{-1}\left\{\tan\left(6\pi-\frac{\pi}{3}\right)\right\}$$

$$=\cot^{-1}\left\{\tan\left(\frac{-\pi}{3}\right)\right\}$$

$$=\frac{\pi}{2}-\tan^{-1}\left\{\tan\left(\frac{-\pi}{3}\right)\right\}=\frac{\pi}{2}+\frac{\pi}{3}$$

$$=\frac{5\pi}{6}$$

$$\cos^{-1}\left\{\frac{1}{\sqrt{2}}\left(\cos\frac{9\pi}{10}-\sin\frac{9\pi}{10}\right)\right\}$$

$$=\cos^{-1}\left\{\cos\left(\frac{9\pi}{10}+\frac{\pi}{4}\right)\right\}=\cos^{-1}\left\{\cos\left(\frac{23\pi}{20}\right)\right\}$$

$$=\cos^{-1}\left\{\cos\left(2\pi-\frac{17\pi}{20}\right)\right\}=\cos^{-1}\left(\cos\frac{17\pi}{20}\right)=\frac{17\pi}{20}$$

$$\tan^{-1}\left(\frac{1+\tan\frac{7\pi}{12}}{1-\tan\frac{7\pi}{12}}\right)=\tan^{-1}\left\{\tan\left(\frac{7\pi}{12}+\frac{\pi}{4}\right)\right\}$$

$$=\tan^{-1}\left(\tan\frac{5\pi}{6}\right)$$

$$=\tan^{-1}\left\{\tan\left(\pi-\frac{\pi}{6}\right)\right\}$$

$$=\tan^{-1}\left(\tan\frac{-\pi}{6}\right)=\frac{-\pi}{6}$$

2. (a),(d) Let S denote the given expression. Then

$$S=\sin^{-1}\frac{1}{\sqrt{5}}+\cos^{-1}\frac{3}{\sqrt{10}}+\tan^{-1}\frac{4}{3}$$

$$=\tan^{-1}\frac{1}{2}+\tan^{-1}\frac{1}{3}+\tan^{-1}\frac{4}{3}$$

$$=\tan^{-1}\left(\frac{\frac{1}{2}+\frac{1}{3}}{1-\frac{1}{2}\cdot\frac{1}{3}}\right)+\tan^{-1}\frac{4}{3}$$

$$=\tan^{-1}1+\tan^{-1}\frac{4}{3}$$

$$=\pi+\tan^{-1}\left(\frac{1+\frac{4}{3}}{1-\frac{4}{3}}\right)=\pi-\tan^{-1}7$$

Since $\cos^{-1}\left(\frac{-1}{5\sqrt{2}}\right)=\pi-\cos^{-1}\left(\frac{1}{5\sqrt{2}}\right)=\pi-\tan^{-1}7,$

(a) is also correct. However, $\sin^{-1}\left(\frac{-7}{5\sqrt{2}}\right)=$

$-\sin^{-1}\left(\frac{1}{5\sqrt{2}}\right)=-\tan^{-1}7$. Therefore, (c) is incorrect.

3. (d) Let S denote the given expression. Then

$$S=\sqrt{1+x^2}\left[\left\{x\cos\left(\cot^{-1}x\right)+\sin\left(\cot^{-1}x\right)\right\}^2-1\right]^{1/2}$$

$$=\sqrt{1+x^2}\left[\left\{x\cos\cos^{-1}\left(\frac{x}{\sqrt{x^2+1}}\right)+\sin\sin^{-1}\left(\frac{1}{\sqrt{x^2+1}}\right)\right\}^2-1\right]^{1/2}$$

$$=\sqrt{1+x^2}\left[\left\{\frac{x^2}{\sqrt{x^2+1}}+\frac{1}{\sqrt{x^2+1}}\right\}^2-1\right]^{1/2}$$

$$=\sqrt{1+x^2}\left[\left\{\sqrt{x^2+1}\right\}^2-1\right]^{1/2}=x\sqrt{1+x^2}$$

4. (c) The given equation reduces to

$$\cos^{-1}\frac{1}{\sqrt{x^2+x+1}}+\sin^{-1}\sqrt{x^2+x+1}=\frac{\pi}{2}$$

$$\Rightarrow \quad \frac{1}{\sqrt{x^2+x+1}}=\sqrt{x^2+x+1}$$

$$\Rightarrow \quad x^2+x+1=1$$

$\Rightarrow \quad x^2+x=0$ gives $x=-1,0$. Hence two real solutions.

5. (c),(d) The given equation reduces to

$$\sum_1^{\infty}x^{k+1}-x\sum_1^{\infty}\left(\frac{x}{2}\right)^k=2\sum_1^{\infty}\left(\frac{-x}{2}\right)^{k+1}+x\sum_1^{\infty}\left(\frac{-x}{3}\right)^k$$

$$\Rightarrow \quad \frac{x^2}{1-x}-x\left(\frac{\frac{x}{2}}{1-\frac{x}{2}}\right)=2\left(\frac{\frac{x^2}{4}}{1+\frac{x}{2}}\right)+x\left(\frac{\frac{-x}{3}}{1+\frac{x}{3}}\right)$$

$$\Rightarrow \quad \frac{x^2}{1-x}-\frac{x^2}{2-x}=\frac{x^2}{2+x}-\frac{x^2}{3+x}$$

$$\Rightarrow \quad \frac{x^2}{x^2-3x+2}=\frac{x^2}{x^2+5x+6}$$

$\Rightarrow \quad x^2(8x+4)=0$ gives $x=-1/2,0$

6. (c) The given equation reduces to

$$\sin\sin^{-1}\left(\frac{1}{\sqrt{(x+1)^2+1}}\right)=\cos\cos^{-1}\left(\frac{1}{\sqrt{1+x^2}}\right)$$

$$\Rightarrow \quad \frac{1}{\sqrt{(x+1)^2+1}}=\frac{1}{\sqrt{1+x^2}}$$

$$\Rightarrow \quad (x+1)^2+1=1+x^2$$

$\Rightarrow \quad 2x+1=0$ gives $x=-1/2$

7. (b),(d) We have

$$A=3\tan^{-1}\left(\frac{1}{2\sqrt{2}}\right)+\tan^{-1}\left(\frac{1}{3}\right)$$

$$<3\tan^{-1}\left(\sqrt{2}-1\right)+\tan^{-1}\left(\sqrt{2}-1\right)$$

$$=4\times 22.5^\circ=90^\circ$$

$$B=2\tan^{-1}\left(2\sqrt{2}-1\right)>2\tan^{-1}\left(\sqrt{3}\right)=120^\circ$$

8. (b),(c),(d) We have

$$\frac{6}{11}>\frac{1}{2}\Rightarrow\sin^{-1}\left(\frac{6}{11}\right)>\sin^{-1}\left(\frac{1}{2}\right)=30^\circ\Rightarrow A>90^\circ$$

$$\frac{4}{9}<\frac{1}{2}\Rightarrow\cos^{-1}\left(\frac{4}{9}\right)>\cos^{-1}\left(\frac{1}{2}\right)=60^\circ\Rightarrow B>180^\circ$$

Hence $\sin B<0$, $\cos(A+B)>0$ and $\cos B<0$.

9. (c) From the figure, we see that the graph of the two functions intersects at three points.

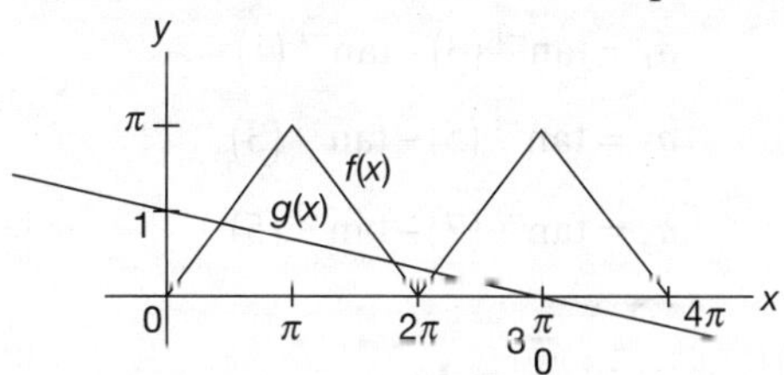

10. (c) The nth term of the series is

$$a_n=\tan^{-1}\left(\frac{4}{4n^2+3}\right)=\tan^{-1}\left(\frac{4}{4+(2n+1)(2n-1)}\right)$$

$$=\tan^{-1}\left(\frac{1}{1+\left(n+\frac{1}{2}\right)\left(n-\frac{1}{2}\right)}\right)$$

$$=\tan^{-1}\left(\frac{\left(n+\frac{1}{2}\right)-\left(n-\frac{1}{2}\right)}{1+\left(n+\frac{1}{2}\right)\left(n-\frac{1}{2}\right)}\right)$$

$$=\tan^{-1}\left(n+\frac{1}{2}\right)-\tan^{-1}\left(n-\frac{1}{2}\right)$$

Thus, we have

$$a_1 = \tan^{-1}\left(\frac{3}{2}\right) - \tan^{-1}\left(\frac{1}{2}\right)$$

$$a_2 = \tan^{-1}\left(\frac{5}{2}\right) - \tan^{-1}\left(\frac{3}{2}\right)$$

$$a_3 = \tan^{-1}\left(\frac{7}{2}\right) - \tan^{-1}\left(\frac{5}{2}\right)$$

....

....

$$a_n = \tan^{-1}\left(n+\frac{1}{2}\right) - \tan^{-1}\left(n-\frac{1}{2}\right)$$

Hence, the required sum is

$$S = \lim_{n\to+\infty} \tan^{-1}\left(n+\frac{1}{2}\right) - \tan^{-1}\left(\frac{1}{2}\right) = \frac{\pi}{2} - \tan^{-1}\left(\frac{1}{2}\right)$$

11. (c) The nth term of the series is

$$a_n = \tan^{-1}\left(\frac{1}{2n^2}\right) = \tan^{-1}\left(\frac{2}{4n^2}\right)$$

$$= \tan^{-1}\left(\frac{2}{1+(4n^2-1)}\right)$$

$$= \tan^{-1}\left(\frac{(2n+1)-(2n-1)}{1+(2n+1)(2n-1)}\right)$$

$$= \tan^{-1}(2n+1) - \tan^{-1}(2n-1)$$

Thus, we have

$$a_1 = \tan^{-1}(3) - \tan^{-1}(1)$$

$$a_2 = \tan^{-1}(5) - \tan^{-1}(3)$$

$$a_3 = \tan^{-1}(7) - \tan^{-1}(5)$$

....

....

$$a_n = \tan^{-1}(2n+1) - \tan^{-1}(2n-1)$$

Hence, the required sum is

$$S = \lim_{n\to+\infty} \tan^{-1}(2n+1) - \tan^{-1}(1) = \frac{\pi}{2} - \frac{\pi}{4} = \frac{\pi}{4}$$

12. (a) The nth term of the series is

$$a_n = \tan^{-1}\left(\frac{1}{n^2+n+1}\right) = \tan^{-1}\left(\frac{(n+1)-n}{1+n(n+1)}\right)$$

$$= \tan^{-1}(n+1) - \tan^{-1}(n)$$

Thus, we have

$$a_1 = \tan^{-1}(2) - \tan^{-1}(1)$$

$$a_2 = \tan^{-1}(3) - \tan^{-1}(2)$$

$$a_3 = \tan^{-1}(4) - \tan^{-1}(3)$$

....

....

$$a_n = \tan^{-1}(n+1) - \tan^{-1}(n)$$

Their sum is

$$S = \tan^{-1}(n+1) - \tan^{-1}(1) = \tan^{-1}\left(\frac{n}{n+2}\right)$$

Now, let $x = \frac{1}{2}\cos^{-1}\left(\frac{24}{145}\right) \Rightarrow \cos(2x) = \frac{24}{145}$. Then

$$\tan x = \sqrt{\frac{1-\cos(2x)}{1+\cos(2x)}} = \sqrt{\frac{121}{169}} = \frac{11}{13}$$

$$\Rightarrow \quad x = \tan^{-1}\left(\frac{11}{13}\right)$$

Thus, we have

$$\tan^{-1}\left(\frac{n}{n+2}\right) = \tan^{-1}\left(\frac{11}{13}\right)$$

$$\Rightarrow \quad n = 11$$

13. (d) The given equation reduces to

$$\left(\tan^{-1}x\right)^2 + (a+\pi)\tan^{-1}x - \frac{\pi^2}{2} = 0$$

$$\left[\text{Putting } \cot^{-1}x = \frac{\pi}{2} - \tan^{-1}x\right]$$

$$\Rightarrow \quad \tan^{-1}x = \frac{-(a+\pi) \pm \sqrt{(a+\pi)^2 + 2\pi^2}}{2}$$

The solutions will not be real if

$$\frac{-(a+\pi) - \sqrt{(a+\pi)^2 + 2\pi^2}}{2} < \frac{-\pi}{2} \text{ and}$$

$$\frac{-(a+\pi) + \sqrt{(a+\pi)^2 + 2\pi^2}}{2} > \frac{\pi}{2}$$

$$\Rightarrow \quad \sqrt{(a+\pi)^2 + 2\pi} > -a \text{ and}$$

$$\sqrt{(a+\pi)^2 + 2\pi} > a + 2\pi$$

$$\Rightarrow \quad 2a\pi + 3\pi^2 > 0 \text{ and } 2a\pi + 3\pi^2 > 4a\pi + 4\pi^2$$

$$\Rightarrow \quad 2a\pi > -3\pi^2 \text{ and } 2a\pi < -\pi^2$$

$$\Rightarrow \quad a > \frac{-3\pi}{2} \text{ and } a < \frac{-\pi}{2}$$

14. (d) Let us insert $x = \cos t$. The function reduces to

$$f(x) = t + \cos^{-1}\left(\frac{\cos t + \sin t}{\sqrt{2}}\right), 0 < t < \pi/4$$

$$\Rightarrow \quad f(x) = t + \cos^{-1}\left\{\cos\left(t - \frac{\pi}{4}\right)\right\}, 0 < t < \pi/4$$

Now $-\frac{\pi}{4} < t - \frac{\pi}{4} < 0$. Hence

$$f(x) = t + \frac{\pi}{4} - t = \frac{\pi}{4}$$

$$\left[\cos^{-1}(\cos\theta) = -\theta \text{ if } -\pi/4 < \theta < 0\right]$$

15. (b) Let us insert $x = \cos t$. The function reduces to

$$f(x) = \begin{cases} a\pi - b\cos^{-1}\{\cos(2t)\}, \pi/2 \le t \le \pi \\ c\cos^{-1}\{\cos(2t)\}, 0 \le t \le \pi/2 \end{cases}$$

$$\Rightarrow \quad f(x) = \begin{cases} a\pi - b(2\pi - 2t), \pi \le 2t \le 2\pi, \\ \text{therefore } \cos^{-1}\{\cos(2t)\} = 2\pi - 2t \\ c(2t), 0 \le 2t \le \pi, \text{ therefore} \\ \cos^{-1}\{\cos(2t)\} = 2t \end{cases}$$

$$\Rightarrow \quad f(x) = \begin{cases} (a-2b)\pi + 2b\cos^{-1}x, -1 \le t \le 0 \\ 2c\cos^{-1}x, 0 \le t \le 1 \end{cases}$$

Now $f(x) = \cos^{-1}x$ if

$a - 2b = 0, 2b = 1$, and $2c =$ gives $a = 1, b = c = 1/2$.

Hence $a + b + c = 2$.

16. (b) Since the greatest value of $\sin^{-1}\theta$ is $\pi/2$, $\sin^{-1}a + \sin^{-1}b + \sin^{-1}c = 3\pi/2$ is possible only if each one of them equals $\pi/2$.

$\Rightarrow \quad a = b = c = 1$

And $f(x+y) = f(x)f(y) \Rightarrow f(x) = a^x$

$f(1) = 2$. Therefore $a = 2 \Rightarrow f(x) = 2^x$

Hence

$$\{f(1)\}^a + \{f(2)\}^b + \{f(3)\}^c = 2^1 + 2^2 + 2^3 = 14.$$

17. (a) Taking cos of both sides, the given equation reduces to

$$\Rightarrow \quad \left(\frac{2}{3x}\right)\left(\frac{3}{4x}\right) - \sqrt{1 - \frac{4}{9x^2}}\sqrt{1 - \frac{9}{16x^2}} = 0$$

$$\Rightarrow \quad \sqrt{9x^2 - 4}\sqrt{16x^2 - 9} = 6$$

$$\Rightarrow \quad 144x^4 - 81x^2 - 64x^2 + 36 = 36$$

[Squaring both sides]

$$\Rightarrow \quad 144x^4 = 145x^2$$

$$\Rightarrow \quad x = 0, \pm\frac{\sqrt{145}}{12}$$

Since $x > 3/4$, the required solution is $x = \frac{\sqrt{145}}{12}$.

18. (a)-(q), (b)-(q), (c)-(p), (d)-(r)

(a) $\sin^{-1}x + \sin^{-1}(y) = \pi$

$\Rightarrow \quad x = \sin(\pi - \sin^{-1}y)$

$\Rightarrow \quad x = \sin(\sin^{-1}y) = y$

Now, putting $x = y$, we get

$2\sin^{-1}x = \pi \Rightarrow x = 1$ and hence $y = 1$

Thus, there is only one solution (1, 1).

(b) $\cos^{-1}x + \cos^{-1}y = 0$

Since $\cos^{-1}x$ function is always non-negative, the sum of two non-negative quantities can be zero only if both are zero. Thus

$\cos^{-1}x = \cos^{-1}y = 0$

$\Rightarrow \quad x = 1$ and $y = 1$

(c) $\operatorname{cosec}^{-1}(xy) + \sec^{-1}1 = \frac{\pi}{2}$

$\Rightarrow \quad \operatorname{cosec}^{-1}(xy) = \frac{\pi}{2}\left[\sec^{-1}1 = 0\right]$

$\Rightarrow \quad xy = 1$

(d) $\sin^{-1}x - \cos^{-1}y = 0$

$\Rightarrow \quad \sin^{-1}x = \sin^{-1}\sqrt{(1-y^2)}$

$\Rightarrow \quad x = \sqrt{(1-y^2)}$

$\Rightarrow \quad x^2 + y^2 = 1 \quad (0 \le x, y \le 1)$

19. (a)-(p), (b)-(q), (c)-(p), (d)-(s)

(a) $\sin^{-1}x + \cos^{-1}y + \cos^{-1}0 = \frac{\pi}{2}$

$\Rightarrow \quad \sin^{-1}x + \cos^{-1}y = 0$

$\Rightarrow \quad xy + \sqrt{(1-x^2)(1-y^2)} = 0$ [Taking sin of both sides]

$\Rightarrow \quad x^2 + y^2 = 1$ (x, y must be of opposite signs)

(b) $\sin^{-1}x + \cos^{-1}y + \cos^{-1}xy = \frac{\pi}{2}$

$\Rightarrow \quad \sin^{-1}x + \cos^{-1}y = \sin^{-1}xy$

$\Rightarrow \quad xy + \sqrt{(1-x^2)(1-y^2)} = xy$ [Taking sin of both sides]

$\Rightarrow \quad (x^2 - 1)(y^2 - 1) = 0$

(c) $\sin^{-1}x + \cos^{-1}y + \cos^{-1}2xy = \frac{\pi}{2}$

$\Rightarrow \quad \sin^{-1}x + \cos^{-1}y = \sin^{-1}2xy$

$\Rightarrow \quad xy+\sqrt{(1-x^2)(1-y^2)}=2xy$ [Taking sin of both sides]

$\Rightarrow \quad (1-x^2)(1-y^2)=x^2y^2$

$\Rightarrow \quad x^2+y^2=1$

(d) $\sin^{-1}2x+\cos^{-1}y+\cos^{-1}2xy=\dfrac{\pi}{2}$

$\Rightarrow \quad \sin^{-1}2x+\cos^{-1}y=\sin^{-1}2xy$

$\Rightarrow \quad 2xy+\sqrt{1-4x^2}\sqrt{1-y^2}=2xy$ [Taking sin of both sides]

$\Rightarrow \quad (4x^2-1)(y^2-1)=0$

20. (a)-(r), (b)-(s), (c)-(p), (d)-(q)

(a) $f(x)=\cos\tan^{-1}\sin\cot^{-1}x$

$=\cos\tan^{-1}\sin\sin^{-1}\left(\dfrac{1}{\sqrt{x^2+1}}\right)$

$=\cos\tan^{-1}\left(\dfrac{1}{\sqrt{x^2+1}}\right)$

$=\cos\cos^{-1}\left(\sqrt{\dfrac{x^2+1}{x^2+2}}\right)=\sqrt{\dfrac{x^2+1}{x^2+2}}$

(b) $f(x)=\dfrac{1}{2}\cos^{-1}\left(\dfrac{1-x}{1+x}\right), 0\le x\le 1$

$=\dfrac{1}{2}\cos^{-1}(\cos 2\theta)$ [Putting $x=\tan^2\theta$]

$=\theta=\tan^{-1}\sqrt{x}$

(c) $f(x)=\cot^{-1}\left(\dfrac{\sqrt{1+\sin x}+\sqrt{1-\sin x}}{\sqrt{1+\sin x}-\sqrt{1-\sin x}}\right), 0<x<\dfrac{\pi}{4}$

$=\cot^{-1}\left(\dfrac{\left|\cos\left(\frac{x}{2}\right)+\sin\left(\frac{x}{2}\right)\right|+\left|\cos\left(\frac{x}{2}\right)-\sin\left(\frac{x}{2}\right)\right|}{\left|\cos\left(\frac{x}{2}\right)+\sin\left(\frac{x}{2}\right)\right|-\left|\cos\left(\frac{x}{2}\right)-\sin\left(\frac{x}{2}\right)\right|}\right)$

$=\cot^{-1}\left(\dfrac{\left\{\cos\left(\frac{x}{2}\right)+\sin\left(\frac{x}{2}\right)\right\}+\left\{\cos\left(\frac{x}{2}\right)-\sin\left(\frac{x}{2}\right)\right\}}{\left\{\cos\left(\frac{x}{2}\right)+\sin\left(\frac{x}{2}\right)\right\}-\left\{\cos\left(\frac{x}{2}\right)-\sin\left(\frac{x}{2}\right)\right\}}\right)$

$=\cot^{-1}\left(\cot\dfrac{x}{2}\right)=\dfrac{1}{2}x$

(d) $f(x)=\tan^{-1}\left(\dfrac{\sqrt{1+x}-\sqrt{1-x}}{\sqrt{1+x}+\sqrt{1-x}}\right), \dfrac{-1}{\sqrt{2}}\le x\le 1$

$=\tan^{-1}\left(\dfrac{|\cos\theta|-|\sin\theta|}{|\cos\theta|+|\sin\theta|}\right)$

[Putting $x=\cos(2\theta), 0\le 2\theta\le\dfrac{3\pi}{4}$]

$=\tan^{-1}\left(\dfrac{\cos\theta-\sin\theta}{\cos\theta+\sin\theta}\right)\left[0\le\theta\le\dfrac{3\pi}{8}\right]$

$=\tan^{-1}\left(\dfrac{1-\tan\theta}{1+\tan\theta}\right)$

$=\tan^{-1}\left(\tan\left(\dfrac{\pi}{4}-\theta\right)\right)$

$=\dfrac{\pi}{4}-\theta=\dfrac{\pi}{4}-\dfrac{1}{2}\cos^{-1}x$

21. (a)-(r), (b)-(s), (c)-(q), (d)-(p)

(a) The equation reduces to

$\tan^{-1}\left(\dfrac{2\cos x}{1-\cos^2 x}\right)=\tan^{-1}(2\operatorname{cosec}x)$

$\Rightarrow \quad \dfrac{2\cos x}{\sin^2 x}=2\operatorname{cosec}x$

$\Rightarrow \quad \dfrac{2\cos x}{\sin^2 x}=2\operatorname{cosec}x$

$\Rightarrow \quad \tan x=1$ gives $x=n\pi+\dfrac{\pi}{4}$

(b) The equation reduces to

$2\tan^{-1}\left(\dfrac{1-x}{1+x}\right)=\tan^{-1}x$

$\Rightarrow \quad \tan^{-1}\left(\dfrac{2\left(\frac{1-x}{1+x}\right)}{1-\left(\frac{1-x}{1+x}\right)^2}\right)=\tan^{-1}x$

$\Rightarrow \quad \dfrac{2(1-x^2)}{4x}=x$

$\Rightarrow \quad 3x^2=1$ gives $x=\dfrac{\pm 1}{\sqrt{3}}$

(c) The equation reduces to

$\sin^{-1}(1-x)=\dfrac{\pi}{2}+2\sin^{-1}x$ [Taking sin of both sides]

$\Rightarrow \quad 1-x=\cos(2\sin^{-1}x)$

$\Rightarrow \quad 1-\sin\theta=\cos(2\theta)$ [Putting $x=\sin\theta$]

$\Rightarrow \quad 2\sin^2\theta-\sin\theta=0$ gives $x=\sin\theta=0, \dfrac{1}{2}$

Only $x=0$ satisfies the given equation.

(d) The equation reduces to

$$\tan^{-1}\left(\frac{\frac{5}{3}x}{1-\frac{2}{3}x^2}\right)=\frac{\pi}{4}$$

$$\Rightarrow \frac{5x}{3-2x^2}=1$$

$\Rightarrow$ $2x^2+5x-3=0$ gives $x=-3, \frac{1}{2}$

Only $x=\frac{1}{2}$ satisfies the given equation.

22. (a) Let $f(x)=\frac{\sqrt{1+x^2}-\sqrt{1-x^2}}{\sqrt{1+x^2}+\sqrt{1-x^2}}, x^2 \le 1$

$$=\frac{1-t}{1+t}=\frac{2}{1+t}-1, \text{ where } t=\sqrt{\frac{1-x^2}{1+x^2}}$$

Now $\frac{1-x^2}{1+x^2}=\frac{2}{1+x^2}-1$ is even and decreasing in $0<x<1$. Hence

$$0 \le \frac{1-x^2}{1+x^2} \le 1$$

$\Rightarrow$ $0 \le t \le 1$

$\Rightarrow$ $1 \le 1+t \le 2$

$\Rightarrow$ $\frac{1}{2} \le \frac{1}{1+t} \le 1$

$\Rightarrow$ $0 \le \frac{2}{1+t}-1 \le 1$

$\Rightarrow$ $0 \le f(x) \le 1$

$\Rightarrow$ $0 \le \tan^{-1}(f(x)) \le \pi/4$

23. (b) We have

$$S=\tan^{-1}\sqrt{\frac{a(a+b+c)}{bc}}+\tan^{-1}\sqrt{\frac{a(a+b+c)}{bc}}+\tan^{-1}\sqrt{\frac{a(a+b+c)}{bc}}$$

$$=\tan^{-1}(ak)+\tan^{-1}(bk)+\tan^{-1}(ck),$$

where $k^2=\frac{a+b+c}{abc}$

$$=\pi+\tan^{-1}\left\{\frac{(a+b)k}{1-abk^2}\right\}+\tan^{-1}(ck)$$

[We have to add π since

$1-abk^2=1-\frac{a+b+c}{c}=-\frac{a+b}{c}<0$]

$$=\pi+\tan^{-1}(-ck)+\tan^{-1}(ck)=\pi.$$

24. (b) Let $\frac{x}{2}=\cos\alpha$ and $x=\cos\beta$. The first function then reduces to

$$\cos^{-1}\left(\frac{x^2}{2}+\sqrt{1-x^2}\sqrt{1-\frac{x^2}{2}}\right)$$

$$=\cos^{-1}(\cos\alpha\cos\beta+\sin\alpha\sin\beta)$$

$$=\cos^{-1}\{\cos(\alpha-\beta)\}=\alpha-\beta \text{ if } 0\le\alpha-\beta\le\pi$$

$$=\cos^{-1}\left(\frac{x}{2}\right)-\cos^{-1}x \text{ if } 0\le\alpha-\beta\le\pi.$$

Solving the LHI, we have

$\alpha \ge \beta$

$\Rightarrow$ $\cos^{-1}\left(\frac{x}{2}\right) \ge \cos^{-1}x$

$\Rightarrow$ $\frac{x}{2} \le x$ [$\cos^{-1}$ is a decreasing function, hence the inequality sign reverses]

$\Rightarrow$ $x \ge 0$.

Solving the RHI, we have $\alpha \le \pi+\beta$, which is always true since α, β are angles lying between 0 and π.

Hence, the two functions are identical for $x \ge 0$.

25. (b) Let $a=\sin\alpha, b=\sin\beta,$ and $c=\sin\gamma$. The equation then reduces to

$\alpha+\beta+\gamma=\pi$

Now, we have

$$S=a\sqrt{1-a^2}+b\sqrt{1-b^2}+c\sqrt{1-c^2}$$

$$=\sin\alpha\cos\alpha+\sin\beta\cos\beta+\sin\gamma\cos\gamma$$

$$=\frac{1}{2}[\sin(2\alpha)+\sin(2\beta)+\sin(2\gamma)$$

$$=\frac{1}{2}[2\sin(\alpha+\beta)\cos(\alpha-\beta)+\sin(2\gamma)$$

$$=\frac{1}{2}[2\sin\gamma\cos(\alpha-\beta)+2\sin\gamma\cos\gamma]$$

[Putting $\alpha+\beta=\pi-\gamma$]

$$=\sin\gamma[\cos(\alpha-\beta)-\cos(\alpha+\beta)]$$

[Putting $\gamma=\pi-\alpha-\beta$]

$$=2\sin\alpha\sin\beta\sin\gamma=2abc$$

26. (a) The given function can be written as

$$f(x) = (\sin^{-1}x)^2 + (\cos^{-1}x)^2$$

$$= (\sin^{-1}x)^2 + \left(\frac{\pi}{2} - \sin^{-1}x\right)^2$$

$$= 2(\sin^{-1}x)^2 - \pi\sin^{-1}x + \frac{\pi^2}{4}$$

$$= 2\left[(\sin^{-1}x)^2 - \frac{\pi}{2}\sin^{-1}x\right] + \frac{\pi^2}{4}$$

$$= 2\left(\sin^{-1}x - \frac{\pi}{4}\right)^2 + \frac{\pi^2}{8}$$

Now, we have

$$-\frac{\pi}{2} \le \sin^{-1}x \le \frac{\pi}{2}$$

$$\Rightarrow \quad -\frac{3\pi}{4} \le \sin^{-1}x - \frac{\pi}{4} \le \frac{\pi}{4}$$

$$\Rightarrow \quad 0 \le \left(\sin^{-1}x - \frac{\pi}{4}\right)^2 \le \frac{9\pi^2}{16}$$

$$\Rightarrow \quad 0 \le 2\left(\sin^{-1}x - \frac{\pi}{4}\right)^2 \le \frac{9\pi^2}{8}$$

$$\Rightarrow \quad \frac{\pi^2}{8} \le 2\left(\sin^{-1}x - \frac{\pi}{4}\right)^2 + \frac{\pi^2}{8} \le \frac{5\pi^2}{4}.$$

Hence, the values of the function lie in the interval $\left[\frac{\pi^2}{8}, \frac{5\pi^2}{4}\right]$

CHAPTER

15 Exponential and Log Functions

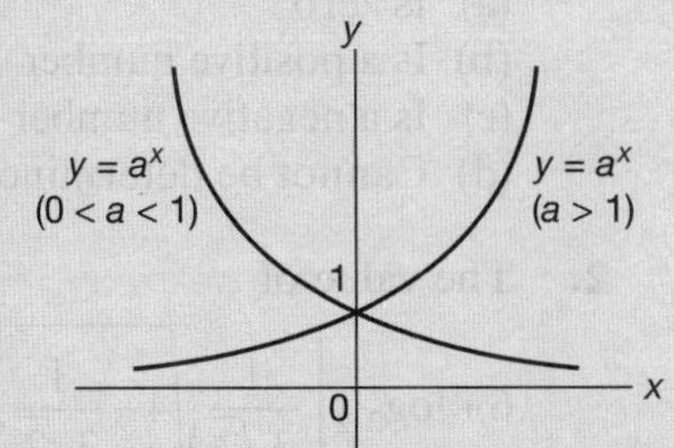

- Exponential function $\{y = a^x \ (a > 0, a \neq 1)\}$: It is a one–one function whose domain is $x \in \mathbf{R}$ and whose range is $y \in (0, +\infty)$.

  For values of $a > 1$, it is a strictly increasing function; it is a strictly decreasing function for $0 < a < 1$.

  Related properties:

  1. $a^{-x} = \dfrac{1}{a^x}$
  2. $a^{x_1} \cdot a^{x_2} = a^{x_1 + x_2}$
  3. $\dfrac{a^{x_1}}{a^{x_2}} = a^{x_1 - x_2}$
  4. $\left(a^{x_1}\right)^{x_2} = a^{x_1 x_2}$

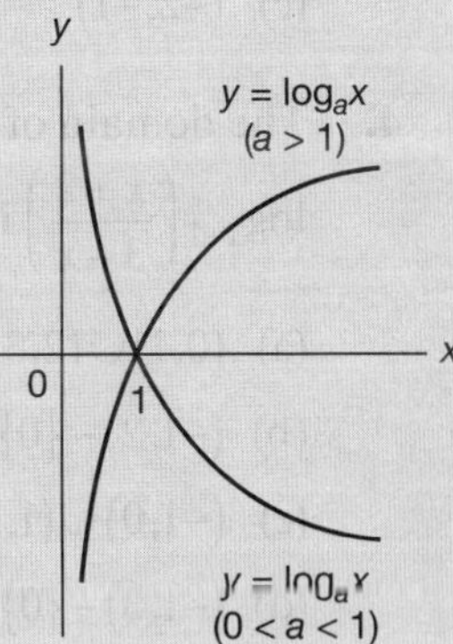

- Log function $\{y = \log_a x \ (a > 0, a \neq 1)\}$: It is the inverse of the exponential function:

$$\log_a \left(a^x\right) = x = a^{\log_a x}$$

$$\log_a b = c \Rightarrow b = a^c$$

  It is a one–one function whose domain is $x \in (0, +\infty)$ and whose range is $y \in \mathbf{R}$.

  For values of $a > 1$, it is a strictly increasing function; it is a strictly decreasing function for $0 < a < 1$.

  The value of $\log_a b$ is positive if both $a, b > 1$ or both $0 < a, b < 1$. The value of $\log_a b$ is negative if one of a, b is greater than 1 while the other lies between 0 and 1.

  Related properties:

  1. $\log_a b = \dfrac{1}{\log_b a}$
  2. $\log_a x_1 + \log_a x_2 = \log_a \left(x_1 x_2\right)$
  3. $\log_a x_1 - \log_a x_2 = \log_a \left(\dfrac{x_1}{x_2}\right)$
  4. $\log_a b = \dfrac{\log_c b}{\log_c a}$
  5. $\log_a \left(x_1^{x_2}\right) = x_2 \log_a x_1$

EXERCISES

1. If $a > b$ and $(\log_b a - 1)(\log_a b - 1) > 0$, then the value of $\dfrac{\log_\pi a^{b-1}}{\log_e b^{a-1}}$:

(a) Is zero
(b) Is a positive number
(c) Is a negative number
(d) Cannot be determined

2. The value of

$$6 + \log_{3/2}\left(\frac{1}{3\sqrt{2}}\sqrt{4 - \frac{1}{3\sqrt{2}}\sqrt{4 - \frac{1}{3\sqrt{2}}\sqrt{4 - \frac{1}{3\sqrt{2}}\cdots\cdots}}}\right)$$

is:

(a) 0 (b) 4
(c) 7 (d) 9

3. If $\log_{0.3}(x-1) \le \log_{0.09}(x-1)$, then x lies in the interval:

(a) $[2, +\infty)$ (b) $(1, 2]$
(c) $(-2, -1)$ (d) None of these

4. The domain of definition of the function $\log_{x+1}\left(\dfrac{x+2}{3-x}\right)$ is:

(a) $(0,1) \cup (2,3)$
(b) $(-1,2) - \{0\}$
(c) $(-1,0) \cup (1,3)$
(d) $(-1,3) - \{0\}$

5. Solve the following equation for x:
$2\log_x a + \log_{ax} a + 3\log_{a^2 x} a = 0,\ (a > 0)$

(a) $a^{-1/2}$ (b) $a^{1/2}$
(c) $a^{-4/3}$ (d) $a^{3/2}$

6. Solve the following equation for x:
$\log_3(5^x - 2^x) = 1 + \log_3(2^x - 3 \cdot 5^x)$

(a) $\dfrac{2}{5}$ (b) $\dfrac{5}{2}$
(c) -1 (d) None of these

7. If $e^{(\sin^2 x + \sin^4 x + \sin^6 x + \ldots)\ln 2}$ satisfies the equation $x^2 - 9x + 8 = 0$, then the value of $\dfrac{\cos x}{\cos x + \sin x}(0 < x < \pi/2)$ is:

(a) $\dfrac{\sqrt{2}+1}{3}$
(b) $\dfrac{\sqrt{2}}{3}$
(c) $\dfrac{\sqrt{2}-1}{2}$
(d) $\dfrac{\sqrt{3}-1}{2}$

8. Solve the following equation for x:
$\log 4 + \left(1 + \dfrac{1}{2x}\right)\log 3 = \log\left(\sqrt[x]{3} + 27\right)$

(a) $1/6$ (b) $1/4$
(c) $1/3$ (d) $1/2$

9. Solve the following equation for x:
$4^{\log_2(\ln x)} = \ln x - \ln^2 x + 1$

(a) e (b) $\dfrac{1}{e^2}$
(c) $\dfrac{1}{e}$ (d) $\dfrac{1}{\sqrt{e}}$

10. If $\dfrac{1}{3}\log_3 M + 3\log_3 N = 1 + \log_{0.008} 5$, then:

(a) $M^9 = \dfrac{9}{N}$
(b) $N^9 = \dfrac{9}{M}$
(c) $M^3 = \dfrac{3}{N}$
(d) $N^9 = \dfrac{3}{M}$

11. The sum of the roots of the equation $x + 1 - 2\log_2(2^x + 3) + 2\log_4(10 - 2^{-x}) = 0$ is:

(a) $\log_2 11$ (b) $\log_2 12$
(c) $\log_2 13$ (d) $\log_2 14$

12. The relation $2^x = 3^y$ represents a:
(a) Straight line with positive slope
(b) Straight line with negative slope
(c) Mutually perpendicular pair of lines
(d) Point

13. Solve the following system of equations for x:
$(2x)^{\ln 2} = (3y)^{\ln 3}$ and $3^{\ln x} = 2^{\ln y}$
(a) $1/6$ (b) 6
(c) $1/2$ (d) 2

14. The least value of the expression $2\log_{10}x - \log_x 0.01$ for $x > 1$ is:
(a) 10 (b) 2
(c) 0.01 (d) None of these

15. If $N = \frac{1}{4}\cdot\frac{2}{6}\cdot\frac{3}{8}\cdot\frac{4}{10}\cdots\frac{30}{62}\cdot\frac{31}{64}$, then $\log_8 N$ equals:
(a) –8 (b) –9
(c) –11 (d) –12

16. The value of $\log_{3/2}\left(\frac{1}{3\sqrt{2}}\sqrt{4-\frac{1}{3\sqrt{2}}\sqrt{4-\frac{1}{3\sqrt{2}}\cdots}}\right)$ is:
(a) –3 (b) –2
(c) 4 (d) 6

17. Solve the following equation for x:
$\frac{6}{5}a^{\log_a x \log_{10} a \log_a 5} - 3^{\log_{10}(x/10)} = 9^{\log_{100} x + \log_4 2}$
(a) $\sqrt[3]{10}$ (b) $\sqrt[5]{10}$
(c) 10 (d) 100

18. If $\frac{\log_a M}{\log_c M} = \frac{\log_a M - \log_b M}{\log_b M - \log_c M}$, then:
(a) $b^2 = 9ac$ (b) $b^2 = 3ac$
(c) $b^2 = 2ac$ (d) $b^2 = ac$

19. If $\log_{175}(5x) = \log_{343}(7x)$, then $\log_{42}\left(x^4 - 2x^2 + 7\right)$ equals:
(a) 1 (b) 2
(c) 3 (d) 4

20. If $\log_2\sqrt{x+1} + \log_{1/2}\sqrt{4-x^2} > -1$, then x lies in the interval:
(a) $(0,2)$
(b) $(-1,2)$
(c) $(-2,-1)$
(d) None of these

21. If $\log_{\frac{x-1}{x+2}}\left\{\log_2\left(\frac{4x+1}{2x-3}\right)\right\} > 0$, then x lies in the interval:
(a) $\left(\frac{-5}{2},-2\right)$
(b) $(-\infty,-2)\cup(1,+\infty)$
(c) $\left(1,\frac{3}{2}\right)$
(d) None of these

22. The equation $x^{\left\{\frac{3}{4}(\log_2 x)^2 + \log_2 x - \frac{5}{4}\right\}} = \sqrt{2}$ has:
(a) Only one real solution
(b) Exactly two real solutions
(c) Exactly three real solutions
(d) None of these

23. Let $\frac{\log\alpha}{3x-5y-z} = \frac{\log\beta}{x+8z} = \frac{\log\gamma}{-x+y-3z}$. If $\log_\alpha a = 2$, $\log_{2\beta}(2b) = 4$, $\log_{4\gamma^2}(16c) = 5$, then the value of abc equals:
(a) 2^7 (b) 2^8
(c) 2^9 (d) 2^{10}

24. P and Q are points on the curves $y = a^x$ and $y = 2a^x$, respectively. If line PQ is parallel to the x-axis and has a length of 6 units, then the value of a is:
(a) $2^{\pm 1/6}$ (b) $3^{\pm 1/6}$
(c) $6^{\pm 1/2}$ (d) $6^{\pm 1/3}$

25. If the equation $2^x + 4^y = 2^y + 4^x$ is solved for y in terms of x, where $x < 0$, then the sum of the solutions is:
(a) $x\log_2(1+2^x)$ (b) $x\log_2(1-2^x)$
(c) $x+\log_2(1+2^x)$ (d) $x+\log_2(1-2^x)$

ANSWER KEYS

1. (b)	**2.** (b)	**3.** (a)	**4.** (d)	**5.** (a),(c)	**6.** (d)	**7.** (d)	**8.** (b),(d)	**9.** (a)	**10.** (b)
11. (a)	**12.** (a)	**13.** (c)	**14.** (d)	**15.** (d)	**16.** (b)	**17.** (d)	**18.** (d)	**19.** (a)	**20.** (a)
21. (d)	**22.** (c)	**23.** (c)	**24.** (a)	**25.** (d)					

SOLUTIONS

1. (b) If we insert $\log_b a = x$, then the given inequality reduces to

$$(x-1)\left(\frac{1}{x}-1\right) > 0 \Rightarrow \frac{(x-1)^2}{x} < 0 \Rightarrow x < 0$$

$\Rightarrow \quad \log_b a < 0 \Rightarrow b < 1$ and $a > 1$ [It is given that $a > b$]

Now $\dfrac{\log_\pi a^{b-1}}{\log_e b^{a-1}} = \dfrac{(b-1)\log_\pi a}{(a-1)\log_e b} = \dfrac{(-\text{ve})(+\text{ve})}{(+\text{ve})(-\text{ve})} > 0.$

2. (b) Let

$$x = \frac{1}{3\sqrt{2}}\sqrt{4-\frac{1}{3\sqrt{2}}\sqrt{4-\frac{1}{3\sqrt{2}}\sqrt{4-\frac{1}{3\sqrt{2}}\ldots\ldots}}}$$

$\Rightarrow \quad x = \dfrac{1}{3\sqrt{2}}\sqrt{4-x}$

$\Rightarrow \quad 18x^2 = 4 - x$

$\Rightarrow \quad 18x^2 + x - 4 = 0$

$\Rightarrow \quad x = \dfrac{-1}{2}, \dfrac{4}{9}$

Since x cannot be –ve, we have

$$6+\log_{3/2}x = 6+\log_{3/2}\left(\frac{4}{9}\right)$$

$$= 6+\log_{3/2}\left(\frac{3}{2}\right)^{-2} = 6-2 = 4$$

3. (a) We have

$$\log_{0.3}(x-1) \le \frac{\log_{0.3}(x-1)}{\log_{0.3}0.09} = \frac{1}{2}\log_{0.3}(x-1)$$

$\Rightarrow \quad 2\log_{0.3}(x-1) \le \log_{0.3}(x-1)$

$\Rightarrow \quad (x-1)^2 \ge x-1$

$\Rightarrow \quad (x-1)(x-2) \ge 0$

$\Rightarrow \quad x \le 1$ or $x \ge 2$

Since $\log_{0.3}(x-1)$ is not defined for $x \le 1$, the required interval is $x \in [2, +\infty)$.

4. (d) The given function is defined for values of x satisfying the following:

$$\frac{x+2}{3-x} > 0 \text{ and } x+1 > 0 \text{ and } x+1 \ne 1$$

$\Rightarrow \quad -2 < x < 3$ and $x > -1$ and $x \ne 0$

Taking the intersection gives

$$-1 < x < 3 \text{ and } x \ne 0$$

5. (a),(c) The given equation reduces to

$$\frac{2}{\log_a x} + \frac{1}{\log_a(ax)} + \frac{3}{\log_a(a^2x)} = 0$$

$\Rightarrow \quad \dfrac{2}{t} + \dfrac{1}{1+t} + \dfrac{3}{2+t} = 0$ [Putting $\log_a x = t$]

$\Rightarrow \quad 6t^2 + 11t + 4 = 0$ gives $t = \dfrac{-1}{2}, \dfrac{-4}{3}$

Hence $x = a^{-1/2}, a^{-4/3}$.

6. (d) The given equation reduces to

$$\log_3\left(\frac{5^x - 2^x}{2^x - 3\cdot 5^x}\right) = 1$$

$\Rightarrow \quad 5^x - 2^x = 3(2^x - 3\cdot 5^x)$

$\Rightarrow \quad 10\cdot 5^x = 4\cdot 2^x$

$$\Rightarrow \quad \left(\frac{5}{2}\right)^x = \frac{2}{5} \text{ gives } x = -1$$

But the LHS and RHS of the given equation are not defined for $x = -1 \Rightarrow$ No solution.

7. (d) We have

$$e^{(\sin^2 x + \sin^4 x + \sin^6 x + \ldots)\ln 2} = e^{\left(\frac{\sin^2 x}{1-\sin^2 x}\right)\ln 2}$$

$$= e^{\tan^2 x \ln 2} = 2^{\tan^2 x}$$

The roots of the given quadratic equation are 1,8. Hence

$$2^{\tan^2 x} = 1,8 \text{ gives } \tan x = 0, \pm\sqrt{3}$$

Since $0 < x < \pi/2$, $\tan x = \sqrt{3}$ only. Hence

$$\frac{\cos x}{\cos x + \sin x} = \frac{\sqrt{3}-1}{2}$$

8. (b),(d) The given equation reduces to

$$\log 4 + \log\left(3^{1+\frac{1}{2x}}\right) = \log\left(3^{\frac{1}{x}} + 27\right)$$

$$\Rightarrow \quad 4\left(3^{1+\frac{1}{2x}}\right) = 3^{\frac{1}{x}} + 27$$

$$\Rightarrow \quad 4 \times 3^{1+\frac{1}{2x}} = 3^{\frac{1}{x}} + 27$$

$$\Rightarrow \quad 12 \times 3^{\frac{1}{2x}} = 3^{\frac{1}{x}} + 27$$

$$\Rightarrow \quad t^2 - 12t + 27 = 0 \text{ gives } t = 3, 9$$

$$\left[\text{Putting } 3^{\frac{1}{2x}} = t\right]$$

Hence $x = \frac{1}{2}, \frac{1}{4}$.

9. (a) The given equation reduces to

$$2^{2\log_2(\ln x)} = \ln x - \ln^2 x + 1$$

$$\Rightarrow \quad 2^{\log_2(\ln^2 x)} = \ln x - \ln^2 x + 1$$

$$\Rightarrow \quad \ln^2 x = \ln x - \ln^2 x + 1$$

$$\Rightarrow \quad 2\ln^2 x - \ln x - 1 = 0 \text{ gives } \ln x = \frac{-1}{2}, 1$$

Since $\log_2(\ln x)$ is not defined for $\ln x = \frac{-1}{2}$, $x = e$ is the only solution.

10. (b) The given equation reduces to

$$\frac{1}{3}\log_3 M + 3\log_3 N = 1 + \frac{\log 5}{\log(5^{-3})} = 1 - \frac{1}{3} = \frac{2}{3}$$

$$\Rightarrow \quad \log_3 M + 9\log_3 N = 2$$

$$\Rightarrow \quad \log_3 M + \log_3 N^9 = 2$$

$$\Rightarrow \quad MN^9 = 9$$

11. (a) The given equation reduces to

$$x + 1 = 2\log_2(2^x + 3) - \log_2(10 - 2^{-x})$$

$$\Rightarrow \quad 2^{x+1} = \frac{(2^x+3)^2}{10 - 2^{-x}}$$

$$\Rightarrow \quad 2y\left(10 - \frac{2}{y}\right) = (y+3)^2 \text{ [Putting } 2^x = y]$$

$$\Rightarrow \quad y^2 - 14y + 11 = 0$$

If $2^\alpha, 2^\beta$ are the roots of the above equation, then

$$2^\alpha \cdot 2^\beta = 11 \Rightarrow \alpha + \beta = \log_2 11.$$

12. (a) The given relation reduces to

$$y = x\log_3 2,$$

which represents a straight line with positive slope.

13. (c) Taking ln on both sides, the given equations reduce to

$$\ln 2 \ln(2x) = \ln 3 \ln(3y)$$

$$\Rightarrow \quad \ln^2 2 + \ln 2 \ln x = \ln^2 3 + \ln 3 \ln y \quad \ldots(1)$$

$$\text{and} \quad \ln 3 \ln x = \ln 2 \ln y \quad \ldots(2)$$

Eliminating $\ln y$ from the above equations, we get

$$\Rightarrow \quad \ln^2 2 + \ln 2 \ln x = \ln^2 3 + \frac{\ln^2 3}{\ln 2}\ln x$$

$$\Rightarrow \quad \left(\ln 2 - \frac{\ln^2 3}{\ln 2}\right)\ln x = \ln^2 3 - \ln^2 2$$

$$\Rightarrow \quad \ln x = -\ln 2 \text{ gives } x = \frac{1}{2}$$

14. (d) Let S denote the given expression. Then

$$S = 2\log_{10} x - \frac{\log_{10}(0.01)}{\log_{10} x} = 2\left(\log_{10} x + \frac{1}{\log_{10} x}\right)$$

Using the inequality $a + \frac{1}{a} \geq 2$ for $a > 0$, we have $S \geq 4$.

15. (d) We have

$$N=\frac{31!}{2^{31}\times 32!}=\frac{1}{2^{31}\times 32}=2^{-36}=8^{-12}$$

Hence $\log_8 N=-12$.

16. (b) Let $x=\frac{1}{3\sqrt{2}}\sqrt{4-\frac{1}{3\sqrt{2}}\sqrt{4-\frac{1}{3\sqrt{2}}\cdots}}$

$\Rightarrow \quad x=\frac{1}{3\sqrt{2}}\sqrt{4-x}$

$\Rightarrow \quad 18x^2+x-4=0$

$\Rightarrow \quad x=\frac{-1}{2},\frac{4}{9}$

The required value is $\log_{3/2}\left(\frac{4}{9}\right)=\log_{3/2}\left(\frac{3}{2}\right)^{-2}$

$=-2.$

17. (d) The given equation reduces to

$$\frac{6}{5}a^{\log_{10}x\log_a 5}-3^{\log_{10}x-1}=9^{\frac{\log_{10}x+1}{2}}$$

$\Rightarrow \quad \frac{6}{5}a^{\log_a 5^u}-\frac{1}{3}3^u=3\cdot 3^u$ [Insert $\log_{10}x=u$]

$\Rightarrow \quad \frac{6}{5}5^u=\frac{10}{3}3^u$

$\Rightarrow \quad \left(\frac{5}{3}\right)^u=\frac{25}{9}$ gives $u=2\Rightarrow x=100$

18. (d) The given equation reduces to

$$\frac{\log_a M}{\log_c M}=\frac{\log_a M-\log_b M}{\log_b M-\log_c M}$$

$\Rightarrow \quad \log_a M\log_M c=\frac{\log_a M\log_M b-1}{1-\log_c M\log_M b}$

$\Rightarrow \quad \log_a c=\frac{\log_a b-1}{1-\log_c b}$

$\Rightarrow \quad \log_a c-\log_a c\log_c b=\log_a b-1$

$\Rightarrow \quad \log_a c-\log_a b=\log_a b-\log_a a$

$\Rightarrow \quad \log_a c+\log_a a=2\log_a b$

$\Rightarrow \quad ac=b^2$

19. (a) Let $\log_{175}(5x)=\log_{343}(7x)=\lambda$

Then $\quad x=\frac{175^\lambda}{5}=\frac{343^\lambda}{7}$

$\Rightarrow \quad \frac{5^{2\lambda}\times 7^\lambda}{5}=\frac{7^{3\lambda}}{7}$

$\Rightarrow \quad 5^{2\lambda-1}=7^{2\lambda-1}$

$\Rightarrow \quad \lambda=1/2$ and hence $x=7^{1/2}$

Now $\quad \log_{42}\left(x^4-2x^2+7\right)=\log_{42}42=1.$

20. (a) We have

$$\log_2\sqrt{x+1}+\log_{1/2}\sqrt{4-x^2}>-1$$

$\Rightarrow \quad \log_2\sqrt{x+1}-\log_2\sqrt{4-x^2}>-1$

$\Rightarrow \quad \log_2\sqrt{\frac{x+1}{4-x^2}}>-1$

$\Rightarrow \quad \sqrt{\frac{x+1}{4-x^2}}>2^{-1}$

$\Rightarrow \quad \frac{x+1}{4-x^2}>\frac{1}{4}$

$\Rightarrow \quad \frac{x+1}{4-x^2}-\frac{1}{4}>0$

$\Rightarrow \quad \frac{4x+x^2}{4-x^2}>0$

$\Rightarrow \quad \frac{x(x+4)}{(x+2)(x-2)}<0\Rightarrow x\in(-4,-2)\cup(0,2)$

Now, the function $\log_2\sqrt{x+1}-\log_2\sqrt{4-x^2}$ is defined for

$$x>-1 \text{ and } -2<x<2$$

$\Rightarrow \quad x\in(-1,2).$

Taking the intersection, we have the required solution set $x\in(0,2)$.

21. (d) Let us first solve the following two inequalities:

First inequality

$$\frac{x-1}{x+2}>1$$

$\Rightarrow \quad \frac{-3}{x+2}>0$

$\Rightarrow \quad x<-2$

Second inequality

$$0<\frac{x-1}{x+2}<1$$

$\Rightarrow \quad \dfrac{x-1}{x+2} > 0$ and $\dfrac{x-1}{x+2} < 1$

$\Rightarrow \quad x \in (-\infty, -2) \cup (1, +\infty)$ and $x > -2$

$\Rightarrow \quad x > 1.$

Now, we shall solve the inequality

$\log_{\frac{x-1}{x+2}}\left\{\log_2\left(\dfrac{4x+1}{2x-3}\right)\right\} > 0$ for the following two cases:

Case 1: If $x < -2$, the given inequality reduces to

$$\log_2\left(\frac{4x+1}{2x-3}\right) > 1$$

$$\Rightarrow \quad \frac{4x+1}{2x-3} > 2$$

$$\Rightarrow \quad \frac{7}{2x-3} > 0 \quad \Rightarrow x > \frac{3}{2}$$

Taking the intersection with $x < -2$ gives no solution.

Case 2: If $x > 1$, the given inequality reduces to

$$\log_2\left(\frac{4x+1}{2x-3}\right) < 1$$

$$\Rightarrow \quad \frac{4x+1}{2x-3} < 2$$

$$\Rightarrow \quad \frac{7}{2x-3} < 0 \quad \Rightarrow x < \frac{3}{2}$$

Taking the intersection with $x > 1$ gives $x \in \left(1, \dfrac{3}{2}\right)$.

However, the function $\log_2\left(\dfrac{4x+1}{2x-3}\right)$ is not defined for $x \in \left(\dfrac{-1}{4}, \dfrac{3}{2}\right)$. Hence, no solution.

22. (c) Taking log on both sides, we get

$$\frac{3}{4}(\log_2 x)^2 + \log_2 x - \frac{5}{4} = \frac{1}{2}\log_x 2$$

$$\Rightarrow \quad \frac{3}{4}y^2 + y - \frac{5}{4} = \frac{1}{2y} \text{ [Putting } \log_2 x = y]$$

$$\Rightarrow \quad 3y^3 + 4y^2 - 5y - 2 = 0$$

$$\Rightarrow \quad (y-1)(y+2)(3y+1) = 0$$

$$\Rightarrow \quad \log_2 x = 1, -2, -1/3$$

$$\Rightarrow \quad x = 2, 2^{-2}, 2^{-1/3}$$

Hence, exactly three real solutions.

23. (c) We have

$$\log_\alpha a = 2, \log_{2\beta}(2b) = 4, \log_{4\gamma^2}(16c) = 5$$

$$\Rightarrow \quad a = \alpha^2, b = \frac{1}{2}(2\beta)^4, c = \frac{1}{16}\left(4\gamma^2\right)^5$$

Then $abc = 2^9\alpha^2\beta^4\gamma^{10}$.

Now, we have

$$\frac{\log\alpha}{3x-5y-z} = \frac{\log\beta}{x+8z} = \frac{\log\gamma}{-x+y-3z} = k \text{ (say)}$$

$$\Rightarrow \quad \log\alpha = k(3x-5y-z)$$

$$\log\beta = k(x+8z)$$

$$\log\gamma = k(-x+y-3z)$$

We see that

$$\log\alpha + 2\log\beta + 5\log\gamma = 0 \Rightarrow \alpha\beta^2\gamma^5 = 1$$

Hence $abc = 2^9\left(\alpha\beta^2\gamma^5\right)^2 = 2^9$.

24. (a) Let the coordinates of the two points be $P\left(\alpha, a^\alpha\right)$ and $Q\left(\beta, 2a^\beta\right)$. Now, since line PQ is parallel to the x-axis, the y coordinates of points P and Q must be the same (see figure.)

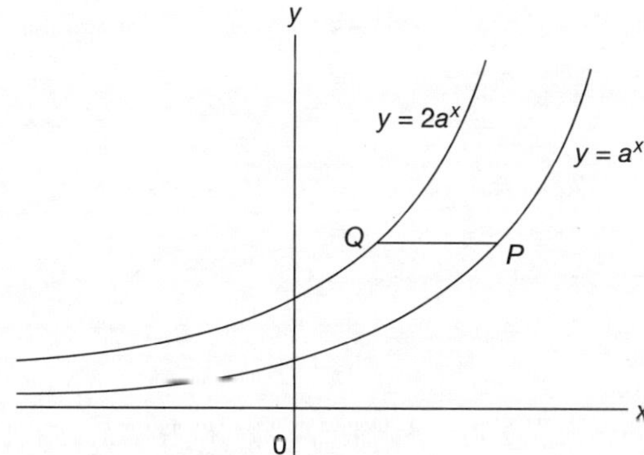

$$\Rightarrow \quad 2a^\beta = a^\alpha$$

And the distance between the points is 6

$$\Rightarrow \quad |\beta - \alpha| = 6$$

Putting $\beta = \alpha \pm 6$ in the first equation, we get

$$2a^{\alpha\pm6} = a^\alpha$$

$$\Rightarrow \quad a^{\pm6} = \frac{1}{2}$$

$$\Rightarrow \quad a = 2^{\pm1/6}$$

25. (d) The given equation reduces to

$$4^y - 2^y + 2^x - 4^x = 0$$

$$\Rightarrow \quad (2^y)^2 - 2^y + 2^x - 4^x = 0$$

The above equation is quadratic in 2^y. If $2^{y_1}, 2^{y_2}$ are the roots of the above equation, then

$$2^{y_1} \cdot 2^{y_2} = 2^x - 4^x$$

$$\Rightarrow \quad 2^{y_1+y_2} = 2^x\left(1-2^x\right)$$

$$\Rightarrow \quad y_1 + y_2 = \log_2\left\{2^x\left(1-2^x\right)\right\}$$

$$= x + \log_2\left(1-2^x\right)$$

CHAPTER

16 Limits and Continuity

- **Indeterminacy of a Function:** If a unique value cannot be assigned to $f(a)$, then $f(x)$ is said to be indeterminate at $x = a$. For example, the function $f(x) = \dfrac{x^2-4}{x-2}$ is indeterminate at $x = 2$ since $f(2) = 0/0$; we say that the function has indeterminacy of the type $0/0$ at $x = 2$.

  Types of Indeterminacy: $0/0 = 0 \cdot \infty = \infty/\infty, 1^\infty, 0^0, \infty^0, \infty - \infty$

- **Limit of a Function**

  1. We say that $f(x)$ has right-hand limit l at $x = a$, and write
  $$\lim_{h \to 0} f(a+h) = l$$
  if, for any number $\epsilon > 0$, there exists a corresponding number $\delta(\epsilon) > 0$ such that $|f(x) - l| < \epsilon$ holds true for all $a < x < a + \delta$.

     We say that $f(x)$ has left-hand limit l at $x = a$, and write
  $$\lim_{h \to 0} f(a-h) = l$$
  if, for any number $\epsilon > 0$, there exists a corresponding number $\delta(\epsilon) > 0$ such that $|f(x) - l| < \epsilon$ holds true for all $a - \delta < x < a$.

     We say that $f(x)$ has limit l at $x = a$, and write
  $$\lim_{x \to a} f(x) = l$$
  if, for any number $\epsilon > 0$, there exists a corresponding number $\delta(\epsilon) > 0$ such that $|f(x) - l| < \epsilon$ holds true for all $|x - a| < \delta$.

  2. We say that $f(x)$ has limit l as $x \to \infty$, and write
  $$\lim_{x \to \infty} f(x) = l$$
  if, for any number $\epsilon > 0$, there exists a corresponding number $N(\epsilon) > 0$ such that $|f(x) - l| < \epsilon$ holds true for all $|x| > N$.

- **Theorems on Limits**

  If $\lim_{x \to a} f(x) = l_1$ and $\lim_{x \to a} g(x) = l_2$, then

  1. $\lim_{x \to a} \{f(x) + g(x)\} = l_1 + l_2$
  2. $\lim_{x \to a} \{f(x) - g(x)\} = l_1 - l_2$
  3. $\lim_{x \to a} \{f(x) \cdot g(x)\} = l_1 \cdot l_2$
  4. $\lim_{x \to a} \dfrac{f(x)}{g(x)} = \dfrac{l_1}{l_2}$ if $l_2 \neq 0$
  5. $\lim_{x \to a} f\{g(x)\} = f(l_2)$
  6. $\lim_{x \to a} f(x)^{g(x)} = l_1^{l_2}$ if $l_1 > 0$ and $l_1 \neq 1$. If there is indeterminacy, express it as $\lim_{x \to a} e^{g(x) \cdot \ln f(x)}$. If l is the limit of the exponent, then the required limit is e^l.

Sandwich Theorem: If $g(x) \le f(x) \le h(x)$ for all x in the neighborhood of $x = a$ and $\lim_{x \to a} g(x) = l = \lim_{x \to a} h(x)$, then

$$\lim_{x \to a} f(x) = l$$

L' Hospital's Theorem: If the function $\dfrac{f(x)}{g(x)}$ has indeterminacy of the type $0/0$ or ∞/∞ at $x = a$, then

$$\lim_{x \to a} \frac{f(x)}{g(x)} = l = \lim_{x \to a} \frac{f'(x)}{g'(x)}$$

- **Some Useful Limits**

1. $\lim_{x \to a} \dfrac{x^n - a^n}{x - a} = na^{n-1}$

   Proof: Indeterminacy is of type (0/0). Hence, using L'Hospital's rule, we have $L = \lim_{x \to 0} \dfrac{nx^{n-1}}{1} = na^{n-1}$

2. $\lim_{x \to 0} \dfrac{\sin x}{x} = 1$

   Proof: Indeterminacy is of type (0/0). Hence, using L'Hospital's rule, we have $L = \lim_{x \to 0} \dfrac{\cos x}{1} = 1$

3. $\lim_{x \to 0} \dfrac{\tan x}{x} = 1$

   Proof: Indeterminacy is of type (0/0). Hence, using L'Hospital's rule, we have $L = \lim_{x \to 0} \dfrac{\sec^2 x}{1} = 1$

4. $\lim_{x \to 0} \dfrac{1 - \cos x}{x^2} = \dfrac{1}{2}$

   Proof: Indeterminacy is of type (0/0). Hence, using L'Hospital's rule, we have $L = \lim_{x \to 0} \dfrac{\sin x}{2x} = \dfrac{1}{2}$

5. $\lim_{x \to 0} (1 + x)^{\frac{1}{x}} = e$

   Proof: Indeterminacy is of type (1^∞). It can be written as $L = \lim_{x \to 0} e^{\frac{\ln(1+x)}{x}}$. Now

$$\lim_{x \to 0} \frac{\ln(1+x)}{x}\left(\frac{0}{0}\right) = \lim_{x \to 0} \frac{\frac{1}{1+x}}{x} = 1$$

   Hence $L = e^1 = e$.

6. $\lim_{x \to 0} \dfrac{a^x - 1}{x} = \ln a$

   Proof: Indeterminacy is of type (0/0). Hence, using L'Hospital's rule, we have $L = \lim_{x \to 0} \dfrac{a^x \ln a}{1} = \ln a$

7. $\lim_{x \to 0} \dfrac{\log_a (1 + x)}{x} = \dfrac{1}{\ln a}$

   Proof: Indeterminacy is of type (0/0). Hence, using L'Hospital's rule, we have $L = \lim_{x \to 0} \dfrac{\frac{1}{\ln a} \cdot \frac{1}{1+x}}{1} = \dfrac{1}{\ln a}$

8. $\lim_{x \to 0^+} x^x = 1$

   Proof: Indeterminacy is of type (0^0). It can be written as $L = \lim_{x \to 0^+} e^{x \ln x}$ Now

$$\lim_{x \to 0^+} x \ln x (0 \cdot \infty) = \lim_{x \to 0^+} \frac{\ln x}{1/x}\left(\frac{0}{0}\right) = \lim_{x \to 0^+} \frac{\frac{1}{x}}{\frac{-1}{x^2}} = \lim_{x \to 0}(-x) = 0$$

   Hence $L = e^0 = 1$.

- **Some Useful Series**

1. $(1+x)^n = 1 + nx + \frac{n(n-1)}{2!}x^2 + \frac{n(n-1)(n-2)}{3!}$
   $x^3 + \ldots$ for $|x| < 1$
2. $\sin x = x - \frac{x^3}{3!} + \frac{x^5}{5!} - \frac{x^7}{7!} + \ldots$ for $x \in \mathbf{R}$
3. $\cos x = 1 - \frac{x^2}{2!} + \frac{x^4}{4!} - \frac{x^6}{6!} + \ldots$ for $x \in \mathbf{R}$
4. $\tan x = x + \frac{x^3}{3} + \frac{2x^5}{15} + \frac{11x^7}{315} + \ldots$ for $x \in \mathbf{R}$
5. $e^x = 1 + x + \frac{x^2}{2!} + \frac{x^3}{3!} + \ldots$ for $x \in \mathbf{R}$
6. $\ln(1+x) = x - \frac{x^2}{2} + \frac{x^3}{3} - \frac{x^4}{4} + \ldots$ for $|x| < 1$

- **Continuity of a Function**: A function $f(x)$ is continuous:

1. At an interior point $x = c$ (point which has left as well as right neighbourhood) if
$$\lim_{x \to a} f(x) = f(c)$$
2. At a left-end point $x = a$ (point which has right neighbourhood only) if
$$\lim_{h \to 0} f(a+h) = f(a)$$
3. At a right-end point $x = b$ (point which has left neighbourhood only) if
$$\lim_{h \to 0} f(b-h) = f(b)$$
4. At all isolated points (points which do not have neighbourhood).
5. On an interval, if it is continuous everywhere in the interval.

EXERCISES

1. Match the columns:

(a) $\lim\limits_{x\to 1}\dfrac{\sqrt{x+8}-\sqrt{7x+2}}{\sqrt{x+3}-\sqrt{5-x}}$ (p) $\dfrac{-1}{8}$

(b) $\lim\limits_{x\to 2}\dfrac{\sqrt[3]{3x+2}-\sqrt[3]{x+6}}{\sqrt{x+7}-3\sqrt{x-1}}$ (q) $\dfrac{1}{5}$

(c) $\lim\limits_{x\to 0}\dfrac{\sqrt[5]{x+1}-1}{x}$ (r) –2

(d) $\lim\limits_{x\to 2}\log_2\left(\dfrac{\sqrt{3+\sqrt{9x+18}}-3}{x-2}\right)$ (s) –3

2. Match the columns:

(a) $\lim\limits_{x\to+\infty}\dfrac{\sqrt{x}+\sqrt[3]{x}-\sqrt[5]{x}}{\sqrt{4x-1}-\sqrt[4]{3x+2}}$ (p) $\dfrac{1}{6}$

(b) $\lim\limits_{x\to\infty}\left(\dfrac{2x^2}{2x-3}-\dfrac{3x^2}{3x-4}\right)$ (q) $\dfrac{1}{2}$

(c) $\lim\limits_{x\to\infty} x\left[\left(\dfrac{x+1}{x}\right)^{1/2}-1\right]$ (r) 1

(d) $\lim\limits_{x\to+\infty} x^{\frac{3}{2}}\left(\sqrt{x^3+1}-\sqrt{x^3-1}\right)$ (s) –1

3. Match the columns:

(a) $\lim\limits_{x\to 0}\dfrac{\sqrt{1-\cos x^2}}{1-\cos x}$ (p) $\dfrac{\pi}{2}$

(b) $\lim\limits_{x\to\frac{\pi}{2}}\dfrac{\sin(x\cos x)}{\cos(x\sin x)}$ (q) $\sqrt{2}$

(c) $\lim\limits_{x\to\frac{\pi}{2}}\dfrac{\tan(3x)}{\tan x}$ (r) 0

(d) $\lim\limits_{x\to\frac{\pi}{3}}\dfrac{\cos\left(x+\frac{\pi}{6}\right)}{(1-2\cos x)^{2/3}}$ (s) $\dfrac{1}{3}$

4. Match the columns:

(a) $\lim\limits_{x\to e^+}(x-e)^{\ln x-1}$ (p) 0

(b) $\lim\limits_{x\to+\infty}\left(\dfrac{x}{2x+1}\right)^x$ (q) 2

(c) $\lim\limits_{x\to 0}\left\{\tan\left(\dfrac{\pi}{4}+x\right)\right\}^{1/x}$ (r) e^{-1}

(d) $\lim\limits_{x\to 1}(\log_2 2x)^{\log_x 4}$ (s) e^2

5. Match the columns:

(a) $\lim\limits_{x\to 0}\dfrac{\ln(2-\cos 2x)}{\ln^2(\sin 3x+1)}$ (p) –4

(b) $\lim\limits_{x\to 0}\dfrac{e^{2x-3x^2}-e^{3x^2-2x}}{\ln(1-x+5x^2)}$ (q) $\dfrac{1}{2}$

(c) $\lim\limits_{n\to\infty}\dfrac{4^{3n-2}-9^{n+1}}{8^{2n-1}-9^{n-1}}$ (r) $\dfrac{2}{9}$

(d) $\lim\limits_{n\to\infty}\dfrac{1}{n\cot^{-1}n}$ (s) Does not exist

6. Match the columns:

(a) $\lim\limits_{x\to 0}\dfrac{8^x-4^x-2^x+1}{x^2}$ (p) 1/2

(b) $\lim\limits_{n\to\infty} n\left[1-n\ln\left(\dfrac{n+1}{n}\right)\right]$ (q) $2\ln^2 2$

(c) $\lim\limits_{x\to+\infty}\dfrac{x^x}{e^x}$ (r) e^2

(d) $\lim\limits_{x\to 1}\dfrac{1-x(1+|1-x|)}{|1-x|}\cos\left(\dfrac{1}{1-x}\right)$ (s) Does not exist

7. Match the columns:

(a) $\lim\limits_{x\to\infty}\left(\dfrac{1^{1/x}+2^{1/x}+3^{1/x}}{3}\right)^{3x}$ (p) 2

(b) $\lim\limits_{n\to\infty}\left(\dfrac{3}{n^3}\sum\limits_{1}^{n} r^2\right)^n$ (q) 6

(c) $\lim\limits_{x\to+\infty} x^{\frac{\ln 2}{1+\ln x}}$ (r) $e^{3/2}$

(d) $\lim\limits_{n\to\infty}\left(a^n+b^n\right)^{\frac{1}{n}}, b<a$ (s) Does not exist

8. Match the columns:

(a) $\lim_{x\to 0}\dfrac{x\tan 2x-2x\tan x}{(1-\cos 2x)^2}$ (p) 1

(b) $\lim_{x\to 0}\dfrac{\sin(2\pi\sec x)}{e^{x^2}-e^{-x^2}}$ (q) $\dfrac{1}{6}$

(c) $\lim_{x\to 0}\dfrac{\ln(1+x+x^2)+\ln(1-x+x^2)}{\sec x-\cos x}$ (r) $\dfrac{\pi}{2}$

(d) $\lim_{x\to 0}\dfrac{\cos(\sin x)-\cos x}{x^4}$ (s) $\dfrac{1}{2}$

9. The value of $\lim_{x\to 1/\alpha}\dfrac{1-\cos(cx^2+bx+a)}{(1-\alpha x)^2}$, where $a\alpha^2+b\alpha+c=0$, is:

(a) $\dfrac{b^2-ac}{\alpha^2}$ (b) $\dfrac{b^2-4ac}{\alpha^2}$

(c) $\dfrac{b^2-4ac}{2\alpha^2}$ (d) $\dfrac{b^2-ac}{2\alpha^2}$

10. The value of $\lim_{x\to 0}\dfrac{1-\cos x\cos 2x\cos 3x}{4x^2}$ is:

(a) $\dfrac{7}{4}$ (b) $\dfrac{5}{4}$

(c) $\dfrac{3}{4}$ (d) $\dfrac{1}{4}$

11. Which of the following limits exist as $x\to 0$? Here, $[x]$ denotes the greatest integer function and $\{x\}=x-[x]$.

(a) $\dfrac{\sin[x]}{x}$ (b) $\dfrac{\sin\{x\}}{x}$

(c) $\dfrac{\sin\{x^2\}}{x^2}$ (d) $\dfrac{\sin\{x^3\}}{x^3}$

12. The integer value of n for which $\lim_{x\to 0}\dfrac{(\cos x-1)(\cos x-e^x)}{x^n}$ is a non-zero finite number is:

(a) 4 (b) 3

(c) 2 (d) 1

13. If $\lim_{x\to 0}\dfrac{e^{\cos(x^n)}-e}{x^m}=\dfrac{-e}{2}$, then the value of $\dfrac{m}{n}$ is:

(a) 1 (b) 2

(c) 3 (d) 4

14. Let $L=\lim_{x\to 0}\dfrac{a-\sqrt{a^2-x^2}-\dfrac{x^2}{4}}{x^4}$. If L is finite, then:

(a) $a=-2, L=\dfrac{1}{64}$

(b) $a=2, L=\dfrac{1}{32}$

(c) $a=2, L=\dfrac{1}{64}$

(d) $a=1, L=\dfrac{1}{32}$

15. If $\lim_{x\to 1}\dfrac{(x-1)^n}{\ln\{\cos^m(x-1)\}}=-1$, then the values of m and n are:

(a) $m=2, n=2$

(b) $m=-2, n=2$

(c) $m=1, n=-1$

(d) $m=-1, n=1$

16. Function $f(x)$ is a cubic polynomial such that $\lim_{x\to 1}\dfrac{f(x)}{(x-1)^2}=-2$. Let $L=\lim_{x\to 3}\{1+f(x)\}^{\frac{1}{x-3}}$. If L exists, then the value of $f(4)-\ln L$ equals:

(a) 3 (b) 4

(c) 5 (d) 6

17. If $\lim_{x\to 0}\dfrac{x(1+a\cos x)-b\sin x}{x^3}=1$, then the values of a and b are:

(a) $a=1, b=\dfrac{3}{2}$

(b) $a=\dfrac{-1}{2}, b=2$

(c) $a=2, b=\dfrac{-1}{2}$

(d) $a=\dfrac{-5}{2}, b=\dfrac{-3}{2}$

18. If $\lim_{x\to -\infty} ax+\sqrt{x^2+bx}=3$, then the values of a and b are:

(a) $a=1, b=-4$

(b) $a=-1, b=-6$

(c) $a=-2, b=6$

(d) $a=1, b=-6$

19. If $\lim_{x\to 1}\left\{\frac{-ax+\sin(x-1)+a}{x+\sin(x-1)-1}\right\}^{\frac{1-x}{1-\sqrt{x}}}=\frac{1}{4}$, then the value of a is:
(a) $a=0$ (b) $a=-1$
(c) $a=1$ (d) $a=2$

20. The function $f(x)=\lim_{n\to+\infty}\frac{(x-1)^{2n}-1}{(x-1)^{2n}+1}$ is discontinuous at:
(a) $x=0$ and 2
(b) $x=0$ only
(c) $x=2$ only
(d) None of these

21. If $\lim_{x\to a}\frac{a^x-x^a}{x^x-a^a}=-1$, then the value of a is:
(a) 1 (b) 0
(c) e (d) $1/e$

22. The value of $\lim_{n\to\infty}n^2\left(x^{\frac{1}{n}}-x^{\frac{1}{n+1}}\right)$, where $x>0$, is:
(a) $\sqrt{1-x^2}$
(b) $x\ln x$
(c) $\ln x$
(d) $(1+x)e^x$

23. Let $f(x)$ be a differentiable function such that $f'(1)=4$ and $f'(2)=6$.

Then $\lim_{h\to 0}\frac{f(2h+2+h^2)-f(2)}{f(h-h^2+1)-f(1)}$ equals:
(a) Does not exist (b) $-3/2$
(c) $3/2$ (d) 3

24. Let $f:\mathbf{R}\to\mathbf{R}$ be a differentiable function such that $f(1)=3$ and $f'(1)=6$. Then $\lim_{x\to 0}\left\{\frac{f(1+x)}{f(1)}\right\}^{1/x}$ equals:
(a) 1 (b) e^2
(c) $e^{1/2}$ (d) e^3

25. The value of $\lim_{x\to\infty}x\left[\tan^{-1}\left(\frac{x+1}{x+2}\right)-\cot^{-1}\left(\frac{x+2}{x}\right)\right]$ is:
(a) $1/2$ (b) 2
(c) $-1/2$ (d) -2

26. Let $f(x)=8x^3+3x$. Then $\lim_{x\to\infty}\frac{f^{-1}(8x)-f^{-1}(x)}{x^{1/3}}$ equals:
(a) -2 (b) 2
(c) $-1/2$ (d) $1/2$

27. If $f(x)=\begin{cases}ax+b, & x<-1\\ x^2+1, & -1\le x<1\\ 3x-1, & x\ge 1\end{cases}$ is continuous everywhere, then the values that ab cannot take are:
(a) -2 (b) 0
(c) 2 (d) -4

28. Let $[x]$ denote the greatest integer less than or equal to x. The points at which the function $f(x)=[x]^2+[x^2]$, $x>0$ is discontinuous, are:
(a) $\{\sqrt{n}\}$, where $n\in\mathbf{N}$
(b) $\{\sqrt{n}\}$, where $n\in\mathbf{N}-\{1\}$
(c) $\{n\}$, where $n\in\mathbf{N}$
(d) $\{n^2\}$, where $n\in\mathbf{N}-\{1\}$

29. Let $[x]$ denote the greatest integer less than or equal to x. The integer points at which the function $f(x)=x\cos\{\pi(x+[x])\}$ is continuous are:
(a) 0 (b) -1
(c) 1 (d) 2

30. Let $f(x)=[x]\sin\left(\frac{\pi}{[x+1]}\right)$, where $[x]$ denotes the greatest integer function. The points of discontinuity of f in its domain are:
(a) $\left\{\frac{1}{n}\right\}$, where $n\in\mathbf{Z}-\{-1,0\}$
(b) $\mathbf{Z}-\{-1,0\}$
(c) $\mathbf{Z}-\{0\}$
(d) $\mathbf{Z}-\{-1\}$

31. Let $f(x)=\left[\frac{6x}{\pi}\right]\cos\left[\frac{3x}{\pi}\right]$, where $[x]$ denotes the greatest integer function. Of the following points, f is continuous at:
(a) $\pi/6$ (b) π
(c) $\pi/3$ (d) $\pi/4$

32. Let $f(x)=[x\sin(\pi x)]$, where $[x]$ denotes the greatest integer function. The correct options are:

(a) f is continuous in $[-1,1]-\{0\}$

(b) f is continuous in $[-1,1]$

(c) f is discontinuous at ± 1

(d) f is continuous at ± 1

33. Let $f(x)=[x-1]\cos\left\{\left(x-\frac{1}{2}\right)\pi\right\}$, where $[x]$ denotes the greatest integer function. Then f is:

(a) Continuous only at $x=1$

(b) Continuous for all real x

(c) Discontinuous only at $x=1$

(d) Discontinuous at all integer values of x, except $x=1$

34. If $0<a,b<1$ and $\tan^{-1}a+\tan^{-1}b=\frac{\pi}{4}$, then the value of $a+b-\frac{a^2+b^2}{2}+\frac{a^3+b^3}{3}+\ldots\infty$ is:

(a) ln6 (b) ln5

(c) ln3 (d) ln2

35. The value of $\sum_{n=1}^{\infty}\frac{n^2+6n+10}{(2n+1)!}$ is:

(a) $\frac{41e}{8}-\frac{19}{8e}+10$ (b) $\frac{41e}{8}+\frac{19}{8e}+10$

(c) $\frac{41e}{8}-\frac{19}{8e}-10$ (d) $\frac{41e}{8}+\frac{19}{8e}-10$

ANSWER KEYS

1. (a)-(r), (b)-(p), (c)-(q), (d)-(s) **2.** (a)-(q), (b)-(p), (c)-(q), (d)-(r) **3.** (a)-(q), (b)-(p), (c)-(s), (d)-(r)
4. (a)-(q), (b)-(p), (c)-(s), (d)-(s) **5.** (a)-(r), (b)-(p), (c)-(s), (d)-(s) **6.** (a)-(q), (b)-(p), (c)-(s), (d)-(s)
7. (a)-(q), (b)-(r), (c)-(p), (d)-(s) **8.** (a)-(s), (b)-(r), (c)-(p), (d)-(q) **9.** (c) **10.** (a) **11.** (c)
12. (b) **13.** (b) **14.** (c) **15.** (a) **16.** (c) **17.** (d) **18.** (d) **19.** (a) **20.** (a) **21.** (a)
22. (c) **23.** (d) **24.** (b) **25.** (a) **26.** (d) **27.** (a),(d) **28.** (b) **29.** (a) **30.** (b) **31.** (d)
32. (b),(c) **33.** (b) **34.** (d) **35.** (a)

SOLUTIONS

1. (a)-(r),(b)-(p),(c)-(q),(d)-(s)

(a) Rationalising the numerator and denominator, we get

$$L=\lim_{x\to1}\frac{(x+8)-(7x+2)}{(x+3)-(5-x)}\times\frac{\sqrt{x+3}+\sqrt{5-x}}{\sqrt{x+8}+\sqrt{7x+2}}$$

$$=\lim_{x\to1}\frac{-6(x-1)}{2(x-1)}\times\frac{\sqrt{x+3}+\sqrt{5-x}}{\sqrt{x+8}+\sqrt{7x+2}}$$

$$=\lim_{x\to1}\frac{-6}{2}\times\frac{\sqrt{1+3}+\sqrt{5-1}}{\sqrt{1+8}+\sqrt{7+2}}=-2$$

(b) Rationalising the numerator and denominator, we get

$$L=\lim_{x\to2}\frac{(3x+2)-(x+6)}{(x+7)-9(x-1)}$$

$$\times\frac{\sqrt{x+7}+3\sqrt{x-1}}{(3x+2)^{2/3}+(3x+2)^{1/3}(x+6)^{1/3}+(x+6)^{2/3}}$$

$$\left[\begin{array}{l}\text{Using } (a-b)(a+b)=a^2-b^2 \text{ for denominator}\\ \text{and } (a-b)(a^2+ab+b^2)=a^3-b^3 \text{ for numerator}\end{array}\right]$$

$$=\lim_{x\to2}\frac{2(x-2)}{-8(x-2)}$$

$$\times\frac{\sqrt{x+7}+3\sqrt{x-1}}{(3x+2)^{2/3}+(3x+2)^{1/3}(x+6)^{1/3}+(x+6)^{2/3}}$$

$$=\lim_{x\to2}\frac{2}{-8}\times\frac{\sqrt{2+7}+3\sqrt{2-1}}{(8)^{2/3}+(8)^{1/3}(8)^{1/3}+(8)^{2/3}}=\frac{-1}{8}$$

(c) Putting $x+1=t$, we have

$$L=\lim_{t\to-1}\frac{t^{1/5}-1}{t-1}=\frac{1}{5}$$

(d) Rationalising the numerator, we get

$$L=\lim_{x\to2}\log_2\left(\frac{\sqrt{9x+18}-6}{x-2}\times\frac{1}{\sqrt{3+\sqrt{9x+18}}+3}\right)$$

$$=\lim_{x\to2}\log_2\left(\frac{9x-18}{x-2}\times\frac{1}{\sqrt{3+\sqrt{9x+18}}+3}\times\frac{1}{6}\right)$$

$$=\log_2\left(\frac{9}{12\times6}\right)=\log_2\left(\frac{1}{8}\right)=-3$$

2. (a)-(q),(b)-(p),(c)-(q),(d)-(r)

(a) Taking $x^{1/2}$ common from the numerator and denominator, we have

$$L=\lim_{x\to+\infty}\frac{1+\frac{1}{x^{1/6}}-\frac{1}{x^{3/10}}}{\sqrt{4-\frac{1}{x}-\sqrt[4]{\frac{3}{x}}+\frac{2}{x^2}}}=\frac{1}{2}$$

(b) Combining the fractions and then taking the highest power of x as common from the numerator and denominator, we have

$$L=\lim_{x\to\infty}\frac{x^2}{(2x-3)(3x-4)}$$

$$=\lim_{x\to2}\frac{1}{\left(2-\frac{3}{x^2}\right)\left(3-\frac{4}{x^2}\right)}=\frac{1}{6}$$

(c) We have

$$L=\lim_{x\to\infty}\frac{\left(1+\frac{1}{x}\right)^{1/2}-1}{\frac{1}{x}}=\lim_{t\to1}\frac{t^{1/2}-1}{t-1}=\frac{1}{2}$$

[Putting $1+\frac{1}{x}=t$]

(d) Rationalising the numerator and then taking the highest power of x as common from the numerator and denominator, we have

$$L=\lim_{x\to+\infty}\frac{2x^{\frac{3}{2}}}{\sqrt{x^3+1}+\sqrt{x^3-1}}$$

$$=\lim_{x\to+\infty}\frac{2}{\sqrt{1+\frac{1}{x^{3/2}}}+\sqrt{1-\frac{1}{x^{3/2}}}}=1$$

3. (a)-(r),(b)-(p),(c)-(s),(d)-(r)

(a) We have

$$L=\lim_{x\to0}\sqrt{\frac{1-\cos x^2}{x^4}\times\frac{x^2}{1-\cos x}}=\frac{1}{\sqrt{2}}\times2=\sqrt{2}$$

(b) We have

$$L=\lim_{x\to\frac{\pi}{2}}\frac{\sin(x\cos x)}{x\cos x}\times\frac{x\cos x}{\cos(x\sin x)}$$

$$=\lim_{x\to\frac{\pi}{2}}\frac{x\cos x}{\cos(x\sin x)}\left(\frac{0}{0}\right)$$

Now, using L'Hospital's rule, we have

$$L=\lim_{x\to\frac{\pi}{2}}\frac{\cos x-x\sin x}{-\sin(x\sin x)[\sin x-x\cos x]}=\frac{\pi}{2}$$

(c) We have

$$L = \lim_{x\to\frac{\pi}{2}} \frac{\tan(3x)}{\tan x} = \lim_{x\to\frac{\pi}{2}} \frac{\frac{3\tan x - \tan^3 x}{1-3\tan^2 x}}{\tan x}$$

$$= \lim_{x\to\frac{\pi}{2}} \frac{3-\tan^2 x}{1-3\tan^2 x} = \lim_{x\to\frac{\pi}{2}} \frac{3\cot^2 x - 1}{\cot^2 x - 3} = \frac{1}{3}.$$

(d) Indeterminacy is of type (0/0). Hence, using L'Hospital's rule, we have

$$L = \lim_{x\to\frac{\pi}{3}} \frac{-\sin\left(x+\frac{\pi}{6}\right)}{\frac{2}{3}(1-2\cos x)^{-1/3} \times 2\sin x}$$

$$= \lim_{x\to\frac{\pi}{3}} \frac{-3\sin\left(x+\frac{\pi}{6}\right)}{4\sin x} \times (1-2\cos x)^{1/3} = 0$$

4. (a)-(q),(b)-(p),(c)-(s),(d)-(s)

(a) Indeterminacy is of type (0^0). It can be written as

$$L = \lim_{x\to e^+} \left\{(x-e)^{(x-e)}\right\}^{\frac{\ln x - 1}{x-e}}$$

Now $\lim_{x\to e^+} (x-e)^{(x-e)} = 1$ and

$$\lim_{x\to e^+} \frac{\ln x - 1}{x-e}\left(\frac{0}{0}\right) = \lim_{x\to e^+} \frac{1/x}{1} = \frac{1}{e}$$

Hence $L = 1^{1/e} = 1$.

(b) It is of type $\left(\frac{1}{2}\right)^{+\infty}$ and hence, the limiting value is 0.

(c) Indeterminacy is of type (1^∞). It can be written as

$$L = \lim_{x\to 0}\left(\frac{1+\tan x}{1-\tan x}\right)^{1/x} = \lim_{x\to 0}\left(1+\frac{2\tan x}{1-\tan x}\right)^{1/x}$$

$$= \lim_{x\to 0}\left\{\left(1+\frac{2\tan x}{1-\tan x}\right)^{\frac{1-\tan x}{2\tan x}}\right\}^{\frac{2\tan x}{x(1-\tan x)}} = e^2$$

(d) Indeterminacy is of type (1^∞). It can be written as

$$L = \lim_{x\to 1}\left\{(1+\log_2 x)^{\frac{1}{\log_2 x}}\right\}^{\log_2 x \times \log_x 4} = e^2$$

5. (a)-(r),(b)-(p),(c)-(s),(d)-(s)

(a) We have

$$L = \lim_{x\to 0} \frac{\ln(1+2\sin^2 x)}{\ln^2(\sin 3x + 1)} \times \frac{\ln(1+2\sin^2 x)}{\ln^2(\sin 3x+1)}$$

$$= \lim_{x\to 0} \frac{2\sin^2 x}{\sin^2(3x)} \quad [\ln(1+x) \sim x \text{ for small } x]$$

$$= \lim_{x\to 0} \frac{2x^2}{9x^2} = \frac{2}{9} \quad [\sin x \sim x \text{ for small } x]$$

(b) We have

$$L = \lim_{x\to 0} \frac{e^{3x^2-2x}\left(e^{4x-6x^2}-1\right)}{\ln\left(1-x+5x^2\right)}$$

$$= \lim_{x\to 0} \frac{4x-6x^2}{-x+5x^2} \quad [e^x - 1 \sim x \text{ and } \ln(1+x) \sim x \text{ for small } x]$$

$$= \lim_{x\to 0} \frac{4-6x}{-1+5x} = -4$$

(c) We have

$$L = \lim_{n\to\infty} \frac{4^{3n-2} - 9^{n+1}}{8^{2n-1} - 9^{n-1}}$$

$$= \lim_{n\to\infty} \frac{\frac{1}{16}(64^n) - 9(9^n)}{\frac{1}{8}(64^n) - \frac{1}{9}(9^n)} = \begin{cases} \lim_{n\to+\infty} \dfrac{\frac{1}{16} - 9\left(\frac{9}{64}\right)^n}{\frac{1}{8} - \frac{1}{9}\left(\frac{9}{64}\right)^n} = \dfrac{1}{2} \\ \lim_{n\to-\infty} \dfrac{\frac{1}{8}\left(\frac{64}{9}\right)^n - 9}{\frac{1}{8}\left(\frac{64}{9}\right)^n - \frac{1}{9}} = 81 \end{cases}$$

Hence, the limit does not exist.

(d) We have

$$L = \lim_{n\to\infty} \frac{1}{n\cot^{-1} n} = \begin{cases} \lim_{n\to+\infty} \dfrac{\frac{1}{n}}{\tan^{-1}\left(\frac{1}{n}\right)} = 1 \\ \lim_{n\to-\infty} \dfrac{\frac{1}{n}}{\pi + \tan^{-1}\left(\frac{1}{n}\right)} = 0 \end{cases}$$

Hence, the limit does not exist.

6. (a)-(q),(b)-(p),(c)-(s),(d)-(s)

(a) Indeterminacy is of type $0/0$. Hence, using L'Hospital's rule, we have

$$L = \lim_{x\to0} \frac{8^x \ln 8 - 4^x \ln 4 - 2^x \ln 2}{2x}\left(\frac{0}{0}\right)$$

$$= \lim_{x\to0} \frac{8^x \ln^2 8 - 4^x \ln^2 4 - 2^x \ln^2 2}{2}$$

$$= \frac{\ln^2 8 - \ln^2 4 - \ln^2 2}{2}$$

$$= \frac{9\ln^2 2 - 4\ln^2 2 - \ln^2 2}{2} = 2\ln^2 2$$

(b) We have

$$L = \lim_{n\to\infty} n\left[1 - n\ln\left(\frac{n+1}{n}\right)\right]$$

$$= \lim_{x\to0} \frac{1 - \frac{\ln(1+x)}{x}}{x} \quad [\text{Putting } 1/n = x]$$

$$= \lim_{x\to0} \frac{x - \ln(1+x)}{x^2}\left(\frac{0}{0}\right)$$

$$= \lim_{x\to0} \frac{1 - \frac{1}{1+x}}{2x} \quad [\text{Using L'Hospital's rule}]$$

$$= \lim_{x\to0} \frac{1}{2(1+x)} = \frac{1}{2}$$

(c) We have

$$L = \lim_{x\to+\infty} \frac{x^x}{e^x} = \lim_{x\to+\infty} \frac{e^{x\ln x}}{e^x}$$

$$= \lim_{x\to+\infty} e^{x(\ln x - 1)} = e^{+\infty} = \text{Does not exist}$$

(d) We have

$$\text{LHL} = \lim_{h\to0} \frac{\text{I} - (1-h)(1+h)}{h}\cos\left(\frac{\text{I}}{h}\right)$$

$$= \lim_{h\to0} h\cos\left(\frac{\text{I}}{h}\right)$$

$= 0\times$ (Number between -1 and 1) $= 0$

$$\text{RHL} = \lim_{h\to0} \frac{\text{I} - (1+h)(1+h)}{h}\cos\left(\frac{\text{I}}{h}\right)$$

$$= \lim_{h\to0} (h+2)\cos\left(\frac{\text{I}}{h}\right)$$

$= 2\times$ (Number between -1 and 1) $=$ Does not exist.

7. (a)-(q),(b)-(p),(c)-(p),(d)-(s)

(a) Indeterminacy is of type (1^∞). It can be written as $L = \lim_{x\to0}\left(\frac{1^x + 2^x + 3^x}{3}\right)^{3/x} = \lim_{x\to0} e^l$, where

$$l = \lim_{x\to0} \frac{3\left[\ln\left(1^x + 2^x + 3^x\right) - \ln 3\right]}{x}$$

$$= \lim_{x\to0} \frac{\frac{3\left[1^x \ln 1 + 2^x \ln 2 + 3^x \ln 3\right]}{1^x + 2^x + 3^x}}{1}$$

[Using L' Hospital's rule]

$= \ln 1 + \ln 2 + \ln 3 = \ln 6$

Hence $L = e^{\ln 6} = 6$.

(b) Indeterminacy is of type (1^∞). It can be written as

$$L = \lim_{n\to\infty}\left\{\frac{(n+1)(2n+1)}{2n^2}\right\}^n$$

$$= \lim_{n\to\infty}\left[\left(1 + \frac{3n+1}{2n^2}\right)^{\frac{2n^2}{3n+1}}\right]^{\frac{3n+1}{2n}} = e^{3/2}$$

(c) Indeterminacy is of type (∞^0). It can be written as $L = \lim_{x\to\infty} x^{\frac{\ln 2}{1+\ln x}} = \lim_{x\to\infty} e^l$, where

$$l = \lim_{x\to\infty} \frac{\ln 2 \ln x}{1+\ln x} = \ln 2 \times \lim_{x\to\infty} \frac{1}{1 + \frac{1}{\ln x}} = \ln 2$$

Hence $L = \lim_{x\to\infty} e^{\ln 2} = 2$.

(d) We have

$$L = \lim_{n\to\infty}\left(a^n + b^n\right)^{\frac{1}{n}} = \begin{cases} \lim_{n\to+\infty} a\left\{1 + \left(\frac{b}{a}\right)^n\right\}^{\frac{1}{n}} = a \\ \lim_{n\to-\infty} b\left\{1 + \left(\frac{a}{b}\right)^n\right\}^{\frac{1}{n}} = b \end{cases}$$

Hence, the limit does not exist.

8. (a)-(s),(b)-(r),(c)-(p),(d)-(q)

(a) We have

$$L = \lim_{x\to0} \frac{x\tan 2x - 2x\tan x}{4\sin^4 x}$$

$$= \lim_{x\to0} \frac{\frac{2\tan x}{1-\tan^2 x} - 2\tan x}{4x^3} \quad [\sin x \sim x \text{ for small } x]$$

$$= \lim_{x\to0} \frac{2\tan^3 x}{4x^3\left(1-\tan^2 x\right)}$$

$$= \lim_{x\to0} \frac{1}{2} \times \frac{\tan^3 x}{x^3} \times \frac{1}{1-\tan^2 x} = \frac{1}{2}$$

(b) We have

$$L=\lim_{x\to 0}\frac{-\sin(2\pi-2\pi\sec x)}{e^{-x^2}\left(e^{2x^2}-1\right)}[\sin x=-\sin(2\pi-x)]$$

$$=\lim_{x\to 0}\frac{2\pi\sec x-2\pi}{2x^2}\ [\sin x\sim x \text{ and } e^x-1\sim x \text{ for small } x]$$

$$=\lim_{x\to 0}\frac{\pi}{\cos x}\times\frac{1-\cos x}{x^2}=\frac{\pi}{2}$$

(c) We have

$$L=\lim_{x\to 0}\frac{\ln\left[\left(1+x+x^2\right)\left(1-x+x^2\right)\right]}{\sin^2 x\sec x}$$

$$=\lim_{x\to 0}\frac{\ln\left(1+x^2+x^4\right)}{\sin^2 x}\left(\frac{0}{0}\right)$$

$$=\lim_{x\to 0}\frac{x^2+x^4}{x^2}\ [\sin x\sim x \text{ and } \ln(1+x)\sim x \text{ for small } x]$$

$$=\lim_{x\to 0}1+x^2=1$$

(d) We have

$$L=\lim_{x\to 0}\frac{-2\sin\left(\dfrac{\sin x+x}{2}\right)\sin\left(\dfrac{\sin x-x}{2}\right)}{x^4}$$

$$=\lim_{x\to 0}\frac{-2(\sin x+x)(\sin x-x)}{4x^4}$$

$[\sin x\sim x$ for small $x]$

$$=\lim_{x\to 0}\frac{x^2-\sin^2 x}{2x^4}\left(\frac{0}{0}\right)=\lim_{x\to 0}\frac{2x-\sin(2x)}{8x^3}\left(\frac{0}{0}\right)$$

$$=\lim_{x\to 0}\frac{2-2\cos(2x)}{24x^2}=\lim_{x\to 0}\frac{\sin^2 x}{6x^2}=\frac{1}{6}$$

9. (c) We have

$$L=\lim_{x\to 1/\alpha}\frac{\left(cx^2+bx+a\right)^2}{2(1-\alpha x)^2}$$

$$\left[1-\cos x\sim\frac{1}{2}x^2 \text{ for small } x\right]$$

$$=\lim_{t\to\alpha}\frac{\left(at^2+bt+c\right)^2}{2t^2(t-\alpha)^2}\ \left[\text{Putting } x=\frac{1}{t}\right]$$

$$=\lim_{t\to\alpha}\frac{a^2(t-\alpha)^2(t-\beta)^2}{2t^2(t-\alpha)^2}$$

$$\left[at^2+bt+c=a(t-\alpha)(t-\beta)\right]$$

$$=\lim_{t\to\alpha}\frac{a^2(t-\beta)^2}{2t^2}=\frac{a^2(\alpha-\beta)^2}{2\alpha^2}$$

$$=\frac{a^2\left[(\alpha+\beta)^2-2\alpha\beta\right]}{2\alpha^2}=\frac{b^2-4ac}{2\alpha^2}$$

10. (a) We have

$$\cos x\cos 2x\cos 3x=\frac{1}{4}[\cos 2x-\cos 4x-\cos 6x]$$

Hence

$$L=\lim_{x\to 0}\frac{3-\cos 2x-\cos 4x-\cos 6x}{16x^2}$$

$$=\lim_{x\to 0}\frac{1}{16}\left[\frac{1-\cos 2x}{x^2}+\frac{1-\cos 4x}{x^2}+\frac{1-\cos 6x}{x^2}\right]$$

$$=\frac{1}{16}\times\frac{4+16+36}{2}=\frac{7}{4}$$

$$\left[1-\cos x\sim\frac{1}{2}x^2 \text{ for small } x\right]$$

11. (c) $[x]=-1$ on the left side and 0 on the right side of 0.

$\{x\}=x+1$ on the left side and x on the right side of 0.

$\{x^2\}=x^2$ on the left as well as right side of 0.

$\{x^3\}=x^3+1$ on the left side and x^3 on the right side of 0.

12. (b) We have

$$L=\lim_{x\to 0}\frac{\cos x-1}{x^2}\times\frac{\cos x-e^x}{x^{n-2}}$$

$$=\lim_{x\to 0}\frac{-1}{2}\times\frac{-\sin x-e^x}{(n-2)x^{n-3}}.\ [(0/0) \text{ type; hence, using L'Hospital's rule}]$$

The numerator approaches a finite number 1. Hence, for a non-zero limit to exist, $n=3$.

13. (b) We have

$$\lim_{t\to 0}\frac{e^{\cos t}-e}{t^c}=\frac{-e}{2}$$

$$\left[\text{Putting } x^n=t \text{ and } \frac{m}{n}=c\right]$$

$$\Rightarrow\quad \lim_{t\to 0}\frac{-e^{\cos t}\sin t}{ct^{c-1}}=\frac{-e}{2}\ [(0/0) \text{ type; hence, using L'Hospital's rule}]$$

$$\Rightarrow\quad \lim_{t\to 0}\frac{\sin t}{t^{c-1}}=\frac{c}{2}$$

$$\Rightarrow\quad c=2.$$

14. (c) We have

$$L=\lim_{x\to 0}\frac{a-\sqrt{a^2-x^2}-\dfrac{x^2}{4}}{x^4}\left(\frac{0}{0}\right)$$

The denominator approaches 0. Hence, for limit to exist, the numerator must also approach 0. Thus $a=\sqrt{a^2}=|a|\Rightarrow a\ge 0$. Now, using L'Hospital's rule, we get

$$L=\lim_{x\to 0}\frac{\dfrac{x}{\sqrt{a^2-x^2}}-\dfrac{x}{2}}{4x^3}$$

$$=\lim_{x\to 0}\frac{2-\sqrt{a^2-x^2}}{8x^2\sqrt{a^2-x^2}}$$

$$=\lim_{x\to 0}\frac{4-a^2+x^2}{x^2}\times\frac{1}{2+\sqrt{a^2-x^2}}\times\frac{1}{8\sqrt{a^2-x^2}}$$

[Rationalising the numerator]

The denominator approaches 0. Hence, for limit to exist, the numerator must also approach 0. Thus $4-a^2=0\Rightarrow a=2$ (taking the positive value only) and $L=\dfrac{1}{8|a|(2+|a|)}=\dfrac{1}{64}$.

15. (a) We have

$$L=\lim_{t\to 0}\frac{t^n}{m\ln(\cos t)}\quad[\text{Putting } x-1=t]$$

$$=\lim_{t\to 0}\frac{nt^{n-1}}{-m\tan t}$$

[(0/0) type; hence, using L'Hospital's rule]

Non-zero limit will exist only if $n-1=1$, and the limiting value in that case is $\dfrac{-n}{m}$, which is given to be –1. Hence $m=2, n=2$.

16. (c) We have

$\lim_{x\to 1}\dfrac{f(x)}{(x-1)^2}=-2\Rightarrow f(x)$ has a factor $(x-1)^2$

$\lim_{x\to 3}\{1+f(x)\}^{\frac{1}{x-3}}$ exists $\Rightarrow f(x)$ has a factor $x-3$

Thus $\quad f(x)=a(x-1)^2(x-3)$

[$f(x)$ is given to be cubic]

Now, the first limit $\lim_{x\to 1}\dfrac{a(x-1)^2(x-3)}{(x-1)^2}=-2$ gives $\alpha=1$.

Then $f(x)=(x-1)^2(x-3)$ and

$$L=\lim_{x\to 3}\{1+f(x)\}^{\frac{1}{f(x)}\cdot\frac{f(x)}{x-3}}=\lim_{x\to 3}e^{\frac{f(x)}{x-3}}$$

$$=\lim_{x\to 3}e^{\frac{(x-1)^2(x-3)}{x-3}}=e^4$$

Now $f(4)=9$ and $\ln L=4$. Hence $f(4)-\ln L=5$.

17. (d) We have

$$L=\lim_{x\to 0}\frac{x(1+a\cos x)-b\sin x}{x^3}\left(\frac{0}{0}\right)$$

$$=\lim_{x\to 0}\frac{(1+a\cos x)-ax\sin x-b\cos x}{3x^2}$$

[Using L'Hospital's rule]

$$=\lim_{x\to 0}\frac{1+(a-b)\cos x-ax\sin x}{3x^2}$$

The denominator approaches 0. Hence, for limit to exist, the numerator should also approach $0\Rightarrow 1+a-b=0$. Now L reduces to

$$L=\lim_{x\to 0}\frac{1-\cos x-ax\sin x}{3x^2}\left(\frac{0}{0}\right)$$

$$=\lim_{x\to 0}\frac{(1-a)\sin x-ax\cos x}{6x}$$

[Using L'Hospital's rule]

$$=\lim_{x\to 0}\frac{(1-a)\sin x}{6x}-\frac{a\cos x}{6}=\frac{1-2a}{6}$$

The value of L is given to be 1. Hence $a=\dfrac{-5}{2}, b=\dfrac{-3}{2}$.

Alternative: We have

$$L=\lim_{x\to 0}\frac{(1+a-b)x+\left(\dfrac{b}{6}-\dfrac{a}{2}\right)x^3}{x^3}$$

$\left[\cos x\sim 1-\dfrac{1}{2}x^2 \text{ and } \sin x\sim x-\dfrac{1}{6}x^3 \text{ for small } x\right]$

Thus, we have $1+a-b=0$ and

$$\frac{b}{6}-\frac{a}{2}=1\Rightarrow a=\frac{-5}{2}, b=\frac{-3}{2}$$

18. (d) We have

$$L = \lim_{x\to-\infty} \frac{(a^2-1)x^2 - bx}{ax - \sqrt{x^2+bx}} \text{ [Rationalising the numerator]}$$

For limit to exist, $a^2 - 1 = 0 \Rightarrow a = \pm 1$. Now L reduces to

$$L = \lim_{x\to-\infty} \frac{-bx}{ax - \sqrt{x^2+bx}}$$

$$= \lim_{x\to-\infty} \frac{-bx}{ax - |x|\sqrt{1+\frac{b}{x}}}$$

$$= \lim_{x\to-\infty} \frac{-b}{a + \sqrt{1+\frac{b}{x}}} = \frac{-b}{a+1}$$

The value of L is given to be 3. Hence $a = 1, b = -6$.

19. (a) The limiting value of the exponent is

$$l_1 = \lim_{x\to 1} 1 + \sqrt{x} - 2. \text{ [Rationalising the denominator]}$$

The limiting value of the base is

$$l_2 = \lim_{t\to 0} \frac{\sin t - at}{\sin t + t} \text{ [Putting } x - 1 = t\text{]}$$

$$= \lim_{t\to 0} \frac{\cos t - a}{\cos t + 1} \text{ [(0/0) type; hence, using L'Hospital's rule]}$$

$$= \frac{1-a}{2}$$

According to the given condition, we have

$$\left(\frac{1-a}{2}\right)^2 = \frac{1}{4}$$

$$\Rightarrow \frac{1-a}{2} = \frac{1}{2} \text{ [Exponential functions are defined only for positive bases]}$$

$$\Rightarrow a = 0$$

20. (a) The given function reduces to

$$f(x) = \begin{cases} -1, & |x-1| < 1 \\ 0, & |x-1| = 1 \\ 1, & |x-1| > 1 \end{cases} = \begin{cases} -1, & 0 < x < 2 \\ 0, & x = 0, 2 \\ 1, & x < 0 \text{ or } x > 2 \end{cases}$$

Hence, the given function is discontinuous at $x = 0$ and 2.

21. (a) We have

$$\lim_{x\to a} \frac{a^x - x^a}{x^x - a^a} = -1$$

$$\Rightarrow \lim_{x\to a} \frac{a^x - x^a}{e^{x\ln x} - a^a} = -1$$

$$\Rightarrow \lim_{x\to a} \frac{a^x \ln a - ax^{a-1}}{e^{x\ln x}(1+\ln x)} = -1$$

[(0/0) type; hence, using L'Hospital's rule]

$$\Rightarrow \frac{\ln a - 1}{\ln a + 1} = -1 \Rightarrow \ln a = 0 \Rightarrow a = 1$$

22. (c) We have

$$L = \lim_{t\to 0} \frac{x^t - x^{\frac{t}{t+1}}}{t^2} \text{ [Inserting } 1/n = t\text{]}$$

$$= \lim_{t\to 0} x^{\frac{t}{t+1}} \times \frac{x^{\frac{t^2}{t+1}} - 1}{t^2}$$

$$= \lim_{t\to 0} x^{\frac{t}{t+1}} \times \frac{x^{\frac{t^2}{t+1}} - 1}{\frac{t^2}{t+1}} \times \frac{1}{t+1} = \ln x$$

23. (d) We have

$$L = \lim_{h\to 0} \frac{f(2h+2+h^2) - f(2)}{f(h-h^2+1) - f(1)} \left(\frac{0}{0}\right)$$

$$= \lim_{h\to 0} \frac{(2+2h) f'(2h+2+h^2)}{(1-2h) f'(h-h^2+1)}$$

[Using L'Hospital's rule]

$$= \frac{2f'(2)}{f'(1)} = -1$$

24. (b) Indeterminacy is of type 1^∞. It can be written as

$$L = \lim_{x\to 0} e^{\frac{\ln\{f(1+x)\} - \ln\{f(1)\}}{x}}$$

The exponent, say l, has indeterminacy of type $(0/0)$. Hence, using L'Hospital's rule, we have

$$l = \lim_{x\to 0} \frac{\frac{f'(1+x)}{f(1+x)}}{1} = \frac{f'(1)}{f(1)} = 2.$$

Hence $L = e^2$.

25. (a) We have

$$L = \lim_{x\to\infty} \frac{\tan^{-1}\left(\frac{x+1}{x+2}\right) - \tan^{-1}\left(\frac{x}{x+2}\right)}{1/x} \left(\frac{0}{0}\right)$$

$$= \lim_{t \to 1} \frac{\tan^{-1}(t) - \tan^{-1}(2t-1)}{\frac{t-1}{1-2t}}$$

$$\left[\text{Putting } \frac{x+1}{x+2} = t\right]$$

$$= \lim_{t \to 1} (1-2t) \frac{\tan^{-1}(t) - \tan^{-1}(2t-1)}{t-1}$$

$$= \lim_{t \to 1} (1-2t) \times \frac{\frac{1}{1+t^2} - \frac{2}{1+(2t-1)^2}}{1}$$

[Using L'Hospital's rule]

$$= 1/2$$

26. (d) For large x, the function $f(x) = 8x^3 + 3x \sim 8x^3$. Thus $f^{-1}(x) = \frac{1}{2}x^{1/3}$. Hence

$$L = \lim_{x \to \infty} \frac{\frac{1}{2}(8x)^{1/3} - \frac{1}{2}(x)^{1/3}}{x^{1/3}} = \frac{1}{2}$$

27. (a),(d) The function is already continuous at $x = 1$, since $f(1) = f(1^+) = f(1^-) = 2$. For continuity at $x = -1$, $b - a = 2$.

Then $ab = a(a+2) = (a+1)^2 - 1 \geq -1$

28. (b) The given function has been defined on $x > 0$. It may have discontinuities at all such points where x or x^2 is an integer.

$$\Rightarrow \quad x = \{\sqrt{n}\}, \text{ where } n \in \mathbf{N}$$

Let us check for continuity at $x = \sqrt{n}$. We have

$$f(\sqrt{n}) = [\sqrt{n}]^2 - n$$

$$\lim_{h \to 0} f(\sqrt{n} + h)$$

$$= \lim_{h \to 0} \left([\sqrt{n} + h]^2 - [n + h(2\sqrt{n} + h)] \right)$$

$$= [\sqrt{n}]^2 - n$$

and

$$\lim_{h \to 0} f(\sqrt{n} - h) = \lim_{h \to 0} \left([\sqrt{n} - h]^2 - [n - h(2\sqrt{n} - h)] \right)$$

$$= \begin{cases} [\sqrt{n}]^2 - (n-1) \text{ if } \sqrt{n} \neq \text{integer} \\ (\sqrt{n} - 1)^2 - (n-1) \text{ if } \sqrt{n} = \text{integer} \end{cases}$$

We see that the three values will be equal only for $n = 1$. Hence, the function is discontinuous at

$$x = \{\sqrt{n}\}, \text{ where } n \in \mathbf{N} - \{1\}.$$

29. (a) At any integer, say $x = k$, we have

$$f(k) = k \cos\{2k\pi\} = k$$

$$\lim_{h \to 0} f(k+h) = k \cos\{2k\pi\} = k$$

and $$\lim_{h \to 0} f(k-h) = k \cos\{(2k-1)\pi\} = -k$$

We see that the three values will be equal only for $k = 0$.

30. (b) Since $[x+1] = [x] + 1$, the given function can be written as

$$f(x) = [x] \sin\left(\frac{\pi}{[x]+1}\right),$$

which is defined for $x \in \mathbf{R} - [-1, 0)$.

At any integer, say $x = k\ (k \neq -1)$, we have

$$f(k) = k \sin\left(\frac{\pi}{k+1}\right)$$

$$\lim_{h \to 0} f(k+h) = k \sin\left(\frac{\pi}{k+1}\right)$$

and $$\lim_{h \to 0} f(k-h) = (k-1) \sin\left(\frac{\pi}{k}\right)$$

We see that the three values do not match, so there is a discontinuity at all integers. However, since the function is not defined on the left side of $x = 0$, for checking continuity at 0, we only need to compare $f(0)$ with the RHL value. Since these two values are equal, the function is continuous at 0.

31. (d) The given function is defined on **R**. It may have discontinuities at points where $\frac{6x}{\pi}$ or $\frac{3x}{\pi}$ is an integer.

$$\Rightarrow \quad x = \frac{m\pi}{6} \text{ or } \frac{n\pi}{3}, \text{ where } m \text{ and } n \text{ are integers}$$

$$\Rightarrow \quad x = \frac{k\pi}{6}, \text{ where } k \text{ is an integer}$$

Let us check for continuity at $x = \frac{k\pi}{6}$, where k is an integer. We have

$$f\left(\frac{k\pi}{6}\right)=k\cos\left[\frac{k}{2}\right]$$

$$\lim_{h\to 0} f\left(\frac{k\pi}{6}+h\right)=\lim_{h\to 0}\left[k+\frac{\pi}{6}h\right]\cos\left[\frac{k}{2}+\frac{3}{\pi}h\right]$$

$$=k\cos\left[\frac{k}{2}\right]$$

and

$$\lim_{h\to 0} f\left(\frac{k\pi}{6}-h\right)=\lim_{h\to 0}\left[k-\frac{\pi}{6}h\right]\cos\left[\frac{k}{2}-\frac{3}{\pi}h\right]$$

$$=\begin{cases}(k-1)\cos\left(\dfrac{k}{2}-1\right), \text{ if } k \text{ is even}\\ (k-1)\cos\left[\dfrac{k}{2}\right], \text{ if } k \text{ is odd}\end{cases}$$

We see that the three values do not match, so there is a discontinuity at all such points.

Only $\frac{\pi}{4}$ does not belong to the above set.

32. (b),(c) The given function is even. For $0 \le x \le 1$, we have

$$0 \le \pi x \le \pi$$

$$\Rightarrow \quad 0 \le \sin(\pi x) \le 1$$

$$\Rightarrow \quad 0 \le x\sin(\pi x) \le 1$$

$$\Rightarrow \quad [x\sin(\pi x)]=0$$

$$\Rightarrow \quad f(x)=0,\ x\in[0,1]$$

$$\Rightarrow \quad f(x)=0,\ x\in[-1,1] \text{ since } f \text{ is even.}$$

Hence, f is continuous in $[-1,1]$.

Now, we have

$$\lim_{h\to 0} f(1+h)=\lim_{h\to 0}[(1+h)\sin(\pi+\pi h)]$$

$$=\lim_{h\to 0}[-(1+h)\sin(\pi h)]$$

$$=\lim_{h\to 0}[-(1+h)\pi h]=-1$$

[Using $\sin x \sim x$ if x is small]

We have already seen that $\lim_{h\to 0} f(1-h)=0=f(1)$. Thus, f is discontinuous at $x=1$ and hence also at $x=-1$, since f is even. Hence, f is discontinuous at $x=\pm 1$.

33. (b) The given function that can be written as $f(x) = [x - 1]\sin(\pi x)$ is defined on **R**. It may have discontinuities at points where $x - 1$ is an integer $\Rightarrow$ where x is an integer. Let us check for continuity at $x = k$, where k is an integer. We have

$$f(k)=[k-1]\sin(\pi x)=0$$

$$\lim_{h\to 0} f(k+h)=\lim_{h\to 0}[k-1+h]\sin(k\pi+\pi h)$$

$$=(k-1)\sin(k\pi)=0$$

and

$$\lim_{h\to 0} f(k-h)=\lim_{h\to 0}[k-1-h]\sin(k\pi-\pi h)$$

$$=(k-2)\sin(k\pi)=0$$

We see that the three values match, so there is continuity at all such points. Hence, f is continuous for all real x.

34. (d) We have

$$\tan^{-1}\left(\frac{a+b}{1-ab}\right)=\frac{\pi}{4}$$

$$\Rightarrow \quad a+b=1-ab$$

$$\Rightarrow \quad (1+a)(1+b)=$$

Hence, we have

$$S=\left(a-\frac{a^2}{2}+\frac{a^3}{3}-\ldots\right)+\left(b-\frac{b^2}{2}+\frac{b^3}{3}-\ldots\right)$$

$$=\ln(1+a)+\ln(1+b)$$

$$=\ln\{(1+a)(1+b)\}=\ln 2$$

35. (a) Let $S=\sum_{n=1}^{\infty}\frac{n^2+6n+10}{(2n+1)!}$. Putting $2n+1=k$, we have

$$S=\sum_{n=1}^{\infty}\frac{n^2+6n+10}{(2n+1)!}$$

$$=\sum_{k=3,5,7,\ldots}^{\infty}\frac{\frac{(k-1)^2}{4}+3(k-1)+10}{k!} \quad \left[\text{Putting } 2n+1=k\right]$$

$$=\frac{1}{4}\sum_{k=3,5,7,\ldots}^{\infty}\frac{k^2+10k+29}{k!}$$

$$=\frac{1}{4}\sum_{k=3,5,7,\ldots}^{\infty}\frac{k(k-1)+11k+29}{k!}$$

$$=\frac{1}{4}\sum_{k=3,5,7,\ldots}^{\infty}\left[\frac{1}{(k-2)!}+\frac{11}{(k-1)!}+\frac{29}{k!}\right]$$

$$=\frac{1}{4}\left[\left(1+\frac{1}{3!}+\frac{1}{5!}+\ldots\right)+11\left(\frac{1}{2!}+\frac{1}{4!}+\ldots\right)\right.$$

$$\left.+29\left(\frac{1}{3!}+\frac{1}{5!}+\ldots\right)\right]$$

Now, using the series

$$e^x = 1 + x + \frac{x^2}{2!} + \frac{x^3}{3!} + \ldots$$

and $$e^{-x} = 1 - x + \frac{x^2}{2!} - \frac{x^3}{3!} + \ldots,$$ we have

$$S = \frac{1}{4}\left[\left(\frac{e-e^{-1}}{2}\right) + 11\left(\frac{e+e^{-1}-2}{2}\right) + 29\left(\frac{e-e^{-1}-2}{2}\right)\right]$$

$$= \frac{1}{4}\left[\frac{41e}{2} - \frac{19}{2e} + 40\right] = \frac{41e}{8} - \frac{19}{8e} + 10$$

CHAPTER

17 Investigating Functions

- A rule f from set A to set B is called a function if it assigns a unique element $f(x)$ in B to every element in A. In simpler words, a function is a computer program that gives a unique output in B for every element in A. In this definition, set A is a subset of the domain of f and set B contains $f(A)$. Hence, there may be elements in B having no pre-image in A but every element in A must have an image in B.
- A function is even symmetric about $x = 0$ if $f(-x) = f(x)$; it is odd symmetric about $x = 0$ if $f(-x) = -f(x)$. A function is even symmetric about $x = \frac{c}{2}$ if $f(c-x) = f(x)$; it is odd symmetric about $x = \frac{c}{2}$ if $f(c-x) = -f(x)$.
- To find whether $f : A \to B$ is one–one or many–one:
  1. Start with the proposition that there are two distinct values x_1, x_2 in the domain of f such that $f(x_1) = f(x_2)$. On further simplification, if it reduces to $x_1 = x_2$, then $f : A \to B$ is one one; otherwise, it is many–one.
  2. Draw the graph of $y = f(x)$. If no horizontal line intersects the curve more than once, then $f : A \to B$ is one–one; otherwise, it is many–one.
  3. For a continuous function, check its monotonicity; if the function monotonically increases/decreases, then it is one–one; otherwise, it is many–one.
- To find out whether $f : A \to B$ is onto or into: First find the range $f(A)$ and then compare it with the co-domain B. If $f(A) = B$, then $f : A \to B$ is onto; if $f(A) \subset B$, then $f : A \to B$ is into.
- To find the range of $f(x)$ over a domain A:
  1. Let $y = f(x)$. Express x in terms of y as $x = g(y)$. Since $x \in A$, the values of y for which $g(y) \in A$ is the required range.
  2. Find the intervals in which $f(x)$ increases/decreases using the sign of the first derivative. Find the range of extreme values for each monotonic interval; their union is the range of $f(x)$ over domain A.
- To find the inverse of $f : A \to B$: For inverse to exist, $f : A \to B$ must be bijective (one–one and onto). If it is bijective, then let $y = f(x)$ and express x in terms of y as $x = g(y)$. Now, $g(x) : B \to A$ is the inverse function.
- Drawing the graph of a function:
  1. Find the domain of the function, if it is not given.
  2. Find out if the function is even/odd/periodic. If it is even/odd, you need to plot only one half, say $x \geq 0$; the other half is its mirror image in the y axis if it is an even function, and the negative of its mirror image in the y-axis if it is an odd function. If it is periodic, you need to plot in only one periodic interval and then repeat the plot.
  3. Once you have decided upon the interval where you have to plot the graph, find the intervals in which $f(x)$ increases/decreases using the sign of the first derivative. Find the extreme values for each monotonic interval; now plot each interval by connecting the two extremes.
- Some useful tips for curve plotting: Suppose you already know the graph of $y = f(x)$.
  1. The graph of $y - \beta = f(x - \alpha)$ is obtained by translating the graph of $y = f(x)$ by α units along the $+x$-axis and by β units along the $+y$-axis.

2. The graph of $y = -f(x)$ is obtained by taking the mirror image of the graph of $y = f(x)$ in the x-axis.
3. The graph of $y = |f(x)|$ is obtained by taking the mirror image of the negative portion (lying below the x-axis) of the graph of $y = f(x)$ in the x-axis; the portion lying the above the x-axis is drawn as it is.
4. The graph of $y = f(|x|)$ is obtained by deleting the portion of the graph of $y = f(x)$ that lies to the left of the y-axis, and then taking the mirror image of the remaining portion in the y-axis.

EXERCISES

1. A periodic function f satisfies the relation $f(x-4)+f(x+4)=f(x)$ for every $x \in \mathbf{R}$. The period of f is:
(a) 8 (b) 12
(c) 16 (d) 24

2. A periodic function f satisfies the relation $f(x)+f(x+3)+f(x+6)+\ldots+f(x+42)=\text{constant}$ for every $x \in \mathbf{R}$. The period of f is:
(a) 81 (b) 45
(c) 9 (d) 1

3. Let f be a continuous function defined for $1 \le x \le 3$. If $f(x)$ takes rational values for all x and $f(2)=10$, then $f(1.5)$ equals:
(a) 1 (b) 1.5
(c) 3 (d) 10

4. If f is a linear function which maps $(-1,1)$ onto $(0,2)$, then $f(x)$ equals:
(a) $x-1$ (b) $-x+1$
(c) $x+1$ (d) None of these

5. Match the functions with their range:
(a) $|x|+|-x|$ (p) $\mathbf{Z}$
(b) $[x]+[-x]$ (q) $\{0\}$
(c) $[-x]-[x]$ (r) $[0,+\infty)$
(d) $\sqrt{x}+\sqrt{-x}$ (s) $\{-1,0\}$

6. The domain and range of the function $f(x)=\sqrt{\sin^{-1}(2x)+\dfrac{\pi}{6}}$ are:
(a) $x \in \left[\dfrac{-1}{4},\dfrac{1}{2}\right]$ and $f(x) \in \left[0,\sqrt{\dfrac{2\pi}{3}}\right]$
(b) $x \in \left[0,\dfrac{1}{4}\right]$ and $f(x) \in \left[0,\sqrt{\dfrac{\pi}{3}}\right]$
(c) $x \in \left[\dfrac{-1}{4},0\right]$ and $f(x) \in \left[0,\sqrt{\dfrac{\pi}{6}}\right]$
(d) $x \in \left[\dfrac{-1}{4},\dfrac{1}{2}\right]$ and $f(x) \in \left[0,\sqrt{\dfrac{\pi}{3}}\right]$

7. Let $f:\mathbf{R}\to\mathbf{R}$ be any function. If we define $g:\mathbf{R}\to\mathbf{R}$, where $g(x)=\dfrac{1}{f(x)}$, then g is:
(a) Onto if f is onto
(b) One–one if f is one–one
(c) Continuous if f is continuous
(d) Differentiable if f is differentiable

8. Let f be an even function defined on the interval $(-5,5)$. If the equation $f(x)=f\left(\dfrac{x+1}{x+2}\right)$ has four real roots, then their sum is:
(a) -1 (b) -2
(c) -4 (d) $-2\sqrt{5}$

9. Let f be a real-valued and differentiable function in its domain such that $f(x+y)=\dfrac{f(x)+f(y)}{1-f(x)f(y)}$ and $f'(0)=3$. Then:
(a) $\lim\limits_{x\to 0}\dfrac{f(x)}{f\left(\dfrac{x}{3}\right)}=3$
(b) $f(1)>f\left(\dfrac{1}{2}\right)$
(c) $f\left(\dfrac{\tan^{-1}x}{3}\right)$ is one–one
(d) $f(x)$ has period $\dfrac{\pi}{3}$

10. If $f(x)=\sin x+\cos x$ and $g(x)=x^2-1$, then $gof(x)$ is invertible in the domain:

(a) $\left[0,\frac{\pi}{2}\right]$ (b) $\left[\frac{\pi}{4},\frac{3\pi}{4}\right]$

(c) $\left[\frac{-\pi}{2},\frac{\pi}{2}\right]$ (d) $[0,\pi]$

11. If the function $f:[a,+\infty)\to[b,+\infty)$ is defined by $f(x)=2^{x(x-1)}$, then the minimum values of a and b so that $f(x)$ is invertible are:

(a) 0 and 1 (b) 0 and 1

(c) 2^{-1} and 2^{-4} (d) 2 and 2^4

12. If $f:[1,+\infty)\to[2,+\infty)$ is given by $f(x)=x+\frac{1}{x}$, then $f^{-1}(x)$ equals:

(a) $\frac{x+\sqrt{x^2-4}}{2}$ (b) $\frac{x}{1+x^2}$

(c) $\frac{x-\sqrt{x^2-4}}{2}$ (d) None of these

13. Consider the function $f(x)=\frac{b-x}{1-bx}, x\in[0,1]$, where $0<b<1$. Then $f^{-1}(x)$ equals:

(a) $\frac{b+x}{1+bx}, x\in[0,b]$ (b) $\frac{1+bx}{b+x}, x\in[-b,1]$

(c) $\frac{1-bx}{b-x}, x\in[b,1]$ (d) $\frac{b-x}{1-bx}, x\in[-1,b]$

14. Let $f(x)$ be defined as $2^x+2^{f(x)}=1$. Then $f^{-1}(x)$ equals:

(a) $\frac{2^x}{1-2^x}, x\in(0,1)$

(b) $\log_2(1-2^x), x\in(-\infty,0)$

(c) $\log_2\left(\frac{2^x}{1-2^x}\right), x\in(-\infty,0)$

(d) None of these

15. Suppose $f(x)=(x+1)^2, x\ge-1$. If $g(x)$ is the function whose graph is a reflection of the graph of $f(x)$ in the line $y=x$, then $g(x)$ equals:

(a) $\sqrt{x}-1, x\ge0$ (b) $\frac{1}{(x+1)^2}, x>-1$

(c) $\sqrt{x+1}, x\ge-1$ (d) $-\sqrt{x}-1, x\ge0$

16. If $g\{f(x)\}=|\sin x|$ and $f\{g(x)\}=\sin^2\sqrt{x}$, then:

(a) $f(x)=\sin^2 x, g(x)=\sqrt{x}$

(b) $f(x)=|\sin x|, g(x)=x^2$

(c) $f(x)=x^2, g(x)=\sin\sqrt{x}$

(d) f and g cannot be determined

17. If $f(x)=(x+1)^2-1, x\ge-1$, then the set $\{x:f(x)=f^{-1}(x)\}$ is:

(a) $\{-1,0\}$ (b) $\{-1,0,1\}$

(c) $\{0,1,\pm\sqrt{3}\}$ (d) $\{\ \}$

18. Let $f(x)=\frac{ax}{x+1}, x\ne-1$. Then the function $fof(x)$ will be identically equal to x, if a equals:

(a) $\sqrt{2}$ (b) -1

(c) 1 (d) $-\sqrt{2}$

19. Let $g(x)=1+x-[x]$ and $f(x)=\begin{cases}-1, & x<0\\ 0, & x=0\\ 1, & x>0\end{cases}$. Then the range of the function $fog(x)-gof(x)$ is:

(a) $\{-1,1\}$ (b) $\{-1,0,1\}$

(c) $[-1,1]$ (d) $\{0\}$

20. Let $f(x)=x^2$ and $g(x)=\sin x$. Then the set of all x satisfying the equation $fogogof(x)=gogof(x)$ is:

(a) $\pm\sqrt{n\pi}, n=0,1,2,\ldots$

(b) $\pm\sqrt{n\pi}, n=1,2,3,\ldots$

(c) $\frac{\pi}{2}+2n\pi, n=0,\pm1,\pm2,\ldots$

(d) $2n\pi, n=1,2,3,\ldots$

21. The domain of definition of the function $f(x)=\sin^{-1}\left\{\frac{8\times3^{x-2}}{1-3^{2(x-1)}}\right\}$ is:

(a) $(-\infty,-1)\cup(1,+\infty)$ (b) $(-\infty,0)\cup(0,+\infty)$

(c) $[2,+\infty)$ (d) $(-\infty,0]\cup[2,+\infty)$

22. Arrange the numbers $2^{800},3^{600},5^{400},6^{200}$ in decreasing order, beginning with the greatest and ending with the smallest:

(a) $2^{800},3^{600},5^{400},6^{200}$ (b) $6^{200},3^{600},5^{400},2^{800}$

(c) $3^{600},5^{400},2^{800},6^{200}$ (d) $5^{400},3^{600},2^{800},6^{200}$

23. Let a, b be two arbitrary real numbers satisfying $a^2 + b^2 = 10$. The largest possible value of $|a + 2b|$ is:
(a) $5\sqrt{2}$ (b) $2\sqrt{5}$
(c) 5 (d) 10

24. The number of real solutions of $1 + |e^x - 1| = e^x(e^x - 2)$ is:
(a) 0 (b) 1
(c) 2 (d) 4

25. The number of real solutions of $3^x - (\ln 2)x - 1 = 0$ is:
(a) 0 (b) 1
(c) 2 (d) 4

26. The number of real solutions of $x^2 - 2x = [x+1]$ is:
(a) 0 (b) 1
(c) 2 (d) 4

27. The number of real solutions of $e^{\sin x} - |\sin x| = 0$ in $x \in [0, 2\pi]$ is:
(a) 0 (b) 1
(c) 2 (d) 4

28. For all $x \in (0,1)$, the correct statements from the following are:
(a) $e^x \le 1 + x$ (b) $\ln(1+x) \le x$
(c) $\sin x \ge x$ (d) $\ln x \ge x$

29. The number of real solutions of $\log_4(x-1) = \log_2(x-3)$ is:
(a) 0 (b) 1
(c) 2 (d) 4

30. The set of all real numbers x for which $x^2 - |x+2| + x > 0$ is:
(a) $|x| > 2$ (b) $|x| > \sqrt{2}$
(c) $|x| > 1$ (d) $(\sqrt{2}, +\infty)$

31. The number of solutions of $xe^{\sin x} - \cos x = 0$ in $x \in \left(0, \frac{\pi}{2}\right)$ is:
(a) 0 (b) 1
(c) 2 (d) 4

32. The number of real solutions of
$2\cos\left(\frac{x^2 + x}{6}\right) = 2^x + 2^{-x}$ is:
(a) 0 (b) 1
(c) 2 (d) 4

33. Let $f(x) = \frac{x^2 - 1}{x^2 + 1}$. Then the least value of $f(x)$:
(a) Does not exist because $f(x)$ is unbounded
(b) Does not exist even though $f(x)$ is unbounded
(c) Is equal to 1
(d) Is equal to -1

34. If $f(x) = x^2 + 2bx + 2c^2$ and $g(x) = -x^2 - 2cx + b^2$ such that $\min f(x) > \max g(x)$, then:
(a) $0 < c < b\sqrt{2}$ (b) $|c| < |b|\sqrt{2}$
(c) $|c| > |b|\sqrt{2}$ (d) None of these

35. If $f(x) = \sin^2 x + \sin^2\left(x + \frac{\pi}{3}\right) + \cos x \cos\left(x + \frac{\pi}{3}\right)$ and $g\left(\frac{5}{4}\right) = 1$, then:
(a) $g\{f(x)\} = 1$ (b) $f\{g(x)\} = \frac{5}{4}$
(c) $f\left(\frac{5}{4}\right) > f(1)$ (d) $f'\left(\frac{5}{4}\right) > f'(1)$

36. Let $A = \{(x, y) : x^2 + y^4 \le 1\}$ and $B = \{(x, y) : x^4 + y^6 \le 1\}$. Then:
(a) $B \subseteq A$
(b) $A \subseteq B$
(c) $A - B, B - A$ and $A \cap B$ are non-empty
(d) None of these

37. The domain of definition of the function $f(x) = \log_2 \log_x (x^2 - 9x + 9)$ is:
(a) $(8, +\infty)$ (b) $(0, +\infty) - \{1, 8\}$
(c) $(1, 8)$ (d) $(0, 1)$

38. Consider the function $f(x) = (\sqrt{3}\cos x + \sin x)(\sin x + \cos x)$. The correct statements among the following are:
(a) Mean value of $f(x) = 0$
(b) $f(x)$ has period π
(c) $f(x)$ is a constant function
(d) $f(x)$ is always positive

39. The range of the function $f(x) = \frac{x^2 + x + 2}{x^2 + x + 1}$ is:
(a) $(1, +\infty)$ (b) $(1, 11/7]$
(c) $(1, 7/3]$ (d) $(1, 7/11]$

40. Let $f(x)=\dfrac{\tan x}{\tan 3x}$. The set of values that f does not take is:

(a) $[0,3]$ (b) $\left[\frac{1}{3},3\right]$

(c) $\left[0,\frac{1}{3}\right]$ (d) $\left[\frac{1}{3},\frac{2}{3}\right]$

41. If $f(x)=2\tan^{-1}\left(e^{-x}\right)-\frac{\pi}{2}$, then $f(x)$ is:

(a) Even and increasing on **R**
(b) Even and decreasing on **R**
(c) Odd and increasing on **R**
(d) Odd and decreasing on **R**

42. Intervals in which function $f(x)=\tan^{-1}(\sin x+\cos x)$ increases are:

(a) $\left(\frac{-\pi}{2},\frac{\pi}{2}\right)$ (b) $\left(\frac{\pi}{8},\frac{5\pi}{4}\right)$

(c) $\left(0,\frac{\pi}{8}\right)$ (d) $\left(\frac{-5\pi}{8},\frac{-\pi}{8}\right)$

43. The range of the function $f(x)=\sqrt{\log_{0.3}\left|\frac{x-2}{x}\right|}$ is:

(a) $\left[0,\frac{1}{3}\right]\cup[1,+\infty)$ (b) $[0,1]-\left\{\frac{1}{3}\right\}$

(c) $[0,1]$ (d) $[0,+\infty)$

44. The function $f(x)=ax+b\sin x$ will be one–one iff:

(a) $|a|=|b|$ (b) $|a|<|b|$

(c) $|a|>|b|$ (d) None of these

ANSWER KEYS

1. (d) **2.** (b) **3.** (d) **4.** (b),(c) **5.** (a)-(r),(b)-(s),(c)-(p),(d)-(q) **6.** (a) **7.** (b) **8.** (c)
9. (a),(c),(d) **10.** (b) **11.** (c) **12.** (a) **13.** (d) **14.** (b) **15.** (a) **16.** (a) **17.** (a)
18. (b) **19.** (d) **20.** (a) **21.** (d) **22.** (c) **23.** (a) **24.** (b) **25.** (c) **26.** (b) **27.** (c)
28. (b) **29.** (b) **30.** (b) **31.** (b) **32.** (a) **33.** (d) **34.** (c) **35.** (a),(b) **36.** (b) **37.** (a)
38. (b) **39.** (c) **40.** (b) **41.** (d) **42.** (c),(d) **43.** (d) **44.** (c)

SOLUTIONS

1. (d) Given $f(x-4)+f(x+4)=f(x)$ ...(1)

Putting $x+4$ for x, we have

$$f(x)+f(x+8)=f(x+4) \quad ...(2)$$

From (1) and (2), we have $f(x+8)=-f(x-4)$.

Putting $x+4$ for x, we have

$$f(x+12)=-f(x) \quad ...(3)$$

Putting $x+12$ for x, we have

$$f(x+24)=-f(x+12) \quad ...(4)$$

From (3) and (4), we have

$$f(x+24)=f(x)$$

Hence, the period equals 24.

2. (b) Given

$$f(x)+f(x+3)+f(x+6)+...+f(x+42)=\text{constant}$$

Putting $x+3$ for x, we have

$$f(x+3)+f(x+6)+f(x+9)+...+f(x+45)=\text{constant}$$

Subtracting the two, we have $f(x)-f(x+45)=0$.

Hence, the period equals 5.

3. (d) Between any two rational numbers, howsoever close, there exist an infinite number of irrational numbers. A continuous function cannot take two rational values without taking irrational values.

Hence, the given function must be a constant function.

4. (b),(c) The graph of the function is a straight line joining points (–1,0) and $(1,2)\Rightarrow x+1$

or a straight line joining points (–1,2) and $(1,0)\Rightarrow -x+1$

5. (a)-(r),(b)-(s),(c)-(p),(d)-(q)

(a) $|x|+|-x|=2|x|$

Hence range $=[0,+\infty]$.

(b) $[x]+[-x]=[I+f]+[-I-f]$

$$=\begin{cases} I+(-I)=0, & f=0 \\ I+(-I-1)=-1, & f\neq 0 \end{cases}$$

Hence range $=\{-1,0\}$.

(c) $[-x]-[x]=[-I-f]-[I+f]$

$$=\begin{cases} (-I)-(I)=-2I, & f=0 \\ (-I-1)-(I)=-2I-1, & f\neq 0 \end{cases}$$

Hence range = $\mathbf{Z}$ (set of all integers).

(d) $\sqrt{x}+\sqrt{-x}$ is defined only for $x=0$.

Hence range $=\{0\}$.

6. (a) The given function is defined for values of x satisfying

$$|2x|\le 1 \Rightarrow \frac{-1}{2}\le x\le \frac{1}{2}$$

and

$$\sin^{-1}(2x)\ge \frac{-\pi}{6}\Rightarrow 2x\ge \sin\left(\frac{-\pi}{6}\right)\Rightarrow x\ge \frac{-1}{4}$$

Intersection gives domain $=\left[\frac{-1}{4},\frac{1}{2}\right]$.

Since the function is strictly increasing, its range

$$=\left[f\left(\frac{-1}{4}\right),f\left(\frac{1}{2}\right)\right]=\left[0,\sqrt{\frac{2\pi}{3}}\right]$$

7. (b) If f is onto, it will be zero for some x and g will not be defined for that x. Hence, (a) is incorrect.

If f is one–one, then $f(x_2)=f(x_1)\Rightarrow x_2=x_1$. In that case, $g(x_2)=g(x_1)\Rightarrow f(x_2)=f(x_1)\Rightarrow x_2=x_1$.

Hence, (b) is correct.

If f is continuous and is not zero for any x, then g will be continuous, but if f is zero for some x, then g will have a discontinuity. Hence, (c) is incorrect.

The derivative function of g is $g'(x)=\frac{-f'(x)}{f^2(x)}$. We see that g' will not exist if f equals zero, even if f' exists. Hence, (d) is incorrect.

8. (c) The given equation reduces to

$$\frac{x+1}{x+2}=\pm x$$

$$\Rightarrow \quad x^2+x-1=0 \text{ or } x^2+3x+1=0.$$

Sum of the roots $=(-1)+(-3)=-4$

9. (a),(c),(d) The given condition is satisfied by the family of functions $f(x)=\tan(cx)$. The condition $f'(0)=3$ is satisfied only if $c=3$. Hence $f(x)=\tan(3x)$.

(a) $\lim_{x\to0}\dfrac{f(x)}{f\left(\dfrac{x}{3}\right)}=\lim_{x\to0}\dfrac{\tan(3x)}{\tan x}=3$. Hence correct.

(b) $f(1)=\tan3<0$ since 3 lies in the second quadrant, whereas $f\left(\dfrac{1}{2}\right)=\tan\left(\dfrac{3}{2}\right)>0$, since $3/2$ lies in the first quadrant. Hence incorrect.

(c) $f\left(\dfrac{\tan^{-1}x}{3}\right)=\tan\left(\tan^{-1}x\right)=x$, which is one–one. Hence correct.

(d) $f(x)$ has period $\dfrac{\pi}{3}$. Hence correct.

10. (b) We have

$$gof(x)=(\sin x+\cos x)^2-1=\sin(2x)$$

It is a periodic function having period π. The maximum interval over which it is monotonic (increasing/decreasing) is $\pi/2$.
Options (c) and (d) are definitely incorrect since they have lengths greater than $\pi/2$. Option (a) is also incorrect as the function increases in $(0,\pi/4)$ and then decreases in $(\pi/4,\pi/2)$. Option (b) is correct as the function monotonically decreases in $(\pi/4,3\pi/4)$.

11. (c) The given function can be written as

$$f(x)=2^{\left(x-\frac{1}{2}\right)^2-\frac{1}{4}}$$

We see that $f(x)$ decreases in $(-\infty,1/2)$ and increases in $(1/2,+\infty)$. For invertibility, the function must be one–one and onto.

Hence, we must choose $a=\dfrac{1}{2}$ and $b=f\left(\dfrac{1}{2}\right)=2^{-4}$.

12. (a) The first derivative $f'=1-\dfrac{1}{x^2}$ is always positive, for $x>1\Rightarrow f$ strictly increases in the given domain $[1,+\infty)$ and the range of f is $[f(1),f(+\infty))=[2,+\infty)$. Hence, f is one–one and onto $\Rightarrow$ Invertible.
To find its inverse, let

$$y=x+\frac{1}{x},\ \text{where}\ x\in[1,+\infty),\ y\in[2,+\infty)$$

$$\Rightarrow\quad x^2-yx+1=0$$

$$\Rightarrow\quad x=\frac{y\pm\sqrt{y^2-4}}{2}$$

Since $x\ge1$, the only choice is

$$x=\frac{y+\sqrt{y^2-4}}{2}$$

Now, substituting x for y, we get the inverse function

$$f^{-1}(x)=\frac{x+\sqrt{x^2-4}}{2},\ x\in[2,+\infty)$$

13. (d) The given function can be written as

$$f=\frac{b^2-bx}{b(1-bx)}=\frac{b^2-1+1-bx}{b(1-bx)}=\frac{1-b^2}{b(bx-1)}+\frac{1}{b}$$

Since $\dfrac{1-b^2}{b}$ is a positive number and $bx-1$ is an increasing function, f strictly decreases in the given domain $[0,1]$. Hence, f is one–one $\Rightarrow$ Invertible.
The range of f is $[f(1),f(0)]=[-1,b]$.
To find its inverse, let

$$y=\frac{b-x}{1-bx}$$

$$\Rightarrow\quad x=\frac{b-y}{1-by},\ \text{where}\ x\in[0,1],\ y\in[-1,b]$$

Now, substituting x for y, we get the inverse function

$$f^{-1}(x)=\frac{b-x}{1-bx},\ x\in[-1,b]$$

14. (b) The given function can be written as

$$f(x)=\log_2\left(1-2^x\right)$$

The function is defined for values of x satisfying $2^x<1\Rightarrow x<0$. Also, the function is strictly decreasing since $f'(x)<0$. Hence, it is one–one $\Rightarrow$ Invertible.
We see that interchanging the positions of x and $f(x)$ does not change the given relation. This means that the graph of the given relation is symmetrical about the line $y=x$ and hence, the inverse of the given function is identically equal to the function itself. That is

$$f^{-1}(x)=\log_2\left(1-2^x\right),\ x\in(-\infty,0)$$

15. (a) The given function is strictly increasing and its range is $[f(-1),f(+\infty))=[0,+\infty)$. The function g is the inverse of f.
To find g, let

$$y=(x+1)^2,\ \text{where}\ x\in[-1,+\infty),\ y\in[0,+\infty)$$

$$\Rightarrow\quad x=-1\pm\sqrt{y}$$

Since $x \geq -1$, we have only one choice

$$x = -1+\sqrt{y}$$

Now, substituting x for y, we get the inverse function

$$g(x) = -1+\sqrt{x}, x \in [0,+\infty)$$

16. (a) In option (a), $f\{g(x)\} = \sin^2\sqrt{x}$ and

$$g\{f(x)\} = \sqrt{\sin^2 x} = |\sin x|$$

17. (a) Since f and f^{-1} can intersect only along the line $y = x$, solving the equation $f(x) = f^{-1}(x)$ is the same as solving the equation $f(x) = x$.

$\Rightarrow \quad (x+1)^2 - 1 = x$ gives $x = -1, 0$

18. (b) We have

$$fof(x) = \frac{af}{f+1} = \frac{a\left(\dfrac{ax}{x+1}\right)}{\dfrac{ax}{x+1}+1} = \frac{a^2x}{(a+1)x+1},$$

which will be identically equal to x if $a = -1$.

19. (d) We have

$$gof(x) = 1+f-[f] = \begin{cases} 1, & x<0 \\ 1, & x=0 \\ 1, & x>0 \end{cases} = 1, x \in \mathbf{R}$$

and $\quad fog(x) = \begin{cases} -1, & g<0 \\ 0, & g=0 \\ 1, & g>0 \end{cases} = 1, \; x \in \mathbf{R}$

[Since $g = 1+\{x\} > 0$ always]

Hence $\quad fog(x) - gof(x) = 0, x \in \boldsymbol{R}$.

20. (a) The given equation can be written as

$$\{\sin\sin(x^2)\}^2 = \sin\sin(x^2) \left[t^2 = t \Rightarrow t = 0,1\right]$$

$\Rightarrow \quad \sin\sin(x^2) = 0, 1$

$\Rightarrow \quad \sin(x^2) = n\pi, \frac{\pi}{2}+2n\pi$, where $n = 0, \pm 1, \pm 2, \ldots$

Since $|\sin x| \leq 1$, the only solution is

$$\sin(x^2) = 0$$

$\Rightarrow \quad x^2 = n\pi, n = 0, 1, 2, \ldots$

$\Rightarrow \quad x = \pm\sqrt{n\pi}, n = 0, 1, 2, \ldots$

21. (d) The given function is defined for values of x satisfying

$$\left|\frac{8\times 3^{x-2}}{1-3^{2(x-1)}}\right| \leq 1$$

$\Rightarrow \quad \left|\frac{8}{9}(3^x)\right| \leq \left|1-\frac{1}{9}(3^{2x})\right|$

$\Rightarrow \quad 64t^2 \leq (9-t^2)^2$ [Putting $3^x = t$ and squaring both sides]

$\Rightarrow \quad t^4 - 82t^2 + 81 \geq 0$

$\Rightarrow \quad (t^2-1)(t^2-1) \geq 0$

$\Rightarrow \quad 3^{2x} \leq 1$ or $3^{2x} \geq 81$

$\Rightarrow \quad x \leq 0$ or $x \geq 2$

22. (c) The given numbers can be written as $2^{800}, 3^{600}, 5^{400}, 6^{200} = 16^{200}, 27^{200}, 25^{200}, 6^{200}$.

Now, they can be easily arranged in descending order.

23. (a) Let $a = \sqrt{10}\cos t$ and $b = \sqrt{10}\sin t$. Then

$$|a+2b| = \sqrt{10}\,|\cos t + 2\sin t| \leq \sqrt{10}\sqrt{5} = \sqrt{50}$$

24. (b) The given equation can be written as

$$1+|t| = (t+1)(t-1) \text{ [Putting } e^x - 1 = t]$$

$\Rightarrow \quad t^2 - |t| - 2 = 0$

Taking two cases:

$t < 0 \Rightarrow t^2 + t - 2 = 0$ gives $t = -2$

or $\quad t \geq 0 \Rightarrow t^2 - t - 2 = 0$ gives $t = 2$

Hence, we have

$$e^x - 1 = \pm 2$$

$\Rightarrow \quad e^x = -1, 3$ gives only one solution $x = \ln 3$.

25. (c) From the graph, we can see that there are two solutions. At $x = 0$, the slope of 3^x is $\ln 3$, which is greater than the slope of the line $(\ln 2)x+1$.

26. (b) The given equation can be written as

$$x^2 - 2x = [x]+1$$

$\Rightarrow \quad (x-1)^2 - 2 = [x]$

The graph of the function $(x-1)^2 - 2$ is a parabola with concavity along the +ve y-axis and vertex at $(1,-2)$. From the graph, we can see that there is only one solution.

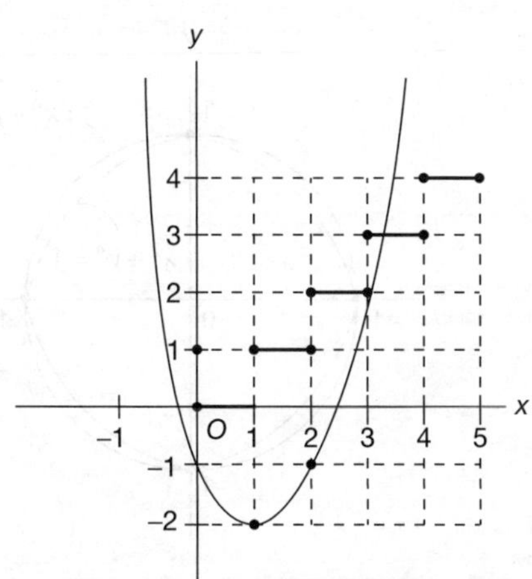

27. (c) The figure shows the graph of three functions: $\sin x$, $e^{\sin x}$ and $|\sin x|$. The function $e^{\sin x}$ has the same monotonocity and period as the $\sin x$ function. From the graph, we see that the functions $e^{\sin x}$ and $|\sin x|$ intersect at two distinct points. Hence, two solutions.

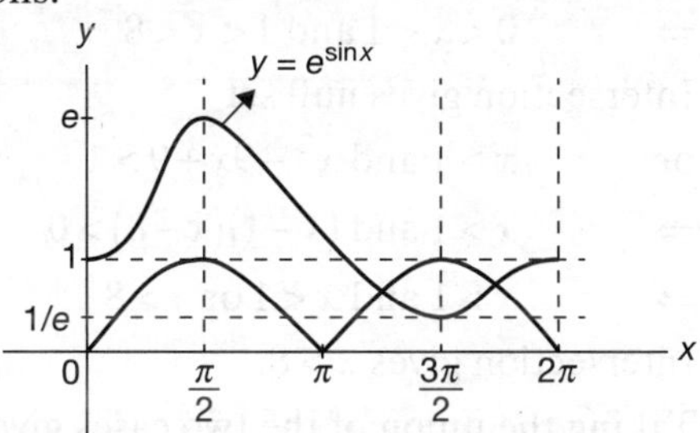

28. (b) From the graph, we can see that $\ln(1+x) \le x$. At $x = 0$, their slopes are equal, and hence they touch each other at the origin.

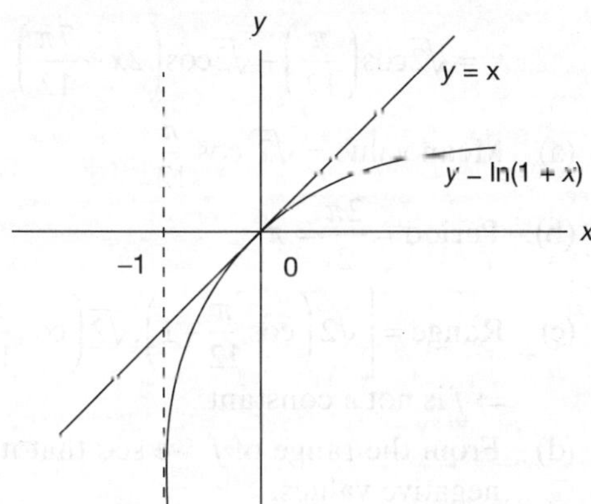

29. (b) The given equation can be written as

$$\frac{\log_2(x-1)}{\log_2 4} = \log_2(x-3)$$

$\Rightarrow \quad \log_2(x-1) = 2\log_2(x-3)$

$\Rightarrow \quad \log_2(x-1) = \log_2(x-3)^2$

$\Rightarrow \quad x-1 = (x-3)^2$

$\Rightarrow \quad x^2 - 7x + 10 = 0$ gives $x = 2, 5$

However, $x = 2$ is not acceptable to $\log_2(x-3)$. Hence, there is only one solution.

30. (b) Let us take two cases:

$x < -2$

$\Rightarrow \quad x^2 + x + 2 + x > 0$

$\Rightarrow \quad (x+1)^2 + 1 > 0$ true $\forall\, x \in \boldsymbol{R}$.

Intersection gives $x < -2$

or $\quad x \ge -2$

$\Rightarrow \quad x^2 - x - 2 + x \ge 0$

$\Rightarrow \quad x^2 \ge 2$ true $\forall |x| \ge \sqrt{2}$

Intersection gives $x \in \left[-2, -\sqrt{2}\,\right] \cup \left[\sqrt{2}, +\infty\right]$.

Taking the union of the two solution sets gives $x \in \left[-\infty, -\sqrt{2}\,\right] \cup \left[\sqrt{2}, +\infty\right]$.

31. (b) In the interval $x \in \left(0, \frac{\pi}{2}\right)$, the function $xe^{\sin x}$ strictly increases from 0 to $\frac{\pi e}{2}$, whereas the $\cos x$ function strictly decreases from 1 to 0. The graphs of the two functions will intersect once in this interval. Hence, there is only one solution.

32. (b) The function $f(x) = 2^x + 2^{-x}$ is an even function. It decreases strictly in $(-\infty, 0)$ and then increases strictly in $(0, +\infty)$. Its least value is 2. On the other hand, the greatest value of the function $2\cos\left(\frac{x^2+x}{6}\right)$ is 2.

Their graphs can meet only at $x = 0$. Hence, there is only one solution.

33. (d) The given function is even and it can be written as

$$f(x) = \frac{x^2-1}{x^2+1} = 1 - \frac{2}{x^2+1}$$

Thus, $f(x)$ decreases in $(-\infty, 0)$ and increases in $(0, +\infty)$.

Also $\lim_{x\to\infty} f(x) = 1$ and $f(0) = -1$. Hence, the range of $f(x)$ is $[-1, 1)$. Thus, $f(x)$ is bounded and its least value equals -1.

34. (c) The minima of the quadratic function

$$f(x) = x^2 + 2bx + 2c^2 = (x+b)^2 + 2c^2 - b^2$$

occurs at $x = -b$ and its minimum value is

$f_{\min} = -b^2 + 2c^2$

The maxima of the quadratic function

$$g(x) = -x^2 - 2cx + b^2 = c^2 + b^2 - (x+c)^2$$

occurs at $x = -c$ and its maximum value is $g_{\max} = c^2 + b^2$

According to the given condition, we have

$$-b^2 + 2c^2 > c^2 + b^2$$

$$\Rightarrow \quad c^2 > 2b^2$$

$$\Rightarrow \quad |c| > |b|\sqrt{2}$$

35. (a),(b) The given function can be written as

$$f(x) = \frac{1}{2}(1 - \cos 2x) + \frac{1}{2}\left\{1 - \cos\left(2x + \frac{2\pi}{3}\right)\right\}$$

$$+ \frac{1}{2}\left\{\cos\frac{\pi}{3} + \cos\left(2x + \frac{\pi}{3}\right)\right\}$$

$$= \frac{5}{4} - \frac{1}{2}\left\{\cos 2x + \cos\left(2x + \frac{2\pi}{3}\right) - \cos\left(2x + \frac{\pi}{3}\right)\right\}$$

$$= \frac{5}{4} - \frac{1}{2}\left\{\cos 2x + \cos\left(2x + \frac{2\pi}{3}\right)\right.$$

$$\left. + \cos\left(2x + \frac{4\pi}{3}\right)\right\} = \frac{5}{4}$$

Hence $g\{f(x)\} = g\left(\frac{5}{4}\right) = 1$ and also $f\{g(x)\} = \frac{5}{4}$.

36. (b) Writing $-x$ in place of x or $-y$ in place of y does not change the relations $x^2 + y^4 = 1$ or $x^4 + y^6 = 1$. This means their graphs will be symmetric about the y-axis as well as the x-axis.

Both the relations are defined for $-1 \le x \le 1$. Let us plot their graphs in the first quadrant $(0 < x < 1, y > 0)$. In this region, for any given x, let y_A and y_B be the ordinates corresponding to $x^2 + y^4 = 1$ and $x^4 + y^6 = 1$, respectively. Then $y_A = \sqrt[4]{1 - x^2}$ and $y_B = \sqrt[6]{1 - x^4}$.

For $0 < x < 1$, we have

$$x^2 > x^4$$

$$\Rightarrow \quad 1 - x^2 < 1 - x^4$$

$$\Rightarrow \quad \sqrt[4]{1 - x^2} < \sqrt[4]{1 - x^4} < \sqrt[6]{1 - x^4}$$

$$[\text{Here } 0 < 1 - x^4 < 1]$$

$$\Rightarrow \quad y_A < y_B$$

Now, from the graph, we can see that the region defined by A is contained in the region defined by B.

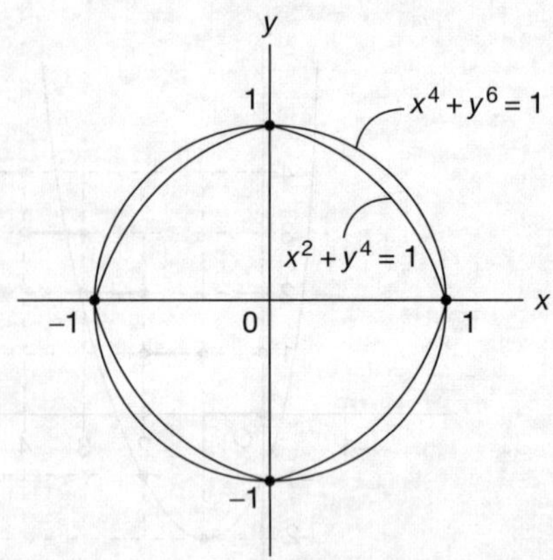

37. (a) The function is defined for values of x satisfying

$$\log_x(x^2 - 9x + 1) > 0$$

Now, two cases arise:

$$0 < x < 1 \text{ and } x^2 - 9x + 9 < 1$$

$$\Rightarrow \quad 0 < x < 1 \text{ and } (x-1)(x-8) < 0$$

$$\Rightarrow \quad 0 < x < 1 \text{ and } 1 < x < 8$$

Intersection gives null set

or $\quad x > 1 \text{ and } x^2 - 9x + 9 > 1$

$$\Rightarrow \quad x > 1 \text{ and } (x-1)(x-8) > 0$$

$$\Rightarrow \quad x > 1 \text{ and } x < 1 \text{ or } x > 8$$

Intersection gives $x > 8$.

Taking the union of the two cases gives $x > 8$.

38. (b) The given function can be written as

$$f(x) = 2\sqrt{2}\sin\left(x + \frac{\pi}{3}\right)\sin\left(x + \frac{\pi}{4}\right)$$

$$= \sqrt{2}\cos\left(\frac{\pi}{12}\right) - \sqrt{2}\cos\left(2x + \frac{7\pi}{12}\right)$$

(a) Mean value = $\sqrt{2}\cos\frac{\pi}{12}$

(b) Period = $\frac{2\pi}{2} = \pi$

(c) Range = $\left[\sqrt{2}\left(\cos\frac{\pi}{12} - 1\right), \sqrt{2}\left(\cos\frac{\pi}{12} + 1\right)\right]$

$\Rightarrow f$ is not a constant.

(d) From the range of f, we see that it also takes negative values.

39. (c) The given function can be written as

$$f(x) = 1 + \frac{1}{x^2 + x + 1} = 1 + \frac{1}{\left(x + \frac{1}{2}\right)^2 + \frac{3}{4}}$$

We see that $f(x)$ increases in $(-\infty,-1/2)$ and decreases in $(-1/2,+\infty)$. The greatest value of the function is $f\left(\frac{-1}{2}\right)=\frac{7}{3}$ and its least value is $f(\infty)=1$.

Hence range $=\left(1,\frac{7}{3}\right]$.

40. (b) The given function can be written as

$$f(x)=\frac{1-3\tan^2 x}{3-\tan^2 x}(\tan x\neq 0)$$
$$=3+\frac{8}{\tan^2 x-3}(\tan x\neq 0)$$

The function has period π and is also even. We only need to analyse it in the interval $(0,\pi/2)$. Since $\tan^2 x$ strictly increases in this interval, $f(x)$ will strictly decrease in this interval.
We see that f is not defined at $x=\pi/3$.

In the interval $\left(0,\frac{\pi}{3}\right)$, the function takes values

$$\left(f\left(\frac{\pi^-}{3}\right),f(0^+)\right)=\left(-\infty,\frac{1}{3}\right)$$

In the interval $\left(\frac{\pi}{3},\frac{\pi}{2}\right)$, the function takes values

$$\left(f\left(\frac{\pi^-}{2}\right),f\left(\frac{\pi^+}{3}\right)\right)=(3,+\infty)$$

Hence, the set of values that the function does not take is $\left[\frac{1}{3},3\right]$.

41. (d) The given function is decreasing on **R** since e^{-x} is a decreasing function and $\tan^{-1}x$ is an increasing function.
Also, we have

$$f(x)+f(-x)=2\{\tan^{-1}(e^{-x})+\tan^{-1}(e^{x})\}-\pi$$
$$=2\times\frac{\pi}{2}-\pi=0$$

Hence, $f(x)$ is odd.

42. (c),(d) The given function

$$f(x)=\tan^{-1}(\sin x+\cos x)=\tan^{-1}\left\{\sqrt{2}\sin\left(x+\frac{\pi}{4}\right)\right\}$$

Since $\tan^{-1}$ is an increasing function, $f(x)$ increases when $\sin\left(x+\frac{\pi}{4}\right)$ increases. That is, when

$$\frac{-\pi}{2}+2n\pi<x+\frac{\pi}{4}<\frac{\pi}{2}+2n\pi$$
$$\Rightarrow\ \frac{-3\pi}{4}+2n\pi<x<\frac{\pi}{4}+2n\pi$$

The shaded portion in the figure represents this interval.

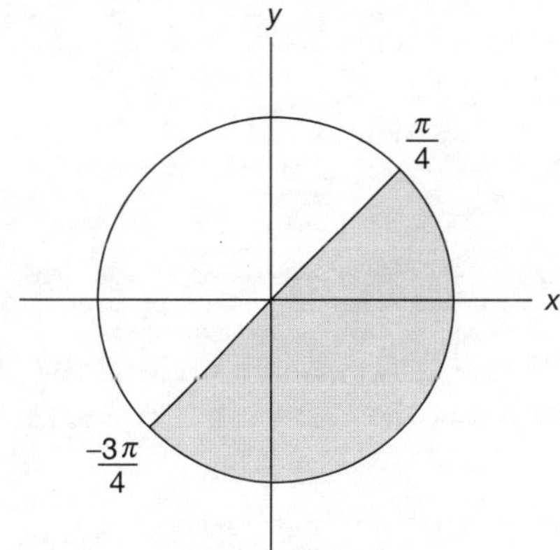

43. (d) The given function is defined for values of x satisfying

$$\log_{0.3}\left|\frac{x-2}{x}\right|\geq 0 \text{ and } \left|\frac{x-2}{x}\right|>0$$
$$\Rightarrow\ \left|\frac{x-2}{x}\right|\leq 1 \text{ and } \left|\frac{x-2}{x}\right|\neq 0$$
$$\Rightarrow\ |x-2|\leq|x| \text{ and } x\neq 2$$
$$\Rightarrow\ x^2-4x+4\leq x^2 \text{ and } x\neq 2$$
$$\Rightarrow\ x\geq 1 \text{ and } x\neq 2$$

Now, the function can be written as

$$f(x)=\begin{cases}\sqrt{\log_{0.3}\left(\frac{2}{x}-1\right)}, & 1\leq x<2\\ \sqrt{\log_{0.3}\left(1-\frac{2}{x}\right)}, & x>2\end{cases}$$

We can see that $f(x)$ increases in $[1,2)$ and decreases in $(2,+\infty)$.
[$1/x$ is a decreasing function, $\log_{0.3}x$ is a decreasing function, and $\sqrt{x}$ is an increasing function.]

In the interval $[1,2)$, the range is

$$\left[f(1), f\left(2^-\right)\right) = [0,+\infty)$$

In the interval $(2,+\infty)$, the range is

$$\left(f(+\infty), f\left(2^+\right)\right) = (0,+\infty)$$

Taking the union, we have the required range as $[0,+\infty)$.

44. (c) The first derivative of the function is

$$f'(x) = a + b\cos x$$

It is a continuous function, so it will be one–one if it is either strictly increasing or strictly decreasing $\Rightarrow f'$ is either always positive or always negative. This will be possible if $|a| > |b|$.

CHAPTER

18 Differentiation

- **Derivative of a Function:** The right-hand derivative of a function $f(x)$ at any point x is defined as

$$f'(x^+) = \lim_{h\to 0} \frac{f(x+h)-f(x)}{h}$$

The left-hand derivative of a function $f(x)$ at any point x is defined as

$$f'(x^-) = \lim_{h\to 0} \frac{f(x)-f(x-h)}{h}$$

A function $f(x)$ is said to be differentiable at any point x if the right-hand and left-hand derivatives exist and are equal; the derivative function in that case is denoted as $f'(x)$ or df/dx. A function is non-diffferentiable at points of discontinuity or kink. Geometrically, the derivative function represents the slope of the tangent to the curve $y = f(x)$. A positive value of $f'(x)$ at any point x would mean an increasing graph of $f(x)$ at that point, and a negative value of $f'(x)$ at any point x would mean a decreasing graph of $f(x)$ at that point.

- **Derivatives of Elementary Functions**

Function	Derivative	Function	Derivative
1. x^n $(n \in \mathbf{Q})$	nx^{n-1}	10. $\tan^{-1} x$	$\frac{1}{1+x^2}$
2. $\sin x$	$\cos x$	11. $\text{cosec}^{-1} x$	$\frac{-1}{\lvert x\rvert\sqrt{x^2-1}}$
3. $\cos x$	$-\sin x$	12. $\sec^{-1} x$	$\frac{1}{\lvert x\rvert\sqrt{x^2-1}}$
4. $\tan x$	$\sec^2 x$	13. $\cot^{-1} x$	$\frac{-1}{1+x^2}$
5. $\text{cosec}x$	$-\text{cosec}x \cot x$	14. a^x $(a>0, a\neq 1)$	$a^x \ln a$
6. $\sec x$	$\sec x \tan x$	15. $\log_a x$ $(a>0, a\neq 1)$	$\frac{1}{x\ln a}$
7. $\cot x$	$-\text{cosec}^2 x$		
8. $\sin^{-1} x$	$\frac{1}{\sqrt{1-x^2}}$		
9. $\cos^{-1} x$	$\frac{-1}{\sqrt{1-x^2}}$		

- **Theorems on Derivatives:** If $u(x)$ and $v(x)$ are differentiable functions, then

1. $\{ku\}' = ku'$, where k is some constant.
2. $\{u+v\}' = u' + v'$ (sum rule).
3. $\{uv\}' = vu' + uv'$ (product rule).
4. $\left\{\frac{u}{v}\right\}' = \frac{vu' - uv'}{v^2}$ (quotient rule).

Derivative of a Composite Function: If $y = f(u)$ is a differentiable function of u and a differentiable function of x, then

$$\frac{d\{f(u)\}}{dx} = \frac{df}{du} \times \frac{du}{dx} \text{ (chain rule)}$$

Derivative of a Function Raised to the Power of Another Function: If $y = u^v (u > 0, u \neq 1)$, where u and v are differentiable functions of x, then

$$\frac{dy}{dx} = u^v \ln u \frac{dv}{dx} + vu^{v-1} \frac{du}{dx}$$

Derivative of an Inverse Function: If $y = f(x)$ has an inverse function $x = g(y)$ and $dy/dx \neq 0$, then

$$\frac{dy}{dx} = \frac{1}{dx/dy}$$

Derivative of a Parametrically Represented Function: If $y = f(t)$ and $x = g(t)$, where f and g are differentiable functions of t, define y as a single-valued continuous function of x, then

$$\frac{dy}{dx} = \frac{f'(t)}{g'(t)}$$

EXERCISES

1. The number of points where the function $f(x) =$ max of or equal to $\{|\tan x|, \cos|x|\}$ is non-differentiable in the interval $(-\pi, \pi)$ is:
(a) 6 (b) 5
(c) 4 (d) 3

2. The function $f(x) = (x^2 - 1)|x^2 - 3x + 2| + \cos|x|$ is not differentiable at x equal to:
(a) –1 (b) 2
(c) 1 (d) 0

3. Let $f(x) = |\sin x - \ln 2|$ and $g(x) = fof(x)$. Then the correct statements from the following are:
(a) $g'(0^-) = 1$
(b) $g'(0^+) = -\cos(\ln 2)$
(c) $g'(0) = -\cos(\ln 2)$
(d) $g'(0) = \cos(\ln 2)$

4. Let $f : \left[\frac{-1}{2}, 2\right] \to \mathbf{R}$ and $g : \left[\frac{-1}{2}, 2\right] \to \mathbf{R}$ be functions defined as $f(x) = [x^2 - 3]$ and $g(x) = |x| f(x) + |4x - 7| f(x)$, where $[x]$ denotes the greatest integer function. Then the correct statements from the following are:
(a) f is discontinuous at exactly 3 points
(b) g is discontinuous at exactly 4 points
(c) f is not differentiable at exactly 3 points
(d) g is not differentiable at exactly 3 points

5. Consider the function $f(x) = e^{ax} + e^{bx}$. If $f''(x) - 2f'(x) - 15f(x)$ is identically equal to 0, then the value of ab is:
(a) –10 (b) 30
(c) 5 (d) –15

6. Let $[x]$ denote the greatest integer less than or equal to x. The LHD of the function $f(x) = [x]\sin(\pi x)$ at $x = k$, where k is any integer, is:
(a) $(-1)^k (k-1)\pi$
(b) $(-1)^{k-1} (k-1)\pi$
(c) $(-1)^k k\pi$
(d) $(-1)^{k-1} k\pi$

7. Let $f : \mathbf{R} \to \mathbf{R}$ be a function defined as $f(x) = a\cos(|x^3 - x|) + b|x|\sin(|x^3 + x|)$, where $a, b \in \mathbf{R}$. Then the correct statements from the following are:
(a) f is differentiable at $x = -1$ for any value of a and b
(b) f is differentiable at $x = 0$ only if $b = 0$
(c) f is differentiable at $x = 1$ for any value of a and b
(d) None of these

8. Let $f(x)=\begin{cases} x^2\left|\cos\left(\frac{\pi}{x}\right)\right|, x\neq 0 \\ 0, x=0 \end{cases}$. Then:

(a) f is differentiable at both $x=0$ and at $x=2$
(b) f is differentiable at $x=0$ but not differentiable at $x=2$
(c) f is not differentiable at $x=0$ but differentiable at $x=2$
(d) f is not differentiable at both $x=0$ and at $x=2$

9. If $x^a y^b=(x+y)^{a+b}$, where a,b are constants, then $\frac{dy}{dx}$ equals:

(a) $\frac{y}{x}$ (b) $\frac{x}{y}$
(c) $\frac{y}{x+y}$ (d) $\frac{x}{x+y}$

10. Let $f(x)=\log_x(\ln x)$. Then $f'(e)$ equals:

(a) e (b) $\frac{1}{e}$
(c) e^2 (d) $\frac{1}{e^2}$

11. If $\ln(x+y)=2xy$, then $y'(0)$ equals:

(a) -1 (b) 0
(c) 1 (d) 2

12. If $xe^{xy}=y+\sin^2 x$, then $y'(0)$ equals:

(a) -1 (b) 0
(c) 1 (d) 2

13. If $x\cos y+y\cos x=\pi$, then $y''(0)$ equals:

(a) -1 (b) $-\pi$
(c) 1 (d) π

14. If $x^{\cos y}+y^{\cos x}-2$, then $y'(1)$ equals:

(a) -1 (b) 0
(c) 1 (d) 2

15. If $y=(1+x^2)(1+x^4)\ldots(1+x^{2^n})$, then $y''(0)$ equals:

(a) -1 (b) 0
(c) 1 (d) 2

16. The derivative of $\sec^{-1}\left(\frac{1}{2x^2-1}\right)$ with respect to $\sqrt{1-x^2}$ at $x=\frac{-1}{2}$ equals:

(a) -1 (b) 1
(c) -2 (d) 4

17. Let $f(x)=\sin\left\{\tan^{-1}\left(\frac{\sin x}{\sqrt{\cos 2x}}\right)\right\}, \frac{-\pi}{4}<x<\frac{\pi}{4}$.

Then the value of $\frac{d\{f(x)\}}{d(\tan x)}$ is:

(a) -1 (b) 1
(c) -2 (d) 0

18. If $x=\sin 2t(1+\cos 2t)$ and $y=\cos 2t(1-\cos 2t)$, then the value of $\frac{dy}{dx}$ at $t=\frac{\pi}{3}$ is:

(a) 0 (b) 1
(c) $\sqrt{2}$ (d) $\sqrt{3}$

19. If $t(1+x^2)=x$ and $x^2+t^2=y$, then the value of $\frac{dy}{dx}$ at $x=2$ is:

(a) $\frac{488}{125}$ (b) $\frac{88}{25}$
(c) $\frac{248}{225}$ (d) None of these

20. If $e^x=\frac{\sqrt{1+t}-\sqrt{1-t}}{\sqrt{1+t}+\sqrt{1-t}}$ and $\tan\frac{y}{2}=\sqrt{\frac{1-t}{1+t}}$, then the value of $\frac{dy}{dx}$ at $t=\frac{1}{2}$ is:

(a) $\frac{2}{3}$ (b) $\frac{-1}{2}$
(c) 2 (d) None of these

21. Let $F(x)=f(x)g(x)h(x)$ for all real x, where $f(x)$, $g(x)$ and $h(x)$ are differentiable functions. If at some point x_0, $F'(x_0)=21F(x_0)$, $f'(x_0)=4f(x_0)$, $g'(x_0)=-7g(x_0)$ and $h'(x_0)=kh(x_0)$, then the value of k is:

(a) -17 (b) -13
(c) 24 (d) 31

22. The second derivative $\frac{d^2x}{dy^2}$ is identically equal to:

(a) $\left(\frac{d^2y}{dx^2}\right)^{-1}$ (b) $\left(\frac{d^2y}{dx^2}\right)^{-1}\left(\frac{dy}{dx}\right)^{-3}$
(c) $\frac{d^2y}{dx^2}\left(\frac{dy}{dx}\right)^{-2}$ (d) $-\frac{d^2y}{dx^2}\left(\frac{dy}{dx}\right)^{-3}$

23. If $x = f(t)$ and $y = g(t)$, then $\dfrac{d^2y}{dx^2}$ equals:

(a) $\dfrac{g''}{f''}$

(b) $\dfrac{f'g'' - g'f''}{(f')^3}$

(c) $\dfrac{g'' + f''}{(f')^2}$

(d) $\dfrac{f'g''}{g'f''}$

24. Consider the function $g(x) = f(|x|) - \sqrt{\dfrac{1-\cos(2x)}{2}}$, where $f(x)$ is a differentiable function on **R**. If $f'(0) = 1$, then:

(a) $g'(0) = 0$

(b) $g'(0) = 1$

(c) $g'(0) = -1$

(d) $g'(0)$ does not exist

25. If $f(x) = \cos^{-1}\left(\dfrac{x^{-1} - x}{x^{-1} + x}\right)$, then $f'(x)$ is:

(a) Odd (b) Even
(c) Periodic (d) None of these

26. If $f(x) = x^3 + e^{x/2}$ and $g(x) = f^{-1}(x)$, then $g'(1)$ equals:

(a) –1 (b) 1
(c) 2 (d) 3

27. Let $F(x) = f^2\left(\dfrac{x}{2}\right) + g^2\left(\dfrac{x}{2}\right)$, where $f''(x) = -f(x)$ and $g(x) = f'(x)$. If $F(5) = 1$, then $F(10)$ equals:

(a) –1 (b) 1
(c) 2 (d) 3

28. If $y\sqrt{1+x} + x\sqrt{1+y} = 0, y \neq x$, then:

(a) $(1+x)^2 y' + 1 = 0$

(b) $x^2 y' + x + 1 = 0$

(c) $xy' + x^2 + 1 = 0$

(d) $xy' + x^2 + x = 0$

29. If $y = \cos\left(3\cos^{-1}x\right), x \in [-1,1] - \left\{\pm\dfrac{\sqrt{3}}{2}\right\}$, then $\dfrac{(x^2-1)y'' + xy'}{y}$ equals:

(a) 9 (b) –7
(c) –6 (d) 0

30. If $y = \sin^{-1}\left(x\sqrt{1-x} - \sqrt{x}\sqrt{1-x^2}\right), x \in [0,1]$, then $y'\left(\dfrac{1}{2}\right)$ equals:

(a) $\dfrac{2-\sqrt{3}}{3}$

(b) $\dfrac{\sqrt{3}-2}{\sqrt{3}}$

(c) $\dfrac{2+\sqrt{3}}{\sqrt{3}}$

(d) $\dfrac{2-\sqrt{3}}{\sqrt{3}}$

31. Let $f(x) = x^3 + x$ and $g(x) = f^{-1}(x)$. If the value of $g''(-2)$ is of the form $\dfrac{a}{b}$, where a and b are co-prime, then the value of $b - 9a$ is:

(a) 3 (b) 5
(c) 7 (d) 9

32. Let $f(x) = \begin{cases} x\left(\dfrac{e^{1/x} - e^{-1/x}}{e^{1/x} + e^{-1/x}}\right), & x \neq 0 \\ 0, & x = 0 \end{cases}$. Then the correct statements from the following are:

(a) f is continuous at $x = 0$

(b) f is not continuous at $x = 0$

(c) f is differentiable at $x = 0$

(d) f is not differentiable at $x = 0$

33. Let $f(x) = [\cos x + \sin x], 0 < x < 2\pi$, where $[x]$ represents the greatest integer function. The number of points where the function is non-differentiable is:

(a) 6 (b) 5
(c) 4 (d) 3

34. Let $f,g,h:\mathbf{R}\to\mathbf{R}$ be three differentiable function such that $f(x)=x^3+3x+2$, $g(f(x))=x$ and $h(g(g(x)))=x$. Then:

(a) $3g'(2)=8$

(b) $h(0)=16$

(c) $h'(1)=666$

(d) $h(g(3))=36$

35. Let $g:\mathbf{R}\to\mathbf{R}$ be a differentiable function with $g(0)=0$, $g'(0)=0$. Let $f(x)=\begin{cases}\frac{x}{|x|}g(x), & x\neq 0\\ 0, & x=0\end{cases}$ and $h(x)=e^{|x|}$, $x\in\mathbf{R}$. Then the correct statements from the following are:

(a) f is differentiable at $x=0$

(b) h is differentiable at $x=0$

(c) foh is differentiable at $x=0$

(d) hof is differentiable at $x=0$

ANSWER KEYS

1. (c)	**2.** (b)	**3.** (d)	**4.** (b),(c)	**5.** (d)	**6.** (a)	**7.** (a),(c)	**8.** (b)	**9.** (a)	**10.** (b)
11. (c)	**12.** (c)	**13.** (d)	**14.** (a)	**15.** (d)	**16.** (d)	**17.** (b)	**18.** (d)	**19.** (a)	**20.** (b)
21. (c)	**22.** (d)	**23.** (b)	**24.** (a)	**25.** (a)	**26.** (c)	**27.** (b)	**28.** (a)	**29.** (a)	**30.** (d)
31. (b)	**32.** (a), (d)	**33.** (b)	**34.** (b),(c)	**35.** (a),(d)					

SOLUTIONS

1. (c) The figure shows the graph of the given function

$f(x)$ = max of or equal to {|tan$x$|, cos|x|}

Note that cos|x| = cos$x$ since cos is an even function.

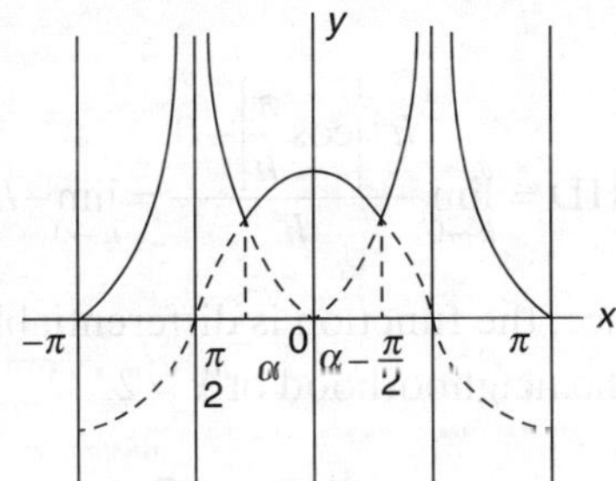

We can see that there are two points $x=\pm\pi/2$ where the function is discontinuous. There are two points $x=\pm\alpha$ where the function is continuous, but the LHD and RHD do not match. Hence, there are four points where the function is non-differentiable.

2. (b) The given function can be written as

$$f(x)=\begin{cases}(x^2-1)(x^2-3x+2)+\cos x, & x<1\\ -(x^2-1)(x^2-3x+2)+\cos x, & 1\le x\le 2\\ (x^2-1)(x^2-3x+2)+\cos x, & x>2\end{cases}$$

Then

$$f'(x)=\begin{cases}(x^2-1)(2x-3)+2x(x^2-3x+2)-\sin x, & x<1\\ -(x^2-1)(2x-3)-2x(x^2-3x+2)-\sin x, & 1<x<2\\ (x^2-1)(2x-3)+2x(x^2-3x+2)-\sin x, & x>2\end{cases}$$

The function is continuous everywhere, but the LHD and RHD do not match at one point, $x=2$.

3. (d) The function $f(x)=|\sin x-\ln 2|$ and its derivative can be written as

$$f(x)=\begin{cases}\ln 2-\sin x, & \sin x\le \ln 2\\ \sin x-\ln 2, & \sin x\ge \ln 2\end{cases}$$

and $f'(x)=\begin{cases}-\cos x, & \sin x<\ln 2\\ \cos x, & \sin x>\ln 2\end{cases}$

The derivative of $g(x)=fof(x)$ is

$$g'(x)=f'\{f(x)\}\times f'(x).$$

Thus $g'(0)=f'(\ln 2)\times f'(0)$ since $f(0)=\ln 2$.

Now $f'(0)=-\cos 0=-1$ since $\sin 0<\ln 2$ and $f'(\ln 2)=-\cos(\ln 2)$ since $\sin(\ln 2)<\ln 2$. Hence $g'(0)=\cos(\ln 2)$.

4. (b),(c) The given functions can be written as

$$f(x)=\begin{cases}-3, & -1/2\le x<1\\ -2, & 1\le x<\sqrt{2}\\ -1, & \sqrt{2}\le x<\sqrt{3}\\ 0, & \sqrt{3}\le x<2\\ 1, & x=2\end{cases}$$

and $$g(x)=\begin{cases}(7-5x)f(x), -1/2\le x\le 0\\ (7-3x)f(x), 0\le x\le 7/4\\ (5x-7)f(x), 7/4\le x\le 2\end{cases}$$

$$=\begin{cases}-3(7-5x), & -1/2\le x<0\\ -3(7-3x), & 0\le x<1\\ -2(7-3x), & 1\le x<\sqrt{2}\\ -1(7-3x), & \sqrt{2}\le x<\sqrt{3}\\ 0, & \sqrt{3}\le x<7/4\\ 0, & 7/4\le x<2\\ (5x-7), & x=2\end{cases}$$

The function f is discontinuous at $x=1,\sqrt{2},\sqrt{3},2$ (four points) and non-differentiable at $x=1,\sqrt{2},\sqrt{3}$ (three points).

The function g is discontinuous at $x=1,\sqrt{2},\sqrt{3},2$ (four points) and non-differentiable at $x=0,1,\sqrt{2},\sqrt{3}$ (four points).

5. (d) We have

$$f(x)=e^{ax}+e^{bx},\ f'(x)=ae^{ax}+be^{bx} \text{ and}$$
$$f''(x)=a^2e^{ax}+b^2e^{bx}$$

Then

$$f''(x)-2f'(x)-15f(x)=(a^2-2a-15)e^{ax}$$
$$+(b^2-2b-15)be^{bx}$$

The above expression will be identically equal to 0 if

$$a^2-2a-15=0 \text{ and } b^2-2b-15=0$$

$\Rightarrow$ a and b are roots of

$$x^2-2x-15=0\Rightarrow ab=-15$$

6. (a) At any integer, say $x=k$

$$\text{LHD}=\lim_{h\to o}\frac{[k]\sin(\pi k)-[k-h]\sin(\pi k-\pi h)}{h}$$

$$=\begin{cases}\lim\limits_{h\to 0}\dfrac{-(k-1)\sin(\pi h)}{h} \text{ if } k \text{ is odd}\\ \lim\limits_{h\to 0}\dfrac{(k-1)\sin(\pi h)}{h} \text{ if } k \text{ is even}\end{cases}$$

$$=\begin{cases}\lim\limits_{h\to 0}-\pi(k-1) \text{ if } k \text{ is odd}\\ \lim\limits_{h\to 0}\pi(k-1) \text{ if } k \text{ is even}\end{cases}=(-1)^k(k-1)\pi$$

7. (a),(c) Since cos is an even function, the given function can be written as $f(x)=a\cos(x-x^3)+b|x|\sin\{|x|(x^2+1)\}$.

In the neighborhood of $x=0$, $f(x)=a\cos(x-x^3)+bx\sin(x^3+x)$, which is differentiable at $x=0$ for any value of a and b. Hence, option (a) is correct.

In the neighborhood of $x=1$, $f(x)=a\cos(x-x^3)+bx\sin(x^3+x)$, which is differentiable at $x=1$ for any value of a and b. Hence, option (b) is incorrect.

In the neighborhood of $x=-1$, $f(x)=a\cos(x-x^3)+bx\sin(x^3+x)$, which is differentiable at $x=-1$ for any value of a and b. Hence, option (c) is correct.

8. (b) At $x=0$

$$\text{LHD}=\lim_{h\to 0}\frac{0-h^2\left|\cos\frac{\pi}{h}\right|}{h}=\lim_{h\to 0}-h\left|\cos\frac{\pi}{h}\right|=0$$

and

$$\text{RHD}=\lim_{h\to 0}\frac{h^2\left|\cos\frac{\pi}{h}\right|-0}{h}=\lim_{h\to 0}-h\left|\cos\frac{\pi}{h}\right|=0$$

Hence, the function is differentiable at $x=0$.

In the neighborhood of $x=2$,

$$f(x)=\begin{cases}-x^2\cos\dfrac{\pi}{x}, x\le 2\\ x^2\cos\dfrac{\pi}{x}, x\ge 2\end{cases}$$

and $$f'(x)=\begin{cases}-2x\cos\dfrac{\pi}{x}-\pi\sin\dfrac{\pi}{x}, x<2\\ 2x\cos\dfrac{\pi}{x}+\pi\sin\dfrac{\pi}{x}, x>2\end{cases}$$

The function is continuous but not differentiable at $x=2$ since LHD $=-\pi$ and RHD $=\pi$

9. (a) Differentiating both sides with respect to x, we get

$$\Rightarrow \quad ax^{a-1}y^b + bx^a y^{b-1}y' = (a+b)(x+y)^{a+b-1}(1+y')$$

$$\Rightarrow \quad x^a y^b\left(\frac{a}{x}+\frac{b}{y}y'\right) = (a+b)(x+y)^{a+b}\left(\frac{1+y'}{x+y}\right)$$

$$\Rightarrow \quad \frac{a}{x}+\frac{b}{y}y' = \frac{a+b}{x+y}(1+y')$$

$$\Rightarrow \quad \left(\frac{b}{y}-\frac{a+b}{x+y}\right)y' = \frac{a+b}{x+y}-\frac{a}{x}$$

$$\Rightarrow \quad \frac{bx-ay}{y(x+y)}y' = \frac{bx-ay}{x(x+y)}$$

$$\Rightarrow \quad y' = \frac{y}{x}$$

10. (b) The given function can be written as $f(x) = \frac{\ln(\ln x)}{\ln x}$

Then $f'(x) = \dfrac{\ln x \cdot \frac{1}{x\ln x} - \ln(\ln x)\cdot\frac{1}{x}}{\ln^2 x} = \dfrac{1-\ln(\ln x)}{x\ln^2 x}$

Hence $f'(e) = \frac{1}{e}$.

11. (c) The given relation is $\ln(x+y) = 2xy$. Putting $x=0$ gives $y=1$.
Differentiating throughout with respect to x, we get

$$\frac{1+y'}{x+y} = 2(y+xy')$$

Putting $x=0$ and $y=1$ gives $y'(0)=1$.

12. (c) The given relation is $xe^{xy} = y+\sin^2 x$. Inserting $x=0$ gives $y=0$.
Differentiating throughout with respect to x, we get

$$e^{xy} + xe^{xy}(y+xy') = y' + 2\sin x\cos x.$$

Putting $x=0$ and $y=0$ gives $y'(0)=1$.

13. (d) The given relation is $x\cos y + y\cos x = \pi$. Inserting $x=0$ gives $y=\pi$.
Differentiating throughout with respect to x, we get

$$\cos y - x\sin y\, y' + y'\cos x - y\sin x = 0$$

$$\Rightarrow \quad (\cos x - x\sin y)y' + \cos y - y\sin x = 0$$

Putting $x=0$ and $y=\pi$ gives $y'(0)=-1$.
Differentiating again, we get

$$(\cos x - x\sin y)y'' + (-\sin x - \sin y - x\cos y\, y')y'$$
$$-\sin y\, y' - \cos x\, y' - y\cos x = 0.$$

Putting $x=0, y=\pi$, and $y'=-1$ gives $y'(0)=\pi$.

14. (a) The given relation is $x^{\cos y} + y^{\cos x} = 2$. Putting $x=1$ gives $y=1$.
Differentiating throughout with respect to x, we get

$$\cos y\, x^{\cos y-1} + x^{\cos y}\ln x(-\sin y\, y') +$$
$$\cos x\, y^{\cos x-1}y' + y^{\cos x}\ln y(-\sin x) = 0$$

Putting $x=1$ and $y=1$ gives $y'(1)=-1$.

15. (d) The given relation is

$$\Rightarrow \quad y = (1+x^2)(1+x^4)\ldots(1+x^{2^n})$$

$$\Rightarrow \quad y = 1+x^2+x^4+x^6+\ldots+x^{2^n}.$$

Differentiating throughout with respect to x, we get

$$y' = 2x+4x^3+6x^5+\ldots.$$

Differentiating again, we have

$$y'' = 2+12x^2+30x^4+\ldots.$$

Putting $x=0$ gives $y''(0)=2$.

16. (d) Let $f(x) = \sec^{-1}\left(\frac{1}{2x^2-1}\right) = \cos^{-1}(2x^2-1)$ and $g(x) = \sqrt{1-x^2}$. Then

$$f'(x) = \frac{-4x}{\sqrt{1-(2x^2-1)^2}} \text{ and } g'(x) = \frac{-x}{\sqrt{1-x^2}}$$

Hence

$$\frac{df}{dg} = \frac{f'}{g'} = \frac{4\sqrt{1-x^2}}{\sqrt{1-(2x^2-1)^2}} = \frac{4\sqrt{1-x^2}}{\sqrt{4x^2-4x^4}} = \frac{2}{|x|}$$

Putting $x = \frac{-1}{2}$ gives $\left(\frac{df}{dg}\right)_{x=-1/2} = 4.$

17. (b) The given function can be written as

$$f(x) = \sin\left\{\sin^{-1}\left(\frac{\sin x}{\sqrt{\sin^2 x + \cos 2x}}\right)\right\}$$

$$= \sin\{\sin^{-1}(\tan x)\} = \tan x$$

Then $\dfrac{d\{f(x)\}}{d(\tan x)} = 1.$

18. (d) Differentiating, we get

$$\frac{dy}{dt} = -2\sin 2t(1-\cos 2t) + \cos 2t(2\sin 2t)$$

$$= 4\sin 2t\cos 2t - 2\sin 2t = 2[\sin 4t - \sin 2t]$$

and $\dfrac{dx}{dt} = 2\cos 2t(1+\cos 2t) + \sin 2t(-2\sin 2t)$

$$= 2\cos^2 2t - 2\sin^2 2t + 2\cos 2t$$

$$= 2[\cos 4t + \cos 2t].$$

Hence, we have

$$\frac{dy}{dx} = \frac{dy/dt}{dx/dt}$$

$$= \frac{\sin 4t - \sin 2t}{\cos 4t + \cos 2t}$$

Putting $t = \dfrac{\pi}{3}$, we have

$$\left(\frac{dy}{dx}\right)_{t=\pi/3} = \frac{\sin\left(\frac{4\pi}{3}\right) - \sin\left(\frac{2\pi}{3}\right)}{\cos\left(\frac{4\pi}{3}\right) + \cos\left(\frac{2\pi}{3}\right)}$$

$$= \frac{-2\sin\left(\frac{\pi}{3}\right)}{-2\cos\left(\frac{\pi}{3}\right)}$$

$$= \tan\left(\frac{\pi}{3}\right) = \sqrt{3}$$

19. (a) Eliminating t from the two relations, we have

$$y = x^2 + \frac{x^2}{(1+x^2)^2}$$

Differentiating throughout with respect to x, we get

$$\frac{dy}{dx} = 2x + \frac{2x(1+x^2)^2 - x^2(1+x^2)4x}{(1+x^2)^4}$$

$$= 2x + \frac{2x(1-x^2)}{(1+x^2)^3}$$

Putting $x = 2$ gives $\left(\dfrac{dy}{dx}\right)_{x=2} = \dfrac{488}{125}.$

20. (b) Eliminating t from the two relations, we have

$$e^x = \frac{1-\tan\frac{y}{2}}{1+\tan\frac{y}{2}}$$

$$= \tan\left(\frac{\pi}{4} - \frac{y}{2}\right)$$

Differentiating throughout with respect to x, we get

$$e^x = \sec^2\left(\frac{\pi}{4} - \frac{y}{2}\right) \times \frac{-y'}{2}$$

$$\Rightarrow \quad y' = \frac{-2e^x}{1+\tan^2\left(\frac{\pi}{4} - \frac{y}{2}\right)}$$

$$= \frac{-2e^x}{1+e^{2x}}$$

When $t = \dfrac{1}{2}$, $e^x = \dfrac{\sqrt{3}-1}{\sqrt{3}+1} = 2 - \sqrt{3}$. Putting this value gives

$$\left(\frac{dy}{dx}\right)_{t=1/2} = \frac{-1}{2}.$$

21. (c) Taking natural log on both sides, we have

$$\ln F = \ln f + \ln g + \ln h.$$

Differentiating throughout with respect to x, we get

$$\frac{F'}{F} = \frac{f'}{f} + \frac{g'}{g} + \frac{h'}{h}$$

At $x = x_0$, we have

$$21 = 4 - 7 + k$$

$$\Rightarrow \quad k = 24$$

22. (d) We have

$$\frac{d^2x}{dy^2} = \frac{d}{dy}\left(\frac{dx}{dy}\right)$$
$$= \frac{d}{dy}\left(\frac{1}{y'}\right)$$
$$= \frac{d}{dx}\left(\frac{1}{y'}\right) \times \frac{dx}{dy}$$
$$= \frac{y''}{-(y')^2} \times \frac{1}{y'}$$
$$= \frac{y''}{-(y')^3}$$

23. (b) We have

$$\frac{d^2y}{dx^2} = \frac{d}{dx}\left(\frac{dy}{dx}\right)$$
$$= \frac{d}{dx}\left(\frac{g'}{f'}\right)$$
$$= \frac{d}{dt}\left(\frac{g'}{f'}\right) \times \frac{dt}{dx}$$
$$= \frac{f'g'' - g'f''}{(f')^2} \times \frac{1}{f'}.$$

24. (a) The given function reduces to $g(x) = f(|x|) - |\sin x|$. The RHD and LHD at $x = 0$, are, respectively,

$$g'(0^+) = \lim_{h\to 0} \frac{g(h) - g(0)}{h}$$
$$= \lim_{h\to 0} \frac{f(h) - \sin h - f(0)}{h}$$
$$= \lim_{h\to 0} \frac{f(h) - f(0)}{h} - \frac{\sin h}{h}$$
$$= f'(0) - 1 = 0$$

and

$$g'(0^-) = \lim_{h\to 0} \frac{g(0) - g(-h)}{h}$$
$$= \lim_{h\to 0} \frac{f(0) - f(h) + \sin h}{h}$$
$$= \lim_{h\to 0} \frac{f(h) - f(0)}{h} + \frac{\sin h}{h}$$
$$= -f'(0) + 1 = 0$$

Hence $g'(0) = 0$.

25. (a) The given function can be written as

$$f(x) = \cos^{-1}\left(\frac{1 - x^2}{1 + x^2}\right)$$

Since $f(x)$ is even, $f'(x)$ will be odd.

26. (c) We have

$$f(x) = x^3 + e^{x/2} \text{ and } f'(x) = 3x^2 + \frac{1}{2}e^{x/2}$$

Solving for $f(x) = 1$ gives $x = 0$. Now

$$g'(1) = \frac{1}{f'(0)} = 2$$

27. (b) The functions satisfying the given differential equations are

$$f(x) = A\sin(x + B) \text{ and } g(x) = A\cos(x + B),$$

where A, B are arbitrary constants.

Then $\quad F(x) = \left\{f\left(\frac{x}{2}\right)\right\}^2 + \left\{g\left(\frac{x}{2}\right)\right\}^2 = A^2$

(a constant function)

Hence $F(10) = F(5) = 1$.

28. (a) We have

$$y\sqrt{1+x} = -x\sqrt{1+y}$$
$$\Rightarrow \quad y^2(1+x) = x^2(1+y)$$
$$\Rightarrow \quad (x-y)(x+y+xy) = 0$$
$$\Rightarrow \quad x + y + xy = 0 \quad [y \neq x, \text{given}]$$
$$\Rightarrow \quad y = \frac{-x}{1+x}$$

Differentiating throughout with respect to x, we have

$$y' = \frac{-1}{(1+x)^2}$$
$$\Rightarrow \quad (1+x)^2 y' + 1 = 0$$

29. (a) Putting $x = \cos\theta$, the given relation reduces to

$$y = \cos(3\theta) = 4\cos^3\theta - 3\cos\theta$$
$$= 4x^3 - 3x.$$

Differentiating twice successively with respect to x, we have

$$y' = 12x^2 - 3$$

and $\quad y'' = 24x$

Hence, we have

$$\frac{(x^2-1)y'' + xy'}{y} = \frac{24x(x^2-1) + x(12x^2-3)}{4x^3-3x}$$

$$= \frac{36x^3 - 27x}{4x^3 - 3x} = 9$$

30. (d) Putting $x = \sin\alpha$ and $\sqrt{x} = \sin\beta$, we have

$$y = \sin^{-1}\left(\sin\alpha\sqrt{1-\sin^2\beta} - \sin\beta\sqrt{1-\sin^2\alpha}\right)$$

$$\Rightarrow \quad y = \sin^{-1}(\sin\alpha\cos\beta - \sin\beta\cos\alpha) = \alpha - \beta$$

$$\Rightarrow \quad y = \sin^{-1}x - \sin^{-1}\sqrt{x}$$

Differentiating throughout with respect to x, we have

$$y' = \frac{1}{\sqrt{1-x^2}} - \frac{1}{2\sqrt{x}\sqrt{1-x}}$$

Hence $\quad y'\left(\frac{1}{2}\right) = \frac{2-\sqrt{3}}{\sqrt{3}}.$

31. (b) We have

$$f(x) = x^3 + x,\ f'(x) = 3x^2 + 1 \text{ and}$$
$$f''(x) = 6x.$$

Solving the equation $f(x) = -2$ gives $x = -1$. Thus, we have

$$f(-1) = -2,\ f'(-1) = 4 \text{ and}$$
$$f''(-1) = -6.$$

Now, we have $g\{f(x)\} = x$. Differentiating with respect to x, we have

$$g'\{f(x)\}f'(x) = 1$$

Putting $x = -1$ gives

$$g'(-2) = \frac{1}{f'(-1)} = \frac{1}{4}.$$

Differentiating again, we have

$$g''\{f(x)\}\{f'(x)\}^2 + g'\{f(x)\}f''(x) = 0$$

Putting $x = -1$, we have

$$g''\{-2\}\{f'(-1)\}^2 + g'\{-2\}f''(-1) = 0$$

$$\Rightarrow \quad 16g''(-2) + \frac{-6}{4} = 0$$

$$\Rightarrow \quad g''(-2) = \frac{3}{32}$$

Hence $a = 3$, $b = 32$, and $b - 9a = 5$.

32. (a), (d) We have

$$\lim_{x\to 0} x\left(\frac{e^{\frac{1}{x}} - e^{\frac{-1}{x}}}{e^{\frac{1}{x}} + e^{\frac{-1}{x}}}\right) = \lim_{x\to 0} x\left(\frac{1 - e^{\frac{-2}{x}}}{1 + e^{\frac{-2}{x}}}\right)$$

$$= 0 \times \left(\frac{1-0}{1+0}\right) = 0 = f(0)$$

Hence, f is continuous at $x = 0$.

At $x = 0$

$$\text{LHD} = \lim_{h\to 0}\frac{f(0) - f(-h)}{h}$$

$$= \lim_{h\to 0}\left(\frac{e^{\frac{-1}{h}} - e^{\frac{1}{h}}}{e^{\frac{-1}{h}} + e^{\frac{1}{h}}}\right)$$

$$= \lim_{h\to 0}\left(\frac{e^{\frac{-2}{h}} - 1}{e^{\frac{-2}{h}} + 1}\right)$$

$$= \left(\frac{0-1}{0+1}\right) = -1$$

and

$$\text{RHD} = \lim_{h\to 0}\frac{f(h) - f(0)}{h}$$

$$= \lim_{h\to 0}\left(\frac{e^{\frac{1}{h}} - e^{\frac{-1}{h}}}{e^{\frac{1}{h}} + e^{\frac{-1}{h}}}\right)$$

$$= \lim_{h\to 0}\left(\frac{1 - e^{\frac{-2}{h}}}{1 + e^{\frac{-2}{h}}}\right)$$

$$= \left(\frac{1-0}{1+0}\right) = 1$$

Hence, f is not differentiable at $x = 0$.

33. (b) The given function can be written as

$$f(x) = \left[\sqrt{2}\sin\left(x + \frac{\pi}{4}\right)\right]$$

This function has discontinuities at all points where $g(x)=\sqrt{2}\sin\left(x+\frac{\pi}{4}\right)$ returns integer values. As x varies from 0 to 2π, that is one phasor cycle, the function $g(x)$ returns integer values $\{1,0,-1\}$ at the points given by

$$\sqrt{2}\sin\left(x+\frac{\pi}{4}\right)=1$$

$$\Rightarrow \quad x=0,\frac{\pi}{2}$$

$$\sqrt{2}\sin\left(x+\frac{\pi}{4}\right)=0$$

$$\Rightarrow \quad x=\frac{3\pi}{4},\frac{7\pi}{4}$$

$$\sqrt{2}\sin\left(x+\frac{\pi}{4}\right)=-1$$

$$\Rightarrow \quad x=\pi,\frac{3\pi}{2}$$

Hence, leaving $x=0$, which is an end point of the domain of $f(x)$, there are 5 points of non-differentiability.

34. (b),(c) We have

$$f(x)=x^3+3x+2,\ g(f(x))=x$$

and $\quad h(g(g(x)))=x.$

Differentiating with respect to x, we have

$$f'(x)=3x^2+3, \qquad \ldots(1)$$

$$g'(f(x))f'(x)=1 \qquad \ldots(2)$$

and $\quad h'(g(g(x)))g'(g(x))g'(x)=1 \qquad \ldots(3)$

Solving for $f(x)=2$, we have $x=0$. Hence, using relation (2), we have

$$g'(2)f'(0)=1$$

$$\Rightarrow \quad 3\,g'(2)=1$$

$\Rightarrow$ Option (a) is incorrect.

Solving for $g(g(x))=0$, we have

$$g(x)=g^{-1}(0)$$
$$=f(0)=2$$

$$\Rightarrow \quad x=g^{-1}(2)$$
$$=f(2)=16$$

Hence $\quad h(0)=h(g(g(16)))$
$$=16$$

$\Rightarrow$ Option (b) is correct.

Solving for $g(g(x))=1$, we have

$$g(x)=g^{-1}(1)$$
$$=f(1)=6$$

$$\Rightarrow \quad x=g^{-1}(1)$$
$$=f(6)=236$$

Hence, using relation (3), we have

$$h'(1)g'(6)g'(236)=1$$

$$\Rightarrow \quad h'(1)\times\frac{1}{f'(1)}\times\frac{1}{f'(6)}=1$$

$$\Rightarrow \quad h'(1)\times\frac{1}{6}\times\frac{1}{111}=1$$

$$\Rightarrow \quad h'(1)=666$$

$\Rightarrow$ Option (c) is correct.

Solving for $g(x)=3$, we have

$$x=g^{-1}(3)=f(3)=38$$

Hence $h(g(3))=h(g(g(38)))=38$

$\Rightarrow$ Option (d) is incorrect.

35. (a),(d) We have

$$f(x)=\begin{cases}-g(x), & x<0\\ 0, & x=0\\ g(x), & x>0\end{cases}$$

and $\quad f'(x)=\begin{cases}-g'(x), & x<0\\ g'(x), & x>0\end{cases}$

At $x=0$, f is continuous since $g(0)=0$, and also differentiable since $g'(0)=0$. Thus $f'(0)=0$

Now $\quad h(x)=\begin{cases}e^{-x}, & x<0\\ 1, & x=0\\ e^{x}, & x>0\end{cases}$

and $\quad h'(x)=\begin{cases}-e^{-x}, x<0\\ e^{x}, x>0\end{cases}$

We see that h is continuous but not differentiable at $x=0$, since LHD $=-1$ and RHD $=1$.

Now $\quad foh(x)=\begin{cases}-goh(x), h(x)<0\\ 0, h(x)=0\\ goh(x), h(x)>0\end{cases}$

$= goh(x)$

since $h(x)$ is always positive and

$$foh'(x)=goh'(x)\times h'(x)$$

We see that foh is not differentiable at $x=0$ since h is not differentiable at $x=0$.

Now $\quad hof(x)=\begin{cases}e^{-f(x)}, f(x)<0\\ 1, f(x)=0\\ e^{f(x)}, f(x)>0\end{cases}$

and $\quad hof'(x)=\begin{cases}-f'(x)e^{-f(x)}, f(x)<0\\ f'(x)e^{f(x)}, f(x)>0\end{cases}$

We see that hof is continuous and differentiable at $x=0$ since LHD = RHD = 0. Thus $hof'(0)=0$.

CHAPTER

19 Application of Derivatives

- **Fermat's Theorem:** Let a function $f(x)$ be defined on a certain interval and have a maximum or a minimum value at some interior point $x = c$ in the interval. If there exists a derivative $f'(c)$ at $x = c$, then $f'(c) = 0$.
- **Rolle's Theorem:** If a function $f(x)$ is
  - continuous in $[a,b]$
  - differentiable in (a,b)
  - $f(a) = f(b)$

  then there exists at least one point c in the interval (a,b) such that $f'(c) = 0$.
- **Lagrange's Mean Value Theorem**: If a function $f(x)$ is
  - continuous in $[a,b]$
  - differentiable in (a,b)

  then there exists at least one point c in the interval (a,b) such that $f'(c) = \dfrac{f(b)-f(a)}{b-a}$.

  In other words, there exists at least one point where the instantaneous rate of change of the function equals the average rate of change of the function in the interval $[a,b]$; hence the name.

  Corollary: If m and M, are, respectively, the least and greatest values of $f'(x)$ in the interval $[a,b]$, then

$$m \le \frac{f(b)-f(a)}{b-a} \le M$$

$$\Rightarrow f(a) + m(b-a) \le f(b) \le f(a) + M(b-a)$$

- **Monotonocity and Concavity:** The sign of the first derivative $f'(x)$ determines whether the function $f(x)$ is increasing or decreasing in an interval. The function is increasing in intervals where $f'(x) > 0$; the function is decreasing in intervals where $f'(x) < 0$.

  The sign of the second derivative $f''(x)$ determines whether the graph of the function $f(x)$ is concave upwards or concave downwards in an interval. The graph is concave upwards in intervals where $f''(x) > 0$; the graph is concave downwards in intervals where $f''(x) < 0$.
- **Maxima and Minima:** A function may attain extreme values (maxima or minima) at interior points where $f'(x) = 0$ or $f'(x)$ does not exist; these points are collectively called the critical points. An end point may also be a point of extrema if it exists.

  Conditions for the existence of extrema at a critical point $x = c$:

  1. If $x = c$ is a point where $f'(c) = 0$ or there is a kink, the function has an extrema if $f'(x)$ changes sign as x changes from $c-h$ to $c+h$ (h is a small +ve number). It is a point of maxima if $f'(x)$ changes sign from +ve to −ve, that is, if $f''(x) < 0$; it is a point of minima if $f'(x)$ changes sign from −ve to +ve, that is, if $f''(x) > 0$.
  2. If $x = c$ is a point where the function is discontinuous, then it is a point of maxima if $f(c) \ge \max\{f(c^-), f(c^+)\}$, and a point of minima if $f(c) \le \min\{f(c^-), f(c^+)\}$. If $f(c)$ lies in between $f(c^-), f(c^+)$, then it is not a point of extrema.

EXERCISES

1. Let $f:[-1,1]\to\left[\frac{\pi}{4},\frac{3\pi}{4}\right]$ be a function defined by $f(x)=\tan^{-1}x+\cos^{-1}x$. Then $f(x)$ is:
   (a) One–one and onto
   (b) One–one but not onto
   (c) Onto but not one–one
   (d) Neither one–one nor onto

2. The number of real solutions of $e^x-x^2=0$ is:
   (a) 0 (b) 1
   (c) 2 (d) 4

3. If $f(x)=|x-2|$ and $g(x)=f\{f(x)\}$, then:
   (a) $g(x)$ increases on $(0,+\infty)$
   (b) $g'(x)$ does not exist at $x=\{0,2,4\}$
   (c) $\int_{-\infty}^{x} g(x)dx$ increases on $\mathbf{R}$
   (d) $g(x)$ has two extrema

4. If $f(x)=x^5+bx^3+cx+d$ and $b^2<2c$, then:
   (a) $f(x)=0$ has exactly one root
   (b) $f(x)$ has one maxima
   (c) $f(x)$ decreases on $\mathbf{R}$
   (d) $f(x)$ is bounded

5. The values of m for which the equation $e^x-mx=0$ has only one real solution are:
   (a) $m=3$ (b) $m=e$
   (c) $m=2$ (d) $m<0$

6. If $f(x)=\sin x(\sin x+\sin 3x)$, then:
   (a) $f(x)\geq 0$ only when $x\geq 0$
   (b) $f(x)\leq 0$ for all real x
   (c) $f'(x)>0$ in $\left(\pi,\frac{5\pi}{4}\right)$
   (d) $f'(x)<0$ in $\left(-\pi,\frac{-\pi}{2}\right)$

7. The function $f(x)=\sin^4 x+\cos^4 x$ is increasing in:
   (a) $\left(0,\frac{\pi}{8}\right)$ (b) $\left(\frac{\pi}{4},\frac{3\pi}{8}\right)$
   (c) $\left(\frac{3\pi}{8},\frac{5\pi}{8}\right)$ (d) $\left(\frac{5\pi}{8},\frac{3\pi}{4}\right)$

8. Let $f(x)=xe^{x(1-x)}, x\in\mathbf{R}$. The incorrect options are:
   (a) $f(x)$ increases on $\left(\frac{-1}{2},1\right)$
   (b) $f(x)$ has one extrema
   (c) $f(x)$ decreases on $\left(\frac{-3}{2},\frac{-1}{2}\right)$
   (d) $\lim_{x\to\infty} f(x)=0$

9. Let $f(x)=(1+b^2)x^2+2bx+1$ and $m(b)$ be the minimum value of $f(x)$. As b varies, the range of $m(b)$ is:
   (a) $[0,1]$ (b) $\left[0,\frac{1}{2}\right]$
   (c) $\left[\frac{1}{2},1\right]$ (d) $(0,1]$

10. The points on the curve $y^3+3x^2=12y$ where the tangent is vertical are:
   (a) $\left(\frac{\pm\sqrt{3}}{2},-2\right)$ (b) $\left(0,\frac{\sqrt{3}}{2}\right)$
   (c) $\left(\frac{\pm 1}{\sqrt{3}},0\right)$ (d) $\left(\frac{\pm 4}{\sqrt{3}},2\right)$

11. The function $f(x)=p|x|-qx^2$, where p,q are constants, has:
   (a) 1 maxima and 2 minima if $p>0$ and $q>0$
   (b) 2 maxima and 1 minima if $p<0$ and $q<0$
   (c) 1 minima if $p>0$ and $q<0$
   (d) 1 maxima if $p<0$ and $q>0$

12. The number of real solutions of $\sqrt[4]{97-x}+\sqrt[4]{x}=5$ is:
   (a) 0 (b) 1
   (c) 2 (d) 4

13. Let $h(x)=f(x)-f^2(x)+f^3(x), x\in\mathbf{R}$. Then:
   (a) $h(x)$ increases whenever $f(x)$ increases
   (b) $h(x)$ increases whenever $f(x)$ decreases
   (c) $h(x)$ decreases whenever $f(x)$ decreases
   (d) Nothing can be said in general

14. If $f(x)=\dfrac{x}{\sin x}$ and $g(x)=\dfrac{x}{\tan x}$, then for $x\in(0,1)$:

(a) Both $f(x)$ and $g(x)$ are increasing

(b) Both $f(x)$ and $g(x)$ are decreasing

(c) $f(x)$ is increasing and $g(x)$ is decreasing

(d) $f(x)$ is decreasing and $g(x)$ is increasing

15. Intervals in which at least one maxima of the function $f(x)=\cos^2 x+\sin x$ lies are:

(a) $\left(\dfrac{-\pi}{2},\dfrac{\pi}{2}\right)$ (b) $\left(\dfrac{\pi}{8},\dfrac{5\pi}{4}\right)$

(c) $\left(0,\dfrac{\pi}{8}\right)$ (d) $\left(\dfrac{3\pi}{8},\dfrac{5\pi}{8}\right)$

16. Let $f(x)=\begin{cases}|x|, x<0\\ e^x, x\geq 0\end{cases}$, $g(x)=x^2$. Consider the function $h:\mathbf{R}\to[0,+\infty)$ given by $h(x)=\begin{cases} gof(x), x<0\\ gof(x)-1, x\geq 0\end{cases}$. Then $h(x)$ is:

(a) Continuous everywhere and one–one

(b) Continuous and differentiable everywhere

(c) Onto but not one–one

(d) Continuous everywhere but not differentiable at $x=0$

17. Let $f(x)=x\cos\dfrac{1}{x}, x\geq 1$. Then the correct statements from the following are:

(a) For at least one x in $(1,+\infty)$, $f(x+2)-f(x)<2$

(b) For all x in $(1,+\infty)$, $f(x+2)-f(x)>2$

(c) $f(x)$ is increasing in $(1,+\infty)$

(d) $f'(x)$ is increasing in $(1,+\infty)$

18. Let $f(x)$ be a quadratic function which is positive for all real x. If $g(x)=f(x)+f'(x)+f''(x)$, then for any real x:

(a) $g(x)<0$ (b) $g(x)>0$

(c) $g(x)=0$ (d) $g(x)\geq 0$

19. The function $f(x)$ is a second-degree polynomial function with $f(0)=0$ and $f(1)=1$. Also, $f'(x)>0$ for all $x\in[0,1]$. Then $f(x)$ is:

(a) $ax+(1-a)x^2, a\in\mathbf{R}$

(b) $ax+(1-a)x^2, a\in(0,2)-\{1\}$

(c) $ax+(1-a)x^2, a\in(-1,1)-\{0\}$

(d) No such polynomial

20. Let $g(x)=\ln\{f(x)\}$, where $f(x)$ is a twice differentiable positive function on $(0,+\infty)$ such that $f(x+1)=xf(x)$. Then, for $n=1,2,3,\ldots$ the value of $g''\left(n+\dfrac{1}{2}\right)-g''\left(\dfrac{1}{2}\right)$ equals:

(a) $-4\left\{1+\dfrac{1}{9}+\dfrac{1}{25}+\ldots+\dfrac{1}{(2n-1)^2}\right\}$

(b) $4\left\{1+\dfrac{1}{9}+\dfrac{1}{25}+\ldots+\dfrac{1}{(2n-1)^2}\right\}$

(c) $-4\left\{1+\dfrac{1}{9}+\dfrac{1}{25}+\ldots+\dfrac{1}{(2n+1)^2}\right\}$

(d) $4\left\{1+\dfrac{1}{9}+\dfrac{1}{25}+\ldots+\dfrac{1}{(2n+1)^2}\right\}$

21. Let $f(x)=\dfrac{\ln(\pi+x)}{\ln(e+x)}$. Then:

(a) $f(x)$ decreases in $(0,+\infty)$

(b) $\lim_{x\to+\infty} f(x)=2$

(c) $f(x)$ increases in $(0,+\infty)$

(d) $\lim_{x\to+\infty} f'(x)=0$

22. In the interval $[-1,1]$, Lagrange's mean value theorem is not applicable to:

(a) $f(x)=\begin{cases}\dfrac{1}{2}-x, x<\dfrac{1}{2}\\ \left(\dfrac{1}{2}-x\right)^2, x\geq\dfrac{1}{2}\end{cases}$

(b) $f(x)=\begin{cases}\dfrac{\sin x}{x}, x\neq 0\\ 1, \quad x=0\end{cases}$

(c) $f(x)=x|x|$

(d) $f(x)=|x|^3$

23. The function $f(x)$ is a cubic polynomial function with $f(-1)=9$, and minima at $x=1$. Also, the equation $f(x)=0$ has twice repeated roots at $x=2$. Then:

(a) $f(x)=0$ has a real root in $(0,1)$

(b) $f(x)$ has minima at $x=2$

(c) $\lim\limits_{x\to\infty}\dfrac{f(x)}{x^3}=\dfrac{-2}{3}$

(d) $f(x)>0$ on $(1/2,2)$

24. Let $f(x)=\begin{cases} e^x, & 0\le x\le 1\\ 2-e^{x-1}, & 1<x\le 2 \text{ and}\\ x-e, & 2<x\le 3\end{cases}$

$g(x)=\int_0^x f(t)dt, 0\le x\le 3$. Then $g(x)$ has:

(a) Maxima at $x=1$ and minima at $x=e$

(b) Maxima at $x=1+\ln 2$ and minima at $x=e$

(c) No maxima

(d) No minima

25. The function $f(x)$ is a twice differentiable polynomial such that $f(1)=1, f(2)=4$ and $f(3)=9$. Then:

(a) There exists at least one $x\in(1,2)$ such that $f''(x)=3$

(b) There exists at least one $x\in(2,3)$ such that $f'(x)=5=f''(x)$

(c) $f''(x)=2$ for every $x\in\mathbf{R}$

(d) There exists at least one $x\in(1,3)$ such that $f''(x)=2$

26. Let $f'(x)=\dfrac{192x^3}{2+\sin^4(\pi x)}$, $x\in\mathbf{R}$ with $f\left(\dfrac{1}{2}\right)=0$. If $m<\int_{1/2}^{1} f(x)dx<M$, then the possible values of m and M are:

(a) $m=12, M=24$ (b) $m=\dfrac{1}{4}, M=\dfrac{3}{4}$

(c) $m=12, M=18$ (d) $m=1, M=12$

27. Let $f(x)$ be a non-constant twice differentiable function defined on $\mathbf{R}$ such that $f(x)=f(1-x)$ and $f'\left(\dfrac{1}{4}\right)=0$. Then:

(a) $f''(x)$ vanishes at least twice in $(0,1)$

(b) $f'\left(\dfrac{1}{2}\right)=0$

(c) $\int_{-1/2}^{1/2} f\left(x+\dfrac{1}{2}\right)\sin x\, dx=0$

(d) $\int_0^{1/2} f(x)e^{\sin(\pi x)}dx=\int_{1/2}^{1} f(1-x)e^{\sin(\pi x)}dx$

28. In the interval $[0,1]$, the function $f(x)=x^{25}(1-x)^{75}$ has maxima at:

(a) 0 (b) $\dfrac{1}{4}$

(c) $\dfrac{1}{3}$ (d) $\dfrac{1}{2}$

29. If $f(x)=\begin{cases} x^a\ln x, & 0<x\le 2\\ 0, & x=0\end{cases}$, then the values of a for which Rolle's theorem will be applicable to $f(x)$ on the interval $[0,1]$ are:

(a) -1 (b) 0

(c) 2 (d) 3

30. Let $f(x)=\dfrac{x^2-ax+1}{x^2+ax+1}$, where $0<a<2$. The correct statements among the following are:

(a) $(2+a)^2 f''(1)+(2-a)^2 f''(-1)=0$

(b) $(2+a)^2 f'(1)+(2-a)^2 f'(-1)=1$

(c) Range of $f(x)$ is $\left[\dfrac{2-a}{2+a},\dfrac{2+a}{2-a}\right]$

(d) The function $f(x)$ is odd

31. Let $f(x)=|px-q|+r|x|$, where $p,q,r>0$. The function will have minima at $x=0$ if:

(a) $p>q$ (b) $r>q$

(c) $r>p$ (d) $p=q>r$

32. Let $f(x)=x+\ln x-x\ln x, x>0$. The correct options are:

(a) $f(x)=0$ for some $x\in(1,e)$

(b) $f(x)$ increases on (e,e^2)

(c) $f'(x)$ decreases on $(0,1)$

(d) $f'(x)=0$ for some $x \in (1,e)$

33. Function $f(x)$ is a fourth-degree polynomial having extrema at $x=1$ and $x=2$ and $\lim_{x\to 0}\left(1+\frac{f(x)}{x^2}\right)=2$. Then $f(2)$ equals:

(a) -1 (b) 0
(c) 1 (d) 2

34. Let $f(x)$ be a function defined on **R** such that $f'(x)=(x-1)(x-2)^2(x-3)^3(x-4)^4$. If $g(x)$ is a function defined on **R** such that $f(x)=\ln\{g(x)\}$, then the number of points at which $g(x)$ has maxima is:

(a) 1 (b) 3
(c) 2 (d) 4

35. Let $f(x)=(x^p-1)-p(x-1)$, $x>0$. If $p>1$, then

(a) $f(x)$ is increasing in $(0,+\infty)$

(b) $f(x)$ is decreasing in $(0,+\infty)$

(c) $f(x)\ge 0$ in $(0,+\infty)$

(d) $f(x)$ takes both positive and negative values in $(0,+\infty)$

36. The greatest value of the function $f(x)=2x^3-15x^2+36x-48$ in set $A=\{x: x^2+20\le 9x\}$ is:

(a) 5 (b) 7
(c) 64 (d) 125

37. Let $f(x)$ and $g(x)$ be two differentiable functions such that $f'(x)\le g'(x)$ for all $x<1$ and $f'(x)>g'(x)$ for all $x>1$. The correct statements among the following are:

(a) If $f(1)\ge g(1)$, then $f(x)\ge g(x)$ for all x

(b) If $f(1)\le g(1)$, then $f(x)\le g(x)$ for all x

(c) If $f(1)\ge g(1)$, then $f(x)\le g(x)$ for all x

(d) If $f(1)\le g(1)$, then $f(x)\ge g(x)$ for all x

38. Let $f(x)$ be a second-degree polynomial function such that $f(-2)=f(2)$. If the real numbers a,b,c are in AP, then $f'(a), f'(b), f'(c)$ are:

(a) In AP (b) In GP
(c) In HP (d) Equal

39. The greatest possible volume of a right-circular cone that can be inscribed inside a hollow sphere of volume V_0 is:

(a) $\frac{8}{27}V_0$ (b) $\frac{4}{27}V_0$

(c) $\frac{16}{81}V_0$ (d) $\frac{32}{81}V_0$

40. The greatest possible volume of a right circular cone having slant length L is

(a) $\frac{\pi}{3\sqrt{3}}L^3$ (b) $\frac{2\pi}{3\sqrt{3}}L^3$

(c) $\frac{\pi}{9\sqrt{3}}L^3$ (d) $\frac{2\pi}{9\sqrt{3}}L^3$

41. If a, b, c are three distinct numbers in G.P., and $a+b+c=kb$, then k cannot take the value

(a) -2 (b) -3
(c) 4 (d) 2

42. The number of distinct real roots of the equation $x^4-4x^3+12x^2+x-1=0$ is:

(a) 1 (b) 2
(c) 4 (d) 0

43. Consider the function $f(x)=4ax^2+\frac{1}{x}$, $a\in\mathbf{R}$. The minimum value of a for which $f(x)\ge 1$ for all $x>0$ is:

(a) $\frac{1}{25}$ (b) $\frac{1}{27}$

(c) $\frac{1}{32}$ (d) $\frac{1}{54}$

44. The functions $f:\mathbf{R}\to(0,+\infty)$ and $g:\mathbf{R}\to\mathbf{R}$ are twice differentiable. It is given that $f'(2)=g(2)=0, f''(2)\ne 0$, and $g'(2)\ne 0$. If $\lim_{x\to 2}\frac{f(x)g(x)}{f'(x)g'(x)}=1$, then:

(a) f has minima at $x=2$

(b) f has maxima at $x=2$

(c) $f''(2)>f(2)$

(d) $f''(2)=f(2)$

45. The range of the function $f(x)=\frac{\sqrt{3}\sin x}{2+\cos x}$ is:

(a) $\left[-1,\frac{-\sqrt{3}}{2}\right]$ (b) $[-1,1]$

(c) $\left[\frac{-\sqrt{3}}{2},1\right]$ (d) $\left[\frac{-3}{\sqrt{2}},\frac{3}{\sqrt{2}}\right]$

46. The function $f(x)=x+\sin(2x)$, $x\in(0,2\pi)$ attains maxima at:

(a) $x=\frac{\pi}{3},\frac{4\pi}{3}$ (b) $x=\frac{2\pi}{3},\frac{4\pi}{3}$

(c) $x=\frac{2\pi}{3},\frac{5\pi}{3}$ (d) $x=\frac{\pi}{3},\frac{2\pi}{3}$

47. Consider the function $f:\mathbf{R}\to\mathbf{R}$ given by $f(x)=x^5-5x+a, (a\in\mathbf{R})$. Then:

(a) $f(x)=0$ has three distinct real roots if $a>4$

(b) $f(x)=0$ has three distinct real roots if $-4<a<4$

(c) $f(x)=0$ has only one real root if $a<-4$

(d) $f(x)=0$ has only one real root if $-4<a<4$

48. Consider the function $f:\left(\frac{-\pi}{2},\frac{\pi}{2}\right)\to\mathbf{R}$ given by $f(x)=\ln^3(\sec x+\tan x)$. Then:

(a) $f(x)$ is odd and onto

(b) $f(x)$ is odd and invertible

(c) $f(x)$ is not odd but onto

(d) $f(x)$ is not odd but one–one

49. The number of points in the interval $\left(-\sqrt{13},\sqrt{13}\right)$ where the function $f(x)=\sin(x^2)+\cos(x^2)$ attains maxima is:

(a) 0 (b) 2

(c) 4 (d) 6

50. Let $f(x)=\frac{x^2-6x+5}{x^2-5x+6}$. If $1<x<2$, then:

(a) $0<f(x)<1$ (b) $f(x)<0$

(c) $f(x)>0$ (d) $f(x)<1$

51. The correct statements regarding the function $f(x)=\frac{\sin 5x}{\sin^5 x}$, $x\in(0,\pi)$ are:

(a) $f(x)=2$ has no roots

(b) $f(x)=1$ has two roots

(c) $f(x)=0$ has three roots

(d) $f(x)=-4$ has two roots

52. Let

$S=\left\{t\in\mathbf{R}: f(x)=|x-\pi|\left(e^{|x|}-1\right)\sin|x| \text{ is not differentiable at } t\right\}$.

Then set S equals:

(a) $\varnothing$ (b) $\{0\}$

(c) $\{\pi\}$ (d) $\{0,\pi\}$

53. Let $f(x)=x^2+\frac{1}{x^2}$ and $g(x)=x-\frac{1}{x}$ be defined for $x>0, x\neq 1$. If $h(x)=\frac{f(x)}{g(x)}$, then the local minimum value of $h(x)$ is:

(a) 3 (b) -3

(c) $2\sqrt{2}$ (d) $-2\sqrt{2}$

54. Let $f,g:[-1,2]\to\mathbf{R}$ be continuous functions which are twice differentiable in the interval $(-1,2)$. The values of f and g at points $-1,0$ and 2 are given in the following table:

	$x=-1$	$x=0$	$x=2$
$f(x)$	3	6	0
$g(x)$	0	1	-1

$(f-3g)''$ never vanishes in each of the intervals $(-1,0)$ and $(0,2)$. Then the correct statements from the following are:

(a) $(f-3g)'=0$ has exactly three solutions in $(-1,0)\cup(0,2)$

(b) $(f-3g)'=0$ has exactly one solution in $(-1,0)$

(c) $(f-3g)'=0$ has exactly one solution in $(0,2)$

(d) $(f-3g)'=0$ has exactly four solutions in $(-1,0)\cup(0,2)$

55. A point on the hypotenuse of a right-angled triangle is at a distance a, b from the other two sides of the triangle. The minimum length of the hypotenuse is:

(a) $\left(a^{2/3}+b^{2/3}\right)^{3/2}$

(b) $\left(a^{1/3}+b^{1/3}\right)^{3/2}$

(c) $\left(a^{2/3}+b^{2/3}\right)^{5/2}$

(d) $\left(a^{1/3}+b^{1/3}\right)^{5/2}$

56. The largest area of a rectangle whose base is on the x-axis and which has two of its vertices lying on the curve $y=e^{-x^2}$ is:

(a) $\sqrt{\frac{2}{e}}$ (b) $\sqrt{\frac{e}{2}}$

(c) $\frac{\sqrt{2}}{e}$ (d) $\frac{\sqrt{e}}{2}$

57. A cylindrical container is to be made from certain solid material with the following constraints. It has a fixed inner volume of V_0 mm^3, a 2-mm-thick solid wall and is open at the top. The bottom of the container is a solid circular disc of thickness 2 mm and is of radius equal to the outer radius of the container. If the volume of the material used to make the container is minimum when the inner radius of the container is 10 mm, then the value of $\frac{V_0}{250\pi}$ is:

(a) 4 (b) 5

(c) 6 (d) 7

58. Match the functions given in the left column with the corresponding number of extrema in the right column:

(a) $\left(1-\frac{x^2}{a^2}\right)^2$	(p) 0
(b) $\frac{x}{a}-\frac{x^3}{3a^3}$	(q) 1
(c) $\frac{x^2}{a^2}e^{\frac{-x^2}{a^2}}$	(r) 2
(d) $\frac{x^2}{a^2}-\frac{x^3}{3a^3}$	(s) 3

ANSWER KEYS

1. (a)	**2.** (b)	**3.** (b),(c)	**4.** (a)	**5.** (b),(d)	**6.** (c)	**7.** (b)
8. (b)	**9.** (d)	**10.** (d)	**11.** (c),(d)	**12.** (c)	**13.** (a),(c)	**14.** (c)
15. (a),(b)	**16.** (c),(d)	**17.** (b),(c)	**18.** (b)	**19.** (b)	**20.** (a)	**21.** (a), (d)
22. (a)	**23.** (a),(c)	**24.** (b)	**25.** (d)	**26.** (d)	**27.** (a),(b),(c),(d)	**28.** (b)
29. (c),(d)	**30.** (a),(c)	**31.** (c)	**32.** (c),(d)	**33.** (b)	**34.** (a)	**35.** (c)
36. (b)	**37.** (a)	**38.** (a)	**39.** (a)	**40.** (d)	**41.** (d)	**42.** (b)
43. (b)	**44.** (a),(d)	**45.** (b)	**46.** (a)	**47.** (b),(c)	**48.** (a),(b)	**49.** (c)
50. (b)	**51.** (d)	**52.** (a)	**53.** (c)	**54.** (b),(c)	**55.** (a)	**56.** (a)
57. (a)	**58.** (a)-(s), (b)-(r), (c)-(s), (d)-(r)					

SOLUTIONS

1. (a) The given function $f:[-1,-1]\rightarrow\left[\frac{\pi}{4},\frac{3\pi}{4}\right]$ and its derivative are, respectively,

$$f(x)=\tan^{-1}x+\cos^{-1}x$$

and $$f'(x)=\frac{1}{1+x^2}-\frac{1}{\sqrt{1-x^2}}=\frac{\sqrt{1-x^2}-\left(1+x^2\right)}{\left(1+x^2\right)\sqrt{1-x^2}}$$

Let us solve the inequality $f'(x)>0$

$\Rightarrow\quad \sqrt{1-x^2}>1+x^2$

$\Rightarrow\quad 1-x^2>x^4+2x^2+1$

$\Rightarrow\quad x^4+3x^2<0$, which is never true.

Thus, we see that $f'(x)$ is always negative. Therefore, $f(x)$ is decreasing on $[-1,-1]$ $\Rightarrow$ One–one.

Also $f(-1)=\frac{-\pi}{4}+\pi=\frac{3\pi}{4}$, and $f(1)=\frac{\pi}{4}+0=\frac{\pi}{4}$.

Hence, range of $f(x)$ is $\left[\frac{\pi}{4},\frac{3\pi}{4}\right]$ which is equal to the given co-domain $\Rightarrow$ Onto.

2. (b) From the graphs of the two functions e^x and x^2, we can see that they will intersect once in the negative x region.
To analyse in the positive x region, let us consider the function

$$f(x)=e^x-x^2, x>0.$$

Then $f'(x)=e^x-2x$ and $f''(x)=e^x-2$.

The second derivative changes sign from –ve to +ve at $x=\ln 2$. Hence, the least value of the first derivative is $f'(\ln 2)=2(1-\ln 2)>0$. Thus, the first derivative is always positive $\Rightarrow f$ is strictly increasing.

Now, since $f(0)>0 \Rightarrow f$ is always greater than 0. Hence, there is no solution of $f=0$ in the positive x region.

3. (b),(c) We have $f(x)=|x-2|$ and

$$g(x)=f\{f(x)\}=\big||x-2|-2\big|$$

The figure shows the graph of $g(x)$. We can see that option (b) is correct whereas options (a) and (d) are incorrect.

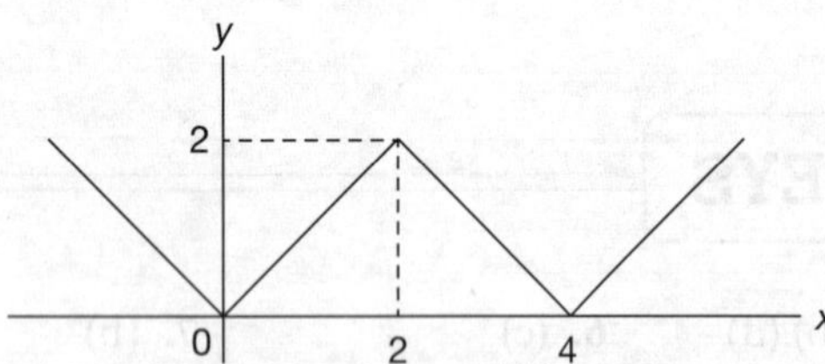

To check option (c), let $h(x)=\int_{-\infty}^{x} g(x)dx$. Then $h'(x)=g(x)$. Since $g(x)$ is always positive, $h(x)$ is increasing on **R**. Hence, option (c) is correct.

4. (a) The given function and its derivative are, respectively,

$$f(x)=x^5+bx^3+cx+d$$

$$f'(x)=5x^4+3bx^2+c$$

The discriminant $D=9b^2-20c<0$ $(b^2<2c$, given), and coefficient of x^4 is +ve; therefore $f'(x)$ is always +ve $\Rightarrow f(x)$ is increasing. Also $f(-\infty)=-\infty$ and $f(+\infty)=+\infty$. Hence, $f(x)$ is unbounded and takes the value 0 only once.

5. (b),(d) From the graphs of e^x and mx, we can see that for $m<0$, there will be only one intersection in the negative x region. Hence, option (d) is correct. For values of $m>0$, the two graphs will not intersect in the negative x region. To analyse in the positive x region, let us consider the function

$$f(x)=e^x-mx, x>0$$

Then $f'(x)=e^x-m$ which changes sign from –ve to +ve at $x=\ln m$.

Thus, the least value of the function is

$$f(\ln m)=m(1-\ln m)$$

$$=\begin{cases} +ve \text{ for } m<e \Rightarrow \text{no solution} \\ 0 \text{ for } m=e \Rightarrow \text{one solution} \\ -ve \text{ for } m>e \Rightarrow \text{two solutions} \end{cases}$$

Hence, option (b) is also correct.

6. (c) The given function can be written as

$$f(x)=\frac{1}{2}(1-\cos 2x)+\frac{1}{2}(\cos 2x-\cos 4x)$$

$$=\frac{1}{2}(1-\cos 4x)=\sin^2(2x)$$

We see that $f(x)\geq 0$ for all real x

$\Rightarrow$ (a), (b) are incorrect.

Also $f'(x)=4\sin 2x\cos 2x=2\sin 4x$.

When $x\in\left(\pi,\frac{5\pi}{4}\right)$, then $4x\in(4\pi,5\pi)$. In this interval, $f'(x)>0 \Rightarrow$ (c) is correct.

When $x\in\left(-\pi,\frac{-\pi}{2}\right)$, then $4x\in(-4\pi,-2\pi)$. In this interval, $f'(x)$ is positive as well as negative $\Rightarrow$ (d) is incorrect.

7. (b) The given function can be written as

$$f(x)=\frac{1}{4}(1-\cos 2x)^2+\frac{1}{4}(1+\cos 2x)^2$$

$$=\frac{1}{2}\{1+\cos^2(2x)\}=\frac{1}{2}+\frac{1}{4}(1+\cos 4x)$$

$$=\frac{3}{4}+\frac{1}{4}\cos 4x.$$

Now $f'(x)=-\sin 4x$. Thus, $f(x)$ is increasing when $f'(x)>0 \Rightarrow \sin 4x<0$. That is, when

$$\pi+2n\pi<4x<2\pi+2n\pi$$

$$\Rightarrow \quad (2n+1)\frac{\pi}{4}<x<(n+1)\frac{\pi}{2}$$

$$\Rightarrow \quad x\in\left(\frac{\pi}{4},\frac{\pi}{2}\right)\cup\left(\frac{3\pi}{4},\pi\right)\cup\left(\frac{5\pi}{4},\frac{3\pi}{2}\right)\cup\left(\frac{7\pi}{4},2\pi\right)$$

Only option (b) lies in the above intervals.

8. (b) The given function and its derivative are, respectively,

$$f(x)=xe^{x(1-x)}$$

and $$f'(x)=e^{x(1-x)}\{1+x(1-2x)\}$$

$$= -2e^{x(1-x)}\left(x+\frac{1}{2}\right)(x-1)$$

$$= \begin{cases} -\text{ve}, x < \frac{-1}{2} \\ +\text{ve}, \frac{-1}{2} < x < 1 \\ -\text{ve}, x > 1 \end{cases}$$

Thus, $f(x)$ increases in $\left(\frac{-1}{2},1\right)$ and decreases otherwise. There are two extrema since $f'(x)$ changes sign twice.

Also $\lim_{x\to\infty}\frac{x}{e^{x^2-x}}\left(\frac{\infty}{\infty}\right) = \lim_{x\to\infty}\frac{1}{e^{x^2-x}(2x-1)} = 0.$

Hence, only option (b) is incorrect.

9. (d) The minima of the quadratic function $f(x) = (1+b^2)x^2 + 2bx + 1$ occurs at $x = \frac{-b}{1+b^2}$ and its minimum value is

$$m = \frac{b^2}{1+b^2} - \frac{2b^2}{1+b^2} + 1 = \frac{1}{1+b^2}$$

The values of $1+b^2$ lie in $[1,+\infty)$. Hence, the values of m will lie in $(0,1]$.

10. (d) The given relation and its derivative are, respectively,

$$y^3 + 3x^2 = 12y$$

and $\quad 3y^2y' + 6x = 12y' \Rightarrow y' = \frac{2x}{4-y^2}$

The tangent will be vertical where $y' = \infty \Rightarrow 4 - y^2 \Rightarrow y = \pm 2$.

Putting $y = 2$ in the equation of the curve gives $x = \frac{\pm 4}{\sqrt{3}}$ whereas $y = -2$ gives no real value for x.

11. (c),(d) The given function can be written as

$$f(x) = \begin{cases} -px - qx^2, x \le 0 \\ px - qx^2, x \ge 0 \end{cases}$$

Its derivative is

$$f'(x) = \begin{cases} -p - 2qx, x < 0 \\ p - 2qx, x > 0 \end{cases}$$

The critical points are points where f' does not exist and where $f' = 0$. That is

$x = 0$ and

$x = \frac{-p}{2q}$ (−ve number), $\frac{p}{2q}$ (+ve number).

If p and q are of opposite signs, $x = 0$ is the only critical point. If $p > 0$, f' changes sign from −ve to +ve at $x = 0 \Rightarrow$ Minima at $x = 0$. If $p < 0$, f' changes sign from +ve to −ve at $x = 0 \Rightarrow$ Maxima at $x = 0$.

If p and q are of the same sign, there are three critical points.

If $p > 0$, then minima at $x = 0$ and hence 2 maxima on either side.

If $p < 0$, then maxima at $x = 0$ and hence 2 minima on either side.

12. (c) The function $f(x) = \sqrt[4]{97-x} + \sqrt[4]{x}$ is defined for $x \in [0,97]$. It is even symmetrical about $x = 97/2$ since $f(x) = f(97-x)$.

Its derivative $f'(x) = \frac{(97-x)^{3/4} - x^{3/4}}{4x^{3/4}(97-x)^{3/4}}$ changes sign from +ve to −ve at $x = 97/2$. Thus, it increases strictly in $[0,97/2]$ and then decreases strictly in $[97/2,97]$. Its range is $[f(0), f(97/2)] = [0, \sqrt[4]{776}]$. Since $5 = \sqrt[4]{625} < \sqrt[4]{776}$, the function will take the value 5 twice, once in $[0,97/2]$ when the function is increasing and once again in $[97/2,97]$ when the function is decreasing. Hence, there are two solutions.

13. (a),(c) The given function and its derivative are, respectively,

$$h(x) = f(x) - f^2(x) + f^3(x)$$

and $\quad h'(x) = f'(x)\left[3f^2(x) - 2f(x) + 1\right]$

We see that $3f^2(x) - 2f(x) + 1$ is always positive since the discriminant $D = -8$ is negative and the coefficient of x^2 is positive. Therefore, $h'(x)$ has the same sign as $f'(x)$.

Therefore, $h(x)$ decreases when $f(x)$ increases, and $h(x)$ decreases when $f(x)$ decreases.

14. (c) The given functions and their derivatives are, respectively,

$$f(x) = \frac{x}{\sin x},\ f'(x) = \frac{\sin x - x\cos x}{\sin^2 x} = \frac{\cos x(\tan x - x)}{\sin^2 x}$$

and

$$g(x) = \frac{x}{\tan x},\ g'(x) = \frac{\tan x - x\sec^2 x}{\tan^2 x} = \frac{\sin x\cos x - x}{\sin^2 x}$$

$$= \frac{\sin 2x - 2x}{2\sin^2 x}$$

For $x \in (0,1)$, we see that $f'(x)$ is positive and $g'(x)$ is negative.

Therefore, $f(x)$ increases and $g(x)$ decreases in $(0,1)$.

15. (a),(b) The given function and its derivative are, respectively,

$$f(x)=\cos^2 x+\sin x$$

and $f'(x)=-2\cos x\sin x+\cos x=-2\cos x\left(\sin x-\frac{1}{2}\right)$

The figure shows the sign scheme for $f'(x)$. We see that $f'(x)$ changes sign from +ve to −ve at $x=\frac{\pi}{6},\frac{5\pi}{6}$. Therefore, $f(x)$ has maxima at these two points.

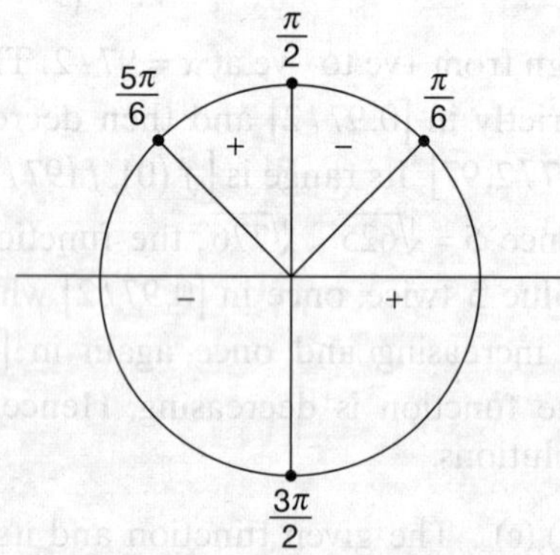

16. (c),(d) The given function can be written as

$$h(x)=\begin{cases} f^2(x), x<0 \\ f^2(x)-1, x\geq 0\end{cases}=\begin{cases} x^2, x<0 \\ e^{2x}-1, x\geq 0\end{cases}$$

Its derivative is

$$h'(x)=\begin{cases} 2x, x<0 \\ 2e^{2x}, x>0\end{cases}$$

We see that $h(x)$ is continuous everywhere but is not differentiable at $x=0$.

It decreases in $(-\infty,0)$ and increases in $(0,+\infty)$
$\Rightarrow$ Function is not one–one.

Its least value is $h(0)=0$. Also $\lim_{x\to-\infty} h(x)=+\infty$ and $\lim_{x\to+\infty} h(x)=+\infty$. Hence, the range is $[0,+\infty)$, which is equal to the given co-domain $\Rightarrow$ Function is onto.

17. (b),(c) The given function and its derivatives are

$$f(x)=x\cos\frac{1}{x}, x\geq 1$$

$$f'(x)=\cos\frac{1}{x}+\frac{1}{x}\sin\frac{1}{x}, x>1$$

and $$f''(x)=\frac{-1}{x^3}\cos\frac{1}{x}, x>1$$

We see that $f''(x)<0$ for all $x>1 \Rightarrow f'(x)$ is decreasing in $(1,+\infty)$.

Its greatest value is $f'(1)=\cos 1+\sin 1$ and its least value is $\lim_{x\to+\infty} f'(x)=1$.

Hence, using Lagrange's mean value theorem, we have

$$1<\frac{f(x+2)-f(x)}{2}<\cos 1+\sin 1 \Rightarrow f(x+2)-f(x)>2$$

Since $f'>0$ (positive slope always), f strictly increases.

18. (b) Let $f(x)=ax^2+bx+c$, where $a>0$, $b^2-4ac<0$.

Its derivatives are

$$f'(x)=2ax+b \text{ and } f''(x)=2a$$

Now, we have

$$g(x)=ax^2+(b+2a)x+c+b+2a$$

Its discriminant $D=(b+2a)^2-4a(c+b+2a)=b^2-4ac-4a^2$ is negative and the coefficient of x^2 is positive. Hence, $g(x)>0$ for any real x.

19. (b) Let us choose the function as $f(x)=ax+(1-a)x^2$, which is the same in all the options; it satisfies the first two conditions, $f(0)=0$ and $f(1)=1$.

Its derivative is $f'(x)=2(1-a)x+a$.

If $a<1$, $f'(x)$ increases and its least value in $[0,1]$ equals $f'(0)=a$. According to the question, $a>0$. The values of a satisfying both inequalities are $0<a<1$.

If $a>1$, $f'(x)$ decreases and its least value in $[0,1]$ equals $f'(1)=2-a$. According to the question, $2-a>0 \Rightarrow a<2$. The values of a satisfying both inequalities are $1<a<2$.

20. (a) The given relation $f(x+1)=xf(x)$ can be written as

$$\ln\{f(x+1)\}=\ln x+\ln\{f(x)\}$$

$$\Rightarrow \qquad g(x+1)=\ln x+g(x)$$

Differentiating twice with respect to x, we have

$$g''(x+1)-g''(x)=\frac{-1}{x^2}$$

Putting $x=\frac{1}{2},\frac{3}{2},\ldots,n\frac{-1}{2}$, we have

$$g''\left(\frac{3}{2}\right)-g''\left(\frac{1}{2}\right)=-4$$

$$g''\left(\frac{5}{2}\right)-g''\left(\frac{3}{2}\right)=\frac{-4}{9}$$

$$\ldots$$

$$g''\left(n+\frac{1}{2}\right)-g''\left(n-\frac{1}{2}\right)=\frac{-4}{(2n-1)^2}$$

Adding the above relations, we have

$$g''\left(n+\frac{1}{2}\right)-g''\left(\frac{1}{2}\right)=-4\left\{1+\frac{1}{9}+\frac{1}{25}+\ldots+\frac{1}{(2n-1)^2}\right\}$$

21. (a),(d) The given function and its derivative are, respectively,

$$f(x)=\frac{\ln(\pi+x)}{\ln(e+x)},\ x>-e,\ x\neq -e+1$$

and $$f'(x)=\frac{\frac{\ln(e+x)}{\pi+x}-\frac{\ln(\pi+x)}{e+x}}{\ln^2(e+x)}$$

$$=\frac{(e+x)\ln(e+x)-(\pi+x)\ln(\pi+x)}{(\pi+x)(e+x)\ln^2(e+x)}$$

$$=\frac{\ln(e+x)^{(e+x)}-\ln(\pi+x)^{(\pi+x)}}{(\pi+x)(e+x)\ln^2(e+x)}$$

Since $e<\pi\to e+x<\pi+x$

$$(e+x)^{(e+x)}<(\pi+x)^{(\pi+x)}\text{ for }x>0.$$

$\Rightarrow$ $f'(x)<0$ for $x>0$

$\Rightarrow$ $f(x)$ decreases in $(0,\infty)$.

Also, we have

$$\lim_{x\to+\infty}f(x)=\lim_{x\to+\infty}\frac{\ln(\pi+x)}{\ln(e+x)}\left(\frac{\infty}{\infty}\right)$$

$$=\lim_{x\to+\infty}\frac{\frac{1}{\pi+x}}{\frac{1}{e+x}}=\lim_{x\to+\infty}\frac{e+x}{\pi+x}=1$$

and $\lim_{x\to+\infty}f'(x)=0$ since $f(x)$ approaches a constant value as x approaches infinity.

22. (a) The function in option (a) is continuous everywhere. Its derivative is

$$f'(x)=\begin{cases}-1,\ x<\frac{1}{2}\\ -2\left(\frac{1}{2}-x\right),\ x>\frac{1}{2}\end{cases}$$

We see that it is not differentiable at $x=1/2$. Hence, Lagrange's mean value theorem is not applicable to this function in the interval $[-1,1]$.

The function in option (b) is continuous everywhere. Its RHD and LHD at $x=0$ are

$$\text{RHD}=\lim_{h\to0}\frac{\frac{\sin h}{h}-1}{h}=\lim_{h\to0}\frac{\sin h-h}{h^2}\left(\frac{0}{0}\right)$$

$$=\lim_{h\to0}\frac{\cos h-1}{2h}=0$$

$$\text{LHD}=\lim_{h\to0}\frac{1-\frac{\sin h}{h}}{h}=\lim_{h\to0}\frac{h-\sin h}{h^2}\left(\frac{0}{0}\right)$$

$$=\lim_{h\to0}\frac{1-\cos h}{2h}=0$$

We see that it is differentiable everywhere. Hence, Lagrange's mean value theorem is applicable to this function in the interval $[-1,1]$.

The function in option (c) and its derivative are, respectively,

$$f(x)=\begin{cases}-x^2,\ x<0\\ x^2,\ x\geq0\end{cases}$$

and $$f'(x)=\begin{cases}-2x,\ x<0\\ 2x,\ x>0\end{cases}$$

We see that it is continuous and differentiable everywhere. Hence, Lagrange's mean value theorem is applicable to this function in the interval $[-1,1]$.

The function in option (c) and its derivative are, respectively,

$$f(x)=\begin{cases}-x^3,\ x<0\\ x^3,\ x\geq0\end{cases}$$

and $$f'(x)=\begin{cases}-3x^2,\ x<0\\ 3x^2,\ x>0\end{cases}$$

We see that it is continuous and differentiable everywhere. Hence, Lagrange's mean value theorem is applicable to this function in the interval $[-1,1]$.

23. (a),(c) Let $f(x)=(x-2)^2(ax+b)$.

Then $\quad f'(x)=a(x-2)^2+2(x-2)(ax+b)$.

Using the conditions $f(-1)=9$ and $f'(1)=0$, we have

$$b-a=1 \text{ and } a+2b=0$$

Solving, we have $a=-2/3, b=1/3$.
Hence, we have

$$f(x)=\frac{-1}{3}(x-2)^2(2x-1) \text{ and}$$

$$f'(x)=\frac{-2}{3}(x-2)^2+\frac{-2}{3}(x-2)(2x-1)$$

Thus, we have the following results:

Roots of $f(x)=0$ are $x=\frac{1}{2},2 \Rightarrow$ (a) is correct.

$f(x)$ has maxima at $x=2$ since f' changes sign from +ve to –ve at $x=2 \Rightarrow$ (b) is incorrect.

$$\lim_{x\to\infty}\frac{f(x)}{x^3}=\frac{-1}{3}\lim_{x\to\infty}\frac{(x-2)^2(2x-1)}{x^3}=\frac{-2}{3}$$

$\Rightarrow$ (c) is correct.
$f(x)<0$ on $(1/2,2) \Rightarrow$ (d) is incorrect.

24. (b) The derivative of $g(x)$ is $g'(x)=f(x)$. Thus, the sign of $g'(x)$ is the same as that of $f(x)$. The figure shows the graph of the function $f(x)$. We see that $f(x)$ changes sign from +ve to –ve at $x=1+\ln 2$ and from –ve to +ve at $x=e$. Hence, $g(x)$ has maxima at $x=1+\ln 2$ and minima at $x=e$.

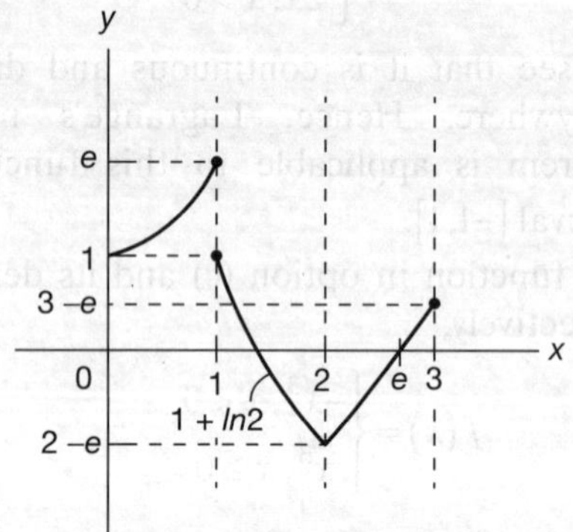

25. (d) Let $g(x)=f(x)-x^2$.

Then $\quad g(1)=0, g(2)=0$, and $g(3)=0$.

From Rolle's theorem, $g'(x)=f'(x)-2$ vanishes at least once in $(1,2)$ and at least once in $(2,3)$. Again, from Rolle's theorem, $g''(x)=f''(x)-2$ vanishes at least once between the points where $g'(x)=0$. Hence, there exists at least one $x\in(1,3)$ such that $f''(x)=2$.

26. (d) In the interval $x\in\left(\frac{1}{2},1\right)\Rightarrow \pi x\in\left(\frac{\pi}{2},\pi\right)$, the function $\sin^4(\pi x)$ decreases, which means $\frac{1}{2+\sin^4(\pi x)}$ increases, and the function $192x^3$ increases. Hence $f'(x)$ increases. Thus, we have

$$f'\left(\frac{1}{2}\right)<f'(x)<f'(1)$$

$$\Rightarrow \quad 8<f'(x)<96$$

Now, using the value of $f\left(\frac{1}{2}\right)$, we can estimate the value of $f(1)$:

$$8<\frac{f(1)-f\left(\frac{1}{2}\right)}{1-\frac{1}{2}}<96$$

$$\Rightarrow \quad 4<f(1)<48$$

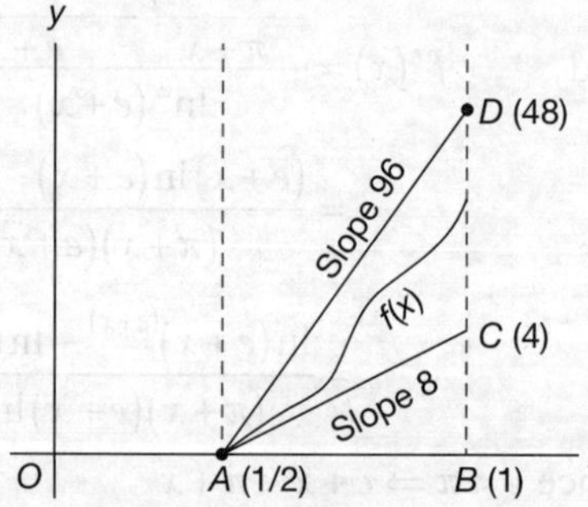

The graph of $f(x)$ lies between the lines AC and AD (see figure), and the area under the graph in the interval $\left(\frac{1}{2},1\right)$ lies between the areas of the triangles ΔABC and ΔABD. Hence, we have

$$\frac{1}{2}\times AB\times BC<\int_{1/2}^{1}f(x)dx<\frac{1}{2}\times AB\times BD$$

$$\Rightarrow \quad \frac{1}{2}\times\frac{1}{2}\times 4<\int_{1/2}^{1}f(x)dx<\frac{1}{2}\times\frac{1}{2}\times 48$$

$$\Rightarrow \quad 1<\int_{1/2}^{1}f(x)dx<12$$

27. (a),(b),(c),(d) The given relation is

$$f(x)=f(1-x)$$

Differentiating with respect to x, we have

$$f'(x)=-f'(1-x)$$

Putting $x=\frac{1}{2}$, we have $f'\left(\frac{1}{2}\right)=0$. It is also given that $f'\left(\frac{1}{4}\right)=0$. Putting $x=\frac{1}{4}$, we have $f'\left(\frac{3}{4}\right)=0$. Hence, by Rolle's theorem, $f''(x)=0$ at least once in $\left(\frac{1}{4},\frac{1}{2}\right)$ and at least once in $\left(\frac{1}{2},\frac{3}{4}\right)$, that is, at least twice in $(0,1)$.

Using properties of definite integration in option (c), we have

$$I=\int_{-1/2}^{1/2} f\left(x+\frac{1}{2}\right)\sin x\,dx=\int_{-1/2}^{1/2} f\left(-x+\frac{1}{2}\right)\sin(-x)\,dx$$

Putting $x+\frac{1}{2}$ for x in the given relation, we get $f\left(x+\frac{1}{2}\right)=f\left(-x+\frac{1}{2}\right)$.

Hence

$$2I=\int_{-1/2}^{1/2}\left\{f\left(x+\frac{1}{2}\right)-f\left(-x+\frac{1}{2}\right)\right\}\sin x\,dx=0\Rightarrow I=0$$

In option (d), let us insert $1-x=t$ in the RHS. Then, we have

$$\text{RHS}=\int_{1/2}^{0}-f(t)e^{\sin\pi(1-t)}\,dt=\int_{0}^{1/2}f(t)e^{\sin\pi t}\,dt=\text{LHS}.$$

28. (b) The given function and its derivative are, respectively,

$$f(x)=x^{25}(1-x)^{75},\ x\in[0,1]$$

and

$$f'(x)=25x^{24}(1-x)^{75}-75x^{25}(1-x)^{74}$$

$$=-100x^{24}(1-x)^{74}\left(x-\frac{1}{4}\right)$$

Since $f'(x)$ changes sign from +ve to −ve at $x=\frac{1}{4}$, $f(x)$ has maxima at this point.

29. (c),(d) The given function and its derivative are, respectively,

$$f(x)=\begin{cases}x^a\ln x, & 0<x\le 2\\ 0, & x=0\end{cases}$$

and

$$f'(x)=x^{a-1}(a\ln x+1),\ 0<x\le 2$$

We see that $f(0)=0=f(1)$.

The RHL value of the function at $x=0$ is

$$f\left(0^+\right)=\lim_{h\to 0}h^a\ \ln h=\lim_{h\to 0}\frac{\ln h}{h^{-a}}\left(\frac{\infty}{\infty}\right)\text{ if } a>0$$

$$=\lim_{h\to 0}\frac{1/h}{-ah^{-a-1}}=\lim_{h\to 0}\frac{h^a}{-a}=0\text{ if } a>0$$

30. (a),(c) The given function and its derivatives are

$$f(x)=\frac{x^2-ax+1}{x^2+ax+1},\text{ where } 0<a<2$$

$$f'(x)=\frac{2a\left(x^2-1\right)}{\left(x^2+ax+1\right)^2}$$

and

$$f''(x)=\frac{4ax\left(-x^2+ax+3\right)}{\left(x^2+ax+1\right)^3}$$

Now $f'(1)=0=f'(-1), f''(1)=\frac{4a}{(2+a)^2}$

and $f''(-1)=\frac{-4a}{(2-a)^2}$

Hence $(2+a)^2 f''(1)+(2-a)^2 f''(-1)=0$

$\Rightarrow$ (a) is correct

$$(2+a)^2 f'(1)+(2-a)^2 f'(-1)=0$$

$\Rightarrow$ (b) is incorrect.

The function has extrema at $x=\pm 1$. Now $f(-1)=\frac{2+a}{2-a}$ and $f(1)=\frac{2-a}{2+a}$. Also $\lim_{x\to\infty}f(x)=1$.

Hence, the range is $\left[\frac{2-a}{2+a},\frac{2+a}{2-a}\right]\Rightarrow$ (c) is correct

Since $f(-x)\neq -f(x)$, the function is not odd

$\Rightarrow$ (d) is incorrect.

31. (c) The given function can be written as

$$f(x)=\begin{cases}-(p+r)x+q, & x<0\\ (r-p)x+q, & 0\le x\le \frac{q}{p}\\ (p+r)x-q, & x>\frac{q}{p}\end{cases}$$

Its derivative is

$$f'(x)=\begin{cases}-(p+r), & x<0\\ (r-p), & 0<x<\frac{q}{p}\\ (p+r), & x>\frac{q}{p}\end{cases}$$

For minima at $x = 0$, $f'(x)$ must change sign from −ve to +ve. The LHD is already −ve. For RHD to be +ve, $r > p$.

32. (c),(d) The given function and its derivatives are, respectively,

$$f(x) = x + \ln x - x\ln x$$

$$f'(x) = \frac{1}{x} - \ln x$$

From the graphs of the functions $\frac{1}{x}$ and $\ln x$, we see that $f'(x)$ changes sign from +ve to −ve at $x = \alpha$, where $1 < \alpha < e$. Therefore, $f(x)$ increases on $(0, \alpha)$ and decreases on $(\alpha, +\infty)$.

$f''(x)$ is always −ve $\Rightarrow$ $f'(x)$ decreases monotonically.

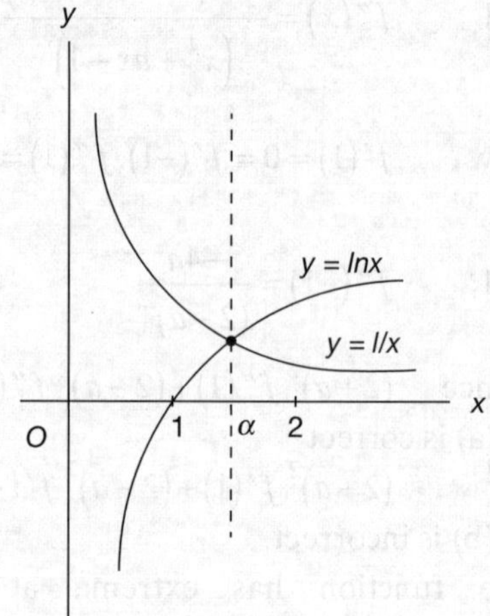

Also, we have

$$f(0^+) = \lim_{x\to 0} x + \ln x - \frac{\ln x}{1/x} = 0 - \infty + 0 = -\infty$$

$$f(+\infty) = \lim_{x\to 0} x + \ln x - x\ln x = \infty + \infty - \infty \cdot \infty = -\infty$$

$$[a + b < ab \text{ for } a, b > 1]$$

and $\quad f(1) = 1 = f(e)$, and $f(e) = 2 - e^2 < 0$

Thus, $f(x) = 0$ for some x in the intervals $(0,1)$ and (e, e^2).

Also $f''(x) = -\frac{x+1}{x^2} < 0$ in the entire domain $(x > 0) \Rightarrow f'$ decreases monotonically.

Thus, options (c), (d) are correct.

33. (b) We have

$$\lim_{x\to 0} \frac{f(x)}{x^2} = 1 \Rightarrow f(x) = x^2(ax^2 + bx + 1)$$

Now $\quad f'(x) = 4ax^3 + 3bx^2 + 2x$

Using the conditions $f'(1) = 0 = f'(2)$, we have

$$4a + 3b + 2 = 0 \text{ and } 8a + 3b + 1 = 0$$

Solving gives $a = \frac{1}{4}$, $b = -1$. Thus,

$$f(x) = x^2\left(\frac{1}{4}x^2 - x + 1\right) \text{ and hence } f(2) = 0.$$

34. (a) We have $g(x) = e^{f(x)}$. The function $g(x)$ will attain maxima whenever $f(x)$ attains maxima, since the exponential function is an increasing function.

We see that $f'(x)$ changes sign from +ve to −ve at $x = 1$ only. Hence maxima occurs at $x = 1$.

35. (c) The given function and its derivative are, respectively,

$$f(x) = (x^p - 1) - p(x - 1), x > 0, p > 1$$

and $\quad f'(x) = p(x^{p-1} - 1)$

For $p > 1$, the function x^{p-1} is strictly increasing in the interval $(0, +\infty)$. Therefore, $f'(x)$ changes sign at $x = 1$ only. At $x = 1$, $f'(x)$ changes sign from −ve to +ve $\Rightarrow$ Minima. The least value of the function in $(0, +\infty)$ is $f(1) = 0$. Hence $f(x) \geq 0$ in $(0, +\infty)$.

36. (b) Solving the inequality in set A, we have

$$x^2 - 9x + 20 \leq 0$$

$$\Rightarrow \quad (x - 4)(x - 5) \leq 0$$

$$\Rightarrow \quad 4 \leq x \leq 5$$

The given function and its derivative are, respectively,

$$f(x) = 2x^3 - 15x^2 + 36x - 48$$

and $\quad f'(x) = 6x^2 - 30x + 36 = 6(x - 2)(x - 3)$

In the interval $[4,5]$, $f'(x)$ is always +ve $\Rightarrow f(x)$ is increasing. Hence, the greatest value of the function in $[4,5]$ is $f(5) = 7$.

37. (a) Let $h(x) = f(x) - g(x)$. Its derivative $h'(x) = f'(x) - g'(x)$ changes sign from –ve to +ve at $x = 1 \Rightarrow$ Minima at $x = 1$. The least value of the function is $h(1) = f(1) - g(1)$. Thus, we have

$$h(x) \geq h(1) \text{ for all } x$$

$$\Rightarrow \quad f(x) - g(x) \geq f(1) - g(1) \text{ for all } x$$

If $f(1) \geq g(1)$, then $f(x) - g(x) \geq 0$ for all x.

38. (a) The function is given to be quadratic and even. The function may be chosen as $f(x) = px^2 + q$. Its derivative is $f'(x) = 2px + q$.
Now, we have

$$f'(a) = 2pa + q,\ f'(b) = 2pb + q$$

and $\quad f'(c) = 2pc + q$

We can see that if a, b, c are in AP, then $f'(a), f'(b), f'(c)$ are also in AP.

39. (a)

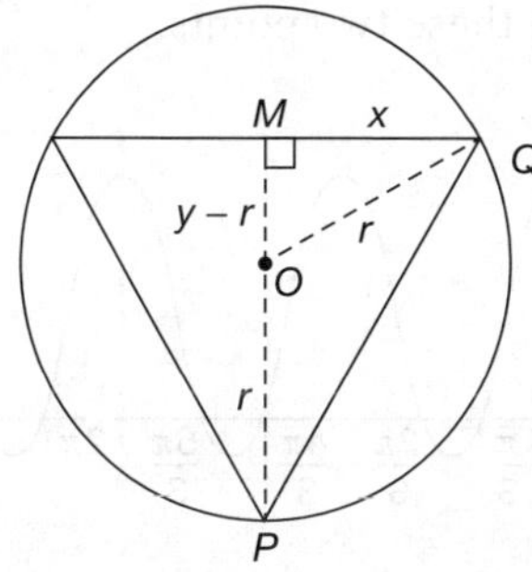

Let x, y be the radius and height of a cone, respectively. If r is the radius of the sphere (see figure), then

$$x^2 = r^2 - (y-r)^2 = 2ry - y^2$$

The volume of the cone is given by

$$V = \frac{1}{3}\pi x^2 y = \frac{1}{3}\pi\left(2ry^2 - y^3\right).$$

Now $\quad \dfrac{dV}{dy} = \dfrac{1}{3}\pi\left(4ry - 3y^2\right) = -\pi y\left(y - \dfrac{4r}{3}\right).$

The derivative changes sign from +ve to −ve at $y = \frac{4r}{3} \Rightarrow$ V attains maxima at $y = \frac{4r}{3}$. Hence, the maximum possible volume of the cone is

$$V_{\max} = \frac{32}{81}\pi r^3 = \frac{8}{27} \times \frac{4}{3}\pi r^3 = \frac{8}{27}V_0$$

40. (d) Let x, y be the radius and height of the cone, respectively. If L is the slant height of the cone, then

$$x^2 + y^2 = L^2.$$

The volume of the cone is given by

$$V = \frac{1}{3}\pi x^2 y = \frac{1}{3}\pi(L^2 - y^2)y = \frac{1}{3}\pi(L^2 y - y^3)$$

Now $\quad \dfrac{dV}{dy} = \dfrac{1}{3}\pi(L^2 - 3y^2) = -\pi\left(y + \dfrac{L}{\sqrt{3}}\right)\left(y - \dfrac{L}{\sqrt{3}}\right)$

The derivative changes sign from +ve to −ve at $y = \frac{L}{\sqrt{3}} \Rightarrow V$ attains maxima at $y = \frac{L}{\sqrt{3}}$. Hence, the maximum possible volume of the cone is

$$V_{\max} = \frac{1}{3}\pi\left(\frac{L^3}{\sqrt{3}} - \frac{L^3}{3\sqrt{3}}\right) = \frac{2\pi}{9\sqrt{3}}L^3$$

41. (d) If x be the common ratio of the G.P., then the given condition $a + b + c = kb$ can be written as

$$\frac{b}{x} + b + bx = kb$$

$$\Rightarrow \quad k = x + \frac{1}{x} + 1$$

Let us analyze the function $f(x) = x + \frac{1}{x}$. It is an odd function defined for $x \in R - \{0\}$. Now

$$\frac{df}{dx} = 1 - \frac{1}{x^2} = \frac{(x+1)(x-1)}{x^2}$$

Let us analyze the function for $x > 0$. The derivative changes sign from −ve to +ve at $x = 1 \Rightarrow f$ decreases in (0, 1), and then increases in $(1, +\infty)$. Now, $f(0^+) = \infty = f(+\infty)$ and $f(1) = 2$. The graph of $f(x)$ can now be drawn (see fig.) from the above information. Note that we didn't have to analyze the function for $x < 0$; we just used the fact it is an odd function. The range of $f(x)$ is $(-\infty, -2]$ U $[2, +\infty)$.
Thus, k can have values lying in the interval $(-\infty, -1]$ U $[3, +\infty)$. Hence k cannot take the value 2.

42. (b) Let $f(x) = x^4 - 4x^3 + 12x^2 + x - 1$.

Then $\quad f'(x) = 4x^3 - 12x^2 + 24x + 1$

and $\quad f''(x) = 12x^2 - 24x + 24 = 12\left(x^2 - 2x + 2\right)$

We see that $f''(x)$ is always +ve $\Rightarrow f'(x)$ is increasing and hence $f(x)$ is concave upwards. Also $f(-\infty) = +\infty$, $f(+\infty) = +\infty$, and $f(0) = -1$. The figure shows the graph of $f(x)$ Hence, the function takes the value 0 only twice.

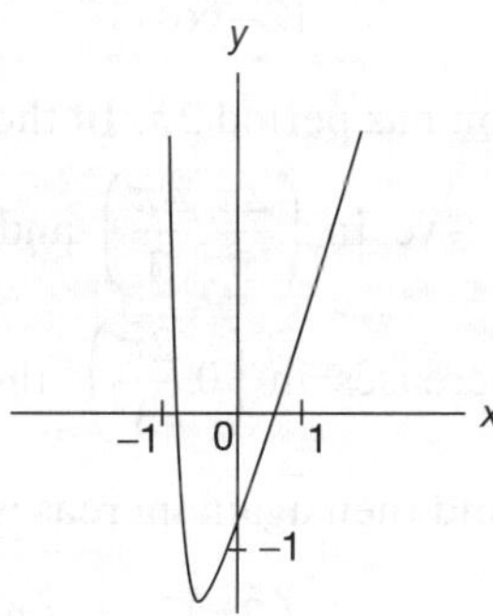

43. (b) The given function and its derivative are

$$f(x) = 4ax^2 + \frac{1}{x}$$

and $\quad f'(x) = 8ax - \dfrac{1}{x^2} = \dfrac{8a\left(x^3 - \dfrac{1}{8a}\right)}{x^2}.$

We see that $f'(x)$ changes sign from –ve to +ve at $x = \dfrac{1}{(8a)^{1/3}}$ if $a > 0$. For $a < 0$, the required condition $f(x) \geq 1$ for all $x > 0$ is not possible.

Hence, $f(x)$ has minima at $x = \dfrac{1}{(8a)^{1/3}}$ if $a > 0$. The required condition will be satisfied if

$$f_{\min} \geq 1 \Rightarrow \frac{4a}{(8a)^{2/3}} + (8a)^{1/3} \geq 1 \Rightarrow \frac{3}{2}(8a)^{1/3} \geq 1 \Rightarrow a \geq \frac{1}{27}.$$

44. (a),(d) We have

$$\lim_{x \to 2} \frac{f(x)g(x)}{f'(x)g'(x)} = 1$$

$$\Rightarrow \lim_{x \to 2} \frac{f'(x)g(x) + f(x)g'(x)}{f''(x)g'(x) + f'(x)g''(x)} = 1$$

[Using L'Hospital's rule]

$$\Rightarrow \frac{f(2)}{f''(2)} = 1 \;[\text{Putting } f'(2) = g(2) = 0]$$

$$\Rightarrow f''(2) = f(2)$$

Since $f(2) > 0$, $f''(2) > 0$. Thus, f has minima at $x = 2$.

45. (b) The given function and its derivative are, respectively,

$$f(x) = \frac{\sqrt{3}\sin x}{2 + \cos x}$$

and $\quad f'(x) = \dfrac{2\sqrt{3}\left(\cos x + \dfrac{1}{2}\right)}{(2 + \cos x)^2}$

The function has period 2π. In the interval $[0, 2\pi]$, $\cos x + \dfrac{1}{2}$ is –ve in $\left(\dfrac{2\pi}{3}, \dfrac{4\pi}{3}\right)$ and +ve otherwise

$\Rightarrow f(x)$ increases in $\left(0, \dfrac{2\pi}{3}\right)$, then decreases in $\left(\dfrac{2\pi}{3}, \dfrac{4\pi}{3}\right)$ and then again increases in $\left(\dfrac{4\pi}{3}, 2\pi\right)$.

Now, $\quad f(0) = 0, f\left(\dfrac{2\pi}{3}\right) = 1, f\left(\dfrac{4\pi}{3}\right) = -1$ and $f(2\pi) = 0$. Hence, range is $[-1, 1]$.

46. (a) The given function and its derivative are, respectively,

$$f(x) = x + \sin 2x, x \in (0, 2\pi)$$

and $\quad f'(x) = 2\left(\cos 2x + \dfrac{1}{2}\right)$

The figure shows the graph of $y = \cos 2x$ and $y = \dfrac{-1}{2}$. In the interval $[0, 2\pi]$, $\cos 2x + \dfrac{1}{2}$ changes sign from +ve to –ve at $x = \dfrac{\pi}{3}, \dfrac{4\pi}{3} \Rightarrow f(x)$ has maxima at these two points.

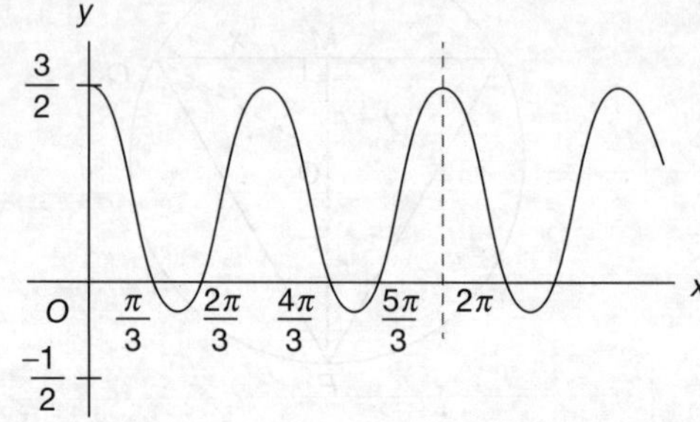

47. (b),(c) The given function and its derivative are, respectively,

$$f(x) = x^5 - 5x + a$$

and $\quad f'(x) = 5x^4 - 5 = 5(x^2 + 1)(x + 1)(x - 1)$

We see that $f'(x)$ is –ve in $(-1, 1)$ and +ve otherwise $\Rightarrow f(x)$ increases in $(-\infty, -1)$, then decreases in $(-1, 1)$ and then again increases in $(1, +\infty)$. Also $\lim_{x \to -\infty} f(x) = -\infty$, $\lim_{x \to +\infty} f(x) = +\infty$.

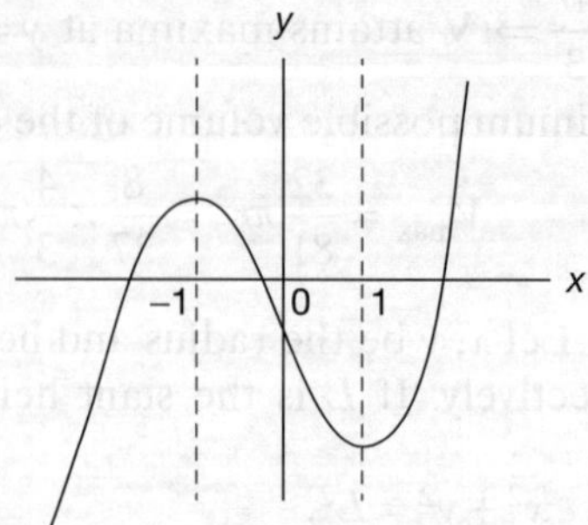

The figure shows the graph of the function. It will cut the x-axis at three distinct points if

$$f(-1) = 4 + a > 0 \Rightarrow a > -4$$

and $\quad f(1) = -4 + a < 0 \Rightarrow a < 4.$

For any other value of a, the graph will cut the x-axis only once.

48. (a),(b) We have

$$f(-x) = \ln^3(\sec x - \tan x) = \ln^3\left(\frac{1}{\sec x + \tan x}\right)$$
$$= -\ln^3(\sec x + \tan x) = -f(x).$$

Hence, the function is odd.

The given function and its derivative are, respectively,

$$f(x) = \ln^3(\sec x + \tan x)$$

and $$f'(x) = 3\ln^2(\sec x + \tan x) \times \frac{1}{\sec x + \tan x} \times (\sec x \tan x + \sec^2 x)$$
$$= 3\ln^2(\sec x + \tan x)\sec x$$

We see that $f'(x)$ is +ve in $\left(\frac{-\pi}{2}, \frac{\pi}{2}\right)$

$\Rightarrow f(x)$ increases in $\left(\frac{-\pi}{2}, \frac{\pi}{2}\right)$

Now, $f\left(\frac{\pi^-}{2}\right) = \ln^3(\infty + \infty) = +\infty$ and since $f(x)$ is odd, $f\left(\frac{-\pi^+}{2}\right) = -\infty$. Hence, range is **R**.

The function is strictly increasing and its range equals the given co-domain. Therefore, the function is one–one and onto $\Rightarrow$ Invertible.

49. (c) The given function can be written as

$$f(x) = \sqrt{2}\sin\left(x^2 + \frac{\pi}{4}\right), x \in \left(-\sqrt{13}, \sqrt{13}\right)$$

The function is even, so we need to analyze only in the interval $\left(0, \sqrt{13}\right)$. In this interval, the function attains maxima at

$$x^2 + \frac{\pi}{4} = \frac{\pi}{2} + 2n\pi$$

$$\Rightarrow \quad x^2 - \frac{\pi}{4} + 2n\pi = \frac{\pi}{4}, \frac{9\pi}{4}$$

[The other values are greater than 13]

Hence, the function has 4 maxima in $\left(-\sqrt{13}, \sqrt{13}\right)$.

50. (b) The given function and its derivative are, respectively,

$$f(x) = \frac{x^2 - 6x + 5}{x^2 - 5x + 6} = \frac{(x-1)(x-5)}{(x-2)(x-3)}$$

and $$f'(x) = \frac{x^2 + 2x - 11}{\left(x^2 - 5x + 6\right)^2} = \frac{(x-\alpha)(x-\beta)}{\left(x^2 - 5x + 6\right)^2},$$

where $\alpha = -1 - 2\sqrt{3} = -4.46$ and $\beta = -1 + 2\sqrt{3} = 2.46$.

We see that $f'(x)$ is –ve in $(-4.46, 2.46)$ and +ve otherwise $\Rightarrow f(x)$ decreases in the interval $(1,2)$.

Now $f\left(1^+\right) = 0$ and $f\left(2^-\right) = -\infty$.

Hence, $f(x) < 0$ in the interval $(1,2)$.

51. (d) The period of the given function is 2π. But its fundamental period is π, since $f(x+\pi) = f(x)$. In this interval, the function and its derivative are, respectively,

$$f(x) = \frac{\sin 5x}{\sin^5 x}, x \in (0, \pi) \text{ and}$$

$$f'(x) = \frac{\sin^5 x(5\cos 4x) - \left(5\sin^4 x \cos x\right)\sin 5x}{\sin^{10} x}$$
$$= \frac{-5\sin 4x}{\sin^6 x}$$

In the interval $(0, \pi)$, we see that $f'(x)$ is –ve in $\left(0, \frac{\pi}{4}\right) \cup \left(\frac{\pi}{2}, \frac{3\pi}{4}\right)$ and +ve in $\left(\frac{\pi}{4}, \frac{\pi}{2}\right) \cup \left(\frac{3\pi}{4}, \pi\right)$

$\Rightarrow f(x)$ decreases in $\left(0, \frac{\pi}{4}\right)$, then increases in $\left(\frac{\pi}{4}, \frac{\pi}{2}\right)$, then decreases in $\left(\frac{\pi}{2}, \frac{3\pi}{4}\right)$ and then increases in $\left(\frac{3\pi}{4}, \pi\right)$.

Now, we have

$$f\left(0^+\right) = \lim_{x\to 0}\frac{\sin 5x}{\sin^5 x} = \lim_{x\to 0}\frac{5\cos 5x}{5\sin^4 x \cos x} = +\infty$$

$$f\left(\pi^-\right) = \lim_{h\to 0}\frac{\sin 5(\pi - h)}{\sin^5(\pi - h)} = \lim_{h\to 0}\frac{\sin 5h}{\sin^5 h} = +\infty$$

$$f\left(\frac{\pi}{4}\right) = f\left(\frac{3\pi}{4}\right) = -4, \text{ and } f\left(\frac{\pi}{2}\right) = 1$$

Hence, range is $[-4, +\infty)$. Now, we can plot the graph of $f(x)$. From the graph, we see that $f(x) = 2$ has two roots, $f(x) = 1$ has three roots, $f(x) = 0$ has four roots and $f(x) = -4$ has two roots.

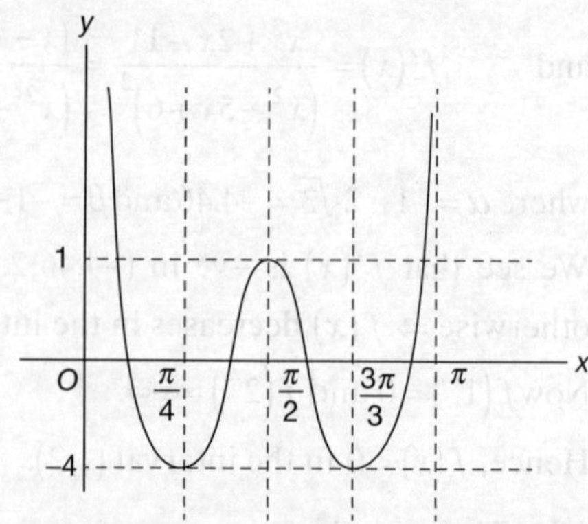

52. (a) The function $f(x)$ is continuous everywhere since all the functions used are of continuous nature. We need to check differentiability only at two points, namely, $x = 0, \pi$.

In a close neighborhood of $x = 0$, we have

$$f(x) = \begin{cases} -(\pi - x)(e^{-x} - 1)\sin x, & -h \le x \le 0 \\ (\pi - x)(e^{x} - 1)\sin x, & 0 \le x \le h \end{cases}$$

and

$$f'(x) = \begin{cases} (e^{-x} - 1)\sin x + (\pi - x)e^{-x}\sin x \\ \quad -(\pi - x)(e^{-x} - 1)\cos x, & -h < x < 0 \\ -(e^{x} - 1)\sin x + (\pi - x)e^{x}\sin x \\ \quad +(\pi - x)(e^{x} - 1)\cos x, & 0 < x < h \end{cases}$$

Now $f'(0^-) = 0$ and $f'(0^+) = 0$. Hence, $f(x)$ is differentiable at $x = 0$.

In a close neighborhood of $x = \pi$, we have

$$f(x) = \begin{cases} (\pi - x)(e^{x} - 1)\sin x, & \pi - h \le x \le \pi \\ (x - \pi)(e^{x} - 1)\sin x, & \pi \le x \le \pi + h \end{cases}$$

and

$$f'(x) = \begin{cases} -(e^{x} - 1)\sin x + (\pi - x)e^{x}\sin x \\ \quad +(\pi - x)(e^{x} - 1)\cos x, & \pi - h < x < \pi \\ (e^{x} - 1)\sin x + (x - \pi)e^{x}\sin x \\ \quad +(x - \pi)(e^{x} - 1)\cos x, & \pi < x < \pi + h \end{cases}$$

Now $f'(\pi^-) = 0$ and $f'(\pi^+) = 0$. Hence, $f(x)$ is differentiable at $x = \pi$.

This means $f(x)$ is differentiable everywhere. Hence $S = \varnothing$.

53. (c) The function $h(x)$ can be written as

$$h = \frac{f}{g} = \frac{g^2 + 2}{g} = g + \frac{2}{g}$$

Then

$$h' = g' - \frac{2g'}{g^2} = g'\left(\frac{g^2 - 2}{g^2}\right) = \left(1 + \frac{1}{x^2}\right)\frac{(g + \sqrt{2})(g - \sqrt{2})}{g^2}$$

We see that h' changes sign from −ve to +ve when $g(x) = \sqrt{2} \Rightarrow h(x)$ has local minima where $g(x) = \sqrt{2} \Rightarrow x - \dfrac{1}{x} = \sqrt{2}$ (only one solution in the interval $x > 1$).

The local minimum value of $h(x)$ equals $\sqrt{2} + \dfrac{2}{\sqrt{2}} = 2\sqrt{2}$.

54. (b),(c) Let us consider the function $h = f - 3g$. Then $h' = (f - 3g)'$ and $h'' = (f - 3g)''$.

We see that $h(-1) = h(0) = h(2) = 3$. Hence, by Rolle's theorem, h' vanishes at at least two points, one in each of the two intervals $(-1, 0)$ and $(0, 2)$.

Now h' satisfies the conditions of Rolle's theorem between these two points. Hence, h'' will vanish at least once between these two points. Since it is given that h'' does not vanish in $(-1, 0)$ and $(0, 2)$, it means that it vanishes at 0.

If h'' does not vanish in any interval, it means it is always +ve or always −ve in that interval. This means h' does not repeat its values in that interval (it increases strictly or decreases strictly).

Hence, we conclude that $h' = 0$ has exactly one solution in $(-1, 0)$ and one solution in $(0, 2)$.

55. (a) Let us choose the two perpendicular sides of the triangle as our coordinate axes (see figure). The equation of the hypotenuse can now be written as

$$y - b = m(x - a), \text{ where } m < 0$$

Its x and y intercepts are, respectively

$$B = \left(a - \frac{b}{m}, 0\right) \text{ and } C = (0, b - am)$$

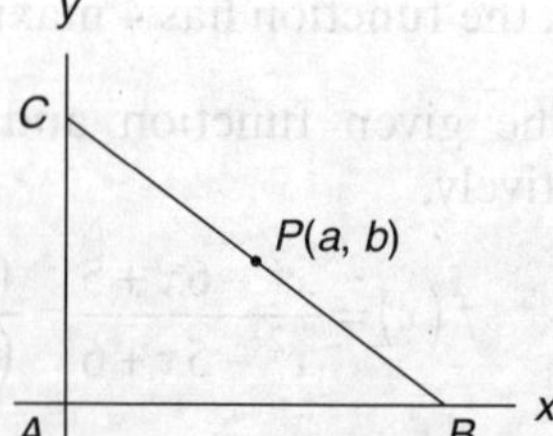

Length L of the hypotenuse BC is given by

$$L^2 = \left(a - \frac{b}{m}\right)^2 + (b - am)^2$$

Let $f(m) = \left(a - \frac{b}{m}\right)^2 + (b - am)^2$. Its derivative is

$$f'(m) = 2\left(a - \frac{b}{m}\right)\left(\frac{b}{m^2}\right) - 2(b - am)a$$

$$= \frac{2\left[(am - b)b + (am - b)am^3\right]}{m^3}$$

$$= \frac{2(am - b)(am^3 + b)}{m^3}$$

$$= \frac{2a^2(m - \alpha^3)(m^3 + \alpha^3)}{m^3}, \text{ where } \alpha^3 = \frac{b}{a}$$

$$= \frac{2a^2(m - \alpha^3)(m + \alpha)(m^2 - \alpha m + 1)}{m^3}$$

From the sign scheme (see figure) of $f'(m)$, we see that it changes sign from –ve to +ve at $m = -\alpha, \alpha^3 \Rightarrow f(m)$ has two local minima. But, since m can only take negative values, we take

$$m = -\alpha = -\left(\frac{b}{a}\right)^{1/3}$$

$$\begin{array}{ccccccc} - & & + & & - & & + \\ & -\alpha & & 0 & & \alpha^3 & \end{array}$$

Hence, the minimum length of the hypotenuse is

$$L_{\min}^2 = \left(a + a^{\frac{1}{3}}b^{\frac{2}{3}}\right)^2 + \left(b + a^{\frac{2}{3}}b^{\frac{1}{3}}\right)^2$$

$$= a^{2/3}\left(a^{2/3} + b^{2/3}\right)^2 + b^{2/3}\left(a^{2/3} + b^{2/3}\right)^2$$

$$= \left(a^{2/3} + b^{2/3}\right)^3$$

$$\Rightarrow L_{\min} = \left(a^{2/3} + b^{2/3}\right)^{3/2}$$

56. (a)

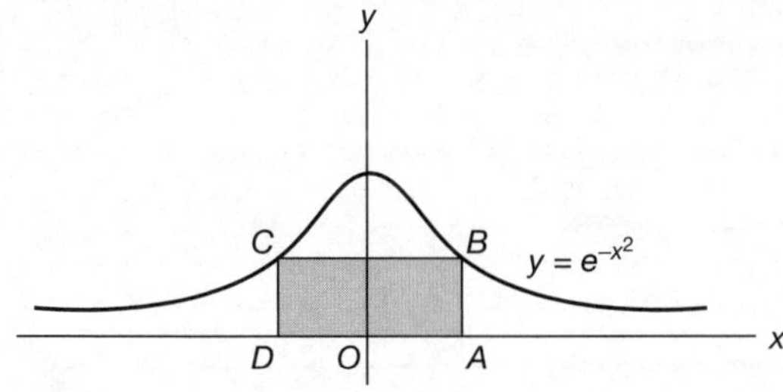

From the figure, we can see that the rectangle is symmetrically placed about the y-axis. Let us choose the coordinates of its vertices as $(\pm x, 0)$ and $\left(\pm x, e^{-x^2}\right)$. Then its area is given by

$$A(x) = 2xe^{-x^2}$$

Its derivative is

$$A'(x) = 2e^{-x^2}\left(1 - 2x^2\right) = -4e^{-x^2}\left(x + \frac{1}{\sqrt{2}}\right)\left(x - \frac{1}{\sqrt{2}}\right).$$

We see that A' changes sign from +ve to –ve at $x = 1/\sqrt{2} \Rightarrow$ Maxima.

Hence, maximum area is

$$A_{\max} = 2 \times \frac{1}{\sqrt{2}} \times e^{-1/2} = \sqrt{\frac{2}{e}}$$

57. (a) Let x be the inner radius and y be the inner height of the container. Then $V_0 = \pi x^2 y$. The volume of the material used to make the container is given by the function

$$f(x) = \pi(x+2)^2 y - V_0 + \pi(x+2)^2 2$$

$$= \frac{(x+2)^2}{x^2} V_0 - V_0 + \pi(x+2)^2 2$$

$$\left[\text{Putting } y = \frac{V_0}{\pi x^2}\right]$$

$$= 4V_0\left(\frac{1}{x} + \frac{1}{x^2}\right) + 2\pi(x+2)^2$$

Then $\quad f'(x) = -4V_0\left(\frac{1}{x^2} + \frac{2}{x^3}\right) + 4\pi(x+2).$

According to the given condition, $f'(10) = 0$. This gives $V_0 = 1000\pi$. Hence $\frac{V_0}{250\pi} = 4$.

58. (a)-(s), (b)-(r), (c)-(s), (d)-(r)

(a) We have

$$f' = -\frac{4x}{a^2}\left(1 - \frac{x^2}{a^2}\right) = \frac{4}{a^4}x(x+a)(x-a)$$

There are three extrema since f' changes sign at $x = -a, 0, a$.

(b) We have $f' = \frac{1}{a} - \frac{x^2}{a^3} = \frac{-1}{a^2}(x+a)(x-a).$

There are two extrema since f' changes sign at $x = -a, a$.

(c) We have

$$f' = \frac{2x}{a^2}\left(1 - \frac{x^2}{a^2}\right)e^{\frac{-x^2}{a^2}} = -\frac{2}{a^4}x(x-a)(x+a)e^{\frac{-x^2}{a^2}}$$

There are three extrema since f' changes sign at $x = -a, 0, a$.

(d) We have $f' = \frac{2x}{a^2} - \frac{x^2}{a^3} = -\frac{1}{a^3}x(x-2a)$

There are two extrema since f' changes sign at $x = 0, 2a$.

CHAPTER

20 Indefinite Integration

- **Anti-derivative of a Function:** A function $g(x)$ is called the anti-derivative of the function $f(x)$ in the interval $[a,b]$ if at all points in the interval, $g'(x) = f(x)$. In that case, $g(x)+C$ (where C is any arbitrary constant) is called the indefinite integral (due to the indefiniteness of the value of C) of $f(x)$ and is written as

$$\int f(x)dx = g(x)+C$$

An indefinite integral is a family of curves $y = g(x)+C$ all having the same differential equation $y' = f(x)$.

Differentiation and integration are inverse mathematical operations. The derivative of the integral of $f(x)$ is $f(x)$ itself:

$$\frac{d}{dx}\left(\int f(x)dx\right) = f(x)$$

The integral of the derivative of $f(x)$ is $f(x)$ itself:

$$\left(\int \frac{df(x)}{dx}dx\right) = f(x)$$

- **Theorems on Anti-derivatives**

1. $\int kf(x)dx = k\int f(x)dx$, where k is some constant.
2. $\int \{f(x)+g(x)\}dx = \int f(x)dx + \int g(x)dx$.
3. If $\int f(x)dx = g(x)+C$, then $\int f(ax+b)dx = \frac{1}{a}g(ax+b)+C$.

- **Anti-derivatives of Elementary Functions**

Function	*Anti-derivative*
1. $x^n \ (n \in \mathbf{Q})$	$\begin{cases} \frac{x^{n+1}}{n+1}+C \text{ if } n \neq -1 \\ \ln\lvert x\rvert + C \text{ if } n = -1 \end{cases}$
2. $\sin x$	$-\cos x + C$
3. $\cos x$	$\sin x + C$
4. $\tan x$	$\ln\lvert\sec x\rvert + C$
5. $\operatorname{cosec} x$	$-\ln\lvert\operatorname{cosec} x + \cot x\rvert + C = \ln\left\lvert\tan\left(\frac{x}{2}\right)\right\rvert + C$
6. $\sec x$	$\ln\lvert\sec x + \tan x\rvert + C = \ln\left\lvert\tan\left(\frac{x}{2}+\frac{\pi}{4}\right)\right\rvert + C$
7. $\cot x$	$\ln\lvert\sin x\rvert + C$

8. $\dfrac{1}{\sqrt{1-x^2}}$	$\sin^{-1}x+C=-\cos^{-1}x+C$
9. $\dfrac{1}{1+x^2}$	$\tan^{-1}x+C=-\cot^{-1}x+C$
10. $\dfrac{1}{x\sqrt{x^2-1}}$	$\sec^{-1}\lvert x\rvert+C=-\text{cosec}^{-1}\lvert x\rvert+C$
11. $a^x\ (a>0, a\neq 1)$	$\dfrac{a^x}{\ln a}+C$
12. $\ln x$	$x(\ln x-1)+C$

- **Methods of Integration**

  1. *Method of Substitution*: To find the indefinite integral $\int f(x)dx$, we may find it convenient to substitute x with another variable, say $\varphi(t)$. In that case, the integral reduces to $\int f(x)dx=\int f\{\varphi(t)\}\varphi'(t)dt$.

  2. *Method of Integration by Parts*: To find the indefinite integral $\int f(x)g(x)dx$, we have

  $$\int f(x)g(x)dx=f(x)\int g(x)dx-\int f'(x)\left[\int g(x)dx\right]dx$$

  Some useful integrals using parts:

  – $\int e^x\{f(x)+f'(x)\}dx=e^x f(x)+C$

  – $\int e^{ax}\sin(bx+c)dx=\dfrac{e^{ax}}{\sqrt{a^2+b^2}}\sin\left(bx+c-\tan^{-1}\dfrac{b}{a}\right)+C$

  – $\int e^{ax}\cos(bx+c)dx=\dfrac{e^{ax}}{\sqrt{a^2+b^2}}\cos\left(bx+c-\tan^{-1}\dfrac{b}{a}\right)+C$

- **Integration of Rational Algebraic Functions:** A function of the type $\dfrac{f(x)}{g(x)}$, where $f(x)$ and $g(x)$ are both polynomials, is called a rational algebraic function. Such functions can be expressed as the sum of partial fractions of two types

  $$\frac{L}{(ax+b)^n}\text{ and }\frac{Lx+M}{\left(ax^2+bx+c\right)^n}\ \left(b^2<4ac\right)$$

  We already know the integral of the first type of fraction. To integrate the second type of fraction, express the numerator as $Lx+M=\lambda(2ax+b)+\mu$. Hence, we have

  $$\int\frac{Lx+M}{\left(ax^2+bx+c\right)^n}dx=\int\frac{\lambda(ax+b)}{\left(ax^2+bx+c\right)^n}dx+\int\frac{\mu}{\left(ax^2+bx+c\right)^n}dx$$

The first integral is of the type $\int \frac{dy}{y^n}$. The second integral ax^2+bx+c, whose discriminant b^2-4ac is negative, can be expressed as $(\alpha x+\beta)^2+k^2$; it then reduces to the type $I_n=\int \frac{dy}{\left(y^2+k^2\right)^n}$. For $n=1$ and 2, it can be integrated using the substitution $y=k\tan\theta$. For $n>2$, we have the following reduction formula:

$$I_{n+1}=\frac{1}{2nk^2}\frac{y}{\left(y^2+k^2\right)^n}+\frac{2n-1}{2nk^2}I_n$$

Two useful integrals:

– $\int \frac{x^2+1}{x^4+1}dx=\frac{1}{\sqrt{2}}\tan^{-1}\left(\frac{x^2-1}{\sqrt{2}x}\right)+C$

– $\int \frac{x^2-1}{x^4+1}dx=\frac{1}{\sqrt{2}}\ln\left(\frac{x^2-\sqrt{2}x-1}{x^2-\sqrt{2}x+1}\right)+C$

- **Integration of Trigonometric Functions**

1. For integrals of the type

$$\int R(\sin x)\cos x\,dx \text{ or } \int R(\cos x)\sin x\,dx$$

where R stands for the rational function of its arguments, use substitution $\sin x=t$ in the first case and $\cos x=t$ in the second case.

2. For integrals of the type

$$\int R(\tan x)dx \text{ or } \int R(\cot x)\sin x\,dx$$

where R stands for the rational function of its arguments, use substitution $\tan x=t$ in the first case and $\cot x=t$ in the second case.

3. For integrals of the type

$$\int R(\sin x,\cos x)dx$$

where R stands for the rational function of its arguments, use substitution

$$\tan\left(\frac{x}{2}\right)=t,\ \sin x=\frac{2t}{1+t^2},\ \cos x=\frac{1-t^2}{1+t^2},\ \text{and } dx=\frac{2\,dt}{1+t^2}$$

4. For integrals of the type

$$\int \sin^m x\cos^n x\,dx$$

substitute as follows:

– If m is an odd positive integer, insert $\cos x=t$.

– If n is an odd positive integer, insert $\sin x=t$.

– If m and n are both odd positive integers, insert $\sin x$ or $\cos x=t$.

– If m and n are both even positive integers, simplify the function as the sum of sines and cosines of multiple angles using

$$\sin^2 x=\frac{1-\cos 2x}{2} \text{ and } \cos^2 x=\frac{1+\cos 2x}{2}$$

5. For integrals of the type

$$\int \tan^m x \sec^n x \, dx$$

substitute as follows:

- If n is an even positive integer, insert $\tan x = t$.
- If n is an odd and m is also an odd positive integer, insert $\sec x = t$.
- If n is an odd and m is an even positive integer, the function reduces to odd powers of $\sec x$; now use parts.

6. For integrals of the type

$$\int \frac{\cos x + \sin x}{1 - \sin x \cos x} dx \text{ or } \int \frac{\cos x - \sin x}{1 - \sin x \cos x} dx$$

For the first integral, use substitution $\sin x - \cos x = t$, $(\cos x + \sin x)dx = dt$ and $\sin x \cos x = \frac{1-t^2}{2}$.

For the first integral, use substitution $\sin x + \cos x = t$, $(\cos x - \sin x)dx = dt$ and $\sin x \cos x = \frac{t^2-1}{2}$.

- **Integration of Irrational Algebraic Functions:** If the integrand involves expressions such as

$$\sqrt{a^2 - x^2}, \sqrt{x^2 + a^2}, \sqrt{x^2 - a^2}, \sqrt{\frac{a-x}{a+x}}$$

the suggested substitutions are, respectively,

$$x = a \sin\theta, x = a \tan\theta, x = a \sec\theta, \text{ and } x = a \cos 2\theta$$

Six useful integrals:

- $\int \frac{1}{\sqrt{a^2 - x^2}} dx = \sin^{-1}\left(\frac{x}{a}\right) + C$
- $\int \frac{1}{\sqrt{x^2 + a^2}} dx = \ln\left|x + \sqrt{x^2 + a^2}\right| + C$
- $\int \frac{1}{\sqrt{x^2 - a^2}} dx = \ln\left|x + \sqrt{x^2 - a^2}\right| + C$
- $\int \sqrt{a^2 - x^2} \, dx = \frac{1}{2} x \sqrt{a^2 - x^2} + \frac{a^2}{2} \sin^{-1}\left(\frac{x}{a}\right) + C$
- $\int \sqrt{x^2 + a^2} \, dx = \frac{1}{2} x \sqrt{x^2 + a^2} + \frac{a^2}{2} \ln\left|x + \sqrt{x^2 + a^2}\right| + C$
- $\int \sqrt{x^2 - a^2} \, dx = \frac{1}{2} x \sqrt{x^2 - a^2} - \frac{a^2}{2} \ln\left|x + \sqrt{x^2 - a^2}\right| + C$

1. Integrals of the type

$$\int \frac{1}{\sqrt{ax^2 + bx + c}} dx \text{ and } \int \sqrt{ax^2 + bx + c} \, dx$$

can be reduced to one of the above six integrals.

2. Integrals of the type

$$\int \frac{Ax+B}{\sqrt{ax^2+bx+c}}dx \text{ and } \int (Ax+B)\sqrt{ax^2+bx+c}\,dx$$

can be evaluated by first expressing $Ax+B=\lambda(2ax+b)+\mu$ and then splitting the integral into two integrals, both of which are known integrals.

3. Integrals of the type

$$\int \frac{1}{(Ax+B)^n\sqrt{ax^2+bx+c}}dx\,(n\in \mathbf{N})$$

can be evaluated using the substitution $Ax+B=\dfrac{1}{t}$.

4. Integrals of the type

$$\int R\left(x, x^{a_1/b_1}, x^{a_2/b_2}, \ldots, x^{a_n/b_n}\right)dx$$

can be evaluated using the substitution $x=t^k$, where $k=\text{LCM}(b_1, b_2, \ldots, b_n)$.

5. Integrals of the type

$$\int f\left(x+\sqrt{x^2+k}\right)dx \text{ or } \int f\left(x-\sqrt{x^2+k}\right)dx$$

can be evaluated using the substitution $x+\sqrt{x^2+k}=t$ and $x-\sqrt{x^2+k}=t$, respectively.

EXERCISES

1. $\int \frac{1-x^7}{x(1+x^7)}dx$ equals:

(a) $\frac{2}{7}\ln(1+x^2)+\ln|x|+C$

(b) $\ln|x|-\frac{2}{7}\ln(1-x^7)+C$

(c) $\ln|x|-\frac{2}{7}\ln(1+x^7)+C$

(d) $\ln|x|+\frac{2}{7}\ln(1-x^7)+C$

2. $\int \frac{x}{\sqrt{1+x^2+\sqrt{(1+x^2)^3}}}dx$ equals:

(a) $\frac{1}{2}\ln(1+\sqrt{1+x^2})+C$

(b) $2\sqrt{1+\sqrt{1+x^2}}+C$

(c) $2(1+\sqrt{1+x^2})+C$

(d) $\frac{-2}{3(1+\sqrt{1+x^2})^{3/2}}+C$

3. $\int \frac{x^4(1-x)^4}{1+x^2}dx$ equals:

(a) $\frac{1}{7}x^7-\frac{1}{3}x^6+x^5-\frac{2}{3}x^3+4x+4\tan^{-1}x+C$

(b) $\frac{1}{7}x^7-\frac{1}{3}x^6+x^5+\frac{1}{3}x^3+4x-4\tan^{-1}x+C$

(c) $\frac{1}{7}x^7-\frac{4}{3}x^6+x^5+\frac{1}{3}x^3+4x+4\tan^{-1}x+C$

(d) $\frac{1}{7}x^7-\frac{2}{3}x^6+x^5-\frac{4}{3}x^3+4x-4\tan^{-1}x+C$

4. $\int \frac{x^2(1-\ln x)}{\ln^4 x-x^4}dx$ equals:

(a) $\frac{1}{2}\ln\left|\frac{x}{\ln x}\right|-\frac{1}{4}\ln(\ln^2 x-x^2)+C$

(b) $\frac{1}{4}\ln\left|\frac{\ln x-x}{\ln x+x}\right|-\frac{1}{2}\tan^{-1}\left(\frac{\ln x}{x}\right)+C$

(c) $\frac{1}{4}\ln\left|\frac{\ln x+x}{\ln x-x}\right|+\frac{1}{2}\tan^{-1}\left(\frac{\ln x}{x}\right)+C$

(d) $\frac{1}{4}\ln\left|\frac{\ln x+x}{\ln x-x}\right|-\frac{1}{4}\tan^{-1}\left(\frac{\ln x}{x}\right)+C$

5. $\int \frac{ax^{a+2b-1}-bx^{b-1}}{x^{2a+2b}+2x^{a+b}+1}dx$ equals:

(a) $\frac{-x^a}{x^{a+b}+1}+C$ (b) $\frac{x^b}{x^{a+b}+1}+C$

(c) $\frac{-x^b}{x^{a+b}+1}+C$ (d) $\frac{x^a}{x^{a+b}+1}+C$

6. If $x\in\left(\frac{\pi}{2},\pi\right)$, then $\int\sqrt{1+2\cot x(\cot x+\operatorname{cosec} x)}\,dx$ equals:

(a) $2\ln\left(\cos\frac{x}{2}\right)+C$

(b) $-2\ln\left(\sin\frac{x}{2}\right)+C$

(c) $\frac{1}{2}\ln\left(\sin\frac{x}{2}\right)+C$

(d) $2\ln\left(\sin\frac{x}{2}\right)+C$

7. $\int \frac{e^{\tan^{-1}x}}{1+x^2}\left[\left(\sec^{-1}\sqrt{1+x^2}\right)^2+\cos^{-1}\left(\frac{1-x^2}{1+x^2}\right)\right]dx$ equals:

(a) $e^{\tan^{-1}x}\left(\tan^{-1}x\right)^2+C$

(b) $e^{\tan^{-1}x}\left(\sec^{-1}x\right)^2+C$

(c) $e^{\tan^{-1}x}\left(\tan^{-1}\sqrt{1+x^2}\right)^2+C$

(d) $e^{\tan^{-1}x}\left(\cos^{-1}\sqrt{1+x^2}\right)^2+C$

8. $\int e^{\tan\theta}(\sec\theta-\sin\theta)d\theta$ equals:

(a) $-e^{\tan\theta}\sin\theta+C$ (b) $-e^{\tan\theta}\cot\theta+C$

(c) $e^{\tan\theta}\sec\theta+C$ (d) $e^{\tan\theta}\cos\theta+C$

9. $\int \frac{1}{\cos(x-a)\cos(x-b)} dx$ equals:

(a) $\frac{1}{\cos(b-a)} \ln\left|\frac{\cos(x-b)}{\cos(x-a)}\right| + C$

(b) $\frac{1}{\sin(b-a)} \ln\left|\frac{\cos(x-b)}{\cos(x-a)}\right| + C$

(c) $\frac{1}{\cos(b-a)} \ln\left|\frac{\sin(x-b)}{\sin(x-a)}\right| + C$

(d) $\frac{1}{\sin(b-a)} \ln\left|\frac{\sin(x-b)}{\sin(x-a)}\right| + C$

10. $\int (x^{3m} + x^{2m} + x^m)(2x^{2m} + 3x^m + 6)^{\frac{1}{m}} dx$ equals:

(a) $\frac{1}{6m}(x^{3m} + x^{2m} + 6x^m)^{1+\frac{1}{m}} + C$

(b) $\frac{1}{6(m+1)}(2x^{3m} + 3x^{2m} + 6x^m)^{1+\frac{1}{m}} + C$

(c) $\frac{1}{2m}(2x^{3m} + 3x^{2m} + x^m)^{\frac{1}{m}} + C$

(d) $\frac{1}{3m}(x^{3m} + x^{2m} + 6x^m)^{\frac{1}{m}} + C$

11. $\int \frac{1}{1+\sin x} dx$ equals:

(a) $\frac{-2}{1+\tan(x/2)} + C$ (b) $\tan\left(\frac{x}{2} + \frac{\pi}{4}\right) + C$

(c) $\tan\left(\frac{x}{2} - \frac{\pi}{4}\right) + C$ (d) None of these

12. $\int \frac{\sin x - x\cos x}{x(x+\sin x)} dx$ equals:

(a) $-\ln\left(1 + \frac{\sin x}{x}\right) + C$

(b) $(\sin x - x)\ln\left(1 + \frac{\cos x}{x}\right) + C$

(c) $(\cos x - x)\ln\left(1 + \frac{\sin x}{x}\right) + C$

(d) None of these

13. $\int \frac{1}{x^2(1+x^4)^{3/4}} dx$ equals:

(a) $\left(\frac{1+x^4}{x^4}\right)^{1/4} + C$ (b) $-\left(\frac{1+x^4}{x^4}\right)^{1/4} + C$

(c) $(x^4+1)^{1/4} + C$ (d) $-(x^4+1)^{1/4} + C$

14. $\int \sqrt{x + \sqrt{x^2+2}}\, dx$ equals:

(a) $\frac{2}{3}\left(\sqrt{x^2+2}+x\right)^{-3/2} - \left(\sqrt{x^2+2}-x\right)^{-1/2} + C$

(b) $\frac{2}{3}\left(\sqrt{x^2+2}+x\right)^{3/2} + \sqrt{2}\left(\sqrt{x^2+2}-x\right)^{1/2} + C$

(c) $\frac{1}{3}\left(\sqrt{x^2+2}+x\right)^{-3/2} - \left(\sqrt{x^2+2}-x\right)^{1/2} + C$

(d) $\frac{1}{3}\left(\sqrt{x^2+2}+x\right)^{3/2} - \sqrt{2}\left(\sqrt{x^2+2}-x\right)^{1/2} + C$

15. $\int \tan x \tan 2x \tan 3x\, dx$ equals:

(a) $\frac{1}{3}\ln|\sec 3x| + \frac{1}{2}\ln|\sec 2x| - \ln|\sec x| + C$

(b) $\frac{1}{3}\ln|\sec 3x| + \frac{1}{2}\ln|\sec 2x| + \ln|\sec x| + C$

(c) $\frac{1}{3}\ln|\sec 3x| - \frac{1}{2}\ln|\sec 2x| - \ln|\sec x| + C$

(d) $\frac{1}{3}\ln|\sec 3x| - \frac{1}{2}\ln|\sec 2x| + \ln|\sec x| + C$

16. $\int \frac{1}{(x+1)\sqrt{x^2+x-1}} dx$ equals:

(a) $\sin^{-1}\left\{\frac{x^2+x-1}{\sqrt{3}(x+1)}\right\} + C$

(b) $\cos^{-1}\left\{\frac{x+3}{\sqrt{5}(x+1)}\right\} + C$

(c) $\tan^{-1}\sqrt{\frac{x+1}{x^2+x-1}} + C$

(d) $\sec^{-1}\left(\frac{x+3}{x^2+x-1}\right) + C$

17. $\int \frac{2x^{12}+5x^9}{(x^5+x^3+1)^3} dx$ equals:

(a) $\frac{-x^{10}}{2(x^5+x^3+1)^2}+C$

(b) $\frac{x^5}{2(x^5+x^3+1)^2}+C$

(c) $\frac{x^{10}}{2(x^5+x^3+1)^2}+C$

(d) $\frac{-x^5}{2(x^5+x^3+1)^2}+C$

18. $\int \frac{1}{x\sqrt{1-x^3}} dx$ equals:

(a) $\frac{2}{3}\ln\left(\frac{\sqrt{1-x^3}-1}{\sqrt{1-x^3}-1}\right)+C$

(b) $\frac{1}{6}\ln\left(\frac{\sqrt{1-x^3}+1}{\sqrt{1-x^3}-1}\right)+C$

(c) $\frac{1}{3}\ln\left(\frac{\sqrt{1-x^3}-1}{\sqrt{1-x^3}+1}\right)+C$

(d) $\frac{2}{3}\ln\left(\frac{\sqrt{1-x^3}+1}{\sqrt{1-x^3}-1}\right)+C$

19. $\int \frac{(a^x-b^x)^2}{a^x b^x} dx$ equals:

(a) $\frac{1}{\ln a}\left(\frac{a}{b}\right)^x - \frac{1}{\ln b}\left(\frac{b}{a}\right)^x - x + C$

(b) $\frac{1}{\ln b}\left(\frac{a}{b}\right)^x - \frac{1}{\ln a}\left(\frac{b}{a}\right)^x + x + C$

(c) $\left(\frac{a}{b}\right)^x + \left(\frac{b}{a}\right)^x - \frac{1}{\ln(b/a)}x + C$

(d) $\frac{1}{\ln(a/b)}\left\{\left(\frac{a}{b}\right)^x - \left(\frac{b}{a}\right)^x\right\} - 2x + C$

20. $\int \left\{\left(\frac{x}{e}\right)^x + \left(\frac{e}{x}\right)^x\right\} \ln x dx$ equals:

(a) $\left(\frac{x}{e}\right)^x - \left(\frac{e}{x}\right)^x + C$

(b) $(x^x - e^x)\ln x + C$

(c) $\left(\frac{x}{e}\right)^x \ln x + C$

(d) $\frac{x^x - e^x}{\ln x} + C$

21. $\int \left(\frac{\ln x - 1}{\ln^2 x + 1}\right)^2 dx$ equals:

(a) $\frac{\ln x - x}{\ln x + 1} + C$

(b) $\frac{\ln x}{\ln^2 x + 1} + C$

(c) $\frac{x}{\ln x + 1} + C$

(d) $\frac{x}{\ln^2 x + 1} + C$

22. $\int \frac{\cos x}{1+\sin 2x} dx$ equals:

(a) $\frac{1}{4\sqrt{2}}\ln\left(\frac{\sin x - \cos x + \sqrt{2}}{\sin x - \cos x - \sqrt{2}}\right) - \frac{1}{2(\sin x + \cos x)} + C$

(b) $\frac{1}{4\sqrt{2}}\ln\left(\frac{\sin x - \cos x - \sqrt{2}}{\sin x - \cos x + \sqrt{2}}\right) + \frac{1}{2(\sin x + \cos x)} + C$

(c) $\frac{1}{4\sqrt{2}}\ln\left(\frac{\sin x + \cos x + \sqrt{2}}{\sin x + \cos x - \sqrt{2}}\right) - \frac{1}{2(\sin x - \cos x)} + C$

(d) $\frac{1}{4\sqrt{2}}\ln\left(\frac{\sin x + \cos x - \sqrt{2}}{\sin x + \cos x + \sqrt{2}}\right) + \frac{1}{2(\sin x - \cos x)} + C$

ANSWER KEYS

1. (c)	**2.** (b)	**3.** (d)	**4.** (b)	**5.** (c)	**6.** (d)	**7.** (a)	**8.** (d)	**9.** (b)
10. (b)	**11.** (a),(c)	**12.** (a)	**13.** (b)	**14.** (d)	**15.** (c)	**16.** (b)	**17.** (c)	**18.** (c)
19. (d)	**20.** (a)	**21.** (d)	**22.** (a)					

SOLUTIONS

1. (c) $$I=\frac{1}{7}\int\frac{(1-x^7)(7x^6dx)}{x^7(1+x^7)}=\frac{1}{7}\int\frac{1-t}{t(1+t)}dt$$

$\left[\text{Insert } x^7=t \text{ and } 7x^6dx=dt\right]$

Now $$\frac{1-t}{t(1+t)}=\frac{1+t-2t}{t(1+t)}=\frac{1}{t}-\frac{2}{1+t}$$

Hence

$$I=\frac{1}{7}\left[\ln|t|-2\ln|1+t|\right]+C=\ln|x|-\frac{2}{7}\ln(1+x^7)+C$$

2. (b) $$I=\int\frac{x\,dx}{\sqrt{1+x^2+\sqrt{(1+x^2)^3}}}$$

$\left[\text{Insert } 1+x^2=t^2 \text{ and } xdx=tdt\right]$

$$=\int\frac{t\,dt}{\sqrt{t^2+t^3}}=\int\frac{dt}{\sqrt{1+t}}$$

$$=2\sqrt{1+t}+C=2\sqrt{1+\sqrt{1+x^2}}+C$$

3. (d) $$I=\int\frac{x^4(1-4x+6x^2-4x^3+x^4)}{(1+x^2)}dx$$

$$=\int\frac{x^8-4x^7+6x^6-4x^5+x^4}{x^2+1}dx$$

$$=\int\left(x^6-4x^5+5x^4-4x^2+4-\frac{4}{x^2+1}\right)dx$$

$$=\frac{1}{7}x^7-\frac{2}{3}x^6+x^5-\frac{4}{3}x^3+4x-4\tan^{-1}x+C$$

4. (b) $$I=\int\frac{x^2(1-\ln x)}{\ln^4 x-x^4}dx=\int\frac{\left(\frac{1-\ln x}{x^2}\right)dx}{\left(\frac{\ln x}{x}\right)^4-1}$$

$\left[\text{Insert } \frac{\ln x}{x}=t \text{ and } \frac{1-\ln x}{x^2}dx=dt\right]$

$$=\int\frac{1}{t^4-1}dt=\int\frac{1}{(t-1)(t+1)(t^2+1)}dt$$

Now

$$\frac{1}{(t-1)(t+1)(t^2+1)}=\frac{1}{4}\left(\frac{1}{t-1}-\frac{1}{t+1}\right)-\frac{1}{2}\left(\frac{1}{t^2+1}\right)$$

Hence

$$I=\frac{1}{4}\ln\left|\frac{t-1}{t+1}\right|-\frac{1}{2}\tan^{-1}\left(\frac{\ln x}{x}\right)+C$$

$$=\frac{1}{4}\ln\left|\frac{\ln x-x}{\ln x+x}\right|-\frac{1}{2}\tan^{-1}\left(\frac{\ln x}{x}\right)+C$$

5. (c)

$$I=\int\frac{ax^{a+2b-1}-bx^{b-1}}{x^{2a+2b}+2x^{a+b}+1}dx=\int\frac{ax^{a-1}\quad bx^{-b-1}}{x^{2a}+2x^{a-b}+x^{-2b}}dx$$

$$=\int\frac{ax^{a-1}-bx^{-b-1}}{(x^a+x^{-b})^2}dx=\frac{-1}{x^a+x^{-b}}+C=\frac{-x^b}{x^{a+b}+1}+C$$

6. (d)

$$I=\int\sqrt{\text{cosec}^2x-\cot^2x+2\cot^2x+2\text{cosec}x\cot x}\,dx$$

$$=\int\sqrt{\text{cosec}^2x+\cot^2x+2\text{cosec}x\cot x}\,dx$$

$$=\int\sqrt{(\text{cosec}x+\cot x)^2}\,dx=\int|\text{cosec}x+\cot x|\,dx$$

$$= \int \left|\cot\frac{x}{2}\right| dx = \int \cot\frac{x}{2}\, dx$$

$$\left[\text{For } x \in \left(\frac{\pi}{2}, \pi\right), \cot\frac{x}{2} > 0\right]$$

$$= 2\ln\left(\sin\frac{x}{2}\right) + C. \left[\text{For } x \in \left(\frac{\pi}{2}, \pi\right), \sin\frac{x}{2} > 0\right]$$

7. (a)

$$I = \int e^t \left[\left(\sec^{-1}\sqrt{1+\tan^2 t}\right)^2 + \cos^{-1}\left(\frac{1-\tan^2 t}{1+\tan^2 t}\right)\right] dt$$

$$\left[\text{Insert } \tan^{-1} x = t \text{ and } \frac{1}{1+x^2} dx = dt\right]$$

$$= \int e^t \left(t^2 + 2t\right) dt = e^t t^2 + C$$

$$= e^{\tan^{-1} x}\left(\tan^{-1} x\right)^2 + C$$

8. (d) $I = \int e^t \left(\frac{1}{\sqrt{1+t^2}} - \frac{t}{\left(1+t^2\right)^{3/2}}\right) dt$

$$\left[\text{Insert } \tan\theta = t \text{ and } \sec^2\theta d\theta = dt\right]$$

$$= e^t \frac{1}{\sqrt{1+t^2}} + C = e^{\tan\theta}\cos\theta + C$$

9. (b) $I = \frac{1}{\sin(b-a)} \int \frac{\sin\{(x-a)-(x-b)\}}{\cos(x-a)\cos(x-b)} dx$

$$= \frac{1}{\sin(b-a)} \int \frac{\sin\{(x-a)-(x-b)\}}{\cos(x-a)\cos(x-b)} dx$$

$$= \frac{1}{\sin(b-a)} \int \left\{\frac{\sin(x-a)}{\cos(x-a)} - \frac{\sin(x-b)}{\cos(x-b)}\right\} dx$$

$$= \frac{1}{\sin(b-a)} \ln\left|\frac{\cos(x-b)}{\cos(x-a)}\right| + C$$

10. (b)

$$I = \int x\left(x^{3m-1} + x^{2m-1} + x^{m-1}\right)\left(2x^{2m} + 3x^m + 6\right)^{\frac{1}{m}} dx$$

$$= \int \left(x^{3m-1} + x^{2m-1} + x^{m-1}\right)\left(2x^{3m} + 3x^{2m} + 6x^m\right)^{\frac{1}{m}} dx$$

$$\left[\begin{array}{l}\text{Insert } 2x^{3m} + 3x^{2m} + 6x^m = u \\ \text{and } 6m\left(x^{3m-1} + x^{2m-1} + x^{m-1}\right) dx = du\end{array}\right]$$

$$= \frac{1}{6m} \int u^{1/m} du = \frac{u^{1+\frac{1}{m}}}{6(m+1)}$$

$$= \frac{1}{6(m+1)}\left(2x^{3m} + 3x^{2m} + 6x^m\right)^{1+\frac{1}{m}} + C$$

11. (a),(c)

$$I = \int \frac{1}{1+\frac{2t}{1+t^2}} \cdot \frac{2\,dt}{1+t^2} \left[\text{Insert } \tan(x/2) = t\right]$$

$$= \int \frac{2}{t^2+1+2t} dt = \int \frac{2}{(t+1)^2} dt$$

$$= \frac{-2}{t+1} + C = \frac{-2}{1+\tan(x/2)} + C.$$

Note that

$$\tan\left(\frac{x}{2} - \frac{\pi}{4}\right) = \frac{\tan(x/2)-1}{\tan(x/2)+1} = 1 + \frac{-2}{1+\tan(x/2)}$$

Hence, both (a), (c) are correct.

12. (a) $I = \int \frac{\sin x - x\cos x}{x^2\left(1+\frac{\sin x}{x}\right)} dx$

$$= \int \frac{-1}{t} dt$$

$$\left[\text{Insert } 1 + \frac{\sin x}{x} = t \text{ and } \frac{x\cos x - \sin x}{x^2} dx = dt\right]$$

$$= -\ln\left(1 + \frac{\sin x}{x}\right) + C$$

13. (b)

$$I = \int \frac{1}{x^2\left(1+x^4\right)^{3/4}} dx = \int \frac{1}{x^5\left(1+\frac{1}{x^4}\right)^{3/4}} dx$$

$$= \int \frac{-1}{4t^{3/4}} dt \left[\text{Insert } 1 + \frac{1}{x^4} = t \text{ and } \frac{-4}{x^5} dx = dt\right]$$

$$= -\left(1 + \frac{1}{x^4}\right)^{1/4} + C$$

14. (d) Insert $\sqrt{x^2+2} + x = t^2$ …(1)

Then $\left(\frac{x}{\sqrt{x^2+2}} + 1\right) dx = 2t\,dt \Rightarrow dx = \frac{2\sqrt{x^2+2}}{t} dt$

Now, rationalising equation (1), we have

$$\frac{2}{\sqrt{x^2+2}-x}=t^2 \Rightarrow \sqrt{x^2+2}-x=\frac{2}{t^2} \quad \ldots(2)$$

Adding equations (1) and (2), we have

$$2\sqrt{x^2+2}=t^2+\frac{2}{t^2}$$

Then $dx=\dfrac{2\sqrt{x^2+2}}{t}dt=\left(t+\dfrac{2}{t^3}\right)dt.$

Hence $I=\displaystyle\int t\left(t+\frac{2}{t^3}\right)dt=\frac{1}{3}t^3-\frac{2}{t}+C$

$$=\frac{1}{3}\left(\sqrt{x^2+2}+x\right)^{3/2}-\sqrt{2}\left(\sqrt{x^2+2}-x\right)^{1/2}+C$$

15. (c) We have

$$\tan 3x=\frac{\tan 2x+\tan x}{1-\tan 2x\tan x}$$

$\Rightarrow \quad \tan 3x-\tan x\tan 2x\tan 3x=\tan 2x+\tan x$

$\Rightarrow \quad \tan x\tan 2x\tan 3x=\tan 3x-\tan 2x-\tan x$

Hence $I=\displaystyle\int(\tan 3x-\tan 2x-\tan x)dx$

$$=\frac{1}{3}\ln|\sec 3x|-\frac{1}{2}\ln|\sec 2x|-\ln|\sec x|+C$$

16. (b) $I=\displaystyle\int\frac{1}{(x+1)\sqrt{x^2+x-1}}dx$

$$=\int\frac{1}{(x+1)\sqrt{(x+1)^2-(x+1)-1}}dx$$

$$=\int\frac{t}{\sqrt{\frac{1}{t^2}-\frac{1}{t}-1}}\cdot\frac{-1}{t^2}dt$$

$$\left[\text{Insert } x+1=\frac{1}{t} \text{ and } dx=\frac{-1}{t^2}dt\right]$$

$$=\int\frac{-1}{\sqrt{1-t-t^2}}dt=\int\frac{-1}{\sqrt{\frac{5}{4}-\left(t+\frac{1}{2}\right)^2}}dt$$

$$=\cos^{-1}\left\{\frac{t+\frac{1}{2}}{\sqrt{5}/2}\right\}+C=\cos^{-1}\left\{\frac{x+3}{\sqrt{5}(x+1)}\right\}+C$$

17. (c) $I=\displaystyle\int\frac{\frac{2}{x^3}+\frac{5}{x^6}}{\left(1+\frac{1}{x^2}+\frac{1}{x^5}\right)^3}dx$

$$=\int\frac{-1}{t^3}dt\left[\text{Insert } 1+\frac{1}{x^2}+\frac{1}{x^5}=t\right]$$

$$=\frac{1}{2t^2}+C=\frac{x^{10}}{2\left(x^5+x^3+1\right)^2}+C$$

18. (c) $I=\dfrac{1}{3}\displaystyle\int\frac{3x^2}{x^3\sqrt{1-x^3}}dx$

$$=\frac{1}{3}\int\frac{2}{t^2-1}dt\left[\text{Insert } 1-x^3=t^2\right]$$

$$=\frac{1}{3}\int\left(\frac{1}{t-1}-\frac{1}{t+1}\right)dt=\frac{1}{3}\ln\left(\frac{\sqrt{1-x^3}-1}{\sqrt{1-x^3}+1}\right)+C$$

19. (d) $I=\displaystyle\int\frac{a^{2x}-2a^xb^x+b^{2x}}{a^xb^x}dx$

$$=\int\left(c^x+c^{-x}-2\right)dx, \text{ where } c=\frac{a}{b}$$

$$=\frac{1}{\ln c}\left\{c^x-c^{-x}\right\}-2x+C$$

$$=\frac{1}{\ln(a/b)}\left\{\left(\frac{a}{b}\right)^x-\left(\frac{b}{a}\right)^x\right\}-2x+C$$

20. (a)

$$I-\int\left(t+\frac{1}{t}\right)\frac{1}{t}dt$$

$$\left[\text{Insert }\left(\frac{x}{e}\right)^x=t \Rightarrow x(\ln x-1)=\ln t \Rightarrow \ln x\,dx=\frac{1}{t}dt\right]$$

$$=\int\left(1+\frac{1}{t^2}\right)dt=t-\frac{1}{t}+C=\left(\frac{x}{e}\right)^x-\left(\frac{e}{x}\right)^x+C$$

21. (d) $I=\displaystyle\int\frac{(t-1)^2}{(t^2+1)^2}e^t dt$

$$\left[\text{Insert } \ln x=t \Rightarrow x=e^t \Rightarrow dx=e^t dt\right]$$

$$=\int\left(\frac{-2t}{(t^2+1)^2}+\frac{1}{t^2+1}\right)e^t dt=\frac{e^t}{t^2+1}+C=\frac{x}{\ln^2 x+1}+C$$

22. (a)

$$I = \int \frac{\cos x}{1+\sin 2x} dx$$

$$= \frac{1}{2}\int \left(\frac{\cos x + \sin x}{1+\sin 2x} + \frac{\cos x - \sin x}{1+\sin 2x} \right) dx = \frac{1}{2}(I_1 + I_2)$$

Putting $\sin x - \cos x = t$, $(\cos x + \sin x)dx = dt$, and $\sin 2x = 1 - t^2$, we have

$$I_1 = \int \frac{1}{2-t^2} dt = \frac{-1}{2\sqrt{2}} \int \left(\frac{1}{t-\sqrt{2}} - \frac{1}{t+\sqrt{2}} \right) dt$$

$$= \frac{1}{2\sqrt{2}} \ln \left(\frac{t+\sqrt{2}}{t-\sqrt{2}} \right) = \frac{1}{2\sqrt{2}} \ln \left(\frac{\sin x - \cos x + \sqrt{2}}{\sin x - \cos x - \sqrt{2}} \right)$$

Putting $\sin x + \cos x = t$, $(\cos x - \sin x)dx = dt$, and $\sin 2x = t^2 - 1$, we have

$$I_2 = \int \frac{1}{t^2} dt = \frac{-1}{t} = \frac{-1}{\sin x + \cos x}$$

Hence, we have

$$I = \frac{1}{4\sqrt{2}} \ln \left(\frac{\sin x - \cos x + \sqrt{2}}{\sin x - \cos x - \sqrt{2}} \right) - \frac{1}{2(\sin x + \cos x)} + C$$

CHAPTER

21 Definite Integration

- **Newton–Leibnitz Theorem:** If $g(x)$ is one of the anti-derivatives of the function $f(x)$ and is continuous on $[a,b]$, then

$$\int_a^b f(x)dx = |g(x)|_a^b = g(b)-g(a)$$

The definite integral is the area of the region surrounded by the curve $y=f(x)$, the x-axis and the ordinates $x=a, x=b$. Here, a and b are called the lower and upper limits, respectively, of the definite integral.

- **Theorems on Definite Integrals**

1. $\int_a^b f(x)dx = \int_a^b f(t)dt$
2. $\int_a^a f(x)dx = 0$
3. $\int_a^b f(x)dx = -\int_b^a f(x)dx$
4. $(b-a)f_{\min} \le \int_a^b f(x)dx \le (b-a)f_{\max}$
5. If $f(x)\le g(x)$ for all x in $[a,b]$, then $\int_a^b f(x)dx \le \int_a^b g(x)dx$
6. $\left|\int_a^b f(x)dx\right| \le \int_a^b |f(x)|dx$

- **Properties of Definite Integrals**

1. $\int_a^b f(x)dx = \int_a^b f(a+b-x)dx$. Hence, we can always write

$$\int_a^b f(x)dx = \frac{1}{2}\int_a^b \{f(x)+f(a+b-x)\}dx$$

2. $$\int_a^b f(x)dx = \begin{cases} 2\int_a^{\frac{a+b}{2}} f(x)dx \text{ if } f(x)=f(a+b-x) \\ 0 \text{ if } f(x)=-f(a+b-x) \end{cases}$$

3. If $f(x)$ is periodic having period T, then $\int_a^{a+nT} f(x)dx = n\int_0^T f(x)dx$, where $n \in \mathbf{N}$

- **Two Useful Definite Integrals**

1. $\int_0^{\pi/2} \ln(\sin x)dx = -\frac{\pi}{2}\ln 2$

2. $$\int_a^{\pi/2} \sin^p x \cos^q x\, dx = \begin{cases} \dfrac{(p-1)(p-3)\ldots(q-1)(q-3)\ldots}{(p+q)(p+q-2)\ldots}\cdot\dfrac{\pi}{2} \text{ if } p,q \text{ are both even} \\ \dfrac{(p-1)(p-3)\ldots(q-1)(q-3)\ldots}{(p+q)(p+q-2)\ldots} \text{ otherwise} \end{cases}$$

EXERCISES

1. Let $I=\int_1^{16}\tan^{-1}\sqrt{\sqrt{x}-1}\,dx$. Then I equals:

(a) $6\pi+\sqrt{3}$ (b) $5\pi-\sqrt{3}$

(c) $\frac{5\pi}{3}-\sqrt{3}$ (d) $\frac{16\pi}{3}-2\sqrt{3}$

2. If $I(m,n)=\int_0^1 t^m(1+t)^n\,dt$, then the expression for $I(m,n)$ in terms of $I(m+1,n-1)$ is:

(a) $\frac{2^n}{m+1}-\frac{n}{m+1}I(m+1,n-1)$

(b) $\frac{-n}{m+1}I(m+1,n-1)$

(c) $\frac{2^n}{m+1}+\frac{n}{m+1}I(m+1,n-1)$

(d) $\frac{n}{m+1}I(m+1,n-1)$

3. Let $I=\int_{e^{-1}}^{e^2}\left|\frac{\ln x}{x}\right|dx$. Then I equals:

(a) $\frac{3}{2}$ (b) $\frac{5}{2}$

(c) 3 (d) 5

4. Let $f(x)=xg(x)$ for all $x\in\mathbf{R}$. Suppose $g(1)=0$ and $g(3)=-4$. If $\int_1^3 x^2g'(x)dx=-12$ and $\int_1^3 x^3g''(x)dx=40$, then the correct statements are:

(a) $9f'(3)+f'(1)-32=0$

(b) $\int_1^3 f(x)dx=12$

(c) $9f'(3)-f'(1)+32=0$

(d) $\int_1^3 f(x)dx=-12$

5. Let $f(x)=\left[x^2-\frac{1}{4}\right]$, where $[\square]$ denotes the greatest integer function. Then the value of $\int_{-1/2}^{1}|x|f(x)dx$ equals:

(a) 0 (b) -1

(c) $\frac{-2}{3}$ (d) $\frac{-1}{4}$

6. Let $I=\int_{-\pi}^{\pi}\frac{\cos^2 x}{1+a^x}dx$, where $a>0$. Then I equals:

(a) π (b) $a\pi$

(c) $\pi/2$ (d) 2π

7. Let $I=\int_{-\sqrt{2}}^{\sqrt{2}}\frac{xf(x^2)}{2+f(x+1)}dx+\int_{-\sqrt{2}}^{\sqrt{2}}\ln\left(\frac{1+xf(x^2)}{1-xf(x^2)}\right)dx$, where $f(x)=[x]$ is the greatest integer function. Then I equals:

(a) $-3/8$ (b) 0

(c) $-2\ln 2$ (d) $1/4$

8. Let $I=\int_0^{\sin^2 x}\sin^{-1}\sqrt{t}\,dt+\int_0^{\cos^2 x}\cos^{-1}\sqrt{t}\,dt$. Then I equals:

(a) π (b) $\pi/2$

(c) $\pi/3$ (d) $\pi/4$

9. Let $T>0$ be a real number. Suppose f is a continuous function such that for all $x\in\mathbf{R}$, $f(x+T)=f(x)$. If $I=\int_0^T f(x)dx$, then $\int_3^{3+3T}f(2x)dx$ equals:

(a) $3I/2$ (b) I

(c) $3I$ (d) $6I$

10. Let $I=\int_0^1 4x^3\frac{d^2}{dx^2}\left\{\left(1-x^2\right)^5\right\}dx$. Then I equals:

(a) 1 (b) -1

(c) 2 (d) -2

11. Let $\frac{d}{dx}\{f(x)\}=\frac{e^{\sin x}}{x}, x>0$. If $\int_1^4\frac{2e^{\sin(x^2)}}{x}dx=f(k)-f(1)$, then one of the possible values of k is:

(a) 0 (b) 1

(c) 8 (d) 16

12. If for non-zero $x, af(x)+bf\left(\frac{1}{x}\right)=\frac{1}{x}-5$, where $a \neq b$, then $\int_1^2 f(x)dx$ equals:

(a) $\frac{1}{a^2-b^2}\left(a\ln 2-5a+\frac{7}{2}b\right)$

(b) $\frac{1}{a^2-b^2}\left(a\ln 2+7a+\frac{5}{2}b\right)$

(c) $\frac{1}{a^2-b^2}\left(a\ln 2-7a+\frac{5}{2}b\right)$

(d) $\frac{1}{a^2-b^2}\left(a\ln 2-2a+\frac{5}{7}b\right)$

13. Let $I=\int_0^{2\pi}\frac{x\sin^{2n}x}{\sin^{2n}x+\cos^{2n}x}dx$, where $n \in \mathbf{N}$. Then I equals:

(a) π^2 (b) $-\pi^2$
(c) π (d) $-\pi$

14. If $I_n=\int_{-\pi}^{\pi}\frac{\sin(nx)}{(1+\pi^x)\sin x}dx$, where $n \in \mathbf{N}$, then:

(a) $I_n=I_{n+2}$ (b) $\sum_{m=1}^{10} I_{2m+1}=10\pi$
(c) $\sum_{m=1}^{10} I_{2m}=10\pi$ (d) $I_n=I_{n+1}$

15. Let $I=\int_0^x\frac{1}{\sqrt{t(x-t)}}dt$. Then I equals:

(a) π (b) $\frac{\pi}{2}$
(c) $\frac{\pi}{3}$ (d) 0

16. Let $I=\int_0^{\pi/2}\ln(\tan x+\cot x)\,dx$. Then I equals:

(a) $\frac{\pi}{4}\ln 3$ (b) $\pi\ln 2$
(c) $\frac{\pi}{8}\ln 3$ (d) $\frac{\pi}{2}\ln 2$

17. Let f be a real-valued function defined on $[-\pi,\pi]$ given by $f(x)=\frac{\sin\left(\frac{9x}{2}\right)}{\sin\left(\frac{x}{2}\right)}, x \neq 0$ and $f(0)=9$. Then $\frac{2}{\pi}\int_{-\pi}^{\pi}f(x)\,dx$ equals:

(a) 6 (b) 5
(c) 4 (d) 3

18. Let $[x]$ denote the greatest integer function. Let f be a real-valued function, given by

$$f(x)=\begin{cases}x-[x], & \text{if } [x] \text{ is even}\\ 1+[x]-x, & \text{if } [x] \text{ is odd}\end{cases}$$

Then $\frac{\pi^2}{10}\int_{-10}^{10}f(x)\cos(\pi x)\,dx$ equals:

(a) $-\pi$ (b) $2-\pi$
(c) 3π (d) -4

19. Let $I=\int_0^1\frac{x^4(1-x)^4}{1+x^2}dx$. Then I equals:

(a) $\frac{22}{7}-\pi$ (b) $\frac{2}{105}$
(c) $\frac{71}{15}-\frac{3\pi}{2}$ (d) 0

20. Let $I=\int_0^{\pi/2}\frac{\sin^{n-2}x}{(1+\cos x)^n}dx$, where $n \in \boldsymbol{Q}, n>1$. Then I equals:

(a) $\frac{n-1}{n+1}$ (b) $\frac{n}{n^2+1}$
(c) $\frac{n+1}{n-1}$ (d) $\frac{n}{n^2-1}$

21. Let a, b, c be non-zero real numbers such that

$$\int_0^1(1+\cos^8 x)(ax^2+bx+c)dx=$$

$$\int_0^2(1+\cos^8 x)(ax^2+bx+c)dx$$

Then $ax^2+bx+c=0$ has:
(a) No root in $(0,2)$
(b) At least one root in $(1,2)$
(c) Two roots in $(0,2)$
(d) No real root

22. If $g(x)=\int_0^x \cos^4 t\, dt$, then $g(x+\pi)$ equals:
(a) $g(x)+g(\pi)$ (b) $g(x)-g(\pi)$
(c) $g(x)\cdot g(\pi)$ (d) $\frac{g(x)}{g(\pi)}$

23. Let $I=\int_{\pi/4}^{3\pi/4} \frac{x}{1+\sin x}dx$. Then I equals:
(a) $\pi(\sqrt{2}-1)$ (b) $\pi(\sqrt{2}+1)$
(c) $\pi(2\sqrt{2}-1)$ (d) $\pi(\sqrt{2}+2)$

24. If $\int_a^b \{f(x)-3x\}dx=a^2-b^2$, then the value of $f(\pi/6)$ equals:
(a) $\frac{\pi}{6}$ (b) $\frac{2\pi}{3}$
(c) $\frac{\pi}{3}$ (d) $\frac{\pi}{2}$

25. Let $f(x)=7\tan^8 x+7\tan^6 x-3\tan^4 x-3\tan^2 x$. Then $\int_0^{\pi/4} xf(x)dx$ equals:
(a) $\frac{1}{6}$ (b) $\frac{2}{3}$
(c) $\frac{1}{3}$ (d) $\frac{1}{12}$

26. Let $I=\int_{\sqrt{\ln 2}}^{\sqrt{\ln 3}} \frac{x\sin(x^2)}{\sin(x^2)+\sin(\ln 6-x^2)}dx$. Then I equals:
(a) $\frac{1}{4}\ln\left(\frac{3}{2}\right)$ (b) $\frac{1}{2}\ln\left(\frac{3}{2}\right)$
(c) $\ln\left(\frac{3}{2}\right)$ (d) $\frac{1}{6}\ln\left(\frac{3}{2}\right)$

27. Let $f(x)=x^4+x^2+1$. Then $\int_{-1}^{1} f(\sin x)f'(\sin x)dx$ equals:
(a) 0 (b) 1
(c) π (d) $\frac{1}{\pi}$

28. Let $I=\int_0^{\pi/2} \frac{2+\sin x}{1+\cos x}e^{x/2}dx$. Then I equals:
(a) $e^{\pi/2}$ (b) $e^{\pi/4}$
(c) $2e^{\pi/2}$ (d) $2e^{\pi/4}$

29. Let $I=\int_0^{\pi/2} \sin(2x)\tan^{-1}(\sin x)dx$. Then I equals:
(a) $\frac{3\pi}{8}-1$ (b) $\frac{3\pi}{4}-\frac{1}{2}$
(c) $\frac{\pi}{2}-1$ (d) $\frac{\pi}{4}-\frac{1}{2}$

30. Let $I=\int_{1/3}^{1} \frac{(x-x^3)^{\frac{1}{3}}}{x^4}dx$. Then I equals:
(a) 3 (b) 5
(c) 4 (d) 6

31. Suppose f, f', f'' are continuous on $[1,e]$ and $f'(e)=f(e)=f(1)=1$. If $\int_1^e \frac{f(x)}{x^2}dx=\frac{1}{2}$, then $\int_1^e f''(x)\ln x\, dx$ equals:
(a) $\frac{5}{2}-\frac{1}{e}$ (b) $\frac{3}{2}-\frac{1}{e}$
(c) $\frac{1}{2}-\frac{1}{e}$ (d) $1-\frac{1}{e}$

32. Let $I=\int_{-\sqrt{3}/2}^{\sqrt{3}/2} \frac{x^5+x^2}{\sqrt{1-x^2}}dx$. Then I equals:
(a) 0 (b) $\frac{\pi}{2}+\frac{\sqrt{3}}{4}$
(c) $\frac{\pi}{3}-\frac{\sqrt{3}}{4}$ (d) $\pi-\sqrt{3}$

33. If $I_n = \int_1^e (\log x)^n \, dx$, where $n \in \mathbf{N}$, then the value of $I_{10} - 90I_8$:

(a) $-10e$ (b) $-9e$
(c) $11e$ (d) $7e$

34. Let f be a function such that for every real x, $f(a + b + 1 - x) = f(x)$ where a, b are some fixed positive real numbers. Then $\frac{1}{a+b}\int_a^b x\{f(x)+f(x+1)\}dx$ equals:

(a) $\int_{a+1}^{b+1} f(x)dx$ (b) $\int_{a+1}^{b+1} f(x+1)$
(c) $\int_{a-1}^{b-1} f(x)dx$ (d) $\int_{a-1}^{b-1} f(x+1)dx$

35. Let f be a function such that for every real x, $f(2-x)=f(2+x)$ and also $f(4-x)=f(4+x)$. If $\int_0^2 f(x)dx = 5$, then the value of $\int_{10}^{50} f(x)dx$ equals:

(a) 50 (b) 80
(c) 100 (d) 120

36. Let $I = \int_0^1 \frac{\ln(1+x)}{1+x^2}dx$. Then I equals:

(a) 1 (b) $\frac{\pi}{8}\ln 2$
(c) $\frac{\pi}{2}\ln 2$ (d) $\frac{\pi}{2}$

37. If $I_n = \int_0^1 (1-x^a)^n \, dx$, where $n \in \mathbf{N}$, then the ratio $\frac{I_n}{I_{n+1}}$ equals:

(a) $n+\frac{1}{(n-1)a}$ (b) $1+\frac{1}{(n-1)a}$
(c) $\frac{n+1}{(n-1)a}$ (d) $1+\frac{1}{(n+1)a}$

38. Let $I_n = \int_0^{\pi/2} \cos^n x \cos(nx)dx$, where $n \in \mathbf{N}$. Then $I_1, I_2, I_3, \ldots$ are in:

(a) AP (b) GP
(c) HP (d) None of these

39. Let $I_n = \int_0^{\pi/4} \tan^n x \, dx$, where $n \in \mathbf{N}$. Then $I_2 + I_4, I_3 + I_5, I_4 + I_6$ are in:

(a) AP (b) GP
(c) HP (d) None of these

40. Let $I = \int_0^{\pi} [\tan x]dx$, where [ ] denotes the greatest integer function. Then I equals:

(a) $-\pi/2$ (b) $-\pi/4$
(c) -1 (d) 0

41. Consider the function $f(x) = x^3 - \frac{3}{2}x^2 + x + \frac{1}{4}$. Let $f_1(x) = f(x)$ and for $n \geq 1$, $f_{n+1}(x) = f_n\{f(x)\}$. Then:

(a) $\int_0^1 f_{2020}(x)dx = 1$ (b) $\int_0^1 f_{2020}(x)dx = 1/2$
(c) $\int_0^1 f_{2020}(x)dx = 1/4$ (d) $\int_0^1 f_{2020}(x)dx = 0$

ANSWER KEYS

1. (d)	**2.** (a)	**3.** (b)	**4.** (c),(d)	**5.** (d)	**6.** (c)	**7.** (a)	**8.** (d)	**9.** (c)
10. (c)	**11.** (d)	**12.** (a)	**13.** (a)	**14.** (a),(b)	**15.** (a)	**16.** (b)	**17.** (c)	**18.** (d)
19. (a)	**20.** (d)	**21.** (b)	**22.** (a)	**23.** (a)	**24.** (a)	**25.** (d)	**26.** (a)	**27.** (a)
28. (d)	**29.** (c)	**30.** (d)	**31.** (b)	**32.** (c)	**33.** (b)	**34.** (a), (d)	**35.** (c)	**36.** (b)
37. (d)	**38.** (b)	**39.** (c)	**40.** (a)	**41.** (b)				

SOLUTIONS

1. (d) $I=\int_0^{\pi/3}\theta d\left(\sec^4\theta\right)\left[\text{Insert } x=\sec^4\theta\right]$

$$=\left|\theta\sec^4\theta\right|_0^{\pi/3}-\int_0^{\pi/3}\sec^4\theta d\theta$$

$$=\frac{16\pi}{3}-\int_0^{\pi/3}\left(\tan^2\theta+1\right)\sec^2\theta d\theta$$

$$=\frac{16\pi}{3}-\left|\tan\theta+\frac{1}{3}\tan^3\theta\right|_0^{\pi/3}=\frac{16\pi}{3}-2\sqrt{3}$$

2. (a)

$$I(m,n)=\left|\frac{t^{m+1}}{m+1}(1+t)^n\right|_0^1-\frac{n}{m+1}\int_0^1 t^{m+1}(1+t)^{n-1}\,dt$$

$$=\frac{2^n}{m+1}-\frac{n}{m+1}I(m+1,n-1)$$

3. (b) $I=\int_{e^{-1}}^{1}\frac{-\ln x}{x}dx+\int_1^{e^2}\frac{\ln x}{x}dx$

$$=\left|\frac{-\ln^2 x}{2}\right|_{e^{-1}}^{1}+\left|\frac{\ln^2 x}{2}\right|_1^{e^2}=\frac{5}{2}$$

4. (c),(d) We have $f(x)=xg(x)$ and $f'(x)=g(x)+xg'(x)$

Then $\int_1^3 x^2g'(x)dx=-12$

$$\Rightarrow\quad \left|x^2g(x)\right|_1^3-2\int_1^3 xg(x)dx=-12$$

$$\Rightarrow\quad -36-2\int_1^3 f(x)dx=-12\left[\text{Using } f(x)=xg(x)\right]$$

$$\Rightarrow\quad \int_1^3 f(x)dx=-12 \text{ and } \int_1^3 x^3g''(x)dx=40$$

$$\Rightarrow\quad \left|x^3g'(x)\right|_1^3-3\int_1^3 x^2g'(x)dx=40$$

$$\Rightarrow\quad \left|x^2(f'-g)\right|_1^3+36=40\left[\text{Using } xg'(x)=f'(x)-g(x)\right]$$

$$\Rightarrow\quad 9f'(3)+36-f'(1)+36=40$$

$$\Rightarrow\quad 9f'(3)-f'(1)+32=0$$

5. (d) The given function can be written as

$$f(x)=\begin{cases}-1, & -1/2\le x<1/2\\ 0, & 1/2\le x\le 1\end{cases}$$

Hence $\int_{-1/2}^{1}|x|f(x)dx=-\int_{-1/2}^{1/2}|x|dx+\int_{1/2}^{1}0\,dx$

$$=-2\int_0^{1/2}x\,dx=\frac{-1}{4}$$

6. (c) $I=\frac{1}{2}\int_{-\pi}^{\pi}\left(\frac{\cos^2x}{1+a^x}+\frac{\cos^2x}{1+a^{-x}}\right)dx$

$$\left[\text{Using property }\int_a^b f(x)dx=\frac{1}{2}\int_a^b\{f(x)+f(a+b-x)\}dx\right]$$

$$=\frac{1}{2}\int_{-\pi}^{\pi}\left(\frac{\cos^2x}{1+a^x}+\frac{a^x\cos^2x}{1+a^x}\right)dx$$

$$=\frac{1}{2}\int_{-\pi}^{\pi}\cos^2x\,dx=\frac{\pi}{2}$$

7. (a) $I=\int_{-\sqrt{2}}^{\sqrt{2}}\frac{x\left[x^2\right]}{2+[x+1]}dx+\int_{-\sqrt{2}}^{\sqrt{2}}\ln\left(\frac{1+x\left[x^2\right]}{1-x\left[x^2\right]}\right)dx$

$$=\int_{-\sqrt{2}}^{\sqrt{2}}\frac{x\left[x^2\right]}{3+[x]}dx+0\left[\ln\left(\frac{1+x\left[x^2\right]}{1-x\left[x^2\right]}\right)\text{ is odd}\right]$$

$$=\int_{-\sqrt{2}}^{-1}\frac{x}{3-2}dx+\int_{-1}^{0}\frac{0}{3-1}dx++\int_0^1\frac{0}{3+0}dx+\int_1^{\sqrt{2}}\frac{x}{3+1}dx$$

$$=\frac{-1}{2}+\frac{1}{8}=\frac{-3}{8}$$

8. (d) $I=\int_0^x\theta\sin(2\theta)d\theta-\int_{\pi/2}^{x}\theta\sin(2\theta)d\theta$

$$\left[\text{Insert } t=\sin^2\theta \text{ and } \cos^2\theta\text{, respectively}\right]$$

$$= \int_0^x \theta\sin(2\theta)d\theta + \int_x^{\pi/2} \theta\sin(2\theta)d\theta$$

$$= \int_0^{\pi/2} \theta\sin(2\theta)d\theta$$

$$= \left|-\theta\frac{\cos(2\theta)}{2}\right|_0^{\pi/2} + \left|\frac{\sin(2\theta)}{4}\right|_0^{\pi/2} = \frac{\pi}{4}$$

9. (c)

$$I' = \frac{1}{2}\int_6^{6+6T} f(y)dy \left[\text{Insert } 2x = y \text{ and } dx = \frac{1}{2}dy\right]$$

$$= \frac{1}{2}\times 6\int_0^T f(y)dy = 3I$$

10. (c)

$$I = \left|4x^3\frac{d}{dx}\left\{\left(1-x^2\right)^5\right\}\right|_0^1 - \int_0^1 12x^2\frac{d}{dx}\left\{\left(1-x^2\right)^5\right\}dx$$

[Using parts]

$$= 0 - \left|12x^2\left(1-x^2\right)^5\right|_0^1 + \int_0^1 24x\left(1-x^2\right)^5 dx$$

[Using parts]

$$= -12\int_1^0 t^5 dt \left[\text{Insert } 1-x^2 = t \text{ and } -2x\,dx = dt\right]$$

$$= -2\left|t^6\right|_1^0 = 2$$

11. (d) $I = \int_1^{16} \frac{e^{\sin t}}{t}dt \left[\text{Insert } x^2 = t \text{ and } 2x\,dx = dt\right]$

$$= \left|f(t)\right|_1^{16} = f(16) - f(1)$$

Hence $k = 16$.

12. (a) The given relation is $af(x) + bf\left(\frac{1}{x}\right) = \frac{1}{x} - 5$.

Putting $1/x$ for x, we have $af\left(\frac{1}{x}\right) + bf(x) = x - 5$.

Eliminating $f\left(\frac{1}{x}\right)$ from the two relations, we have

$$f(x) = \frac{1}{a^2-b^2}\left[a\left(\frac{1}{x}-5\right) - b(x-5)\right]$$

Now $\int_1^2 f(x)dx = \frac{1}{a^2-b^2}\left|a(\ln x - 5x) - b\frac{(x-5)^2}{2}\right|_1^2$

$$= \frac{1}{a^2-b^2}\left(a\ln 2 - 5a + \frac{7}{2}b\right)$$

13. (a)

$$I = \frac{1}{2}\int_0^{2\pi}\left(\frac{x\sin^{2n}x}{\sin^{2n}x+\cos^{2n}x} + \frac{(2\pi-x)\sin^{2n}x}{\sin^{2n}x+\cos^{2n}x}\right)dx$$

$$\left[\text{Using property } \int_a^b f(x)dx = \frac{1}{2}\int_a^b \{f(x)+f(a+b-x)\}dx\right]$$

$$= \pi\int_0^{2\pi}\frac{\sin^{2n}x}{\sin^{2n}x+\cos^{2n}x}dx$$

$$= 2\pi\int_0^{\pi}\frac{\sin^{2n}x}{\sin^{2n}x+\cos^{2n}x}dx \left[\text{Since } f(x) = f(2\pi-x)\right]$$

$$= 4\pi\int_0^{\pi/2}\frac{\sin^{2n}x}{\sin^{2n}x+\cos^{2n}x}dx \left[\text{Since } f(x) = f(\pi-x)\right]$$

$$= \frac{1}{2}\times 4\pi\int_0^{\pi/2}\left(\frac{\sin^{2n}x}{\sin^{2n}x+\cos^{2n}x} + \frac{\cos^{2n}x}{\cos^{2n}x+\sin^{2n}x}\right)dx$$

$$\left[\text{Using property } \int_a^b f(x)dx = \frac{1}{2}\int_a^b \{f(x)+f(a+b-x)\}dx\right]$$

$$= 2\pi\int_0^{\pi/2} 1\,dx = \pi^2.$$

14. (a),(b) $I_n = \frac{1}{2}\int_{-\pi}^{\pi}\left(\frac{\sin(nx)}{\left(1+\pi^x\right)\sin x} + \frac{\sin(nx)}{\left(1+\pi^{-x}\right)\sin x}\right)dx$

$$\left[\text{Using property } \int_a^b f(x)dx = \frac{1}{2}\int_a^b \{f(x)+f(a+b-x)\}dx\right]$$

$$= \frac{1}{2}\int_{-\pi}^{\pi}\left(\frac{\sin(nx)}{(1+\pi^x)\sin x} + \frac{\pi^x \sin(nx)}{(1+\pi^x)\sin x}\right)dx$$

$$= \frac{1}{2}\int_{-\pi}^{\pi}\frac{\sin(nx)}{\sin x}dx$$

$$= 2\int_{0}^{\pi}\frac{\sin(nx)}{\sin x}dx \left[\frac{\sin(nx)}{\sin x} \text{ is even}\right]$$

Now $\quad I_{n+2} - I_n = \int_0^{\pi}\frac{\sin(n+2)x - \sin nx}{\sin x}dx$

$$= \int_0^{\pi} 2\cos(n+1)x\,dx$$

$$= \frac{2}{n+1}\left|\sin(n+1)x\right|_0^{\pi} = 0$$

$\Rightarrow \quad I_{n+2} = I_n, I_0 = 0, I_1 = \pi, I_2 = 0, I_3 = \pi, \ldots$

Hence $\sum_{m=1}^{10} I_{2m+1} = 10 I_3 = 10\pi$ and $\sum_{m=1}^{10} I_{2m} = 10 I_2 = 0.$

15. (a) $I = \int_0^x \frac{1}{\sqrt{t(x-t)}}dt = \int_0^x \frac{1}{\sqrt{\frac{x^2}{4} - \left(t - \frac{x}{2}\right)^2}}dx$

$$= \left|\sin^{-1}\left(\frac{t - \frac{x}{2}}{\frac{x}{2}}\right)\right|_0^x = \sin^{-1}(1) - \sin^{-1}(-1) = \pi$$

16. (b)

$$I = \int_0^{\pi/2}\ln(\tan x + \cot x)dx = \int_0^{\pi/2}\ln\left(\frac{1}{\sin x\cos x}\right)dx$$

$$= \int_0^{\pi/2}\ln\left(\frac{2}{\sin 2x}\right)dx$$

$$= \int_0^{\pi/2}\left[\ln 2 - \ln(\sin 2x)\right]dx$$

$$= \frac{\pi}{2}\ln 2 - \frac{1}{2}\int_0^{\pi}\ln(\sin t)dt \text{ [Putting } 2x = t]$$

$$= \frac{\pi}{2}\ln 2 - \int_0^{\pi/2}\ln(\sin t)dt \;[f(t) = f(\pi - t)]$$

$$= \frac{\pi}{2}\ln 2 + \frac{\pi}{2}\ln 2 = \pi\ln 2. \left[\int_0^{\pi/2}\ln(\sin t)dt = \frac{\pi}{2}\ln 2\right]$$

17. (c) $I = \frac{4}{\pi}\int_0^{\pi}\frac{\sin\left(\frac{9x}{2}\right)}{\sin\left(\frac{x}{2}\right)}dx \left[\frac{\sin\left(\frac{9x}{2}\right)}{\sin\left(\frac{x}{2}\right)} \text{ is even}\right]$

$$= \frac{8}{\pi}\int_0^{\pi/2}\frac{\sin(9t)}{\sin t}dt \text{ [Insert } x = 2t \text{ and } dx = 2\,dt]$$

$$= \frac{1}{2}\times\frac{8}{\pi}\int_0^{\pi/2}\left(\frac{\sin(9t)}{\sin t} + \frac{\cos(9t)}{\cos t}\right)dt$$

$$= \frac{8}{\pi}\int_0^{\pi/2}\frac{\sin(10t)}{\sin(2t)}dt$$

$$\left[\text{Using property } \int_a^b f(x)dx = \frac{1}{2}\int_a^b\{f(x) + f(a+b-x)\}dx\right]$$

$$= \frac{4}{\pi}\int_0^{\pi}\frac{\sin(5y)}{\sin y}dy \text{ [Insert } 2t = y \text{ and } 2\,dt = dy]$$

$$= \frac{8}{\pi}\int_0^{\pi/2}\frac{\sin(5y)}{\sin y}dy\,[f(y) = f(\pi - y)]$$

$$= \frac{1}{2}\times\frac{8}{\pi}\int_0^{\pi/2}\left(\frac{\sin(5y)}{\sin y} + \frac{\cos(5y)}{\cos y}\right)dt$$

$$= \frac{8}{\pi}\int_0^{\pi/2}\frac{\sin(6y)}{\sin(2y)}dt$$

$$\left[\text{Using property } \int_a^b f(x)dx = \frac{1}{2}\int_a^b\{f(x) + f(a+b-x)\}dx\right]$$

$$= \frac{4}{\pi}\int_0^{\pi}\frac{\sin(3u)}{\sin u}dy \text{ [Insert } 2y = u \text{ and } 2\,dy = du]$$

$$= \frac{8}{\pi}\int_0^{\pi/2}\frac{\sin(3u)}{\sin u}dy\,[f(y) = f(\pi - y)]$$

$$= \frac{1}{2}\times\frac{8}{\pi}\int_0^{\pi/2}\left(\frac{\sin(3u)}{\sin u} - \frac{\cos(3u)}{\cos u}\right)du$$

$$= \frac{8}{\pi}\int_0^{\pi/2}\frac{\sin(2u)}{\sin(2u)}du$$

$$\left[\text{Using property} \int_a^b f(x)dx = \frac{1}{2}\int_a^b \{f(x)+f(a+b-x)\}dx\right]$$

$$= \frac{8}{\pi}\times\frac{\pi}{2} = 4$$

18. (d) The function $f(x)$ is periodic, having period equal to 2. The function $\cos(\pi x)$ is also periodic, having period equal to 2. Thus, the function $f(x)\cos(\pi x)$ is periodic, having period equal to 2. Hence, we have

$$I = 10\times\frac{\pi^2}{10}\int_0^2 f(x)\cos(\pi x)dx$$

$$= \pi^2\int_0^2 g(x)dx, \text{ where}$$

$$g(x) = \begin{cases} x\cos(\pi x), & 0<x<1 \\ (2-x)\cos(\pi x), & 1<x<2 \end{cases}$$

$$= 2\pi^2\int_0^1 x\cos(\pi x)\,dx\,[g(x)=g(2-x)]$$

$$= 2\pi^2\left|x\frac{\sin(\pi x)}{\pi} + \frac{\cos(\pi x)}{\pi^2}\right|_0^1 \text{ [Using parts]}$$

$$= -4$$

19. (a) $I = \int_0^1 \frac{x^8-4x^7+6x^6-4x^5+x^4}{x^2+1}dx$

$$= \int_0^1 \left(x^6-4x^5+5x^4-4x^2+4-\frac{4}{x^2+1}\right)dx$$

$$= \left|\frac{1}{7}x^7 - \frac{4}{6}x^6 + x^5 - \frac{4}{3}x^3 + 4x - 4\tan^{-1}x\right|_0^1$$

$$= \frac{1}{7} - \frac{4}{6} + 1 - \frac{4}{3} + 4 - \pi = \frac{22}{7} - \pi$$

20. (d) Using the substitution $\tan\left(\frac{x}{2}\right) = t$, the integral reduces to

$$I = \int_0^1 \left(\frac{2t}{1+t^2}\right)^{n-2}\left(\frac{1+t^2}{2}\right)^n \frac{2dt}{1+t^2}$$

$$= \frac{1}{2}\int_0^1 (1+t^2)t^{n-2}dt$$

$$= \frac{1}{2}\int_0^1 (t^{n-2}+t^n)dt$$

$$= \frac{1}{2}\left|\frac{t^{n-1}}{n-1} + \frac{t^{n+1}}{n+1}\right|_0^1 = \frac{n}{n^2-1}$$

21. (b) Let $f(x) = (1+\cos^8 x)(ax^2+bx+c)$. From the given relation, we

$$\int_0^1 f(x)dx = \int_0^2 f(x)dx$$

$$\Rightarrow \int_0^1 f(x)dx = \int_0^1 f(x)dx + \int_1^2 f(x)dx$$

$$\Rightarrow \int_1^2 f(x)dx = 0$$

Thus, $f(x)$ must take negative as well as positive values in (1,2). Since $1+\cos^8 x$ is always positive, ax^2+bx+c must take negative as well as positive values in (1,2). Hence, $ax^2+bx+c=0$ will have at least one root in (1,2).

22. (a) $g(x+\pi) = \int_0^{x+\pi} \cos^4 t\,dt$

$$= \int_0^x \cos^4 t\,dt + \int_x^{x+\pi} \cos^4 t\,dt$$

$$= \int_0^x \cos^4 t\,dt + \int_0^\pi \cos^4 t\,dt\,[\cos^4 t \text{ has period } \pi]$$

$$= g(x) + g(\pi)$$

23. (a) $I = \frac{1}{2}\int_{\pi/4}^{3\pi/4}\left[\frac{x}{1+\sin x} + \frac{\pi - x}{1+\sin(\pi - x)}\right]dx$

$$\left[\text{Using property} \int_a^b f(x)dx = \frac{1}{2}\int_a^b \{f(x)+f(a+b-x)\}dx\right]$$

$$= \frac{\pi}{2}\int_{\pi/4}^{3\pi/4} \frac{1}{1+\sin x}dx$$

$$= \frac{\pi}{2}\int_{\sqrt{2}-1}^{\sqrt{2}+1} \frac{1}{1+\frac{2t}{1+t^2}}\cdot\frac{2dt}{1+t^2}\left[\text{Insert } \tan\left(\frac{x}{2}\right)=t\right]$$

$$= \pi\int_{\sqrt{2}-1}^{\sqrt{2}+1}\frac{1}{(1+t)^2}dt = \pi\left|\frac{-1}{1+t}\right|_{\sqrt{2}-1}^{\sqrt{2}+1}$$

$$= \pi\left(\frac{1}{\sqrt{2}}-\frac{1}{\sqrt{2}+2}\right) = \pi\left(\sqrt{2}-1\right)$$

24. (a) $\int_a^b \{f(x)-3x\}dx = a^2-b^2$

$$\Rightarrow \int_a^b f(x)dx - \frac{3}{2}(b^2-a^2) = a^2-b^2$$

$$\Rightarrow \int_a^b f(x)dx = \frac{1}{2}(b^2-a^2)$$

$$\Rightarrow f(x) = x$$

Hence $f\left(\frac{\pi}{6}\right) = \frac{\pi}{6}$

25. (d) We have $f(x) = 7\tan^6 x\sec^2 x - 3\tan^2 x\sec^2 x$. Then

$$\int_0^{\pi/4} xf(x)dx = \left|x\left(\tan^7 x - \tan^3 x\right)\right|_0^{\pi/4} - \int_0^{\pi/4}\left(\tan^7 x-\tan^3 x\right)dx$$

$$= 0 - \int_0^{\pi/4}\tan^3 x\left(\tan^2 x - 1\right)\sec^3 x\,dx$$

$$= \int_0^1 \left(t^3-t^5\right)dt \text{ [Insert } \tan x = t \text{ and } \sec^3 x\,dx = dt]$$

$$= \left|\frac{t^4}{4}-\frac{t^6}{6}\right|_0^1 = \frac{1}{12}$$

26. (a) $I = \frac{1}{2}\int_{\ln 2}^{\ln 3}\frac{\sin t}{\sin t + \sin(\ln 6 - t)}dt$

$\left[\text{Insert } x^2 = t \text{ and } 2x\,dx = dt\right]$

$$= \frac{1}{2}\times\frac{1}{2}\int_{\ln 2}^{\ln 3}\left[\frac{\sin t}{\sin t + \sin(\ln 6-t)} + \frac{\sin(\ln 6 - t)}{\sin(\ln 6-t)+\sin t}\right]dt$$

$$\left[\text{Using property } \int_a^b f(x)dx = \frac{1}{2}\int_a^b\{f(x)+f(a+b-x)\}dx\right]$$

$$= \frac{1}{4}\int_{\ln 2}^{\ln 3} 1\,dt = \frac{1}{4}\ln\left(\frac{3}{2}\right)$$

27. (a) We have

$$f(\sin x)f'(\sin x) = \left(\sin^4 x + \sin^2 x + 1\right)\left(4\sin^3 x + 2\sin x\right)$$

We see that $f(\sin x)f'(\sin x)$ is odd. Therefore

$$\int_{-1}^{1} f(\sin x)f'(\sin x)dx = 0$$

28. (d)

$$I = 2\int_0^{\pi/2}\frac{2+\sin(2t)}{1+\cos(2t)}e^t\,dt \text{ [Insert } x = 2t \text{ and } dx = 2\,dt]$$

$$= 2\int_0^{\pi/4}\frac{1+\sin t\cos t}{\cos^2 t}e^t dt$$

$$= 2\int_0^{\pi/4}\left(\tan t + \sec^2 t\right)e^t\,dt = 2\left|e^t\tan t\right|_0^{\pi/4} = 2e^{\pi/4}$$

29. (c) $I = \int_0^{\pi/4} 2t\tan t\sec^2 t\,dt$ [Insert $\sin x = \tan t$ and $\cos x\,dx = \sec^2 t\,dt$]

$$= \left|2t\frac{\tan^2 t}{2}\right|_0^{\pi/4} - \int_0^{\pi/4}\tan^2 t\,dt \text{ [Using parts]}$$

$$= \frac{\pi}{4} - \left|\tan t - t\right|_0^{\pi/4} = \frac{\pi}{2}-1$$

30. (d) $I = \int_0^{\pi/4}\left(\frac{1}{x^2}-1\right)^{1/3}\cdot\frac{1}{x^3}dx$

$$= \frac{-1}{2}\int_8^0 t^{1/3}dt\left[\text{Insert } \frac{1}{x^2}-1 = t \text{ and } \frac{-2}{x^3}dx = dt\right]$$

$$= \frac{-1}{2}\left|\frac{t^{4/3}}{4/3}\right|_8^0 = 6$$

31. (b) $I = \left|f'(x)\ln x\right|_1^e - \int_1^e f'(x)\cdot\frac{1}{x}dx$ [Using parts]

$$= f'(e) - \left| f(x) \cdot \frac{1}{x} \right|_1^e - \int_1^e f'(x) \cdot \frac{-1}{x^2} dx \text{ [Using parts]}$$

$$= f'(e) - \frac{1}{e} f(e) + f(1) - \frac{1}{2} = \frac{3}{2} - \frac{1}{e}$$

32. (c) $I = \frac{1}{2} \int_{-\sqrt{3}/2}^{\sqrt{3}/2} \left[\frac{x^5 + x^2}{\sqrt{1-x^2}} + \frac{-x^5 + x^2}{\sqrt{1-x^2}} \right] dx$

$$\left[\text{Using property} \int_a^b f(x) dx = \frac{1}{2} \int_a^b \{ f(x) + f(a+b-x) \} dx \right]$$

$$= \int_{-\sqrt{3}/2}^{\sqrt{3}/2} \frac{x^2}{\sqrt{1-x^2}} dx$$

$$= 2 \int_0^{\sqrt{3}/2} \frac{x^2}{\sqrt{1-x^2}} dx \left[\frac{x^2}{\sqrt{1-x^2}} \text{ is even} \right]$$

$$= 2 \int_0^{\pi/3} \sin^2 \theta d\theta \text{ [Insert } x = \sin\theta \text{ and } dx = \cos\theta d\theta]$$

$$= \int_0^{\pi/3} (1 - \cos 2\theta) d\theta = \left| \theta - \frac{\sin(2\theta)}{2} \right|_0^{\pi/3} = \frac{\pi}{3} - \frac{\sqrt{3}}{4}$$

33. (b) $I_n = \int_1^e (\log x)^n dx = \left| x(\log x)^n \right|_1^e - n \int_1^e (\log x)^{n-1} dx$

$$\Rightarrow \quad I_n = e - nI_{n-1}$$

Putting n 1 for n, we have

$$I_{n-1} = e - (n-1) I_{n-2}$$

Now eliminating I_{n-1} from the above relations, we have

$$\Rightarrow \quad I_n - n(n-1) I_{n-2} = (1-n)e$$

Putting $n = 10$ gives $I_{10} - 90 I_8 = -9e$

34. (a),(d) The condition $f(a+b+1-x) = f(x)$ can also be written as $f(a+b-x) = f(x+1)$.

Let $I = \frac{1}{a+b} \int_a^b x \{ f(x) + f(x+1) \} dx$. Then, by the property of definite integration

$$I = \frac{1}{a+b} \int_a^b (a+b-x) \{ f(a+b-x) + f(a+b-x+1) \} dx$$

$$= \frac{1}{a+b} \int_a^b (a+b-x) \{ f(x+1) + f(x) \} dx$$

Adding the two values of I, we have

$$2I = \frac{1}{a+b} \int_a^b (a+b) \{ f(x) + f(x+1) \} dx$$

$$= \int_a^b f(x) dx + \int_a^b f(x+1) dx$$

The above result can now be simplified in two ways:

$$2I = \int_a^b f(a+b-x) dx + \int_a^b f(x+1) dx$$

$$= \int_a^b f(x+1) dx + \int_a^b f(x+1) dx = 2 \int_a^b f(x+1) dx$$

$$\Rightarrow \quad I = \int_a^b f(x+1) dx \qquad (1)$$

$$\text{or} \quad 2I = \int_a^b f(x) dx + \int_a^b f(a+b-x+1) dx$$

$$= \int_a^b f(x) dx + \int_a^b f(x) dx = 2 \int_a^b f(x) dx$$

$$\Rightarrow \quad I = \int_a^b f(x) dx \qquad (2)$$

If we substitute $x+1 = t$ in result (1), I reduces to

$$I = \int_{a+1}^{b+1} f(t) dt \Rightarrow \text{Option (a) is correct.}$$

If we substitute $x = t+1$ in result (2), I reduces to

$$I = \int_{a-1}^{b-1} f(t+1) dt \Rightarrow \text{Option (d) is correct.}$$

35. (c) The condition $f(2-x) = f(2+x)$ can be written as $f(x) = f(4-x)$.

The condition $f(4-x) = f(4+x)$ can be written as $f(x) = f(8-x)$

Taking together, we have $f(4-x) = f(8-x)$. Putting t for $4-x$, reduces it to $f(t) = f(4+t)$. Thus, f is periodic, having period 4.

The condition $f(2-x) = f(2+x)$ also means the function is symmetric about $x = 2$. Thus

$$\int_0^4 f(x)dx = 2\int_0^2 f(x)dx = 10$$

Hence $\displaystyle\int_{10}^{50} f(x)dx = 10\int_0^4 f(x)dx = 100$

36. (b) $I = \displaystyle\int_0^{\pi/4} \ln(1+\tan\theta)d\theta$ [put $x = \tan\theta$]

$$= \frac{1}{2}\int_0^{\pi/4}\left[\ln(1+\tan\theta)+\ln\{1+\tan(\pi/4-\theta)\}\right]d\theta$$

$$\left[\text{Using property } \int_a^b f(x)dx = \frac{1}{2}\int_a^b \{f(x)+f(a+b-x)\}dx\right]$$

$$= \frac{1}{2}\int_0^{\pi/4}\left[\ln(1+\tan\theta)+\ln\left\{\frac{2}{1+\tan\theta}\right\}\right]d\theta$$

$$= \frac{1}{2}\int_0^{\pi/4}\ln 2\, d\theta = \frac{\pi}{8}\ln 2$$

37. (d) $I_{n+1} = \displaystyle\int_0^1 (1-x^a)^{n+1} dx$

$$= \left|x(1-x^a)^{n+1}\right|_0^1 + (n+1)a\int_0^1 x^a(1-x^a)^n dx$$

$$= (n+1)a\int_0^1 (x^a-1+1)(1-x^a)^n dx$$

$$= (n+1)a[-I_{n+1}+I_n] \Rightarrow I_{n+1}\left\{1+\frac{1}{(n+1)a}\right\} = I_n$$

38. (b) $I_n = \displaystyle\int_0^{\pi/2} \cos^n x\cos nx\, dx$

$$= \left|\cos^n x\left(\frac{\sin nx}{n}\right)\right|_0^{\pi/2} + \int_0^{\pi/2}\cos^{n-1}x\sin x\sin nx\, dx$$

$$= \int_0^{\pi/2}\cos^{n-1}x[\cos(n-1)x-\cos x\cos nx]dx$$

$$= I_{n-1} - I_n \Rightarrow \frac{I_n}{I_{n-1}} = \frac{1}{2}$$

Hence $I_1, I_2, I_3, \ldots$ are in GP.

39. (c) $I_n = \displaystyle\int_0^{\pi/4}\tan^n x\, dx = \int_0^{\pi/4}(\sec^2 x-1)\tan^{n-2}x\, dx$

$$= \int_0^{\pi/4}\tan^{n-2}x\sec^2 x\, dx - I_{n-2}$$

$$= \left|\frac{\tan^{n-1}x}{n-1}\right|_0^{\pi/4} - I_{n-2} = \frac{1}{n-1} - I_{n-2}$$

$$\Rightarrow \quad I_n + I_{n-2} = \frac{1}{n-1}$$

Now $I_2+I_4 = \frac{1}{3}$, $I_3+I_5 = \frac{1}{4}$, $I_4+I_6 = \frac{1}{5}$

Hence $I_2+I_4, I_3+I_5, I_4+I_6$ are in HP.

40. (a) $I = \dfrac{1}{2}\displaystyle\int_0^{\pi}([\tan x]+[\tan(\pi-x)])dx$

$$\left[\text{Using property } \int_a^b f(x)dx = \frac{1}{2}\int_a^b \{f(x)+f(a+b-x)\}dx\right]$$

$$= \frac{1}{2}\int_0^{\pi}([\tan x]+[-\tan x])dx$$

Now

$$[x]+[-x] = [I+f]+[-I-f] = \begin{cases} I+(-I) \text{ if } f=0 \\ I+(-I-1) \text{ otherwise}\end{cases}$$

$$= \begin{cases} 0 \text{ if } x = \text{integer} \\ -1 \text{ otherwise}\end{cases}$$

Hence $I = \dfrac{1}{2}\displaystyle\int_0^{\pi}(-1)dx = -\pi/2.$

41. (b) $I = \dfrac{1}{2}\displaystyle\int_0^1 \{f_{2020}(x)+f_{2020}(1-x)\}dx$

$$\left[\text{Using property } \int_a^b f(x)dx = \frac{1}{2}\int_a^b \{f(x)+f(a+b-x)\}dx\right]$$

Now

$$f(x)+f(1-x) = \left(x^3-\frac{3}{2}x^2+x+\frac{1}{4}\right)$$
$$+\left((1-x)^3-\frac{3}{2}(1-x)^2+(1-x)+\frac{1}{4}\right) = 1$$

Then $\quad f_2(x)+f_2(1-x) = f\{f(x)\}+f\{f(1-x)\}$

$$= f\{f(x)\}+f\{1-f(x)\}$$
$$= f\{t\}+f\{1-t\} = 1$$

Proceeding similarly, we can show that

$$f_3(x)+f_3(1-x) = 1$$

......

$$f_{2020}(x)+f_{2020}(1-x) = 1$$

Hence $I = \dfrac{1}{2}\displaystyle\int_0^1 (1)dx = 1/2.$

CHAPTER

22 Differentiation of an Integral

- **The Fundamental Theorem:** If f is continuous on $[a,b]$, then the function $F(x)=\int_a^x f(t)\,dt$ has a derivative at every point on $[a,b]$ and is given by

$$F'(x)=\frac{d}{dx}\left(\int_a^x f(t)\,dt\right)=f(x)$$

- **Leibnitz's Rule**

$$\frac{d}{dx}\left(\int_{u(x)}^{v(x)} f(t)\,dt\right)=f\{v(x)\}\frac{dv}{dx}-f\{u(x)\}\frac{du}{dx}$$

EXERCISES

1. Let $f:\mathbf{R}\to\mathbf{R}$ be a differentiable function such that $f(x)=\int_0^x f(t)\,dt$. Then $f(\ln 5)$ equals:

(a) 0 (b) 1

(c) 4 (d) 5

2. The value of $\lim_{x\to 0}\frac{1}{x^3}\int_0^x \frac{t\ln(1+t)}{t^4+4}\,dt$ is:

(a) 0 (b) $\frac{1}{12}$

(c) $\frac{1}{24}$ (d) $\frac{1}{64}$

3. If $\int_0^x f(t)\,dt = x+\int_x^1 t\,f(t)\,dt$, then $f(1)$ equals:

(a) $\frac{1}{2}$ (b) 0

(c) -1 (d) $\frac{-1}{2}$

4. Let $f(x)=\int_2^x \sqrt{2-t^2}\,dt$. Then the real roots of the equation $x^2-f'(x)=0$ are:

(a) ± 1 (b) $\pm\frac{1}{\sqrt{2}}$

(c) $\pm\frac{1}{\sqrt{3}}$ (d) 0,1

5. If $\int_0^{t^2} x\,f(x)\,dx=\frac{2}{5}t^2$, then $f\left(\frac{4}{25}\right)$ equals:

(a) $\frac{2}{5}$ (b) -1

(c) $\frac{5}{2}$ (d) $\frac{-4}{25}$

6. Let $f:(0,+\infty)\to\mathbf{R}$ be a differentiable function and $F(x)=\int_0^x f(t)\,dt$. If $F(x^2)=x^2(1+x)$, then $f(4)$ equals:

(a) 2 (b) 4

(c) $\frac{5}{4}$ (d) 7

7. If $f(x)=\int_{x^2}^{x^2+1} e^{-t^2}dt$, then $f(x)$ increases in:

(a) $(-2,2)$ (b) No such interval
(c) $(0,+\infty)$ (d) $(-\infty,0)$

8. The function $f(x)=\int_{-1}^{x} t(t-1)(t-2)^3(t-3)^5(e^t-1)dt$ has local minima at x equal to:

(a) 0 (b) 1
(c) 2 (d) 3

9. Let f be a non-negative function defined on $[0,1]$. If $\int_0^x \sqrt{1-\{f'(t)\}^2}\,dt=\int_0^x f(t)dt$ and $f(0)=0$, then:

(a) $f\left(\frac{1}{2}\right)<\frac{1}{2}$ and $f\left(\frac{1}{3}\right)>\frac{1}{3}$

(b) $f\left(\frac{1}{2}\right)>\frac{1}{2}$ and $f\left(\frac{1}{3}\right)>\frac{1}{3}$

(c) $f\left(\frac{1}{2}\right)<\frac{1}{2}$ and $f\left(\frac{1}{3}\right)<\frac{1}{3}$

(d) $f\left(\frac{1}{2}\right)>\frac{1}{2}$ and $f\left(\frac{1}{3}\right)<\frac{1}{3}$

10. Let $g(x)=\int_1^{e^x}\frac{f'(t)}{1+t^2}dt$, where $f(x)=\frac{x^2-ax+1}{x^2+ax+1}$ $(0<a<2)$. Then the correct statements from the following are:

(a) $g'(x)$ is positive on $(-\infty,0)$ and negative on $(0,+\infty)$
(b) $g'(x)$ is negative on $(-\infty,0)$ and positive on $(0,+\infty)$
(c) $g'(x)$ changes sign on both $(-\infty,0)$ and $(0,+\infty)$
(d) $g'(x)$ does not change sign on $(-\infty,0)$

11. Let f be a real-valued function defined on $(-1,1)$ such that $e^{-x}f(x)=2+\int_0^x\sqrt{1+t^4}\,dt$. If g is the inverse function of f, then the value of $g'(2)$ is:

(a) 1 (b) $\frac{1}{3}$
(c) $\frac{1}{2}$ (d) $\frac{1}{e}$

12. Let f be a real-valued function defined on $(0,+\infty)$ as $f(x)=\ln x+\int_0^x\sqrt{1+\sin t}\,dt$. Then the correct statements from the following are:

(a) $f''(x)$ exists for all $x\in(0,+\infty)$
(b) $f'(x)$ exists and is continuous for all $x\in(0,+\infty)$
(c) There exists $\alpha>1$ such that $|f'(x)|<|f(x)|$ for all $x\in(\alpha,+\infty)$
(d) There exists $\beta>0$ such that $|f'(x)|+|f(x)|\le\beta$ for all $x\in(\beta,+\infty)$

13. If $f(x)=\begin{cases}5x+1, & x\le 2\\ \int_0^x(5+|1-y|)dy, & x>2\end{cases}$, then the correct statements from the following are:

(a) f is discontinuous at $x=2$
(b) f is continuous and differentiable everywhere
(c) f is continuous everywhere but not differentiable at $x=1$
(d) f is continuous everywhere but not differentiable at $x=2$

14. The value of $\lim_{x\to0}\frac{\int_0^{x^2}\cos(t^2)dt}{x\sin x}$ is:

(a) 1 (b) −1
(c) 2 (d) −2

15. Let $f:(0,+\infty)\to\mathbf{R}$ be given by $f(x)=\int_{1/x}^{x}\frac{e^{-\left(t+\frac{1}{t}\right)}}{t}dt$. Then the correct statements from the following are:

(a) f is increasing on $(1,+\infty)$
(b) f is decreasing on $(0,1)$
(c) $f(x)+f\left(\frac{1}{x}\right)=0$ for all $x\in(0,+\infty)$
(d) $f(2^x)$ is an odd function on $\mathbf{R}$

16. Let $f(x)=\int_0^x(1+t^3)^{-1/2}dt$. If $g(x)$ is the inverse function of $f(x)$, then the value of $\frac{g''(y)}{g^2(y)}$ is:

(a) $\frac{3}{2}$ (b) $\frac{-1}{2}$
(c) −1 (d) $\frac{5}{2}$

17. Let $f:\mathbf{R}\to\mathbf{R}$ be a continuous odd function which vanishes at exactly one point and $f(1)=\frac{1}{2}$. Suppose $F(x)=\int_{-1}^{x} f(t)\,dt$ and $G(x)=\int_{-1}^{x} t\left|fof(t)\right|dt$. If $\lim_{x\to 1}\frac{F(x)}{G(x)}=\frac{1}{14}$, then the value of $f\left(\frac{1}{2}\right)$ is:

(a) –7 (b) 7

(c) –2 (d) 2

18. Let $F(x)=\int_{x}^{x^2+\frac{\pi}{6}} 2\cos^2 t\,dt$ for all $x\in\mathbf{R}$ and $f:\left[0,\frac{1}{2}\right]\to[0,+\infty)$ be a continuous function. For $\alpha\in\left[0,\frac{1}{2}\right]$, if $F'(\alpha)+2$ equals the area of the region bounded by $x=0$, $y=0$, $y=f(x)$ and $x=\alpha$, then $f(0)$ is:

(a) $\frac{3}{2}$ (b) $\frac{-1}{2}$

(c) –1 (d) 3

ANSWER KEYS

1. (a)	**2.** (b)	**3.** (a)	**4.** (a)	**5.** (c)	**6.** (b)	**7.** (d)	**8.** (b),(d)	**9.** (c)
10. (b),(d)	**11.** (b)	**12.** (b),(c)	**13.** (d)	**14.** (a)	**15.** (a),(c),(d)	**16.** (a)	**17.** (b)	**18.** (d)

SOLUTIONS

1. (a) Differentiating both sides with respect to x, we have

$$f'(x) = f(x)$$

$$\Rightarrow \quad f(x) = Ce^x$$

Since $f(0) = \int_0^0 f(t)\,dt = 0, C = 0.$

Hence, the particular solution is $f(x) = 0$. Now $f(\ln 5) = 0.$

2. (b) We have

$$L = \lim_{x\to 0} \frac{1}{x^3}\int_0^x \frac{t\ln(1+t)}{t^4+4}\,dt \left(\frac{0}{0}\right)$$

$$= \lim_{x\to 0} \frac{x\ln(1+x)}{3x^2(x^4+4)} \text{ [Using L'Hospital's rule]}$$

$$= \lim_{x\to 0} \frac{1}{3(x^4+4)} \cdot \frac{\ln(1+x)}{x} = \frac{1}{12}$$

3. (a) Differentiating both sides with respect to x, we have

$$f(x) = 1 - xf(x)$$

$$\Rightarrow \quad f(x) = \frac{1}{1+x}$$

Hence $f(1) = \frac{1}{2}$.

4. (a) Differentiating both sides with respect to x, we have

$$f'(x) = \sqrt{2-x^2}$$

Now solving the equation $x^2 - f'(x) = 0$, we have

$$\Rightarrow \quad \sqrt{2-x^2} = x^2$$

$$\Rightarrow \quad x^4 + x^2 - 2 = 0 \text{ gives } x = \pm 1.$$

5. (c) Differentiating both sides with respect to x, we have

$$t^2 f(t^2)\cdot 2t = \frac{4}{5}t$$

$$\Rightarrow \quad f(t^2) = \frac{2}{5t^2}$$

Hence $f\left(\frac{4}{25}\right) = \dfrac{2}{5\left(\frac{4}{25}\right)} = \frac{5}{2}$

6. (b) Differentiating both the equations throughout with respect to x, we have

$$F'(x) = f(x) \qquad \text{...(1)}$$

and $\quad 2xF'(x^2) = 2x + 3x^2 \qquad$ ...(2)

From the above equations, we have

$$2xf(x^2) = 2x + 3x^2$$

$$\Rightarrow \quad f(x^2) = 1 + \frac{3}{2}x$$

Hence $f(4) = 1 + \frac{3\times 2}{2} = 4$

7. (d) Differentiating both sides with respect to x, we have

$$f'(x) = 2xe^{-(x^2+1)^2} - 2xe^{-(x^2)^2}$$

$$= \frac{2x\left\{e^{(x^2)^2} - e^{(x^2+1)^2}\right\}}{e^{(x^2)^2}e^{(x^2+1)^2}}$$

$$\Rightarrow \quad f'(x) \text{ is } \begin{cases} +\text{ve if } x<0 \\ -\text{ve if } x>0 \end{cases}$$

$$\left[e^{(x^2)^2} - e^{(x^2+1)^2} < 0 \text{ for all } x\right]$$

Hence $f(x)$ increases in $(-\infty, 0)$.

8. (b),(d) Differentiating both sides with respect to x, we have

$$f'(x)=(e^x-1)x(x-1)(x-2)^3(x-3)^5$$

$$\Rightarrow \quad f'(x) \text{ is} \begin{cases} -\text{ve if } x<1 \\ +\text{ve if } 1<x<2 \\ -\text{ve if } 2<x<3 \\ +\text{ve if } x>3 \end{cases} \left[(e^x-1)x>0 \text{ for all } x\right]$$

Since $f(x)$ changes sign from –ve to +ve at $x=1$ and 3, it has minima at these two points.

9. (c) Differentiating both sides with respect to x, we have

$$f(x)=\sqrt{1-\{f'(x)\}^2}$$

$$\Rightarrow \quad \{f'(x)\}^2+\{f(x)\}^2=1$$

$$\Rightarrow \quad f(x)=\sin(x+C)$$

Since $f(0)=0$, $C=0$. Hence, the particular solution is $f(x)=\sin(x)$. Since $\sin x<x$ for all $x>0$, $f\left(\frac{1}{2}\right)<\frac{1}{2}$ and $f\left(\frac{1}{3}\right)<\frac{1}{3}$

10. (b),(d) Differentiating both the equations throughout with respect to x, we have

$$g'(x)=e^x\cdot\frac{f'(e^x)}{1+e^{2x}} \quad \ldots(1)$$

and
$$f'(x)=\frac{2a(x^2-1)}{(x^2+ax+1)^2} \quad \ldots(2)$$

From the above equations, we have

$$g'(x)=\frac{e^x}{1+e^{2x}}\cdot\frac{2a(e^{2x}-1)}{(e^{2x}+ae^x+1)^2}$$

$$=\frac{2ae^x(e^x-1)(e^x+1)}{(e^{2x}+1)(e^{2x}+ae^x+1)^2}$$

$$\Rightarrow \quad g'(x) \text{ is} \begin{cases} -\text{ve if } x<0 \\ +\text{ve if } x>0 \end{cases}$$

11. (b) From the given relation, we see that $f(0)=2 \Rightarrow g(2)=0$ since g and f are inverse functions of each other. Hence $g'(2)=\frac{1}{f'(0)}$.

Differentiating both sides of the given relation with respect to x, we have

$$e^{-x}\{f'(x)-f(x)\}=\sqrt{1+x^4}$$

Putting $x=0$, we have

$$f'(0)-f(0)=1$$

$$\Rightarrow \quad f'(0)=f(0)+1=3$$

Hence $g'(2)=\frac{1}{3}$.

12. (b),(c) Differentiating the given relation twice successively with respect to x, we have

$$f'(x)=\frac{1}{x}+\sqrt{1+\sin x}$$

and
$$f''(x)=\frac{-1}{x^2}+\frac{\cos x}{2\sqrt{1+\sin x}}$$

We see that $f''(x)$ does not exist when $\sin x=-1$. Hence (a) is incorrect.

However, $f'(x)$ exists and is continuous for all $x\in(0,+\infty)$. Hence (b) is correct.

For $x>1$, $f'(x)$ is bounded whereas $f(x)$ increases without bound. Hence (c) is also correct.

The function $|f'(x)|+|f(x)|$ does not have an upper bound since $f(x)$ is unbounded. Hence (d) is incorrect.

13. (d) The given function can be written as

$$f(x)=\begin{cases} 5x+1, & x\le 2 \\ \int_0^1 (6-y)\,dy+\int_1^x (4+y)\,dy, & x>2 \end{cases}$$

$$\Rightarrow \quad f(x)=\begin{cases}5x+1, & x\le 2\\ 1+4x+\frac{1}{2}x^2, & x>2\end{cases}$$

Differentiating with respect to x, we have

$$f'(x)=\begin{cases}5, & x<2\\ 4+x, & x>2\end{cases}$$

We can see that f is continuous everywhere but is not differentiable at $x = 2$.

14. (a) We have

$$L=\lim_{x\to 0}\frac{\int_0^{x^2}\cos(t^2)\,dt}{x\sin x}$$

$$=\lim_{x\to 0}\frac{\int_0^{x^2}\cos(t^2)\,dt}{x^2}\left(\frac{0}{0}\right)[\sin x\sim x]$$

$$=\lim_{x\to 0}\frac{2x\cos(x^4)}{2x}\ \text{[Using L'Hospital's rule]}$$

$$=1$$

15. (a),(c),(d) Differentiating both sides with respect to x, we have

$$f'(x)=\frac{e^{-\left(x+\frac{1}{x}\right)}}{x}\cdot 1-\frac{e^{-\left(\frac{1}{x}+x\right)}}{1/x}\cdot\frac{-1}{x^2}=\frac{2e^{-\left(x+\frac{1}{x}\right)}}{x}$$

$$\Rightarrow \quad f'(x)\text{ is }\begin{cases}-\text{ve if } x<0\\ +\text{ve if } x>0\end{cases}$$

Thus, f is increasing on $(0,+\infty)$. Hence, (a) is correct but (b) is incorrect.

$$\text{Now } f\left(\frac{1}{x}\right)=\int_x^{1/x}\frac{e^{-\left(t+\frac{1}{t}\right)}}{t}\,dt=-f(x).$$

Hence (c) is correct.

Now, putting 2^x in place of x in the above result, we see that $f(2^{-x})=-f(2^x)$. Hence (d) is correct.

16. (a) We have

$$f(x)=\int_0^x\left(1+t^3\right)^{-1/2}dt$$

$$\Rightarrow \quad f\{g(x)\}=\int_0^{g(x)}\left(1+t^3\right)^{-1/2}dt$$

$$\Rightarrow \quad x=\int_0^{g(x)}\left(1+t^3\right)^{-1/2}dt$$

Differentiating with respect to x, we have

$$1=\left(1+g^3\right)^{-1/2}g'$$

$$\Rightarrow \quad (g')^2=1+g^3$$

Differentiating again with respect to x, we have

$$2g'g''=3g^2g'$$

$$\Rightarrow \quad \frac{g''(y)}{g^2(y)}=\frac{3}{2}$$

17. (b) We see that $F(1)=0=G(1)$, since both the integrands are odd. Then

$$\lim_{x\to 1}\frac{F(x)}{G(x)}=\frac{1}{14}$$

$$\Rightarrow \quad \lim_{x\to 1}\frac{F'(x)}{G'(x)}=\frac{1}{14}\ \text{[By L'Hospital's rule]}$$

$$\Rightarrow \quad \lim_{x\to 1}\frac{f(x)}{x\,|fof(x)|}=\frac{1}{14}$$

$$\Rightarrow \quad \frac{f(1)}{|fof(1)|}=\frac{1}{14}$$

$$\Rightarrow \quad \frac{f(1)}{\left|f\left(\frac{1}{2}\right)\right|}=\frac{1}{14}\Rightarrow\left|f\left(\frac{1}{2}\right)\right|=7$$

If f is odd and vanishes at only one point, then that point is $x = 0$. Since $f(1)$ is positive, it means $f(x)$ is positive for all $x > 0$. Hence $f\left(\frac{1}{2}\right) = 7$.

18. (d) We have

$$\int_0^{\alpha} f(x)\,dx = F'(\alpha) + 2$$

Differentiating with respect to α, we have $f(\alpha) = F''(\alpha)$.

Now

$$F''(x) = 4\cos^2\left(x^2 + \frac{\pi}{6}\right)$$

$$= 8x^2\cos\left(x^2 + \frac{\pi}{6}\right)\sin\left(x^2 + \frac{\pi}{6}\right) + 2\cos x \sin x$$

Hence $\quad f(0) = F''(0) = 4\cos^2\left(\frac{\pi}{6}\right) = 3.$

CHAPTER

23 Area Between Curves

- Suppose we need to find the area enclosed between two curves $y = f(x)$ and $y = g(x)$, shown in the figure. Subdivide the region into thin vertical strips. The area of one such strip is

$$dA = (y_2 - y_1)dx = \{f(x) - g(x)\}dx$$

and the total area is given by $A = \int_a^b \{f(x) - g(x)\}dx$

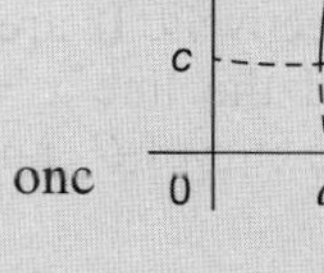

Alternative: Subdivide the region into thin horizontal strips. The area of one such strip is

$$dA = (x_2 - x_1)dy = \{g^{-1}(y) - f^{-1}(y)\}dy$$

and the total area is given by $A = \int_a^b \{g^{-1}(y) - f^{-1}(y)\}dy$

EXERCISES

1. Area of the region bounded by the curves $y^2 = x, 2y + 3 = x$ and the x-axis in the 1st quadrant is:

(a) 9 (b) $\frac{27}{4}$

(c) 18 (d) $\frac{15}{2}$

2. Consider the function $f(x) = [x^2 - 2x - 2]$ where $[\square]$ denotes the greatest integer function. The area of the region bounded by the curve $y = f(x)$ and the x-axis between the ordinates $x = 1$ to $x = 3$ is:

(a) $-1 + \sqrt{2} - \sqrt{3}$

(b) $1 + \sqrt{2} - \sqrt{3}$

(c) $-1 - \sqrt{2} - \sqrt{3}$

(d) $1 - \sqrt{2} - \sqrt{3}$

3. The triangle formed by the tangent to the curve $y = x^2 + bx - b$ at the point $(1, 1)$ and the coordinate axes lies in the 1st quadrant. If its area is 2 sq. unit, then the value of b is:

(a) –4 (b) 3

(c) –3 (d) 1

4. Area of the region $\left\{(x, y) : \sqrt{|x+3|} \le y \le \frac{1}{5}(x+9)\right\}$ is:

(a) $\frac{6}{5}$ (b) $\frac{4}{3}$

(c) $\frac{5}{3}$ (d) $\frac{3}{2}$

5. Area of the region bounded by the curve $y = f(x)$, the x-axis and the lines $x = 1, x = b$ is $(b-1)\sin(3b+4)$. Then $f(x)$ is:

(a) $(x-1)\sin(3x+4)$

(b) $\sin(3x+4)$

(c) $\sin(3x+4) + 3(x-1)\cos(3x+4)$

(d) None of these

6. Area of the region bounded by the curve $y = e^x$, the y-axis and the line $y = e$ is:
(a) $e-1$
(b) $\int_1^e \ln(y)dy$
(c) 1
(d) $\int_1^e \ln(e+1-y)dy$

7. For $a > 0$, let the curves $C_1 : y^2 = ax$ and $C_2 : x^2 = ay$ intersect at origin O and a point P. Let the line $x = b$ intersect the chord OP and the x-axis at points Q and R, respectively. If area of triangle ΔOQR equals 1/2, and the line $x = b$ bisects the area bounded by the curves C_1 and C_2, then a satisfies the equation:
(a) $x^6 - 6x^3 - 2 = 0$ (b) $x^6 - 4x^3 + 2 = 0$
(c) $x^6 - 4x^3 - 2 = 0$ (d) $x^6 - 4x^3 + 2 = 0$

8. The region bounded by $y = \frac{3}{2}\sqrt{x}, x = 1, x = 4, y = 0$ is divided into two equal halves by the straight line $y = mx$. Then the value of m is:
(a) $\frac{7}{15}$ (b) $\frac{5}{7}$
(c) $\frac{1}{6}$ (d) $\frac{3}{5}$

9. Area of the region bounded by the curves $y = \cos x$, $y = \sin x$ between $x = \frac{\pi}{4}, x = \frac{3\pi}{2}$ is:
(a) 1 (b) 2
(c) $\sqrt{2}$ (d) $2\sqrt{2}$

10. Area of the region bounded by the curves $y = \sqrt{\frac{1+\sin x}{\cos x}}, y = \sqrt{\frac{1-\sin x}{\cos x}}$ and the lines $x = 0$, $x = \frac{\pi}{4}$ is:
(a) $\int_0^{\sqrt{2}-1} \frac{t}{(1+t^2)\sqrt{1-t^2}}dt$
(b) $\int_0^{\sqrt{2}-1} \frac{4t}{(1+t^2)\sqrt{1-t^2}}dt$
(c) $\int_0^{\sqrt{2}+1} \frac{4t}{(1+t^2)\sqrt{1-t^2}}dt$
(d) $\int_0^{\sqrt{2}+1} \frac{t}{(1+t^2)\sqrt{1-t^2}}dt$

11. Let $f(x)$ be a function defined on **R** such that $f'(x) = f'(1-x)$ for all $x \in [0,1]$. If $f(0) = 1$ and $f(1) = 41$, then $\int_0^1 f(x)dx$ equals:
(a) $\sqrt{41}$ (b) 21
(c) 41 (d) 42

12. If the area of the region bounded by the curve $y = x - x^2$ and the line $y = mx$ is $9/2$ sq. unit, then m equals:
(a) −4 (b) −2
(c) 2 (d) 4

13. Area of the region bounded by the parabola $(y-2)^2 = x-1$, the tangent to the parabola at the point $(2,3)$ and the x-axis is:
(a) 4 (b) 6
(c) 7 (d) 9

14. Area of the region bounded by the circles $x^2 + y^2 = a^2$ and $x^2 + y^2 - 2ax = 0$ is:
(a) $\left(\frac{\pi}{3} + \frac{\sqrt{3}}{2}\right)a^2$
(b) $\left(\frac{\pi}{3} - \frac{1}{2\sqrt{3}}\right)a^2$
(c) $\left(\frac{2\pi}{3} + \frac{1}{\sqrt{3}}\right)a^2$
(d) $\left(\frac{2\pi}{3} - \frac{\sqrt{3}}{2}\right)a^2$

15. Let $I = \int_0^1 \frac{\sin x}{\sqrt{x}}dx$ and $J = \int_0^1 \frac{\cos x}{\sqrt{x}}dx$. Then the correct statements from the following are:

(a) $I > \frac{2}{3}$ and $J < 2$

(b) $I > \frac{2}{3}$ and $J > 2$

(c) $I < \frac{2}{3}$ and $J < 2$

(d) $I < \frac{2}{3}$ and $J > 2$

16. Area of the region bounded by the curves $x + 2y^2 = 0$ and $x + 3y^2 = 1$ is:

(a) $\frac{1}{3}$ (b) $\frac{2}{3}$

(c) $\frac{4}{3}$ (d) $\frac{5}{3}$

17. Area of the region bounded by the curves $y = \ln|x|$ and $y - |\ln|x|| $ is:

(a) 4 (b) 6

(c) 7 (d) 9

18. Let the straight line $x = b$ divide the region enclosed by $y = (1-x)^2$, $y = 0$ and $x = 0$ into two parts $R_1\,(0 \le x \le b)$ and $R_2\,(b \le x \le 1)$. Let A_1 and A_2 denote their respective areas. If $A_1 - A_2 = \frac{1}{4}$, then b equals:

(a) $\frac{3}{4}$ (b) $\frac{1}{2}$

(c) $\frac{1}{3}$ (d) $\frac{1}{4}$

19. Area of the region $\{(x,y) : y^2 \ge 2x\}$ and $\{(x,y) : x^2 + y^2 \le 4x\}$ is:

(a) $2\pi - \frac{4\sqrt{2}}{3}$

(b) $2\pi - \frac{8\sqrt{2}}{3}$

(c) $2\pi - \frac{8}{3}$

(d) $2\pi - \frac{16}{3}$

20. Let $f : [-1,2] \to [0,+\infty)$ be a continuous function such that $f(x) = f(1-x)$ for all $x \in [-1,2]$. Let $A_1 = \int_{-1}^{2} x f(x)\,dx$ and $A_2 = \int_{-1}^{2} f(x)\,dx$. Then:

(a) $A_1 = 2A_2$

(b) $A_1 = 3A_2$

(c) $2A_1 = A_2$

(d) $3A_1 = A_2$

21. Let $g(x) = \int_0^x f(t)\,dt$, where f is such that $\frac{1}{2} \le f(t) \le 1$ for $t \in [0,1]$ and $0 \le f(t) \le \frac{1}{2}$ for $t \in [1,2]$. Then $g(2)$ satisfies the inequality:

(a) $\frac{-3}{2} \le g(2) < \frac{1}{2}$

(b) $\frac{1}{2} < g(2) \le \frac{3}{2}$

(c) $\frac{3}{2} < g(2) \le \frac{5}{2}$

(d) $2 \le g(2) \le 4$

22. Let $g(x)$ be a continuous and differentiable function satisfying the condition $|g(x) - g(y)| \le |x - y|$ for every $x, y \in [2,10]$. Let m be the greatest possible value of $\left|\int_2^{10} g(x)\,dx - 8g(x)\right|$ for $x \in [2,10]$. Then $m - 30$ equals:

(a) 8 (b) 7

(c) 3 (d) 2

23. Let $f(x)$ be a continuous and differentiable function on $x \in [1/2, 1]$. If $f(x) \le f'(x) \le 2f(x)$ and $f(1/2) = 1$, then the value of $\int_{1/2}^{1} f(x)\,dx$ cannot be equal to:

(a) $\sqrt{e}$ (b) $\frac{e-1}{2}$

(c) $\sqrt{e} - \frac{1}{2}$ (d) $e - 2$

24. Area of the region $\left\{(x,y):16^{y^2+2x}\le\frac{1}{8}\right\}$ and $\left\{(x,y):16^{x^2+2y}\le\frac{1}{8}\right\}$ is:

(a) $\frac{1}{6}$ (b) $\frac{2}{3}$

(c) $\frac{3}{8}$ (d) $\frac{5}{12}$

25. Let $f(x)$ be a continuous and one–one function on **R** which intersects the x-axis at $x=a$. If $\forall t\in\mathbf{R}$, area bounded by $y=f(x), x=a-t, x=a$ and the x-axis is equal to the area bounded by $y=f(x), x=a, x=a+t$ and the x-axis. Then $\int_{-\lambda}^{\lambda} f^{-1}(x)dx$ equals:

(a) $\frac{1}{2}a\lambda$ (b) $\frac{3}{2}a\lambda$

(c) $a\lambda$ (d) $2a\lambda$

ANSWER KEYS

1. (a)	**2.** (c)	**3.** (c)	**4.** (d)	**5.** (c)	**6.** (b),(c),(d)	**7.** (d)	**8.** (a)	**9.** (d)
10. (b)	**11.** (b)	**12.** (b),(d)	**13.** (d)	**14.** (d)	**15.** (c)	**16.** (c)	**17.** (a)	**18.** (b)
19. (d)	**20.** (c)	**21.** (b)	**22.** (d)	**23.** (a),(c)	**24.** (a)	**25.** (d)		

SOLUTIONS

1. (a) The two curves intersect in the 1st quadrant at the point (9, 3), as shown in the figure.

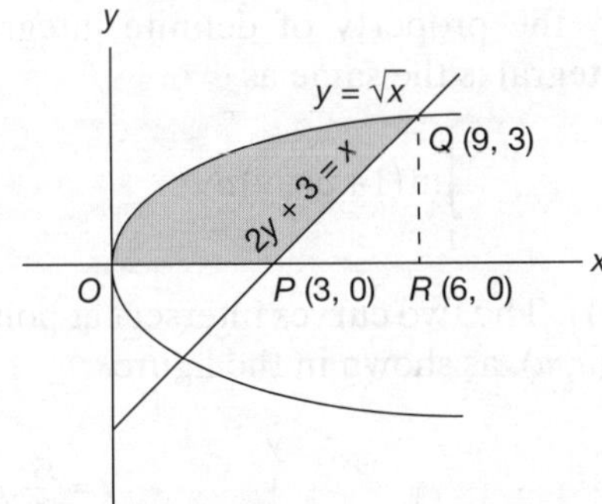

The x intercept of the line is 3. Area of $\Delta PQR = \frac{1}{2}\times 3\times 6 = 9$. Area of the enclosed region is

$$A = \int_0^9 \sqrt{x}\,dx - 9 = \left|\frac{2}{3}x^{3/2}\right|_0^9 - 9 = 9$$

2. (c) The given function can be written as $f(x) = [x^2 - 2x] - 2$. Now consider the function $g(x) = x^2 - 2x$. Its graph is a concave upward parabola that intersects the x-axis at $x = 0, 2$.

It takes the value –1 at $x^2 - 2x = -1 \Rightarrow x = 1$

It takes the value 1 at $x^2 - 2x = 1 \Rightarrow x = 1 \pm \sqrt{2}$

It takes the value 2 at $x^2 - 2x = 2 \Rightarrow x = 1 \pm \sqrt{3}$

It takes the value 3 at $x^2 - 2x = 3 \Rightarrow x = -2, 3$

Let $\alpha = 1 + \sqrt{2}$ and $\beta = 1 + \sqrt{3}$. The function $[g(x)]$ can now be written as

$$[g(x)] - \begin{cases} -1, 1 \le x < 2 \\ 0, 2 \le x < \alpha \\ 1, \alpha \le x < \beta \\ 2, \beta \le x < 3 \end{cases}$$

The function $f(x) = [g(x)] - 2$ can now be written as

$$f(x) = \begin{cases} -3, 1 \le x < 2 \\ -2, 2 \le x < \alpha \\ -1, \alpha \le x < \beta \\ 0, \beta \le x < 3 \end{cases}$$

Hence, the required area is

$$\int_1^3 f(x)dx = (-3)(2-1) + (-2)(\alpha - 2) + (-1)(\beta - \alpha)$$

$$= (-3) + (-2)(\sqrt{2} - 1) + (-1)(\sqrt{3} - \sqrt{2})$$

$$= -1 - \sqrt{2} - \sqrt{3}$$

3. (c) The first derivative of the given function is $f'(x) = 2x + b$. Slope of the tangent at the point $(1,1)$ is $f'(1) = 2 + b$. Equation of the tangent is

$$y - 1 = (2 + b)(x - 1)$$

The intercepts of this line are

$$y\text{-intercept} = -(b+1) \text{ and } x\text{-intercept} = \frac{b+1}{b+2}$$

It is given that the intercepts are positive. Then

$$b + 1 < 0 \text{ and } b + 2 < 0$$

$$\Rightarrow \quad b < -2$$

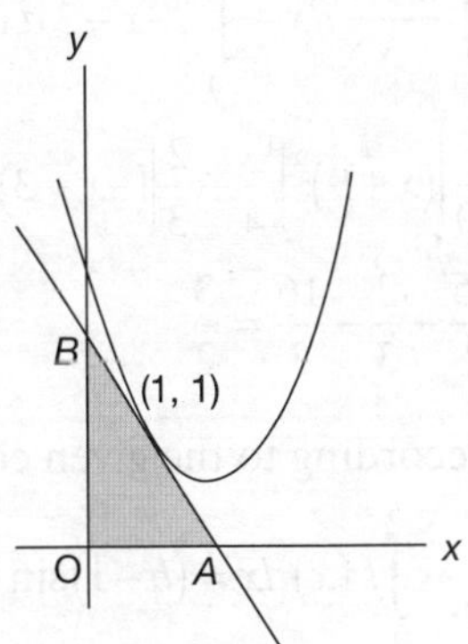

Area of triangle ΔOAB (see figure) is given to be 2. Hence

$$\frac{1}{2}\times\left|\frac{b+1}{b+2}\right|\times|b+1| = 2 \Rightarrow \frac{(b+1)^2}{-(b+2)} = 4$$

$$\Rightarrow \quad b^2 + 6b + 9 = 0 \text{ gives } b = -3$$

4. (d)

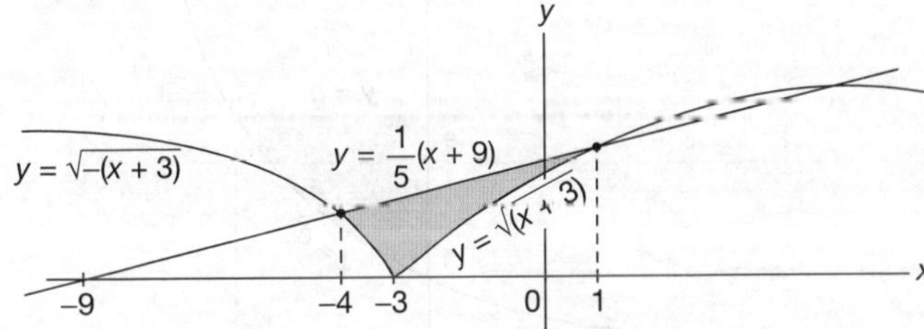

The figure shows the graphs of the relations $y = \sqrt{|x+3|}$ and $y = \frac{1}{5}(x+9)$.

Solving the equation $\sqrt{x+3} = \frac{1}{5}(x+9)$ for $x + 3 \ge 0$, we have

$$x^2 - 7x + 6 = 0 \Rightarrow x = 1, 6$$

Solving the equation $\sqrt{-x-3} = \frac{1}{5}(x+9)$ for $x + 3 \le 0$, we have

$$x^2 + 43x + 156 = 0 \Rightarrow x = -4, -39$$

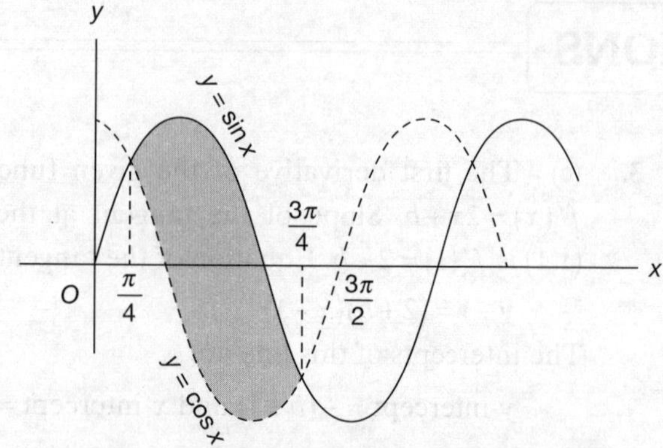

The figure shows the enclosed region. Its area is

$$A = \int_{-4}^{1} \frac{x+9}{5} dx - \int_{-4}^{-3} \sqrt{-x-3}\, dx - \int_{-3}^{1} \sqrt{x+3}\, dx$$

$$= \frac{1}{10}\left|(x+9)^2\right|_{-4}^{1} - \frac{2}{3}\left|(-x-3)^{3/2}\right|_{-3}^{-4} - \frac{2}{3}\left|(x+3)^{3/2}\right|_{-3}^{1}$$

$$= \frac{15}{2} - \frac{2}{3} - \frac{16}{3} = \frac{3}{2}$$

5. (c) According to the given condition, we have

$$\int_{1}^{b} f(x)dx = (b-1)\sin(3b+4)$$

Differentiating both sides with respect to b, we have

$$f(b) = \sin(3b+4) + 3(b-1)\cos(3b+4)$$

Hence $\quad f(x) = \sin(3x+4) + 3(x-1)\cos(3x+4)$

6. (b),(c),(d)

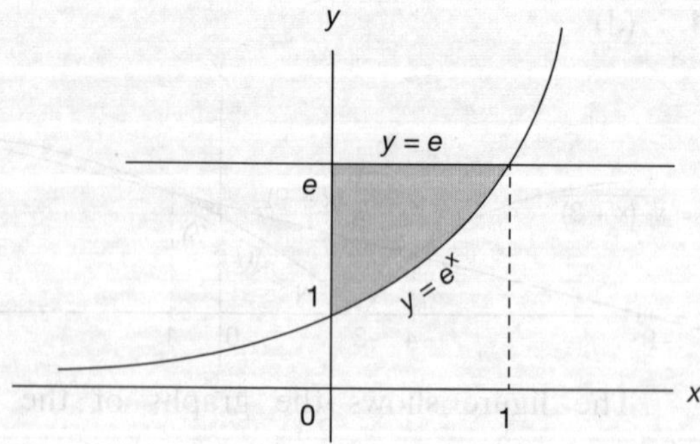

The curve and the line intersect at the point $(1, e)$. The figure shows the enclosed region. If we subdivide the region into vertical strips, then its area is

$$A = \int_{0}^{1} \left(e - e^x\right)dx = \left|ex - e^x\right|_{0}^{1} = 1$$

The curve intersects the y-axis at 1. If we subdivide the region into horizontal strips, then the expression for area is

$$A = \int_{1}^{e} \ln y\, dy$$

By the property of definite integrals, the above integral is the same as

$$\int_{1}^{e} \ln(1+e-y)dy$$

7. (d) The two curves intersect at points $O(0, 0)$ and $P(a, a)$, as shown in the figure.

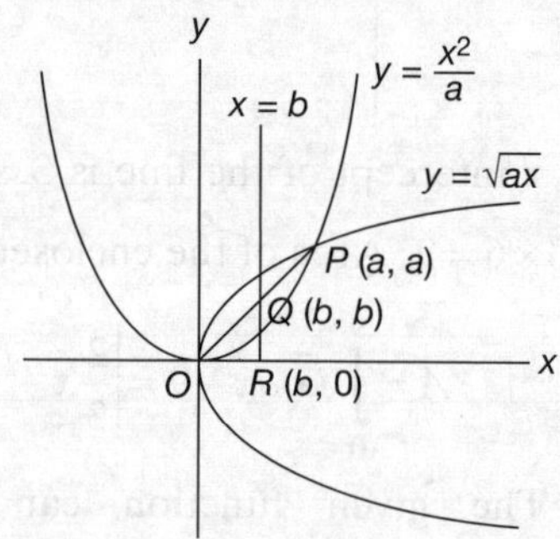

The equation of the chord OP is $y = x$. Hence, the line $x = b$ intersects the chord OP at $Q(b, b)$.

It is given that the area of triangle ΔOQR equals 1/2. Thus, we have

$$\frac{1}{2}b^2 = \frac{1}{2}$$

$$\Rightarrow \quad b = 1$$

Also, it is given that the line $x = b$ bisects the area bounded by the curves C_1 and C_2. Thus, we have

$$\int_{0}^{a}\left(\sqrt{ax} - \frac{x^2}{a}\right)dx = 2\int_{0}^{b}\left(\sqrt{ax} - \frac{x^2}{a}\right)dx$$

$$\Rightarrow \sqrt{a}\left(\frac{2}{3}a^{3/2}\right) - \frac{1}{a}\left(\frac{a^3}{3}\right) = 2\sqrt{a}\left(\frac{2}{3}b^{3/2}\right) - \frac{2}{a}\left(\frac{b^3}{3}\right)$$

$$\Rightarrow a^2 = 4\sqrt{a} - \frac{2}{a} \qquad \text{[Putting } b = 1\text{]}$$

$$\Rightarrow a^3 - 4a^{3/2} + 2 = 0$$

$$\Rightarrow x^6 - 4x^3 + 2 = 0 \qquad \text{[Putting } a = x^2\text{]}$$

8. (a) We have

$$\int_{1}^{4} \frac{3}{2}\sqrt{x}\, dx = 7$$

and $\int_1^4 mx\,dx = \frac{15m}{2}$

Now $\frac{15m}{2} = \frac{7}{2} \Rightarrow m = \frac{7}{15}$.

9. (d) The figure shows the enclosed region.

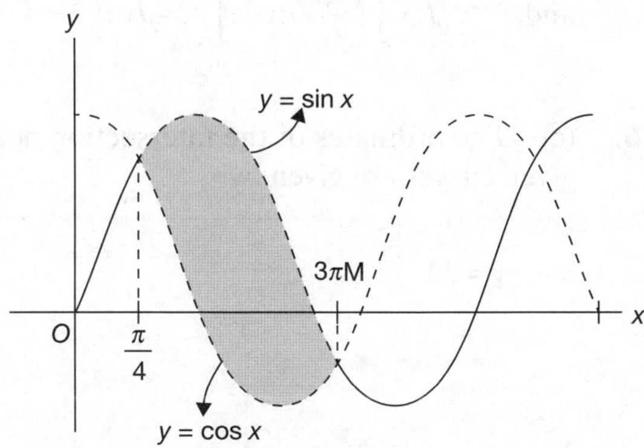

Its area is

$$A = \int_{\pi/4}^{5\pi/4} (\sin x - \cos x)\,dx = \left|-\cos x - \sin x\right|_{\pi/4}^{5\pi/4} = 2\sqrt{2}$$

10. (b) The required area is

$$A = \int_0^{\pi/4} \left(\sqrt{\frac{1+\sin x}{\cos x}} - \sqrt{\frac{1-\sin x}{\cos x}} \right) dx$$

$$= \int_0^{\pi/4} \left(\sqrt{\frac{1+\tan(x/2)}{1-\tan(x/2)}} - \sqrt{\frac{1-\tan(x/2)}{1+\tan(x/2)}} \right) dx$$

$$= \int_0^{\pi/4} \frac{2\tan(x/2)}{\sqrt{1 \quad \tan^2(x/2)}}\,dx$$

$$= \int_0^{\sqrt{2}-1} \frac{4t}{(1+t^2)\sqrt{1-t^2}}\,dt$$

$$\left[\text{Insert } \tan\left(\frac{x}{2}\right) = t \text{ and } dx = \frac{2\,dt}{1+t^2}\right]$$

11. (b) Integrating the given relation $f'(x) = f'(1-x)$ on both sides, we have

$$f(x) + f(1-x) = C$$

Using the conditions $f(0) = 1$and $f(1) = 41$, we get $C = 42$. Hence, we have

$$f(x) + f(1-x) = 42$$

Now, by the property of definite integrals, the required integral is

$$I = \frac{1}{2}\int_0^1 \{f(x) + f(1-x)\}\,dx$$

$$= \frac{1}{2}\int_0^1 42\,dx = 21$$

12. (b),(d)

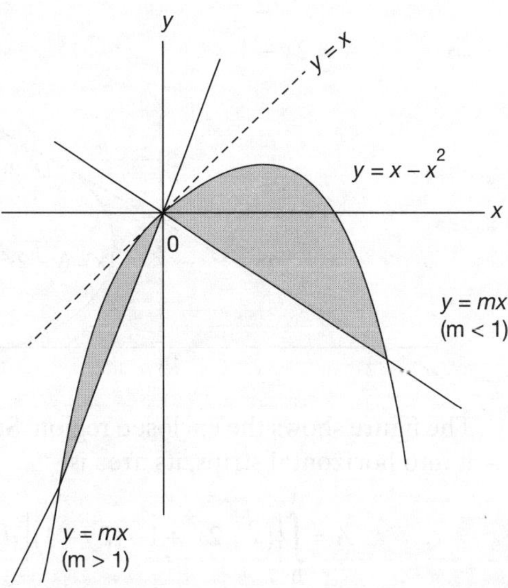

The figure shows the graph of $y = x - x^2$, which is an inverted parabola cutting the x-axis at $x = 0, 1$. The equation of its tangent at $x = 0$ is $y = x$. Depending upon whether $m < 1$ or $m > 1$, the two possible regions are shown in the figure. The abscissa of the intersection points of the given curve and the line are given by

$$x - x^2 = mx$$

$$\Rightarrow \quad x^2 = (1-m)x$$

$$\Rightarrow \quad x = 0, 1-m$$

The expressions for the enclosed area are, respectively,

$$\int_{1-m}^{0} \left(x - x^2 - mx\right)dx \text{ and } \int_0^{1-m} \left(x - x^2 - mx\right)dx$$

Since the area is given to be 9/2, we have

$$\pm\int_0^{1-m} \left(x - x^2 - mx\right)dx = 9/2$$

$$\Rightarrow \quad \left|\frac{1-m}{2}x^2 - \frac{1}{3}x^3\right|_0^{1-m} = \pm 9/2$$

$$\Rightarrow \quad \frac{1}{6}(1-m)^3 = \pm 9/2$$

$$\Rightarrow \quad (1-m)^3 = \pm 27 \text{ gives } m = -2, 4$$

13. (d) Differentiating throughout, we have $2(y-2)y' = 1$. Slope of the tangent at the point $(2,3)$ is $y'(2,3) = 1/2$. Equation of the tangent is

$$y - 3 = \frac{1}{2}(x-2)$$

$$\Rightarrow \quad x = 2y - 4$$

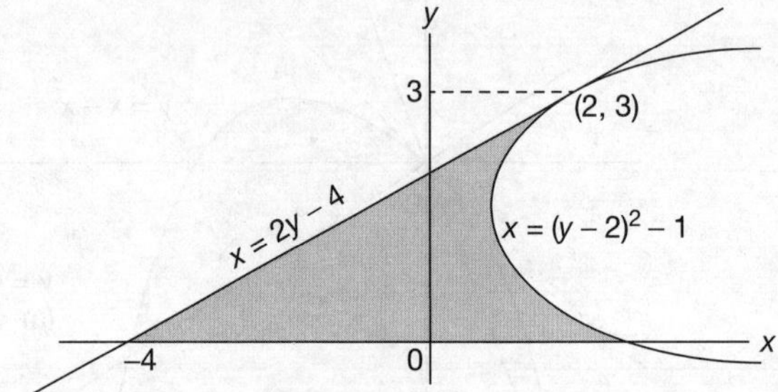

The figure shows the enclosed region. Sub-dividing it into horizontal strips, its area is

$$A = \int_0^3 \left\{(y-2)^2 + 1 - (2y-4)\right\} dy$$

$$= \left|\frac{1}{3}(y-2)^3 - y^2 + 5y\right|_0^3 = 9$$

14. (d) The given circles intersect at points $P\left(\frac{a}{2}, \frac{\sqrt{3}a}{2}\right)$ and $Q\left(\frac{a}{2}, \frac{-\sqrt{3}a}{2}\right)$. The parametric equations representing the circle $x^2 + y^2 = a^2$ are $x = a\cos\theta$ and $y = a\sin\theta$. The required area is

$$A = 2\int_{\pi/3}^{0} 2a\sin\theta\, d(a\cos\theta)$$

$$= 4a^2 \int_0^{\pi/3} \sin^2\theta\, d\theta$$

$$= 2a^2 \int_0^{\pi/3} (1-\cos 2\theta)\, d\theta$$

$$= 2a^2 \left|\theta - \frac{\sin 2\theta}{2}\right|_0^{\pi/3}$$

$$= \left(\frac{2\pi}{3} - \frac{\sqrt{3}}{2}\right)a^2$$

15. (c) $$I = \int_0^1 \frac{\sin x}{\sqrt{x}}\, dx < \int_0^1 \frac{x}{\sqrt{x}}\, dx$$

$$= \int_0^1 \sqrt{x}\, dx = \frac{2}{3}$$

and $$J = \int_0^1 \frac{\cos x}{\sqrt{x}}\, dx < \int_0^1 \frac{1}{\sqrt{x}}\, dx = 2$$

16. (c) The ordinates of the intersection point of the given curves are given by

$$-2y^2 = 1 - 3y^2$$

$$\Rightarrow \quad y = \pm 1$$

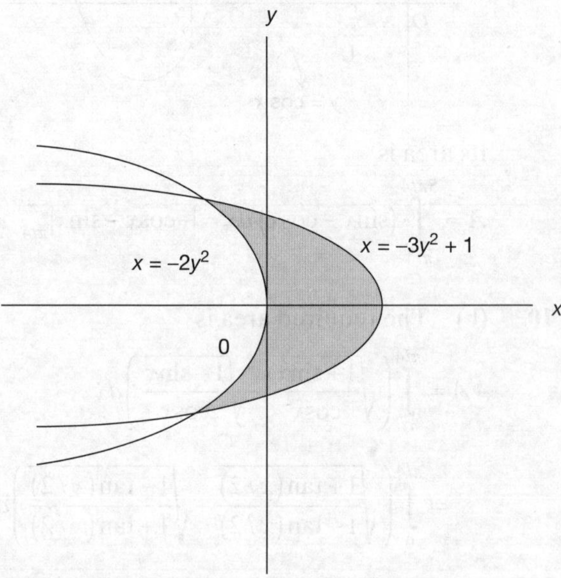

The figure shows the enclosed region. Sub-dividing it into horizontal strips, its area is

$$A = \int_{-1}^{1} \left\{(1-3y^2) - (-2y^2)\right\} dy$$

$$= \left|y - \frac{1}{3}y^3\right|_{-1}^{1} = \frac{4}{3}$$

17. (a) The relation $y = \ln|x|$ is even. Hence, its graph consists of two parts. The positive half is simply the graph of $y = \ln x$, and the negative half is its mirror image in the y-axis. To draw the graph of $y = |\ln|x||$, we take the upper part of the graph of $y = \ln|x|$ as it is, and the mirror image of its lower part, in the x-axis.

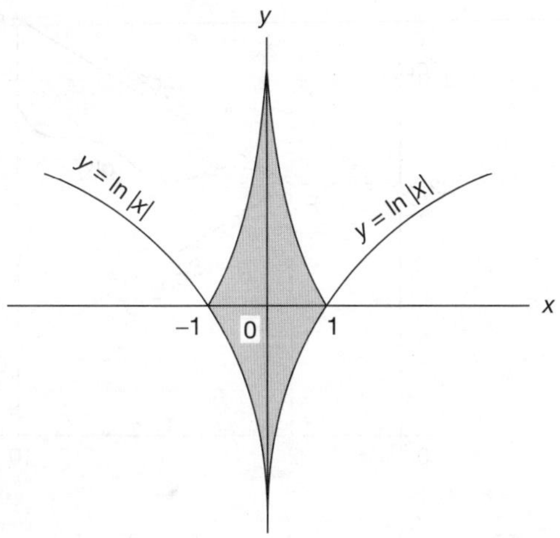

The figure shows the enclosed region. Its area is

$$A = 4\int_0^1 -\ln x\, dx$$

$$= 4\left|-x\ln x + x\right|_0^1$$

$$= 4\left(1 - \lim_{x\to 0^+} x\ln x\right) = 4$$

$$\left[\lim_{x\to 0^+} x\ln x = \lim_{x\to 0^+}\frac{\ln x}{\frac{1}{x}} = \lim_{x\to 0}\frac{\frac{1}{x}}{\frac{-1}{x^2}} = \lim_{x\to 0} -x = 0\right]$$

18. (b) The figure shows the regions R_1, R_2. It is given that $A_1 - A_2 = \frac{1}{4}$. Hence, we have

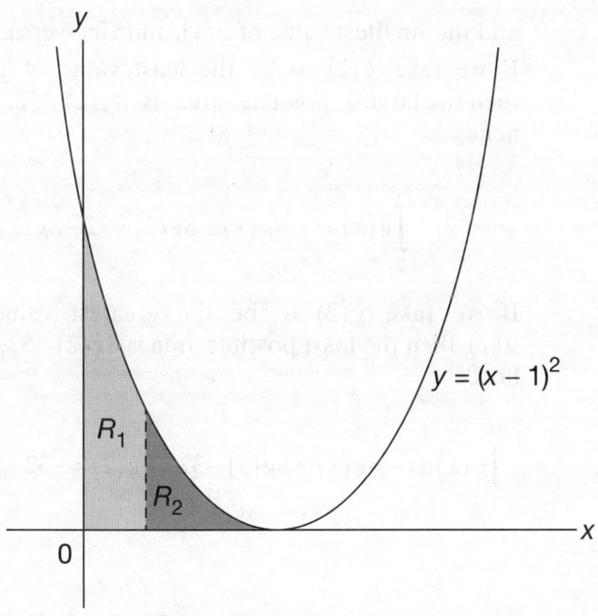

$$\int_0^b (x-1)^2\, dx - \int_b^1 (x-1)^2\, dx = \frac{1}{4}$$

$$\Rightarrow \quad \left|\frac{1}{3}(x-1)^3\right|_0^b - \left|\frac{1}{3}(x-1)^3\right|_b^1 = \frac{1}{4}$$

$$\Rightarrow \quad \frac{(b-1)^3 + 1}{3} - \frac{-(b-1)^3}{3} = \frac{1}{4}$$

$$\Rightarrow \quad (b-1)^3 = \frac{-1}{8} \text{ gives } b = \frac{1}{2}$$

19. (d)

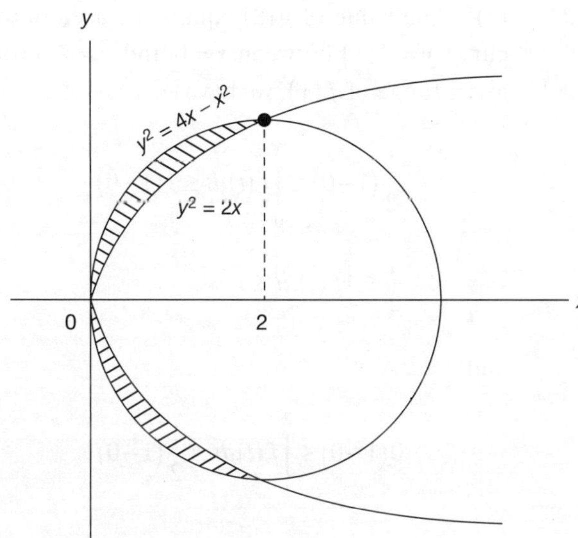

The figure shows the region. The parabola and circle intersect at $(2, \pm 2)$. Its area is

$$A = 2\int_0^2 \left(\sqrt{4x - x^2} - \sqrt{2x}\right)dx$$

$$= 2\int_0^2 \sqrt{4-(x-2)^2}\, dx - \frac{16}{3}$$

$$= 2\int_{-\pi/2}^{0} 4\cos^2\theta\, d\theta - \frac{16}{3} \quad [\text{Putting } x - 2 = 2\sin\theta]$$

$$= 4\int_{-\pi/2}^{0} (1+\cos(2\theta))\, d\theta - \frac{16}{3}$$

$$= 4\left|\theta + \frac{1}{2}\sin(2\theta)\right|_{-\pi/2}^{0} - \frac{16}{3} = 2\pi - \frac{16}{3}$$

20. (c) By the property of definite integrals, we have

$$A_1 = \frac{1}{2}\int_{-1}^{2}\{xf(x)+(1-x)f(1-x)\}dx$$

$$= \frac{1}{2}\int_{-1}^{2}\{xf(x)+(1-x)f(x)\}dx$$

$$[\text{Given } f(x) = f(1-x)]$$

$$= \frac{1}{2}\int_{-1}^{2}f(x)dx = \frac{1}{2}A_2$$

21. (b) The value of $g(2)$ equals the area under the curve $y = f(x)$ between $x = 0$ and $x = 2$. From the given range of $f(x)$, we have

$$\frac{1}{2}(1-0) \le \int_0^1 f(t)dt \le 1(1-0)$$

$$\Rightarrow \quad \frac{1}{2} \le \int_0^1 f(t)dt \le 1$$

and

$$0(1-0) \le \int_1^2 f(t)dt \le \frac{1}{2}(1-0)$$

$$\Rightarrow \quad 0 \le \int_1^2 f(t)dt \le \frac{1}{2}$$

Adding the two inequalities, we have

$$\frac{1}{2} \le g(2) \le \frac{3}{2}.$$

22. (d) The condition $\left|\frac{g(x)-g(y)}{x-y}\right| \le 1 \Rightarrow |\text{slope}| \le 1 \Rightarrow$ $-1 \le \text{slope} \le 1$. In that case, we have

$$-1 \le \frac{g(10)-g(2)}{10-2} \le 1$$

$$\Rightarrow \quad g(2)-8 \le g(10) \le g(2)+8$$

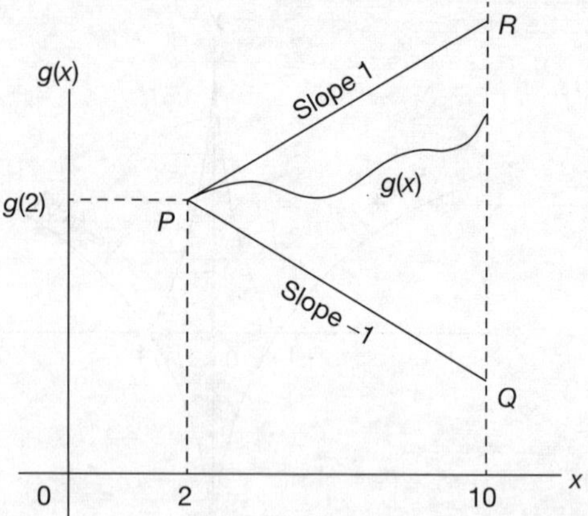

The graph of $g(x)$, therefore, lies between the two straight lines PQ, PR (see figure), and the area under the graph lies between

$$\Rightarrow \quad 8\left(\frac{g(2)+g(2)-8}{2}\right) \le \int_2^{10} g(x)dx \le 8\left(\frac{g(2)+g(2)+8}{2}\right)$$

$$\Rightarrow \quad 8g(2)-32 \le \int_2^{10} g(x)dx \le 8g(2)+32$$

The extreme values of $\int_2^{10} g(x)dx - 8g(x)$ are obtained by taking the greatest value of $\int_2^{10} g(x)dx$ and the smallest value of $g(x)$, and vice-versa.

If we take $g(2)$ to be the least value of $g(x)$, then the largest possible area is $8g(2)+32$, and hence

$$\int_2^{10} g(x)dx - 8g(x) \le 8g(2)+32-8g(2) = 32$$

If we take $g(2)$ to be the greatest value of $g(x)$, then the least possible area is $8g(2)-32$, and hence

$$\int_2^{10} g(x)dx - 8g(x) \ge 8g(2)-32-8g(2) = -32$$

Hence, the greatest value of $\left|\int_2^{10} g(x)dx - 8g(x)\right|$, that is, $m = 32$. Hence $m - 30 = 2$.

23. (a),(c) From the condition $f'(x) = 2f(x)$ and $f(1/2) = 1$, we have

$$f(x) = e^{2x-1}$$

From the condition $f'(x) = f(x)$ and $f(1/2) = 1$, we have

$$f(x) = e^{x-1/2}$$

Then the area under the curve lies between

$$\int_{1/2}^{1} e^{x-1/2}\,dx \le \int_{1/2}^{1} f(x)dx \le \int_{1/2}^{1} e^{2x-1}\,dx$$

$$\Rightarrow \quad \sqrt{e} - 1 \le \int_{1/2}^{1} f(x)dx \le \frac{e-1}{2}$$

$$\Rightarrow \quad 0.65 \le \int_{1/2}^{1} f(x)dx \le 0.86$$

The numbers $\sqrt{e} = 1.65$ and $\sqrt{e} - \frac{1}{2} = 1.15$ do not belong to this interval.

24. (a) We have

$$16^{y^2+2x} \le \frac{1}{8}$$

$$\Rightarrow \quad 2^{4(y^2+2x)} \le 2^{-3}$$

$$\Rightarrow \quad y^2 + 2x \le \frac{-3}{4}$$

$$\Rightarrow \quad y^2 \le -2\left(x + \frac{3}{8}\right)$$

Similarly, we have

$$16^{x^2+2y} \le \frac{1}{8}$$

$$\Rightarrow \quad 2^{4(x^2+2y)} \le 2^{-3}$$

$$\Rightarrow \quad x^2 + 2y \le \frac{-3}{4}$$

$$\Rightarrow \quad x^2 \le -2\left(y + \frac{3}{8}\right)$$

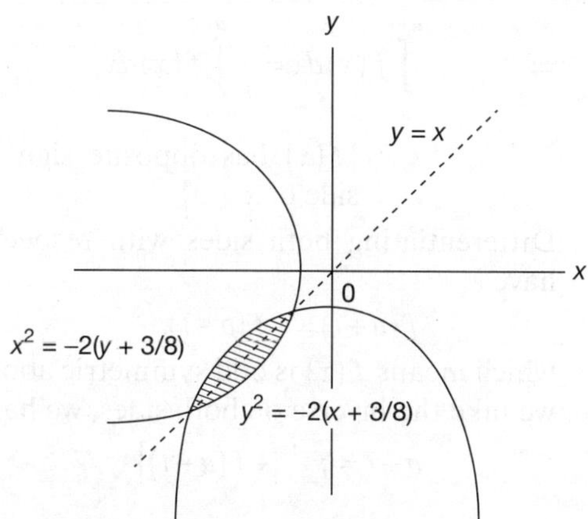

The required area (see figure) is the region bounded by the parabolas $y^2 = -2\left(x + \frac{3}{8}\right)$ and $x^2 = -2\left(y + \frac{3}{8}\right)$.

We can see that the two curves are symmetric about the line $y = x$ (interchanging x and y in one equation gives the other equation). Hence, their intersection points lie on the line $y = x$.

Putting $y = x$ in any one equation gives $x = \frac{-3}{2}$ and $x = \frac{-1}{2}$.

From the two equations, we have

$$y_1 = -\sqrt{-2x - \frac{3}{4}}$$

and $$y_2 = \frac{-x^2}{2} - \frac{3}{8}$$

The required area is

$$A = \int_{-3/2}^{-1/2} (y_2 - y_1)dx$$

$$= \int_{-3/2}^{-1/2} \left(\frac{-x^2}{2} - \frac{3}{8} + \sqrt{-2x - \frac{3}{4}}\right)dx$$

$$= \left|\frac{-x^3}{6} - \frac{3}{8}x - \frac{1}{3}\left(-2x - \frac{3}{4}\right)^{3/2}\right|_{-3/2}^{-1/2} = \frac{1}{6}$$

25. (d) From the given condition, we have

$$\left|\int_a^{a+t} f(x)dx\right| = \left|\int_{a-t}^{a} f(x)dx\right|$$

$$\Rightarrow \quad \int_a^{a+t} f(x)dx = -\int_{a-t}^{a} f(x)dx$$

[$f(x)$ has opposite signs on either side of $x = a$]

Differentiating both sides with respect to t, we have

$$f(a+t) = -f(a-t),$$

which means $f(x)$ is odd symmetric about $x = a$. If we take the inverse on both sides, we have

$$a+t = f^{-1}\{-f(a-t)\}$$

Now, let $f(a-t) = x \Rightarrow t = a - f^{-1}(x)$. The above equation then reduces to

$$a + a - f^{-1}(x) = f^{-1}(-x)$$

$$\Rightarrow \quad f^{-1}(x) + f^{-1}(-x) = 2a$$

Now, by the property of definite integrals, we have

$$\int_{-\lambda}^{\lambda} f^{-1}(x)dx = \int_{-\lambda}^{\lambda} f^{-1}(-x)dx$$

Hence, we have

$$\int_{-\lambda}^{\lambda} f^{-1}(x)dx = \int_{-\lambda}^{\lambda} \frac{f^{-1}(x)+f^{-1}(-x)}{2}dx$$

$$= \int_{-\lambda}^{\lambda} a\,dx = 2a\lambda$$

CHAPTER

24 Sum of a Series and Definite Integral

- **Definite Integral as the Limit of a Sum:** Suppose we have to find the area enclosed under the curve $y = f(x)$ between the ordinates $x = a$ and $x = b$ (see figure). We subdivide the region into n vertical strips, each of width $h = \frac{b-a}{n}$. Here, n is very large so h is very small. The area under the curve can now be written as

$$A = hf(a+h) + hf(a+2h) + \ldots + + hf\{a+rh\}$$

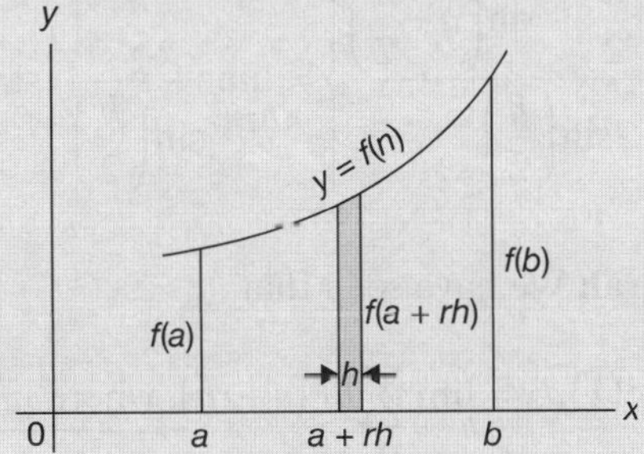

Thus, we have the following result:

$$\int_a^b f(x)\,dx = \lim_{h\to 0}\sum_1^n hf(a+rh), \text{ where } nh = b-a$$

Note: Since each term $hf(a+rh)$ in the series approaches zero, addition or subtraction of a certain finite number of terms will not affect the limit.

Example 1: Evaluate $\int_a^b x^2 dx$ as the limit of a sum.

Solution: We have

$$\int_a^b x^2 dx = \lim_{h\to 0}\sum_1^n h(a+rh)^2, \text{ where } nh = b-a$$

$$= \lim_{h\to 0}\left[ha^2\sum_1^n 1 + 2ah^2\sum_1^n r + h^3\sum_1^n r^2\right] = \lim_{h\to 0}\left[nha^2 + 2ah^2\frac{n(n+1)}{2} + h^3\frac{n(n+1)(2n+1)}{6}\right]$$

$$= \lim_{n\to\infty}\left[a^2(b-a) + a(b-a)^2\frac{n(n+1)}{n^2} + (b-a)^3\frac{n(n+1)(2n+1)}{6n^3}\right]$$

$$= \lim_{n\to\infty}\left[a^2(b-a) + a(b-a)^2 + \frac{1}{3}(b-a)^3\right] = \frac{1}{3}\left(b^3 - a^3\right)$$

Example 2: Evaluate $\int_a^b \cos x\, dx$ as the limit of a sum.

Solution: We have

$$\int_a^b \cos x\, dx = \lim_{h\to 0}\sum_1^n h\cos(a+rh), \text{ where } nh = b-a = \lim_{h\to 0} h\left[\cos(a+h) + \cos(a+2h) + \ldots + \cos(a+nh)\right]$$

Now, let $S = \cos(a+h)+\cos(a+2h)+\ldots+\cos(a+nh)$. Multiplying both sides by $2\sin\left(\frac{h}{2}\right)$, we have

$$\left(2\sin\left(\frac{h}{2}\right)\right)S = 2\sin\left(\frac{h}{2}\right)\cos(a+h)+2\sin\left(\frac{h}{2}\right)\cos(a+2h)+\ldots+2\sin\left(\frac{h}{2}\right)\cos(a+nh)$$

$$= \sin\left(a+\frac{3h}{2}\right)-\sin\left(a+\frac{h}{2}\right)+\sin\left(a+\frac{5h}{2}\right)-\sin\left(a+\frac{3h}{2}\right)+\ldots+\sin\left(a+\frac{(2n+1)h}{2}\right)-\sin\left(a+\frac{(2n-1)h}{2}\right)$$

$$= \sin\left(a+\frac{(2n+1)h}{2}\right)-\sin\left(a+\frac{h}{2}\right) = \sin\left(a+nh+\frac{h}{2}\right)-\sin\left(a+\frac{h}{2}\right) = \sin\left(b+\frac{h}{2}\right)-\sin\left(a+\frac{h}{2}\right)$$

Hence, we have

$$\int_a^b \cos x\, dx = \lim_{h\to 0} h\left\{\frac{\sin\left(b+\frac{h}{2}\right)-\sin\left(a+\frac{h}{2}\right)}{2\sin\left(\frac{h}{2}\right)}\right\} = \lim_{h\to 0}\frac{\frac{h}{2}}{\sin\left(\frac{h}{2}\right)}\left\{\sin\left(b+\frac{h}{2}\right)-\sin\left(a+\frac{h}{2}\right)\right\} = \sin b-\sin a$$

- **Limit of a Sum as a Definite Integral:** We have seen that

$$\int_a^b f(x)dx = \lim_{h\to 0}\sum_1^n hf(a+rh), \text{ where } nh = b-a$$

Changing h to $\frac{b-a}{n}$, the series reduces to

$$\lim_{h\to 0}\sum_1^n hf(a+rh) = (b-a)\lim_{n\to\infty}\frac{1}{n}\sum_1^n f\left\{a+(b-a)\frac{r}{n}\right\}$$

Substituting $x = a+(b-a)t$ and $dx = (b-a)dt$, the integral reduces to

$$\int_a^b f(x)dx = (b-a)\int_0^1 f\{a+(b-a)t\}dt$$

Equating the two, we have

$$\lim_{n\to\infty}\frac{1}{n}\sum_1^n f\left\{a+(b-a)\frac{r}{n}\right\} = \int_0^1 f\{a+(b-a)t\}dt$$

Thus, we have the following result:

$$\lim_{n\to\infty}\frac{1}{n}\sum_1^n f\left(\frac{r}{n}\right) = \int_0^1 f(x)dx$$

EXERCISES

1. The value of $\lim_{n\to\infty}\sum_1^n \frac{n}{\left(n^2+r^2\right)^{1/2}}$ is:

(a) $\ln\left(\sqrt{2}+1\right)$ (b) $\ln\left(\sqrt{2}-1\right)$

(c) $\ln\left(\sqrt{3}+1\right)$ (d) $\ln\left(\sqrt{3}-1\right)$

2. The value of

$$\lim_{n\to\infty}\left[\frac{1}{n}+\frac{n}{(n+1)^2}+\frac{n}{(n+2)^2}+\ldots+\frac{n}{(2n-1)^2}\right] \text{ is:}$$

(a) 2 (b) 1

(c) $\frac{1}{2}$ (d) $\frac{3}{2}$

3. The value of

$$\lim_{n\to\infty}\left[\frac{1}{n}+\frac{\sqrt{n}}{\sqrt{(n+2)^3}}+\frac{\sqrt{n}}{\sqrt{(n+4)^3}}+\frac{\sqrt{n}}{\sqrt{(n+8)^3}}+\ldots n\,\text{terms}\right]$$

is:

(a) $\frac{1}{\sqrt{2}}$ (b) $1-\frac{1}{\sqrt{2}}$

(c) $\frac{1}{\sqrt{3}}$ (d) $1-\frac{1}{\sqrt{3}}$

4. The value of

$$\lim_{n\to\infty}\left[\frac{1}{n}+\frac{1}{\sqrt{n^2-1^2}}+\frac{1}{\sqrt{n^2-2^2}}+\frac{1}{\sqrt{n^2-3^2}}+\ldots n\text{ terms}\right]$$

is:

(a) $\frac{3\pi}{2}$ (b) $\frac{\pi}{2}$

(c) $\frac{\pi}{3}$ (d) $\frac{\pi}{4}$

5. The value of $\lim_{n\to\infty}\frac{1+\sqrt[3]{2}++\sqrt[3]{3}+\ldots+\sqrt[3]{n-1}}{\sqrt[3]{n^4}}$ is:

(a) $\frac{1}{2}$ (b) $\frac{3}{4}$

(c) $\frac{1}{3}$ (d) $\frac{2}{3}$

6. The value of

$$\lim_{n\to\infty}\left[\frac{n+1}{n^2+1^2}+\frac{n+2}{n^2+2^2}+\frac{n+3}{n^2+3^2}+\ldots n\text{ terms}\right]$$ is:

(a) $\frac{\pi}{4}+\frac{1}{2}\ln 2$ (b) $\frac{\pi}{2}+\frac{1}{2}\ln 2$

(c) $\frac{\pi}{4}+\ln 2$ (d) $\frac{\pi}{2}+\ln 2$

7. The value of $\lim_{n\to\infty}\prod_{1}^{n}\left(\frac{n+r}{n}\right)^{1/n}$ is:

(a) $\frac{1}{e}$ (b) $1-\frac{1}{e}$

(c) $\frac{4}{e}$ (d) $1+\frac{1}{e}$

ANSWER KEYS

1. (a) **2.** (c) **3.** (d) **4.** (b) **5.** (b) **6.** (a) **7.** (c)

SOLUTIONS

1. (a) We have

$$\lim_{n\to\infty}\sum_{1}^{n}\frac{n}{\left(n^2+r^2\right)^{1/2}}=\lim_{n\to\infty}\frac{1}{n}\sum_{1}^{n}\frac{1}{\sqrt{1+(r/n)^2}}$$

$$=\int_0^1\frac{1}{\sqrt{1+x^2}}dx=\left|\ln\left|x+\sqrt{1+x^2}\right|\right|_0^1$$

$$=\ln\left(\sqrt{2}+1\right)$$

2. (c) We have

$$\lim_{n\to\infty}\left[\frac{1}{n}+\frac{n}{(n+1)^2}+\frac{n}{(n+2)^2}+\ldots+\frac{n}{(2n-1)^2}\right]$$

$$=\lim_{n\to\infty}\sum_{0}^{n-1}\frac{n}{(n+r)^2}=\lim_{n\to\infty}\sum_{1}^{n}\frac{n}{(n+r)^2}$$

[Adding or omitting a few terms does not affect the limit]

$$=\lim_{n\to\infty}\frac{1}{n}\sum_{1}^{n}\frac{1}{\left(1+\frac{r}{n}\right)^2}$$

$$=\int_0^1\frac{1}{(1+x)^2}dx=\left|\frac{-1}{1+x}\right|_0^1=\frac{1}{2}$$

3. (d) We have

$$\lim_{n\to\infty}\left[\frac{1}{n}+\frac{\sqrt{n}}{\sqrt{(n+2)^3}}+\frac{\sqrt{n}}{\sqrt{(n+4)^3}}+\frac{\sqrt{n}}{\sqrt{(n+8)^3}}+\ldots n\text{ terms}\right]$$

$$= \lim_{n\to\infty} \sum_{0}^{n-1} \frac{\sqrt{n}}{\sqrt{(n+2r)^3}} = \lim_{n\to\infty} \sum_{1}^{n} \frac{\sqrt{n}}{\sqrt{(n+2r)^3}}$$

[Adding or omitting a few terms does not affect the limit]

$$= \lim_{n\to\infty} \frac{1}{n} \sum_{1}^{n} \frac{1}{\left(1+\frac{2r}{n}\right)^{3/2}}$$

$$= \int_0^1 \frac{1}{(1+2x)^{3/2}} dx = \left|\frac{(1+2x)^{-1/2}}{2(-1/2)}\right|_0^1$$

$$= \left|\frac{1}{\sqrt{1+2x}}\right|_1^0 = 1 - \frac{1}{\sqrt{3}}$$

4. (b) We have

$$\lim_{n\to\infty}\left[\frac{1}{n} + \frac{1}{\sqrt{n^2-1^2}} + \frac{1}{\sqrt{n^2-2^2}} + \frac{1}{\sqrt{n^2-3^2}} + \ldots n \text{ terms}\right]$$

$$= \lim_{n\to\infty} \sum_{0}^{n-1} \frac{1}{\sqrt{n^2-r^2}} = \lim_{n\to\infty} \sum_{1}^{n} \frac{1}{\sqrt{n^2-r^2}}$$

[Adding or omitting a few terms does not affect the limit]

$$= \lim_{n\to\infty} \frac{1}{n} \sum_{1}^{n} \frac{1}{\sqrt{1-\left(\frac{r}{n}\right)^2}} = \int_0^1 \frac{1}{\sqrt{1-x^2}} dx$$

$$= \left|\sin^{-1} x\right|_0^1 = \left|\frac{1}{\sqrt{1+2x}}\right|_1^0 = \frac{\pi}{2}$$

5. (b) We have

$$\lim_{n\to\infty} \frac{1+\sqrt[3]{2}++\sqrt[3]{3}+\ldots+\sqrt[3]{n-1}}{\sqrt[3]{n^4}}$$

$$= \lim_{n\to\infty} \sum_{1}^{n-1} \frac{\sqrt[3]{r}}{\sqrt[3]{n^4}} = \lim_{n\to\infty} \sum_{1}^{n} \frac{\sqrt[3]{r}}{\sqrt[3]{n^4}}$$

[Adding or omitting a few terms does not affect the limit]

$$= \lim_{n\to\infty} \frac{1}{n} \sum_{1}^{n} \sqrt[3]{\frac{r}{n}}$$

$$= \int_0^1 \sqrt[3]{x}\, dx = \left|\frac{x^{4/3}}{4/3}\right|_0^1 = \frac{3}{4}\left|x^{4/3}\right|_1^0 = \frac{3}{4}$$

6. (a) We have

$$\lim_{n\to\infty}\left[\frac{n+1}{n^2+1^2} + \frac{n+2}{n^2+2^2} + \frac{n+3}{n^2+3^2} + \ldots n \text{ terms}\right]$$

$$= \lim_{n\to\infty} \sum_{1}^{n} \frac{n+r}{n^2+r^2}$$

$$= \lim_{n\to\infty} \frac{1}{n} \sum_{1}^{n} \frac{1+\frac{r}{n}}{1+\left(\frac{r}{n}\right)^2}$$

$$= \int_0^1 \frac{1+x}{1+x^2} dx = \int_0^1 \frac{1}{1+x^2} dx + \frac{1}{2}\int_0^1 \frac{2x}{1+x^2} dx$$

$$= \left|\tan^{-1} x\right|_0^1 + \frac{1}{2}\left|\ln|1+x^2|\right|_0^1 = \frac{\pi}{4} + \frac{1}{2}\ln 2$$

7. (c) Let $S = \lim_{n\to\infty} \prod_{1}^{n} \left(\frac{n+r}{n}\right)^{1/n}$. Then, we have

$$S = \lim_{n\to\infty}\left[\left(\frac{n+1}{n}\right)\left(\frac{n+2}{n}\right)\left(\frac{n+3}{n}\right)\ldots\left(\frac{n+n}{n}\right)\right]^{1/n}$$

Taking log both sides, we have

$$\ln S = \lim_{n\to\infty} \frac{1}{n}\left[\ln\left(\frac{n+1}{n}\right) + \ln\left(\frac{n+2}{n}\right) + \ldots + \ln\left(\frac{n+n}{n}\right)\right]$$

$$= \lim_{n\to\infty} \frac{1}{n} \sum_{1}^{n} \ln\left(1+\frac{r}{n}\right)$$

$$= \int_0^1 \ln(1+x)\, dx = \int_1^2 \ln t\, dt = \left|t\ln t - t\right|_1^2$$

$$= 2\ln 2 - 1 = \ln 4 - \ln e = \ln\left(\frac{4}{e}\right)$$

Hence $S = \frac{4}{e}$.

CHAPTER

25 Differential Equations

- An equation involving variables and their derivatives is called a differential equation. If the equation involves a single independent variable, it is called an **ordinary** differential equation; a differential equation involving more than one independent variable is called a **partial** differential equation.

  The **order** of a differential equation is the order of the highest derivative that occurs in the equation. The **degree** of a differential equation is the degree of the highest ordered derivative in the equation. The degree of a differential equation is defined only if the equation is a polynomial equation in derivatives $y', y'', y''',\ldots$ etc.

  An equation of the first order and first degree can be written as
$$M(x,y)dx+N(x,y)dy=0$$

- Solving a differential equation means obtaining a relation between the variables. Such a relation which, apart from the variables, also contains arbitrary constants is called the **primitive** of the differential equation. A differential equation of order n has a primitive containing n essential arbitrary constants.

  The primitive of a differential equation is also called the **general solution** of the equation. It represents the equation of a family of curves, and a **particular solution** is the equation of a particular curve of the family.

- **Variable Separable Form:** In the differential equation $M\,dx+N\,dy=0$, the variables are said to be separated if M is a function of x only and N is a function of y only. The primitive of such a differential equation may be obtained by integration.

- **Homogeneous Differential Equations:** A function $f(x,y)$ is called a homogeneous function of degree n if
$$f(\lambda x,\lambda y)=\lambda^n f(x,y)$$
  The differential equation $M\,dx+N\,dy=0$ is said to be homogeneous if M and N are both homogeneous and of the same degree. The substitution
$$y=vx \text{ and } dy=v\,dx+x\,dv$$
  reduces the differential equation to the variable separable form.

- ***M* and *N* are Linear but not Homogeneous:** In the differential equation $M\,dx+N\,dy=0$, suppose $M=a_1x+b_1y+c_1$ and $N=a_2x+b_2y+c_2$, where both c_1, c_2 are not equal to zero.

  If $\frac{a_1}{a_2}=\frac{b_1}{b_2}$, then the substitution
$$a_1x+b_1y=v \text{ and } dy=\frac{dv-a_1dx}{b_1}$$
  reduces the differential equation to the variable separable form.

  If $\frac{a_1}{a_2}\neq\frac{b_1}{b_2}$, then the substitution
$$x=x'+h,\ y=x'+k \text{ and } dx=dx',\ dy=dy'$$
  where h,k satisfy the equations $a_1h+b_1k+c_1=0$ and $a_2h+b_2k+c_2=0$, reduces the differential equation to $(a_1x'+b_1y')dx'+(a_2x'+b_2y')dy'=0$, which is of homogeneous form.

- **Exact Differential Equations:** The differential equation $M\,dx+N\,dy=0$ is said to be exact if $\frac{\partial M}{\partial y}=\frac{\partial N}{\partial x}$. In that case, the differential equation has a solution of the type $\mu(x,y)=C$, where
$$\frac{\partial\mu}{\partial x}=M \text{ and } \frac{\partial\mu}{\partial y}=N$$

The function μ can be found using the above equations. The first equation gives

$$\mu = \int^{x} M\,dx + \phi(y),$$

where the function ϕ can be found using the second equation

$$\frac{\partial}{\partial y}\left(\int^{x} M\,dx\right) + \frac{d\phi}{dy} = N$$

- **Linear Differential Equations:** The differential equation $\frac{dy}{dx} + yP(x) = Q(x)$, which is linear in y and y', is called a linear differential equation, linear in y. Its integrating factor is IF $= e^{\int P\,dx}$, and its solution is

$$ye^{\int P\,dx} = \int\left(Qe^{\int P\,dx}\right)dx + C$$

Other equations which are reducible to the linear form:

1. $f'(y)\frac{dy}{dx} + f(y)P(x) = Q(x)$

   The substitution $f(y) = u$ reduces the equation to linear form: $\frac{du}{dx} + uP(x) = Q(x)$.

2. $\frac{dy}{dx} + yP(x) = y^nQ(x)$

   The equation can be rearranged as $y^{-n}\frac{dy}{dx} + y^{-n+1}P(x) = y^nQ(x)$. The substitution $y^{-n+1} = u$ reduces the equation to linear form: $\frac{du}{dx} + u(1-n)P(x) = (1-n)Q(x)$.

EXERCISES

1. The order and degree of the differential equation $(y''')^{1/2} + x^2(y'')^3 - x\cos y = 0$ are:
   (a) 3rd order, 1st degree (b) 2nd order, 3rd degree
   (c) 3rd order, 6th degree (d) None of these

2. Consider the family of curves $y^2 = 2C\left(x + \sqrt{C}\right)$, where C is an arbitrary constant. The order and degree of the differential equation representing these curves are:
   (a) 1st order, 2nd degree (b) 1st order, 3rd degree
   (c) 2nd order, 1st degree (d) None of these

3. Consider the family of curves $y = Ae^{2x} + Be^x + C$, where A, B, C are arbitrary constants. The differential equation representing these curves is:
   (a) $3y''' - 2y'' + y' = 0$ (b) $2y''' - y'' + y' = 0$
   (c) $y''' - y'' + 2y' = 0$ (d) $y''' - 3y'' + 2y' = 0$

4. Consider the family of circles having a fixed radius r. The differential equation representing these curves is:
   (a) $(y'')^2 - r^2\left\{(1+(y')^2\right\} = 0$
   (b) $(y'')^2 - r^2\left\{(1+(y')^2\right\}^2 = 0$
   (c) $r^2(y'')^2 - \left\{(1+(y')^2\right\}^3 = 0$
   (d) $r^2(y'')^2 - \left\{(1+(y')^2\right\}^2 = 0$

5. Consider the family of circles whose centres lie on the line $y = x$. If this family is represented by the differential equation $Py'' + Qy' + 1 = 0$, then:

(a) $P+Q=1-x+y+y'+(y')^2$
(b) $P=y-x$
(c) $P-Q=x+y-y'-(y')^2$
(d) $P=y+x$

6. A normal drawn at any point P on a curve meets the x-axis at Q. If PQ is of constant length c, the differential equation representing these curves is:
(a) $y^2(y')^2+1-c^2y^2=0$
(b) $y^2(y')^2+y^2-c^2=0$
(c) $(y')^2-y^2+c^2=0$
(d) $(y')^2+y^2-c^2=0$

7. The differential equation $\frac{dy}{dx}=\frac{\sqrt{1-y^2}}{y}$ represents a family of circles with:
(a) Variable radius and a fixed centre at $(0,1)$
(b) Variable radius and a fixed centre at $(0,-1)$
(c) Fixed radius and a variable centre along the x-axis
(d) Fixed radius and variable centre along the y-axis

8. Let f be a real-valued differentiable function on **R** such that $f(1)=1$. If the y intercept of the tangent at any point P on the curve $y=f(x)$ is equal to the cube of the abscissa of P, then $f(-3)$ equals:
(a) -1 (b) 0 (c) 3 (d) 9

9. A curve $y=f(x)$ passes through $(1,1)$ and the tangent at any point P on the curve cuts the x-axis at A and y-axis at B such that $BP:AP=3:1$. Then:
(a) Equation of the curve is $xy'-3y=0$
(b) Normal at $(1,1)$ is $x+3y=4$
(c) Curve passes through $\left(2,\frac{1}{8}\right)$
(d) Equation of the curve is $xy'+3y=0$

10. If $(1+t)\frac{dy}{dt}=ty-1$ and $y(0)=-1$, then $y(1)$ equals:
(a) $e+\frac{1}{2}$ (b) $\frac{1}{2}$ (c) $e-\frac{1}{2}$ (d) $\frac{-1}{2}$

11. Let $y(x)$ be a solution of the differential equation $(1+e^x)y'+ye^x=1$. If $y(0)=2$, then the correct statements from the following are:
(a) $y(-4)=0$
(b) $y(-2)=0$
(c) $y(x)$ has a critical point in the interval $(-1,0)$
(d) $y(x)$ has a critical point in the interval $(-2,-1)$

12. The general solution of the differential equation $x\frac{dy}{dx}=y(\ln y-\ln x+1)$ is:
(a) $y+Ce^x=0$ (b) $y=xe^{Cx}$
(c) $y+xe^{Cx}=0$ (d) $y=e^{Cx}$

13. If $f'(x)-\tan x f(x)=\int_{-\pi/6}^{\pi/6} f(x)dx$ and $f(0)=1$, then $f(\pi/3)-\sqrt{3}\ln 3$ equals:
(a) 1 (b) 2
(c) 3 (d) 4

14. Solution of the differential equation $\frac{dy}{dx}=\frac{2}{x+y}$ is $x+y+2=$ ___:
(a) 1 (b) 0
(c) $Ce^{y/2}$ (d) $\frac{4}{3}$

15. The general solution of the differential equation $\cos x\, dy=y(\sin x-y)dx,\ 0<x<\frac{\pi}{2}$ is:
(a) $y\tan x=\sec x+C$ (b) $y\sec x=\tan x+C$
(c) $\sec x=y(\tan x+C)$ (d) $\tan x=y(\sec x+C)$

16. A solution of the differential equation $\left(\frac{dy}{dx}\right)^2-x\frac{dy}{dx}+y=0$ is:
(a) $y=2$ (b) $y=2x$
(c) $y=2x-4$ (d) $y=2x^2-4$

17. Let $f(x)$ be a differentiable function on the interval $(0,\infty)$ such that $f(1)=1$ and $\lim_{t\to x}\frac{t^2f(x)-x^2f(t)}{t-x}=1$ for all $x\in(0,\infty)$. Then $f(x)$ equals:
(a) $\frac{1}{3x}+\frac{2x^2}{3}$ (b) $\frac{-1}{3x}+\frac{2x^2}{3}$
(c) $\frac{-1}{x}+\frac{4x^2}{3}$ (d) $\frac{1}{x}-\frac{x^2}{3}$

18. Intervals contained in the domain of definition of non-zero solutions of the differential equation $(x-3)^2y'+y=0$ are:
(a) $\left(\frac{-\pi}{2},\frac{\pi}{2}\right)$ (b) $\left(0,\frac{\pi}{2}\right)$
(c) $\left(\frac{\pi}{8},\frac{5\pi}{4}\right)$ (d) $\left(0,\frac{\pi}{8}\right)$

19. If $8\sqrt{x}\sqrt{9+\sqrt{x}}\,dy = \left(\sqrt{4+\sqrt{9+\sqrt{x}}}\right)^{-1} dx$ and $y(0)=\sqrt{7}$, then $y(256)$ equals:

(a) 16 (b) 9
(c) 3 (d) 1

20. If $\left(xy^3 + x^2y^7\right)\dfrac{dy}{dx} = 1$ and $y\left(\dfrac{1}{4}\right) = 1$, then $\left(\dfrac{dy}{dx}\right)_{y=-1}$ equals:

(a) $\dfrac{4}{3}$ (b) $\dfrac{-4}{3}$

(c) $\dfrac{16}{5}$ (d) $\dfrac{-16}{5}$

21. The differential equation of a curve in parametric form is $\dfrac{dx}{dt} = \tan x$, $\dfrac{dy}{dt} = -\sin^2 x$. If the curve passes through $\left(\dfrac{\pi}{2}, 0\right)$, then the equation of the curve in rectangular coordinates is:

(a) $y = \dfrac{1}{2}\cos^2 x$ (b) $y = \sin(2x)$

(c) $y = \cos(2x) + 1$ (d) $y = \sin^2 x - 1$

22. If $\dfrac{dy}{dx} = 2x^3\sqrt{y} - 4xy$ and $y(0) = 0$, then $y(1)$ equals:

(a) $\dfrac{1}{4e^2}$ (b) $\dfrac{1}{e}$

(c) $e^{1/2}$ (d) $e^{3/2}$

23. If $2\dfrac{dy}{dx} = \sqrt{y^2 - 4}$ and $y(0) = 2$, then the correct statements from the following are:

(a) $y(x)$ is an even function
(b) $y(x)$ is an odd function
(c) $y(2) = e + \dfrac{1}{e}$
(d) $y'' = y$

ANSWER KEYS

1. (a)	**2.** (b)	**3.** (d)	**4.** (c)	**5.** (a),(b)	**6.** (b)	**7.** (c)	**8.** (d)	**9.** (c),(d)
10. (d)	**11.** (a),(c)	**12.** (b)	**13.** (b)	**14.** (b),(c)	**15.** (c)	**16.** (c)	**17.** (a)	**18.** (a),(b),(d)
19. (c)	**20.** (d)	**21.** (a)	**22.** (a)	**23.** (a),(c)				

SOLUTIONS

1. (a) The given differential equation can be written as

$$(y''')^{1/2} = x\cos y - x^2(y'')^3$$

$$\Rightarrow \quad y''' = \left(x\cos y - x^2(y'')^3\right)^2$$

which is 3rd order, 1st degree.

2. (b) Differentiating throughout with respect to x, we have

$$yy' = C$$

Putting the value of C in the given differential relation, we have

$$y^2 = 2xyy' + 2(yy')^{3/2}$$

$$\Rightarrow \quad 8(yy')^3 = \left(y^2 - 2xyy'\right)^2$$

which is 1st order, 3rd degree.

3. (d) The given relation and its three successive derivatives are

$$Ae^{2x} + Be^x + C = y \quad \ldots(1)$$

$$2Ae^{2x} + Be^x = y' \quad \ldots(2)$$

$$4Ae^{2x} + Be^x = y'' \quad \ldots(3)$$

$$8Ae^{2x} + Be^x = y''' \quad \ldots(4)$$

The arbitrary constants can be eliminated from the last three equations:

$$\begin{vmatrix} 2A & B & y' \\ 4A & B & y'' \\ 8A & B & y''' \end{vmatrix} = 0$$

$$\Rightarrow \quad \begin{vmatrix} 1 & 1 & y' \\ 2 & 1 & y'' \\ 4 & 1 & y''' \end{vmatrix} = 0$$

$$\Rightarrow \quad y''' - 3y'' + 2y' = 0$$

4. (c) Equation of the family of circles having a fixed radius r is

$$(x-A)^2+(y-B)^2=r^2 \quad \ldots(1)$$

Its two successive derivatives are

$$x-A+(y-B)y'=0 \quad \ldots(2)$$

and $$1+(y')^2+(y-B)y''=0 \quad \ldots(3)$$

From equations (2) and (3), we have

$$y-B=-\frac{1+(y')^2}{y''}$$

and $$x-A=\frac{y'\{1+(y')^2\}}{y''}$$

Putting these values in equation (1), we have

$$r^2(y'')^2-\{(1+(y')^2\}^3=0$$

5. (a),(b) Equation of the family of circles having centres on the line $y=x$ is

$$(x-A)^2+(y-A)^2=B \quad \ldots(1)$$

Its two successive derivatives are

$$x-A+(y-A)y'=0 \quad \ldots(2)$$

and $$1+(y')^2+(y-A)y''=0 \quad \ldots(3)$$

Eliminating A from equations (2) and (3), we have

$$\frac{x+yy'}{y'+1}=\frac{yy''+(y')^2+1}{y''}$$

$$\Rightarrow \quad xy''=yy''+(y')^3+(y')^2+y'+1$$

$$\Rightarrow \quad (y-x)y''+\{(y')^2+y'+1\}y'+1=0$$

$$\Rightarrow \quad P=y-x \text{ and } Q=(y')^2+y'+1$$

6. (b) Let $P(h,k)$ be any point on the curve and p be the slope of the tangent to the curve at P. Equation of the normal at P is

$$y-k=\frac{-1}{p}(x-h)$$

It meets the x-axis at $Q(pk+h,0)$. According to the given condition $PQ=c$, we have

$$(pk)^2+k^2=c^2$$

Now, substituting (x,y) for (h,k) and y' for p, the required differential equation is

$$y^2(y')^2+y^2-c^2=0$$

7. (c) Separating the variables and integrating both sides, we have

$$\int\frac{y}{\sqrt{1-y^2}}dy=\int dx$$

$$\Rightarrow \quad -\sqrt{1-y^2}=x+C$$

$$\Rightarrow \quad (x+C)^2+y^2=1$$

8. (d) Let $P(h,k)$ be any point on the curve and p be the slope of the tangent to the curve at P. Equation of the tangent at P is

$$y-k=p(x-h)$$

It meets the y-axis at $Q(0,k-ph)$. According to the given condition, we have

$$k-ph=h^3$$

Now, substituting (x,y) for (h,k) and y' for p, the required differential equation is

$$xy'=y-x^3$$

$$\Rightarrow \quad \frac{dy}{dx}+\left(\frac{-1}{x}\right)y=-x^2$$

$$\Rightarrow \quad y\left(\frac{1}{x}\right)=\int -x\,dx+C$$

$$\left[\text{IF}=e^{\int\frac{-1}{x}dx}=e^{-\ln x}=\frac{1}{x}\right]$$

$$\Rightarrow \quad y=\frac{-1}{2}x^3+Cx$$

Since $y(1)=1$, $C=\frac{3}{2}$. Hence, the particular solution is $y=\frac{-1}{2}x^3+\frac{3}{2}x$. Now $y(-3)=\frac{27}{2}-\frac{9}{2}=9$.

9. (c),(d) Let $P(h,k)$ be any point on the curve and p be the slope of the tangent to the curve at P. Equation of the tangent at P is

$$y-k=p(x-h)$$

It meets the x-axis at $A\left(h-\frac{k}{p},0\right)$ and the y-axis at $B(0,k-ph)$. According to the given condition $BP:AP=3:1$, we have

$$k=\frac{3(0)+1(k-ph)}{3+1}$$

$$\Rightarrow \quad ph+3k=0$$

Now, substituting (x, y) for (h, k) and y' for p, the required differential equation is $xy'+3y=0$. Hence (d) is correct.

Now, $y'(1,1)=-3$. Equation of the normal at $(1,1)$ is

$$y-1=\frac{1}{3}(x-1) \Rightarrow x-3y+2=0$$

Hence (b) is incorrect.

Separating the variables and integrating both sides, we have

$$\int \frac{1}{y}dy+\int \frac{3}{x}dx=0$$

$\Rightarrow \quad \ln y+3\ln x=\ln C$

$\Rightarrow \quad yx^3=C$

Since the curve passes through $(1,1)$, $C=1$. Hence, the equation of the curve is $yx^3=1$. We see that the curve passes through $\left(2, \frac{1}{8}\right)$. Hence (c) is correct.

10. (d) The given differential equation can be written as

$$\frac{dy}{dt}+\left(\frac{-t}{1+t}\right)y=\frac{1}{1+t}$$

$$y(1+t)e^{-t}=\int e^{-t}\,dt+C$$

$$\left[\text{IF}=e^{\int \frac{-t}{1+t}dt}=e^{-t+\ln(1+t)}=(1+t)e^{-t}\right]$$

$\Rightarrow \quad y(1+t)e^{-t}=-e^{-t}+C$

Since $y(0)=-1$, $C=0$.

Hence, the particular solution is $y=\frac{-1}{1+t}$. Now $y(1)=\frac{-1}{2}$.

11. (a),(c) The given differential equation can be written as

$$\frac{dy}{dx}+\left(\frac{e^x}{1+e^x}\right)y=\frac{1}{1+e^x}$$

$\Rightarrow \quad y\left(1+e^x\right)=\int 1\,dx+C$

$$\left[\text{IF}=e^{\int \frac{e^x}{1+e^x}dx}=e^{\ln\left(1+e^x\right)}=1+e^x\right]$$

$\Rightarrow \quad y\left(1+e^x\right)=x+C$

Since $y(0)=2$, $C=4$.

Hence, the particular solution is $y=\frac{x+4}{1+e^x}$. Now $y(-4)=0$.

Critical point is the point where $y'=0$

$\Rightarrow \quad ye^x=1$ [Putting $y'=0$ in the given differential equation]

$\Rightarrow \quad \frac{x+4}{1+e^x}=e^{-x}$

$\Rightarrow \quad x+4=e^{-x}+1$

$\Rightarrow \quad x+3=e^{-x}$

At $x=-1$, the graph of e^{-x} lies above the graph of $x+3$, and at $x=0$, the graph of e^{-x} lies below the graph of $x+3$. This means that they do intersect at some point in the interval $(-1,0)$. Hence, the equation $y'=0$ does have a solution in this interval.

12. (b) The given differential equation can be written as

$$\frac{dy}{dx}=\frac{y}{x}\left(\ln\frac{y}{x}+1\right)$$

$\Rightarrow \quad v+x\frac{dv}{dx}=v(\ln v+1)$

[Put $y=vx$ and $dy=v\,dx+x\,dv$]

$\Rightarrow \quad x\frac{dv}{dx}=v\ln v$

$\Rightarrow \quad \int \frac{1}{v\ln v}dv-\int \frac{1}{x}dx=0$

$\Rightarrow \quad \ln(\ln v)-\ln(x)=\ln C$

$\Rightarrow \quad \ln\left(\frac{\ln v}{x}\right)=\ln C$

$\Rightarrow \quad \ln v=Cx$

$\Rightarrow \quad v=e^{Cx}$

$\Rightarrow \quad y=xe^{Cx}$

13. (b) The given differential equation can be written as

$$\frac{df}{dx}-\tan x f=a, \text{ where } a=\int_{-\pi/6}^{\pi/6} f(x)dx$$

$$f\cos x=\int a\cos x\,dx+C$$

$$\left[\text{IF}=e^{\int -\tan x\,dx}=e^{\ln(\cos x)}=\cos x\right]$$

$\Rightarrow \quad f\cos x=\int a\cos x\,dx+C$

$\Rightarrow \quad f\cos x=a\sin x+C$

$\Rightarrow \quad f(x)=a\tan x+C\sec x$

Since $f(0)=1$, $C=1$, and hence

$$f(x)=a\tan x+\sec x$$

Now $a=\int_{-\pi/6}^{\pi/6} f(x)dx = a\int_{-\pi/6}^{\pi/6}\tan x\,dx+\int_{-\pi/6}^{\pi/6}\sec x\,dx$

$$=0+2\left|\ln(\sec x+\tan x)\right|_0^{\pi/6}$$

$$=2\ln\left(\sqrt{3}\right)=\ln 3$$

Thus $f(x)=(\ln 3)\tan x+\sec x$. Hence

$$f(\pi/3)-\sqrt{3}\ln 3=2$$

14. (b),(c) The given differential equation can be written as

$$\frac{dx}{dy}+\left(\frac{-1}{2}\right)x=\frac{1}{2}y$$

$$\Rightarrow \quad xe^{-y/2}=\int\frac{1}{2}ye^{-y/2}dy+C$$

$$\left[\text{IF}=e^{\int\frac{-1}{2}dy}=e^{-y/2}\right]$$

$$\Rightarrow \quad xe^{-y/2}=-(y+2)e^{-y/2}+C$$

$$\Rightarrow \quad x+y+2=Ce^{y/2}$$

Hence (b), (c) are correct.

15. (c) The given differential equation can be written as

$$\frac{-1}{y^2}\frac{dy}{dx}+\frac{1}{y}\left(\frac{\sin x}{\cos x}\right)=\frac{1}{\cos x}$$

$$\Rightarrow \quad \frac{du}{dx}+\left(\frac{\sin x}{\cos x}\right)u=\frac{1}{\cos x}$$

$$\left[\text{Put}\ \frac{1}{y}=u \text{ and } \frac{-1}{y^2}\frac{dy}{dx}=\frac{du}{dx}\right]$$

$$\Rightarrow \quad u\sec x=\int\sec^2 x\,dx+C$$

$$\left[\text{IF}=e^{\int\frac{\sin x}{\cos x}dx}=e^{\ln(\sec x)}=\sec x\right]$$

$$\Rightarrow \quad u\sec x=\tan x+C$$

$$\Rightarrow \quad \sec x=y(\tan x+C)$$

16. (c) Check all the options.

17. (a) We have

$$\lim_{t\to x}\frac{t^2f(x)-x^2f(t)}{t-x}=1$$

$$\Rightarrow \quad \lim_{t\to x}\frac{(t^2-x^2)f(t)}{t-x}-\frac{x^2\{f(t)-f(x)\}}{t-x}=1$$

$$\Rightarrow \quad 2xf(x)-x^2f'(x)=1$$

$$\Rightarrow \quad \frac{dy}{dx}+\left(\frac{-2}{x}\right)y=\frac{-1}{x^2}\left[\text{let } f(x)=y\right]$$

$$\Rightarrow \quad y\left(\frac{1}{x^2}\right)=\int\frac{-1}{x^4}dx+C$$

$$\left[\text{IF}=e^{\int\frac{-2}{x}dx}=e^{-2\ln x}=\frac{1}{x^2}\right]$$

$$\Rightarrow \quad y\left(\frac{1}{x^2}\right)=\frac{1}{3x^3}+C$$

Since $y(1)=1$, $C=\frac{2}{3}$. Hence, the particular solution is $y=\frac{1}{3x}+\frac{2x^2}{3}$.

18. (a),(b),(d) Separating the variables and integrating both sides, we have

$$\int\frac{1}{y}dy+\int\frac{1}{(x-3)^2}dx=0$$

$$\Rightarrow \quad \ln y-\frac{1}{x-3}=\ln C$$

$$\Rightarrow \quad \ln\left(\frac{y}{C}\right)=\frac{1}{x-3}$$

$$\Rightarrow \quad y=Ce^{\frac{1}{x-3}}$$

The domain of definition of the above solution is $x\in\mathbf{R}-\{3\}$.

19. (c) The given differential equation can be written as

$$dy=\frac{dt}{2\sqrt{t+4}}\left[\text{Put } 9+\sqrt{x}=t^2 \text{ and } \frac{1}{2\sqrt{x}}dx=2t\,dt\right]$$

$$\Rightarrow \quad y=\sqrt{t+4}+C=\sqrt{4+\sqrt{9+\sqrt{x}}}+C$$

Since $y(0)=\sqrt{7}, C=0$. $y(256)=3$.

20. (d) The given differential equation can be written as

$$\frac{dx}{dy}-y^3x=y^7x^2$$

$$\Rightarrow \quad \frac{-1}{x^2}\frac{dx}{dy}+y^3\frac{1}{x}=-y^7$$

$$\Rightarrow \quad \frac{du}{dy}+y^3u=-y^7$$

$$\left[\text{Put}\ \frac{1}{x}=u \text{ and } \frac{-1}{x^2}\frac{dx}{dy}=\frac{du}{dy}\right]$$

$\Rightarrow \quad ue^{y^4/4} = -\int y^7 e^{y^4/4} dy + C$

$$\left[\text{IF} = e^{\int y^3 dy} = e^{y^4/4}\right]$$

$\Rightarrow \quad ue^{y^4/4} = -\int 4te^t dt + C$

$$\left[\text{Put } y^4 = 4t \text{ and } y^3 = dt\right]$$

$\Rightarrow \quad ue^{y^4/4} = -4(t-1)e^t + C$

$\Rightarrow \quad \frac{1}{x}e^{y^4/4} = (4-y^4)e^{y^4/4} + C$

Since $y\left(\frac{1}{4}\right) = 1$, $C = e^{1/4}$. Hence, the particular solution is $\frac{1}{x} = 4 - y^4 + e^{(1-y^4)/4}$. Now, when $y = -1$, $x = \frac{1}{4}$. Hence

$$\left(\frac{dy}{dx}\right)_{y=-1} = \frac{1}{\frac{1}{4}(-1)^3 + \left(\frac{1}{4}\right)^2(-1)^7} = \frac{-16}{5}$$

21. (a) We have

$$\frac{dy}{dx} = \frac{-\sin^2 x}{\tan x} = -\frac{1}{2}\sin(2x)$$

$\Rightarrow \quad y = \frac{1}{4}\cos(2x) + C$

Since $y\left(\frac{\pi}{2}\right) = 0$, $C = \frac{1}{4}$. Hence, the particular solution is $y = \frac{1}{4}\cos(2x) + \frac{1}{4} = \frac{1}{2}\cos^2 x$.

22. (a) The given differential equation can be written as

$$\frac{1}{\sqrt{y}}\frac{dy}{dx} + 4x\sqrt{y} = 2x^3$$

$\Rightarrow \quad \frac{du}{dx} + 2xu = 2x^3 \left[\text{Insert } 2\sqrt{y} = u\right.$

$$\left.\text{and } \frac{1}{\sqrt{y}}\frac{dy}{dx} = \frac{du}{dx}\right]$$

$\Rightarrow \quad ue^{x^2} = \int 2x^3 e^{x^2} dx + C \left[\text{IF} = e^{\int 2x\,dx} = e^{x^2}\right]$

$\Rightarrow \quad ue^{x^2} = \int te^t dt + C$

$$\left[\text{Insert } x^2 = t \text{ and } 2x\,dx = dt\right]$$

$\Rightarrow \quad ue^{x^2} = (t-1)e^t + C$

$\Rightarrow \quad 2\sqrt{y}e^{x^2} = (x^2-1)e^{x^2} + C$

Since $y(0) = 0$, $C = 1$, and hence, the particular solution is $2\sqrt{y} = x^2 - 1 + e^{-x^2}$. Now $y(1) = \frac{1}{4e^2}$.

23. (a),(c) The given differential equation can be written as

$$\int \frac{1}{\sqrt{y^2-4}} dy = \frac{1}{2}\int dx$$

$\Rightarrow \quad \ln\left|y + \sqrt{y^2-4}\right| = \frac{1}{2}x + \text{constant}$

$\Rightarrow \quad y + \sqrt{y^2-4} = Ce^{x/2}$

Since $y(0) = 2$, $C = 2$. Hence, the particular solution is $y + \sqrt{y^2-4} = 2e^{x/2}$. If we rationalise the left-hand-side, we have $y - \sqrt{y^2-4} = 2e^{-x/2}$. Now adding these two equations, we get

$$y = e^{x/2} + e^{-x/2}$$

Now, we can see that $y(x) = y(-x) \Rightarrow y(x)$ is an even function, and $y(2) = e + \frac{1}{e}$.

Differentiating twice, we have

$$y'' = \frac{1}{4}\left(e^{x/2} + e^{-x/2}\right) = \frac{1}{4}y$$

Hence, options (a) and (c) are correct.

PART III

COORDINATE GEOMETRY

CHAPTER

26 Straight Line

- **Distance Formula:** The distance between points $A(x_1, y_1)$ and $B(x_2, y_2)$ is

$$AB = \sqrt{(x_2 - x_1)^2 + (y_2 - y_1)^2}$$

- **Section Formula:** If P is a point on the line joining points $A(x_1, y_1)$ and $B(x_2, y_2)$, such that $PA : PB = m : n$, then

$$P = \left(\frac{mx_2 \pm nx_1}{m \pm n}, \frac{my_2 \pm ny_1}{m \pm n}\right)$$

The + sign gives the internal point; the – sign gives the external point.

- **Slope:** The slope of a line is $\tan\theta$, where θ is the angle that the line makes with the +ve direction of the x-axis. If $A(x_1, y_1)$ and $B(x_2, y_2)$ are any two points on the line, then

$$\text{Slope of} = \tan\theta = \frac{y_2 - y_1}{x_2 - x_1}$$

Three points A, B and C are collinear if slope of AB = slope of AC.

- **Angle Between Two Lines:** The acute angle θ between two lines with slopes m_1 and m_2 is given by

$$\tan\theta = \left|\frac{m_1 - m_2}{1 + m_1 m_2}\right|$$

Two lines are parallel if $m_1 = m_2$ and perpendicular if $m_1 m_2 = -1$.

The slope m of the angular bisectors of two lines with slopes m_1 and m_2 can be found by solving the equation

$$\frac{m_1 - m}{1 + mm_1} = \frac{m - m_2}{1 + mm_2}$$

- **Equation of a Line:** The equation of a line with slope m and passing through the point $A(x_1, y_1)$ is

$$y - y_1 = m(x - x_1)$$

Equation of a line passing through the points $A(x_1, y_1)$ and $B(x_2, y_2)$ is

$$y - y_1 = \left(\frac{y_2 - y_1}{x_2 - x_1}\right)(x - x_1)$$

Equation of a line with slope m and y intercept c is

$$y = mx + c$$

Equation of a line with x intercept a and y intercept b is

$$\frac{x}{a} + \frac{y}{b} = 1$$

Equation of a line whose perpendicular distance from the origin is p, and the angle made by the normal with the $+x$ direction is α is

$$x\cos\alpha + y\sin\alpha = p$$

- Two given lines $a_1x+b_1y+c_1=0$ and $a_2x+b_2y+c_2=0$ represent

$$\text{Identical lines if } \frac{a_1}{a_2}=\frac{b_1}{b_2}=\frac{c_1}{c_2}$$

$$\text{Parallel lines if } \frac{a_1}{a_2}=\frac{b_1}{b_2}\neq\frac{c_1}{c_2}$$

$$\text{Perpendicular lines if } a_1a_2+b_1b_2=0$$

- Three given lines $a_1x+b_1y+c_1=0, a_2x+b_2y+c_2=0$ and $a_3x+b_3y+c_3=0$ are concurrent if

$$\begin{vmatrix} a_1 & b_1 & c_1 \\ a_2 & b_2 & c_2 \\ a_3 & b_3 & c_3 \end{vmatrix}=0$$

- Slope m of a line inclined at angle α to a given line with slope m_0: $m=\dfrac{m_0\pm\tan\alpha}{1\mp m_0\tan\alpha}$.

  The + sign gives the slope for anticlockwise inclination; the – sign gives the slope for clockwise inclination.

- **Perpendicular Distance:** The perpendicular distance AM of a point $A(x_1, y_1)$ from the line $L(x, y)\equiv ax+by+c=0$ is given by

$$AM=\frac{|L(x_1, y_1)|}{\sqrt{a^2+b^2}}$$

  Perpendicular distance d between two parallel lines $ax+by+c_1=0$ and $ax+by+c_2=0$ is given by

$$d=\frac{|c_2-c_1|}{\sqrt{a^2+b^2}}$$

- **Relative Position:** The relative position of a point $P(x_1, y_1)$ with respect to the line $L(x, y)\equiv ax+by+c=0$:

$$\text{If } \frac{L(x_1, y_1)}{b}>0\Rightarrow \text{Point } P \text{ lies above line } L.$$

$$\text{If } \frac{L(x_1, y_1)}{b}<0\Rightarrow \text{Point } P \text{ lies below line } L.$$

  The ratio in which the line $L(x, y)\equiv ax+by+c=0$ divides the line joining two points $A(x_1, y_1)$ and $B(x_2, y_2)$:

$$\frac{PB}{PA}=-\frac{L(x_2, y_2)}{L(x_1, y_1)}$$

- **Angular Bisectors:** The angular bisectors of the two given lines $L_1(x, y)\equiv a_1x+b_1y+c_1=0$ and $L_2(x, y)\equiv a_2x+b_2y+c_2=0$: If the above equations are written such that the constants c_1 and c_2 are of the same sign, then

$$a_1a_2+b_1b_2<0\Rightarrow \text{Angle containing the origin is acute}$$

$$a_1a_2+b_1b_2>0\Rightarrow \text{Angle containing the origin is obtuse}$$

  Equations of the angular bisectors are

$$\frac{L_1(x, y)}{\sqrt{a_1^2+b_1^2}}=\pm\frac{L_2(x, y)}{\sqrt{a_2^2+b_2^2}}$$

  The + sign corresponds to the angular bisector of the angle which contains the origin; the – sign corresponds to the angular bisector of the angle which does not contain the origin.

- **Family of Lines:**
  1. Equation of any line passing through a given point $A(x_1, y_1)$ can be written as
  $$y - y_1 = \lambda(x, -x_1)$$
  2. Equation of any line of a given slope m can be written as
  $$y = mx + \lambda$$
  3. Equation of any line passing through the intersection point of two given lines $L_1(x, y) = 0$ and $L_2(x, y) = 0$ can be written as
  $$L_1(x, y) + \lambda L_2(x, y) = 0$$
- **Triangle:** For a triangle whose vertices are $A(x_1, y_1), B(x_2, y_2)$ and $C(x_3, y_3)$:

$$\text{Area of the triangle} = \text{mod of } \frac{1}{2}\begin{vmatrix} x_1 & y_1 & 1 \\ x_2 & y_2 & 1 \\ x_3 & y_3 & 1 \end{vmatrix}$$

$$\text{Centroid } G = \left(\frac{x_1 + x_2 + x_3}{3}, \frac{y_1 + y_2 + y_3}{3}\right)$$

$$\text{Incentre } I = \left(\frac{ax_1 + bx_2 + cx_3}{a+b+c}, \frac{ay_1 + by_2 + cy_3}{a+b+c}\right)$$

The circumcentre is the intersection point of the perpendicular bisectors of the sides of the triangle. The orthocentre is the intersection point of the three perpendiculars drawn from the vertices to their opposite sides. For a right-angled triangle, the mid-point of the hypotenuse is the circumcentre; the right-angled vertex is the orthocentre.

For any triangle, its circumcentre C, its centroid G and its orthocentre H are collinear points and G divides the line joining C and H in the ratio $1:2$.

- **Parallelogram:** The area of a parallelogram is given by

$$\text{Area of a parallelogram} = \frac{p_1 p_2}{\sin \alpha},$$

where p_1, p_2 are the perpendicular distances between the two sets of parallel sides and α is the acute angle between its adjacent sides.

EXERCISES

1. Consider the triangle with vertices $(0,0), (0,21)$ and $(21,0)$. The number of integral points (points with integer coordinates) in the interior of this triangle is:
(a) 133 (b) 190
(c) 233 (d) 105

2. Consider the lines $2ax + 4ay + b = 0$ and $5cx + 2cy + d = 0$, where $a, b, c, d \in \mathbf{R}$. If these two lines intersect in the fourth quadrant at a point which is equidistant from the coordinate axes, then:
(a) $2ac - 3bd = 0$ (b) $2ad + 3bc = 0$
(c) $2ad - 3bc = 0$ (d) $2ac + 3bd = 0$

3. The number of integer values of m for which the abscissa of the intersection point of the lines $3x + 4y = 9$ and $y = mx + 1$ is also an integer is:
(a) 2 (b) 0
(c) 4 (d) 1

4. Area of the parallelogram formed by the lines $y = mx$, $y = mx + 1$, $y = nx$ and $y = nx + 1$ equals:
(a) $\dfrac{|m+n|}{(m-n)^2}$ (b) $\dfrac{2}{|m+n|}$
(c) $\dfrac{1}{|m+n|}$ (d) $\dfrac{1}{|m-n|}$

5. The straight lines $x + y = 0$, $3x + y = 0$ and $x + 3y - 4 = 0$ form a triangle which is:
(a) Isosceles (b) Equilateral
(c) Right-angled (d) None of these

6. Equation of a line which passes through the point $(-1,-2)$ and makes an intercept of length 3 between the lines $4x+3y=3$ and $4x+3y=12$ is:
(a) $24y+7x+55=0$ (b) $x+1=0$
(c) $11y+6x+28=0$ (d) $\sqrt{3}y+x+2\sqrt{3}=0$

7. The points $A(p,0)$, $B(1,4)$ and $C(5,6)$ are the vertices of a triangle. If $\angle ABC$ is obtuse, then the greatest integral value of p is:
(a) 3 (b) 2
(c) 1 (d) 0

8. If the vertices of a triangle are rational points (points with rational coordinates), then the triangle cannot be:
(a) Right-angled (b) Isosceles
(c) Equilateral (d) None of these

9. Two sides of a rhombus are along $x-y+1=0$ and $7x-y-5=0$. If its diagonals intersect at $(-1,3)$, then which of the following is a vertex of the rhombus?
(a) $(-3,-8)$ (b) $(-4,-3)$
(c) $\left(\frac{-10}{3},\frac{-7}{3}\right)$ (d) $(-3,4)$

10. If the straight line $ax+by+c=0$ divides the line joining points $A(-1,2)$, $B(3,-1)$ externally in the ratio $2:3$, then it passes through the fixed point:
(a) $(-3,5)$ (b) $(-9,8)$
(c) $(4,-3)$ (d) $(6,-5)$

11. A rod of length 3 units moves such that its ends A and B always lie on the lines $3x-y+4=0$ and $y+2=0$, respectively. The locus of point P which divides AB internally in the ratio $2:1$ is:
(a) $x^2-xy+4y^2+6y-8=0$
(b) $x^2+3xy+y^2+11x+14=0$
(c) $x^2-2xy+5y^2+16y+12=0$
(d) $2x^2-2xy+y^2+6y+12=0$

12. Lines $L_1: y-x=0$ and $L_2: 2x+y=0$ intersect the line $L_3: y+2=0$ at P and Q, respectively. The bisector of the acute angle between L_1 and L_2 intersects L_3 at R. Then $PR:RQ$ equals:
(a) $2:1$ (b) $\sqrt{2}+1:2$
(c) $2\sqrt{2}:\sqrt{5}$ (d) $3:\sqrt{2}$

13. If the point $P=(a,a^2)$, where $a\in R$ lies above $L_1: 2y-x=0$ and below $L_2: 2y-3x=0$, then a belongs to the set:
(a) $a\in\left(0,\frac{1}{2}\right)$ (b) $a\in(3,+\infty)$
(c) $a\in\left(\frac{1}{2},\frac{3}{2}\right)$ (d) $a\in\left(-3,\frac{-1}{2}\right)$

14. Let $O(0,0)$, $A(2,0)$ and $B(1,1/\sqrt{3})$ be the vertices of a triangle. Let R be the region consisting of all points P inside ΔOAB which satisfy $d(P,OA)\le\min\{d(P,OB),d(P,AB)\}$, where d denotes the distance of point P from the corresponding line. Area of the region R is:
(a) $\sqrt{3}$ (b) $\sqrt{3}$
(c) $2+\sqrt{3}$ (d) $2-\sqrt{3}$

15. A variable triangle ΔABC is such that A is at $(1,2)$, whereas B and C lie on the line $y=x+\lambda$ (where λ is a variable). Then the locus of the orthocentre of ΔABC is:
(a) $x^2=y-1$ (b) $x+y=3$
(c) $(x-1)^2+y^2=4$ (d) $2x-y=0$

16. The point $(-3,8)$ undergoes the following transformations successively: Reflection about the line $x+y=0$, translation of 10 units parallel to the line $4x+3y+1=0$ in the direction of decreasing ordinates, and rotation through angle $\pi/4$ in the anti-clockwise direction about the origin. The final position of the point is:
(a) $\left(\frac{7}{\sqrt{2}},\frac{-3}{\sqrt{2}}\right)$ (b) $\left(\frac{3}{\sqrt{2}},\frac{-1}{\sqrt{2}}\right)$
(c) $\left(\frac{1}{\sqrt{2}},\frac{-3}{\sqrt{2}}\right)$ (d) $\left(\frac{3}{\sqrt{2}},\frac{-7}{\sqrt{2}}\right)$

17. Let $0<\alpha<\frac{\pi}{2}$ be a fixed angle. If $P=(\cos\theta,\sin\theta)$ and $Q=(\cos(\alpha-\theta),\sin(\alpha-\theta))$, then Q is obtained from P by:
(a) Clockwise rotation around the origin through an angle α
(b) Anti-clockwise rotation around the origin through an angle α
(c) Reflection in the line through the origin with slope $\tan\alpha$
(d) Reflection in the line through the origin with slope $\tan\left(\frac{\alpha}{2}\right)$

18. Consider points $A=(2,0)$ and $B=(0,2)$. If P is a point lying on the line $2x+3y+1=0$ such that $|PB-PA|$ is greatest, then P equals:

(a) $\left(\frac{7}{2},\frac{-8}{3}\right)$ (b) $\left(\frac{1}{2},\frac{-2}{3}\right)$

(c) $\left(\frac{-1}{5},\frac{-1}{5}\right)$ (d) $(7,-5)$

19. A triangle has vertices at $(a\cos t, a\sin t)$, $(b\sin t, -b\cos t)$ and $(1,0)$, where t is a parameter. The locus of the centroid of these triangles is:

(a) $(x-3a)^2+y^2=a^2+b^2$

(b) $9x^2+9y^2=a^2+b^2-1$

(c) $(x-1)^2+y^2=9(a^2+b^2)$

(d) $(3x-1)^2+9y^2=a^2+b^2$

20. Let $A(2,-3)$ and $B(-2,1)$ be the vertices of a triangle ABC. If the centroid of this triangle moves on the line $2x+3y=1$, the locus of the vertex C is:

(a) $x+3y=-2$ (b) $3x-y=2$

(c) $2x+3y=9$ (d) $x-2y=1$

21. If the distance between points $A(x_1,y_1)$ and $B(x_2,y_2)$ is defined as $d=|x_1-x_2|+|y_1-y_2|$, then the locus of point P lying in the first quadrant and equidistant from the origin and $(3,2)$ is:

(a) $y=2.5(x\geq 3)$

(b) $x-y=0.5(0\leq x\leq 3 \text{ and } y\geq 2)$

(c) $x=0.5(y\geq 2)$

(d) $x+y=2.5(0\leq x\leq 3 \text{ and } 0\leq y\leq 2)$

22. The locus of the orthocentre of a triangle formed by the lines $(1+p)x-py+p(1+p)=0$, $(1+q)x-qy+q(1+q)=0$ and $y=0$, where p and q are real numbers $(p\neq q)$, is:

(a) A hyperbola (b) A parabola

(c) An ellipse (d) A straight line

23. The sides of a quadrilateral are given by $|x+y|+|x-y|=4$. Its area is:

(a) 16 (b) 8

(c) 4 (d) 2

24. Area of the triangle formed by the intersection of a line parallel to the x-axis and passing through $P(h,k)$, with the lines $y=x$ and $x+y=2$ is $4h^2$. The locus of point P is:

(a) $y=1\pm x$ (b) $y=1\pm 2x$

(c) $y=-1\pm 2x$ (d) None of these

25. If $4a^2+9b^2-c^2+12ab=0$, then the family of straight lines $ax+by+c=0$ passes through the fixed point:

(a) $(-2,-3)$ or $(2,3)$ (b) $(-2,-3)$ or $(0,0)$

(c) $(2,3)$ or $(0,0)$ (d) None of these

26. If a light ray coming along the line $3x+4y=5$ is reflected from the line $ax+by=1$ and travels along the line $5x-12y=10$, then:

(a) $a=\frac{64}{115}, b=\frac{112}{15}$ (b) $a=\frac{14}{15}, b=\frac{72}{15}$

(c) $a=\frac{64}{115}, b=\frac{-8}{115}$ (d) $a=\frac{64}{15}, b=\frac{-14}{15}$

27. Two rays $x+y=|a|$ and $ax-y=1$ intersect each other in the first quadrant if $a\in(a_0,+\infty)$. The value of a_0 is:

(a) -1 (b) 1

(c) 0 (d) 2

28. If $y=(a-b)x^2+(b-c)x+(c-a)$ touches the x-axis, then the line $ax+by+c=0$:

(a) Passes through a fixed point

(b) Is a family of parallel lines

(c) Data is insufficient

(d) None of these.

29. One side of an equilateral triangle lies along the line $x+y=1$. If the circumcentre of the triangle lies at the origin, then the equation of the other two sides of the triangle is:

(a) $y+1=(2\pm\sqrt{3})(x+1)$

(b) $y+1=(1\pm\sqrt{3})(x+1)$

(c) $y+1=(\sqrt{3}+2)(x+1)$

(d) $y+1=(\sqrt{3}\pm 1)(x+1)$

30. The vertices B and C of a triangle ABC lie on the lines $3y=4x$ and $y=0$, respectively, and the side BC passes through $\left(\frac{2}{3},\frac{2}{3}\right)$. If $ABOC$ is a rhombus, O being the origin, the equation of BC and coordinates of A are, respectively:

(a) $2x+y-1=0, \left(\frac{6}{5},\frac{2}{5}\right)$

(b) $2x+y-2=0, \left(\frac{8}{5},\frac{4}{5}\right)$

(c) $x+2y-2=0, \left(\frac{4}{5},\frac{8}{5}\right)$

(d) $x+y-2=0, \left(\frac{4}{5},\frac{4}{5}\right)$

31. Locus of the mirror image of the point (4, 3) about the variable line $y = mx + 2$ is:
(a) $x^2 + y^2 - 4y - 13 = 0$ (b) $x^2 + y^2 - 4y - 21 = 0$
(c) $x^2 + y^2 - 4x - 5 = 0$ (d) $x^2 + y^2 - 25 = 0$

32. A man starts walking from point $P(1,2)$ and reaches point $Q(3,4)$, touching the x-axis at point R, such that $PR + RQ$ is minimum. The coordinates of R are:
(a) $(5,0)$ (b) $\left(\frac{5}{3},0\right)$
(c) $\left(\frac{3}{2},0\right)$ (d) $(2,0)$

33. Two equal sides of an isosceles triangle are $7x - y + 3 = 0$ and $x + y - 3 = 0$. If the third side passes through $(1,-10)$, then its equation is:
(a) $3x + y + 7 = 0$ (b) $x + 3y + 30 = 0$
(c) $x - 3y - 31 = 0$ (d) $3x - y - 33 = 0$

34. Consider the family of straight lines $\sqrt{a}x + \sqrt{b}y + \sqrt{c} = 0, (a > b > c > 0)$ such that $\frac{a}{\sqrt{bc}} + 2 = \frac{\sqrt{b}}{\sqrt{c}} + \frac{\sqrt{c}}{\sqrt{b}}$. Equation of the straight line belonging to this family that is farthest from the point $P(3,-2)$ is:
(a) $2x - y - 3 = 0$ (b) $2x - y + 3 = 0$
(c) $x - 2y - 3 = 0$ (d) $x - 2y + 3 = 0$

35. Let L be the line belonging to the family of straight lines $(a+2b)x + (a-b)y + a - 7b = 0$, $a, b \in \mathbf{R}$, and farthest from the point $(-13, 7)$.
Then the equation of the line L is:
(a) $3x - 2y - 12 = 0$ (b) $x + 4y + 10 = 0$
(c) $4x - y - 5 = 0$ (d) $3x - 5y - 21 = 0$

36. The range of t for which the points $(t, 2+t)$ and $\left(\frac{3}{2}t, t^2\right)$ lie on opposite sides of the line $2x + 3y = 6$ is:
(a) $(-2, 1)$ (b) $(-\infty,-2)\cup(0,1)$
(c) $(-2,0)\cup(1,+\infty)$ (d) $(-1,0)\cup(2,+\infty)$

37. Let ABC be a triangle with $AB = AC$. D is the mid-point of BC, E is the foot of the perpendicular from D to AC, and F is the mid-point of DE. If θ is the acute angle between lines AF and BE, then the value of $4\sin\theta$ equals:
(a) 4 (b) 3
(c) $3\sqrt{2}$ (d) $2\sqrt{3}$

38. The sides of a rhombus $OABC$ (O is the origin) are along the lines $\sqrt{3}y = x$ and $y = \sqrt{3}x$. If the rhombus lies in the 1st quadrant and has an area of 2 sq. units, then the possible coordinates of B are:
(a) $\left(1+\sqrt{3}, 1+\sqrt{3}\right)$ (b) $\left(2-\sqrt{3}, 2-\sqrt{3}\right)$
(c) $\left(\sqrt{3}-1, \sqrt{3}-1\right)$ (d) None of these

39. The vertices of a triangle ABC are $A(1,3), B(2,3)$ and $C(t, 2t+3)$, where $t \in \mathbf{Z}$. If the greatest integer less than or equal to the triangle's area equals 5 sq. units, then the possible coordinates of C are:
(a) $(2,7)$ (b) $(5,13)$
(c) $\left(\frac{-11}{2},-8\right)$ (d) $(-3,-3)$

40. A variable line through $P(-1,2)$ meets the coordinate axes at A and B. A point Q is now chosen on the line such that PA, PQ, PB are in harmonic progression and A, Q, B lie on the same side of P. Then the locus of Q is:
(a) $y = 2x + 1$ (b) $2y = x + 1$
(c) $2y = x$ (d) $y = 2x$

41. Two sides of a rhombus are parallel to $y = \sqrt{3}x$ and $\sqrt{3}y = x$. The diagonals of the rhombus intersect at (1,2). If one vertex of the rhombus lies on the y-axis, then the possible values of its ordinate are:
(a) 1 (b) 2
(c) 3 (d) 4

42. A variable line through $P(2,3)$ meets the coordinate axes at A and B. If O is the origin, and the rectangle $OAPB$ is completed, then the locus of P is:
(a) $3x + 2y = 6$ (b) $2x + 3y = xy$
(c) $3x + 2y = xy$ (d) $3x + 2y = 6xy$

43. A triangle has two of its sides along the lines $y = mx$ and $y = nx$, where m,n are the roots of the equation $3x^2 + 10x + 1 = 0$. If $H(6,2)$ is the orthocentre of the triangle, then the equation of its third side is:
(a) $x - 3y + 4 = 0$ (b) $x - 3y + 3 = 0$
(c) $3x + y + 2 = 0$ (d) $3x + y + 1 = 0$

44. The angular bisectors of the lines $2mx + (3-m)y + 1 = 0$ and $x + 2my + 1 - m = 0$ intersect the x-axis to form a triangle. Then the locus of the orthocentre of the triangle is:
(a) $2x^2 - xy + 6y^2 + 2y + 1 = 0$
(b) $6x^2 - xy + 2y^2 + 2y + 1 = 0$
(c) $2x^2 - xy + 6y^2 + 2x + 1 = 0$
(d) $6x^2 - xy + 2y^2 + 2x + 1 = 0$

ANSWER KEYS

1. (b)	**2.** (b)	**3.** (a)	**4.** (d)	**5.** (a)	**6.** (a),(b)	**7.** (b)	**8.** (c)	**9.** (b),(d)
10. (b)	**11.** (c)	**12.** (c)	**13.** (c)	**14.** (d)	**15.** (b)	**16.** (d)	**17.** (d)	**18.** (d)
19. (d)	**20.** (c)	**21.** (c),(d)	**22.** (d)	**23.** (a)	**24.** (b)	**25.** (a)	**26.** (c)	**27.** (b)
28. (a)	**29.** (a)	**30.** (b)	**31.** (a)	**32.** (b)	**33.** (a),(c)	**34.** (a)	**35.** (a)	**36.** (b)
37. (a)	**38.** (a)	**39.** (b)	**40.** (d)	**41.** (a),(c)	**42.** (c)	**43.** (d)	**44.** (c)	

SOLUTIONS

1. (b) On the line $x = 1$, there are 19 such points, namely, $(1,1),(1,2),\ldots(1,19)$.
On the line $x = 2$, there are 18 such points, namely, $(2,1),(2,2),\ldots(2,18)$.
…
On the line $x = 19$, there is 1 such point, $(19,1)$.
Hence, the total number of such points is

$$19+18+\ldots+2+1=\frac{19(19+1)}{2}=190.$$

2. (b) Let $(h,-h)$ be their intersection point. Then, we have

$-2ah+b=0$ and $3ch+d=0$.

Eliminating h gives $2ad+3bc=0$.

3. (a) The x coordinate of the intersection point of the given lines is $\frac{5}{3+4m}$.
It will be an integer iff

$$3+4m=\pm1,\pm5 \text{ gives } m=\frac{-1}{2},-1,\frac{1}{2},-2$$

Hence, there are only two integer values of m.

4. (d) Perpendicular distances between the two parallel sides

$$p_1=\frac{1}{\sqrt{1+m^2}} \text{ and } p_2=\frac{1}{\sqrt{1+n^2}}$$

Angle between two adjacent sides of the parallelogram

$$\tan\theta=\frac{|m-n|}{|1+mn|}$$

$$\Rightarrow \quad \sin\theta=\frac{|m-n|}{\sqrt{(m-n)^2+(1+mn)^2}}$$

$$=\frac{|m-n|}{\sqrt{(1+m^2)(1+n^2)}}$$

Area of the parallelogram $=\frac{p_1p_2}{\sin\theta}=\frac{1}{|m-n|}$.

5. (a) Slopes of the three sides in descending order are $\frac{-1}{3},-1,-3$. The angles of the triangle are

$$\tan\alpha=\frac{-\frac{1}{3}+1}{1+\frac{1}{3}}=\frac{1}{2},\ \tan\beta=\frac{-1+3}{1+3}=\frac{1}{2}$$

and $$\tan\gamma=\frac{-3+\frac{1}{3}}{1+1}=\frac{-4}{3}$$

Hence, the given triangle is isosceles.

6. (a),(b) The perpendicular distance between the two parallel lines is $\frac{12}{5}$. The line which makes an intercept of length 3 must be inclined at angle θ (see figure) with the parallel lines such that

$$3\cos\theta=\frac{12}{5}\Rightarrow\cos\theta=\frac{4}{5}\Rightarrow\tan\theta=\frac{3}{4}.$$

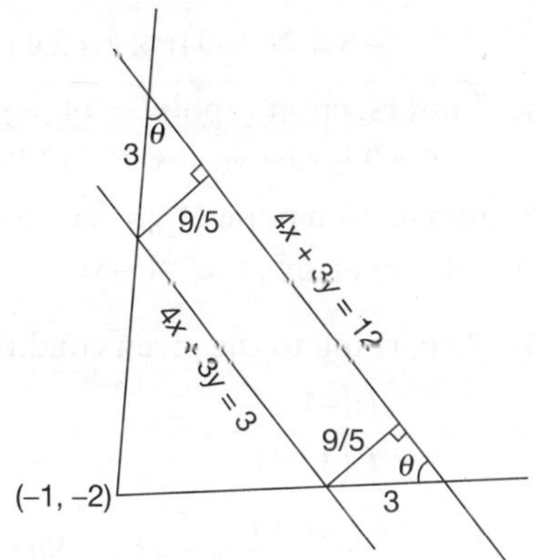

The slopes of the required lines will be

$$\frac{\frac{-4}{3}+\tan\theta}{1-\frac{-4}{3}\tan\theta}=\frac{-7}{24} \text{ and } \frac{\frac{-4}{3}-\tan\theta}{1+\frac{-4}{3}\tan\theta}=\infty$$

Equations of the required lines will be

$$\frac{y+2}{x+1}=\frac{-7}{24},\infty$$

$\Rightarrow$ $24y+7x+55=0$ and $x+1=0$

7. (b) Slope of $=\frac{4}{1-p}$ and slope of $BC=\frac{1}{2}$.

If $\angle ABC$ is obtuse, then

$$\frac{\frac{1}{2}-\frac{4}{1-p}}{1+\frac{2}{1-p}}<0\Rightarrow\frac{p+7}{p-3}<0$$

$\Rightarrow$ $-7<p<3$

Hence, the greatest integral value of p is 2.

8. (c) Area of an equilateral triangle of side a equals $\frac{\sqrt{3}}{4}a^2$, which is an irrational number, whereas area of a triangle with rational vertices will be rational. Hence, by contradiction, a triangle with rational vertices cannot be equilateral.

9. (b),(d) Intersection point of the given lines $x-y+1=0$ and $7x-y-5=0$ is $A=(1,2)$.
Let the opposite vertex be $C=(h,k)$. Then

$\frac{h+1}{2}=-1$ gives $h=-3$

and $\frac{k+2}{2}=3$ gives $k=4$. Hence $C=(-3,4)$.

Slope of diagonal AC is $-1/2$. Hence, slope of the other diagonal BD equals 2.
Equation of diagonal BD is

$$y-3=2(x+1)\Rightarrow y=2x+5$$

The intersection point of $y=2x+5$ and $7x-y-5=0$ is one vertex $B=(2,9)$.
The intersection point of $y=2x+5$ and $x-y+1=0$ is the other vertex $D=(-4,-3)$.

10. (b) According to the given condition, we have

$$-\frac{L(-1,2)}{L(3,-1)}=-\frac{2}{3}$$

$$\Rightarrow\quad\frac{-a+2b+c}{3a-b+c}=\frac{2}{3}\Rightarrow c=9a-8b$$

Equation of the line can now be written as

$$ax+by+9a-8b=0$$

$$\Rightarrow\quad a(x+9)+b(y-8)=0$$

This represents a family of lines all passing through the point $(-9,8)$.

Alternative: The point which divides AB externally in the ratio $2:3$ is $P(-9,8)$. All these lines will pass through P.

11. (c) Let $A=(a,3a+4)$, $B=(b,-2)$ and $P=(h,k)$. Then

$$3h=2b+a \text{ and } k=a$$

$$\Rightarrow\quad a=k \text{ and } b=\frac{3h-k}{2}$$

Now $AB=3$, hence

$$(a-b)^2+(3a+6)^2=9$$

$$\Rightarrow\quad\frac{9}{4}(h-k)^2+9(k+2)^2=9$$

$$\Rightarrow\quad(h-k)^2+4(k+2)^2=4$$

$$\Rightarrow\quad x^2-2xy+5y^2+16y+12=0$$

12. (c)

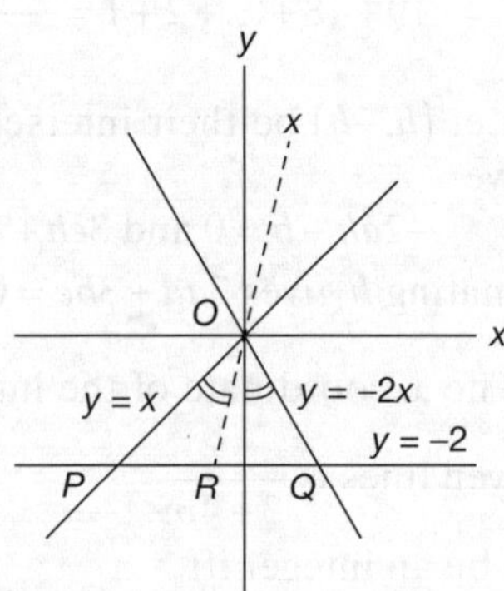

The coordinates of points P and Q are $(-2,-2)$ and $(1,-2)$, respectively (see figure). Since OR is the angular bisector of $\angle POQ$

$$\frac{PR}{QR}=\frac{OP}{OQ}=\frac{2\sqrt{2}}{\sqrt{5}}$$

13. (c) Point (a,a^2) must satisfy the inequalities

$$a^2>\frac{1}{2}a\Rightarrow a\left(a-\frac{1}{2}\right)>0\Rightarrow a\in(\in-\infty,0)\cup\left(\frac{1}{2},+\infty\right)$$

and $$a^2<\frac{3}{2}a\Rightarrow a\left(a-\frac{3}{2}\right)<0\Rightarrow a\in\left(0,\frac{3}{2}\right).$$

Intersection of the two solution sets gives $a\in\left(\frac{1}{2},\frac{3}{2}\right)$.

14. (d)

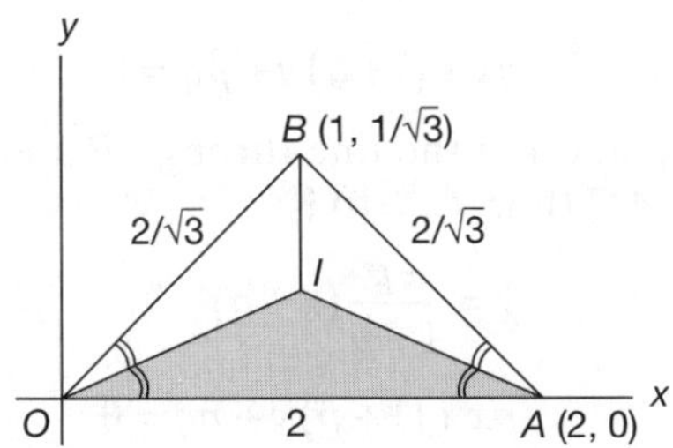

The figure shows the lengths of the sides of the triangle. Let I be the intersection point of the internal angular bisectors of ΔOAB. Then

$$I=\left(\frac{2\sqrt{3}(2)+2\sqrt{3}(0)+2(1)}{2\sqrt{3}+2\sqrt{3}+2},\right.$$

$$\left.\frac{2\sqrt{3}(0)+2\sqrt{3}(0)+2(1/\sqrt{3})}{2\sqrt{3}+2\sqrt{3}+2}\right)$$

$$=\left(1,\frac{1}{2+\sqrt{3}}\right)=\left(1,2-\sqrt{3}\right)$$

According to the given condition, point P is nearest to line OA. All points lying inside ΔOIA satisfy this condition. Hence, area of the required region is

$$\text{Area}=\frac{1}{2}\times 2\times\left(2-\sqrt{3}\right)=\left(2-\sqrt{3}\right)$$

15. (d) Equation of the altitude through $A(1,2)$ and perpendicular to side BC (line $y=x+\lambda$) is

$$x+y=3$$

The orthocentre of ΔABC will always lie on the above line. Hence, this is the required locus.

16. (d) The first transformation takes $P(-3,8)$ to $Q(-8,3)$. The second transformation takes it to $R(-8+10\cos\theta, 3-10\sin\theta)$, where $\tan\theta=\frac{4}{3}\Rightarrow\cos\theta=\frac{3}{5},\sin\theta=\frac{4}{5}$ (see figure), that is, $R(-2,-5)$. The third transformation takes it to, say $S(h,k)$.

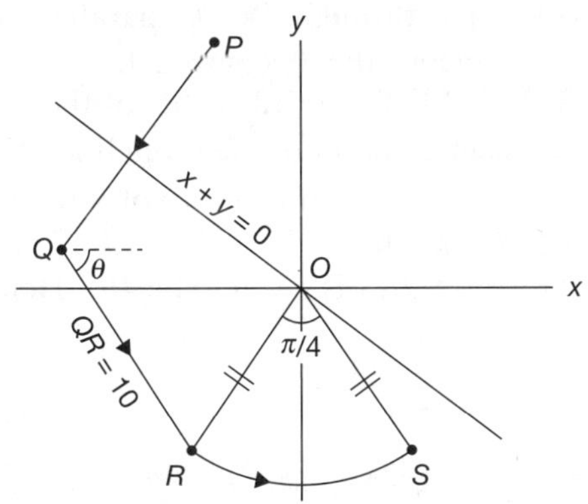

From the figure, we see that $OR=OS$. Hence

$$h^2+k^2=2^2+5^2=29$$

Slope of $OS=\frac{k}{h}$, slope of $OR=\frac{5}{2}$ and angle between them is $\frac{\pi}{4}$. Hence

$$\frac{\frac{k}{h}-\frac{5}{2}}{1+\frac{5k}{2h}}=\tan\left(\frac{\pi}{4}\right)\Rightarrow k=\frac{-7}{3}h$$

Solving the two equations gives $h=\frac{3}{\sqrt{2}}$ and $k=\frac{-7}{\sqrt{2}}$.

17. (d) Lines OP and OQ are inclined at angles θ and $\alpha-\theta$, respectively, to the x-axis. The angular bisector of OP and OQ is inclined at angle $\frac{\alpha-\theta+\theta}{2}=\frac{\alpha}{2}$ to the x-axis.

Hence, P and Q are reflections in the line through the origin having slope $\tan\left(\frac{\alpha}{2}\right)$.

18. (d) For any triangle, we know that the difference between any two sides is less than the third side. Hence $|PB-PA|\le AB$. The greatest value equals $AB=2\sqrt{2}$ when P is collinear with AB. In that case, P is the intersection point of the given line with the line joining A and B, that is, $x+y=2$. Hence $P=(7,-5)$.

19. (d) Let (h,k) be the coordinates of the centroid. Then

$$h=\frac{a\cos t+b\sin t+1}{3}\text{ and }k=\frac{a\sin t-b\cos t+0}{3}$$

$\Rightarrow\quad 3h-1=a\cos t+b\sin t$ and $3k=a\cos t-b\sin t$.

Squaring and adding eliminates t, and hence the required locus is

$$(3x-1)^2+(3y)^2=a^2+b^2$$

20. (c) Let (h,k) be the coordinates of the vertex C. Then the centroid of ΔABC is

$$G=\left(\frac{h}{3},\frac{k-2}{3}\right)$$

Since G lies on the line $2x+3y=1$

$$2\left(\frac{h}{3}\right)+3\left(\frac{k-2}{3}\right)=1$$

Hence, the required locus is $2x+3y=9$.

21. (c),(d) Let $P=(x,y)$. Then according to the given condition, we have

$$|x|+|y|=|x-3|+|y-2|$$

Let us divide the first quadrant into four regions

Region I ($0\le x\le 3$ and $0\le y\le 2$)

In this region, the above equation reduces to

$$x+y=3-x+2-y\Rightarrow x+y=2.5$$

Region II ($0\le x\le 3$ and $y\le 2$)

In this region, the above equation reduces to

$$x+y=3-x+y-2\Rightarrow x=0.5$$

Region III ($x\le 3$ and $0\le y\le 2$)

In this region, the above equation reduces to

$$x+y=x-3+2-y\Rightarrow y=-0.5$$

(no such point in this region)

Region IV ($x\le 3$ and $y\le 2$)

In this region, the above equation reduces to

$$x+y=x-3+y-2\Rightarrow 1=-5$$

(no such point in this region)

This figure shows the required locus.

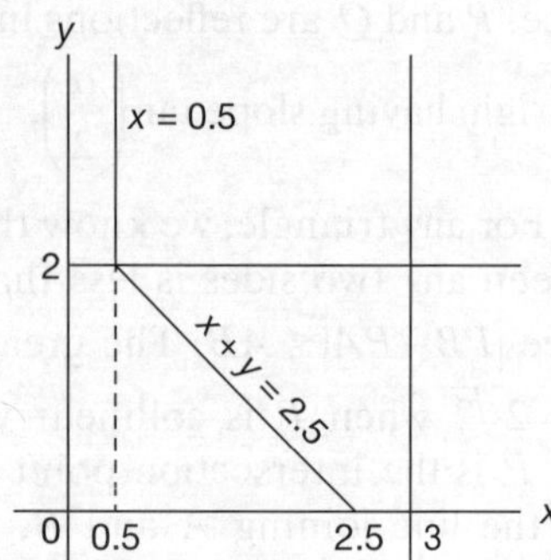

22. (d)

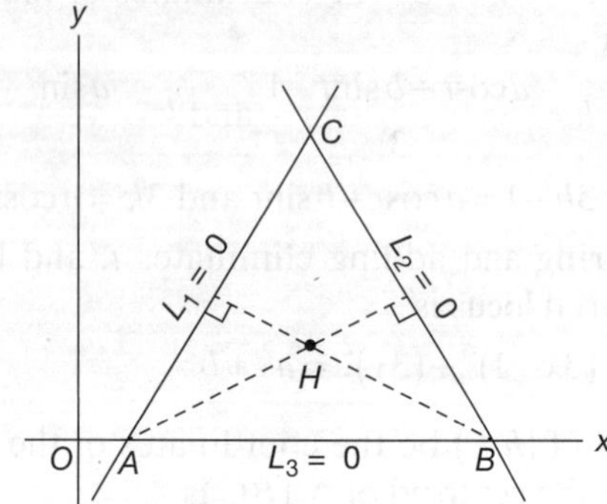

Let us name the given lines as

$$L_1\equiv(1+p)x-py+p(1+p)=0$$

$$L_2\equiv(1+q)x-py+q(1+q)=0$$

and $L_2\equiv y=0$

The two vertices of the triangle are $A(-p,0)$ and $B(-q,0)$ (see figure).

Equation of the line through A and perpendicular to BC (line $L_2=0$) is

$$y=\frac{-q}{1+q}(x+p)$$

$$\Rightarrow\quad qx+(1+q)y+pq=0 \qquad \ldots(1)$$

Equation of the line through B and perpendicular to AC (line $L_1=0$) is

$$y=\frac{-p}{1+p}(x+q)$$

$$\Rightarrow\quad px+(1+p)y+pq=0 \qquad \ldots(2)$$

Orthocentre is the intersection point of the above lines. To find its locus, we need to eliminate p,q from the above equations.

Subtracting the two equations eliminates p,q and gives the required locus $x+y=0$, which is a straight line.

23. (a)

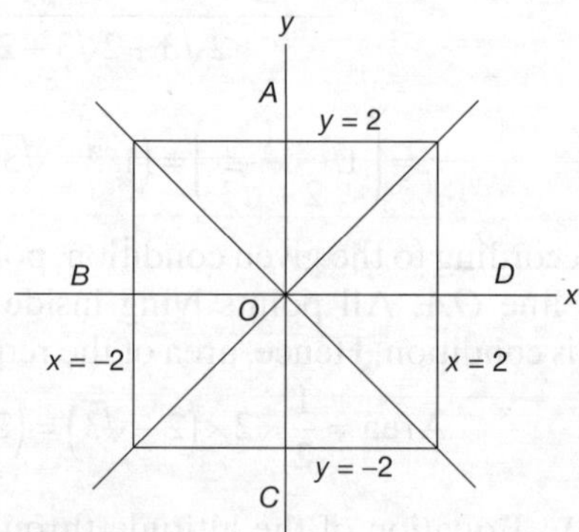

Let us divide the xy plane into four regions using lines $y=\pm x$ (see figure). The given equation $|x+y|+|x-y|=4$ reduces to

Region $A:(x+y)+(y-x)=4\Rightarrow y=2$

Region $B:-(x+y)+(y-x)=4\Rightarrow x=-2$

Region $C:-(x+y)+(x-y)=4\Rightarrow y=-2$

Region $D:(x+y)+(x-y)=4\Rightarrow x=2$

Hence, the area of the enclosed region $=4\times 4=16$.

24. (b) Line through $P(h,k)$ parallel to the x-axis: $y=k$ meets the two given lines at $Q(k,k)$ and $R(2-k,k)$. The third vertex of the triangle is the intersection point of the given lines, that is, $S(1,1)$. The perpendicular distance of S from the line QR is $SM=|k-1|$.

Area of ΔQRS is given to be $4h^2$. Hence

$$\frac{1}{2}\times QR\times SM=4h^2$$

$$\Rightarrow\quad \frac{1}{2}|2k-2||k-1|=4h^2$$

$$\Rightarrow \quad (k-1)^2 = 4h^2$$

Hence, the required locus

$$(y-1)^2 = 4x^2$$

$$\Rightarrow \quad y = 1 \pm 2x$$

25. (a) The given relation reduces to

$$c^2 = (2a+3b)^2$$

$$\Rightarrow \quad c = \pm(2a+3b)$$

Equation of the line reduces to

$$a(x+2)+b(y+3)=0 \text{ or } a(x-2)+b(y-3)=0,$$

which represents a family of lines passing through $(-2,-3)$ or $(2,3)$.

26. (c) The mirror lies along the angular bisector of the incident ray and the reflected ray. The angular bisectors are

$$\frac{3x-4y-5}{5} = \pm\frac{5x-12y-10}{13}$$

$$\Rightarrow \quad 64x-8y-115=0 \text{ and } 14x+112y-15=0$$

Comparing with equation $ax+by=1$, we have

$$a=\frac{64}{115}, b=\frac{-8}{115} \text{ or } a=\frac{14}{15}, b=\frac{112}{15}$$

27. (b) Intersection point of the two rays is $P\left(\frac{1+|a|}{1+a}, \frac{a|a|-1}{1+a}\right)$.

If point P lies in the first quadrant, then

$$1+a>0 \text{ and } a|a|>1$$

$$\Rightarrow \quad a>-1 \text{ and } a^2>1 \ (a \text{ must be +ve})$$

$$\Rightarrow \quad a>1.$$

Hence $a_0 = 1$.

28. (a) Putting $y=0$ in the second-degree equation, we have

$$(a-b)x^2+(b-c)x+(c-a)=0$$

Since the curve touches the x-axis, the roots of the above quadratic must be identical. Equating the discriminants of the above quadratic to zero gives

$$b+c=2a.$$

Equation of the given line reduces to

$$\left(\frac{b+c}{2}\right)x+by+c=0.$$

$$\Rightarrow \quad b(x+2y)+c(x+2)=0$$

which passes through the fixed point $(-2,1)$.

29. (a) The perpendicular distance $OM = \frac{1}{\sqrt{2}}$ (see figure).

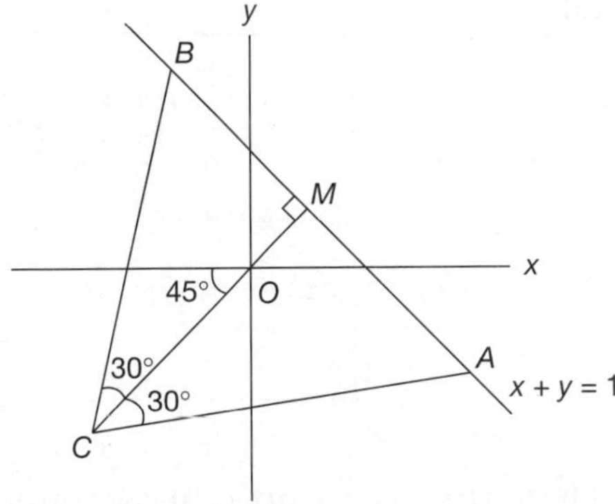

The circumcentre O is also the centroid since the triangle is equilateral. Therefore, vertex C lies on the line $y=x$ at distance $2\times OM=\sqrt{2}$ from the origin.

Hence $C=\left(-\sqrt{2}\cos45°, -\sqrt{2}\sin45°\right)=(-1,-1)$

The other two sides of the triangle pass through C and are inclined at angle 30° to the line $y=x$. Hence their equations

$$y+1=\left(\frac{1\pm\tan30°}{1\mp\tan30°}\right)(x+1)$$

$$\Rightarrow \quad y+1=\left(2\pm\sqrt{3}\right)(x+1)$$

30. (b) Let $B=(3h,4h)$. Since $OC=OB=5h$, let $C=(5h,0)$ (see figure).

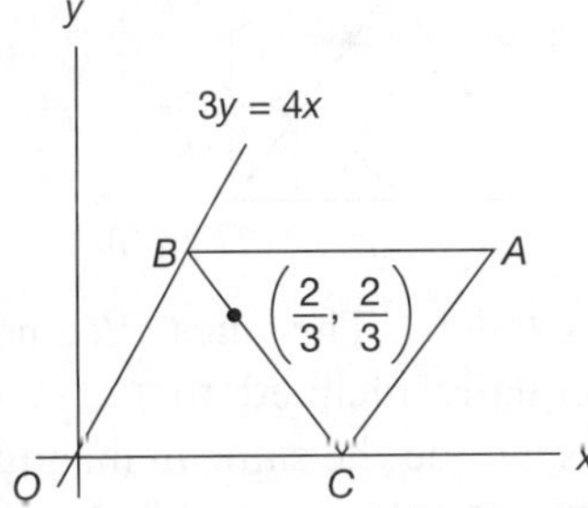

The points B, C and $\left(\frac{2}{3},\frac{2}{3}\right)$ are collinear

$$\frac{4h}{3h-5h}=\frac{2/3}{2/3-5h} \text{ gives } h=\frac{1}{5}$$

Hence $B=\left(\frac{3}{5},\frac{4}{5}\right), C=(1,0)$ and equation of $BC: 2x+y-2=0$.

Now, let $A=\left(a,\frac{4}{5}\right)$. Diagonals OA and BC are perpendicular. Hence

$$\frac{4/5}{a}\times(-2)=-1 \text{ gives } a=\frac{8}{5}$$

Hence $A=\left(\frac{8}{5},\frac{4}{5}\right)$.

31. (a)

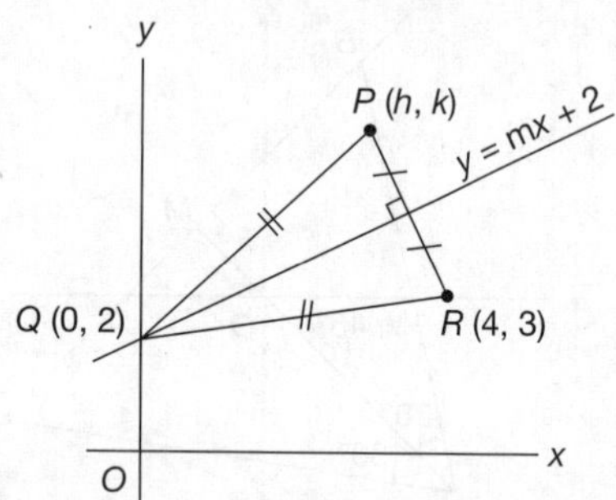

The mirror line $y = mx + 2$ passes through the fixed point $Q(0,2)$. The given point $R(4,3)$ maintains a fixed distance from Q as the value of m changes. Hence, the image point $P(h,k)$ satisfies the condition $QP = QR$.

$$\Rightarrow \quad h^2 + (k-2)^2 = 4^2 + (3-2)^2$$

Hence, the required locus

$$x^2 + y^2 - 4y - 13 = 0$$

32. (b)

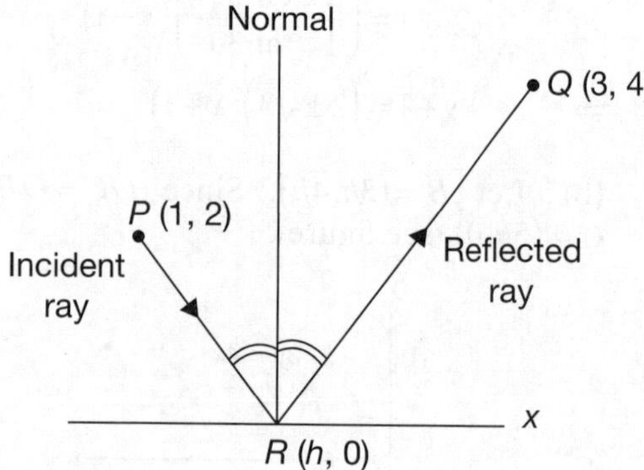

Let $R = (h,0)$. The lines PR and QR (see figure) are equally inclined to the x-axis. Thus, their slopes will be the same in magnitude but opposite in sign. Hence

$$\frac{2}{1-h} = -\frac{4}{3-h} \text{ gives } h = \frac{5}{3}$$

Hence $R = \left(\frac{5}{3}, 0\right)$.

33. (a), (c) Slopes of the two given lines are –1 and 7. The third side is equally inclined to these two sides. Let m be the slope of the third side. Then

$$\frac{7-m}{1+7m} = \frac{m+1}{1-m}$$

$$\Rightarrow \quad 3m^2 + 8m - 3 = 0 \text{ gives } m = -3, \frac{1}{3}$$

Since the third side passes through (1, –10), its possible equations are $3x + y + 7 = 0$ and $x - 3y - 31 = 0$.

34. (a) Simplifying the given relation $\frac{a}{\sqrt{bc}} + 2 = \frac{\sqrt{b}}{\sqrt{c}} + \frac{\sqrt{c}}{\sqrt{b}}$, we have

$$a + 2\sqrt{bc} = b + c$$

$$\Rightarrow \quad \left(\sqrt{b} - \sqrt{c}\right)^2 = a$$

$$\Rightarrow \quad \sqrt{b} - \sqrt{c} = \sqrt{a} \text{ [given } b > c]$$

Equation of the family of lines can now be written as

$$\left(\sqrt{b} - \sqrt{c}\right)x + \sqrt{b}y + \sqrt{c} = 0$$

$$\Rightarrow \quad \sqrt{b}(x+y) - \sqrt{c}(x-1) = 0$$

which always passes through the point $Q(1,-1)$. The line belonging to this family and farthest from the point $P(3,-2)$ is the line perpendicular to PQ. The slope of PQ is $-1/2$. Hence, the required equation is

$$y + 1 = 2(x-1)$$

$$\Rightarrow \quad 2x - y - 3 = 0$$

35. (a) The given equation can be written as $a(x+y+1) + b(2x-y-7) = 0$, which represents a family of straight lines passing through the fixed point $(2,-3)$.
The line passing through the point $(2,-3)$ and farthest from the point $(-13,7)$ is the one which is the normal to the line joining these two points. Hence, the equation of the required line L is

$$y + 3 = \frac{3}{2}(x-2)$$

$$\Rightarrow \quad 3x - 2y - 12 = 0$$

36. (b) Points lie on opposite sides of the given line. Hence

$$\{2t + 3(2+t) - 6\}\left\{2\left(\frac{3}{2}t\right) + 3t^2 - 6\right\}\frac{k}{2} < 0$$

$$\Rightarrow \quad t\left(t^2 + t - 2\right) < 0$$

$$\Rightarrow \quad t(t-1)(t+2) < 0$$

$$\Rightarrow \quad t \in (-\infty, -2) \cup (0,1)$$

37. (a) Let us chose D as our origin, x-axis along BC and the y-axis along AD (see figure). Now, if we choose $AD = h$ and $\angle ACD = \alpha$, then $CD = h\cot\alpha, DE = h\cos\alpha$ and $\angle EDC = 90° - \alpha$.

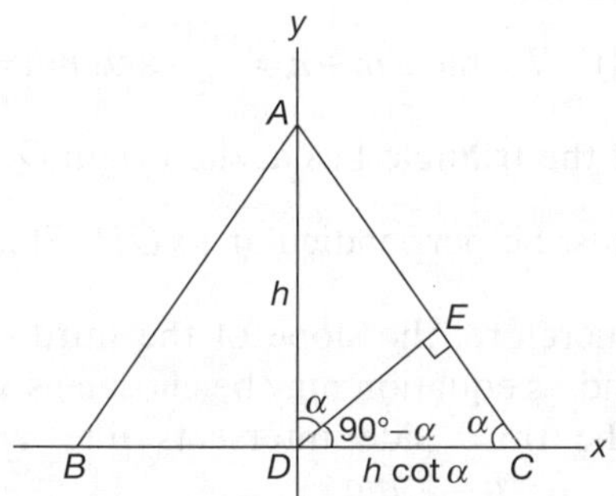

The coordinates of the various points are

$A(0,h), B(-h\cot\alpha,0), E(h\cos\alpha\sin\alpha, h\cos^2\alpha)$,

$F\left(\frac{1}{2}h\cos\alpha\sin\alpha, \frac{1}{2}h\cos^2\alpha\right)$.

Now, we have

$$\text{slope of } BE = \frac{\cos\alpha\sin\alpha}{\sin^2\alpha+1}$$

and slope of $AF = \frac{\cos^2\alpha-2}{\cos\alpha\sin\alpha} = -\frac{\sin^2\alpha+1}{\cos\alpha\sin\alpha}$

We see that the product of their slopes is –1, which means the angle between them is $\theta = 90°$. Hence $4\sin\theta = 4$.

38. (a)

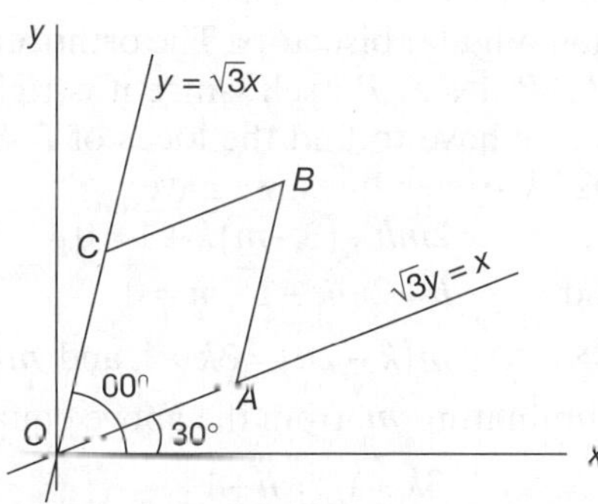

Let a be the side length of the rhombus. From the figure, we see that

$$\text{Area of } OABC = 2 \times \text{Area of } \Delta OAC$$
$$= 2\times\frac{1}{2}a^2\sin 30° = \frac{1}{2}a^2,$$

which is given to be 2; therefore $a = 2$.

Hence $C = (a\cos 30° + a\cos 60°, a\sin 30° + a\sin 60°)$

$$= \left(\frac{\sqrt{3}+1}{2}a, \frac{\sqrt{3}+1}{2}a\right)$$

39. (b)

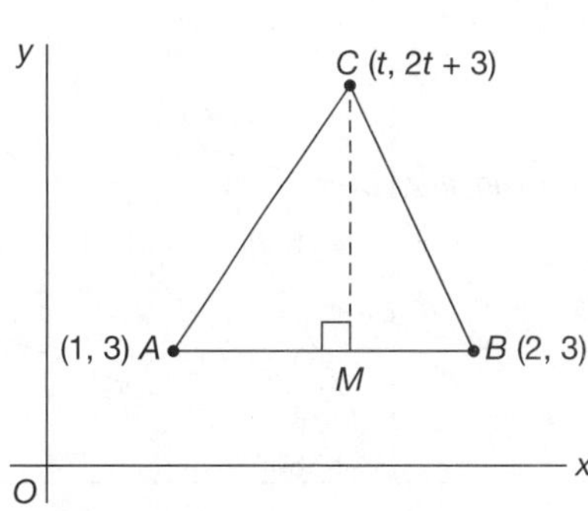

From the figure, we see that

$$\text{Area of } \Delta ABC = \frac{1}{2}\times CM\times AB = \frac{1}{2}\times|2t|\times 1 = |t|$$

According to the question

$$[|t|] = 5$$

$\Rightarrow \quad 5 \le |t| < 6$

The only integer values in this interval are $t = \pm 5$. Hence, the correct option is $(5,13)$.

40. (d) Let t be the angle made by a variable line through $(-1,2)$. Let A, B be its y intercept and x intercept, respectively. Then point Q will lie somewhere between A and B. The coordinates of points A, Q, B can be written as

$$A(-1+PA\cos t, 2+PA\sin t)$$
$$Q(-1+PQ\cos t, 2+PQ\sin t)$$
$$B(-1+PB\cos t, 2+PB\sin t)$$

If A is the y intercept and B is the x intercept, then

$$-1+PA\cos t = 0 \Rightarrow \frac{1}{PA} = \cos t$$

and $\quad 2+PB\sin t = 0 \Rightarrow \frac{1}{PB} = \frac{-1}{2}\sin t$

Since PA, PQ, PB are in harmonic progression, we have

$$\frac{2}{PQ} = \frac{1}{PA}+\frac{1}{PB} = \cos t - \frac{1}{2}\sin t$$

$\Rightarrow \quad PQ\cos t - \frac{1}{2}PQ\sin t = 2$

If (h,k) are the coordinates of Q, then

$$-1+PQ\cos t = h \text{ and } 2+PQ\sin t = k$$

Hence $\quad h+1-\frac{1}{2}(k-2) = 2 \Rightarrow k = 2h.$

41. (a), (c)

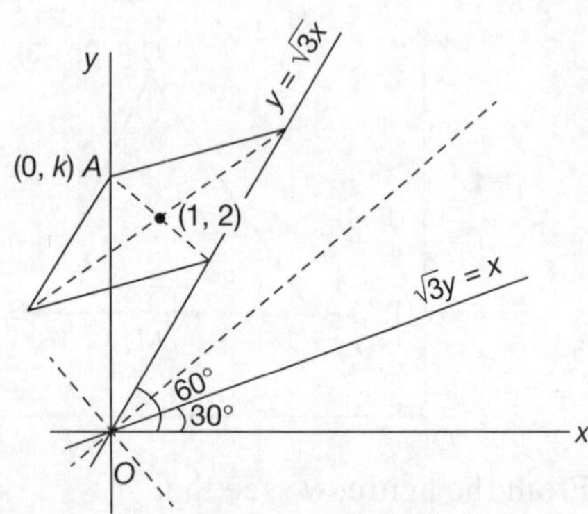

The diagonals will be parallel to the angular bisectors of the sides of the rhombus. The two given lines are inclined at angles 60° and 30° to the x-axis. Hence their angular bisectors will be inclined at 45° and 135° to the x-axis and their slopes will be ±1.

Let $A=(0,k)$. The line joining A and $(1,2)$ should have slope equal to ±1. Thus, we have

$$\frac{2-k}{1}=\pm 1$$

$$\Rightarrow \quad k=1,3$$

42. (c) Let $y-3=m(x-2)$ be a variable line through $(2,3)$. Let $A(h,0)$ and $B(0,k)$ be its x intercept and y intercept, respectively. Then

$$-3=m(h-2) \text{ and } k-3=-2m$$

The coordinates of P will be (h,k). Eliminating m, we have

$$(h-2)(k-3)=6$$

$$\Rightarrow \quad 3h+2k=hk$$

Hence, the required locus of P is

$$3x+2y=xy$$

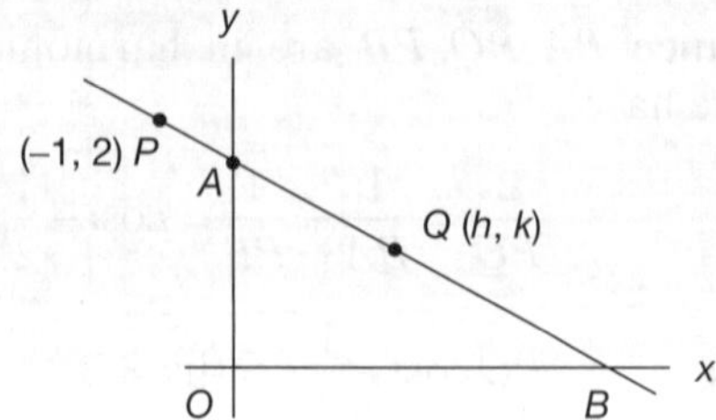

43. (d) We have $m+n=\frac{-10}{3}$ and $mn=\frac{1}{3}$. One vertex of the triangle lies at the origin O. The third side must be perpendicular to OH. Slope of OH is $\frac{1}{3}$. Therefore, the slope of the third side will be –3, and its equation may be chosen as $y=-3x+c$. The third side intersects line $y=mx$ at point $A=\left(\frac{c}{m+3},\frac{mc}{m+3}\right)$. Now line AH must be perpendicular to line $y=nx$. Thus, we have

$$\frac{\frac{mc}{m+3}-2}{\frac{c}{m+3}-6}=\frac{-1}{n}$$

$$\Rightarrow \quad \frac{m(c-2)-6}{-6m+c-18}=\frac{-1}{n}$$

$$\Rightarrow \quad mn(c-2)-6(m+n)=18-c$$

$$\Rightarrow \quad \frac{1}{3}(c-2)+20=18-c \text{ gives } c=-1$$

Hence, the equation of the third side is $3x+y+1=0$.

44. (c) Let $P(h,k)$ be the intersection point of the two given lines $2mx+(3-m)y+1=0$ and $x+2my+1-m=0$. Let A,B be the x intercepts of their angular bisectors. The orthocentre of triangle ΔPAB lies at P itself, since it is right-angled at P. So, we have to find the locus of P. Since P lies on the two given lines, we have

$$2mh+(3-m)k+1=0$$

and

$$h+2mk+1-m=0$$

$$\Rightarrow \quad m(k-2h)=3k+1 \text{ and } m(1-2k)=h+1$$

Eliminating m from the above equations, we have

$$\frac{3k+1}{k-2h}=\frac{h+1}{1-2k}$$

$$\Rightarrow \quad 2h^2-hk+6k^2+2h+1=0$$

Hence, the required locus is

$$2x^2-xy+6y^2+2x+1=0$$

CHAPTER

27 Circle

- **Equation of a Circle:** The equation of a circle with centre at $O(0,0)$ and radius a is
$$x^2 + y^2 = a^2$$
The parametric representation of this circle is
$$x = a\cos\theta \text{ and } y = a\sin\theta$$
The equation of a general tangent to this circle is
$$y = mx \pm a\sqrt{1+m^2} \text{ at point } P = \left(\frac{-am}{\pm\sqrt{1+m^2}}, \frac{a}{\pm\sqrt{1+m^2}}\right)$$
For a circle with centre at $C(\alpha, \beta)$ and radius a, all the above equations can be obtained by writing $x-\alpha$ in place of x and $y-\beta$ in place of y.

- **Equation of a Circle Passing Through Three Given Points:** For any three given points P, Q, R, a unique circle can be drawn passing through them provided they are non-collinear. If the points are non-collinear, they will form a triangle. The circumcentre of this triangle lies on the intersection of the perpendicular bisectors of the three sides of the triangle. The centre C can be found by finding the intersection point of any two perpendicular bisectors. Once the centre is found, the radius is the distance of C from any one of the three given points. Once the centre $C(\alpha, \beta)$ and the radius r are known, the equation of the circle can be written as $(x-\alpha)^2 + (y-\beta)^2 = r^2$.

- **Equation of a Circle Passing Through Two Given Points:** For any two given points $P(x_1, y_1)$ and $Q(x_2, y_2)$, an infinite number of circles of various radii can be drawn passing through them. However, the smallest circle that can be drawn passing through them is the one for which PQ is its diameter. The equation of this circle is
$$(x-x_1)(x-x_2)+(y-x_1)(y-x_2)=0$$

- **General Equation of a Circle:** The general equation of a circle is a second-degree equation whose Coefficient of x^2 = Coefficient of y^2 and Coefficient of $xy = 0$
The general equation $S(x, y) \equiv x^2 + y^2 + 2gx + 2fy + c = 0$, which can also be written as
$$(x+g)^2 + (y+f)^2 = g^2 + f^2 - c,$$
represents a circle with centre at $C(-g, -f)$ and radius $r = \sqrt{g^2 + f^2 - c}$.

- **Length of a Tangent:** From a given point $P(x_1, y_1)$, two tangents of equal length can be drawn to a given circle $S(x, y) = 0$, provided the point lies outside the circle. The length of these tangents equals $\sqrt{S(x_1, y_1)}$. The value of $S(x_1, y_1)$ is positive or negative depending on whether $P(x_1, y_1)$ lies outside or inside the circle.

- **Radical Axis of Two Circles:** For two circles $S_1(x, y) \equiv x^2 + y^2 + 2g_1x + 2f_1y + c_1 = 0$ and $S_2(x, y) \equiv x^2 + y^2 + 2g_2x + 2f_2y + c_2 = 0$, the equation of their radical axis (locus of points from where tangents to both the circles are equal in length) is
$$S_1(x, y) - S_2(x, y) = 0$$
The radical axis is a line perpendicular to the line joining the centres of the two circles. For two intersecting circles, the common chord is their radical axis; for two touching circles, the common tangent at the contact point is their radical axis.

- **Intersection Points of a Line and a Circle:** Consider a given line $L(x, y) \equiv lx + my + n = 0$ and a given circle $S(x, y) \equiv x^2 + y^2 + 2gx + 2fy + c = 0$. Writing the equation of the line in slope-intercept form $y = \frac{-l}{m}x + \frac{-n}{m}$ and substituting it in the equation of the circle gives a quadratic in x. Solving the quadratic gives the x coordinates of the intersection points. The corresponding y coordinates are now obtained by inserting these x values in the equation of the line.

  Condition for tangency: The given line may be a tangent or a secant or a non-intersecting line depending upon whether the quadratic obtained above in x gives only one real solution, two real solutions or imaginary solutions, respectively.

  This method is used for checking whether a given line is a tangent to any given second-degree curve. For circles, however, there is a simpler way to check tangency. First find the perpendicular distance, say p, between the line and the centre of the circle, and then compare it with the radius, say r, of the circle. The given line is a tangent if $p = r$, a secant if $p < r$, and a non-intersecting line if $p > r$.

- **Intersection Points of Two Circles:** Consider two given circles $S_1(x, y) = 0$ and $S_2(x, y) = 0$. Their intersection points will lie on the common chord $S_1(x, y) - S_2(x, y) = 0$. So, we need to find the intersection points of the common chord and any one of the two given circles. The problem, therefore, reduces to finding the intersection points of a line and a circle.

- **Equation of a Tangent to a Circle from a Point:** From any given point $P(x_1, y_1)$, two tangents can be drawn to a given circle having its centre at $C(\alpha, \beta)$ and radius r. To find their equations, begin by choosing them as $y - y_1 = m(x - x_1)$. Now the value of m can be found by using the tangency condition, that is, the perpendicular distance between this line and $C(\alpha, \beta)$ must equal r. Thus, we have

  $$\frac{|m(\alpha - x_1) - (\beta - y_1)|}{\sqrt{1 + m^2}} = r$$

  Squaring and rearranging gives a quadratic in m.

  $$\left\{(\alpha - x_1)^2 - r^2\right\}m^2 - 2(\alpha - x_1)(\beta - y_1)m + \left\{(\beta - y_1)^2 - r^2\right\} = 0$$

  Solving the above quadratic gives the values of m, and hence the equations of the required tangents.

  The above obtained quadratic in m gives only one real solution or two real solutions or imaginary solutions depending upon whether the given point P lies on the given circle or outside the given circle or inside the given circle, respectively.

- **Relative Positioning of Two Circles:** Consider two given circles, one circle of radius r_1 centred at $C_1(\alpha_1, \beta_1)$ and another circle of radius r_2 centred at $C_2(\alpha_2, \beta_2)$. Then we have the following conditions:

  $C_1C_2 > r_1 + r_2 \Rightarrow$ Circles are non-intersecting and not lying inside each other

  $C_1C_2 = r_1 + r_2 \Rightarrow$ Circles touch each other externally

  $C_1C_2 = |r_1 - r_2| \Rightarrow$ Circles touch each other internally

  $|r_1 - r_2| < C_1C_2 < r_1 + r_2 \Rightarrow$ Circles intersect at two distinct points

  $C_1C_2 < |r_1 - r_2| \Rightarrow$ One circle lies completely inside the other circle

- **Common Tangents of Two Circles:** Consider one circle of radius r_1 having its centre at $C_1(\alpha_1, \beta_1)$ and another circle of radius r_2 having its centre at $C_2(\alpha_2, \beta_2)$.

  Case 1: If one circle lies completely inside the other circle, then there is no common tangent.

  Case 2: If the circles touch each other internally, there is only one common tangent and its equation is $S_1(x, y) - S_2(x, y) = 0$.

Case 3: If the circles intersect at two distinct points, there are two common tangents, both of which are direct tangents.

Case 4: If the circles touch each other externally, there are three common tangents. One tangent is at the contact point of the circles, and its equation is $S_1(x, y) - S_2(x, y) = 0$. The other two tangents are direct tangents.

Case 5: If the circles are non-intersecting and not lying inside each other, there are four common tangents, two direct and two cross tangents.

Equations of the direct and cross tangents: Let P and Q, respectively, be the external and internal points dividing the line joining the centres in the ratio $r_1 : r_2$. The two direct tangents pass through the external point P and the two cross tangents pass through the internal point Q. Now, finding the equation of a line passing through P and touching any one of the two circles will give the equations of the direct tangents. Similarly, finding the equation of a line passing through Q and touching any one of the two circles will give the equations of the cross tangents.

- **Lengths of the Common Tangents:**

  Length of the cross tangents = $\sqrt{(C_1C_2)^2 - (r_1 + r_2)^2}$

  Length of the direct tangents = $\sqrt{(C_1C_2)^2 - (r_1 - r_2)^2}$

  For two externally touching circles, the length of the cross tangents = 0 and the length of the direct tangents = $\sqrt{4r_1r_2}$.

- **Orthogonal Circles:** Two circles $x^2 + y^2 + 2g_1x + 2f_1y + c_1 = 0$ and $x^2 + y^2 + 2g_2x + 2f_2y + c_2 = 0$ cut each other orthogonally if $2g_1g_2 + 2f_1f_2 = c_1 + c_2$

  Two circles with centres at C_1, C_2 and radii r_1, r_2 will intersect at two distinct points if $|r_1 - r_2| < C_1C_2 < r_1 + r_2$; they will touch each other internally if $C_1C_2 = |r_1 - r_2|$ and externally if $C_1C_2 = r_1 + r_2$.

- **Family of Circles**

  1. The equation of any circle passing through the intersection points of a given circle $S = 0$ and a given line $L = 0$ can be written as
  $$S + \lambda L = 0$$
  2. The equation of any circle passing through the intersection points of two given circles $S_1 = 0$ and $S_2 = 0$ can be written as
  $$S_1 + \lambda S_2 = 0$$
  3. The equation of any circle passing through the two given points $A(x_1, y_1)$ and $B(x_2, y_2)$ can be written as
  $$(x - x_1)(x - x_2) + (y - y_1)(y - y_2) + \lambda \begin{vmatrix} x & y & 1 \\ x_1 & y_1 & 1 \\ x_2 & y_2 & 1 \end{vmatrix} = 0$$
  4. The equation of any circle touching a given line $L = 0$ at a point $P(x_1, y_1)$ on the line, can be written as
  $$(x - x_1)^2 + (y - y_1)^2 + \lambda L = 0$$

- **The General Second-Degree Equation:** The general second-degree equation $S(x, y) \equiv ax^2 + 2hxy + by^2 + 2gx + 2fy + c = 0$ represents

  A circle if $a = b$ and $h = 0$ or

  A pair of straight lines if $\begin{vmatrix} a & h & g \\ h & b & f \\ g & f & c \end{vmatrix} = 0$

  If it is neither a circle nor a pair of straight lines, then it will represent

  A parabola if $h^2 - ab = 0$

  An ellipse if $h^2 - ab < 0$

  A hyperbola if $h^2 - ab > 0$

- **For All Second-Degree Curves $S(x, y) = 0$:**
  1. Equation of the tangent at a point $P(x_1, y_1)$ on the curve is $T(x, y) = 0$
  2. Equation of the chord of contact, of the point $P(x_1, y_1)$ is $T(x, y) = 0$
  3. Equation of the chord whose mid-point is $P(x_1, y_1)$ is $T(x, y) = S(x_1, y_1)$
  4. Equation of the pair of tangents that can be drawn from the point $P(x_1, y_1)$ is $T^2(x, y) = S(x, y)S(x_1, y_1)$

  Here $T(x, y)$ stands for the tangent format obtained by substituting xx_1 for x^2, $(xy_1 + yx_1)$ for $2xy$, yy_1 for y^2, $(x + x_1)$ for $2x$, and $(y + y_1)$ for $2y$:
  $$T(x, y) \equiv axx_1 + h(xy_1 + yx_1) + byy_1 + g(x + x_1) + f(y + y_1) + c = 0$$

EXERCISES

1. S_1 and S_2 are two concentric circles of area 12 sq. units and 3 sq. units, respectively. From a point A on circle S_1, chords AB and AC are drawn touching circle S_2. Area of the triangle ABC is:

(a) $\dfrac{9}{\pi}$ (b) $\dfrac{3\sqrt{3}}{2\pi}$

(c) $\dfrac{9\sqrt{3}}{\pi}$ (d) $\dfrac{3\sqrt{3}}{\pi}$

2. A circle is inscribed in an equilateral triangle of side a. Area of the largest rectangle that can be inscribed in this circle is:

(a) $\dfrac{1}{2}a^2$ (b) $\dfrac{1}{3}a^2$

(c) $\dfrac{1}{4}a^2$ (d) $\dfrac{1}{6}a^2$

3. If P and Q are the points of intersection of the circles $2x^2 + 2y^2 + 5x + p^2 + 5 = 0$ and $x^2 + y^2 + 2x + 5y + p^2 + p = 0$, then a circle can be drawn passing through the points P, Q and $(4, 1)$ for:

(a) All values of p
(b) Exactly one value of p
(c) All except two values of p
(d) All except one value of p

4. The centres of the four circles shown in figure are collinear. PQR is a common tangent and the length of the tangent segments are $PQ = 1$ unit, $QR = 2$ units. The area of the shaded region is:

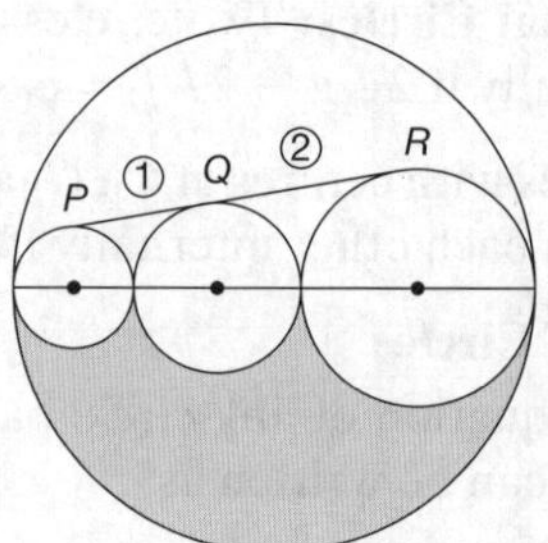

(a) $\dfrac{8\pi}{3}$ (b) $\dfrac{7\pi}{4}$

(c) $\dfrac{9\pi}{2}$ (d) $\dfrac{6\pi}{5}$

5. Let $ABCD$ be a quadrilateral of area 18 sq. units with side AB parallel to CD, $AB = 2 \times CD$ and AD perpendicular to both AB and CD. If a circle is drawn touching all the sides of the quadrilateral, then its radius is:

(a) 3 (b) $5/2$

(c) 2 (d) 1

6. Area of the triangle formed by the tangents from an external point (h, k) to the circle $x^2 + y^2 = a^2$ and the chord of contact is:

(a) $\dfrac{a(h^2 + k^2 - a^2)}{\sqrt{h^2 + k^2}}$ (b) $\dfrac{a(h^2 + k^2 - a^2)}{2\sqrt{h^2 + k^2}}$

(c) $\dfrac{a(h^2 + k^2 - a^2)^{3/2}}{(h^2 + k^2)}$ (d) $\dfrac{a(h^2 + k^2 - a^2)^{3/2}}{2(h^2 + k^2)}$

7. $A(5,-2), B(1,1)$ are two fixed points. If point P moves such that $PA = 2 \times PB$, then the maximum area of ΔPAB is:
(a) $5\sqrt{3}$ (b) $15/2$
(c) $8\sqrt{2}$ (d) $25/3$

8. If the chord $y - x - b = 0$ subtends 60° on the major segment of the circle $x^2 + y^2 = a^2$, then the value of b/a is:
(a) ± 1 (b) $\pm\sqrt{2}$
(c) $\pm\frac{1}{\sqrt{2}}$ (d) $\pm\frac{1}{2}$

9. A variable circle of fixed radius a passes through the origin and cuts the coordinate axes at points A and B. Locus of the centroid of triangle OAB is:
(a) $4x^2 + 4y^2 = 9a^2$ (b) $9x^2 + 9y^2 = 4a^2$
(c) $3x^2 + 3y^2 = 4a^2$ (d) $x^2 + y^2 = 4a^2$

10. The centre of a circle passing through (0, 0) and (1, 0) and touching the circle $x^2 + y^2 = 9$ is:
(a) $\left(\frac{1}{2}, \frac{\sqrt{3}}{2}\right)$ (b) $\left(\frac{1}{2}, \frac{1}{\sqrt{2}}\right)$
(c) $\left(\frac{3}{2}, \frac{1}{2}\right)$ (d) $\left(\frac{1}{2}, \sqrt{2}\right)$

11. The circle passing through the point (–1, 0) and touching the y-axis at $(0,2)$ also passes through the point:
(a) $\left(\frac{-3}{2}, 0\right)$ (b) $\left(\frac{-5}{2}, 2\right)$
(c) $\left(\frac{-3}{2}, \frac{5}{2}\right)$ (d) $(-4, 0)$

12. From the point $A(0,3)$ on the circle $x^2 + 4x + (y-3)^2 = 0$, a chord AB is drawn and extended to a point M such that $AM = 2 \times AB$. The locus of M is:
(a) $x^2 + y^2 - 8x - 6y + 9 = 0$
(b) $x^2 + y^2 + 8x - 6y + 9 = 0$
(c) $x^2 + y^2 + 8x + 6y - 9 = 0$
(d) $x^2 + y^2 - 8x + 6y - 9 = 0$

13. If $P(h,k)$ is a point on the circle $x^2 + y^2 - 14x - 6y - 6 = 0$, then the greatest value of $3h + 4k$ is:
(a) 73 (b) 67
(c) 65 (d) 54

14. Let P be a variable point and $Q = (1,0)$ be a fixed point on the circle $x^2 + y^2 = 1$. The tangents to the circle at points P and Q meet at point R. The normal to the circle at P meets the line through R drawn parallel to the x-axis, at point S. The locus of S passes through the points:
(a) $\left(\frac{1}{3}, \frac{1}{\sqrt{3}}\right)$ (b) $\left(\frac{1}{4}, \frac{1}{2}\right)$
(c) $\left(\frac{1}{3}, \frac{-1}{\sqrt{3}}\right)$ (d) $\left(\frac{1}{4}, \frac{-1}{2}\right)$

15. Let $P = \left(\sqrt{2}, 1\right)$ be a point on the circle $S: x^2 = y^2 = 3$. Tangent to the circle S at point P touches two circles S_1 and S_2 at points R_1 and R_2, respectively $(PR_1 > PR_2)$. If the circles S_1 and S_2 have equal radii $2\sqrt{3}$ and their respective centres Q_1 and Q_2 both lie on the y-axis, then:
(a) $Q_1Q_2 = 12$ (b) area of $\Delta PQ_1Q_2 = 4\sqrt{2}$
(c) $R_1R_2 = 4\sqrt{6}$ (d) $PR_1 : PR_2 = 3:1$

16. Two vertices of an equilateral triangle are $(-1,0)$ and $(1,0)$, and its third vertex lies above the x-axis. Equation of its circumcircle is:
(a) $x^2 + y^2 - \sqrt{3}x - 1 = 0$
(b) $2x^2 + 2y^2 - 2y - 1 = 0$
(c) $\sqrt{3}x^2 + \sqrt{3}y^2 - 2y - \sqrt{3} = 0$
(d) $x^2 + y^2 - \sqrt{3}x - 1 = 0$

17. Consider the circles $x^2 + y^2 - 12x + 35 = 0$ and $x^2 + y^2 - 4y + 3 = 0$. The sum of the y intercepts of their common tangents is:
(a) $11/3$ (b) $3\sqrt{10}$
(c) $4\sqrt{3}$ (d) $33/4$

18. If one of the diameters of the circle $x^2 + y^2 - 2x - 6y + 6 = 0$ is a common chord with a circle having its centre at (2, 1), Then the radius of that circle is:
(a) $\sqrt{3}$ (b) 2 (c) 3 (d) $2\sqrt{2}$

19. The chords of contact of tangents from three points A, B, C to the circle $x^2 + y^2 = a^2$ are concurrent. Then A, B, C will be:
(a) Collinear (b) Vertices of a triangle
(c) Concyclic (d) None of these

20. Triangle PQR is inscribed in the circle $x^2 + y^2 = 25$. If $(3, 4)$ and $(-4, 3)$ are the coordinates of P and R, respectively, then $\angle PQR$ equals:
(a) $\pi/2$ (b) $\pi/3$ (c) $\pi/4$ (d) $\pi/6$

21. If the tangent at point P on the circle $x^2+y^2+6x+6y-2=0$ meets the straight line $5x-2y+6=0$ at a point Q on the y-axis, then the length of PQ is:

(a) 4 (b) $2\sqrt{5}$
(c) 5 (d) $3\sqrt{5}$

22. If the sum of the squares of the lengths of the chords intercepted by the line $x+y=n\,(n\in\mathbf{N})$ on the circle $x^2+y^2=4$ is $11k$, then k equals:

(a) 2 (b) 3
(c) 4 (d) 5

23. Let L_1 be a straight line passing through the origin and L_2 be the straight line $x+y=1$. If the intercepts made by the circle $x^2+y^2-x+3y=0$ on L_1 and L_2 are equal, then the equation representing L_1 is:

(a) $x+y=0$ (b) $x-y=0$
(c) $x+7y=0$ (d) $x-7y=0$

24. Tangents drawn from $P(1,8)$ to the circle $x^2+y^2-6x-4y-11=0$ touch the circle at A and B. Equation of the circumcircle of triangle PAB is:

(a) $x^2+y^2+4x-6y+19=0$
(b) $x^2+y^2-4x-10y+19=0$
(c) $x^2+y^2-2x+6y-29=0$
(d) $x^2+y^2-6x-4y+19=0$

25. In a rectangle $ABCD$, the coordinates of A and B are $(1,2)$ and $(3,6)$, respectively, and some diameter of the circle circumscribing $ABCD$ has the equation $3x+y-6=0$. Area of rectangle $ABCD$ is:

(a) 16 (b) $2\sqrt{10}$
(c) $2\sqrt{5}$ (d) 20

26. The centres of two circles S_1 and S_2, each of unit radii, are at a distance of 6 units from each other. Let P be the mid-point of the line segment joining the centres of S_1 and S_2, and S be a circle touching circles S_1 and S_2 externally. If a common tangent to S_1 and S_2 passing through P is also a tangent to S, then the radius of the circle S is:

(a) 4 (b) $5\sqrt{2}$
(c) 6 (d) 8

27. Consider a family of straight lines $ax+by-49=0$, where $a^2+b^2=1$. Then this family of lines will always touch the circle:

(a) $x^2+(y\pm 7)^2=49$ (b) $(x\pm 7)^2+y^2=49$
(c) $x^2+y^2=49^2$ (d) None of these

28. A straight line through the vertex P of a triangle PQR intersects the side QR at the point S and the circumcircle of the triangle PQR at the point T. If S is not the centre of the circumcircle, then:

(a) $\frac{1}{PS}+\frac{1}{ST}<\frac{2}{\sqrt{QS\cdot SR}}$

(b) $\frac{1}{PS}+\frac{1}{ST}>\frac{2}{\sqrt{QS\cdot SR}}$

(c) $\frac{1}{PS}+\frac{1}{ST}<\frac{4}{QR}$

(d) $\frac{1}{PS}+\frac{1}{ST}>\frac{4}{QR}$

29. A circle passing through the origin cuts the straight lines $x^2-y^2=0$ at points A and B. If the abscissae of A and B are roots of the equation $x^2+ax+b=0$, then the equation of the circle is:

(a) $x^2+y^2+ax\pm y\sqrt{a^2-4b}=0$
(b) $x^2+y^2+ax\pm by=0$
(c) $x^2+y^2\pm x\sqrt{a^2-4b}+ay=0$
(d) $x^2+y^2\pm ax+by=0$

30. The straight line $2x-3y=1$ divides the circular region $x^2+y^2\le 6$ into two parts. If $S=\left\{\left(2,\frac{3}{4}\right),\left(\frac{5}{2},\frac{3}{4}\right),\left(\frac{1}{4},\frac{-1}{4}\right),\left(\frac{1}{8},\frac{1}{4}\right)\right\}$, then the number of points in S lying inside the smaller part is:

(a) 1 (b) 2
(c) 3 (d) 4

31. Tangents are drawn at points A and B on the circle $x^2+y^2=a^2$ whose parametric angles differ by $2\pi/3$. The locus of the intersection point of these tangents is:

(a) $x^2+y^2=\frac{3}{2}a^2$ (b) $x^2+y^2=\frac{4}{3}a^2$
(c) $x^2+y^2=2a^2$ (d) None of these

32. From the origin, chords are drawn to the circle $(x-1)^2+y^2=1$. Equation of the locus of the mid-point of these chords is:

(a) $x^2+y^2-x=0$ (b) $x^2+y^2-x-y=0$
(c) $x^2+y^2-x+y=0$ (d) None of these

33. AB is the diameter of circle S_1 of radius 6 units. S_2 is a circle of radius 3 units which touches S_1

internally at B. If chord AC of circle S_1 touches circle S_2, then the length of AC is:

(a) $6\sqrt{3}$ (b) $6\sqrt{2}$

(c) $8\sqrt{2}$ (d) 8

34. Equation of the circle which cuts each of the three circles $x^2+y^2=4, (x-1)^2+y^2=4$ and $x^2+(y-2)^2=4$ orthogonally is:

(a) $x^2+y^2-x-2y+4=0$

(b) $x^2+y^2+x-2y+4=0$

(c) $x^2+y^2+x+2y+4=0$

(d) $x^2+y^2-x+2y+4=0$

35. Let AB be a fixed chord of a circle of given radius, subtending a right angle at the centre. Then the locus of the centroid of the triangle PAB as P moves on the circle is:

(a) A parabola (b) A circle

(c) An ellipse (d) A pair of straight lines

36. Consider the circles $S_1: x^2+y^2=64$ and S_2 with radius 10. If the centre of S_2 lies on the line $y=x$, and the length of the common chord of S_1 and S_2 is 16, then the centre of circle S_2 is:

(a) $\left(\frac{3}{\sqrt{2}}, \frac{3}{\sqrt{2}}\right)$ (b) $\left(\frac{4}{\sqrt{2}}, \frac{4}{\sqrt{2}}\right)$

(c) $\left(\frac{6}{\sqrt{2}}, \frac{6}{\sqrt{2}}\right)$ (d) $\left(\frac{8}{\sqrt{2}}, \frac{8}{\sqrt{2}}\right)$

37. Three distinct points A, B and C are given in the xy plane such that the ratio of the distance of any one of them from the point $(1,0)$ to the distance from the point $(-1,0)$ is equal to $1/3$. The circumcentre of triangle ABC is at:

(a) $\left(\frac{3}{4}, \frac{1}{4}\right)$ (b) $\left(\frac{1}{2}, -1\right)$

(c) $\left(-1, \frac{1}{4}\right)$ (d) $\left(\frac{5}{4}, 0\right)$

38. Consider a circle of radius 2, and two parallel chords subtending angles $2\pi/k$ and π/k at the centre of the circle. If the distance between the chords is $\sqrt{3}+1$, the value of k is:

(a) 1 (b) 2

(c) 3 (d) 4

39. The locus of the mid-point of the chord of contact of tangents drawn from points lying on the straight line $4x-5y=20$ to the circle $x^2+y^2=9$ is:

(a) $20(x^2+y^2)-36x+45y=0$

(b) $20(x^2+y^2)+36x-45y=0$

(c) $36(x^2+y^2)-20x+45y=0$

(d) $36(x^2+y^2)+20x-45y=0$

40. The radius of the smallest circle passing through the point $(8,4)$ and cutting the circle $x^2+y^2-40=0$ orthogonally is:

(a) $\sqrt{3}$ (b) $\sqrt{5}$

(c) $2\sqrt{3}$ (d) $\sqrt{7}$

41. Equation of a circle passing through $(1,1)$ and touching the circle $x^2+y^2+4x-6y-3=0$ at the point $(2,3)$ is:

(a) $x^2+y^2-x-y=0$

(b) $x^2+y^2-3y+1=0$

(c) $x^2+y^2+x-6y+3=0$

(d) $x^2+y^2-x-2y+1=0$

42. Equation of a circle that touches the line $y=x$ at the origin and bisects the circumference of the circle $x^2+y^2+2y-3=0$ is:

(a) $x^2+y^2-2x-y=0$

(b) $x^2+y^2-2y=0$

(c) $x^2+y^2-x+2y=0$

(d) $x^2+y^2-5x+5y=0$

43. A circle passes through the vertex C of a rectangle $ABCD$ and touches its sides AB and AD at M and N, respectively. If the distance from C to the line segment MN equals 5, then the area of rectangle $ABCD$ is:

(a) 35 (b) 25

(c) 20 (d) 15

44. Two circles of radii r_1 and r_2 are drawn touching the x-axis at A and B, respectively. The circles also touch each other externally at P. The circumradius of triangle ΔAPB equals:

(a) $\frac{r_1^2+r_2^2}{\sqrt{r_1 r_2}}$ (b) $\sqrt{r_1 r_2}$

(c) $\frac{r_1+r_2}{2}$ (d) $\frac{r_1 r_2}{r_1+r_2}$

45. Three circles of radii a,b,c $(a<b<c)$ touch each other externally. If there exists a tangent common to all the three circles, then:

(a) $\sqrt{a}\left(\sqrt{b}+\sqrt{c}\right)=\sqrt{bc}$

(b) $\sqrt{a}\left(\sqrt{b}+\sqrt{c}\right)=b+c$

(c) $a\left(b^2+c^2\right)=\sqrt{b^3c^3}$

(d) $a(b+c)=bc$

46. A circle S of radius 1 is inscribed in an equilateral triangle PQR. The points of contact of S with the sides PQ, QR and RP are D, E and F, respectively. The line PQ is given by the equation $\sqrt{3}x+y-6=0$ and the point D is $\left(\frac{3\sqrt{3}}{2},\frac{3}{2}\right)$. Further, it is given that the origin and the centre I of S are on the same side of the line PQ. Match the columns:

(a) R	(p) $\left(\sqrt{3}/2, 3/2\right)$
(b) E	(q) $\left(\sqrt{3}, 0\right)$
(c) F	(r) $(0,0)$
(d) I	(s) $\left(\sqrt{3}, 1\right)$

ANSWER KEYS

1. (c)	**2.** (d)	**3.** (d)	**4.** (b)	**5.** (c)	**6.** (c)	**7.** (d)	**8.** (c)	**9.** (b)
10. (d)	**11.** (d)	**12.** (b)	**13.** (a)	**14.** (a),(c)	**15.** (a),(c),(d)	**16.** (c)	**17.** (d)	**18.** (c)
19. (a)	**20.** (c)	**21.** (c)	**22.** (a)	**23.** (b),(c)	**24.** (b)	**25.** (a)	**26.** (d)	**27.** (c)
28. (b),(d)	**29.** (a)	**30.** (b)	**31.** (d)	**32.** (a)	**33.** (c)	**34.** (a)	**35.** (b)	**36.** (c)
37. (d)	**38.** (c)	**39.** (a)	**40.** (b)	**41.** (c)	**42.** (d)	**43.** (b)	**44.** (b)	**45.** (a)

46. (a)-(r), (b)-(p), (c)-(q), (d)-(s)

SOLUTIONS

1. (c)

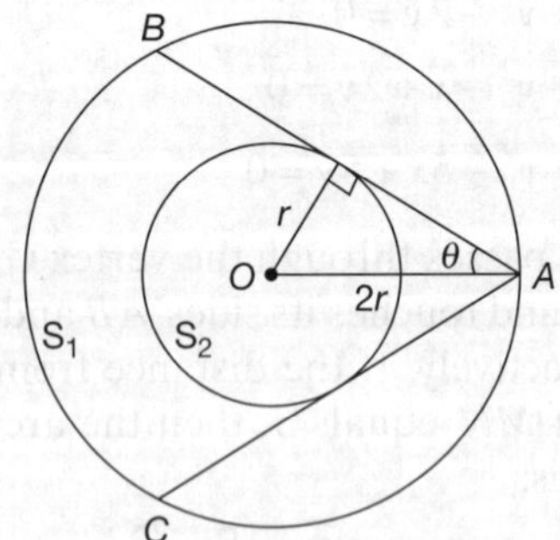

If the radius of the inner circle is r, then the radius of the outer circle is $2r$ since its area is four times that of the outer circle. Here $\pi r^2=3$.

From the figure, we see that

$$\sin\theta=\frac{r}{2r}=\frac{1}{2}\Rightarrow\theta=\pi/6$$

Thus $\angle BAC=2\theta=\pi/3$

and $AB=AC=2\times 2r\cos\left(\frac{\pi}{6}\right)=2\sqrt{3}r$

Hence,

$$\text{Area of }\Delta ABC=\frac{1}{2}\times AB\times AC\times\sin(\angle BAC)$$

$$=6r^2\sin\left(\frac{\pi}{3}\right)=3\sqrt{3}r^2=\frac{9\sqrt{3}}{\pi}$$

2. (d) For an equilateral triangle of side a, radius of the incircle

$$r=\frac{1}{3}a\sin(60^\circ)=\frac{a}{2\sqrt{3}}$$

The largest rectangle that can be inscribed inside a circle is a square whose diagonals are of length $2r$ and whose area $=\frac{1}{2}(2r)^2=\frac{1}{6}a^2$.

3. (d) The intersection points P and Q of the two circles lie on their common chord. The given equations are

$$2x^2+2y^2+5x+p^2+5=0 \quad \ldots(1)$$

and $$x^2+y^2+2x+5y+p^2+p=0 \quad \ldots(2)$$

Multiplying the second equation by 2 and then subtracting from the first equation, gives the equation of the common chord as

$$x-10y-p^2-2p+5=0 \qquad \ldots(3)$$

A circle can be drawn passing through points P, Q and $(4,1)$ only if the three points are non-collinear. That is, if the point $(4,1)$ does not lie on the common chord given by equation (3)

$$\Rightarrow \quad 4-10-p^2-2p+5 \neq 0$$

$$\Rightarrow \quad p^2+2p+1 \neq 0$$

$$\Rightarrow \quad (p+1)^2 \neq 0$$

$$\Rightarrow \quad p \neq -1$$

Hence, p can take all values except one value.

4. (b) Let a, b, c $(a<b<c)$ be the radii of the three inscribed circles. Then, we have the following equations:

$$PQ=\sqrt{(b+a)^2:(b-a)^2}\sqrt{4ab} \rightarrow 4ab=1 \qquad \ldots(1)$$

$$QR=\sqrt{4bc} \Rightarrow 4bc=4 \qquad \ldots(2)$$

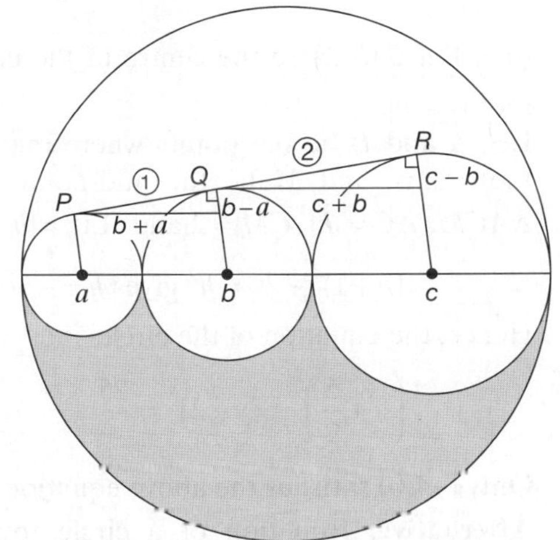

From similar triangles (see figure), we have

$$\frac{c+b}{b+a}=2 \Rightarrow c-b=2a \qquad \ldots(3)$$

Solving the above equations gives $c=4a, b=2a$, and $a=\frac{1}{2\sqrt{2}}$.

Now, the required area is

$$A=\frac{1}{2}\left[\pi(a+b+c)^2-\pi\left(a^2+b^2+c^2\right)\right]$$

$$=\frac{\pi}{2}\left[28a^2\right]=\frac{7\pi}{4}$$

5. (c) Let $CD=x$ and $AB=2x$. Let the radius of the circle $= y$ and hence $AD=2y$ (see figure).

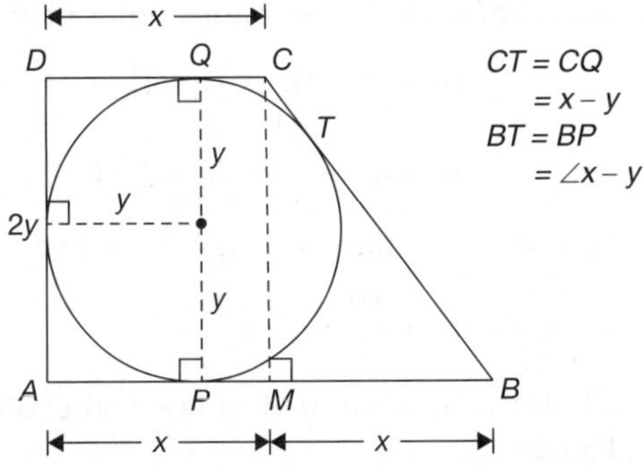

In ΔCMB, $CM=2y$, $BM=x$ and $CB=CT+BT=CQ+BP=x-y+2x-y=3x-2y$. Hence

$$x^2+(2y)^2=(3x-2y)^2 \Rightarrow 2x=3y$$

Also, area of the trapezium $ABCD$ equals 18. Hence

$$\frac{1}{2}(2x+x)\times 2y=18 \Rightarrow xy=6$$

Solving the two equations gives $y=2$.

6. (c)

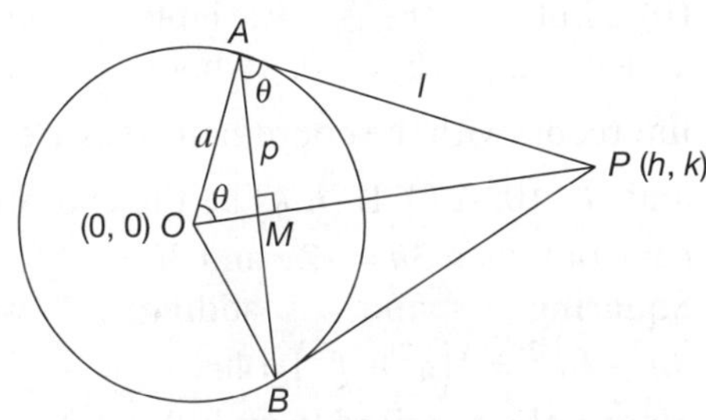

Let O be the centre and PA, PB be the two tangents from point P. Let M be the mid-point of the chord AB (see figure). Then

$$OA=a, OP=\sqrt{h^2+k^2}$$

and $PA=\sqrt{h^2+k^2-a^2}=l$ (say).

Now, length of $AM=p$ (say) is given by

$$p\times OP=OA\times PA$$

$$\rightarrow \quad p=\frac{al}{\sqrt{h^2+k^2}}$$

Hence, area of ΔPAB is

$$\text{Area}=\frac{1}{2}(PA\times AB\sin\theta)$$

$$=\frac{1}{2}\left(l\times 2p\times\frac{p}{a}\right)=\frac{p^2 l}{a}$$

$$=\frac{al^3}{h^2+k^2}=\frac{a\left(h^2+k^2-a^2\right)^{3/2}}{h^2+k^2}$$

7. (d) Let (h, k) be the coordinates of P. Then

$$(h-5)^2+(k+2)^2=4\left[(h-1)^2+(k-1)^2\right]$$

$$\Rightarrow \quad h^2+k^2+\frac{2}{3}h-4k-7=0$$

Hence, P moves on a circle of radius $=\sqrt{\frac{1}{9}+4+7}=\frac{10}{3}$.

Thus, the maximum height of P above AB is $10/3$. Hence

$$\text{Maximum area}=\frac{1}{2}\times AB\times\frac{10}{3}=\frac{25}{3}$$

8. (c) The chord subtends 120° at the centre of the circle. The perpendicular distance of the chord from the centre of the circle= $a\cos 60°=a/2$.

Using distance formula, the perpendicular distance $=\frac{|b|}{\sqrt{2}}$.

Equating the two values gives $\frac{b}{a}=\pm\frac{1}{\sqrt{2}}$.

9. (b) Let the variable circle be $x^2+y^2+2gx+2fy=0$, where $g^2+f^2=a^2$. Its intercepts with the coordinate axes are $A=(-2g,0)$ and $B=(0,-2f)$. If (h,k) be the coordinates of the centroid, then $3h=-2g$ and $3k=-2f$.

Squaring and adding, we have $9h^2+9k^2=4\left(g^2+f^2\right)=4a^2$.

Hence, the required locus is $9x^2+9y^2=4a^2$.

10. (d) The centre will lie on the perpendicular bisector of line joining $(0,0)$ and $(1,0)$, that is, $x=1/2$. Hence, the coordinates of the centre can be chosen as $C(1/2,k)$ and its radius as $r=\sqrt{\left(\frac{1}{2}\right)^2+k^2}$. Centre of the given circle is at $O(0,0)$ and its radius is $R=3$.

Now, if the circles touch each other (in this case, they can only touch internally since the points $(0,0)$ and $(1,0)$ lie inside the given circle), then $OC=R-r$, that is

$$\sqrt{\left(\frac{1}{2}\right)^2+k^2}=3-\sqrt{\left(\frac{1}{2}\right)^2+k^2}$$

$$\Rightarrow \quad 4\left(\frac{1}{4}+k^2\right)=9 \text{ gives } k=\pm\sqrt{2}$$

Hence, the coordinates of the centre of the required circle is $C\left(\frac{1}{2},\pm\sqrt{2}\right)$.

Alternative: Equation of a circle passing through $(0,0)$ and $(1,0)$ can be chosen as

$$x(x-1)+y^2+\lambda y=0$$

$$\Rightarrow \quad x^2+y^2-x+\lambda y=0$$

Its centre is at $C\left(\frac{1}{2},\frac{-\lambda}{2}\right)$ and its radius is $r=\frac{\sqrt{1+\lambda^2}}{2}$.

Centre of the given circle is at $O(0,0)$ and its radius is $R=3$.

Now, if the circles touch each other (in this case they can only touch internally since the points $(0,0)$ and $(1,0)$ lie inside the given circle), then $OC=R-r$, that is

$$\frac{\sqrt{1+\lambda^2}}{2}=3-\frac{\sqrt{1+\lambda^2}}{2}$$

$$\Rightarrow \quad 1+\lambda^2=9 \text{ gives } \lambda=\pm2\sqrt{2}$$

Hence, the coordinates of the centre of the required circle is $C\left(\frac{1}{2},\pm\sqrt{2}\right)$.

11. (d) Let $C(h,2)$ be the centre of the circle. Then radius $=|h|$.

Let A and B be the points where the circle cuts the x-axis, and M be the mid-point of AB. In ΔACM, $AC=|h|$, $CM=2$ and $AM=|h+1|$. Then

$$(h+1)^2+2^2=h^2 \text{ gives } h=-5/2$$

Hence, the equation of the circle

$$\left(x+\frac{5}{2}\right)^2+(y-2)^2=\frac{25}{4}$$

Only $(-4,0)$ satisfies the above equation.

Alternative: Equation of a circle touching the y-axis at $(0,2)$ can be chosen as

$$x^2+(y-2)^2+\lambda x=0$$

Since it passes through $(-1,0)$, $\lambda=5$. Hence, the equation of the circle is

$$x^2+(y-2)^2+5x=0.$$

Only $(-4,0)$ satisfies the above equation.

12. (b) Let $M(h,k)$ be the point whose locus is to be found. Then mid-point of AM is $\left(\frac{h}{2},\frac{k+3}{2}\right)$. It lies on the given circle. Hence

$$\frac{h^2}{4}+2h+\frac{(k-3)^2}{4}=0$$

$$\Rightarrow \quad h^2+k^2+8h-6k+9=0$$

13. (a) Equation of the circle in standard form is

$$(x-7)^2+(y-3)^2=64$$

The coordinates of any point on this circle can be chosen as $P(7+8\cos\theta, 3+8\sin\theta)$

Let $\quad S=3(7+8\cos\theta)+4(3+8\sin\theta)$

$$=33+8(3\cos\theta+4\sin\theta)$$

The greatest value of the function is $33+8\times5=73$.

14. (a),(c) Let $P=(\cos\theta, \sin\theta)$. Equation of the tangent to the circle at P is $x\cos\theta+y\sin\theta=1$. Equation of the tangent at $Q(1,0)$ is $x=1$. Their intersection point is at

$$R\left(1, \frac{1-\cos\theta}{\sin\theta}\right)=(1, \tan(\theta/2))$$

Equation of the normal to the circle at P is $y=x\tan\theta$. Equation of the line through R drawn parallel to the x-axis is $y=\tan(\theta/2)$.

If their intersection point is $S=(h,k)$, then

$$k=h\tan\theta \text{ and } k=\tan(\theta/2)$$

Using the identity $\tan\theta=\dfrac{2\tan(\theta/2)}{1-\tan^2(\theta/2)}$, we have

$$\frac{k}{h}=\frac{2k}{1-k^2}\Rightarrow 1-k^2=2h$$

The points given in options (a), (c) satisfy the above equation.

15. (a),(c),(d)

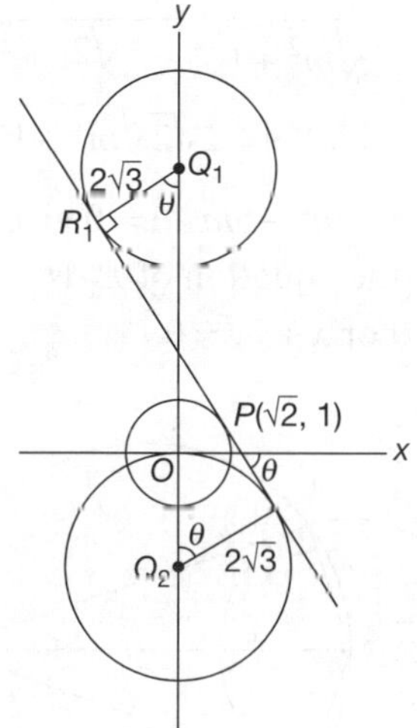

Equation of tangent to the circle at $P(\sqrt{2},1)$ is $\sqrt{2}x+y-3=0$. Slope of this line is $-\sqrt{2}$. Hence $\tan\theta=\sqrt{2}\Rightarrow\sin\theta=\dfrac{\sqrt{2}}{\sqrt{3}}, \cos\theta=\dfrac{1}{\sqrt{3}}$ (see figure).

Let $(0, k)$ be the coordinates of the centres of the circles S_1 and S_2. Then

$$\frac{|k-3|}{\sqrt{3}}=2\sqrt{3}\Rightarrow k=-3, 9$$

$$\Rightarrow \quad Q_1=(0,9) \text{ and } Q_2=(0,-3)$$

Hence $Q_1Q_2=9+3=12\Rightarrow$ Option (a) is correct.

Area of $\Delta PQ_1Q_2=\dfrac{1}{2}\times\sqrt{2}\times12=6\sqrt{2}$

$\Rightarrow$ Option (b) is incorrect.

The coordinates of R_1 and R_2 are

$$R_1=\left(0-2\sqrt{3}\sin\theta, 9-2\sqrt{3}\cos\theta\right)=\left(-2\sqrt{2},7\right)$$

and $R_2=\left(0+2\sqrt{3}\sin\theta, -3+2\sqrt{3}\cos\theta\right)=\left(2\sqrt{2},-1\right)$

Hence $R_1R_2=4\sqrt{6}\Rightarrow$ Option (c) is correct.

Now $PR_1=3\sqrt{6}$ and $PR_2=\sqrt{6}$. Hence $PR_1:PR_2=3:1\Rightarrow$ Option (d) is correct.

16. (c) Length of the side of the equilateral triangle is $a=2$.

Radius of the circumcircle is $r=\dfrac{2}{3}(a\sin60^\circ)=\dfrac{2}{\sqrt{3}}$.

The centre lies on the perpendicular bisector of line joining $A(1,0)$ and $B(-1,0)$, that is, $x=0$. Hence, coordinates of the centre can be chosen as $C(0,k)$.

The value of k can be found from the equation

$$CA=r$$

$$\Rightarrow \quad \sqrt{k^2+1}=\frac{2}{\sqrt{3}} \text{ gives } k=\frac{1}{\sqrt{3}}$$

Hence, the equation of the circumcircle

$$x^2+\left(y-\frac{1}{\sqrt{3}}\right)^2=\frac{4}{3}$$

$$\Rightarrow \quad \sqrt{3}x^2+\sqrt{3}y^2-2y-\sqrt{3}=0$$

17. (d)

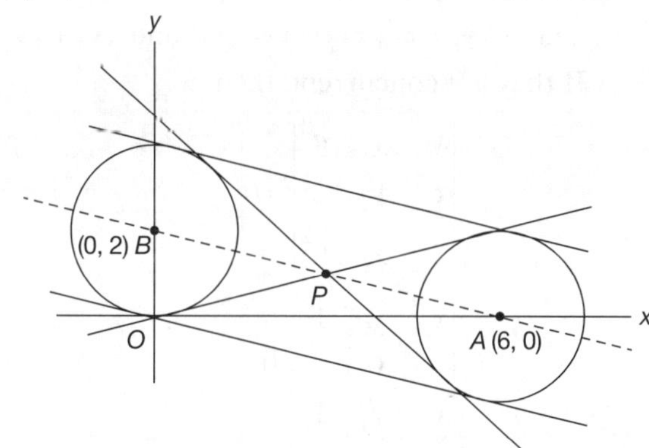

The given circles are of the same radius $=1$ with centres at $A(6,0)$ and $B(0,2)$.

There will be four common tangents (see figure), two of which will be parallel to the line joining their centres, that is, of slope $= -1/3$. Let us choose their equations as $x+3y=c$. Using tangency condition, we have $\frac{|c-6|}{\sqrt{10}} = 1 \Rightarrow c = 6 \pm \sqrt{10}$. Thus, the equations of these two tangents are $x+3y = 6 \pm \sqrt{10}$. The other two common tangents will pass through the point which divides AB internally in the ratio $1:1$, that is, through the point $P(3,1)$. Let us choose their equations as $y-1 = m(x-3)$. Using tangency condition, we have $\frac{|3m+1|}{\sqrt{1+m^2}} = 1 \Rightarrow m = 0, -3/4$.

Thus, the equations of these two tangents are $y=1$ and $3x+4y=13$.

Hence, sum of the y intercepts

$$= \frac{6+\sqrt{10}}{3} + \frac{6-\sqrt{10}}{3} + 1 + \frac{13}{4} = \frac{33}{4}$$

18. (c)

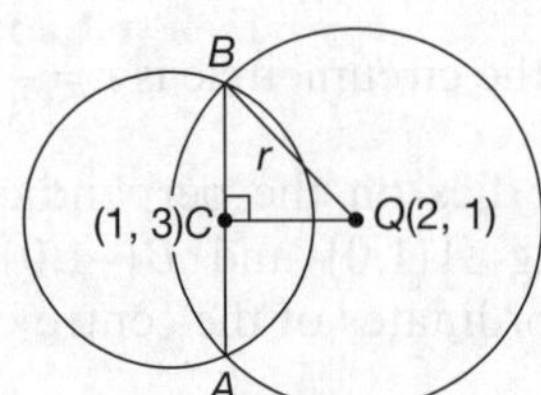

The given circle has centre at $C(1,3)$ and radius $= \sqrt{1^2+3^2-6} = 2$. The mid-point of the common chord AB is at $C(1,3)$. Let r be the radius of the required circle (see figure). Then

$$r^2 = BC^2 + QC^2 = 2^2 + (2-1)^2 + (1-3)^2 = 9$$

Hence $r = 3$.

19. (a) Let $A = (x_1, y_1)$, $B = (x_2, y_2)$ and $C = (x_3, y_3)$. Equations of their chords of contacts are, respectively,

$$xx_1 + yy_1 = a^2,\ xx_2 + yy_2 = a^2 \text{ and } xx_3 + yy_3 = a^2$$

If they are concurrent, then

$$\begin{vmatrix} x_1 & y_1 & a^2 \\ x_2 & y_2 & a^2 \\ x_3 & y_3 & a^2 \end{vmatrix} = 0$$

$$\Rightarrow \begin{vmatrix} x_1 & y_1 & 1 \\ x_2 & y_2 & 1 \\ x_3 & y_3 & 1 \end{vmatrix} = 0$$

$\Rightarrow$ A, B and C are collinear points.

20. (c) The line OP makes angle 53° with the +ve x-axis and line OR makes angle 37° with the –ve x-axis. Hence $\angle POR = 90°$.
If a chord subtends angle θ at the centre, it subtends $\theta/2$ at any point on the major segment of the circle. Hence $\angle POR = 45°$.

21. (c) The y intercept of the given line is $Q(0,3)$. Hence $PQ = \sqrt{S(0,3)} = \sqrt{3^2+18-2} = 5$.

22. (a) The family of lines $x+y=n$ will intersect the circle $x^2+y^2=4$ only if $\frac{n}{\sqrt{2}} \le 2 \Rightarrow n \le 2.8$. So, there are only two chords, namely, $x+y=1$ and $x+y=2$. Their perpendicular distances from the centre $(0,0)$ of the circle are $\frac{1}{\sqrt{2}}$ and $\frac{2}{\sqrt{2}} = \sqrt{2}$, respectively. The radius of the circle is 2. Lengths of the two chords are, respectively,

$$2\sqrt{2^2 - \frac{1}{2}} = \sqrt{14} \text{ and } 2\sqrt{2^2-2} = \sqrt{8}$$

Hence $\quad 11k = 14 + 8 = 22 \Rightarrow k = 2$.

23. (b),(c) The given circle has its centre at $C\left(\frac{1}{2}, \frac{-3}{2}\right)$.

Let $L_1 : y = mx$. The intercepts will be equal if the perpendicular distances from the centre of the circle are equal

$$\frac{\left|\frac{m}{2} + \frac{3}{2}\right|}{\sqrt{m^2+1}} = \frac{\left|\frac{1}{2} - \frac{3}{2} - 1\right|}{\sqrt{2}}$$

$$\Rightarrow \quad |m+3| = 2\sqrt{2}\sqrt{m^2+1}$$

$$\Rightarrow \quad 7m^2 - 6m - 1 = 0 \text{ gives } m = -1/7, 1$$

Hence, the equation of L_1 is
$x - y = 0$ or $x + 7y = 0$.

24. (b)

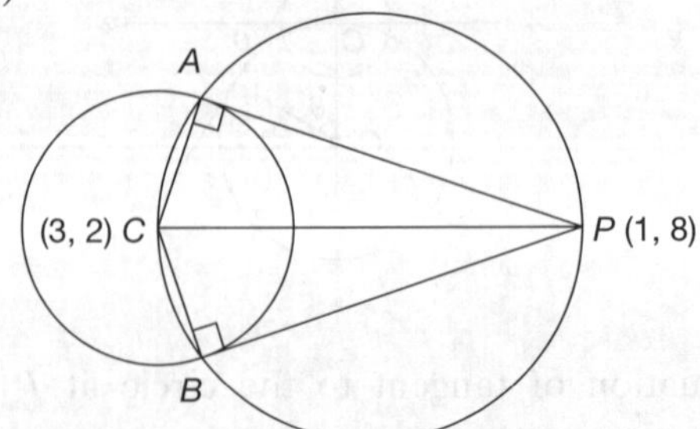

The given circle has its centre at $C(3,2)$. The circumcircle of ΔPAB passes through C, and PC is its diameter (see figure). Hence, the equation of this circle

$$(x-3)(x-1)+(y-2)(y-8)=0$$
$$\Rightarrow \quad x^2+y^2-4x-10y+19=0$$

25. (a) Slope of $AB=2$ and its mid-point is at $M(2,4)$. Equation of the perpendicular bisector of AB

$$y-4=\frac{-1}{2}(x-2)$$
$$\Rightarrow \quad x+2y-10=0$$

It intersects the given diameter $3x+y-6=0$ at point $P\left(\frac{2}{5},\frac{24}{5}\right)$.

Length of the rectangle is

$$AB=\sqrt{(3-1)^2+(6-2)^2}=2\sqrt{5}$$

Width of the rectangle is

$$2\times MP=2\times\sqrt{\left(2-\frac{2}{5}\right)^2+\left(4-\frac{24}{5}\right)^2}=\frac{8}{\sqrt{5}}$$

Area of the rectangle $=2\sqrt{5}\times\frac{8}{\sqrt{5}}=16$

26. (d)

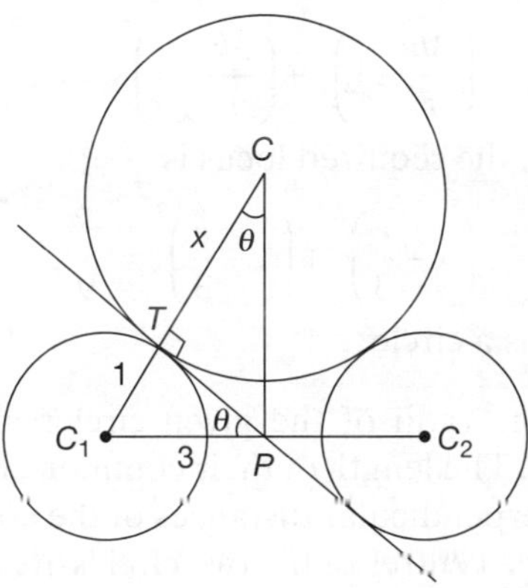

Let x be the radius of the required circle.
Let $\angle C_1PT=\theta$. Then $\angle C_1CP=\theta$ (see figure).

From ΔC_1PT, $\sin\theta=\frac{C_1T}{PT}=\frac{1}{3}$.

From ΔC_1CP, $\sin\theta=\frac{PC_1}{CC_1}=\frac{3}{x+1}$.

Equating the two values gives $x=8$.

27. (c) Equation of the given line in slope-intercept form

$$y=\frac{-a}{b}x+\frac{49}{b}.$$

Let $a=-bm$. Substituting in the given relation $a^2+b^2=1$, we have

$$b^2\left(m^2+1\right)=1$$
$$\Rightarrow \quad \frac{1}{b}=\pm\sqrt{m^2+1}$$

Equation of the given line reduces to

$$y=mx\pm 49\sqrt{m^2+1}$$

The above line is a general tangent to the circle

$$x^2+y^2=49^2$$

28. (b),(d) For any two positive numbers a and b, we know that $a+b>2\sqrt{ab}$. Hence

$$\frac{1}{PS}+\frac{1}{ST}>\frac{2}{\sqrt{PS\cdot ST}}=\frac{2}{\sqrt{QS\cdot SR}}$$

[Property of circle $PS\cdot ST=QS\cdot QR$]

Similarly, we have

$$\Rightarrow \quad QR=QS+SR>2\sqrt{QS\cdot SR}$$
$$\Rightarrow \quad \frac{2}{\sqrt{QS\cdot SR}}>\frac{4}{QR}$$
$$\Rightarrow \quad \frac{1}{PS}+\frac{1}{ST}>\frac{4}{QR}$$

29. (a) The two lines are $x-y=0$ and $x+y=0$. Let $A=(\alpha,\alpha)$ and $B=(\beta,-\beta)$ be the points on the two lines, respectively. Since $\angle AOB=90°$, AB is a diameter of the circle. Hence, its equation is

$$(x-\alpha)(x-\beta)+(x-\alpha)(x+\beta)=0$$
$$\Rightarrow \quad x^2+y^2-(\alpha+\beta)x+(\beta-\alpha)y=0$$
$$\Rightarrow \quad x^2+y^2+ax\pm y\sqrt{a^2-4b}=0$$

30. (b)

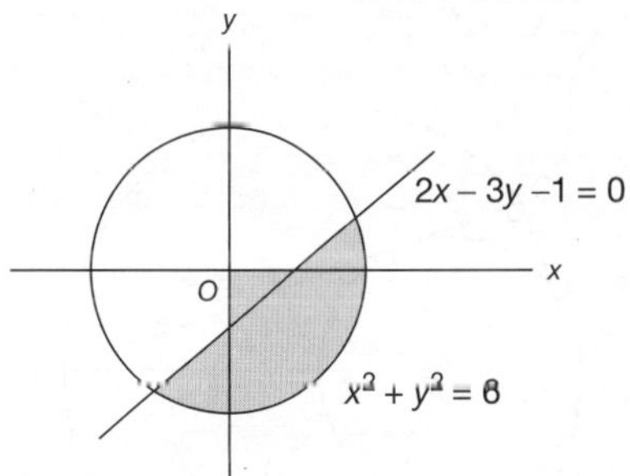

The smaller region (see figure) consists of points lying below the line and inside the circle. Hence, this region is represented by

$$y<\frac{2x-1}{3} \text{ and } x^2+y^2<6$$

Only the first two points in set S satisfy both inequalities.

31. (d)

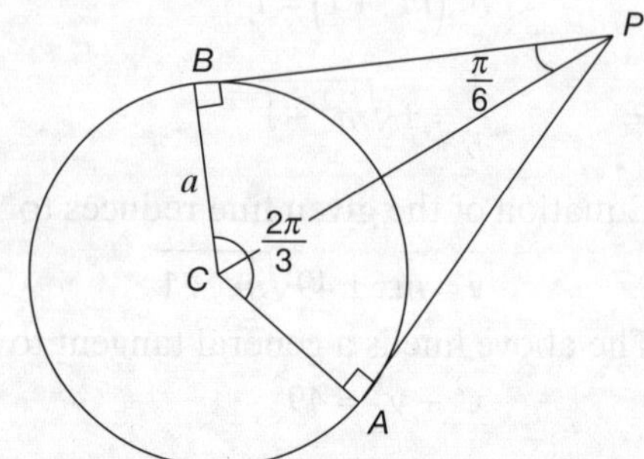

The figure shows a pair of points A and B on the given circle, whose parametric angles differ by $2\pi/3$. The tangents drawn at these points are mutually inclined at $\pi/3$. Their intersection point P lies at a fixed distance $CP = \dfrac{a}{\sin(\pi/6)} = 2a$ from the centre $C(0,0)$ of the given circle.

Hence, the required locus is a circle of radius $2a$ entered at C, that is, $x^2 + y^2 = 4a^2$.

32. (a) The given circle has its centre at $C(1,0)$. Let $y = mx$ be a chord passing through the origin. Let $P(h,k)$ be the mid-point of this chord. Then

$$k = mh$$

Also, CP is perpendicular to the chord. Hence

$$\frac{k}{h-1} = \frac{-1}{m}$$

Eliminating m from the above equations gives

$$k^2 + h(h-1) = 0$$

Hence, the required locus

$$x^2 + y^2 - x = 0$$

33. (c)

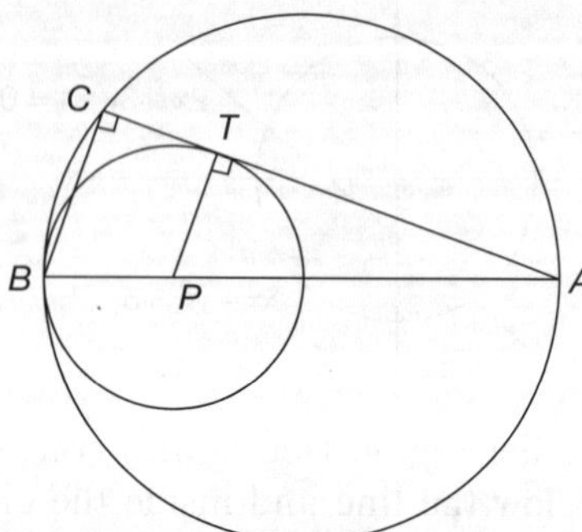

Let P be the centre of the smaller circle and T be the point where the chord AC touches the smaller circle (see figure). Then $\angle ATP = 90°$ and $\angle ACB = 90°$. Now, $\Delta ATP \sim \Delta ACB$. Hence

$$\frac{AC}{AB} = \frac{AT}{AP} = \frac{\sqrt{AP^2 - AT^2}}{AP}$$

$$\Rightarrow \quad \frac{AC}{12} = \frac{\sqrt{9^2 - 3^2}}{9} \text{ gives } AC = 8\sqrt{2}$$

34. (a) Let the equation of the circle be $x^2 + y^2 + 2gx + 2fy + c = 0$.

Using orthogonality condition with each of the three given circles $x^2 + y^2 - 4 = 0$, $x^2 + y^2 - 2x - 3 = 0$ and $x^2 + y^2 - 4y = 0$, we have

$$c - 4 = 0,\ -2g = c - 3, \text{ and } -4f = c$$

$$\Rightarrow \quad c = 4,\ g = -1/2,\ f = -1$$

Hence, the equation of the circle is $x^2 + y^2 - x - 2y + 4 = 0$.

35. (b) Let us choose the fixed points A and B as $(r,0)$ and $(0,r)$, respectively. Let $P(r\cos\theta, r\sin\theta)$ be any point on the given circle. If $M(h,k)$ is the centroid of ΔPAB, then

$$h = \frac{r(1+\cos\theta)}{3} \text{ and } k = \frac{r(1+\sin\theta)}{3}$$

Eliminating θ from the above equations gives

$$\left(\frac{3h}{r} - 1\right)^2 + \left(\frac{3k}{r} - 1\right)^2 = 1$$

Hence, the required locus is

$$\left(x - \frac{r}{3}\right)^2 + \left(y - \frac{r}{3}\right)^2 = \frac{r^2}{9},$$

which is a circle.

36. (c) The radii of the given circles are $r_1 = 8$ and $r_2 = 10$. The length of their common chord is $l = 16$. The perpendicular distances of the common chord from the centres of the two circles are, respectively,

$$\sqrt{r_1^2 - \left(\frac{l}{2}\right)^2} = 0 \text{ and } \sqrt{r_2^2 - \left(\frac{l}{2}\right)^2} = 6$$

The distance between the centres of the two circles is therefore $0 + 6 = 6$. Centre of S_2 is at distance 6 from centre $(0,0)$ of S_1 along the line $y = x$, that is, along $\pi/4$ with the +ve x_axis. Hence its coordinates

$$(0 + 6\cos 45°, 0 + 6\sin 45°) = \left(\frac{6}{\sqrt{2}}, \frac{6}{\sqrt{2}}\right)$$

37. (d) The two given· points are $A(1,0)$ and $B(-1,0)$. The question requires finding the locus of such points P which satisfy the condition $PA : PB = 1 : 3$. Hence the required locus

$$\sqrt{(x-1)^2 + y^2} = \frac{1}{3}\sqrt{(x+1)^2 + y^2}$$

$$\Rightarrow \quad x^2+y^2-\frac{5}{2}x+1=0$$

We see that the locus is a circle centred at $\left(\frac{5}{4},0\right)$.

38. (c) The perpendicular distances of the two chords from the centre of the circle are

$$d_1=2\cos\left(\frac{\pi}{k}\right) \text{ and } d_2=2\cos\left(\frac{\pi}{2k}\right)$$

Since the two chords are parallel, the perpendicular distance between them is d_1+d_2 which is given to be $\sqrt{3}+1$. Hence

$$2\cos\left(\frac{\pi}{k}\right)+2\cos\left(\frac{\pi}{2k}\right)=\sqrt{3}+1$$

$$\Rightarrow \quad \cos\left(\frac{\pi}{k}\right)+\cos\left(\frac{\pi}{2k}\right)=\frac{\sqrt{3}}{2}+\frac{1}{2} \text{ gives } k=3$$

39. (a) Equation of the chord whose mid-point is $P(h,k)$

$$hx+ky-9=h^2+k^2-9$$

$$\Rightarrow \quad hx+ky=h^2+k^2$$

Let $Q\left(t,\frac{4t-20}{5}\right)$ be any point on the given line.

Equation of the chord of contact of Q with the given circle

$$tx+\frac{4t-20}{5}y=9$$

For the two equations to be identical

$$\frac{t}{h}=\frac{4t-20}{5k}=\frac{9}{h^2+k^2}$$

$$\Rightarrow \quad t=\frac{9h}{h^2+k^2} \text{ and } 4t-20=\frac{45k}{h^2+k^2}$$

Eliminating t gives the required locus

$$20\left(x^2+y^2\right)-36x+45y=0$$

40. (b) Let the equation of the required circle be

$$x^2+y^2+2gx+2fy+c=0$$

It is orthogonal to the circle $x^2+y^2-40=0$

$$c=40$$

It passes through the point $(8,4)$

$$2g+f+15=0$$

The above equation shows that the centre $(-g,-f)$ lies on the line

$$2x+y-15=0$$

Of all circles passing through (8, 4) and having centres on the above line, the smallest radius is the perpendicular distance of $(8,4)$ from the above line, that is, $\sqrt{5}$.

41. (c) Equation of the tangent to the given circle at point $(2,3)$

$$2x+3y+2(x+2)-3(y+3)-3=0$$

$$\Rightarrow \quad x-2=0.$$

Equation of a family of circles touching the given circle at point $(2,3)$

$$x^2+y^2+4x-6y-3+\lambda(x-2)=0$$

The required circle passes through $(1,1)$

$$1+1+4-6-3-\lambda=0 \text{ gives } \lambda=-3$$

Hence, the equation of the required circle

$$x^2+y^2+x-6y+3=0$$

42. (d) Equation of a family of circles touching the line $y=x$ at the origin

$$x^2+y^2+\lambda(x-y)=0$$

Equation of the common chord of the given circle and the above circle

$$\lambda x-(\lambda+2)y+3=0$$

If the common chord bisects the circumference of the given circle, it must pass through its centre $(0,-1)$

$$\lambda+2+3=0 \text{ gives } \lambda=-5$$

Hence, the equation of the required circle

$$x^2+y^2-5x+5y=0$$

43. (b) Let us choose our reference frame as shown in the figure. Let $AB=a$ and $AD=b$ be the lengths of the sides of the rectangle. Then $C=(a,b)$. Let the centre of the circle be $P=(h,h)$.

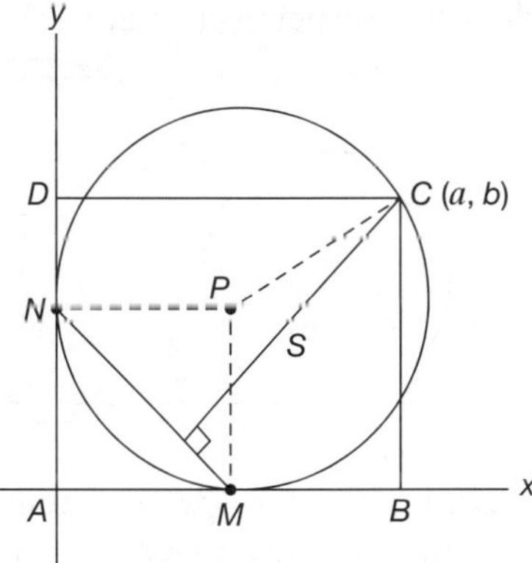

Then radius of the circle is $PM=PN=h \Rightarrow PC=h$. Hence

$$(a-h)^2+(b-h)^2=h^2$$

$$\Rightarrow \quad a^2+b^2+h^2-2h(a+b)=0 \quad \ldots(1)$$

Equation of line MN is $x+y=h$. Distance of C from MN is given to be 5 .

$$\Rightarrow \quad |a+b-h| = 5\sqrt{2}$$

$$\Rightarrow \quad a^2+b^2+h^2+2ab-2h(a+b) = 50 \quad \ldots(2)$$

Subtracting the above equations, we have $ab = 25$, which is the area of rectangle $ABCD$.

44. (b)

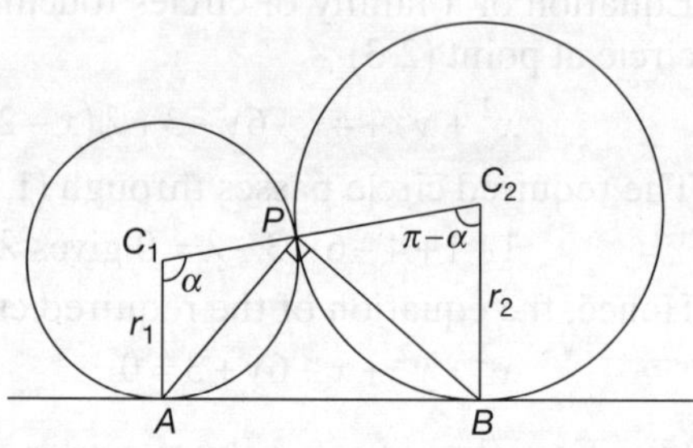

The triangle ΔAPB is right-angled at P. This can be easily proved:

Let C_1 and C_2 be the centres of the two circles. In the trapezium AC_1C_2B, if we choose $\angle AC_1C_2 = \alpha$, then $\angle AC_1C_2 = \pi-\alpha$. Now, since the triangles ΔAC_1P and ΔBC_2P are both isosceles, $\angle APC_1 = \dfrac{\pi-\alpha}{2}$ and $\angle BPC_2 = \dfrac{\alpha}{2}$. Now,

$$\angle APB = \pi - (\angle APC_1 + \angle BPC_2) = \pi/2.$$

In that case, the circumcentre lies on the hypotenuse AB and the circumradius equals $AB/2$. Now $AB = \sqrt{(r_1+r_2)^2-(r_1-r_2)^2} = 2\sqrt{r_1r_2}$.

Hence, the circumradius equals $\sqrt{r_1r_2}$.

45. (a) Let A, B, C be the centres of the circles of radii a, b, c, respectively. Let

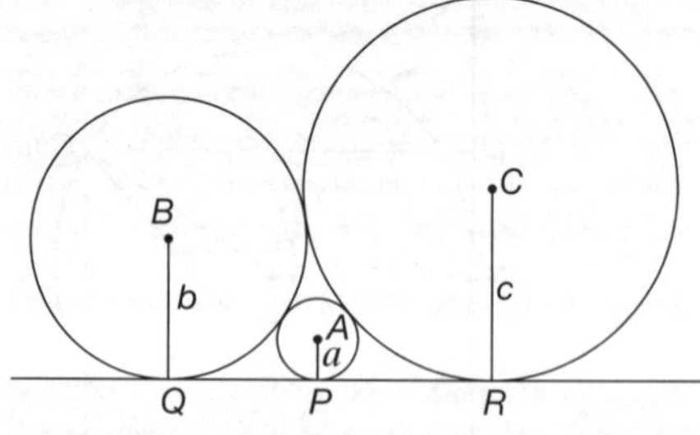

P, Q, R be their respective contact points with the common tangent (see figure). Now, using the formula for the length of a direct tangent, we have

$$QP = \sqrt{(b+a)^2-(b-a)^2} = 2\sqrt{ab}$$

$$PR = \sqrt{(c+a)^2-(c-a)^2} = 2\sqrt{ac}$$

$$QR = \sqrt{(c+b)^2-(c-b)^2} = 2\sqrt{bc}$$

Now $QP+PR = QR$. Hence, we have

$$\sqrt{ab}+\sqrt{ac} = \sqrt{bc} \Rightarrow \sqrt{a}\left(\sqrt{b}+\sqrt{c}\right) = \sqrt{bc}$$

46. (a)-(r), (b)-(p), (c)-(q), (d)-(s) Radius of the incircle is 1. If a is the side length of the equilateral triangle, then

$$\frac{1}{3}a\sin 60° = 1 \text{ gives } a = 2\sqrt{3}$$

Points P and Q are at distance $\sqrt{3}$ on either side of D. Hence

$$P = \left(\frac{3\sqrt{3}}{2}+\sqrt{3}\cos 60°, \frac{3}{2}-\sqrt{3}\sin 60°\right) = \left(2\sqrt{3}, 0\right)$$

$$\text{and } Q = \left(\frac{3\sqrt{3}}{2}-\sqrt{3}\cos 60°, \frac{3}{2}+\sqrt{3}\sin 60°\right) = \left(\sqrt{3}, 3\right)$$

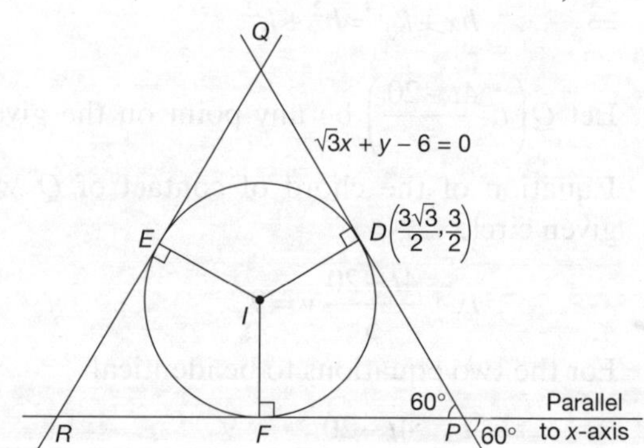

Point R is at distance $2\sqrt{3}$ to the left of P along the –ve direction of the x-axis. Hence (see figure)

$$R = \left(2\sqrt{3}-2\sqrt{3}, 0\right) = (0,0)$$

Points E and F are the mid-points of QR and PR, respectively. Hence

$$E = \left(\frac{\sqrt{3}}{2}, \frac{3}{2}\right) \text{ and } F = \left(\sqrt{3}, 0\right)$$

The incentre of an equilateral triangle coincides with its centroid. Hence

$$I = \left(\sqrt{3}, 1\right)$$

CHAPTER

28 Parabola

- **Equation of the Parabola:** The equation of the parabola with vertex at $O(0,0)$, distance between focus and vertex equal a, and axis along the x-axis is

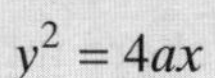

$$y^2 = 4ax$$

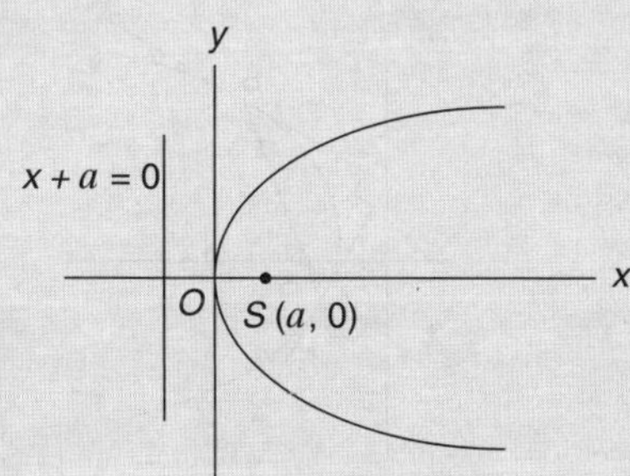

A few quantities related to the parabola:

$$\text{Focus: } S = (a,0)$$

$$\text{Directrix: } x + a = 0$$

$$\text{Extremities of latus-rectum: } (a, \pm 2a)$$

$$\text{Focal distance: } SP = |x + a|$$

- **Parametric Representation:** The parametric representation of this parabola is

$$x = at^2 \text{ and } y = 2at$$

Equation of a general tangent to this parabola is

$$y = mx + \frac{a}{m} \text{ at point } P = \left(\frac{a}{m^2}, \frac{2a}{m}\right)$$

Equation of a general normal to this parabola is

$$y = mx - 2am - am^3 \text{ at point } P = \left(am^2, -2am\right)$$

Useful result: Tangents drawn at points $P\left(at_1^2, 2at_1\right)$ and $Q\left(at_2^2, 2at_2\right)$ intersect at point $R\left(at_1t_2, a\left(t_1 + t_2\right)\right)$.

- **Some Properties of the Parabola:**
  1. If the tangent and normal at any point P of a parabola meet the axis at A and B, respectively, then $SA - SB = SP$, where S is the focus.

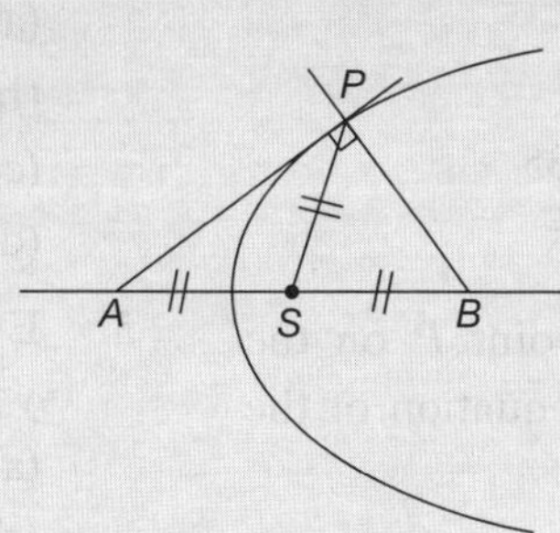

2. If the tangent at any point P of a parabola meets the directrix at Q, then PQ subtends a right angle at the focus.

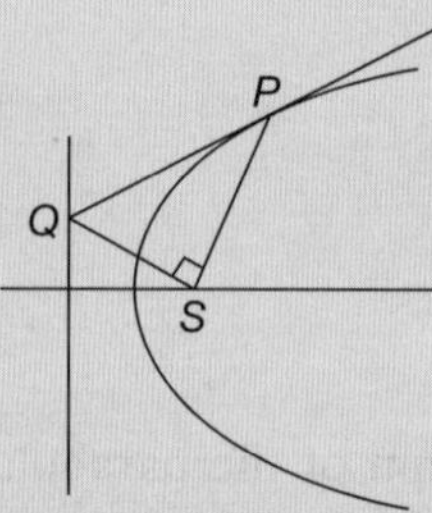

3. Tangents at the extremities of any focal chord intersect at right angles on the directrix.

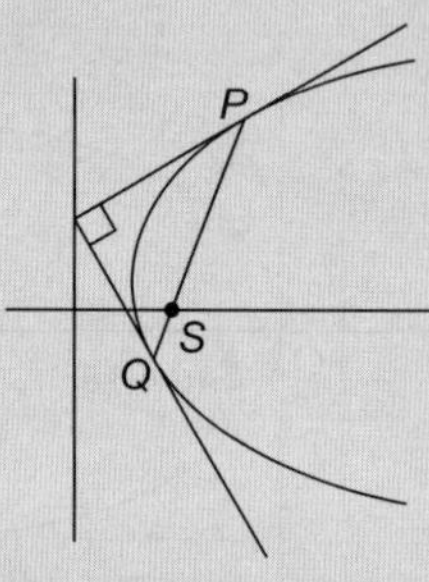

4. A line through the focus S and perpendicular to the tangent at any point P will intersect at a point which lies on the tangent at the vertex.

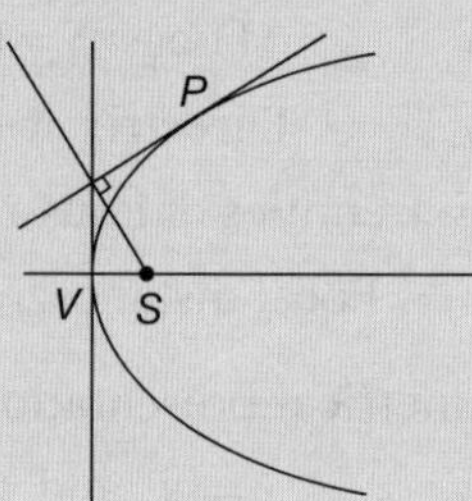

EXERCISES

1. If the line $x-1=0$ is the directrix of the parabola $y^2-kx+4y+12=0$, then one of the values of k is:
(a) $1/8$ (b) 8
(c) 4 (d) $1/4$

2. The locus of the vertices of the family of parabolas $x=\frac{a^3}{3}y^2+\frac{a^2}{2}y-2a$ is:
(a) $4xy=3$ (b) $16xy=35$
(c) $64xy=105$ (d) $6xy=25$

3. If $x-2y=c$ is the normal at a point P on the parabola $x^2-2x+y=0$, then the equation of the tangent to the parabola at point P is:
(a) $3x-y-6=0$ (b) $2x+y-4=0$
(c) $6x+y-12=0$ (d) $x-4y-2=0$

4. If the angle between the pair of tangents drawn from a point P to the parabola $y^2=4x$ is $\pi/3$, then the locus of P is:
(a) $x^2-y^2+x+3=0$
(b) $x^2-2y^2+3x+1=0$
(c) $3x^2-y^2+10x+3=0$
(d) $x^2-y^2+6x+1=0$

5. Equation of the common tangent to the parabola $y^2=8x$ and $xy=-1$ is:
(a) $3y=x+3$ (b) $2y=x+2$
(c) $y=x+2$ (d) $y=-x+1$

6. The curve described parametrically by $x = t^2 + t + 1$ and $y = t^2 - t + 1$ represents:
(a) A hyperbola (b) An ellipse
(c) A parabola (d) A pair of straight lines

7. The tangent (having non-zero slope) common to the parabolas $y = -(x-2)^2$ and $y = x^2$ touches the circle $17x^2 + 17y^2 - 34x - 68y + 81 = 0$ at point:
(a) $\left(\frac{18}{17}, \frac{22}{17}\right)$ (b) $\left(\frac{25}{17}, \frac{32}{17}\right)$
(c) $\left(\frac{21}{17}, \frac{41}{17}\right)$ (d) $\left(\frac{22}{17}, \frac{28}{17}\right)$

8. The shortest distance between the parabolas $y^2 = x - 1$ and $x^2 = y - 1$ is:
(a) $\frac{5\sqrt{2}}{4}$ (b) $\frac{2\sqrt{2}}{4}$
(c) $\frac{\sqrt{2}}{4}$ (d) $\frac{3\sqrt{2}}{4}$

9. The locus of the centre of circles passing through the fixed point $(0, b)$ and cutting an intercept of fixed length $2a$ on the x-axis is a parabola with directix $y + 1 = 0$. Then the value of $a^2 / 2b$ is:
(a) 1 (b) 2
(c) 3 (d) 4

10. The sides of an equilateral triangle ΔABC touch the parabola $y^2 = 4x$. Then the points A, B, C lie on:
(a) $y^2 = (x+1)^2 + 4x$
(b) $y^2 = 3(x+1)^2 + x$
(c) $y^2 = 3(x+1)^2 + 4x$
(d) $y^2 = (x+1)^2 + x$

11. AB, AC are tangents to the parabola $y^2 = 4ax$. If p_1, p_2, p_3 are lengths of the perpendiculars from A, B, C on any tangent to the parabola, then p_2, p_1, p_3 are in:
(a) AP (b) GP
(c) HP (d) None of these

12. Let S be the focus of the parabola $y^2 = 8x$ and let PQ be the common chord of the circle $x^2 + y^2 - 2x - 4y = 0$ and the given parabola. Area of the triangle PQS is:
(a) 4 (b) $3/2$
(c) 5/4 (d) $4/5$

13. Normal to the parabola $y^2 = 4ax$ at point $A(\lambda, \lambda)$, meets the parabola again at B. Angle subtended by chord AB at the focus of the parabola is
(a) $\pi/2$ (b) $\pi/3$
(c) $\pi/4$ (d) $\pi/6$

14. Let A and B be two distinct points on the parabola $y^2 = 4x$. A circle is drawn with AB as its diameter and touching the axis of the parabola. If the radius of this circle is r, then the possible values of the slope of line AB are:
(a) $\pm\frac{1}{r}$ (b) $\pm\frac{2}{r}$
(c) $\pm\frac{r}{2}$ (d) None of these

15. Consider two parabolas P_1 and P_2 whose vertices coincide with the origin and their foci are at $S_1(2,0)$ and $S_2(-4,0)$, respectively. If m_1 is the slope of a tangent to P_1 passing through S_2, and m_2 is the slope of a tangent to P_2 passing through S_1, then the value of $\frac{1}{m_1^2} + m_2^2$ is:
(a) 4 (b) 5
(c) 7 (d) 8

16. A circle is given by $x^2 + (y-1)^2 = 1$. The locus of the centre of a circle that externally touches the given circle and the x-axis is:
(a) A straight line
(b) A circle with radius = 2
(c) A parabola with latus-rectum = 4
(d) None of these

17. If l denotes the length of the semi-latus rectum of a parabola and SP, SQ denote the segments of any focal chord PQ, S being the focus, then SP, l, SQ are in the relation:
(a) HP (b) GP
(c) AP (d) $l^2 = SP^2 + SQ^2$

18. A tangent and a normal drawn at any point Q on the parabola $y^2 = 4x$ meet the axis of the parabola at points M and N, respectively. The locus of the centroid of triangle QMN is another parabola whose directrix is:
(a) $x = 2/3$ (b) $x = 1/3$
(c) $x = -1/3$ (d) $x = 0$

19. Let curve C be the mirror image of the parabola $y^2 = 4x$ with respect to the line $x + y + 4 = 0$. If A and B are the intersection points of C with the line $y = -5$, then the distance between A and B is:
(a) 8 (b) 6
(c) 4 (d) 2

20. $P(0,2)$ is a point on the line $4y-3x-8=0$. If this line intersects the parabola $x^2+y-4=0$ at points A and B, then $PA \cdot PB$ equals:

(a) 3 (b) $\sqrt{2}$

(c) $\frac{25}{8}$ (d) $\frac{13}{\sqrt{5}}$

21. Let P and Q be two distinct points on the parabola $y^2=2x$ such that a circle with PQ as diameter passes through the vertex O of the parabola. If P lies in the first quadrant and the area of ΔOPQ is $3\sqrt{2}$, then coordinates of P are:

(a) $(4,2\sqrt{2})$ (b) $(9,3\sqrt{2})$

(c) $\left(\frac{1}{4},\frac{1}{\sqrt{2}}\right)$ (d) $(1,\sqrt{2})$

22. The radius of the smallest circle touching the parabola $4x^2+4y-17=0$ and the lines $y=|x|$ is:

(a) $2(\sqrt{2}-1)$ (b) $1/\sqrt{2}$

(c) $\sqrt{2}+1$ (d) $\sqrt{2}$

23. Consider a parabola whose latus-rectum is of length l. The locus of the mid-points of its focal chords is another parabola with latus-rectum of length:

(a) l (b) $l/2$

(c) $l/3$ (d) $l/4$

24. The tangent and normal are drawn at $P(16, 16)$ on the parabola $y^2=16x$, which intersects the axis of the parabola at A and B, respectively. If C is the circumcentre of ΔPAB and $\angle CPB=\theta$, then the value of $\tan\theta$ is:

(a) $1/2$ (b) 2

(c) 3 (d) $4/3$

25. AB is a double ordinate of the parabola $y^2=4x$. Tangents drawn to the parabola at A and B meet the y-axis at A_1 and B_1, respectively. If the area of the trapezium AA_1B_1B is 24 sq. units, then the angle subtended by A_1B_1 at the focus of the parabola equals:

(a) $2\tan^{-1}(2)$ (b) $2\tan^{-1}(3)$

(c) $\tan^{-1}(\sqrt{2}+1)$ (d) $\tan^{-1}(\sqrt{3}+1)$

26. Let P be the point on the parabola $y^2=4x$ nearest to the centre C of the circle $x^2+y^2-4x-16y+64=0$. Let Q be the point on the circle dividing CP internally. Then the correct statements from the following are:

(a) $CP=4\sqrt{5}$

(b) $CQ:QP=\sqrt{5}+1:4$

(c) Slope of the tangent to the circle at $Q=1/2$

(d) x intercept of the normal to the parabola at $P=4$

27. The circle $x^2+y^2=9$ and the parabola $y^2=8x$ intersect at P and Q in the first and fourth quadrants, respectively. Tangents to the circle at P and Q intersect the x-axis at R, and tangents to the parabola at P and Q intersect the x-axis at S. Match the columns:

(a) Length of PQ	(p) $3\sqrt{3}$
(b) $\frac{\text{Area of } \Delta PQR}{\text{Area of } \Delta PQS}$	(q) 4
(c) Radius of circumcircle of ΔPRS	(r) $4\sqrt{2}$
(d) Radius of incircle of ΔPQR	(s) 2

ANSWER KEYS

1. (c) **2.** (c) **3.** (b) **4.** (c) **5.** (c) **6.** (c) **7.** (b) **8.** (d) **9.** (a)
10. (c) **11.** (b) **12.** (a) **13.** (a) **14.** (b) **15.** (a) **16.** (a), (c) **17.** (a) **18.** (b)
19. (c) **20.** (c) **21.** (a),(d) **22.** (d) **23.** (b) **24.** (b) **25.** (a) **26.** (b),(c)
27. (a)-(r), (b)-(q), (c)-(p), (d)-(s)

SOLUTIONS

1. (c) Equation of the given ellipse in standard form

$$(y+2)^2 = k\left(x-\frac{8}{k}\right)$$

Equation of its directrix is

$$x-\frac{8}{k}+\frac{k}{4}=0$$

Comparing with the given equation $x-1=0$

$$\frac{8}{k}-\frac{k}{4}=1$$

$\Rightarrow$ $k^2-4k+32=0$ gives $k=-8,4$

2. (c) For the parabola $x=ay^2+by+c$, the vertex is at $\left(\frac{-D}{4a},\frac{-b}{2a}\right)$

If (h,k) are the coordinates of the vertices of the given parabola, then

$$h=-\frac{\frac{a^4}{4}+\frac{8a^3}{3}}{\frac{4a^3}{3}}=-\frac{35a}{16}$$

and $k=-\dfrac{\frac{a^2}{2}}{\frac{2a^3}{3}}=-\dfrac{3}{4a}$

Multiplying the two equations, we have

$$hk=\frac{105}{64}$$

Hence, the required locus is $64xy=105$.

3. (b) Equation of the general normal to the parabola $(x-1)^2=-(y-1)$ is

$$x-1=m(y-1)-2am-am^3$$

and the coordinates of the foot of the normal are $\left(-2am+1,\ am^2+1\right)$, where $a=-1/4$.

For the given normal $(x=2y+c)$, $m=2$. Putting the values of a and m, we have the foot of this normal as $(2,0)$.

Equation of the tangent at this point

$$2x-(x+2)+\frac{y}{2}=0\Rightarrow 2x+y-4=0$$

4. (c) Let $P(h,k)$ be one such point whose locus is to be found. Equation of the general tangent to the given parabola

$$y=mx+\frac{1}{m}$$

Since the tangent passes through $P(h,k)$

$$k=mh+\frac{1}{m}$$

$\Rightarrow$ $hm^2-km+1=0$

If m_1 and m_2 are the roots of this equation, then

$$m_1+m_2=\frac{k}{h},\ m_1m_2=\frac{1}{h}$$

and $|m_1-m_2|=\dfrac{\sqrt{k^2-4h}}{h}$

If the angle between the tangents is $\pi/6$, then

$$\sqrt{3}=\left|\frac{m_1-m_2}{1+m_1m_2}\right|=\frac{\sqrt{k^2-4h}}{h+1}$$

$\Rightarrow$ $3h^2-k^2+10h+3=0$

5. (c) Equation of the general tangent to the given parabola

$$y=mx+\frac{2}{m}$$

Its intersection with the curve $xy = -1$ is given by

$$x\left(mx + \frac{2}{m}\right) = -1$$

$$\Rightarrow \quad m^2x^2 + 2x + m = 0$$

For tangency, the roots of the above quadratic equations must be identical

$$D = 0 \Rightarrow 4 - 4m^3 = 0 \text{ gives } m = 1$$

Hence, the equation of the common tangent

$$y = x + 2$$

6. (c) Subtracting the two equations, we have $2t = x - y$. Putting this value in the first equation, we have

$$4x = (x-y)^2 + 2(x-y) + 4$$

$$\Rightarrow \quad x^2 - 2xy + y^2 - 2x - 2y + 4 = 0$$

Comparing with the general second-degree equation $ax^2 + 2hxy + by^2 + 2gx + 2fy + c = 0$, we have $a = b = 1, c = 4, f = g = h = -1$.

The equation does not represent a circle since $h \neq 0$.

It does not represent a pair of straight lines since

$$\begin{vmatrix} 1 & -1 & -1 \\ -1 & 1 & -1 \\ -1 & -1 & 4 \end{vmatrix} = 3 - 5 - 2 \neq 0$$

Now, $h^2 - ab = 0 \Rightarrow$ It represents a parabola.

7. (b) Equation of the general tangent to the given parabolas

$$x = my + \frac{1}{4m} \text{ and } x - 2 = m'y - \frac{1}{4m'}$$

For the two equations to be identical

$$m' = m \text{ and } 2 - \frac{1}{4m'} = \frac{1}{4m}$$

$$\Rightarrow \quad 2 - \frac{1}{4m} = \frac{1}{4m} \text{ gives } m = \frac{1}{4}$$

Hence, the equation of the common tangent is $4x - y - 4 = 0$. Let (h,k) be the point where this tangent touches the given circle $17x^2 + 17y^2 - 34x - 68y + 81 = 0$. Then the equation of the tangent should be identical to:

$$17hx + 17ky - 17(x+h) - 34(y+k) + 81 = 0$$

$$\Rightarrow \quad 17(h-1)x + 17(k-2)y - 17h - 34k + 81 = 0$$

Comparing with $4x - y - 4 = 0$, we have

$$\frac{17(h-1)}{4} = \frac{17(2-k)}{1} = \frac{17h + 34k - 81}{4}$$

$$\Rightarrow \quad h = \frac{25}{17} \text{ and } k = \frac{32}{17}$$

8. (d)

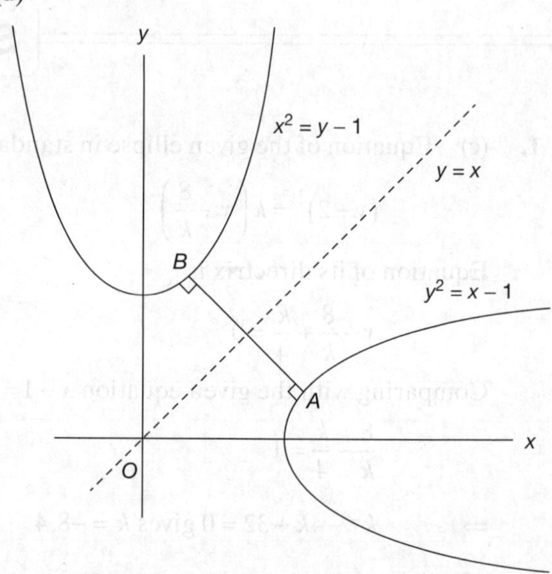

The shortest distance between the two curves is along the common normal AB (see figure). Equations of general normals to the given parabolas $y^2 = x - 1$ and $x^2 = y - 1$ are, respectively,

$$y = m(x-1) - \frac{1}{2}m - \frac{1}{4}m^3 \Rightarrow y = mx - \frac{3}{2}m - \frac{1}{4}m^3$$

and $\quad x = m'(y-1) - \frac{1}{2}m' - \frac{1}{4}m'^3$

$$\Rightarrow y = \frac{1}{m'}x + \frac{3}{2} + \frac{1}{4}m'^2$$

The coordinates of their foot are, respectively,

$$A\left(\frac{1}{4}m^2 + 1, \frac{-1}{2}m\right) \text{ and } B\left(\frac{-1}{2}m', \frac{1}{4}m'^2 + 1\right)$$

For the above equations to be identical, we have

$$\frac{1}{m'} = m \text{ and } -\frac{3}{2}m - \frac{1}{4}m^3 = \frac{3}{2} + \frac{1}{4}m'^2$$

$$\Rightarrow \quad -\frac{3}{2}m - \frac{1}{4}m^3 = \frac{3}{2} + \frac{1}{4m^2}$$

$$\Rightarrow \quad m^5 + 6m^3 + 6m^2 + 1 = 0 \text{ gives } m = -1$$

Hence $A = \left(\frac{5}{4}, \frac{1}{2}\right)$ and $B = \left(\frac{1}{2}, \frac{5}{4}\right)$. The minimum distance between the parabolas is

$$AB = \frac{3\sqrt{2}}{4}$$

Alternative: We can see that the two parabolas are symmetric about the line $y = x$. Hence, the slope of the common normal must be -1.
Equation of the general normal to the parabola $y^2 = x - 1$ is $y = m(x-1) - \frac{1}{2}m - \frac{1}{4}m^3$ and the coordinates of its foot are $A\left(\frac{1}{4}m^2 + 1, \frac{-1}{2}m\right)$.
Putting $m = -1$, we have $A = \left(\frac{5}{4}, \frac{1}{2}\right)$. This normal at A will intersect the other parabola normally at point $B = \left(\frac{1}{2}, \frac{5}{4}\right)$.
The minimum distance between the parabolas is $AB = \frac{3\sqrt{2}}{4}$.

9. (a) Let us choose the x intercepts as $A(t, 0)$ and $B(t + 2a, 0)$. Let $C(h, k)$ be the centre of the circle passing through A, B and the fixed point $P(0, b)$. Then

$$CA = CB \Rightarrow h = t + a$$

and $$CA = CP \Rightarrow h^2 + (k-b)^2 = (h-t)^2 + k^2$$

Putting $h = t + a$ in the second equation, we have

$$h^2 = 2bk + a^2 - b^2.$$

Thus, the required locus is

$$x^2 = 2b\left(y + \frac{a^2 - b^2}{2b}\right)$$

It is a parabola with directrix $y + \frac{a^2 - b^2}{2b} + \frac{b}{2} = 0 \Rightarrow y + \frac{a^2}{2b} = 0$. Comparing with the given equation $y + 1 = 0$, we have $\frac{a^2}{2b} = 1$.

10. (c) Let the sides AB, BC, CA touch the parabola $y^2 = 4x$ at points $P(t_1^2, 2t_1), Q(t_2^2, 2t_2)$ and $R(t_3^2, 2t_3)$, respectively. Let $A = (h, k)$. Then

$$h = t_1 t_3 \quad \ldots(1)$$

and $$k = t_1 + t_3 \quad \ldots(2)$$

The slopes of the sides AB, BC, CA are $\frac{1}{t_1}, \frac{1}{t_2}, \frac{1}{t_3}$, respectively. Since the triangle is equilateral, we have

$$\left|\frac{\frac{1}{t_1} - \frac{1}{t_3}}{1 + \frac{1}{t_1 t_3}}\right| = \sqrt{3}$$

$$\Rightarrow \quad |t_3 - t_1| = \sqrt{3}|t_3 t_1 + 1| \quad \ldots(3)$$

From equations (2) and (3), we have

$$|t_3 - t_1| = \sqrt{3}|h + 1| \quad \ldots(4)$$

Now squaring and subtracting (2) and (4), we have

$$4t_1 t_3 = k^2 - 3(h+1)^2$$

$$\Rightarrow \quad 4h = k^2 - 3(h+1)^2$$

Hence, the points A, B, C lie on $y^2 = 3(x+a)^2 + 4ax$.

11. (b) Let $B = (at_1^2, 2at_1), C = (at_2^2, 2at_2)$ and $A = (at_1t_2, a(t_1 + t_2))$. Let $y = mx + \frac{a}{m}$ be any tangent to the parabola. Then

$$p_1 = \frac{\left|mat_1t_2 - a(t_1 + t_2) + \frac{a}{m}\right|}{\sqrt{1 + m^2}}$$

$$= \frac{a\left|m^2 t_1 t_2 - m(t_1 + t_2) + 1\right|}{m\sqrt{1 + m^2}}$$

$$= \frac{a\left|(mt_1 - 1)(mt_2 - 1)\right|}{m\sqrt{1 + m^2}}$$

$$p_2 = \frac{\left|mat_1^2 - 2at_1 + \frac{a}{m}\right|}{\sqrt{1+m^2}}$$
$$= \frac{a\left|m^2t_1^2 - 2mt_1 + 1\right|}{m\sqrt{1+m^2}} = \frac{a(mt_1 - 1)^2}{m\sqrt{1+m^2}}$$

and $$p_3 = \frac{\left|mat_2^2 - 2at_2 + \frac{a}{m}\right|}{\sqrt{1+m^2}}$$
$$= \frac{a\left|m^2t_2^2 - 2mt_2 + 1\right|}{m\sqrt{1+m^2}} = \frac{a(mt_2 - 1)^2}{m\sqrt{1+m^2}}$$

We see that $p_1^2 = p_2p_3$. Hence p_2, p_1, p_3 are in GP.

12. (a) Focus of the given parabola is at $S(2,0)$. Intersection point of $y^2 = 8x$ and

$x^2 + y^2 - 2x - 4y = 0$ is given by

$$\left(\frac{y^2}{8}\right)^2 + y^2 - 2\left(\frac{y^2}{8}\right) - 4y = 0$$

$\Rightarrow$ $y\left(y^3 + 48y - 256\right) = 0$ gives $y = 0, 4$ and corresponding $x = 0, 2$.

The points are $P(0,0)$ and $Q(2,4)$.

Area of the triangle PQS

$$= \frac{1}{2} \times PS \times \text{Distance of } Q \text{ from } PS = \frac{1}{2} \times 2 \times 4 = 4$$

13. (a) If $A(\lambda, \lambda)$ lies on $y^2 = 4ax$, then $\lambda^2 = 4a\lambda \Rightarrow \lambda = 4a$.

However, $\lambda = 0$ is not acceptable, since the normal at $(0,0)$ does not meet the parabola again. Now, equation of normal at $A(4a, 4a)$ is

$$y = -2x + 12a$$

The normal meets the parabola again at point B (say), whose abscissa is given by

$$(2x - 12a)^2 = 4ax$$

$\Rightarrow$ $x^2 - 13ax + 36a^2 = 0$ gives $x = 4a, 9a$

Hence $B(9a, -6a)$. The focus is at $S(a,0)$. The slopes of SA and SB are, respectively, $4/3$ and $-3/4$. Hence, the angle between SA and SB is $\pi/2$.

14. (b)

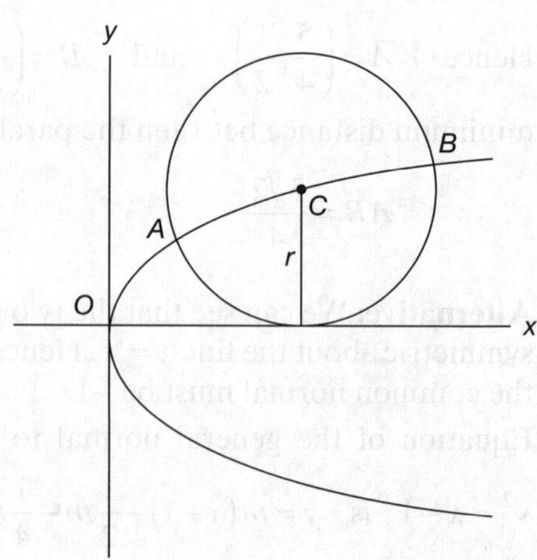

Let $A = \left(t_1^2, 2t_1\right)$ and $B = \left(t_2^2, 2t_2\right)$ (see figure).

Centre of circle having AB as diameter is $C = \left(\frac{t_1^2 + t_2^2}{2}, t_1 + t_2\right)$.

Since the circle touches the x-axis, $|t_1 + t_2| = r$.

Now, slope of $AB = \frac{2(t_1 - t_2)}{t_1^2 - t_2^2} = \frac{2}{t_1 + t_2} = \frac{2}{\pm r}$.

15. (a) Equations of the parabolas P_1 and P_2 are $y^2 = 8x$ and $y^2 = -16x$.

A tangent to the parabola P_1 can be chosen as $y = m_1x + \frac{2}{m_1}$. If it passes through $S_2(-4, 0)$, then

$$-4m_1 + \frac{2}{m_1} = 0 \Rightarrow \frac{1}{m_1^2} = 2.$$

A tangent to the parabola P_2 can be chosen as $y = m_2x - \frac{4}{m_2}$. If it passes through $S_1(2,0)$, then

$$2m_2 - \frac{4}{m_2} = 0 \Rightarrow m_2^2 = 2.$$

Hence $\frac{1}{m_1^2} + m_2^2 = 4$.

16. (a),(c) The given circle has its centre at $C(0,1)$ and radius $= 1$.

Let $P(h,k)$ be the centre of the variable circle. Since it touches the x-axis, its radius $= |k|$.

The two circles touch each other externally. Hence, the distance between their centres must equal to the sum of their radii

$$\sqrt{h^2+(k-1)^2} = |k|+1 = \pm k+1$$

$\Rightarrow \quad h^2+k^2+1-2k = k^2+1\pm 2k$

$\Rightarrow \quad h^2 = 4k$ or $h = 0$

Hence, the locus is a parabola with latus-rectum = 4 and a straight line.

17. (a) Let us consider a focal chord through the focus $S(a,0)$ of the parabola $y^2 = 4ax$. If the focal chord is inclined at some angle θ to the x-axis, then any point on this focal chord may be chosen as $P(a+r\cos\theta, r\sin\theta)$, where $SP = |r|$ (r is a parameter). If P lies on the parabola, then

$$(r\sin\theta)^2 = 4a(a+r\cos\theta)$$

$\Rightarrow \quad (\sin^2\theta)r^2-(4a\cos\theta)r-4a^2 = 0$

$\Rightarrow \quad (\sin^2\theta)r^2-(2l\cos\theta)r-l^2 = 0$

[$l = 2a$ is the semi-latus rectum]

$\Rightarrow \quad r = \dfrac{(1+\cos\theta)l}{\sin^2\theta}, \dfrac{-(1-\cos\theta)l}{\sin^2\theta}$

Thus, the focal chord cuts the ellipse at two points P, Q (say) such that

$$SP = \frac{(1+\cos\theta)l}{\sin^2\theta} \text{ and } SQ = \frac{(1-\cos\theta)l}{\sin^2\theta}$$

18. (b) Let $Q(t^2,2t)$ be an arbitrary point on the parabola $y^2 = 4x$. Equation of the tangent and normal at A are, respectively,

$$y = \frac{1}{t}x+t \text{ and } y = -tx+2t+t^3$$

They intersect the x-axis at $M(-t^2,0)$ and $N(t^2+2,0)$.

Let $P(h,k)$ be the centroid of ΔQMN. Then

$$h = \frac{t^2+2}{3} \text{ and } k = \frac{2t}{3}$$

Eliminating t gives the locus $y^2 = \frac{4}{3}\left(x-\frac{2}{3}\right)$.

Directrix of the above parabola is $x-\frac{2}{3}+\frac{1}{3} = 0 \Rightarrow x = \frac{1}{3}$.

19. (c)

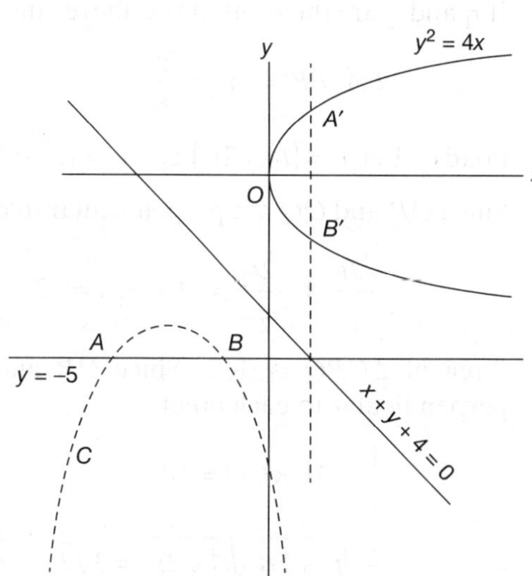

The figure shows the parabola $y^2 = 4x$ and its mirror image curve C in the line $x + y + 4 = 0$. Let AB be the intercept of the line $y = -5$ and the mirror image curve C. Let us first find the mirror image of the line $y = -5$ in the line $x + y + 4 = 0$; its intercept $A'B'$ with the parabola $y^2 = 4x$ has the same length as its intercept AB with curve C.

Let $P(t,-5)$ be any point on the line $y = -5$ and $Q(h,k)$ be its mirror image in the line $x+y+4 = 0$. Then

$$\left(\frac{h+t}{2}\right)+\left(\frac{k-5}{2}\right)+4 = 0 \text{ and } \frac{k+5}{h-t} = 1$$

$\Rightarrow \quad h+k+t+3 = 0$ and $h-k-t-5 = 0$

Adding the two equations, we have $h = 1$. Hence, the equation of the mirror image of line $y = -5$ in the line $x+y+4 = 0$ is $x = 1$.

It intersects the given parabola $y^2 = 4x$ at points $A'(1, 2)$ and $B'(1, -2)$. Hence $A'B' = 4$.

20. (c) The point $P(0,2)$ lies on the given line. Any point on this line may be chosen as $Q(r\cos\theta, 2+r\sin\theta)$, where $|r|$ represents the distance between P and Q and $\tan\theta = \frac{3}{4}$ is the slope of the line. Hence $Q = \left(\frac{4r}{5}, 2+\frac{3r}{5}\right)$.

Since Q also lies on the given parabola $x^2+y-4 = 0$

$$\left(\frac{4r}{5}\right)^2+2+\frac{3r}{5}-4 = 0$$

$\Rightarrow \quad 16r^2+15r-50 = 0$

If r_1 and r_2 are the roots of the above equation, then

$$PA \cdot PB = |r_1 r_2| = \frac{25}{8}$$

21. (a),(d) Let $P = (t_1^2, \sqrt{2}t_1)$ and $Q = (t_2^2, \sqrt{2}t_2)$.

Since OP and OQ are perpendicular to each other

$$\frac{\sqrt{2}t_1}{t_1^2} \times \frac{\sqrt{2}t_2}{t_2^2} = -1 \Rightarrow t_1 t_2 = -2$$

Area of ΔOPQ is $3\sqrt{2}$. Since OP and OQ are perpendicular to each other

$$\frac{1}{2} \times OP \times OQ = 3\sqrt{2}$$

$$\Rightarrow \quad \frac{1}{2}\sqrt{t_1^4 + 2t_1^2}\sqrt{t_2^4 + 2t_2^2} = 3\sqrt{2}$$

$$\Rightarrow \quad t_1^2 t_2^2 (t_1^2 + 2)(t_2^2 + 2) = 72$$

$$\Rightarrow \quad t_1^2 + t_2^2 = 5 \quad [\text{Using } t_1 t_2 = -2]$$

$$\Rightarrow \quad t_1 + t_2 = \pm\sqrt{t_1^2 + t_2^2 + 2t_1 t_2} = \pm 1$$

$$\Rightarrow \quad t_1 - \frac{2}{t_1} = \pm 1$$

$\Rightarrow \quad t_1^2 \pm t_1 - 2 = 0$ gives $t_1 = 1, 2$ (Taking positive values).

Hence $P = (1, \sqrt{2})$ or $(4, 2\sqrt{2})$.

22. (d)

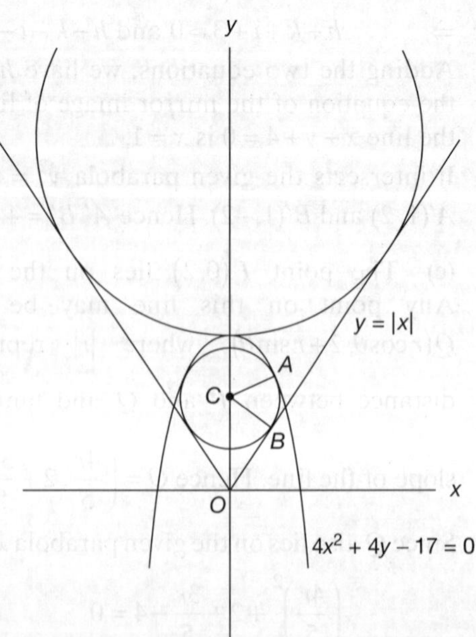

From the figure, we see that there are two such circles. Let $P = (h, k)$ be the point in the 1st quadrant, where the smaller circle touches the parabola $4x^2 + 4y - 17 = 0$.

Equation of the tangent to the parabola at point P is

$$4hx + 2(y + k) - 17 = 0 \Rightarrow \text{slope} = -2h$$

Hence, the equation of the normal to the parabola at point P is

$$y - k = \frac{1}{2h}(x - h)$$

The above normal intersects the y-axis at $Q = \left(0, k - \frac{1}{2}\right)$, which is the centre of the circle. Now, the distance PQ must equal the perpendicular distance of Q from the line $y = x$. Hence, we have

$$\sqrt{h^2 + \frac{1}{4}} = \frac{\left|k - \frac{1}{2}\right|}{\sqrt{2}}$$

$$\Rightarrow \quad \frac{17}{4} - k + \frac{1}{4} = \frac{1}{2}\left(k - \frac{1}{2}\right)^2$$

$$\left[\text{Using } 4h^2 + 4k - 17 = 0\right]$$

$$\Rightarrow \quad 9 - 2k = k^2 - k + \frac{1}{4}$$

$$\Rightarrow \quad k^2 + k - \frac{35}{4} = 0 \text{ gives } k = \frac{5}{2}$$

(Taking the positive value).

Hence, the radius of the required circle is $\frac{\left|k - \frac{1}{2}\right|}{\sqrt{2}} = \sqrt{2}$.

23. (b) Let the equation of the parabola be $y^2 = lx$. Extremities of any arbitrary focal chord can be chosen as $P = \left(\frac{l}{4}t_1^2, \frac{l}{2}t_1\right)$ and $Q = \left(\frac{l}{4}t_2^2, \frac{l}{2}t_2\right)$, where $t_1 t_2 = -1$.

Let $P(h, k)$ be the mid-point of PQ. Then

$$8h = l(t_1^2 + t_2^2) \text{ and } 4k = l(t_1 + t_2)$$

Squaring the second equation, we have

$$16k^2 = l^2(t_1^2 + t_2^2) + 2lt_1 t_2 = 8lh - 2l$$

$$\Rightarrow \quad k^2 = \frac{l}{2}(h - 4)$$

Hence, the locus is a parabola with latus-rectum of length $l/2$.

24. (b) The triangle ΔPAB is right-angled at P. Hence, its cicumcentre C is the mid-point of the hypotenuse AB, which coincides with focus of the parabola. Hence $C=(4,0)$. Now $CB=CP=|16+4|=20$. Hence $B=(4+20,0)=(24,0)$.

Now slope of $BP=\dfrac{16}{16-24}=-2$ and slope of $CP=\dfrac{16}{16-4}=4/3$.

Hence $\quad \tan\theta=\dfrac{-2-\frac{4}{3}}{1-\frac{8}{3}}=2.$

25. (a)

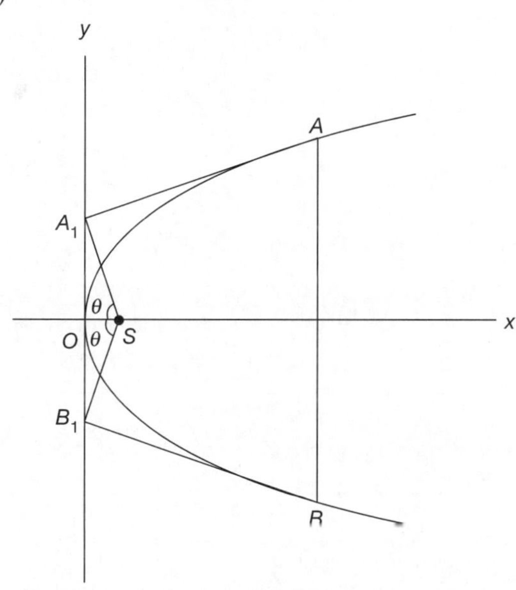

Let $A=(t^2,2t)$ and $B=(t^2,-2t)$ (see figure).

Equation of the tangent to the parabola at A is $y=\dfrac{1}{t}x+t$. It meets the y axis at $A_1=(0,t)$.

Similarly, the tangent to the parabola at B meets the y-axis at $B_1=(0,-t)$.

Area of trapezium AA_1B_1B is given to be 24. Hence, we have

$$\frac{1}{2}(4t+2t)t^2=24$$

$\Rightarrow \qquad t^3=8$ gives $t=2$

Hence $A_1=(0,2)$ and $B_1=(0,-2)$. The focus is at $S=(1,0)$. The angle subtended by A_1B_1 at the focus is $2\theta=2\tan^{-1}\left(\dfrac{A_1O}{SO}\right)=\tan^{-1}(2)$.

26. (b),(c)

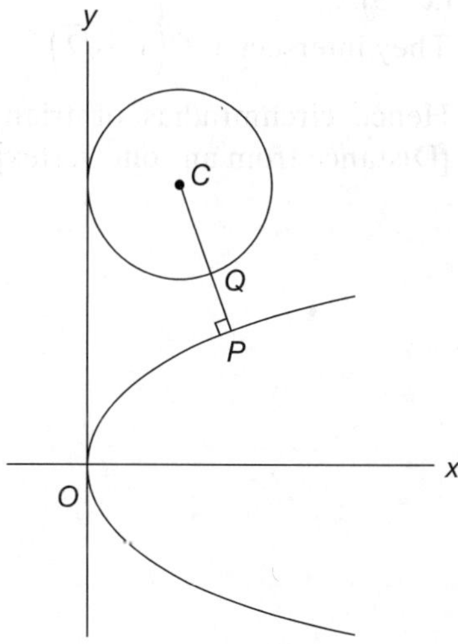

Equation of general tangent to the parabola $y^2=4x$ is

$$y=mx-2m-m^3 \text{ at point } P\left(m^2,-2m\right)$$

If P is nearest to the circle, then the normal at P must pass through the centre $S=(2,8)$ of the circle. Thus, we have

$$8=-m^3 \text{ gives } m=-2\Rightarrow P=(4,4)$$

Now $\qquad SP=\sqrt{(2-4)^2+(8-4)^2}=2\sqrt{5}$

and $\qquad SQ=$ radius of circle $=2$

$\Rightarrow \qquad QP=SP-PQ=2\left(\sqrt{5}-1\right)$

$\Rightarrow \qquad SQ:QP=\dfrac{1}{\sqrt{5}-1}=\dfrac{\sqrt{5}+1}{4}$

Line SP is the normal to the parabola at P. Its equation is $y=-2x+12$. Its x intercept is 6. Tangent to the circle at Q is perpendicular to SP. Hence its slope is $1/2$.

27. (a)-(r),(b)-(q),(c)-(p),(d)-(s) The given curves intersect at $P\left(1,2\sqrt{2}\right)$ and $Q\left(1,-2\sqrt{2}\right)$.

Tangent to the circle at $P: x+2\sqrt{2}y=9$ intersects the x-axis at $R(9,0)$.

Tangent to the parabola at $P: 2\sqrt{2}y=4(x+1)$ intersects the x-axis at $S(-1,0)$.

(a) Length of $PQ = 4\sqrt{2}$.

(b) $\dfrac{\text{Area of } PQR}{\text{Area of } PQS} = \dfrac{MR}{MS} = \dfrac{8}{2} = 4.$

(c) Perpendicular bisector of SR is $x = 4$.
Perpendicular bisector of PR is $y - \sqrt{2} = 2\sqrt{2}(x-5)$.
They intersect at $C\left(4, -\sqrt{2}\right)$.

Hence circumradius of triangle $PRS = 3\sqrt{2}$ [Distance from any one vertex].

(d) Coordinates of the incentre of triangle PQR

$$I = \frac{6\sqrt{2}\times 1 + 6\sqrt{2}\times 1 + 4\sqrt{2}\times 9}{6\sqrt{2} + 6\sqrt{2} + 4\sqrt{2}} = (3,0)$$

Hence in-radius of triangle $PQR = 2$ [Perpendicular distance from any one side].

CHAPTER

29 Ellipse

- **Equation of the Ellipse:** The equation of the ellipse with centre at $O(0,0)$, semi-major axis a along the x-axis, and semi-minor axis b along the y-axis is

$$\frac{x^2}{a^2}+\frac{y^2}{b^2}=1$$

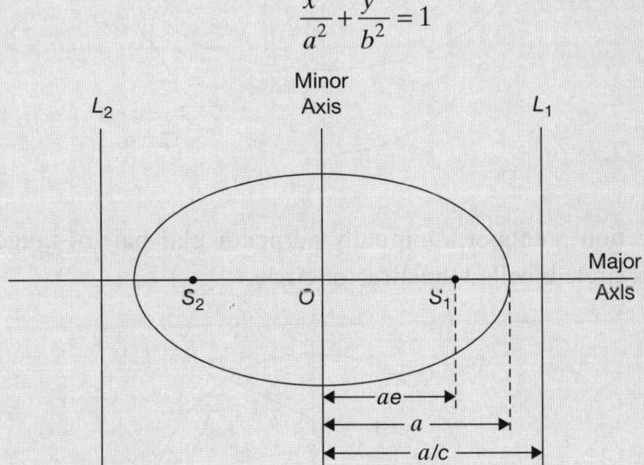

A few quantities related to the ellipse:

$$\text{Eccentricity: } e=\sqrt{1-b^2/a^2}$$

$$\text{Foci: } S=(\pm ae,0)=\left(\pm\sqrt{a^2-b^2},0\right)$$

$$\text{Directrices: } x=\pm\frac{a}{e}=\pm\frac{a^2}{\sqrt{a^2-b^2}}$$

$$\text{Extremities of latus-rectum: } \left(\pm ae,\pm b^2/a\right)=\left(\pm\sqrt{a^2-b^2},\pm b^2/a\right)$$

$$\text{Focal distances: } S_1P=a-ex,\ S_2P=a+ex;\ S_1P+S_2P=2a$$

- **Parametric Representation:** The parametric representation of this ellipse is

$$x=a\cos\theta \text{ and } y=b\sin\theta$$

Equation of a general tangent to this ellipse is

$$y=mx\pm\sqrt{a^2m^2+b^2} \text{ at point } P=\left(\frac{a^2m}{\pm\sqrt{a^2m^2+b^2}},\frac{b^2}{\pm\sqrt{a^2m^2+b^2}}\right)$$

Tangents with positive y intercepts touch the ellipse above the x-axis, and vice-versa.

Equation of a general normal to this ellipse is

$$\frac{x-x_1}{x_1/a^2}=\frac{y-y_1}{y_1/b^2} \text{ at point } P=(x_1,y_1) \text{ or}$$

$$(a\sec\theta)x-(b\operatorname{cosec}\theta)y=a^2-b^2 \text{ at point } P=(a\cos\theta,b\sin\theta)$$

- **Some Properties of the Ellipse:**

1. If S_1N_1 and S_2N_2 are perpendiculars from the foci upon the tangent at any point P of the ellipse, then N_1 and N_2 lie on the auxiliary circle and $S_1N_1 \cdot S_2N_2 = b^2$.

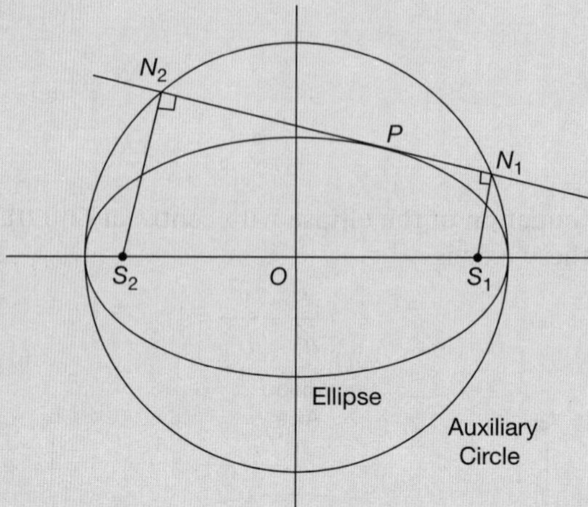

2. The locus of intersection points of a mutually perpendicular pair of tangents of the ellipse is the circle $x^2 + y^2 = a^2 + b^2$; this circle is called the director circle.

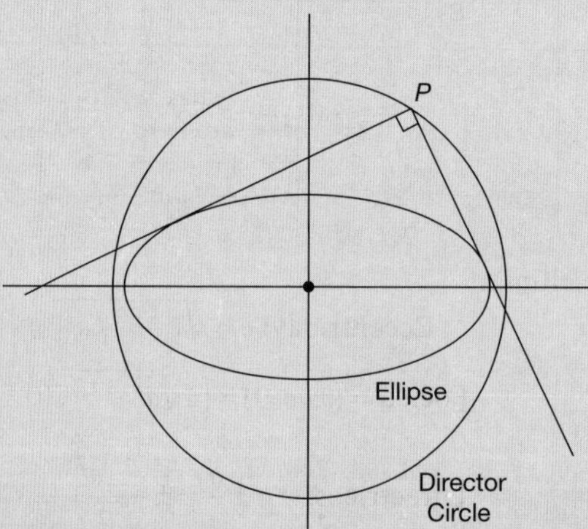

3. If the tangent at any point P of an ellipse meets the directrix at Q, then PQ subtends a right angle at the nearer focus.

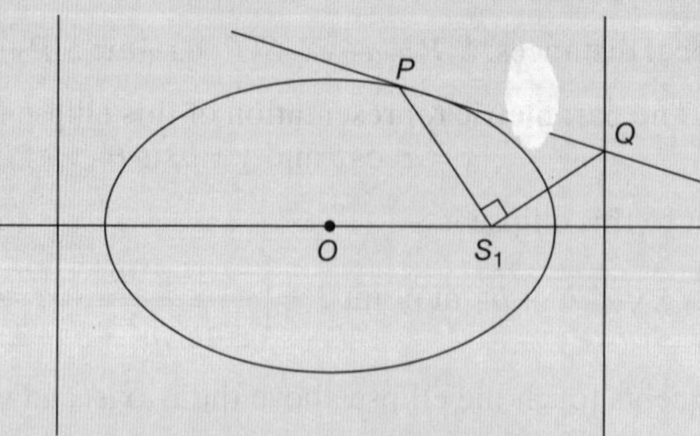

EXERCISES

1. Area of the quadrilateral formed by the tangents at the end points of the latus-rectum of the ellipse $5x^2+9y^2-10x-18y-31=0$ is:
(a) 12 (b) 18
(c) 24 (d) 27

2. Ellipses E_1, E_2 are drawn such that the minor axis of E_2 coincides with the major axis of E_1, and the foci of E_2 coincides with the extremities of the minor axis of E_1. If e is their eccentricity, then $(2e+1)^2$ equals:
(a) 5 (b) 4
(c) 3 (d) None of these

3. An ellipse having foci at $(\pm 1,0)$ and eccentricity $1/3$ intersects a parabola having its vertex at the origin and focus at $(1,0)$ at point M in the first quadrant and at point N in the fourth quadrant. If the tangent to the ellips, and the normal to the parabola at point M meet the x-axis at points Q and R, respectively, then the ratio of the area of the triangle MNQ to area of the triangle MNR is:
(a) $7:4$ (b) $8:5$
(c) $8:3$ (d) $9:4$

4. A tangent is drawn to the ellipse $x^2+27y^2=27$ at the point $(3\sqrt{3}\cos\theta, \sin\theta)$, where $\theta \in (0, \pi/2)$. Let $S(\theta)$ denote the sum of the intercepts made by the tangent on the coordinate axes. The value of θ for which S is minimum is:
(a) $\pi/8$ (b) $\pi/6$
(c) $\pi/4$ (d) $\pi/3$

5. The common tangent to the parabola $y^2=8x$ and the ellipse $15x^2+4y^2=60$ touches the ellipse at point:
(a) $\left(\frac{-2}{5}, \frac{12}{\sqrt{10}}\right)$ (b) $\left(\frac{-1}{\sqrt{3}}, \frac{3\sqrt{5}}{2}\right)$
(c) $\left(\frac{-2}{3}, \frac{2\sqrt{10}}{\sqrt{3}}\right)$ (d) $\left(\frac{-1}{2}, \frac{15}{4}\right)$

6. The line passing through the extremity A of the major axis and extremity B of the minor axis of the ellipse $x^2+9y^2=9$ meets its auxiliary circle at the point M. Area of the triangle with vertices at A, M and the origin O is:
(a) $31/10$ (b) $29/10$
(c) $27/10$ (d) $21/10$

7. The normal at a point P on the ellipse $x^2+4y^2=16$ meets the x-axis at Q. If M is the mid-point of the segment PQ, then the locus of M intersects the latus-rectum of the given ellipse at the points:
(a) $\left(\pm\frac{3\sqrt{5}}{2}, \pm\frac{2}{7}\right)$ (b) $\left(\pm\frac{3\sqrt{5}}{2}, \pm\frac{\sqrt{19}}{4}\right)$
(c) $\left(\pm 2\sqrt{3}, \pm\frac{1}{7}\right)$ (d) $\left(\pm 2\sqrt{3}, \pm\frac{4\sqrt{3}}{7}\right)$

8. In a triangle ΔABC, vertices $B=(2,0)$ and $C=(8,0)$. If vertex A moves in such a way that $4\tan\left(\frac{B}{2}\right)\tan\left(\frac{C}{2}\right)=1$, then the locus of A is:
(a) $\frac{(x-5)^2}{25}+\frac{y^2}{16}=1$ (b) $\frac{(x-5)^2}{81}+\frac{y^2}{45}=1$
(c) $\frac{(x-5)^2}{64}+\frac{y^2}{25}=1$ (d) None of these

9. A tangent to the ellipse $\frac{x^2}{25}+\frac{y^2}{16}=1$ meets the coordinate axes at A and B. If the points A, B and the origin form the vertices of an isoceles triangle, then the length of AB is:
(a) $\sqrt{41/2}$ (b) $\sqrt{41}$
(c) $\sqrt{82}$ (d) $\sqrt{164}$

10. If the normal from point $(h,2)$ to the ellipse $\frac{x^2}{6}+\frac{y^2}{3}-1$ is perpendicular to the line $x+y=3$, the value of h is:
(a) 1 (b) 2
(c) 3 (d) 4

11. Two sets are defined as follows:
$A=\{(a,b)\in \mathbf{R}\times\mathbf{R} : |a-5|<1 \text{ and } |b-5|<1\}$ and
$B=\{(a,b)\in \mathbf{R}\times\mathbf{R} : 4(a-6)^2+9(b-5)^2 \le 36\}$.
Then the correct statements from the following are:
(a) $A\subset B$
(b) $B\subset A$
(c) $A\cap B=\varnothing$
(d) Neither $A\subset B$ nor $B\subset A$

12. If the curves $y^2 = 6x, 9x^2 + by^2 = 1$ intersect each other at right angles, then the value of b is:
(a) 4 (b) 6
(c) $7/2$ (d) $9/2$

13. Let E_1 and E_2 be two ellipses whose centres are at the origin. Their major axes lie along the x-axis and y-axis, respectively. Let S be the circle $x^2 + (y-1)^2 = 2$. The straight line $x + y = 3$ touches S, E_1 and E_2 at points P, Q and R, respectively. If $PQ = PR = \frac{2\sqrt{2}}{3}$ and e_1, e_2 are the eccentricities of E_1, E_2, respectively, then:
(a) $e_1^2 + e_2^2 = \frac{43}{40}$ (b) $e_1 e_2 = \frac{\sqrt{7}}{2\sqrt{10}}$
(c) $\left|e_1^2 - e_2^2\right| = \frac{5}{8}$ (d) $e_1 e_2 = \frac{\sqrt{3}}{4}$

14. If the normal at any point $P(\theta)$ to the ellipse $\frac{x^2}{14} + \frac{y^2}{5} = 1$ intersects it again at point $Q(2\theta)$, then $\cos\theta$ equals:
(a) $\frac{3}{4}$ (b) $\frac{3}{5}$
(c) $\frac{-1}{3}$ (d) $\frac{-2}{3}$

15. If l denotes the length of the semi-latus rectum of an ellipse and SP, SQ denote the segments of any focal chord PQ, S being the focus, then SP, l, SQ are in the relation:
(a) HP (b) GP
(c) AP (d) $l^2 = SP^2 + SQ^2$

ANSWER KEYS

1. (d) **2.** (a) **3.** (d) **4.** (b) **5.** (d) **6.** (c) **7.** (c) **8.** (a) **9.** (c)
10. (a),(c) **11.** (a) **12.** (d) **13.** (a),(b) **14.** (d) **15.** (a)

SOLUTIONS

1. (d) Equation of the given ellipse in standard form

$$\frac{(x-1)^2}{9} + \frac{(y-1)^2}{5} = 1$$

To find the area of the quadrilateral formed by the tangents drawn at the extremities of the latus-rectum, let us translate our coordinate axes to the centre of the ellipse (note that the area of the quadrilateral does not change by this transformation).

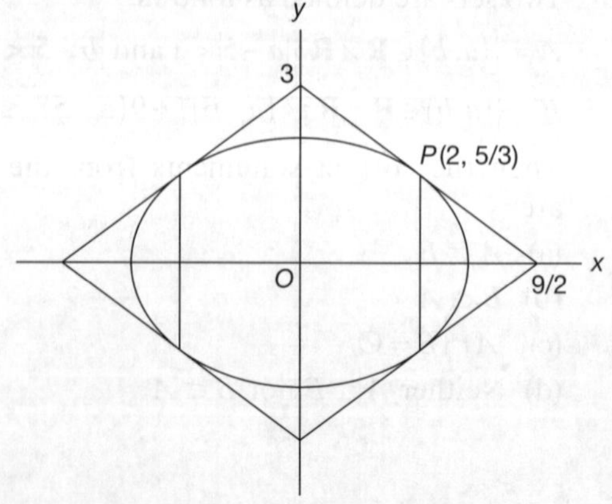

Equation of the ellipse now reduces to

$$\frac{x^2}{9} + \frac{y^2}{5} = 1$$

The extremity of its latus-rectum (in the 1st quadrant) is

$$P\left(\sqrt{a^2 - b^2}, \frac{b^2}{a}\right) = P\left(2, \frac{5}{3}\right)$$

Equation of tangent at this point

$$\frac{2x}{9} + \frac{(5/3)y}{5} = 1$$

The intercepts of the above tangent are

$$x\text{-intercept} = \frac{9}{2} \text{ and } y\text{-intercept} = 3$$

Hence, the area of the quadrilateral is

$$\text{Area} = 4\left(\frac{1}{2} \times \frac{9}{2} \times 3\right) = 27$$

2. (a) Let a, b be the semi-major and semi-minor axis, respectively, of E_1. Then

$$b = a\sqrt{1 - e^2} \qquad \ldots(1)$$

Let a', a be the semi-major and semi-minor axis, respectively, of E_2. Then

$$a = a'\sqrt{1-e^2} \quad \text{...(2)}$$

Also, since the foci of E_2 coincides with the extremities of the minor axis of E_1, we have

$$b = a'e \quad \text{...(3)}$$

From equations (2) and (3)

$$\frac{b}{a} = \frac{e}{\sqrt{1-e^2}}$$

Now using equation (1), we have

$$\sqrt{1-e^2} = \frac{e}{\sqrt{1-e^2}}$$

$$\Rightarrow \quad e^2 + e - 1 = 0 \text{ gives } e = \frac{\sqrt{5}-1}{2}$$

Hence $(2e+1)^2 = 5$.

3. (d) For the ellipse, $ae = 1, e = 1/3 \Rightarrow a = 3$ and $b = 3\sqrt{1-\frac{1}{9}} = 2\sqrt{2}$.

Hence, the equation of the ellipse is

$$\frac{x^2}{9} + \frac{y^2}{8} = 1$$

For the parabola, $a = 1$. Hence, the equation of the parabola is $y^2 = 4x$.

The abscissa of their intersection points M and N are given by

$$\frac{x^2}{9} + \frac{4x}{8} = 1 \Rightarrow x = 3/2$$

(The other root is –ve, hence unacceptable)

Hence $M = \left(\frac{3}{2}, \sqrt{6}\right)$ and $N = \left(\frac{3}{2}, -\sqrt{6}\right)$

Equation of the tangent to the ellipse at point M is given by $\frac{(3/2)x}{9} + \frac{\sqrt{6}y}{8} = 1$.

The x intercept of the above tangent is $Q = (6, 0)$.

Equation of the normal to the parabola at point M is given by $y - \sqrt{6} = -\frac{\sqrt{6}}{2}\left(x - \frac{3}{2}\right)$.

The x intercept of the above normal is $R = \left(\frac{7}{2}, 0\right)$.

Now, from the figure, we see that

$$\text{Area of triangle } MNQ = \frac{1}{2} \times MN \times \left(6 - \frac{3}{2}\right) = \frac{9}{4} MN$$

$$\text{Area of triangle } MNR = \frac{1}{2} \times MN \times \left(\frac{7}{2} - \frac{3}{2}\right) = MN.$$

Hence, the required ratio is $9:4$.

4. (b) Equation of tangent at the given point

$$\frac{x\cos\theta}{3\sqrt{3}} + \frac{y\sin\theta}{1} = 1$$

The intercepts of the above tangent are

x intercept $= 3\sqrt{3}\sec\theta$ and y intercept $= \operatorname{cosec}\theta$.

Sum of the intercepts

$$S(\theta) = 3\sqrt{3}\sec\theta + \operatorname{cosec}\theta$$

The derivative function

$$S'(\theta) = 3\sqrt{3}\sec\theta\tan\theta - \operatorname{cosec}\theta\cot\theta$$

Solving for $S'(\theta) = 0$, we have

$$\tan\theta = \frac{1}{\sqrt{3}} \Rightarrow \theta = \frac{\pi}{6}$$

5. (d) Equation of general tangents to the parabola $y^2 = 8x$ and the ellipse $\frac{x^2}{4} + \frac{y^2}{15} = 1$ are, respectively,

$$y = mx + \frac{2}{m} \text{ and } y = mx \pm \sqrt{4m^2 + 15}$$

The two equations will be identical if

$$\frac{4}{m^2} = 4m^2 + 15 \text{ gives } m = \pm 1/2$$

The contact point of the tangent with the ellipse is

$$P = \left(\frac{-4m}{\pm\sqrt{4m^2+15}}, \frac{15}{\pm\sqrt{4m^2+15}}\right)$$

Putting $m = \pm 1/2$ gives $P = \left(\frac{-1}{\pm 2}, \frac{15}{\pm 4}\right)$. From the figure, we can see that the contact points lie in the second and third quadrants. Hence, the contact points are $\left(\frac{-1}{2}, \frac{\pm 15}{4}\right)$.

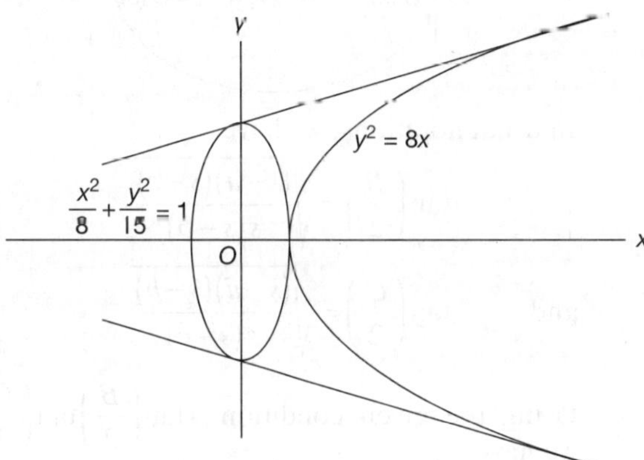

6. (c) Equation of AB

$$\frac{x}{3} + y = 1$$

Intersection of AB with the auxiliary circle $x^2 + y^2 = 9$

$$9(y-1)^2 + y^2 = 9 \Rightarrow y = 0, \frac{9}{5}$$

The ordinate of M is $9/5$. Hence, the area of ΔOMN

$$\frac{1}{2} \times OA \times MN = \frac{1}{2} \times 3 \times \frac{9}{5} = \frac{27}{10}$$

7. (c) Equation of the normal at some point $P(4\cos\theta, 2\sin\theta)$

$$(4\sec\theta)x - (2\operatorname{cosec}\theta)y = 12$$

It intersects the x-axis at $Q(3\cos\theta, 0)$. If $M(h,k)$ is the mid-point, then

$$h = \frac{7}{2}\cos\theta \text{ and } k = \sin\theta$$

Eliminating θ, we obtain the desired locus

$$\frac{x^2}{49/4} + \frac{y^2}{1} = 1$$

Equation of latus-rectum of the given ellipse $x = \pm\sqrt{16-4} = \pm 2\sqrt{3}$.

Intersection points of the above latus-rectum with the locus of M are $\left(\pm 2\sqrt{3}, \pm\frac{1}{7}\right)$.

8. (a)

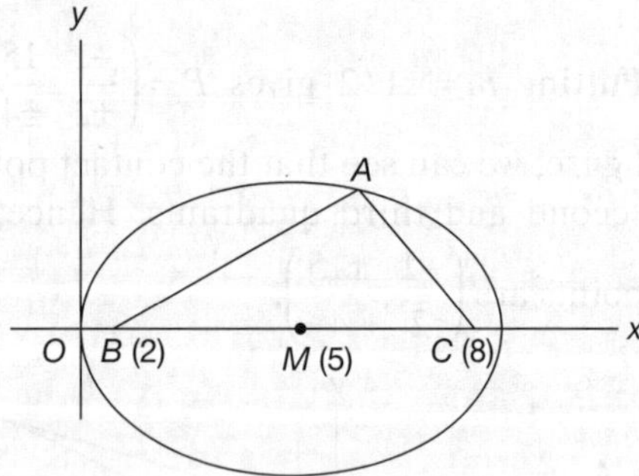

In usual notations, we have

$$\tan\left(\frac{B}{2}\right) = \sqrt{\frac{(s-a)(s-c)}{s(s-b)}}$$

and $$\tan\left(\frac{C}{2}\right) = \sqrt{\frac{(s-a)(s-b)}{s(s-c)}}$$

Using the given condition $4\tan\left(\frac{B}{2}\right)\tan\left(\frac{C}{2}\right) = 1$, we have

$$\frac{s-a}{s} = \frac{1}{4} \Rightarrow s = \frac{4}{3}a \Rightarrow \frac{a+b+c}{2} = \frac{4}{3}a$$

$$\Rightarrow \quad b + c = \frac{5}{3}a = 10 \qquad [a = BC = 6, \text{ given}]$$

$$\Rightarrow \quad AB + BC = 10.$$

Thus, the locus of A is an ellipse with foci at $B(2,0)$ and $C(8,0)$ and major axis = 10 (see figure). The centre of the ellipse is at the mid-point of BC, that is, $M(5,0)$; its semi-major axis is $a = 5$ and eccentricity is $c = BC/10 = 3/5$. Therefore, semi-minor axis is $b = a\sqrt{1-c^2} = 4$. Hence, the equation of the ellipse is

$$\frac{(x-5)^2}{25} + \frac{y^2}{16} = 1$$

9. (c) Equation of a general tangent to the given ellipse

$$y = mx \pm \sqrt{25m^2 + 16}$$

For intercepts to be the same, the coefficients of x and y must be the same in magnitude. Hence $m = \pm 1$. Equation of the tangent reduces to

$$y = \pm x \pm \sqrt{41}$$

The magnitude of its x and y intercepts are each equal to $\sqrt{41}$. Hence, the length of the intercept = $\sqrt{82}$.

10. (a),(c)

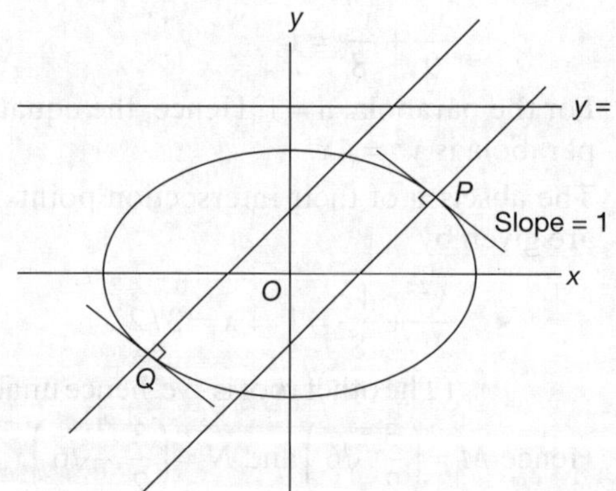

Slope of the line $x + y = 3$ is -1. Hence, the slope of the required normal is $1 \Rightarrow$ slope of tangent $= -1$.

For the ellipse $\frac{x^2}{6} + \frac{y^2}{3} = 1$, the contact point of a tangent with slope m is

$$P = \left(\frac{-a^2 m}{\pm\sqrt{a^2m^2 + b^2}}, \frac{b^2}{\pm\sqrt{a^2m^2 + b^2}}\right)$$

Putting $m = -1$ gives contact points $P(2, 1)$ and $Q(-2, -1)$ (see figure).

Equations of the normals at these points are

$$y - 1 = x - 2 \text{ and } y + 1 = x + 2 \Rightarrow y = x \pm 1$$

Now, if $(h, 2)$ is a point on these normals, then

$$h = 2 \pm 1 = 1, 3$$

11. (a) Set A is represented by all points lying inside the square

$$4 < x < 6, 4 < y < 6$$

Set B is represented by all points lying on or inside the ellipse

$$\frac{(x-6)^2}{9} + \frac{(y-5)^2}{4} = 1$$

The centre of the ellipse is at $(6,5)$. Its x coordinates belong to $6-3 < x < 6+3 \Rightarrow 3 < x < 9$ and its y coordinates belong to $5-2 < y < 5+2 \Rightarrow 3 < y < 7$.
The four corners of the square are $(6,4)$, $(6,6)$ and $(4,4)$, $(4,6)$.
The line $x = 6$ meets the ellipse at $y = 5 \pm 2 = 3, 7$. Thus, the right corners $(6,4)$, $(6,6)$ of the square lie inside the ellipse.
The line $x = 4$ meets the ellipse at $y = 5 \pm \frac{2\sqrt{5}}{3} = 3.5, 6.5$. Thus, the left corners $(4,4)$, $(4,6)$ of the square lie inside the ellipse.
Hence, the entire square lies inside the ellipse $\Rightarrow A \subset B$.

12. (d) Slope of the tangent to the curves is given by

$$y' = \frac{3}{y}, \; y' = -\frac{9x}{by}$$

If the two curves intersect at (h,k), then

$$k^2 = 6h \qquad \ldots(1),$$

$$9h^2 + bk^2 = 1 \qquad \ldots(2)$$

Also, if they intersect at right angles, then

$$\frac{3}{k} \times \frac{-9h}{bk} = -1 \Rightarrow bk^2 = 27 \qquad \ldots(3)$$

From equations (1) and (3), we have $b = 9/2$.

13. (a),(b)

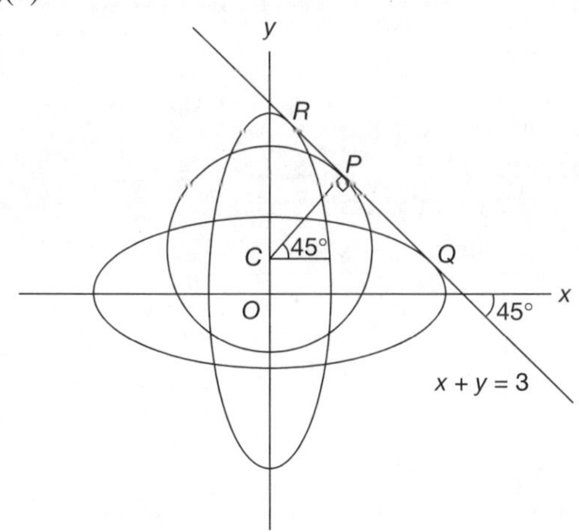

Centre of the circle is at $C(0,1)$ and its radius is $CP = \sqrt{2}$. The line CP is perpendicular to the line $x + y = 3$. Hence, CP has slope $1 \Rightarrow CP$ makes angle $45°$ with the x-axis. Thus, the coordinates of point P are

$$P = \left(0 + \sqrt{2}\cos 45°, 1 + \sqrt{2}\sin 45°\right) = (1,2).$$

It is given that $PQ = PR = \frac{2\sqrt{2}}{3}$. Thus, the coordinates of Q and R are

$$Q = \left(1 + \frac{2\sqrt{2}}{3}\cos 45°, 2 - \frac{2\sqrt{2}}{3}\sin 45°\right) = \left(\frac{5}{3}, \frac{4}{3}\right)$$

$$R = \left(1 - \frac{2\sqrt{2}}{3}\cos 45°, 2 + \frac{2\sqrt{2}}{3}\sin 45°\right) = \left(\frac{1}{3}, \frac{8}{3}\right)$$

If a and b are the semi-major and semi-minor axes, respectively, of E_1, then the contact point of its tangent is given by $\left(\frac{-a^2m}{\pm\sqrt{a^2m^2+b^2}}, \frac{b^2}{\pm\sqrt{a^2m^2+b^2}}\right)$.
Putting $m = -1$ and comparing with the coordinates of $Q\left(\frac{5}{3}, \frac{4}{3}\right)$, we have

$$\frac{a^2}{\sqrt{a^2+b^2}} = \frac{5}{3}, \; \frac{b^2}{\sqrt{a^2+b^2}} = \frac{4}{3}$$

Hence $\quad \frac{b^2}{a^2} = \frac{4}{5} \Rightarrow e_1^2 = 1 - \frac{4}{5} = \frac{1}{5}.$

Similarly, comparing with the coordinates of $R\left(\frac{1}{3}, \frac{8}{3}\right)$, we have

$$\frac{b^2}{a^2} = \frac{8}{1} \Rightarrow e_2^2 = 1 - \frac{1}{8} = \frac{7}{8}$$

In this case, a and b are the semi-minor and semi-major axes, respectively, of E_2.
Now, we can see that options (a) and (b) are correct.

14. (d) Equation of the tangent to the ellipse $\frac{x^2}{14} + \frac{y^2}{5} = 1$ at point $P(\theta) = \left(\sqrt{14}\cos\theta, \sqrt{5}\sin\theta\right)$ is

$$\frac{x\cos\theta}{\sqrt{14}} + \frac{y\sin\theta}{\sqrt{5}} = 1.$$

Slope of the tangent $= -\frac{\sqrt{5}\cos\theta}{\sqrt{14}\sin\theta}$.

Slope of the normal$= \frac{\sqrt{14}\sin\theta}{\sqrt{5}\cos\theta}$.

Slope of line joining points $P(\theta)$ and $Q(2\theta)$ equals $\frac{\sqrt{5}(\sin 2\theta - \sin\theta)}{\sqrt{14}(\cos 2\theta - \cos\theta)}$.

Equating the two, we have

$$\frac{\sqrt{5}(\sin 2\theta - \sin\theta)}{\sqrt{14}(\cos 2\theta - \cos\theta)} = \frac{\sqrt{14}\sin\theta}{\sqrt{5}\cos\theta}$$

$$\Rightarrow \quad 5\cos\theta(\sin 2\theta - \sin\theta) = 14\sin\theta(\cos 2\theta - \cos\theta)$$

$$\Rightarrow \quad 5\cos\theta\sin 2\theta - 14\sin\theta\cos 2\theta + 9\sin\theta\cos\theta = 0$$

$$\Rightarrow \quad 5(\cos\theta\sin 2\theta - \sin\theta\cos 2\theta) - 9\sin\theta(\cos 2\theta - \cos\theta) = 0$$

$$\Rightarrow \quad 5\sin\theta = 9\sin\theta(\cos 2\theta - \cos\theta)$$

$$\Rightarrow \quad \cos 2\theta - \cos\theta = \frac{5}{9}$$

$$\Rightarrow \quad 2\cos^2\theta - \cos\theta - \frac{14}{9} = 0 \text{ gives } \cos\theta = \frac{-2}{3}$$

15. (a) Let us consider a focal chord through the focus $S(ae, 0)$ of the ellipse $\frac{x^2}{a^2} + \frac{y^2}{b^2} = 1$. If the focal chord is inclined at some angle θ to the x-axis, then any point on this focal chord may be chosen as $P(ae + r\cos\theta, r\sin\theta)$, where $SP = |r|$ (r is a parameter). If P lies on the ellipse, then

$$\frac{(ae + r\cos\theta)^2}{a^2} + \frac{(r\sin\theta)^2}{b^2} = 1$$

$$\Rightarrow \quad e^2 + \left(\frac{\cos^2\theta}{a^2} + \frac{\sin^2\theta}{b^2}\right)r^2 + \left(\frac{2e\cos\theta}{a}\right)r - 1 = 0$$

$$\Rightarrow \quad \left(\frac{\cos^2\theta}{a^2} + \frac{\sin^2\theta}{b^2}\right)r^2 + \left(\frac{2e\cos\theta}{a}\right)r - \frac{b^2}{a^2} = 0$$

$$\left[1 - e^2 = b^2/a^2\right]$$

$$\Rightarrow \quad \left(\frac{b^2\cos^2\theta}{a^2} + \sin^2\theta\right)r^2 + \left(\frac{2eb^2\cos\theta}{a}\right)r - \frac{b^4}{a^2} = 0$$

$$\Rightarrow \quad \left((1 - e^2)\cos^2\theta + \sin^2\theta\right)r^2 + (2el\cos\theta)r - l^2 = 0$$

[$l = b^2/a$ is the semi-latus rectum]

$$\Rightarrow \quad (1 - e^2\cos^2\theta)r^2 + (2el\cos\theta)r - l^2 = 0$$

$$\Rightarrow \quad r = \frac{l}{1 + e\cos\theta}, \frac{-l}{1 - e\cos\theta}$$

Thus, the focal chord cuts the ellipse at two points P, Q (say) such that

$$SP = \frac{l}{1 + e\cos\theta} \text{ and } SQ = \frac{l}{1 - e\cos\theta}$$

Now, we can see that

$$\frac{1}{SP} + \frac{1}{SQ} = \frac{2}{l} \Rightarrow \text{HP}$$

CHAPTER

30 Hyperbola

- **Equation of Hyperbola:** The equation of a hyperbola with centre at $O(0,0)$, semi-transverse axis a along the x-axis and semi-conjugate axis b along the y-axis is

$$\frac{x^2}{a^2}-\frac{y^2}{b^2}=1$$

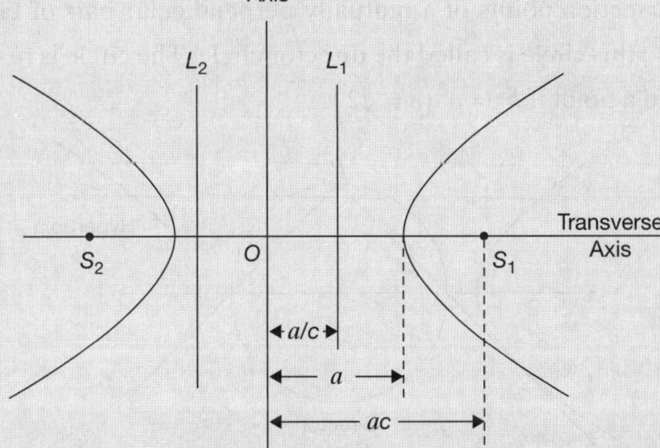

A few quantities related to the hyperbola:

$$\text{Eccentricity: } e=\sqrt{1+b^2/a^2}$$

$$\text{Foci: } S=(\pm ae,0)=\left(\pm\sqrt{a^2+b^2},0\right)$$

$$\text{Directrices: } x=\pm\frac{a}{e}=\pm\frac{a^2}{\sqrt{a^2+b^2}}$$

$$\text{Length of latus-rectum} = 2b^2/a$$

$$\text{Focal distances: } S_1P=ex-a,\ S_2P=ex+a;\ |S_1P-S_2P|=2a$$

- **Parametric Representation:** The parametric representation of this hyperbola is

$$x=a\sec\theta \text{ and } y=b\tan\theta$$

Equation of a general tangent to this hyperbola is

$$y=mx\pm\sqrt{a^2m^2-b^2} \text{ at point } P=\left(\frac{-a^2m}{\pm\sqrt{a^2m^2-b^2}},\frac{-b^2}{\pm\sqrt{a^2m^2-b^2}}\right)$$

Tangents with positive y intercepts touch the hyperbola below the x-axis, and vice-versa.

Equation of a general normal to this hyperbola is

$$\frac{x-x_1}{x_1/a^2}=\frac{y-y_1}{-y_1/b^2} \text{ at point } P=(x_1,y_1) \text{ or}$$

$$(a\cos\theta)x+(b\cot\theta)y=a^2+b^2 \text{ at point } P=(a\sec\theta, b\tan\theta)$$

- **Some Properties of the Hyperbola:**

1. If S_1N_1 and S_2N_2 are perpendiculars from the foci upon the tangent at any point P of the hyperbola, then N_1 and N_2 lie on the auxiliary circle and $S_1N_1 \cdot S_2N_2 = b^2$.

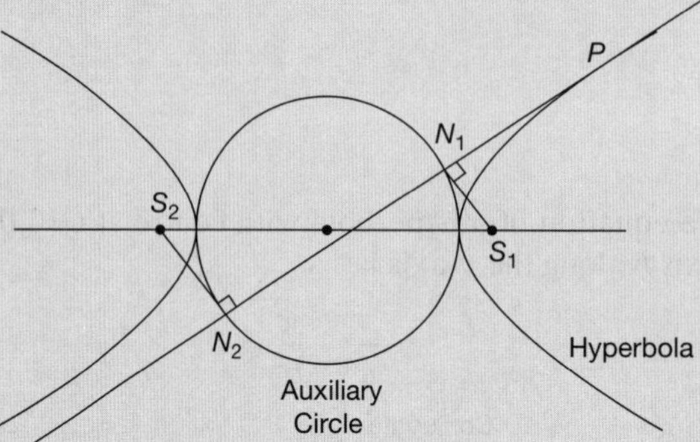

2. The locus of the intersection points of a mutually perpendicular pair of tangents of the hyperbola is the circle $x^2 + y^2 = a^2 - b^2$; this circle is called the director circle. The circle is real if $b^2 < a^2$ $(e < \sqrt{2})$, imaginary if $b^2 > a^2$ $(e > \sqrt{2})$, and a point if $b^2 = a^2 \left(e = \sqrt{2}\right)$.

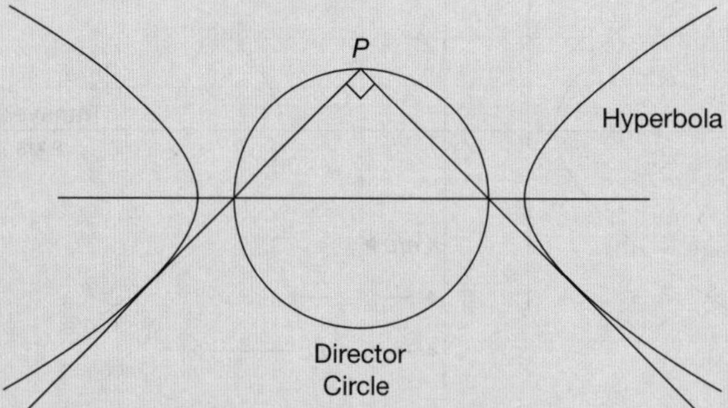

3. If the tangent at any point P of a hyperbola meets the directrix at Q, then PQ subtends a right angle at the nearer focus.

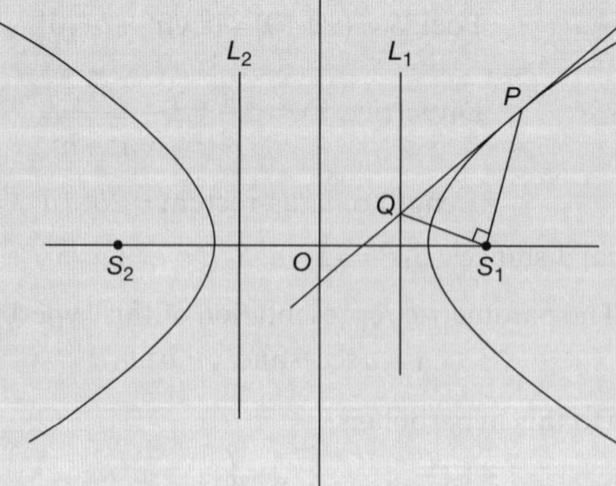

- **Equation of Conjugate Hyperbola:** The equation of a conjugate hyperbola is

$$\frac{x^2}{a^2} - \frac{y^2}{b^2} = -1$$

- **Equation of Pair of Asymptotes:** The equation of a pair of asymptotes is:

$$\frac{x^2}{a^2} - \frac{y^2}{b^2} = 0$$

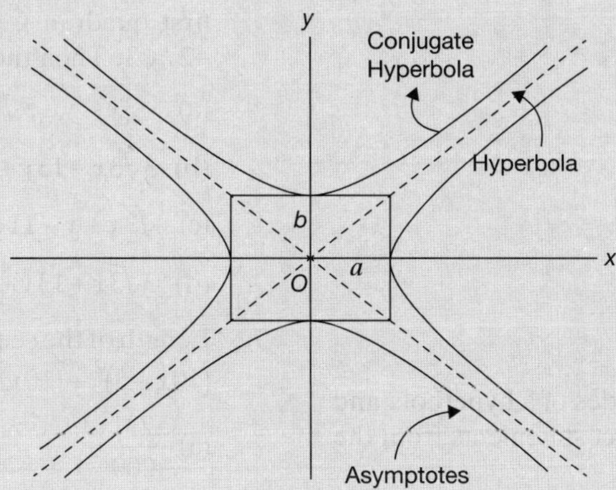

If $b = a$, the pair of asymptotes are mutually perpendicular; the hyperbola is called a rectangular hyperbola.

EXERCISES

1. If the latus-rectum of a hyperbola forms an equilateral triangle with one vertex at the centre of the hyperbola, then the eccentricity of the hyperbola equals:

(a) $\frac{\sqrt{11}+1}{2\sqrt{5}}$

(b) $\frac{\sqrt{11}-1}{2\sqrt{5}}$

(c) $\frac{\sqrt{13}+1}{2\sqrt{3}}$

(d) $\frac{\sqrt{13}-1}{2\sqrt{3}}$

2. If e and e' are the eccentricities of a hyperbola and its conjugate, then the correct statements from the following are:

(a) $ee' \geq 2$

(b) $1 < ee' \leq 2$

(c) $\frac{1}{e^2}+\frac{1}{e'^2}=1$

(d) $\frac{e}{e'}=\frac{e^2-1}{e'^2-1}$

3. If the eccentricity of the hyperbola

$\frac{x^2}{\cos^2\theta}-\frac{y^2}{\sin^2\theta}=1\left(0<\theta<\frac{\pi}{2}\right)$ is greater than 2, then the length of its latus-rectum lies in the interval:

(a) $(3,+\infty)$ (b) $(2,3)$

(c) $(1,3/2]$ (d) $(3/2,2]$

4. If the angle between the asymptotes of a hyperbola is 30°, then its eccentricity is:

(a) $\sqrt{7\pm 3\sqrt{3}}$ (b) $\sqrt{4\pm\sqrt{3}}$

(c) $\sqrt{5\pm\sqrt{3}}$ (d) $\sqrt{8\pm 4\sqrt{3}}$

5. If $x=9$ is a chord of contact of the hyperbola $x^2-y^2=9$, then the equation of the corresponding pair of tangents is:

(a) $9x^2-8y^2+18x-9=0$

(b) $9x^2-8y^2+18x+9=0$

(c) $9x^2-8y^2-18x+9=0$

(d) $9x^2-8y^2-18x-9=0$

6. A ray emanating from point $P(5,0)$ is incident on the hyperbola $9x^2-16y^2=144$ at point M (in the first quadrant), where the slope of the normal is $-2/\sqrt{3}$. Then the equation of the reflected ray is:

(a) $\sqrt{3}x-y-5\sqrt{3}=0$

(b) $3\sqrt{3}x-13y+15\sqrt{3}=0$

(c) $\sqrt{3}x+y-11\sqrt{3}=0$

(d) $3\sqrt{3}x+13y+63\sqrt{3}=0$

7. Length of the semi-transverse axis of the hyperbola $(10x-5)^2+(10y-2)^2=9(3x+4y-7)^2$ is:

(a) $\frac{231}{200}$ (b) $\frac{297}{200}$

(c) $\frac{335}{250}$ (d) $\frac{282}{250}$

8. A hyperbola and an ellipse, both centred at the origin, have the same foci on the x-axis, and they intersect at $(2,2)$. If the eccentricity of the ellipse is $1/2$, then the eccentricity of the hyperbola is:

(a) $\sqrt{7/6}$ (b) $\sqrt{7/5}$

(c) $\sqrt{7/4}$ (d) $\sqrt{7/3}$

9. Let $P(a\sec\alpha, b\tan\alpha)$ and $Q(a\sec\beta, b\tan\beta)$, where $\alpha+\beta=\pi/2$ are two points on the hyperbola $\frac{x^2}{a^2}-\frac{y^2}{b^2}=1$. If (h,k) is the point of intersection of the normals at P and Q, then k equals:

(a) $\frac{a^2+b^2}{2}$

(b) $-\frac{a^2+b^2}{a}$

(c) $\frac{a^2+b^2}{a}$

(d) $-\frac{a^2+b^2}{b}$

10. An ellipse has eccentricity $1/2$ and one focus at the point $P(1/2,1)$. Its corresponding directrix is the tangent nearer to point P and common to the circle $x^2+y^2=1$ and the hyperbola $x^2-y^2=1$. The equation of the ellipse is:

(a) $\frac{\left(x-\frac{1}{3}\right)^2}{1/9}+\frac{(y-1)^2}{1/12}=1$

(b) $\frac{(x-1)^2}{1/4}+\frac{(y-1)^2}{1/12}=1$

(c) $\frac{\left(x-\frac{1}{2}\right)^2}{1/4}+\frac{\left(y-\frac{1}{3}\right)^2}{1/9}=1$

(d) $\frac{(x-1)^2}{1/12}+\frac{\left(y-\frac{1}{4}\right)^2}{1/16}=1$

11. An ellipse intersects the hyperbola $2x^2-2y^2=1$ orthogonally. The eccentricity of the ellipse is reciprocal to that of the hyperbola. If the axes of the ellipse are along the coordinate axes, then the equation of the ellipse is:

(a) $x^2+2y^2=2$

(b) $2x^2+y^2=2$

(c) $x^2+2y^2=4$

(d) $2x^2+y^2=4$

12. Equation $\frac{x^2}{(\sin\sqrt{2}-\sin\sqrt{3})^2}-\frac{y^2}{(\cos\sqrt{2}-\cos\sqrt{3})^2}=1$ represents a hyperbola having:

(a) Eccentricity $<\sqrt{2}$

(b) Eccentricity $>\sqrt{2}$

(c) Director circle with radius = 2

(d) Perpendicular pair of asymptotes

13. Equation of a common tangent with positive slope to the curves $x^2+y^2-8x=0$ and $\frac{x^2}{9}-\frac{y^2}{4}=1$ is:

(a) $2x-\sqrt{5}y-4=0$ (b) $2x-\sqrt{5}y+4=0$

(c) $3x-2\sqrt{5}y+8=0$ (d) $2\sqrt{5}x-3y+4=0$

14. The tangent and normal to the hyperbola $xy=c^2$ at a point, respectively, cut off intercepts a_1, a_2 on the x-axis and b_1, b_2 on the y-axis. Then $a_1a_2+b_1b_2$ equals:

(a) 0 (b) 1

(c) 2 (d) 3

15. The line $2x+y=1$ is tangent to the hyperbola $\frac{x^2}{a^2}-\frac{y^2}{b^2}=1$. If this line passes through the point of intersection of one of the directrices and the x-axis, then the eccentricity of the hyperbola is:

(a) 2 (b) 1

(c) $\sqrt{2}$ (d) $\sqrt{3}$

16. Let a hyperbola pass through the foci of the ellipse $\frac{x^2}{25}+\frac{y^2}{16}=1$. The transverse and conjugate axis of the hyperbola coincides with the major and minor axis, respectively, of the given ellipse. Also, the product of their eccentricities is 1. Equation of the directrices of the hyperbola is:

(a) $x=\pm\frac{9}{5}$ (b) $x=\pm\frac{16}{5}$

(c) $x=\pm\frac{9}{16}$ (d) None of these

17. Consider the hyperbola $\frac{y^2}{a^2}-\frac{x^2}{b^2}=1$ and the ellipse $\frac{x^2}{a^2}+\frac{y^2}{b^2}=1$. If the hyperbola has no perpendicular pair of tangents, then the number of tangents common to the ellipse and the hyperbola are:

(a) 1 (b) 2

(c) 4 (d) None of these

18. Suppose a, b are real numbers such that $ab\neq 0$, which of the following four figures represent the equation $(y-ax-b)(bx^2+ay^2-ab)=0$?

(a)

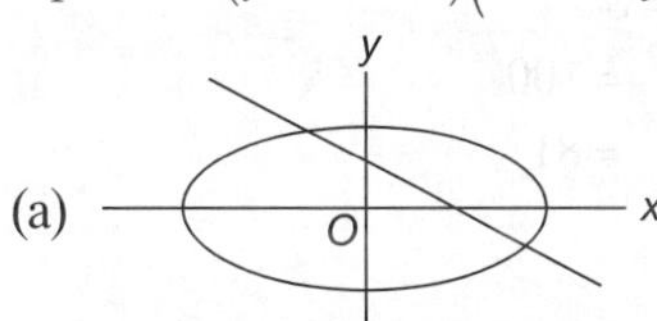

(b)

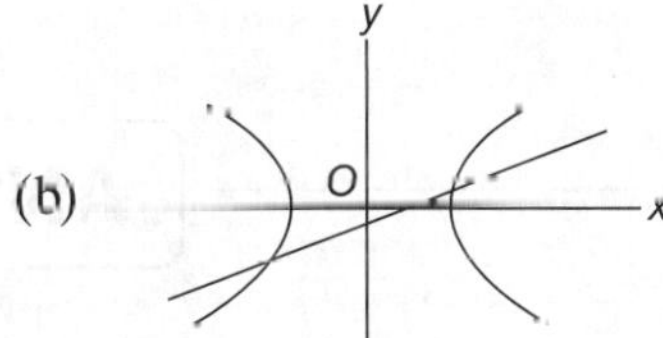

(c)

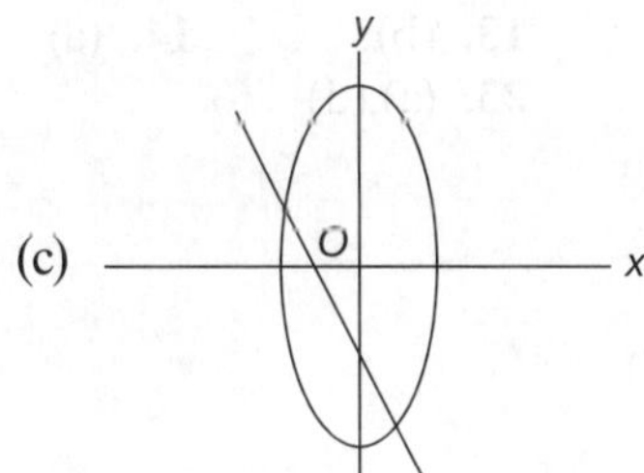

(d)

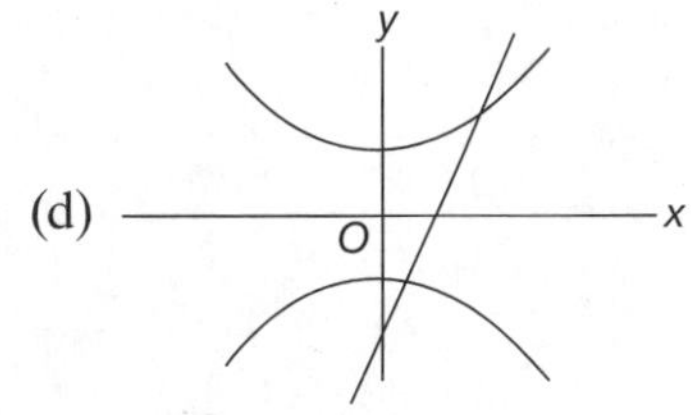

19. Points $P(a\sec\alpha, b\tan\alpha)$ and $Q(a\sec\beta, b\tan\beta)$ are the ends of a focal chord of the hyperbola $\frac{x^2}{a^2}-\frac{y^2}{b^2}=1$. If e is the eccentricity of the hyperbola, then $\frac{1-e}{1+e}$ equals:

(a) $\cos\left(\frac{\alpha-\beta}{2}\right)$

(b) $\tan\left(\frac{\alpha}{2}\right)\tan\left(\frac{\beta}{2}\right)$

(c) $\sin\left(\frac{\alpha}{2}\right)\sin\left(\frac{\beta}{2}\right)$

(d) $\cos\left(\frac{\alpha+\beta}{2}\right)$

20. Let $P(6,3)$ be a point on the hyperbola $H:\frac{x^2}{a^2}-\frac{y^2}{b^2}=1$. The normal at point P intersects the x-axis at $(9,0)$. The hyperbola H and an ellipse E have reciprocal eccentricities, and the same latus-rectum. Then the equation of the ellipse is:

(a) $9x^2+20y^2=100$

(b) $2x^2+6y^2=81$

(c) $81x^2+90y^2=100$

(d) $10x^2+18y^2=81$

21. Tangents are drawn to the hyperbola $4x^2-y^2=36$ from the point $P(0,3)$. If these tangents touch the hyperbola at points Q and R, then area of ΔPQR is:

(a) $45\sqrt{5}$ (b) $48\sqrt{5}$

(c) $54\sqrt{3}$ (d) $60\sqrt{3}$

22. The curves $x^2+y^2-8x=0$ and $4x^2-9y^2=36$ intersect at points A and B. Equation of the circle with AB as diameter is:

(a) $x^2+y^2-24x+12=0$

(b) $x^2+y^2+12x+24=0$

(c) $x^2+y^2-12x+24=0$

(d) $x^2+y^2-24x-12=0$

23. Consider the hyperbola $H: x^2-y^2=1$ and a circle S with centre at $N(x_2,0)$. Suppose H and S touch each other at $P(x_1,y_1)$ with $x_1>1$ and $y_1>0$. The common tangent to H and S at P meets the x-axis at M. If (l,m) is the centroid of the triangle ΔPMN, then:

(a) $\frac{dl}{dx_1}=1-\frac{1}{3x_1^2}$

(b) $\frac{dm}{dx_1}=\frac{x_1}{\sqrt{x_1^2-1}}$

(c) $\frac{dl}{dx_1}=\frac{1}{3}$

(d) $\frac{dm}{dy_1}=\frac{1}{3}$

ANSWER KEYS

1. (c)	**2.** (a),(c)	**3.** (a)	**4.** (d)	**5.** (c)	**6.** (b)	**7.** (d)	**8.** (d)	**9.** (d)	**10.** (a)
11. (a)	**12.** (b)	**13.** (b)	**14.** (a)	**15.** (a)	**16.** (a)	**17.** (d)	**18.** (b)	**19.** (b)	**20.** (b)
21. (a)	**22.** (c)	**23.** (a),(d)							

SOLUTIONS

1. (c) The vertices of the triangle are (0, 0), $\left(ae, \frac{-b^2}{a}\right), \left(ae, \frac{b^2}{a}\right)$. If the triangle is equilateral, then

$$\frac{b^2/a}{ae} = \tan 30^\circ$$

$$\Rightarrow \quad \frac{b^2}{a^2} = \frac{e}{\sqrt{3}}$$

$$\Rightarrow \quad \sqrt{3}\left(e^2 - 1\right) = e$$

$$\Rightarrow \quad \sqrt{3}e^2 - e - \sqrt{3} = 0 \text{ gives } e = \frac{\sqrt{13}+1}{2\sqrt{3}}$$

2. (a),(c) $\quad e^2 = 1 + \frac{b^2}{a^2}$

$$= \frac{a^2+b^2}{a^2}$$

and $\quad e'^2 = 1 + \frac{a^2}{b^2}$

$$= \frac{a^2+b^2}{b^2}$$

Hence $\quad \frac{1}{e^2} + \frac{1}{e'^2} = 1.$

Also $\quad ee' = \frac{a^2+b^2}{a^2}$

$$= \frac{a}{b} + \frac{b}{a} \geq 2$$

3. (a) The eccentricity is greater than 2. Hence

$$e^2 > 4$$

$$\Rightarrow \quad 1 + \frac{\sin^2\theta}{\cos^2\theta} > 4$$

$$\Rightarrow \quad \cos^2\theta < 1/4$$

$$\Rightarrow \quad \cos\theta < 1/2$$

$$\Rightarrow \quad \frac{\pi}{3} < \theta < \frac{\pi}{2}$$

Now, the length of the latus-rectum is

$$l = \frac{2\sin^2\theta}{\cos\theta} = 2\sin\theta\tan\theta$$

The above function is an increasing function in $\frac{\pi}{3} < \theta < \frac{\pi}{2}$. Hence, we have

$$l \in \left(2\sin\frac{\pi}{3}\tan\frac{\pi}{3}, 2\sin\frac{\pi}{2}\tan\frac{\pi}{2}\right) = (3, +\infty)$$

4. (d) Slope of the asymptotes is $\pm\frac{b}{a} = \pm m$ (say). Now

$$\left|\frac{2m}{1-m^2}\right| = \tan 30^\circ = \frac{1}{\sqrt{3}}$$

$$\Rightarrow \quad \left(m^2-1\right)^2 = 12m^2$$

$$\Rightarrow \quad m^4 - 14m^2 + 1 = 0 \text{ gives } m^2 = 7 \pm 4\sqrt{3}$$

The possible values of e are

$$e = \sqrt{1+\frac{b^2}{a^2}} = \sqrt{1+m^2} = \sqrt{8 \pm 4\sqrt{3}}.$$

5. (c) Let (h,k) be the point whose chord of contact is $x = 9$. The equation of the chord of contact should be identical to $hx - ky - 9 = 0$.Comparing the two, we have $h = 1, k = 0$.

Equation of the corresponding pair of tangents is

$$(x-9)^2 = -8\left(x^2 - y^2 - 9\right)\left[T^2 = S(x,y)S(1,0)\right]$$

$$\Rightarrow \quad 9x^2 - 8y^2 - 18x + 9 = 0$$

6. (b) Equation of the hyperbola can be written as $\frac{x^2}{16} - \frac{y^2}{9} = 1.$

Slope of the tangent is $\sqrt{3}/2$. The contact point is

$$M\left(\frac{-a^2m}{\pm\sqrt{a^2m^2-b^2}}, \frac{-b^2}{\pm\sqrt{a^2m^2-b^2}}\right) =$$

$$\left(-8, -3\sqrt{3}\right), \left(8, 3\sqrt{3}\right) \quad [a = 4, b = 3]$$

It is given that M lies in the first quadrant. Hence $\left(8, 3\sqrt{3}\right)$.

Slope of the incident ray $PM = \frac{3\sqrt{3}}{8-5} = \sqrt{3}$. Let the slope of the reflected ray be m. Then, equating the angles that the incident and the reflected rays make with the normal, we have

$$\frac{m+\frac{2}{\sqrt{3}}}{1-\frac{2m}{\sqrt{3}}}=\frac{\frac{-2}{\sqrt{3}}-\sqrt{3}}{1+\left(\frac{-2}{\sqrt{3}}\right)\sqrt{3}}=\frac{5}{\sqrt{3}}$$

$\Rightarrow \quad \sqrt{3}m+2=5-\frac{10m}{\sqrt{3}}$ gives $m=\frac{3\sqrt{3}}{13}$

Hence, the equation of the reflected ray is

$$y-3\sqrt{3}=\frac{3\sqrt{3}}{13}(x-8)$$

$\Rightarrow \quad 3\sqrt{3}x-13y+15\sqrt{3}=0$

7. (d) Equation of the given hyperbola can be written as

$$100\left(x-\frac{1}{2}\right)^2+100\left(y-\frac{1}{5}\right)^2=9(3x+4y-7)^2$$

$$\Rightarrow \quad \sqrt{\left(x-\frac{1}{2}\right)^2+\left(y-\frac{1}{5}\right)^2}=\frac{3}{2}\times\frac{|3x+4y-7|}{5}$$

It represents a hyperbola with eccentricity $e=3/2$, focus $S=(1/2,1/5)$, and the corresponding directrix $3x+4y-7=0$.

If a is the semi-major axis, then

$ae-\frac{a}{e}=$ Distance between directrix and focus

$$\Rightarrow \quad \frac{5}{6}a=\frac{\left|\frac{3}{2}+\frac{4}{5}-7\right|}{5}=\frac{47}{50} \text{ gives } a=\frac{282}{250}$$

8. (d) Let the equation of the ellipse be

$$\frac{x^2}{a^2}+\frac{y^2}{a^2(1-1/4)}=1 \text{ [Eccentricity}=1/2\text{, given]}$$

$$\Rightarrow \quad \frac{x^2}{a^2}+\frac{y^2}{3a^2/4}=1$$

Using the condition that it passes through (2,2), we have $a^2=28/3$.

Let the equation of the hyperbola be

$$\frac{x^2}{c^2}-\frac{y^2}{c^2(e^2-1)}=1$$

Using the condition that its foci coincides with that of the ellipse, we have

$$ce=\frac{1}{2}a$$

$$\Rightarrow \quad ce=\sqrt{\frac{7}{3}} \qquad \text{...(1)}$$

Using the condition that it passes through (2,2), we have

$$\frac{4}{c^2}-\frac{4}{c^2(e^2-1)}=1$$

$$\Rightarrow \quad \frac{e^2-2}{e^2-1}=\frac{c^2}{4} \qquad \text{...(2)}$$

Eliminating c^2 from equations (1) and (2), we have

$$\Rightarrow \quad \frac{e^2-2}{e^2-1}=\frac{7}{12e^2}$$

$\Rightarrow \quad 12e^4-31e^2+7=0$ gives $e^2=\frac{7}{3}$

9. (d) Equation of the normal at P

$$(a\cos\alpha)x+(b\cot\alpha)y=a^2+b^2 \qquad \text{...(1)}$$

Equation of the normal at Q

$$(a\cos\beta)x+(b\cot\beta)y=a^2+b^2$$

$$\Rightarrow \quad (a\sin\alpha)x+(b\tan\alpha)y=a^2+b^2 \qquad \text{...(2)}$$

$$\left[\beta=\frac{\pi}{2}-\alpha\right]$$

Multiplying equation (1) by $\sin\alpha$, equation (2) by $\cos\alpha$, and then subtracting the two eliminates x and gives $y=-\left(\frac{a^2+b^2}{b}\right)$.

10. (a) There are two common tangents $x=\pm1$. The one nearer to (1/2, 1) is $x=1$.

Equation of the ellipse with focus at $(1/2,1)$, directrix $x=1$ and eccentricity $1/2$ is

$$\sqrt{\left(x-\frac{1}{2}\right)^2+(y-1)^2}=\frac{1}{2}|x-1|$$

$$\Rightarrow \quad (2x-1)^2+4(y-1)^2=(x-1)^2$$

$$\Rightarrow \quad 3x^2-2x+4(y-1)^2=0$$

$$\Rightarrow \quad 3\left(x-\frac{1}{3}\right)^2+4(y-1)^2=\frac{1}{3}$$

$$\Rightarrow \quad \frac{\left(x-\frac{1}{3}\right)^2}{1/9}+\frac{(y-1)^2}{1/12}=1$$

11. (a) Eccentricity of the given hyperbola $=\sqrt{2}$. Thus eccentricity of the ellipse$=1/\sqrt{2}$.

Let the equation of the ellipse be

$$\frac{x^2}{a^2}+\frac{y^2}{a^2\left(1-\frac{1}{2}\right)}=1$$

$$\Rightarrow \quad x^2+2y^2=a^2$$

Solving for the intersection of the above ellipse and the given hyperbola $2x^2-2y^2=1$ gives

$$x^2=\frac{a^2+1}{3} \text{ and } y^2=\frac{2a^2-1}{6}$$

Slope of tangents are given by

$$y'=-\frac{x}{2y} \text{ for points on the ellipse}$$

and $\quad y'=\frac{x}{y}$ for points on the hyperbola

At their intersection point, the product of slopes $=-1$. Hence

$$\frac{x^2}{2y^2}=1$$

$$\Rightarrow \quad \frac{a^2+1}{3}=2\times\frac{2a^2-1}{6} \text{ gives } a^2=2$$

Hence, the equation of the ellipse is $x^2+2y^2=2$.

12. (b) Let $a=\sin\sqrt{2}-\sin\sqrt{3}$ and $b=\cos\sqrt{2}-\cos\sqrt{3}$. It is clear from the phasor diagram (see figure) that

$$\left|\cos\sqrt{2}-\cos\sqrt{3}\right|>\left|\sin\sqrt{2}-\sin\sqrt{3}\right|$$

$$\Rightarrow \quad b>a$$

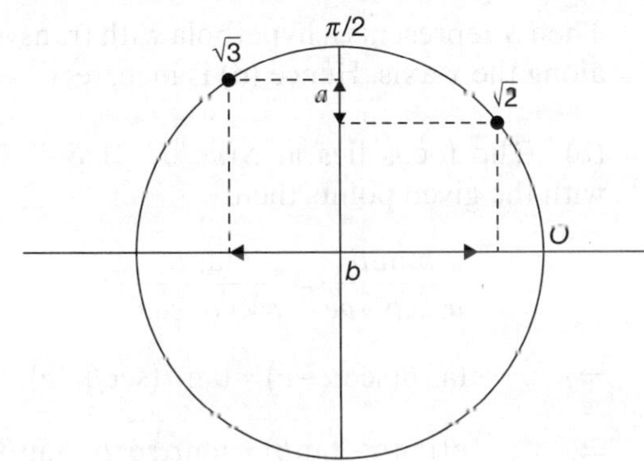

Hence, the equation represents a hyperbola with eccentricity $>\sqrt{2}$.

The director circle is imaginary; it is real when $b<a$.

The pair of asymptotes are not perpendicular; they are perpendicular when $a=b$.

13. (b)

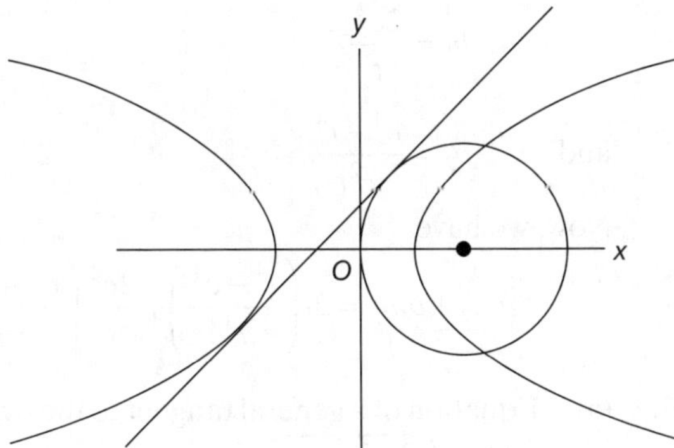

Equation of the given circle can be written as $(x-4)^2+y^2-16$. Equation of a general tangent to this circle is

$$y=m(x-4)+4\sqrt{1+m^2}$$

$$[y\text{-intercept is positive (see figure)}]$$

Equation of a general tangent to the given hyperbola is

$$y=mx+\sqrt{9m^2-4}$$

For these tangents to be identical

$$-4m+4\sqrt{1+m^2}=\sqrt{9m^2-4}$$

From the given options, only $m=2/\sqrt{5}$ satisfies the above equation. Hence, the equation of the common tangent is

$$y=\frac{2}{\sqrt{5}}x+\frac{4}{\sqrt{5}}$$

$$\Rightarrow \quad 2x-\sqrt{5}y+4=0$$

14. (a) Let $\left(t,\frac{c^2}{t}\right)$ be any point on the hyperbola $xy=c^2$. Equations of the tangent and normal at this point are, respectively,

$$\frac{c^2}{t}x+ty=2c^2$$

and $\quad y-\frac{c^2}{t}=\frac{t^2}{c^2}(x-t)$

Their intercepts on the x-axis are, respectively,

$$a_1=2t$$

and $\quad a_2 = \dfrac{t^4 - c^4}{t^3}$

Their intercepts on the y-axis are, respectively,

$$b_1 = \frac{2c^2}{t}$$

and $\quad b_2 = \dfrac{c^4 - t^4}{c^2 t}$

Now, we have

$$a_1 a_2 + b_1 b_2 = 2t\left(\frac{t^4 - c^4}{t^3}\right) + \frac{2c^2}{t}\left(\frac{c^4 - t^4}{c^2 t}\right) = 0$$

15. (a) Equation of a general tangent to the hyperbola is $y = mx \pm \sqrt{a^2m^2 - b^2}$.

Comparing with the given equation $m = -2$ and

$$4a^2 - b^2 = 1$$

$$\Rightarrow \quad 4a^2 - a^2(e^2 - 1) = 1$$

$$\Rightarrow \quad a^2(5 - e^2) = 1$$

Also, the given line passes through $(a/e, 0)$; it cannot pass through $(-a/e, 0)$. Hence

$$\frac{2a}{e} = 1$$

$$\Rightarrow \quad 4a^2 = e^2.$$

Solving the above equations gives $e = 2$.

16. (a) Eccentricity of the given ellipse $= \sqrt{1 - \dfrac{16}{25}} = 3/5$.

Thus eccentricity of the hyperbola $= 5/3$

According to the given condition, the vertex of the hyperbola coincides with the focus of the ellipse. Hence, the semi-transverse axis of the hyperbola is

$$a = \sqrt{25 - 16} = 3$$

Equation of the directrices of the hyperbola is

$$x = \pm\frac{a}{e}$$

$$= \pm\frac{9}{5}$$

17. (d) Points from where a perpendicular pair of tangents can be drawn to the hyperbola $\dfrac{y^2}{a^2} - \dfrac{x^2}{b^2} = 1$, lie on the circle $x^2 + y^2 = a^2 - b^2$.

According to the question, there is no such point, which means $a^2 < b^2$ (the circle is imaginary).

Now, the equation of general tangent to the ellipse is

$$y = mx \pm \sqrt{a^2m^2 + b^2}$$

And the equation of general tangent to the hyperbola is

$$x = my \pm \sqrt{a^2m^2 - b^2}$$

$$\Rightarrow \quad y = tx \pm \sqrt{a^2 - b^2t^2}.$$

The two equations will be identical if

$$t = m \text{ and } a^2m^2 + b^2 = a^2 - b^2t^2.$$

$$\Rightarrow \quad a^2m^2 + b^2 = a^2 - b^2m^2 \text{ [Eliminating } t\text{]}$$

$\Rightarrow \quad m = \pm\sqrt{\dfrac{a^2 - b^2}{a^2 + b^2}}$ which is imaginary since

$$a^2 < b^2$$

Hence, no common tangents.

18. (b) The given equation represents a second-degree curve $S: \dfrac{x^2}{a} + \dfrac{y^2}{b} = 1$ and a straight line with slope a, y intercept b.

In the figure, (a), $a < 0, b > 0$.

Then S represents a hyperbola with transverse axis along the y-axis. Hence (a) is incorrect.

In the figure, (b), $a > 0, b < 0$.

Then S represents a hyperbola with transverse axis along the x-axis. Hence (b) is correct.

In the figure, (c), $a < 0, b < 0$.

Then S represents nothing. Hence (c) is incorrect.

In the figure, (d), $a > 0, b < 0$.

Then S represents a hyperbola with transverse axis along the x-axis. Hence (d) is incorrect.

19. (b) The focus lies at $S(ae, 0)$. If S is collinear with the given points then

$$\frac{b\tan\beta}{a\sec\beta - ae} = \frac{b\tan\alpha}{a\sec\alpha - ae}$$

$$\Rightarrow \quad \tan\beta(\sec\alpha - e) = \tan\alpha(\sec\beta - e)$$

$$\Rightarrow \quad e(\tan\alpha - \tan\beta) = \tan\alpha\sec\beta - \tan\beta\sec\alpha$$

$$\Rightarrow \quad e\sin(\alpha - \beta) = \sin\alpha - \sin\beta$$

[Multiplying both sides by $\cos\alpha\cos\beta$]

$$\Rightarrow \quad e = \frac{\cos\left(\dfrac{\alpha+\beta}{2}\right)}{\cos\left(\dfrac{\alpha-\beta}{2}\right)}$$

$$\Rightarrow \qquad \frac{1-e}{1+e} = \frac{\cos\left(\frac{\alpha-\beta}{2}\right) - \cos\left(\frac{\alpha+\beta}{2}\right)}{\cos\left(\frac{\alpha-\beta}{2}\right) + \cos\left(\frac{\alpha+\beta}{2}\right)}$$

$$= \tan\left(\frac{\alpha}{2}\right)\tan\left(\frac{\beta}{2}\right)$$

20. (b) Equation of the normal to the hyperbola $\frac{x^2}{a^2} - \frac{y^2}{b^2} = 1$ at $P(6,3)$ is

$$\frac{x-6}{6/a^2} = \frac{y-3}{-3/b^2}$$

Its x-intercept equals 9, and hence

$$\frac{b^2}{a^2} = \frac{1}{2} \qquad \ldots(1)$$

Also, $P(6,3)$ lies on the hyperbola $\frac{x^2}{a^2} - \frac{y^2}{b^2} = 1$. Hencc

$$\frac{36}{a^2} - \frac{9}{b^2} = 1 \qquad \ldots(2)$$

Solving the two equations gives $a^2 = 18$ and $b^2 = 9$. Hence

$$\text{eccentricity} = \sqrt{1 + b^2/a^2} = \sqrt{3/2}$$

and $\qquad$ latus-rectum $= \frac{2b^2}{a} = \sqrt{18}$

Then eccentricity of the required ellipse is $\sqrt{2/3}$ and latus-rectum $= \sqrt{18}$. Let the equation of the required ellipse be

$$\frac{x^2}{c^2} + \frac{x^2}{c^2\left(1 - \frac{2}{3}\right)} = 1$$

$$\Rightarrow \qquad \frac{x^2}{c^2} + \frac{y^2}{\frac{c^2}{3}} = 1$$

Its latus-rectum equals $\sqrt{18}$, hence

$$\frac{2c^2/3}{c} = \sqrt{18}$$

$$\Rightarrow \qquad c = \frac{9}{\sqrt{2}}$$

Hence, the equation of the required ellipse is

$$x^2 + 3y^2 = \frac{81}{2}$$

$$\Rightarrow \qquad 2x^2 + 6y^2 = 81$$

21. (a) Equation of the general tangent to the hyperbola $\frac{x^2}{9} - \frac{y^2}{36} = 1$ is

$$y = mx + \sqrt{9m^2 - 36}.$$

[y-intercept is given as positive]

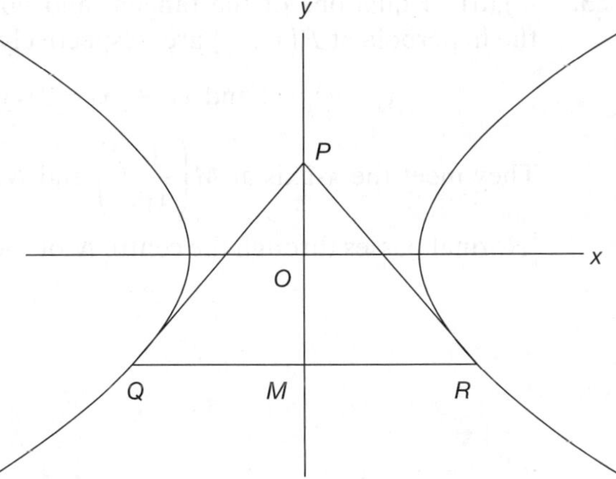

If it passes through $P(0,3)$ (see figure), then

$$3 = \sqrt{9m^2 - 36} \text{ gives } m = \pm\sqrt{5}.$$

Coordinates of the contact points are

$$\left(\frac{-9m}{\sqrt{9m^2-36}}, \frac{-36}{\sqrt{9m^2-36}}\right) = (-3m, -12)$$

Thus, the contact points are

$$Q\left(-3\sqrt{5}, -12\right) \text{ and } R\left(3\sqrt{5}, -12\right)$$

Hence, the area of ΔPQR is

$$\text{Area} = \frac{1}{2} \times QR \times PM$$

$$= \frac{1}{2} \times 6\sqrt{5} \times (12 + 3)$$

$$= 45\sqrt{5}$$

22. (c) Putting $y^2 = 8x - x^2$ in the equation $4x^2 - 9y^2 = 36$, we have

$$13x^2 - 72x - 36 = 0 \text{ gives } x = \frac{-6}{13}, 6$$

The value $x = \frac{-6}{13}$ does not give a real value for y.

The value $x = 6$ gives $y = \pm 2\sqrt{3}$. Hence, the intersection points are $\left(6, \pm 2\sqrt{3}\right)$.

Now, equation of the circle with these points as diameter is

$$(x-6)^2+(y-2\sqrt{3})(y+2\sqrt{3})=0$$

$$\Rightarrow \quad x^2+y^2-12x+24=0$$

23. (a),(d) Equations of the tangent and normal to the hyperbola at $P(x_1, y_1)$ are, respectively,

$$xx_1-yy_1=1 \text{ and } xy_1+yx_1=2x_1y_1$$

They meet the x-axis at $M\left(\frac{1}{x_1},0\right)$ and $N(2x_1,0)$.

[Normal passes through the centre N of the circle]

Now $\quad l=x_1+\frac{1}{3x_1}$

and $\quad m=\frac{y_1}{3}=\frac{\sqrt{x_1^2-1}}{3}$.

$$\left[x_1^2-y_1^2=1\right]$$

Hence, we have $\frac{dl}{dx_1}=1-\frac{1}{3x_1^2}$

and $\quad \frac{dm}{dy_1}=\frac{1}{3}, \frac{dm}{dx_1}=\frac{x_1}{3\sqrt{x_1^2-1}}$

CHAPTER

31 3D Geometry

Plane

- Distance between points $A(x_1, y_1, z_1)$ and $B(x_2, y_2, z_2)$ is

$$AB = \sqrt{(x_2 - x_1)^2 + (y_2 - y_1)^2 + (z_2 - z_1)^2}$$

- **Section Formula:** If P is a point on the line joining points $A(x_1, y_1, z_1)$ and $B(x_2, y_2, z_2)$, such that $PA : PB = m : n$, then

$$P = \left(\frac{mx_2 \pm nx_1}{m \pm n}, \frac{my_2 \pm ny_1}{m \pm n}, \frac{mz_2 \pm nz_1}{m \pm n}\right)$$

  The + sign gives the internal point; the – sign gives the external point.

- If α, β, γ are the angles that a line makes with the +ve directions of the x, y and z axes, respectively, then $\cos\alpha$, $\cos\beta$, $\cos\gamma$ are called the direction cosines of the line. If we denote the direction cosines as l, m, n, then $l^2 + m^2 + n^2 = 1$. If a, b, c are the direction ratios, then the direction cosines are

$$\frac{a}{\sqrt{a^2 + b^2 + c^2}}, \frac{b}{\sqrt{a^2 + b^2 + c^2}}, \frac{c}{\sqrt{a^2 + b^2 + c^2}}$$

  The direction ratios of a line joining two points $A(x_1, y_1, z_1)$ and $B(x_2, y_2, z_2)$ are

$$x_2 - x_1, y_2 - y_1, z_2 - z_1$$

- The acute angle θ between two lines with direction cosines l_1, m_1, n_1 and l_2, m_2, n_2, is given by

$$\cos\theta = |l_1 l_2 + m_1 m_2 + n_1 n_2|$$

  Two lines are parallel if $\frac{l_1}{l_2} = \frac{m_1}{m_2} = \frac{n_1}{n_2}$ and perpendicular if $l_1 l_2 + m_1 m_2 + n_1 n_2 = 0$.

  The direction ratios of the angular bisectors of two lines with direction cosines l_1, m_1, n_1 and l_2, m_2, n_2 are $l_1 \pm l_2, m_1 \pm m_2, n_1 \pm n_2$.

- The projection length of a line joining two points $A(x_1, y_1, z_1)$, and $B(x_2, y_2, z_2)$ along a line with direction cosines l, m, n equals

$$|l(x_2 - x_1) + m(y_2 - y_1) + n(z_2 - z_1)|$$

  In terms of direction ratios a, b, c, the projection length equals

$$\frac{|a(x_2 - x_1) + b(y_2 - y_1) + c(z_2 - z_1)|}{\sqrt{a^2 + b^2 + c^2}}$$

- **Equation of a Plane:**

  1. Equation of a plane passing through points $A(x_1, y_1, z_1)$, $B(x_2, y_2, z_2)$, and $C(x_3, y_3, z_3)$ is

$$\begin{vmatrix} x - x_1 & y - y_1 & z - z_1 \\ x_2 - x_1 & y_2 - y_1 & z_2 - z_1 \\ x_3 - x_1 & y_2 - y_1 & z_3 - z_1 \end{vmatrix} = 0$$

2. Equation of a plane with x intercept a, y intercept b and z intercept c is
$$\frac{x}{a}+\frac{y}{b}+\frac{z}{c}=1$$
3. Equation of a plane whose perpendicular distance from the origin is p and the normal has direction cosines l,m,n is
$$lx+my+nz=p.$$

- The acute angle θ between two planes $a_1x+b_1y+c_1z+d_1=0$ and $a_2x+b_2y+c_2z++d_2=0$ is given by
$$\cos\theta=\frac{|a_1a_2+b_1b_2+c_1c_2|}{\sqrt{a_1^2+b_1^2+c_1^2}\sqrt{a_2^2+b_2^2+c_2^2}}$$
- The two equations represent
$$\text{Identical planes if } \frac{a_1}{a_2}=\frac{b_1}{b_2}=\frac{c_1}{c_2}=\frac{d_1}{d_2}$$
$$\text{Parallel lines if } \frac{a_1}{a_2}=\frac{b_1}{b_2}=\frac{c_1}{c_2}\neq\frac{d_1}{d_2}$$
$$\text{Perpendicular planes if } a_1a_2+b_1b_2+c_1c_2=0$$
- Perpendicular distance AM of a point $A(x_1, y_1, z_1)$ from the plane $L(x, y, z)\equiv ax+by+cz+d=0$ is given by
$$AM=\frac{|L(x_1, y_1, z_1)|}{\sqrt{a^2+b^2+c^2}}$$
Perpendicular distance d between two parallel planes $ax+by+cz+d_2=0$ and $ax+by+cz+d_2=0$ is given by
$$d=\frac{|d_2-d_1|}{\sqrt{a^2+b^2+c^2}}$$
- Two points $A(x_1, y_1, z_1)$ and $B(x_2, y_2, z_2)$ lie on the same side or opposite sides of the plane $L(x, y, z)\equiv ax+by+cz+d=0$, respectively, as
$$L(x_1, y_1, z_1)L(x_2, y_2, z_2)>0 \text{ or } L(x_1, y_1, z_1)\,L(x_2, y_2, z_2)<0$$
The ratio in which the plane $L(x, y, z)\equiv ax+by+cz+d=0$ divides the line joining two points $A(x_1, y_1, z_1)$ and $B(x_2, y_2, z_2)$ is
$$\frac{PB}{PA}=-\frac{L(x_2, y_2, z_2)}{L(x_1, y_1, z_1)}$$
- **Family of Planes:**

1. Equation of any plane passing through a given point $A(x_1, y_1, z_1)$ can bewritten as
$$a(x-x_1)+b(y-y_1)+c(z-z_1)=0 \ (a, b, c \text{ are variables}).$$
2. Equation of any plane perpendicular to a line with given direction ratios a, b, c can be written as
$$ax+by+cz+d=0 \ (d \text{ is a variable}).$$
3. Equation of any plane passing through the line of intersection of two given planes $L_1(x, y, z)=0$ and $L_2(x, y, z)=0$ can be written as
$$L_1(x, y, z)+\lambda L_2(x, y, z)=0 \ (\lambda \text{ is a variable}).$$
4. Equation of any plane parallel to the z axis (perpendicular to the xy plane) can be written as
$$ax+by+c=0 \ (a, b, c \text{ are variables}).$$

Similarly, equation of any plane parallel to the x-axis or the y-axis can be written as $ay+bz+c=0$ and $ax+bz+c=0$, respectively.

5. Equation of any plane containing the line $\frac{x-x_1}{l}=\frac{y-y_1}{m}=\frac{z-z_1}{n}$ can be written as

$$a(x-x_1)+b(y-y_1)+c(z-z_1)=0, \text{ where}$$
$$al+bm+cn=0 \ (a, b, c \text{ are variables}).$$

Right Line

- **Equation of a Line:**

1. Equation of a line with direction ratios a, b, c and passing through the point $A(x_1, y_1, z_1)$ is

$$\frac{x-x_1}{a}=\frac{y-y_1}{b}=\frac{z-z_1}{c}$$

2. Equation of a line passing through the points $A(x_1, y_1, z_1)$ and $B(x_2, y_2, z_2)$ is

$$\frac{x-x_1}{x_2-x_1}=\frac{y-y_1}{y_2-y_1}=\frac{z-z_1}{z_2-z_1}$$

3. Equation of a line formed by the intersection of two given planes $a_1x+b_1y+c_1z+d_1=0$ and $a_2x+b_2y+c_2z+d_2=0$ can be found by first finding two points which lie on both planes, and then using the above equation.

- Perpendicular distance AM of a point $A(x_2, y_2, z_2)$ from the line $\frac{x-x_1}{a}=\frac{y-y_1}{b}=\frac{z-z_1}{c}$:

First, find the projection of the line joining the points $A(x_2, y_2, z_2)$, and $B(x_1, y_1, z_1)$ along the direction cosines a,b,c

$$BM=\frac{|a(x_2-x_1)+b(y_2-y_1)+c(z_2-z_1)|}{\sqrt{a^2+b^2+c^2}}$$

Now, the perpendicular distance AM is given by $AM=\sqrt{AB^2-BM^2}$.

- The line $\frac{x-x_1}{l}=\frac{y-y_1}{m}=\frac{z-z_1}{n}$ and the plane $ax+by+cz+d=0$ are coplanar iff

$$al+bm+cn=0 \text{ and } ax_1+by_1+cz_1+d=0.$$

- The lines $\frac{x-x_1}{a_1}=\frac{y-y_1}{b_1}=\frac{z-z_1}{c_1}$ and $\frac{x-x_2}{a_2}=\frac{y-y_2}{b_2}=\frac{z-z_2}{c_2}$ are coplanar iff

$$\begin{vmatrix} x_2-x_1 & y_2-y_1 & z_2-z_1 \\ a_1 & b_1 & c_1 \\ a_2 & b_2 & c_2 \end{vmatrix}=0$$

- The lines $\frac{x-x_1}{a_1}=\frac{y-y_1}{b_1}=\frac{z-z_1}{c_1}$ and $\frac{x-x_2}{a_2}=\frac{y-y_2}{b_2}=\frac{z-z_2}{c_2}$ intersect each other iff

$$\begin{vmatrix} x_2-x_1 & y_2-y_1 & z_2-z_1 \\ a_1 & b_1 & c_1 \\ a_2 & b_2 & c_2 \end{vmatrix}=0$$

- Three planes $a_1x+b_1y+c_1z+d_1=0$, $a_2x+b_2y+c_2z+d_2=0$, and $a_3x+b_3y+c_3z+d_3=0$ intersect on the same line iff

$$\begin{vmatrix} a_1 & b_1 & c_1 \\ a_2 & b_2 & c_2 \\ a_3 & b_3 & c_3 \end{vmatrix}=0$$

- Equation of a plane containing the line $\frac{x-x_1}{a_1}=\frac{y-y_1}{b_1}=\frac{z-z_1}{c_1}$ and parallel to the line $\frac{x-x_2}{a_2}=\frac{y-y_2}{b_2}=\frac{z-z_2}{c_2}$ is given by

$$\begin{vmatrix} x-x_1 & y-y_1 & z-z_1 \\ a_1 & b_1 & c_1 \\ a_2 & b_2 & c_2 \end{vmatrix}=0$$

- The shortest distance between two lines $\frac{x-x_1}{a_1}=\frac{y-y_1}{b_1}=\frac{z-z_1}{c_1}$ and $\frac{x-x_2}{a_2}=\frac{y-y_2}{b_2}=\frac{z-z_2}{c_2}$:

Method 1
First, find the equation of the plane which contains line 1 and is parallel to line 2. Now, the required shortest distance is the perpendicular distance of the plane from any point, say (x_2, y_2, z_2), on line 2.
Method 2
First, find the direction ratios a, b, c of the line which is perpendicular to both the two given lines, by solving the equations

$$aa_1+bb_1+cc_1=0 \text{ and } aa_2+bb_2+cc_2=0$$

Now, the required shortest distance is the projection of the line joining the points $A(x_1, y_1, z_1)$, and $B(x_2, y_2, z_2)$ along the direction ratios a, b, c.

EXERCISES

1. If the lines $L_1: \frac{x+1}{2}=\frac{y+1}{3}=\frac{z-1}{c}$ and $L_2: \frac{x+3}{1}=\frac{y+6}{2}=\frac{z}{1}$ intersect, the equation of the plane containing the two lines is:
(a) $x-y-z+1=0$ (b) $2x+y-z+1=0$
(c) $3x-y-z+3=0$ (d) $x-y+2z+5=0$

2. Consider the lines $L_1: \frac{x+1}{1}=\frac{y+2}{1}=\frac{z+1}{2}$ and $L_2: \frac{x-3}{1}=\frac{y+2}{2}=\frac{z-3}{3}$. The distance of their intersection point from the plane passing through the points $(-8,1,1), (2,-2,3)$ and $(-4,-1,1)$ is:
(a) $2/3$ (b) $1/3$
(c) 1 (d) 2

3. The plane through the intersection of the planes $x+y+z-1=0$ and $2x+3y-z+4=0$ and parallel to the y-axis also passes through the point:
(a) $(-3,0,-1)$ (b) $(-3,1,1)$
(c) $(3,3,-1)$ (d) $(3,2,1)$

4. The direction ratios of a line passing through $(-4,3,1)$, parallel to the plane $x+2y-z-5=0$, and intersecting the line $\frac{x+1}{-3}=\frac{y-3}{2}=\frac{z-2}{-1}$ are:
(a) 2, 1, 4 (b) 1, 1, 3
(c) 3, −1, 1 (d) −1, 1, 1

5. From a point $P(a,a,a)$, perpendiculars PQ and PR are drawn to the lines $y=x, z=1$ and $y=-x, z=-1$. If $\angle QPR=90°$, then a equals:
(a) $\sqrt{2}$ (b) -1
(c) 1 (d) $-\sqrt{2}$

6. Let P be the plane equidistant from the planes $x+y-1=0$ and $z=0$. A line L with positive direction cosines passes through the point $A(2,-1,1)$ and makes equal angles with the coordinate axes. The line L meets the plane P at points:
(a) $(3-\sqrt{2}, -\sqrt{2}, 2-\sqrt{2})$
(b) $(2+\sqrt{2}, -\sqrt{2}, \sqrt{2}-1)$
(c) $(2-\sqrt{2}, \sqrt{2}, 2+\sqrt{2})$
(d) $(1-\sqrt{2}, -2-\sqrt{2}, -\sqrt{2})$

7. Equation of the plane containing the straight line $\frac{x}{2}=\frac{y}{3}=\frac{z}{4}$ and perpendicular to the plane containing the straight lines $\frac{x}{3}=\frac{y}{4}=\frac{z}{2}$ and $\frac{x}{4}=\frac{y}{2}=\frac{z}{3}$ is:
(a) $x+2y-z=0$ (b) $3x+2y-2z=0$
(c) $x-2y+z=0$ (d) $5x+2y-4z=0$

8. If the distance between the parallel planes $ax-2y+2z=d$ and the plane containing the lines $\frac{x-2}{2}=\frac{y-2}{3}=\frac{z-3}{4}$ and $\frac{x-2}{2}=\frac{y-3}{4}=\frac{z-4}{5}$ is 2, then the value of $|d|$ is:
(a) 2 (b) –3
(c) –1 (d) 6

9. A plane whose perpendicular distance from the origin is unity meets the coordinate axes at points A, B, C. Let $G(\alpha,\beta,\gamma)$ be the centroid of ΔABC. Then $\frac{1}{\alpha^2}+\frac{1}{\beta^2}+\frac{1}{\gamma^2}$ equals:
(a) 7 (b) 8
(c) 9 (d) 10

10. Let (x, y, z) be any point on the line passing through (x_0, y_0, z_0) and parallel to the vector $\mathbf{i}+\mathbf{j}+\mathbf{k}$. If $x_0+y_0=2$, and z_0 is some fixed real number, then (x, y, z) lies on the plane normal to the vector:
(a) $\mathbf{i}+\mathbf{j}-2\mathbf{k}$ (b) $\mathbf{i}+\mathbf{j}+2\mathbf{k}$
(c) $\mathbf{i}+\mathbf{j}-\mathbf{k}$ (d) $\mathbf{i}+\mathbf{j}+\mathbf{k}$

11. Consider the lines $L_1:\frac{x+1}{3}=\frac{y+2}{1}=\frac{z+1}{2}$ and $L_2:\frac{x-2}{1}=\frac{y+2}{2}=\frac{z-3}{3}$. The shortest distance between L_1 and L_2 is:
(a) 0 (b) $\frac{17}{\sqrt{3}}$
(c) $\frac{41}{5\sqrt{3}}$ (d) $\frac{17}{5\sqrt{3}}$

12. If the line $\frac{x-4}{1}=\frac{y-2}{1}=\frac{z-k}{n}$ lies in the plane $2x-4y+z=7$, then its reflection in the plane $x-y+z=1$ is:
(a) $\frac{x}{-1}=\frac{y+2}{7}=\frac{z+1}{2}$ (b) $\frac{x+2}{-1}=\frac{y-1}{1}=\frac{z}{5}$
(c) $\frac{x}{1}=\frac{y}{3}=\frac{z-1}{-2}$ (d) $\frac{x-2}{2}=\frac{y}{3}=\frac{z-1}{3}$

13. A plane perpendicular to the yz plane, passing through the point $(1,1,1)$ and inclined at 45° to the plane $2x+y+2z+1=0$ is represented by:
(a) $2y+z-3=0$ (b) $y+z-2=0$
(c) $y-2z+1=0$ (d) $y+7z-8=0$

14. Consider the planes $P_1: y=0$ and $P_2: x+z-1=0$. Let P_3 be a plane passing through the intersection line of the planes P_1 and P_2. If the distance of point (0, 1, 0) from P_3 is 1 and the distance of point (α,β,γ) from P_3 is 2, then:
(a) $2\alpha+\beta+2\gamma+2=0$ (b) $2\alpha-\beta+2\gamma+4=0$
(c) $2\alpha+\beta-2\gamma-10=0$ (d) $2\alpha-\beta+2\gamma-8=0$

15. Consider the planes $P_1: x+2y-z+1=0$ and $P_2: 2x-y+z-1=0$. Let L be a straight line passing through the origin and parallel to the planes P_1 and P_2. Let M be the locus of the foot of the perpendiculars drawn from the points on line L to plane $P_3: x+y-z+1=0$. From the following points, those which lie on M are:
(a) $\left(\frac{-1}{3}, 1, \frac{5}{3}\right)$ (b) $\left(\frac{-1}{3}, \frac{-5}{3}, -1\right)$
(c) $\left(\frac{-1}{3}, \frac{5}{6}, 0\right)$ (d) $\left(\frac{-1}{3}, 0, \frac{-1}{6}\right)$

16. Plane P_1 is parallel to the vectors $\mathbf{i}+\mathbf{j}+\mathbf{k}$ and $2\mathbf{k}$. Plane P_2 is parallel to the vectors $\mathbf{i}+\mathbf{j}$ and $\mathbf{i}-\mathbf{k}$. Then the acute angle between the vector $\mathbf{i}+\mathbf{j}-\sqrt{2}\mathbf{k}$, and the line of intersection of the planes P_1, P_2 is:
(a) $\pi/8$ (b) $\pi/6$
(c) $\pi/4$ (d) $\pi/3$

17. Reflection of the plane $2x-3y+4z-3=0$ in the plane $x-y+z-3=0$ is:
(a) $4x-3y+z-15=0$ (b) $4x-3y+2z-15=0$
(c) $3x-2y+z-5=0$ (d) $3x-2y+z+5=0$

18. The length of the projection of the line segment joining the points $A(5,-1,4)$ and $B(4,-1,3)$ on the plane $x+y+z-7=0$ is:
(a) $\frac{2}{\sqrt{3}}$ (b) $\frac{2}{3}$
(c) $\frac{2}{\sqrt{3}}$ (d) $\frac{\sqrt{2}}{\sqrt{3}}$

19. If L_1 is the intersection line of the planes $2x-2y+3z-2=0$, $x-y+z+1=0$ and L_2 is the intersection line of the planes $x+2y-z-3=0$, $3x-y+2z-1=0$, then the distance of the origin from the plane containing the lines L_1 and L_2 is:
(a) $\frac{1}{4\sqrt{2}}$ (b) $\frac{1}{3\sqrt{2}}$
(c) $\frac{1}{2\sqrt{2}}$ (d) $\frac{1}{\sqrt{2}}$

20. Line L passes through the origin and is perpendicular to $L_1:(3+t)\mathbf{i}+(-1+2t)\mathbf{j}+(4+2t)\mathbf{k}$ and $L_2:(3+2s)\mathbf{i}+(3+2s)\mathbf{j}+(2+s)\mathbf{k}$, where $t, s \in \mathbf{R}$.

Then the points on L_2 at a distance of $\sqrt{17}$ from the intersection point of the lines L and L_1 are:

(a) $\left(\frac{-1}{3}, \frac{-4}{3}, \frac{2}{3}\right)$ (b) $(-1,-1,0)$

(c) $(2, 1, 1)$ (d) $\left(\frac{7}{9}, \frac{7}{9}, \frac{8}{9}\right)$

21. A line with direction ratios 2, 1, 2 meets the lines $L_1 : x = y + a = z$ and $L_2 : x + a = 2y = 2z$ at points A and B, respectively. Their coordinates are:

(a) $A = (3a, 2a, 3a), B = (a, a, 2a)$

(b) $A = (2a, 3a, 3a), B = (2a, a, a)$

(c) $A = (3a, 3a, 3a), B = (a, a, a)$

(d) $A = (3a, 2a, 3a), B = (a, a, a)$

22. If the projection of the line $L_1 : \frac{x}{2} = \frac{y-1}{2} = \frac{z-1}{1}$ on a plane P is the line $L_2 : \frac{x}{1} = \frac{y-1}{1} = \frac{z-1}{-1}$, then the distance of plane P from the origin is:

(a) $\sqrt{2}$ (b) $\sqrt{3/2}$

(c) $\sqrt{3}$ (d) $\sqrt{6}$

ANSWER KEYS

1. (c)	**2.** (c)	**3.** (d)	**4.** (c)	**5.** (b)	**6.** (a),(d)	**7.** (c)	**8.** (d)	**9.** (c)
10. (a)	**11.** (d)	**12.** (a)	**13.** (b),(d)	**14.** (b),(d)	**15.** (a),(b)	**16.** (c)	**17.** (b)	**18.** (d)
19. (b)	**20.** (b),(d)	**21.** (d)	**22.** (b)					

SOLUTIONS

1. (c)

$$L_1 : \frac{x+1}{2} = \frac{y+1}{3} = \frac{z-1}{c} \text{ and } L_2 : \frac{x+3}{1} = \frac{y+6}{2} = \frac{z}{1}$$

If the two lines intersect, then

$$\begin{vmatrix} -3+1 & -6+1 & -1 \\ 2 & 3 & c \\ 1 & 2 & 1 \end{vmatrix} = 0 \text{ gives } c = 3$$

Equation of the plane containing the two lines is

$$\begin{vmatrix} x+1 & y+1 & z-1 \\ 2 & 3 & 3 \\ 1 & 2 & 1 \end{vmatrix} = 0$$

$$\Rightarrow \quad 3x - y - z + 3 = 0.$$

2. (c) Equations of the two lines in parametric form are

$$(t-1, t-2, 2t-1) \text{ and } (s+3, 2s-2, 3s+3)$$

At their intersection point, we have

$$t-1 = s+3, t-2 = 2s-2, \text{ and } 2t-1 = 3s+3.$$

Solving gives $t = 8, s = 4$. Hence, the intersection point is $(7, 6, 15)$.

Equation of the plane containing the points $(-8,1,1), (2,-2,3)$, and $(-4,-1,1)$ is

$$\begin{vmatrix} x+8 & y-1 & z-1 \\ 2+8 & -2-1 & 3-1 \\ -4+8 & -1-1 & 1-1 \end{vmatrix} = 0$$

$$\Rightarrow \quad \begin{vmatrix} x+8 & y-1 & z-1 \\ 10 & -3 & 2 \\ 4 & -2 & 0 \end{vmatrix} = 0$$

$$\Rightarrow \quad x + 2y - 2z + 8 = 0$$

Its perpendicular distance from $(7,6,15)$ is

$$\frac{|7+12-30+8|}{\sqrt{1^2+2^2+2^2}} = 1$$

3. (d) Equation of the plane passing through the intersection of the two given planes can be written as

$$x + y + z - 1 + \lambda(2x + 3y - z + 4) = 0$$

(λ is a variable).

$$\Rightarrow \quad (1+2\lambda)x + (1+3\lambda)y + (1 = \lambda)z + (-1+4\lambda) = 0.$$

Since the above plane is parallel to the y-axis

$$1 + 3\lambda = 0 \text{ gives } \lambda = -1/3$$

Putting the above value of λ gives the equation of the required plane as

$$x + 4z - 7 = 0$$

Only point $(3, 2, 1)$ lies on the above plane.

4. (c) Equation of line passing through passing through $(-4, 3, 1)$ can be written as

$$\frac{x+4}{a} = \frac{y-3}{b} = \frac{z-1}{c}$$

If it is parallel to the plane $x + 2y - z - 5 = 0$, then

$$a + 2b - c = 0 \qquad \text{...(1)}$$

If it intersects the line $\frac{x+1}{-3} = \frac{y-3}{2} = \frac{z-2}{-1}$, then

$$\begin{vmatrix} -1+4 & 3-3 & 2-1 \\ a & b & c \\ -3 & 2 & -1 \end{vmatrix} = 0$$

$$\Rightarrow \quad \begin{vmatrix} 3 & 0 & 1 \\ a & b & c \\ 3 & -2 & 1 \end{vmatrix} = 0$$

$$\Rightarrow \quad a + 2b - 3c = 0 \qquad \text{...(2)}$$

From the above equations, we have

$$\frac{a}{3} = \frac{b}{-1} = \frac{c}{1}$$

Hence, the direction ratios of the required line are $3, -1, 1$.

5. (b) Equations of the two lines in symmetric form are

$$L_1 : \frac{x}{1} = \frac{y}{1} = \frac{z-1}{0}$$

$$L_2 : \frac{x}{1} = \frac{y}{-1} = \frac{z+1}{0}$$

Since Q lies on L_1, its coordinates may be chosen as $(t, t, 1)$. If PQ is perpendicular to L_1, then

$$1(a-t) + 1(a-t) = 0 \text{ gives } t = a \Rightarrow Q = (a, a, 1)$$

Since R lies on L_2, its coordinates may be chosen as $(t, -t, -1)$. If PR is perpendicular to L_2, then

$$1(a-t) - 1(a+t) = 0 \text{ gives } t = 0 \Rightarrow R = (0, 0, -1)$$

The direction ratios of PQ and PR are, respectively, $0,0,a-1$ and $a,a,a+1$. If PQ and PR are perpendicular, then

$$(a-1)(a+1)=0 \text{ gives } a=\pm 1$$

For $a=1$, P coincides with Q. Hence, it is not acceptable.

6. (a),(d) Points on plane P will be equidistant from the two given planes. Hence, equation of plane P is given by

$$\frac{|x+y-1|}{\sqrt{2}}=\frac{|z|}{1}$$

$$\Rightarrow \quad x+y\pm\sqrt{2}z-1=0$$

Equation of the line is

$$\frac{x-2}{1}=\frac{y+1}{1}=\frac{z-1}{1}$$

Any point on this line can be chosen as $(2+t,-1+t,1+t)$. If this point also lies on the plane $x+y\pm\sqrt{2}z-1=0$, then

$$(2+t)+(-1+t)\pm\sqrt{2}(1+t)-1=0 \text{ gives } t=-\sqrt{2}\pm 1$$

Hence, the intersection points are

$$\left(3-\sqrt{2},-\sqrt{2},2-\sqrt{2}\right) \text{ and } \left(1-\sqrt{2},-2-\sqrt{2},-\sqrt{2}\right).$$

7. (c) Let l,m,n be the direction ratios of the normal to the plane which contains the lines $\frac{x}{3}=\frac{y}{4}=\frac{z}{2}$ and $\frac{x}{4}=\frac{y}{2}=\frac{z}{3}$. Then

$$3l+4m+2n=0 \text{ and } 4l+2m+3n=0$$

$$\Rightarrow \quad \frac{l}{8}=\frac{m}{-1}=\frac{n}{-10}$$

Equation of a plane containing the line $\frac{x}{2}=\frac{y}{3}=\frac{z}{4}$ can be chosen as $ax+by+cz=0$, where

$$2a+3b+4c=0$$

Also, the required plane is perpendicular to the given plane. Therefore

$$8a-b-10c=0$$

Solving the above equations gives

$$\frac{a}{1}=\frac{b}{-2}=\frac{c}{1}$$

Hence, the equation of the required plane

$$x-2y+z=0$$

8. (d) Equation of the plane containing the given lines is

$$\begin{vmatrix} x-2 & y-3 & z-4 \\ 2 & 3 & 4 \\ 2 & 4 & 5 \end{vmatrix}=0$$

$$\Rightarrow \quad -1(x-2)-2(y-3)+2(z-4)=0$$

$$\Rightarrow \quad -x-2y+2z=0$$

The given plane $ax-2y+2z=d$ will be parallel to the above plane if $a=-1$. Perpendicular distance between the planes is given to be 2. Hence

$$\frac{|d|}{\sqrt{1^2+2^2+2^2}}=2 \text{ gives } |d|=6$$

9. (c) Let $A=(a,0,0)$, $B=(0,b,0)$ and $C=(0,0,c)$. Then equation of the plane through A, B and C is

$$\frac{x}{a}+\frac{y}{b}+\frac{z}{c}=1$$

Its perpendicular distance from the origin is given to be 1. Hence

$$\frac{1}{a^2}+\frac{1}{b^2}+\frac{1}{c^2}=1$$

The centroid of ΔABC is at $\left(\frac{a}{3},\frac{b}{3},\frac{c}{3}\right)$. Therefore $\alpha=\frac{a}{3}, \beta=\frac{b}{3}, \gamma=\frac{c}{3}$. Hence

$$\frac{1}{\alpha^2}+\frac{1}{\beta^2}+\frac{1}{\gamma^2}=9\left(\frac{1}{a^2}+\frac{1}{b^2}+\frac{1}{c^2}\right)=9.$$

10. (a) Equation of the line is

$$\frac{x-x_0}{1}=\frac{y-y_0}{1}=\frac{z-z_0}{1}$$

For any point (x,y,z) on this line $x=x_0+t, y=y_0+t, z=z_0+t$.

Also, it is given that $x_0+y_0=2$. Eliminating x_0, y_0 and t from the above equations, we have

$$x+y=x_0+y_0+2t=2+2t=2+2(z-z_0)$$

$$\Rightarrow \quad x+y-2z=2-2z_0$$

which represents a plane whose normal is along $\mathbf{i}+\mathbf{j}-2\mathbf{k}$.

11. (d) Equation of the plane containing line $L_1: \frac{x+1}{3}=\frac{y+2}{1}=\frac{z+1}{2}$ and parallel to line $L_2: \frac{x-2}{1}=\frac{y+2}{2}=\frac{z-3}{3}$ is

$$\begin{vmatrix} x+1 & y+2 & z+1 \\ 3 & 1 & 2 \\ 1 & 2 & 3 \end{vmatrix}=0$$

$$\Rightarrow \quad x+7y-5z+10=0$$

Now, the shortest distance between the two lines equals the perpendicular distance of any point on line L_2, say $(2,-2,3)$ from the above plane:

$$\frac{|2-14-15+10|}{\sqrt{1^2+7^2+5^2}}=\frac{17}{5\sqrt{3}}$$

Alternative: Let a,b,c be the ratios of the direction perpendicular to both the given lines. Then

$$3a+b+2c=0 \text{ and } 1a+2b+3c=0$$

$$\Rightarrow \quad \frac{a}{-1}=\frac{b}{-7}=\frac{c}{5}$$

Line L_1 passes through $A(-1,-2,-1)$ and line L_2 passes through $(2,-2,3)$. The shortest distance between the two lines is the projection of AB along a,b,c:

$$\frac{|-1(2+1)-7(-2+2)+5(3+1)|}{\sqrt{1^2+7^2+5^2}}=\frac{17}{5\sqrt{3}}$$

12. (a) If the given line lies in the given plane, then the point $(4,2,k)$ must satisfy the equation of the plane

$$8-8+k=0 \text{ gives } k=7$$

Also, the line and the normal to the plane should be mutually perpendicular

$$2-4+n=0 \text{ gives } n=2$$

To find its reflection in the plane $x-y+z=1$, we need to find the reflection of any two points on this line in this plane. One convenient point is the point of intersection of the line and the plane.

Any point on this line can be chosen as $(t+4, t+2, 2t+7)$. If it lies on the given plane, then

$$t+4-t-2+2t+7=1 \text{ gives } t=-4$$

and hence their intersection point is $M(0,-2,-1)$. Now, if we choose $t=-2$, then a point on the line is $P(2,0,3)$. Let its reflection in the given plane be $Q(a,b,c)$. Then the mid-point of PQ will lie on the given plane, and line PQ will be parallel to the normal to the given plane.

$$\frac{a+2}{2}-\frac{b+0}{2}+\frac{c+3}{2}-1\rightarrow a-b+c+3=0 \quad \ldots(1)$$

$$\text{and} \quad \frac{a-2}{1}=\frac{b}{-1}=\frac{c-3}{1} \quad \ldots(2)$$

Solving the above equations, we have

$$a=\frac{-2}{3}, b=\frac{8}{3}, c=\frac{1}{3}.$$

Now, the reflection is the line joining the points $M(0,-2,-1)$ and $Q\left(\frac{-2}{3},\frac{8}{3},\frac{1}{3}\right)$, that is

$$\frac{x}{-1}=\frac{y+2}{7}=\frac{z+1}{2}$$

13. (b),(d) Equation of a plane passing through $(1,1,1)$ and perpendicular to the yz plane can be chosen as $a(y-1)+(z-1)=0$.

The direction ratios of the normal to the above plane are $0,a,1$ and those for the given plane $2x+y+2z+1=0$ are $2,1,2$.

The angle between these planes is given to be 45°. Hence

$$\frac{|a+2|}{3\sqrt{1+a^2}}=\frac{1}{\sqrt{2}}$$

$$\Rightarrow \quad 7a^2-8a+1=0 \text{ gives } a=\frac{1}{7},1$$

Hence, the equation of the required plane is

$$y+7z-8=0 \text{ or } y+z-2=0$$

14. (b),(d) Equation of a plane P_3 passing through the intersection line of the planes P_1 and P_2 can be chosen as $x+z-1+ay=0$.

The distance of point $(0,1,0)$ from P_3 is 1. Hence

$$\frac{a-1}{\sqrt{1+1+a^2}}=1\Rightarrow a=\frac{-1}{2}$$

Hence, the equation of the plane P_3 is $2x-y+2z-2=0$.

The distance of point (α,β,γ) from P_3 is 2. Hence

$$\frac{2\alpha-\beta+2\gamma-2}{\sqrt{4+1+4}}=2$$

$$\Rightarrow \quad 2\alpha-\beta+2\gamma+4=0 \text{ or } 2\alpha-\beta+2\gamma-8=0.$$

15. (a),(b) Equation of line L can be chosen as $\frac{x}{a}=\frac{y}{b}=\frac{z}{c}$, where $a+2b-c=0$ and $2a-b+c=0$

$$\Rightarrow \quad \frac{a}{1}=\frac{b}{-3}=\frac{c}{-5}$$

Hence, the equation of L is $\frac{x}{1}=\frac{y}{-3}=\frac{z}{-5}$.

Any point on line L can be chosen as $A(t,-3t,-5t)$. Let $M(\alpha,\beta,\gamma)$ be the foot of the perpendicular dropped from point A to the plane $P_3: x+y-z+1=0$. Then

$\alpha+\beta-\gamma+1=0$ and

$$\frac{\alpha-t}{1}=\frac{\beta+3t}{2}=\frac{\gamma+5t}{-1}=r(\text{say})$$

Now, putting $\alpha=r+t, \beta=2r-3t, \gamma=-r-5t$ in the first equation gives $=-t-\frac{1}{3}$. Hence

$$\alpha=\frac{-1}{3}, \beta=-5t-\frac{2}{3}, \gamma=-4t-\frac{1}{3}$$

Eliminating t, we have

$$\frac{\alpha+\frac{1}{3}}{0}=\frac{\beta+\frac{1}{3}}{1}=\frac{\gamma-\frac{1}{3}}{1}$$

Now, putting (x,y,z) in place of (α,β,γ) gives the required locus as

$$\frac{x+\frac{1}{3}}{0}=\frac{y+\frac{1}{3}}{1}=\frac{z-\frac{1}{3}}{1}$$

Only points in options (a) and (b) satisfy the above equation.

16. (c) If a,b,c be the direction ratios of a normal to the plane P_1, then

$$a+b+c=0$$

and $\quad c=0 \Rightarrow a,b,c=1,-1,0$

If a',b',c' be the direction ratios of a normal to the plane P_2, then

$$a'+b'=0$$

and $\quad a'-c'=0 \Rightarrow a',b',c'=1,-1,1.$

If l,m,n be the direction ratios of the line of intersection of the two planes, then

$$l-m=0$$

and $\quad l-m+n=0 \Rightarrow l,m,n=1,1,0.$

The acute angle between this line and the vector $\mathbf{i}+\mathbf{j}-\sqrt{2}\mathbf{k}$ is given by

$$\cos\theta=\frac{|1+1+0|}{\sqrt{2}\sqrt{4}}=\frac{1}{\sqrt{2}} \Rightarrow \theta=\pi/4$$

17. (b) If $A(u,v,w)$ be any point on the given plane, then

$$2u-3v+4w-3=0 \qquad \ldots(1)$$

If $B(f,g,h)$ be the image point of $A(u,v,w)$ in the plane $x-y+z=3$, then

$$\frac{u+f}{2}-\frac{v+g}{2}+\frac{w+h}{2}-3=0$$ [Mid-point of AB lies on the plane $x-y+z=3$]

$$\Rightarrow \quad u-v+w+f-g+h-6=0 \qquad \ldots(2)$$

and $\quad \frac{u-f}{1}=\frac{v-g}{-1}=\frac{w-h}{1}$ [AB is normal to the plane $x-y+z=3$]

$\Rightarrow \quad u=f+t, v=g-t, w=h+t \ldots(3)$. [For some t]

Putting the above values in equations (1) and (2), we have

$$2f-3g+4h-3=-9t$$

and $\quad 2f-2g+2h-6=-3t$

Eliminating t, we have

$$4f-3g+2h-15=0.$$

Hence, the equation of the image plane is

$$4x-3y+2z-15=0.$$

18. (d) The direction ratios of line AB is 1,0,1 and that of a normal to the plane $x+y+z-7=0$ is 1,1,1. If θ is the acute angle between these two directions, then

$$\cos\theta=\frac{|1+0+1|}{\sqrt{2}\sqrt{3}}=\frac{\sqrt{2}}{\sqrt{3}}$$

The projection of AB on the given plane

$$=AB\sin\theta=\sqrt{2}\times\frac{1}{\sqrt{3}}=\frac{\sqrt{2}}{\sqrt{3}}$$

19. (b) Two points on line L_1 are $A(0,5,4)$ and $B(-5,0,4)$. Hence, the equation of L_1 is

$$\frac{x}{1}=\frac{y-5}{1}=\frac{z-4}{0} \qquad \ldots(1)$$

Two points on line L_2 are $C\left(\frac{5}{7},\frac{8}{7},0\right)$ and $D\left(\frac{7}{5},0,\frac{-8}{5}\right)$. Hence, the equation of L_2 is

$$\frac{x-\frac{5}{7}}{-\frac{24}{35}}=\frac{y-\frac{8}{7}}{\frac{8}{7}}=\frac{z}{\frac{8}{5}}$$

$$\Rightarrow \quad \frac{x-\frac{5}{7}}{-3}=\frac{y-\frac{8}{7}}{5}=\frac{z}{7} \qquad \ldots(2)$$

Equation of the plane containing lines L_1 and L_2 is

$$\begin{vmatrix} x & y-5 & z-4 \\ 1 & 1 & 0 \\ -3 & 5 & 7 \end{vmatrix} = 0$$

$\Rightarrow \quad -7x+7(y-5)-8(z-4)=0$

$\Rightarrow \quad 7x-7y+8z+3=0$

Distance of the origin from the above plane

$$= \frac{3}{\sqrt{7^2+7^2+8^2}}$$

$$= \frac{1}{3\sqrt{2}}$$

20. (b),(d) Equations of the given lines in symmetric form are

$$L_1: \frac{x-3}{1} = \frac{y+1}{2} = \frac{z-4}{2}$$

and $$L_2: \frac{x-3}{2} = \frac{y-3}{2} = \frac{z-2}{1}$$

Equation of line L can be chosen as $\frac{x}{a} = \frac{y}{b} = \frac{z}{c}$, where

$$a+2b+2c=0$$

and $$2a+2b+c=0$$

$\Rightarrow \quad \frac{a}{-2} = \frac{b}{3} = \frac{c}{-2}.$

Hence, the equation of L is $\frac{x}{2} = \frac{y}{-3} = \frac{z}{2}$

Any point on lines L_1 and L can be chosen as $(3+t,-1+2t,4+2t)$ and $(2r,-3r,2r)$. At the point of intersection, we have

$3+t=2r, -1+2t=-3r$, and

$4+2t=5r$

$\Rightarrow \quad r=1, t=-1$

Hence, the intersection point of lines L_1 and L is $P(2,-3,2)$.

Now, any point on line L_2 can be chosen as $(3+2s, 3+2s, 2+s)$. If the distance of this point from P is $\sqrt{17}$, then

$$(1+2s)^2+(6+2s)^2+s^2=17$$

$\Rightarrow \quad 9s^2+28s+20=0$ gives $s=-2, \frac{-10}{9}$

Hence, there are two such points, $(-1,-1,0)$ and $\left(\frac{7}{9},\frac{7}{9},\frac{8}{9}\right)$.

21. (d) Equation of the two lines in symmetric form are

$$L_1: \frac{x}{1} = \frac{y+a}{1} = \frac{z}{1},$$

$$L_2: \frac{x+a}{2} = \frac{y}{1} = \frac{z}{1}$$

Since A lies on L_1, its coordinates may be chosen as $(t,t-a,t)$.

Since B lies on L_2, its coordinates may be chosen as $(2r-a,r,r)$.

If direction ratios of AB are $2,1,2$, then

$$\frac{t-2r+a}{2} = \frac{t-r-a}{1} = \frac{t-r}{2}$$

$\Rightarrow \quad t=3a$ and $r=a$

Hence $A=(3a,2a,3a)$, $B=(a,a,a)$.

22. (b)

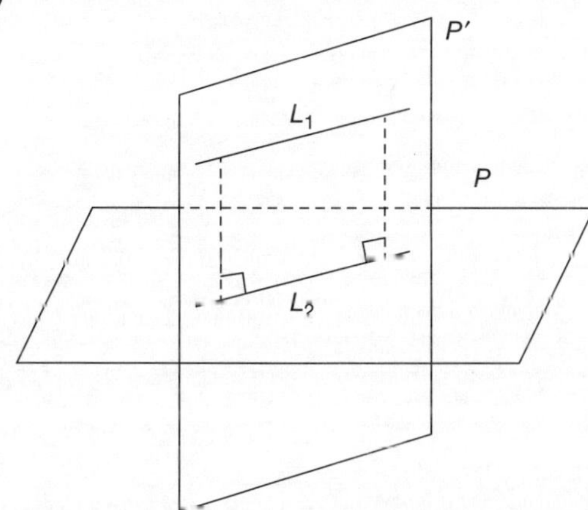

Let P' represent the plane containing the two given lines. Then equation of P' is

$$\begin{vmatrix} x & y-1 & z-1 \\ 2 & 2 & 1 \\ 1 & 1 & -1 \end{vmatrix} = 0$$

$$\Rightarrow \quad x - y + 1 = 0$$

Now, the plane P is perpendicular to the plane P' and contains line L_2 (see figure). Hence, the equation of plane P is given by

$$ax + b(y-1) + c(z-1) = 0, \text{ where}$$

$$a - b = 0$$

and $\quad a + b - c = 0$

$$\Rightarrow \quad \begin{vmatrix} x & y-1 & z-1 \\ 1 & -1 & 0 \\ 1 & 1 & -1 \end{vmatrix} = 0$$

$$\Rightarrow \quad x + y + 2z - 3 = 0$$

Now, the distance of plane P from the origin is

$$\frac{3}{\sqrt{1^2 + 1^2 + 2^2}} = \frac{\sqrt{3}}{\sqrt{2}}.$$

Appendix A: Previous Years' JEE Main Questions and Solutions

Only One Correct Option

- Each question has **FOUR** options. **ONLY ONE** of these four options is the correct answer.
- For each question, choose the option corresponding to the correct answer.
- The answer to each question will be evaluated according to the following marking scheme:

Full Marks: +3	If ONLY the correct option is chosen;
Zero Marks: 0	If none of the options is chosen (i.e. the question is unanswered);
Negative Marks: –1	In all other cases

1. The number of elements in the set $\{x \in \mathbf{R}: (|x| - 3)\,|x + 4| = 6\}$ is:
(a) 3 (b) 2
(c) 4 (d) 1

2. Let a vector $\alpha\hat{i} + \beta\hat{j}$ be obtained by rotating the vector $\sqrt{3}\hat{i} + \hat{j}$ by an angle of 45° about the origin in the counterclockwise direction in the first quadrant. Then the area of the triangle having vertices (α, β), $(0, \beta)$ and (0,0) is:
(a) $\frac{1}{2}$ (b) 1
(c) $\frac{1}{\sqrt{2}}$ (d) $2\sqrt{2}$

3. If for $a > 0$, the feet of perpendiculars from the points $A(a, -2a, 3)$ and $B(0, 4, 5)$ on the plane $lx + my + nz = 0$ are points $C(0, -a, -1)$ and D, respectively, then the length of line segment CD is:
(a) $\sqrt{31}$ (b) $\sqrt{41}$
(c) $\sqrt{55}$ (d) $\sqrt{66}$

4. Consider three observations a, b and c such that $b = a + c$. If the standard deviation of $a + 2$, $b + 2$, $c + 2$ is d, then which of the following is true?
(a) $b^2 = 3(a^2 + c^2) + 9d^2$
(b) $b^2 = a^2 + c^2 + 3d^2$
(c) $b^2 = 3(a^2 + c^2 + d^2)$
(d) $b^2 = 3(a^2 + c^2) - 9d^2$

5. If for $x \in \left(0, \frac{\pi}{2}\right)$, $\log_{10}\sin x + \log_{10}\cos x = -1$ and $\log_{10}(\sin x + \cos x) = \frac{1}{2}(\log_{10}n - 1)$, $n > 0$, then the value of n is:
(a) 20 (b) 12
(c) 9 (d) 16

6. Let $A = \begin{bmatrix} i & -i \\ -i & i \end{bmatrix}, i = \sqrt{-1}$. Then the system of linear equations $A^8\begin{bmatrix} x \\ y \end{bmatrix} = \begin{bmatrix} 8 \\ 64 \end{bmatrix}$ has:
(a) A unique solution
(b) Infinitely many solutions
(c) No solution
(d) Exactly two solutions

7. If the three normals drawn to the parabola, $y^2 = 2x$ pass through the point $(a, 0)$ $a \neq 0$, then a must be greater than:
(a) $\frac{1}{2}$ (b) $-\frac{1}{2}$
(c) –1 (d) 1

8. Let the position vectors of two points P and Q be $3\check{i} - \check{j} + 2\check{k}$ and $\check{i} + 2\check{j} - 4\check{k}$, respectively. Let R and S be two points such that the direction ratios of lines PR and QS are (4, –1, 2) and (–2, 1, –2), respectively. Let lines PR and QS intersect at T. If the vector $\overline{TA}$ is perpendicular to both $\overline{PR}$ and $\overline{QS}$ and the length of vector $\overline{TA}$ is $\sqrt{5}$ units, then the modulus of a position vector of A is:
(a) $\sqrt{482}$ (b) $\sqrt{171}$
(c) $\sqrt{5}$ (d) $\sqrt{227}$

9. Let the functions $f: \mathbf{R} \to \mathbf{R}$ and $g: \mathbf{R} \to \mathbf{R}$ be defined as:

$$f(x) = \begin{cases} x + 2, & x < 0 \\ x^2, & x \geq 0 \end{cases} \text{ and } g(x) = \begin{cases} x^3 & x < 1 \\ 3x - 2, & x \geq 1 \end{cases}$$

Then the number of points in **R** where $fog(x)$ is NOT differentiable are:
(a) 3 (b) 1
(c) 0 (d) 2

10. Let a complex number z, $|z| \neq 1$ satisfy $\log_{\frac{1}{\sqrt{2}}}\left\{\frac{|z|+1}{(|z|-1)^2}\right\} \leq 2$. Then the greatest value of $|z|$ is:

(a) 8 (b) 7
(c) 6 (d) 5

11. Let P be a plane $lx + my + nz = 0$ containing the line, $\frac{1-x}{1} = \frac{y+4}{2} = \frac{z+2}{3}$. If plane P divides the line segment AB joining points $A(-3, -6, 1)$ and $B(2, 4, -3)$ in the ratio k: 1 then the value of k is:

(a) 1.5 (b) 3
(c) 2 (d) 4

12. The range of $a \in \mathbf{R}$ for which the function $f(x) = (4a-3)(x + \log_e 5) + 2(a-7)\cot\left(\frac{x}{2}\right)\sin^2\left(\frac{x}{2}\right)$, $x \neq 2n\pi$, $n \in \mathbf{N}$ has critical points is:

(a) $(-3, 1)$ (b) $\left[-\frac{4}{3}, 2\right]$
(c) $[1, \infty)$ (d) $(-\infty, -1]$

13. A pack of cards has one card missing. Two cards are drawn randomly and are found to be spades. The probability that the missing card is not a spade is:

(a) $\frac{3}{4}$ (b) $\frac{52}{867}$
(c) $\frac{39}{50}$ (d) $\frac{22}{425}$

14. Let $[x]$ denote greatest integer less than or equal to x. If for $n \in \mathbf{N}$, $(1 - x + x^3)^n = \sum_{j=0}^{3n} a_j x^j$, then $\sum_{j=0}^{\left[\frac{3n}{2}\right]} a_{2j} + 4\sum_{j=0}^{\left[\frac{3n-1}{2}\right]} a_{2j} + 1$ is equal to:

(a) 2 (b) 2^{n-1}
(c) 1 (d) n

15. If $y = y(x)$ is the solution of the differential equation $\frac{dy}{dx} + 2y\tan x = \sin x$, $y\left(\frac{\pi}{3}\right) = 0$, then the maximum value of the function $y(x)$ over **R** is:

(a) 8 (b) $\frac{1}{2}$
(c) $-\frac{15}{4}$ (d) $\frac{1}{8}$

16. The locus of the midpoints of the chord of the circle $x^2 + y^2 = 25$, which is tangent to the hyperbola $\frac{x^2}{9} - \frac{y^2}{16} = 1$, is:

(a) $(x^2 + y^2)^2 - 16x^2 + 9y^2 = 0$
(b) $(x^2 + y^2)^2 - 9x^2 + 144y^2 = 0$
(c) $(x^2 + y^2)^2 - 9x^2 - 16y^2 = 0$
(d) $(x^2 + y^2)^2 - 9x^2 + 16y^2 = 0$

17. The number of roots of the equation $(81)^{\sin^2 x} + (81)^{\cos^2 x} = 30$ in the interval $[0, \pi]$ is:

(a) 3 (b) 4
(c) 8 (d) 2

18. Let $S_k = \sum_{r=1}^{k} \tan^{-1}\left(\frac{6^r}{2^{2r+1} + 3^{2r+1}}\right)$. Then the value of $\lim_{k\to\infty} S_k$ is:

(a) $\tan^{-1}\left(\frac{3}{2}\right)$ (b) $\frac{\pi}{2}$
(c) $\cot^{-1}\left(\frac{3}{2}\right)$ (d) $\tan^{-1}(3)$

19. The locus of the midpoint of the line segment joining the focus of parabola $y^2 = 4ax$ to a point moving on it is a parabola, the equation of whose directrix is:

(a) $y = 0$ (b) $x = 0$
(c) $x = a$ (d) $y = a$

20. There are 6 Indians and 8 foreigners. A committee is to be formed with at least 2 Indians, such that the number of foreigners is twice the number of Indians. The total number of ways of forming the committee is equal to:

(a) 1625 (b) 1050
(c) 1400 (d) 575

21. There are two positive numbers p and q such that $p + q = 2$ and $p^4 + q^4 = 272$. The quadratic equation whose roots are p and q is:

(a) $x^2 - 2x + 2 = 0$ (b) $x^2 - 2x + 135 = 0$
(c) $x^2 - 2x + 16 = 0$ (d) $x^2 - 2x + 130 = 0$

22. A fair die is tossed n times. If the probability of getting an odd number twice is equal to that of getting an even number thrice, then the probability of getting an odd number, odd number of times is:

(a) $\frac{1}{3}$ (b) $\frac{1}{6}$
(c) $\frac{1}{2}$ (d) $\frac{1}{8}$

23. Population P of a town at time t is given by the differential equation $\frac{dP}{dt} = 0.5P - 450$, $P(0) = 850$. The time when the population of the town becomes zero is:
(a) $\ell n9$ (b) $3\ell n4$
(c) $2\ell n18$ (d) $\ell n18$

24. The value of $(-{}^{15}C_1 + 2.\ {}^{15}C_2 - 3\ {}^{15}C_3 + \ldots\ldots -15\ {}^{15}C_{15}) + ({}^{14}C_1 + {}^{14}C_3 + \ldots\ldots + {}^{14}C_{11})$ is:
(a) $2^{16} - 14$ (b) $2^{13} - 14$
(c) $2^{13} - 13$ (d) 2^{14}

25. The tangent at point $P(t, t^3)$ of curve $y = x^3$ meets the curve again at Q. Then the ordinate of the point which divides PQ internally in the ratio 1 : 2 is:
(a) 0 (b) $2t^3$
(c) $-2t^3$ (d) $8t$

26. Let $f(x) = \frac{4x^3 - 3x^2}{6} - 2\sin x + (2x - 1)\cos x$. Then $f(x)$:
(a) Decreases in $\left[\frac{1}{2}, \infty\right)$
(b) Increases in $\left[\frac{1}{2}, \infty\right)$
(c) Decreases in$(-\infty, \infty)$
(d) Increases in $\left(-\infty, \frac{1}{2}\right]$

27. The area of the region bounded by the circle $x^2 + y^2 = 36$ and the convex side of the parabola $y^2 = 9x$ is:
(a) $12\pi + 3\sqrt{3}$ (b) $36\pi + 3\sqrt{3}$
(c) $24\pi - 3\sqrt{3}$ (d) $24\pi - 3\sqrt{3}$

28. If f:**R**→**R** is a function defined by $f(x) = [x - 1]\cos\left(\frac{2x-1}{2}\right)\pi$, where$[x]$ denotes the greatest integer function, then f is:
(a) Continuous for every real x.
(b) Discontinuous only at $x = 1$.
(c) Discontinuous only at non-zero integral values of x.
(d) Continuous only at $x = 1$.

29. Consider the family of lines such that the AM of the reciprocal of the x- and y-intercepts is $\frac{1}{4}$. Which of the following points lie on any of these lines:
(a) (2, 2) (b) (4, 4)
(c) (1, 1) (d) All of the above

30. If $I = \int \frac{\cos\theta - \sin\theta}{\sqrt{8 - \sin 2\theta}}\, d\theta = a\sin^{-1}\left(\frac{\sin\theta + \cos\theta}{b}\right) + C$, then the ordered pair (a, b) is:
(a) (1, 3) (b) (3, 1)
(c) (1, 1) (d) (–1, 3)

31. Let f: **R**→**R**, $f(x) = 2x - 1$ and $g(x) = \frac{x - \frac{1}{2}}{x - 1}$. Then $fog(x)$ is:
(a) One-one, onto (b) Many-one, onto
(c) One-one, into (d) Many-one, into

32. The value of $\lim_{x\to 0^+} \frac{\int_0^{x^2} \sin\sqrt{t}\, dt}{x^3}$ is:
(a) $\frac{1}{15}$ (b) $\frac{2}{3}$
(c) 3 (d) 2

33. The values of k and m such that the system of equations $3x + 2y - kz = 10$, $x - 2y + 3z = 3$, $x + 2y - 3z = 5m$ is inconsistent is:
(a) $k = 3$ and $m \neq \frac{7}{10}$ (b) $k = 3$ and $m = \frac{7}{10}$
(c) $k \neq 3$ and $m = \frac{7}{10}$ (d) $k = 2$ and $m \neq \frac{7}{10}$

34. The value of ${}^{n+1}C_2 + 2\,({}^2C_2 + {}^3C_2 + \ldots\ldots + {}^nC_2)$ is:
(a) $\frac{n(n+1)(2n-1)}{6}$ (b) $\frac{n(n+1)(2n+1)}{6}$
(c) $\frac{(n-1)n(n+1)}{6}$ (d) $\frac{n(n+1)}{2}$

35. If A and B are subsets of $X = \{1,2,3,4,5\}$, then the probability that $n(A \cap B) = 2$ is:
(a) $\frac{65}{2^7}$ (b) $\frac{65}{2^9}$
(c) $\frac{35}{2^9}$ (d) $\frac{135}{2^9}$

36. Given $f(0) = 1$, $f(2) = e^2$ and $f'(x) = f'(2 - x)$. Then the value of $\int_0^2 f(x)dx$ is:
(a) $1 - e^2$ (b) $1 + e^2$
(c) e (d) e^2

37. A curve $y = f(x)$ passing through the point (1,2) satisfies the differential equation $x\frac{dy}{dx} + y = bx^4$ such that $\int_1^2 f(y)dy = \frac{62}{5}$. Then the value of b is:

(a) 10 (b) 11
(c) $\frac{32}{5}$ (d) $\frac{62}{5}$

38. The area of the region defined by $5x^2 \le y \le 2x^2 + 9$ is:
(a) $6\sqrt{3}$ (b) $12\sqrt{3}$
(c) $18\sqrt{3}$ (d) $9\sqrt{3}$

39. The value of $\tan\left(\frac{1}{4}\sin^{-1}\frac{\sqrt{63}}{8}\right)$ is:
(a) $\frac{1}{\sqrt{7}}$ (b) $\frac{1}{\sqrt{5}}$
(c) $\frac{2}{\sqrt{3}}\frac{dP}{dt} = 0$ (d) None of these

40. The value of $\int_1^3 [x^2 - 2x - 2]dx$ is: ([ ] denotes greatest integer function)
(a) -4 (b) -5
(c) $-1-\sqrt{2}-\sqrt{3}$ (d) $1-\sqrt{2}-\sqrt{3}$

41. A is a 3×3 square matrix and B is a 3×3 skew-symmetric matrix and X is a 3×1 matrix. Then the equation $(A^2B^2 - B^2A^2)\,X = O$ (where O is a null matrix) has:
(a) Infinite number of solutions
(b) No solution
(c) Exactly one solution
(d) Exactly two solutions

42. If $\begin{vmatrix} f(x) & f'(x) \\ f'(x) & f''(x) \end{vmatrix} = 0$, $f(0) = 1$ and $f'(0) = 2$, then $f(1)$ belongs to the interval:
(a) [6, 9] (b) [9, 12]
(c) [8, 10] (d) [5, 7]

43. The point on the curve $y = x^2 + 4$ which is nearest to the line $y = 4x - 1$ is:
(a) (2,8) (b) (1,5)
(c) (3,13) (d) (–1,5)

44. Let $f(x) = \begin{cases} -55x & ; \quad x < -5 \\ 2x^3 - 3x^2 - 120x & ; \quad -5 \le x < 4 \\ 2x^3 - 3x^2 - 36x + 10 & ; \quad x \ge 4 \end{cases}$

Then the interval in which $f(x)$ is monotonically increasing is:
(a) $(-5, -4) \cup (4, \infty)$ (b) $(-\infty, -4) \cup (5, \infty)$
(c) $(-5, 4) \cup (5, \infty)$ (d) $(-5, -4) \cup (3, \infty)$

45. If a, b, c are in AP, and the centroid of the triangle with vertices (a, c), (a, b), $(2, b)$ is $\left(\frac{10}{3}, \frac{7}{3}\right)$, and α, β are roots of the equation $ax^2 + bx + 1 = 0$, then $\alpha^2 + \beta^2 - \alpha\beta$ equals:
(a) $-\frac{71}{256}$ (b) $\frac{71}{256}$
(c) $\frac{69}{256}$ (d) $-\frac{69}{256}$

46. Let $A = \begin{bmatrix} 0 & \tan\frac{\theta}{2} \\ -\tan\frac{\theta}{2} & 0 \end{bmatrix}$ and $(I + A)\,(I - A)' = \begin{bmatrix} a & -b \\ b & a \end{bmatrix}$, then the value of $13(a^2 + b^2)$ is:
(a) $26\sec^2\frac{\theta}{2}$ (b) $13\tan^4\frac{\theta}{2}$
(c) $26\tan^2\frac{\theta}{2}$ (d) $13\sec^4\frac{\theta}{2}$

47. Let $L_1: (2-i)z = 4i + (2+i)\bar{z}$ and $L_2: (2+i)z = (i-2)\bar{z}$ intersect at a point A. If a circle is drawn centred at A and touching the line $(i-1)z + (1+i)\bar{z} + 2i = 0$, the radius of the circle is:
(a) $\frac{3}{2\sqrt{2}}$ (b) $\frac{1}{\sqrt{2}}$
(c) $3\sqrt{2}$ (d) $\frac{1}{3\sqrt{2}}$

48. The value of
$$\int \frac{\sin\theta\sin 2\theta(\sin^6\theta + \sin^4\theta + \sin^2\theta)\sqrt{2\sin^4\theta + 3\sin^2\theta + 6}}{1-\cos 2\theta}\,d\theta$$
equals:
(a) $\frac{1}{6}[2\cos^6\theta + 9\cos^4\theta - 18\cos^2\theta + 11]^{3/2} + C$
(b) $\frac{1}{18}[-2\cos^6\theta + 9\cos^4\theta - 18\cos^2\theta + 11]^{3/2} + C$
(c) $\frac{1}{18}[2\cos^6\theta - 9\cos^5\theta - 18\cos^2\theta + 11]^{3/2} + C$
(d) $\frac{1}{18}[-2\cos^6\theta - 9\cos^5\theta - 18\cos^2\theta + 11]^{3/2} + C$

49. If $\vec{a} = \hat{i} + \hat{j} - \hat{k}$, $\vec{b} = \hat{i} + \hat{j}$, $\vec{c} = \hat{i} - 2\hat{j} - \hat{k}$ and $\vec{r} \times \vec{a} = \vec{c} \times \vec{a}$, $\vec{r} \cdot \vec{b} = 0$, then $\vec{r} \cdot \vec{a}$ is equal to:
(a) $\frac{1}{2}$ (b) $\frac{3}{2}$
(c) $-\frac{3}{2}$ (d) $-\frac{1}{2}$

50. Let f and g be functions defined from $\mathbf{N} \to \mathbf{N}$ such that $f(n+1) = f(n) + f(1)$. Then the correct statement from the following is:
(a) f is one-one
(b) f is onto$\Rightarrow f(x) = x$
(c) If fog is one-one then g is onto
(d) If fog is onto, then g is onto

51. If the curves $\frac{x^2}{a} + \frac{y^2}{b} = 1$ and $\frac{x^2}{c} + \frac{y^2}{d} = 1$ cut each other orthogonally, then:
(a) $a - b = c - d$ (b) $ab = \frac{c+d}{a+b}$
(c) $a + b = c + d$ (d) $ab = \frac{c-d}{a-b}$

52. Let S: $\sin 2\theta + \tan 2\theta > 0$, $\theta \in [0, 2\pi]$. Then the complete set of values of θ which satisfy S is:
(a) $\left(0, \frac{\pi}{4}\right) \cup \left(\frac{\pi}{2}, \frac{3\pi}{4}\right) \cup \left(\pi, \frac{5\pi}{4}\right) \cup \left(\frac{3\pi}{2}, \frac{7\pi}{4}\right)$
(b) $\left[0, \frac{\pi}{4}\right] \cup \left[\frac{\pi}{2}, \frac{3\pi}{4}\right] \cup \left[\pi, \frac{5\pi}{4}\right] \cup \left[\frac{3\pi}{2}, \frac{7\pi}{4}\right]$
(c) $\left(0, \frac{\pi}{2}\right) \cup \left(\frac{3\pi}{2}, \frac{5\pi}{4}\right)$
(d) None of these

53. Let the quadratic equation be $ax^2 + bx + c = 0$, where a, b, c are obtained by rolling a dice thrice. The probability that the equation has equal roots is:
(a) $\frac{5}{216}$ (b) $\frac{1}{72}$
(c) $\frac{1}{36}$ (d) $\frac{3}{216}$

54. Let $f(x)$ be a polynomial of 6th degree with leading co-efficient unity, and $\lim_{x\to 0} \frac{f(x)}{x^3} = 1$. Also, $x = -1$ and $x = 1$ are points of extremas of $f(x)$. Then the value of $5f(2)$ is:
(a) 144 (b) 146
(c) 148 (d) 150

55. The slope of the tangent at any point on a curve is given by $\frac{dy}{dx} = \frac{x^2 - 4x + y + 8}{(x-2)}$ and the curve passes through the origin. Then which of the following points also lie on the curve:
(a) (2, 4) (b) (2, –4)
(c) (–2, –4) (d) (3, 1)

56. The number of points where $f(x) = |2x + 1| - 3|x + 2| + |x^2 + x - 2|$ is non-differentiable is:
(a) 2 (b) 3
(c) 4 (d) 0

57. The value of $\lim_{n\to\infty} \left(1 + \frac{1 + \frac{1}{2} + \frac{1}{3} + \ldots + \frac{1}{n}}{n^2}\right)^n$ is:
(a) $\frac{1}{e}$ (b) 1
(c) 0 (d) $\frac{1}{e^2}$

58. The direction cosines of two lines satisfy the relations: $l + m = n$ and $l^2 + m^2 = n^2$. If α is the angle between them, then the value of $\sin^4\alpha + \cos^4\alpha$ is:
(a) $\frac{3}{4}$ (b) $\frac{5}{8}$
(c) $\frac{1}{2}$ (d) $\frac{3}{8}$

59. Let $f(x) = x^3 - ax^2 + bx + 1$ be defined in [1, 2]. Rolle's theorem is applied on $f(x)$ in [1,2] such that $f'\left(\frac{4}{3}\right) = 0$. Then the ordered pair (a, b) is:
(a) (–5, 8) (b) (5, 8)
(c) (5, –8) (d) (–5, –8)

60. The value of $\int_{-\pi/2}^{\pi/2} \frac{\cos^2 x}{1+3^x} dx$ is:
(a) $\frac{\pi}{4}$ (b) $\frac{\pi}{2}$
(c) $\frac{\pi}{8}$ (d) $\frac{\pi}{3}$

61. The value of $\lim_{x\to 0} 2\left\{\frac{\sqrt{3}\sin\left(\frac{\pi}{6}+x\right) - \cos\left(\frac{\pi}{6}+x\right)}{\sqrt{3}x(\sqrt{3}\cos x - \sin x)}\right\}$ is:
(a) $\frac{4}{3}$ (b) $\frac{2}{\sqrt{3}}$
(c) $\frac{2}{3}$ (d) $\frac{4}{\sqrt{3}}$

62. If $x - y = 0$, $x + 2y = 3$ and $2x + y = 6$ are three lines forming a triangle, then the triangle is:
(a) Isosceles (b) Right angled
(c) Equilateral (d) None of these

63. The number of integral values of k for which the equation $3 \sin x + 4 \cos x = k + 1$ has a solution is:
(a) 13 (b) 6
(c) 8 (d) 11

64. The number of 7-digit numbers in which the sum of the digits is 10 and the digits can take 1, 2, 3 values is:
(a) 77 (b) 42
(c) 60 (d) 35

65. The number of solutions of the equation $4(x-1)=\log_2(x-3)$ is:
(a) 0 (b) 1
(c) 2 (d) 4

66. If A is a symmetric matrix of order 2, and the sum of the diagonal elements of A^2 is 1, where the elements of the matrix are integers, then the number of such matrices is:
(a) 4 (b) 6
(c) 8 (d) 5

67. The maximum value of the slope of a tangent to the curve $y=\frac{x^4}{2}-5x^3+18x^2+6$ is at the point:
(a) (2,2) (b) (2,46)
(c) $\left(1,\frac{39}{2}\right)$ (d) (1,0)

68. The value of $\begin{vmatrix}(a+1)(a+2) & (a+1) & 1\\ (a+2)(a+3) & (a+2) & 1\\ (a+3)(a+4) & (a+3) & 1\end{vmatrix}$ is:
(a) –2 (b) 2
(c) 0 (d) 1

69. If $\frac{\sin^{-1}x}{a}=\frac{\cos^{-1}x}{b}=\frac{\tan^{-1}y}{c}$, then the value of $\cos\left(\frac{\pi c}{a+b}\right)$ is:
(a) $\frac{1+y^2}{1-y^2}$ (b) $\frac{2y}{1+y^2}$
(c) $\frac{1-y^2}{1+y^2}$ (d) $\frac{y}{1+y^2}$

70. The value of $\mathbf{a}\times(\mathbf{a}\times(\mathbf{a}\times(\mathbf{a}\times\mathbf{b})))$ is:
(a) $|\vec{a}|^4\vec{b}$ (b) $-|\vec{a}|^4\vec{b}$
(c) $|\vec{a}|^2\vec{b}$ (d) $-|\vec{a}|^2\vec{b}$

71. If $|f(x)-f(y)|\le|(x-y)^2|\ \forall\ x, y\in\mathbf{R}$ and $f(0)=1$, then:
(a) $f(x)=0\ \forall\ x\in\mathbf{R}$ (b) $f(x)>0\ \forall\ x\in\mathbf{R}$
(c) $f(x)<0\ \forall\ x\in\mathbf{R}$ (d) $f(x)$ can take any value

72. The value of $1+\frac{2}{3}+\frac{7}{3^2}+\frac{12}{3^3}\ldots\ldots\infty$ is:
(a) $\frac{13}{4}$ (b) $\frac{13}{2}$
(c) $\frac{11}{4}$ (d) $\frac{11}{2}$

73. The maximum value of the term independent of t in the expansion of $\left(tx^{1/5}+\frac{(1-x)^{1/10}}{t}\right)^{10}$ is:
(a) $56\sqrt{3}$ (b) $\frac{56}{\sqrt{3}}$
(c) 56 (d) $28\sqrt{3}$

74. The value of $\sum_{n=1}^{n=100}\int_{n-1}^{n}e^{x-[x]}dx$ is:
(a) $100(e-1)$ (b) $100\,e$
(c) 100 (d) $100\,(1-e)$

75. The sum of the 2nd and 6th terms of an increasing GP is $\frac{25}{2}$, and the product of the 3rd and the 5th terms is 25. Then sum of the 4th, 6th and 8th terms is:
(a) 30 (b) 35
(c) 20 (d) 22

76. If points $P(1,5,35)$, $Q(7,5,2)$, $R(1,\lambda,7)$, $S(2\lambda,1,2)$ are coplanar, then the sum of all the possible values of λ is:
(a) $\frac{39}{5}$ (b) $\frac{17}{2}$
(c) $\frac{-39}{5}$ (d) $\frac{-17}{2}$

77. The distance between the line $\mathbf{r}=2\mathbf{i}-2\mathbf{j}+3\mathbf{k}+\lambda(\mathbf{i}-\mathbf{j}+4\mathbf{k})$ and the plane $\mathbf{r}\cdot(\mathbf{i}+5\mathbf{j}+\mathbf{k})=5$ is:
(a) $\frac{7}{9}$ (b) $\frac{10}{3\sqrt{3}}$
(c) $\frac{5}{3}$ (d) $\frac{8}{\sqrt{3}}$

78. A tetrahedron has vertices at $O(0,0,0)$, $A(1,2,1)$, $B(2,1,3)$ and $C(-1,1,2)$. Then the angle between the faces OAB and ABC is:
(a) 30° (b) 90°
(c) $\cos^{-1}\left(\frac{17}{31}\right)$ (d) $\cos^{-1}\left(\frac{19}{35}\right)$

79. If $f(x)=\int_0^x e^t f(t)dt + e^x$, then $f(x)$ is equal to:

(a) $2e^{e^x-1}$ (b) $2e^{e^x-1}+1$

(c) $e^{e^x-1}+1$ (d) $2e^{e^x-1}-1$

80. A 7-digit number is formed using digits 3, 3, 4, 4, 4, 1, 1 (by taking all at a time). The probability that the number is even is:

(a) $\frac{2}{7}$ (b) $\frac{3}{7}$

(c) $\frac{5}{14}$ (d) $\frac{3}{14}$

81. If A_1 and A_2 are areas of regions defined as

A_1:$y=\sin x$, $y=\cos x$ and the y-axis in the I[st] quadrant

A_2:$y=\sin x$, $y=\cos x$ and the x-axis and $x=\frac{\pi}{2}$.

Then the correct statement from the following is:

(a) $A_1 : A_2 = 1:\sqrt{2}; A_1 + A_2 = 1$

(b) $A_1 : A_2 = \sqrt{2}:1; A_1 + A_2 = \sqrt{2}+1$

(c) $A_1 : A_2 = 1:2; A_1 + A_2 = 2$

(d) $A_1 : A_2 = 1:2; A_1 + A_2 = 1$

82. Consider the circle $(x-1)^2+(y-1)^2=1$ and the points $A(1, 4)$, $B(1, -5)$. If P is a point on the circle such that $(PA)+(PB)$ is maximum, then P, A, B lie on:

(a) Ellipse (b) Hyperbola

(c) Straight line (d) None of these

83. If a triangle is inscribed in a circle of radius r, then which of the following triangles has the maximum area?

(a) Equilateral triangle with height $2r/3$

(b) Right-angled triangle with sides $2r$, r

(c) Equilateral triangle with height $\sqrt{3}r$

(d) Isoceles triangle with base $2r$

84. If $\vec{a}_1 = x\hat{i}-\hat{j}+\hat{k}$, $\vec{a}_2=\hat{i}+y\hat{j}+z\hat{k}$ are collinear vectors, then a unit vector which is parallel to $x\hat{i}+y\hat{j}+z\hat{k}$ is:

(a) $\frac{1}{\sqrt{3}}(\hat{i}-\hat{j}+\hat{k})$ (b) $\frac{\hat{i}+\hat{j}+\hat{k}}{\sqrt{3}}$

(c) $\frac{1}{\sqrt{2}}(\hat{j}-\hat{k})$ (d) $\frac{\hat{i}-\hat{j}-\hat{k}}{\sqrt{3}}$

85. Let the prime factors of a natural number be $N=2^x 3^y 5^z$, where $y+z=5$, $\frac{1}{y}+\frac{1}{z}=\frac{5}{6}$, $y>z$. The number of odd divisors of N including 1 is:

(a) 4 (b) 6

(c) 12 (d) 16

86. The slope of the tangent to a curve $y=f(x)$ is given by $\frac{dy}{dx}=\frac{xy^2+y}{x}$ and the curve passes through the point $(-2, 3)$. If the curve meets the line $L=0$ at the point $(3, k)$, then the value of k is:

(a) $\frac{-11}{19}$ (b) $\frac{-18}{19}$

(c) $\frac{-11}{29}$ (d) $\frac{11}{19}$

87. A function $f(k)$ is defined from $A \to A$, where $A = \{1, 2, 3, 4, \ldots, 10\}$, such that

$f(k)=\begin{cases} k+1, & k \in \text{odd} \\ k, & k \in \text{even} \end{cases}$. If $gof(x) = f(x)$, then the number mapping of $g(x)$ from $A \to A$ is:

(a) ${}^{10}C_5$ (b) 10^5

(c) 5^5 (d) 5!

88. The foot of the perpendicular from the point (3, 4, 1) on the line of intersection of the planes $x+2y+z-6=0$ and $y+2z=4$ is:

(a) $\left(\frac{10}{7},\frac{12}{7},\frac{8}{7}\right)$ (b) $\left(\frac{10}{7},\frac{-12}{7},\frac{8}{7}\right)$

(c) $\left(\frac{10}{7},\frac{-12}{7},\frac{-8}{7}\right)$ (d) $\left(\frac{-10}{7},\frac{12}{7},\frac{8}{7}\right)$

89. From the point $A(3, 2)$, a line is drawn to any point on the circle $x^2+y^2=1$. If the locus of the midpoint of this line segment is a circle, then its radius is:

(a) $\frac{\sqrt{13}}{2}$ (b) $\frac{1}{2}$

(c) $\frac{\sqrt{11}}{2}$ (d) $\sqrt{11}$

90. Given $f(x)=\sin^{-1}x$, $g(x)=\frac{x^2-x-2}{2x^2-x-6}$, $x \neq 2$, and $g(2)=\lim_{x\to 2} g(x)$. Then the domain of definition of $fog(x)$ is:

(a) $(-\infty, -2] \cup \left[-\frac{4}{3}, \infty\right)$

(b) $(-\infty, -1] \cup [2, \infty)$

(c) $\left[-2, -\frac{4}{3}\right]$

(d) $(-\infty, 2)$

91. Let $f(n)=a^n+b^n$. If $\begin{vmatrix} 3 & 1+f(1) & 1+f(2) \\ 1+f(1) & 1+f(2) & 1+f(3) \\ 1+f(2) & 1+f(3) & 1+f(4) \end{vmatrix}$ $=k(1-a)^2(1-b)^2(a-b)^2$ for every $a,b\neq 0$, then k equals:

(a) –1 (b) 1

(c) ab (d) $\frac{1}{ab}$

92. Let $ABCD$ be a parallelogram such that $\mathbf{AB}=\mathbf{q}$, $\mathbf{AD}=\mathbf{p}$, and $\angle BAD$ is an acute angle. If $\mathbf{r}$ is the vector that coincides with the altitude directed from B to the side AD, then $\mathbf{r}$ is:

(a) $\mathbf{r}=\mathbf{q}-\left(\frac{\mathbf{p}\cdot\mathbf{q}}{\mathbf{p}\cdot\mathbf{p}}\right)\mathbf{p}$ (b) $\mathbf{r}=-3\mathbf{q}+\left(\frac{\mathbf{p}\cdot\mathbf{q}}{\mathbf{p}\cdot\mathbf{p}}\right)3\mathbf{p}$

(c) $\mathbf{r}=3\mathbf{q}-\left(\frac{\mathbf{p}\cdot\mathbf{q}}{\mathbf{p}\cdot\mathbf{p}}\right)3\mathbf{p}$ (d) $\mathbf{r}=-\mathbf{q}+\left(\frac{\mathbf{p}\cdot\mathbf{q}}{\mathbf{p}\cdot\mathbf{p}}\right)\mathbf{p}$

93. The value of $\lim\limits_{y\to 0}\frac{(x+y)\sec(x+y)-x\sec x}{y}$ is:

(a) $\sec x(1+x\tan x)$ (b) $\sec x(1-x\tan x)$

(c) $\tan x(1+x\sec x)$ (d) $\tan x(1-x\sec x)$

94. If $f(x)=x^n$ is a differentiable function having property $f(x+y)=f(x)+f(y)+y^2x+x^2y$ and $\lim\limits_{x\to 0}\frac{f(x)}{x}=0$, then the value of $f'(-1)$ is:

(a) 0 (c) –1

(c) 1 (d) –2

95. If the integral $\int_0^{10}\frac{[\sin 2\pi x]}{e^{x-[x]}}dx=\alpha e^{-1}+\beta e^{-\frac{1}{2}}+\gamma$, where α, β, γ are integers and $[x]$ denotes the greatest integer function, then the value of $\alpha+\beta+\gamma$ is:

(a) 0 (c) 20

(c) 25 (d) 10

96. Let $y=y(x)$ be the solution of the differential equation $\cos x(3\sin x+\cos x+3)\,dy=(1+y\sin x(3\sin x+\cos x+3))dx$, $0\leq x\leq\frac{\pi}{2}$, $y(0)=0$. Then the value of $y\left(\frac{\pi}{3}\right)$ is:

(a) $2\log_e\left(\frac{2\sqrt{3}+9}{6}\right)$ (c) $2\log_e\left(\frac{2\sqrt{3}+10}{11}\right)$

(c) $2\log_e\left(\frac{\sqrt{3}+7}{2}\right)$ (d) $2\log_e\left(\frac{3\sqrt{3}-8}{4}\right)$

97. The value of $\sum_{r=0}^{6}\left({}^6C_r\cdot{}^6C_{6-r}\right)$ is equal to:

(a) 1124 (c) 1324

(c) 1024 (d) 924

98. Let $S_n=\frac{[r]+[2r]+[3r]+\ldots+[nr]}{n^2}$, where r is a non-zero real number and $[r]$ denotes the greatest integer less than or equal to r. Then the value of $\lim\limits_{n\to\infty}S_n$ is:

(a) $\frac{r}{2}$ (c) r

(c) $2r$ (d) 0

99. The number of solutions of the equation $\sin^{-1}\left[x^2+\frac{1}{3}\right]+\cos^{-1}\left[x^2-\frac{2}{3}\right]=x^2$, for $x\in[-1,1]$, is:

($[x]$ denotes the greatest integer less than or equal to x)

(a) 2 (c) 0

(c) 4 (d) Infinite

100. The number of solutions of the equation $x+2\tan x=\frac{\pi}{2}$ in the interval $[0,2\pi]$ is:

(a) 3 (c) 4

(c) 2 (d) 5

101. The sides AB, BC and CA of a triangle ABC have 3, 5 and 6 interior points, respectively. The total number of triangles that can be constructed using these points as vertices is:

(a) 364 (c) 240

(c) 333 (d) 360

102. If x, y, z are in arithmetic progression with common difference d, $x^1\,3d$, and the determinant of the matrix $\begin{bmatrix} 3 & 4\sqrt{2} & x \\ 4 & 5\sqrt{2} & y \\ 5 & k & z \end{bmatrix}$ is zero, then the value of k^2 is:

(a) 72 (c) 12

(c) 36 (d) 6

103. Two tangents are drawn from a point P to the circle $x^2+y^2-2x.\,4y+4=0$, such that the angle between these tangents is $\tan^{-1}\left(\frac{12}{5}\right)$, where

$\tan^{-1}\left(\frac{12}{5}\right) \in (0, \pi)$. If the centre of the circle is denoted by C and these tangents touch the circle at points A and B, then the ratio of the areas of ΔPAB and ΔCAB is:

(a) 11 : 4 (c) 9 : 4
(c) 3 :1 (d) 2 : 1

104. Let L be a tangent line to the parabola $y^2 = 4x - 20$ at $P(6, 2)$. If L is also a tangent to the ellipse $\ldots + 9\int_0^1 e^t\, dt$, then the value of b is:

(a) 11 (c) 14
(c) 16 (d) 20

105. The value of the limit $\lim_{\theta \to 0} \frac{\tan(\pi \cos^2 \theta)}{\sin(2\pi \sin^2 \theta)}$ is:

(a) $2 - x = t$ (b) $-\frac{1}{4}$
(c) 0 (d) $\frac{1}{4}$

106. Let the tangent to the circle $x^2 + y^2 = 25$ at the point $R(3, 4)$ meet the x-axis and y-axis at points P and Q, respectively. If r is the radius of the circle passing through the origin O and having centre at the incentre of the triangle OPQ, then the value of r^2 is:

(a) $\frac{529}{64}$ (b) $\frac{125}{72}$
(c) $\frac{625}{72}$ (d) $\frac{585}{66}$

107. If the equation of the plane passing through the mirror image of a point $P(2, 3, 1)$ with respect to line $\frac{x+1}{2} = \frac{y-3}{1} = \frac{z+2}{-1}$ and containing the line $\frac{x-2}{3} = \frac{1-y}{2} = \frac{z+1}{1}$ is $\alpha x + \beta y + \gamma z = 24$, then $\alpha + \beta + \gamma$ is equal to:

(a) 20 (c) 19
(c) 18 (d) 21

108. The inverse of $y = 5^{\log x}$ is:

(a) $x = 5^{\log y}$ (c) $x = y^{\log 5}$
(c) $x = y^{\frac{1}{\log y}}$ (d) $x = 5^{\frac{1}{\log y}}$

109. The line $2x - y + 1 = 0$ is a tangent to the circle at the point $P(2, 5)$ and the centre of the circle lies on $x - 2y = 4$. Then the radius of the circle is:

(a) $3\sqrt{5}$ (c) $5\sqrt{3}$
(c) $5\sqrt{4}$ (d) $4\sqrt{5}$

110. The value of $4 + \cfrac{1}{5 + \cfrac{1}{4 + \cfrac{1}{5 + \cfrac{1}{4 + \ldots\ldots \infty}}}}$ is:

(a) $2 + \frac{2}{5}\sqrt{30}$ (b) $2 + \frac{4}{\sqrt{5}}\sqrt{30}$
(c) $5x^2 - 20x - 4 = 0$ (d) $5 + \frac{2}{5}\sqrt{30}$

111. The value of $\lim_{x \to 0^+} \frac{\cos^{-1}(x - [x]^2) \cdot \sin^{-1}(x - [x]^2)}{x - x^3}$, where $[x]$ denotes the greatest integer less than or equal to x, is:

(a) π (c) 0
(c) $\frac{\pi}{4}$ (d) $\frac{\pi}{2}$

112. Let $I = \int_1^{10} \frac{[x]e^{[x]}}{e^{x-1}} dx$, where x is the greatest integer less than or equal to the x function. Then the value of I is:

(a) <9(e+1) (c) 45(e+1)
(c) <9(e-1) (d) 45(e-1)

113. If $x + 2y = 12$ is a differentiable function having property $f\left(\frac{x}{y}\right) = \frac{f(x)}{f(y)}\ \forall x, y \neq 0$ and $f'(1) = 3$, then the value of $f(-1)$ is:

(a) <0 (c) –1
(c) <1 (d) –2

114. Let $y = y(x)$ be the solution of the differentiable equation $\frac{dy}{dx} = (y+1)\left\{(y+1)e^{\frac{x^2}{2}} - x\right\}, 0 < x < 2.1$ with $y(2) = 0$. Then the value of $y'(1)$ is:

(a) $\frac{e^{1/2}}{(1+e^2)^2}$ (c) $\frac{3e^{3/2}}{(1+e^2)^2}$
(c) $\frac{-3e^{1/2}}{(1+e^2)^2}$ (d) $\frac{-e^{3/2}}{(1+e^2)^2}$

115. Let $f:\mathbf{R}-\{3\}\to\mathbf{R}-\{1\}$ be defined as $f(x)=\dfrac{x-2}{x-3}$ and $g:\mathbf{R}\to\mathbf{R}$ be defined as $g(x)=2x-3$. Then the sum of the values of x for which $f^{-1}(x)+g^{-1}(x)=\dfrac{13}{2}$ is:

(a) 2 (c) 3
(c) 5 (d) 7

116. The value of $\lim\limits_{x\to\infty} 6x^2\ln\left(x\cot^{-1}x\right)$ is:

(a) 1 (b) 2
(c) −1 (d) −2

117. If $f(x)=\begin{cases}0, & -1\le x<0\\ 1, & x=0\\ 2, & 0<x\le 1\end{cases}$ and $F(x)=\int_{-1}^{x} f(x)\,dx$, then the correct statements from the following are:

(a) f is discontinuous at $x=0$
(b) f is continuous and differentiable everywhere
(c) f is discontinuous and non-differentiable at $x=0$
(d) f is continuous everywhere but not differentiable at $x=0$

Numerical Value Answer

- The answer to each question is a **NUMERICAL VALUE.**
- For each question, enter the correct numerical value of the answer using the mouse and the on-screen virtual numeric keypad in the place designated to enter the answer. If the numerical value has more than two decimal places, truncate/round-off the value to TWO decimal places.
- The answer to each question will be evaluated according to the following marking scheme:

Full Marks: +4 If ONLY the correct numerical value is entered;
Zero Marks: 0 In all other cases

1. Consider an arithmetic series and a geometric series having four initial terms from the set {11,8, 21, 16, 26, 32, 4}. If the last terms of the series are the maximum possible four-digit numbers, then the number of common terms in these two series is equal to ______.

2. Let $f:(0,\ 2)\to\mathbf{R}$ be defined as $f(x)=\log_2\left(1+\tan\left(\dfrac{\pi x}{4}\right)\right)$.

Then $\lim\limits_{n\to\infty}\dfrac{2}{n}\left(f\left(\dfrac{1}{n}\right)+f\left(\dfrac{2}{n}\right)+\ldots+f(1)\right)$ is equal to ______.

3. Let $ABCD$ be a square of side of unit length. Let a circle C_1 centred at A with unit radius be drawn. Another circle C_2 which touches C_1 and the lines AD and AB that are tangent to it is also drawn. Let a tangent line from the point C to the circle C_2 meet the side AB at E. If the length of EB is $\alpha+\sqrt{3}\beta$, where α, β are integers, then $\alpha+\beta$ is equal to ______.

4. If the normal to the curve $y(x)=\int_0^x (2t^2-15t+10)dt$ at a point (a, b) is parallel to the line $x+3y+5=0$, $a>1$, then the value of $|a+6b|$ is equal to ______.

5. Let the curve $y=y(x)$ be the solution of the differential equation $\dfrac{dy}{dx}=2(x+1)$. If the numerical value of the area bounded by the curve $y=y(x)$ and the x-axis is $\dfrac{4\sqrt{8}}{3}$, then the value of $y(1)$ is equal to ______.

6. Let $f:\mathbf{R}\to\mathbf{R}$ be a continuous function such that $f(x)+f(x+1)=2$, for all $x\in\mathbf{R}$. If $I_1=\int_0^8 f(x)dx$ and $I_2=\int_{-1}^3 f(x)dx$, then the value of I_1+2I_2 is equal to ______.

7. Let z and w be two complex numbers such that $w=z\bar{z}-2z+2$, $\left|\dfrac{z+i}{z-3i}\right|=1$ and $Re(w)$ has minimum value. Then, the minimum value of $n\in\mathbf{N}$ for which w^n is real is equal to ______.

8. Of the three independent events B_1, B_2 and B_3, the probability that only B_1 occurs is α, only B_2 occurs is β, and only B_3 occurs is γ. Let the probability p that none of the events B_1, B_2 or B_3 occurs satisfy the equations $(\alpha-2\beta)\,p=\alpha\beta$ and $(\beta-3\gamma)\,p=2\beta\gamma$. All the given probabilities are assumed to lie in the interval (0, 1).

Then $\dfrac{\text{Probability of occurrence of } B_1}{\text{Probability of occurrence of } B_3}$ is equal to ______.

9. Vector $\vec{c}$ is coplanar with vectors $\vec{a}=-\check{i}+\check{j}+\check{k}$ and $\vec{b}=2\check{i}+\check{k}$. If $\vec{a}\cdot\vec{c}=7$ and $c\perp b$, then the value of $2\left|\vec{a}+\vec{b}+\vec{c}\right|^2$ is equal to ______.

10. Let $P = \begin{bmatrix} 3 & -1 & -2 \\ 2 & 0 & \alpha \\ 3 & -5 & 0 \end{bmatrix}$, where $\alpha \in \mathbf{R}$. Suppose $Q = [q_{ij}]$ is a matrix such that $PQ = kI$, where $k \in \mathbf{R}$, $k \neq 0$ and I is an identity matrix of order 3. If $q_{23} = -\dfrac{k}{8}$ and $\det(Q) = \dfrac{k^2}{2}$, then the value of $k^2 + \alpha^2$ is equal to_____.

11. If $z + \alpha|z - 1| + 2i = 0$, $z \in \mathbf{C}$ and $\alpha \in \mathbf{R}$, then the value of $4[(\alpha_{max})^2 + (\alpha_{min})^2]$ is equal to _____.

12. Let $A = \{x : x \text{ is 3 digit number}\}$
$B = \{x : x = 9K + 2, k \in I\}$
$C : \{x : x = 9K + \ell, k \in I, \ell \in I, 0 < \ell < 9\}$
If the sum of elements in $A \cap (B \cup C)$ is 274×400, then ℓ is equal to_____.

13. The least value of α such that $\dfrac{4}{\sin x} + \dfrac{1}{1 - \sin x} = \alpha$ has at least one solution in $x \in \left(0, \dfrac{\pi}{2}\right)$ is equal to_____.

14. If $\int_{-a}^{a} \left(|x| + |x - 2|\right) dx = 22, a > 2$, then the value of $\int_{-a}^{a} \left(x + [x]\right) dx$ is equal to_____.
([ ] represents greatest integer function)

15. Given $a + \alpha = 1$, $b + \beta = 2$, and $af(x) + \alpha f\left(\dfrac{1}{x}\right) = bx + \dfrac{\beta}{x}$, then the value of $\dfrac{f(x) + f\left(\dfrac{1}{x}\right)}{x + \dfrac{1}{x}}$ is equal to_____.

16. If the maximum value of the variance of 10 elements is 10, in which 9 values are 1 and one value is k (k is an integer), then the greatest value of k is equal to_____.

17. The distance of $P(x, y)$ from (5,0) is thrice the distance of $P(x, y)$ from (–5,0). If the locus of P is a circle with radius r, then the value of $4r^2$ is equal to_____.

18. Four numbers whose sum is $\dfrac{65}{12}$ are in GP. The sum of their reciprocals is $\dfrac{65}{18}$ and the product of the first three of them is 1. If the third term is α, then the value of 2α is equal to_____.

19. There are 10 students $S_1, S_2, \ldots\ldots S_{10}$. Three groups G_1, G_2, G_3 are to be formed such that each group has at least 1 member, and group G_3 has at most 3 members. The number of ways of forming the groups is equal to_____.

20. At point $P(5, 7)$ on the circle $(x - 2)^2 + (y - 3)^2 = 25$, a tangent and a normal are drawn. If the area of the triangle formed by the tangent, the normal, and the x axis is λ, then 24λ is equal to_____.

21. If $A = \begin{bmatrix} x & y & z \\ y & z & x \\ z & x & y \end{bmatrix}$, $A^2 = I$ and $xyz = 2$, $x + y + z > 0$, then the value of $x^3 + y^3 + z^3$ is equal to_____.

22. If $x^2 - 2(3k - 1)x + 8k^2 - 7 > 0$ $\forall x \in \mathbf{R}$, then the integral value of k is equal to_____.

23. The chance that a missile is intercepted is $\dfrac{1}{3}$. If the missile is not intercepted, the chance that it hits the target is $\dfrac{3}{4}$. If three missiles are fired at the same target, the probability that all three missiles hit the target is equal to_____.
(Assume that the launches of missiles are independent events)

24. Numbers between 100 and 1000 are formed, using the digits 1, 2, 3, 4, 5 (no repetition) such that they are divisible by 3 or 5. The total number of such numbers is equal to_____.

25. If $30\,{}^{30}C_0 + 29\,{}^{30}C_1 + 28\,{}^{30}C_2 + \ldots\ldots + {}^{30}C_{29} = n(2^m)$, then the value of $(m + n)$ is equal to_____.

26. If $x^3 - 2x^2 + 2x - 1 = 0$ has roots α, β, γ, then the value of $(\alpha^{162} + \beta^{162} + \gamma^{162})$ is equal to_____.

27. The area bounded by the curve $y = \big||x - 1| - 2\big|$ with the x-axis is equal to_____.

28. The number of solutions of $\sqrt{3}\cos^2 x = (\sqrt{3} - 1)\cos x + 1$ in $x \in \left[0, \dfrac{\pi}{2}\right]$ is equal to_____.

29. In the given figure, $AD = 13$, $DE = 1$, AD bisects angle $\angle BAC$ and BC is perpendicular to AD. Then the area of triangle ABC is equal to_____.

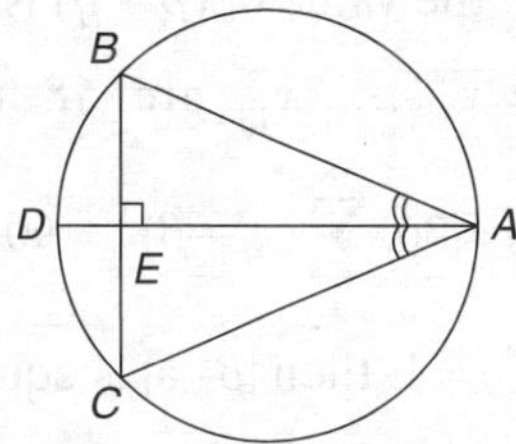

30. The difference between the degree and the order of the differential equation, corresponding to the family of curves $y^2 = a(x+\sqrt{2})$, is equal to______.

31. A plane passes through the points $P(\lambda, 2, 1)$ and $Q(4, -2, 2)$. Also, it is perpendicular to the line joining the points $A(-2, 23, 18)$ and $B(-1, 29, 16)$. Then the value of $\left(\frac{\lambda}{11}\right)^2 - \frac{4\lambda}{11} - 4$ is equal to______.

32. Bacteria is increasing at a rate proportional to their number N at time t. At $t = 0$, the number of bacteria is $N_0 = 1000$, and after 2 hours, the number of bacteria increases by 20%. If at $t = \frac{k}{\ell n \frac{5}{6}}$ the number of bacteria is 2000, then the value of $\left(\frac{k}{\ln 2}\right)^2$ is equal to______.

33. If **a**, **b**, **c** are three non-collinear vectors such that $\mathbf{a}\times\mathbf{b} = \mathbf{b}\times\mathbf{c} = \mathbf{c}\times\mathbf{a}$, then the value of $|\mathbf{a}+\mathbf{b}+\mathbf{c}|$ is equal to______.

34. If the slope of the common tangent to the curves $4x^2 + 9y^2 = 36$ and $4x^2 + 4y^2 = 31$ is m, then m^2 is equal to______.

35. If $A = \begin{bmatrix} 1 & 0 & 0 \\ 0 & 2 & 0 \\ 3 & 0 & -1 \end{bmatrix}$ and $A^{20} + \alpha A^{19} + \beta A = \begin{bmatrix} 1 & 0 & 0 \\ 0 & 4 & 0 \\ 0 & 0 & 1 \end{bmatrix}$ then the value of $(\alpha - \beta)$ is equal to______.

36. The normal drawn to a curve at any point passes through a fixed point (a, b). The curve passes through the points $(3, -3)$ and $(4, -2\sqrt{2})$. If $a - 2\sqrt{2}b = 3$, then the value of $(a^2 + b^2 + ab)$ is equal to______.

37. Let $z (z \in \mathbf{C})$ satisfy $|z + 5| \le 5$ and $z(1 + i) + \bar{z}(1 - i) \ge -10$. If the maximum value of $|z + 1|^2$ is $\alpha + \beta\sqrt{2}$; then the value of $(\alpha + \beta)$ is equal to______.

38. $-16, 8, -4, 2$ ...... is a sequence, whose AM and GM of the pth and q^{th} terms are the roots of $4x^2 - 9x + 5 = 0$. Then the value of $(p + q)$ is equal to______.

39. If $x_1, x_2, x_3 \ldots\ldots x_{18}$ are 18 terms such that $\sum_1^{18}(x_i - \alpha) = 36, \sum_1^{18}(x_i - \beta)^2 = 90$, and variance$(s^2) = 1$, then $|\beta - \text{a}|$ is equal to______.

40. Let $P_n = a^n + b^n (n \in \mathbf{N})$, where $\alpha + \beta = 1, a\beta = -1$. If $P_{n-1} = 11$ and $P_{n+1} = 29$, then P_n^2 is equal to______.

41. The number of four-digit numbers whose HCF with 18 is 3 equals______.

42. The image of the point $(1, 0, -1)$ in the plane $4x - 5y + 2z = 8$ is (α, β, γ). Then the value of $15(\alpha + \beta + \gamma)$ is equal to______.

43. If $f(x) = 2x^5 + 5x^4 + 10x^3 + 10x^2 + 10x + 10$ and all real roots of $f(x)$ lie in the interval $(-\alpha, -\alpha + 1)$, then α is equal to______.

44. The figure shows a regular octagon $ABCDEFGH$ with centre coinciding with the origin O. If $\mathbf{AB} + \mathbf{AC} + \mathbf{AD} + \mathbf{AE} + \mathbf{AF} + \mathbf{AG} + \mathbf{AH} = x(\mathbf{AO})$, then x is equal to______.

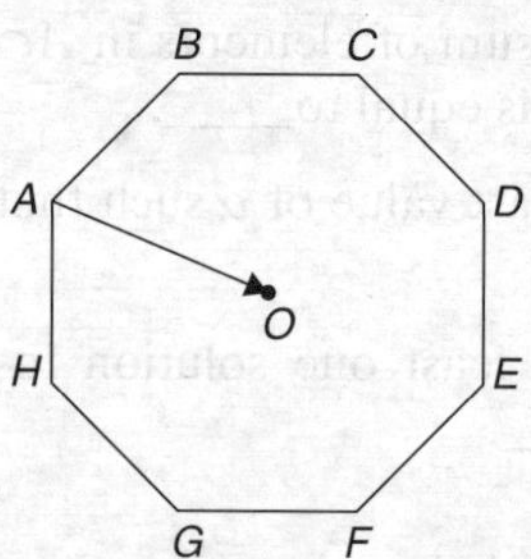

45. The curve $x^2 + y^2 - 4x - 4y + 4 = 0$ is inscribed in a triangle which has two sides along the coordinate axes. If the locus of the circumcentre of the triangle is $x + y - xy + \alpha\sqrt{x^2 + y^2}$, then α is equal to______.

46. If $1, \log_{10}(4^x - 2), \log_{10}\left(4^x + \frac{18}{5}\right)$ are in AP for some real number x, then the value of the determinant $\begin{vmatrix} 2\left(x - \frac{1}{2}\right) & x - 1 & x^2 \\ 1 & 0 & x \\ x & 1 & 0 \end{vmatrix}$ is equal to______.

47. Let the function $f: [-1, 1] \to \mathbf{R}$ be defined as $f(x) = ax^2 + bx + c$, where $a, b, c \in \mathbf{R}$, such that $f(-1) = 2$, $f'(-1) = 1$ and the maximum value of $f^2(x)$ is $\frac{1}{2}$. If $f(x) \le a$, then the least value of a is equal to______.

48. Let the function $f : [-3, 1] \to \mathbf{R}$ be defined as $f(x) = \begin{cases} \min\{(x+6), x^2\}, & -3 \le x \le 0 \\ \max\{\sqrt{x}, x^2\}, & 0 \le x \le 1 \end{cases}$. If the area bounded by $y = f(x)$ and the x-axis is A, then the value of $6A$ is equal to______.

49. Let tan*a*, tan*b*, tan*g* be the slopes of three line segments OA, OB, OC, respectively, where O is the origin. If the circumcentre of ΔABC coincides with the origin and its orthocentre lies on the y-axis, then the value of $\left(\frac{\cos 3\alpha + \cos 3\beta + \cos 3\gamma}{\cos\alpha\cos\beta\cos\gamma}\right)^2$ is equal to ______.

50. Consider a set of $3n$ numbers having variance 4. In this set, the mean of the first $2n$ numbers is 6 and the mean of the remaining n numbers is 3. A new set is constructed by adding 1 to each of the first $2n$ numbers, and subtracting 1 from each of the remaining n numbers. If the variance of the new set is k, then $9k$ is equal to ______.

51. Let the coefficients of the third, fourth and fifth terms in the expansion of $\left(x + \frac{a}{x^2}\right)^n$, $x^1 0$, be in the ratio 12 : 8 : 3. Then the term independent of x in the expansion is equal to ______.

52. Let $\vec{x}$ be a vector in the plane containing vectors $\vec{a} = 2\breve{i} - \breve{j} + \breve{k}$ and $\vec{b} = \breve{i} + 2\breve{j} - \breve{k}$. If the vector $\vec{x}$ is perpendicular to $(3\breve{i} + 2\breve{j} - \breve{k})$ and its projection on $\vec{a}$ is $\frac{17\sqrt{6}}{3}$, then the value of $|\vec{x}|^2$ is equal to ______.

53. Let $I_n = \int^{e} x^{19}(\log|x|)^n\,dx$, where $n\hat{I}N$. If$(20)I_{10} = aI_9 + bI_8$, for natural numbers a and b, then $a–b$ is equal to ______.

54. Let P be an arbitrary point having sum of the squares of the distance from the planes $x + y + z = 0$, $lx–nz = 0$, and $x– 2y + z = 0$, equal to 9. If the locus of the point P is $x^2 + y^2 + z^2 = 9$, then the value of $l–n$ is equal to ______.

55. If the function $f(x) = \frac{\cos(\sin x) - \cos x}{x^4}$ is continuous at each point in its domain and $f(0) = \frac{1}{k}$, then k is equal to ______.

56. If $f(x) = \sin\left\{\cos^{-1}\left(\frac{1-2^{2x}}{1+2^{2x}}\right)\right\}$ and $f'(x) = -\frac{b}{a}\ln 2$, where $a = 4$ and $b = 0$ when $x = 0$, then the minimum value of $|a^2–b^2|$ is equal to ______.

57. If $A = \begin{bmatrix} 2 & 3 \\ 0 & -1 \end{bmatrix}$, then the value of $\det(A^4) + \det(A^{10}–(\text{adj}(2A))^{10})$ is equal to______.

58. If [ ] represents the greatest integer function, then the value of $\left|\int_0^{\sqrt{\frac{\pi}{2}}} \left[[x^2] - \cos x\right]dx\right|$ is equal to______.

59. If $\lim_{x\to\infty}\left(1 + \frac{a}{x} - \frac{4}{x^2}\right)^{2x} = e^3$, then the value of $2a$ is equal to______.

60. If the fourth term in the expansion of $\left(x + x^{\log_2 x}\right)^7$ is 4480, then the value of x is equal to______.

ANSWER KEYS

Only One Correct Option

1. (b)	**2.** (a)	**3.** (d)	**4.** (d)	**5.** (b)	**6.** (c)	**7.** (d)	**8.** (b)	**9.** (b)	**10.** (b)
11. (c)	**12.** (b)	**13.** (c)	**14.** (c)	**15.** (d)	**16.** (d)	**17.** (b)	**18.** (c)	**19.** (b)	**20.** (a)
21. (c)	**22.** (c)	**23.** (c)	**24.** (b)	**25.** (c)	**26.** (b)	**27.** (c)	**28.** (a)	**29.** (a)	**30.** (a)
31. (c)	**32.** (b)	**33.** (a)	**34.** (b)	**35.** (d)	**36.** (b)	**37.** (a)	**38.** (b)	**39.** (a)	**40.** (c)
41. (a)	**42.** (a)	**43.** (a)	**44.** (a)	**45.** (a)	**46.** (d)	**47.** (d)	**48.** (b)	**49.** (b)	**50.** (c)
51. (a)	**52.** (a)	**53.** (a)	**54.** (a)	**55.** (b)	**56.** (b)	**57.** (b)	**58.** (b)	**59.** (b)	**60.** (a)
61. (c)	**62.** (a)	**63.** (d)	**64.** (a)	**65.** (a)	**66.** (a)	**67.** (b)	**68.** (a)	**69.** (c)	**70.** (a)
71. (b)	**72.** (a)	**73.** (a)	**74.** (a)	**75.** (b)	**76.** (b)	**77.** (b)	**78.** (d)	**79.** (d)	**80.** (b)
81. (a)	**82.** (c)	**83.** (c)	**84.** (a)	**85.** (c)	**86.** (b)	**87.** (b)	**88.** (b)	**89.** (b)	**90.** (a)
91. (b)	**92.** (d)	**93.** (a)	**94.** (c)	**95.** (a)	**96.** (b)	**97.** (d)	**98.** (a)	**99.** (b)	**100.** (b)
101. (c)	**102.** (a)	**103.** (b)	**104.** (b)	**105.** (a)	**106.** (c)	**107.** (b)	**108.** (b)	**109.** (a)	**110.** (a)
111. (d)	**112.** (d)	**113.** (b)	**114.** (d)	**115.** (c)	**116.** (c)	**117.** (d)			

Numerical Value Answer

1. 3	**2.** 1	**3.** 1	**4.** 406	**5.** 2	**6.** 16	**7.** 4	**8.** 6	**9.** 75	**10.** 17
11. 10	**12.** 5	**13.** 9	**14.** –3	**15.** 2	**16.** 11	**17.** 56.25	**18.** 3	**19.** 31650	
20. 1225	**21.** 7	**22.** 3	**23.** 0.125	**24.** 32	**25.** 59	**26.** 3	**27.** 4	**28.** 1	
29. 41.56	**30.** 2	**31.** 8	**32.** 4	**33.** 0	**34.** 3	**35.** –4	**36.** 9	**37.** 48	**38.** 10
39. 4	**40.** 324	**41.** 1000	**42.** 4	**43.** 2	**44.** 8	**45.** 1	**46.** 2	**47.** 2	**48.** 4
49. 144	**50.** 98	**51.** 15	**52.** 486	**53.** 1	**54.** 1	**55.** 6	**56.** 16	**57.** 16	**58.** 1
59. 3	**60.** 2								

SOLUTIONS

Only One Correct Option

1. (b) For $x \le -4$, the equation reduces to

$$(x+3)(x+4)=6$$

$$\Rightarrow \quad x^2+7x+6=0$$

$$\Rightarrow x=-6,-1$$

In this interval, $x=-6$ is an acceptable solution.

For $-4<x\le 0$, the equation reduces to

$$-(x+3)(x+4)=6$$

$$\Rightarrow \quad x^2+7x+18=0$$

No solution in this interval.

For $x>0$, the equation reduces to

$$(x-3)(x+4)=6$$

$$\Rightarrow \quad x^2+x-18=0$$

$$\Rightarrow \quad x=\frac{-1\pm\sqrt{73}}{2}$$

In this interval, $x=\dfrac{-1+\sqrt{73}}{2}$ is an acceptable solution.

So there are two solutions, and hence, two elements in the set.

2. (a) The figure shows the given vector $\mathbf{OQ}=\sqrt{3}\mathbf{i}+\mathbf{j}$ and the rotated vector $\mathbf{OP}=\alpha\mathbf{i}+\beta\mathbf{j}$. Note that $\mathbf{OP}$ makes angle 15° with the y-axis and that

$$OP=OQ=\sqrt{\left(\sqrt{3}\right)^2+(1)^2}=2$$

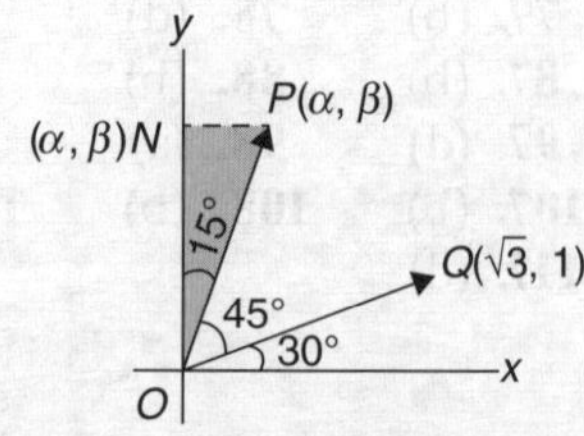

Hence, area of the triangle ΔPNO is

$$\text{Area}=\frac{1}{2}\times PN\times ON$$

$$=\frac{1}{2}\times 2\sin(15°)\times 2\cos(15°)=\sin(30°)=\frac{1}{2}$$

3. (d)

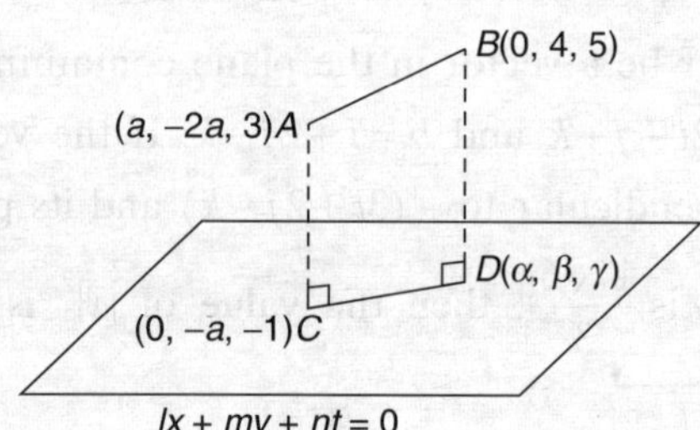

Direction ratios of AC are $a,-a,4$. AC is perpendicular to the plane $lx+my+nz=0$. Thus, we have

$$\frac{l}{a}=\frac{m}{-a}=\frac{n}{4} \tag{1}$$

Point $C(0,-a,-1)$ lies on the given plane. Thus, we have

$$am+n=0 \tag{2}$$

From equation (1), let $l,m,n=at,-at,4t$. Putting in equation (4), we have

$$a(-at)+(4t)=0$$

$$\Rightarrow \quad a^2-4=0 \text{ gives } a=2\ [a>0,\text{ given}]$$

Hence, $C=(0,-2,-1)$ and the equation of the plane is

$$ax-ay+4z=0$$

$$\Rightarrow \quad x-y+2z=0$$

Let $D=(\alpha,\beta,\gamma)$. Now BD is perpendicular to the above plane. Thus, we have

$$\frac{\alpha}{1}=\frac{\beta-4}{-1}=\frac{\gamma+5}{2} \tag{3}$$

Point D lies on the given plane. Thus, we have

$$\alpha-\beta+2\gamma=0 \quad (4)$$

From equation (3), let $\alpha,\beta,\gamma=t,4-t,2t+5$. Putting in equation (4), we have

$$t-(4-t)+2(2t+5)=0$$

$$\Rightarrow \quad 6t+6=0 \text{ gives } t=-1$$

Hence, $D=(-1,5,3)$ and

$$CD=\sqrt{1^2+7^2+4^2}=\sqrt{66}$$

4. (d) We have $\sigma^2=\dfrac{\sum x^2}{N}-\left(\dfrac{\sum x}{N}\right)^2$

$$\Rightarrow d^2=\frac{(a+2)^2+(b+2)^2+(c+2)^2}{3}-\left(\frac{a+b+c+6}{3}\right)^2$$

$$\Rightarrow 9d^2=3\left[(a+2)^2+(b+2)^2+(c+2)^2\right]-(a+b+c+6)^2$$

$$\Rightarrow 9d^2=3\left[a^2+b^2+c^2+4a+4b+4c+12\right]-(2a+2c+6)^2 \quad [\text{Putting } b=a+c]$$

$$\Rightarrow 9d^2=3\left[a^2+b^2+c^2+8a+8c+12\right]-4(a+c+3)^2 \quad [\text{Putting } b=a+c]$$

$$\Rightarrow 9d^2=3\left[a^2+b^2+c^2+8a+8c+12\right]-4\left[a^2+c^2+2ac+6a+6b+9\right]$$

$$\Rightarrow 9d^2=3\left[a^2+b^2+c^2+8a+8c+12\right]-4\left[b^2+6a+6c+9\right]$$

$$\Rightarrow 9d^2=3\left(a^2+c^2\right)-b^2$$

$$\Rightarrow b^2=3\left(a^2+c^2\right)-9d^2$$

5. (b) We have

$$\log_{10}(\sin x)+\log_{10}(\cos x)=-1$$

$$\Rightarrow \quad \log_{10}(\sin x\cos x)=-1$$

$$\Rightarrow \quad \sin x\cos x=1/10$$

Now, we have

$$\log_{10}n-1=\log_{10}(\sin x+\cos x)^2$$

$$\Rightarrow \quad \log_{10}n=\log_{10}10+\log_{10}(1+2\sin x\cos x)$$

$$\Rightarrow \quad \log_{10}n=\log_{10}10+\log_{10}\left(\frac{12}{10}\right)$$

$$\Rightarrow \quad \log_{10}n=\log_{10}12$$

$$\Rightarrow \quad n=12$$

6. (c) We have $A=i\begin{bmatrix}1 & -1\\ -1 & 1\end{bmatrix}$. Then

$$A^2=i^2\begin{bmatrix}1 & -1\\ -1 & 1\end{bmatrix}\begin{bmatrix}1 & -1\\ -1 & 1\end{bmatrix}=i^2\begin{bmatrix}2 & -2\\ -2 & 2\end{bmatrix}=2iA$$

$$A^3=(2iA)A=2iA^2=(2i)^2A$$

$$\ldots\ldots\ldots$$

$$A^8=(2i)^7A=(2i)^7i\begin{bmatrix}1 & -1\\ -1 & 1\end{bmatrix}=112\begin{bmatrix}1 & -1\\ -1 & 1\end{bmatrix}$$

Now, the given equation reduces to

$$112\begin{bmatrix}1 & -1\\ -1 & 1\end{bmatrix}\begin{bmatrix}x\\ y\end{bmatrix}=\begin{bmatrix}8\\ 64\end{bmatrix}$$

$$\Rightarrow x-y=\frac{8}{112} \text{ and } x-y=\frac{-64}{112}$$

$$\Rightarrow \frac{8}{112}=\frac{-64}{112}$$

Hence, no solution.

7. (d) The equation of a normal to the parabola $y^2=2x$ can be chosen as

$$y=mx-m-\frac{1}{2}m^3$$

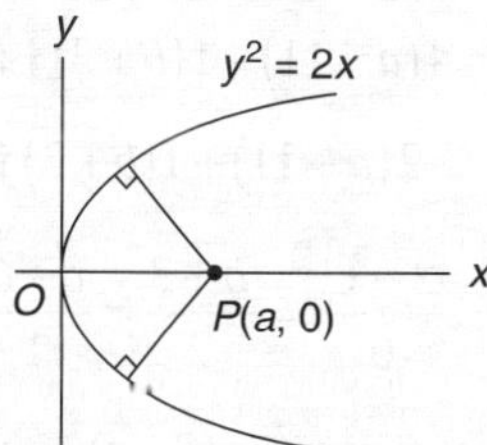

If the normal passes through the point $P(a,0)$ (see figure), then

$$m(a-1)-\frac{1}{2}m^3=0$$

$$\Rightarrow \quad m\left[m^3-2(a-1)\right]=0$$

$$\Rightarrow \quad m=0, m=\pm\sqrt{2(a-1)}$$

Hence, for three real normals, $a-1>0 \Rightarrow a>1$.

8. (b) Let the position vector of T be $\mathbf{OT}=\alpha\mathbf{i}+\beta\mathbf{j}+\gamma\mathbf{k}$. Then, we have (see figure)

$$\frac{\alpha-3}{4}=\frac{\beta+1}{-1}=\frac{\gamma-2}{2} \quad (1)$$

and $$\frac{\alpha-1}{-2}=\frac{\beta-2}{1}=\frac{\gamma+4}{-2} \quad (2)$$

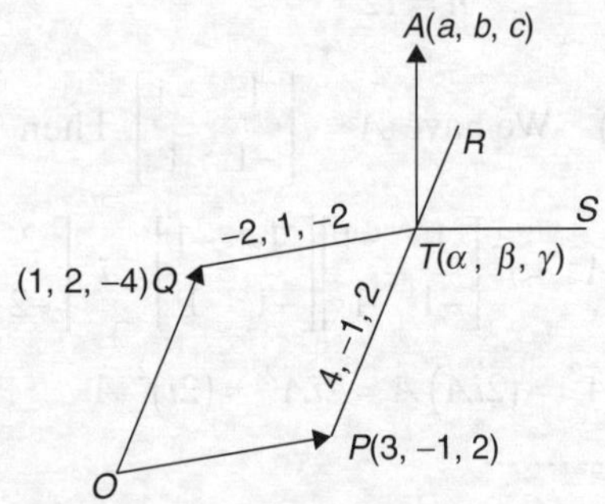

From equations (1) and (2), let (α,β,γ) equal $(4m+3,-m-1,2m+2)$ and $(-2n+1,n+2,-2n-4)$, respectively. Thus, we have

$$4m+3=-2n+1 \quad (3)$$

$$-m-1=n+2 \quad (4)$$

and $$2m+2=-2n-4 \quad (5)$$

Equations (4) and (5) are the same. Solving equations (3) and (4) gives $m=2, n=-5$. Hence, $(\alpha,\beta,\gamma)=(11,-3,6)$.

Let the position vector of A be $\mathbf{OA}=a\mathbf{i}+b\mathbf{j}+c\mathbf{k}$. Then

$$\mathbf{TA}=(a-11)\mathbf{i}+(b+3)\mathbf{j}+(c-6)\mathbf{k}$$

Since **TA** is perpendicular to **PT** and **QT**, we have

$$4(a-11)-1(b+3)\mathbf{j}+2(c-6)=0$$

and $$-2(a-11)+1(b+3)\mathbf{j}-2(c-6)=0$$

$$\Rightarrow \quad \frac{\alpha-11}{0}=\frac{b+3}{2}=\frac{c-6}{1} \quad (6)$$

Also $$(a-11)^2+(b+3)^2+(c-6)^2=\left(\sqrt{5}\right)^2 \quad (7)$$

From equation (6), let $a-11, b+3, c-6=0, 2t, t$. Putting in equation (7), we have

$$0^2+(2t)^2+t^2=5$$

$$\Rightarrow \quad 5t^2=5 \text{ gives } t=\pm 1$$

$$\Rightarrow \quad a-11, b+3, c-6=0, 2, 1 \text{ or } 0, -2, -1$$

$$\Rightarrow \quad a, b, c=11, -1, 7 \text{ or } 11, -4, 5$$

Hence, we have

$$OA=\sqrt{a^2+b^2+c^2}=\sqrt{171} \text{ or } \sqrt{162}$$

9. (b) We have

$$fog(x)=\begin{cases} g+2, & g<0 \\ g^2, & g\ge 0\end{cases}$$

$$=\begin{cases} x^3+2, & x^3<0,\ x<1 \Rightarrow x<0 \\ 3x, & 3x-2<0,\ x\ge 1 \Rightarrow \text{no } x \\ \left(x^3\right)^3, & x^3\ge 0,\ x<1 \Rightarrow 0\le x<1 \\ (3x-2)^2, & 3x-2\ge 0,\ x\ge 1 \Rightarrow x\ge 1\end{cases}$$

$$=\begin{cases} x^3+2, & x<0 \\ x^6, & 0\le x<1 \\ (3x-2)^2, & x\ge 1\end{cases}$$

and $$\{fog(x)\}'=\begin{cases} 3x^2, & x<0 \\ 6x^5, & 0<x<1 \\ 6(3x-2), & x\ge 1\end{cases}$$

There is discontinuity at $x=0$. The function is differentiable everywhere else.

10. (b) We have

$$\frac{|z|+1}{(|z|-1)^2}\le\left(\frac{1}{\sqrt{2}}\right)^2=\frac{1}{2}$$

$$\Rightarrow \quad (|z|-1)^2\ge 2|z|+2$$

$$\Rightarrow \quad |z|^2-4|z|-21\ge 0$$

$$\Rightarrow \quad (|z|+3)(|z|-7)\ge 0$$

$$\Rightarrow \quad |z|\ge 7$$

11. (c) The plane $lx+my+nz=0$ contains the line $\frac{x-1}{-1}=\frac{y+4}{2}=\frac{z+2}{3}$. Then, we have

$$-l+2m+3n=0 \quad (1)$$

and $$l-4m-2n=0 \quad (2)$$

$$\Rightarrow \quad \frac{l}{8}=\frac{m}{1}=\frac{n}{2}$$

Hence, equation of the plane is $L(x,y,z)=8x+y+2z=0$. The ratio in which this plane divides the line joining points $A(-3,-6,1)$ and $B(2,4,-3)$ is given by

$$k=-\frac{L(-3,-6,1)}{L(2,4,-3)}=-\frac{-24-6+2}{16+4-6}=2.$$

12. (b) We have

$$f'(x)=(4a-3)+(a-7)\cos x$$

Critical points are points where $f'(x)=0$ vanishes. That is, where

$$(4a-3)+(a-7)\cos x=0$$

$$\Rightarrow \quad \cos x = \frac{3-4a}{a-7}$$

For the above equation to have a real solution, we have

$$\left|\frac{3-4a}{a-7}\right| \le 1$$

$$\Rightarrow \quad (3-4a)^2 \le (a-7)^2$$

$$\Rightarrow \quad 15a^2 - 10a - 40 \le 0$$

$$\Rightarrow \quad 3a^2 - 2a - 8 \le 0$$

$$\Rightarrow \quad 3\left(a+\frac{4}{3}\right)(a-2) \le 0$$

$$\Rightarrow \quad -\frac{4}{3} \le a \le 2$$

13. (c) Let us define the events E = missing card is a spade, and F = drawing two spades. Then, we have

$$P(F) = P(E)P(F|E) + P(E')P(F|E)$$

$$= \frac{1}{4} \times \frac{^{12}C_2}{^{51}C_2} + \frac{3}{4} \times \frac{^{13}C_2}{^{51}C_2} = \frac{1}{4} \times \frac{12\times 11}{51\times 50} + \frac{3}{4} \times \frac{13\times 12}{51\times 50}$$

$$= \frac{33}{51\times 50} + \frac{117}{51\times 50} = \frac{150}{51\times 50}$$

We have to find the probability that the missing card is not a spade (E') if two spades were drawn (F). The required probability is

$$P(E'|F) = \frac{P(E'\cap F)}{P(F)} = \frac{\frac{117}{51\times 50}}{\frac{150}{51\times 50}} = \frac{117}{150} = \frac{39}{50}$$

14. (c) Putting $x = 1$ and $x = -1$ in the given series, we have

$$a_0 + a_1 + a_2 + a_3 + \ldots + a_{3n} = 1 \quad (1)$$

and $$a_0 - a_1 + a_2 - a_3 + \ldots + (-1)^{3n} a_{3n} = 0 \quad (2)$$

Adding the two equations, we have

$$2(a_0 + a_2 + a_4 + \ldots) = 1$$

$$\Rightarrow \quad \sum a_{2j} = \frac{1}{2}$$

Subtracting the two equations, we have

$$2(a_1 + a_3 + a_5 + \ldots) = 0$$

$$\Rightarrow \quad \sum a_{2j+1} = 0$$

Hence, we have

$$2\sum a_{2j} + 4\sum a_{2j+1} = 1.$$

15. (d) For the given differential equation $\frac{dy}{dx} + 2y\tan x = \sin x$, we have

$$\text{IF} = e^{2\int \tan x\, dx} = e^{2\ln(\sec x)} = \sec^2 x$$

The general solution is

$$y\left(\frac{1}{\cos^2 x}\right) = \int \frac{\sin x}{\cos^2 x} dx$$

$$\Rightarrow \quad y\left(\frac{1}{\cos^2 x}\right) = \frac{1}{\cos x} + C$$

$$\Rightarrow \quad y = \cos x + C\cos^2 x$$

Using $y\left(\frac{\pi}{3}\right) = 0$ gives $C = -2$. Hence, the particular solution is

$$y = \cos x - 2\cos^2 x$$

Now, we have

$$y' = -\sin x + 4\sin x\cos x = 4\sin x\left(\cos x - \frac{1}{4}\right)$$

and $$y'' = 4\cos x\left(\cos x - \frac{1}{4}\right) - 4\sin^2 x$$

The critical points are where $\sin x = 0$ or $\cos x = \frac{1}{4}$. Putting these values in y'', we have

$$y''(\sin x = 0) = 4\left(1 - \frac{1}{4}\right) > 0 \Rightarrow \text{points of minima}$$

and $y''\left(\cos x = \frac{1}{4}\right) = -4\left(1 - \frac{1}{16}\right) < 0$

$\Rightarrow$ points of maxima.

Hence, the maximum value of y is

$$y_{\max} = y\left(\cos x = \frac{1}{4}\right) = \frac{1}{4} - \frac{2}{16} = \frac{1}{8}$$

16. (d) Let $P(h, k)$ be the point whose locus is to be found. Equation of the chord of the circle $x^2 + y^2 = 25$ whose midpoint is P is

$$xh + yk = h^2 + k^2$$

$$\Rightarrow \quad y = \left(\frac{-h}{k}\right)x + \frac{h^2 + k^2}{k} \quad (1)$$

Equation of the general tangent to the hyperbola $\frac{x^2}{9} - \frac{y^2}{16} = 1$ is

$$y = mx \pm \sqrt{9m^2 - 16} \quad (2)$$

If the above chord touches the hyperbola, then equations (1) and (2) must be identical. Thus, we have

$$\Rightarrow \quad m = \frac{-h}{k} \text{ and } \pm\sqrt{9m^2 - 16} = \frac{h^2 + k^2}{k}$$

Eliminating m, we have

$$\frac{9h^2}{k^2} - 16 = \frac{(h^2 + k^2)^2}{k^2}$$

Now putting (x, y) in place of (h, k) gives the required locus as

$$(x^2 + y^2)^2 = 9x^2 - 16y^2$$

17. (b) Let us put $\sin^2 x = t$. The given equation then reduces to

$$81^t + 81^{1-t} = 30, 0 \le t \le 1$$

The figure shows the graph of the function $f(t) = 81^t + 81^{1-t}$. The graph is symmetric about the line $t = 1/2$ since $f(t) = f(1-t)$.

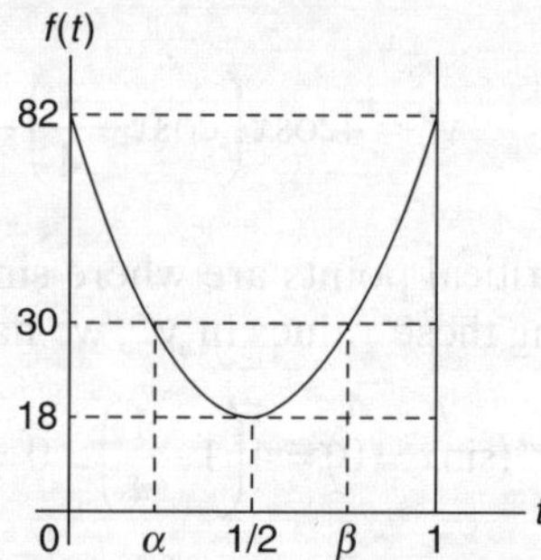

We see that $f(t)$ takes the value 30 for two values $t = \alpha, \beta$ (say), that is, $\sin x = \sqrt{\alpha}, \sqrt{\beta}$. Each equation gives two values of x in the interval $0 \le x \le \pi$. Hence, there are four solutions.

18. (c) The general term of the series can be simplified as

$$\tan^{-1}\left(\frac{6^r}{2^{2r+1} + 3^{2r+1}}\right) = \tan^{-1}\left(\frac{\frac{1}{2}\left(\frac{3}{2}\right)^r}{1 + \left(\frac{3}{2}\right)^{2r+1}}\right)$$

$$= \tan^{-1}\left(\frac{\left(\frac{3}{2} - 1\right)\left(\frac{3}{2}\right)^r}{1 + \left(\frac{3}{2}\right)^{2r+1}}\right) = \tan^{-1}\left(\frac{\left(\frac{3}{2}\right)^{r+1} - \left(\frac{3}{2}\right)^r}{1 + \left(\frac{3}{2}\right)^{2r+1}}\right)$$

$$= \tan^{-1}\left(\frac{3}{2}\right)^{r+1} - \tan^{-1}\left(\frac{3}{2}\right)^r$$

Thus, we have

$$S_k = \sum_{r=1}^{k}\left\{\tan^{-1}\left(\frac{3}{2}\right)^{r+1} - \tan^{-1}\left(\frac{3}{2}\right)^r\right\}$$

$$= \left\{\tan^{-1}\left(\frac{3}{2}\right)^2 - \tan^{-1}\left(\frac{3}{2}\right)\right\} + \left\{\tan^{-1}\left(\frac{3}{2}\right)^3 - \tan^{-1}\left(\frac{3}{2}\right)^2\right\} + \ldots$$

$$\ldots + \left\{\tan^{-1}\left(\frac{3}{2}\right)^{k+1} - \tan^{-1}\left(\frac{3}{2}\right)^k\right\}$$

$$= \tan^{-1}\left(\frac{3}{2}\right)^{k+1} - \tan^{-1}\left(\frac{3}{2}\right)$$

Thus, we have

$$\lim_{k\to\infty} S_k = \lim_{k\to\infty}\left\{\tan^{-1}\left(\frac{3}{2}\right)^{k+1} - \tan^{-1}\left(\frac{3}{2}\right)\right\}$$

$$= \frac{\pi}{2} - \tan^{-1}\left(\frac{3}{2}\right) = \cot^{-1}\left(\frac{3}{2}\right)$$

19. (b) Let $P(at^2, 2at)$ be any point on the parabola $y^2 = 4ax$. The focus of the parabola is at $P(a, 0)$. Let $M(h, k)$ be the midpoint of PS. Then

$$at^2 + a = 2h \text{ and } 2at + 0 = 2k.$$

Eliminating t from the above equations, we have

$$\left(\frac{k}{a}\right)^3 = \frac{2h - a}{a}$$

Putting (x, y) in place of (h, k), we get the required locus as

$$y^2 = a(2x - a)$$

$$\Rightarrow \quad y^2 = 4\left(\frac{a}{2}\right)\left(x - \frac{a}{2}\right)$$

The locus is a parabola, and its directrix is

$$x - \frac{a}{2} + \frac{a}{2} = 0 \Rightarrow x = 0$$

20. (a) The committees can be formed in the following ways:

$$(2I, 4F) \text{ or } (3I, 6F) \text{ or } (4I, 8F)$$

The total number of ways of forming the committees is

$$N = {}^6C_2 \cdot {}^8C_4 + {}^6C_3 \cdot {}^8C_6 + {}^6C_4 \cdot {}^8C_8$$
$$= (15\times 70) + (20\times 28) + (15\times 1) = 1625$$

21. (c) We have

$$\left(p^2+q^2\right)^2 - 2p^2q^2 = 272$$
$$\Rightarrow \quad \left\{(p+q)^2 - 2pq\right\}^2 - 2p^2q^2 = 272$$
$$\Rightarrow \quad (4-2pq)^2 - 2p^2q^2 = 272$$
$$\Rightarrow \quad 2p^2q^2 - 8pq - 256 = 0$$
$$\Rightarrow \quad p^2q^2 - 4pq - 128 = 0$$
$$\Rightarrow \quad pq = -8, 16$$

The acceptable solution is $pq = 16$ since p, q are given to be positive numbers. Hence, the required quadratic equation is

$$x^2 - (p+q)x + pq = 0$$
$$\Rightarrow \quad x^2 - 2x + 16 = 0$$

22. (c) In any single throw of the die $P(\text{odd}) = P(\text{even}) = 1/2$.
According to the given condition, we have
$P(\text{two odds in } n \text{ trials}) = P(\text{three evens in } n \text{ trials})$

$$\Rightarrow \quad {}^nC_2\left(\frac{1}{2}\right)^n = {}^nC_3\left(\frac{1}{2}\right)^n$$
$$\Rightarrow \quad {}^nC_2\left(\frac{1}{2}\right)^n = {}^nC_3 \Rightarrow n = 5$$

Hence, in $n = 5$ tosses, the probability of getting an odd number for odd number of times is

$P(\text{odds for odd number of times})$
$= P(1\text{ time odd}) + P(3\text{ times odd}) + P(5\text{ times odd})$

$$= {}^5C_1\left(\frac{1}{2}\right)^5 + {}^5C_3\left(\frac{1}{2}\right)^5 + {}^5C_5\left(\frac{1}{2}\right)^5 = \frac{16}{2^5} = \frac{1}{2}$$

23. (c) Solving the given differential equation, we have

$$\frac{dP}{dt} = \frac{1}{2}(P-900)$$
$$\Rightarrow \quad \int \frac{dP}{P-900} = \frac{1}{2}\int dt$$
$$\Rightarrow \quad \ln|P-900| = \frac{1}{2}t + C$$

Using $P(0) = 850$ gives $C = \ln(50)$. Hence, the particular solution is

$$\ln|P-900| = \frac{1}{2}t + \ln(50)$$

The population will reduce to zero at time τ given by

$$\ln(900) = \frac{1}{2}\tau + \ln(50)$$
$$\Rightarrow \quad \tau = 2\ln\left(\frac{900}{50}\right) = 2\ln(18)$$

24. (b) We have

$$S_1 = \sum_{r=1}^{15}(-1)^r\, r\, {}^{15}C_r$$
$$= 15\sum_{r=1}^{15}(-1)^r\, {}^{14}C_{r-1} \quad \left[\text{Using } \frac{15}{r}\times {}^{14}C_{r-1} = {}^{15}C_r\right]$$
$$= 15\sum_{k=0}^{14}(-1)^r\, {}^{14}C_k = 0$$

and $S_2 = {}^{14}C_1 + {}^{14}C_3 + {}^{14}C_5 + \ldots + {}^{14}C_{11}$

$$= \left({}^{14}C_1 + {}^{14}C_3 + {}^{14}C_5 + \ldots + {}^{14}C_{11} + {}^{14}C_{13}\right) - {}^{14}C_{13}$$
$$= 2^{13} - 14$$

Hence, $S_1 + S_2 = 2^{13} - 14$.

Alternative: The value of S_1 can also be found as follows:

We have

$$(1-x)^{15} = \sum_0^{15}(-1)^r\, {}^{15}C_r x^r$$

and. $-15(1-x)^{14} = \sum_1^{15}(-1)^r\, r\, {}^{15}C_r x^{r-1}$ [Differentiating]

Now, putting $x = 1$ gives $S_1 = 0$.

25. (c) Equation of the tangent to the curve $y = x^3$ at the point $P(t, t^3)$ is

$$y - t^3 = 3t^2(x-t)$$

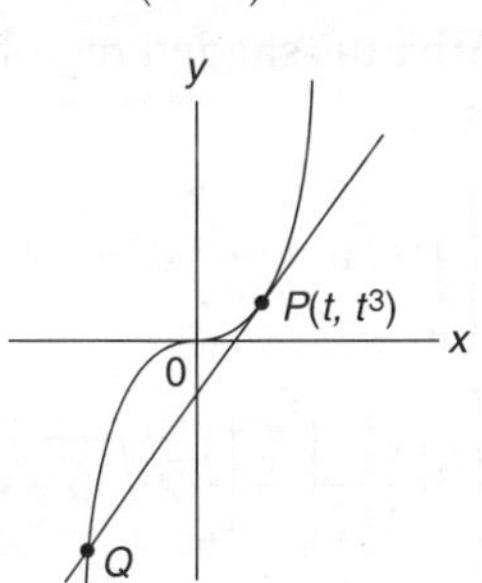

The above tangent meets the curve $y = x^3$ again at point Q (see figure) whose abscissa is given by

$$x^3 - t^3 = 3t^2(x-t)$$

$$\Rightarrow \quad (x-t)(x^2 - xt + t^2) = 3t^2(x-t)$$

$$\Rightarrow \quad (x-t)(x^2 - xt - 2t^2) = 0$$

$$\Rightarrow \quad (x-t)(x-t)(x+2t) = 0$$

$$\Rightarrow \quad x = -2t \; [x = t \text{ is the abscissa of } P]$$

Hence, $Q = (-2t, -8t^3)$ and the ordinate of the required point is

$$\frac{1(-8t^3) + 2(t^3)}{1+2} = -2t^3$$

26. (b) We have $f'(x) = 2x^2 - x - (2x-1)\sin x$

$$= (2x-1)(x - \sin x)$$

Since $2x-1$ changes sign at $x = 1/2$ and $x - \sin x$ changes sign at $x = 0$, the sign-scheme of $f'(x)$ is as shown below.

$$\underset{0}{+ \;|}\; - \;\underset{1/2}{|\; +}$$

Hence, $f(x)$ increases in the interval $[1/2, +\infty)$.

27. (c) Solving the equations, $x^2 + y^2 = 36$ and $y^2 = 9x$, we get

$$x^2 + 9x - 36 = 0 \Rightarrow x = -12, 3$$

The acceptable solution is $x = 3$ (see figure), which is the abscissa of both points P and Q.

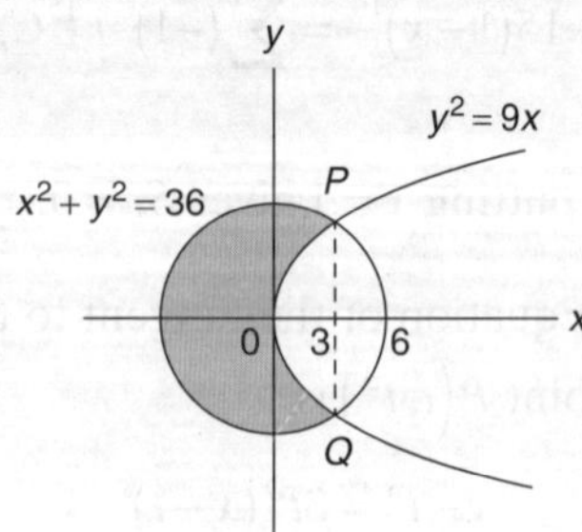

Area of the un-shaded region bounded by the two curves is

$$A' = 2\left[\int_0^3 \sqrt{9x}\, dx + \int_3^6 \sqrt{36 - x^2}\, dx\right]$$

$$= 2\left[3\left|\frac{x^{3/2}}{3/2}\right|_0^3 + \left|\frac{1}{2}x\sqrt{36-x^2} + 18\sin^{-1}\left(\frac{x}{6}\right)\right|_3^6\right]$$

$$= 2\left[6\sqrt{3} - \frac{9\sqrt{3}}{2} + 18\left(\frac{\pi}{2}\right) - 18\left(\frac{\pi}{6}\right)\right] = 3\sqrt{3} + 12\pi$$

Hence, area of the shaded region bounded by the two curves is

$$A = 36\pi - A' = 24\pi - 3\sqrt{3}$$

28. (a) We only need to check the continuity of the given function at integer points. Let us check continuity at $x = k$, where k is some integer. Then, we have

$$\text{LHL} = \lim_{h\to 0} f(k-h) = \lim_{h\to 0}[k-1-h] \cos\left(\frac{2k-1-2h}{2}\right)\pi$$

$$= (k-1)\cos\left(\frac{2k-1}{2}\right)\pi = 0,$$

$$\text{RHL} = \lim_{h\to 0} f(k+h) = \lim_{h\to 0}[k-1+h]cos\left(\frac{2k-1+2h}{2}\right)\pi$$

$$= (k-2)\cos\left(\frac{2k-1}{2}\right)\pi = 0,$$

and $\quad f(k) = [k-1]cos\left(\dfrac{2k-1}{2}\right)\pi = 0$

Hence, $f(x)$ is continuous for every real x.

29. (a) Let the equation of the line be $\frac{x}{a} + \frac{y}{b} = 1$. Then, we have

$$\frac{\frac{1}{a} + \frac{1}{b}}{2} = \frac{1}{4}v \Rightarrow \frac{1}{a} + \frac{1}{b} = \frac{1}{2} \qquad (1)$$

Putting $\frac{1}{b} = \frac{1}{2} - \frac{1}{a}$, the equation of the line reduces to

$$\frac{x}{a} + y\left(\frac{1}{2} - \frac{1}{a}\right) = 1$$

$$\Rightarrow \quad \frac{1}{a}(x-y) + \frac{1}{2}y - 1 = 0 \qquad (2)$$

The above equation represents a family of straight lines passing through the fixed point given by

Putting $\frac{1}{b} = \frac{1}{2} - \frac{1}{a}$, the equation of the line reduces to

$$x - y = 0 \text{ and } \frac{1}{2}y - 1 = 0 \Rightarrow (2,2)$$

We can check that this family of lines cannot pass through $(1, 1)$ or $(4, 4)$. If we put $(1, 1)$ in equation (2), we get $a = 2$, and then from equation (1), we get $b = \infty$. We can similarly check for the point $(4, 4)$.

30. (a) Putting $\sin\theta+\cos\theta=t, 1+\sin(2\theta)=t^2$ and $(\sin\theta+\cos\theta)d\theta=dt$, the integral reduces to

$$I=\int\frac{dt}{\sqrt{8-(t^2-1)}}=\int\frac{dt}{\sqrt{9-t^2}}$$

$$=\sin^{-1}\left(\frac{t}{3}\right)+C=\sin^{-1}\left(\frac{\sin\theta+\cos\theta}{3}\right)+C$$

Hence, $a=1, b=3$.

31. (c) We have

$$fog(x)=2g(x)-1=2\left(\frac{x-\frac{1}{2}}{x-1}\right)$$

$$=\frac{x}{x-1}=1+\frac{1}{x-1}$$

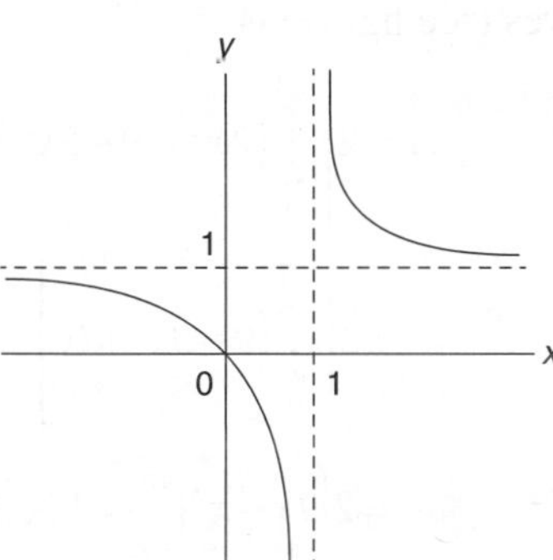

The figure shows the graph of $fog(x)$. We can see that no horizontal line cuts the graph more than once ⇒ one-one. Also, we can see that the range is $\mathbf{R}-\{1\}$ which is a subset of the given co-domain $\mathbf{R}$ → into.

32. (b) We have

$$L=\lim_{x\to0^+}\frac{\int_0^{x^2}\sin\sqrt{t}\,dt}{x^3}\left(\frac{0}{0}\right)$$

$$=\lim_{x\to0^+}\frac{\sin\sqrt{x^2}\cdot 2x}{3x^2}\quad\text{[Using L'Hospital's rule]}$$

$$=\lim_{x\to0^+}\frac{2\sin x}{3x}=\frac{2}{3}$$

33. (a) For the given system of equations, we have

$$D=\begin{vmatrix}0 & 2 & -k\\ 1 & -2 & 3\\ 1 & 2 & -3\end{vmatrix}=4(3-k),$$

$$D_1=\begin{vmatrix}10 & 2 & -k\\ 3 & -2 & 3\\ 5m & 2 & -3\end{vmatrix}=0,$$

$$D_2=\begin{vmatrix}0 & 10 & -k\\ 1 & 3 & 3\\ 1 & 5m & -3\end{vmatrix}=6(7-10m),$$

and $$D_3=\begin{vmatrix}0 & 2 & 10\\ 1 & -2 & 3\\ 1 & 2 & 5m\end{vmatrix}=4(7-10m)$$

For no solution, $D=0$ and at least one of D_1, D_2, D_3 must not be zero. Hence, the system of equations has no solution if $k=3$ and $m\neq 7/10$.

34. (b) We have

$$S={}^2C_2+{}^3C_2+{}^4C_2+\ldots+{}^nC_2=$$

$$=\text{Coefficient of } x^2 \text{ in}\left[(1+x)^2+(1+x)^3+\ldots+(1+x)^n\right]$$

$$=\text{Coefficient of } x^2 \text{ in}\frac{1}{x}\left[\frac{(1+x)^2\left\{(1+x)^{n-1}-1\right\}}{(1+x)-1}\right]$$

$$=\text{Coefficient of } x^3 \text{ in}\left[\frac{(1+x)^{n+1}-(1+x)^2}{x}\right]$$

$$=\text{Coefficient of } x^3 \text{ in}\left[(1+x)^{n+1}-(1+x)^2\right]={}^{n+1}C_3$$

Thus, we have

$${}^{n+1}C_2+2S={}^{n+1}C_2+{}^{n+1}C_3+{}^{n+1}C_3$$

$$={}^{n+2}C_3+{}^{n+1}C_3$$

$$=\frac{(n+2)(n+1)n}{6}+\frac{(n+1)n(n-1)}{6}$$

$$=\frac{n(n+1)(2n+1)}{6}$$

35. (d) The number of subsets of X equals 2^5. The sample space S consists of all possible pairs of subsets. Thus $n(S)=2^5\times2^5=2^{10}$.

Let us consider the case when $A=\{1,2,\ldots\}$ and $B=\{1,2,\ldots\}$ have two common elements, say 1, 2. Now, we can put 3 in set A, or in set B, or neither. Similarly we have three choices for elements 4 and 5. So, we have 3^3 such pairs of sets $A=\{1,2,\ldots\}$ and $B=\{1,2,\ldots\}$.

Now that we have ${}^5C_2$ choices for the two common elements, the total number of subset pairs having two common elements is $n(E) = {}^5C_2 \times 3^3 = 270$.

Hence, the required probability is

$$P(E) = \frac{270}{2^{10}} = \frac{135}{2^9}$$

36. (b) Integrating the given equation $f'(x) = f'(2-x)$, we have

$$f(x) = -f(2-x) + C$$

Putting $x = 0$, we get $C = f(0) + f(2) = 1 + e^2$. Thus, we have

$$f(x) + f(2-x) = 1 + e^2 \quad (1)$$

Hence, we have

$$\int_0^2 f(x)dx = \frac{1}{2}\int_0^2 \{f(x) + f(2-x)\}dx \text{ [By property]}$$

$$\Rightarrow \quad = \frac{1}{2}\int_0^2 (1+e^2)dx = 1 + e^2$$

$$\Rightarrow \quad f(x) + f(2-x) = 1 + e^2$$

37. (a) The given differential equation can be written as

$$\frac{dy}{dx} + \frac{y}{x} = bx^3$$

Its IF $= e^{\int \frac{dx}{x}} = e^{\ln x} = x$. Thus, the general solution is

$$yx = b\int x^4 dx + C = \frac{b}{5}x^5 + C$$

$$\Rightarrow \quad y = \frac{b}{5}x^4 + \frac{C}{x}$$

Putting (1,2), we get

$$b + 5C = 10 \quad (1)$$

Now, using the other given condition, we have

$$\int_1^2 \left(\frac{b}{5}x^4 + \frac{C}{x}\right)dx = \frac{62}{5}$$

$$\Rightarrow \quad \frac{b}{5}\left(\frac{2^5 - 1^5}{5}\right) + C\ln 2 = \frac{62}{5}$$

$$\Rightarrow \quad \frac{31b}{25} + C\ln 2 = \frac{62}{5}$$

$$\Rightarrow \quad b + \left(\frac{25\ln 2}{31}\right)C = 10 \quad (2)$$

Solving equations (1) and (2) gives $C = 0$ and $b = 10$.

38. (b) Solving the equations $y = 5x^2$ and $y = 2x^2 + 9$, we get

$$3x^2 = 9 \Rightarrow x = \pm\sqrt{3}$$

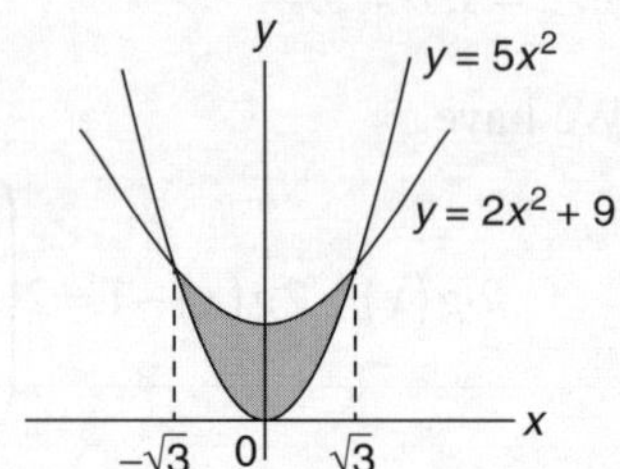

Area of the shaded region bounded by the two curves (see figure) is

$$A = 2\left[\int_0^{\sqrt{3}} (2x^2 + 9 - 5x^2)dx\right]$$

$$= 2\left[\int_0^{\sqrt{3}} (9 - 3x^2)dx\right]$$

$$= 2\left|9x - x^3\right|_0^{\sqrt{3}} = 12\sqrt{3}$$

39. (a) Let $\sin^{-1}\frac{\sqrt{63}}{8} = x \Rightarrow \sin x = \frac{\sqrt{63}}{8}$ and $\cos x = \frac{1}{8}$. Now, we have

$$\cos\left(\frac{x}{2}\right) = \sqrt{\frac{1+\cos x}{2}} = \sqrt{\frac{1+\frac{1}{8}}{2}} = \frac{3}{4}$$

Hence, we have

$$\tan\left(\frac{x}{4}\right) = \sqrt{\frac{1-\cos\left(\frac{x}{2}\right)}{1+\cos\left(\frac{x}{2}\right)}} = \sqrt{\frac{1-\frac{3}{4}}{1+\frac{3}{4}}} = \frac{1}{\sqrt{7}}$$

40. (c) We have

$$I = \int_1^3 \left[x^2 - 2x - 2\right]dx$$

$$= \int_1^3 \left[(x-1)^2 - 3\right]dx$$

$$= \int_1^3 (-3)dx + \int_1^3 \left[(x-1)^2\right]dx$$

$$= -6 + \int_0^2 \left[t^2\right]dt$$

$$= -6 + \int_0^1 0dt + \int_1^{\sqrt{2}} 1dt + \int_{\sqrt{2}}^{\sqrt{3}} 2dt + \int_{\sqrt{3}}^2 3dt$$

$$= -6 + \int_0^1 0dt + \int_1^{\sqrt{2}} 1dt + \int_{\sqrt{2}}^{\sqrt{3}} 2dt + \int_{\sqrt{3}}^2 3dt$$

$$= -6 + \left(\sqrt{2}-1\right) + 2\left(\sqrt{3}-\sqrt{2}\right) + 3\left(2-\sqrt{3}\right)$$

$$= -1 - \sqrt{2} - \sqrt{3}$$

41. (a) We have

$A' = A$ and $B' = -B$

Now, let $P = A^2B^2 - B^2A^2$. Then, we have

$$|P| = \left|A^2B^2 - B^2A^2\right| = \left|\left(A^2B^2 - B^2A^2\right)'\right|$$

$$= \left|\left(A^2B^2\right)' - \left(B^2A^2\right)'\right|$$

$$= \left|\left(B^2\right)'\left(A^2\right)' - \left(A^2\right)'\left(B^2\right)'\right|$$

$$= \left|(B')^2(A')^2 - (A')^2(B')^2\right|$$

$$= \left|B^2A^2 - A^2B^2\right|$$

$$= |-P| = -|P| \quad \text{[Since } P \text{ is third order]}$$

$$\Rightarrow \quad 2|P| = 0 \Rightarrow |P| = 0.$$

Hence, the equation $PX = O$ has infinite solutions.

42. (a) We have

$$f(x)f''(x) - \{f'(x)\}^2 = 0$$

$$\Rightarrow \quad d\left(\frac{f'(x)}{f(x)}\right) = 0$$

$$\Rightarrow \quad \frac{f'(x)}{f(x)} = k$$

Putting $x = 0$, we get $k = \dfrac{f'(0)}{f(0)} = 2$. Thus, we have

$$f'(x) = 2f(x)$$

$$\Rightarrow \quad f(x) = Ce^{2x}$$

Putting $x = 0$, we get $C = f(0) = 1$. Thus, we have

Thus, $f(x) = e^{2x}$ and hence $f(1) = e^2$.

43. (a)

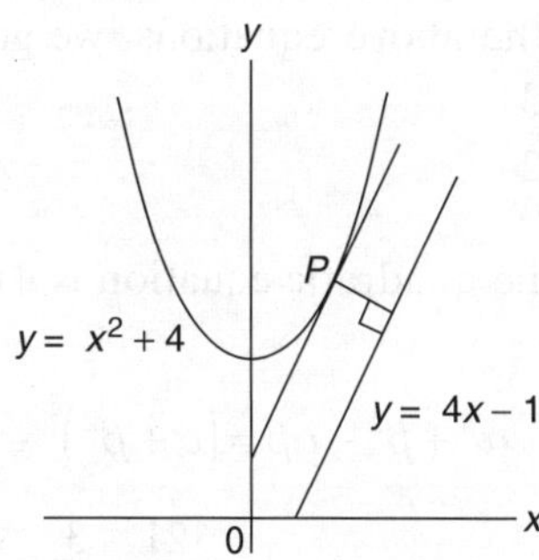

The figure shows the nearest point $P(h,k)$ on the parabola $y = x^2 + 4$. The tangent at P must be parallel to the line $y = 4x - 1$. Thus, we have

$$y'(h,k) = 4.$$

$$\Rightarrow \quad 2h = 4 \text{ gives } h = 2$$

Hence $P = \left(2, 2^2 + 4\right) = (2, 8)$.

44. (a) We have

$$f'(x) = \begin{cases} -55, & x < -5 \\ 6\left(x^2 - x - 20\right), & -5 < x < 4 \\ 6\left(x^2 - x - 6\right), & x > 4 \end{cases}$$

$$= \begin{cases} -55, & x < -5 \\ 6(x+4)(x-5), & -5 < x < 4 \\ 6(x+2)(x-3), & x > 4 \end{cases}$$

The function $6(x+2)(x-3)$ is always positive for $x > 4$.

The function $6(x+4)(x-5)$ changes sign, as shown below.

+ −4 − 5 +

Note that in the interval $-5 < x < 4$, it changes sign only at $x = -4$

Thus, the sign scheme for $f'(x)$ is as shown below.

− −5 + −4 − 4 +

Hence, $f(x)$ monotonically increases in the interval $(-5, -4) \cup (4, +\infty)$.

45. (a) We have

$$a+c=2b, \frac{2a+2}{3}=\frac{10}{3} \text{ and } \frac{2b+c}{3}=\frac{7}{3}$$

Solving the above equations, we get $a=4$, $b=\frac{11}{4}$ and $c=\frac{3}{2}$.

Hence, the quadratic equation is $4x^2+\frac{11}{4}x+1=0$ and

$$\alpha^2+\beta^2-\alpha\beta=(\alpha+\beta^2)^2-3\alpha\beta$$

$$=\frac{121}{256}-\frac{3}{4}=\frac{-71}{256}$$

46. (d) We have

$$A=\begin{bmatrix} 0 & \tan\frac{\theta}{2} \\ -\tan\frac{\theta}{2} & 0 \end{bmatrix} \text{ and } I=\begin{bmatrix} 1 & 0 \\ 0 & 1 \end{bmatrix}$$

Then, we have

$$I+A=\begin{bmatrix} 1 & \tan\frac{\theta}{2} \\ -\tan\frac{\theta}{2} & 1 \end{bmatrix} \text{ and}$$

$$I-A=\begin{bmatrix} 1 & -\tan\frac{\theta}{2} \\ \tan\frac{\theta}{2} & 1 \end{bmatrix}$$

Now, we have

$$(I+A)(I+A)'=\begin{bmatrix} 1 & \tan\frac{\theta}{2} \\ -\tan\frac{\theta}{2} & 1 \end{bmatrix}\begin{bmatrix} 1 & \tan\frac{\theta}{2} \\ -\tan\frac{\theta}{2} & 1 \end{bmatrix}$$

$$=\begin{bmatrix} 1-\tan^2\frac{\theta}{2} & 2\tan\frac{\theta}{2} \\ -2\tan\frac{\theta}{2} & 1-\tan^2\frac{\theta}{2} \end{bmatrix}$$

Thus, $a=1-\tan^2\frac{\theta}{2}$ and $b=-2\tan\frac{\theta}{2}$. Hence, we have

$$13(a^2+b^2)=13\left\{\left(1-\tan^2\frac{\theta}{2}\right)^2+\left(2\tan\frac{\theta}{2}\right)^2\right\}$$

$$=13\left(1-\tan^2\frac{\theta}{2}\right)^2=13\sec^4\frac{\theta}{2}$$

47. (d) Putting $z=x+iy$, the equations of the two lines reduce to

Line L_1:

$$2(z-\bar{z})-i(z+\bar{z})=4i$$

$$\Rightarrow \quad i(4y)-i(2x)=4i$$

$$\Rightarrow \quad 2y-x=2$$

Line L_2:

$$2(z+\bar{z})+i(z-\bar{z})=0$$

$$\Rightarrow \quad 4x-2y=0$$

$$\Rightarrow \quad y=2x$$

Line L_3:

$$i(z+\bar{z})-(z-\bar{z})+2i=0$$

$$\Rightarrow \quad i(2x)-i(2y)+2i=0$$

$$\Rightarrow \quad x-y+1=0$$

Lines L_1 and L_2 intersect at the point $A\left(\frac{2}{3},\frac{4}{3}\right)$. The required circle has its centre at A and touches line L_3. Thus, radius r of the circle is the perpendicular distance of A from line L_3.

Hence, $$r=\frac{\left|\frac{2}{3}-\frac{4}{3}+1\right|}{\sqrt{2}}=\frac{1}{3\sqrt{2}}$$

48. (b) We have

$$I=\int\frac{2\sin^2\theta(\sin^6\theta+\sin^4\theta+\sin^2\theta)\sqrt{2\sin^4\theta+3\sin^2\theta+6}}{2\sin^2\theta}\cos\theta d\theta$$

$$=\int(t^6+t^4+t^2)\sqrt{2t^4+3t^2+6}\,dt \text{ [Put } \sin\theta=t]$$

$$=\int(t^5+t^3+t)\sqrt{2t^6+3t^4+6t^2}\,dt$$

$$=\frac{1}{12}\int\sqrt{u}\,du \text{ [Put } 2t^6+3t^4+6t^2=u]$$

$$=\frac{1}{18}u^{3/2}+C=\frac{1}{18}(2\sin^6\theta+3\sin^4\theta+6\sin^2\theta)+C$$

Since all the options are in powers of $\cos\theta$, we need to express our result in powers of $\cos\theta$. Hence, we have

$$I=\frac{1}{18}\sin^2\theta(2\sin^4\theta+3\sin^2\theta+6)+C$$

$$=\frac{1}{18}(1-\cos^2\theta)\left[2(1-\cos^2\theta)^2+3(1-\cos^2\theta)+6\right]+C$$

$$=\frac{1}{18}(1-\cos^2\theta)\left[2\cos^4\theta-7\cos^2\theta+11\right]+C$$

$$= \frac{1}{18}\left(-2\cos^6\theta + 9\cos^2\theta - 18\cos^2\theta + 11\right) + C$$

49. (b) We have

$$\mathbf{r} \times \mathbf{a} = \mathbf{c} \times \mathbf{a}$$

$$\Rightarrow \quad (\mathbf{r} - \mathbf{c}) \times \mathbf{a} = 0$$

$$\Rightarrow \quad \mathbf{r} - \mathbf{c} = m\mathbf{a}$$

$$\Rightarrow \quad \mathbf{r} = m\mathbf{a} + \mathbf{c} = (m+1)\mathbf{i} + (m-2)\mathbf{j} - (m+1)\mathbf{k}$$

It is given that $\mathbf{r} \cdot \mathbf{b} = 0$. Thus, we have

$$(m+1) + (m-2) = 0 \text{ gives } m = \frac{1}{2}$$

Thus $\mathbf{r} = \frac{3}{2}\mathbf{i} - \frac{3}{2}\mathbf{j} - \frac{3}{2}\mathbf{k}$, and hence

$$\mathbf{r} \cdot \mathbf{a} = \frac{3}{2} - \frac{3}{2} + \frac{3}{2} = \frac{3}{2}$$

50. (c) Given $f(n+1) = f(n) + f(1)$. Thus, we have

$$f(2) = 2f(1)$$

$$f(3) = f(2) + f(1) = 3f(1),$$

$$f(4) = f(3) + f(1) = 4f(1),$$

$$\ldots$$

$$\Rightarrow \quad f(n) = nf(1).$$

Similarly $g(n) = ng(1)$.

(a) Since f is increasing $\Rightarrow f$ is one-one. Hence, option (a) is true.

(b) Onto f means its range equals **N**, which is possible only if $f(1) = 1$. So f onto $\Rightarrow f(1) = 1 \Rightarrow f(n) = n$. Hence, option (b) true.

(c) Since f, g are both increasing functions, fog is one-one. But this does not imply that g is onto. For g to be onto, its range should be **N**, which is possible only if $g(1) = 1$. Hence, option (c) is not true.

(d) Onto fog means its range equals **N**, which is possible only if $f(1) = 1$ and $g(1) = 1$. That is, if both f and g are onto. Hence, option (d) is true.

51. (a) Differentiating $\frac{x^2}{a} + \frac{y^2}{b} = 1$, we have

$$\frac{2x}{a} + \frac{2yy'}{b} = 1$$

$$\Rightarrow \quad y' = -\frac{bx}{ay}$$

Differentiating $\frac{x^2}{c} + \frac{y^2}{d} = 1$, we have

$$\frac{2x}{c} + \frac{2yy'}{d} = 1$$

$$\Rightarrow \quad y' = -\frac{dx}{cy}$$

At the intersection point, say $P(x, y)$, the tangents are perpendicular. Thus, we have

$$\left(\frac{-bx}{ay}\right)\left(\frac{-dx}{cy}\right) = -1$$

$$\Rightarrow \quad bdx^2 = -acy^2 \tag{1}$$

Also $P(x, y)$ lies on the two curves $\frac{x^2}{a} + \frac{y^2}{b} = 1$ and $\frac{x^2}{c} + \frac{y^2}{d} = 1$. Subtracting these two equations, we have

$$\left(\frac{1}{a} - \frac{1}{c}\right)x^2 + \left(\frac{1}{b} - \frac{1}{d}\right)y^2 = 0$$

$$\Rightarrow \quad \left(\frac{c-a}{ac}\right)x^2 = -\left(\frac{d-b}{bd}\right)y^2 \tag{2}$$

Dividing equations (1) and (2), we have

$$c - a = d - b$$

$$\Rightarrow \quad a - b = c - d$$

52. (a) We have

$$\sin 2\theta + \tan 2\theta > 0$$

$$\Rightarrow \quad \tan 2\theta (1 + \cos 2\theta) > 0$$

$$\Rightarrow \quad \tan 2\theta > 0 \text{ [since } 1 + \cos 2\theta > 0 \text{ for every real } \theta]$$

$$\Rightarrow \quad 2\theta \in \left(0, \frac{\pi}{2}\right) \cup \left(\pi, \frac{3\pi}{2}\right) \cup \left(2\pi, \frac{5\pi}{2}\right) \cup \left(3\pi, \frac{7\pi}{2}\right)$$

$$\Rightarrow \quad \theta \in \left(0, \frac{\pi}{4}\right) \cup \left(\frac{\pi}{2}, \frac{3\pi}{4}\right) \cup \left(\pi, \frac{5\pi}{4}\right) \cup \left(\frac{3\pi}{2}, \frac{7\pi}{4}\right)$$

53. (a) Since $a, b, c \in \{1, 2, 3, \ldots, 6\}$, the number of elements in the sample space is $n(S) = 6^3 = 216$.

For real roots $b^2 = 4ac \Rightarrow ac = \frac{b^2}{4}$.

If $b = 2$, then $ac = 1 \Rightarrow (a, c) = (1, 1)$.

If $b = 4$, then $ac = 4 \Rightarrow (a, c) = (1, 4), (2, 2), (4, 1)$.

If $b = 5$, then $ac = 9 \Rightarrow (a, c) = (3, 3)$.

The total number of favourable choices equals 5.

Hence, the required probability equals $\frac{5}{216}$.

54. (a) Using the conditions leading to coefficient unity and $\lim_{x\to 0}\frac{f(x)}{x^3}=1$, we have

$$f(x)=x^6+ax^5+bx^4+x^3$$

and $$f'(x)=6x^5+5ax^4+4bx^3+3x^2$$

Since $x=-1,1$ are points of extrema of $f(x)$, it means $f'(x)=0$ at these points. Thus, we have

$$5a-4b=3 \text{ and } 5a+4b=-9$$

$$\Rightarrow \quad a=\frac{-3}{5}, b=\frac{-3}{2}$$

Thus, $f(x)=x^6-\frac{3}{5}x^5-\frac{3}{2}x^4+x^3$ and hence

$$5f(2)=2\left(64-\frac{96}{5}-24+8\right)=144$$

55. (b) The given differential equation can be written as

$$\frac{dy}{dx}=\frac{(x-2)^2+y+4}{x-2}=x-2+\frac{y+4}{x-2}$$

$$\Rightarrow \quad \frac{dy}{dx}-\frac{1}{x-2}(y+4)=x-2$$

Putting $y+4=u$, we have

$$\frac{du}{dx}-\frac{u}{x-2}=x-2$$

Its integrating factor is

$$\Rightarrow \quad \text{IF}=e^{-\int\frac{dx}{x-2}}=e^{-\ln(x-2)}=\frac{1}{x-2}$$

The general solution is

$$u\left(\frac{1}{x-2}\right)=\int 1dx$$

$$\Rightarrow \quad u\left(\frac{1}{x-2}\right)=x+C$$

$$\Rightarrow y+4=(x-2)(x+C)$$

It passes through $(0,0)$, therefore $C=-2$. Hence, the particular solution is

$$y+4=(x-2)^2$$

We can see that the point $(2,-4)$ lies on the above curve.

56. (b) The given function $f(x)=|2x+1|-3|x+2|+|x^2+x-2|$ is non-differentiable at points where

$$2x+1=0,\ x+2=0, \text{ and } x^2+x-2=0$$

$$\Rightarrow \quad x=\frac{-1}{2},\ x=-2, \text{ and } x=-2,1$$

Hence, $f(x)$ is non-differentiable at three points $x=-2, \frac{-1}{2}, 1$.

57. (b) Let $\delta=\frac{1+\frac{1}{2}+\frac{1}{3}+\ldots+\frac{1}{n}}{n^2}$. Then the given limit can be written as

$$L=\lim_{\substack{n\to\infty\\ \delta\to 0}}(1+\delta)^n=\lim_{\substack{n\to\infty\\ \delta\to 0}}(1+\delta)^{\frac{1}{\delta}\times n\delta}=\lim_{\substack{n\to\infty\\ \delta\to 0}}e^{n\delta}$$

Now, we have

$$l=\lim_{\substack{n\to\infty\\ \delta\to 0}}n\delta=\lim_{n\to\infty}\frac{1+\frac{1}{2}+\frac{1}{3}+\ldots+\frac{1}{n}}{n}$$

$$=\lim_{n\to\infty}\frac{1}{n}+\frac{1}{2n}+\frac{1}{3n}+\ldots+\frac{1}{n^2}=0$$

Hence, $L=e^0=1$.

58. (b) The direction cosines l, m, n satisfy the following equations:

$$l+m=n \quad (1)$$

$$l^2+m^2=n^2 \quad (2)$$

and $$l^2+m^2+n^2=1 \quad (3)$$

From equations (2) and (3), we have

$$2n^2=1 \Rightarrow n=\pm\frac{1}{\sqrt{2}}$$

Squaring equation (1) and then subtracting equation (2), we have

$$lm=0$$

Thus, the possible direction cosines of the two lines are

$$0, \frac{1}{\sqrt{2}}, \frac{1}{\sqrt{2}} \text{ and } \frac{1}{\sqrt{2}}, 0, \frac{1}{\sqrt{2}} \left[\text{If we choose } n=\frac{1}{\sqrt{2}}\right]$$

$$\text{or } 0, \frac{-1}{\sqrt{2}}, \frac{-1}{\sqrt{2}} \text{ and } \frac{-1}{\sqrt{2}}, 0, \frac{-1}{\sqrt{2}} \left[\text{If we choose } n=\frac{-1}{\sqrt{2}}\right]$$

The angle α between the two lines is given by

$$\cos\alpha=l_1l_2+m_1m_2+n_1n_2$$

$$=0+0+\frac{1}{2}=\frac{1}{2} \text{ [Same in either case]}$$

Hence, we have

$$\sin^4\alpha + \cos^4\alpha = \left(1-\frac{1}{4}\right)^2 + \left(\frac{1}{4}\right)^2 = \frac{5}{8}$$

59. (b) If Rolle's Theorem is applicable on $f(x) = x^3 - ax^2 + bx + 1$ in the interval $[0,1]$, then we have

$$f(1) = f(2)$$

$$\Rightarrow \quad 1 - a + b + 1 = 8 - 4a + 2b + 1$$

$$\Rightarrow \quad 3a - b = 7 \qquad (1)$$

Now $f'(x) = 3x^2 - 2ax + b$. It is given that $f'\left(\frac{4}{3}\right) = 0$. Thus, we have

$$\frac{16}{3} - \frac{8}{3}a + b = 0$$

$$\Rightarrow \quad 8a - 3b = 16 \qquad (2)$$

Solving equations (1) and (2), we get $a - 5$, $b - 8$.

60. (a) We have

$$I = \frac{1}{2}\left[\int_{-\pi/2}^{\pi/2} \frac{\cos^2 x}{1+3^x}dx + \int_{-\pi/2}^{\pi/2} \frac{\cos^2 x}{1+3^{-x}}dx\right] \text{ [By property]}$$

$$= \frac{1}{2}\left[\int_{-\pi/2}^{\pi/2} \frac{\cos^2 x}{1+3^x}dx + \int_{-\pi/2}^{\pi/2} \frac{3^x\cos^2 x}{1+3^x}dx\right]$$

$$= \frac{1}{2}\left[\int_{-\pi/2}^{\pi/2} \cos^2 x dx\right]$$

$$= \frac{1}{2}\times 2\left[\int_{0}^{\pi/2} \cos^2 x dx\right] \text{ [Even function]}$$

$$= \frac{1}{2}\int_{0}^{\pi/2} (1+\cos 2x)dx$$

$$= \frac{1}{2}\left|x + \frac{\sin 2x}{2}\right|_0^{\pi/2} = \frac{\pi}{4}$$

61. (c) We have

$$L = \lim_{x\to 0} \frac{\sqrt{3}\sin\left(\frac{\pi}{6}+x\right) - \cos\left(\frac{\pi}{6}+x\right)}{\sqrt{3}x\left(\sqrt{3}\cos x - \sin x\right)}$$

$$= \lim_{x\to 0} \frac{2\sin\left(\frac{\pi}{6}+x-\frac{\pi}{6}\right)}{\sqrt{3}x\left(\sqrt{3}\cos x - \sin x\right)}$$

$$= \lim_{x\to 0} \frac{\sin x}{x} \times \frac{2}{\sqrt{3}\left(\sqrt{3}\cos x - \sin x\right)} = \frac{2}{3}$$

62. (a) The given lines are $L_1 : x - y = 0$, $L_2 : x + 2y = 3$, $L_3 : 2x + y = 6$. Their intersection points are

$$A(2,2), B(1,1), C(3,0)$$

Now $\quad AB = \sqrt{2}, BC = \sqrt{5}, AC = \sqrt{5}$

Hence, the triangle ΔABC is isosceles.

63. (d) We have

$$-\sqrt{3^2+4^2} \le 3\sin x + 4\cos x \le \sqrt{3^2+4^2}$$

$$\Rightarrow \quad -5 \le k+1 \le 5$$

$$\Rightarrow \quad -6 \le k \le 4$$

64. (a) Case I: 1, 1, 1, 1, 1, 2, 3

Number of ways $= \frac{7!}{5!} = 42$

Case II: 1, 1, 1, 1, 2, 2, 2

Number of ways $= \frac{7!}{4!3!} = 35$

Hence, total number of ways $= 42 + 35 = 77$.

65. (a)

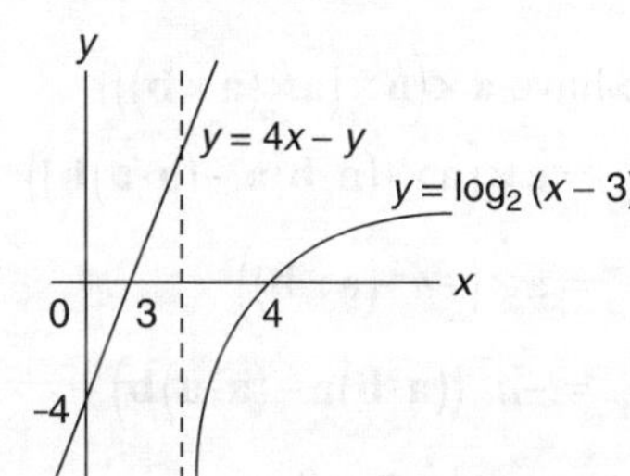

From the figure, we can see that the two curves $y = 4(x-1)$ and $y = \log_2(x-3)$ have no intersection points.

Hence, the given equation has no solution.

66. (a) Let $A - \begin{bmatrix} a & b \\ b & c \end{bmatrix}$. Then

$$A^2 = \begin{bmatrix} a & b \\ b & c \end{bmatrix}\begin{bmatrix} a & b \\ b & c \end{bmatrix} = \begin{bmatrix} a^2+b^2 & ab+bc \\ ab+bc & b^2+c^2 \end{bmatrix}$$

From the given condition, we have

$$\Rightarrow \quad a^2 + 2b^2 + c^2 - 1$$

$$\Rightarrow \quad b = 0 \text{ and } a^2 + c^2 = 1 \text{ [}a, b, c\text{ are integers]}$$

$$\Rightarrow \quad b = 0 \text{ and } (a,c) = (1,0),(0,1),(-1,0),(0,-1)$$

Hence, there are 4 such matrices.

67. (b) The slope m at any point is given by

$$m = \frac{dy}{dx} = 2x^3 - 5x^2 + 36x$$

Now, we have

$$\frac{dm}{dx} = 6x^2 - 10x + 36 = 6(x-2)(x-3)$$

$$\begin{array}{ccc} + & & + \\ \hline & 2 & 3 \end{array}$$

From the above sign scheme, we can see that m has maximum value at $x = 2$. Hence, the required point is $(2, 46)$.

68. (a) We have

$$D = \begin{vmatrix} (a+1)(a+2) & a+1 & 1 \\ 2(a+2) & 1 & 0 \\ 2(a+3) & 1 & 0 \end{vmatrix} \begin{matrix} R_2 \to R_2 - R_1 \\ R_3 \to R_3 - R_1 \end{matrix}$$

$$= 2(a+2) - 2(a+3) = -2$$

69. (c) Let $\sin^{-1} x = at, \cos^{-1} x = bt, \tan^{-1} y = ct$. Then, we have

$$at + bt = \frac{\pi}{2} \Rightarrow t = \frac{\pi}{2(a+b)}$$

Now, we have

$$\cos\left(\frac{\pi c}{a+b}\right) = \cos(2ct) = \frac{1-\tan^2(ct)}{1+\tan^2(ct)} = \frac{1-y^2}{1+y^2}$$

70. (a) We have $\mathbf{a} \times (\mathbf{a} \times (\mathbf{a} \times (\mathbf{a} \times \mathbf{b})))$

$$= \mathbf{a} \times (\mathbf{a} \times ((\mathbf{a} \cdot \mathbf{b})\mathbf{a} - (\mathbf{a} \cdot \mathbf{a})\mathbf{b}))$$

$$= \mathbf{a} \times (-a^2 (\mathbf{a} \times \mathbf{b}))$$

$$= -a^2 ((\mathbf{a} \cdot \mathbf{b})\mathbf{a} - (\mathbf{a} \cdot \mathbf{a})\mathbf{b})$$

$$= a^4 \mathbf{b} \; [\mathbf{a} \cdot \mathbf{b} = 0 \text{ given}]$$

71. (b) We have $\left|\dfrac{f(x) - f(y)}{x - y}\right| \le |x - y|$

$$\Rightarrow \lim_{y \to x} \left|\frac{f(x) - f(y)}{x - y}\right| = \lim_{y \to x} |x - y| \; \text{[Taking limit both sides]}$$

$$\Rightarrow |f'(x)| \le 0$$

$$\Rightarrow f'(x) = 0$$

$$\Rightarrow f(x) = C$$

$f(0) = 1$, therefore $C = 1$. Hence, $f(x) = 1$.

72. (a) This is an arithmetic-geometric series. We have

$$S = 1 + \frac{2}{3} + \frac{7}{3^2} + \frac{12}{3^3} + \ldots \infty \quad (1)$$

and $$\frac{1}{3} S = \frac{1}{3} + \frac{2}{3^2} + \frac{7}{3^3} + \frac{12}{3^4} + \ldots \infty \quad (2)$$

Subtracting equation(2) from equation (1), we have

$$\frac{2}{3} S = 1 + \frac{1}{3} + \frac{5}{3^2} + \frac{5}{3^3} + \frac{5}{3^4} + \ldots \infty$$

$$\Rightarrow \frac{2}{3} S = \frac{4}{3} + \frac{5}{3^2}\left(\frac{1}{1 - \frac{1}{3}}\right) = \frac{4}{3} + \frac{5}{6} = \frac{13}{6}$$

$$\Rightarrow S = \frac{13}{4}$$

73. (a) The general term of the binomial is

$$T_{r+1} = {}^{10}C_r \, x^{\frac{10-r}{5}} (1-x)^{\frac{r}{10}} t^{10-2r}$$

The term will be independent of t if $r = 5$, and the corresponding term is

$$T_6 = {}^{10}C_5 \, x\sqrt{1-x}$$

Now, we have

$$\frac{d(T_6)}{dx} = {}^{10}C_5 \left(\sqrt{1-x} - \frac{x}{2\sqrt{1-x}}\right)$$

$$= {}^{10}C_5 \left(\frac{2-3x}{2\sqrt{1-x}}\right) = {}^{10}C_5 \left(\frac{-3\left(x - \frac{2}{3}\right)}{2\sqrt{1-x}}\right)$$

The derivative changes sign from +ve to −ve at $x = 2/3 \Rightarrow T_6$ has maximum value at $x = 2/3$. Hence, we have

$$(T_6)_{max} = {}^{10}C_5 \left(\frac{2}{3}\right)\left(\frac{1}{3}\right)^{1/2} = 56\sqrt{3}$$

74. (a) We have

$$I = \sum_{n=1}^{100} \int_{n-1}^{n} e^{\{x\}} dx$$

$$= \int_0^1 e^{\{x\}} dx + \int_1^2 e^{\{x\}} dx + \ldots \int_{99}^{100} e^{\{x\}} dx$$

$$= 100 \int_0^1 e^x dx \; [\{x\} \text{ is a periodic function}]$$

$$= 100(e - 1)$$

75. (b) Let a be the first term, and r be the common ratio. Then, we have

$$ar + ar^5 = \frac{25}{2} \quad (1)$$

and $$(ar^2)(ar^4) = 25 \Rightarrow ar^3 = 5 \quad (2)$$

Dividing equations (1) and (2), we have

$$\frac{r + r^5}{r^3} = \frac{5}{2}$$

$$\Rightarrow \quad 2r^4 - 5r^2 + 2 = 0 \text{ gives } r^2 = \frac{1}{2}, 2$$

Only $r^2 = 2$ is acceptable since the GP is given to be increasing.

Hence, we have

$$ar^3 + ar^5 + ar^7 = ar^3\left(1 + r^2 + r^4\right)$$

$$= 5(1 + 2 + 4) = 35$$

76. (b) The points $P(1,5,35), Q(7,5,2), R(1,\lambda,7), S(2\lambda,1,2)$ are given to be coplanar. Thus, we have

$$\begin{vmatrix} 7-1 & 5-5 & 2-35 \\ 1-1 & \lambda-5 & 7-35 \\ 2\lambda-1 & 1-5 & 2-35 \end{vmatrix} = 0$$

$$\Rightarrow \quad \begin{vmatrix} 6 & 0 & -33 \\ 0 & \lambda-5 & -28 \\ 2\lambda-1 & 1-5 & -33 \end{vmatrix} = 0$$

$$\Rightarrow \quad 6(-33\lambda + 53) + 33\left(2\lambda^2 - 11\lambda + 5\right) = 0$$

$$\Rightarrow \quad 2(-33\lambda + 53) + 11\left(2\lambda^2 - 11\lambda + 5\right) = 0$$

$$\Rightarrow \quad 22\lambda^2 - 187\lambda + 161 = 0.$$

Hence, sum of the roots $= \dfrac{187}{22} = \dfrac{17}{2}$.

77. (b) The given line is along the vector $\mathbf{a} = \mathbf{i} - \mathbf{j} + 4\mathbf{k}$, and the normal to the given plane is along the vector $\mathbf{p} = \mathbf{i} + 5\mathbf{j} + \mathbf{k}$. We see that $\mathbf{a} \cdot \mathbf{p} = 0$, which implies that the line is parallel o the plane.

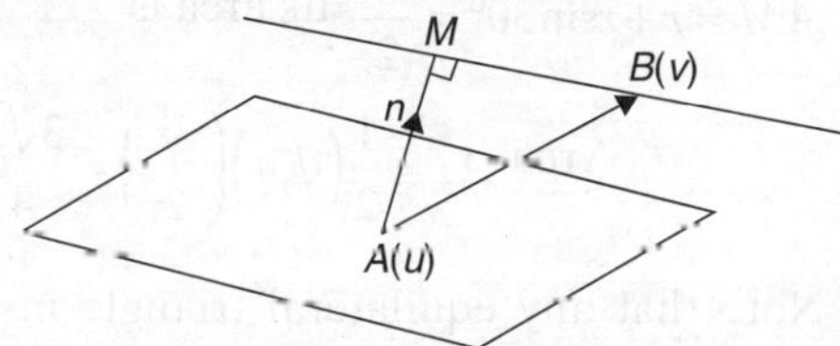

We choose a point A on the plane having position vector $\mathbf{u} = 0\mathbf{i} + 1\mathbf{j} + 0\mathbf{k}$, and a point B on the line having position vector $\mathbf{v} = 2\mathbf{i} - 2\mathbf{j} + 3\mathbf{k}$ (see figure). Then

$$\mathbf{AB} = \mathbf{v} - \mathbf{u} = 2\mathbf{i} - 3\mathbf{j} + 3\mathbf{k}$$

The unit vector along the normal to the plane is

$$\mathbf{n} = \frac{1}{3\sqrt{3}}(\mathbf{i} + 5\mathbf{j} + \mathbf{k})$$

Hence, the perpendicular distance between the line and the plane is

$$AM = |\mathbf{AB} \cdot \mathbf{n}| = \left|\frac{2 - 15 + 3}{3\sqrt{3}}\right| = \frac{10}{3\sqrt{3}}$$

78. (d) Equation of the face OAB is

$$\begin{vmatrix} x & y & z \\ 1 & 2 & 1 \\ 2 & 1 & 3 \end{vmatrix} = 0$$

$$\Rightarrow \quad 5x - y - 3z = 0 \qquad (1)$$

Equation of the face ABC is

$$\begin{vmatrix} x-1 & y-2 & z-1 \\ 2-1 & 1-2 & 3-1 \\ -1-1 & 1-2 & 2-1 \end{vmatrix} = 0$$

$$\Rightarrow \quad \begin{vmatrix} x-1 & y-2 & z-1 \\ 1 & -1 & 2 \\ -2 & -1 & 1 \end{vmatrix} = 0$$

$$\Rightarrow \quad (x-1) - 5(y-1) - 3(z-1) = 0$$

$$\Rightarrow \quad x - 5y - 3z + 7 = 0 \qquad (2)$$

The direction ratios of the normals to the faces OAB and ABC are

$5, -1, -3$ and $1, -5, -3$. Hence, the angle θ between the two faces, is given by

$$\cos\theta = \frac{5 + 5 + 9}{\sqrt{5^2 + 1^2 + 3^2}\sqrt{1^2 + 5^2 + 3^2}} = \frac{19}{35}$$

$$\Rightarrow \theta = \cos^{-1}\left(\frac{19}{35}\right)$$

79. (d) Differentiating both sides, we have

$$\frac{df}{dx} = e^x f(x) + e^x$$

$$\Rightarrow \quad \frac{df}{f(x) + 1} = e^x dx$$

$$\Rightarrow \quad \int \frac{df}{f(x) + 1} = \int e^x dx$$

$$\Rightarrow \quad \ln|f(x) + 1| = e^x + C$$

From the given equation, we can see that $f(0) = 1$. Using this, we get $C = \ln 2 - 1$. Thus, the particular solution is

$$\ln|f(x) + 1| = e^x + \ln 2 - 1$$

$$\Rightarrow f(x) = 2e^{e^x - 1} - 1$$

80. (b) Total number of seven-digit numbers that can be formed is

$$n(S) = \frac{7!}{2!3!2!}$$

The seven-digit number will be even if there is a 4 in the units place. The total number of such numbers is

$$n(E) = \frac{6!}{2!2!2!}$$

Hence, the required probability is

$$P(E) = \frac{n(E)}{n(S)} = \frac{6!}{2!2!2!} \times \frac{2!3!2!}{7!} = \frac{3}{7}$$

81. (a)

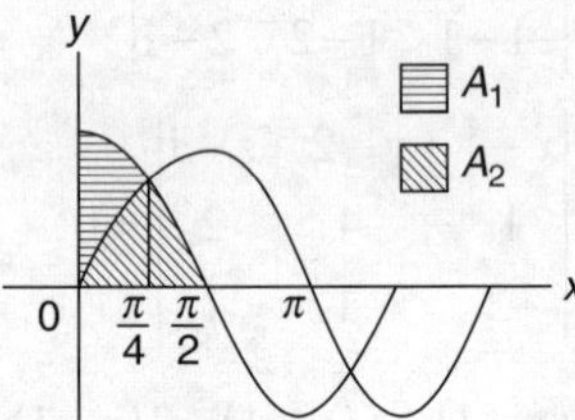

We have (see figure)

$$A_1 + A_2 = \int_0^{\pi/2} \cos x dx = |\sin x|_0^{\pi/2} = 1$$

and $$A_2 = \int_0^{\pi/4} (\cos x - \sin x) dx$$

$$= |\sin x + \cos x|_0^{\pi/4} = \sqrt{2} - 1$$

From the above results, we get $A_1 = 1 - A_2 = 2 - \sqrt{2}$. Hence, we have

$$\frac{A_1}{A_2} = \frac{\sqrt{2}-1}{2-\sqrt{2}} = \frac{1}{\sqrt{2}}$$

82. (c)

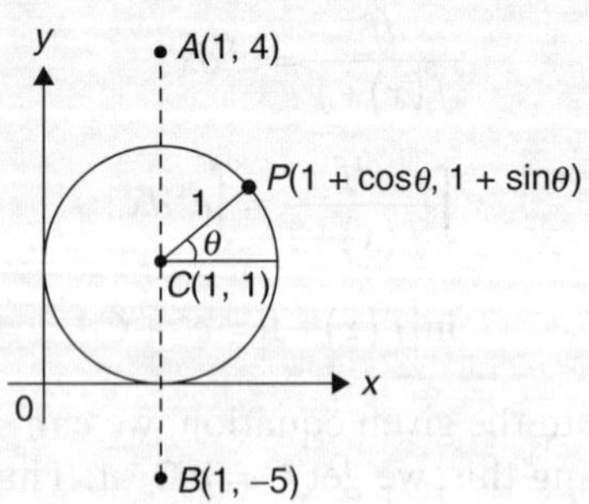

An arbitrary point on the circle (see figure) can be chosen as $P(1+\cos\theta, 1+\sin\theta)$. Now

$$(PA)^2 = (\cos\theta)^2 + (\sin\theta - 3)^2 = 10 - 6\sin\theta$$

and $$(PB)^2 = (\cos\theta)^2 + (\sin\theta + 6)^2 = 37 + 12\sin\theta$$

Thus, we have

$$(PA)^2 + (PB)^2 = 47 + 6\sin\theta$$

We see that $(PA)^2 + (PB)^2$ attains its maximum value when $\theta = \frac{\pi}{2}$. Hence, points P, A, B lie on a straight line.

83. (c) The figure shows a right-angled triangle with side lengths $2r, r$. Its area is

$$\text{Area } A_1 = \frac{1}{2}(2r)(r) = r^2$$

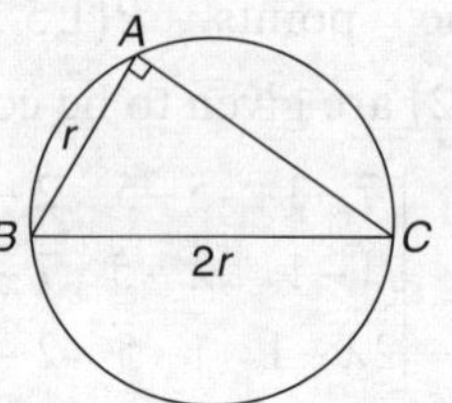

The figure shows an isoceles triangle with base length $2r$. In this case, side BC is the diameter, and therefore, height of the triangle equals r. Its area is

$$\text{Area } A_2 = \frac{1}{2}(2r)(r) = r^2$$

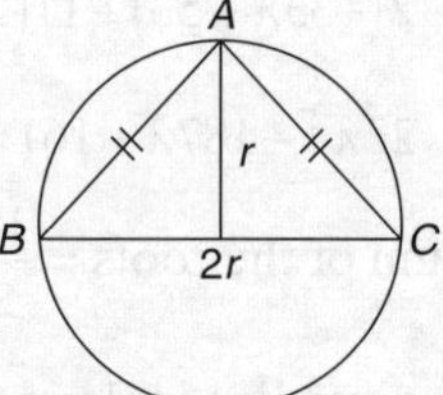

The figure shows an equilateral triangle. Its side length is $BC = 2r\cos 30° = \sqrt{3}r$, and its height is $AM = r + r\sin 30° = \frac{3r}{2}$. Its area is

$$\text{Area } A_3 = \frac{1}{2}(\sqrt{3}r)\left(\frac{3r}{2}\right) = \frac{3\sqrt{3}}{4}r^2$$

Note that any equilateral triangle inscribed in a circle of radius r will have height $\frac{3r}{2}$. So the triangle mentioned in option (a) is not possible.

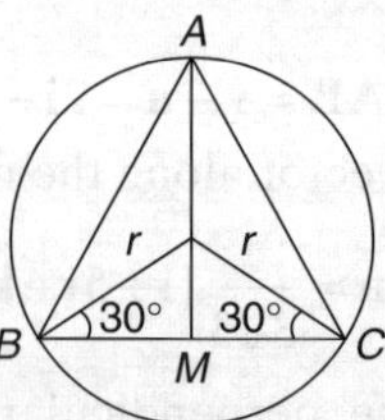

Hence, the greatest area is A_3.

84. (a) If **a** and **b** are collinear vectors, then

$$\frac{x}{1}=\frac{-1}{y}=\frac{1}{z}=t \text{ (say)}$$

Now, a unit vector parallel to vector $\mathbf{a}=x\mathbf{i}+y\mathbf{j}+z\mathbf{k}=t\mathbf{i}-t\mathbf{j}+t\mathbf{k}$ is

$$\mathbf{n}=\frac{t\mathbf{i}-t\mathbf{j}+t\mathbf{k}}{\sqrt{t^2+t^2+t^2}}=\frac{\mathbf{i}-\mathbf{j}+\mathbf{k}}{\sqrt{3}}$$

85. (c) Solving the given equations $y+z=5$ and $\frac{1}{y}+\frac{1}{z}=\frac{5}{6}$ gives $y=3, z=2$. Then $N=2^x3^35^2$. The odd divisors are numbers of the type 3^m5^n, where $m=0,1,2,3$ and $n=0,1,2$.

Hence, the total number of odd divisors $=4\times 3=12$.

86. (b) Solving the given differential equation, we have

$$xdy=\left(xy^2-y\right)dx$$

$$\Rightarrow \quad \frac{xdy-ydx}{y^2}=xdx$$

$$\Rightarrow \quad -d\left(\frac{x}{y}\right)=d\left(\frac{x^2}{2}\right)$$

$$\Rightarrow \quad -\frac{x}{y}=\frac{x^2}{2}+C$$

It passes through $(-2,3)$, therefore $C=\frac{-4}{3}$. Thus, the curve is

$$-\frac{x}{y}=\frac{x^2}{2}-\frac{4}{3}$$

If it passes through $(3,k)$, then

$$-\frac{3}{y}=\frac{9}{2}-\frac{4}{3} \text{ gives } k=\frac{-18}{19}$$

87. (b) We have

$$f(1)=f(2)=2,$$

$$f(3)=f(4)=4,$$

$$\ldots$$

$$\Rightarrow \quad f(x)\in\{2,4,6,\ldots\text{all even numbers}\}.$$

Thus, we have

$$g\{f(x)\}=f(x)\Rightarrow g(x)=x, \text{ where } x \text{ is even}.$$

The figure shows the mapping of $g(x)$ from A to A. For a function to be defined, all elements in the domain must have a corresponding image in the co-domain.

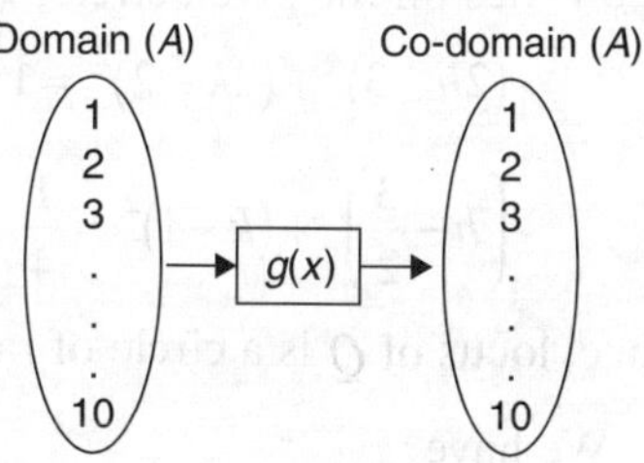

The elements $2,4,6,8,10$ in the domain have fixed images, namely, $2,4,6,8,10$, respectively. The remaining five elements $1,3,5,7,9$ in the domain can be paired with any one of the ten elements in the co-domain.

Hence, the number of mappings of the function $g(x): A\to A$ is

$$10\times10\times10\times10\times10=10^5$$

88. (b) The equations of the planes are $x+2y+z=6$ and $y+2z=4$.

Putting $z=0$ in both equations and solving gives $x=-2, y=4$.

Putting $y=0$ in both equations and solving gives $x=4, z=2$.

Thus, we have two points $(-2,4,0)$ and $(4,0,2)$ lying on the intersection line. Thus, its equation is

$$\frac{x+2}{-6}=\frac{y-4}{4}=\frac{z}{-2}$$

$$\Rightarrow \quad \frac{x+2}{3}=\frac{y-4}{-2}=\frac{z}{1}$$

Let $M(3t-2,4-2t,t)$ be any point on the above line. The direction ratios of PM where P is the given point $P(3,4,1)$, are $3t-5, -2t, t-1$. If PM is perpendicular to the above line, then

$$3(3t-5)-2(-2t)+1(t-1)=0 \text{ gives } t=\frac{8}{7}$$

Hence, the required point is $M\left(\frac{10}{7},\frac{12}{7},\frac{8}{7}\right)$.

89. (b)

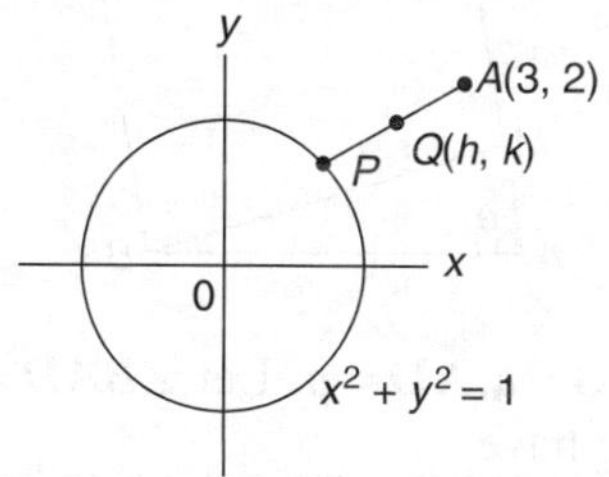

Given point $A(3,2)$. Let $Q(h,k)$ be the midpoint of AP (see figure). Then

$$P=(2h-3,2k-2)$$

Since P lies on the given circle, we have

$$(2h-3)^2+(2k-2)^2=1$$

$$\Rightarrow \quad \left(h-\frac{3}{2}\right)^2+(k-1)^2=\frac{1}{4}$$

Hence, locus of Q is a circle of radius $=1/2$.

90. (a) We have

$$g(x)=\lim_{x\to 2}\frac{x^2-x-2}{2x^2-x-6}=\lim_{x\to 2}\frac{x+1}{2x+3}=\frac{3}{7}$$

The domain of $fog(x)$ is given by

$$\left|\frac{x^2-x-2}{2x^2-x-6}\right|\le 1$$

$$\Rightarrow \quad \left|\frac{x+1}{2x+3}\right|\le 1$$

$$\Rightarrow \quad (x+1)^2\le(2x+3)^2$$

$$\Rightarrow \quad 3x^2+10x+8\ge 0$$

$$\Rightarrow \quad 3(x+2)\left(x+\frac{4}{3}\right)\ge 0$$

$$\Rightarrow \quad x\in(-\infty,-2]\cup[-4/3,+\infty)$$

91. (b) Since it is identically true for every $a,b\ne 0$, let us put $a=2,b=-1$. Thus, we have

$$36k=\begin{vmatrix}3 & 1+1 & 1+5\\ 1+1 & 1+5 & 1+7\\ 1+5 & 1+7 & 1+17\end{vmatrix}$$

$$\Rightarrow \quad 36k=\begin{vmatrix}3 & 2 & 6\\ 2 & 6 & 8\\ 6 & 8 & 18\end{vmatrix}=4\begin{vmatrix}3 & 2 & 6\\ 1 & 3 & 4\\ 3 & 4 & 9\end{vmatrix}$$

$$\Rightarrow \quad 9k=3(27-16)+2(12-9)+6(4-9)=9$$

$$\Rightarrow \quad k=1$$

92. (d)

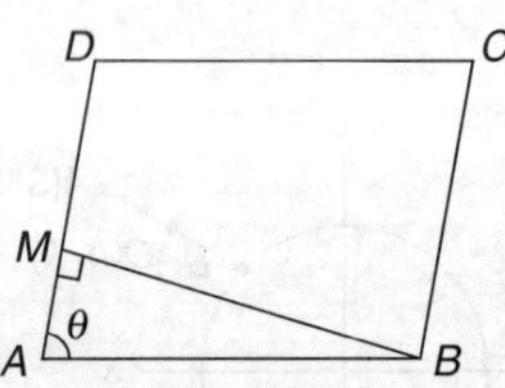

Given $\mathbf{AB}=\mathbf{q},\mathbf{AD}=\mathbf{p}$. Let $\angle BAD=\theta$ (see figure). Then, we have

$$AM=AB\cos\theta=q\left(\frac{\mathbf{p}\cdot\mathbf{q}}{pq}\right)=\frac{\mathbf{p}\cdot\mathbf{q}}{p}$$

A unit vector parallel to AM is $\mathbf{n}=\dfrac{\mathbf{p}}{p}$. Then, we have

$$\mathbf{AM}=(AM)\mathbf{n}=\left(\frac{\mathbf{p}\cdot\mathbf{q}}{pq}\right)\frac{\mathbf{p}}{p}=\left(\frac{\mathbf{p}\cdot\mathbf{q}}{p^2}\right)\mathbf{p}$$

Hence, we have

$$\mathbf{BM}=\mathbf{AM}-\mathbf{AB}$$

$$=\left(\frac{\mathbf{p}\cdot\mathbf{q}}{p^2}\right)\mathbf{p}-q=\left(\frac{\mathbf{p}\cdot\mathbf{q}}{\mathbf{p}\cdot\mathbf{p}}\right)\mathbf{p}-q$$

93. (a) We have

$$L=\lim_{y\to 0}\frac{(x+y)\sec(x+y)-x\sec x}{y}$$

$$=\lim_{y\to 0}\frac{(x+y)\cos x-x\cos(x+y)}{y\cos(x+y)\cos x}$$

$$=\lim_{y\to 0}\frac{x\cos x(1-\cos y)+y\cos x+x\sin x\sin y}{y\cos(x+y)\cos x}$$

$$=\lim_{y\to 0}\frac{1}{\cos(x+y)}\left[\left(\frac{1-\cos y}{y}\right)x+1+\left(\frac{\sin y}{y}\right)x\tan x\right]$$

$$=\lim_{y\to 0}\frac{1}{\cos(x+y)}\left[y\left(\frac{1-\cos y}{y^2}\right)x+1+\left(\frac{\sin y}{y}\right)x\tan x\right]$$

$$=\sec x\left[0\left(\frac{x}{2}\right)+1+x\tan x\right]$$

$$=\sec x(1+x\tan x).$$

Note that the above limit is the derivative of the function $x\sec x$.

94. (c) We have

$$f'(x)=\lim_{h\to 0}\frac{f(x+h)-f(x)}{h}$$

$$=\lim_{h\to 0}\frac{f(x)+f(h)+h^2x+x^2h-f(x)}{h}$$

$$\left[\text{Given } f(x+y)=f(x)+f(y)+y^2x+x^2y\right]$$

$$=\lim_{h\to 0}\frac{f(h)}{h}+h+x^2=x^2$$

Now solving the above differential equation, we have

$$f(x)=\frac{x^3}{3}+C$$

It is given that $\lim_{x\to 0}\dfrac{f(x)}{x}=0$. Therefore $C=0$ and $f(x)=\dfrac{x^3}{3}$.

Hence, $f'(-1)=1$.

95. (a) The function $\sin(2\pi x)$ is a periodic function with period 1. Thus, in the interval $[0, 1]$ we have

$$[\sin(2\pi x)] = \begin{cases} 0, 0 \le x \le \frac{1}{2} \\ -1, \frac{1}{2} < x < 1 \end{cases}$$

The function $e^{x-[x]} = e^{\{x\}}$ is also a periodic function with period 1. In the interval $[0, 1]$ we have $e^{\{x\}} = e^x$

Thus, the integrand is also periodic with period 1. In the interval $[0, 1]$, the integrand reduces to

$$\frac{[\sin(2\pi x)]}{e^{x-[x]}} = \begin{cases} 0, 0 \le x \le \frac{1}{2} \\ -e^{-x}, \frac{1}{2} < x < 1 \end{cases}$$

Thus, we have

$$\int_0^{10} \frac{[\sin(2\pi x)]}{e^{x-[x]}} dx = 10\int_0^1 \frac{[\sin(2\pi x)]}{e^{x-[x]}} dx$$

$$= -10\int_{1/2}^{1} e^{-x} dx$$

$$= 10\left(e^{-1} - e^{-1/2}\right)$$

Thus $\alpha = 10, \beta = -10, \gamma = 0$ and hence $\alpha + \beta + \gamma = 0$.

96. (b) The given differential equation can be written as

$$\frac{dy}{dx} - y\tan x = \frac{1}{\cos x(3\sin x + \cos x + 3)}$$

The integrating factor is

$$\text{IF} = e^{-\int \tan x\, dx} = e^{\ln(\cos x)} = \cos x$$

Thus, the general solution is

$$y\cos x = \int \frac{1}{3\sin x + \cos x + 3} dx + C$$

$$\Rightarrow \quad y\cos x = \int \frac{1}{\frac{6t}{1+t^2} + \frac{1-t^2}{1+t^2} + 3} \times \frac{2dt}{1+t^2} + C$$

$$\left[\text{Put } \tan\left(\frac{x}{2}\right) = t\right]$$

$$\Rightarrow \quad y\cos x = \int \frac{1}{t^2 + 3t + 2} dt + C$$

$$\Rightarrow \quad y\cos x = \int \left(\frac{1}{t+1} - \frac{1}{t+2}\right) dt + C$$

$$\Rightarrow \quad y\cos x = \ln\left|\frac{\tan\left(\frac{x}{2}\right)+1}{\tan\left(\frac{x}{2}\right)+2}\right| + C$$

The condition $y(0) = 0$ gives $C = \ln 2$. Thus, we have

$$y = \sec x \ln\left(2\left|\frac{\tan\left(\frac{x}{2}\right)+1}{\tan\left(\frac{x}{2}\right)+2}\right|\right)$$

Hence, we have

$$y\left(\frac{\pi}{3}\right) = 2\ln\left(2\left|\frac{\frac{1}{\sqrt{3}}+1}{\frac{1}{\sqrt{3}}+2}\right|\right)$$

$$= 2\ln\left(\frac{2\sqrt{3}+2}{2\sqrt{3}+1}\right) = 2\ln\left(\frac{2\sqrt{3}+10}{11}\right)$$

97. (d) The given series is

$$S = {}^6C_0\,{}^6C_6 + {}^6C_1\,{}^6C_5 + \ldots + {}^6C_6\,{}^6C_0$$

We have

$$(1+x)^6 = {}^6C_0 + {}^6C_1x + {}^6C_2x^2 + \ldots + {}^6C_6x^6$$

Now squaring both sides, we have

$$(1+x)^{12} = \left({}^6C_0 + {}^6C_1x + {}^6C_2x^2 + \ldots + {}^6C_6x^6\right) \times \left({}^6C_0 + {}^6C_1x + {}^6C_2x^2 + \ldots + {}^6C_6x^6\right)$$

We can see that

$$S = \text{coeff of } x^6 \text{ in } (1+x)^{12}$$

$$= {}^{12}C_6 = 924$$

98. (a) Let $S_n = \dfrac{[r]+[2r]+[3r]+\ldots+[nr]}{n^2}$. Then we can see that

$$\frac{(r-1)+(2r-1)+\ldots+(nr-1)}{n^2} \le S_n \le \frac{r+2r+\ldots+nr}{n^2}$$

$$\Rightarrow \quad \frac{rn(n+1)}{2n^2} - \frac{n}{n^2} \le S_n \le \frac{rn(n+1)}{2n^2}$$

$$\Rightarrow \quad \frac{r}{2}\left(1+\frac{1}{n}\right) - \frac{1}{n} \le S_n \le \frac{r}{2}\left(1+\frac{1}{n}\right)$$

$$\Rightarrow \quad \lim_{n\to\infty} \frac{r}{2}\left(1+\frac{1}{n}\right) - \frac{1}{n} \le \lim_{n\to\infty} S_n \le \lim_{n\to\infty} \frac{r}{2}\left(1+\frac{1}{n}\right)$$

Hence, $\lim\limits_{n\to\infty} S_n = \dfrac{r}{2}$.

99. (b) When $x \in [-1, 1]$, then $x^2 \in [0, 1]$. Let

$$f(x) = \sin^{-1}\left[x^2 + \frac{1}{3}\right] + \cos^{-1}\left[x^2 - \frac{2}{3}\right]$$

The function can be written as

$$f(x) = \begin{cases} \sin^{-1}(0) + \cos^{-1}(-1), 0 \le x^2 < \dfrac{2}{3} \\ \sin^{-1}(1) + \cos^{-1}(0), \dfrac{2}{3} \le x \le 1 \end{cases}$$

$$= \begin{cases} \pi, 0 \le x^2 < \dfrac{2}{3} \\ \pi, \dfrac{2}{3} \le x \le 1 \end{cases}$$

Thus LHS $= \pi$ (always), whereas the $0 \le \text{RHS} \le 1$ (always). Hence, no real solution is possible.

100. (b) Let $f(x) = x + 2\tan x$. Then, we have

$$f'(x) = 1 + 2\sec^2 x$$

In the interval $x \in [0, 2\pi]$, $f(x)$ has discontinuities at $x = \frac{\pi}{2}, \frac{3\pi}{2}$. Since $f'(x) > 0$ (always), we conclude that $f(x)$ is a piecewise increasing function.

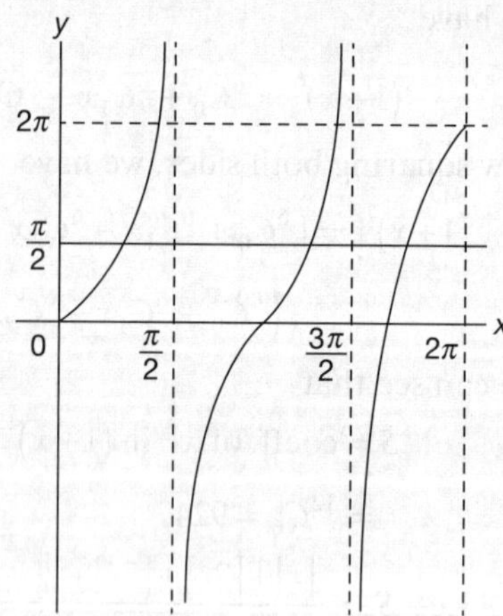

The figure shows the graphs of $y = f(x)$ and the horizontal line $y = \frac{\pi}{2}$. We can see that they intersect at three points. Hence, the given equation has three solutions.

101. (c) We can choose the points for drawing the triangle in the following ways.
Case I: One point from each side.

Number of ways $= {}^3C_1 \times {}^5C_1 \times {}^6C_1 = 90$

Case II: Two points from any one side, and one point from any one of the other two sides.

$$\text{Number of ways } = {}^3C_2\left({}^5C_1 + {}^6C_1\right) + {}^5C_2\left({}^3C_1 + {}^6C_1\right) + {}^6C_2\left({}^3C_1 + {}^5C_1\right)A$$

$$= 33 + 90 + 120 = 243$$

Hence, total number of ways $= 90 + 243 = 333$.

102. (a) We have

$$D = \begin{vmatrix} 3 & 4\sqrt{2} & x \\ 4 & 5\sqrt{2} & y \\ 5 & k & z \end{vmatrix}$$

$$= \begin{vmatrix} 3 & 4\sqrt{2} & x \\ 1 & \sqrt{2} & d \\ 1 & k - 5\sqrt{2} & d \end{vmatrix} \begin{matrix} R_3 \to R_3 - R_2 \\ R_2 \to R_2 - R_1 \end{matrix}$$

$$= \begin{vmatrix} 3 & 4\sqrt{2} & x \\ 1 & \sqrt{2} & d \\ 0 & k - 6\sqrt{2} & 0 \end{vmatrix} R_3 \to R_3 - R_2$$

$$= x\left(k - 6\sqrt{2}\right) + d\left(18\sqrt{2} - 3k\right)$$

$$= (x - 3d)\left(k - 6\sqrt{2}\right)$$

It is given that $D = 0$ and $x \ne 3d$. Thus $k = 6\sqrt{2}$ and hence $k^2 = 72$.

103. (b)

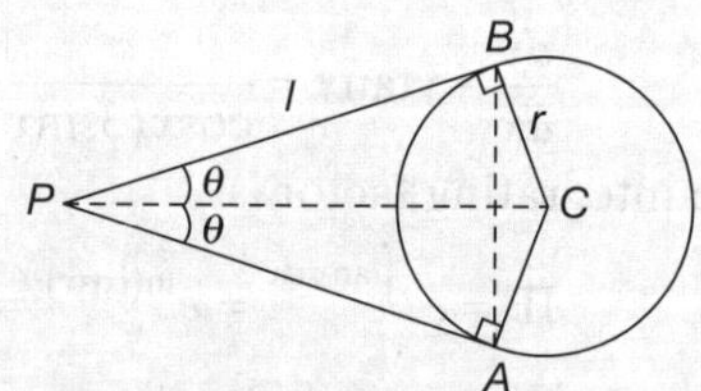

Let l be the length of the tangent and r be the radius of the given circle (see figure). Let $\angle APB = 2\theta$. Then $\angle ACB = \pi - 2\theta$. Now area of ΔPAB and ΔCAB are

$$A_1 = \frac{1}{2} l^2 \sin(2\theta)$$

and $$A_2 = \frac{1}{2} r^2 \sin(\pi - 2\theta) = \frac{1}{2} r^2 \sin(2\theta).$$

Thus, the ratio of the two areas is

$$\frac{A_1}{A_2} = \frac{l^2}{r^2} = \cot^2\theta.$$

It is given that $\tan(2\theta) = \frac{12}{5}$. Then, we have

$$\frac{2\tan\theta}{1-\tan^2\theta}=\frac{12}{5}$$

$\Rightarrow \qquad 12\tan^2\theta+10\tan\theta-12=0$ gives $\tan\theta=\frac{2}{3}$

Hence, $\frac{A_1}{A_2}=\cot^2\theta=\frac{9}{4}$

104. (b) Equation of the tangent to the parabola $y^2=4x-20$ at the point $P(6,2)$ is

$$2y=2(x+6)-20$$

$$\Rightarrow \qquad y=x-4 \qquad (1)$$

Equation of any tangent to the ellipse $\frac{x^2}{2}+\frac{y^2}{b}=1$ is

$$y=mx\pm\sqrt{2m^2+b} \qquad (2)$$

For the two equations to be identical, we have

$$m=1 \text{ and } \sqrt{2m^2+b}=4.$$

Hence, $2+b=16\Rightarrow b=14$.

105. (a) We have

$$L=\lim_{x\to 0}\frac{\tan\left(\pi\cos^2\theta\right)}{\sin\left(2\pi\sin^2\theta\right)}\left(\frac{0}{0}\right)$$

$$=\lim_{x\to 0}\frac{\tan\left(\pi-\pi\sin^2\theta\right)}{\sin\left(2\pi\sin^2\theta\right)}$$

$$=\lim_{x\to 0}\frac{-\tan\left(\pi\sin^2\theta\right)}{\sin\left(2\pi\sin^2\theta\right)}$$

$$=\lim_{x\to 0}\frac{-\pi\sin^2\theta}{2\pi\sin^2\theta}=\frac{-1}{2}$$

$$\left[\sin\delta\sim\delta,\ \tan\delta\sim\delta \text{ if } \delta \text{ is small}\right]$$

106. (c)

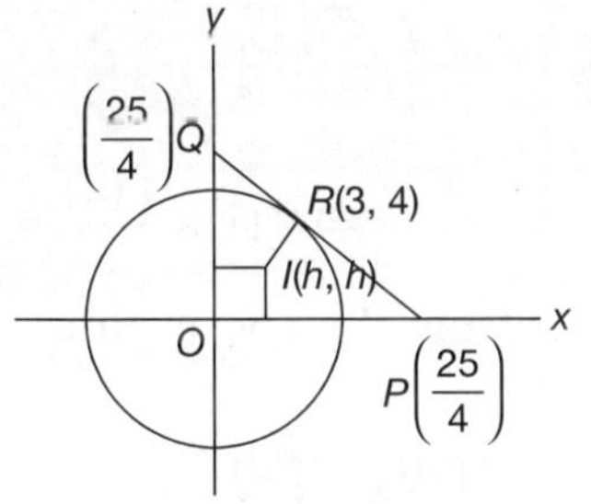

Equation of the tangent to the circle $x^2+y^2=25$ at the point $R(3,4)$ is

$$3x+4y=25 \qquad (1)$$

Its x- and y- intercepts are

$$P\left(\frac{25}{3},0\right) \text{ and } Q\left(\frac{25}{4},0\right)$$

The incentre I of ΔOPQ must be equidistant from its three sides. So let us choose its coordinates as $I(h,h)$. Now the distance of I from the tangent PQ must also be h. Thus, we have

$$\frac{|3h+4h-25|}{\sqrt{3^2+4^2}}=h$$

$\Rightarrow \qquad 7h-25=-5h$ gives $h=\frac{25}{12}$

$$\left[3h+4h-25<0 \text{ since } I \text{ lies below the tangent}\right]$$

The circle having radius at $I\left(\frac{25}{12},\frac{25}{12}\right)$ and passing through the origin O will have radius

$$r=OI=\frac{25\sqrt{2}}{12}$$

Hence, $r^2=\frac{625}{72}$.

107. (b) Let the image of the point $P(2,3,1)$ in the line $\frac{x+1}{2}=\frac{y-3}{1}=\frac{z+2}{-1}$ be the point $Q(u,v,w)$. Then PQ must be perpendicular to the line, that is

$$2(u-2)+1(v-3)-1(w-1)=0$$

$$\Rightarrow \qquad 2u+v-w=6 \qquad (1)$$

And the mid-point $M\left(\frac{u+2}{2},\frac{v+3}{2},\frac{w+1}{2}\right)$ must lie on the line, that is

$$\frac{\frac{u+2}{2}+1}{2}=\frac{\frac{v+3}{2}-3}{1}=\frac{\frac{w+1}{2}+2}{-1}$$

$$\Rightarrow \qquad \frac{u+4}{2}=\frac{v-3}{1}=\frac{w+5}{-1} \qquad (2)$$

From equation (2), we can choose $Q(u,v,w)=(2t-4,t+3,-t-5)$. Putting these values in equation (1), we have

$$2(2t-4)+(t+3)-(-t-5)=6$$

$\Rightarrow \qquad 6t=6$ gives $t=1$

Thus, we have the image point as $Q(-2,4,-6)$. Now equation of the plane which contains Q and also contains the line $\frac{x-2}{3}=\frac{y-1}{-2}=\frac{z+1}{1}$ is given by

$$\begin{vmatrix} x-2 & y-1 & z+1 \\ -2-2 & 4-1 & -6+1 \\ 3 & -2 & 1 \end{vmatrix} = 0$$

$$\Rightarrow \begin{vmatrix} x-2 & y-1 & z+1 \\ -4 & 3 & -5 \\ 3 & -2 & 1 \end{vmatrix} = 0$$

$$\Rightarrow \quad -7(x-2)-11(y-1)-(z+1)=0$$

$$\Rightarrow \quad 7x+11y+z=24$$

Thus $\alpha=7, \beta=11, \gamma=1$ and hence $\alpha+\beta+\gamma=19$.

108. (b) The given relation is $y=5^{\log x}$. Interchanging x, y gives the inverse relation as

$$x=5^{\log y}=y^{\log 5}\left[a^{\log b}=b^{\log a}\right]$$

109. (a) Equation of the normal to the circle at point $A(2,5)$ can be chosen as

$$x+2y=c$$

Since it passes through $A(2,5)$, $c=12$ and hence the equation of the normal is $x+2y=12$. Intersection of the normal and the line $x-2y=4$ gives the centre of the circle as $C(6,2)$. Hence, the radius of the circle is

$$CA=\sqrt{(6-2)^2+(2-5)^2}=\sqrt{45}=3\sqrt{5}$$

110. (a) Let the given expression be equal to x. Then, we have

$$\Rightarrow \quad x=4+\cfrac{1}{5+\cfrac{1}{x}}$$

$$\Rightarrow \quad x-4=\frac{x}{5x+1}$$

$$\Rightarrow \quad (x-4)(5x+1)=x$$

$$\Rightarrow \quad 5x^2-20x-4=0$$

$$\Rightarrow \quad x=\frac{20\pm\sqrt{480}}{10}=2+\frac{2}{5}\sqrt{30} \text{ [}x\text{ cannot be –ve]}$$

111. (d) We have

$$L=\lim_{x\to 0^+}\frac{\cos^{-1}\left(x-[x]^2\right)\sin^{-1}\left(x-[x]^2\right)}{x-x^3}\left(\frac{0}{0}\right)$$

$$=\lim_{x\to 0^+}\frac{\cos^{-1}x\sin^{-1}x}{x-x^3}$$

$$=\lim_{x\to 0^+}\frac{\sin^{-1}x}{x}\times\frac{\cos^{-1}x}{1-x^2}$$

$$=1\times\frac{\pi/2}{1}=\frac{\pi}{2}$$

112. (d) We have

$$I=\int_1^2\frac{e}{e^{x-1}}dx+\int_2^3\frac{2e^2}{e^{x-1}}dx+\int_1^2\frac{3e^3}{e^{x-1}}dx+\ldots$$

$$\ldots+\int_1^2\frac{9e^9}{e^{x-1}}dx$$

$$=\int_1^2 e^{2-x}dx+2\int_2^3 e^{3-x}dx+3\int_1^2 e^{4-x}dx+\ldots$$

$$\ldots+9\int_1^2 e^{9-x}dx$$

Putting $2-x=t$ in the first integral, $3-x=t$ in the second integral, and so on, we have

$$I=\int_0^1 e^t dt+2\int_0^1 e^t dt+3\int_0^1 e^t dt+\ldots+9\int_0^1 e^t dt$$

$$=45\int_0^1 e^t dt=45(e-1)$$

113. (b) We have

$$f'(x)=\lim_{h\to 0}\frac{f(x+h)-f(x)}{h}$$

$$=\lim_{h\to 0}\frac{\frac{f(x+h)}{f(x)}-1}{h}\times f(x)$$

$$=\lim_{h\to 0}\frac{f\left(\frac{x+h}{h}\right)-1}{h}\times f(x)$$

$$\left[\text{Given } f\left(\frac{x}{y}\right)=\frac{f(x)}{f(y)}\right]$$

$$=\lim_{h\to 0}\frac{f\left(1+\frac{h}{x}\right)-1}{\frac{h}{x}}\times\frac{f(x)}{x}$$

$$=f'(1)\times\frac{f(x)}{x}=\frac{3f(x)}{x}$$

Now solving the above differential equation, we have

$$\int\frac{df}{f}-3\int\frac{dx}{x}=0$$

$$\Rightarrow \quad \ln f-3\ln x=\text{constant}$$

$\Rightarrow \quad \ln\left(\frac{f}{x^3}\right) = \text{constant}$

$\Rightarrow \quad f(x) = Cx^3$

It is given that $f'(1) = 3$; therefore $C = 1$ and $f(x) = x^3$.

Hence, $f(-1) = -1$.

Alternative. The property $\left(\frac{x}{y}\right) = \frac{f(x)}{f(y)}$ is satisfied by the family of functions $f(x) = x^n$.

It is given that $f'(1) = 3$, and therefore $C = 1$ and $f(x) = x^3$.

Hence, $f(-1) = -1$.

114. (d) The given differential equation can be written as

$$\frac{dy}{dx} = (y+1)^2 e^{\frac{x^2}{2}} - x(y+1)$$

$$\Rightarrow \quad \frac{1}{(y+1)^2}\frac{dy}{dx} + \frac{x}{y+1} = e^{\frac{x^2}{2}}$$

Putting $\frac{1}{y+1} = u$ and $\frac{-1}{(y+1)^2}\frac{dy}{dx} = \frac{du}{dx}$, it reduces to

$$\frac{du}{dx} - xu = -e^{\frac{x^2}{2}}$$

Now, we have $\text{I.F.} = e^{\int -x dx} = e^{\frac{-x^2}{2}}$. Thus, the solution is

$$ue^{\frac{-x^2}{2}} = -\int 1 dx + C$$

$$\Rightarrow \quad u = (C-x)e^{\frac{x^2}{2}}$$

$$\Rightarrow \quad \frac{1}{y+1} = (C-x)e^{\frac{x^2}{2}}$$

Using the condition $y(2) = 0$ gives

$$(C-2)e^2 = 1 \Rightarrow C = e^{-2} + 2.$$

Now the given differential equation can be written as

$$\frac{dy}{dx} = \frac{1}{(C-x)e^{\frac{x^2}{2}}}\left\{\frac{1}{(C-x)} - x\right\} \text{ where } C = e^{-2} + 2.$$

Hence, we have

$$y'(1) = \frac{1}{(C-1)e^{\frac{1}{2}}}\left\{\frac{1}{(C-1)} - 1\right\}$$

$$= \frac{1}{(e^{-2}+1)e^{\frac{1}{2}}}\left\{\frac{1}{(e^{-2}+1)} - 1\right\}$$

$$= \frac{e^2}{(1+e^2)e^{\frac{1}{2}}}\left\{\frac{e^2}{1+e^2} - 1\right\}$$

$$= \frac{e^{3/2}}{(1+e^2)}\left\{\frac{-1}{1+e^2}\right\} = \frac{-e^{3/2}}{(1+e^2)^2}$$

115. (c) The given relation is $y = \frac{x-2}{x-3}$. Interchanging x, y gives the inverse relation as

$$x = \frac{y-2}{y-3} \Rightarrow y = \frac{3x-2}{x-1}$$

Thus $\quad f^{-1}(x) = \frac{3x-2}{x-1}.$

Similarly, the other given relation is $y = 2x - 3$. Interchanging x, y gives the inverse relation as

$$x = 2y - 3 \Rightarrow y = \frac{x+3}{2}$$

Thus $\quad g^{-1}(x) = \frac{x+3}{2}.$

Now, we have

$$f^{-1}(x) + g^{-1}(x) = \frac{13}{2}$$

$$\Rightarrow \quad \frac{3x-2}{x-1} + \frac{x+3}{2} = \frac{13}{2}$$

$$\Rightarrow \quad 6x - 4 + x^2 + 2x - 3 = 13x - 13$$

$$\Rightarrow \quad x^2 - 5x + 6 = 0$$

Hence, sum of the roots = 5.

116. (c) Let $x = \cot y$. Then, we have

$$L = 6\lim_{y\to 0}\frac{\ln\left(\frac{y}{\tan y}\right)}{\tan^2 y}$$

$$= 6\lim_{y\to 0}\frac{\ln\left(1 + \frac{y - \tan y}{\tan y}\right)}{\frac{y - \tan y}{\tan y}} \times \frac{y - \tan y}{\tan^3 y}$$

$$= 6\lim_{\delta\to 0}\frac{\ln(1+\delta)}{\delta}\times\lim_{y\to 0}\frac{y-\tan y}{y^3}\times\frac{y^3}{\tan^3 y}$$

$$= 6\lim_{y\to 0}\frac{y-\tan y}{y^3}\left(\frac{0}{0}\right)$$

$$= 6\lim_{y\to 0}\frac{1-\sec^2 y}{3y^2} \quad \text{[Using L'Hospital's rule]}$$

$$= 2\lim_{y\to 0}\frac{\cos^2 y-1}{y^2}\times\frac{1}{\cos^2 y}$$

$$= 2\times\frac{-1}{2}\times 1 = -1$$

117. (d) The function $F(x)$ can be written as

$$F(x)=\begin{cases}\int_{-1}^{x} 0\,dx, & -1\le x<0\\ \int_{-1}^{0} 0\,dx+\int_{0}^{x} 2\,dx, & 0<x\le 1\end{cases}$$

$$\Rightarrow \quad F(x)=\begin{cases}0, -1\le x<0\\ 2x, 0<x\le 1\end{cases}$$

Differentiating with respect to x, we have

$$F'(x)=\begin{cases}0, -1<x<0\\ 2, 0<x<1\end{cases}$$

We can see that F is continuous everywhere but not differentiable at $x=0$.

Numerical Value Answer

1. The AP and GP are

AP : 11, 16, 21, 26, ………, 9996

and GP : 4, 8, 16, 32, 64, 128, 256, 1012, 2024, 2048, 4096, 8152.

The general term for the arithmetic and the geometric progression are

$$\text{AP}: a_n = 11+5(n-1) = 5n+6$$

and $$\text{GP}: g_m = 4\times 2^{m-1} = 2^{m+1}$$

The terms will be common if

$g_m = 5n+6 \Rightarrow$ terms of the GP having last digit 1 or 6

$\Rightarrow$ 16, 256, 4096

Hence, three common terms.

2. The given infinite series can be written as

$$S = 2\int_0^1 \log_2\left(1+\tan\frac{\pi x}{4}\right)dx$$

$$= \frac{8}{\pi}\int_0^{\pi/4}\log_2(1+\tan t)\,dt \quad \left[\text{Putting } \frac{\pi x}{4}=t\right]$$

From the property of definite integrals, we also have

$$S = \frac{8}{\pi}\int_0^{\pi/4}\log_2\left(1+\tan\left(\frac{\pi}{4}-t\right)\right)dt$$

$$= \frac{8}{\pi}\int_0^{\pi/4}\log_2\left(1+\frac{1-\tan t}{1+\tan t}\right)dt$$

$$= \frac{8}{\pi}\int_0^{\pi/4}\log_2\left(\frac{2}{1+\tan t}\right)dt$$

Adding the two results, we have

$$2S = \frac{8}{\pi}\int_0^{\pi/4}\left(\log_2(1+\tan t)+\log_2\left(\frac{2}{1+\tan t}\right)\right)dt$$

$$\Rightarrow \quad 2S = \frac{8}{\pi}\int_0^{\pi/4}\log_2 2\,dt = \frac{8}{\pi}\times\frac{\pi}{4} = 2$$

$$\Rightarrow \quad S = 1.$$

3.

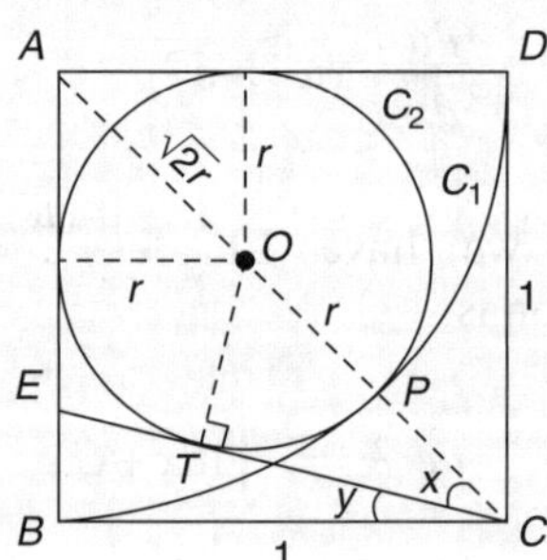

Let O be the centre and r be the radius of circle C_2 (see figure).

Then $AO=\sqrt{2}r, OP=r$. Thus, we have

$$AO+OP=AP$$

$$\Rightarrow \quad \sqrt{2}r+r=1$$

$$\Rightarrow \quad r=\frac{1}{\sqrt{2}+1}=\sqrt{2}-1$$

Also $AC=\sqrt{2}$ and hence

$$CO = AC-\sqrt{2}r = \sqrt{2}-\sqrt{2}(\sqrt{2}-1) = 2(\sqrt{2}-1)$$

In triangle ΔCOT, let $\angle TOC = x$. Then, we have

$$\sin x = \frac{OT}{CO} = \frac{r}{2\left(\sqrt{2}-1\right)} = \frac{1}{2} \Rightarrow x = 30°$$

Then $\angle EOB = y = 45° - 30°$. Hence, we have

$$EB = BC \times \tan y = 1 \times \tan(45° - 30°)$$

$$= \frac{1 - \dfrac{1}{\sqrt{3}}}{1 + \dfrac{1}{\sqrt{3}}} = \frac{\sqrt{3}-1}{\sqrt{3}+1} = 2 - \sqrt{3}$$

Hence $\alpha = 2, \beta = -1 \Rightarrow \alpha + \beta = 1$.

4. From the given definite integral, we have

$$y = \frac{2}{3}x^3 - \frac{15}{2}x^2 + 10x$$

Differentiating the above equation, we have

$$y' = 2x^2 - 15x + 10$$

It is given that point (a, b) lies on the above curve, and slope of the normal at (a, b) is $\frac{-1}{3}$. Thus, we have

$$b = \frac{2}{3}a^3 - \frac{15}{2}a^2 + 10a \quad (1)$$

and $$3 = 2a^2 - 15a + 10 \quad (2)$$

From equation (2), we have

$$2a^2 - 15a + 7 = 0 \text{ gives } a = \frac{1}{2}, 7$$

Only $a = 7$ is the acceptable solution since it is given that $a > 1$. Putting this value in equation (1) gives $6b = 4a^3 - 45a^2 + 60a = -413$.

Hence, $|a + 6b| = |7 - 413| = 406$.

5. The general solution of the given differential equation is

$$y = x^2 + 2x + C$$

Its graph is a concave upward parabola (see figure) having x-intercepts, say $x = a, b\,(b > a)$.

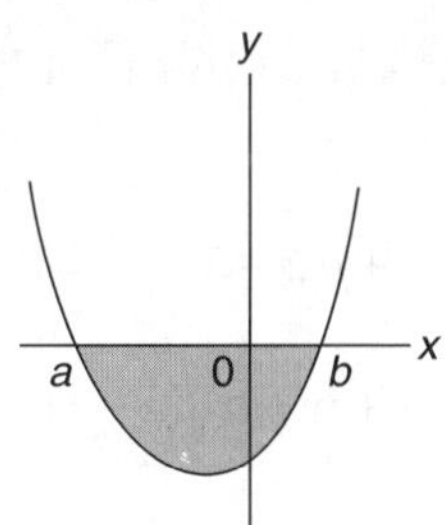

Area of the shaded region is given to be $\frac{4\sqrt{8}}{3}$. Thus, we have

$$-\int_a^b \left(x^2 + 2x + C\right)dx = \frac{4\sqrt{8}}{3}$$

$$\Rightarrow \quad \frac{b^3 - a^3}{3} + b^2 - a^2 + C(b - a) = -\frac{4\sqrt{8}}{3}$$

$$\Rightarrow \quad (b - a)\left[\left(a^2 + b^2 + ab\right) + 3(a + b) + 3C\right] = -4\sqrt{8}$$

Since a, b are the roots of the equation $x^2 + 2x + C = 0$

$$a + b = -2, ab = C. \text{ Then}$$

$$a^2 + b^2 = (a + b)^2 - 2ab = 4 - 2C$$

and $b - a = \sqrt{(a + b)^2 - 4ab} = \sqrt{4 - 4C} = 2\sqrt{1 - C}$

Putting these values in the above equation, we have

$$\Rightarrow \quad 2\sqrt{1 - C}\left[(4 - C) - 6 + 3C\right] = -4\sqrt{8}$$

$$\Rightarrow \quad 2\sqrt{1 - C}\,(2C - 2) = -4\sqrt{8}$$

$$\Rightarrow \quad \sqrt{1 - C}\,(1 - C) = 2\sqrt{2} \text{ gives } C = -1$$

Thus, the particular solution is $y = x^2 + 2x - 1$ and hence $y(1) = 2$.

6. Given $f(x) + f(x + 1) = 2 \quad (1)$

Putting $x - 1$ in place of x, it reduces to

$$f(x - 1) + f(x) = 2 \quad (2)$$

Subtracting the two equations, we have

$$f(x - 1) = f(x + 1)$$

$$\Rightarrow \quad f(x) = f(x + 2) \text{ [Putting } x + 1 \text{ in place of } x]$$

$$\Rightarrow \quad f(x) \text{ has period 2}$$

The given integrals can now be written as

$$I_1 = \int_0^8 f(x)dx = 4\int_0^2 f(x)dx$$

and $I_2 = \int_{-1}^3 f(x)dx = 2\int_0^2 f(x)dx$

Thus, we have

$$I_1 + 2I_2 = 8\int_0^2 f(x)dx$$

Now, we have

$$\int_0^2 f(x)dx = \int_0^1 f(x)dx + \int_1^2 f(x)dx$$

$$= \int_0^1 f(x)dx + \int_0^1 f(t+1)dt$$

[Put $x-1=t$]

$$= \int_0^1 \{f(x)+f(x+1)\}dx$$

$$= \int_0^1 2dx = 2$$

Hence, $I_1 + 2I_2 = 8\times 2 = 16$.

7. The given equation $\left|\frac{z+i}{z-3i}\right| = 1$ can be simplified as

$$|x+i(y+1)| = |x+i(y-3)|$$

$$\Rightarrow \quad x^2+(y+1)^2 = x^2+(y-3)^2$$

$$\Rightarrow \quad 2y+1 = -6y+9 \Rightarrow y=1$$

Simplifying the given expression $w = z\bar{z} - 2z + 2$, we have

$$w = x^2+y^2-2x+2-i(2y)$$

$$= x^2-2x+3+2i \text{ [Putting } y=1]$$

Now $\text{Re}(w) = x^2-2x+3 = (x-1)^2+2$ has a minimum value 2. Thus

$$w = 2-2i = 2\sqrt{2}e^{-i(\pi/4)}$$

Now $w^n = (2\sqrt{2})^n e^{-i(n\pi/4)}$. For w^n to be real, its argument should be a multiple of π. Hence, the minimum natural value of n for w^n to be real is 4.

8. Let $P(B_1) = x, P(B_2) = y$ and $P(B_3) = z$. Then, we have

$$x(1-y)(1-z) = \alpha, \quad (1)$$

$$y(1-x)(1-z) = \beta \quad (2)$$

$$z(1-x)(1-y) = \gamma \quad (3)$$

and $\quad (1-x)(1-y)(1-z) = p \quad (4)$

Putting the above results in the given relations $(\alpha-2\beta)p = \alpha\beta$ and $(\alpha-3\gamma)p = 2\beta\gamma$, we have $x = 2y$ and $y = 3z$. Hence, we have $x = 6z \Rightarrow \frac{x}{z} = 6$.

9. Let $\quad \mathbf{c} = m\mathbf{a}+n\mathbf{b} = (-m+2n)\mathbf{i}+(m)\mathbf{j}+(m+n)\mathbf{k}$.

Then, we have

$$\mathbf{a}\cdot\mathbf{c} = 7$$

$$\Rightarrow \quad m-2n+m+m+n = 7$$

$$\Rightarrow \quad 3m-n = 7 \quad (1)$$

and $\quad \mathbf{b}\cdot\mathbf{c} = 7$

$$\Rightarrow \quad -2m+4n+m+n = 7$$

$$\Rightarrow \quad m = 5n \quad (2)$$

Solving equations (1) and (2) gives $m = 5/2$ and $n = 1/2$, Thus

$$\mathbf{c} = \frac{-3}{2}\mathbf{i}+\frac{5}{2}\mathbf{j}+3\mathbf{k}$$

Hence, we have

$$2|\mathbf{a}+\mathbf{b}+\mathbf{c}|^2 = 2\left|\frac{-1}{2}\mathbf{i}+\frac{7}{2}\mathbf{j}+5\mathbf{k}\right|^2$$

$$= 2\left(\frac{1}{4}+\frac{49}{4}+25\right) = 75$$

10. We have $PQ = kI \Rightarrow Q = kP^{-1} = \frac{k}{|P|}\text{adj}.P$. Thus

$$Q = \frac{k}{12\alpha+20}\begin{bmatrix} \cdots & \cdots & \cdots \\ \cdots & \cdots & -(3\alpha+4) \\ \cdots & \cdots & \cdots \end{bmatrix}.$$

Since $q_{23} = \frac{-k}{8}$

$$\frac{-k(3\alpha+4)}{12\alpha+20} = \frac{-k}{8}$$

$$\Rightarrow \quad 2(3\alpha+4) = 3\alpha+5 \text{ gives } \alpha = -1.$$

Also $|Q| = \frac{k^2}{2}$, therefore

$$|Q| = \frac{k^2}{2}$$

$$\Rightarrow \quad \frac{k^3}{|P|} = \frac{k^2}{2}$$

$$\Rightarrow \quad k = \frac{1}{2}(12\alpha+20) = 4.$$

Hence, $k^2+\alpha^2 = 16+1 = 17$.

11. We have

$$z+\alpha|z-1|+2i = 0$$

$$\Rightarrow \quad x+iy+\alpha\sqrt{(x-1)^2+y^2}+2i = 0$$

$$\Rightarrow \quad x+\alpha\sqrt{(x-1)^2+y^2}=0 \text{ and } y+2=0$$

$$\Rightarrow \quad x^2=\alpha^2\left\{(x-1)^2+4\right\} \text{ and } y=-2$$

$$\Rightarrow \quad x^2=\alpha^2\left(x^2-2x+5\right) \text{ and } y=-2$$

Thus, we have

$$\alpha^2=\frac{x^2}{x^2-2x+5}$$

$$\Rightarrow \quad \frac{d\left(\alpha^2\right)}{dx}=\frac{\left(x^2-2x+5\right)2x-x^2(2x-2)}{\left(x^2-2x+5\right)^2}$$

$$=\frac{-2x(x-5)}{\left(x^2-2x+5\right)^2}$$

– + –
0 5

From the sign scheme, we see that α^2 decreases in $(-\infty,0)$, then increases in $(0,5)$, and then again increases in $(0,+\infty)$. Now

$$\lim_{x\to\infty}\alpha^2=1, \alpha^2(0)=0, \text{ and } \alpha^2(5)=\frac{5}{4}$$

Thus, $\alpha^2\in\left[0,\frac{5}{4}\right]\Rightarrow\alpha\in\left[\frac{-\sqrt{5}}{2},\frac{\sqrt{5}}{2}\right]$.

Hence, we have

$$4\left[\alpha_{max}^2+\alpha_{min}^2\right]=4\left(\frac{5}{4}+\frac{5}{4}\right)=10$$

12. We have

$$A\cap B=\{\text{3-digit numbers of the form } 9k+2\}$$
$$=\{101,110,119,\ldots,992\}$$

and $A\cap C=\{\text{3-digit numbers of the form } 9k+l\}$

$$=\{99+l,108+l,117+l,\ldots,990+l\}$$

Thus, we have

$$n(A\cap B)=100\left(\frac{101+992}{2}\right)=50\times1093$$

and

$$n(A\cap C)=100\left(\frac{99+l+990+l}{2}\right)=50\times(1089+2l)$$

Note that $A\cap B$ and $A\cap C$ are disjoint sets. Thus, we have

$$n\{A\cap(B\cup C)\}=n\{(A\cap B)\cup(A\cap C)\}$$
$$=n(A\cap B)+n(A\cap C)$$
$$=50\times(2182+2l)$$

Using the given condition, we have

$$50\times(2182+2l)=274\times400 \text{ gives } l=5.$$

13. Let $f(t)=\frac{4}{t}+\frac{1}{1-t}=\frac{4-3t}{t-t^2}$ where $t=\sin x$. Then, we have

$$f'(t)=\frac{-3\left(t-t^2\right)-(1-2t)(4-3t)}{\left(t-t^2\right)^2}$$

$$=\frac{-\left(3t^2-8t+4\right)}{\left(t-t^2\right)^2}=\frac{-3\left(t-\frac{2}{3}\right)(t-2)}{\left(t-t^2\right)^2}$$

– + –
2/3 2

According to the question, $x\in\left[0,\frac{\pi}{2}\right]\Rightarrow t\in[0,1]$.

From the sign scheme, we see that in this interval of t, the function $f(t)$ has a minima at $t=\frac{2}{3}$. Thus, we have

$$f_{min}=f\left(\frac{2}{3}\right)=\frac{4-3\left(\frac{2}{3}\right)}{\left(\frac{2}{3}\right)-\left(\frac{2}{3}\right)^2}=9$$

Hence, α should be at least equal to 9.

14. The given integral

$$\int_{-a}^{a}\left(|x|+|x-2|\right)dx=22, a>2 \text{ reduces to}$$

$$\int_{-a}^{0}(-2x+2)dx+\int_{0}^{2}(2)dx+\int_{2}^{a}(2x-2)dx=22$$

$$\Rightarrow \quad \left|-x^2+2x\right|_{-a}^{0}+\left|2x\right|_{9}^{2}+\left|x^2-2x\right|_{2}^{a}=22$$

$$\Rightarrow \quad a^2+2a+4+a^2-2a=22$$

$$\Rightarrow \quad a^2=9 \text{ gives } a=3$$

Thus, we have

$$\int_{-3}^{3}(x+[x])dx=\int_{-3}^{3}x\,dx+\int_{-3}^{3}[x]dx$$

$$=0+[-3-2-1+0+1+2]=-3$$

15. We have

$$af(x)+\alpha f\left(\frac{1}{x}\right)=bx+\frac{\beta}{x} \qquad (1)$$

Putting x in place of $1/x$, we have

$$af\left(\frac{1}{x}\right)+\alpha f(x)=\frac{b}{x}+\beta x \quad (2)$$

Now adding equations (1) and (2), we have

$$(a+\alpha)\left\{f(x)+f\left(\frac{1}{x}\right)\right\}=(b+\beta)\left\{x+\frac{1}{x}\right\}$$

$$\Rightarrow \quad \frac{f(x)+\frac{1}{f(x)}}{x+\frac{1}{x}}=\frac{b+\beta}{a+\alpha}=2$$

16. Given $\sigma^2<10$. Thus, we have

$$\frac{\sum x^2}{N}-\left(\frac{\sum x}{N}\right)^2<10$$

$$\Rightarrow \quad \frac{9+k^2}{10}-\left(\frac{9+k}{10}\right)^2<10$$

$$\Rightarrow \quad (90+10k^2)-(k^2+18k+81)<1000$$

$$\Rightarrow \quad (k-1)^2<\frac{1000}{9}$$

$$\Rightarrow \quad k<1+\frac{10\sqrt{10}}{3}=11.54$$

Hence, maximum integral value of k is 11.

17. We have

$$\sqrt{(x-5)^2+y^2}=3\sqrt{(x+5)^2+y^2}$$

$$\Rightarrow \quad x^2+y^2-10x+25=9\{x^2+y^2+10x+25\}$$

$$\Rightarrow \quad 8x^2+8y^2+100x+200=0$$

$$\Rightarrow \quad x^2+y^2+\frac{25}{2}x+25=0$$

Thus, the locus of P is a circle at centre $\left(\frac{-25}{4},0\right)$ and radius $=\sqrt{\left(\frac{25}{4}\right)^2-25}=\frac{15}{4}$.

Hence, $4r^2=4\left(\frac{15}{4}\right)^2=56.25$.

18. Let the four numbers be a, ar, ar^2, ar^3. Then, we have

$$a+ar+ar^2+ar^3=\frac{65}{12} \quad (1)$$

$$\frac{1}{a}+\frac{1}{ar}+\frac{1}{ar^2}+\frac{1}{ar^3}=\frac{65}{18}$$

$$\Rightarrow \quad \frac{1+r+r^2+r^3}{ar^3}=\frac{65}{18} \quad (2)$$

and $\quad a^3r^3=1 \quad (3)$

Dividing equation (1) by equation (2), we have

$$a^2r^3=\frac{3}{2} \quad (4)$$

Solving equations (3) and (4), we get $a=\frac{2}{3}$ and $=\frac{3}{2}$.

Hence, $2\alpha=2ar^2=2\left(\frac{2}{3}\right)\left(\frac{3}{2}\right)^2=3$.

19. When G_3 has 1 member, the groups G_1, G_2 can have any of the following pairs of members: $(1,8),(2,7),\ldots,(8,1)$. Number of such groups is

$$N_1={}^{10}C_1\left({}^9C_1+{}^9C_2+{}^9C_3+\ldots+{}^9C_8\right)$$
$$=10(2^9-2)=10\times 510=5100$$

When G_3 has 2 members, the groups G_1, G_2 can have any of the following pairs of members: $(1,7),(2,6),\ldots,(7,1)$. Number of such groups is

$$N_2={}^{10}C_2\left({}^8C_1+{}^8C_2+{}^8C_3+\ldots+{}^8C_7\right)$$
$$=45(2^8-2)=45\times 254=11430$$

When G_3 has 3 members, the groups G_1, G_2 can have any of the following pairs of members: $(1,6),(2,5),\ldots,(6,1)$. Number of such groups is

$$N_3={}^{10}C_3\left({}^7C_1+{}^7C_2+{}^7C_3+\ldots+{}^7C_6\right)$$
$$=120(2^7-2)=120\times 126=15120.$$

Hence, total number of such groups is $N_1+N_2+N_3=31650$.

20.

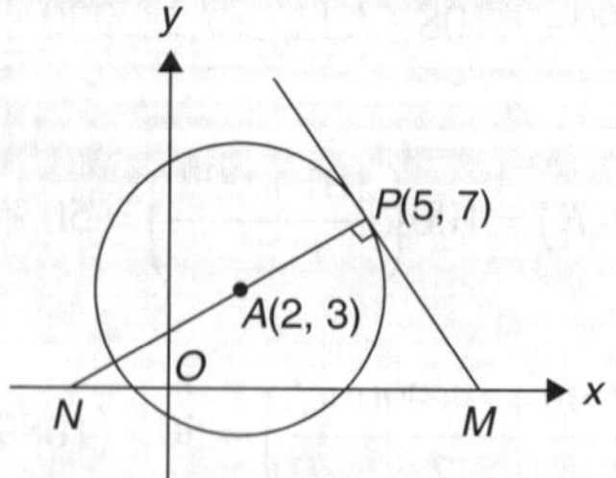

Equation of the tangent at $P(5,7)$ is

$$(x-2)(5-2)+(y-3)(7-3)=25$$

$$\Rightarrow \quad 3x+4y-43=0$$

Equation of the normal at $P(5,7)$ is

$$y-7=\frac{4}{3}(x-5)$$

$\Rightarrow \quad 4x-3y+1=0$

The x-intercepts of the tangent and the normal are $M\left(\frac{43}{3},0\right)$ and $N\left(\frac{-1}{4},0\right)$. Now, area of the triangle ΔPMN is

$$\lambda=\frac{1}{2}\times MN\times 7=\frac{1}{2}\times\left(\frac{43}{3}+\frac{1}{4}\right)\times 7=\frac{1225}{24}$$

Hence, $24\lambda=1225$.

21. We have

$$[A]^2=\begin{bmatrix} x & y & z\\ y & z & x\\ z & x & y\end{bmatrix}\begin{bmatrix} x & y & z\\ y & z & x\\ z & x & y\end{bmatrix}$$

$$=\begin{bmatrix} x^2+y^2+z^2 & xy+yz+zx & xy+yz+zx\\ xy+yz+zx & x^2+y^2+z^2 & xy+yz+zx\\ xy+yz+zx & xy+yz+zx & x^2+y^2+z^2\end{bmatrix}$$

Given $[A]^2=I$, we have

$$x^2+y^2+z^2=1 \text{ and } xy+yz+zx=0$$

Now, we have

$$(x+y+z)^2=x^2+y^2+z^2+2(xy+yz+zx)=1$$

$\Rightarrow \quad x+y+z=1$ [since $x+y+z>0$]

Now, we have

$$(x+y+z)^3=x^3+y^3+z^3+3(xy+yz+zx)(x+y+z)-3xyz$$

$\Rightarrow \quad 1=x^3+y^3+z^3-6$ [$xyz=2$, given]

$\Rightarrow \quad x^3+y^3+z^3=7$

22. For the given inequality to be true, the discriminant must be negative. That is

$$4(3k-1)^2-4\left(8k^2-7\right)<0$$

$\Rightarrow \quad k^2-6k+8<0$

$\Rightarrow \quad (k-4)(k-2)<0$

$\Rightarrow \quad 2<k<4$

Hence the integral value of k is 3.

23. The probability of any one missile hitting the target is

$$P(\text{hitting target})=P(\text{not intercepted})\times P(\text{hitting}\mid\text{not intercepted})$$

$$=\frac{2}{3}\times\frac{3}{4}=\frac{1}{2}$$

Hence, probability of all three missiles hitting the target $=\left(\frac{1}{2}\right)^3=0.125$.

24. We have to form numbers lying between 100 and 1000, meaning three-digit numbers.

Case I: Numbers divisible by 5 must have 5 in the units place. The remaining two places can be filled using 1, 2, 3, 4 in ${}^4C_2\times 2!=12$ ways.

Case II: Numbers divisible by 3 must have digits that add up to multiples of 3. The possible options are

sum of digits 6: (1,2,3)

sum of digits 9: (2,3,4),(1,3,5)

sum of digits 12: (3,4,5)

Thus, the total number of numbers divisible by 3 is $4\times 3!=24$. But note that out of these 24 numbers that are divisible by 3, there are $2\times 2!=4$ numbers which are also divisible by 5.

Hence, the required number is $12+24-4=32$.

25. We have

$$S=\sum_{k=0}^{30}(30-k)\,{}^{30}C_k$$

$$=\sum_{r=0}^{30} r\,{}^{30}C_{30-r} \quad [\text{Putting } 30-k=r]$$

$$=\sum_{r=0}^{30} r\,{}^{30}C_r$$

Now, we have

$$(1+x)^{30}=\sum_{r=0}^{30}{}^{30}C_r x^r$$

and $30(1+x)^{29}=\sum_{r=0}^{30} r\,{}^{30}C_r x^{r-1}$ [Differentiating]

Now, putting $x=1$ gives $S=30\cdot 2^{29}$

Thus, $n=39, m=29$ and hence $m+n=59$

26. The given equation can be written as

$$(x-1)\left(x^2-x+1\right)=0$$

$\Rightarrow \quad x=1,-\omega,-\omega^2$

Hence, we have

$$S=1^{162}+(-\omega)^{162}+\left(-\omega^2\right)^{162}$$

$$=1+\left(\omega^3\right)^{54}+\left(\omega^3\right)^{108}=1+1+1=3$$

27. The figure shows the graph of the curve $y = ||x-1|-2|$

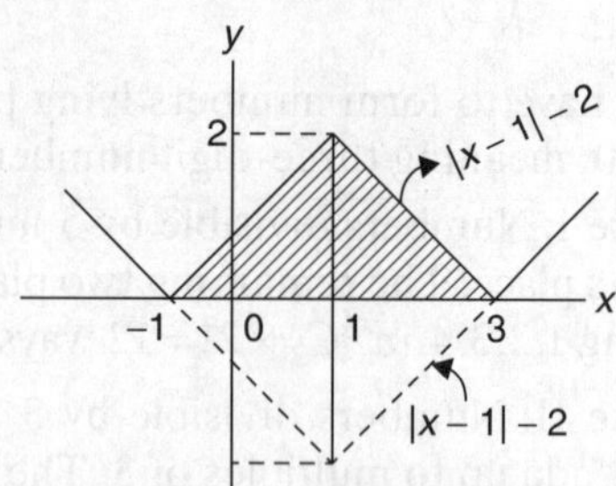

Hence, area of the shaded region is

$$\text{Area} = \frac{1}{2}\times 4\times 2 = 4.$$

28. Solving the given equation, we have

$$\cos x = \frac{(\sqrt{3}-1)\pm\sqrt{(\sqrt{3}-1)^2+4\sqrt{3}}}{2\sqrt{3}}$$

$$= \frac{(\sqrt{3}-1)\pm(\sqrt{3}+1)}{2\sqrt{3}} = \frac{-1}{\sqrt{3}}, 1.$$

Since $x \in \left(0, \frac{\pi}{2}\right)$, the only acceptable solution is $\cos x = 1$. Hence, $x = 0$ is the only solution.

29.

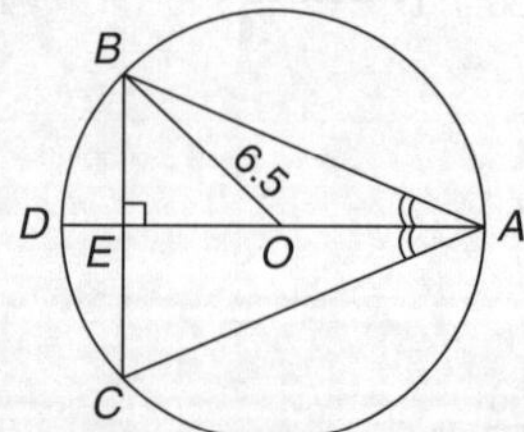

Let O be the midpoint of AD. Since AD bisects $\angle BAC$ and is perpendicular to BC, $BE = CE$. This means that AD is the perpendicular bisector of chord BC. Thus, AD is a diameter and O is the centre of the circle.

Then $OB = OD = \frac{13}{2} = 6.5$ and

$$OE = OD - DE = 6.5 - 1 = 5.5$$

$$\Rightarrow \quad BE = \sqrt{6.5^2 - 5.5^2} = 2\sqrt{3}$$

Hence, area of triangle ΔABC is

$$\text{Area} = \frac{1}{2}\times AE\times BC = \frac{1}{2}\times(5.5+6.5)\times 4\sqrt{3}$$

$$= 24\sqrt{3} = 41.56$$

30. The given equation is

$$y^2 = a\left(x+\sqrt{a}\right) \quad (1)$$

Differentiating the above equation, we have

$$2yy' = a \quad (2)$$

Now eliminating a from equations (1) and (2), we have

$$y^2 = 2yy'\left(x+\sqrt{2yy'}\right)$$

$$\Rightarrow \quad y - 2xy' = 2y'\sqrt{2yy'}$$

$$\Rightarrow \quad (y-2xy')^2 = 8y(y')^3$$

The above differential equation is of order 1 and degree 3. Hence, the difference between them is 2.

31. The direction ratios of lines AB and PQ are $1, 6, -2$ and $\lambda - 4, 4, -1$.

Since they are perpendicular, we have

$$\lambda - 4 + 24 + 2 = 0 \text{ gives } \lambda = -22$$

$$\text{Hence, } \left(\frac{\lambda}{11}\right)^2 - \frac{4\lambda}{11} - 4 = 4 + 8 - 4 = 8.$$

32. We have $\frac{dN}{dt} = \lambda N$

$$\Rightarrow \quad N = N_0 e^{\lambda t} = 1000 e^{\lambda t}$$

At $t = 2$, it is given that $N = 1.2N_0 = 1200$. Thus, we have

$$1200 = 1000e^{2\lambda} \text{ gives } = \frac{\ln(6/5)}{2}$$

Now it is given that $N = 2000$ at time $= \frac{k}{\ln(5/6)}$. Thus, we have

$$2000 = 1000e^{\lambda t}$$

$$\Rightarrow \quad \lambda t = \ln 2$$

$$\Rightarrow \quad \frac{\ln(6/5)}{2}\times\frac{k}{\ln(5/6)} = \ln 2$$

$$\Rightarrow \quad \frac{k}{\ln 2} = -2$$

$$\text{Hence, } \left(\frac{k}{\ln 2}\right)^2 = 4$$

33. We have $\mathbf{a}\times\mathbf{b} = \mathbf{b}\times\mathbf{c}$

$$\Rightarrow \quad (\mathbf{a}\times\mathbf{b}) + (\mathbf{c}\times\mathbf{b}) = 0$$

$$\Rightarrow \quad (\mathbf{a}+\mathbf{c})\times\mathbf{b} = 0$$

$$\Rightarrow \quad \mathbf{a}+\mathbf{c} = l\mathbf{b}$$

$$\Rightarrow \quad \mathbf{a}+\mathbf{b}+\mathbf{c} = (l+1)\mathbf{b} \quad (1)$$

Similarly, we have

$$\mathbf{b}\times\mathbf{c} = \mathbf{c}\times\mathbf{a}$$

$\Rightarrow \quad (\mathbf{b}\times\mathbf{c})+(\mathbf{a}\times\mathbf{c})=0$

$\Rightarrow \quad (\mathbf{a}+\mathbf{b})\times\mathbf{c}=0$

$\Rightarrow \quad \mathbf{a}+\mathbf{b}+\mathbf{c}=(m+1)\mathbf{c}$ (2)

and $\quad \mathbf{c}\times\mathbf{a}=\mathbf{a}\times\mathbf{b}$

$\Rightarrow \quad (\mathbf{c}\times\mathbf{a})+(\mathbf{b}\times\mathbf{a})=0$

$\Rightarrow \quad (\mathbf{b}+\mathbf{c})\times\mathbf{a}=0$

$\Rightarrow \quad \mathbf{b}+\mathbf{c}=n\mathbf{a}$

$\Rightarrow \quad \mathbf{a}+\mathbf{b}+\mathbf{c}=(n+1)\mathbf{a}$ (3)

Equation (1) implies $\mathbf{a}+\mathbf{b}+\mathbf{c}$ is parallel to vector $\mathbf{b}$. Equation (1) implies $\mathbf{a}+\mathbf{b}+\mathbf{c}$ is parallel to vector $\mathbf{b}$. Equation (2) implies $\mathbf{a}+\mathbf{b}+\mathbf{c}$ is parallel to vector $\mathbf{c}$. Equation (3) implies $\mathbf{a}+\mathbf{b}+\mathbf{c}$ is parallel to vector $\mathbf{a}$. Since $\mathbf{a},\mathbf{b},\mathbf{c}$ are given to be non-collinear, this is possible only if $\mathbf{a}+\mathbf{b}+\mathbf{c}=0$.

34. Equation of a general tangent to the ellipse $\frac{x^2}{9}+\frac{y^2}{4}=1$ is

$$y=mx\pm\sqrt{9m^2+4} \quad (1)$$

Equation of a general tangent to the circle $x^2+y^2=\frac{31}{4}$ is

$$y=mx\pm\sqrt{\frac{31}{4}m^2+\frac{31}{4}} \quad (2)$$

The above equations will represent the same tangent if

$$9m^2+4=\frac{31}{4}m^2+\frac{31}{4} \text{ gives } m^2=3.$$

35. We have

$$A=\begin{bmatrix}1&0&0\\0&2&0\\3&0&-1\end{bmatrix}$$

$$A^2=\begin{bmatrix}1&0&0\\0&2&0\\3&0&-1\end{bmatrix}\begin{bmatrix}1&0&0\\0&2&0\\3&0&-1\end{bmatrix}=\begin{bmatrix}1&0&0\\0&4&0\\0&0&1\end{bmatrix}$$

$$A^3=\begin{bmatrix}1&0&0\\0&2&0\\3&0&-1\end{bmatrix}\begin{bmatrix}1&0&0\\0&4&0\\0&0&1\end{bmatrix}=\begin{bmatrix}1&0&0\\0&8&0\\0&0&-1\end{bmatrix}$$

$$A^4=\begin{bmatrix}1&0&0\\0&2&0\\3&0&-1\end{bmatrix}\begin{bmatrix}1&0&0\\0&8&0\\0&0&-1\end{bmatrix}=\begin{bmatrix}1&0&0\\0&16&0\\0&0&1\end{bmatrix}$$

...

...

$$A^{19}=\begin{bmatrix}1&0&0\\0&2^{19}&0\\3&0&-1\end{bmatrix} \text{ and } A^{20}=\begin{bmatrix}1&0&0\\0&2^{20}&0\\3&0&1\end{bmatrix}$$

Now, we have

$$A^{20}+\alpha A^{19}+\beta A=$$

$$\begin{bmatrix}1+\alpha+\beta&0&0\\0&2^{20}+\alpha 2^{19}+2\beta&0\\3\alpha+3\beta&0&1-\alpha-\beta\end{bmatrix}$$

Comparing it with $\begin{bmatrix}1&0&0\\0&4&0\\0&0&1\end{bmatrix}$, we have

$$\alpha+\beta=0 \text{ and } 2^{20}+\alpha 2^{19}+2\beta=4$$

Solving the above equations, we have

$$2^{20}+\alpha\left(2^{19}-2\right)=4$$

$$\Rightarrow \quad \alpha=\frac{4-2^{20}}{2^{19}-1}=-2 \text{ and } \beta=2$$

Hence, $\alpha-\beta=-4$.

36. Let $P(h,k)$ be any point on the curve and p be the slope of the tangent to the curve at point P. Then equation of the normal to the curve at point P is

$$y-k=\frac{-1}{p}(x-h)$$

Since the normal passes through (a,b)

$$b-k=\frac{-1}{p}(a-h)$$

$$\Rightarrow \quad (k-b)p+h-a=0$$

Now, putting (x,y) in place of (h,k) and $\frac{dy}{dx}$ in place of p, we get the differential equation of the curve as

$$(y-b)\frac{dy}{dx}+x-a=0$$

Solving the differential equation, we have

$$(x-a)dx+(y-b)dy=0$$

$$\Rightarrow \quad \frac{1}{2}x^2-ax+\frac{1}{2}y^2-by+C=0$$

$$\Rightarrow \quad ax+by-C=\frac{x^2+y^2}{2}$$

Since the curve passes through $(3,-3)$ and $(4,-2\sqrt{2})$, we have

$$3a-3b-C=9 \quad (1)$$

and $$4a-2\sqrt{2}b-C=12 \quad (2)$$

Also, it is given that

$$a-2\sqrt{2}b=3 \quad (3)$$

Subtracting equation (1) from equation (2), we have

$$a+\left(3-2\sqrt{2}\right)b=3 \quad (4)$$

Solving equations (3) and (4) gives $a=3, b=0$. Hence, we have

$$a^2+b^2+ab=9$$

37. The inequality $|z+5|\le 4$ represents a point lying inside the circle centred at $z=-5$ and of radius equal to 4. Putting $z=x+iy$, the other inequality reduces to

$$(x+iy)(1+i)+(x-iy)(1-i)\ge -10$$

$$\Rightarrow \quad x-y+5\ge 0$$

$$\Rightarrow \quad y\le x+5$$

The above inequality represents points lying below the line $y=x+5$. The shaded region (see figure) represents points satisfying both the inequalities.

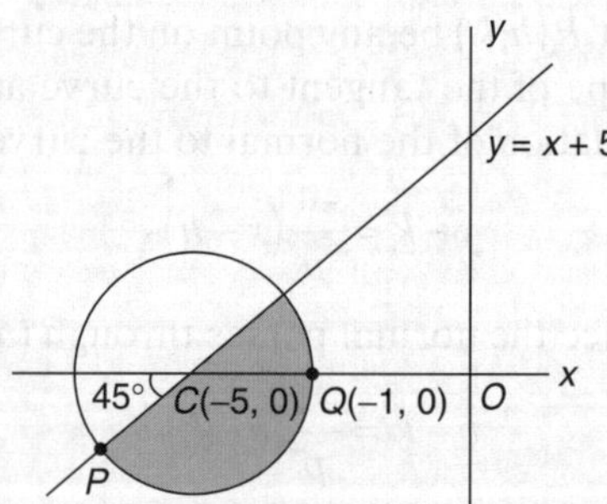

The quantity $|z+1|$ represents the distance between a point z and the point $Q(-1,0)$. The point which lies in the shaded region and is farthest from Q is the point

$$P(-5-4\cos 45°, 0-4\cos 45°)=\left(-5-2\sqrt{2},-2\sqrt{2}\right)$$

Thus, the greatest value of $|z+1|^2$ is

$$(PQ)^2=\left(4+2\sqrt{2}\right)^2+\left(2\sqrt{2}\right)^2=32+16\sqrt{2}$$

Thus, $\alpha=32, \beta=16$ and hence $\alpha+\beta=48$.

38. The pth and the qth terms of the given series $-16,8,-4,2,\ldots$ are

$$t_p=-16\left(\frac{-1}{2}\right)^{p-1} \text{ and } t_q=-16\left(\frac{-1}{2}\right)^{q-1}$$

The roots of the quadratic equation $4x^2-9x+5=0$ are $1, 5/4$. The AM and GM of t_p and t_q are

$$\sqrt{t_pt_q}=1 \text{ and } \frac{t_p+t_q}{2}=\frac{5}{4} \text{ [AM > GM]}$$

$$\Rightarrow \quad 16^2\left(\frac{-1}{2}\right)^{p+q-2}=1$$

$$\Rightarrow \quad (-2)^8=(-2)^{p+q-2}$$

$$\Rightarrow \quad p+q-2=8$$

$$\Rightarrow \quad p+q=10$$

39. The equation $\sum_{i=1}^{18}(x_i-\alpha)=36$ reduces to

$$\sum_{i=1}^{18}x_i-18\alpha=36$$

$$\Rightarrow \quad \sum_{i=1}^{18}x_i=18(\alpha+2)$$

$$\Rightarrow \quad \frac{\sum_{i=1}^{18}x_i}{18}=\alpha+2$$

The equation $\sum_{i=1}^{18}(x_i-\beta)^2=90$ reduces to

$$\sum_{i=1}^{18}x_i^2-2\beta\sum_{i=1}^{18}x_i+18\beta^2=90$$

$$\Rightarrow \quad \sum_{i=1}^{18}x_i^2-36\beta(\alpha+2)+18\beta^2=90$$

$$\Rightarrow \quad \sum_{i=1}^{18}x_i^2=18\left\{5-\beta^2+2\beta(\alpha+2)\right\}$$

$$\Rightarrow \quad \frac{\sum_{i=1}^{18}x_i^2}{18}=5-\beta^2+2\beta(\alpha+2)$$

It is given that variance$\left(\sigma^2\right)=1$. Thus, we have

$$\frac{\sum x^2}{N}-\left(\frac{\sum x}{N}\right)^2=1$$

$$\Rightarrow \quad 5-\beta^2+2\beta(\alpha+2)-(\alpha+2)^2=1$$

$$\Rightarrow \quad \alpha^2+\beta^2-2\alpha\beta+4\alpha-4\beta=0$$

$$\Rightarrow \quad (\alpha-\beta)^2+4(\alpha-\beta)=0$$

$$\Rightarrow \quad (\alpha-\beta)(\alpha-\beta+4)=0$$

$$\Rightarrow \quad \alpha-\beta=-4 \; [\alpha \neq \beta, \text{ given}]$$

Hence, $\beta-\alpha=4$.

40. Given $\alpha+\beta=1$ and $\alpha\beta=-1$. Thus, α,β are the roots of the quadratic equation $x^2-x-1=0$. Therefore, we have

$$\alpha^2-\alpha-1=0 \quad (1)$$

and $$\beta^2-\beta-1=0 \quad (2)$$

Multiplying equation (1) by α^{n-1} and equation (2) by β^{n-1}, we have

$$\alpha^{n+1}-\alpha^n-\alpha^{n-1}=0 \quad (3)$$

and $$\beta^{n+1}-\beta^n-\beta^{n-1}=0 \quad (4)$$

Adding equations (3) and (4), we have

$$P_{n+1}-P_n-P_{n-1}=0$$

$$\Rightarrow \quad P_n=P_{n+1}-P_{n-1}=29-11=18$$

Hence, $P_n^2=324$.

41. The prime factors of 18 are 2,3,3. Thus, the required four-digit numbers must be divisible by 3 but not be divisible by 2,9.

Odd four-digit numbers divisible by 3 are 1005,1011,1017,…. The total number n of such numbers is given by

$$1005+(n-1)6 \leq 9999$$

$$\Rightarrow \quad n \leq 1+\frac{9999-1005}{6} \Rightarrow n=1500$$

Odd four-digit numbers divisible by 9 are 1017,1035,1053,…. The total number m of such numbers is given by

$$1017+(m-1)18 \leq 9999$$

$$\Rightarrow \quad m \leq 1+\frac{9999-1015}{18} \Rightarrow m=500$$

Hence, the required number of four-digit numbers is $1500-500=1000$.

42. The line joining points $P(1,0,-1)$ and $Q(\alpha,\beta,\gamma)$ must be perpendicular to the plane $4x-5y+2z=8$. Thus, we have

$$\frac{\alpha-1}{4}=\frac{\beta}{-5}=\frac{\gamma+1}{2} \quad (1)$$

Let the midpoint of PQ, that is, $M\left(\frac{\alpha+1}{2},\frac{\beta}{2},\frac{\gamma-1}{2}\right)$ lie on the plane. Thus, we have

$$4\left(\frac{\alpha+1}{2}\right)-5\left(\frac{\beta}{2}\right)+2\left(\frac{\gamma-1}{2}\right)=8$$

$$\Rightarrow \quad 4\alpha-5\beta+2\gamma=14 \quad (2)$$

From equation (1), let $\alpha=4t+1, \beta=-5t, \gamma=2t-1$. Putting in equation (2), we have

$$4(4t+1)-5(-5t)+2(2t-1)=14 \text{ gives } =\frac{4}{15}$$

Thus, $\alpha=\frac{31}{15}, \beta=\frac{-20}{15}, \gamma=\frac{-7}{15}$. Hence, we have

$$15(\alpha+\beta+\gamma)=4$$

43. We have

$$f'(x)=10\left(x^4+2x^3+3x^2+2x+1\right)$$

$$=10x^3\left(x^2+2x+3+\frac{2}{x}+\frac{1}{x^2}\right)$$

$$=10x^3\left\{\left(x+\frac{1}{x}\right)^2+2\left(x+\frac{1}{x}\right)+1\right\}$$

$$=10x^3\left(x+\frac{1}{x}+1\right)^2$$

We see that $f'(x)>0 \; \forall x \in \mathbf{R} \Rightarrow f(x)$ is an increasing function.

Now, we can see that $f(-2)=-34<0$ and $f(-1)=3>0$. Thus, $f(x)$ has exactly one real zero in $(-2,-1)$. Hence, $\alpha=2$.

44. Let position vectors of $A,B,C,\ldots,H$ be $\mathbf{a},\mathbf{b},\mathbf{c},\ldots,\mathbf{h}$, respectively. Then, we have

$$\frac{\mathbf{a}+\mathbf{b}+\mathbf{c}+\ldots+\mathbf{h}}{8}=0$$

$$\Rightarrow \quad \mathbf{a}+\mathbf{b}+\mathbf{c}+\ldots+\mathbf{h}=0 \quad (1)$$

Now, we have

$$\mathbf{AB}+\mathbf{AC}+\mathbf{AD}+\mathbf{AE}+\mathbf{AF}+\mathbf{AG}+\mathbf{AH}$$

$$=(\mathbf{b}-\mathbf{a})+(\mathbf{c}-\mathbf{a})+(\mathbf{d}-\mathbf{a})+\ldots+(\mathbf{h}-\mathbf{a})$$

$$=(\mathbf{b}+\mathbf{c}+\ldots+\mathbf{h})-7\mathbf{a}$$

$$=-\mathbf{a}-7\mathbf{a}=-8\mathbf{a} \; \text{[Using equation (1)]}$$

$$=-8(\mathbf{OA})=8(\mathbf{AO})$$

Hence, $x=8$.

45. The given curve is a circle having its centre at $C(2,2)$ and radius $=2$. The circle is inscribed inside the triangle ΔOAB. The circumcentre of triangle ΔOAB lies at the midpoint of AB.

Let $P(h,k)$ be the midpoint of AB. Then, we have $A(2h,0), B(0,2k)$ and the equation of line AB as

$$\frac{x}{2h}+\frac{y}{2k}=1$$

$$\Rightarrow \quad kx+hy-2hk=0 \tag{1}$$

Since the above line touches the given circle, we have

$$\frac{|2k+2h-2hk|}{\sqrt{h^2+k^2}}=2$$

In the equation $2k+2h-2hk<0$, the point $C(2,2)$ lies below the line AB. Thus, the above equation reduces to

$$k+h-hk=-\sqrt{h^2+k^2}$$

Now, putting (x,y) in place of (h,k), we get the required locus as

$$x+y-xy+\sqrt{x^2+y^2}=0$$

Hence, $\alpha=1$.

46. We have

$$1+\log_{10}\left(4^x+\frac{18}{5}\right)=2\log_{10}\left(4^x-2\right)$$

$$\Rightarrow \quad \log_{10}10+\log_{10}\left(4^x+\frac{18}{5}\right)=\log_{10}\left(4^x-2\right)^2$$

$$\Rightarrow \quad 10\left(4^x+\frac{18}{5}\right)=\left(4^x-2\right)^2$$

$$\Rightarrow \quad 4^{2x}-14\times4^x-32=0$$

$$\Rightarrow \quad 4^x=\frac{14\pm\sqrt{14^2+128}}{2}=16 \text{ gives } x=2$$

Hence, we have

$$D=\begin{vmatrix}3&1&4\\1&0&2\\2&1&0\end{vmatrix}=-6+4+4=2$$

47. We have

$$f(x)=ax^2+bx+c$$

$$f'(x)=2ax+b,$$

and $\quad f''(x)=2a$

Using the given conditions $f(-1)=2, f'(-1)=1$, and $f''(x)_{max}=\frac{1}{2}$, we have

$$a-b+c=2 \tag{1}$$

$$-2a+b=1 \tag{2}$$

and $\quad 2a=\frac{1}{2} \qquad (3)$

Solving the above equations, we have $a=\frac{1}{4}, b=\frac{3}{2}, c=\frac{13}{4}$. Thus, we have

$$f(x)=\frac{1}{4}x^2+\frac{3}{2}x+\frac{13}{4}$$

and $\quad f'(x)=\frac{1}{2}(x+3)$

In the interval $x\in[-1,1]$ we can see that $f'(x)>0 \Rightarrow f(x)$ increases in this interval. Thus, in this interval $f(x)\le f(1)=5$. Hence, $\alpha=5$.

48.

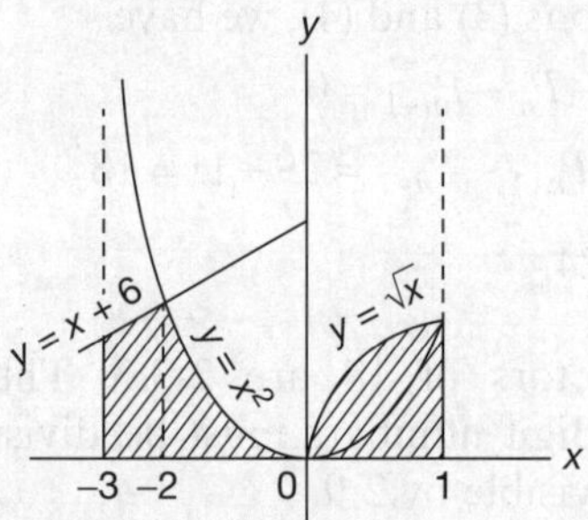

The figure shows the graph of the given function. Thus, we have

$$A=\int_{-3}^{-2}(x+6)\,dx+\int_{-2}^{0}x^2\,dx+\int_{0}^{1}\sqrt{x}\,dx$$

$$=\left|\frac{(x+6)^2}{2}\right|_{-3}^{-2}+\left|\frac{x^3}{3}\right|_{-2}^{0}+\left|\frac{x^{3/2}}{3/2}\right|_{0}^{1}$$

$$=\frac{16-9}{2}+\frac{8}{3}+\frac{2}{3}=\frac{41}{6}$$

Hence, $6A=41$.

49. Let R be the radius of the circumcircle of ΔABC. Then the coordinates of the vertices of ΔABC can be written as

$$A(R\cos\alpha, R\sin\alpha), A(R\cos\beta, R\sin\beta), A(R\cos\gamma, R\sin\gamma)$$

It is known that the circumcentre, the centroid and the orthocentre of any triangle are collinear. In this question, it is given that the circumcentre is at the origin and the orthocentre lies on the y-axis. So we conlude that the centroid must also be on the y-axis $\Rightarrow$ abscissa of the centroid must equal zero. Thus, we have

$$\frac{R}{3}(\cos\alpha+\cos\beta+\cos\gamma)=0$$

The above equation is true only if, α, β, γ are in AP with a common difference of $\frac{2\pi}{3}$. Therefore, we can choose the angles as

$$\beta-\frac{2\pi}{3}, \beta, \beta+\frac{2\pi}{3}$$

Thus, we have

$$S=\frac{\cos 3\alpha+\cos 3\beta+\cos 3\gamma}{\cos\alpha\cos\beta\cos\gamma}$$

$$=\frac{\cos(3\beta-2\pi)+\cos 3\beta+\cos(3\beta+2\pi)}{\cos\left(\beta-\frac{2\pi}{3}\right)\cos\beta\cos\left(\beta+\frac{2\pi}{3}\right)}$$

$$=\frac{\cos 3\beta+\cos 3\beta+\cos 3\beta}{\frac{1}{2}\left\{\cos 2\beta+\cos\left(\frac{4\pi}{3}\right)\right\}\cos\beta}$$

$$=\frac{6\cos 3\beta}{\left(\cos 2\beta-\frac{1}{2}\right)\cos\beta}$$

$$=\frac{6\cos 3\beta}{\cos 2\beta\cos\beta-\frac{1}{2}\cos\beta}$$

$$=\frac{6\cos 3\beta}{\frac{1}{2}(\cos 3\beta+\cos\beta)-\frac{1}{2}\cos\beta}$$

$$=\frac{6\cos 3\beta}{\frac{1}{2}\cos 3\beta}=12$$

Hence, $S^2=144$.

50. We have

$$\frac{\sum_1^{2n} x}{2n}=6 \text{ and } \frac{\sum_{2n+1}^{3n} x}{n}=3$$

$$\Rightarrow \quad \sum_1^{2n} x=12n \text{ and } \sum_{2n+1}^{3n} x=3n$$

$$\Rightarrow \quad \sum_1^{3n} x=15n$$

Also, we have

$$\frac{\sum_1^{3n} x^2}{3n}-\left(\frac{\sum_1^{3n} x}{3n}\right)^2=4$$

$$\Rightarrow \quad \frac{\sum_1^{3n} x^2}{3n}-5^2=4$$

$$\Rightarrow \quad \sum_1^{3n} x^2=87n$$

After the changes in the data, we have

$$\sum_1^{3n} y=\sum_1^{2n}(x+1)+\sum_{2n+1}^{3n}(x-1)$$

$$=\sum_1^{3n} x+2n-n$$

$$=15n+n=16n$$

and
$$\sum_1^{3n} y^2=\sum_1^{2n}(x+1)^2+\sum_{2n+1}^{3n}(x-1)^2$$

$$=\sum_1^{3n} x^2+2\sum_1^{2n} x-2\sum_{2n+1}^{3n} x+2n+n$$

$$=87n+2(12n)-2(3n)+3n=108n$$

Thus, the variance k of the new data is given by

$$k=\frac{\sum_1^{3n} y^2}{3n}-\left(\frac{\sum_1^{3n} y}{3n}\right)^2$$

$$=\frac{108n}{3n}-\left(\frac{16n}{3n}\right)^2=\frac{324}{9}-\frac{256}{9}=\frac{66}{9}$$

Hence, $9k=68$.

51. The $(r+1)^{th}$ term in the expansion of the given binomial is

$$T_{r+1}={}^nC_r x^{n-r}\left(\frac{a}{x^2}\right)^r={}^nC_r a^r x^{n-2r} \tag{1}$$

It is given that the coefficients of the terms T_3, T_4, T_5 are in the ratio 12 : 8 : 3. Thus, we have

$$\frac{{}^nC_2 a^2}{12}=\frac{{}^nC_3 a^3}{8}=\frac{{}^nC_4 a^4}{3}$$

$$\Rightarrow \quad \frac{{}^nC_2}{12}=\frac{{}^nC_3 a}{8}=\frac{{}^nC_4 a^2}{3} \tag{2}$$

Eliminating a^2 from equation (2), we have

$$\frac{{}^nC_2}{12}\times\frac{{}^nC_4 a^2}{3}=\left(\frac{{}^nC_3 a}{8}\right)^2$$

$$\Rightarrow \quad \frac{{}^nC_2\,{}^nC_4}{\left({}^nC_3\right)^2} = \frac{9}{16}$$

$$\Rightarrow \quad \frac{\frac{n(n-1)}{2} \times \frac{n(n-1)(n-2)(n-3)}{24}}{\left(\frac{n(n-1)(n-2)}{6}\right)^2} = \frac{9}{16}$$

$$\Rightarrow \quad \frac{n-3}{n-2} = \frac{3}{4} \text{ gives } n = 6.$$

Now putting the value of n in equation (2), we have

$$\frac{{}^6C_2}{12} = \frac{{}^6C_3 a}{8}$$

$$\Rightarrow \quad a = \frac{8 \times 15}{12 \times 20} = \frac{1}{2}$$

Now from equation (1), we can see that the term is independent of x when $r = \frac{n}{3} = 2$. Thus, the term independent of x is

$$k = {}^nC_2 a^2 = {}^6C_2\left(\frac{1}{2}\right)^2 = \frac{15}{4}$$

Hence, $4k = 15$.

52. $\vec{x}$ is coplanar with $\vec{a} = 2\hat{i} - \hat{j} + \hat{k}$ and $\vec{b} = \hat{i} + 2\hat{j} - \hat{k}$; therefore we can choose $\vec{x} = m\vec{a} + n\vec{b}$, that is

$$\vec{x} = (2m+n)\hat{i} + (-m+2n)\hat{j} + (m-n)\hat{k}$$

It is given that $\vec{x}$ is perpendicular to $3\hat{i} + 2\hat{j} - \hat{k}$. Thus, we have

$$3(2m+n) + 2(-m+2n) - 1(m-n) = 0$$

$$\Rightarrow \quad 3m + 8n = 0 \Rightarrow n = \frac{-3}{8}m$$

Using the above result, we can now write $\vec{x}$ as

$$\vec{x} = \left(\frac{13m}{8}\right)\hat{i} + \left(\frac{-14m}{8}\right)\hat{j} + \left(\frac{11m}{8}\right)\hat{k}$$

It is also given that the projection of $\vec{x}$ on $\vec{a}$ is $\frac{17\sqrt{6}}{2}$. Thus, we have

$$\frac{|\vec{x} \cdot \vec{a}|}{|\vec{a}|} = \frac{17\sqrt{6}}{2}$$

$$\Rightarrow \quad \frac{\frac{26m}{8} + \frac{14m}{8} + \frac{11m}{8}}{\sqrt{2^2 + 1^2 + 1^2}} = \frac{17\sqrt{6}}{2}$$

$$\Rightarrow \quad \frac{51m}{8} = 51 \text{ gives } m = 8.$$

Thus $\vec{x} = 13\hat{i} - 14\hat{j} + 11\hat{k}$, and hence $|\vec{x}|^2 = 13^2 + 14^2 + 11^2 = 486$.

53. We have

$$I_{10} = \int_1^e x^{19} (\ln x)^{10}\, dx$$

$$\Rightarrow \quad I_{10} = \left|\frac{x^{20}}{20}(\ln x)^{10}\right|_1^e - \frac{1}{20}\int_1^e x^{20}\, \frac{10(\ln x)^9}{x}\, dx$$

$$\Rightarrow \quad I_{10} = \frac{e^{20}}{20} - \frac{10}{20}\int_1^e x^{19} (\ln x)^9\, dx$$

$$\Rightarrow \quad 20 I_{10} = e^{20} - 10 I_9 \qquad (1)$$

Similarly, we have

$$I_9 = \int_1^e x^{19} (\ln x)^9\, dx$$

$$\Rightarrow \quad I_9 = \left|\frac{x^{20}}{20}(\ln x)^9\right|_1^e - \frac{1}{20}\int_1^e x^{20}\, \frac{9(\ln x)^8}{x}\, dx$$

$$\Rightarrow \quad I_9 = \frac{e^{20}}{20} - \frac{9}{20}\int_1^e x^{19} (\ln x)^8\, dx$$

$$\Rightarrow \quad 20 I_9 = e^{20} - 9 I_8 \qquad (2)$$

Subtracting equation (2) from equation (1), we have

$$20 I_{10} - 20 I_9 = 9 I_8 - 10 I_9$$

$$\Rightarrow \quad 20 I_{10} = 10 I_9 + 9 I_8$$

Thus $\alpha = 10$, $\beta = 9$, and hence $\alpha - \beta = 1$.

54. Let us choose a point $P(3, 0, 0)$ on $x^2 + y^2 + z^2 = 9$. Then according to the question sum of the squares of the distance of P from the planes $x + y + z = 0, lx - nz = 0, x - 2y + z = 0$ must equal 9. Thus, we have

$$\left(\frac{3}{\sqrt{3}}\right)^2 + \left(\frac{3l}{\sqrt{l^2 + n^2}}\right)^2 + \left(\frac{3}{\sqrt{6}}\right)^2 = 9$$

$$\Rightarrow \quad \frac{9l^2}{l^2 + n^2} = \frac{9}{2}$$

$$\Rightarrow \quad l^2 = n^2 \text{ gives } l = \pm n$$

If we choose $l = n$, the equations of the three planes are $x + y + z = 0, x - z = 0, x - 2y + z = 0$. We can see that these planes do give the desired locus:

$$\left(\frac{x+y+z}{\sqrt{3}}\right)^2+\left(\frac{x-z}{\sqrt{2}}\right)^2+\left(\frac{x-2y+z}{\sqrt{6}}\right)^2=9$$

$$\Rightarrow \quad 2(x+y+z)^2+3(x-z)^2+(x-2y+z)^2=54$$

$$\Rightarrow \quad 6\left(x^2+y^2+z^2\right)=54$$

$$\Rightarrow \quad x^2+y^2+z^2=9$$

If we choose $l=-n$, the equations of the three planes are $x+y+z=0$, $x+z=0$, $x-2y+z=0$. We can see that these planes do not give the desired locus:

$$\left(\frac{x+y+z}{\sqrt{3}}\right)^2+\left(\frac{x+z}{\sqrt{2}}\right)^2+\left(\frac{x-2y+z}{\sqrt{6}}\right)^2=9$$

$$\Rightarrow \quad 2(x+y+z)^2+3(x+z)^2+(x-2y+z)^2=54$$

$$\Rightarrow \quad 6\left(x^2+y^2+z^2\right)+12xz=54$$

$$\Rightarrow \quad x^2+y^2+z^2+2xz=9$$

Thus $l=n$ is the only solution, and hence $l-n=0$.

55. For continuity at $x=0$, $f(0)=\lim_{x\to\infty} f(x)$. Thus, we have

$$\frac{1}{k}=\lim_{x\to 0}\frac{\cos(\sin x)-\cos x}{x^4}$$

$$=\lim_{x\to 0}\frac{-2\sin\left(\frac{\sin x+x}{2}\right)\sin\left(\frac{\sin x-x}{2}\right)}{x^4}$$

$$=\lim_{x\to 0}\frac{-2\left(\frac{\sin x+x}{2}\right)\left(\frac{\sin x-x}{2}\right)}{x^4}$$

$$[\sin\delta\sim\delta \text{ if } \delta \text{ is small}]$$

$$=\lim_{x\to 0}\frac{x^2-\sin^2 x}{2x^4}\left(\frac{0}{0}\right)$$

$$=\lim_{x\to 0}\frac{2x-\sin(2x)}{8x^3}\left(\frac{0}{0}\right)$$

$$=\lim_{x\to 0}\frac{2-2\cos(2x)}{24x^2}\left(\frac{0}{0}\right)$$

$$=\lim_{x\to 0}\frac{4\sin^2 x}{24x^2}=\frac{1}{6}$$

Hence, $k=6$.

56. The given function can be written as

$$f(x)=\sin\left\{\cos^{-1}\left(\frac{1-2^{2x}}{1+2^{2x}}\right)\right\}$$

$$=\sin\left\{\sin^{-1}\sqrt{1-\left(\frac{1-2^{2x}}{1+2^{2x}}\right)^2}\right\}$$

$$=\frac{\sqrt{\left(1+2^{2x}\right)^2-\left(1-2^{2x}\right)^2}}{1+2^{2x}}$$

$$=\frac{2\times 2^x}{1+2^{2x}}=\frac{2}{2^x+2^{-x}}$$

The derivative of $f(x)$ is

$$f'(x)=-\frac{2\left(2^x-2^{-x}\right)\ln 2}{\left(2^x+2^{-x}\right)^2}$$

Thus $a=\left(2^x+2^{-x}\right)^2, b=2\left(2^x-2^{-x}\right)$. Note that $a=4$ and $b=0$ when $x=0$. Then, we have

$$a^2=\left(2^x+2^{-x}\right)^4=2^{4x}+4\cdot 2^{2x}+6+4\cdot 2^{-2x}+2^{-4x}$$

$$\text{and } b^2=4\left(2^x-2^{-x}\right)^2=4\left(2^{2x}-2+2^{-2x}\right)$$

Hence, we have

$$\left|a^2-b^2\right|=\left|2^{4x}+2^{-4x}+14\right|$$

Now using the identity AM $\geq$ GM, we have

$$\frac{2^{4x}+2^{-4x}}{2}\geq\sqrt{2^{4x}\times 2^{-4x}}$$

$$\Rightarrow \quad 2^{4x}+2^{-4x}\geq 2$$

Hence, $\left|a^2-b^2\right|\geq 16$.

57. We have

$$A^2=\begin{bmatrix}2 & 3\\ 0 & -1\end{bmatrix}\begin{bmatrix}2 & 3\\ 0 & -1\end{bmatrix}=\begin{bmatrix}4 & 3\\ 0 & 1\end{bmatrix}$$

$$A^3=\begin{bmatrix}2 & 3\\ 0 & -1\end{bmatrix}\begin{bmatrix}4 & 3\\ 0 & 1\end{bmatrix}=\begin{bmatrix}8 & 9\\ 0 & -1\end{bmatrix}$$

$$A^4=\begin{bmatrix}2 & 3\\ 0 & -1\end{bmatrix}\begin{bmatrix}8 & 9\\ 0 & -1\end{bmatrix}=\begin{bmatrix}16 & 15\\ 0 & 1\end{bmatrix}$$

$$A^5=\begin{bmatrix}2 & 3\\ 0 & -1\end{bmatrix}\begin{bmatrix}16 & 15\\ 0 & 1\end{bmatrix}=\begin{bmatrix}32 & 33\\ 0 & -1\end{bmatrix}$$

$$\ldots\ \ldots\ \ldots$$

$$A^n=\begin{bmatrix}2^n & 2^n-(-1)^n\\ 0 & (-1)^n\end{bmatrix}$$

$$\text{Thus} \quad A^{10}=\begin{bmatrix}2^{10} & 2^{10}-1\\ 0 & 1\end{bmatrix}.$$

Now, we have

$$\{\text{adj}(2A)\}^{10} = \{2^{2-1}\text{adj}A\}^{10}$$

$$\left[\text{Using adj}(kA) = k^{n-1}\text{adj}(A)\right]$$

$$= 2^{10}\{\text{adj}A\}^{10} = 2^{10}\text{adj}(A^{10})$$

$$= 2^{10}\begin{bmatrix} 1 & 1-2^{10} \\ 0 & 2^{10} \end{bmatrix} = \begin{bmatrix} 2^{10} & 2^{10}-2^{20} \\ 0 & 2^{20} \end{bmatrix}$$

$$\Rightarrow \quad A^{10} - \{\text{adj}(2A)\}^{10} = \begin{bmatrix} 2^{10} & 2^{10}-1 \\ 0 & 1 \end{bmatrix} - \begin{bmatrix} 2^{10} & 2^{10}-2^{20} \\ 0 & 2^{20} \end{bmatrix}$$

$$= \begin{bmatrix} 0 & 2^{20}-1 \\ 0 & 1-2^{20} \end{bmatrix}$$

Hence, we have

$$|A^4| - \left|A^{10} - \{\text{adj}(2A)\}^{10}\right|$$

$$= \begin{vmatrix} 16 & 15 \\ 0 & 1 \end{vmatrix} - \begin{vmatrix} 0 & 2^{20}-1 \\ 0 & 1-2^{20} \end{vmatrix} = 16.$$

58. We have

$$I = \int_0^{\sqrt{\frac{\pi}{2}}} \left[[x^2] - \cos x\right] dx$$

$$= \int_0^1 [-\cos x]\,dx + \int_1^{\sqrt{\frac{\pi}{2}}} [1-\cos x]\,dx$$

$$= \int_0^1 (-1)\,dx + \int_1^{\sqrt{\frac{\pi}{2}}} (0)\,dx = -1$$

Hence, $|I| = 1$.

59. We have

$$L = \lim_{x\to\infty}\left(1 + \frac{a}{x} - \frac{4}{x^2}\right)^{2x}$$

$$= \lim_{t\to 0}\left(1 + at - 4t^2\right)^{\frac{2}{t}}$$

$$= \lim_{t\to 0}\left(1 + at - 4t^2\right)^{\frac{1}{at-4t^2}\times\frac{2(at-4t^2)}{t}}$$

$$= \lim_{t\to 0}\left\{\left(1 + at - 4t^2\right)^{\frac{1}{at-4t^2}}\right\}^{2(a-4t)}$$

$$= e^{2a}\left[\lim_{\delta\to 0}(1+\delta)^{\frac{1}{\delta}} = 1\right]$$

Equating it with e^3 gives $a = 3/2$. Hence, $2a = 3$.

60. It is given that $T_4 = 4480$. Thus, we have

$$^7C_3 x^4 x^{3\log_2 x} = 4480$$

$$\Rightarrow \quad x^{4+3\log_2 x} = \frac{4480}{35} = 108$$

Now since $x \in \mathbf{N}$, by trial we get $x = 2$.

Appendix B: Previous Years' JEE Advanced Questions and Solutions

QUESTIONS

Only One Correct Option

- Each question has **FOUR** options. **ONLY ONE** of these four options is the correct answer.
- For each question, choose the option corresponding to the correct answer.
- The answer to each question will be evaluated according to the following marking scheme:

Full Marks: +3	If ONLY the correct option is chosen;
Zero Marks: 0	If none of the options is chosen (i.e. the question is unanswered);
Negative Marks: –1	In all other cases

1. Suppose a, b denote the distinct real roots of the quadratic polynomial $x^2 + 20x - 2020$ and suppose c, d denote the distinct complex roots of the quadratic polynomial $x^2 - 20x + 2020$. Then the value of $ac(a-c)+ad(a-d)+bc(b-c)+bd(b-d)$ is:

(a) 0 (b) 8000
(c) 8080 (d) 16000

2. If the function $f:\mathbf{R}\to\mathbf{R}$ is defined by $f(x)=|x|(x-\sin x)$, then which of the following statements is **TRUE**?

(a) f is one–one, but **NOT** onto
(b) f is onto, but **NOT** one–one
(c) f is **BOTH** one–one and onto
(d) f is **NEITHER** one–one **NOR** onto

3. Let the functions $f:\mathbf{R}\to\mathbf{R}$ and $g:\mathbf{R}\to\mathbf{R}$ be defined by

$$f(x)=e^{x-1}-e^{-|x-1|} \text{ and } g(x)=\frac{1}{2}(e^{x-1}+e^{1-x}).$$

Then the area of the region in the first quadrant bounded by the curves $y=f(x)$, $y=g(x)$ and $x=0$ is:

(a) $(2-\sqrt{3})+\frac{1}{2}(e-e^{-1})$
(b) $(2+\sqrt{3})+\frac{1}{2}(e-e^{-1})$
(c) $(2-\sqrt{3})+\frac{1}{2}(e+e^{-1})$
(d) $(2+\sqrt{3})+\frac{1}{2}(e+e^{-1})$

4. Let a, b and λ be positive real numbers. Suppose P is an end point of the latus rectum of the parabola $y^2=4\lambda x$, and suppose the ellipse $\frac{x^2}{a^2}+\frac{y^2}{b^2}=1$ passes through the point P. If the tangents to the parabola and the ellipse at the point P are perpendicular to each other, then the eccentricity of the ellipse is:

(a) $\frac{1}{\sqrt{2}}$ (b) $\frac{1}{2}$
(c) $\frac{1}{3}$ (d) $\frac{2}{5}$

5. Let C_1 and C_2 be two biased coins such that the probabilities of getting heads in a single toss are $\frac{2}{3}$ and $\frac{1}{3}$, respectively. Suppose α is the number of heads that appear when C_1 is tossed twice, independently, and suppose β is the number of heads that appear when C_2 is tossed twice, independently. Then the probability that the roots of the quadratic polynomial $x^2-\alpha x+\beta$ are real and equal is:

(a) $\frac{40}{81}$ (b) $\frac{20}{81}$
(c) $\frac{1}{2}$ (d) $\frac{1}{4}$

6. Consider all rectangles lying in the region $\left\{(x,y)\in \mathbf{R}\times\mathbf{R}: 0\le x\le \frac{\pi}{2} \text{ and } 0\le y\le 2\sin(2x)\right\}$ and having one side on the x-axis. The area of the rectangle that has the maximum perimeter among all such rectangles is:

(a) $\frac{3\pi}{2}$ (b) π

(c) $\frac{\pi}{2\sqrt{3}}$ (d) $\frac{\pi\sqrt{3}}{2}$

7. Let S be the set of all complex numbers z satisfying $|z-2+i|\ge\sqrt{5}$. If the complex number z_0 is such that $\frac{1}{|z_0-1|}$ is the maximum of the set $\left\{\frac{1}{|z-1|}: z\in S\right\}$, then the principal argument of $\frac{4-z_0-\bar{z}_0}{z_0-\bar{z}_0+2i}$ is:

(a) $\frac{\pi}{2}$ (b) $\frac{\pi}{4}$

(c) $\frac{\pi}{2}$ (d) $\frac{3\pi}{4}$

8. Let

$$M=\begin{bmatrix}\sin^4\theta & -1-\sin^2\theta\\ 1+\cos^2\theta & \cos^4\theta\end{bmatrix}=\alpha I+\beta M^{-1},$$

where $\alpha=\alpha(\theta)$ and $\beta=\beta(\theta)$ are real numbers, and I is the 2×2 identity matrix. If

α^* is the minimum of the set $\{\alpha(\theta):\theta\in[0,2\pi)\}$ and

β^* is the minimum of the set $\{\beta(\theta):\theta\in[0,2\pi)\}$,

then the value of $\alpha^*+\beta^*$ is:

(a) $-\frac{37}{16}$ (b) $-\frac{31}{16}$

(c) $-\frac{29}{16}$ (d) $-\frac{17}{16}$

9. A line $y = mx + 1$ intersects the circle $(x-3)^2+(y+2)^2=25$ at points P and Q. If the mid-point of the line segment PQ has x-coordinate $-\frac{3}{5}$, then which one of the following options is correct?

(a) $-3\le m<-1$ (b) $2\le m<4$

(c) $4\le m<6$ (d) $6\le m<8$

10. The area of the region $\{(x,y): xy\le 8, 1\le y\le x^2\}$ is:

(a) $16\log_e 2-\frac{14}{3}$ (b) $8\log_e 2-\frac{14}{3}$

(c) $16\log_e 2-6$ (d) $8\log_e 2-\frac{7}{3}$

One or More Correct Options

- Each question has **FOUR** options. **ONE OR MORE THAN ONE** of these four options(s) is(are) correct answer(s).
- For each question, choose the option(s) corresponding to (all) the correct answer(s).
- The answer to each question will be evaluated according to the following marking scheme:

Full Marks: +4	If only (all) the correct option(s) is(are) chosen;
Partial Marks: +3	If all the four options are correct but ONLY three options are chosen;
Partial Marks: +2	If three or more options are correct but ONLY two options are chosen, both of which are correct;
Partial Marks: +1	If two or more options are correct but ONLY one option is chosen and it is a correct option;
Zero Marks: 0	If none of the options is chosen (i.e. the question is unanswered);
Negative Marks: –2	In all other cases

1. Let the function $f:\mathbf{R}\to\mathbf{R}$ be defined by $f(x)=x^3-x^2+(x-1)\sin x$ and $g:\mathbf{R}\to\mathbf{R}$ be an arbitrary function. Let $fg:\mathbf{R}\to\mathbf{R}$ be the product function defined by $fg(x)=f(x)g(x)$. Then which of the following statements is/are true?

(a) If g is continuous at $x = 1$, then fg is differentiable at $x = 1$

(b) If fg is differentiable at $x = 1$, then g is continuous at $x = 1$

(c) If g is differentiable at $x = 1$, then fg is differentiable at $x = 1$

(d) If fg is differentiable at $x = 1$, then g is differentiable at $x = 1$

2. Let M be a 3×3 invertible matrix with real entries and let I denote the 3×3 identity matrix. If M^{-1} = adj(adj$M$), then which of the following statements is/are always true?

(a) $M = I$ (b) $\det M = 1$

(c) $M^2 = 1$ (d) $(\text{adj}M)^2 = I$

3. Let S be the set of all complex numbers z satisfying $|z^2+z+1|=1$. Then which of the following statements is/are true?

(a) $\left|z+\frac{1}{2}\right| \le \frac{1}{2}$ for all $z \in S$

(b) $|z| \le 2$ for all $z \in S$

(c) $\left|z+\frac{1}{2}\right| \ge \frac{1}{2}$ for all $z \in S$

(d) The set S has exactly four elements

4. Let x, y and z be positive real numbers. Suppose x, y and z are the lengths of the sides of a triangle opposite to its angles X, Y and Z, respectively. If

$$\tan\frac{X}{2}+\tan\frac{Z}{2}=\frac{2y}{x+y+z},$$

then which of the following statements is/are true?

(a) $2Y = X + Z$ (b) $Y = X + Z$

(c) $\tan\frac{X}{2}=\frac{x}{y+z}$ (d) $x^2+z^2-y^2 = xz$

5. Let L_1 and L_2 be the following straight lines:

$$L_1: \frac{x-1}{1}=\frac{y}{-1}=\frac{z-1}{3} \text{ and } L_2: \frac{x-1}{-3}=\frac{y}{-1}=\frac{z-1}{1}$$

Suppose the straight line

$$L: \frac{x-\alpha}{l}=\frac{y-1}{m}=\frac{z-\gamma}{-2}$$

lies in the plane containing L_1 and L_2 and passes through the point of intersection of L_1 and L_2. If the line L bisects the acute angle between the lines L_1 and L_2, then which of the following statements is/are true?

(a) $\alpha - \gamma = 0$ (b) $l + m = 2$

(c) $\alpha - \gamma = 1$ (d) $l - m = 0$

6. Which of the following inequalities is/are true?

(a) $\int_0^1 x\cos x\,dx > \frac{3}{8}$ (b) $\int_0^1 x\sin x\,dx \ge \frac{3}{10}$

(c) $\int_0^1 x^2\cos x\,dx \ge \frac{1}{2}$ (d) $\int_0^1 x^2\sin x\,dx \ge \frac{2}{9}$

7. Let b be a non-zero real number. Suppose $f: \mathbf{R} \to \mathbf{R}$ is a differentiable function such that $f(0) = 1$. If the derivative f' of f satisfies the equation

$$f' = \frac{f(x)}{b^2+x^2}$$

for all $x \in \mathbf{R}$, then which of the following statements is/are true?

(a) If $b > 0$, then f is an increasing function

(b) If $b < 0$, then f is a decreasing function

(c) $f(x)f(-x) = 1$ for all $x \in \mathbf{R}$

(d) $f(x) - f(-x) = 0$ for all $x \in \mathbf{R}$

8. Let a and b be positive real numbers such that $a > 1$ and $b < a$. Let P be a point in the first quadrant that lies on the hyperbola $\frac{x^2}{a^2}-\frac{y^2}{b^2}=1$. Suppose the tangent to the hyperbola at P passes through the point $(1,0)$ and suppose the normal to the hyperbola at P cuts off equal intercepts on the coordinate axes. Let Δ denote the area of the triangle formed by the tangent at P, the normal at P and the x-axis. If e denotes the eccentricity of the hyperbola, then which of the following statements is/are true?

(a) $1 < e < \sqrt{2}$ (b) $\sqrt{2} < e < 2$

(c) $\Delta = a^4$ (d) $\Delta = b^4$

9. Let $f: \mathbf{R} \to \mathbf{R}$ and $g: \mathbf{R} \to \mathbf{R}$ be functions satisfying $f(x+y) = f(x)+f(y)+f(x)f(y)$ and $f(x) = xg(x)$ for all $(x, y) \in \mathbf{R}$. If $\lim_{x\to 0} g(x) = 1$, then which of the following statements is/are true?

(a) f is differentiable at every $x \in \mathbf{R}$

(b) If $g(0) = 1$, then g is differentiable at every $x \in \mathbf{R}$

(c) The derivative $f'(1)$ is equal to 1

(d) The derivative $f'(0)$ is equal to 1

10. Let $\alpha, \beta, \gamma, \delta$ be real numbers such that $\alpha^2+\beta^2+\gamma^2 \ne 0$ and $\alpha + \gamma = 1$. Suppose the point $(3, 2, -1)$ is the mirror image of the point $(1, 0, -1)$ with respect to the plane $\alpha x + \beta y + \gamma z = \delta$. Then which of the following statements is/are true?

(a) $\alpha + \beta = 2$ (b) $\delta - \gamma = 3$

(c) $\delta + \beta = 4$ (d) $\alpha + \beta + \gamma = \delta$

11. Let a and b be positive real numbers. Suppose $\overrightarrow{PQ} = a\hat{i} + b\hat{j}$ and $\overrightarrow{PS} = a\hat{i} - b\hat{j}$ are adjacent sides of a parallelogram $PQRS$. Let $\vec{u}$ and $\vec{v}$ be the projection vectors of $\vec{w} = \hat{i} + \hat{j}$ along $\overrightarrow{PQ}$ and $\overrightarrow{PS}$, respectively. If $|\vec{u}| + |\vec{v}| = |\vec{w}|$ and if the area of the parallelogram $PQRS$ is 8, then which of the following statements is/are true?

(a) $a + b = 4$

(b) $a - b = 2$

(c) The length of the diagonal PR of the parallelogram $PQRS$ is 4

(d) $\vec{w}$ is an angle bisector of the vectors $\overrightarrow{PQ}$ and $\overrightarrow{PS}$

12. For non-negative integers s and r, let

$$\binom{s}{r} = \begin{cases} \dfrac{s!}{r!(s-r)!} & \text{if } r \le s \\ 0 & \text{if } r > s \end{cases}$$

For positive integers m and n, let

$$g(m, n) = \sum_{p=0}^{m+n} \frac{f(m, n, p)}{\binom{n+p}{p}},$$

where for any non-negative integer p,

$$f(m, n\ p) = \sum_{i=0}^{p} \binom{m}{i}\binom{n+i}{p}\binom{p+n}{p-i}$$

Then which of the following statements is/are true?

(a) $g(m, n) = g(n, m)$ for all positive integers m, n
(b) $g(m, n+1) = g(m+1, n)$ for all positive integers m, n
(c) $g(2m, 2n) = 2g(m, n)$ for all positive integers m, n
(d) $g(2m, 2n) = (g(m, n))^2$ for all positive integers m, n

13. Let α and β be the roots of $x^2 - x - 1 = 0$, with $\alpha > \beta$, for all positive integers n. Define

$$a_n = \frac{\alpha^n - \beta^n}{\alpha - \beta} \qquad n \geq 1$$

$$b_1 = 1 \quad \text{and} \quad b_n = a_{n-1} + a_{n+1}, \quad n \geq 2$$

Then, which of the following options is/are correct?

(a) $\alpha_1 + \alpha_2 + \alpha_3 + \cdots + \alpha_n = \alpha_{n+2} - 1$ for all $n \geq 1$
(b) $\sum_{n=1}^{\infty} \frac{\alpha_n}{10^n} = \frac{10}{89}$
(c) $b_n = \alpha^n + \beta^n$ for all $n \geq 1$
(d) $\sum_{n=1}^{\infty} \frac{b_n}{10^n} = \frac{8}{89}$

14. Let

$$M = \begin{bmatrix} 0 & 1 & a \\ 1 & 2 & 3 \\ 3 & b & 1 \end{bmatrix} \text{ and adj } M = \begin{bmatrix} -1 & 1 & -1 \\ 8 & -6 & 2 \\ -5 & 3 & -1 \end{bmatrix},$$

where a and b are real numbers. Which of the following options is/are correct?

(a) $a + b = 3$
(b) $(\text{adj} M)^{-1} + \text{adj} M^{-1} = -M$
(c) $\det(\text{adj } M^2) = 81$
(d) If $M\begin{bmatrix} \alpha \\ \beta \\ \gamma \end{bmatrix} = \begin{bmatrix} 1 \\ 2 \\ 3 \end{bmatrix}$, then $\alpha - \beta + \gamma = 3$

15. There are three bags B_1, B_2 and B_3. Bag B_1 contains 5 red and 5 green balls, B_2 contains 3 red and 5 green balls, and B_3 contains 5 red and 3 green balls. Bags B_1, B_2 and B_3 have probabilities $\frac{3}{10}, \frac{3}{10}$ and $\frac{4}{10}$, respectively, of being chosen. A bag is selected at random and a ball is chosen at random from the bag. Then, which of the following options is/are correct?

(a) Probability that the chosen ball is green, given that the selected bag is B_3, equals $\frac{3}{8}$
(b) Probability that the chosen ball is green equals $\frac{39}{80}$
(c) Probability that the selected bag is B_3, given that the chosen ball is green, equals $\frac{5}{13}$
(d) Probability that the selected bag is B_3 and the chosen ball is green equals $\frac{3}{10}$

16. In a non–right-angled triangle ΔPQR, let p, q and r denote the lengths of the sides opposite the angles at P, Q and R, respectively. The median from R meets the side PQ at S, the perpendicular from P meets the side QR at E, and RS and PE intersect at O. If $p = \sqrt{3}$, $q = 1$ and the radius of the circumcircle of the ΔPQR equals 1, then which of the following options is/are correct?

(a) Length of $RS = \frac{\sqrt{7}}{2}$
(b) Area of $\Delta SOE = \frac{\sqrt{3}}{12}$
(c) Length of $OE = \frac{1}{6}$
(d) Radius of incircle of $\Delta PQR = \frac{\sqrt{3}}{2}(2 - \sqrt{3})$

17. Define the collections $\{E_1, E_2, E_3, \ldots\}$ of ellipses and $\{R_1, R_2, R_3, \ldots\}$ of rectangles as follows:

$E_1 : \frac{x^2}{9} + \frac{y^2}{4} = 1$

R_1 : rectangle of largest area, with sides parallel to the axes, inscribed in E_1

E_n: ellipse $\frac{x^2}{a_n^2} + \frac{y^2}{b_n^2} = 1$ of largest area inscribed in R_{n-1}, $n > 1$

R_n: rectangle of largest area, with sides parallel to the axes, inscribed in E_n, $n > 1$

Then, which of the following options is/are correct?

(a) The eccentricities of E_{18} and E_{19} are NOT equal

(b) $\sum_{n=1}^{N}$ (area of R_n) < 24, for each positive integer **N**

(c) The length of the latus rectum of E_9 is 1/6

(d) The distance of a focus from the centre in E_9 is $\sqrt{5}/32$

18. Let $f : \mathbf{R} \to \mathbf{R}$ be given by

$$f(x) = \begin{cases} x^5 + 5x^4 + 10x^3 + 10x^2 + 3x + 1, & x < 0; \\ x^2 - x + 1, & 0 \le x < 1; \\ \frac{2}{3}x^3 - 4x^2 + 7x - \frac{8}{3}, & 1 \le x < 3; \\ (x-2)\log_e(x-2) - x + \frac{10}{3}, & x \ge 3. \end{cases}$$

Then, which of the following options is/are correct?

(a) f is increasing on $(-\infty, 0)$

(b) f' has a local maximum at $x = 1$

(c) f is onto

(d) f' is NOT differentiable at $x = 1$

19. Let Γ denote a curve $y = y(x)$ that is in the first quadrant and let the point (1, 0) lie on it. Let the tangent to Γ at a point P intersect the y-axis at Y_P. If PY_P has length 1 for each point P on Γ, then which of the following options is/are correct?

(a) $y = \log_e\left(\frac{1+\sqrt{1-x^2}}{x}\right) - \sqrt{1-x^2}$

(b) $xy' + \sqrt{1-x^2} = 0$

(c) $y = -\log_e\left(\frac{1+\sqrt{1-x^2}}{x}\right) + \sqrt{1-x^2}$

(d) $xy' - \sqrt{1-x^2} = 0$

20. Let L_1 and L_2 denote the lines

$\vec{r} = \hat{i} + \lambda(-\hat{i} + 2\hat{j} + 2\hat{k}),\ \lambda \in \mathbf{R}$ and

$\vec{r} = \mu(2\hat{i} - \hat{j} + 2\hat{k}),\ \mu \in \mathbf{R}$

respectively. If L_3 is a line that is perpendicular to both L_1 and L_2 and cuts both of them, then which of the following options describe(s) L_3?

(a) $\vec{r} = \frac{2}{9}(4\hat{i} + \hat{j} + \hat{k}) + t(2\hat{i} + 2\hat{j} - \hat{k}), t \in \mathbf{R}$

(b) $\vec{r} = \frac{2}{9}(2\hat{i} - \hat{j} + 2\hat{k}) + t(2\hat{i} + 2\hat{j} - \hat{k}), t \in \mathbf{R}$

(c) $\vec{r} = \frac{1}{3}(2\hat{i} + \hat{k}) + t(2\hat{i} + 2\hat{j} - \hat{k}), t \in \mathbf{R}$

(d) $\vec{r} = t(2\hat{i} + 2\hat{j} - \hat{k}), t \in \mathbf{R}$

21. Let

$$P_1 = I = \begin{bmatrix} 1 & 0 & 0 \\ 0 & 1 & 0 \\ 0 & 0 & 1 \end{bmatrix},\ P_2 = \begin{bmatrix} 1 & 0 & 0 \\ 0 & 0 & 1 \\ 0 & 1 & 0 \end{bmatrix},\ P_3 = \begin{bmatrix} 0 & 1 & 0 \\ 1 & 0 & 0 \\ 0 & 0 & 1 \end{bmatrix},$$

$$P_4 = \begin{bmatrix} 0 & 1 & 0 \\ 0 & 0 & 1 \\ 1 & 0 & 0 \end{bmatrix},\ P_5 = \begin{bmatrix} 0 & 0 & 1 \\ 1 & 0 & 0 \\ 0 & 1 & 0 \end{bmatrix},\ P_6 = \begin{bmatrix} 0 & 0 & 1 \\ 0 & 1 & 0 \\ 1 & 0 & 0 \end{bmatrix}$$

and $X = \sum_{k-1}^{6} P_k \begin{bmatrix} 2 & 1 & 3 \\ 1 & 0 & 2 \\ 3 & 2 & 1 \end{bmatrix} P_k^T$,

where P_k^T denotes the transpose of the matrix P_k. Then, which of the following options is/are correct?

(a) If $X\begin{bmatrix} 1 \\ 1 \\ 1 \end{bmatrix} = \alpha\begin{bmatrix} 1 \\ 1 \\ 1 \end{bmatrix}$, then $\alpha = 30$

(b) X is a symmetric matrix

(c) The sum of the diagonal entries of X is 18

(d) $X - 30I$ is an invertible matrix

22. Let $x \in \mathbf{R}$ and let

$$P = \begin{bmatrix} 1 & 1 & 1 \\ 0 & 2 & 2 \\ 0 & 0 & 3 \end{bmatrix},\ Q = \begin{bmatrix} 2 & x & x \\ 0 & 4 & 0 \\ x & x & 6 \end{bmatrix} \text{ and } R = PQP^{-1}.$$

Then which of the following option is/are correct?

(a) There exists a real number x such that $PQ = QP$.

(b) $\det R = \det\begin{bmatrix} 2 & x & x \\ 0 & 4 & 0 \\ x & x & 5 \end{bmatrix} + 8$, for all $x \in \mathbf{R}$

(c) For $x = 0$, if $R\begin{bmatrix} 1 \\ a \\ b \end{bmatrix} = 6\begin{bmatrix} 1 \\ a \\ b \end{bmatrix}$, then $a + b = 5$

(d) For $x = 1$, there exists a unit vector $\alpha\hat{i} + \beta\hat{j} + \gamma\hat{k}$ for which $R\begin{bmatrix} \alpha \\ \beta \\ \gamma \end{bmatrix} = \begin{bmatrix} 0 \\ 0 \\ 0 \end{bmatrix}$

23. For non-negative integers n, let

$$f(n)=\frac{\sum_{k=0}^{n}\sin\left(\frac{k+1}{n+2}\pi\right)\sin\left(\frac{k+2}{n+2}\pi\right)}{\sum_{k=0}^{n}\sin^2\left(\frac{k+1}{n+2}\pi\right)}$$

Assuming $\cos^{-1}x$ takes values in $[0, \pi]$, which of the following options is/are correct?

(a) $f(4)=\frac{\sqrt{3}}{2}$

(b) $\lim_{n\to\infty} f(n)=\frac{1}{2}$

(c) If $\alpha=\tan(\cos^{-1} f(6))$, then $\alpha^2+2\alpha-1=0$

(d) $\sin(7\cos^{-1} f(5))=0$

24. Let $f:\mathbf{R}\to\mathbf{R}$ be a function. We say that f has

PROPERTY 1: If $\lim_{h\to 0}\frac{f(h)-f(0)}{\sqrt{|h|}}$ exists and is finite, and

PROPERTY 2: If $\lim_{h\to 0}\frac{f(h)-f(0)}{h^2}$ exists and is finite.

Then, which of the following option is/are correct?

(a) $f(x)=|x|$ has PROPERTY 1

(b) $f(x)=x^{2/3}$ has PROPERTY 1

(c) $f(x)=x|x|$ has PROPERTY 2

(d) $f(x)=\sin x$ has PROPERTY 2

25. Let $f(x)=\frac{\sin \pi x}{x^2}$, $x>0$.

Let $x_1<x_2<x_3<\cdots<x_n<\cdots$ be all the points of local maximum of f and $y_1<y_2<y_3<\cdots<y_n<\cdots$ be all the points of local minimum of f. Then, which of the following options is/are correct?

(a) $x_1<y_1$

(b) $x_{n+1}-x_n>2$ for every n

(c) $x_n\in\left(2n, 2n+\frac{1}{2}\right)$ for every n

(d) $|x_n-y_n|>1$ for every n

26. For $a\in\mathbf{R}$, $|a|>1$, let

$$\lim_{n\to\infty}\left(\frac{1+\sqrt[3]{2}+\cdots+\sqrt[3]{n}}{n^{7/3}\left(\frac{1}{(an+1)^2}+\frac{1}{(an+2)^2}+\cdots+\frac{1}{(an+n)^2}\right)}\right)=54.$$

Then the possible value(s) of α is/are:

(a) –9 (b) – 6
(c) 7 (d) 8

27. Let $f:\mathbf{R}\to\mathbf{R}$ be given by $f(x)=(x-1)(x-2)(x-5)$.

Define $F(x)=\int_0^x f(t)dt$, $x>0$.

Then which of the following options is/are correct?

(a) F has a local minimum at $x=1$

(b) F has a local maximum at $x=2$

(c) F has two local maxima and one local minimum in $(0,\infty)$

(d) $F(x)\neq 0$ for all $x\in(0,5)$

28. Three lines

$L_1:\vec{r}=\lambda\hat{i},\ \lambda\in\mathbf{R}$,

$L_2:\vec{r}=\hat{k}+\mu\hat{j},\ \mu\in\mathbf{R}$ and

$L_3:\vec{r}=\hat{i}+\hat{j}+v\hat{k},\ v\in\mathbf{R}$

are given. For which point(s) Q on L_2 can we find a point P on L_1 and a point R on L_3 so that P, Q and R are collinear?

(a) $\hat{k}-\frac{1}{2}\hat{j}$ (b) $\hat{k}$

(c) $\hat{k}+\frac{1}{2}\hat{j}$ (d) $\hat{k}+\hat{j}$

Single Digit Answer

- The answer to each question is a **SINGLE DIGIT INTEGER** ranging from 0 TO 9, **BOTH INCLUSIVE**
- For each question, enter the correct integer corresponding to the answer using the mouse and the on-screen virtual numeric keypad in the place designated to enter the answer.
- The answer to each question will be evaluated according to the following marking scheme:

Full Marks: +3 If ONLY the correct integer is entered;
Zero Marks: 0 If the question is unanswered;
Negative Marks: –1 In all other cases

1. For a complex number z, let Re(z) denote the real part of z. Let S be the set of all complex numbers z satisfying $z^4-|z|^4=4iz^2$, where $i=\sqrt{-1}$. Then the minimum possible value of $|z_1-z_2|^2$, where $z_1, z_2\in S$ with $\text{Re}(z_1)>0$ and $\text{Re}(z_2)<0$, is _____.

2. The probability that a missile hits a target successfully is 0.75. In order to destroy the target completely, at least three successful hits are required. Then the minimum number of missiles that have to be fired so that the probability of completely destroying the target is not less than 0.95 is _______.

3. Let O be the centre of the circle $x^2 + y^2 = r^2$, where $r > \frac{\sqrt{5}}{2}$. Suppose PQ is a chord of this circle and the equation of the line passing through P and Q is $2x + 4y = 5$. If the centre of the circumcircle of the triangle OPQ lies on the line $x + 2y = 4$, then the value of r is _______.

4. The trace of a square matrix is defined to be the sum of its diagonal entries. If A is a 2×2 matrix such that the trace of A is 3 and the trace of A^3 is –18, then the value of the determinant of A is _______.

5. Let the functions $f : (-1, 1) \to \mathbf{R}$ and $g : (-1, 1) \to (-1, 1)$ be defined by

$$f(x) = |2x - 1| + |2x + 1| \text{ and } g(x) = x - [x],$$

where $[x]$ denotes the greatest integer less than or equal to x. Let $fog : (-1, 1) \to \mathbf{R}$ be the composite function defined by $fog(x) = f(g(x))$. Suppose c is the number of points in the interval (–1, 1) at which fog is not continuous, and suppose d is the number of points in the interval (–1, 1) at which fog is not differentiable. Then the value of $c + d$ is _____.

6. The value of the limit

$$\lim_{x \to \frac{\pi}{2}} \frac{4\sqrt{2}(\sin 3x + \sin x)}{\left(2 \sin 2x \sin \frac{3x}{2} + \cos \frac{5x}{2}\right) - \left(\sqrt{2} + \sqrt{2} \cos 2x + \cos \frac{3x}{2}\right)}$$

is ______.

Numerical Value Answer

- The answer to each question is a **NUMERICAL VALUE.**
- For each question, enter the correct numerical value of the answer using the mouse and the on screen virtual numeric keypad in the place designated to enter the answer. If the numerical value has more than two decimal places, truncate/round-off the value to TWO decimal places.
- The answer to each question will be evaluated according to the following marking scheme:

Full Marks: +4 If ONLY the correct numerical value is entered;

Zero Marks: 0 In all other cases

1. Let m be the minimum possible value of $\log_3(3^{y_1} + 3^{y_2} + 3^{y_3})$, where y_1, y_2, y_3 are real numbers for which $y_1 + y_2 + y_3 = 9$. Let M be the maximum possible value of $(\log_3 x_1 + \log_3 x_2 + \log_3 x_3)$, where x_1, x_2, x_3 are positive real numbers for which $x_1 + x_2 + x_3 = 9$. Then the value of $\log_2(m^3) + \log_3(M^2)$ is __________.

2. Let $a_1, a_2, a_3, \ldots$ be a sequence of positive integers in arithmetic progression with common difference 2. Also, let $b_1, b_2, b_3, \ldots$ be a sequence of positive integers in geometric progression with common ratio 2. If $a_1 = b_1 = c$, then the number of all possible values of c, for which the equality

$$2(a_1 + a_2 + \cdots + a_n) = b_1 + b_2 + \cdots + b_n$$

holds for some positive integer n is ______.

3. Let $f : [0, 2] \to \mathbb{R}$ be the function defined by

$$f(x) = (3 - \sin(2\pi x)) \sin\left(\pi x - \frac{\pi}{4}\right) - \sin\left(3\pi x + \frac{\pi}{4}\right).$$

If $\alpha, \beta \in [0, 2]$ are such that $\{x \in [0, 2] : f(x) \geq 0\} = [\alpha, \beta]$, then the value of $\beta - \alpha$ is _____.

4. In a triangle PQR, let $\vec{a} = \overrightarrow{QR}$, $\vec{b} = \overrightarrow{RP}$ and $\vec{c} = \overrightarrow{PQ}$.

If $|\vec{a}| = 3$, $|\vec{b}| = 4$ and $\frac{\vec{a} \cdot (\vec{c} - \vec{b})}{\vec{c} \cdot (\vec{a} - \vec{b})} = \frac{|\vec{a}|}{|\vec{a}| + |\vec{b}|}$,

then the value of $|\vec{a} \times \vec{b}|^2$ is ______.

5. For a polynomial $g(x)$ with real coefficients, let m_g denote the number of distinct real roots of $g(x)$. Suppose S is the set of polynomials with real coefficients defined by

$$S = \{(x^2 - 1)^2 (a_0 + a_1 x + a_2 x^2 + a_3 x^3) : a_0, a_1, a_2, a_3 \in \mathbf{R}\}.$$

For a polynomial f, let f' and f'' denote its first and second order derivatives, respectively. Then the minimum possible value of $(m_{f'} + m_{f''})$, where $f \in S$, is _______.

6. Let e denote the base of the natural logarithm. The value of the real number a for which the right-hand limit

$$\lim_{x \to 0^+} \frac{(1 - x)^{\frac{1}{x}} - e^{-1}}{x^a}$$

is equal to a non-zero real number is _______.

7. An engineer is required to visit a factory for exactly four days during the first 15 days of every month and it is mandatory that no two visits take place on consecutive days. Then the number of all possible ways in which such visits to the factory can be made by the engineer during June 1–15, 2021 is _______.

8. In a hotel, four rooms are available. Six persons are to be accommodated in these four rooms in such a way that each of these rooms contains at least one person and at most two persons. Then the number of all possible ways in which this can be done is _______.

9. Two fair dice, each with faces numbered 1,2,3,4,5 and 6, are rolled together and the sum of the numbers on the faces is observed. This process is repeated till the sum is either a prime number or a perfect square. Suppose the sum turns out to be a perfect square before it turns out to be a prime number. If p is the probability that this perfect square is an odd number, then the value of $14p$ is _______.

10. Let the function $f:[0,1]\to\mathbf{R}$ be defined by

$$f(x)=\frac{4^x}{4^x+2}.$$

Then the value of

$$f\left(\frac{1}{40}\right)+f\left(\frac{2}{40}\right)+f\left(\frac{3}{40}\right)+\cdots+f\left(\frac{39}{40}\right)-f\left(\frac{1}{2}\right)$$

is _______.

11. Let $f:\mathbf{R}\to\mathbf{R}$ be a differentiable function such that its derivative f' is continuous and $f(\pi)=-6$. If $F:[0,\pi]\to\mathbf{R}$ is defined by $F(x)=\int_0^x f(t)\,dt$, and if

$$\int_0^{\pi}(f'(x)+F(x))\cos x\,dx=2$$

then the value of $f(0)$ is _______.

12. Let the function $f:[0,\pi]\to\mathbf{R}$ be defined by

$$f(\theta)=(\sin\theta+\cos\theta)^2+(\sin\theta-\cos\theta)^4.$$

Suppose the function f has a local minimum at θ precisely when $\theta\in\{\lambda_1\pi,\ldots,\lambda_r\pi\}$, where $0<\lambda_1<\cdots<\lambda_r<1$. Then the value of $\lambda_1+\cdots+\lambda_r$ is _______.

13. Let $\omega\neq 1$ be a cube root of unity. Then, the minimum of the set

$\{|a+b\omega+c\omega^2|^2 : a,b,c$ distinct non-zero integers$\}$

equals ____.

14. Let $AP(a;d)$ denote the set of all the terms of an infinite arithmetic progression with first term a and common difference $d>0$. If

$$AP(1;3)\cap AP(2;5)\cap AP(3;7)=AP(a;d)$$

Then $a+d$ equals ___.

15. Let S be the sample space of all 3×3 matrices with entries from the set $\{0,1\}$. Let the events E_1 and E_2 be given by

$E_1=\{A\in S:\ \det A=0\}$ and

$E_2=\{A\in S: \text{sum of entries of } A \text{ is } 7\}.$

If a matrix is chosen at random from S, then the conditional probability $P(E_1/E_2)$ equals _____.

16. Let the point B be the reflection of the point $A(2,3)$ with respect to the line $8x-6y-23=0$. Let Γ_A and Γ_B be circles of radii 2 and 1 with centres A and B, respectively. Let T be the common tangent to the circles Γ_A and Γ_B such that both the circles are on the same side of T. If C is the point of intersection of T and the line passing through A and B, then the length of the line segment AC is ____.

17. If $I=\dfrac{2}{\pi}\displaystyle\int_{-\pi/4}^{\pi/4}\frac{dx}{(1+e^{\sin x})(2-\cos 2x)}$, then $27\ I^2$ equals _____.

18. Three lines are given by

$\vec{r}=\lambda\hat{i},\lambda\in\mathbf{R}$

$\vec{r}=\mu(\hat{i}+\hat{j}),\mu\in\mathbf{R}$ and

$\vec{r}=v(\hat{i}+\hat{j}+\hat{k}),v\in\mathbf{R}.$

Let the lines cut the plane $x+y+z=1$ at the points A, B and C, respectively. If the area of the triangle ABC is Δ, then the value of $(6\Delta)^2$ equals _____.

19. Suppose

$$\det\begin{vmatrix}\sum_{k=0}^{n}k & \sum_{k=0}^{n}{}^nC_k\,k^2\\ \sum_{k=0}^{n}{}^nC_k\,k & \sum_{k=0}^{n}{}^nC_k\,3^k\end{vmatrix}=0$$

holds for some positive integer n, then $\displaystyle\sum_{k=0}^{n}\frac{{}^nC_k}{k+1}$ equals _____.

20. Five persons A, B, C, D and E are seated in a circular arrangement. If each of them is given a hat of one of the three colours red, blue and green, then the number of ways of distributing the hats such that the persons seated in adjacent seats get different coloured hats is _____.

21. Let $|X|$ denotes the number of elements in a set X. Let $S = \{1, 2, 3, 4, 5, 6\}$ be a sample space, where each element is equally likely to occur. If A and B are independent events associated with S, then the number of ordered pairs (A, B) such that $1 \le |B| < |A|$, equals______.

22. The value of

$$\sec^{-1}\left(\frac{1}{2}\sum_{k=0}^{10}\sec\left(\frac{7\pi}{12}+\frac{k\pi}{2}\right)\sec\left(\frac{7\pi}{12}+\frac{(k+1)\pi}{2}\right)\right)$$

in the interval $\left[-\frac{\pi}{4}, \frac{3\pi}{4}\right]$ equals ___.

23. The value of the integral

$$\int_0^{\pi/2} \frac{3\sqrt{\cos\theta}}{(\sqrt{\cos\theta}+\sqrt{\sin\theta})^5}\, d\theta$$

equals ____.

24. Let $\vec{a} = 2\hat{i} + \hat{j} - \hat{k}$ and $\vec{b} = \hat{i} + 2\hat{j} + \hat{k}$ be two vectors. Consider a vector $\vec{c} = \alpha\vec{a} + \beta\vec{b}$, $\alpha, \beta \in \mathbf{R}$. If the projection of $\vec{c}$ on the vector $(\vec{a}+\vec{b})$ is $3\sqrt{2}$, then the minimum value of $(\vec{c} - (\vec{a}\times\vec{b}))\cdot\vec{c}$ equals ____.

Match the Lists

- Each List-Match set has **TWO (02)** Multiple Choice Questions.
- Each List-Match set has two lists: **List I** and **List II**.
- **FOUR** options are given in each Multiple Choice Question based on **List I** and **List II** and **ONLY ONE** of these four options satisfies the condition asked in the Multiple Choice Question.
- The answer to each question will be evaluated according to the following marking scheme:

Full Marks: +3 If ONLY the correct option is chosen;
Zero Marks: 0 If none of the options is chosen (i.e. the question is unanswered);
Negative Marks: –1 In all other cases

Paragraph: Let $f(x) = \sin(\pi\cos x)$ and $g(x) = \cos(2\pi\sin x)$ be two functions defined for $x > 0$. Define the following sets whose elements are written in increasing order:

$$X = \{x : f(x) = 0\},\quad Y = \{x : f'(x) = 0\},$$
$$Z = \{x : g(x) = 0\},\quad W = \{x : g'(x) = 0\}.$$

List I contains the sets X, Y, Z and W. List II contains some information regarding these sets.

List I	**List II**
(I) X	(P) $\supseteq\left\{\frac{\pi}{2}, \frac{3\pi}{2}, 4\pi, 7\pi\right\}$
(II) Y	(Q) An arithmetic progression
(III) Z	(R) NOT an arithmetic progression
(IV) W	(S) $\supseteq\left\{\frac{\pi}{6}, \frac{7\pi}{6}, \frac{13\pi}{6}\right\}$
	(T) $\supseteq\left\{\frac{\pi}{3}, \frac{2\pi}{3}, \pi\right\}$
	(U) $\supseteq\left\{\frac{\pi}{6}, \frac{3\pi}{4}\right\}$

Answer Q.1 and Q.2 by appropriately matching the lists based on the information given in the paragraph.

1. Which of the following is the only CORRECT combination?
(a) (I), (P), (R) (b) (II), (Q), (T)
(c) (I), (Q), (U) (d) (II), (R), (S)

2. Which of the following is the only CORRECT combination?
(a) (III), (R), (U) (b) (IV), (P), (R), (S)
(c) (III), (P), (Q), (U) (d) (IV), (Q), (T)

Paragraph: Let the circles $C_1 : x^2 + y^2 = 9$ and $C_2 : (x-3)^2 + (y-4)^2 = 16$ intersect at the points X and Y. Suppose that another circle $C_3 : (x-h)^2 + (y-k)^2 = r^2$ satisfies the following conditions:

(i) Centre of C_3 is collinear with the centres of C_1 and C_2
(ii) C_1 and C_2 both lie inside C_3
(iii) C_3 touches C_1 at M and C_2 at N

Let the line through X and Y intersect C_3 at Z and W, and let a common tangent of C_1 and C_3 be a tangent to the parabola $x^2 = 8\alpha y$. There are some expressions given in List I whose values are given in List II below:

List I	**List II**
(I) $2h + k$	(P) 6
(II) $\dfrac{\text{Length of } ZW}{\text{Length of } XY}$	(Q) $\sqrt{6}$
(III) $\dfrac{\text{Area of triangle } MZN}{\text{Area of triangle } ZMW}$	(R) $\dfrac{5}{4}$
(IV) α	(S) $\dfrac{21}{5}$
	(T) $2\sqrt{6}$
	(U) $\dfrac{10}{3}$

Answer Q.3 and Q.4 by appropriately matching the lists based on the information given in the paragraph.

3. Which of the following is the only CORRECT combination?
(a) (I), (S) (b) (I), (U)
(c) (II), (Q) (d) (II), (T)

4. Which of the following is the only INCORRECT combination?
(a) (I), (P) (b) (IV), (U)
(c) (III), (R) (d) (IV), (S)

ANSWER KEYS

Only One Correct Option

1. (d) **2.** (c) **3.** (a) **4.** (a) **5.** (b) **6.** (c) **7.** (a) **8.** (c) **9.** (b) **10.** (d)

One or More Correct Options

1. (a),(c) **2.** (b) **3.** (b),(c) **4.** (b) **5.** (a),(d)
6. (a),(b) **7.** (a),(c) **8.** (a),(d) **9.** (a),(d) **10.** (a),(b)
11. (a),(c) **12.** (a),(b),(d) **13.** (a),(b),(c) **14.** (a),(b),(d) **15.** (a),(b)
16. (a),(c),(d) **17.** (b),(c) **18.** (b),(c) **19.** (a),(b) **20.** (a),(b),(c)
21. (a),(b),(c) **22.** (c) **23.** (a),(c),(d) **24.** (a),(b) **25.** (b),(c),(d)
26. (a),(d) **27.** (a),(b),(d) **28.** (a),(c)

Single Digit Answer

1. 8 **2.** 6 **3.** 2 **4.** 5 **5.** 4 **6.** 8

Numerical Value Answer

1. 8 **2.** 1 **3.** 1 **4.** 108 **5.** 3 **6.** 1 **7.** 429 **8.** 1080 **9.** 7
10. 19.17 **11.** 4 **12.** 0.5 **13.** 1.5 **14.** 262 **15.** 0.5 **16.** 10 **17.** 4 **18.** 0.75
19. 4 **20.** 30 **21.** 186 **22.** 2.62 **23.** 0.5 **24.** 18

Match the Lists

1. (b) **2.** (b) **3.** (c) **4.** (c)

SOLUTIONS

Only One Correct Option

1. (d) From the given quadratic equations, we have

$$a + b = -20,\ ab = -2020$$

and $c + d = 20,\ cd = 2020$

Now, we have

$$S = ac(a - c) + ad(a - d) + bc(b - c) + bd(b - d)$$
$$= a[ac - c^2 + ad - d^2] + b[bc - c^2 + bd - d^2]$$
$$= a[a(c + d) - (c^2 + d^2)] + b[b(c + d) - (c^2 + d^2)]$$
$$= (a^2 + b^2)(c + d) - (a + b)(c^2 + d^2)$$
$$= 20[a^2 + b^2 + c^2 + d^2]$$
$$= 20[(a + b)^2 - 2ab + (c + d)^2 - 2cd]$$
$$= 20[400 + 4040 + 400 - 4040] = 16000$$

2. (c) The given function $f(x) = |x|(x - \sin x)$ is defined for $x \in \mathbf{R}$ and is odd since

$$f(-x) = |-x|(-x - \sin(-x))$$
$$= |x|(-x + \sin x) = -f(x)$$

Let us analyse the function for $x \geq 0$. We have

$$f(x) = x^2 - x\sin x,$$
$$f'(x) = 2x - x\cos x - \sin x$$

and $f''(x) = 2 + x\sin n - 2\cos x$

$$= x\sin x + 4\sin^2\left(\frac{x}{2}\right)$$

Now $f'' \geq 0\ \forall x \geq o \Rightarrow f'$ is increasing in $(0, +\infty)$.
Since $f'(0) = 0 \Rightarrow f' \geq 0\ \forall\ x \geq 0 \Rightarrow f$ is increasing in $(0, +\infty)$
Since $f(0) = 0 \Rightarrow f \geq 0\ \forall\ x \geq 0$
Also $f(+\infty) = +\infty \Rightarrow f(x)$ increases from o to $+\infty$ for $x \in (o, +\infty)$.
Since f is odd, we can infer that $f(x)$ increases from $-\infty$ to 0 for $x \in (-\infty, 0)$.
Thus, f is an increasing function and its range is **R** $\Rightarrow f$: **R** $\to$ **R** is one–one and onto.

3. (a) The function $f(x)$ can be written as

$$f(x) = \begin{cases} o, x \leq 1 \\ e^{x-1} - e^{-x+1}, x \geq 1 \end{cases}$$

The figure shows the graphs of the two functions, $f(x)$ and $g(x)$. Their intersection point $x = \alpha$ is given by

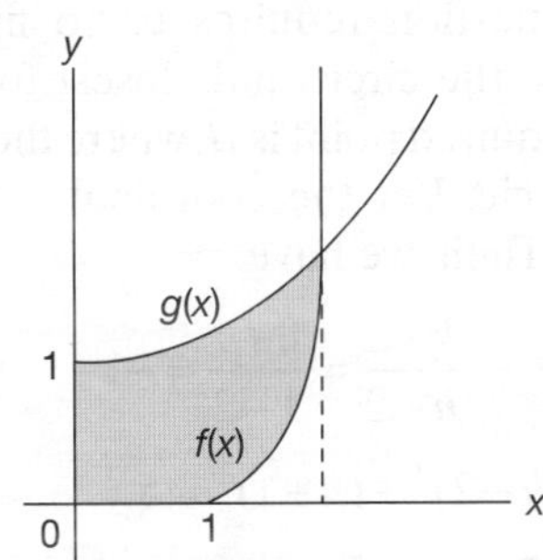

$$e^{x-1} - e^{1-x} = \frac{e^{x-1} + e^{1-x}}{2}$$

$\Rightarrow \quad e^{x-1} - 3e^{1-x}$

$\Rightarrow \quad e^{2(x-1)} = 3$

$\Rightarrow \quad x = 1 \pm \frac{1}{2}\ln 3$

$\Rightarrow \quad x = 1 + \ln\sqrt{3}$

Hence, area of the shaded region is

$$A = \int_0^\alpha \{g(x) - f(x)\}dx$$

$$= \int_0^1 \left(\frac{e^{x-1} + e^{1-x}}{2}\right)dx$$

$$+ \int_1^\alpha \left(\frac{e^{x-1} + e^{1-x}}{2} - e^{x-1} + e^{1-x}\right)dx$$

$$= \frac{1}{2}\left|e^{x-1} - e^{1-x}\right|_0^1 + \int_1^\alpha \left(\frac{-e^{x-1} + 3e^{1-x}}{2}\right)dx$$

$$= \frac{1}{2}(e - e^{-1}) + \frac{1}{2}\left|-e^{x-1} - 3e^{1-x}\right|^{1+\ln\sqrt{3}}$$

$$= \frac{1}{2}(e - e^{-1}) + \frac{1}{2}\left|e^{x-1} + 3e^{1-x}\right|_{1+\ln\sqrt{3}}^{1}$$

$$= \frac{1}{2}(e - e^{-1}) + \frac{1}{2}(4 - e^{\ln\sqrt{3}} + 3e^{-\ln\sqrt{3}})$$

$$= \frac{1}{2}(e - e^{-1}) + \frac{1}{2}\left(4 - \sqrt{3} - \frac{3}{\sqrt{3}}\right)$$

$$= \frac{1}{2}(e - e^{-1}) + (2 - \sqrt{3})$$

4. (a) The intersection point of the parabola and the ellipse is $P(\lambda, 2\lambda)$.
Differentiating $y^2 = 4\lambda x$, we have

$$2yy' = 4\lambda \Rightarrow y' = \frac{2\lambda}{y}$$

Thus, the slope of the tangent to the parabola at point P is

$$y_1^1 = \frac{2\lambda}{2\lambda} = 1$$

Differentiating $\frac{x^2}{a^2} + \frac{y^2}{b^2} = 1$, we have

$$\frac{2x}{a^2} + \frac{2yy'}{b^2} = 0 \Rightarrow y' = -\frac{b^2x}{a^2y}$$

Thus, the slope of the tangent to the ellipse at point P is

$$y_2^1 = -\frac{b^2\lambda}{a^2(2\lambda)} = -\frac{b^2}{2a^2}$$

Since the two tangents are given to be perpendicular

$$y_1^1 \times y_2^1 = -1$$

$\Rightarrow \quad \frac{-b^2}{2a^2} = -1$

$\Rightarrow \quad \frac{a^2}{b^2} = \frac{1}{2}$

Hence, eccentricity of the ellipse is

$$e = \sqrt{1 - \frac{a^2}{b^2}} = \sqrt{1 - 1/2} = \frac{1}{\sqrt{2}}$$

5. (b) The roots of $x^2 - \alpha x + \beta = 0$ will be real and equal if $\alpha^2 = 4\beta$. Since α, β can only take the values 0, 1, 2, the condition $\alpha^2 = 4\beta$ can be satisfied if Event $A = (\alpha = 0$ and $\beta = 0)$ or Event $B = (\alpha = 2$ and $\beta = 1)$.

Now, we have

$$P(A) = P\{(TT \text{ in } C_1) \text{ and } (TT \text{ in } C_2)\}$$

$$= \left(\frac{1}{3}\times\frac{1}{3}\right)\times\left(\frac{2}{3}\times\frac{2}{3}\right) = \frac{4}{81}$$

and $P(B) = P\{(HH \text{ in } C_1) \text{ and } (HT \text{ or } TH \text{ in } C_2)\}$

$$= \left(\frac{2}{3}\times\frac{2}{3}\right)\times\left[\left(\frac{1}{3}\times\frac{2}{3}\right)+\left(\frac{2}{3}\times\frac{1}{3}\right)\right]$$

$$= \frac{4}{9}\times\frac{4}{9} = \frac{16}{81}$$

Hence, the required probability is

$P(A \text{ or } B) = P(A) + P(B)$ [A and B are mutually exclusive]

$$= \frac{4}{81}+\frac{16}{81} = \frac{20}{81}$$

6. (c) The figure shows the graph of $y = 2\sin(2x)$ and a rectangle $ABCD$ inscribed inside the graph and the x-axis. Let $OA = x$ and $AB = y = 2\sin(2x)$.

Then $AD = 2\left(x-\frac{\pi}{4}\right) = 2x-\frac{\pi}{2}$

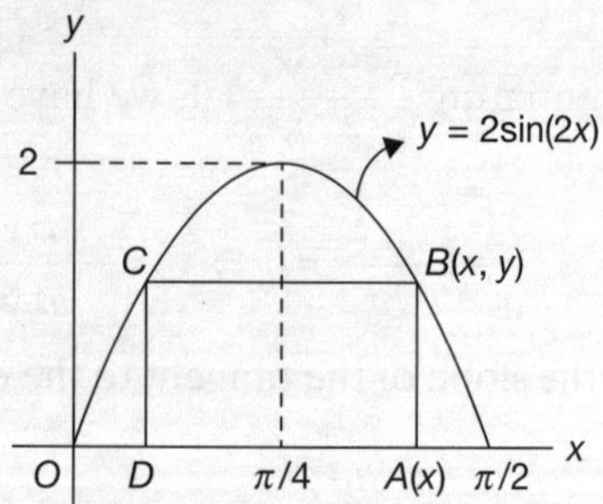

Thus, the perimeter of the rectangle is

$$P = 2\left(2x-\frac{\pi}{2}\right)+2y$$

$$= 4x - \pi + 4\sin(2x)$$

The maximum value of P occurs where $\frac{dP}{dx} = 0$. That is, where

$$4 + 8\cos(2x) = 0$$

$$\Rightarrow \quad \cos 2x = -\frac{1}{2} \Rightarrow x = \frac{\pi}{3}$$

Hence, the corresponding area of the rectangle is

$$A = \left(2x-\frac{\pi}{2}\right)y = \left(2x-\frac{\pi}{2}\right)\times 2\sin(2x)$$

$$= \left(\frac{2\pi}{3}-\frac{\pi}{2}\right)\times 2\sin\left(\frac{2\pi}{3}\right)$$

$$= \frac{\pi}{6}\times\sqrt{3} = \frac{\pi}{2\sqrt{3}}$$

7. (a)

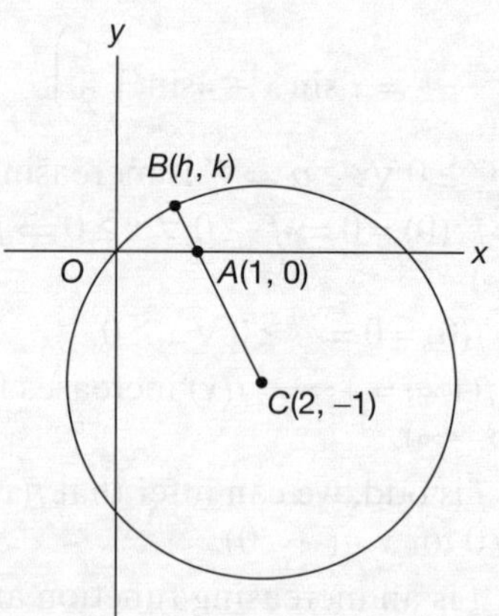

The inequality $|z-2+i| \geq \sqrt{5}$ represents points lying on or outside the circle centred at $C(2,-1)$ having radius $\sqrt{5}$ (see figure). The expression $|z-1|$ represents the distance between points having complex representation z and 1. Maximum value of $\frac{1}{|z-1|}$ occurs when $|z-1|$ is minimum.

The question requires us to find a point on or outside the circle and closest to the point $A(1,0)$. The required point is B, where the line CA intersects the circle. Let the coordinates of the point B be (h,k). Then, we have

$$\frac{k+1}{h-2} = \frac{0+1}{1-2} = -1 \quad (1)$$

and $(h-2)^2 + (h+1)^2 = 5$ (2)

Then the complex representation of point B will be $z_0 = h + ik$, and the given expression will reduce to

$$\frac{4-z_0-\overline{z_0}}{z_0-\overline{z_0}+2i} = \frac{4-2h}{2ik+2i} = \frac{2-h}{i(k+1)} = \left(\frac{h-2}{k+1}\right)i = -i$$

[Using equation (1)]

Now, the principal argument of $-i$ is $\text{Arg}(-i) = \pi$. Note that we did not need to solve equations (1), (2) and find the values of h,k.

8. (c) The given equation $M = \alpha I + \beta M^{-1}$ can be written as

$$M^2 = \alpha M + \beta I \quad (1)$$

Now, let $\sin^2\theta = a$ and $\cos^2\theta = b$. Then, we have

$$M^2 = \begin{bmatrix} a^2 & -1-a \\ 1+b & b^2 \end{bmatrix}\begin{bmatrix} a^2 & -1-a \\ 1+b & b^2 \end{bmatrix}$$

$$= \begin{bmatrix} a^4-(1+a)(1+b) & -(1+a)(a^2+b^2) \\ (1+b)(a^2+b^2) & b^4-(1+a)(1+b) \end{bmatrix}$$

$$= \begin{bmatrix} a^2(a^2+b^2)-a^2b^2 \\ -(1+a)(1+b) & -(1+a)(a^2+b^2) \\ (1+b)(a^2+b^2) & b^2(a^2+b^2)-a^2b^2 \\ & -(1+a)(1+b) \end{bmatrix}$$

$$= \begin{bmatrix} a^2(a^2+b^2) & -(1+a)(a^2+b^2) \\ (1+b)(a^2+b^2) & b^2(a^2+b^2) \end{bmatrix}$$

$$+ \begin{bmatrix} -a^2b^2-(1+a)(1+b) & 0 \\ 0 & -a^2b^2-(1+a)(1+b) \end{bmatrix}$$

$$= (a^2+b^2)M + \{-a^2b^2-(1+a)(1+b)\}I \quad (2)$$

Comparing equations (1) and (2), we have

$$\alpha = a^2+b^2 = \sin^4\theta + \cos^4\theta$$

and $\beta = -a^2b^2-(1+a)(1+b)$

$$= -\left[\sin^4\theta\cos^4\theta + (1+\sin^2\theta)(1+\cos^2\theta)\right]$$

Simplifying the two expressions, we have

$$\alpha = (\sin^2\theta\cos^4\theta)^2 - 2\sin^2\theta\cos^2\theta$$

$$= 1 - 2\left(\frac{1-\cos 2\theta}{2}\right)\left(\frac{1+\cos 2\theta}{2}\right)$$

$$= 1 - \frac{1}{2}(1-\cos^2 2\theta) = 1 - \frac{1}{2}\sin^2 2\theta \quad (3)$$

and

$$\beta = -\left[\left(\frac{\sin 2\theta}{2}\right)^4 + \left(1+\frac{1-\cos 2\theta}{2}\right)\left(1+\frac{1+\cos 2\theta}{2}\right)\right]$$

$$= -\left[\frac{1}{16}\sin^4 2\theta + \frac{1}{4}(3-\cos 2\theta)(3+\cos 2\theta)\right]$$

$$= -\frac{1}{16}\left[\sin^4 2\theta + 4(9-\cos^2 2\theta)\right]$$

$$= -\frac{1}{16}\left[\sin^4 2\theta + 4(8+\sin^2 2\theta)\right]$$

$$= -\frac{1}{16}\left[\sin^4 2\theta + 4\sin^2 2\theta + 32\right]$$

$$= -\frac{1}{16}\left[(\sin^2 2\theta + 2)^2 + 28\right] \quad (4)$$

From equations (3) and (4), the minimum values of α and β are, respectively

$$\alpha' = 1 - \frac{1}{2} = \frac{1}{2} \text{ and } \beta' = -\frac{1}{16}\left[(1+2)^2+28\right] = -\frac{37}{16}$$

Hence, $\alpha' + \beta' = \frac{1}{2} - \frac{37}{16} = -\frac{29}{16}$.

9. (b) The equation of the given circle is $(x-3)^2+(y+2)^2-25=0$. Let the coordinates of the mid-point of the chord PQ be $M\left(\frac{-3}{5}, k\right)$. Then the equation of the chord PQ is

$$(x-3)\left(\frac{-3}{5}-3\right) + (y+2)(k+2) - 25$$

$$= \left(\frac{-3}{5}-3\right)^2 + (k+2)^2 - 25$$

$$\Rightarrow \frac{-18}{5}(x-3) + (k+2)(y+2) = \left(\frac{18}{5}\right)^2 + (k+2)^2 \quad (1)$$

It is also given that the equation of the chord PQ is

$$y = mx + 1 \quad (2)$$

Since $M\left(\frac{-3}{5}, k\right)$ lies on this chord, we have

$$k = \frac{-3}{5}m + 1 \quad (3)$$

Comparing the slopes of the equations (1) and (2) of chord PQ, we have

$$m = \frac{18}{5(k+2)} \quad (4)$$

From equations (3) and (4), we have

$$5m(k+2) = 18$$

$$\Rightarrow \quad 5m\left(\frac{-3}{5}m + 1 + 2\right) = 18$$

$$\Rightarrow \quad -3m^2 + 15m = 18$$

$$\Rightarrow \quad m^2 - 5m + 6 = 0 \text{ gives } m = 2, 3.$$

10. (d)

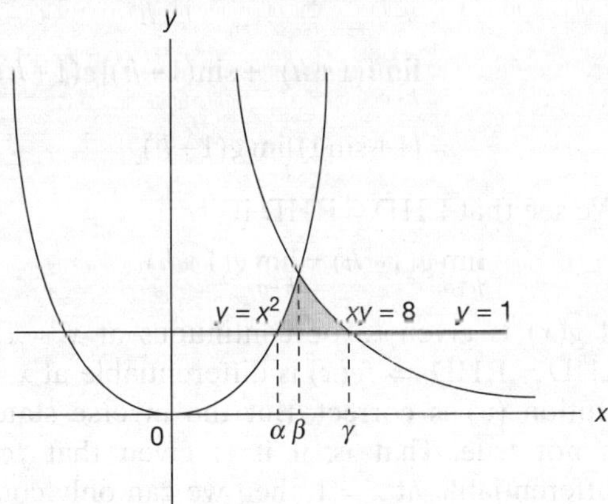

We have to find the area of the shaded region (see figure). The x-coordinates α, β, γ of the intersection points are, respectively

$$\alpha^2 = 1 \Rightarrow \alpha = 1,\ \beta^2 = \frac{8}{\beta} \Rightarrow \beta = 2, \text{ and } \frac{\gamma}{8} = 1 \Rightarrow \gamma = 8$$

Hence, the required area is

$$A = \int_1^2 (x^2 - 1)dx + \int_2^8 \left(\frac{8}{x} - 1\right)dx$$

$$= \left|\frac{x^3}{3} - x\right|_1^2 + |8\ \ln x - x|_2^8$$

$$= \left(\frac{8}{3} - 2\right) - \left(\frac{1}{3} - 1\right) + (8\ln 8 - 8) - (8\ln 2 - 2)$$

$$= 24\ln 2 - 8\ln 2 - 6 = 16\ln 2 - 6$$

One or More Correct Options

1. (a), (c) The function $fg(x)$ can be written as

$$fg(x) = f(x)\ g(x)$$
$$= [x^3 - x^2 + (x - 1)\sin x]\ g(x)$$
$$= (x - 1)\ (x^2 + \sin x)\ g(x)$$

Let us write the left-hand and the right-hand derivatives of the function $fg(x)$ at $x = 1$. Using first principle, we have

$$\text{LHD} = \lim_{h \to o} \frac{fg(1) - fg(1-h)}{h}$$

$$= \lim_{h \to 0} \frac{0 - (-h)\{(1-h)^2 + \sin(1-h)\}g(1-h)}{h}$$

$$= \lim_{h \to o}\{(1-h)^2 + \sin(1-h)\}g(1-h)$$

$$= (1 + \sin 1)\lim_{h \to o} g(1-h)$$

and $\text{RHD} = \lim_{h \to o} \dfrac{fg(1+h) - fg(1)}{h}$

$$= \lim_{h \to o} \frac{h\{(1+h)^2 + \sin(1+h)\}g(1+h) - 0}{h}$$

$$= \lim_{h \to o}\{(1+h)^2 + \sin(1+h)\}g(1+h)$$

$$= (1 + \sin 1)\lim_{h \to o} g(1+h)$$

We see that LHD = RHD if

$$\lim_{h \to o} g(1-h) = \lim_{h \to o} g(1+h)$$

If $g(x)$ is given to be continuous at $x = 1$, then LHD = RHD $\Rightarrow fg(x)$ is differentiable at $x = 1 \Rightarrow$ Option (a) is correct. But the inverse statement is not true. That is, if it is given that $fg(x)$ is differentiable at $x = 1$, then we can only conclude that $\lim_{h \to o} g(1-h) = \lim_{h \to o} g(1+h)$, which is not enough to conclude continuity of $g(x)$ at $x = 1 \Rightarrow$ Option B is incorrect.

Similarly if $g(x)$ is given to be differentiable at $x = 1$, it implies that $g(x)$ is given to be continuous at $x = 1$, then LHD = RHD $\Rightarrow fg(x)$ is differentiable at $x = 1 \Rightarrow$ Option (c) is correct. But the inverse statement again is not true. That is, if it is given that $fg(x)$ is differentiable at $x = 1$, then we can only conclude that $\lim_{h \to o} g(1-h) = \lim_{h \to o} g(1+h)$, which is not enough to conclude different ability of $g(x)$ at $x = 1 \Rightarrow$ Option (d) is incorrect.

2. (b) We have

$$M^{-1} = \text{adj}(\text{adj}M)$$
$$\Rightarrow \quad I = \text{adj}\ (\text{adj}M) \times M$$
$$\Rightarrow \quad I(\text{adj}M) = \text{adj}M \times \text{adj}\ (\text{adj}M) \times M$$
$$\Rightarrow \quad \text{adj}M = |\text{adj}M|\, I \times M$$
$$\Rightarrow \quad \text{adj}M = |M|^2\, M$$
$$\Rightarrow \quad |M|I = |M|^2\, M^2$$
$$\Rightarrow \quad \frac{1}{|M|} I = M^2$$

Now taking determinant of both sides, we have

$$\frac{1}{|M|^3} = |M|^2$$
$$\Rightarrow \quad |M|^5 = 1$$
$$\Rightarrow \quad |M| = 1$$

3. (b), (c) The set S can be written as

$$|z^2 + z + 1| = 1$$
$$\Rightarrow \quad \left|\left(z + \frac{1}{2}\right)^2 + \frac{3}{4}\right| = 1$$

Using the inequality $||z_1| - |z_2|| \le |z_1 + z_2| \le |z_1| + |z_2|$, we have

$$\left|\left|\left(z + \frac{1}{2}\right)^2\right| - \frac{3}{4}\right| \le 1 \le \left|\left(z + \frac{1}{2}\right)^2\right| + \frac{3}{4}$$

Solving the RHI, we have

$$\left|\left(z + \frac{1}{2}\right)^2\right| \ge \frac{1}{4} \quad (1)$$

Solving the LHI, we have

$$-1 \le \left|\left(z + \frac{1}{2}\right)^2\right| - \frac{3}{4} \le 1$$

$$\Rightarrow \quad -\frac{1}{4} \le \left|\left(z + \frac{1}{2}\right)^2\right| \le \frac{7}{4} \quad (2)$$

Intersection of inequalities (1) and (2) gives

$$\frac{1}{4} \le \left|\left(z+\frac{1}{2}\right)^2\right| \le \frac{7}{4}$$

$$\Rightarrow \quad \frac{1}{2} \le \left|z+\frac{1}{2}\right| \le \frac{\sqrt{7}}{2} \qquad (3)$$

Hence, option (c) is correct

From LHI of inequality (3), we have

$$\frac{1}{2} \le \left|z+\frac{1}{2}\right| \le |z| + \frac{1}{2}$$

$$\Rightarrow \quad |z| \ge 0 \qquad (4)$$

From RHI of inequality (3), we have

$$\left||z|-\frac{1}{2}\right| \le \left|z+\frac{1}{2}\right| \le \frac{\sqrt{7}}{2}$$

$$\Rightarrow \quad -\frac{\sqrt{7}}{2} \le |z| - \frac{1}{2} \le \frac{\sqrt{7}}{2}$$

$$\Rightarrow \quad \frac{1-\sqrt{7}}{2} \le |z| \le \frac{\sqrt{7}+1}{2} \qquad (5)$$

Intersection of inequalities (4) and (5) gives

$$0 \le |z| \le \frac{\sqrt{7}+1}{2} \le 2 \qquad (6)$$

Hence, option (b) is correct.

4. (b) We have

$$\tan\left(\frac{X}{2}\right) + \tan\left(\frac{Z}{2}\right) = \frac{2y}{x+y+z}$$

$$\Rightarrow \quad \frac{r}{s-x} + \frac{r}{s-z} = \frac{2y}{2s}$$ [r is the radius of the incircle and s is the semi-perimeter]

$$\Rightarrow \quad \frac{r(2s-x-z)}{(s-x)(s-z)} = \frac{y}{s}$$

$$\Rightarrow \quad \frac{ry}{(s-x)(s-z)} = \frac{y}{s}$$

$$\Rightarrow \quad rs = (s-x)(s-z) \qquad (1)$$

$$\Rightarrow \quad \sqrt{s(s-x)(s-y)(s-z)} = (s-x)(s-z)$$

$$\Rightarrow \quad \sqrt{\frac{(s-x)(s-z)}{s(s-y)}} = 1$$

$$\Rightarrow \quad \tan\left(\frac{Y}{2}\right) = 1$$

$$\Rightarrow \quad Y = 90^\circ$$

$$\Rightarrow \quad X + Z = 90^\circ = Y$$

Hence, option (b) is correct.

If $Y = 90^\circ$, then $x^2 + z^2 - y^2 = 2xz\cos 90^\circ = 0$. Hence, option (d) is incorrect.

Now, we here

$$\tan\left(\frac{X}{2}\right) = \frac{r}{s-x} = \frac{s-z}{s} \qquad \text{[From equation (1)]}$$

$$= \frac{2s-2z}{2s} = \frac{x+y-z}{x+y+z}$$

Hence, option (c) is incorrect.

5. (a), (b) If the three lines are coplanar, then we have

$$\begin{vmatrix} 1 & -1 & -3 \\ -3 & -1 & 1 \\ l & m & -2 \end{vmatrix} = 0$$

$$\Rightarrow \quad 2 - m + 6 - l + 3(3m-2) = 0$$

$$\Rightarrow \quad l - 2m = 2 \qquad (1)$$

The direction cosines of lines L_1 and L_2 are, respectively

$$\frac{1}{\sqrt{11}}, \frac{-1}{\sqrt{11}}, \frac{-3}{\sqrt{11}} \text{ and } \frac{-3}{\sqrt{11}}, \frac{-1}{\sqrt{11}}, \frac{1}{\sqrt{11}}$$

The direction ratios of their angular bisectors are

$$\frac{1-3}{\sqrt{11}}, \frac{-1-1}{\sqrt{11}}, \frac{-3+1}{\sqrt{11}} = \frac{-2}{\sqrt{11}}, \frac{-2}{\sqrt{11}}, \frac{-2}{\sqrt{11}} = 1, 1, 1$$

and

$$\frac{1+3}{\sqrt{11}}, \frac{-1+1}{\sqrt{11}}, \frac{-3-1}{\sqrt{11}} = \frac{4}{\sqrt{11}}, \frac{0}{\sqrt{11}}, \frac{-4}{\sqrt{11}} = 1, 0, -1.$$

If line L_3 is an angular bisector, then

$$\frac{l}{1} = \frac{m}{1} = \frac{-2}{1} \Rightarrow l = m = -2,$$

or

$$\frac{l}{1} = \frac{m}{0} = \frac{-2}{-1} \Rightarrow l = 2, m = 0.$$

If line L_3 passes through the intersection point (1, 0, 1) of lines L_1 and L_2, then we have

$$\frac{1-\alpha}{l} = \frac{-1}{m} = \frac{1-\gamma}{-2} \qquad (4)$$

If we use $l = m = -2$, we have

$$\frac{1-\alpha}{-2} = \frac{-1}{-2} = \frac{1-\gamma}{-2} \Rightarrow \alpha = l = 2.$$

If we use $l = 2, m = 0$, we have

$$\frac{1-\alpha}{2} = \frac{-1}{0} = \frac{1-\gamma}{-2} \Rightarrow \text{No solution}$$

Thus, the possible values are

$$l = m = -2 \text{ and } \alpha = \gamma = 2.$$

Hence, options (a) and (d) are correct.

6. (a), (b) We have

$$I_1 = \int_0^1 x\cos x\,dx = |\sin x + \cos x|_0^1$$

$$= \sin 1 + \cos 1 - 1 = 0.38 \geq \frac{3}{8}$$

⇒ Option (a) is correct.

$$I_2 = \int_0^1 x\sin x\,dx = |-x\cos x + \sin x|_0^1$$

$$= \sin 1 - \cos 1 = 0.3011 \geq \frac{3}{10}$$

⇒ Option (b) is correct.

$$I_3 = \int_0^1 x^2 \cos x dx = |x^2 \sin x|_0^1 - 2\int_0^1 x \sin x dx$$

$$= \sin 1 - 2(\sin 1 - \cos 1)$$

$$= 2\cos 1 - \sin 1 = 0.239 \leq \frac{1}{2}$$

⇒ Option (c) is incorrect.

$$I_3 = \int_0^1 x^2 \sin x dx = |-x^2 \cos x|_0^1 + 2\int_0^1 x \cos x dx$$

$$= -\cos 1 + 2(\sin 1 + \cos 1 - 1)$$

$$= 2\sin 1 + \cos 1 - 2 = 0.22 \leq \frac{2}{9}$$

⇒ Option (d) is incorrect.

7. (a), (c) Solving the given differential equation, we have

$$\int \frac{df}{f} = \int \frac{dx}{x^2 + b^2}$$

$$\Rightarrow \quad \ln f = \frac{1}{b}\tan{-1}\left(\frac{x}{b}\right) + \text{constant}$$

Since $f(0) = 1$, constant = 0. Hence, we have

$$\ln f = \frac{1}{b}\tan^{-1}\left(\frac{x}{b}\right)$$

$$\Rightarrow \quad f(x) = e^{\frac{1}{b}\tan^{-1}\left(\frac{x}{b}\right)}$$

Replacing b with $-b$ does not change the function since

$$\frac{1}{-b}\tan^{-1}\left(\frac{x}{-b}\right) = \frac{1}{b}\tan^{-1}\left(\frac{x}{b}\right)$$

Hence, whatever be the sign of b, the function $f(x)$ is an increasing function since $\frac{1}{b}\tan^{-1}\left(\frac{x}{b}\right)$ is an increasing function and e^x is also an increasing function ⇒ Option (a) is correct.

Now, we have

$$f(-x) = e^{\frac{1}{b}\tan^{-1}\left(\frac{-x}{b}\right)} = e^{\frac{-1}{b}\tan^{-1}\left(\frac{x}{b}\right)} = \frac{1}{f(x)}.$$

$$\Rightarrow \quad f(-x)\, f(x) = 1 \Rightarrow \text{Option (c) is correct}$$

8. (a), (d) Let $P = (h, k)$. Equation of the tangent at P is

$$\frac{xh}{a^2} - \frac{yk}{b^2} = 1 \qquad (1)$$

Since the tangent passes through $A(1, 0)$, we have

$$h = a^2$$

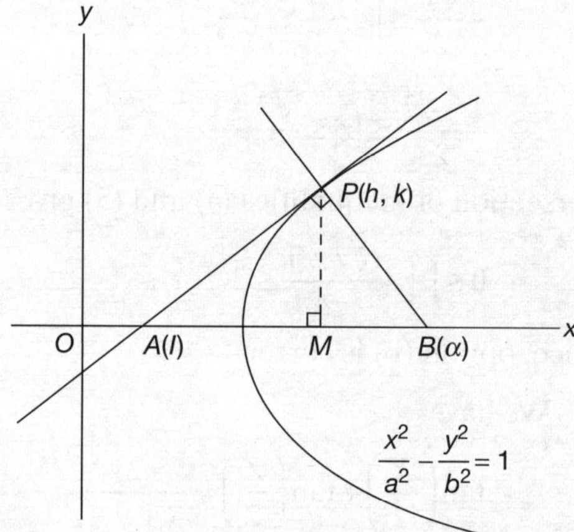

Since (h, k) lies on the hyperbola, we have

$$\frac{h^2}{a^2} - \frac{k^2}{b^2} = 1$$

$$\Rightarrow \quad \frac{a^4}{a^2} - \frac{k^2}{b^2} = 1$$

$$\Rightarrow \quad \frac{k^2}{b^2} = a^2 - 1$$

$$\Rightarrow \quad k = b\sqrt{a^2 - 1}$$

Hence, $P = \left(a^2, b\sqrt{a^2 k}\right)$.

From equation (1), slope of the tangent at P is $\frac{b^2 h}{a^2 k}$.

Thus, slope of the normal at P is $\frac{-a^2 k}{b^2 h}$. Hence, equation of the normal at P is

$$y - k = \frac{b^2 h}{a^2 k}(n - h) \qquad (2)$$

The x- and y-intercepts of the normal are

$$\alpha = \frac{a^2k^2}{b^2h} + h = \frac{a^2b^2(a^2-1)}{b^2a^2} + a^2 = 2a^2 - 1$$

and $\beta = k + \frac{b^2h}{a^2k} = b\sqrt{a^2-1} + \frac{ba^2}{\sqrt{a^2-1}} = \frac{b(2a^2-1)}{\sqrt{a^2-1}}$

It is given that the intercepts are equal. Thus, we have

$$2a^2 - 1 = \frac{b(2a^2-1)}{\sqrt{a^2-1}}$$

$\Rightarrow \quad a^2 - 1 = b^2 \qquad (3)$

Now, area of the triangle ΔAPB is

$$\Delta APB = \frac{1}{2} \times AB \times PM$$

$$= \frac{1}{2}(\alpha - 1)k = \frac{1}{2}(2a^2 - 2)b\sqrt{a^2-1}$$

$$= b(a^2-1)^{3/2} = b(b^2)^{3/2} = b^4$$

[Using result (3)]

The eccentricity of a hyperbola is $e = \sqrt{1 + \frac{b^2}{a^2}}$, which is always greater than 1. In this question $b < a$, hence, $e < \sqrt{2}$. Thus, we have $1 < e < \sqrt{2}$.

9. (a), (d) Let us find the left-hand and right-hand derivatives of $f(x)$ at any $x \in \mathbf{R}$. Using first principle, we have

$$\text{RHD} = \lim_{h\to 0} \frac{f(x+h) - f(x)}{h}$$

$$= \lim_{h\to 0} \frac{[f(x) + f(h) + f(x)f(h)] - f(x)}{h}$$

$$= \lim_{h\to 0} [1 + f(x)] \frac{f(h)}{h}$$

$$= [1 + f(x)] \lim_{h\to 0} g(h) = 1 + f(x)$$

$$\text{and LHD} = \lim_{h\to 0} \frac{f(x) - f(x-h)}{h}$$

$$= \lim_{h\to 0} \frac{f(x) - [f(x) + f(-h) + f(x)f(-h)]}{h}$$

$$= \lim_{h\to 0} [1 + f(x)] \frac{f(-h)}{-h}$$

$$= [1 + f(x)] \lim_{h\to 0} g(-h) = 1 + f(x)$$

Since LHD = RHD for every $x \in \mathbf{R}$, f is differentiable everywhere $\Rightarrow$ Option (a) is correct.

Now, solving the differential equation $f'(x) = 1 + f(x)$, we have

$$\int \frac{df}{1+f} = \int dx$$

$\Rightarrow \quad \ln|1 + f| = x + \text{constant} \qquad (1)$

Now since $\lim_{h\to 0} g(x) - \lim_{h\to 0} \frac{f(x)}{x} - 1$, we conclude that $f(0) = 0$; otherwise a finite limit cannot exist as the denominator approaches zero.

Using $f(0) = 0$ in equation (1) gives constant = 0. Hence, we have

$$f(x) = e^x - 1 \text{ and } f'(x) = e^x$$

Hence $f'(1) = e \Rightarrow$ Option (c) is incorrect, and $f'(0) = 1 \Rightarrow$ Option (d) is correct.

Now, we have

$$g(x) = \frac{f(x)}{x} = \frac{e^x - 1}{x} \text{ and } g'(x) = \frac{xe^x - (e^x - 1)}{x^2}$$

We see that $g'(0)$ does not exist $\Rightarrow$ Option (b) is incorrect.

10. (a), (b), (c) If points A and B are mirror images in the plane $\alpha x + \beta y + \gamma z = \delta$, then the following two conditions must be satisfied.

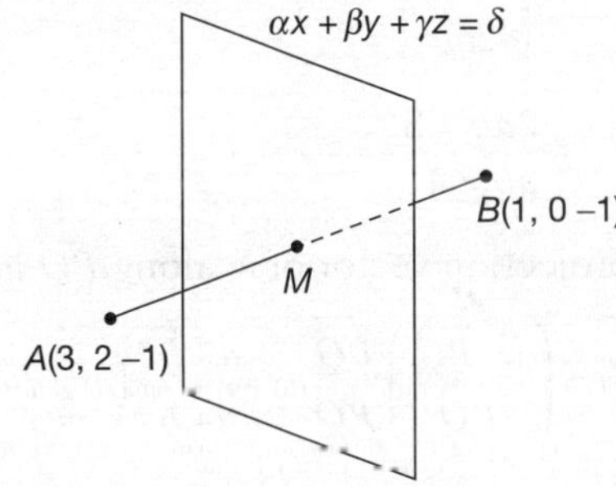

Condition 1: Line AB must be normal to the plane. So the direction ratios of AB, that is, $3 - 1, 2 - 0, -1 + 1 = 2, 2, 0 = 1, 1, 0$ must be identical to the ratios α, β, y. Thus, we have

$$\frac{\alpha}{1} = \frac{\beta}{1} = \frac{y}{0}$$

If is given that $\alpha + y = 1$. Solving together, we have

$$\alpha = 1, \beta = 1, y = 0$$

Condition 2: Mid-point of AB, that is, M (2, 1, 0) must lie on the plane. Thus, we have

$$2\alpha + \beta = \delta$$

Putting $\alpha = 1 = \beta$ gives $\delta = 3$

Now that we have the value of α, β, y and δ, we can see that

$\alpha + \beta = 2 \Rightarrow$ Option (a) is correct.

$\delta - y = \beta \Rightarrow$ Option (b) is correct.
$\delta + \beta = 4 \Rightarrow$ Option (c) is correct.
$\alpha + \beta + y = 2 \neq \delta \Rightarrow$ Option (d) is incorrect.

11. (a), (d) The vectors $\overrightarrow{PQ} = a\hat{i} + b\hat{j}$ and $\overrightarrow{PQ} = a\hat{i} - b\hat{j}$ have the same magnitude $\sqrt{a^2 + b^2}$ and are inclined at the same angle $\tan^{-1}(b/a)$ with the x-axis, one in the clockwise sense and the other in the counter-clockwise sense (see figure).

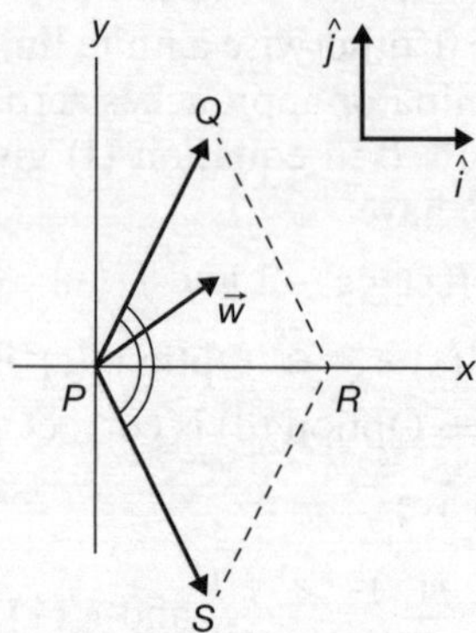

Area of the rectangle $PQRS$ is given to be 8. Hence, we have

$$|\overrightarrow{PQ} \times \overrightarrow{PS}| = 8$$

$$\Rightarrow \quad |(a\hat{i} + b\hat{j}) \times (a\hat{i} - b\hat{j})| = 8$$

$$\Rightarrow \quad |-2ab\hat{k}| = 8$$

$$\Rightarrow \quad 2ab = 8$$

$$\Rightarrow \quad ab = 4 \qquad (1)$$

The projection vector of $\vec{w}$ along $\overrightarrow{PQ}$ is

$$\vec{u} = \left(\frac{\vec{w} \cdot \overrightarrow{PQ}}{PQ}\right)\frac{\overrightarrow{PQ}}{PQ} = \frac{a+b}{a^2+b^2}(a\hat{i} + b\hat{j})$$

The projection vector of $\vec{w}$ along $\overrightarrow{PS}$ is

$$\vec{v} = \left(\frac{\vec{w} \cdot \overrightarrow{PS}}{PS}\right)\frac{\overrightarrow{PS}}{PS} = \frac{a-b}{a^2+b^2}(a\hat{i} - b\hat{j})$$

If is given that $|\vec{u}| + |\vec{v}| = |\vec{w}|$. Hence, we have

$$\frac{a+b}{\sqrt{a^2+b^2}} + \frac{a-b}{\sqrt{a^2+b^2}} = \sqrt{2}$$

$$\Rightarrow \quad \frac{2a}{\sqrt{a^2+b^2}} = \sqrt{2}$$

$$\Rightarrow \quad 2a^2 = a^2 + b^2$$

$$\Rightarrow \quad a^2 = b^2$$

$\Rightarrow \quad a = b$ –(2) [a, b are given to be positive real numbers]

From equations (1) and (2), we have $a = b = 2 \Rightarrow$ Option (a) is correct and option (b) is incorrect.

The diagonal $\overrightarrow{PR}$ equals $\overrightarrow{PQ} + \overrightarrow{PS}$. Hence, we have

$|\overrightarrow{PR}| = |\overrightarrow{PQ} + \overrightarrow{PS}| = 2a = 4 \Rightarrow$ Option (c) is correct.

From the figure, we can see that the angular bisectors of $\overrightarrow{PQ}$ and $\overrightarrow{PS}$ lie along the $\hat{i}$ and $\hat{j}$ vectors $\Rightarrow$ Option (d) is incorrect.

12. (a), (b), (d) We have

$$g(m,n) = \sum_{p=0}^{m+n}\sum_{i=o}^{p} \frac{\binom{mn}{i}\binom{m+i}{p}\binom{p+n}{p-i}}{\binom{n+p}{p}}$$

$$= \sum_{p=0}^{m+n}\sum_{i=0}^{p}\binom{m}{i}\frac{(n+i)!}{p!(n+i-p)!} \times \frac{(p+n)!}{(p-i)!(n+i)!} \times \frac{n!\,p!}{(n+p)!}$$

$$= \sum_{p=0}^{m+n}\sum_{i=0}^{p}\binom{m}{i}\frac{n!}{(n+i-p)!(p-i)!}$$

$$= \sum_{p=0}^{m+n}\sum_{i=0}^{p}\binom{m}{i}\binom{n}{p-i}$$

Now, we have

$$\sum_{i=0}^{p}\binom{m}{i}\binom{n}{p-i} = \binom{m}{0}\binom{n}{p} + \binom{m}{1}\binom{n}{p-1} + \binom{m}{2}\binom{n}{p-2} + \text{-----} + \binom{m}{p}\binom{n}{o}$$

= coefficient of x^p in $(1 + x)^m (1 + x)^n$
= coefficient of x^p in $(1 + x)^{m+n}$

$$= \binom{m+n}{p}$$

Now, we have

$$g(m,n) = \sum_{p=0}^{m+n}\binom{m+n}{p} = \binom{m+n}{0} + \binom{m+n}{1} + \binom{m+n}{2} + \text{---} + \binom{m+n}{m+n}$$

$$= 2^{m+n}$$

Hence, we have

$g(n, m) = 2^{n+m} = g(m, n) \Rightarrow$ Option (a) is correct.

$g(m, n + 1) = 2^{m+n+1} = g(n, m + 1) \Rightarrow$ Option (b) is correct.

$g(2m, 2n) = 2^{2m + 2n} = (2^{m+n})^2 = (g(m, n))^2 \Rightarrow$ Option (d) is correct but option (c) is incorrect.

13. (a),(b),(c) Since α, β are the roots of the quadratic equation $x^2 - x - 1 = 0$, we have

$$\alpha + \beta = 1 \text{ and } \alpha\beta = -1$$

(a) We have

$$\sum_1^n a_n = \sum_1^n \left(\frac{\alpha^n - \beta^n}{\alpha - \beta}\right) = \frac{1}{\alpha - \beta}\left[\sum_1^n \alpha^n - \sum_1^n \beta^n\right]$$

$$= \frac{1}{\alpha - \beta}\left[\frac{\alpha(\alpha^n - 1)}{\alpha - 1} - \frac{\beta(\beta^n - 1)}{\beta - 1}\right]$$

$$= \frac{1}{\alpha - \beta}\left[\frac{(\alpha^{n+1} - \alpha)(\beta - 1) - (\beta^{n+1} - \beta)(\alpha - 1)}{(\alpha - 1)(\beta - 1)}\right]$$

$$= \frac{1}{\alpha - \beta}\left[\frac{(\beta\alpha^{n+1} - \alpha^{n+1} - \alpha\beta + \alpha) - (\alpha\beta^{n+1} - \beta^{n+1} - \alpha\beta + \beta)}{\alpha\beta - (\alpha + \beta) + 1}\right]$$

$$= \frac{\alpha\beta(\alpha^n - \beta^n) - (\alpha^{n+1} - \beta^{n+1}) + (\alpha - \beta)}{-(\alpha - \beta)}$$

[Putting $\alpha + \beta = 1$ and $\alpha\beta = -1$]

$$= \frac{\alpha^n - \beta^n}{\alpha - \beta} + \frac{\alpha^{n+1} - \beta^{n+1}}{\alpha - \beta} - 1$$

$$\Rightarrow a_1 + a_2 + a_3 + \ldots + +a_{n-1} + a_n = a_n + a_{n+1} - 1$$

$$\Rightarrow a_1 + a_2 + a_3 + \ldots + a_{n-1} = a_{n+1} - 1$$

Putting $n + 1$ in place of n in the above equation, we have

$$a_1 + a_2 + a_3 + \ldots + +a_{n-1} + a_n = a_{n+2} - 1$$

$\Rightarrow$ Option (a) is correct.

(b) We have

$$\sum_1^\infty \frac{a_n}{10^n} = \frac{1}{\alpha - \beta}\left[\sum_1^\infty \frac{\alpha^n}{10^n} - \sum_1^\infty \frac{\beta^n}{10^n}\right]$$

$$= \frac{1}{\alpha - \beta}\left[\frac{\frac{\alpha}{10}}{1 - \frac{\alpha}{10}} - \frac{\frac{\beta}{10}}{1 - \frac{\beta}{10}}\right]$$

$$= \frac{1}{\alpha - \beta}\left[\frac{\alpha}{10 - \alpha} - \frac{\beta}{10 - \beta}\right]$$

$$= \frac{1}{\alpha - \beta}\left[\frac{(10\alpha - \alpha\beta) - (10\beta - \alpha\beta)}{100 - 10(\alpha + \beta) + \alpha\beta}\right]$$

$$= \frac{1}{\alpha - \beta}\left[\frac{10(\alpha - \beta)}{89}\right] \text{[Putting } \alpha + \beta = 1 \text{ and } \alpha\beta = -1\text{]}$$

$= \frac{10}{89} \Rightarrow$ Option (b) is correct.

(c) We have

$$b_n = a_{n-1} + a_{n+1} = \frac{\alpha^{n-1} - \beta^{n-1}}{\alpha - \beta} + \frac{\alpha^{n+1} - \beta^{n+1}}{\alpha - \beta}$$

$$= \frac{\left(\frac{\alpha^n}{\alpha} - \frac{\beta^n}{\beta}\right) + (\alpha^{n+1} - \beta^{n+1})}{\alpha - \beta}$$

$$= \frac{\alpha\beta^n - \beta\alpha^n + \alpha^{n+1} - \beta^{n+1}}{\alpha - \beta} \quad \text{[Putting } \alpha\beta = -1\text{]}$$

$$= \frac{\alpha(\alpha^n + \beta^n) - \beta(\alpha^n + \beta^n)}{\alpha - \beta}$$

$= \alpha^n + \beta^n \Rightarrow$ Option (c) is correct.

(d) We have

$$\sum_1^\infty \frac{b_n}{10^n} = \left[\sum_1^\infty \frac{\alpha^n}{10^n} + \sum_1^\infty \frac{\beta^n}{10^n}\right]$$

$$= \frac{\frac{\alpha}{10}}{1 - \frac{\alpha}{10}} + \frac{\frac{\beta}{10}}{1 - \frac{\beta}{10}}$$

$$= \frac{\alpha}{10 - \alpha} + \frac{\beta}{10 - \beta}$$

$$= \frac{(10\alpha - \alpha\beta) + (10\beta - \alpha\beta)}{100 - 10(\alpha + \beta) + \alpha\beta}$$

$$= \frac{10(\alpha + \beta) - 2\alpha\beta}{89} \text{ [Putting } \alpha + \beta = 1 \text{ and } \alpha\beta = -1\text{]}$$

$= \frac{12}{89} \Rightarrow$ Option (d) is incorrect.

14. (a),(b),(d) We have

$$M \text{ adj.} M = |M| I$$

$$\Rightarrow \begin{bmatrix} 0 & 1 & a \\ 1 & 2 & 3 \\ 3 & b & 1 \end{bmatrix}\begin{bmatrix} -1 & 1 & -1 \\ 8 & -6 & 2 \\ -5 & 3 & -1 \end{bmatrix} = |M| I$$

$$\Rightarrow \begin{bmatrix} 8 - 5a & 3a - 6 & 2 - a \\ 0 & -2 & 0 \\ 8b - 8 & 6 - 6b & 2b - 4 \end{bmatrix} = |M|\begin{bmatrix} 1 & 0 & 0 \\ 0 & 1 & 0 \\ 0 & 0 & 1 \end{bmatrix}$$

$$\Rightarrow -2\begin{bmatrix} \frac{5}{2}a-4 & 3-\frac{3}{2}a & \frac{1}{2}a-1 \\ 0 & 1 & 0 \\ 4-4b & 3b-3 & 2-b \end{bmatrix} = |M|\begin{bmatrix} 1 & 0 & 0 \\ 0 & 1 & 0 \\ 0 & 0 & 1 \end{bmatrix}$$

Comparing the two sides, we have

$$|M| = -2, a = 2, b = 1$$

(a) Thus, we have

$$a+b=3 \Rightarrow \text{Option (a) is correct.}$$

(b) Simplifying the given equation, we have

$$(\text{adj.}M)^{-1} + \text{adj.}M^{-1} = -M$$

$$\Rightarrow I + \text{adj.}M\text{adj.}M^{-1} = -M\text{adj.}M$$

$$\Rightarrow I + \text{adj.}M(\text{adj.}M)^{-1} = -|M|I \quad [\text{Putting } |M| = -2]$$

$$\Rightarrow I + I = -|M|I$$

$$\Rightarrow 2I = -|M|I$$

$$\Rightarrow |M| = -2 \text{ which is true} \Rightarrow \text{Option (b) is correct.}$$

(c) We have

$$M^2\text{adj.}M^2 = |M^2|I = |M|^2 I = 4I$$

$$\Rightarrow \text{adj.}M^2 = (M^{-1})^2 4I$$

$$\Rightarrow |\text{adj.}M^2| = |M^{-1}|^2 |4I| = \frac{1}{|M|^2} \times 4^3 = 16$$

$\Rightarrow$ Option (c) is incorrect.

(d) We have

$$M\begin{bmatrix} \alpha \\ \beta \\ \gamma \end{bmatrix} = \begin{bmatrix} 1 \\ 2 \\ 3 \end{bmatrix}$$

$$\Rightarrow \begin{bmatrix} 0 & 1 & 2 \\ 1 & 2 & 3 \\ 3 & 1 & 1 \end{bmatrix}\begin{bmatrix} \alpha \\ \beta \\ \gamma \end{bmatrix} = \begin{bmatrix} 1 \\ 2 \\ 3 \end{bmatrix}$$

$$\Rightarrow \quad \beta + 2\gamma = 1 \quad (1)$$

$$\alpha + 2\beta + 3\gamma \quad (2)$$

$$3\alpha + \beta + \gamma = 3 \quad (3)$$

Solving the above equations gives $\alpha = 1, \beta = -1, \gamma = 1$. Hence $\alpha - \beta + \gamma = 3 \Rightarrow$ Option (d) is correct.

15. (a),(b)

(a) We have

$$P(G \mid B_3) = P(\text{chosing a green ball from } B_3) = \frac{3}{8}$$

$\Rightarrow$ Option (a) is correct.

(b) We have

$$P(G) = P(B_1)P(G \mid B_1) + P(B_2)P(G \mid B_2)$$
$$P(B_3)P(G \mid B_3)$$

$$= \left(\frac{3}{10} \times \frac{1}{2}\right) + \left(\frac{3}{10} \times \frac{5}{8}\right) + \left(\frac{4}{10} \times \frac{3}{8}\right) = \frac{39}{80}$$

$\Rightarrow$ Option (b) is correct.

(c) We have

$$P(B_3 \mid G) = \frac{P(B_3 \cap G)}{P(G)}$$

$$= \frac{\frac{4}{10} \times \frac{3}{8}}{\left(\frac{3}{10} \times \frac{1}{2}\right) + \left(\frac{3}{10} \times \frac{5}{8}\right) + \left(\frac{4}{10} \times \frac{3}{8}\right)} = \frac{4}{13}$$

$\Rightarrow$ Option (c) is incorrect.

(d) We have

$$P(B_3 \cap G) = \frac{4}{10} \times \frac{3}{8} = \frac{3}{20} \Rightarrow \text{Option (d) is incorrect.}$$

16. (a),(c),(d)

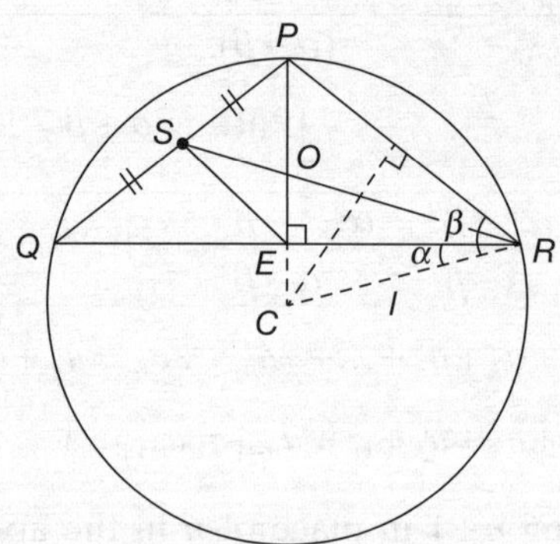

Lengths of the chords RP and RQ are given to be $q = 1$ and $p = \sqrt{3}$, respectively. Also, the radius of the circumcircle is given to be $l = 1$. Let $\angle CRQ = \alpha$ and $\angle CRP = \beta$ (see figure). Then, we have

$$\cos\alpha = \frac{p/2}{l} = \frac{\sqrt{3}}{2} \Rightarrow \alpha = 30°$$

$$\text{and } \cos\beta = \frac{q/2}{l} = \frac{1}{2} \Rightarrow \beta = 60°$$

Thus, $\angle PRQ = \beta - \alpha = 30°$ and hence, we have

$$PQ = \sqrt{p^2 + q^2 - 2pq\cos 30°}$$

$$= \sqrt{1 + 3 - 2\sqrt{3}\left(\frac{\sqrt{3}}{2}\right)} = 1$$

Now, since $PQ = PR = 1 \Rightarrow \Delta PQR$ is isosceles and hence $\angle RPQ = 180° - (30° + 30°) = 120°$.

(a) In ΔPRS, we have $PR = 1$, $PS = \frac{1}{2}(PQ) = \frac{1}{2}$ and $\angle RPS = 120°$. Hence

$$RS = \sqrt{1+\frac{1}{4}-2(1)\left(\frac{1}{2}\right)\cos 120°} = \sqrt{\frac{5}{4}+\frac{1}{2}} = \frac{\sqrt{7}}{2}$$

$\Rightarrow$ Option (a) is correct.

(b) Since S and E are the respective mid-points of the sides PQ and QR, side SE is parallel to side $PR \Rightarrow \angle SEQ = \angle PRQ = 30°$ and hence $\angle SEP = 90° - 30° = 60°$. Also, length $SE = \frac{1}{2}(PR) = \frac{1}{2}$ and $= \frac{1}{3}(PE) = \frac{1}{3}(PR\sin 30°) = \frac{1}{6}$. Hence, area of triangle ΔSOE is

$$\text{Area} = \frac{1}{2}(OE)(SE)\sin 60° = \frac{1}{2}\left(\frac{1}{6}\right)\left(\frac{1}{2}\right)\left(\frac{\sqrt{3}}{2}\right) = \frac{\sqrt{3}}{48}$$

$\Rightarrow$ Option (b) is incorrect.

(c) Length of $OE = \frac{1}{3}(PE) = \frac{1}{3}(PR\sin 30°) = \frac{1}{6}$.

$\Rightarrow$ Option (c) is correct.

(d) Area and semi-perimeter of ΔPQR are, respectively

$$\text{Area} = \frac{1}{2}pq\sin 30° = \frac{1}{2}(\sqrt{3})(1)\left(\frac{1}{2}\right) = \frac{\sqrt{3}}{4}$$

and $s = \dfrac{1+1+\sqrt{3}}{2} = \dfrac{2+\sqrt{3}}{2}$

The radius of the incircle is given by

$$\text{Radius} = \frac{\Delta}{s} = \frac{\sqrt{3}}{4}\times\frac{2}{2+\sqrt{3}} = \frac{\sqrt{3}}{2}(2-\sqrt{3})$$

$\Rightarrow$ Option (d) is correct.

17. (b),(c)

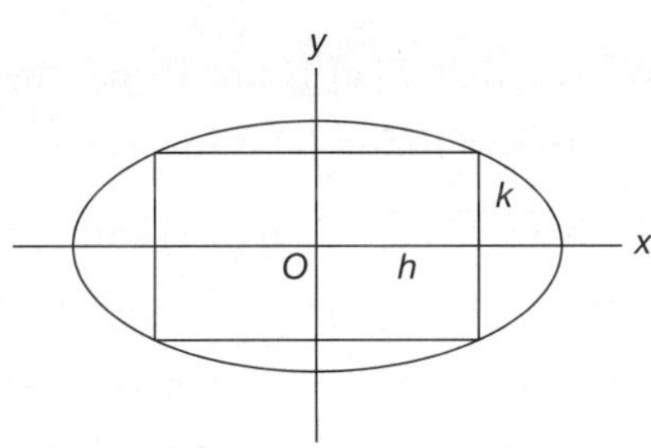

Let us consider a rectangle of width $2h$ and height $2k$ (see figure) where

$$\frac{h^2}{a^2}+\frac{k^2}{b^2} = 1 \Rightarrow k = \frac{b}{a}\sqrt{a^2-h^2}$$

Hence, area of the rectangle is

$$A = 4hk = \frac{4b}{a}h\sqrt{a^2-h^2} \tag{1}$$

The maximum value of A occurs where $dA/dh = 0$. That is where

$$\sqrt{a^2-h^2} - \frac{h^2}{\sqrt{a^2-h^2}} = 0$$

$$\Rightarrow \quad a^2 - h^2 = h^2 n$$

$$\Rightarrow \quad 2h^2 = a^2 \text{ gives } h = \frac{a}{\sqrt{2}}$$

Putting in the equation gives the maximum area as

$$A = 4\left(\frac{a}{\sqrt{2}}\right)\left(\frac{b}{\sqrt{2}}\right)$$

The major axis and minor axis lengths of ellipse E_2 inscribed inside this rectangle will be $\frac{a}{\sqrt{2}}, \frac{b}{\sqrt{2}}$, respectively. Generalising the result, we can see that the major axis and minor axis lengths of ellipse E_n will be $a_n = \dfrac{a}{(\sqrt{2})^{n-1}}$, $b_n = \dfrac{b}{(\sqrt{2})^{n-1}}$, respectively.

(a) Eccentricity of the ellipse E_n is

$$e_n = \sqrt{1-\frac{b_n^2}{a_n^2}} = \sqrt{1-\frac{b^2}{a^2}} = \sqrt{1-\frac{4}{9}} = \frac{\sqrt{5}}{3}$$

We see that the eccentricity is the same for all the ellipses $\Rightarrow$ Option (a) is incorrect.

(b) Area of rectangle R_n is

$$A_n = 4a_nb_n = \frac{4ab}{(\sqrt{2})^{2n}} = \frac{24}{2^n}$$

Hence, we have

$$\sum_1^N A_n = 24\sum_1^N \frac{1}{2^n} = 24\times\frac{\frac{1}{2}\left(1-\frac{1}{2^N}\right)}{1-\frac{1}{2}} = 24\left(1-\frac{1}{2^N}\right)$$

We see that $\sum_1^N A_n < 24$ for any $N \Rightarrow$ Option (b) is correct.

(c) Length of the latus rectum of the ellipse E_n is

$$L_n = \frac{2b_{n-1}^2}{a_{n-1}} = \frac{2b^2}{a}\frac{1}{(\sqrt{2})^{n-1}} = \frac{8}{3(\sqrt{2})^{n-1}}$$

For ellipse E_9, we have

$$L_9 = \frac{8}{3\left(\sqrt{2}\right)^8} = \frac{1}{6} \Rightarrow \text{Option (c) is correct.}$$

(d) Distance between the centre and the focus for the ellipse E_n is

$$D_n = a_{n-1}e_{n-1} = \frac{a}{\left(\sqrt{2}\right)^{n-1}} \times \frac{\sqrt{5}}{3} = \frac{\sqrt{5}}{\left(\sqrt{2}\right)^{n-1}}$$

For ellipse E_9, we have

$$D_9 = \frac{\sqrt{5}}{\left(\sqrt{2}\right)^8} = \frac{\sqrt{5}}{16} \Rightarrow \text{Option (d) is incorrect.}$$

18. (b),(c) The given function is

$$f(x) = \begin{cases} x^5 + 5x^4 + 10x^3 + 10x^2 + 3x + 1, x < 0 \\ x^2 - x + 1, 0 \le x < 1 \\ \frac{2}{3}x^3 - 4x^2 + 7x - \frac{8}{3}, 1 \le x < 3 \\ (x-2)\ln(x-2) - x + \frac{10}{3}, x \ge 3 \end{cases}$$

We see that $f(0^-) = 1 = f(0^+)$, $f(1^-) = 1 = f(1^+)$, and $f(3^-) = 1/3 = f(3^+)$. This means that the given function is continuous everywhere.

The derivative of the given function is

$$f'(x) = \begin{cases} 5x^4 + 20x^3 + 30x^2 + 20x + 3, x < 0 \\ 2x - 1, 0 < x < 1 \\ 2x^2 - 8x + 7, 1 < x < 3 \\ \ln(x-2), x > 3 \end{cases}$$

We see that $f'(0^-) = 3$ whereas $f'(0^+) = -1$, $f'(1^-) = 1 = f'(1^+)$, and $f'(3^-) = 1$ whereas $f'(3^+) = 0$. This means that the given function is differentiable everywhere, except at $x = 0, 3$.

Let us now analyse each segment of $f'(x)$ one by one: In the interval $x < 0$, we have

$$f''(x) = 20x^3 + 60x^2 + 60x + 20 = 20(x+1)^3$$

We see that $f''(x)$ changes sign from $-$ve to +ve at $x = -1$. This means that $f'(x)$ has a local minima at $x = -1$, that is, $f'(-1) = -4$. Also, we have $f'(-\infty) = +\infty$, $f'(-2) = 3$ and $f'(0) = 3$. Hence, $f'(x)$ equals zero once in $(-2, -1)$ and once between $(-1, 0)$. This means that $f(x)$ has a local maxima somewhere in $(-2, -1)$, and a local minima somewhere in $(-1, 0)$.

In the interval $0 < x < 1$, we have

$$f'(x) = 2\left(x - \frac{1}{2}\right)$$

We see that $f'(x)$ is $-$ve in $\left(0, \frac{1}{2}\right)$ and +ve in $\left(\frac{1}{2}, 1\right)$.

This means that $f(x)$ has a local minima at $= \frac{1}{2}$.

In the interval $1 < x < 3$, we have

$$f'(x) = 2(x-2)^2 - 1 \Rightarrow f'(x) = 0 \text{ at } x = 2 \pm \frac{1}{\sqrt{2}}$$

We see that $f'(x)$ is +ve in $\left(1, 2 - \frac{1}{\sqrt{2}}\right)$, $-$ve in $\left(2 - \frac{1}{\sqrt{2}}, 2 + \frac{1}{\sqrt{2}}\right)$, and then again +ve in $\left(2 + \frac{1}{\sqrt{2}}, 1\right)$. This means that $f(x)$ has a local maxima at $x = 2 - \frac{1}{\sqrt{2}}$, and a local minima at $x = 2 + \frac{1}{\sqrt{2}}$.

In the interval $x > 3$, we have

$$f'(x) = \ln(x-2) \Rightarrow f'(x) = 0 \text{ at } x = 3$$

We see that $f'(x)$ is +ve everywhere. This means that $f(x)$ strictly increases in this interval.

Now, we can draw the graph of $f(x)$ (see figure).

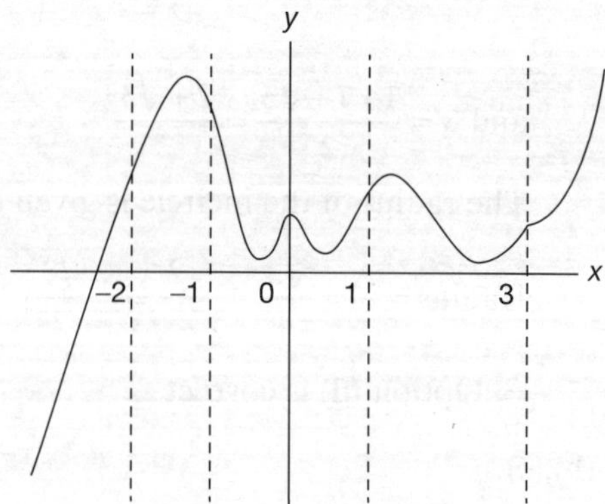

(a) We see that $f(x)$ is not strictly increasing in $(-\infty, 0) \Rightarrow$ Option (a) is incorrect.

(b) We have $f''(x) = 2$ in $(0,1)$ and $f''(x) = 4x - 8$ in $(1,3)$. Thus, $f''\left(1^-\right) = 2$ and $f''\left(1^+\right) = -8$. We see that $f''(x)$ changes sign from +ve to $-$ve at $x = 1$. This means $f'(x)$ has a local maxima at $x = 1 \Rightarrow$ Option (b) is correct.

(c) We see from the graph that the range of $f(x)$ is $\mathbf{R}$, which matches with the given co-domain. This means $f:\mathbf{R}\to\mathbf{R}$ is onto $\Rightarrow$ Option (c) is correct.

(d) We have already seen that $f'(1^-)=1=f'(1^+)$. This means $f(x)$ is differentiable at $x=1\Rightarrow$ Option (d) is incorrect.

19. (a),(b) Let $P(h,k)$ be any point on the curve, and p be the slope of the tangent at that point. Then equation of the tangent at P is $y-k=p(x-h)$, and its y-intercept is $Y_P=(0,k-ph)$. According to the given condition, we have $PY_P=1$. That is

$$h^2-p^2h^2=1$$

$$\Rightarrow\quad ph=\pm\sqrt{1-h^2}$$

Putting (x,y) in place of (h,k) and y' in place of p, we have the differential equation as

$$xy'\pm\sqrt{1-x^2}=0 \qquad (1)$$

Separating the variables of equation (1) and then integrating, we have

$$\int dy=\mp\int\frac{\sqrt{1-x^2}}{x}dx$$

$$\Rightarrow\quad y=\pm\int\frac{\sin^2\theta}{\cos\theta}d\theta$$

[Put $x=\cos\theta$ and $dx=-\sin\theta d\theta$]

$$\Rightarrow\quad y=\pm\int\frac{1-\cos^2\theta}{\cos\theta}d\theta$$

$$\Rightarrow\quad y=\pm\int(\sec\theta-\cos\theta)d\theta$$

$$\Rightarrow\quad y=\pm\left[\ln|\sec\theta+\tan\theta|-\sin\theta+C\right]$$

$$\Rightarrow\quad y=\pm\left[\ln\left|\frac{1+\sqrt{1-x^2}}{x}\right|-\sqrt{1-x^2}+C\right]$$

Now using the condition $y(1)=0$ gives $C=0$. Hence, the solutions of equation (1) are

$$y=\pm\left[\ln\left(\frac{1+\sqrt{1-x^2}}{x}\right)-\sqrt{1-x^2}\right]-(2)$$ [mod sign can be removed since $x>0$]

The above equation is defined for $0<x\le 1$. Since the curve is given to lie in the first quadrant, y must be +ve for every $0<x\le1$. To confirm this, let us write equation (2) as

$$y=\pm\left[\ln\left(1+\sqrt{1-x^2}\right)-\ln x-\sqrt{1-x^2}\right]$$

For every $0<x\le1$, the first two terms inside the square bracket, that is, $\ln\left(1+\sqrt{1-x^2}\right)$ and $-\ln x$ both return non-negative values. The third term $-\sqrt{1-x^2}$ returns negative values but they are small in magnitude compared to the positive sum of the first two terms. Thus, all the terms add up to a positive value.

Hence, the required curve and the corresponding differential equation are, respectively

$$y=\ln\left(\frac{1+\sqrt{1-x^2}}{x}\right)-\sqrt{1-x^2}$$

and $\quad xy'+\sqrt{1-x^2}=0$

20. (a),(b),(c) Let the equation of line L_3 be chosen as

$$\mathbf{r}=(l\mathbf{i}+m\mathbf{j}+n\mathbf{k})+t(a\mathbf{i}+b\mathbf{j}+c\mathbf{k})$$

where $l\mathbf{i}+m\mathbf{j}+n\mathbf{k}$ is the position vector of any point on the line $a\mathbf{i}+b\mathbf{j}+c\mathbf{k}$ is a vector parallel to the line.

The two given lines are

$$L_1:\mathbf{r}=\mathbf{i}+\lambda(-\mathbf{i}+2\mathbf{j}+2\mathbf{k})$$

and $\quad L_2:\mathbf{r}=\mu(2\mathbf{i}-\mathbf{j}+2\mathbf{k})$

Since L_3 is perpendicular to both L_1 and L_2, we have

$$-a+2b+2c=0 \qquad (1)$$

and $$2a-b+2c=0 \qquad (2)$$

Thus, we have

$$\frac{a}{6}=\frac{b}{6}=\frac{c}{-3}$$

$$\Rightarrow\quad \frac{a}{2}=\frac{b}{2}=\frac{c}{-1}$$

Thus, the equation of line L_3 can now be written as

$$\mathbf{r}=(l\mathbf{i}+m\mathbf{j}+n\mathbf{k})+t(2\mathbf{i}+2\mathbf{j}-\mathbf{k})$$

Since L_3 intersects both L_1 and L_2, we have $l+2t=-1,\ m+2t=2,\ n-t=2$ for some t, and $l+2t=2\mu,\ m+2t=-\mu,\ n-t=2\mu$ for some t, Eliminating t from the two sets of equations, we have

$$2l-m+2n=2 \qquad (3)$$

and $$l-2m-2n=0 \qquad (4)$$

Equations (3) and (4) can be further reduced to

$l-m=\frac{2}{3}-(5)$ [Adding equations (3) and (4)]

and $m+2n=\frac{2}{3}-(6)$ [Subtracting equation (3) from $2\times$ equation (4)]

The values of l, m, n in options (a), (b) and (c) satisfy the above equations.

21. (a),(b),(c) Let $M=\begin{bmatrix}2&1&3\\1&0&2\\3&2&1\end{bmatrix}$. Then, we have

$$P_1MP_1^T=\begin{bmatrix}1&0&0\\0&1&0\\0&0&1\end{bmatrix}\begin{bmatrix}2&1&3\\1&0&2\\3&2&1\end{bmatrix}\begin{bmatrix}1&0&0\\0&1&0\\0&0&1\end{bmatrix}$$

$$=\begin{bmatrix}2&1&3\\1&0&2\\3&2&1\end{bmatrix}\begin{bmatrix}1&0&0\\0&1&0\\0&0&1\end{bmatrix}=\begin{bmatrix}2&1&3\\1&0&2\\3&2&1\end{bmatrix}$$

$$P_2MP_2^T=\begin{bmatrix}1&0&0\\0&0&1\\0&1&0\end{bmatrix}\begin{bmatrix}2&1&3\\1&0&2\\3&2&1\end{bmatrix}\begin{bmatrix}1&0&0\\0&0&1\\0&1&0\end{bmatrix}$$

$$=\begin{bmatrix}2&1&3\\3&2&1\\1&0&2\end{bmatrix}\begin{bmatrix}1&0&0\\0&0&1\\0&1&0\end{bmatrix}=\begin{bmatrix}2&3&1\\3&1&2\\1&2&0\end{bmatrix}$$

$$P_3MP_3^T=\begin{bmatrix}0&1&0\\1&0&0\\0&0&1\end{bmatrix}\begin{bmatrix}2&1&3\\1&0&2\\3&2&1\end{bmatrix}\begin{bmatrix}0&1&0\\1&0&0\\0&0&1\end{bmatrix}$$

$$=\begin{bmatrix}1&0&2\\2&1&3\\3&2&1\end{bmatrix}\begin{bmatrix}0&1&0\\1&0&0\\0&0&1\end{bmatrix}=\begin{bmatrix}0&1&2\\1&2&3\\2&3&1\end{bmatrix}$$

$$P_4MP_4^T=\begin{bmatrix}0&1&0\\0&0&1\\1&0&0\end{bmatrix}\begin{bmatrix}2&1&3\\1&0&2\\3&2&1\end{bmatrix}\begin{bmatrix}0&0&1\\1&0&0\\0&1&0\end{bmatrix}$$

$$=\begin{bmatrix}1&0&2\\3&2&1\\2&1&3\end{bmatrix}\begin{bmatrix}0&0&1\\1&0&0\\0&1&0\end{bmatrix}=\begin{bmatrix}0&2&1\\2&1&3\\1&3&2\end{bmatrix}$$

$$P_5MP_5^T=\begin{bmatrix}0&0&1\\1&0&0\\0&1&0\end{bmatrix}\begin{bmatrix}2&1&3\\1&0&2\\3&2&1\end{bmatrix}\begin{bmatrix}0&1&0\\0&0&1\\1&0&0\end{bmatrix}$$

$$=\begin{bmatrix}3&2&1\\2&1&3\\1&0&2\end{bmatrix}\begin{bmatrix}0&1&0\\0&0&1\\1&0&0\end{bmatrix}=\begin{bmatrix}1&3&2\\3&2&1\\2&1&0\end{bmatrix}$$

$$P_6MP_6^T=\begin{bmatrix}0&0&1\\0&1&0\\1&0&0\end{bmatrix}\begin{bmatrix}2&1&3\\1&0&2\\3&2&1\end{bmatrix}\begin{bmatrix}0&0&1\\0&1&0\\1&0&0\end{bmatrix}$$

$$=\begin{bmatrix}3&2&1\\2&0&1\\2&1&3\end{bmatrix}\begin{bmatrix}0&0&1\\0&1&0\\1&0&0\end{bmatrix}=\begin{bmatrix}1&2&3\\2&0&1\\3&1&2\end{bmatrix}$$

Adding all the above matrices, we have

$$X=\sum_{k=1}^{6}P_kMP_k^T=\begin{bmatrix}2&1&3\\1&0&2\\3&2&1\end{bmatrix}+\begin{bmatrix}2&3&1\\3&1&2\\1&2&0\end{bmatrix}+\begin{bmatrix}0&1&2\\1&2&3\\2&3&1\end{bmatrix}+\begin{bmatrix}0&2&1\\2&1&3\\1&3&2\end{bmatrix}$$

$$+\begin{bmatrix}1&3&2\\3&2&1\\2&1&0\end{bmatrix}+\begin{bmatrix}1&2&3\\2&0&1\\3&1&2\end{bmatrix}=\begin{bmatrix}6&12&12\\12&6&12\\12&12&6\end{bmatrix}.$$

(a) Thus, we have

$$X\begin{bmatrix}1\\1\\1\end{bmatrix}=\begin{bmatrix}6&12&12\\12&6&12\\12&12&6\end{bmatrix}\begin{bmatrix}1\\1\\1\end{bmatrix}=\begin{bmatrix}30\\30\\30\end{bmatrix}$$

$$=30\begin{bmatrix}1\\1\\1\end{bmatrix}\Rightarrow\alpha=30$$

$\Rightarrow$ Option (a) is correct.

(b) We can see that X is a symmetric matrix $\Rightarrow$ Option (b) is correct.

(c) We can see that the sum of the diagonal entries of X equals $6+6+6=18\Rightarrow$ Option (c) is correct.

(d) We have

$$X-30I=\begin{bmatrix}6&12&12\\12&6&12\\12&12&6\end{bmatrix}-\begin{bmatrix}30&0&0\\0&30&0\\0&0&30\end{bmatrix}$$

$$=\begin{bmatrix}-24&12&12\\12&-24&12\\12&12&-24\end{bmatrix}$$

Now, we have

$$|X-30I|=\begin{bmatrix}0&0&0\\12&-24&12\\12&12&-24\end{bmatrix}=0$$

$[R_1 \to R_1+R_2+R_3]$

This means $X-30I$ is not invertible $\Rightarrow$ Option (d) is incorrect.

22. (c) The given matrix is $P=\begin{bmatrix}1&1&1\\0&2&2\\0&0&3\end{bmatrix}$. Then its determinant is $|P|=6$.

The transpose and the adjoint matrix of P are, respectively

$$P'=\begin{bmatrix}1&0&0\\1&2&0\\1&2&3\end{bmatrix} \text{ and adj.} P=\begin{bmatrix}6&-3&0\\0&3&-2\\0&0&2\end{bmatrix}$$

Thus, the inverse matrix of P is

$$P^{-1}=\frac{1}{6}\begin{bmatrix}6&-3&0\\0&3&-2\\0&0&2\end{bmatrix}$$

Now, the matrix $R=PQP^{-1}$ is

$$R=\frac{1}{6}\begin{bmatrix}1&1&1\\0&2&2\\0&0&3\end{bmatrix}\begin{bmatrix}2&x&x\\0&4&0\\x&x&6\end{bmatrix}\begin{bmatrix}6&-3&0\\0&3&-2\\0&0&2\end{bmatrix}$$

$$=\frac{1}{6}\begin{bmatrix}x+2&2x+4&x+6\\2x&2x+8&12\\3x&3x&18\end{bmatrix}\begin{bmatrix}6&-3&0\\0&3&-2\\0&0&2\end{bmatrix}$$

$$=\frac{1}{6}\begin{bmatrix}6x+12&3x+6&-2x+4\\12x&24&-4x+8\\18x&0&-6x+36\end{bmatrix}$$

(a) We have

$$PQ=\begin{bmatrix}1&1&1\\0&2&2\\0&0&3\end{bmatrix}\begin{bmatrix}2&x&x\\0&4&0\\x&x&6\end{bmatrix}=\begin{bmatrix}x+2&2x+4&x+6\\2x&2x+8&12\\3x&3x&18\end{bmatrix}$$

and

$$QP=\begin{bmatrix}2&x&x\\0&4&0\\x&x&6\end{bmatrix}\begin{bmatrix}1&1&1\\0&2&2\\0&0&3\end{bmatrix}=\begin{bmatrix}2&2x+2&5x+2\\0&8&8\\x&3x&3x+18\end{bmatrix}$$

We can see that the second row, third column entries of the above two matrices, can never be equal. This means PQ and QP cannot be equal for any value of $x \Rightarrow$ Option (a) is incorrect.

(b) The LHS of the given equation is

$$\text{LHS}=\frac{1}{6^3}\begin{vmatrix}6x+12&3x+6&-2x+4\\12x&24&-4x+8\\18x&0&-6x+36\end{vmatrix}$$

$$=\frac{(6)(3)(-2)}{6^3}\begin{vmatrix}x+2&x+2&x-2\\2x&8&2x-4\\3x&0&-6x+36\end{vmatrix}$$

$$=\frac{-(2)(3)}{6}\begin{vmatrix}x+2&x+2&x-2\\x&4&x-2\\x&0&-2x+18\end{vmatrix}$$

$$=-\begin{vmatrix}2&x-2&0\\x&4&x-2\\x&0&-2x+18\end{vmatrix} \quad [R_1 \to R_1-R_2]$$

$$=-\left[2(-8x+72)+(x-2)(x^2-2x)\right]$$

$$=-\left[x^3-4x^2-12x+144\right]$$

The LHS of the given equation is

$$\text{RHS}=\begin{vmatrix}2&x&x\\0&4&0\\x&x&6\end{vmatrix}+8=48-4x^2+8=56-4x^2$$

Now, the two sides will be equal only for values of x which satisfy the equation

$$x^3-4x^2-12x+144=4x^2-56$$

$\Rightarrow \quad x^3-8x^2-12x+200=0 \Rightarrow$ Option (b) is incorrect.

(c) Solving the given equation $R(0)\begin{bmatrix}1\\a\\b\end{bmatrix}=6\begin{bmatrix}1\\a\\b\end{bmatrix}$, we have

$$\frac{1}{6}\begin{bmatrix}12&6&4\\0&24&8\\0&0&36\end{bmatrix}\begin{bmatrix}1\\a\\b\end{bmatrix}=6\begin{bmatrix}1\\a\\b\end{bmatrix}$$

$$\Rightarrow \quad \begin{bmatrix}12+6a+4b\\24a+8b\\36b\end{bmatrix}=\begin{bmatrix}36\\36a\\36b\end{bmatrix}$$

$$\Rightarrow \quad 12+6a+4b=36 \text{ and } 24a+8b=36a$$

$$\Rightarrow \quad 3a+2b=12\cdots(1) \text{ and } 3a=2b\cdots(2)$$

Solving equations (1) and (2) gives $a=2, b=3$. Hence, $a+b=5 \Rightarrow$ Option (c) is correct.

(d) Solving the given equation $R(1)\begin{bmatrix}\alpha\\\beta\\\gamma\end{bmatrix}=\begin{bmatrix}0\\0\\0\end{bmatrix}$, we have

$$\frac{1}{6}\begin{bmatrix}18 & 9 & 2\\12 & 24 & 4\\18 & 0 & 30\end{bmatrix}\begin{bmatrix}\alpha\\\beta\\\gamma\end{bmatrix}=\begin{bmatrix}0\\0\\0\end{bmatrix}$$

$\Rightarrow 18\alpha+9\beta+2\gamma=0\cdots(1),\ 12\alpha+24\beta+4\gamma=0\cdots(2),$ and $18\alpha+30\gamma=0\cdots(3).$

The above homogeneous system of equations has a unique solution $\alpha=\beta=\gamma=0$, since $\begin{vmatrix}18 & 9 & 2\\12 & 24 & 4\\18 & 0 & 30\end{vmatrix}\neq 0.$

Now, $\alpha^2+\beta^2+\gamma^2\neq 1\Rightarrow$ Option (d) is incorrect.

23. (a),(c),(d) Let us denote the numerator and the denominator of the given function $f(n)$ as S_1 and S_2, respectively. Then, we have

$$S_1=\sum_{k=0}^{n}\sin(k+1)\theta\sin(k+2)\theta,\ \text{where } \theta=\frac{\pi}{n+2}$$

$$=\frac{1}{2}\sum_{k=0}^{n}\left[\cos\theta-\cos(2k+3)\theta\right]$$

$$=\left(\frac{1}{2}\cos\theta\right)(n+1)-\frac{1}{2}\begin{bmatrix}\cos(3\theta)+\cos(5\theta)+\cos(7\theta)\\+\ldots(n+1)\text{terms}\end{bmatrix}$$

$$=\frac{n+1}{2}\cos\theta-\frac{1}{2}\text{Re}\begin{bmatrix}e^{i(3\theta)}+e^{i(5\theta)}+e^{i(7\theta)}\\+\ldots(n+1)\text{terms}\end{bmatrix}$$

$$=\frac{n+1}{2}\cos\theta-\frac{1}{2}\text{Re}\left[\frac{e^{i(3\theta)}\left(e^{i(n+1)2\theta}-1\right)}{e^{i(2\theta)}-1}\right]$$

$$=\frac{n+1}{2}\cos\theta-\frac{1}{2}\text{Re}\left[\frac{e^{i(3\theta)}\left(e^{i(-2\theta)}-1\right)}{e^{i(2\theta)}-1}\right]$$

$$\left[(n+1)2\theta=(n+2)2\theta-2\theta=2\pi-2\theta\right]$$

$$=\frac{n+1}{2}\cos\theta-\frac{1}{2}\text{Re}\left[\frac{e^{i\theta}\left(1-e^{i(2\theta)}\right)}{e^{i(2\theta)}-1}\right]$$

$$=\frac{n+1}{2}\cos\theta-\frac{1}{2}\text{Re}\left(-e^{i\theta}\right)$$

$$=\frac{n+1}{2}\cos\theta+\frac{1}{2}\cos\theta=\frac{n+2}{2}\cos\theta$$

and $S_2=\sum_{k=0}^{n}\sin^2(k+1)\theta$ where $\theta=\frac{\pi}{n+2}$

$$=\frac{1}{2}\sum_{k=0}^{n}\left[1-\cos(2k+2)\theta\right]$$

$$=\frac{1}{2}(n+1)-\frac{1}{2}\begin{bmatrix}\cos(2\theta)+\cos(4\theta)+\cos(6\theta)\\+\ldots(n+1)\text{terms}\end{bmatrix}$$

$$=\frac{n+1}{2}-\frac{1}{2}\text{Re}\left[e^{i(2\theta)}+e^{i(4\theta)}+e^{i(6\theta)}+\ldots(n+1)\text{terms}\right]$$

$$=\frac{n+1}{2}-\frac{1}{2}\text{Re}\left[\frac{e^{i(2\theta)}\left(e^{i(n+1)2\theta}-1\right)}{e^{i(2\theta)}-1}\right]$$

$$=\frac{n+1}{2}-\frac{1}{2}\text{Re}\left[\frac{e^{i(2\theta)}\left(e^{i(-2\theta)}-1\right)}{e^{i(2\theta)}-1}\right]$$

$$\left[(n+1)2\theta=(n+2)2\theta-2\theta=2\pi-2\theta\right]$$

$$=\frac{n+1}{2}-\frac{1}{2}\text{Re}\left[\frac{1-e^{i(2\theta)}}{e^{i(2\theta)}-1}\right]$$

$$=\frac{n+1}{2}-\frac{1}{2}\text{Re}(-1)$$

$$=\frac{n+1}{2}+\frac{1}{2}=\frac{n+2}{2}.$$

Thus, we have

$$f(n)=\frac{S_1}{S_2}=\cos\theta=\cos\left(\frac{\pi}{n+2}\right).$$

(a) Now $f(4)=\cos\left(\frac{\pi}{6}\right)=\frac{\sqrt{3}}{2}\Rightarrow$ Option (a) is correct.

(b) Now $\lim_{n\to\infty}f(n)=\lim_{n\to\infty}\cos\left(\frac{\pi}{n+2}\right)=\cos 0=1$
$\Rightarrow$ Option (b) is incorrect.

(c) Now

$$\alpha=\tan\left(\cos^{-1}f(6)\right)=\tan\left(\cos^{-1}\cos\left(\frac{\pi}{8}\right)\right)$$

$$=\tan\frac{\pi}{8}=\sqrt{2}-1$$

We can see that $\sqrt{2}-1$ is a root of $\alpha^2+2\alpha-1=0$
$\Rightarrow$ Option (c) is correct.

(d) Now

$$\sin\left(7\cos^{-1}f(5)\right)=\sin\left(7\cos^{-1}\cos\left(\frac{\pi}{7}\right)\right)=\sin\pi=0$$

$\Rightarrow$ Option (d) is correct.

24. (a),(b)

(a) For $f(x)=|x|$, we have

Property 1: $\lim\limits_{h\to 0}\dfrac{|h|}{\sqrt{|h|}}=\lim\limits_{h\to 0}\sqrt{|h|}=0$

$\Rightarrow$ Option (a) is correct.

(b) For $f(x)=x^{2/3}$, we have

Property 1: $\lim\limits_{h\to 0}\dfrac{h^{2/3}}{\sqrt{|h|}}=\begin{cases}\lim\limits_{h\to 0}-|h|^{1/6}, h<0=0\\ \lim\limits_{h\to 0}|h|^{1/6}, h>0=0\end{cases}$

$\Rightarrow$ Option (b) is correct.

(c) For $f(x)=x|x|$, we have

Property 2: $\lim\limits_{h\to 0}\dfrac{h|h|}{h^2}=\lim\limits_{h\to 0}\dfrac{|h|}{h}\begin{cases}-1, h<0\\ 1, h>0\end{cases}$

$\Rightarrow$ Option (c) is incorrect.

(d) For $f(x)=|x|$, we have

Property 2: $\lim\limits_{h\to 0}\dfrac{\sinh}{h^2}=\text{dne}$ $\Rightarrow$ Option (d) is incorrect.

25. (b),(c),(d) The figure shows the graph of the given function $f(x)=\dfrac{\sin(\pi x)}{x^2}, x>0$. The function oscillates with decreasing amplitude, and it cuts the x-axis where $\sin(\pi x)=0 \Rightarrow x=1,2,3,\ldots$. Also $f(0^+)=+\infty$ and $f(+\infty)=0$.

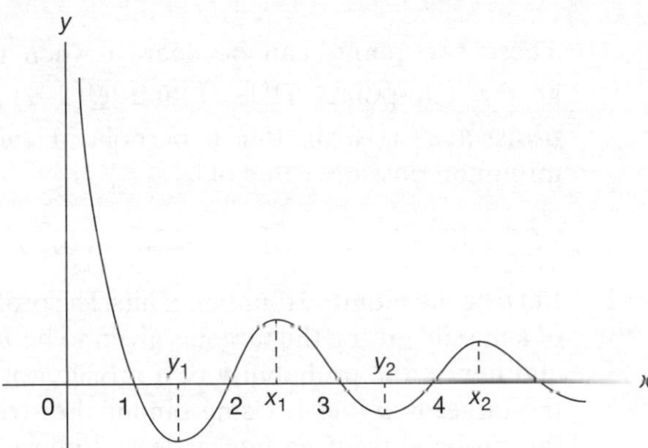

The derivative of $f(x)$ is

$$f'(x)=\frac{x^2\pi\cos(\pi x)-2x\sin(\pi x)}{x^4}$$

The troughs and crests on the graph occur at points where $f'(x)=0$, that is, at points given by

$$x^2\pi\cos(\pi x)=2x\sin(\pi x)$$

$$\Rightarrow \qquad \tan(\pi x)=\frac{\pi x}{2} \qquad (1)$$

The values of x satisfying equation (1) lie on the intersection of the graphs of $\tan(\pi x)$ and $\dfrac{\pi x}{2}$ (see figure).

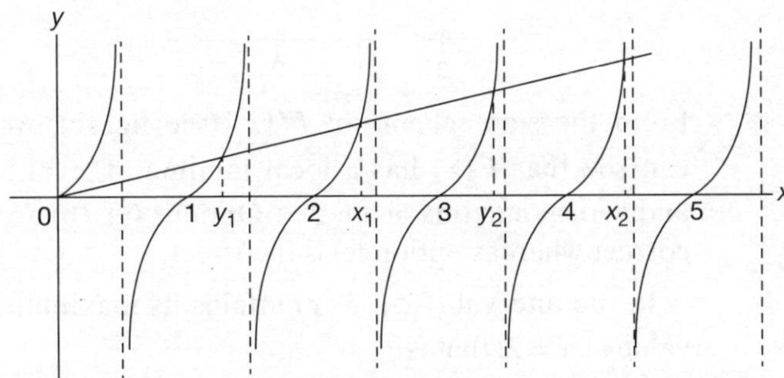

From the graph of $f(x)$, we can see that $y_1<x_1 \Rightarrow$ Option (a) is incorrect.

From the graphs of $\tan(\pi x)$ and $\dfrac{\pi x}{2}$, we can see that the distance between any two successive intersections $|x_n-y_n|>1$ and the distance between any two alternate intersections $|x_{n+1}-x_n|>2$. We can also see that $2<x_1<2.5, 4<x_1<4.5, \ldots 2n<x_n<2n+\dfrac{1}{2}$

$\Rightarrow$ Options (b), (c), (d) are correct.

26. (a),(d) We have

$$L=\lim_{n\to\infty}\frac{\sum_1^n r^{1/3}}{n^{7/3}\sum_1^n(\alpha n+r)^{-2}}=\lim_{n\to\infty}\frac{\frac{1}{n}\sum_1^n\left(\frac{r}{n}\right)^{1/3}}{\frac{1}{n}\sum_1^n\left(\alpha+\frac{r}{n}\right)^{-2}}$$

The numerator can be written as

$$\int_0^1 x^{1/3}dx=\left|\frac{x^{4/3}}{4/3}\right|_0^1=\frac{3}{4}$$

The denominator can be written as

$$\int_0^1\frac{1}{(\alpha+x)^2}dx=\left|\frac{-1}{\alpha+x}\right|_0^1=\frac{-1}{\alpha+1}+\frac{1}{\alpha}=\frac{1}{\alpha(\alpha+1)}$$

It is given that $L=54$. Hence, we have

$$\frac{3}{4}\alpha(\alpha+1)=54$$

$\Rightarrow \alpha^2+\alpha-72=0$ gives $\alpha=-9,8 \Rightarrow$ Options (a), (d) are correct.

27. (a),(b),(d) The given function and its derivative are, respectively

$$F(x)=\int_0^x (x-1)(x-2)(x-5)dx$$

and $F'(x)=(x-1)(x-2)(x-5)$

$$\begin{array}{cccc} & - & + & - \\ 0 & 1 & 2 & 5 \end{array}$$

From the sign scheme of $F'(x)$ (see figure), we can see that $F(x)$ has a local minima at $x=1,5$ and a local maxima at $x=2 \Rightarrow$ Options (a), (b) are correct whereas option (c) is incorrect.

In the interval $(0,5)$, $F(x)$ attains its maximum value at $x=2$, that is

$$F_{\max}=\int_0^2 (x-1)(x-2)(x-5)dx$$

$$=\int_0^2 \left(x^3-8x^2+17x-10\right)dx$$

$$=\left|\frac{1}{4}x^4-\frac{8}{3}x^3+\frac{17}{2}x^2-10x\right|_0^2=-\frac{9}{4}.$$

Thus, we see that in the interval $(0,5)$, $F(x)<\frac{-9}{4}<0$ $\Rightarrow$ Option (d) is correct.

28. (a),(c) The points P, Q and R are, respectively

$$\lambda\mathbf{i},\ \mu\mathbf{j}+\mathbf{k}, \text{ and } \boldsymbol{i}+\boldsymbol{j}+\nu\mathbf{k}.$$

The three points will be collinear if vectors

$$\mathbf{PQ}=-\lambda\mathbf{i}+\mu\mathbf{j}+\mathbf{k} \text{ and } \mathbf{PR}=(1-\lambda)\mathbf{i}+\mathbf{j}+\nu\mathbf{k}$$

are parallel. That is

$$\frac{\lambda-1}{\lambda}=\frac{1}{\mu}=\frac{\nu}{1}$$

(a) For $\mu=\frac{-1}{2}$, we have $\lambda=1/3$ and $\nu=-2$ $\Rightarrow$ Option (a) is correct.

(b) For $\mu=0$, we do not get values for λ,ν $\Rightarrow$ Option (b) is incorrect.

(c) For $\mu=\frac{1}{2}$, we have $\lambda=1$ and $\nu=2 \Rightarrow$ Option (c) is correct.

(d) For $\mu=1$, we do not get a value for $\lambda \Rightarrow$ Option (d) is incorrect.

Single Digit Answer

1. The given equation can be written as

$$z^4-|z|^4=4iz^2$$

$$\Rightarrow \quad z^4-z^2\bar{z}^2=4iz^2$$

$$\Rightarrow \quad z^2(z^2-\bar{z}^2)=4iz^2$$

$$\Rightarrow \quad z^2-\bar{z}^2=4i \text{ or } z=0$$

Putting $z=x+iy$, the above equation reduces to

$$(x+iy)^2-(x-iy)^2=4i$$

$$\Rightarrow \quad (x^2-y^2+2ixy)=(x^2-y^2-2ixy)=4i$$

$$\Rightarrow \quad 4ixy=4i$$

$$\Rightarrow \quad xy=1$$

Thus, all z satisfying the above equation lie on the hyperbola $xy=1$ (see figure). Now according to the question, z_1 is a point on the curve lying in the first quadrant and z_2 is a point on the curve lying in the second quadrant.

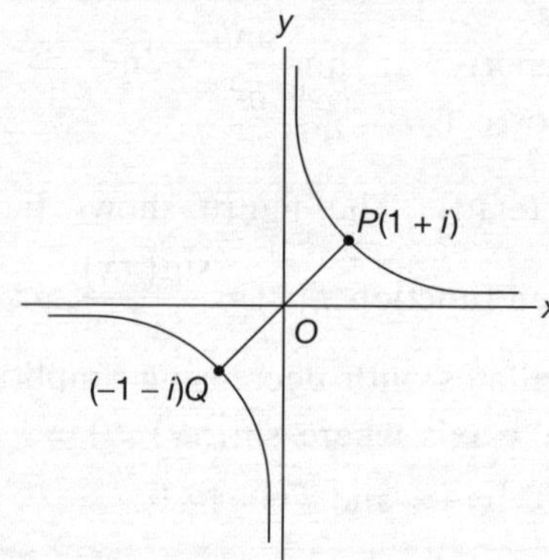

These two points can be nearest when they lie at the end-points $P(1+i)$ and $Q(1-i)$ of the transverse axis of the hyperbola. Hence, the minimum possible value of $|z_1-z_2|^2$ is

$$PQ=|(1+i)-(-1-i)|^2=|2+2i|^2=(2\sqrt{2})^2=8$$

2. Let n be the required number of hits. The probability of a missile hitting the target is given to be $p=3/4$, and hence, the probability of a missile not hitting the target is $p=1/4$. Using binomial distribution, the probability of getting at least three hits in n firings is

$$1-\left[{}^nC_0\left(\frac{1}{4}\right)^n+{}^nC_1\left(\frac{3}{4}\right)\left(\frac{1}{4}\right)^{n-1}+{}^nC_2\left(\frac{3}{4}\right)^2\left(\frac{1}{4}\right)^{n-2}\right]$$

$$=1-\frac{1}{4^n}\left[1+3n+\frac{9n(n-1)}{2}\right]=1-\frac{9n^2-3n+2}{2\times 4^n}$$

According to the question, we have

$$1-\frac{9n^2-3n+2}{2\times 4^n}\geq 0.95$$

$$\Rightarrow \quad \frac{9n^2-3n+2}{2\times 4^n}\leq 0.05$$

$$\Rightarrow \quad 4^n \geq 10(9n^2 - 3n + 2) \text{ gives } n \geq 6$$

3. Let $P(h, k)$ be one of the intersection points of the line $2x + 4y = 5$ and the circle $x^2 + y^2 = r^2$ (see figure). Then, we have

$$2h + 4k = 5 \qquad (1)$$

and $$h^2 + k^2 = r^2 \qquad (2)$$

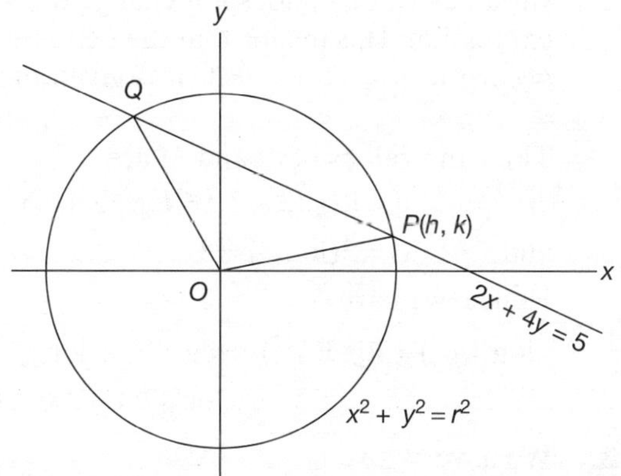

To find the circumcentre of ΔOPQ, let us find the perpendicular bisectors of sides PQ and OP; their intersection point will be the circumcentre.

Slope of line PQ is $-1/2$. The perpendicular bisector of PQ passes through the origin and has slope 2. Thus, its equation is

$$y = 2x \qquad (3)$$

Slope of line OP is k/h and its mid-point is $\left(\frac{h}{2},\frac{k}{2}\right)$

The perpendicular bisector of OP passes through $\left(\frac{h}{2},\frac{k}{2}\right)$ and has slope $-h/k$. Thus, its equation is

$$y-\frac{k}{2}=-\frac{h}{k}\left(x-\frac{h}{2}\right)$$

$$\Rightarrow \quad hx+ky=\frac{h^2+x^2}{2}$$

$$\Rightarrow \quad hx+ky=\frac{r^2}{2} \qquad (4)$$

Solving equations (3) and (4) gives the coordinates of the circumcentre as

$$x=\frac{r^2}{2h+4k} \text{ and } x=\frac{2r^2}{2h+4k}$$

$$\Rightarrow \quad x=\frac{r^2}{5} \text{ and } y=\frac{2r^2}{5} \quad \text{[Using equation (1)]}$$

Now it is given that the circumcentres lies on the line $x + 2y = 4$. Hence, we have

$$\frac{r^2}{5}+\frac{4r^2}{5}=4$$

$$\Rightarrow \quad r^2 = 4 \text{ gives } r = 2$$

4. Let $A=\begin{bmatrix} a & b \\ c & d \end{bmatrix}$

Then $A^2=\begin{bmatrix} a & b \\ c & d \end{bmatrix}\begin{bmatrix} a & b \\ c & d \end{bmatrix}=\begin{bmatrix} a^2+bc & ab+bd \\ ac+cd & bc+d^2 \end{bmatrix}$

and $A^3=\begin{bmatrix} a & b \\ c & d \end{bmatrix}\begin{bmatrix} a^2+bc & ab+bd \\ ac+cd & bc+d^2 \end{bmatrix}$

$$=\begin{bmatrix} a^3+2abc+bcd & \ldots \\ \ldots & abc+2bcd+d^3 \end{bmatrix}$$

Now according to the question, we have

$$a + d = 3 \qquad (1)$$

and $$a^3 + d^3 + 3abc + 3bcd = -18 \qquad (2)$$

Now subtracting equation (2) from the cube of equation (1), we have

$$(a^3 + 3a^2d + 3ad^2 + d^3)$$
$$- (a^3 + d^3 + 3abc + 3bcd) = 27 + 18$$

$$\Rightarrow \quad 3ad(a + d) - 3bc(a + d) = 45$$

$$\Rightarrow \quad 3(a + d)(ad - bc) = 45$$

$$\Rightarrow \quad 9|A| = 45 \text{ gives } |A| = 5$$

5. The function $f(x)$ can be written as

$$f(x)=\begin{cases} -(2x-1)-(2x+1), & x\leq \frac{-1}{2} \\ -(2x-1)+(2x+1), & \frac{-1}{1}\leq x\leq \frac{1}{2} \\ (2x-1)+(2x+1), & x\geq \frac{1}{2} \end{cases}$$

$$\Rightarrow \quad f(x)=\begin{cases} -4x, & x\leq \frac{-1}{2} \\ 2, & \frac{-1}{2}\leq x\leq \frac{1}{2} \\ 4x, & x\geq \frac{1}{2} \end{cases}$$

The function $g(x) = x - [x] = \{x\}$ is a periodic function. Its values lie between [0, 1] and they repeat with period 1. Hence $fog(x)$ will also be periodic with period 1.

Thus, the graph of $fog(x)$ will be the same in (–1, 0) as in (0, 1). So let us analyse $fog(x)$ in (0, 1). Then we can copy the graph and paste the same in (–1, 0).

Thus, we have

$$fog(x) = \begin{cases} -4g, g \le -1/2 \\ 2, \frac{-1}{2} \le g \le \frac{1}{2} \\ 4g, g \ge \frac{1}{2} \end{cases}$$

$$\Rightarrow \quad fog(x) = \begin{cases} 2, 0 \le g \le \frac{1}{2} \\ 4g, \frac{1}{2} \le g < 1 \end{cases}$$

[Value of g always lies between (0, 1)]

$$\Rightarrow \quad fog(x) = \begin{cases} 2, 0 \le g \le \frac{1}{2} \\ 4x, \frac{1}{2} \le g < 1 \end{cases} \quad [g(x) = x \text{ in } [0, 1)]$$

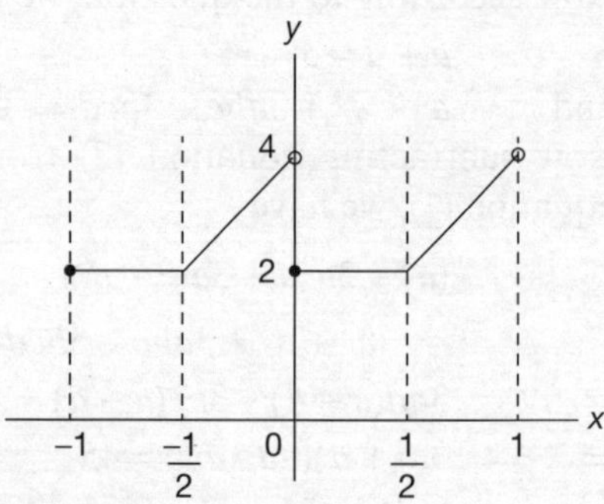

The figure shows the graph of $fog(x)$. In the interval (–1, 1), there is one point of discontinuity and three points of non-differentiability. Hence, the required answer is $1 + 3 = 4$.

6. We have

$$L = \lim_{x\to\pi/2} \frac{4\sqrt{2}(\sin 3x + \sin x)}{\left(2\sin 2x \sin\frac{3x}{2} + \cos\frac{5x}{2}\right) - \left(\sqrt{2} + \sqrt{2}\cos 2x + \cos\frac{3x}{2}\right)}$$

$$= \lim_{x\to\pi/2} \frac{8\sqrt{2}\sin 2x \cos x}{2\sin 2x \sin\frac{3x}{2} + \left(\cos\frac{5x}{2} - \cos\frac{3x}{2}\right) - \sqrt{2}(1+\cos 2x)}$$

$$= \lim_{x\to\pi/2} \frac{8\sqrt{2}\sin zx \cos x}{2\sin 2x \sin\frac{2x}{2} - 2\sin 2x \sin\frac{x}{2} - 2\sqrt{2}\cos^2 x}$$

$$= \lim_{x\to\pi/2} \frac{8\sqrt{2}\sin 2x \cos x}{4\sin 2x \cos x \sin\frac{x}{2} - 2\sqrt{2}\cos^2 x}$$

$$= \lim_{x\to\pi/2} \frac{16\sqrt{2}\sin x \cos^2 x}{8\sin x \cos^2 x \sin\frac{x}{2} - 2\sqrt{2}\cos^2 x}$$

$$= \lim_{x+\pi/2} \frac{16\sqrt{2}\sin x}{8\sin x \sin\frac{x}{2} - 2\sqrt{2}} = \frac{16\sqrt{2}}{\frac{8}{\sqrt{2}} - 2\sqrt{2}} = 8$$

Numerical Value Answer

1. We see that interchanging the positions of the variables y_1, y_2, y_3 does not change the value of the expression. This means that the extreme values will occur for $y_1 = y_2 = y_3 = 3$ (it is given that $y_1 + y_2 + y_3 = 9$).

Thus, the values of m and M are

$$m = \log_3(3 \times 3^3) = \log_3(3^4) = 4$$

and $\quad M = 3(\log_3 3) = 3$

Hence, we have

$$\log_2(m^3) + \log 3(M^2) = \log_2(4^3) + \log_3(3^2) = \log_2(2^6) + 2 = 6 + 2 = 8$$

2. We have

$$2(a_1 + a_2 + \ldots + a_n) = b_1 + b_2 + \ldots b_n$$

$$\Rightarrow \quad 2 \times \frac{n}{2}[2c + (n-1)2] = c\left(\frac{2^n - 1}{2-1}\right)$$

$$\Rightarrow \quad 2nc + 2n(n-1) = (2n - 1)C$$

$$\Rightarrow \quad c = \frac{2n(n-1)}{2^n - 2n - 1} \quad n = 1, 2, 3, \ldots \quad (1)$$

Now, since c is an integer

$$2^n - 2n - 1 \le 2n^2 - 2n$$

$$\Rightarrow \quad 2^n \le 2n^2 + 1$$

$$\Rightarrow \quad n \le 6$$

Now, putting $n = 1, 2, 3, 4, 5, 6 \ldots$ in equation (1), we get an integer value for c only for $n = 3$. All other values of n give non-integer values of c. Hence, there is only one possible value of c.

3. The given function can be written as

$$f(x) = (3 - \sin(2\pi x))\sin\left(\pi x - \frac{\pi}{4}\right) - \sin\left(3\pi x + \frac{\pi}{4}\right)$$

$$= \left(3 - \sin\left(2\left(\pi x - \frac{\pi}{4}\right) + \frac{\pi}{2}\right)\right)\sin\left(\pi x - \frac{\pi}{4}\right) - \sin\left(3\left(\pi x - \frac{\pi}{4}\right) + \pi\right)$$

$$= (3 - \cos(2\theta))\sin\theta + \sin(3\theta) \quad \left[\text{Putting } \pi x - \frac{\pi}{4} = \theta\right]$$
$$= (3 - \cos(2\theta))\sin\theta + (3 - 4\sin^2\theta)\sin\theta$$
$$= \sin\theta[6 - \cos(2\theta) - 4\sin^2\theta]$$
$$= \sin\theta[6 - \cos(2\theta) - 2(1 - \cos(2\theta)]$$
$$= \sin\theta(\cos(2\theta) + 4)$$

Note that $4 + \cos(2\theta)$ is always positive since $-1 \le \cos(2\theta) \le 1 \Rightarrow 3 \le 4 + \cos(2\theta) \le 5$. Thus, $f(x)$ is positive when $\sin\theta$ is positive, negative when $\sin\theta$ is negative, and zero when $\sin\theta$ is zero.

Now, when $0 \le x \le 2$, then

$$0 \le \pi x \le 2\pi$$
$$\Rightarrow \quad -\frac{\pi}{4} \le \pi x - \frac{\pi}{4} \le -\frac{\pi}{4} + 2\pi$$
$$\Rightarrow \quad \frac{-\pi}{4} \le \theta \le -\frac{\pi}{4} + 2\pi$$

Within this internal, $\sin\theta > 0$ when

$$0 < \theta < \pi$$
$$\Rightarrow \quad 0 < \pi x - \frac{\pi}{4} < \pi$$
$$\Rightarrow \quad \frac{\pi}{4} < \pi x < \frac{5\pi}{4}$$
$$\Rightarrow \quad \frac{1}{4} < x < \frac{5}{4}$$

Thus, $\alpha = \frac{1}{4}$ and $\beta = \frac{5}{4}$. Hence $\beta - \alpha = 1$.

4. We have

$$\overline{PQ} + \overline{QR} + \overline{RP} = 0$$
$$\Rightarrow \quad \vec{a} + \vec{b} + \vec{c} = 0$$

Using the given condition, we have

$$\frac{\vec{a}\cdot(\vec{c}-\vec{b})}{\vec{c}\cdot(\vec{a}-\vec{b})} = \frac{\vec{a}}{\vec{a}+\vec{b}} = \frac{3}{7} \quad [a = 3,\ b = 4, \text{ given}]$$
$$\Rightarrow \quad 7\vec{a}\cdot(\vec{a}+2\vec{b}) = 3(\vec{a}+\vec{b})\cdot(\vec{a}-\vec{b})$$
$$[\text{Putting } \vec{c} = -\vec{a} - \vec{b}\,]$$
$$\Rightarrow \quad 7a^2 + 14\vec{a}\cdot\vec{b} = 3(a^2 - b^2)$$
$$\Rightarrow \quad \vec{a}\cdot\vec{b} = -\frac{4a^2 + 3b^2}{14} = -\frac{36+48}{14} = -6$$
$$\Rightarrow \quad ab\cos C = -6$$
$$\Rightarrow \quad \cos C = -\frac{6}{ab} = -\frac{6}{12} = -\frac{1}{2} \text{ gives } = \frac{2\pi}{3}$$

Hence, we have

$$\left|\vec{a}\times\vec{b}\right|^2 = (ab\sin C)^2 = \left[12\sin\left(\frac{2\pi}{3}\right)\right]^2 = \left(1\times\frac{\sqrt{3}}{2}\right)^2 = 108$$

5. We have

$$f = (x^2 - 1)^2 P_3 \qquad [P_3 = a_0 + a_1x + a_2x^2 + a_3x^3 \text{ is a third-degree polynomial}]$$

Differentiating twice with respect to x, we have

$$f' = 2x(x^2 - 1)P_3 + (x^2 - 1)^2(a_1 + 2a_2x + 3a_3x^2)$$
$$= (x^2 - 1)P_4 \qquad [P_4 \text{ is a fourth-degree polynomial}]$$

and
$$f'' = 2xP_4 + (x^2 - 1)(2a_2 + 6a_3x^2)$$
$$= P_5\ [P_5 \text{ is a fifth-degree polynomial}]$$

The function $(x^2 - 1)P_4$ will definitely have two zeros at $x = \pm 1$. About P_4, we only know that it may have no zeros, two zeros or four zeros. Thus, f' has at least two zeros.

The function P_5 may have one zero, three zeros or five zeros. Thus, f'' has at least one zero. Hence, $m_{f'} + m_{f''} = 2 + 1 = 3$.

6. We have

$$L = \lim_{x\to0}\frac{(1-x)^{\frac{1}{x}} - e^{-1}}{x^a}$$
$$= \lim_{x\to0}\frac{e^{\frac{\ln(1-x)}{x}} - e^{-1}}{x^a}$$
$$= \frac{1}{e}\lim_{x\to0}\frac{e^{\frac{x+\ln(1-x)}{x}} - 1}{x^a}$$

Let us first evaluate

$$l = \lim_{x\to0}\frac{x+\ln(1-x)}{x}\left(\frac{0}{0}\right)$$
$$= \lim_{x\to0}\frac{1+\frac{-1}{1-x}}{1}$$
$$= \lim_{x\to0}\frac{-x}{1-x} = 0$$

Now, we can write L as

$$L = \frac{1}{e}\lim_{x\to0}\frac{e^l - 1}{l}\times\frac{l}{x^a}$$
$$= \frac{1}{e}\lim_{l\to0}\frac{e^l - 1}{l}\times\lim_{x\to0}\frac{x+\ln(1-x)}{x^{a+1}}\left(\frac{0}{0}\right)$$

$$= \frac{1}{e}\lim_{x\to 0}\frac{1+\frac{-1}{1-x}}{(a+1)x^a}$$

$$= \frac{1}{e}\lim_{x\to 0}\frac{-x}{(a+1)x^a(1-x)}$$

$$= \frac{1}{e}\lim_{x\to 0}\frac{-x^{1-a}}{(a+1)(1-x)}$$

The value of L will be non-zero if $a = 1$, and in that case, $L = -1/2e$.

7. Total number of ways of visiting 4 days out of 15 days is ${}^{15}c_4 = \frac{15\times14\times13\times12}{4\times3\times2} = 1365.$

From the above number, we have to subtract those ways which include consecutive visitations. Let

$A = 4$ consecutive visitations

$B = 3$ consecutive visitations $+1$ non-consecutive visitations

$C = 2$ consecutive visitations $+2$ non-consecutive visitations

$D = 2$ consecutive visitations $+1$ non-consecutive visitations

Now 4 consecutive visitations can be done on days (1, 2, 3, 4) or (2, 3, 4, 5) or… (14, 13, 14, 15). Hence, $n(A) = 14$

Three consecutive visits can be done on days (1, 2, 3) or (2, 3, 4) or … (13, 14, 15). That is, in 13 ways. The fourth visit has to be non-consecutive. So if he visits on days (1, 2, 3), he has 11 choices (from day 4 to day 15) for his fourth visit. If he visits on days (2, 3, 4), he has 10 choices for his fourth visit, and so on. Hence, $n(B) = 11 + (10\times11) + 11 = 132.$

Two consecutive visits can be done on days (1, 2) or (2, 3)… or (14, 15), that is, in 14 ways. If he visits on days (1, 2), he has 11 choices (from (4, 5) to (14, 15)) for his other two consecutive visits. If he visits on days (2, 3), he has 10 choices (from (5, 6) to (14, 15)) for his other two consecutive visits. If he visits on days (3, 4), he has 9 choices for his other two consecutive visits, and so on. Hence, $n(c) = 11 + 10 + (9\times10) + 10 + 11 = 132.$

Two consecutive visits can be done on days (1, 2) or (2, 3)… or (14, 15), that is, in 14 ways. If we visits on days (1, 2), he has 12 days (from day 4 to day 15) for choosing his other two non-consecutive visits, which can be done in ${}^{12}c_2 - 11$ ways (we have subtracted the 11 consecutive choices (4, 8) or (5, 6)… or (14, 15)). If he visits on days (2, 3), he has 11 days (from day 5 to day 14) for choosing his other two non-consecutive visits, which can be done in ${}^{11}c_2 - 10$ ways. If he visits on days (3, 4), he has 11 days (day 1 or day 6 to 15) for choosing his other two non-consecutive visits, which can be done in ${}^{11}c_2 - 9$ ways, and so on. Hence, $n(D) = ({}^{12}c_2 - 11) + ({}^{11}c_2 - 10) + 10({}^{11}c_2 - 11) = 55 + 45 + (10 \times 46) + 45 + 55 = 660.$

Hence, the required number of ways

$= 1365 - (12 + 132 + 132 + 660) = 429$

8. The six people can be put up in groups of 1, 1, 2, 2 in the four rooms. These groups can be formed in $\frac{{}^6c_2 \times {}^4c_2 \times {}^2c_2}{2!\times 2!} = \frac{15\times6\times2}{4} = 45$ ways. The $2! \times 2!$ in the denominator appears because there are two identical groups (groups of 1, 1 and groups of 2, 2). Now the four rooms can be allotted to the four groups in $4! = 24$ ways. Hence, the required number of ways is $45 \times 24 = 1080$.

9. Let us define the following events:

A(sum is a prime number) = {2, 3, 5, 7, 11}

B(sum is a perfect square) = {4, 9}

The question is on conditional probability. It is given that event B occurred before event A occurred. This means the sum of the numbers on the two dice is either 4 or 9. So this is our sample space. Then the probability that the number is odd is $p = \frac{1}{2}$ (only one of the two numbers is odd).

Hence $14p = 7$.

10. We have

$$S = f\left(\frac{1}{40}\right) + f\left(\frac{2}{40}\right) + f\left(\frac{3}{40}\right) + \ldots + f\left(\frac{39}{40}\right) - f\left(\frac{1}{2}\right)$$

$$= \sum_{r=1}^{40} f\left(\frac{r}{40}\right) - f(1) - f\left(\frac{1}{2}\right)$$

$$= 40\times\frac{1}{40}\sum_{r=1}^{40} f\left(\frac{r}{40}\right) - \frac{2}{3} - \frac{1}{2}$$

$$= 40\int_0^1 f(x)dx - \frac{5}{6}$$

Now, we have

$$\int_0^1 f(x)dx = \int_0^1 \frac{4^x}{4^x 2}dx$$

$$= \frac{1}{\ln 4}\int_3^6 \frac{dt}{t} \quad [\text{Put } 4^x + 2 = t \text{ and } 4^x \ln 4\, dx = dt]$$

$$= \frac{1}{\ln 4}|\ln t|_3^6 = \frac{1}{2\ln 2} \times \ln 2 = \frac{1}{2}$$

Hence, we have

$$S = 40\left(\frac{1}{2}\right) - \frac{5}{6} = 20 - 0.83 = 19.17$$

11. It is given that

$$F(x) = \int_0^x f(t)dx \quad \Rightarrow \quad F'(x) = f(x)$$

Hence, we have

$$\int_0^\pi (f' + F)\cos x dx = 2$$

$$\Rightarrow \quad \int_0^\pi f' \cos x\, dx + \int_0^\pi F \cos x\, dx = 2$$

$$\Rightarrow \quad \int_0^\pi f' \cos x dx + |F \sin x|_0^\pi - \int_0^\pi F' \sin x dx = 2$$

[Using parts]

$$\Rightarrow \quad \int_0^\pi f' \cos x\, dx - \int_0^\pi f \sin x\, dx = 2$$

[Using $F' = f$]

$$\Rightarrow \quad \int_0^\pi f' \cos x\, dx + |f \cos x|_0^\pi - \int_0^\pi f' \cos x\, dx = 2$$

[Using parts]

$\Rightarrow \quad -f(\pi) - f(0) = 2$

$\Rightarrow \quad 6 - f(0) = 2 \qquad [f(\pi) = -6, \text{ given}]$

$\Rightarrow \quad f(0) = 4$

12. The given function can be written as

$f(\theta) = (\sin\theta + \cos\theta)^2 + (\sin\theta - \cos\theta)^4$

$= 1 + \sin 2\theta + (1 - \sin 2\theta)^2$

$= \sin^2 2\theta - \sin 2\theta + 2$

Differentiating with respect to θ, we have

$$f'(\theta) = (2\sin 2\theta)(2\cos 2\theta) - 2\cos 2\theta$$

$$= 4\cos 2\theta\left(\sin 2\theta - \frac{1}{2}\right)$$

In the internal $\theta \in (\theta, \pi)$, $\cos 2\theta$ changes sign at $2\theta = \frac{\pi}{2}, \frac{3\pi}{2} \Rightarrow \theta = \frac{\pi}{4}, \frac{3\pi}{4}$ and $\sin 2\theta - \frac{1}{2}$ changes sign at $2\theta = \frac{\pi}{6}, \frac{5\pi}{6} \Rightarrow \theta = \frac{\pi}{12}, \frac{5\pi}{12}$.

The figure shows the sign scheme for the function $f'(\theta)$. Minima for $f(\theta)$ occurs where $f'(\theta)$ changes sign from –ve to +ve. Thus, there are two local minimas at $\theta = \frac{\pi}{12}, \frac{5\pi}{12}$

Hence, we have $\lambda_1 + \lambda_2 = \frac{1}{12} + \frac{5}{12} = 0.5.$

13. We have

$$\left|a + b\omega + c\omega^2\right|^2 = \left(a + b\omega + c\omega^2\right)\left(\overline{a + b\omega + c\omega^2}\right)$$

$$= \left(a + b\omega + c\omega^2\right)\left(a + b\bar{\omega} + c\overline{\omega^2}\right)$$

$$= \left(a + b\omega + c\omega^2\right)\left(a + b\omega^2 + c\omega\right)$$

$$= a^2 + b^2 + c^2 + ab\left(\omega + \omega^2\right) + ab\left(\omega + \omega^2\right) + bc\left(\omega^2 + \omega^4\right) + ca\left(\omega + \omega^2\right)$$

$$= a^2 + b^2 + c^2 - ab - bc - ca$$

[using $\omega + \omega^2 = -1$ and $\omega^4 = \omega$]

$$= \frac{1}{2}\left[(a - b)^2 + (b - c)^2 + (c - a)^2\right]$$

Since a, b, c are distinct non-zero integers, the minimum value of the above expression is

$$\frac{1}{2}[1 + 1 + 1] = 1.5$$

14. The terms of the sequences $AP(1;3), AP(2;5)$ and $AP(3;7)$ are, respectively, given by

$$1 + 3(l - 1) = 3l - 2 \qquad (1)$$

$$2 + 5(m - 1) = 5m - 3 \qquad (2)$$

$$3 + 7(n - 1) = 7n - 4 \qquad (3)$$

The terms of the three sequences will be equal when

$$3l - 2 = 5m - 3 = 7n - 4$$

$\Rightarrow \quad 3l+1=5m$ and $3l+2=7n$

$\Rightarrow \quad 3l+1$ must be a multiple of 5 and $3l+2$ must be a multiple of 7

The conditions are separately satisfied for values $l=8,18,28,38,\ldots$. Putting these values and checking, we get the values that satisfy both the conditions as $l=18,88,158,\ldots$. Putting these values in equation (1) gives the terms common to all the three sequences as $52,262,472,\ldots$.

So the first term and the common difference of the sequence of the common terms are, respectively

$$a=52 \text{ and } d=210$$

Hence, $a+d=262$.

15. We have

$$P(E_1|E_2)=\frac{P(E_1\cap E_2)}{P(E_2)}=\frac{n(E_1\cap E_2)}{n(E_2)} \quad (1)$$

Now event $E_2=\{A:\text{sum of entries of } A \text{ is } 7\}$
$=\{A: A \text{ has seven 1s and two 0s}\}$.

Thus, we have

$$n(E_2)={}^9C_2=36$$

Now event $E_1\cap E_2=\{A:\text{sum of entries of } A \text{ is 7 and } \det A=0\}$. This is possible when {six 1s are arranged in any two rows and the remaining row is filled with 0,0,1} or {six 1s are arranged in any two columns and the remaining column is filled with 0,0,1}. Thus, we have

$$n(E_1\cap E_2)=2\left({}^3C_1\times\frac{3!}{2!}\right)=18$$

[Choose one row or column for 0, 0, 1 and then arrange]

We can also see that when the two 0s are placed in two different rows as well as two different columns, then $\det A\neq 0$ (as shown below):

$$\begin{vmatrix}0&1&1\\1&1&0\\1&1&1\end{vmatrix}=-1 \text{ or } \begin{vmatrix}0&1&1\\1&1&1\\1&1&0\end{vmatrix}=1$$

Hence, the required probability is

$$P(E_1|E_2)=\frac{n(E_1\cap E_2)}{n(E_2)}=\frac{18}{36}=0.5$$

16.

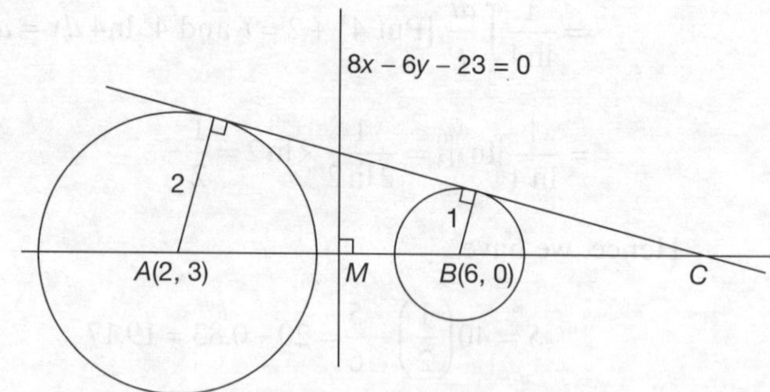

Let point $B(h,k)$ be the mirror image of point $A(2,3)$ with respect to the line $8x-6y-23=0$. Then the line joining AB must be perpendicular to the given line, and the mid-point $M\left(\frac{h+2}{2},\frac{k+3}{2}\right)$ of A, B must lie on the given line (see figure). Thus, we have the following equations:

$$\frac{k-3}{h-2}=-\frac{6}{8}\Rightarrow 3h+4k=18 \quad (1)$$

and $8\left(\frac{h+2}{2}\right)-6\left(\frac{k+3}{2}\right)=23\Rightarrow 4h-3k=18 \quad (2)$

Solving equations (1) and (2) gives $h=6, k=0$.

Now, the point C divides the line joining $A(2,3)$, $B(6,0)$ externally in the ratio $2:1$. Thus, we have

$$C=\left(\frac{2(6)-1(2)}{2-1},\frac{2(0)-1(3)}{2-1}\right)=(10,-3)$$

Hence, distance between points A,C is

$$AC=\sqrt{(2-10)^2+(2+3)^2}=10$$

17. Using the property

$$\int_a^b f(x)\,dx=\frac{1}{2}\int_a^b\{f(x)+f(a+b-x)\}\,dx,$$

We have

$$I=\int_{-\pi/4}^{\pi/4} f(x)\,dx=\frac{1}{2}\int_{-\pi/4}^{\pi/4}\{f(x)+f(-x)\}\,dx$$

$$=\frac{2}{\pi}\times\frac{1}{2}\int_{-\pi/4}^{\pi/4}\left(\begin{array}{l}\dfrac{1}{(1+e^{\sin x})(2-\cos 2x)}\\ +\dfrac{1}{(1+e^{-\sin x})(2-\cos 2x)}\end{array}\right)dx$$

$$= \frac{1}{\pi}\int_{-\pi/4}^{\pi/4}\left(\frac{1}{(1+e^{\sin x})(2-\cos 2x)} + \frac{e^{\sin x}}{(1+e^{\sin x})(2-\cos 2x)}\right)dx$$

$$= \frac{1}{\pi}\int_{-\pi/4}^{\pi/4}\left(\frac{1}{2-\cos 2x}\right)dx$$

$$= \frac{2}{\pi}\int_{0}^{\pi/4}\left(\frac{1}{2-\cos 2x}\right)dx \qquad [1-\cos 2x \text{ is even}]$$

$$= \frac{2}{\pi}\int_{0}^{1}\frac{1}{2-\frac{1-t^2}{1+t^2}}\times\frac{dt}{1+t^2}$$

$$\left[\text{Put } \tan x = t \text{ and } dx = \frac{dt}{1+t^2}\right]$$

$$= \frac{2}{\pi}\int_{0}^{1}\left(\frac{1}{3t^2+1}\right)dt$$

$$= \frac{2}{\pi}\left|\frac{\tan^{-1}(\sqrt{3}t)}{\sqrt{3}}\right|_0^1 = \frac{2}{\pi\sqrt{3}}\times\frac{\pi}{3} = \frac{2}{3\sqrt{3}}$$

Hence, $27I^2 = 4$.

18. The equation of the given plane is $x+y+z=1$. The coordinates of point A, which lies on line 1, can be chosen as $A=(\lambda,0,0)$. If it intersects with the given plane, then

$$\lambda = 1 \Rightarrow A = (1,0,0)$$

The coordinates of point B, which lies on line 2, can be chosen as $B=(\mu,\mu,0)$. If it intersects with the given plane, then

$$\mu+\mu=1 \Rightarrow \mu=\frac{1}{2} \Rightarrow B=\left(\frac{1}{2},\frac{1}{2},0\right)$$

The coordinates of point C, which lies on line 3, can be chosen as $C=(\nu,\nu,\nu)$. If it intersects with the given plane, then

$$\nu+\nu+\nu=1 \Rightarrow \nu=\frac{1}{3} \Rightarrow C=\left(\frac{1}{3},\frac{1}{3},\frac{1}{3}\right)$$

Area of the triangle ΔABC is given by

$$\Delta = \frac{1}{2}|\mathbf{AB}\times\mathbf{AC}|$$

Here $\mathbf{AB} = \frac{-1}{2}\mathbf{i}+\frac{1}{2}\mathbf{j}+0\mathbf{k} = \frac{1}{2}(-\mathbf{i}+\mathbf{j})$ and

$\mathbf{AC} = \frac{-2}{3}\mathbf{i}+\frac{1}{3}\mathbf{j}+\frac{1}{3}\mathbf{k} = \frac{1}{3}(-2\mathbf{i}+\mathbf{j}+\mathbf{k})$. Then

$$\mathbf{AB}\times\mathbf{AC} = \frac{1}{6}\begin{vmatrix}\mathbf{i} & \mathbf{j} & \mathbf{k}\\ -1 & 1 & 0\\ -2 & 1 & 1\end{vmatrix} = \frac{1}{6}(\mathbf{i}+\mathbf{j}+\mathbf{k})$$

Thus, we have

$$\Delta = \frac{1}{2}|\mathbf{AB}\times\mathbf{AC}| = \frac{1}{2}\times\frac{1}{6}\sqrt{1^2+1^2+1^2} = \frac{1}{4\sqrt{3}}$$

Hence, we have

$$(6\Delta)^2 = 36\times\frac{1}{48} = 0.75$$

19. Let us first determine the four entries of the given determinant.

The entry S_{11} is

$$S_{11} = \sum_{0}^{n} k = \frac{n(n+1)}{2}$$

The entry S_{22} is

$$S_{22} = \sum_{0}^{n} {}^nC_k 3^k = (1+3)^n = 4^n = 2^{2n}$$

To find the entries S_{21} and S_{21}, consider the binomial series

$$(1+x)^n = \sum_{0}^{n} {}^nC_k x^k \qquad (1)$$

Differentiating equation (1) with respect to x, we have

$$n(1+x)^{n-1} = \sum_{0}^{n} k\,{}^nC_k x^{k-1} \qquad (2)$$

Multiplying equation (2) with x and then differentiating, we have

$$nx(1+x)^{n-1} = \sum_{0}^{n} k\,{}^nC_k x^{k} \qquad \text{[Multiplying with } x]$$

$$n\left[(1+x)^{n-1}+(n-1)x(1+x)^{n-2}\right]=\sum_{0}^{n}k^2\,{}^nC_kx^{k-1} \quad (3)$$

[Differentiating]

Putting $x=1$ in equation (2) gives

$$S_{21}=n2^{n-1}$$

Putting $x=1$ in equation (2) gives

$$S_{12}=n\left[2^{n-1}+(n-1)2^{n-2}\right]$$
$$=n2^{n-2}\left[2+(n-1)\right]=n(n+1)2^{n-2}$$

Now, according to the question, $\det A=0$. Thus, we have

$$S_{11}S_{22}=S_{12}S_{21}$$

$$\Rightarrow \frac{n(n+1)}{2}\times 2^{2n}=n2^{n-1}\times n(n+1)2^{n-2} \text{ gives } n=4$$

20. Let us denote the red, green and blue hats by the alphabets R, G, B, respectively. We can distribute the hats in the following ways:

Case I: We can give R to one person and then give B, G, B, G to the other four persons in any one of two ways. Now, since R can be given to any one of the five persons, this distribution can be done in $5\times 2=10$ ways.

Case II: We can give G to one person and then give B, R, B, R to the other four persons. As discussed in case I, this distribution can be done in $5\times 2=10$ ways.

Case III: We can give B to one person and then give G, R, G, R to the other four persons. As discussed in case I, this distribution can be done in $5\times 2=10$ ways.

Hence, the distribution can be done in a total number of $10+10+10=30$ ways.

21. If $|A|=6$, then $|B|=1, 2, 3, 4$ or 5. Number of such sets is

$$N_1={}^6C_1+{}^6C_2+{}^6C_3+{}^6C_4+{}^6C_5$$
$$=6+15+20+15+6=62$$

If $|A|=5$, then $|B|=1, 2, 3,$ or 4. Number of such sets is

$$N_2={}^6C_1+{}^6C_2+{}^6C_3+{}^6C_4=6+15+20+15=56$$

If $|A|=4$, then $|B|=1, 2,$ or 3. Number of such sets is

$$N_3={}^6C_1+{}^6C_2+{}^6C_3=6+15+20=41$$

If $|A|=3$, then $|B|=1$ or 2. Number of such sets is

$$N_4={}^6C_1+{}^6C_2=6+15=21$$

If $|A|=2$, then $|B|=1$. Number of such sets is

$$N_5={}^6C_1=6$$

Hence, the total number of required ordered pairs $=62+56+41+21+6=186$.

22. Let us first find the value of the series

$$S=\sum_{0}^{10}\sec\left(\frac{7\pi}{12}+\frac{k\pi}{2}\right)\sec\left(\frac{7\pi}{12}+\frac{(k+1)\pi}{2}\right)$$

$$=-\sum_{0}^{10}\sec\left(\frac{7\pi}{12}+\frac{k\pi}{2}\right)\operatorname{cosec}\left(\frac{7\pi}{12}+\frac{k\pi}{2}\right)$$

$$=-\sum_{0}^{10}\frac{1}{\sin\left(\frac{7\pi}{12}+\frac{k\pi}{2}\right)\cos\left(\frac{7\pi}{12}+\frac{k\pi}{2}\right)}$$

$$=-\sum_{0}^{10}\frac{2}{\sin\left(\frac{7\pi}{6}+k\pi\right)}$$

$$=-\sum_{0}^{10}\frac{2}{\sin\left(\pi-\frac{\pi}{6}+k\pi\right)}$$

$$=2\sum_{0}^{10}\frac{1}{\sin\left(k\pi-\frac{\pi}{6}\right)} \quad \left[\text{Using } \sin(\pi+\theta)=-\sin\theta\right]$$

Now, we have

$$\sin\left(k\pi-\frac{\pi}{6}\right)=\begin{cases}-\sin\left(\frac{\pi}{6}\right)=-\frac{1}{2}, \text{ if } k \text{ is even}\\ \sin\left(\frac{\pi}{6}\right)=\frac{1}{2}, \text{ if } k \text{ is odd}\end{cases}$$

$$\Rightarrow \frac{1}{\sin\left(k\pi-\frac{\pi}{6}\right)}=\begin{cases}-2, \text{ if } k \text{ is even}\\ 2, \text{ if } k \text{ is odd}\end{cases}$$

The series S has 11 terms out of which 6 have even ks, and five have odd ks. Hence, we have

$$S = 2[6(-2)+5(2)] = -4$$

$$\Rightarrow \quad \sec^{-1}\left(\frac{1}{2}S\right) = \sec^{-1}(-2) = \cos^{-1}\left(\frac{-1}{2}\right)$$

$$= \pi - \cos^{-1}\left(\frac{1}{2}\right) = \frac{5\pi}{6} = 2.62$$

23. Using property

$$\int_a^b f(x)dx = \frac{1}{2}\int_a^b \{f(x)+f(a+b-x)\}dx,$$

we have

$$I = \int_0^{\pi/2} f(\theta)d\theta = \frac{1}{2}\int_0^{\pi/2} \{f(\theta)+f(\pi/2-\theta)\}d\theta$$

$$= \frac{1}{2}\int_0^{\pi/2}\left(\frac{3\sqrt{\cos\theta}}{\left(\sqrt{\cos\theta}+\sqrt{\sin\theta}\right)^5} + \frac{3\sqrt{\sin\theta}}{\left(\sqrt{\cos\theta}+\sqrt{\sin\theta}\right)^5}\right)d\theta$$

$$= \frac{3}{2}\int_0^{\pi/2} \frac{1}{\left(\sqrt{\cos\theta}+\sqrt{\sin\theta}\right)^4}d\theta$$

$$= \frac{3}{2}\int_0^{\pi/2} \frac{\sec^2\theta}{\left(1+\sqrt{\tan\theta}\right)^4}d\theta$$

$$= \frac{3}{2}\int_1^{\infty} \frac{2(t-1)}{t^4}dt$$

$$\left[\text{Put } \tan\theta = (t-1)^2 \text{ and } \sec^2\theta d\theta = 2(t-1)dt\right]$$

$$= 3\int_1^{\infty}\left(\frac{1}{t^3}-\frac{1}{t^4}\right)dt$$

$$= 3\left|\left(\frac{-1}{2t^2}\right)-\left(\frac{-1}{3t^3}\right)\right|_1^{\infty} = 3\left|\left(\frac{1}{2t^2}\right)-\left(\frac{1}{3t^3}\right)\right|_{\infty}^{1}$$

$$= 3\left(\frac{1}{2}-\frac{1}{3}\right) - 0.5$$

24. Given $\mathbf{a} = 2\mathbf{i}+\mathbf{j}-\mathbf{k}$ and $\mathbf{b} = \mathbf{i}+2\mathbf{j}+\mathbf{k}$. Then, we have

$$\mathbf{a}+\mathbf{b} = 3\mathbf{i}+3\mathbf{j} \text{ and } \mathbf{a}\times\mathbf{b} = \begin{vmatrix} \mathbf{i} & \mathbf{j} & \mathbf{k} \\ 2 & 1 & -1 \\ 1 & 2 & 1 \end{vmatrix} = 3\mathbf{i}-3\mathbf{j}+3\mathbf{k}$$

Now, $\mathbf{c} = \alpha\mathbf{a}+\beta\mathbf{b} = (2\alpha+\beta)\mathbf{i}+(\alpha+2\beta)\boldsymbol{j}+(-\alpha+\beta)\boldsymbol{k}$. It is given that the projection of $\mathbf{c}$ on $\mathbf{a}+\mathbf{b}$ is $3\sqrt{2}$. Thus, we have

$$\frac{\mathbf{c}\cdot(\mathbf{a}+\mathbf{b})}{|\mathbf{a}+\mathbf{b}|} = 3\sqrt{2}$$

$$\Rightarrow \quad \frac{1}{3\sqrt{2}}[3(2\alpha+\beta)+3(\alpha+2\beta)] = 3\sqrt{2}$$

$$\Rightarrow \quad 9(\alpha+\beta) = 18$$

$$\Rightarrow \quad \alpha+\beta = 2 \qquad (1)$$

Now putting $\beta = 2-\alpha$, we have

$$\mathbf{c} = (\alpha+2)\mathbf{i}+(4-\alpha)\boldsymbol{j}+(2-2\alpha)\boldsymbol{k}$$

Then, we have

$$(\mathbf{c}-(\mathbf{a}\times\mathbf{b}))\cdot\mathbf{c} = ((\alpha-1)\mathbf{i}+(7-\alpha)\boldsymbol{j}-(2\alpha+1)\boldsymbol{k})\cdot((\alpha+2)\mathbf{i}+(4-\alpha)\boldsymbol{j}+(2-2\alpha)\boldsymbol{k})$$

$$= (\alpha-1)(\alpha+2)+(7-\alpha)(4-\alpha)+(2\alpha+1)(2\alpha-2)$$

$$= 6\alpha^2 - 12\alpha + 24 = 6(\alpha-1)^2 + 18$$

Hence, the minimum value of $(\mathbf{c}-(\mathbf{a}\times\mathbf{b}))\cdot\mathbf{c}$ is 18.

Match the Lists

1. (b) The given function $f(x)$ and its derivative $f'(x)$ are, respectively

$$f(x) = \sin(\pi\cos x)$$

and $\quad f'(x) = -\pi\cos(\pi\cos x)\sin x$

The elements of set X are given by

$$\sin(\pi\cos x) = 0$$

$$\Rightarrow \quad \cos x = 0, \pm 1$$

$$\Rightarrow \quad x = \left\{0, \frac{\pi}{2}, \pi, \frac{3\pi}{2}\right\} \text{ [Principal solutions]}$$

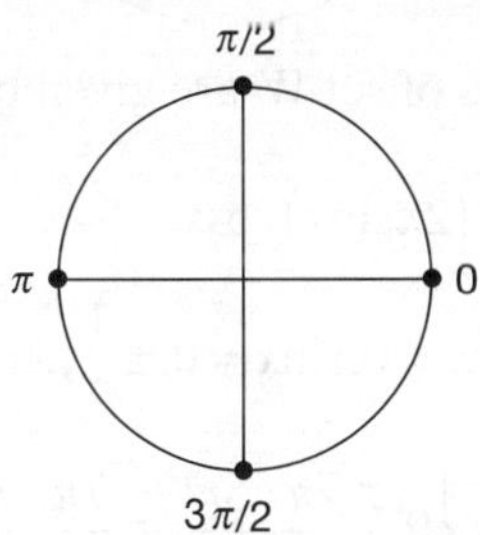

The elements of set Y are given by

$$\cos(\pi\cos x)\sin x = 0$$

$$\Rightarrow \quad \sin x = 0, \cos x = \pm\frac{1}{2}$$

$$\Rightarrow \quad x = \left\{0, \frac{\pi}{3}, \frac{2\pi}{3}, \pi, \frac{4\pi}{3}, \frac{5\pi}{3}\right\} \text{ [Principal solutions]}$$

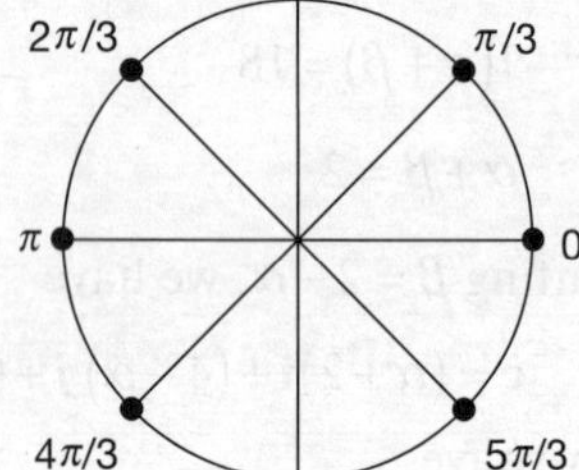

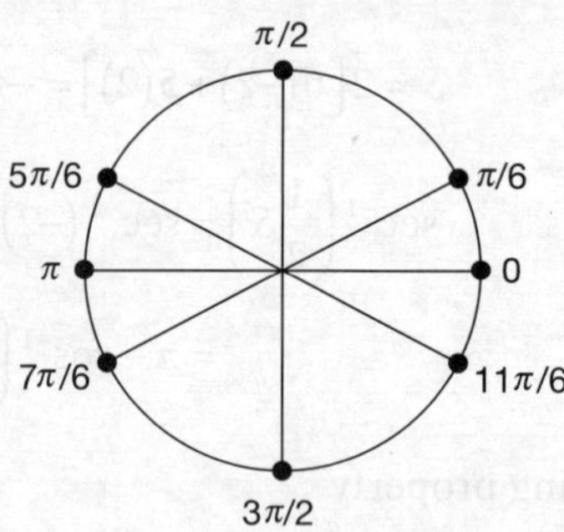

Hence, the only correct match is option (b) II – Q,T.

2. (b) The given function $g(x)$ and its derivative $g'(x)$ are, respectively

$$g(x) = \cos(2\pi\sin x)$$

and $$g'(x) = -2\pi\sin(2\pi\sin x)\cos x$$

The elements of set Z are given by

$$\cos(2\pi\sin x) = 0$$

$$\Rightarrow \quad \sin x = \pm\frac{1}{4}$$

$$\Rightarrow \quad x = \{\theta, \pi-\theta, \pi+\theta, 2\pi-\theta\} \text{ [Principal solutions]}$$

where $\theta = \sin^{-1}\left(\frac{1}{4}\right)$

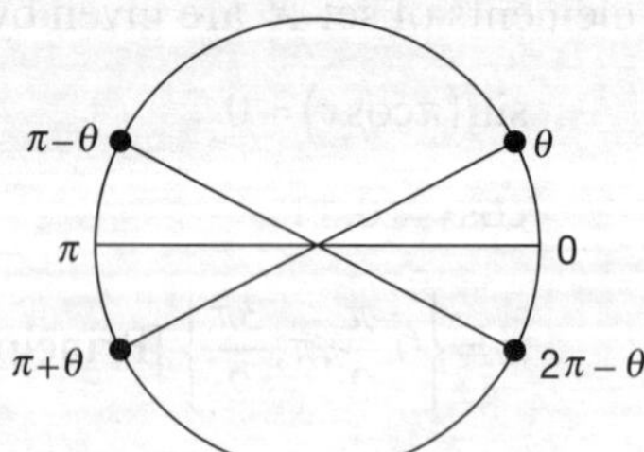

The elements of set W are given by

$$\sin(2\pi\sin x)\cos x = 0$$

$$\Rightarrow \quad \cos x = 0, \sin x = 0, \pm\frac{1}{2}, \pm 1$$

$$\Rightarrow \quad x = \left\{0, \frac{\pi}{6}, \frac{\pi}{2}, \frac{5\pi}{6}, \pi, \frac{7\pi}{6}, \frac{3\pi}{2}, \frac{11\pi}{6}\right\}$$

[Principal solutions]

Hence, the only correct match is option (b) IV – P,R,S.

3. (c)

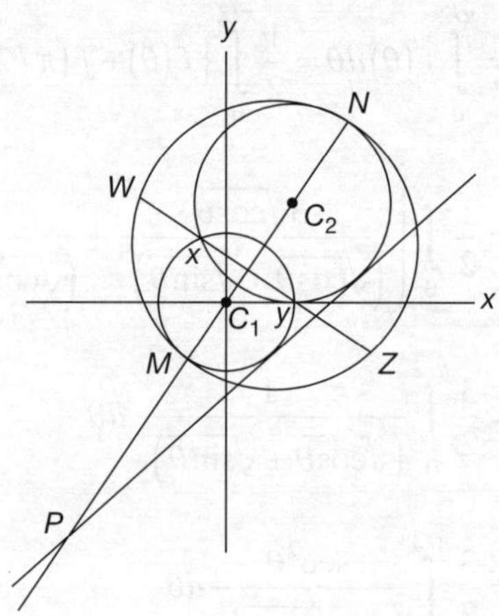

The circle $x^2 + y^2 = 9$ is of radius $r_1 = 3$ and has its centre at $C_1(0,0)$. The circle $(x-3)^2 + (y-4)^2 = 16$ is of radius $r_2 = 4$ and has its centre at $C_2(3,4)$.

The distance between the centres is $C_1C_2 = \sqrt{3^2 + 4^2} = 5$. The length $MN = r_1 + C_1C_2 + r_2 = 3 + 5 + 4 = 12$. The radius of circle C_3 is $r_3 = \frac{1}{2}(MN) = 6$. The centre of circle C_3 lies on line MN at a distance of $r_3 - r_1 = 6 - 3 = 3$ from the origin. The line MN is inclined at angle θ with the x-axis such that $\tan\theta = \frac{4}{3}$. Thus, $C_3 = (3\cos\theta, 3\sin\theta) = \left(\frac{9}{5}, \frac{12}{5}\right)$. Hence, we have

$$2h + k = \frac{18}{5} + \frac{12}{5} = 6$$

Equation of the common chord XY is

$$\left(x^2 + y^2 - 9\right) - \left(x^2 + y^2 - 6x - 8y + 9\right) = 0$$

$$\Rightarrow \qquad 3x+4y-9=0$$

Perpendicular distance of $C_2(3,4)$ from line XY is $=\dfrac{|3(3)+4(4)-9|1}{\sqrt{3^2+4^2}}=\dfrac{16}{5}$. Thus, we have

Length of

$$XY = 2\sqrt{r_2^2-a^2}$$
$$=2\sqrt{4^2-\left(\frac{16}{5}\right)^2}$$
$$=\frac{2}{5}\sqrt{20^2-16^2}$$
$$=\frac{24}{5}$$

Perpendicular distance of $C_3\left(\dfrac{9}{5},\dfrac{12}{5}\right)$ from line XY is $=\dfrac{\left|3\left(\frac{9}{5},\right)+4\left(\frac{12}{5}\right)-9\right|1}{\sqrt{3^2+4^2}}=\dfrac{6}{5}$. Thus, we have

Length of

$$ZW = 2\sqrt{r_3^2-b^2}=2\sqrt{6^2-\left(\frac{6}{5}\right)^2}$$
$$=\frac{2}{5}\sqrt{30^2-6^2}=\frac{24\sqrt{6}}{5}$$

Hence, we have

$$\frac{\text{Length of } ZW}{\text{Length of } XY}=\sqrt{6}$$

Hence, the only correct match is option (c) II – Q.

4. (c)

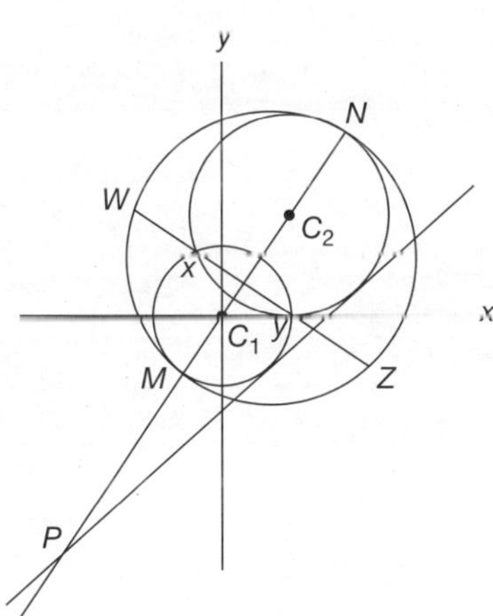

Equation of the common chord XY is

$$\left(x^2+y^2-9\right)-\left(x^2+y^2-6x-8y+9\right)=0$$
$$\Rightarrow \qquad 3x+4y-9=0$$

Length of MN is 12, and length of ZW is $\dfrac{24\sqrt{6}}{5}$. Hence, we have

Area of ΔMZN is

$$\frac{1}{2}(MN)\left(\frac{ZW}{2}\right)=\frac{1}{2}\times 12\times\frac{12\sqrt{6}}{5}$$
$$=\frac{12^2\sqrt{6}}{10}$$

Perpendicular distance of $C_1(0,0)$ from line XY is $\dfrac{|3(0)+4(0)-9|1}{\sqrt{3^2+4^2}}=\dfrac{9}{5}$. Thus, the perpendicular distance of point M from line XY is

$$h=r_1+c=3+\frac{9}{5}=\frac{24}{5}.$$

Hence, we have

Area of ΔZMW is

$$\frac{1}{2}(ZW)h=\frac{1}{2}\times\frac{24\sqrt{6}}{5}\times\frac{24}{5}$$
$$=\frac{24^2\sqrt{6}}{50}$$

Hence, we have

$$\frac{\text{Area of } \Delta MZN}{\text{Area of } \Delta ZMW}=\frac{12^2\sqrt{6}}{10}\times\frac{50}{24^2\sqrt{6}}$$
$$=\frac{5}{4}$$

The circles C_1, C_2 have two common tangents. However, the parabola $x^2=8\alpha y$, which has vertex at the origin and concavity along the y-axis, can touch only one of the two common tangents (see figure). This common tangent passes through the point P that divides line joining $C_1(0,0)$ and $C_2(3,4)$ externally in the ratio $3:4$, that is, $P=(-9,-12)$. The equation of this tangent will be $y+12=m(x+9)$. Its perpendicular distance from $C_1(0,0)$ must equal to $r_1=3$. Thus, we have

$$\frac{|9m-12|}{\sqrt{m^2+1}}=3$$

$$\Rightarrow \quad (3m-4)^2 = m^2+1$$

$$\Rightarrow \quad 8m^2 - 24m + 15 = 0 \text{ gives } m = \frac{6 \pm \sqrt{6}}{4}$$

The required common tangent is the one with the lesser slope, hence we take $= \frac{6-\sqrt{6}}{4}$.

Now, equation of the tangent to the parabola $x^2 = 8\alpha y$ must be of the type $x = ty + \frac{2\alpha}{t}$.

Comparing with the equation $y + 12 = m(x+9)$

$\Rightarrow x = \frac{1}{m}y + \frac{12}{m} - 9$, we have

$$t = \frac{1}{m}$$

and $$\frac{12}{m} - 9 = \frac{2\alpha}{t}$$

$$\Rightarrow \quad \frac{12}{m} - 9 = 2m\alpha \quad \text{[Eliminating } t\text{]}$$

$$\Rightarrow \quad \alpha = \frac{12-9m}{2m^2}$$

Now, putting the value of $m = \frac{6-\sqrt{6}}{4} = 0.887$ gives $\alpha = 2.55$.

Hence, the only correct match is option (c) (III), (*R*).